A
BLAKE
DICTIONARY

Frontispiece. S. Foster Damon
(Courtesy of the John Hay Library, Brown University)

A

BLAKE

DICTIONARY

The Ideas and Symbols of William Blake

Revised Edition
with a new foreword
and annotated bibliography
by Morris Eaves

S. Foster Damon

University Press of New England
Hanover and London

Published by
University Press of New England
One Court Street, Lebanon, NH 03766
www.upne.com

Printed in the United States of America
10 9 8 7

CIP data appear at the end of the book

ISBN-13: 978-0-87451-436-0
ISBN-10: 0-87451-436-3

Cover Illustration: Detail of "The goddess bursts . . . ," from *The Complaint and the Consolation: Or Night Thoughts* by Edward Young, 1797. Engraving by William Blake. Reproduced by permission of the Huntington Library, San Marino, California.

FOR

GEOFFREY KEYNES

to whom all Blake lovers are
indebted permanently

*Forgive what you do not approve, & love me
for this energetic exertion of my talent.*

BLAKE · JERUSALEM 3

Contents

Foreword *Blake as Conceived:*
Lessons in Endurance by Morris Eaves   ix
Acknowledgments   xxiii
Introduction   xxv
A Blake Dictionary   1
Illustrations by Blake and Maps   between 460–61
Index by Morris Eaves   461

Foreword

The study of Blake inevitably leads to controversy; the reader of this dictionary might never guess that there was anything but an agreed orthodoxy. ("Guides to a New Language," 3 October 1968)

S FOSTER DAMON was the young Turk of Blake studies when *William Blake: His Philosophy and Symbols* was published in 1924. He was "the patriarch of Blake studies" (Bloom rev., 24) when *A Blake Dictionary: The Ideas and Symbols of William Blake* was published in 1965. As I write this preface, *Philosophy and Symbols* is more than 63 years old, *A Blake Dictionary* more than 22, and Damon has been dead since 1971. It's fair to ask what *A Blake Dictionary* is good for at this late hour. Though Damon loved to pore over patriarchal tomes himself, he would have understood that people entering strange territory want up-to-date guidebooks. When I started getting serious about Blake, my guides were Northrop Frye's *Fearful Symmetry* (1947), David Erdman's *Blake: Prophet against Empire* (1954), and Damon's *Dictionary*. That was 1968, after all, and the *Dictionary* was nearly new. But today I'd still endorse my own experience: if Blake is where you're going, Frye, Erdman, and Damon should be your guides. As an introductory offer they remain unbeatable.

To understand the power of the *Dictionary* in this durable trio, we start with the recognition that Damon's lifetime coincided with the incorporation of Blake into legitimate fields of study. The process began well before Damon arrived on the scene and may continue indefinitely, but the crucial decades were those bracketed by Damon's Blake books. From the 1920s through the 1960s, various factors cooperated to assign to the name "William Blake" a set of attributes and a location in history. The rough consensus achieved during Damon's lifetime is by and large the one we are still operating with today—that consensus leads us to expect to find William Blake at home in one of the six slots allotted to the so-called major English romantic poets in standard textbooks devoted to the standard subject of English romantic poetry.

To the extent that the Blake of Damon's *Philosophy and Symbols* is the same as the Blake of the *Dictionary* in most essentials, the *Dictionary* is an annotated index to its own predecessor. The sustained equilibrium in the meaning of "Blake" that made it possible for a book published in 1965 to represent a book published in 1924 has less to do with the consistency of the author than with the consistency of the scholarly institutions within which he operated. Not that he or they never changed or never learned anything new during all those years. But the fact that the Blake whom Damon calls to memory for his *Dictionary* is very largely the same Blake whom Damon had first assembled for his *Philosophy and Symbols* four decades earlier confirms not just Damon's stubborn faith in his own critical powers but also the capacity of institutions to remember what they need to remember and to build on that memory while staunchly forgetting what they need to forget.

"Damon's . . . *Philosophy and Symbols* (1924) has been the foundation stone on which all modern interpretations of Blake have built" (Bateson rev., 25). Having laid the foundation in the 1920s, it was only proper for Damon the pioneer to return to it in the 1960s with a late scholarly tribute to his own work. By then a flourishing temple of Blake studies had appeared, occupied by a mostly academic staff that some observers (not I) have identified as the middle management of a veritable Blake industry. As a scholarly resource, Damon's *Dictionary* has stood up as well as it has for as long as it has because it belongs to that collective effort. Some reviewers pointed out what they saw as a discrepancy between the impersonality of a proper dictionary and the "eccentric and occasionally oracular" (Erdman rev., 607) personality of this one. Damon himself played up the independence that made his compilation *A*, not *The*, *Blake Dictionary*: "It is not the intention of this book to compile digests of the works of other scholars or to confute their theories. I have felt it better to make a new start and to attempt to present fresh evaluations of Blake's symbols" (see p. xxviii). To the contrary, the nucleus of the *Dictionary* is precisely a digest of Damon's ideas that had become common property over the years. Damon expanded, and occasionally changed this digest under the influence of other scholars' ideas that he had found congenial. Consequently, even as he insisted on his independence, he regularly acknowledged his institutional position with gestures toward scholarly posterity: "When a final answer has not been possible, I have tried to assemble the material for others to work on" (p. xxviii; also xxvii). Many of the parts of other scholars' works that Damon refused to digest were, after all, the peripheral parts for which no consensus yet existed. And his own attempts at "new" starts and "fresh evaluations" are, for the most part, simply the parts of the *Dictionary* one must learn to ignore. Fortunately, those are few, and they usually advertise their own peculiarity.

The best reason for studying Damon is neither to acquire a real English Blake from the bowels of history nor a curiosity Blake from the fascinating mind of an eccentric scholar but to acquire the Blake that unglamorously satisfies the rules and requirements of our institutions of artistic memory, in which Damon lived and thrived. He later said it himself, with a bit of irony and unmistakable pride: "At last, Blake was academically respectable" ("How I Discovered Blake," 3)—made respectable by an academic whose work of Blake scholarship had been rejected by Harvard as too inconsequential to merit a Ph.D. Thus what we have before us in the *Dictionary* is undeniably a sturdy Blake, well crafted for the very purpose of being remembered, read, taught, and written about within our institutions of reading, teaching, and writing. Of course, despite its endurance, we would never want to mistake this brilliantly conceived Blake for the only conceivable Blake. Nor, however, can we pretend that we presently know *how* to conceive any other Blake of comparable usefulness. In short, the essence of the Blake who materializes in the pages of Damon's *Dictionary* is nothing less than the presently indispensable Blake. And only that indispensability makes it matter in the least that the *Dictionary* is "a rich treasury embodying the results of a lifetime of masterly and devoted research into every aspect of Blake's work and thought" (Pinto rev., 153). Yes, the treasury is rich. Equally important, it is the coin of the realm.

Needless to say, Damon's academically respectable Blake did not come from nowhere. Even by 1924 the way had been well prepared. The single most important event in the history of Blake's reputation had already occurred. It was, essentially, a solution to the problem of Blake's double mastery of words and pictures, which made it very difficult to achieve a good fit between Blake's works and the structures that commit poets and painters to different kinds of institutional memory. Today's academic division between departments of art and departments of English reflects and extends a separation with an extensive history both inside and outside institutions of higher education. Though it has become routine in the later twentieth century to celebrate Blake's magnificent twofold achievement in art and literature, that boast could only begin to register effectively at a certain ripe and recent historical moment. Until then, for all practical purposes Blake's doubleness was a kind of duplicity, an indigestible alliance, like a dessert combined with an entrée.

Blake died, after all, in 1827 as an engraver and painter in a circle that included mainly engravers, painters, and buyers of art. He was barely known to the writers such as Wordsworth and Coleridge with whom he is now yoked in anthologies of English romantic poetry. Although Blake died an engraver/painter virtually unknown to his poet contemporaries, a fundamental change in Blake's reputation occurred when history found a way to conclude that he is essentially a poem-maker rather than a picture-maker. The change began to come on strongly in the last quarter of the nineteenth century, with the efforts of Algernon Charles Swinburne, William Michael Rossetti, and others to produce editions of Blake's poems. Since many of those "poems" were originally crafted as "illuminated books" in "illuminated printing"—usually relief-etched and watercolored combinations of text and design—they were doomed to run afoul of the institutional standards for poetic legibility. The first duty of an editor is to present poems. We all know what poems look like: in such an edition pictures may be present as ornaments and illustrations but not as integral poetic ingredients.

Blake the printmaker and painter was not forgotten, however; in some narrow circles his art was even revered. But on the larger cultural stage the emphasis was steadily shifting from the visual element in his work to the verbal, and the memories of his literary and artistic work were being stored ever more systematically in separate cultural compartments. The institutions of literacy edited the illuminated books into poems, lowering the visual component to the status of the ornamental and the dispensable. Meanwhile, the institutions of imagery operated by art historians, collectors, and curators looked past the illuminated books—the mainstay, curiously, of Blake's literary reputation—toward the categories of Blake's oeuvre where pictures rather than words are primary, because there he most clearly conforms to the conventional definition of a visual artist.

These moves to separate words from images were portentous. On the side of the literary institutions, where most of the action was, the decision to regard the component of visual design in Blake's product as a separate rather than integral part of his work had the curious effect of transforming the design component from a disadvantage (how does one reproduce these illuminated plates for consumption; having reproduced them, how does one read them?) to a minor advantage. As long as Blake's visual art did not have to be coordinated systematically with the verbal in the process of interpreting, the visual art could signal his surplus creativity—his difference from the norm and even from the five romantic poets to whom his future was beginning to be tied. Thus, as long as the illuminated books did not have to be reproduced *as* illuminated books, as long as they could be edited, printed, interpreted, and taught as poems, the visual element of the work could serve handily as a kind of place-holder in accounts of Blake, marking his difference from the rest of his poetic family. Meanwhile, in the practice of literary criticism the visual element could have the (diminished) role of an optional rhetorical opportunity rather than a haunting, forbidding obligation that no practicing critic would know how to live up to. Moreover, as the burden of responsibility for Blake's reputation shifted from the institutions of art history and art collecting to the institutions of literary history and criticism, some major impediments to a favorable appraisal of Blake, such as the entrenched orthodox standards of drawing, became much more manageable. After all, the literary types in whose hands Blake's fortunes lay cared little and knew less about such orthodoxies.

It was not for nothing, then, that Foster Damon traced the beginning of his serious study of Blake to a literary edition: "The present study of the philosophy and symbols of William Blake was begun ten years ago, when Dr. Sampson's edition of *Blake's Poetic Works* made most of the texts accessible in their correct form" (*Philosophy and Symbols*, vii). Sampson's edition had in fact first been published in 1905 but Damon used the "Oxford Edition" of 1913, 1914, and later printings. In any event, we can see from his comment how Sampson's meticulous edition had helped codify a concept of Blake the poet. Now the question would be, what kind of poet? Answer: a sort of modernist. Damon's "ten years ago" had been around 1914, one of the three years when the older William Butler Yeats and the younger Ezra Pound spent the winter at Stone Cottage in Sussex together, plotting the next stage in the history of modern poetry. "Philosophy and symbols" had already become part of that history and were destined to become much more important parts with Yeats's increasing devotion to the kind of philosophical symbolism that culminated in *A Vision* (1925). Blake had already influenced the development of Yeats's symbolism, and Yeats with his collaborator Edwin J. Ellis had edited Blake's complete works with two volumes of commentary in 1893. Damon once called the first volume "unreadable" ("How I Discovered Blake," 2). Indeed it took a Foster Damon to write a readable replacement for Yeats and Ellis. But that should not be taken to suggest that we can understand Damon's Blake without understanding the decisive alliance between Blake's literary fortunes and the fortunes of modernism.

Blake's system-making, his blend of psychology with religion, his exalted claims for the powers of art, the difficulty of his work, and his failure to win an audience in his lifetime are only a few of the several factors that cooperated to make him a potential artist-hero and guardian angel of a significant filament of modern poetry. Blake and modernism belong together, not necessarily on the strand that was spare and taut in its verbal standards, but on the mythopoeic strand that wanted to make poetry the cult-object for an elite society of initiates who would deal only in the deepest, most significant kinds of knowledge of which the world at large was unworthy. This helps to explain why Damon's Blake is "definitely a mystic," which Damon says he discovered by reading William James's *Varieties of Religious Experience* ("How I Discovered Blake," 2). We would hardly be the first to notice that Damon's Blake is a mystic of a particularly artistic persuasion, for whom the traditional goal of seeing the face of God becomes a vision of imagination—a magico-aesthetic mysticism closer to the Order of the Golden Dawn, the late nineteenth-century occultists, and poets like William Butler Yeats than to the author of *The Cloud of Unknowing*.

This is not the place to trace the affiliations with modernism that helped shape an academically respectable Blake, one who was not only a mystic but also, as Damon's title advertises, a philosopher and symbolist. In the game of institutionalization, finding powerful metaphors is an important maneuver, and Damon's three favorites, Blake as mystic, philosopher, and symbolist, had all the right connections at the time. But in the long run Blake-mystic and, to a large extent, Blake-symbolist, at least, fell away as inadequate anachronisms. Their historical connections with the period of Blake's discovery, the roughly 50 years from 1875 to 1925, became more apparent than their connections with Blake's texts. But a variety of other, analogous terms have had to be brought in as substitutes, simply because *some* mode of identification is required.

The metaphors continue to shift, but, so far, the general need that they try to satisfy has changed much less. R. P. Blackmur once expressed that need well in his essay on "A Critic's Job of Work," which uses Damon's own *Philosophy and Symbols* as an example of that job properly done: ". . . Mr. Damon made Blake exactly what he seemed least to be, perhaps the most intellectually consistent of the greater poets in English" (quoted by Morton D. Paley in Damon, "How I Discovered Blake," 3n). Blackmur registers precisely the combination of surprise and relief that has become characteristic of Blake's reputation or, we might say, characteristic of the narrative that is told repeatedly to justify his inclusion among the "greater poets." At least in the twentieth century, the surprise of discovering a poet who is consistent has been a reliable part of the stories that readers tell about their relationships with Blake, and the juxtapositions of surprise, discovery, poetry, and consistency have been basic indices of his place in our literary institutions.

In discussing the literary elements in the growth of Blake's reputation, I would not want to give the impression that Damon's *Philosophy and Symbols* eliminated Blake's art from consideration. To some extent, especially by comparison with the literary scholars who would come later, he did the opposite. The last section of *Philosophy and Symbols* commented, however briefly, on each plate of the illuminated books, while other books on Blake often left the designs unmentioned. But Damon segregated the designs into little clusters under the heading "decorations," interpreted them as extensions of meanings gleaned first from the poetry, and relegated them to the back of his book where they can easily be forgotten. The best evidence of their forgettability comes with the *Dictionary*, where Damon eliminates the design component of illuminated printing as a subject of systematic discussion. The justification for doing so, in a presumably unabridged Blake dictionary that one literary-minded reviewer called "extraordinarily comprehensive" (Bateson rev., 25), is left implicit. It is again, of course, the metaphor that made most twentieth-century advances in the study of Blake possible: Blake is a poet. And he is that kind of poet who uses words as "tools . . . to rouse with thought" (*Philosophy and Symbols*, xi); he is a philosopher. As Damon said emphatically, "*Jerusalem*, as pure poetry, is obviously inferior to the *Songs of Innocence*. . . . *Blake was not trying to make literature*. Truth, not pleasure, is the object of all his writings" (his emphasis; *Philosophy and Symbols*, 63).

As Damon indicated, to find Blake the thinker one travels well beyond *Songs of Innocence* ("The lyrics are in every anthology; yet professors of literature wonder if the epics are worth reading!" *Philosophy and Symbols*, ix) into the territory of the "epics" (as *Jerusalem* can be termed only if considered a literary work), where thought takes precedence over pleasure—as it must, if Blake is to be taken seriously enough to deserve his place beside Wordsworth and Coleridge. Damon passed this version of Blake the philosopher into literary history, where it was eventually taken up by Northrop Frye, who depended fundamentally upon the model of Blake designed by Damon. The Blake of Frye's *Fearful Symmetry* (1947) is even more exclusively a writer than Damon's, and an even more profound and consistent thinker. Frye's Blake is no longer a mystic (the appeal of that metaphor had dissolved in the mists of modernism) but he is very much a philosopher. When Damon combined philosophy and symbolism he got mysticism; when Frye combined them he got myth. Myth, for Frye, is not unlike mysticism for Damon: both are terms for thinking at a particularly profound level that in previous centuries would have been identified with religion. Damon would not refuse to allow that Blake was a Christian, but he knew he had to be an especially appealing kind of Christian, a "Gnostic" Christian, said Damon (*Philosophy and Symbols*, xi), or a mystic. Frye went a step further by relentlessly exploiting the implications of a new metaphor: religion, deeply considered and thawed out, is poetry. Both draw on the same myths. Blake's revelations as a thinker, then, are myths that reveal the fundamental nature of poetry itself.

David Erdman, the third member of our trio of resources, came in to do a job that desperately needed doing by the mid-1950s. He relied heavily on the Damon and Frye's Blake, the philosophically consistent thinker more poet than painter and more interested in truth than pleasure, as the basis for *Blake: Prophet against Empire* (1954). Erdman's great revision in the licensed image of Blake involved little change at the base. Damon and Frye's Blake was a man of universal ideas; we learn to read him by reading through a confusing welter of particulars into general patterns of thought. Erdman's Blake we read in reverse, back from those general patterns of thought into particulars, and then we use the particulars to align the patterns with everyday events in London. Erdman's work augmented the impression already established of a *profound* Blake, whose concern, though with everyday events, was with the most elevated aspect of those events: liberty, justice, fraternity, equality. In bringing him down to earth, Erdman paradoxically managed to create an even more formidable Blake, a both–and rather than an either–or thinker whose poems could deliver simultaneously profound truths about poetry and equally profound reactions to local events. And, like Damon and Frye, Erdman reinforced the element of surprise in discovering again a consistent thinker, this time a consistent social and political thinker, where before we saw none. When Damon returned with his *Dictionary* two decades after Frye's book and a decade after Erdman's, he had no trouble recognizing the Blake he found. This augmented, fortified, and considerably refined Blake, though now a celebrity much in demand to ornament the books of scientists, literary theorists, theologians, and philosophers, was still recognizably the Blake whom Damon had introduced to the academy in the 1920s, now ready to be represented by a scholarly instrument as impartial and consensual as a dictionary.

From our vantage point more than two decades later, we can now see that Damon's *Dictionary* arrived just in time to signal the end of an era of definition and the beginning of an era of rapid consolidation and codification—with, certainly, some evolution. As many significant additions to our knowledge of Blake as there have been over the years since the *Dictionary*, most have been additions to the base. One important alternative image has been a changing, as opposed to a consistent, Blake. We might speculate about what motivated the creators of a monolithically stable Blake. Perhaps it was the need to hold a difficult subject still long enough to get a focused likeness, and, more important, the need to deny the possibility that Blake might be intellectually erratic, even insane. If so, then a consistent Blake was the required precursor of any (memorable) Blake less consistent. The way for a Blake who changes his ideas significantly over the course of his life was already prepared for to some extent by Erdman, whose focus on political ideology almost necessarily brought change into the picture, though it must be said that Erdman's Blake is notable for his stubborn refusal to change with the tides of English opinion on the French Revolution—and in that way belongs in the family with Damon's and Frye's.

The more important product of our new knowledge is a Blake more in line with the historically situated engraver and painter. (Consequently, I have devoted most of the space in the annotated bibliography [see pp. xix–xx] to this aspect of Blake scholarship.) Although the advances in understanding Blake as an artist have been major, nonetheless they have chiefly proceeded from the prior understanding of Blake as a writer and remain subsidiary. The main categories of analysis have been preserved. In fact, with a very few notable exceptions, most of the scholarship on Blake's visual art has been done by English professors working out of their areas of specialization. Understandably, they have eased the difficulties of their transition by importing their literary understanding of Blake. In their terms, Blake the artist works by analogy alongside Blake the writer. Meanwhile, the position of Blake among the art historians has not altered profoundly in recent years. He has greater name recognition among them and perhaps somewhat greater respectability, and, at last, has engendered a relatively complete kit of scholarly tools for art historians (see the bibliography). Even after these modifications to the scholarly base, however, so far no rumblings in recent art history suggest an imminent change comparable to Blake's twentieth-century ascendancy among the romantic poets.

The nineteenth century made it impossible for readers of the twentieth to "discover"

Wordsworth or Keats. The same fate may befall Blake in the twenty-first century. W. J. T. Mitchell's often cited article on "Dangerous Blake" recognized the sobersidedness and the unmitigated sublimity that was characteristic of the established Blake. Mitchell's prophecy that "we are about to rediscover the dangerous Blake, the angry, flawed, Blake, the crank . . . the ingrate, the sexist, the madman, the religious fanatic, the tyrannical husband, the second-rate draughtsman" (410−11) seemed a symptom not only of the need to reinstitute surprise in the Blake canon but also of a fear that a Blake who can't surprise his readers may not be able to hold his place. In the half-decade since Mitchell's article, though progress has continued, no new era has begun. Meanwhile, however, the consolidated Blake holds his own, along with Frye's *Fearful Symmetry*, Erdman's *Blake: Prophet against Empire*, and Damon's *Blake Dictionary*, to make them the oldest surviving threesome in literary studies of comparable influence, and, to my knowledge, the best. Not that there is any reason to suppose that we have seen our last Blake. Like all such "figures," as we call them, in the history of the arts, Blake is one name that can cover many mutable and even incompatible things. Literary critics and art historians have called many Blakes to our attention and will call many more. Many are called, but few are chosen.

University of Rochester   MORRIS EAVES

Annotated Bibliography

Works Cited in the Preface

Bateson, F. W. "Blake and the Scholars: II." Rev. of *A Blake Dictionary*. *New York Review of Books* 28 Oct. 1965: 24−25.

Blackmur, R. P. "A Critic's Job of Work." *The Double Agent: Essays in Craft and Elucidation*. New York: Arrow, 1935. 269−302.

Bloom, Harold. "Foster Damon and William Blake." Rev. of *A Blake Dictionary*. *New Republic* 5 June 1965: 24−25.

Damon, S. Foster. "How I Discovered Blake." *Blake Newsletter* 1 (winter 1967−68): 2−3.

———. *William Blake: His Philosophy and Symbols*. Boston: Houghton Mifflin, 1924.

Ellis, Edwin J., and William Butler Yeats, eds. *The Works of William Blake, Poetic, Symbolic, and Critical*. 3 vols. London: B. Quaritch, 1893.

Erdman, David V. *William Blake: Prophet against Empire*. 3rd ed. Princeton, N.J.: Princeton University Press, 1977 [1st ed. 1954].

Erdman, David V. Rev. of *A Blake Dictionary*. *Journal of English & Germanic Philology* 65 (1966): 606−12.

Frye, Northrop. *Fearful Symmetry: A Study of William Blake*. Princeton, N.J.: Princeton University Press, 1947.

"Guides to a New Language." Rev. of *A Blake Dictionary*. *Times Literary Supplement* 3 Oct. 1968: 1098.

Mitchell, W. J. T. "Dangerous Blake." *Studies in Romanticism* 21 (1982): 410–16.
Pinto, Vivian de Sola. Rev. of *A Blake Dictionary. Modern Language Review* 65 (1970): 153–55.
Sampson, John, ed. *The Poetical Works of William Blake.* London: Oxford University Press, 1913 (and later printings).
Yeats, William Butler. *A Vision.* London: T. Werner Laurie, Ltd., 1925.

Further Information on S. Foster Damon

Blake Newsletter 1.3 (15 Dec. 1967).   (The issue is devoted to Damon.)
Rosenfeld, Alvin H., ed. *William Blake: Essays for S. Foster Damon.* Providence, R.I.: Brown University Press, 1969. (See especially Rosenfeld's preface, Malcolm Cowley's "S. Foster Damon: The New England Voice," and Ernest D. Costa and Elizabeth C. Wescott's bibliography of works by Damon.)
Rosenfeld, Alvin H., and Barton Levi St. Armand, eds. *A Birthday Garland for S. Foster Damon: Tributes Collected in Honor of His Seventy-Fifth Birthday, February 22, 1968.* Providence, R.I.: privately printed, 1968. (The volume includes tributes by numerous students, friends, admirers, and former students, including poet e. e. cummings, composer Virgil Thomson, and mystery writer Colin Wilson, among others.)

Biography

Bentley, G. E., Jr. *Blake Records.* Oxford: Clarendon, 1969. (A rich source of contemporary accounts of Blake arranged, as far as possible, in chronological order. *Blake Records* can be read profitably as a continuous narrative.)
Gilchrist, Alexander. *Life of William Blake, "Pictor Ignotus."* 2nd ed. 2 vols. London: Macmillan & Co., 1880. (Gilchrist's biography [1st ed. 1863] is the platform from which Blake's twentieth-century reputation was launched. Although Gilchrist has distinct biases and some of the events he reports are mythical, no twentieth-century narrative of Blake's life has so far managed to replace this one. Ruthren Todd's Everyman edition of the Gilchrist biography [rev. ed., London: Dent, 1945] is particularly useful.)

Edition

Erdman, David V., ed. (with commentary by Harold Bloom). *The Complete Poetry and Prose of William Blake.* Berkeley and Los Angeles: University of California Press, 1982 (and later printings). (In the *Dictionary*, Damon uses an earlier edition by Geoffrey Keynes. Erdman's edition, which as far as possible follows Blake's spelling, capitalization, and punctuation, is the current standard.)

A Selection of Facsimiles

Bain, Iain, David Chambers, and Andrew Wilton, eds. *The Wood Engravings of William Blake for Thornton's Virgil.* London: British Museum, 1977. (These are modern impressions printed directly from Blake's own wood blocks from the British Museum collection.)

Blake Trust facsimiles. Several decades ago the Blake Trust was formed with the objective of issuing superior (and expensive) facsimiles of Blake's work. Through the Trianon Press in Paris the Trust published a series of very fine volumes (too many to list here, chiefly but not exclusively the illuminated books) that are now in libraries throughout the world. Trianon Press and Oxford University Press later collaborated in issuing inexpensive facsimiles of the *Songs of Innocence and of Experience* and *The Marriage of Heaven and Hell*. (These are still in print.) Though the Trianon Press no longer exists, the Blake Trust recently published a facsimile of Blake's Job watercolors and engravings and is planning future projects.

Erdman, David V. (with Donald Moore), ed. *The Notebook of William Blake: A Photographic and Typographic Facsimile*. Rev. ed. New York: Readex, 1977 [1st ed. Clarendon, 1973]. (An ingenious piece of editing in which each page of the notebook—an important source of Blake's writings and designs—is represented by a photograph of the page and [on the facing page] a translation of the handwriting into type. With extensive commentary.)

Essick, Robert N., and Morton D. Paley, eds. *Robert Blair's* The Grave *Illustrated by William Blake: A Study with Facsimile*. London: Scolar, 1982. (One of the clearest signals of the misalignment between Blake's career and his subsequent reputation lies in the fact that his engravings for Blair's *Grave* were probably the works for which he was best known in his lifetime.)

Grant, John E., Edward J. Rose, and Michael J. Tolley, with David V. Erdman, coordinating ed. *William Blake's Designs for Edward Young's* Night Thoughts. Oxford: Clarendon, 1980. (This volume reproduces all 537 watercolor designs and the far fewer engravings based on them. The project calls for a second volume of interpretive commentary, as yet unpublished.)

Keynes, Geoffrey, ed. *The Marriage of Heaven and Hell*. London: Oxford University Press (with Trianon), 1975.

Keynes, Geoffrey, ed. *Songs of Innocence and of Experience*. London: Oxford University Press (with Trianon), 1970. (These are the Oxford University Press/Trianon collaborations just mentioned.)

Magno, Cettina Tramontano, and David V. Erdman. *The Four Zoas by William Blake: A Photographic Facsimile of the Manuscript with Commentary on the Illuminations*. Lewisburg, Penn.: Bucknell University Press, 1987. (A special feature of the Magno/Erdman facsimile is its attempt to recover pictorial details, many of them sexual, that have been heretofore indecipherable. The lengthy commentary offers interpretations of the designs.)

Songs of Innocence. New York: Dover, 1972, and *Songs of Experience*. New York: Dover, 1984. (Inexpensive facsimiles of Blake's illuminated books have been hard to come by. These two paperback editions by Dover are reasonably accurate, readily available, and cheap.)

Songs of Innocence and *Songs of Experience*. Manchester, England: Manchester Etching Workshop, 1983. (For those interested in the processes by which Blake produced the illuminated books, this is by far the most useful facsimile available. It is unfortunately rare, since only 40 colored copies and 35 monochrome copies were made. The printer/publisher took special care in duplicating Blake's printing, inking, and coloring. Joseph Viscomi, one of the most knowledgeable scholars of Blake's printmaking processes, played a role in the production of the facsimile and wrote an accompanying pamphlet, *The Art of William Blake's Illuminated Prints*.)

Miscellaneous Aids to Study

Erdman, David V., et al. *A Concordance to the Writings of William Blake*. 2 vols. Ithaca, N.Y.: Cornell University Press, 1967. (Erdman's concordance is keyed to Geoffrey Keynes's edition of Blake [1957 and later printings], which though no longer standard can be found in many libraries.)

Bentley, G. E., Jr. *Blake Books*. Oxford: Clarendon, 1977. (Bentley's subtitle indicates the vast range of work covered: "annotated catalogues of William Blake's writings in illuminated printing, in conventional typography, and in manuscript, and reprints thereof, reproductions of his designs, books with his engravings, catalogues, books he owned, and scholarly and critical works about him." A supplement is underway.)

Blake/An Illustrated Quarterly. Edited by Morris Eaves and Morton D. Paley. Address: Department of English, University of Rochester, Rochester N.Y. 14627. (*Blake* is an international quarterly journal for specialists—whether art historians, literary critics, museum curators, or freelance students of Blake—compiled by specialists: in addition to Eaves and Paley, Nelson Hilton [book review editor], Detlef Doerrbecker [bibliographer], and David Worrall [editor for Great Britain]. *Blake* runs articles, book reviews, news, and comprehensive annual checklists of Blake scholarship and art sales.)

Johnson, Mary Lynn. "William Blake." *The English Romantic Poets: A Review of Research and Criticism*. Ed. Frank Jordan. New York: Modern Language Association, 1985. 113–253. (Johnson's is the most recent and comprehensive bibliographical essay on the subject, and excellent by any standard. Readers looking for guidance in the maze of Blake studies published since Damon's *Dictionary* should begin here. Update with annual bibliographies in *Blake: An Illustrated Quarterly* and *PMLA*.)

Painting and Printmaking

Although certainly Damon was always alert to Blake's artistic side, he had a literary view of that side. One of the most obvious changes in his approach to Blake was the elimination in the *Blake Dictionary* of systematic discussion of the visual component in Blake's illuminated books, which had played a larger part in Damon's *William Blake: His Philosophy and Symbols*. Since the publication of the *Dictionary*, however, knowledge and understanding of Blake's work as painter and printmaker have increased substantially, and long overdue standard works of scholarship, such as Butlin's two-volume catalogue raisonné, have made good scholarship considerably easier to carry out.

Bindman, David. *Blake as an Artist*. Oxford: Phaidon, 1977. (The best art-historical account of the subject, superseding the earlier work by Anthony Blunt, *The Art of William Blake* (1959).

Bindman, David (assisted by Deirdre Toomey). *The Complete Graphic Works of William Blake*. New York: Putnam's, 1978. (In some ways this is an inconvenient book to use. The reproductions of plates from the illuminated books are too small, and one often wants more information about individual works. Nevertheless, the 765 reproductions cover a lot of ground and the annotations are authoritative. Notice that "complete graphic works" does not include works designed by others and only engraved by Blake.)

Butlin, Martin. *The Paintings and Drawings of William Blake*. 2 vols. New Haven: Yale University Press, 1981. (Butlin's catalogue totals more than 1000 pages. The first volume contains the text of entries; the second volume contains reproductions—some color, some monochrome—of most of the items. Note that "paintings and drawings" excludes all of Blake's work as a printmaker.)

Eaves, Morris. *William Blake's Theory of Art*. Princeton, N.J.: Princeton University Press, 1982. (A venerable tradition denies that Blake had coherent theories for his practice. Eaves draws the broad outlines of a theory from Blake's writings and from the literary and art discourses of his time.)

Erdman, David V. *The Illuminated Blake: All of William Blake's Illuminated Works with a Plate-by-Plate Commentary*. Garden City, N.Y.: Doubleday-Anchor, 1974. (The reproductions [monochrome] range from adequate to dismal, but having them all in one volume is exceedingly useful. The commentary ranges from the irrefutable to the incredible, but it can always be counted on as an excellent place to begin.)

Essick, Robert N. *The Separate Plates of William Blake: A Catalogue*. Princeton, N.J.: Princeton University Press, 1983. (Essick's catalogue complements Butlin's catalogue raisonné and Bindman's *Complete Graphic Works* [cited here].)

Essick, Robert N. *William Blake Printmaker*. Princeton, N.J.: Princeton University Press, 1980. (Essick's book, covering the full range of Blake's printmaking, cleared away a logjam of well-intentioned misinformation that had been accumulating for decades and set new terms and high new standards for further discussion. When new information on Blake's graphic work comes in, as it regularly does, it now fits into a coherent base of accurate knowledge. See, for example, the booklet by Viscomi [*Songs*, Manchester Etching Workshop, above].)

Mitchell, W. J. T. *Blake's Composite Art: A Study of the Illuminated Poetry*. Princeton, N.J.: Princeton University Press, 1978. (The most forceful booklength attempt to establish a theory and practice of reading Blake's illuminated books aimed at encompassing both the textual and visual elements of the medium.)

Paley, Morton D. *William Blake*. Oxford: Phaidon, 1978. (A concise alternative to Bindman [above].)

Criticism of the Illuminated Books since Damon's *Dictionary*

The infrastructure of our understanding, and our estimate, of Blake continues to derive from the illuminated books, plus *The Four Zoas*. Here is a highly condensed and unannotated list, only a tiny sample, of critical studies that variously treat the illuminated books and the "myth" extracted from them. Some of the books produced over the last two decades are very much of the school of Damon, some not.

Curran, Stuart, and Joseph A. Wittreich, Jr., eds. *Blake's Sublime Allegory: Essays on* The Four Zoas, Milton, *and* Jerusalem. Madison, Wisc.: University of Wisconsin Press, 1973.

Damrosch, Leopold, Jr. *Symbol and Truth in Blake's Myth*. Princeton, N.J.: Princeton University Press, 1980.

Erdman, David V., and John E. Grant, eds. *Blake's Visionary Forms Dramatic*. Princeton, N.J.: Princeton University Press, 1970.

Fox, Susan. *Poetic Form in Blake's* Milton. Princeton, N.J.: Princeton University Press, 1976.

Hilton, Nelson. *Literal Imagination: Blake's Vision of Words*. Berkeley: University of California Press, 1983.

Hilton, Nelson, and Thomas A. Vogler, eds. *Unnam'd Forms: Blake and Textuality*. Berkeley: University of California Press, 1986.

Johnson, Mary Lynn, and Brian Wilkie. *Blake's* Four Zoas: *The Design of a Dream*. Cambridge, Mass.: Harvard University Press, 1978.

Leader, Zachary. *Reading Blake's* Songs. Boston: Routledge, 1981.

Paley, Morton D. *The Continuing City: William Blake's* Jerusalem. Oxford: Clarendon, 1983.

———. *Energy and the Imagination: A Study of the Development of Blake's Thought*. Oxford: Clarendon, 1970.

Raine, Kathleen. *Blake and Tradition*. Mellon Lectures, 1962. Bollingen Series 35. 2 vols. Princeton, N.J.: Princeton University Press, 1968.

Acknowledgments

THROUGH the years I have been indebted to so many people for information and discussion that I am at a loss to acknowledge them all. Particularly I have been indebted to Sir Geoffrey Keynes, establisher of the Blake text, describer of all known copies of the books, collector of many facts about Blake, and hearty encourager of my efforts; to the late Joseph Wicksteed, whose *Job* taught us all how to read Blake's pictures; to the late Max Plowman, who discovered the basic structures of *The Marriage of Heaven and Hell* and *The Four Zoas*; to Kerrison Preston, contributor of ideas and prompt and precise checker of material in London; to George Goyder, whose publication of all Blake's Biblical pictures made easy their comparison and interpretations; to Dr. Karl Kiralis, discoverer of the structure of *Jerusalem*, for maps of the counties, the loan of his *Jerusalem* index, and many suggestions; to Dr. Merrill Patterson for the use of his discovery that hands and feet have meaning in the fourfold system; to David Erdman, establisher of many facts about Blake, and eager critic of my manuscript pro and con; to G. E. Bentley, Jr., for information about Blake's Blair illustrations and other matters; to Dr. Gershom Scholem and Rabbi William G. Braude for elucidation of the Hebraic material; to the Reverend John D. Elder, ever ready with his concordances; to Dr. Ronald Levinson for the clue to Taylor's mysticism; to Mrs. Norman V. Ballou for information about the correspondence of Horace Scudder, the first American Blake enthusiast; to David Jenkins, the Keeper of Printed Books at the National Library of Wales, who found the source of Blake's "Welch Triades"; to Paul Miner, who took such pains in locating The Green Man and other places Blake knew as a boy; to William Thomas Wilkins III for an important quotation from Athanasius; to the late William A. Jackson, librarian, and Miss Caroline Jakeman, of the Houghton Library; to H. Glenn Brown and other members of the staff of the Brown University Library; to Alvin Rosenfeld, checker of Blake references, who gave me some valuable suggestions; to Catherine Brown and the copy-editing staff of the Brown University Press, whose unflagging application and intelligent criticisms were most welcome in preparing the manuscript for the printer; and particularly to John R. Turner Ettlinger, Curator of the Annmary Brown Memorial, for his maps and diagrams and constant encouragement.

S. FOSTER DAMON

Introduction

E XUBERANCE is Beauty" (*MHH* 10). "Passion & Expression is Beauty Itself" (On Reynolds, *K* 466). "Knowledge of Ideal Beauty is Not to be Acquired. It is Born with us" (On Reynolds, *K* 459). Blake wrote little else about Beauty, although he created it in new forms all his life.

The fact is, Beauty for him was not an end in itself, nor was it a mere by-product. It was a means of communication. Beauty is the spark at contact, marking the mystical union of poet and reader. All art exists at that point and nowhere else. The thrill is the preliminary perception of a Truth, and prophecy of its revelation. I know of no other poet who so constantly wrote passages which give us that thrill while the actual meaning is still quite hidden from the corporeal understanding. A single poem, say "Ah! Sun-Flower," holds one by its mere melody. "Tyger! Tyger! burning bright" fascinates, long before one connects it with Wrath in heaven and Revolution on earth. The "Proverbs of Hell" seem to make sense long before they do. Even in the turbulence and thunder of his most chaotic passages, a paragraph or even a single line will flash and strike like a lightning bolt, illuminating an entire landscape. It is so powerful because it has the force of a new universe behind it.

Blake's basic purpose was the discovery and recording of new truths about the human soul. For him the most exciting thing possible was the discovery of these truths. Hunting for them and warfare over them with other thinkers were the joys of his "eternity" (*Mil* 35:2). His "long resounding strong heroic [lines are] marshall'd in order for the day of Intellectual Battle" (*FZ* i:5). The "Births of Intellect" come to us direct from "the divine Humanity" (*LJ*, *K* 613). "The Treasures of Heaven are . . . Realities of Intellect, from which all the Passions Emanate Uncurbed in their Eternal Glory" (*LJ*, *K* 615). These truths are the only possible basis for genuine belief. With a few trifling exceptions, Blake never wrote a poem or painted a picture without intellectual meaning.

So profound were his researches in the *terra incognita* that he may be hailed as the Columbus of the psyche, in whose course Freud and Jung, among others, were to follow. So novel was everything in this new world that no vocabulary was prepared for him. But these psychic forces were so real that he *had* to name them. Thence arose his special mythology, for these forces were living creatures.

Blake was not content only to record: he wanted to force his reader to think along with him. No great work of art has its meaning on the surface, not

Chaucer's, Shakespeare's, or Milton's. The public has taken these great writers merely as a storyteller, a playwright, an epic-maker, and has been content to enjoy their writings on that level only. For example, *Paradise Lost* has been treated as an epic (but is it really Aristotelean?), as a theological treatise (but is it quite orthodox?), and as Biblical history, though it is no more history than *The Divine Comedy* is a travelogue; but never had it been understood as a study of damnation. Blake was the very first person to know what Milton was writing about. He was determined not to have his own message sidetracked by surface meanings. So he removed the surface meanings.

Blake heartily embraced Thomas Taylor's teaching that the Ancients concealed the Divine Mysteries under symbols. "What is Grand is necessarily obscure to Weak men. That which can be made Explicit to the Idiot is not worth my care. The wisest of the Ancients consider'd what is not too Explicit as the fittest for Instruction because it rouzes the faculties to act. I name Moses, Solomon, Esop, Homer, Plato" (To Trusler, 23 Aug 1799). Even Aesop's easy fables require thought for their application.

Blake's great task was "to open the immortal Eyes of Man inwards, into the Worlds of Thought" (*J* 5:18). A thought is wholly true only the first time it is said. At second hand, it is just that much nearer falsity; and at third hand it may have completely reversed its meaning. "Christs crucifix shall be made an Excuse for Executing Criminals" (*FZ*, end of Night iv, *K* 380, 904). But Blake's reader cannot accept passively what Blake writes, as he cannot understand it. He must dig, participate actively; thus Blake's thought is kept living and his ideas fresh. "[Symbolism] address'd to the Intellectual powers, while it is altogether hidden from the Corporeal Understanding, is My Definition of the Most Sublime Poetry" (To Butts, 6 July 1803).

Therefore, to rouse the Intellectual Powers while baffling the Corporeal Understanding, Blake deliberately confused his prophetic books. He introduced flat contradictions, which can be resolved only when the meaning is understood; then they turn out to be clues. He furnished some definitions. Jerusalem is Liberty, he tells us twice (*J* 26:3; 54:5), but to understand her, you find you have to think out exactly what Liberty really is. Other definitions turn out to be only extended applications. System there is, but it must be discovered. Narrative there is, but it is a dream narrative which does not obey the conventional rules for story-plotting. None of it makes sense until we apply it to the workings of the human mind.

"I give you the end of a golden [intellectual] string, | Only wind it into a ball, | It will lead you in at Heaven's gate | Built in Jerusalem's wall" (*J* 77). Blake scattered his clues broadcast throughout his writings. They form a prodigious jigsaw puzzle. Pieces are missing; pieces which ought to belong don't quite fit. Nevertheless, assembling what we can, we find that not only does a section fit together, but that it also makes amazing good sense which might have been obvious from the first.

Thus Blake, secure behind his symbols in a time of severe thought-control, was free to write whatever he chose. He could say what he thought of George III and all kings; he could prove to his own satisfaction that the Decalogue was not written by the true God; that the Christian cult of chastity had blighted our world for eighteen centuries; and that the congregations of most churches were really worshipping the Devil. Furthermore, he was inciting his readers to agree with him.

But you need not believe a word he says; you will not—indeed, you cannot —until you discover what he is talking about. Even then, you will not believe him unless you know of yourself that he is telling a truth. "Truth can never be told so as to be understood, and not be believ'd" (*MHH* 10). Real faith is the opening of the eyes to self-evident truths; it is not closing them to inconvenient facts.

Blake had no desire to found a new religion. "I know my power," he said, through the mask of Milton, to the great error Satan, "thee to annihilate and be a greater in thy place . . . till one greater comes and smites me as I smote thee" (*Mil* 38:29). He was no authoritarian. He wanted nobody to take anything on his say-so; he challenged opposition, for in the great warfare over ideas, "Opposition is true Friendship" (*MHH* 20). "Religion" was generally a bad word with him; in his millennium, "the dark Religions are departed & sweet Science reigns" (*FZ* ix:855—the last line of the epic).

Every sect is self-limited, whereas Truth is universal. Instead of any religion, Blake wanted the truth—the whole truth including all errors, life including death, the soul including the body, the world of mind including the world of matter, the profound discoveries of the mystics reconciled with the scoffings of the skeptics, heaven and hell married and working together, and in the ultimate heart, Man eternally in the arms of God.

The purpose of this dictionary is to make things easier for his readers by gathering together the clues scattered through his writings. These gatherings most often have shed welcome light. At other times, when the meaning has not made itself clear, I have at least laid out the material for future scholars. Some articles which contain material not readily available are rather extensive. Others, such as those on Painting and Poetry, which might have been whole books, are limited to what Blake himself said on the subject; consequently they may seem inadequate.

As Blake saw everything in human terms, practically anything might be a symbol; but it has not been feasible to write an article on every noun, especially as many of them have little or no symbolic significance. Blake, who was a painter and a poet as well as a mystic, often used objects solely for their poetic values. "Silver," for example, may be only a color ("wash the dusk with silver," *PS*, "To the Evening Star" 10; "[wings] silvery white, shining upon the dark blue sky in silver," *FZ* viii:11), or a sound ("silver voices," *FZ* v:24), or money ("the gold & silver of the Merchant," *J* 64:23). It may indicate temperament ("girls of mild silver or of furious gold," *VDA* 7:24). But eventually and fundamentally, as the metal of Luvah, it signifies Love. It is also convenient to remember that "gold" signifies "intelligence." Winding up the golden ball means using one's head. It is generally safe also to assume that Water is Matter, as in Noah's Flood, but the fountains of the Holy Ghost and the rivers of Eden are not. One must obey common sense. Blake's symbols are not mechanical or inflexible.

I have included some material which might not seem to need explanation to British readers. A foreigner could search in vain for Blake's "Pancrass" in map, atlas, and gazetteer; whereas every Londoner knows that "Pancrass" was a saint, and "St. Pancras" is an important railway station. Moreover, since Blake's day, London has expanded enormously, absorbing and destroying the outlying villages which the boy Blake loved. I have included all Biblical characters and place-names, for even the Biblical scholar cannot always identify quickly such names as Araunah, Eliakim, or Uzzah, and especially those Hebrew terms not used in the King James translation.

As a Blake Concordance is in preparation, I have not included items which have no particular symbolic significance, such as Nerves, Nightingale, and the Nile. I have omitted historical characters in *King Edward the Third* and *The French Revolution*, incidental characters in *Poetical Sketches* and *An Island in the Moon*, and Blake's contemporaries in the arts, such as Sir Joshua Reynolds.

It is not the intention of this book to compile digests of the works of other scholars or to confute their theories. I have felt it better to make a new start and to attempt to present fresh evaluations of Blake's symbols.

But Blake cannot be contained in any dictionary. Even his simplest and clearest statements have vast implications behind them. I have merely untied some knots and shaken out some tangles in the Golden String. When a final answer has not been possible, I have tried to assemble the material for others to work on. The important thing to remember is that he was always writing about the human soul.

Blake is a challenge to every thinking person. He was so far ahead of his times that we are just catching up to him. Many of his once strange theories are now commonplaces to the psychologist. It is not recorded that any of his friends ever asked him to explain anything. No doubt they did, but they got put off. A poet hates to "explain" his work: it should speak for itself. Seemingly his friends tolerated Blake's gnomisms as a harmless and wholly pardonable eccentricity. Yet he could talk freely enough to Crabb Robinson about his general ideas. And no reader today could possibly mistake what Blake believed about such fundamentals as the Holiness of all Life, the Brotherhood of Man, the Forgiveness of Sins, and the God within us.

Brown University   S. FOSTER DAMON

A

BLAKE

DICTIONARY

NOTE   All textual references, unless otherwise indicated, are to *The Complete Writings of William Blake*, edited by Geoffrey Keynes, London and New York, 1957. (It is *not* the "Centenary Edition.") This is the only edition containing all Blake's writings, with numbered lines. I have followed this numbering, which goes by the plates (not by chapters); thus the lines in *Jerusalem*, Chapter iii, " 'Doth Jehovah Forgive a Debt only on condition that it shall | be Payed?' " will be located as *J* 61:17. However, in the cases of *Tiriel* and *The Four Zoas*, which Blake never published, and which consequently have no plate numbers, references are given by section and line; thus a line from Night the Ninth of *The Four Zoas*, "But in the Wine Presses the Human Grapes sing not nor dance," is located as *FZ* ix:748. In quotations from Blake's prose, and from poems whose titles do not appear in the Table of Contents of *The Complete Writings*, I have given the Keynes pagination. Names are usually spelled as Blake himself spelled them.

It will be noted that I have sometimes disagreed with Sir Geoffrey's reading of the text; and like all Blake scholars, I have felt free to repunctuate in the interest of clarity.

Abbreviations

Ahan   The Book of Ahania
AllR   All Religions are One
Am   America, a Prophecy
Aug   Auguries of Innocence

Bentley   G. E. Bentley, Jr., Vala, Oxford, 1963
Bishop   Morchard Bishop, Blake's Hayley, London, 1951
Blunt   Anthony Blunt, The Art of William Blake, New York, 1959
BoL   The Book of Los
Bryant   Jacob Bryant, A New System, 3rd ed., London, 1807

Chron   Chronicles
Col   Colossians
Cor   Corinthians
CR   Crabb Robinson, in Arthur Symons, William Blake, New York, 1907

Damon   S. Foster Damon, William Blake, His Philosophy and Symbols, London and New York, 1924
DesC   A Descriptive Catalogue
Deut   Deuteronomy

EG   The Everlasting Gospel
Ellis and Yeats   E. J. Ellis and W. B. Yeats, eds., The Works of William Blake, London, 1893
Eph   Ephesians
Epig   Epigrams, Verses, and Fragments from The Note-Book (ca. 1808–11)
Erd   David V. Erdman, Blake, Prophet Against Empire, Princeton, 1954
Eur   Europe, a Prophecy
Exod   Exodus
Ezek   Ezekiel

FQ   Spenser, The Faerie Queene
FR   The French Revolution
Frye   Northrop Frye, Fearful Symmetry, Princeton, 1947
FZ   The Four Zoas

Gal   Galatians
Gen   Genesis
Geof   Geoffrey of Monmouth, Historia Britonum
GhA   The Ghost of Abel
Gil   Alexander Gilchrist, Life of William Blake, London, 1st ed., 1863; 2nd ed., 1880 (2nd ed. referred to unless otherwise specified)
Gleckner   Robert F. Gleckner, The Piper and the Bard, Detroit, 1959
GoP   The Gates of Paradise
Goyder   George Goyder, Introduction to William Blake's Illustrations to the Bible, Geoffrey Keynes, comp., London, 1957

Harper   George Mills Harper, The Neoplatonism of William Blake, Chapel Hill, 1961
Heb   Hebrews

Illustr Job   Illustrations of The Book of Job Invented & Engraved by William Blake
IslM   An Island in the Moon

J   Jerusalem
Josh   Joshua

K   Geoffrey Keynes, ed., The Complete Writings of William Blake, London and New York, 1957
K Census   Geoffrey Keynes and Edwin Wolf II, comps., William Blake's Illuminated Books: A Census, New York, 1953
K Studies   Geoffrey Keynes, Blake Studies, London, 1949

Lam   Lamentations
Laoc   Laocoön plate
LJ   A Vision of the Last Judgment
"LJ"   "A Vision of the Last Judgment," Rosenwald version as reproduced and keyed in the Illustrations at the end of this book

Malkin   Benjamin Heath Malkin, A Father's Memoirs of his Child, London, 1806
Marg Vala   H. M. Margoliouth, ed., Vala, Blake's Numbered Text, Oxford, 1956
Marg WB   H. M. Margoliouth, William Blake, Oxford, 1951
Matt   Matthew
MHH   The Marriage of Heaven and Hell
Mil   Milton, a Poem
Miner   Paul Miner, "William Blake's London Residences," New York Public Library Bulletin, November 1958

NNR   There is No Natural Religion
Numb   Numbers

On Swed DL   Annotations to Swedenborg's Wisdom of Angels Concerning Divine Love and Divine Wisdom
On Swed DP   Annotations to Swedenborg's The Wisdom of Angels Concerning Divine Providence

Phil   Philippians
PL   Milton, Paradise Lost
PS   Poetical Sketches
PubA   Public Address

Rev   Revelation
Roe   Albert S. Roe, Blake's Illustrations to the Divine Comedy, Princeton, 1953
Rom   Romans

Sam   Samuel
SoE   Songs of Experience
SoI   Songs of Innocence
SoL   The Song of Los
Song of Sol   The Song of Solomon
Symons   Arthur Symons, William Blake, New York, 1907

Thel   The Book of Thel
Thess   Thessalonians
Tir   Tiriel
To Butts   Letter to Thomas Butts

Ur   The Book of Urizen

VDA   Visions of the Daughters of Albion

Wilson   Mona Wilson, The Life of William Blake, London, 1927

Illustrations by Blake and Maps are at the end of the Dictionary.

A

ABARIM is a mountain range east of the Dead Sea. From Mount Abarim, Moses beheld the Promised Land (*Numb* xxvii:12).

It is one of the six mountains surrounding Palestine which are equated with Milton's Sixfold Emanation, his three wives and his three daughters (*Mil* 17:16).

ABEL, the second child of Adam and Eve, was killed by his brother Cain.

Blake was not interested in the victim of this first of murders, but he was very much interested in the result: the desire for vengeance on the criminal, which became the *lex talionis*, "life for life" (*Exod* xxi:23), a law abrogated by the Forgiveness of Sins. This voice of Abel's blood crying to the Lord (*Gen* iv:10) Blake personified as the "ghost of Abel," which Eve instantly recognized as not the real Abel at all (*GhA* 13), who she perceives is still living, though terribly afflicted.

Therefore, in *A Vision of the Last Judgment* (*K* 606), "Abel kneels on a bloody cloud descriptive of those Churches before the flood, that they were fill'd with blood & fire & vapour of smoke." See Illustrations.

In the painting illustrating Hervey's *Meditations Among the Tombs* (see Illustrations), both Abel and Cain flee from the Serpent, as though Adam and Eve's division of things into Good and Evil were carried out in their progeny.

ABERDEEN is a county of Scotland which, with Berwick and Dumfries, is assigned to Judah (*J* 16:54). With the rest of Scotland it is assigned to Bowen (*J* 71:46).

The ABOMINATION OF DESOLATION is a mysterious apocalyptic phrase used by Daniel (ix:27; xi:31; xii:11), and quoted by Jesus: "But when ye shall see the abomination of desolation, spoken of by Daniel the prophet, standing where it ought not, (let him that readeth understand,) then let them that be in Judaea flee to the mountains" (*Mark* xiii:14; *Matt* xxiv:15–16).

"This is the Spectre of Man, the Holy Reasoning Power, and in its Holiness is closed the Abomination of Desolation" (*J* 10:15). It is also "State Religion, which is the source of all Cruelty" (On Watson, *K* 393). It is the enemy of Holy Generation, birthplace of the Lamb (*J* 7:70). But it is also the flesh: "These are the Sexual Garments, the Abomination of Desolation, hiding the Human Lineaments as with an Ark & Curtains, which Jesus rent & now shall wholly purge away with Fire till Generation is swallow'd up in Regeneration" (*Mil* 41:25).

ABRAHAM (Abram), the great patriarch, was born in Ur, a city of Chaldea. Under divine command, he fled with his family from the idolaters to Canaan, where God promised him that he should be father to a great nation, and changed his name from Abram ("father of elevation") to Abraham ("father of multitudes").

According to Blake, Abraham was born into that primitive religion of human sacrifice which Blake called Druidism (*J* 27). He fled from Chaldea "in fire" of inspiration (*SoL* 3:16), "shaking his goary locks" (*J* 15:28). Evidently his locks became "goary" from the human sacrifices of Chaldea, and were not a reminiscence of Banquo's ghost. To Blake, his flight meant his renunciation of such sacrifices (as exemplified by his substitution of a ram for Isaac), which started a new era in religion.

"Abraham was called to succeed the Druidical age, which began to turn allegoric and mental signification into corporeal command, whereby human sacrifice would have depopulated the earth" (*DesC* V, *K* 578). Even until his time the "blood & fire & vapour of smoke" of the earlier churches were not extinguished (*LJ*, *K* 606).

Thus in the cycle of the Twenty-seven Churches, Abraham is the twenty-first, and the first of the last septenary, "the Male Females" of Moral Virtue (*Mil* 37:41; *J* 75: 16). Los created him as one of the prophets to offset the Satanic kings (*J* 73:41). His children were the Hebrew Church (*LJ*, *K* 610), and he himself was an ancestor of Jesus (*J* 27). Reuben, however, "enroots his brethren in the narrow Canaanite" (the merchants) "from the Limit Noah to the Limit Abram" (the preceding cycle of the Twenty-seven Churches); but in Abram's loins, "Reuben in his Twelve-fold majesty & beauty shall take refuge as Abraham flees from Chaldea" (*J* 15:25–28).

Jerusalem, Plate 15, depicts the flight of Abram from Chaldea, opposed by the vegetated Reuben.

An ABSTRACTION is a generalization based on reality, but which when substituted for reality becomes hostile to humanity. In Blake's writings, "abstract" usually can be translated "non-human." It is "opposed to the Visions of Imagination" (*J* 74:26).

Orthodox religion is such an abstraction. Priesthood "enslav'd the vulgar by attempting to realize or abstract the mental deities from their objects" (*MHH* 11). The parson with his "nets & gins & traps" surrounds the farmer "with cold floods of abstraction, and with forests of solitude" in order to take his money and build "castles and high spires, where kings & priests may dwell"

(*VDA* 5:18). "And this is the manner of the Sons of Albion in their strength: they take the Two Contraries which are call'd Qualities, with which every Substance is clothed: they name them Good & Evil; from them they make an Abstract, which is a Negation not only of the Substance from which it is derived, a murderer of its own Body, but also a murderer of every Divine Member: it is the Reasoning Power, an Abstract objecting power that Negatives every thing. This is the Spectre of Man, the Holy Reasoning Power, and in its Holiness is closed the Abomination of Desolation" (*J* 10:7).

As abstractions are the invention of logic, Urizen is the great abstracter. At the very beginning he is "unknown, abstracted" (*Ur* 3:6), and at the end, Albion bids him "come forth from slumbers of thy cold abstraction" (*FZ* ix:129). Fuzon, in denouncing Urizen, calls him "this abstract nonentity" (*Ahan* 2:11). "The Human Abstract" (*SoE*) describes the origin and growth of his Tree of Mystery. When Orc begins to reptilize under Urizen's influence, he turns "affection into fury, & thought into abstraction" (*FZ* vii:155).

Blake learned early from Lavater (*K* 86) that "all abstraction is temporary folly"; and he complained later to Butts (11 Sept 1801) that "my Abstract folly hurries me often away while I am at work, carrying me over Mountains & Valleys, which are not Real, in a Land of Abstraction where Spectres of the Dead wander."

ACHITOPHEL ("Ahithophel" in the King James Version) was the wise counsellor of King David. However, he conspired against him with Absalom, and when he knew that the conspiracy had failed, he hanged himself (*II Sam* xvii:23). Blake ranked him with Caiaphas, Pilate, and Judas: "Achitophel is also here with the cord in his hand" (*LJ*, *K* 608).

ADAH, a Cainite, was one of the two wives of Lamech, the first polygamist (*Gen* iv:19). Blake listed her as the eleventh daughter of Los and Enitharmon, in the line from

Ocalythron to Mary (*FZ* viii:365). In the revised list of the Maternal Line, she is a daughter of Vala, second in the line from Cainah to Mary (*J* 62:9).

ADAM ("red earth") was the first human being. His creation was a comparatively late episode in the general fall of man (Albion). "Satan & Adam & the whole World was Created by the Elohim" in Albion's "Chaotic State of Sleep" (*J* 27).

In Blake's day, the first two chapters of *Genesis* were read as a consecutive tale, not as two independent accounts of the same event. Consequently, there were two stages of Adam's creation: the first, when he was made in the image of God (*Gen* i:27); the second, when he was made of the dust (*Gen* ii:7). Later, the Lord was to repent "that he had made Adam (of the Female, the Adamah) & it grieved him at his heart" (*Laoc, K* 776—revised from *Gen* vi:6; see ADAMAH).

Adam originally contained both sexes. Blake confused Crabb Robinson on this point by talking of "a union of sexes in man as in Ovid, an androgynous state" (*CR* 263, 296). This theory, which Blake might have got from Plato, seemed indicated by the text "And God created man in his own image, in the image of God created he him; male and female created he them" (*Gen* i: 27). The sexes were not separated until the creation of Eve, when Adam was "divided into Male and Female" (Blake's MS. *Genesis*, Chap. ii; *Damon* 221). But it was Jesus himself who divided the sexes in creating Eve (*J* 35 [31], illustr.) that "Himself may in process of time be born Man to redeem" (*J* 42:34).

Blake made much of the statement that the Elohim was the creator of Adam, for he was not the supreme Jehovah (*CR* 298), but was only the third Eye of God. See ELOHIM. "[The Eternals] sent Elohim, who created Adam to die for Satan. Adam refus'd, but was compell'd to die by Satan's arts" (*FZ* viii:401). But first the merciful Jesus fixed two limits to the Fall. "The Divine hand found the Two Limits, first of Opacity, then

of Contraction. Opacity was named Satan, Contraction was named Adam" (*Mil* 13: 20). This event took place between the failure of the second Eye and before the coming of the third. Jesus found these two limits in Albion's bosom "while yet those two beings were not born nor knew of good or Evil" (*FZ* iv:271–74). They are to be found in every individual man (*J* 42:30; see also *J* 35:1; 73:28).

On the Laocoön plate, Satan and Adam are the two sons of Yod, "the Angel of the Divine Presence" (*K* 775). Adam is thus the younger brother of Satan. Their relationship is shown most clearly in the illustration on *Milton* 33. The "Mundane Egg" (*Mil* 25:42) is superimposed on the four flaming Zoas, and is divided into two parts. The lower part, labelled "Satan," is mostly in the sphere of Urizen; the infernal flames reach into the upper part, labelled "Adam." Thus Adam is the conscious mind and Satan the subconscious, the source of Energy. See MUNDANE EGG. As the two sons of Laocoön, they are entwined with the serpents of Good and Evil, which also are killing their father. Adam struggles with the serpent labelled "Good"; and the name of his first wife, Lilith, is written there. See LILITH.

Adam and Eve remained in the state of Innocence until the Serpent persuaded Eve to eat the fruit of the forbidden Tree of the Knowledge of Good and Evil, promising her that "ye shall be as gods [*Elohim*—judges], knowing good and evil" (*Gen* iii: 5). The Original Sin therefore was judging others by moral values.

After she had persuaded Adam to eat also, they were instantly ashamed of their nakedness. Shame was the first sign of Experience; the second was hiding from God. Their first two children exhibited their error, for Cain was evil and Abel was good. The evil slew the good. For Adam, who contained all the souls of future mankind, according to rabbinical tradition, contained warring elements: he is "Peleg ['division'] & Joktan ['who is made small,' his brother], & Esau & Jacob, & Saul & David" (*J* 73:28).

The fallen Adam "is only The Natural Man & not the Soul or Imagination" (*Laoc, K* 776; *Damon* 221); he is Rousseau's Natural Man. He is also the conscious part of the mind. As the Limit of Contraction, he is the lowest point to which man can shrink. In the illustration to Young's *Night Thoughts,* "*Sense* and *Reason* Shew the Door" (iv:136), Blake followed Milton in representing Reason as Adam and Sense as Eve; but he contradicted Young by having them point upwards as well as down, and the door is Gothic, with angels for archivolts.

"Satan & Adam are States Created into Twenty-seven Churches" (*Mil* 32:25). None of these is named for Satan: as Error he includes them all. Adam leads the cycle, being the first of the nine from Adam to Lamech (the father of Noah, who begins the second group). These nine were mighty giants (having lived before the Flood); they were "hermaphroditic," being self-contradictory and unsynthesized (*Mil* 37:36; *J* 13:32; 75:11). "And where Luther ends Adam begins again in Eternal Circle" (*J* 75:24). These churches before the Flood were "fill'd with blood & fire & vapour of smoke; even till Abraham's time the vapor & heat was not extinguish'd; these States Exist now" (*LJ, K* 606).

Adam is the nineteenth son of Los and Enitharmon (*FZ* viii:360); he is preceded by Satan (error), Har (self-love), Ochim (woes), and Ijim (animal lusts). He is the first of the prophets created by Los, to offset the line of kings created by Satan (*J* 73:41). He is reduced to a skeleton by the laws of Urizen, while Noah, the man of vision with whom he is contrasted, becomes leprous (*SoL* 3:6, 10; 7:20). He is equated with Scofield (*J* 7:25, 42); Hand and Scofield in their innocence were united as one man, Adam (*J* 60:16).

In *The Marriage of Heaven and Hell,* Blake prophesied Adam's return into Paradise (*MHH* 3).

The CAVE OF ADAM, obviously meaning the skull, is the place where Reuben sleeps while his senses are being limited (*J* 36:5).

But Blake may also have intended to refer to "the city Adam" (Adamah), which was beside Zaretan, approximately half way between that city and Succoth (*Josh* iii:16).

ADAMAH is a feminine noun meaning "earth," used in *Genesis* vi:6: "And it repented the Lord that he had made man on the earth, and it grieved him at his heart." Blake retranslated this passage: "He repented that he had made Adam (of the Female, the Adamah) & it grieved him at his heart" (*Laoc, K* 776). In other words, the creator of man (the Elohim) repented that he had made man with a mortal body, the mortal body being given by the female.

The ADONA is a river beside which Thel laments (*Thel* 1:4). The name was suggested by the river Adonis, where the Syrian damsels lamented in amorous ditties the annual wounding of Thammuz (*PL* i:450).

AFRICA is the first in the clockwise cycle of the four continents. It is the state of slavery, historically illustrated by Pharaoh's oppression of the Israelites. See EGYPT. The name "Africa" does not occur in the Bible; Blake's statement that its name was originally Egypt (*Ur* 28:10) would signify that the Egyptian bondage typified all slavery.

According to *The Book of Urizen* civilization originated in Africa. Being in the south, it is under Urizen, whose Net of Religion shrank and materialized its inhabitants. "Six days they shrunk up from existence, and on the seventh day they rested, and they bless'd the seventh day, in sick hope, and forgot their eternal life. And their thirty cities divided in form of a human heart. . . . They lived a period of years; then left a noisom body to the jaws of devouring darkness. And their children wept, & built tombs [the pyramids] in the desolate places, and form'd laws of prudence, and call'd them the eternal laws of God. . . . Perswasion was in vain; for the ears of the inhabitants were wither'd & deafen'd & cold, and their eyes could not discern their brethren of other cities" (25:39; 28:1–18). "Africa" is the first of the two sections of *The Song of Los*. "He sung it to four harps at the tables of Eternity. In heart-formed Africa Urizen faded! Ariston shudder'd!" (3:2). The song tells of the enslavement of man by Urizen's laws and religions promulgated by the prophets, "the children of Los." "Black grew the sunny African when Rintrah gave Abstract Philosophy to Brama in the East" (3:10). A résumé of the other religions follows. "Thus the terrible race of Los & Enitharmon gave Laws & Religions to the sons of Har [self-love], binding them more and more to Earth, closing and restraining, till a Philosophy of Five Senses was complete. Urizen wept & gave it into the hands of Newton & Locke" (4:13). Error is now complete, and Revolution is imminent. "Clouds roll heavy upon the Alps round Rousseau & Voltaire . . . The Guardian Prince of Albion burns in his nightly tent" (4:18, 21). This last line is repeated as the first of the narrative of *America*, which continues the tale and the cycle.

A reference to the revolt of the Surinam slaves, described in J. G. Stedman's *Narrative* (1793), appears in *Jerusalem* (45:19): "When Africa in sleep rose in the night of Beulah and bound down the Sun & Moon, his friends cut his strong chains & overwhelm'd his dark machines in fury & destruction, and the Man reviving repented: he wept before his wrathful brethren, thankful & considerate for their well timed wrath."

AGAG was the king of the Amalekites. Samuel ordered Saul to exterminate them all, with their possessions. Saul, however, spared King Agag and the best of the booty. Samuel denounced Saul and hewed Agag in pieces before the Lord in Gilgal (*I Sam* xv).

The Spectre constricts "into Druid Rocks round Canaan, Agag & Aram & Phar[a]oh" (*J* 54:26).

AGRIPPA von Nettesheim (Heinrich Cor-

nelius, 1486–1535) was one of the brilliant men of his generation. He was secretary to Maximilian I, Holy Roman Emperor, who sent him to Paris on a diplomatic mission in 1506, and again in 1510 to England, where he was the guest of Dean Colet. Later he was archivist and historiographer to the Emperor Charles V. He was also physician to the mother of Francis I. As a theologian he attended the council of Pisa in 1511.

He was in trouble with the Church three times. In 1509 he was obliged to resign his lectureship at the University of Dole because of his lectures on Reuchlin's *De verbo mirifice*; in 1515, he was forced from the University of Pavia for his lectures on the *Divine Pimander* of Hermes Trismegistus; and in 1518 he was forced to resign as syndic at Metz because he persistently defended a woman accused of witchcraft.

The Inquisition prevented the publication of his *De occulta philosophia* (1510), which he wrote probably under the influence of his friend the Abbot John Trithemius; but it finally was printed at Antwerp in 1531. It was a system of world philosophy, a synthesis of Christianity, Platonism, and Kabbalism, in which he defended magic as a means for understanding God and Nature. It gave him his popular reputation of being a magician. His *De incertitudine et vanitate scientiarum et artium* (written 1527, pub. 1531) was a satire in which he renounced all the occult arts except alchemy.

Blake in his early days, when searching for significant names for his characters, took "Tiriel" and "Zazel" from the tables of the planets in the *Occult Philosophy* II, xxii. The mysterious "Mne Seraphim" in the first line of *The Book of Thel* was apparently an alteration, in the interest of gender, of "Bne Seraphim" ("Sons of the Seraphim," the intelligencies of Venus) which occurs in the same tables.

AHANIA, or Pleasure, is the Emanation of Urizen. The division of the two is caused by the fact that Urizen, the Abstract Philosopher, has yet to learn "that Enjoyment &

not Abstinence is the food of Intellect" (To Cumberland, 6 Dec 1795).

The original tale of their division and her casting out is told in *The Book of Ahania* (1795). Once she had rejoiced when Urizen returned in the evening, the sweat pouring from his temples, after his sowing the seed of eternal science in the human soul (5:28–36); but when Fuzon's globe of wrath divided Urizen's loins, she became a separate being (2:32). Urizen named her "Sin" and jealously hid her in darkness, where she became a faint shadow, the "mother of Pestilence" (2:43). The poem ends with her splendid lament.

Blake suppressed *The Book of Ahania* and recast her tale in *The Four Zoas* (ii; iii; ix). She is Urizen's "Shadowy Feminine Semblance" (ii:181). They have twelve sons (ii:173, 199), who are the signs of the Zodiac, and three daughters (ii:175, 189), who are the Head, Heart, and Loins (see URIZEN'S DAUGHTERS). But Urizen resents Ahania's influence and does not take her to the nuptial feast of Los and Enitharmon; consequently, "Urizen with faded radiance sigh'd, forgetful of the flowing wine and of Ahania, his Pure Bride; but she was distant far" (i: 436). When he is away, "Trembling, cold, in paling fears she sat, a shadow of Despair; therefore toward the West, Urizen form'd a recess in the wall for fires to glow upon the pale Female's limbs in his absence" (ii:186). When he does return, "Astonish'd & Confounded he beheld her shadowy form now separate . . . Two wills they had, two intellects, & not as in times of old" (ii:203, 206). To divide them further, Los and Enitharmon contrive to let Ahania hear Enion's lament and see her "Spectrous form . . . in the Void, and never from that moment could she rest upon her pillow" (ii:287–90, 383–84, 419, 423–24).

Distressed at Urizen's gloom, Ahania pleads with him: "Why wilt thou look upon futurity, dark'ning present joy?" (iii: 11); he replies that he fears the birth of Orc, "& that Prophetic boy must grow up to command his Prince" (iii:18). Ahania tells him to leave the future to the Eternal One,

and recounts her vision of the Darkening Man worshipping his own shadow, and of the smiting of man by Luvah (iii:27–104). Urizen in fury casts her out. "Shall the feminine indolent bliss, the indulgent self of weariness, the passive idle sleep, the enormous night & darkness of Death set herself up to give her laws to the active masculine virtue? Thou little diminutive portion that dar'st be a counterpart [Emanation], thy passivity, thy laws of obedience & insincerity are my abhorrence. Wherefore hast thou taken that fair form? Whence is this power given to thee? Once thou wast in my breast a sluggish current of dim waters on whose verdant margin a cavern shagg'd with horrid shades, dark, cool & deadly, where I laid my head in the hot noon after the broken clods had wearied me; there I laid my plow, & there my horses fed: and thou hast risen with thy moist locks into a wat'ry image reflecting all my indolence, my weakness & my death, to weigh me down beneath the grave into non Entity" (iii:114).

She falls "into the Caverns of the Grave & places of Human Seed where the impressions of Despair & Hope enroot for ever" (iii:142); there she wanders lamenting. Tharmas flees from her voice while she, with her eyes towards Urizen, bewails the state of the fallen Man (viii:487–532).

But at the Last Judgment, once Urizen gives up his attempt to control the other Zoas and the future, he is instantly restored to his pristine glory, and Ahania returns, only to die of joy, for Urizen's work is not yet done. He is to plow in the winter; then she shall awake every spring (ix:179–219). After the plowing, she rises like the harvest moon, and takes her place by Urizen at the feast (ix:344–53). When the Harvest and Vintage are done, she and the other three Emanations leave the feast and go to their looms.

Other references in *The Four Zoas*: Enitharmon deceives Los by assuming Ahania's form, then blames him for embracing her (ii:324, 328); Vala tells Tharmas that Enitharmon, Ahania, and Enion have hidden Luvah in the form of Orc (vii *b*:248).

In *Milton* 19:41, Ahania, rent apart into a desolate night, laments.

In *Jerusalem* 14:10–12, Los sees the four Emanations; Ahania, Enion, and Vala (but not Enitharmon) are described as three evanescent shades.

AHOLIAB and Bezaleel were divinely appointed to build the Ark, the Mercy Seat, the Tabernacle, and its furniture (*Exod* xxxi:1–11). The two are mentioned in "If it is True what the Prophets write" (*K* 543), as real artists whose works are preferable to the Roman and Greek gods.

AIR, one of the four Elements, is assigned to Urizen. It is materialized as Urizen's son Thiriel, the first to appear, "astonish'd at his own existence, like a man from a cloud born" (*Ur* 23:12).

Once Blake seems to touch upon the occult theory, which he could have found in Agrippa or Paracelsus, that nothing is ever lost but is preserved in the Air. "Hast thou forgot that the air listens thro' all its districts, telling the subtlest thoughts shut up from light in chambers of the Moon?" (*FZ* vii *b*:242). Even the subtlest thoughts of love are preserved.

AL-ULRO is the third state of humanity in its repose. It is situated in the loins and seminal vessels (*Mil* 34:12, 15). The first state is Beulah (head), the second is Alla (heart), the third is Al-Ulro, and the fourth is Or-Ulro (the digestive tract). Blake mentions this set of states only this one time.

ALBION is a common poetical name for England. When the Trojans land on the rocky shore of Albion, they call it "mother" (*PS, King Edward the Third* vi:14). Thereafter, through the minor prophecies, Blake used "Albion" simply as the name for England, without reference to gender. About 1793, he added a couple of lines to his engraving, the so-called "Glad Day," in which he gave the name of Albion to the dancing youth who symbolizes the politically awakened England. See ALBION'S DANCE, below.

Eventually Blake learned that "Albion" was the name of the aboriginal giant who conquered the island and renamed it for himself. Neither Geoffrey of Monmouth nor Milton mentions him, but Holinshed does (*Chronicles*, 1577), confusing the classical Albion (a son of Neptune who was killed by Hercules) with the local giant, who was killed by Brut. Camden (*Britannia*, 1586) refers to him, and Camden's admirer Spenser devoted a couple of stanzas to him (*FQ* II.x.11; IV.xi.15–16).

Meanwhile Blake had come to believe that fallen Man is sleeping with his "faded head" laid down "on the rock of eternity, where the eternal lion and eagle remain to devour" (*FR* 96). In *The Four Zoas* he gave the name Albion to the hitherto nameless "Eternal Man" or "Fallen Man" (*FZ* i:477, 485, etc.).

Albion is the father of all mankind (*FZ* ii:43). "He is Albion, our Ancestor, patriarch of the Atlantic Continent, whose History Preceded that of the Hebrews & in whose Sleep, or Chaos, Creation began" (*LJ*, *K* 609; *DesC* V, *K* 578, where he is identified with Atlas). But nothing of his history came from the legends of Holinshed and the others. He corresponds instead to Swedenborg's Grand Man and the Adam Kadmon of the Kabbalists.

Albion's wife is Brittannia (*LJ*, *K* 609; *J* 94:20, 26). When the Zoas changed their situations in the Universal Man, Brittannia "divided into Jerusalem & Vala" (*J* 36:28). Jerusalem is called the daughter of the two (*LJ*, *K* 609), but she is usually known as Albion's Emanation (*J* t.p.). Jesus took her as his bride, giving Vala to Albion as his bride (*J* 20:40; 63:7; 64:19; 65:71). This allocation of Emanations indicates the close bonds between God and Man. But the jealous Albion hid Jerusalem from the Saviour (*J* 4:33) and turned his back on the Divine Vision (*FZ* i:290, 558; ii:2; *J* 4:22, etc.), sinking into his deadly sleep.

This loss of the Divine Vision had terrible consequences. Albion's Emotions (Luvah) usurped the place of his Reason (Urizen) when those two Zoas were fighting over Albion's body sleeping in the holy tent (*FZ* i:484–544). Urizen left Luvah to pour his fury on Albion (*FZ* i:540). Luvah did this when Albion worshipped the "Shadow from his wearied intellect" (*FZ* iii:50). Luvah smote him with boils (*FZ* iii:82), whereupon Albion dismissed him, limiting his senses (iii:83).

Albion's sleep is also a wandering (*FZ* i: 478; v:221). "Now Man was come to the Palm tree & the Oak of Weeping which stand upon the edge of Beulah, & he sunk down from the supporting arms of the Eternal Saviour, who dispos'd the pale limbs of his Eternal Individuality upon the Rock of Ages, Watching over him with Love & Care" (*FZ* i:464). See ROCK OF AGES. Here Albion remains until the Last Judgment. Meanwhile Jesus (the Divine Council) elects the seven Eyes of God to protect the Man, whose inward eyes are "closing from the Divine vision, & all his children wandering outside, from his bosom fleeing away" (*FZ* i:553–59; cf. ii:43). "Turning his Eyes outward to Self, losing the Divine Vision" (*FZ* ii:2), Albion, in a last effort on his couch of death, delivers his sovereignty to Urizen (*FZ* ii:5).

In *The Four Zoas*, Albion does not reappear until the beginning of Night viii, when the Council of God (Jesus) meets "upon the Limit of Contraction to create the fallen Man" (viii:3), who lies upon the Rock, dreaming horrible dreams. "The limit of Contraction now was fix'd & Man began to wake upon the Couch of Death; he sneezed seven times [thus clearing his brain]; a tear of blood dropped from either eye; again he repos'd in the Saviour's arms, in the arms of tender mercy & loving kindness" (viii: 16). Later, Enion reports that Man is "collecting up the scatter'd portions of his immortal body into the Elemental forms of every thing that grows. . . . wherever a grass grows or a leaf buds, The Eternal Man is seen, is heard, is felt, and all his sorrows, till he reassumes his ancient bliss" (viii:562, 581).

The Last Judgment follows immediately upon the death of the physical body. Albion

wakes and laments his fallen state (ix:95–122). He then sits up and calls upon Urizen, to whom he had given his sovereignty when he fell asleep; but Urizen, now the Dragon, cannot answer (ix:123–35). Enraged, Albion blames Urizen as the cause of all the trouble, and threatens to cast him into the Indefinite forever (ix:136–61). Urizen repents, renouncing his attempts to control the other Zoas in fear of futurity, and is instantly rejuvenated (ix:162–93). Albion then tells Urizen of the Incarnation, and of the revolving seasons in Eden (ix: 204–25).

When the Lamb appears, Albion beholds again the Vision of God (ix:286), upon which long ago he had turned his back. He rises from the Rock and goes with Urizen to meet the Lord coming to Judgment, "but the flames repell'd them still to the Rock; in vain they strove to Enter the Consummation together, for the Redeem'd Man could not enter the Consummation" (ix:286–90). There is work to be done first.

The First Day, of Urizen's plowing and sowing, ends with the evening feast. "The Eternal Man also sat down upon the Couches of Beulah, sorrowful that he could not put off his new risen body in mental flames; the flames refus'd, they drove him back to Beulah. His body was redeem'd to be permanent thro' Mercy Divine" (ix:354). Orc has now burned out; Albion gives Luvah and Vala into the hands of Urizen (ix:358). After Urizen's reaping on the Second Day, "the Regenerate Man sat at the feast rejoicing" (ix:587). On the Third Day, Tharmas and Enion are rejuvenated and reunited. "The Eternal Man arose. He welcom'd them to the Feast. . . . And Many Eternal Men sat at the golden feast to see the female form now separate. They shudder'd at the horrible thing" (ix:617–22). These other Eternals "embrac'd the New born Man, calling him Brother, image of the Eternal Father" (ix:643). At the feast after the Fourth Day, the Eternal Man directs Luvah to gather the grapes (ix:693), but at the pressing he "darken'd with sorrow" and summoned Tharmas and Urthona to do their part (ix:693, 772). When Luvah and Vala had slept from exhaustion, they woke and "wept to one another & they reascended to the Eternal Man in woe: he cast them wailing into the world of shadows, thro' the air, till winter is over & gone" (ix:796).

On the Sabbath of the Seventh Day, "Man walks forth from midst of the fires: the evil is all consum'd. . . . The Expanding Eyes of Man behold the depths of wondrous worlds! . . . He walks upon the Eternal Mountains, raising his heavenly voice, conversing with the Animal forms of wisdom night & day . . . in the Vales around the Eternal Man's bright tent, the little Children play among the wooly flocks. . . ." (ix:827-40).

In *Milton*, Albion-Britain is waked from his deadly sleep by the association of the revolutionist Milton with Blake. As he descends, "First Milton saw Albion upon the Rock of Ages, deadly pale outstretch'd and snowy cold, storm cover'd, a Giant form of perfect beauty outstretch'd on the rock in solemn death: the Sea of Time & Space thunder'd aloud against the rock" (15:36-40). Then Milton "fell thro' Albion's heart, travelling outside of Humanity" (20:41). "Albion's sleeping Humanity began to turn upon his Couch, feeling the electric flame of Milton's awful precipitate descent" (20:25). Los calls: "Awake, thou sleeper on the Rock of Eternity! Albion awake! The trumpet of Judgment hath twice sounded [in the American and French Revolutions]: all Nations are awake, but thou art still heavy and dull. Awake, Albion awake! Lo, Orc arises on the Atlantic. Lo, his blood and fire glow on America's shore. Albion turns upon his Couch: he listens to the sounds of War, astonished and confounded: he weeps into the Atlantic deep, yet still in dismal dreams unwaken'd, and the Covering Cherub advances from the East" (23:3-10).

Satan, the Covering Cherub, is Albion's Spectre (32:12; 37:45). The seven Eyes trumpet: "Awake, Albion awake! reclaim thy Reasoning Spectre. Subdue him to the Divine Mercy. Cast him down into the Lake of Los that ever burneth with fire ever &

ever, Amen! Let the Four Zoas awake from Slumbers of Six Thousand Years" (39:10). When Satan appears in his true form, "Then Albion rose up in the Night of Beulah on his Couch of dread repose seen by the visionary eye: his face is toward the east, toward Jerusalem's Gates." His body covers the British Isles: his right hand covers Wales, his right elbow leans on Ireland, his left foot reaches from Windsor to Holloway, his right foot stretches to the Dover cliffs, with the heel "on Canterbury's ruins," and London is between his knees. But his strength fails, "& down with dreadful groans he sunk upon his Couch in moony Beulah" (39:32-52). However, in the mystical moment, "Jesus wept & walked forth from Felpham's Vale clothed in Clouds of blood, to enter into Albion's Bosom, the bosom of death" (42:19).

In *Jerusalem*, the fall and resurrection of Albion are studied in much more detail. The poem opens as Jesus calls on him to return (4:10), but Albion has turned away and in jealousy hidden his Emanation Jerusalem from her divine bridegroom. Blake sees "the Four-fold Man, The Humanity in deadly sleep and its fallen Emanation, The Spectre & its cruel Shadow" (15:6), and he implores the Divine Spirit to sustain him "that I may awake Albion from his long & cold repose" (15:10). "All his Affections [his Sons] now appear withoutside" (19:17). "Albion's Circumference was clos'd: his Center began dark'ning into the Night of Beulah" (19:36).

He flees inward and finds Jerusalem "soft repos'd in the arms of Vala" (19:40). In the colloquy that follows, it is told how Albion embraced Vala, rending her Veil; but although the Lamb gives Vala to Albion as bride, and takes Jerusalem for his own, both Albion and Vala are overwhelmed with guilt. His children and his whole universe are driven forth and separated from him by his disease of shame. "All is Eternal Death unless you can weave a chaste Body over an unchaste Mind!" (21:11). Therefore Albion commits himself to the materialism of the Moral Law, which is Vala's Veil. "He recoil'd: he rush'd outwards: he bore the Veil whole away. . . . He drew the Veil of Moral Virtue, woven for Cruel Laws, and cast it into the Atlantic Deep to catch the Souls of the Dead. He stood between the Palm tree & the Oak of weeping which stand upon the edge of Beulah, and there Albion sunk down in sick pallid languor" (23:20–26). His last words are his curse: "May God, who dwells in this dark Ulro & voidness, vengeance take" (23:38). But his lamentations are stopped suddenly by the appearance of the Saviour. "Dost thou appear before me, who liest dead in Luvah's Sepulcher? Dost thou forgive me, thou who wast Dead & art Alive? Look not so merciful upon me, O thou Slain Lamb of God! I die! I die in thy arms, tho' Hope is banish'd from me" (24:57). Hereafter, all that ensues before Albion's resurrection takes place in his dreams.

When the second chapter opens, the Moral Law is established. "Every ornament of perfection and every labour of love in all the Garden of Eden & in all the golden mountains was become an envied horror and a remembrance of jealousy, and every Act a Crime, and Albion the punisher & judge. . . . All these ornaments are crimes, they are made by the labours of loves, of unnatural consanguinities and friendships horrid to think of when enquired deeply into; and all these hills & valleys are accursed witnesses of Sin. I therefore condense them into solid rocks, stedfast, a foundation and certainty and demonstrative truth, that Man be separate from Man" (28:1–12). "He sat by Tyburn's brook [the gallows], and underneath his heel shot up a deadly Tree: he nam'd it Moral Virtue and the Law of God who dwells in Chaos hidden from the human sight" (28:14). "From willing sacrifice of Self, to sacrifice of (miscall'd) Enemies for Atonement, Albion began to erect twelve Altars . . . He nam'd them Justice and Truth" (28:20–23).

In the rearranged version, Plates 33–37 follow Plate 28, so that Albion's Spectre and Vala appear immediately after Albion sets himself up as Judge. "Turning his back to the Divine Vision, his Spectrous Chaos before his face appear'd, an Unformed Memory" (33:1). The Spectre announces: "I am your Rational Power, O Albion, & that Human Form you call Divine is but a Worm seventy inches long" (33:5). Vala then announces the supremacy of woman (33:48–34:1). While Los tries to get Reuben into the Promised Land, "the Divine hand found the Two Limits, Satan and Adam, in Albion's bosom" (35:1). Los calls on Albion to rouse himself; "Albion fled more indignant, revengeful covering his face and bosom with petrific hardness, and his hands and feet, lest any should enter his bosom & embrace his hidden heart" (37:12–38:3); yet the Saviour follows him, declaring the Universal Family of men in Jesus (38:10–26). Albion flees through the Gate of Los. "Seeing Albion had turn'd his back against the Divine Vision, Los said to Albion: 'Whither fleest thou?' Albion reply'd: 'I die! I go to Eternal Death! . . . God hath forsaken me . . .' " (39:11–23).

Los (now the Spectre of Urthona) and Enitharmon escape from Albion's darkening locks and report how Albion worshipped his own Shadow and cast forth Luvah, who had smitten him with boils (29:28–84; cf. FZ iii:44–104). When Los shows his labors to Albion, Albion sees that his would-be victims are his own affections. Furious, he orders Hand and Hyle to bring Los to justice. "And as Albion built his frozen Altars, Los built the Mundane Shell" (42:78).

The Twenty-eight Cathedral Cities kneel round Albion's Couch of Death (41:24); "with one accord in love sublime, & as on Cherubs' wings, they Albion surround with kindest violence to bear him back against his will thro' Los's Gate to Eden. . . . but Albion dark, repugnant, roll'd his Wheels backward into Non-Entity" (44:1–6).

War breaks out; again Albion utters his last words: " 'Hope is banish'd from me.' These were his last words; and the merciful Saviour in his arms reciev'd him, in the arms of tender mercy, and repos'd the pale limbs of his Eternal Individuality upon the Rock of Ages" (47:18–48:4).

In Chapter iii, Los builds Golgonooza "in the midst of the rocks of the Altars of Albion" (53:17). "But Albion fell down, a Rocky fragment from Eternity hurl'd by his own Spectre, who is the Reasoning Power in every Man, into his own Chaos, which is the Memory between Man & Man. The silent broodings of deadly revenge, springing from the all powerful parental affection, fills Albion from head to foot" (54:6). "Then Albion drew England [Brittannia] into his bosom in groans & tears, but she stretch'd out her starry Night in Spaces against him" (54:27). The Seven Eyes are established (55:30); the Plowing of the Nations begins (55:54). "But Albion fled from the Divine Vision; with the Plow of Nations enflaming, the Living Creatures madden'd, and Albion fell into the Furrow; and the Plow went over him & the Living was Plowed in among the Dead. But his Spectre rose over the starry Plow. Albion fled beneath the Plow till he came to the Rock of Ages, & he took his Seat upon the Rock" (57:12). War impends. "The clouds of Albion's Druid Temples rage in the eastern heaven while Los sat terrified beholding Albion's Spectre, who is Luvah [France], spreading in bloody veins in torments over Europe & Asia, not yet formed" (60:1). War breaks out: "Luvah's Cloud reddening above burst forth in streams of blood upon the heavens" (62:30). In the confusion that follows, Albion takes no part until his final awakening. "Albion cold lays on his Rock . . . England [Brittannia], a Female Shadow . . . lays upon his bosom heavy . . . And the Body of Albion was closed apart from all Nations. . . . Time was Finished! The breath Divine Breathed over Albion beneath the Furnaces & starry Wheels and in the Immortal Tomb. And England, who is Brittannia, awoke from Death on Albion's bosom" (94:1–20). She laments that she has murdered her husband "in Dreams of Chastity & Moral Law . . . with the Knife of the Druid. . . . O all ye Nations of the Earth, behold ye the Jealous Wife!" (94:22–26). Her voice wakes Albion; he rises in wrath and grasps his bow, compelling the Zoas to their proper tasks (95:1–18). Brittannia enters his bosom rejoicing (95:22; 96:2).

Then Jesus appears standing by Albion; they converse; the cloud of the Covering Cherub, who is Albion's Self (96:13), divides them (96:29); but Albion sacrifices himself for Jesus (96:35). Instantly all the terrors are a dream; the Zoas enter Albion's bosom (96:41); and Albion stands by Jesus in heaven, "Fourfold among the Visions of God in Eternity" (96:43). With his fourfold bow he annihilates the Druid Spectre (98:6), and Eternity is achieved in the mystical union of all things.

ALBION'S DANCE (often called "Glad Day") exists in two versions: a line engraving (ca. 1790) and a color print (ca. 1793). The engraving is signed "W. B. 1780," doubtless the date of Blake's original design. Albion, a nude irradiant youth with arms outspread, stands on a high eminence, rising above a black downpour from clouds in the background. Between his feet, a moth flies free of its chrysalis, signifying the new birth. In some copies, beneath is written: "Albion rose from where he labour'd at the Mill with Slaves: Giving himself for the Nations he danc'd the dance of Eternal Death." The subject is political: England rises spiritually above the Industrial Revolution and works for all nations. "Eternal Death" signifies complete self-sacrifice, and Albion's arms are in the position of the crucifixion.

In the color print, the initials, date, month, and inscription cannot be seen. From Albion expands a glory of primary colors.

In 1938 Anthony Blunt identified Albion's posture as that of the "Vitruvian Man." Vitruvius (De architectura, iii) had remarked that man's body is a model of proportion because with arms and legs extended it fits into the perfect geometrical forms, the square and the circle. The Renaissance artists made many attempts to fit the human body into these forms. The earliest known appears in the Trattato d'architettura by Francesco di Giorgio (1439–1502). The best known is that of Leonardo.

The nearest to Blake's is in Scamozzi's *Dell' idea dell' architettura universale* (1615). Blake could well have been impressed with the idea that Man thus represented the Microcosm; however, he disliked geometry, and omitted the geometrical forms from his picture. Later Blunt (*The Art of William Blake*, New York, 1959, p. 33 and plates) made a very convincing case that Blake was also influenced by a Roman bronze of a dancing faun.

The sunburst effect of the picture gave it early the title of "Glad Day," on the erroneous assumption that it was inspired by lines in *Romeo and Juliet* (III.v.9–10): "Night's candles are burnt out, and jocund day | Stands tiptoe on the misty mountain tops." But there are no candles and no mist, nor does the figure stand on tiptoe.

ALBION'S DAUGHTERS, in the *Visions of the Daughters of Albion*, are simply Englishwomen, enslaved in the social mores of their time, who weep over their sorrows and long for the freedom of the body, or "America" (*VDA* 1:1–2). They hear Oothoon's woes "& eccho back her sighs" (2: 20; 5:2; 8:13).

In the three major prophecies, however, the Daughters are twelve; they have names, personalities, and functions. They are listed first in an insertion in *The Four Zoas* (ii:61): Gwendolen, Ragan, Sabrina, Gonorill, Mehetabel, Cordella, Boadicea, Conwenna, Estrild, Gwinefrid, Ignoge, and Cambel, but are not mentioned again in the epic. A revised list appears in *Jerusalem* (5:40–44): Cambel, Gwendolen, Conwenna, Cordella, Ignoge, Gwiniverra, Gwinefred, Gonorill, Sabrina, Estrild, Mehetabel, and Ragan. Gwiniverra has replaced Boadicea, who is later equated with Cambel (*J* 71:23). This order is revised again when the Daughters are paired with the Sons (*J* 71:10–49).

The names, "names anciently remember'd, but now contemn'd as fictions" (*J* 5:38), are derived from Geoffrey of Monmouth's legendary *Historia Britonum* and Milton's *History of Britain*. Gwinefred alone seems to have no source; it is impossible that she could be the virgin martyr, St. Winifred, of the famous well. Mostly, they are a bad lot: queens, leaders of armies, adulteresses and mistresses, jealous wives, faithless daughters, bastard children. "In every bosom they controll our Vegetative powers" (*J* 5:39), for they are all aspects of the sexual strife. "And this is the manner of the Daughters of Albion in their beauty. Every one is threefold in Head & Heart & Reins, & every one has three Gates into the Three Heavens of Beulah, which shine translucent in their Foreheads & their Bosoms & their Loins surrounded with fires unapproachable: but whom they please they take up into their Heavens in intoxicating delight" (*Mil* 5:5–10). Five of them are under Tirzah: Cambel (the "Venus pudica"), Gwendolen, Conwenna, Cordella, and Ignoge; the other seven are under Rahab (*J* 5:40–44). They set up as Female Wills; they torture men; with their charms they infuriate the warriors to battle.

"They are the beautiful Emanations of the Twelve Sons of Albion" (*J* 5:45). When Albion is disintegrating they escape from him after the Sons (*J* 21:7). They come from the four Emanations of the Zoas (*J* 14:11). Albion is horrified when he learns that their childhood was not so innocent as he supposed (*J* 21:19–27).

As men communicate with others by means of their Emanations, the Twelve Daughters in their ideal state often work together and even produce each other. Hand and Hyle share Cambel and Gwendolen (*J* 71:23); Coban's Ignoge adjoins with Gwantoke's children and becomes the mother of Gwantoke's Cordella (*J* 71:28); Breretun's Ragan adjoins to Slade and produces Slade's Gonorill (*J* 71:33); Kox's Estrild joins with Gwantoke's Cordella (*J* 71:43); and Kotope's Sabrina joins with Peachey's Mehetabel (*J* 71:45).

In the apocalypse, "All the Sons & Daughters of Albion [rise] on soft clouds, waking from Sleep" (*J* 96:39).

For details, see BOADICEA, CAMBEL, CONWENNA, CORDELLA, ESTRILD,

GONORILL, GWENDOLEN, GWINE-
FRED, GWINIVERRA, IGNOGE, ME-
HETABEL, RAGAN, SABRINA. See also
ALBION'S SONS below.

ALBION'S SONS escape from his Bosom
when he falls into his deadly sleep (*J* 32:
10). They are his affections (*J* 19:17), or
the States of his Center, or Heart (*J* 71:9).
Their twelve names are Hand, Hyle, Coban, Guantok, Peachey, Brereton, Slade,
Hutton, Scofield, Kox, Kotope, and Bowen.
As eight of these names were derived from
those connected with Blake's trial for treason (Hayley, Quantock, Peachey, Brereton,
Hutton, Scofield, Cock, and Bowen), it may
be assumed that the other four were also
involved, although they have not been identified.

The last four are separated from the
others in the first listing (*J* 5:27); they are
"one" in Scofield, Blake's accuser (*J* 7:47);
and they are the only Sons assigned compass points (*J* 71:40, 43, 45, 48). They are
the Accusers; from which fact one might
assume that the first four are the Execu-
tioners (and Hand is certainly that), and
the middle four are the Judges. However,
this classification is not satisfactory. The
first three (Hand, Hyle, and Coban) are
grouped together six times (*Mil* 19:58;
23:15; *J* 8:41; 9:21; 18:41; 36:15), and are
evidently the Head, Heart, and Loins. The
next three (Guantok, Peachey, and Brereton) have been identified as three of Blake's
judges. This leaves Slade and Hutton un-
classified.

There is a further complication in the
fact that the Twelve Tribes are the spiritual
equivalents of the Twelve Sons. "And above
Albion's Land was seen the Heavenly Canaan as the Substance is to the Shadow,
and above Albion's Twelve Sons were seen
Jerusalem's Sons and all the Twelve Tribes
spreading over Albion. As the Soul is to
the Body, so Jerusalem's Sons are to the
Sons of Albion" (*J* 71:1). Hand, the first
of Albion's Sons, cuts the fibres of Reuben,
the first of the Tribes (*J* 90:25); similarly
Bowen, the last of the Sons, cuts the fibres

from Benjamin, the last Tribe (*J* 90:15).
But the allocation of counties to the Sons
and the Tribes do not correspond. Further
attempts to equate the two lists seem futile.

In their state of Innocence, the "Sons
came to Jerusalem with gifts; she sent them
away with blessings on their hands & on
their feet, blessings of gold and pearl &
diamond" (*J* 24:38). This perfect state,
when they dwell in the various Cathedral
Cities with their Emanations, is described
at length (*J* 71:10-49). But when they become separate from Albion, they rage to
devour his sleeping Humanity (*J* 5:30; 78:
2); they renounce their father and declare
war against him (*J* 18:13, 21), also against
the Saviour (*J* 18:37), the Imagination
(*J* 5:58), Golgonooza and Los's Furnaces
(*J* 5:29), Jerusalem (*J* 18:11), and Erin
(*J* 78:12). See ERIN.

They are Spectres (*J* 65:56; 66:15; 78:
1), having petrified their Emanations (*J*
8:43; 9:1). They have constructed an Abstract Philosophy to war against the Imagination (*J* 5:58). "And this is the manner
of the Sons of Albion in their strength:
they take the Two Contraries which are
call'd Qualities, with which Every Substance is clothed: they name them Good &
Evil; from them they make an Abstract,
which is a Negation not only of the Substance from which it is derived, a murderer
of its own Body, but also a murderer of
every Divine Member: it is the Reasoning
Power, an Abstract objecting power that
Negatives every thing" (*J* 10:7). "The
Spectre is the Reasoning Power in Man, &
when separated from Imagination and closing itself as in steel in a Ratio of the Things
of Memory, It thence frames Laws & Moralities to destroy Imagination, the Divine
Body, by Martyrdoms & Wars" (*J* 74:10).

When Albion establishes his Law, they
flee, being the first Transgressors (*J* 28:23;
48:61), "trembling victims of his Moral
Justice" (*J* 23:34). They assume the Providence of God and "slay" him (*J* 24:56),
and lay him on a golden couch round which
they rear "their Druid Patriarchal rocky
Temples" (*J* 32:14), preaching Vengeance

and "planting these Oaken Groves, Erecting these Dragon Temples" (*J* 25:4).

Although they began by crucifying Vala, whom Nimrod released (*J* 22:2), they soon hail her as their Goddess Virgin-Mother (*J* 18:29), crowning her with gold and giving her power over the Earth, "even to the stars exalting her Throne, to build beyond the Throne of God and the Lamb" (*J* 78: 15–20). "Furious in pride of Selfhood [they] rear their dark Rocks among the Stars of God" (*J* 58:48). They build the druid Stonehenge as Vala's temple, "Natural Religion & its Altars Natural Morality" (*J* 66: 2, 8).

They corrupt the Twenty-four Cathedral Cities, "raging against their Human natures, rav'ning to gormandize the Human majesty and beauty of the Twenty-four, condensing them into solid rocks with cruelty and abhorrence, suspition & revenge" (*J* 19:23; 42:48). However, when the Cities try to save man, they can still curb their Spectres severely (*J* 42:67), which "rage within" (*J* 41:25) and "cry out from the deeps beneath" (*J* 42:57).

The Sons become the twelve pagan gods (*Mil* 37:34; *J* 74:22).

They are murderous towards their Emanations, "the infant Loves & Graces ... infant thoughts & desires," which they petrify (*J* 8:44; 9:2). But Los builds Golgonooza to protect them (*J* 53:23); he dashes in pieces the Sons' "Self-righteousnesses ... lest they destroy the Feminine Affections" (*J* 78:6–8); and he bids the Daughters of Beulah to "separate Albion's Sons gently from their Emanations" (*J* 83:49). This separation is necessary because the Emanations have become Female Wills and the Sons' enemies. The two chief Emanations, "Cambel & Gwendolen wove webs of war & of religion to involve all Albion's sons, and when they had involv'd Eight, their webs roll'd outwards into darkness" (*J* 7:44). Their machinations are described at length later (*J* 80:37–82:79).

The Starry Wheels are the Sons'. See WHEELS. The twelve become "as Three Immense Wheels" (*J* 18:8; 8:34) which as

they turn rend a way into Albion's loins (*J* 18:43). These form the "Satanic Mill" of the Industrial Revolution (*J* 19:19); here the Sons grind the living and the dead "for bread of the Sons of Albion" (*J* 43:50). But Los fixes their systems "permanent, by mathematic power, giving a body to Fals[e]hood that it may be cast off for ever" (*J* 12:12).

The Twelve Sons are "enrooted into every Nation, a mighty Polypus growing from Albion over the whole Earth" (*J* 15: 4). Soon Hand, the selfish Head, absorbs them all (*J* 8:43), and becomes the Polypus. See POLYPUS.

"From these Twelve all the Families of England spread abroad" (*J* 5:33).

In the apocalpyse, "All the Sons & Daughters of Albion [rise] on soft clouds, waking from Sleep" (*J* 96:39).

For further details, see ALBION'S DAUGHTERS, above; also BOWEN, BRERETON, COBAN, GUANTOK, HAND, HUTTON, HYLE, KOTOPE, KOX, PEACHEY, SCOFIELD, SLADE.

ALL RELIGIONS ARE ONE (*ca.* 1788), a small tractate, perhaps Blake's first experiment in his illuminated printing, exists in only one copy.

It affirms that the Imagination ("the Poetic Genius") is "the true Man"; that it creates man's body and the forms of all things; that (allowing for infinite variety) all men are alike in the Poetic Genius; that all sects of philosophy are derived from it, "adapted to the weaknesses of every individual"; that all religions are derived from each nation's different reception of the Poetic Genius; and that the two Testaments "are an original derivation from the Poetic Genius."

Thus early Blake had completed his revolutionary theory of the nature of Man and proclaimed the unity of all true religions.

The influence of Lavater's *Aphorisms* is obvious. The very first two read: "Know, in the first place, that mankind agree in essence, as they do in their limbs and senses. Mankind differ as much in essence as they do in form, limbs, and senses—and only so, and not more." Blake commented: "This is true Christian philosophy far above all abstraction" (*K* 65).

Blake also probably had in mind Spenser's "For soule is forme, and doth the bodie make" (*Hymn to Beauty* 133).

ALLA is the second of the four States of Humanity in its repose; it is situated in the heart (*Mil* 34:12, 14). The other three are Beulah (head); Al-Ulro (loins); and Or-Ulro (digestive tract).

"Multitudes of those who sleep in Alla" are lured down by the war-music of the Covering Cherub, and are absorbed in the Antichrist (*J* 89:58).

ALLAMANDA is the nervous system of the vegetated man. It is constantly associated with Bowlahoola, which combines the respiratory, the circulatory, and the digestive systems; and often with Entuthon-Benython, the flesh and bones.

Allamanda, the nervous system, is the apparatus for giving and receiving communications. On earth it is called "Commerce" and is "the Cultivated land around the city of Golgonooza in the Forests of Entuthon. Here the Sons of Los labour against Death Eternal" (*Mil* 27:42). Here they clothe with flesh the wailing souls yet unbodied and "provide houses & fields" (*Mil* 26:30); here they also build the inward form of every generated body as "a garden of delight & a building of magnificence" (*Mil* 26:32).

"Were it not for Bowlahoola & Allamanda, no Human Form but only a Fibrous Vegetation, a Polypus of soft affections without Thought or Vision, must tremble in the Heavens & Earths thro' all the Ulro space" (*Mil* 24:36). The two are placed on each side of the Globule of Blood and the creative Pulsation (*Mil* 29:25).

See BOWLAHOOLA and ENTUTHON-BENYTHON.

ALLEGORY is a literary device in which abstractions are personified. "Allegories are things that Relate to Moral Virtues. Moral Virtues do not Exist; they are Alle-

gories & dissimulations" (*LJ, K* 614). Allegory is conceived in the intellect and seeks emotional form. Symbolism, however, is a literary device in which psychological realities rise from the subconscious and take sensorial form. Allegory is a riddle, which fails unless it is solved; symbolism is a dream, which fails if its entire meaning is obvious. Allegory is to poetry what dogma is to religion.

As far as I know, Blake was the first English critic to distinguish between the two. "The Last Judgment is not Fable or Allegory, but Vision [symbolism] . . . Vision or Imagination is a Representation of what Eternally Exists, Really & Unchangeably. Fable or Allegory is Form'd by the daughters of Memory. Imagination is surrounded by the daughters of Inspiration, who in the aggregate are call'd Jerusalem. Fable is Allegory, but what Critics call The Fable, is Vision itself. The Hebrew Bible & the Gospel of Jesus are not Allegory, but Eternal Vision or Imagination of All that Exists. Note here that Fable or Allegory is seldom without some Vision. Pilgrim's Progress is full of it, the Greek Poets the same; but Allegory & Vision ought to be known as Two Distinct Things, & so call'd for the Sake of Eternal Life" (*LJ, K* 604).

Whenever Blake uses the word "allegory" (with one or two exceptions) he means something falsified from an original. Thus Enitharmon's doctrine promises eternal life "in an allegorical abode where existence hath never come" (*Eur* 5:7). The economists "fix the price of labour, to invent allegoric riches" (*SoL* 6:17). The religion of chastity reveals "hidden wonders, allegoric of the Generations of secret lust" (*FZ* vii *b*:24). The Tree of Mystery "unfolds in Allegoric fruit" (*FZ* viii:169). "The Atlantic Mountains where Giants dwelt in Intellect [are] now given to stony Druids and Allegoric Generation" (*J* 50:1). Jerusalem, when in the stomach of the Covering Cherub, is bewildered "in allegoric delusion & woe" (*J* 89:45). Dr. Thornton's God "is only an Allegory of Kings & nothing Else" (On Thornton, *K* 789).

Ordinary marriage in this world is the result of Gwendolen's falsehood, which grew till it became "a Space & an Allegory around the Winding Worm" (J 85:1); this is "the little lovely Allegoric Night of Albion's Daughters" (J 88:31). Albion tries to limit Los by "rending the fibres of Brotherhood & in Feminine Allegories inclosing Los" (J 30:18).

The one important exception when Blake used the word with approval seems to have been a slip of the pen. "Allegory address'd to the Intellectual powers, while it is altogether hidden from the Corporeal Understanding, is My Definition of the Most Sublime Poetry" (To Butts, 6 July 1803).

ALLEN was Major-General Ethan Allen (1748–89), an American Revolutionary soldier and author. With Benedict Arnold, he took Fort Ticonderoga in 1775. Later that year he was captured at Montreal, but was exchanged in 1778. In 1779 he published *A Narrative of Col. Ethan Allen's Captivity. Reason the Only Oracle of Man* (1784), his outstanding book, expressed his Deism. He is mentioned in Blake's *America* (14: 2).

"The ALMIGHTY" is the common translation of "Shaddai" in the King James Bible. Blake identified the two when "the Harrow of the Almighty" (Mil 4:1) is also called "the Harrow of Shaddai" (Mil 4:12). Shaddai, in Blake's system, is the Accuser, a fact which sheds light on "the wine of the Almighty" by which Luvah intoxicated Urizen and thus got control of the chariot of light (FZ v:234). See SHADDAI.

But elsewhere Blake did not use the word in this special sense. Truth dwells with "the Almighty Father" (PS, "Samson" 4). "The breath of the Almighty" is likened to "the fury of Poetic Inspiration" (Mil 30: 18). "And the bitter groan of a Martyr's woe | Is an Arrow from the Almighltie's Bow" (J 52:27). The Spectre asserts that "the Almighty hath made me his Contrary" (J 10:56).

Elsewhere again, the Almighty would

seem to be simply the supreme God. The seven Eyes of God (which include Shaddai) are "the Seven Lamps of the Almighty" (FZ i:554). The constellations are "Forty-eight deformed Human Wonders of the Almighty" (Mil 37:54). And in a sarcastic paraphrase of dogmatic theology, Blake even equates him with the evil creator, adding "First God Almighty comes with a Thump on the Head. Then Jesus Christ comes with a balm to heal it" (LJ, K 617).

The ALPS are inhabited by the Swiss, long known as champions of "the Mountain Nymph, sweet Liberty." Rousseau and Voltaire, heralds of the French Revolution, established residences there.

The clouds of the impending Revolution "roll heavy upon the Alps round Rousseau & Voltaire" (SoL 4:18). "Orc, raging in European darkness, arose like a pillar of fire above the Alps" (SoL 7:26). Various mountains, including the Alps, listen to Los's watch-song (J 85:16).

AMALEK, grandson of Esau, was the eponym of the Amalekites, the southernmost of the heathen nations surrounding Palestine. The Amalekites attacked the Israelites on their way from Goshen, and were smitten successively by Joshua, Gideon, Saul, and David.

Blake used the Amalekite females to symbolize the sexual temptations which the outlandish women offered to the sons of Israel. They are daughters of Tirzah; "their various divisions are call'd the daughters of Amalek, Canaan & Moab" (FZ viii:294; cf. J 82:24). Blake often refers to this triad (Mil 24:14; J 29:31; 80:50; 82:24; 83:16; 86:28), which presumably represents the loins (Amalek being South), heart, and head. The Amalekite women are named for the daughters of Zelophehad, and their song (which is also the song of Tirzah) describes their torture of the males (FZ viii: 297–321; expanded in J 67:44–68:9). Los and Enitharmon escape from this triad (J 29:31). When the Hermaphrodite tempts the undergraduate Milton, he says: "The beautiful Amalekites behold the fires of youth bound with the Chain of Jealousy by Los & Enitharmon" (*Mil* 19:37). Los says that the infant Joseph "was sold to the Amalekite who carried him down into Egypt" (*Mil* 24:19).

Amalek is one of the countries which receive Jerusalem's little ones for sacrifices and the delights of cruelty (*J* 5:14). Los "woos" to Amalek to protect his fugitives, and Amalek trembles (*J* 83:16). Reuben enroots "beneath the shining Looms of Albion's daughters in Philistea by the side of Amalek" (*J* 74:45). The Lamb of God stands before Satan "upon the heights of Amalek" (*FZ* viii:270).

Amalek also seems to be one of a quaternary. Los sees "the Amalekite, the Canaanite, the Moabite, the Egyptian" outside of Golgonooza (*J* 13:58); later he says that these same four are "by Demonstrations the cruel Sons of Quality & Negation" (*J* 43: 67).

AMAZONIA was a name sometimes given to the valley of the Amazon River. It is the thirty-first of the Thirty-two Nations which shall protect liberty and govern the rest of the world (*J* 72:42).

AMERICA is the continent of the West, and as such represents the Body and its five senses, especially sex. Just as the Body is now cut off from the rest of the individual by its material form, so America is cut off from the other three continents by the ocean (matter). Historically, America, the birthplace of Orc (Revolution), represents Liberty, especially the liberty of the Body. In the cycle of continents, it is preceded by Africa (slavery) and is followed by Europe and Asia (counter-revolution).

It is to this land of the West that the sex-starved youths and maidens of "Ah! Sun-Flower" (*SoE*) aspire. The Daughters of Albion sigh towards America; and Oothoon seeks for the soft soul of America. But her flight thither is interrupted by Bromion, who claims her soft American plains (*VDA* 1:2, 3, 20).

The outbreak of the American Revolution is symbolized in "A Song of Liberty" (*MHH*). The ominous pause beforehand is felt in England, America, France, and Spain. Orc is born, and confronts Urizen on the Atlantean mountains. Urizen hurls him into the western sea, only to suffer a Satanic fall himself. He promulgates the Ten Commandments, eyeing in dismay Orc, who is destroying curses, law, empire, and sexual repression.

The subsequent separation of the two countries is political as well as spiritual. "Albion clos'd the Western Gate, & shut America out by the Atlantic, for a curse, and hidden horror, and an altar of victims to Sin and Repentance" (*FZ* iii:105). This is also the attitude of Enitharmon, as reported by the mendacious Gwendolen: "But hide America, for a Curse, an Altar of Victims, & a Holy Place," from which Jerusalem is to be cut off (*J* 82:29-34). And America is "clos'd out by the Oaks of the western shore" (*J* 43:6)—the oaks being druidic, and possibly referring by an extension of meaning to the British Navy and the blockade of the War of 1812. Erin unaccountably orders: "Build & prepare a Wall & Curtain for America's shore!" (*J* 49:49).

But underneath the hostility, the basic feeling is love, even envy, of America, and sorrow for the separation. Rintrah and Palamabron see hope in Orc's blood and fire on America's shore (*Mil* 23:6). When Oothoon descends into Beulah, England weeps, and trembles towards America (*Mil* 31:14). Los laments that America is closed apart (*J* 43:69); indeed, the two Americas are his baths of living waters (*J* 58:43). Erin bids Sihon and Og to move back to their own lands and leave the secret coverts of Albion and the hidden places of America (*J* 49:1). Sabrina and Mehetabel shine west over America (*J* 71:45). Jerusalem laments that she no longer sees America, and remembers its golden mountains (*J* 79:53). Los plans to hide the Tribes of Llewellyn there (*J* 83: 59), perhaps from the aggressions of Edward I.

The remaining references to America simply include it as an essential part of the world. Albion trembles in all lands, including "Great America" (*Mil* 14:7). The Loom of Death operates to all four quarters, including "America North & South" (*Mil* 35:17). All countries center in London and Golgonooza, including America (*J* 72:31). See VIPER.

AMERICA, A PROPHECY. *Lambeth, printed by William Blake in the Year 1793*, was the first of Blake's books to name a place in the imprint. To publish where he lived on the title page of so controversial a book, with his name in full for the first time, was an act of defiant courage in 1793, when the counter-revolution was building up, and the government (on May 21) had passed its act against "divers wicked and seditious writings" (*Erd* 197). "I say I shan't live five years, And if I live one it will be a Wonder. June 1793," Blake jotted in his notebook (*K* 187). Five years later he was to write: "To defend the Bible in this year 1798 would cost a man his life. The Beast & the Whore rule without control" (On Watson, *K* 383).

He worked hard to make this book perfect. He engraved four plates, then discarded them. One of them had actually named George III, yet in his final text "the King of England" was obviously that unfortunate monarch. On the second plate of the final text, he eliminated four lines which merely reflected his own personal reactions of rage and shame at the situation.

For the first time, he designated one of his books as "a prophecy." He was no longer attempting to dramatize history, as in *The French Revolution*; instead, he was recording the formula of all revolution, utilizing the American material without regard for chronology. He concentrated particularly on the dramatic events in Boston, Massachusetts, beginning just after the Boston Massacre of 1770 ("the coast glowing with blood from Albion's fiery Prince," *Am* 3:5). See BOSTON. The American patriots convene; Washington warns them

of the increasing tyranny; "Albion's wrathful Prince" threatens them with war ("a dragon form"); whereupon Orc appears and a voice (Paine's?) proclaims the rights of life, liberty, and the pursuit of happiness (6:1–11; see *Erd* 23). Albion's Angel accuses Orc of being the Dragon of *Revelation* (see WOMAN IN THE WILDERNESS); Orc replies that he is the Serpent in Paradise (the Messiah, who tempts man to break the prohibitions—see ORC), proclaiming the holiness of all life and the destruction of the Ten Commandments. The Angel bids the war-trumpets sound, but the thirteen colonies remain silent and refuse the loud alarm. Instead, they meet and renounce their allegiance. The thirteen royal governors and their troops are terrified. Then the Angel sheds diseases on America, thereby enraging its inhabitants; but the diseases recoil dreadfully on the British Isles. Finally the leprous Urizen is manifested. He manages to conceal Orc from European eyes "till Angels & weak men twelve years should govern o'er the strong; and then their end should come, when France reciev'd the Demon's light" (16:14). France, Spain, and Italy in terror strive to shut "the five gates of their law-built heaven" (16:19), but the fires of Orc consume the gates. Thus the poem closes, foretelling the world-wide spread of the American idea.

Ingeniously digging out the historical material embedded in the poem, Erdman has demonstrated that Blake utilized it without regard for chronology. Washington's opening speech, however, occurs at a nonhistorical meeting, which Joel Barlow invented for his *Vision of Columbus* (1787), though he placed it immediately after the battle of Bunker Hill. The meeting of the governors at Bernard's house was also nonhistorical, as Bernard had been recalled in 1769. The voice which proclaims the principles of the Declaration of Independence (probably Paine) precedes the actual Declaration by some eighty lines. The naval bombardments and burning of towns (4:3; 12:10) precede the command to fire (14:3). The king with "aged limbs" was really only thirty-seven. The various surrenders of British arms are compressed into a single act of terror (13:6). Such events as Lexington and Concord, Bunker Hill, Saratoga, and Yorktown are not specified.

Blake continued his tale in *Europe*; then, to make the cycle of continents complete, he wrote "Africa" and "Asia," giving a general title for all four: *The Song of Los.* "Africa," the continent of slavery, ends with the first line of *America*, the continent of revolution and liberty. "Asia" continues the tale of *Europe.*

The "Preludium" of *America* gives a fragment of the myth of Orc: his reaching the age of potency, breaking his fetters, and embracing the Shadowy Female. This "Preludium" is continued in the "Preludium" of *Europe.*

America is, pictorially, the most brilliant of Blake's books. It glows with the colors of sunrise. "Turning over the leaves," wrote Gilchrist (I, 309), "it is sometimes like an increase of light on the retina, so fair and open is the effect of particular pages." But the Revolution is not all the glory which the text implies. Orc, though spiritual in origin and essential to man's progress, operates in the material world by material means. The pictures trace, subtly at first, the degeneration of the revolutionary ideals.

While Orc is still chained under the Tree of Mystery, his sullen imagination crouches, on the level of the Worm, beneath the tree's roots, which vegetate above him in the shape of a copulating couple (Plate 1). He bursts up through the ground in a sunrise (Plate 2). Then, on the first page (Plate 3) of "A Prophecy"—the letters expand into ears of wheat, but are also involved with the ivy-vine of experience—a man soars upward with broken fetters, while below him Albion's Angel blows flames from his war-trumpet, causing a family to flee from its burning home. On the next page (Plate 4) a griffin pursues Urizen, with his books of law and sceptre of dominion, to his downfall; below, men cower among the fallen trunks of the forest of error. The griffin, who must signify War, does not resemble Blake's

other war-dragons, but was probably inspired by the griffin on the masthead of the *Massachusetts Spy*; Paul Revere, the engraver, confronted it with Franklin's snake "Join, or Die."

A Last Judgment (Plate 5) and a Resurrection (Plate 6) follow; but below the rejuvenated man are evil signs: a thistle; a lizard catching a fly; a toad facing a rampant adder. Innocence sleeps by a ram, the protector of the flock, in a sunrise (Plate 7), but the next plate reveals Urizen on high, still dominant. The last five plates are all pessimistic. An old man enters his tomb; Oothoon is torn by an eagle, while a drowned man is devoured by fish; Rahab beneath the sterile Tree preaches materialism to a youth; females, cowering in the intoxicating flames of lust, vegetate; and finally, prostrate Nature prays on the verge of an abyss; behind her is a small forest of vegetated forms; and the colophon entwines thorny plants and snakes. The high ideals of the Revolution have failed.

AMMON was a hostile kingdom east of the Jordan, bounded on the south by Moab (from which it was separated by the Arnon), on the west by Sihon, on the north by Og (from which it was separated by the Jabbok), and on the east by wilderness. It was subdued with great slaughter by Jephthah and finally conquered by David. Molech was worshipped there (*Mil* 37:21). Naamah the Ammonite, a wife of Solomon and the mother of Rehoboam, appears in the "Maternal Line" as an ancestor of Mary (*J* 62:12).

Ammon and five other hostile kingdoms receive Jerusalem's little ones for sacrifice (*J* 5:14). With two others, it is included in Jerusalem's reins (*J* 86:28). Satan's bosom reflects Moab and Ammon on the Arnon (*J* 89:24). Ammon, as one of the seven hostile kingdoms surrounding Jerusalem, finally exists only in the memory and in possibility (*J* 92:23).

AMSTERDAM. The voice of the wandering Reuben echoes in all the cities of the nations, including Amsterdam (*J* 84:14).

ANAK was the son of Arba, founder of the city Kirjath-Arba, or Hebron. The Anakim were giants of terrifying size, whom Joshua conquered and virtually annihilated (*Josh* xi:21-22). Hebron was assigned to Caleb, who expelled from there Anak's three sons, Sheshui, Ahiman, and Talmon (*Josh* xv: 13-14).

Anak, Og, Sihon, and Satan constitute an evil quaternary (*FZ* i:507; *Mil* 22:33), whose function is to oppose Man's progress towards Eternity.

Anak is particularly paired with Og. These two dwell beyond the skies with Chaos and Night, in the seat of Satan; they are set there to prevent Man from passing through the gates in brain and heart and loins, which open into Golgonooza (*Mil* 20:33-40); these are the doors of eternity (*Mil* 31:49). These two "Giants of Albion" were placed there by Jehovah (*J* 49:56).

They are also responsible for the looms, mills, prisons, and workhouses which prevent Man from leading a spiritual life (*J* 13:57).

Luvah erroneously calls Satan, Og, Sihon, and the Anakim the sons of Jerusalem (*FZ* i:507). The two Sons of Los fear that Milton will loose the quaternary on Albion (*Mil* 22:33). The four Sons of Los peruse Albion's tomb in the starry characters of Og and Anak [query: Sihon?] (*J* 73:16). In the Stomach of the Covering Cherub are seen the forces hostile to Israel, including Sihon, Og, and the Anakim (*J* 89:47).

ANANA was Ariston's stolen bride. "Ariston ran forth with bright Anana" (*FZ* frag. *incipit* "Beneath the veil," 6).

ANANTON is mentioned once, as the sixth in the list of the Sons of Los and Enitharmon (*FZ* viii:358). Enanto, the sixth of the Daughters (*FZ* viii:364), whose name closely resembles his, is his Emanation.

ANGEL is the Greek word for "messenger." Blake used the word in the specific sense only once, in expanding *Matthew* i:20, where the Angel of the Lord appears to Joseph in a dream, bidding him marry Mary. In the Bible it is not always easy to be sure whether God himself may not be intended by the word. Blake combined the two: "I heard his voice in my sleep & his Angel in my dream" (*J* 61:16). But anything that speaks of Eternity may be an angel; thus the tiny skylark is "a Mighty Angel" (*Mil* 36: 12; cf. *L'Allegro*, *K* 618).

"Every man's leading propensity ought to be call'd his leading Virtue & his good Angel" (On Lavater, *K* 88). Blake had one (*SoI*, "A Dream" 2; "The Angel that presided o'er my birth," *K* 541); Milton had one (*Mil* 21:52); also the unfortunate heroine of "The Angel" (*SoE*). Angels guard children and give them sleep (*SoI*, "Night" 23 and "A Cradle Song" 7).

Angels also mercifully bring death, particularly to children. The lion of "The Little Girl Lost" and "The Little Girl Found" (*SoI*) is a golden-haired angel who unites Lyca and her parents in his realm. An angel unlocks the coffins of the chimney-sweepers (*SoI*, "The Chimney Sweeper"). Angels receive the spirits of the victims of wolves and tygers (*SoI*, "Night"). "That is a wise tale of the Mahometans—of the Angel of the Lord, who murdered the Infant. . . . Is not every infant that dies of a natural death in reality slain by an Angel?" (*CR* 291).

The guardian spirit of each nation is an angel. Albion's Angel plays a big role in *America* and *Europe*, opposing Orc, while the yet ununited thirteen original colonies have thirteen Angels, their spokesman being Boston's Angel. Erdman identifies the two with Lord Bute and Samuel Adams.

We often call people "angels" without intending more than a compliment, but when Blake did so (as in his letter to Flaxman, 12 Sept 1800), he startles us by meaning it. He was writing about living people when he wrote: "It is not because Angels are Holier than Men or Devils that makes them Angels, but because they do not Expect Holiness from one another, but from God only. The Player is a liar when he says: 'Angels are happier than Men because they are better.' Angels are happier than Men & Devils because they are not always Prying after Good & Evil in one another & eating the Tree of Knowledge for Satan's Gratification" (*LJ, K* 616). The manner is Swedenborgian though the matter is not.

In his anti-Swedenborgian *Marriage of Heaven and Hell*, Blake's Angels are, satirically, the orthodox, "good" people, the contraries of the Devils, who are the unorthodox geniuses, the "evil" upsetters of established orders. When the American Revolution did not spread to England, these "Angels" and weak men governed the strong for twelve years (*Am* 16:14). When materialism succeeded there, "man became an Angel" (*Eur* 10:23). The successful Angel of "I asked a thief" (*K* 163) is of the orthodox, but is hypocritically worldly-wise in succeeding where the honest man failed. However, in "I heard an Angel singing" (*K* 164), the Angel sees only Innocence while his contrary, the Devil, sees only Experience.

The Angels described in *Revelation* of course are active in the pictures of the Last Judgment. One pair binds the Dragon; another, the Harlot; and a third pair opens the Book of Life (*K* 443). Seven empty the vials of the Wrath of God, and another seven blow their trumpets (*K* 444). Seven descend headlong to wake the dead with their trumpets (*K* 607). See Illustrations.

The Fallen Angels, who figure in the sketches for the *Book of Enoch*, are placed in the deserts of Africa (*SoL* 4:20).

The ANGEL OF THE DIVINE PRESENCE is Satan. He appears in the presence of the Lord (*Job* i–ii); in Blake's second illustration to *Job*, he is named and specified. He may take the form of an angel of light (*II Cor* ix:14), and is often mistaken for God. He provoked David to number his people (*I Chron* xxi:1). "The Aged Figure with Wings, having a writing tablet & taking account of the numbers who arise, is That Angel of the Divine Presence mention'd in Exodus, xiv c., 19 v. [as leading the Israelites into the Wilderness] & in other Places;

this Angel is frequently call'd by the Name of Jehovah Elohim, The 'I am' of the Oaks of Albion" (*LJ, K* 610). In a water color, he writes the Decalogue, starting with "Yod," his own name and the first letter of the Divine Name. See YOD. In the Laocoön plate, the central figure is labelled (in Hebrew) "King Jehovah," but immediately above, in smaller letters, Blake wrote in English "The Angel of the Divine Presence." The priest and his sons are entangled in the serpents of Good and Evil. See LAOCOÖN.

In *The Everlasting Gospel* (e:29–42), he is the creator of the body, law, and hell; in his sight, heaven is impure; he rolled all to chaos with the Serpent for its soul. As the creator of the body, he clothed Adam and Eve with coats of skin (To Butts, 6 July 1803).

The Divine Voice, lamenting Albion's fall, says: "I elected Albion for my glory: I gave to him the Nations of the whole Earth. He was the Angel of my Presence, and all the Sons of God were Albion's Sons, and Jerusalem was my joy" (*J* 29:6).

The Angel of the Divine Presence is the first of the Seven Angels of the Presence; and, as the unfallen Lucifer, is the first of the seven Eyes of God.

The ANGELS OF PROVIDENCE in *William Bond* (*K* 434) are the spirits of conventional morality who stand by his sick-bed and drive away the fairies of natural delight; but when they leave, the fairies return and he recovers.

In *Milton*, however, they are spirits of the divine order. The divisions of Time are guarded by "Angels of Providence on duty evermore" (28:60). The larks "all night consult with Angels of Providence & with the Eyes of God all night in slumbers Inspired" (36:4). If this last quotation contains a definition, these Angels are the Eyes of God.

The ANGELS OF THE PRESENCE are the seven Eyes, "which are the seven Spirits of God sent forth into all the earth" (*Rev* v:6). They are the seven spirits before the throne

(*Rev* i:4), the seven lamps (*Rev* iv:5; *FZ* i: 554), and the seven stars (*Rev* i:20; iii:1).

Milton's avowed purpose was to "assert Eternal Providence, | And justifie the wayes of God to men" (*PL* i:25–26); Blake quoted the second of these lines on the title page of his *Milton*. Milton's faith in the divine order (symbolized by the Eyes, the fixed path of Error which leads ultimately to the Truth) was unshakeable; therefore the Seven Angels of the Presence accompany him in his descent from heaven, occasionally giving him glimpses of his essential genius.

They weep when Milton enters his Shadow (14:42) and enter it with him. "Entering, they gave him still perceptions of his Sleeping Body which now arose and walk'd with them in Eden, as an Eighth Image Divine tho' darken'd and tho' walking as one walks in sleep, and the Seven comforted and supported him" (15:4). Various Eternals, "fill'd with rage . . . rend the heavens round the Watchers in a fiery circle and round the Shadowy Eighth: the Eight close up the Couch into a tabernacle and flee with cries down to the Deeps, where Los opens his three wide gates surrounded by raging fires" (20:45–49). The Divine Vision is driven down into the Ulro with "the Seven Starry Ones" (22:1). Milton "oft sat upon the Couch of Death & oft conversed in vision & dream beatific with the Seven Angels of the Presence" (32:1). Lucifer (the first of the Eyes), instructed by the [other?] Seven, replies to Milton's self-recriminations, and tells him: "We are not Individuals but States, Combinations of Individuals. We were Angels of the Divine Presence, & were Druids in Annandale, compell'd to combine into Form by Satan . . . But the Divine Humanity & Mercy gave us a Human Form because we were combin'd in Freedom & holy Brotherhood" (32: 8–15). Ololon reproves the angry Eternals (34:4); Los, Enitharmon, Albion's Sons, and his four Zoas all groan and beg forgiveness from the "Eight Immortal Starry-Ones" guarding the couch (35:30). The Eight rejoice at Ololon's descent (35:34).

When Satan appears, claiming to be God, the Starry Seven burn terrible, "and there went forth from the Starry limbs of the Seven, Forms Human, with Trumpets innumerable, sounding articulate as the Seven spake; and they stood in a mighty Column of Fire" (39:4–8) bidding Albion awake. Finally, "the Fires of Intellect . . . rejoic'd . . . around the Starry Eight; with one accord the Starry Eight became One Man, Jesus the Saviour" (42:9–11), who enters Albion's bosom.

Satan, in his God-like imitated state, also has his Angels: "Seven Angels bear my Name & in those Seven I appear" (38:55). These are doubtless "the Seven Angels of the Seven Churches in Asia, Antichrist Science," who destroyed the work of Jesus and his followers (*Laoc*, *K* 777); these churches, listed in *Revelation* (i:4; ii; iii), are the "seven houses of brick" in the fourth "Memorable Fancy" (*MHH*).

See EYES OF GOD.

ANGLESEA is an island county of North Wales. With Sodor it constitutes the Gate of Zebulun (*J* 16:40). It is also assigned to Peachey (*J* 71:30). Its Latin name was Mona. See MONA.

ANNANDALE is the valley of the river Annan in Dumfries, Scotland, just over the border from England.

The seven Eyes of God "were Angels of the Divine Presence, & were Druids in Annandale, compell'd to combine into Form by Satan" (*Mil* 32:11). At the outbreak of war, "Jehovah stood among the Druids in the Valley of Annandale when the Four Zoas of Albion . . . tremble before the Spectre in the starry Harness of the Plow of Nations" (*J* 63:1). Then "the Flute of summer in Annandale" is "fitted to mortal battle" (*J* 65:15).

ANTAMON symbolizes the male seed. In *Thel* he was simply "the Cloud."

Antamon is fifth in the list of the Sons of Los (*FZ* viii:358). His mother is Enitharmon (*Eur* 14:16). His Emanation is doubtless Elythiria, as she is fifth in the list of the Daughters of Los (*FZ* viii:364), and as her name suggests "ethereal." However, Antamon is chiefly associated with Leutha (sin), who is a rainbow (*Eur* 14:20; *Mil* 12:14).

He is "prince of the pearly dew" (the seed), a "crystal form, floating upon the bosom'd air" (like Thel's fructifying Cloud), with "lineaments of gratified desire" (*Eur* 14:15–19). Enitharmon summons him to her enormous revelry, and says that the "seven churches of Leutha" seek his love—the churches of chained monkeys in *The Marriage of Heaven and Hell*, the seven churches of Asia (*Rev* i:4).

Because of the spread of monasticism, he calls up Leutha from her valleys of delight and gives a loose Bible to Mahomet (*SoL* 3:28).

It is Antamon who makes physical forms for the yet unbodied Spectres. He takes them into his beautiful flexible hands as the sower takes the seed or the artist the clay; he draws with golden pen the indelible line of the immortal form, which the admiring Spectre puts on; then Antamon smiles bright through his windows (*Mil* 28:13–18).

Los once asks Oothoon if she is hiding in Oxford with Antamon (*J* 83:28); perhaps Blake had in mind the Oxonian Shelley, author of "The Cloud," and a notorious propagandist for free love.

The ANTEDILUVIANS were the giants who were destroyed by the Flood. See GIANTS.

"The ANTICHRIST cometh" (*I John* ii: 18). John alone names him, but the false prophet was foretold by Paul and others, and was identified with the Beast (*Rev* xiii; xvii). According to the Church Fathers, he will appear shortly before the Second Coming, will seduce multitudes with his false doctrines and miracles (parodies of the work of Christ), and then be destroyed.

For Blake, the Antichrist is anything opposed to the Everlasting Gospel. "If he had been Antichrist, Creeping Jesus, | He'd have done any thing to please us" (*EG d*:

59–60). The "majestic image of Selfhood ... [is] the Antichrist accursed" (*J* 89:9). He is War: the armies of souls, lured by the war-music of the Dragon, "become One with the Antichrist & are absorb'd in him" (*J* 89:62). He is Science: the works of Jesus and his followers "were destroy'd by the Seven Angels of the Seven Churches in Asia, Antichrist Science" (*Laoc, K* 777). He is Justice: "For what is Antichrist but those | Who against Sinners Heaven close | With Iron bars, in Virtuous State, | And Rhadamanthus at the Gate?" (*EG* supp. 1:11–14). Dante and Swedenborg both claimed "that in this World is the Ultimate of Heaven. This is the most damnable Falshood of Satan & his Antichrist" (On Dante, *K* 785). "The Greek & Roman Classics is the Antichrist" (On Thornton, *K* 786). "The outward Ceremony is Antichrist" (*Laoc, K* 776).

ANTRIM is one of the thirty-two counties of northern Ireland. With the other eight counties of the province of Ulster, it is assigned to "Dan, Asher, & Napthali" (*J* 72:26).

ANYTUS, Melitus, and Lycon, the accusers of Socrates, brought about his execution. They are depicted at the head of *Jerusalem* 93 with the inscription: "Anytus Melitus & Lycon thought Socrates a Very Pernicious Man. So Caiphas thought Jesus." Their downfall is depicted at the head of the next page.

"The Painter hopes that his Friends Anytus Melitus & Lycon will percieve that they are not now in Ancient Greece, & tho' they can use the Poison of Calumny, the English Public will be convinc'd that such a Picture as this Could never be Painted by a Madman or by one in a State of Outrageous manners, as these Bad Men both Print & Publish by all the means in their Power; the Painter begs Public Protection & all will be well" (*PubA, K* 598).

APOLLO was the Greek sun-god. Blake, in his propaganda against neoclassicism in the arts, made much of the fact that Apollo's Muses were the Daughters of Memory and not of Inspiration.

The unfallen Urizen, "Prince of Light," plays Apollo's role in *The Four Zoas*. See URIZEN. Urizen is depicted as Apollo in his sun-chariot in the fourteenth illustration to *Job*. When Blake saw the spiritual sun on Primrose Hill, he distinguished him from Apollo. "*That* (pointing to the sky) that is the Greek Apollo. He is Satan" (*CR* 291). Urizen is also paralleled with Satan.

Los sees Lambeth ruined and given over to "the detestable Gods of Priam, to Apollo" (*Mil* 25:49). Apollo was one of the chief defenders of Priam's city. David Erdman (*Erd* 266–67) shows that there actually was a decayed "Apollo Gardens" in Lambeth.

APOLLYON ("destroyer") is the angel of the bottomless pit (*Rev* ix:11). He is king of the stinging locusts which torment without killing the men unsealed of God.

"On the left hand Apollyon is foiled before the Sword of Michael" (*LJ*, *K* 612). Los defines his work as "giving a body to Fals[e]hood that it may be cast off for ever, with Demonstrative Science piercing Apollyon with his own bow" (*J* 12:13). In Bunyan's *Pilgrim's Progress*, Apollyon nearly overcomes Christian in the Valley of Humiliation, a scene which Blake illustrated dramatically.

The APPENINES (i.e., Apennines) are the backbone of the Italian peninsula. The Alps and the Appenines listen to Los's Watch Song (*J* 85:16).

APULEIUS (2nd cent. A.D.) was the author of the *Golden Ass*, based on a tale in the lost *Metamorphoses* of Lucius of Patras, which Lucian also rewrote. In Apuleius' hands it became the story of a young man's fall into the sensual corruptions of this world, and his salvation by a mystical conversion, in which Isis and Osiris play the parts of Mary and Jesus. It is a pagan *Pilgrim's Progress* written with the sophisticated wit of a Boccaccio. The interpolated tale of Cupid and

Psyche (the key to the whole work) is the last classic myth and the first gothic fairy tale.

"Apuleius's Golden Ass & Ovid's Metamorphosis & others of the like kind are Fable; yet they contain Vision in a sublime degree, being derived from real Vision in More ancient Writings" (*LJ*, *K* 607).

When the rejuvenated Luvah and Vala enter Vala's Garden (*FZ* ix:375–470), the invisible Luvah plays the part of the invisible Cupid in Apuleius' myth.

ARABIA is the ninth of the Thirty-two Nations which shall protect liberty and rule the rest of the world (*J* 72:39). Urizen's poisoned rock (the Decalogue) falls on Mount Sinai in Arabia (*Ahan* 3:46).

ARAM, the son of Cush and the grandson of Noah, was the eponym of the Aramaeans. He is one of the hostile kings whose hearts were hardened: the cold Spectre named Arthur constricts into druid Rocks round Canaan, Agag, Aram, and Pharaoh (*J* 54: 26).

Aram was also the Hebrew name for Syria, one of the heathen lands surrounding Palestine. Hyle peoples Ashur and Aram; Cush is adjoined to Aram (*J* 7:18–19).

ARARAT is a mountain range in Armenia, on the summit of which Noah's ark came to rest.

Here Noah sees Urizen give his laws; he fades and shrinks beneath the waters (*SoL* 3:7, 15); later he is seen there "white as snow" (*SoL* 7:22).

ARAUNAH (or "Ornan") the Jebusite offered David his threshing-floor on Mount Moriah as a site for an altar to Jehovah, and his oxen for the sacrifices, but David insisted on paying for them (*II Sam* xxiv: 18–24; *I Chron* xxi:22–25).

In the "Last Judgment" is "a Figure with a Basket, emptying out the vanities of Riches & Worldly Honours: he is Araunah, the Jebusite, master of the threshing floor" (*LJ*, *K* 607), who is getting rid of the chaff. (See Illustrations.)

The ARCHIEREUS is the office of high priest, one of the six in the religious hierarchy, which remains in spite of the Crucifixion. The six are "twelvefold in Allegoric pomp," being "double, each withoutside of the other, covering eastern heaven"; they are beheld in the revelation of the Covering Cherub (*J* 89:5–9).

ARCHITECTURE is the art of Urizen. It is one of the four eternal arts, and is Science; it alone remains through Mercy (*Mil* 27:56).

For Blake, Gothic architecture, which the boy learned to love in his work at Westminster Abbey, symbolizes true Christianity. "A Gothic Church is representative of true Art" (*LJ*, *K* 610). "Gothic is Living Form . . . Living Form is Eternal Existence" (*On Virgil*).

Classical architecture, especially the dome surmounted by the cross, symbolizes the worldly religion based on Reason.

Druidic architecture symbolizes the primitive religion which sacrifices others.

ARGYLL is a county assigned to Simeon (*J* 16:53). With the rest of Scotland it is assigned to Bowen (*J* 71:46).

ARISTON, king of beauty, anciently built for his stolen bride Anana a pinnacled (Gothic) palace, type of mighty emperies, in the forest of God on the Atlantean hills (*Am* 10:5–10).

He shudders at Los's song of the enslavement of man (*SoL* 3:4).

In the astonishment when a hermaphrodite is formed, Ariston runs forth with bright Anana (*FZ* frag. *incipit* "Beneath the veil" 6).

It is probably a coincidence that Herodotus (VI, 61–66) records an Ariston, king of Sparta, who stole his bride from his best friend.

ARISTOTLE (384–322 B.C.) was the culmination of Greek speculative philosophy and the forerunner of modern science. Blake referred to him once as one of the great lights of antiquity (On Watson, *K* 388), but elsewhere disapproved of him. In the fourth "Memorable Fancy" (*MHH* 20), the poet brings with him from the seven monkey-houses "the skeleton of a body, which in the mill was Aristotle's Analytics [the great opus on logic]. . . . It is but lost time to converse with you whose works are only Analytics." Blake also attacked Aristotle's conception of drama: "Aristotle says Characters are either Good or Bad; now Goodness or Badness has nothing to do with Character . . ." (*On Homer's Poetry*, *K* 778). But he applied Aristotle's definition of poetry, "a Poem of probable impossibilities," to the Bible (On Watson, *K* 390).

The ARK OF NOAH is moon-shaped: it is the love which preserves the man of vision and his family in the flood of materialism. See NOAH.

When Ololon descends as "a Moony Ark" into the fires of Intellect (*Mil* 42:7), love and thought are combined, and Jesus appears.

The ARK OF THE COVENANT was the sacred chest in which were concealed the Tables of the Law. On the lid, between two cherubim with outstretched wings, was the Mercy Seat, the place of the Divine Presence. The Ark was kept in the Holy of Holies behind a veil, so that none but the High Priest might see it.

"Man is the ark of God; the mercy seat is above, upon the ark; cherubims guard it on either side, & in the midst is the holy law; man is either the ark of God or a phantom of the earth & of the water" (On Lavater 533, *K* 82). Later, Blake was impressed by the fact that Mercy had superseded Law. "Jehovah's Finger Wrote the Law: | Then Wept! then rose in Zeal & Awe, | And the Dead Corpse from Sinai's heat | Buried beneath his Mercy Seat. | O Christians, Christians! tell me Why | You rear it on your Altars high" (*GoP*, "Prologue"). The triumphal Chorus at the end of *The Ghost of Abel* ascribes the establishment of the Ark to Jehovah's proclamation of Mercy: "The

Elohim of the Heathen Swore Vengeance for Sin! Then Thou stood'st forth, O Elohim Jehovah! in the midst of the darkness of the Oath, All Clothed in Thy Covenant of the Forgiveness of Sins . . . The Elohim saw their Oath Eternal Fire: they rolled apart trembling over The Mercy Seat, each in his station fixt in the Firmament by Peace, Brotherhood and Love." In the Petworth "Last Judgment," "Behind the Seat & Throne of Christ appears the Tabernacle with its Veil opened . . . & in the midst, the Cross in place of the Ark, with the two Cherubim bowing over it" (To Ozias Humphry, *K* 444). In the Rosenwald drawing, the Cross is replaced by the dove of the Holy Ghost (see Illustrations).

ARMAGH is one of the thirty-two counties of Ireland. With the other counties of Ulster, it is assigned to Dan, Asher, and Naphtali (*J* 72:26).

The ARNON is a river in Jordan, running due west, through a magnificent gorge, into the Dead Sea. It was the boundary between Moab on the south and Sihon and Ammon on the north; later, the boundary between Moab and Reuben.

The Arnon is the symbol of the female genital tract. "The terrors [Spectres] put on their sweet clothing [the body] on the banks of Arnon, whence they plunge into the river of space for a period, till the dread Sleep of Ulro is past" (*FZ* viii:215). The five females and the Shadowy Mother with songs lure "the Sleepers of Beulah down the River Storge [parental affection] (which is Arnon) into the Dead Sea" (*Mil* 34:29).

Milton (forming his philosophy) strives with Urizen (reason) on the Arnon (sex), "even to Mahanaim" (probably about eighty miles north); when Ololon descends she sees them still striving (*Mil* 19:6; 39:53; 40:4).

Mary emanates into Pison and Arnon and Jordan (*J* 61:33). Vala laments from Arnon and Jordan and Euphrates (*J* 80:8). The Covering Cherub's breast reflects "Moab & Ammon on the River Pison [the

river of Paradise which encompassed Havilah], since call'd Arnon" (*J* 89:24).

ARPHAXAD was a son of Shem and grandson of Noah, also an ancestor of Abraham. He is third in the second series of the Twenty-seven Churches, one of the Female Males (*Mil* 37:38; *J* 75:13).

"ART is the Tree of Life. . . . Science is the Tree of Death" (*Laoc, K* 777); thus Blake stated his belief that the humanities should save us, whereas science may kill us. But by "Art" Blake meant a whole mode of life, the life of the imagination, which is that of Jesus. "Jesus & his Apostles & Disciples were all Artists. . . . The Whole Business of Man Is The Arts" (*Laoc, K* 777). The aesthetic response should determine all acts, even the most inconsiderable. Each Zoa has its Art (*Mil* 27:55). "A Poet, a Painter, a Musician, an Architect: the Man Or Woman who is not one of these is not a Christian" (*Laoc, K* 776); anyone who does not develop one of these aspects (though without actually writing, composing, painting, or building) is not living according to the divine plan. "Prayer is the Study of Art. Praise is the Practise of Art. Fasting &c., all relate to Art" (*Laoc, K* 776).

"Christianity is Art & not Money. Money is its Curse" (*Laoc, K* 777). "Where any view of Money exists, Art cannot be carried on" (*Laoc, K* 776). "Works of Art can only be produc'd in Perfection where the Man is either in Affluence or is Above the Care of it. . . . Tho' Art is Above Either, the Argument is better for Affluence than Poverty" (*LJ, K* 612).

Art is essentially the precise telling of truth. "Art can never exist without Naked Beauty displayed" (*Laoc, K* 776; cf. *J* 36: 49). It "cannot exist but in minutely organized Particulars and not in generalizing Demonstrations of the Rational Power" (*J* 55:62). It also gives "a body to Fals[e]hood that it may be cast off forever" (*J* 12:13).

Consequently, great art is always revolutionary. "The grandest Poetry is Immoral" (On Boyd, *K* 412). "Bacon calls Intellectual

Arts Unmanly. Poetry, Painting, Music are in his opinion Useless & so they are for Kings & Wars & shall in the End Annihilate them" (On Bacon, *K* 407). "Art Degraded, Imagination Denied, War Governed the Nations" (*Laoc*, *K* 775). "The Arts & Sciences are the Destruction of Tyrannies or Bad Governments. . . . The Foundation of Empire is Art & Science. Remove them or Degrade them, & the Empire is No More. Empire follows Art & Not Vice Versa as Englishmen suppose" (On Reynolds, *K* 445). "It is not Arts that follow & attend upon Empire, but Empire that attends upon & follows The Arts" (*PubA*, *K* 597).

"There is a class of artists whose whole art and science is fabricated for the purpose of destroying art" (*DesC* III, *K* 573). These are the Generalizers, who work from theory, not from inspiration. "Generalizing Art & Science till Art & Science is lost" (*J* 43: 54). "A pretence of Art to destroy Art" (*J* 43:35). Failures as artists, they may nevertheless attain positions of power, as professors, heads of conservatories, curators, and librarians; then they devote themselves to destroying anything which might challenge their own limited talents.

ARTERY. The pulsation of the artery is the moment of inspiration. A moment equals the pulsation (*Mil* 28:47); every time less than this is equal in period and value to six thousand years (all history until the Millennium). In this moment, a pulsation of the artery, the poet's work is done, and all great events of time start forth and are conceived (*Mil* 28:62–29:3).

ARTHUR was the ninetieth in Geoffrey of Monmouth's list of the mythical kings of Britain. It is now generally accepted that he lived in the sixth century, but so many fables gathered about his name that his existence has been doubted. Geoffrey (who once was supposed to have invented him) wrote up the tales (*Historia Britonum* IX–XI, ii); Malory collected more, and immortalized them; Milton repeated them, but disbelieved in their historicity: "But who Arthur was, and whether ever any such reign'd in *Britain*, hath bin doubted heertofore, and may again with good reason" (*History of Britain*, 1670, pp. 122–23).

King Arthur, the stories go, established the Round Table with its code of war and idealization of womanhood. His queen Gwenever, however, deceived him. He conquered the whole of Europe, including Rome, and established a world-wide reign of justice. His treacherous nephew finally defeated him in a last battle, which extinguished the whole of his knighthood. He himself, sorely wounded, was borne away to the Isle of Avalon, where he was healed and whence some day he will return. Meanwhile the constellation Lyra became known as "Arthur's Lyre" and the Great Bear as "Arthur's Chariot."

Blake wrote: "The stories of Arthur are the acts of Albion, applied to a Prince of the fifth century, who conquered Europe, and held the Empire of the world in the dark age, which the Romans never again recovered." "And all the fables of Arthur and his round table; of the warlike naked Britons; of Merlin; of Arthur's conquest of the whole world; of his death, or sleep, and promise to return again . . . All these things are written in Eden" (*DesC* V, *K* 578, 577).

William Owen [Pughe] wrote: "Arthur is the Great Bear, as the epithet literally implies; and perhaps, this constellation, being so near the pole, and visibly describing a circle in a small place, is the origin of the famous round table" (*Cambrian History*, London, 1803, p. 15). Blake accepted Pughe's theory, because it made a significant symbol: "Arthur was a name for the constellation Arcturus, or Boötes, the keeper of the North Pole" (*DesC* V, *K* 577). For war originates in the polar regions, where the imagination is frozen (see POLAR); and in Arthur's day, war was the basic fact of human society. Arthur, the great conqueror, was the ideal warrior, with the chivalric code which idealized woman. Hence he was the pole-star, round which all society revolved. For that reason, Arthur is one of the kings created by Rahab and Tirzah, against whom Los creates the prophets (*J* 73:36).

Merlin (the enslaved Imagination), Arthur (the enslaved Reason), and Bladud (the enslaved Body) form a triad (*J* 75:2). Arthur is "the cold constrictive Spectre" (*J* 54:25). His idealization of woman has created the Female Will. Enitharmon, declaring that this is Woman's World, creates "secret places, and the masculine names of the places, Merlin & Arthur. A triple Female Tabernacle for Moral Law I weave, that he who loves Jesus may loathe, terrified, Female love, till God himself becomes a Male subservient to the Female" (*J* 88:17). Arthur is also in the power of Vala, who declares: "The Human is but a Worm, & thou, O Male! Thou art thyself Female, a Male, a breeder of Seed, a Son & Husband . . . Go assume Papal dignity, thou Spectre, thou Male Harlot! Arthur, divide into the Kings of Europe in times remote, O Womanborn and Woman-nourish'd & Womaneducated & Woman-scorn'd!" (*J* 64:12–17). When Jerusalem is destroyed, "Bath stood upon the Severn with Merlin & Bladud & Arthur, the Cup of Rahab in his hand" (*J* 75:2).

"In the last Battle of King Arthur, only Three Britons escaped; these were the Strongest Man [the human sublime], the Beautifullest Man [the human pathetic, which was in the wars of Eden divided into male and female], and the Ugliest Man [the human reason]; these three marched through the field unsubdued, as Gods, and the Sun of Britain set, but shall arise again with tenfold splendor when Arthur shall awake from sleep, and resume his dominion over earth and ocean. . . . They were originally one man, who was fourfold; he was self-divided, and his real humanity slain on the stems of generation, and the form of the fourth [Los] was like the Son of God" (*DesC* V, *K* 577–78).

See BLADUD, GWINIVERRA, MERLIN.

ASAPH [i.e., St. Asaph], in Flintshire, Wales, is the twenty-second of the Twenty-four Cathedral Cities (*J* 46:19). It is under Tharmas and York.

ASHER was Jacob's eighth son and the founder of a tribe.

His Gate in Wales is Carnarvonshire (*J* 16:39); his English counties are Sussex, Hampshire, and Berkshire (*J* 16:47); his Scottish counties are Sutherland, Sterling, and Wigtoun (*J* 16:56); and with Dan and Naphtali he shares the Irish counties of Ulster (*J* 72:25).

With his brothers, he was one of the Sons of Los who fled (*FZ* viii:361, 376). With five of his brothers, he rolls apart into Non Entity (*J* 74:50), becoming one of the Lost Tribes.

ASHTAROTH [i.e., Ashtoreth] was the moon-goddess of love, worshipped throughout the Near East. Blake mistook Milton's plural for a singular. He pairs her with Baal (the sun god) as the first two of the Twelve Gods of Asia, the "Monstrous churches of Beulah" (religions based on sex), "the Gods of Ulro dark" (the gods of this world). These two are worshipped in Tyre and Sidon. Beautiful Ashtaroth weaves the veils of pestilence bordered with war, which are worn by the priestesses of Molech (*Mil* 37:16–24).

ASHUR [i.e., Asshur] is another name for Assyria, one of the heathen nations surrounding Palestine.

Hyle has peopled Ashur and Aram (*J* 7:18). Ashur is one of the countries which eventually shall disappear (*J* 92:23).

ASIA, the continent in the East, is the last in the cycle of continents. It rose from the pendulous deep when the arrows of pestilence had flown for forty years round the crucified Fuzon, and Urizen's children felt their skulls harden (*Ahan* 4:41).

The book "Asia" (*SoL* 6–7) continues the story of *Europe*, describing the counterrevolution. The kings of Asia, on hearing the howl from Europe, run out of their webs and dens, to defend their oppressive rule; in the darkness they cry aloud, startled by the fires of Orc. A general resurrection and triumph of the grave closes the book.

Satan stood on the Euphrates and over Asia stretched his pride—a reference to the English acquisitions in Asia (*J* 27:48). Asia is included in Urizen's temple (*J* 58:37). In the time of Innocence, the skiey tent of mankind reached over Asia (*J* 60:17).

World-wide events extend from Europe to Asia (*FZ* ii:59; *Mil* 24:33; 40:18; *J* 8:24; 34:41; 42:76; 49:24; 60:3; 67:7; 68:26; 89:12).

See GODS OF ASIA, under GODS.

ASSYRIA and Egypt were the two great oppressors of Israel. The Great Shepherd assures Jerusalem that her "Sons are lovelier than Egypt or Assyria" (*J* 60:31). Her children are "dash'd upon Egypt's iron floors & the marble pavements of Assyria" (*J* 79:2). Los sees Egypt and Assyria in the reins of the ideal Jerusalem (*J* 86:31).

See ASHUR.

The ASYLUM was the Royal Asylum for Female Orphans, built on the site of the Hercules Tavern, as David Erdman (*Erd* 266) has demonstrated. It stood on the juncture of the New Road and Hercules Road, near Blake's dwelling in Lambeth. "The Asylum given to Hercules, who labour in Tirzah's Looms for bread, who set Pleasure against Duty" (*Mil* 25:49).

ATLANTEAN HILLS or Mountains. See ATLANTIC CONTINENT, under ATLANTIC.

The ATLANTIC is the Western ocean, which separates America from the British Isles. It also separates Ireland from Great Britain. Before the flood (of matter), it was only a narrow sea (*J* 44:14); then it contained the Atlantic Continent, now barred out or actually lost in the Sea of Time and Space.

Albion casts the Veil of Vala into the Atlantic deep (*J* 23:23; 59:2). Orc is seen rising on the Atlantic (*Am* 4:6; *Mil* 23:6; 31:

27). To indicate a sweep across the map, an action may extend from the Atlantic to the Erythrean (*Mil* 29:63; *J* 24:62; 83:22), like the similar sweep from Ireland to Japan.

The ATLANTIC CONTINENT (so Captain Francis Wilford conjectured) once consisted of America and the British Isles, but the Deluge submerged much of it, dividing England from America (Edward B. Hungerford, *Shores of Darkness*, New York, 1941, p. 32). The correspondence of the American and Euro-African shore-lines would have inspired such a theory. Humboldt speculated that the continents might have been a single land-mass divided by an immense torrent from the south.

To Blake, the Atlantic Continent symbolized the original spiritual and intellectual unity of the two countries; indeed, the American idea was the logical development of English libertarian thought. These ideals were lofty, therefore the Atlantic Continent is mountainous. It had "infinite mountains of light now barr'd out by the atlantic sea" (*MHH* 25:8). These mountains are "golden" (*J* 79:54), because gold is the metal of the intellect. They are "vast shady hills between America & Albion's shore, now barr'd out by the Atlantic sea, call'd Atlantean hills, because from their bright summits you may pass to the Golden world" (*Am* 10:5). Giants once dwelt here in Intellect (*J* 50:1); here Blake has his Golden House ("The Caverns of the Grave I've seen," 18, *K* 558). Jerusalem once covered the place (*J* 24:46); but now she beholds no more America's "golden mountains where my Cherubim & Seraphim rejoic'd together among my little-ones" (*J* 79:54).

Albion was "patriarch of the Atlantic Continent, whose History Preceded that of the Hebrews & in whose Sleep, or Chaos, Creation began" (*LJ, K* 609). When Albion gave his loud death groan, "the Atlantic Mountains trembled. Aloft the Moon fled with a cry" (*FZ* ii:41; *J* 27:36).

The thirteen angels of the thirteen American colonies convene in Ariston's palace, "the archetype of mighty Emperies," which

he built in the forest of God on the Atlantean hills (*Am* 10:11). See ARISTON.
After the colonies declare their independence, Albion's forty million angels darken
the Atlantic mountains (*Am* 13:14). Here
the new-born Orc stands before Urizen
(*MHH* 25:8). The Duke of Burgundy asks
indignantly: "Shall . . . these mowers from
the Atlantic mountains mow down all this
great starry harvest of six thousand years?"
(*FR* 89).

Although Jerusalem speaks of the continent as part of America (*J* 79:53), Blake
places it between America and England
(*Am* 10:5), which once were separated only
by a narrow sea (*J* 44:14). Usually it still
exists, but is barred out by the Atlantic
(*MHH* 25:8; *Am* 10:6; *J* 44:14). Blake denies that (like Plato's Atlantis) it has sunk
(*Am* 14:16), only to say elsewhere that it
was actually submerged (*J* 36:38), and
again, that in one night it was "caught up
with the Moon and became an Opake Globe
far distant, clad with moony beams" (*J* 49:
19).

The ATLANTIC VALE is the river valley of
the Thames. It is also called "Lambeth
Vale."
Perhaps the beginning of the Flood is in-
dicated by *Jerusalem* 4:9: "In all the dark
Atlantic vale down from the hills of Surrey
a black water accumulates." Elsewhere,
Blake identified the Atlantic Vale with the
Vale of Rephaim; here Eno extends her
Moment of Time "oblique across the At-
lantic Vale" (*J* 48:32).

ATLAS was a giant, brother of Prometheus
and Epimetheus. With the other Titans, he
warred against Jupiter, and was punished
by being obliged to support the heavens on
his shoulders. His name was given to a
mountain range in northwest Africa. On
this mountain the jealous Jupiter chained
down Prometheus, friend of man and bring-
er of fire, to be tortured by eagles, which
devoured his ever-renewing liver, much as
Oothoon was tortured.

"The giant Albion was Patriarch of the
Atlantic; he is the Atlas of the Greeks, one
of those the Greeks called Titans" (*DesC* V,
*K*578). Orc howls on Mount Atlas, "chain'd
down with the Chain of Jealousy" (*SoL*
3:21).

AYR, a county on the west coast of Scotland, is assigned, with Argyll and Banff, to
Simeon (*J* 16:53). As part of Scotland, it is
also assigned to Bowen (*J* 71:46).

B

BAAL was the sun-god whose consort was Ashtareth, the moon-goddess of love. Under various names they were worshipped in Canaan and throughout the Near East.

Blake places these two first in his list of the Twelve Gods of Asia; as male and female, they head the "Monstrous Churches of Beulah." They are worshipped in Tyre and Sidon (*Mil* 37:20).

The BAALIM were the five rulers of Philistia (*I Sam* vi:16—translated as "the five lords of the Philistines").

"The Seven Kings of Canaan & Five Baalim of Philistea" are seen in the Stomach of the Covering Cherub (*J* 89:46). When Rahab-Babylon manifests, beneath her "the Nations innumerable of Ulro appear'd: the Seven Kingdoms of Canaan & Five Baalim of Philistea into Twelve divided, call'd after the Names of Israel, as they are in Eden" (*Mil* 40:23).

BABEL is the Hebrew word, used in *Genesis*, for Babylon, the Unholy City. It was founded by Nimrod, the first king, on the plain of Shinar (Mesopotamia). Nimrod was also credited with building the blasphemous Tower of Babel ("Nimrod's Tower," To Butts, 6 July 1803), which the jealous God stopped by confusing the tongues of the builders; "therefore is the name of it called Babel, because the Lord did there confound the language of all the earth" (*Gen* xi:9). See NIMROD.

Blake, in associating Babel with Shinar, seems to have followed Bryant in supposing that Shinar was a rival, warring city. The idea probably arose from the Battle of Four Kings against Five, one of whom was Amraphel king of Shinar (*Gen* xiv:1). Babel is therefore a state of primitive warfare. (See BRYANT.)

Druid temples overspread the earth "till Babel, the Spectre of Albion, frown'd over the Nations in glory & war" (*Mil* 6:23). "Hand has peopled Babel & Nineveh" (*J* 7:18). Cush is adjoined to Aram "by the daughter of Babel in a woven mantle of pestilence & war" (*J* 7:20). "Behold what cruelties are practised in Babel & Shinar" (*J* 8:19). "The Spectre saw to Babel & Shinar" (*J* 8:23). Six of Albion's Sons "labour mightily in the Wars of Babel & Shinar" (*J* 8:41). "Babel mocks, saying there is no God nor Son of God" (*J* 60:56). At the Watch Song of Los, "Babel & Shinar look toward the Western Gate, they sit down Silent at his voice" (*J* 85:18).

BABYLON (or Babel) on the Euphrates is the Unholy City, where the God of This World is worshipped. It is the Contrary to Jerusalem. It is Empire, which despoils the Temple and carries the inhabitants off into slavery; therefore it is "represented by a King crowned, Grasping his Sword & his Sceptre" (*LJ, K* 608). Being a state of War, it is also the city of Lust. In *Revelation* (xvii:5) it is the scarlet woman, the great whore, "Mystery, Babylon the Great, the mother of harlots and abominations of the earth." To these epithets Blake added the name Rahab, the harlot of Jericho, who is associated with Babylon (*Psalm* lxxxvii:4) and the Great Dragon (*Isaiah* li:9).

Babylon therefore symbolizes Moral Virtue, the state Rahab. This identification occurs in *The Four Zoas* viii:330; *Milton* 5:27; 22:49; 33:20; 40:17; *Jerusalem* 18:29; 42: 63; 52; 75:1; 75:19; 93:25.

It is the city of Vala, of Natural Religion (*J* 18:29) or Deism (*J* 52), the Goddess Nature (*J* 93:25; *Laoc*, *K* 777). It is the Mother of War (*Mil* 22:49) and companion of the Great Dragon (*Mil* 40:17; *J* 93:25).

It is built by the Spectres of the Dead (*J* 42:63) in the wastes of Moral Law, and founded on Human Desolation. "The Walls of Babylon are Souls of Men, her Gates the Groans of Nations, her Towers are the Miseries of once happy Families, her Streets are paved with Destruction, her Houses built with Death, her Palaces with Hell & the Grave, her Synagogues with Torments of ever-hardening Despair, squar'd & polish'd with cruel skill" (*J* 24: 31).

Babylon sums up the final section of the Twenty-seven Churches, the section beginning with Abraham (*Mil* 37:41; *J* 75: 19). Here Jesus is crucified (*FZ* viii:326); and other crucifixions take place here "with cruel Og," or Justice (*J* 27:22).

The Daughters of Albion also build Babylon (*J* 84:8). Gwendolen entices her sisters there (*J* 82:18). Babylon is their chief desire; the fires of their loins point eastward to Babylon (*J* 82:31, 36). They bind Jerusalem's children in the dungeons there (*FZ* ii:63). Jerusalem herself is bound in the dens (*Mil* 38:27); in the dungeons she works at the mills (*J* 60:39).

The Covering Cherub's Loins "inclose Babylon on Euphrates beautiful and Rome in sweet Hesperia" (*J* 89:38). His Stomach includes all the heathen from Babylon to Rome (*J* 89:48).

Other references: "Whether this is Jerusalem or Babylon we know not" (*FZ* iii: 102). "The whole place of the Covering Cherub, Rome, Babylon & Tyre" (*Mil* 9: 51). Albion views Jerusalem and Babylon (*Mil* 39:48). Hand drives the Daughters of Albion through the streets of Babylon (*J* 21:30). Vala, "art thou not Babylon?" (*J*

34:8). "Why . . . build this Babylon & sacrifice in secret Groves?" (*J* 60:23). "I behold Babylon in the opening Streets of London" (*J* 74:16). "Drawing them away towards Babylon" (*J* 74:31). Gwendolen bids the looms of Enitharmon and the Furnaces of Los create Jerusalem, Babylon, Egypt, and various other places (*J* 82:27). "I see London . . . begging through the Streets of Babylon" (*J* 84:11).

The Divine Voice in the Songs of Beulah calls the self-centered wife a Daughter of Babylon: "When I first Married you, I gave you all my whole Soul. I thought that you would love my loves & joy in my delights, seeking for pleasures in my pleasures, O Daughter of Babylon" (*Mil* 33:2). "O Vala . . . Slay not my little ones, beloved Virgin daughter of Babylon" (*J* 20:22, 27).

"The King of Babylon in Hell" is the title of Blake's illustration to *Isaiah* xiv:9: "Hell from beneath is moved for thee to meet thee at thy coming: it stirreth up the dead for thee, even all the chief ones of the earth; it hath raised up from their thrones all the kings of the nations." The king, wearing the triple tiara, looks backward at a falling figure entwined with a serpent. A nude angel sternly points forward, and holds the chain to which the king's hands are manacled. Before them, in dark flames, huddle three kings, while the armed heads of warriors appear below them.

BACCHUS, the god of intoxication, is among the deities invoked by the warriors (*J* 68:18).

BACON (Francis, first Baron Verulam and Viscount St. Albans, 1561–1621) was the founder of experimental science. He believed that all science should be based on facts established by experiments. Consequently doubt, not faith, was the prime intellectual virtue; and reason, not imagination, was the supreme mental faculty.

When "very Young," Blake read and annotated Burke on the Sublime, Locke on Human Understanding, and Bacon's *Ad-*

vancement of Learning with "Contempt & Abhorrence . . . They mock Inspiration & Vision" (On Reynolds, *K* 476). These books are unfortunately lost, but his annotated copy of Bacon's *Essays* (London, 1798) has been preserved. His marginalia fairly sputter with outrage at Bacon's devotion to monarchy, money, and Reason. "Pretence to Religion to destroy Religion. . . . Bacon put an End to Faith. . . . Man is not Improved by the hurt of another. States are not Improved at the Expense of Foreigners. Bacon has no notion of anything but Mammon. . . . Bacon was a Contemplative Atheist. Evidently an Epicurean. . . . a Lord Chancellor's opinions are as different from Christ as those of Caiphas or Pilate or Herod . . . Bacon hated Talents of all Kinds. . . . Bacon is in his Element on Usury; it is himself & his Philosophy. . . . King James was Bacon's Primum Mobile" (*K* 396–410). In his annotations on Reynolds, Blake was still outraged. "The Great Bacon—he is Call'd: I call him the Little Bacon—says that Every thing must be done by Experiment; his first principle is Unbelief" (*K* 459). "Bacon's Philosophy has Ruin'd England. Bacon is only Epicurus over again" (*K* 456).

In Blake's symbolic system, Bacon is the first of the trinity of Bacon, Newton, and Locke, who were responsible for the materialism of modern times. Therefore his ideal is "to cast off Bacon, Locke & Newton from Albion's covering" (*Mil* 41:5). "Bacon & Newton, sheath'd in dismal steel, their terrors hang like iron scourges over Albion: Reasonings like vast Serpents infold around my limbs" (*J* 15:11). The Spectre asks: "Am I not Bacon & Newton & Locke who teach Humility to Man, who teach Doubt & Experiment?" (*J* 54:17). Voltaire and Rousseau are "Frozen Sons of the feminine Tabernacle of Bacon, Newton & Locke" (*J* 66:14). The Twelve Sons of Albion "combine into Three Forms named Bacon & Newton & Locke in the Oak Groves of Albion which overspread all the Earth" (*J* 70:15). Enitharmon asks: "if Bacon, Newton, Locke deny a Conscience

in Man & the Communion of Saints & Angels, contemning the Divine Vision & Fruition, Worshiping the Deus of the Heathen, The God of This World, & the Goddess Nature, Mystery, Babylon the Great, The Druid Dragon & hidden Harlot, is it not that Signal of the Morning which was told us in the Beginning?" (*J* 93:21).

Yet Blake recognized the essential genius of these men, however misguided they might be on this material plane; therefore, in the final apotheosis, the three scientific philosophers appear in the heavens, counterbalancing the three poets Milton, Shakespeare, and Chaucer (*J* 98:9).

Bacon was buried within the site of Verulam; for that reason Blake substituted "Verulam" for "Canterbury" when he was attacking the materialism of the Established Church. See VERULAM.

BALAAM, son of Beor, though a gentile, was a true prophet and in high repute. When King Balak of Moab sent for him to curse the Israelites, who were advancing under Joshua and Caleb, Balaam repeatedly warned the king: "I cannot go beyond the commandment of the Lord to do either good or bad of my own mind" (*Numb* xxiv: 13—slightly misquoted by Blake, To Trusler, 16 Aug 1799); and thrice he blessed Israel, though under great pressure to curse them (*Numb* xxiii–xxiv).

Yet Balaam soon came to be of bad repute, perhaps because of a disinclination to admit that a true prophet could be a gentile. He was denied any credit for his blessings, on the ground that they had been uttered against his real intent (*Deut* xxiii:5; *Josh* xxiv:10). Moses accused him of counselling the women of Midian to commit whoredom with the Israelites, and therefore ordered all the prisoners to be massacred, except the virgin girls, whom they might keep for themselves (*Numb* xxxi:15–18). Balaam was also accused of prophesying for money (*II Peter* ii:15; *Jude* 11), perhaps because of the customary "rewards of divination" (*Numb* xxxii:7); but the text states flatly that Balaam refused to accept the bribes of Balak, and thus could not have been guilty of simony. John the Divine warned the church in Pergamos that some of its members held "the doctrine of Balaam, who taught Balac [sic] to cast a stumbling block before the children of Israel, to eat things sacrificed unto idols, and to commit fornication" (*Rev* ii:14).

Blake made only two obscure references to Balaam, but they are sufficient to let us understand his interpretation of this historical event. Balaam was obviously a prophet under the constant guidance of God. He did not want to obey Balak: he went to him only at the king's second summons, and then only at God's command. His human reluctance is indicated by "the Lord's" contradictory attitudes: two verses after bidding him go (*Numb* xxii:20), he is angry at him for going (*Numb* xxii:22); then his angel ("an adversary"—Satan?) blocks his way, yet bids him continue (*Numb* xxii:22–35). See ANGEL OF THE DIVINE PRESENCE. Balaam then not only blessed Israel and foretold its glorious future; he also prevented the impending warfare, and even urged fraternization (so we may politely interpret "whoredom"). This intercourse between the lads of Israel and the Moabite women was, to the Jew, an abomination, a pollution of their racial purity; but Blake believed that it prevented war and was an essential step towards the Brotherhood of Man. In his genealogy of Mary, he stressed the outlandish women who were ancestors of Jesus, among whom was Ruth, a Moabite. See MATERNAL LINE. Elsewhere Blake exulted in the mixture of races which had produced the Englishman.

Balaam, then, was a reconciler of enemies. His tears (not mentioned elsewhere) are tears of sorrow over their battlings. "Oshea [Joshua] and Caleb fight: they contend . . . in the terrible Family Contentions of those who love each other. The Armies of Balaam weep—no women come to the field: dead corses lay before them" (*J* 43:37). "Og & Sihon in the tears of Balaam, the Son of Beor, have given their power to Joshua & Caleb" (*J* 49:58).

BALTIMORE, County Cork, is a town on the southern tip of Ireland. "From Rathlin to Baltimore" (*J* 49:4) means from north to south of Ireland.

BANFF is a Scottish county assigned to Simeon (*J* 46:19). With the rest of Scotland, it is also assigned to Bowen (*J* 71:46).

BANGOR, in Carnarvonshire, North Wales, is twenty-third in the list of the Twenty-four Cathedral Cities (*J* 46:19). It is under Tharmas and York.

BAPTISM, instituted by John the Baptist, is one of the two Protestant sacraments. It symbolizes the washing away of sins. It involves the repentance of the sinner (*J* 63: 28), and forgiveness by the Lord. In a wider sense, it is the casting away of error. See SACRAMENTS.

Although Blake's father was a Non-Conformist, he had William baptized at St. James's Church, Piccadilly, before the baby was quite two weeks old. Towards the end of his life, Blake once "expressed the uneasiness he should have felt (had he been a parent) at a child of his dying unbaptized" (*Gil* 1863, I, 330—not in the second edition).

A **BARD** was a Celtic poet-prophet, of great antiquity and authority. Bards were sometimes confused with Druids, but never by Blake. Gray's Bard, the last survivor of the Welsh bards whom Edward III had massacred, confronts the English conqueror on Snowdon, prophesies his doom, and plunges into the Conway. Blake made fourteen illustrations to Gray's poem (about 1800) and later made a single picture (*DesC* IV).

Blake himself was "the Ancient Bard" (*SoI*, "The Voice of the Ancient Bard") and again "the Bard" (*SoE*, "Introduction" 1); and is presumably "the stern Bard" who broke his harp in shame and rage over the American Revolution (*Am* 2: 18–21). Again, the Bard in *Milton* (2:22–14:9), whose inspired song causes Milton to leave heaven to redeem his Emanation, sings of the Hayley-Blake quarrel, then terrified takes refuge in Milton's bosom.

The Bard of Albion, hid in his caves, who is nonetheless smitten by the recoiling plagues of Albion's Angel (*Am* 15:16), might be William Whitehead, the poet laureate during the American Revolution, or James Henry Pye, the laureate when Blake published *America*; but it is hard to believe that Blake was wasting his celestial artillery on such picayunes. It seems much more likely that he was satirizing all English poetry of that period.

The Bard of Oxford, who brings the healing leaves from the Tree of Life to the hostile Albion (*J* 45:30–46:17), might well be Shelley. See BARD OF OXFORD, under OXFORD.

BASHAN constituted the northern part of Palestine east of the Jordan, stretching from Hermon to Gilead (across the Yarmuk). It was ruled by the giant Og when Reuben, Gad, and the eastern half-tribe of Manasseh conquered it, slaughtering the king and all his giant subjects. The land was then assigned to Half Manasseh.

Bashan contained two mountain ranges. The "hill of Bashan" mentioned in *Psalm* lxviii:15 accounts for the inclusion of Bashan among the six mountains around Palestine which are equated with Milton's Sixfold Emanation, his three wives and three daughters (*Mil* 17:16). Blake assigns Bashan to Reuben; either Blake was misled by such passages as *Numbers* xxxii:33 and *Deuteronomy* iii:12, or (since Og symbolizes Justice) he thought of Reuben as living most appropriately in a state of Law. Reuben enroots there (*J* 34:36; 74:42); and though Los keeps sending him across the Jordan, he always returns (*J* 34:43–54; 36:1–4).

Erin bids Sihon and Og return to Bashan and Gilead (*J* 63:43). Canaan hovers over Cheviot from Bashan to Tyre and from Troy to Gaza (*J* 63:43).

BATH was the famous place of mineral springs where society assembled to cure gout, rheumatism, and other ailments. According to legend, King Bladud founded it in 813 B.C., after he had been cured of leprosy by bathing there. The Romans built baths, which have been restored and still function. The bishopric of Wells (named for St. Andrew's Springs, once thought to be curative) was removed to Bath about 1090, but was returned to Wells in 1139, after which the Norman cathedral at Bath was left unfinished and fell to ruins. The bishop's title is "the Bishop of Bath and Wells."

Blake therefore felt entitled to substitute the well-known Bath for Wells in his list of the Twenty-four Cathedral Cities. Bath, in spite of its geographical position, is North, under Urthona and Edinburgh. From it rises the line of important Cities which runs northward. It symbolizes the Brotherhood of Man; as such, this "merciful Son of Heaven" (*J* 45:33) is a reflection of Jesus. Jesus is the great healer: Bath is the "healing City" (*J* 45:1), the "mild Physician of Eternity, mysterious power whose springs are unsearchable & knowledge infinite" (*J* 46:1); yet "benevolent Bath" when it becomes corrupted is "the physician and the poisoner, the best and worst in Heaven and Hell" (*J* 41:1).

Bath is given the prominent place of the Seventh of the Twenty-four Cities (*J* 41:1 — the list is continued *J* 46:1), the first of the second group of six under Urthona. Blake added Plate 45 (and perhaps 41), so that Bath might speak at length; he does so as the spokesman for all Twenty-eight, as in him the preceding Ten "shone manifest a Divine Vision," and the remaining Eighteen combine with them (*J* 45:37).

Bath comes with the others to the dying Albion when Los summons them. Albion is hostile; in vain the Cities try to force him back through Los's Gate into Eden; but compulsion cannot bring salvation. Then Bath, with its "wisdom in midst of Poetic Fervor" (*J* 45:1), speaks with mildness and tears through the Western Porch, lamenting that Albion's Western Gate is closed.

Man's degradation proves that the Individual in Selfhood is nothing: only Jesus can cure his dread disease. Bath calls on God to descend, then bids the bard Oxford to give Albion the healing leaves of the Tree of Life (J 45:30). (When religion fails, only poetry and the other arts can still rouse the imagination and discover the truth.) But Albion turns away, refusing comfort; Oxford faints; Albion dies; and the churches are infected with his disease.

It is then that Bath becomes "the worst in Heaven and Hell," the poisoner. His Spectre was the first to assimilate with Luvah in Albion's mountains, and he took "a triple octave . . . to reduce Jerusalem to twelve, to cast Jerusalem forth upon the wilds," by eliminating the Emanations of the Twenty-four Cities, removing their true inspiration (J 41:1–5; 74:27). When war breaks out, Luvah is crucified on Albion's Tree in Bath (J 65:8). The Daughters of Albion sacrifice their victims; "hence arose from Bath soft deluding odours, in spiral volutions intricately winding over Albion's mountains, a feminine indefinite cruel delusion" (J 65:65). Bath is last seen separate from the other Cities when he stands upon the Severn, with Merlin, Bladud, and Arthur, the Cup of Rahab in his hand (J 75: 2). Then in the resurrection, "the Twenty-four Cities of Albion arise upon their Thrones to Judge the Nations of the Earth" (Mil 42:16).

In his ideal form, Coban (the loins) dwells in Bath (J 71:26).

Several times, Bath appears in a quaternary, but each quaternary is different. The four pillars of Albion's throne are London, Bath, Legions, and Edinburgh (Mil 39:35), but elsewhere Bath is identified with Legions, King Arthur's city (J 41:1). On the front of Albion's bosom are Bath, Oxford, Cambridge, and Norwich (Mil 39:44). The voices of Bath, Canterbury, York, and Edinburgh cry out over the Plow of Nations (J 57:1)—here Bath is substituted for Verulam. Elsewhere, Bath is contrasted with Canterbury when Los cries: "Go thou to Skofield: ask him if he is Bath or if he is Canterbury" (J 17:59)—that is, is Skofield motivated by humanitarianism or moral law? At another time, Los cries: "Bristol & Bath [poetry and humanitarianism], listen to my words, & ye Seventeen, give ear" (J 43:55).

Each of the chief Cathedral Cities has a representative in the flesh. See CATHEDRAL CITIES. Thanks to David Erdman's researches (Erd 440 ff.), we can identify Bath's representative with the Rev. Richard Warner, poet, vigorous pacifist, and the "best known man of letters in Bath." On Fast Day, May 25, 1804, in a time of war fever and thought-control, and undeterred by the unexpected presence of a large body of recruits, he preached his startling sermon, War Inconsistent with Christianity, on the text "Put up again thy sword into his place: for all they that take the sword shall perish with the sword" (Matt xxvi:52). "WAR is the GREATEST CURSE with which a nation can be afflicted." Therefore he urged his countrymen to refuse to bear arms even in the case of an invasion by Napoleon. He repeated his sermon on February 20, 1805. He published it; it sold, and reached a fourth enlarged edition in 1805. And he supplemented his sermon with other publications.

Blake evidently was greatly impressed with the courage of the man who spoke out so bravely in a time of general hysteria, and honored him as the voice of Bath. And this voice of Bath (humanitarianism) inspires Oxford (Shelley), although there is no evidence that the two ever met.

There are no fewer than three plates (41, 45, 46) which begin with the word "Bath," suggesting that each at one time was intended to follow Plate 40. Evidently some of these were insertions, caused, I conjecture, by the news of Shelley's death. Blake consequently included his elegy to Shelley. See BARD OF OXFORD, under OXFORD.

BATHSHEBA, of the daughters of Heth, was a Hittite. She committed adultery with David, but later married him and became the mother of Solomon. Blake names her as the ninth of the Maternal Line, the ancestry of Mary (*J* 62:11).

BATTERSEA, where Blake was married, was a Surrey village whose gardens were noted for producing the finest asparagus, and Blake's father-in-law was a market gardener. Battersea is just across the Thames from Chelsea. Battersea and Chelsea mourn for Cambel and Gwendolen (*J* 21:32). At the death of the Worm, Battersea and Chelsea mourn (*J* 33:13).

BEDFORD is an English county assigned to Zebulun (*J* 16:48). Later it also is assigned to Hutton (*J* 71:36).

BEELZEBOUL is the Greek for "Baalzebub," the Philistine god consulted by King Ahaziah, for which Elisha reproved him. "Beelzeboul" was the prince of the devils, by whose power Jesus was accused of casting out devils. In the Vulgate and the King James translations, the name was rendered "Beelzebub." In *Paradise Lost*, Beelzebub is Satan's chief partner in crime and the second in command.

"The Mills of Satan and Beelzeboul" unwind the threads of the clothing prepared for the Spectres by Enitharmon, and weave them anew in forms of death and despair (*FZ* viii:201, 227–31).

BEHEMOTH ("colossal beast") probably was the hippopotamus seen in the Nile. He is described in *Job* xi:15–23; immediately following is the description of Leviathan. They illustrate the tremendous creative powers of God. The two were constantly paired, and in the writings of the occultists became two of the chief devils.

The two are pictured in Blake's fifteenth illustration of *Job*. God with his left hand points down to the two, who are enclosed in the cloud-barrier limiting the physical world of Job and his friends. The two beasts symbolize the immense powers of the subconscious mind, the unredeemed and warring portion of the psyche. Behemoth stands on the land with the rushes indicative of

Egypt; Leviathan is coiled in the waters below.

The Spectre forms Leviathan and Behemoth, "the War by Sea enormous & the War by Land astounding" (*J* 91:40).

BEHMEN (Jacob [Jakob Böhme], 1575–1624), "The Teutonic Philosopher," was one of the greatest mystics. Born of poor German peasants, he was apprenticed to a shoemaker, who discharged him because for a full week he was in a mystical ecstasy. He became an itinerant cobbler, then settled in Görlitz, where he married and had six children. About 1600, a ray reflected from a polished metal dish filled him with the light of God and opened to him the mysteries of the universe. In 1610, a third "flash" unified his discoveries and drove him to write. In 1612, his manuscript *Aurora* caused him to be banished; but he left the book unfinished and promised to write no more. Then about 1618, he was so driven to write that he produced some thirty other books. In 1623, his *Way to Christ* provoked more persecution, and he was banished again. He died the next year; the local Count had to use pressure to get him buried properly. His statue now stands in the town square.

John Sparrow translated his works into English in 1645–62. Sir Isaac Newton studied the books deeply, and is said to have found his theory of gravitation in them. Behmen's English followers were eventually absorbed into the Society of Friends. The books were republished (Vols. I and II, 1764; Vol. III, 1772; Vol. IV, 1781) with an unfinished dialogue by the Rev. William Law as introduction. This is the edition which Blake read.

"Paracelsus & Behmen appear'd to me" before the American Revolution (To Flaxman, 12 Sept 1800). On December 10, 1825, he told Crabb Robinson that Behmen was "a divinely inspired man." Blake praised, too, Dionysius Freher's figures in Law's translation) as Erdman notes, *Erd* 10, n. 17) as being "very beautiful. Michael Angelo could not have done better" (*CR*

258–59) —not an aesthetic but a philosophical criticism, suggesting that Blake had penetrated the symbolism of the Sistine ceiling. But in *The Marriage of Heaven and Hell*, excited at having discovered the psychological universe, Blake heaped scorn upon those on whose shoulders he was standing. "Any man of mechanical talents may, from the writings of Paracelsus or Jacob Behmen, produce ten thousand volumes of equal value with Swedenborg's, and from those of Dante or Shakespear an infinite number" (*MHH* 22); but this is not so disparaging as might seem, because he actually says that Behmen is a storehouse of ideas, and that he is equal to the greatly admired Swedenborg; and he places him next to two of the greatest poets.

Behmen's writings affected Blake profoundly, a fact generally overlooked, because Behmen is hard reading. Struggling to record his discoveries, he used the vocabulary of Scripture, astrology (although he was a Copernican), and Paracelsus, thus initiating the school which interpreted alchemy mystically; and at times he was driven to invent terms of his own, which he called "the Language of Nature," and which we might call subjective philology.

What influenced Blake most in these difficult writings was Behmen's analysis of the psyche and the interaction of its parts. There are, he saw, three worlds. First of all is the Dark Fire-World, which he called Hell and which has since been named the Subconscious. It contains all the basic impulses—all the deadly sins. Although evil, these are the sources of life itself. Above is the Light World (Heaven). As the evil instincts rise, a certain divine spark transmutes them from Evil to Good. The Deadly Sins become the Virtues: selfishness becomes generosity, lust becomes love, and so on.

These two worlds, Hell and Heaven, are essential to each other; they exist simultaneously in God. Thus there is the Opposition of Contraries in God himself, without which there could be no life.

The third World is the Outer World of Nature. This is a mere "outbirth" of the others, a projection of Man. Behmen has much to say about this "astral" world with its starry wheels, which place Man under the rule of physical laws; but these laws of cause and effect are actually an expression of the spiritual realities underlying them. The human body is part of Nature; the soul within gives it form.

Nature is Law; God is Liberty.

The problem of salvation is that of keeping a harmonious balance of the parts, so that the Dark World is kept down where the Light World can irradiate and temper it. The Fall occurred as a lack of balance, specifically the ambition of Lucifer to dominate the Heart of God (Jesus); then the fire of the Dark World broke loose, and all the disasters followed.

Behmen's discovery of the Three Worlds solved for Blake the question how a God of Love could create a place of everlasting punishment for his children. God is good; all things that proceed from him are good in essence, nor can that essence ever be corrupted. Therefore "Hell," which is of God (and this point bothered Behmen) must be good; and the Life Force proceeding from it (the libido, Blake's "Energy") cannot be ''evil," and far from being everlasting pain, is "Eternal Delight." Everything that lives is holy.

Therefore, in *The Marriage of Heaven and Hell*, Blake used the words "Heaven" and "Hell," "Good" and "Evil," as mere technical terms, without moral meaning of any sort. Behmen had seen clearly but had misunderstood what he saw. His Dark World is indeed the source of life; its flames appear to be "torment and insanity" only to the short-sighted Angels. Behmen's Light World is Blake's restraining force, or "Reason" (the superego), which is not creative, and if not itself restrained may easily become a destructive tyrant.

The three worlds correspond to Milton's (Hell, Heaven, and Earth is the order in which he presents them), also to Swedenborg's; but both sages overlooked the dynamic relationship of the two and retained the old moral values; for which Blake twitted Milton (*MHH* 5–6) and reproved Swedenborg (*Mil* 22:50–54).

It is a temptation to outline here Behmen's entire system—meaningless unless read as psychology—but we must limit ourselves to those points which particularly enlightened Blake or confirmed his ideas.

Behmen placed the Imagination as man's central power; it is the creative force. All things are generated out of the Imagination. He constantly attacks "Reason," which is wholly unable to compete with the directness of actual perception, or Vision.

He believed that the Bible was "inspired" —that is to say, symbolic; it is an expression of the eternal truths of the human soul. He spoke often of the "Veil of Moses," meaning that one should not take him literally. He expressed great scorn of merely "historical Christianity" and the "stone churches" in which a blind and exterior "faith" is imposed. He constantly contrasted the true and invisible church with the outward churches of Cain and Babel.

Man is basically bisexual; therefore in heaven there can be no marriage. The division of the sexes was a result of the Fall, and Behmen, though happily married, unfortunately looked on it as evil. But besides Eve man has a heavenly bride, Sophia or Wisdom; as such she corresponds to Jerusalem, the Bride of the Lamb. She suggests the rabbinical Shekinah, Blake's Emanation, and Jung's Anima.

The activity of the Contraries produces motion in the two Worlds: a contraction, followed by expansion and rotation; their opposed contact produces the divine spark. Urizen's initial activities are this same contraction, expansion, and rotation (*Ur* 3:38, 37, 18), though without producing a spark, only a conflagration.

Another Blakish point: Behmen constantly (and particularly in the *Aurora*) identified the joy of children with the joy of heaven.

BELIAL was apparently not a god at all, but a term of strong opprobrium. No temples were erected for his worship. In *Paradise Lost* he symbolizes the Deadly Sin of Sloth, and is patron of mischief-makers, especially his "sons" who attempted the rape of the angels in Sodom.

Blake names him as ninth of the Twelve Gods of Asia. He is "Belial of Sodom & Gomorrha, obscure Demon of Bribes and secret Assassinations, not worship'd nor ador'd, but with the finger on the lips & the back turned to the light" (*Mil* 37:30).

BELIN was twenty-first of the mythical British kings. He fought with his brother Brennius over their inheritance, but the plea of their mother Conwenna caused them to join forces. They ravaged Gaul and Italy, and captured Rome (Milton—in *History of Britain*—is too patriotic to deny this, but too scholarly not to express a doubt), after which Brennius tyrannized in Italy while Belin returned to Britain, where he built the Tower of London. His reign was marked with justice and peace. His ashes were placed in a golden urn on the top of the Tower (*Geof* III, 1–10; Milton repeats his account).

Blake placed Belin between Bladud and Arthur in his list of kings whom Los opposes (*J* 73:35).

BENJAMIN, the beloved brother of Joseph, was Jacob's last, twelfth son.

As the youngest, Benjamin is frequently associated with Reuben, the eldest, implying the inclusion of all the others. The two are divided "bleeding from Chester's River" (*J* 63:12); they flee and hide in the Valley of the Rephaim (*J* 68:47); Bowen and Conwenna cut the fibres of Benjamin from Chester's River, while Hand and Boadicea cut Reuben apart from the Hills of Surrey (*J* 90:14–25); the Daughters of Albion drink the two (*J* 90:46); Los proclaims that nobody shall assume the characteristics of the two, or of three more brothers and other persons (*J* 90:31).

In the enrooting of the Twelve Brothers, Joseph and Benjamin roll apart in vain; they are fixed in Cabul (*J* 74:56–57).

Benjamin's Gate in Wales is Glamorganshire (*J* 16:41); in England, the counties of Derby, Cheshire, and Monmouth; in Scotland, Kromarty, Murra, and Kirkubriht (*J* 16:58); in Ireland, he shares with Ephraim and Manasseh the counties of the province of Connaut (*J* 72:23). His equivalent among the Sons of Albion is Bowen.

BEOR was the father of Balaam (*J* 49:59).

BERKSHIRE is an English county assigned to Asher (*J* 16:47). It is also assigned to Hutton (*J* 71:37).

BERNARD (Sir Francis, 1712–79), the Royal Governor of Massachusetts (August 1760–July 1769), was so distinguished for rapacity and double-dealing that when he was recalled, Boston gave over the day to public celebrations. He is credited with having been a contributory cause to the Revolution; therefore Blake, appropriately but without regard for chronology, included his name in *America*. The thirteen Royal Governors convene at his home (*Am* 13:2). "Bernard's house" was the famous Province House (1679–1864), successively the residence of ten Royal Governors.

BERWI[C]K is a Scottish county assigned to Judah (*J* 16:54). As a part of Scotland, it is also assigned to Bowen (*J* 71:46).

BERYL is a pale green precious stone, related to the emerald. It was the first stone in the fourth row of the high priest's breastplate, signifying the tribe of Asher (*Exod* xxviii:20) and the eighth foundation stone of the New Jerusalem (*Rev* xxi:20). The wheels beheld by Ezekiel were "like unto the colour of a beryl" (*Ezek* i:16; x:9). It was among the precious stones which clad the Covering Cherub (*Ezek* i:16). The body of the angel who appeared to Daniel (x:6) "was like beryl."

When Orc becomes the Serpent, one of his precious stones is the beryl (*FZ* viii:74), doubtless with reference to the Covering Cherub.

When Albion divides into the sexes, "the Male is a Furnace of beryll; the Female is a golden Loom" (*J* 5:34; 90:27). "Translucent the Furnaces, of Beryll & Emerald immortal, and Seven-fold each within other" (*J* 53:9), suggesting Ezekiel's wheels.

BETH-PEOR. See VALLEY OF PEOR, under PEOR.

BETH RABBIM was Blake's misprint for Bath-rabbim. "Thine eyes [are] like the fishpools in Heshbon, by the gate of Bath-rabbim" (*Song of Sol* vii:4). Gwendolen says of Hyle: "I have nail'd his hands on Beth Rabbim & his hands on Heshbon's Wall" (*J* 82:43).

BETHLEHEM means "house of bread." The famous hospital for the insane ("Bedlam") dates back to 1547; its present building, on Lambeth Road, was erected 1812–15. Los, surveying London for some sign of hope, comes "to Bethlehem, where was builded dens of despair in the house of bread" (*J* 31:25).

BEULAH ("married") was the name given to Palestine when it was restored to God's favor: "thy land [shall be called] Beulah: for the Lord delighteth in thee, and thy land shall be married" (*Isaiah* lxii:4). In *The Pilgrim's Progress*, the land of Beulah is Bunyan's Earthly Paradise, the happy land where the pilgrims live until it is time for them to cross the River of Death. It is celebrated in J. R. Sweeney's popular hymn "O Beulah Land."

In Blake's system, Beulah is the realm of the Subconscious. It is the source of poetic inspiration and of dreams (*FZ* i:20, 99, 246; *Mil* 2:1; *J* 17:27; 36:22; 63:37; 79:74). In Beulah, "Contrarieties are equally True" (*Mil* 30:1; *J* 48:14); and it is now well known that in the Subconscious, love and hate coexist without affecting each other, also tenderness and cruelty, prudishness and lust, cleanliness and filth, and other such split impulses. Here too the sexes are separate. In Eternity, the Individual contains his feminine portion within him; consequently marriage does not exist there. "Humanity is far above sexual organization & the Visions of the Night of Beulah where Sexes wander in dreams of bliss among the Emanations" (*J* 79:73). In Beulah, however, the unions of the sexes are ideal and unrestricted (*J* 30:34–37; 69:14–25; 85: 7–9).

Blake placed Beulah as an intermediary between Eternity and Ulro (this world of Matter). The Lamb created Beulah as a refuge from the gigantic warfare of ideas in Eternity; here flock all those who are exhausted, the weak, the terrified Emanations, to rest in sleep. In spite of the Contrarieties, no disputes occur which would disturb their repose (*FZ* i:94–98; *Mil* 30:1; *J* 48:20).

It is a place of night, lighted by the Moon of Love. It contains hills and vales (*FZ* iv: 89; *Mil* 30:5; *J* 47:10) and caves of sleep (*FZ* ix:627), also streams and rivers (*Mil* 35:50; *J* 4:34; 53:3). It is a land of flowers —i.e., sexual pleasures (*FZ* vii:239; *Mil* 34: 10; *J* 49:47; 55:2; 90:7; 98:21). There are couches for the sleepers (*FZ* ix:354, 558; *Mil* 34:10; *J* 44:35). As the sleepers are often called "the dead," there is a graveyard with grave, urns, tombs, and funeral arks (*FZ* vii *b*:292, 298; *J* 11:2; 89:60). On the verge are the Palm and the Oak of Weeping, between which Albion sinks into the arms of the Saviour, who lays him upon the Rock of Ages (*FZ* i:465; *J* 23:24).

Although a Golden Wall is mentioned once as surrounding Beulah (*FZ* vii:243), it lies open to Eternity. The Eternals can look down into it, descend in a body; and individuals continually enter it, to sleep there.

Beneath Beulah is Ulro (*FZ* i:102; *Mil* 21:7), which is this world of Matter, usually England (*Mil* 11:4; 31:11; *J* 38:35; 85:26), and once Ireland (*J* 48:52). The Thames springs from the rivers of Beulah (*J* 53:3); in fact, the Thames and Medway (married by Spenser) are rivers of Beulah (*J* 4:34).

From Beulah, visions and dreams descend into Ulro. Inspiration may come as a wind which uproots the rocks and hills (*Mil* 7:33) or a winter thunderbolt (*Mil* 15:44). In a cataclysm, the dead can burst through the bottoms of their graves into Ulro (*FZ* vii *b*:298; *J* 89:60). Ololon breaks away from Eternity clear through Beulah into Blake's garden.

But for Generated Man to enter Beulah, special gates are required. Each Daughter of Albion and each Emanation has three: one each in head, heart, and loins (*FZ* viii: 59; *Mil* 5:7); they are called the Three Heavens of Beulah (*Mil* 2:5; 5:7; 20:2; 26:20). Los's city of art, Golgonooza, has four gates, each fourfold, and each of the fourfold has an opening into Beulah. That of the Northern Gate is of gold, silver, brass, and iron (*J* 12:66); those of the Western and Eastern Gates are of stone (*J* 13:9, 16); while the Southern Gate, of four precious stones, is guarded by the mystics Fenelon, Guion, Teresa, Whitefield, and Hervey, "with all the gentle Souls who guide the great Wine-press of Love" (*J* 72: 51). Cf. "And formed into Four precious stones for enterance [*sic*] from Beulah" (*J* 59:1)—a line which does not follow from Plate 58.

The active inhabitants of Beulah are its Daughters, who are Blake's muses—the daughters of direct inspiration, contrasted with the classical muses, who are the daughters of Mnemosyne or Memory (i.e., who get their inspiration from traditions, books, or other secondary sources). Blake invokes "Daughters of Beulah" at the opening of *Milton* (2:1), where he bids them descend down the nerves of his right arm from his brain, where by their ministry the Eternal Great Humanity Divine planted his Paradise. A Daughter stands between every two Moments (*Mil* 28:48; *J* 56:10). Once they are called the Female Emanation (*FZ* iv: 263).

In *The Four Zoas*, when the Circle of Destiny is complete, they give it a space and name it Ulro, then close the Gate of the Tongue (west) in trembling fear (*FZ* i:101– 7). Later, they behold the Saviour descending over Beulah, and worship him, saying that Eternal Death (Albion) is in Beulah; that He alone can resurrect Man, and if they be not granted a hiding place, they will consume at the sight of the wonders of Eternity (*FZ* iv:250–62). When they behold the Polypus (nature) adjoined to Beulah, they mourn, yet put their faith in the resurrection, singing comfortable notes; but they name the descending Spectres "Satan" (*FZ* vii *b*:290–301). They see Enitharmon weaving bodies for these "dead," also the Saviour, whom they worship (*FZ* viii:42). They anoint his feet and wipe them with their hair (*FZ* viii:237).

In *Milton* they stand in mute wonder at the descent of Ololon and her children (30:6). They weep when they hear her lamentation (31:9). The Divine Voice sings in their songs (33:1) — songs of comfortable notes to comfort Ololon (34:1). Many of them accompany Ololon, but on seeing Milton's Shadow, some daughters return trembling (34:20, 47).

In *Jerusalem*, the main function of the Daughters is to protect Liberty. They preserve the idea of freedom when it is lost outwardly. With Vala, Jerusalem redounds from their arms, and they weep as they hold her form, but she arises from their arms (5: 49, 55; 14:33). They snatch her away and hide her in Beulah, then weep for her when she forsakes the place (41:14; 48:19–21). Again they receive her, hold her, and hide her (60:40). They emerge from Los's furnaces with Erin (11:8), who addresses them (48:53–50:18), and they respond (50:23), calling on the Lamb to take away the remembrance of Sin. A Son of Eden is set over each Daughter to guard the wondrous creation in Albion's tomb (72:48). In Beulah, they nurse the Masculine and the Feminine into youth and maiden until the time of sleep is past (79:76). Los addresses them (83:66).

Among the Daughters are Eno (*FZ* i: 222), Leutha (*Mil* 11:28), and Ololon (*Mil* 36:25). As Jerusalem is their sister (*J* 48: 22), she may also be a Daughter.

The Sons of Beulah are mentioned comparatively seldom. In the fall, Tharmas

drew them all into his dread vortex (*FZ* iv: 88). They act as messengers or ambassadors (*FZ* i:476, 481, 550).

Both Albion and Milton leave their Humanities sleeping in Beulah while the rest of their personalities descends into Ulro. Shiloh, the Masculine Emanation of France, dwells among the flowers of Beulah (*J* 49: 47). The Dead of Beulah fall into Ulro by bursting through the bottoms of the graves; they are the Spectres for whom Enitharmon weaves forms so that they can be born into this world.

The CHURCHES OR HEAVENS OF BEULAH are those evil organizations of (or beneath) Beulah, which are divided into "a Double Twelve & Thrice Nine" (*Mil* 37:18). The Double Twelve are Paganism: the Twelve Gods of Asia with their Emanations or Spectres. The Thrice Nine are official Christianity, the Twenty-seven Churches extending from Adam to Luther, then repeating in endless round. The complete list is to be found in *Milton* 37:13–43; the Twenty-seven are listed again in *Jerusalem* 75:10–24, where they are summed up as Rahab. These Twenty-seven are once called "Three" (*Mil* 26:20), probably with reference to the "threefold region, a false brain, a false heart, and false bowels" (*J* 14:5). They are not to be confused with the Three Heavens or Gates into Beulah.

"The Monstrous Churches of Beulah" are "the Gods of Ulro dark" (the gods of this world); they are "monstrous dishumaniz'd terrors, Synagogues of Satan" (*Mil* 37:16–17). The Twenty-seven are situated "in Ulro, Seat of Satan, which is the False Tongue [false doctrine] beneath Beulah: it is the Sense of Touch [sex]" (*Mil* 27:45–46). They are "Self-righteousness conglomerating against the Divine Vision" (*J* 13:52). They are the "threefold region, a false brain, a false heart, and false bowels, altogether composing the False Tongue, beneath Beulah as a wat'ry flame revolving every way" (*J* 14:5) — the materialistic sword of the cherub barring entrance to Eden and the Tree of Life. They are also "a Forest of affliction, growing in seas of sorrow" (*J* 14:8).

Their congregations consist of the "Elect" (the Pharisees); to save them from Eternal Death they must be formed into these churches "that they destroy not the Earth" (*Mil* 25:39). Religious wars are the bloodiest of all wars. Los bends his force against the east (Luvah) lest the "Three Heavens of Beulah should the Creation detroy" (*Mil* 26:20). They sacrifice even Jesus himself (*Mil* 2:15); but breaking through the Central Zone of Death and Hell, he opens Eternity into Time (*J* 75:21).

Ololon, descending into Ulro, rends the Heavens of Beulah with her thunders and lightnings (*Mil* 34:5).

BEZALEEL ("in the shadow of God") and Aholiab were divinely appointed to build the Ark, the Mercy Seat, the Tabernacle, and all its furniture (*Exod* xxxi:1–11).

The two are cited in "If it is True, what the Prophets write" (*K* 543), as proof that the real artist is divinely inspired.

The BIBLE is not to be understood literally as a mere history of past events: this "natural sense" Voltaire was "commissioned by God to expose" (*CR* 267). "The letter killeth, but the spirit giveth life" (*II Cor* iii:6). Therefore Blake read the Bible spiritually, "in its infernal or diabolical sense," as his irony once phrased it (*MHH* 24).

"The Hebrew Bible & the Gospel of Jesus are . . . Eternal Vision or Imagination of All that Exists" (*LJ, K* 604). It applies not only to the dead of the past, but to every Individual now and always. We are all born into Paradise; we all fall and become enslaved; we escape from our bondage only to endure the long trek through the Wilderness, where we come under the Law; our own hearts are the Bethlehem where Jesus is born.

Read this way, the Bible is the whole history of man in this world, "the Woof of Six Thousand Years" (*Mil* 42:15). It has three grand periods: Creation (*Genesis*), Redemption (the Gospels), and Judgment (*Revelation*), written "in the Vision & in

the Prophecy, that we may Foresee & Avoid the terrors of Creation & Redemption & Judgment" (*J* 92:19; cf. *LJ, K* 614).

Blake accepted Swedenborg's list of the books to be read symbolically (for not all of the Bible is inspired). When Albion fell into his deadly sleep, the merciful Saviour, "surrounded with a Cloud . . . builded with immortal labour, of gold & jewels, a sublime Ornament, a Couch of repose with Sixteen pillars, canopied with emblems & written verse, Spiritual Verse, order'd & measur'd: from whence time shall reveal the Five books of the Decalogue: the books of Joshua & Judges, Samuel, a double book, & Kings, a double book, the Psalms & Prophets, the Four-fold Gospel, and the Revelations everlasting. Eternity groan'd & was troubled at the image of Eternal Death!" (*J* 48:4–12). Eno, who reveals the eternity in a grain of sand and in a moment, peruses Albion's tomb, reading the books in the spiritual sense (*J* 48:41). When at the end of *Milton* Jesus appears, "round his limbs the Clouds of Ololon folded as a Garment dipped in blood, written within & without in woven letters, & the Writing is the Divine Revelation in the Litteral expression, a Garment of War" (*Mil* 42:11). The "war" is of course spiritual: "the Word of God [is] the only light of antiquity that remains unperverted by War" (*On Virgil, K* 778).

The Bible is "a Poem of probable impossibilities [Aristotle's phrase], fabricated . . . by Inspiration. . . . Poetry & that poetry inspired" (On Watson, *K* 390, 392). "The Jewish & Christian Testaments are An original derivation from the Poetic Genius" (*AllR* 6). "The Hebrew Bible & the Greek Gospel are Genuine [Vision]" (*LJ, K* 605). "The Old & New Testaments are The Great Code of Art" (*Laoc, K* 777).

"The Whole Bible is fill'd with Imagination & Visions from End to End & not with Moral Virtues; that is the baseness of Plato & the Greeks & all Warriors. The Moral Virtues are continual Accusers of Sin & promote Eternal Wars & Dominency over others" (On Berkeley, *K* 774). "The Gospel is Forgiveness of Sins & has No Moral

Precepts" (On Watson, *K* 395). Blake searched the Bible for examples of the Forgiveness of Sins, and found God's forgiveness of Cain, Jehovah's hiding the Law and placing the Mercy Seat above, Balaam's reconciliation of enemies, Joseph forgiving his brethren, David forgiving Absalom, Job forgiving his children and his "friends," Joseph forgiving Mary, and Jesus forgiving the adulteress.

Although it is "addressed to the Imagination, which is Spiritual Sensation, & but mediately to the understanding, or Reason" (To Trusler, 23 Aug 1799), "the Beauty of the Bible is that the most Ignorant & Simple Minds Understand it Best" (On Thornton, *K* 786). "This sense of the Bible is equally true to all & equally plain to all. . . . If [a man] is good he will abhor wickedness in David or Abraham; if he is wicked he will make their wickedness an excuse for his" (On Watson, *K* 393). Therefore the Caiaphases read black where Blake read white (*EG a*:14).

Ezra and *Isaiah* were the first books which appealed to young Blake (To Flaxman, 12 Sept 1800). Thereafter he quoted or referred to the Bible continually; and the Goyder-Keynes *William Blake's Illustrations to the Bible* (London, 1957) reproduces one hundred and seventy-five pictures, which are often much more than mere illustrations.

The BIBLE OF HELL, Blake wrote, "I have also . . . which the world shall have whether they will or no" (*MHH* 24). This work was obviously a symbolic reading of the Bible, which Blake was determined to publish.

The beginning of such a work may be found in *The Book of Los* and *The Book of Ahania*. Both of them were written in free anapestic trimeter and arranged in double columns; for once they were etched by the ordinary method with the simplest decorations; were published at Lambeth in 1795; then suppressed.

The story of their production and suppression might be something as follows.

Blake had already issued his most elaborate work hitherto: *The First Book of Urizen* (1794). *The Book of Ahania* was certainly intended to be *The Second Book of Urizen*; but Blake erased the word "First" and gave the sequel another title. Now the events of this sequel are paralleled with the events of *Exodus*, whereas *The Book of Urizen*, though it dealt with the beginnings of things, has no such parallels with *Genesis*. Blake then produced *The Book of Los*, which retells the story of *The Book of Urizen*, but with strong parallels from *Genesis*.

At this point Blake became dissatisfied with his *Bible of Hell*, if such it were. He evidently suppressed *The Book of Los* and *The Book of Ahania*, which survived in single copies only, and began recasting his complete myth in a new poem, *The Four Zoas*.

Towards the end of his life he started a new attempt at *The Bible of Hell*, but sketched a few pages only. This consisted of a transcription of the text of *Genesis*, with interpretive chapter-headings and illustrations. See GENESIS.

BILLINGSGATE is the great fish-market on Lower Thames Street, near London Bridge. With "the blast of his Furnace upon fishy Billingsgate," Los shows Cambel the fibres of her beloved (*J* 82:59).

BITUMEN is an inflammable mineral pitch which formed slime-pits in Palestine, where it was used for cementing and caulking. Milton wrote: "A black bituminous gurge | Boiles out from under ground, the mouth of Hell," near Babel, where it was used in the building of the Tower (*PL* xii:41). He also mentioned "that bituminous Lake where Sodom flam'd" (*PL* x:562). Blake placed "the Pits of Bitumen deadly" in the hell outside of Golgonooza (*J* 13:39); he contrasted the "Pits of bitumen ever burning" with Mutual Forgiveness (*J* 43:62); and Jerusalem gets lost in "a dark land of pitch & bitumen" (*J* 79:61).

BLACKHEATH was a common to the

southeast of old London. Alexander Gilchrist (*Gil* I, 7) mentions it as "a favourite day's ramble of later date."

Blake placed it to the East, as one of a quaternary surrounding London, the others being Hounslow, Norwood, and Finchley. The center is London Stone. "From Golgonooza the spiritual Four-fold London eternal, in immense labours & sorrows, ever building, ever falling, thro' Albion's four Forests which overspread all the Earth from London Stone to Blackheath east: to Hounslow west: to Finchley north: to Norwood south" (*Mil* 6:1). Los bends his force against the east, along the valleys of Middlesex from Hounslow to Blackheath (*Mil* 26:19). Malah's courts are on Blackheath; Hoglah weaves the Loom of Death on Highgate over the Thames to Shooter's Hill and thence to Blackheath (*Mil* 35:9,13). Albion orders Los to be brought to justice on London Stone, between Blackheath and Hounslow, between Norwood and Finchley (*J* 42: 51). Los builds the Mundane Shell in the Four Regions of Humanity, east, west, north, and south, till Norwood, Finchley, Blackheath, and Hounslow cover the earth (*J* 42:80).

BLADUD was tenth of the mythical kings of Britain. On being cured of leprosy by bathing in a spring later known as "Bladud's Well," he dedicated it to Minerva and founded the city of Bath there. He was a necromancer. On attempting to fly, he was dashed to pieces on the temple of Apollo.

He is seventh in Blake's list of the kings whom Los demolishes (*J* 73:35). When Rahab triumphs, Bath, holding Rahab's cup, stands upon the Severn with Merlin, Bladud, and Arthur (*J* 75:2), a triad in which Bladud symbolizes the Heart. See BATH.

BLAIR (Robert, 1699–1746) was a Scottish clergyman of distinguished family, independent means, and an uneventful life. The success of Young's *Night Thoughts* (1742) probably suggested the publication of Blair's only poem, *The Grave*, in the following year. It became an established success.

In 1805, Robert Hartley Cromek, ambitious to produce beautiful books, employed Blake to make forty illustrations for the poem, twenty of which Blake was to engrave. Flaxman wrote Hayley enthusiastically of the plan (18 Oct 1805), mentioning among the most striking designs "The Gambols of Ghosts according with their affections previous to the final Judgment" and "A Widow embracing the turf which covers her Husband's Grave." Blake actually produced "about twenty Designs, which pleas'd [Cromek] so well that he, with the same liborality with which he set me about the Drawings, has now set me to Engrave them" (To Hayley, 27 Nov 1805). At this time the Blakes were reduced to living on half a guinea a week; the twenty guineas for the drawings—now only twelve—were most welcome; but the big money was to come from the engraving, as a single plate at the usual rate for the best engraving would have brought more than the price of all the drawings.

However, Cromek distrusted Blake's austere style, and eager for the success of the book commissioned the popular engraver Louis Schiavonetti to do the plates. Blake expressed his rage in a lost letter, but enclosed a new sketch for the dedication, which Cromek indignantly rejected (May 1807) in a scurrilous letter, which even suggested that Blake might withdraw from the project. (See *Wilson*, 187–91.) But Blake did not withdraw.

The finished volume (1808) was indeed handsome. Cromek had worked hard to make it a success. It was dedicated by permission to the queen; there were 589 subscribers; and members of the Royal Academy, headed by West, approved the pictures. But Blake, disappointed of the money he had expected to make, must have regarded the book with strong but contrary emotions. The frontispiece was his own portrait; the dedication was his own poem; here were some of his best designs. But Schiavonetti's name preceded his on the engraved title page; Schiavonetti's sentimental style had enfeebled his designs; and there was an announcement of Stothard's "Canterbury Pilgrims," the idea for which Cromek had stolen from Blake.

Also, Blair's poem was quite antipathetic. His subject was mainly the vanity of human aspirations, in a reiterated echo of Hamlet: "Where are the jesters now? . . . Where the droll, whose very look and gesture was a joke to clapping theatres and shouting crowds?" His setting was that of the mortuary horrors: "the sickly taper . . . glimm'ring through thy low-brow'd misty vaults, furr'd round with mouldy damps and ropey slime." Blake, however, believed that death was no degrading and ironic end, but only an episode in life. The corpse is consumed in a quiet flame. His dead sleep peacefully together in a vault illumined by a clear lamp, which is no sickly taper. At least once, his picture is a flat contradiction of the text: that where the departing soul hovers over the body. Blake's picture is a peaceful scene at dawn; unlike Blair's, his soul is not frantic, shrieking, groaning, weeping blood, and sinking to tremendous ruin. For the rest, the binder had difficulty in placing the pictures appropriately, and was obliged to crowd three of the best together at the end.

The book was a success, although the nudes shocked various persons. After Cromek's death, Rudolph Ackermann, famous for his illustrated books, bought the plates from Cromek's widow for £120, and reissued *The Grave* in 1813. When the text was reset, the successful first edition was reprinted, even to the original impressive list of subscribers. But Blake's part was ostensibly minimized. Although his portrait was still the frontispiece, his name was omitted from the cover-label, and the dedication *To the Queen* was moved from its place of prominence. Biographies of Blair, Schiavonetti, and Cromek were added, but none of Blake. However, some kindlier hand (probably Fuseli's) managed to insert: "The pictorial embellishments in this edition of the poem are perfectly worthy of its subject. The

painter who produced the designs is allowed to possess great powers; his pencil, imbued with the fiery genius and bold correctness of a *Michael Angelo*, is directed by the boundless imagination of a *Dante*."

This underplaying of Blake could be accounted for by a stipulation of Widow Cromek when she sold the plates. But Ackermann, doubtless heeding the protests of Blake's admirers, atoned for this edition by publishing a handsome tall-paper second issue, in which the dedicatory poem was replaced, and the engravings gathered together at the end, in Blake's preferred order. For Blair's poem is formless; whereas Blake was always an organizer. The volume concludes with a note: "These Designs, detached from the Work they embellish, form of themselves a most interesting Poem"; and following Blake's own order of plates, "the regular progression of Man, from his first descent into the Vale of Death, to his last admission into Life eternal, is exhibited." Thus rearranged, without Blair's shallow verse, they constitute one of Blake's Prophetic Books. This attempt to express his ideas through a series of pictures without text was preceded by *The Gates of Paradise* (1793) and followed by *Illustrations of the Book of Job* (1825).

In 1826, the plates were used in Jose Joaquin de Mora's *Meditaciones poeticas*. Ackermann, as part of his plan to familiarize Latin America with European culture, commissioned the political refugee to write twelve poems as "illustraciones de las estampas." A. L. Dick in 1847 and in 1858 published at New York an abridgment of the 1813 edition, with Blake's illustrations reduced and re-engraved.

When Gilchrist's *Life of William Blake* (1863) made the artist's name familiar again, a deposit of prints left over from 1813 came to light, probably in Ackermann's storehouse. Somebody (possibly John Camden Hotton) reissued the books; and when he ran out of portraits, gathered the remaining plates in portfolios. There are no new title pages, no places or dates indicated; but the bindings are in mid-Victorian style, and could not have been made in the first half-century.

In 1963 was issued at Providence *Blake's Grave*, a reproduction of the prints without Blair's text, to emphasize its significance as a Prophetic Book.

BOADICEA was the British queen who led a revolt against the Romans; on being defeated, she took poison, in A.D. 62.

Milton, who took her story from Dion and inserted it in his paraphrase of Geoffrey of Monmouth, was disgusted with her unwomanly actions. "For *Boadicea* and her Daughters ride about in a Chariot, telling the tall Champions as a great encouragement, that with the *Britans* it was usual for Women to be their Leaders. A deal of other fondness they put into her mouth, not worth recital; how she was lash'd, how her Daughters were handl'd, things worthier silence, retirment, and a Vail, then for a Woeman to repeat, as don to hir own person, or to hear repeated before an host of men. The *Greek Historian* setts her in the field on a high heap of turves, in a loose-bodied Gown declaming, a Spear in her hand, a Hare in her bosome, which after a long circumlocution she was to let slip among them for lucks sake, then praying to *Andate the British Goddess*, to talk again as fondly as before." Milton rejects this story, however, as a foreign fabrication to prove that "in *Britain* Woemen were Men, and Men Woemen" (*History of Britain* II).

Blake names her as seventh of the Daughters of Albion (*FZ* ii:62), but on repeating the list in *Jerusalem* 5:43, he substituted Gwiniverra. He identifies Boadicea with Cambel (*J* 71:23). Hand with "double Boadicea" (i.e., Cambel = Boadicea) in cruel pride cuts Reuben apart from the hills of Surrey (*J* 90:24). "Double" suggests Rahab, the "Double Female . . . Religion hid in War" (*J* 89:52).

BOGNOR (Sussex) was too insignificant to be shown in Cary's Atlas of 1787, though he located "Bognor Rocks" directly south of Felpham about a mile out to sea. "It was only some nine years previous to Blake's residence in Sussex that Sir Richard Hotham, the retired hatter, had set Bognor going as a fashionable watering-place. He had found it a sequestered hamlet of smugglers" (*Gil* I, 160). Blake, when arranging for a visit from the Buttses, suggested that they might find Bognor "a pleasant relief from business in the summer" (To Butts, 10 May 1801).

When Albion wakes, "he mov'd his right foot to Cornwall, his left to the Rocks of Bognor. He strove to rise to walk into the Deep" (*Mil* 39:49).

BOHAN was a son of Reuben (*Josh* xv:6), of whom nothing further is known. His Stone marked the division between Judah and Benjamin; but Blake located it across the Jordan in Bashan, which he had assigned to Reuben. See BASHAN.

"Reuben slept in Bashan . . . between Succoth & Zaretan beside the Stone of Bohan" (*J* 34:43). After his incursion into the land of the Hittite, he "return'd to Bashan; in despair he slept on the Stone" (*J* 34:51).

BOILS were the second trial of Job. After Satan had destroyed Job's sons and his property, he returned again and smote the man himself with "sore boils from the sole of his foot unto his crown" (*Job* ii:7). They were the symptoms of that most dreaded of diseases, leprosy.

But to Blake, boils had a spiritual significance. His sixth illustration to *Job* shows Satan (now with scaly loins) emptying with his left hand a vial upon Job's head. The four arrows beneath Satan's right hand indicate that this picture symbolizes the death of the four Senses and the corruption of the fifth, that of Touch or Sex.

When Luvah (love) strove to gain dominion over Albion, the latter was left prostrate, "cover'd with boils from head to foot, the terrible smitings of Luvah" (*FZ* iii:82; *J* 29:64). Albion laments: "The disease of Shame covers me from head to feet. I have no hope. Every boil upon my body is a separate & deadly Sin. Doubt first assail'd me, then Shame took possession of me" (*J* 21:3). "Yet why these smitings of Luvah, the gentlest mildest Zoa?" (*J* 24:52).

BOLINGBROKE (1678–1751) was a famous skeptic and leading Deist, on whose ideas Pope innocently based his *Essay on Man*. Voltaire admired Bolingbroke's *Letters on the Study of History*. "How is this thing, this Newtonian Phantasm, this Voltaire & Rousseau, this Hume & Gibbon & Bolingbroke, this Natural Religion, this impossible absurdity?" (*Mil* 40:11).

BONAPARTE and Byron were the two supermen who obsessed the imagination of the early nineteenth century. Both were individualists who challenged the time-spirit of the Age of Reason. Bonaparte, the self-made man, stopped the disorders of the French Revolution; he spread its principles of Liberty, Equality, and Fraternity through the Continent; he tumbled down the petty kings and abolished the various inquisitions. But in becoming the master of the Continent, he also became the great menace to England. In 1803, during the inevitable hysteria, a soldier, Scofield, accused Blake and his wife of being ardent Bonapartists; Blake was tried for high treason and acquitted.

The next year, Bonaparte betrayed the high hopes of the liberals by crowning himself Emperor. The great liberator had become the tyrant. Beethoven, who had dedicated his *Eroica* to him, erased the dedication. Blake insisted "that the Bonaparte of Italy was killed, and that another was somehow substituted from the exigent want of the name, who was the Bonaparte of the Empire! . . . and a very plausible story he made of it" (*Gil* I, 373).

Among other misdeeds, Bonaparte removed many of the European art treasures to the Louvre. "Let us teach Buonaparte, & whomsoever else it may concern, That it is not Arts that follow & attend upon Empire, but Empire that attends upon & follows The Arts" (*PubA*, *K* 597).

The BOOK OF AHANIA, *Lambeth, Printed by W. Blake, 1795*, exists in a single copy only, now in the Rosenwald Collection. There are some scattered sheets in the Morgan Library and the Yale University Library. For its relationship to *The Book of Urizen* and *The Book of Los*, see BIBLE OF HELL.

As the plot of *The Book of Ahania* continues that of *The [First] Book of Urizen*, it was originally intended to be *The Second Book*, then Blake erased "First" and gave the new book its present title. But even so, Blake was dissatisfied with it, obviously because his ideas were expanding and the myth was changing accordingly. Therefore, in spite of his startling anticipation of Freud's Oedipus complex and the beauty of Ahania's lament, he suppressed the book, never advertising it, but keeping a single copy for himself. Later he rewrote the myth into *The Four Zoas*.

The basic idea was surely suggested by the first part of Plato's *Philebus*, where the relationship of Wisdom and Pleasure is discussed. The main plot of Blake's poem consists of Urizen's (Reason's) division from and rejection of Ahania (Pleasure).

Fuzon, the fire-son of Urizen, revolting against his father's tyranny, molds his wrath into a globe, which pierces Urizen's shield and divides his loins. (This suggests Saturn's castration of his father.) Urizen names his sundered Emanation "Ahania," and hides her, calling her "Sin"; she falls into darkness and becomes the Mother of Pestilence. Urizen then makes a black stone-bow of the ribs of a serpent (Nature) and with a poisoned rock (the Decalogue) smites Fuzon just as he believes that he is now God.

The upas Tree of Mystery (the religion of moral values) had sprung up under Urizen's heel as he worked on his books; he was nearly trapped in the labyrinth but escaped, though he had to leave his Book of Iron (warfare). Now on this Tree he nails Fuzon's living corpse, where for forty years the arrows of pestilence fly round it. Clouds of disease rise about the disorganized Urizen; Los forges nets of iron, in which he snares a few of them. The poem ends with the lament of Ahania, weeping for Urizen round the Tree of Fuzon.

These events occur in the individual soul; they were also manifested in the early history of man. Fuzon's fiery beam (revolt) was the pillar of fire which led the Israelites from Egypt. Urizen's rock (the Decalogue) falls upon Mount Sinai. The forty years of Fuzon's crucifixion are the forty years of the wandering in the wilderness (also the hardening of the skulls), until Asia (the future home of the Israelites) rises from the deep.

Blake suppressed the book probably because of his dissatisfaction with his symbols. Passion (Fuzon) could not possibly be the child of Reason (Urizen); he is merely the element of Fire. Also, it was Jesus, not Fuzon, who was crucified on the Tree of Mystery. Therefore Blake never published his book, and dropped Fuzon entirely from his mythology.

See AHANIA.

The BOOK OF LOS, *Lambeth, Printed by W. Blake, 1795*, exists in a single copy, now in the British Museum. For its relationship to *The Book of Urizen* and *The Book of Ahania*, see BIBLE OF HELL.

The Book of Los retells the story of *The Book of Urizen* from the point of view of Los; but it is also a paraphrase of *Genesis* i. As it ends with the creation of Adam, Blake may have intended this book to precede the other two, for *The Book of Urizen* ends with the enslavement of man in Africa, and *The Book of Ahania* with man's escape into Asia. However, in the beginning, Eternity is already disorganized, Los is already separated from Urizen, and the flames of desire are already loose. The tremendous forging of a form for Urizen in six days is now reduced to Los's binding the sun to Urizen's spine.

The plot concerns the furious efforts of Los (the creative imagination) to give form to the disorganized universe in which he finds himself trapped. The creation is the result of his desperate wrath.

Chapter i, stanzas 1–5, is a prelude in which the aged mother Eno recalls that Golden Age when what are now considered deadly sins were innocent pleasures.

On the first day of *Genesis*, God divided the light from the darkness. Los, bound in a chain and compelled to watch Urizen's shadow, in his fury divides the lightless flames of pestilential desires. As a result, the fires freeze into a solid, which binds in his clear expanding senses (4:4).

On the second day of *Genesis*, the firmament dividing the waters above from the waters below was created. Los rends the black solid and falls until the vacuum becomes the element of water (Chap. ii).

On the third day of *Genesis*, the waters and the land were divided and vegetation began. In the waters, Los develops lungs, and sleep begins. On waking, he starts to grow into an immense fibrous form. Furious, he smites the waters, dividing the heavy, which sinks, from the thin, which rises (Chap. iii).

On the fourth day of *Genesis*, the sun, moon, and stars were created. In Blake's poem, light begins, and Los sees Urizen's spine. Terrified, he makes the tools for forging and begins the binding of Urizen. But first, from the flowing particles of light he makes the sun, which he binds to Urizen's spine (Chap. iv, st. 1–7).

The fifth day of *Genesis*, on which the whales and fishes were created, is omitted from Blake's paraphrase.

The sixth day was that of the creation of Adam. Urizen lies in fierce torments on his glowing bed; then from his brain in a rock and his heart in a fleshy slough flow four rivers (of Eden), and a Form is created, a Human Illusion (Adam). Here the poem ends.

It is possible to consider *The Book of Los* as the prelude to *The Song of Los*, which begins with the newly created Adam, leads up to *America* and *Europe* (the Christian era), then concludes the cycle of the continents. Blake was evidently trying to consolidate his myths; but *The Song of Los* was designed in an entirely different format.

See LOS.

The BOOK OF THEL, *The Author &
Printer Willm Blake, 1789,* was the first, the
simplest, and the most charming of the
prophetic books written and printed by
Blake. It was preceded by *Tiriel,* which
Blake left in manuscript, incorporating a
few lines in his new poem. Both poems use
names from Agrippa's *Occult Philosophy.*

The Book of Thel is best understood as a
rewriting of Milton's *Comus.* Milton's Lady
is a girl on the verge of womanhood, who is
travelling towards her parents' estate. She
gets lost in a forest by night; hears strange
voices, which she exorcizes by invoking her
chastity; meets the evil Comus disguised in
the innocent garb of a shepherd; and goes
with him to his palace, where by the power
of his wand he fixes her in a chair. But she
refuses the cup of actual dissipation; then
her brothers drive Comus away and break
his cup, but neglect to seize his wand. The
maiden Sabrina rises from her stream, and
with a sprinkling of her pure waters releases
the Lady from Comus' charm.

This is the tale of a girl's first infatuation
with an unworthy person, whose true character she discovers only after he has fascinated her. Sabrina, who finally releases her,
is evidently the healing power of Nature.

Blake tells the same story, but in biological terms, not moral ones. Thel is also the
girl on the verge of womanhood. She is still
self-centered, for she dwells in the Vales of
Har. (See HAR.) But it is characteristic of
her years that she is beginning to ponder
the mysteries of life and death. She questions the value of her own virginity (the
Lily); she considers impregnation (the
Cloud) and motherhood (the Clod). The
Cloud, who corresponds to Milton's Comus, is, however, simply the non-moral
principle of the fertilizing male; his moisture
seeks the dew of the flower. All these characters assure Thel that they have purpose,
even though they may not understand it,
and that life consists of self-sacrifice. The
poem comes to a climax when Thel hears
the voices of her awakening senses, especially sex. These are the same voices which
Milton's Lady dismissed so primly. But

Thel is terrified and flees in revulsion back
to the innocent Vales of Har.

Besides Milton and Agrippa, Voltaire
may have influenced one passage. In his
bitter poem on the Lisbon earthquake, he
attacked the popular optimism which taught
that all one's misfortunes are benefits in the
general scheme of things. "Quand la mort
met le comble aux maux que j'ai soufferts, |
Le beau soulagement d'être mangé des
vers!" Blake answered him: "Then if thou
art the food of worms, O virgin of the skies,
| How great thy use, how great thy bless-
ing!" (3:25).

There is also an echo of Young's "O the
soft Commerce! O the tender Tyes | Close-
twisted with the Fibres of the Heart" (*Night
Thoughts,* v:1063–64) in Blake's lines:
"She saw the couches of the dead, & where
the fibrous roots | Of every heart on earth
infixes deep its restless twists" (6:3). See
YOUNG.

Eighteen copies of *The Book of Thel* have
been traced, two of them bound up with its
intellectual sequel, *Visions of the Daughters
of Albion.* The decorations of the text, colored in simple water-color washes, are
straight illustrations. On the title page,
Thel, holding the sheephook of Innocence,
stands beneath the slender trunk of a weeping willow with light spring foliage. She
watches the fertilization of womblike flowers
—a tiny male (the Cloud) reaches to embrace a tiny female. A bud ready to open is
lifting itself at Thel's feet. The tail-piece
symbolizes the innocent sexual play of children. A girl, with a light bridle, guides the
Serpent of Nature; behind her, two baby
boys climb on for the ride. This design is
repeated in *America,* Plate 13.

See THEL.

The [First] BOOK OF URIZEN, *Lambeth,
Printed by Will Blake, 1794,* with twenty-
eight plates in a complete copy, was Blake's
most ambitious production thitherto. Sev-
en copies and a few scattered pages have
been located. From these it is evident that
Blake worked hard over this book, adding or transposing plates, erasing lines,

and painting over figures in the designs.

It was intended to be the first of a series dealing with activities in the supernatural world which caused the creation of the natural world and the early history of mankind. Blake named its sequel *The Book of Ahania* (1795), however, and erased "First" from the title of *The Book of Urizen*. The *Book of Los* (1795) is closely related. All three are written in the unusual meter of free unrhymed anapestic trimeters, which he did not use elsewhere. Then Blake suppressed the two last *Books*, and later recast the entire project as part of *The Four Zoas*. The binding of Urizen is repeated almost verbatim in *The Four Zoas* (iv:215–46) and *Milton* (3:9–27).

The plot describes Urizen's secret deeds in his dark world, then the promulgation of his tyrannic laws; the opposition of Los, who binds him in a human shape; the division of Los through Pity, which is the creation of Enitharmon, and the birth of Orc, Urizen's future opponent; the travels of Urizen through his world, and the birth and cursing of his children; and finally the degeneration of mankind under Urizen's religion.

There are a few obscure references to *Genesis* i. Los creates the form of Urizen in six "ages," and in the seventh, Urizen moves (10:31–13:19). Later, Urizen creates this world and plants the garden of Eden (20:33–41). Under the stultifying net of his religion, men are materialized: "Six days they shrunk up from existence, and on the seventh day they rested" (25:39). In the subsequent *Book of Los*, however, the story is retold with close parallels throughout.

The influence of Behmen is discernible in the first chapter. Creation is the work of opposition and anguish. At the beginning, Urizen contracts, expands, and rotates after the formula of Behmen's Dark World. However, there is no parallel activity in the Light World. The transmuting Spark, which should result from the friction of the two Worlds, may find its equivalent in Los's furnace. But Urizen's Dark World is one of water; the fires all belong to the Light World.

Underlying the first four of the nine chapters (actually there are ten, but two are both numbered "Four," thus keeping the number correspondent to Urizen's "ninefold darkness") is a description of the prenatal forces which produce the human form. These forces are spiritual, because "every Natural Effect has a Spiritual Cause, and Not a Natural; for a Natural Cause only seems: it is a Delusion of Ulro" (*Mil* 26:44). The true causes are the Contraries of Law (Urizen) and the creating Imagination (Los). In self-protection, Urizen forms the womb: "a roof, vast, petrific around on all sides . . . like a womb, where thousands of rivers in veins of blood pour down the mountains to cool the eternal fires" (*Ur* 5:28). The puzzling lake (10:22) is the amniotic fluid. Then the embryo develops into the foetus. Los gives Urizen a human shape: first the skull, spine, and other bones; then the heart and the arterial system; next, nervous system with its four senses, including the tongue and the alimentary system; and finally the foetus moves (10:35–13:19). These "changes" correspond roughly to the third through the sixteenth week of life.

We have learned much about embryology since Blake's day; for example, Van Baer, "the father of modern embryology," did not discover the mammalian ovum until the year of Blake's death. Yet even so, Blake anticipated the modern theory of recapitulation (19:34) and the Oedipus complex (20:9–25).

Urizen first appears as a self-closed shadow of horror, withdrawing from the rest of existence. This concentering has rent him from the side of Los, leaving Los in anguish (6:4), but Urizen does not understand the severing. "First I fought with the fire, consum'd inwards into a deep world within: a void immense, wild, dark & deep, where nothing was . . . & arose on the waters" (4:14–22). He strives with the chaos of amorphous forms, expanding and revolving (3:13–18); then he prepares his weapons of conquest.

As yet, Eternity was eternal life, with no earth or other "globes of attraction" (the solar system). Urizen with a trumpet blast summons the Eternals to hear the promulgation of his laws. He seeks a joy without pain, a solid without fluctuation, whereas the Eternals live in unquenchable burnings (which to him seem like torment) and die (for each other). Urizen has divided dark from light; he has created a solid; he has written his books about the seven deadly sins which inhabit all breasts; and now he reveals the Book of Brass, which would standardize all life under One King, One God, One Law.

The Eternals are furious, especially when the seven deadly sins appear in living creations. Eternity splits (division of Good and Evil). Fires roar down on Urizen's armies; he flees in anguish until he forms a roof to protect himself, and his world appears like a struggling heart.

Los now enters the scene. Urizen has been rent from his side (division of Imagination and Reason), and the wound will not heal. Though Urizen has fallen into a deathlike sleep, Los in fright begins his work at the forge, making traps for the amorphous shapes hurtling about. Then he forges the chains of Time, and Urizen's chaos settles like a lake.

Next, Los gives form to Urizen in seven ages. First, the skeleton; then the heart and its system; then the nerves and the eyes; the ears; the nostrils; the tongue and the digestive system. Urizen's senses are now limited; in the seventh age, he faces West, flinging his arms to North and South.

Urizen (still sleeping) can see only through his eyes; his eternal life is obliterated like a dream. Los's fires decay; he smites a blow from north to south; the two are now enclosed in a cold silent solitude and a dark void.

Los now pities Urizen, and the pity divides Los. His heart takes shape outside himself and becomes Enitharmon. In horror at the sight of "the first female now separate" (18:10), the Eternals shut the two out with a Tent (the material sky, or "Science"). On Enitharmon, Los begets a child, who is a worm, then a serpent, taking

on "many forms of fish, bird & beast" (19: 34), until it is born as the boy Orc (revolt). He is the future opponent of Urizen, who will force him back into the worm and serpent of Eden. The Tent is now finished, and Los beholds Eternity no more.

Los becomes jealous of the boy's affection for his mother, "discerning plain that Orc plotted his death" (FZ v:82). The parents bind Orc down on a mountain top with the chain of Los's jealousy. But at Orc's voice, the dead begin to wake. (At first, the Imagination suppresses the instinct to revolt, yet it cannot be silenced.)

Urizen wakes also, and explores his dens. He forms mathematical instruments, including the compasses, to divide the Abyss beneath (creation of this world), where he plants a garden of fruits (Paradise). His children then emerge from his horrible chaos. His first sons are the four elements: Thiriel (air), Utha (water), Grodna (earth), and Fuzon (fire), the first begotten and last born. His daughters are created from lower forms of life. He curses all his children because neither flesh nor spirit can keep his iron laws one moment. Life now lives upon death (food killed for consumption); he weeps and calls it "Pity."

On high he wanders over his children's cities, drawing after him a cold shadow like a spider's web (religion), which no wings of fire can break.

In six days, his children shrink from existence and reptilize (materialize); on the seventh day they rest in sick hope, and forget eternal life. Their thirty cities divide in the form of a human heart (heart-shaped Africa). No longer able to soar into the infinite at will, they are bound to earth by their narrowing perceptions. They live a number of years, then die, leaving a corpse. They build tombs and develop laws of prudence, which they call the eternal laws of God. They can no longer discern their brothers of other cities (the brotherhood of man is lost).

Fuzon calls together all the remaining children of Urizen; they leave the pendulous earth, naming it Egypt (slavery).

Thus Blake triumphed over the god of

the Age of Reason. He relegated it to its proper place in the human psyche, gave it a human form, analyzed its errors at length, and limited them to time. See URIZEN.

BOSTON, the capital of Massachusetts, was the first town in America to oppose actively the encroachments of the British ministry on its citizens' rights as Englishmen. With the other colonies, it protested vigorously against the Stamp Act (1765) as taxation without representation; it was withdrawn; but two years later a high duty was imposed on tea, which was resented for the same reason. The royal governor Bernard quartered troops on the town in 1768. He was recalled the next year, for rapacity and other misdeeds; but the troops remained until the "Boston Massacre" of 1770, when they fired upon a small crowd, killing five and wounding eight, after which they were withdrawn. In December 1773, three cargoes of the hated tea were to be unloaded, over the protests of fiery town-meetings; but a group of patriots, disguised as Indians, boarded the ships and dumped the tea into the harbor; this event was the famous "Boston Tea Party." The troops were quartered on the town again, and the port was closed, causing great hardship, Boston being a port of entry. In June 1775, the patriots occupied Bunker Hill, which overlooked the town, but were driven away in an exceedingly bloody battle, where the beloved physician, General Warren, was killed. In the action, the town of Charlestown was burned. Finally, Washington's occupation of Dorchester Heights forced the evacuation of Boston in March 1776.

These events are a background for Blake's *America*. Washington and other patriots "meet on the coast glowing with blood" (3:5)—a non-historical convention inspired by the Boston Massacre. "Boston's Angel" makes a vigorous protest and refuses allegiance; Erdman identifies him with Samuel Adams. He also sees a reference to the Tea Party: "The mariners of Boston drop their anchors and unlade" (14:14), though this might refer to the closing of the port. Blake assumes a meeting of the thirteen royal governors in Bernard's house (the Province House). He mentions Warren four times (3:4; 9:11; 12:7; 14:2).

The BOW is a customary weapon for all of Blake's characters. Blake himself has a bow of "burning gold" (gold is the metal signifying intellect) with "Arrows of desire" (*Mil* 1:9), although elsewhere they are "long winged arrows of thought" (*J* 38:14). God has a bow; each arrow is "the bitter groan of a Martyr's woe" (*J* 52:29). Albion has a bow and "arrows of flaming gold" (*J* 95:13),with which he slays the Covering Cherub. "And the Bow is a Male & Female, & the Quiver of the Arrows of Love are the Children of this Bow, a Bow of Mercy & Loving-kindness laying open the hidden Heart in Wars of mutual Benevolence, Wars of Love" (*J* 97:12). It is a fourfold Bow, compounded of the bows of the Zoas.

Satan's black Bow is the exact contrary. It is of hate, not love; of revenge, not mercy; of death, not life. "When Satan first the black bow bent | And the Moral Law from the Gospel rent, | He forg'd the Law into a Sword | And spill'd the blood of Mercy's Lord" (*J* 52:17).

Urizen's black stone-bow (*Ahan* 3:23) is obviously that of Satan. It is made of the ribs of the Serpent of nature; it is poisoned with hatred; it smites the fiery Fuzon, who is then crucified. However, when Urizen is redeemed, his weapon is "a breathing Bow of carved Gold" (*J* 97:8).

BOW ("Old Bow") in Blake's day was a Middlesex village a little to the east of Mile-end Road, which leads to Maldon. (Today it is in the county of London and the borough of Poplar.) It was named "Bow" from the stone arches of its bridge across the river Lea, built by Maud, the wife of Henry I. It was and is commonly known as Stratford-le-Bow. The bridge led to a hamlet also called Stratford.

Los's forge is heard "to Stratford & old Bow & across to the Gardens of Kensington" (*Mil* 6:10). "He heaves the iron cliffs in his rattling chains from Hyde Park to the Alms-houses of Mile-end & old Bow" (*Mil* 6:30). When war broke out, "Jerusalem fell from Lambeth's Vale | Down thro' Poplar & Old Bow, | Thro' Malden & acros[s] the Sea" (*J* 27:41). When Bath's Spectre assimilated with Luvah, he tried "to cast Jerusalem forth upon the wilds to Poplar & Bow, to Malden & Canterbury" (*J* 41:5). After Jerusalem is gone, Albion's Daughters strive to wake "Highgate's heights & Hampsteads . . . Poplar, Hackney & Bow . . . Islington & Paddington & the Brook of Albion's River" (*J* 84:1).

During the poet's perambulation of London, "he came down from Highgate thro' Hackney & Holloway towards London till he came to old Stratford & thence to Stepney" (*J* 31:14).

The BOWELS, a general term for all the organs within the abdomen, are the customary symbol of compassion (*I John* iii:17; *J* 56:34), found throughout the Bible (*Gen* xliii:30; *Col* iii:12; etc.). Paul wrote the Philippians (i:8): "How greatly I long after you all in the bowels of Jesus Christ."

"Tharmas beheld them; his bowels yearn'd over them" (*FZ* iv:6). "All the Regions of Beulah were moved as the tender bowels are moved" (*J* 25:1; cf. *Song of Sol* v:4). The False Tongue has a false brain, heart, and bowels (*J*14:6). Within the Polypus, "the Five Females & the nameless Shadowy Mother" spin the Ulro "from their bowels with songs of amorous delight and melting cadences that lure the Sleepers of Beulah down the River Storge" (*Mil* 34:27).

The Bowels are not to be confused with the Intestines (see OR-ULRO).

BOWEN, a Son of Albion in *Jerusalem*, was originally somebody connected with Blake's trial, but he has never been identified. Herbert Ives conjectures that he might have been the prosecuting attorney; David Erdman, that he was one of the dragoons. Herbert Jenkins discovered a Thomas Barton Bowen on the Law List, who practised on the Home Circuit and Sussex Sessions; it is possible that he assisted at this trial.

Blake's Bowen is the twelfth and last of Albion's Sons. His Emanation is Conwenna (*J* 71:47). In the first listing of Albion's Sons, the last four are separated from the others by a single line: "Scofield, Kox, Kotope and Bowen revolve most mightily upon the Furnace of Los" (*J* 5:27); but usually Bowen acts only in concert with the other eleven Sons. They appear outside Albion; they are Satan's Mills (*J* 19:19). They issue in stern defiance from Albion's bosom and bear him to a golden couch, round which they rear "their Druid Patriarchal rocky Temples" (*J* 32:14). When the Sons disperse at the sight of Reuben, Kotope and Bowen become what they behold, fleeing over the earth (*J* 36:19).

When Scofield (the Accuser) becomes dominant, the three others of the last four, Kox, Kotope, and Bowen, are one in him, a Fourfold Wonder, and they involve the other eight (*J* 7:48)—i.e., the system of justice becomes wholly accusatory. When Los cries out against appropriating the characteristics of others, then Hand, Hyle, Bowen, and Scofield in Selfhood appropriate the Divine Names in a corporeal and ever dying Vegetation and Corruption; mingling with Luvah (in his fallen state of Wrath) in one, they become the Great Satan (*J* 90:40)—that is, when the emotional interpretation of Law sets itself up as God, it becomes Satan.

Eventually, Bowen has a separate function. When all twelve Sons are drinking Luvah (*J* 90:17), and the last four are materializing the divine Vision and becoming Satan (*J* 90:41), Bowen and Conwenna stand on Skiddaw, "cutting the Fibres of Benjamin from Chester's River" (*J* 90:14). He sears the fibres "with hot Iron of his Forge & fixes them into Bones of chalk & Rock [Albion's white cliffs]. Conwenna sat above; with solemn cadences she drew Fibres of life out from the Bones into her golden Loom" (*J*90:19). At the same time, Hand "with double Boadicea in cruel pride cut Reuben apart from the Hills of Surrey" (*J*90:24).

Now, Albion's Sons correspond to the Sons of Israel, who are "as the Soul is to the Body" (*J* 71:4). Hand, the first of Albion's Sons, therefore corresponds to Reuben, the first of Israel's Sons; and Bowen, the last, to Benjamin, also the last. The combination of oldest and youngest Sons suggests an action inclusive of them all.

In his redeemed form, Bowen is given the highest place: he has all Scotland, the Isles, and the two northernmost of the English counties, Northumberland and Cumberland (in which is Mount Skiddaw). Conwenna "shines a triple form over the north with pearly beams gorgeous and terrible. Jerusalem & Vala rejoice in Bowen & Conwenna" (*J* 71:46–49).

"BOWLAHOOLA is the Stomach in every individual man" (*Mil* 24:67); but this definition is only partial, because Bowlahoola also includes the other two motile organs, the heart and lungs (*Mil* 24:58). It is usually paired with Allamanda, the nervous system. Were it not for these two organizations, there could be "No Human Form but only a Fibrous Vegetation, a Polypus of soft affections without Thought or Vision" (*Mil* 24:37). When Blake added Entuthon Benython to this pair (*Mil* 37:59), he anticipated the modern theory of the three basic types: the endomorphs, ectomorphs, and mesomorphs. At any rate, the three constitute human physiology.

All natural effects have a spiritual cause: the motive power of Bowlahoola is none other than the creative imagination. "In Bowlahoola Los's Anvils stand & his Furnaces rage . . . The Bellows are the Animal Lungs: the Hammers the Animal Heart: the Furnaces the Stomach for digestion" (*Mil* 24:51, 58; *J* 53:12). Here he creates bodies for wandering souls (*J* 40:57). All souls must descend to him in Bowlahoola, Allamanda, and Entuthon Benython (*Mil* 37:59); here the spectres choose their affinities; "the various Classes of Men are all mark'd out determinate"; and "so they are born on earth" (*Mil* 26:37, 39).

Los's Sons aid the labors (*Mil* 26:24),

clothing and feeding the formless souls. In Bowlahoola and Allamanda, they build the inward body as a mansion with a garden. Meanwhile, in Cathedron, Enitharmon's Daughters weave the flowers and the furniture (*Mil* 26:34; *J* 49–52). In Bowlahoola and Cathedron, Los makes every moment and space permanent (*J* 75:9).

In one of Blake's riddling definitions, "Bowlahoola is nam'd Law by mortals; Tharmas founded it, because of Satan, before Luban in the City of Golgonooza" (*Mil* 24:48). As "Energy . . . is from the Body" (*MHH* 4), all science is divided into Bowlahoola and Allamanda. The four eternal Arts "become apparent in Time & Space in the Three Professions, Poetry in Religion: Music, Law: Painting, in Physic & Surgery . . . and from these Three, Science derives every Occupation of Men, and Science is divided into Bowlahoola & Allamanda" (*Mil* 27:59–63). These two are placed on either side of the globule sun and the pulsation of the artery (*Mil* 29:25).

When Milton descends from heaven, the fearful Sons beg permission to bring him, chained, to Bowlahoola (*Mil* 23:18) and to throw all vegetated mortals there (*Mil* 24: 40); but Los refuses.

Bowlahoola is not to be confused with Or-Ulro, the intestines.

The BRAIN is a member of the triad of Brain (Head), Heart, and Loins, the threefold division of the vegetated man (*FZ* vii: 354; viii:55; ix:365; etc.).

In the Brain "the Eternal Great Humanity Divine planted his Paradise" (*Mil* 2:8; *FR* 184; *FZ* ix:181). It is the dwelling place of Los and Enitharmon (*FZ* i:302). Its portals open through Beulah to the poet (*FZ* viii:55; *Mil* 2:7). Even the fly has "a brain open to heaven & hell" (*Mil* 20:28).

But in the fall of man, the brain was limited. Oothoon blames the philosophy of Locke (*VDA* 2:32). In the first Age of Urizen's binding, "a roof, shaggy, wild, inclos'd in an orb his fountain of thought" (*Ur* 10:33; *FZ* iv:216). The shadowy sisters of Tirzah (Natural Religion) form "the orbed scull around the brain" (*Mil* 19:52); the Twelve Daughters of Albion in Rahab and Tirzah circumscribe the brain and pierce it with a golden pin (*J* 67:41). Gwendolen cuts round the brain, which bonifies into a Scull (*J* 58:7). Urizen baptizes Milton's brain with the icy water of the Jordan (*Mil* 19:9); the Daughters of Albion baptize their victims similarly (*J* 66:30).

"Each mortal brain is wall'd and moated round within, and Og & Anak watch here ... for in the brain and heart and loins Gates open behind Satan's Seat to the City of Golgonooza" (*Mil* 20:36). See ANAK; OG. The false brain of the Covering Cherub "incloses a reflexion of Eden all perverted" (*J* 89:14).

When Los builds Golgonooza, new heavens and a new earth are opened "within the brain, within the heart, within the loins: a Threefold Atmosphere Sublime, continuous from Urthona's world, but yet having a Limit Twofold named Satan & Adam" (*FZ* vii:381). The vegetated bodies which Enitharmon weaves for the Spectres open "within their hearts & in their loins & in their brain to Beulah" (*FZ* viii:55).

BRAMA, the supreme God of post-Vedic Hindu religion, is the divine reality, of which all things are only a manifestation. The mystical union is an absorption into the divine substance, in which the individual is lost.

When the children of Los give Urizen's laws to the nation, Rintrah (wrath) gives Abstract Philosophy to Brama in the East (*SoL* 3:11).

BRASS is one of the four symbolic metals. Its compass-point is west; of such is the bow of Tharmas made (*J* 97:10). It is the metal of social organization—of the Brotherhood of Man. Therefore, when man rises, regenerated by Revolution, "his feet become like brass" (*Am* 8:16). But in the hands of Urizen, brass is the metal of tyranny.

Of Urizen's four books, the Book of Brass is the most prominent. It contains his laws

for organizing human society. It has been copied by Kings and Priests on earth (*Eur* 11:4). Urizen announces its purpose, which seeking for laws of peace and love would standardize everything under "one King, one God, one Law" (*Ur* 4:34–40). When he unclasps it, he infuriates the Eternals (*Ur* 4:44). He reads from it to his Daughters (*FZ* vii:109–34).

Many other objects are made of brass, such as Urizen's quadrant with which he explores the Abyss (*Ur* 20:38) and the Spectre's compasses with which he divides the Space of Love (*J* 88:47), the red hot girdle which Noah places around her victim's loins (*FZ* viii:312), the gates in every human heart (*Mil* 20:34), the walls of every day and night (*Mil* 28:52), and the Covering Cherub's ribs (*J* 89:36).

Blake often couples brass with iron, because Brotherhood and Imagination must work together. Los binds Urizen with the two metals (*Ur* 8:11; 10:30; *FZ* iv:201, 214); and he builds Golgonooza with the two metals (*J* 10:63). But when the victims of the Industrial Revolution polish brass and iron hour after hour (*FZ* vii *b*:182; *J* 65:24), Blake was being quite literal.

BRAZIL is the last in Blake's list of the Thirty-two Nations who shall dwell in Jerusalem's gates and rule all the rest of the world (*J* 72:42).

BRECKNO[C]KSHIRE, in eastern Wales, is the Gate of Issachar (*J* 16:39).

BRERETON (Brertun) was William Brereton, J.P. of Petworth, an assisting Justice at Blake's trial.

Blake names him as sixth of the Sons of Albion (*J* 5:25; 19:18). His Emanation is Ragan (*J* 71:33). With his brothers, he emerges from Albion's bosom, and they bear him to a golden couch, round which they rear "their Druid Patriarchal rocky Temples" (*J* 32:14). When the Sons flee from Reuben, Brereton and Slade hide in Egypt (*J* 36:17). He is assigned Yorkshire, Durham, and Westmoreland. His Emanation, Ragan, adjoined with Slade and produced the far beaming Gonorill, who became Slade's Emanation (*J* 71:32–35).

BRISTOL, in Somersetshire, is the metropolis of western England, a big seaport a few miles from Bath. Besides the cathedral, it contains Chatterton's church of St. Mary Redcliffe.

"Chatterton never writ those poems! A parcel of fools, going to Bristol!" says the skeptical Quid (*IslM*, Chap. vii).

When the plagues projected against the Americans recoil, "the spotted plague smote Bristol's and the Leprosy London's Spirit, sickening all their bands" of soldiers (*Am* 15:2) —symbolizing the reluctance of those merchant cities hostile to the war.

Bristol is the sixth in Blake's list of the Twenty-four Cathedral Cities, and is under Urizen and Verulam (*J* 40:61). Los bids Bristol and Bath listen to his words (*J* 43: 55). The Polypus' head is in Verulam; his bulk winds through Rochester, Chichester, Exeter, and Salisbury (where his heart is) to Bristol (*J* 67:37).

The BRITON was the original inhabitant of Britain. "What do I see! The Briton, Saxon, Roman, Norman amalgamating . . . into One Nation, the English" (*J* 92:1). Blake believed that such amalgamation was necessary to break down racial barriers and thus produce the Brotherhood of Man.

BRITTANNIA (the Latin spelling preferred by Blake) is the name for England when she is wedded to Albion. "The Aged Woman is Brittannia, the Wife of Albion" (*LJ*, *K* 609). In the early period of confusion when the Zoas are changing places, "England, who is Brittannia, divided into Jerusalem & Vala" (*J* 36:28).

In the middle of *Jerusalem*, after the Spectre has announced himself as God, Albion makes an attempt to draw England into his bosom again; "but she stretch'd out her starry Night in Spaces against him like a long Serpent in the Abyss of the Spectre, which augmented the Night with Dragon wings cover'd with stars, & in the Wings, Jerusalem & Vala appear'd; & above, between the Wings magnificent, the Divine Vision dimly appear'd in clouds of blood weeping" (*J* 54:28).

At the end, England, a deadly Female Shadow, lies heavy upon the sleeping Albion's bosom (94:7). She wakes first, fainting on his body, accusing herself of having murdered him with the knife of the Druid, while she slept in dreams of chastity and moral law. "O England! O all ye Nations of the Earth, behold ye the Jealous Wife!" (*J* 94:25). Albion then opens his eyes and sees her (*J* 95:4). After he has driven the Zoas back to their proper places, "England, who is Brittannia, enter'd Albion's bosom rejoicing" (*J* 95:22; 96:2).

BROAD STREET (now unhappily renamed "Broadwick") was so called because there were few streets of that breadth within the walls before the Great Fire. It is in the Soho district, one brief block north of Golden Square. Blake was born at 28 Broad Street, on the corner of Marshall Street. His father's shop was on the ground floor; after he died in 1784, it was taken over by his oldest son James. William's exhibition of 1809 was held here. The Parker & Blake print-shop was at 27 Broad Street (1784–87); after its failure, William removed one block away to 28 Poland Street (parallel to Marshall Street), where he lived for four years.

"The Corner of Broad Street weeps: Poland Street languishes" (*J* 84:15).

The district suffered in the Gordon riots of 1780. On June 6, Blake was caught in the mob which destroyed Newgate Prison. On the next night, when the rioters were sacking the house of Mr. Donavan in Broad Street, the London Military Association, after failing to stop them, fired, killing four men and wounding fifteen. Nine or ten houses were burned in Great Queen Street nearby, where Blake had been apprenticed to Basire (1772–79).

A decade after Blake's death, Dickens described Golden Square in its decline (*Nicholas Nickleby*, Chap. ii).

BROCKLEY HILLS are now within suburban London, south of the Thames. "Hand had his Furnace on Highgate's heights & it reach'd to Brockley Hills across the Thames" (*J* 90:23).

BROMION is Reason, when used by the poet. He is the fourth of the Sixteen Sons of Los and Enitharmon (*FZ* viii:358). "Loving Science" (*Mil* 24:12), he resembles Urizen; like Urizen, his eternal position is South, but in this world (again like Urizen) he is shifted to the North (*J* 54, diagram). His Cathedral City is Verulam (*J* 74:2–3—but note that Blake reverses the order of the cities). His Emanation is Leutha (*FZ* viii: 363). When the last Twelve Sons (the Tribes) fled from Los, the first Four remained with him and thus never fell into the World of Generation (*Mil* 23:61; *J* 71:51).

Usually, Bromion is mentioned only as one of the Four. They forge the instruments of harvest, "the Plow & Harrow to pass over the Nations" (*Mil* 6:13). Various London suburbs rage loud before Bromion's tongs and poker (*J* 16:2). In the quarrel of Palamabron and Satan, Theotormon and Bromion contend on the side of Satan against their brother (*Mil* 8:30).

In *Jerusalem* 71:51, the Four are described as sons of Jerusalem. They dwell over the four provinces of Ireland, the four universities of Scotland, and in Oxford, Cambridge, and Winchester.

Bromion's biggest part is played in the *Visions of the Daughters of Albion*. When Oothoon is winging her way towards the realm of her true love, Theotormon, Bromion rapes and rejects her; but the two are "bound back to back" in a union of hatred. Oothoon thus becomes the soul caught between Desire (Theotormon) and Law (Bromion). All three lament, and Bromion's lamentation shakes his cavern. The microscope has revealed other worlds, and he begins to wonder about possibilities of life other than those we try to live by. Yet "is there not one law for both the lion and the ox?" and is there not also the traditional Hell "to bind the phantoms of existence from eternal life?" (*VDA* 4:13–24).

The BROTHERHOOD of Man is the only possible solution to the problems of this world. We are all brothers, being all sons of the Father, all one in Jesus, who is in each individual (*John* xvii:21–23). See DIVINE FAMILY. Those who already have realized this brotherhood dwell in Eden. Their city is Jerusalem, the city of peace and liberty. Their influence in the world is that of humanitarianism.

Seen afar, they are one man, Jesus; but seen near to, they are multitudes. The Brotherhood is a brotherhood of Individuals. However united in ultimate purpose, they may be widely diverse in ideas and callings; then they wage the intellectual wars of Eternity, where opposition is true friendship. Without this differentiation of Individuals, the Brotherhood would be a sterile leveling down, a tyranny of the mob.

To achieve this Brotherhood, the "dark religions" of vengeance for sin must be replaced by their contrary, the Everlasting Gospel. "That the Jews assumed a right Exclusively to the benefits of God will be a lasting witness against them & the same will it be against Christians" (On Watson, *K* 389). The various races must be blended, as it was in the ancestry of Jesus (see MATERNAL LINE) and in the formation of the English (*J* 92:1). The different nations must preserve their national characteristics, but unite in a well-balanced league dedicated to the preservation of liberty; it shall rule the rest of the world. See THIRTY-TWO NATIONS, under NATIONS.

Brotherhood, the supreme virtue, is superior to Conjugal Love, which unifies the Individual, whereas Brotherhood unifies Mankind.

BRUTUS (or "Brut"), the first of the mythical kings of Britain, was a great-grandson of Aeneas, through Ascanius and Sylvius. After killing his father accidentally, he was exiled to Greece, where he roused the Trojan captives to such a successful revolt that the defeated king of Greece gave Brutus his daughter Ignoge, a rich dowry, and also a fleet. After ravaging France, Brutus and his Trojans reached Albion, then inhabited only by a few giants, who were easily conquered. Brutus renamed Albion "Britain" after himself, and built the city Troja Nova (Trinovantium, now London), where, having reigned twenty-four years, he died and was buried.

In the last scene of *King Edward the Third* (*PS*), a minstrel sings of the Trojan invasion of the island; and when the giants are all slain, Brutus prophesies that the descendants of the Trojans shall rule the sea, and Liberty shall stand upon the cliffs of Albion.

BRYANT (Jacob, 1715–1804) was the outstanding figure among the mythagogues who flourished in the late eighteenth and early nineteenth centuries. Like all the others, he assumed that the Bible recorded historical facts, and that all other mythologies were perversions and distortions made by the scattered races who had lost touch with the original. Amusing accounts of these mythagogues are to be found in Edward B. Hungerford's *Shores of Darkness* (New York, 1941) and Ruthven Todd's *Tracks in the Snow* (New York, 1947).

Bryant's *New System, or an Analysis, of Ancient Mythology* was published in two volumes, London, 1774, and reissued in three volumes, 1775–76, and again in six volumes, 1807. Opinionated and peppery, unhampered by modern standards of scholarship, and indulging a fantastic philology, Bryant was of the Age of Reason in that he sought to reduce all fables to common sense.

For example: there was a universal tradition of the Flood; therefore all survivors were really Noah and his family. But Bryant did not stop there: indefatigably he jumbled names, myths, symbols, places, and ceremonies, to disentangle the historical facts he believed had been obscured by time. Amongst other things, he identified Noah's Ark with the new moon, which involved many other unexpected identifications. In Volume III alone of the 1807 edition, I find

it on page 62 (with Plate XIV), pages 178 and 183 (where it is the funeral ark of Osiris), page 214 (where the opening of the Ark is the bursting of the Mundane Egg), page 291 (where it is the person styled Rhea and "Damater"), page 308 (the horns of Europa's bull), page 320 (it is now Baal Maon), and page 326.

A number of the plates in the first two editions were signed by James Basire; outstanding among them is a charming vignette of the Ark as a crescent moon, with dove and rainbow. It was suggested by A. G. B. Russell (*Engravings*, 191) that young Blake, then apprenticed to Basire, actually designed and engraved this vignette, an idea accepted by Ruthven Todd and endorsed by Geoffrey Keynes. In *Jerusalem*, the Ark is twice depicted as a crescent moon (Plates 24 and 44). Keynes (*K Studies*, Plates 10–12) reproduces this and other plates from Bryant which might have influenced Blake in his ideas of cosmic eggs and man-headed bulls, and particularly an altar in which the heavy architecture is upheld by two rows of men with arms extended above their heads and crossing each other—a pattern which became the expression of exultation in several designs of Blake, particularly the famous fourteenth illustration of *Job*.

Blake, like everybody else in his day, believed that all myths "are the same thing, as Jacob Bryant and all antiquaries have proved" (*DesC* V, *K* 578); but he disagreed with him when he (Blake) wrote: "The antiquities of every Nation under Heaven, is no less sacred than that of the Jews." Blake doubtless liked Bryant's contempt for the Greeks, and would have disliked his ignoring of the Druids. He followed Bryant in a few points—such as the location of the Erythrean Sea—and his identification of Arthur with Atlas and Boötes was quite in the mythagogue's vein.

BUCKS and BUCKINGHAM are both abbreviations for Buckinghamshire. It is an inland English county which, with the adjacent Oxford and Hertford, is assigned to Gad (*J* 16:47). With the adjacent counties of Warwick, Northhampton, Bedford, Leicester, and Berkshire, it is assigned to Hutton (*J* 71:36).

The BULLS of Luvah symbolize the tremendous force of passion.

They drag the Plow of Ages (*FZ* ii:120), and when war breaks out, "dark & fierce the Bull his rage propagates thro' the warring Earth" (*FZ* vii *b*:109). The loins of the chained Orc, "inwove with silken fires, are like a furnace fierce, as the strong Bull in summer time" (*FZ* v:135); "the bulls of Luvah, breathing fire, bellow on burning pastures round howling Orc" (*FZ* vii:16); yet all their power cannot melt his chain or unroot its fibres (*FZ* v:164).

They cause the sunrise. "Luvah's bulls each morning drag the sulphur Sun out of the Deep; harness'd with starry harness black & shining, kept by black slaves that work all night at the starry harness, Strong and vigorous they drag the unwilling Orb" (*Mil* 21:20; *FZ* v:164).

On the Fourth Day of the Last Judgment, when Luvah is again the prince of love, Albion commands: "Let the Bulls of Luvah tread the Corn & draw the loaded waggon into the Barn while children glean the Ears round the door. Then shall they lift their innocent hands & stroke his furious nose, and he shall lick the little girl's white neck & on her head scatter the perfume of his breath" (*FZ* ix:701).

"The North Gate of Golgonooza, toward generation, has four sculptur'd Bulls, terrific, before the Gate of iron, and iron the Bulls" (*J* 12:61).

BUNYAN'S *Pilgrim's Progress* is an analysis of salvation which is so widely true that it has been edited to fit all the leading religions. Blake, in his attack on allegory, as distinguished from symbolism ("vision"), wrote: "Allegory is seldom without some vision. Pilgrim's Progress is full of it" (*LJ*, 604).

In his later years, Blake made twenty-eight (unfinished) water-color drawings to illustrate the book. As Bunyan explained

his meanings so clearly, and as Blake agreed with them, his illustrations follow the text with his usual detailed precision, and with but a slight symbolic amplification to underscore Bunyan's meaning. Thus Christian sets out under lowering clouds, intent on his book (of the law), and meets Evangelist with his scroll (of inspiration). Bunyan unknowingly had anticipated Blake's contrasting symbols. Blake also contrasts Gothic architecture with the cross-surmounted dome. He added luxuriant grapevines to the crucifixion, and set bishop and king (church and state) as witnesses to Faithful's martyrdom. Otherwise, his symbols are obvious: clouds of despair impend; the flames of wrath break out; the lightnings of disaster threaten; but the sun appears at appropriate moments. The pictures are Blake's most direct illustrations since *Tiriel*.

About 1822 Blake made his engraving of the man sweeping the interpreter's parlor. According to Bunyan, the parlor is the uncleansed heart; the man who raises the dust is the Law, which only revives and increases sin; the maid who allays the dust with her sprinkling is the Gospel. Blake represented the man as a bearded and bat-winged devil; in his clouds of dust imps peep and fly. His maid is a winged angel, letting in light. Blake inscribed a copy: "The parable of the relapsed sinner & her 7 Devils."

In a letter to Hayley (4 Dec 1804), Blake quoted Christian when in the Valley of the Shadow of Death: "I have indeed fought thro' a Hell of terrors and horrors (which none could know but myself) in a divided existence; now no longer divided nor at war with myself, I shall travel on in the strength of the Lord God, as Poor Pilgrim says."

Blake's use of the name "Beulah" for the state next to Eternity may well have been inspired by Bunyan's rapturous description of Beulah, the Earthly Paradise, where his pilgrims dwell before crossing the river of death into Heaven.

BUTE is an insular county of Scotland. With Caithness and Clakmannan, it is assigned to Dan (*J* 16:55). As a part of

Scotland, it is also assigned to Bowen (*J* 71:46).

BYRON and Napoleon were the two supermen who overshadowed the European imagination at the beginning of the nineteenth century. Napoleon was the political hope of mankind as he smashed the Inquisitions and the petty kings, spreading the principles of Liberty, Equality, and Fraternity, until he proclaimed himself Emperor and became the deadly enemy of England. The genius of Byron struck still deeper, at the bases of society itself. He aimed his deadly satire against kings and their ministers, and ridiculed the moral pretensions of his age. Though a lord, with all the privileges of rank, he stood defiantly apart from mankind, an individual, an Ishmael, wrapped in the sinister mystery of his aberration, refusing to conform or pretend to be what he was not.

His most sensational work was *Cain, a Mystery*, published in December 1821. Into this he poured all the bitter broodings wrought by his Calvinist upbringing, for he was born deformed in body and soul: clubfooted, and with that incestuous urge which prevented the possibility of a happy marriage. Past any orthodox doubt, he was predestined to damnation, a Reprobate created to suffer here and in eternity. So now he spoke out, impugning the justice of the Creator, and accusing him of being the author of all evil, of all human suffering, of sin, death, and Hell.

Paine's *Age of Reason* long since had been officially explained away and forgotten; yet enough residue of his ideas remained in the public mind to render it sensitive to Byron's attack on orthodoxy. So shocked was the public that Lord Chancellor Eldon refused it the protection of copyright.

This was the work which Blake answered in his two-page leaflet, *The Ghost of Abel* (1822). It is dedicated to "Lord Byron in the Wilderness" of the forests of the night. Byron, whom he hailed as a true poet (at least, Elijah is there), is the only contemporary poet whom Blake named in his publications.

C

CABUL was originally in the land of Asher, and later was included in Galilee. Solomon gave Hiram twenty cities in Galilee, which Hiram disliked and called the land of Cabul ("displeasing" or "dirty," *I Kings* ix:13).

Joseph and Benjamin rolled apart in vain and were fixed into the Land of Cabul (*J* 74: 57). When Jerusalem is fallen, she is "shrunk to a narrow doleful form in the dark land of Cabul" (*J* 79:63).

CAESAR is a generic name for all the ambitious monarchs and glory-seeking generals who are the sole cause of war (*J* 52). "The Strongest Poison ever known | Came from Caesar's Laurel Crown" (*Aug* 97, *K* 433). Had Jesus played the worldly game, "He had soon been bloody Caesar's Elf, | And at last he would have been Caesar himself" (*EG d*:41).

CAFFRARIA (i.e., Kaffraria) is the country of the Kaffirs, in Africa. It is the twentieth of the Thirty-two Nations who shall protect liberty and rule the rest of the world (*J* 72:40).

The CAGE was one of Blake's earliest symbols. Originally, it signified matrimony. Phoebus "caught me in his silken net, | And shut me in his golden cage" (*PS*, "How sweet I roam'd" 11). "Matrimony's Golden cage" (*IslM*, Chap. ix, "Hail Matrimony" 27).

Later, Blake used the symbol freely to signify any state of mind in which a person may seem hopelessly trapped.

CAIAPHAS (or "Caiphas," as Blake often spelled it), the high priest in Jerusalem, was the chief instigator of the Crucifixion. He is "the dark Preacher of Death, of sin, of sorrow & of punishment: opposing Nature! It is Natural Religion" (*J* 77:18). Caiaphas and Pilate symbolize Church and State, particularly in *The Everlasting Gospel*, where, however, Blake noted, "Caiphas was in his own Mind | A benefactor to Mankind" (*EG a*:11). "Two persons, one in Purple, the other in Scarlet, are descending down the steps into the Pit; these are Caiphas & Pilate—Two States where all those reside who Calumniate & Murder under Pretence of Holiness & Justice. Caiphas has a Blue Flame like a Miter on his head. Pilate has bloody hands that never can be cleansed" (*LJ*, *K* 608; see Illustrations, "LJ" 41, 42).

CAIN, the first child of Adam, was the first murderer. In *The Ghost of Abel* he is depicted stretched upon his brother's corpse in desperate grief. In another picture, he flees clutching his head, while flames break out from him and a black cloud lowers above. In Blake's illuminated *Genesis*, the mark which the Lord set upon him "lest any finding him should kill him" is the kiss of the Forgiveness of Sins.

However, before the seat of Judgment, "Cain, with the flint in his hand with which he slew his brother, [is] falling with the head downward" (*LJ*, *K* 606; see Illustrations, "LJ" No. 27); but here he is the State and not the person.

After the murder, Cain fled to the Land of Nod, where he married and built a city, traditionally evil. "Cain's City built with

Human Blood, not Blood of Bulls & Goats" (*GhA* 45) signifies a society based on human sacrifice.

According to Blake's tracing of the ancestry of Mary, she was descended from Caina; thus Cain was a progenitor of Jesus. See MATERNAL LINE.

The primal sin of Adam and Eve in dividing Good from Evil was reflected in their first two children. In Blake's painting "Meditations Among the Tombs," both Cain and Abel flee from the attacking serpent (see Illustrations).

CAINA or Cainah is Blake's name for Cain's sister-wife. She is thirteenth in the list of the daughters of Los and Enitharmon, where her name follows those of Lamech's two wives (*FZ* viii:365). This list was revised and expanded as the "Maternal Line," or ancestry of Mary; here Cainah heads the list (*J* 62:9).

CAINAN was the great-grandson of Adam, and grandson of Seth. He is fourth in the list of the Twenty-seven Churches; he is in the first group of nine, the "Giants, mighty, Hermaphroditic" (*Mil* 37:36; *J* 75:11).

CAINAN THE SECOND was the great-grandson of Noah and grandson of Shem (*Luke* iii:36; but he is not named in *Genesis* x). He is thirteenth in the list of the Twenty-seven Churches; he is fourth in the second group from Noah to Terah, the "Female-Males" (*Mil* 37:38; *J* 75:13).

CAITHNESS (which Blake also spelled "Caitnes" and "Cathnes") is the northernmost county of Scotland. With Bute and Clakmanan, Caitnes is assigned to Dan (*J* 16:55).

Caithness is one of the two Gates, the northern one, through which all souls descend. With it are named Durness, a coastal town in Sutherland; [the Firth of] Pentland, which lies between Scotland and the Orkneys; and John Groat's House, a famous inn in Caithness (*Mil* 26:15), the idea being to extend the Gate along the northern coast of Scotland.

Enitharmon's looms play from "Caithness in the north" to southernmost England (*J* 83:70). Urizen's world extends from Cornwall to Cathnes (*J* 58:46).

CALEB was a general under Joshua. The two were the only spies who believed that the Israelites could conquer the Promised Land, and they were the only two persons who survived the journey from Sinai into Canaan.

Apparently they were close friends, but Blake uses them as symbols of the inevitable quarrels between friends. "Oshea [so Joshua's name is spelled *Numb* xiii:8] and Caleb fight: they contend in the valleys of Peor, in the terrible Family Contentions of those who love each other" (*J* 43:37). Og and Sihon, moved by Balaam's tears, "have given their power to Joshua & Caleb" (*J* 49:59).

CALVARY (Latin), or Golgotha (Aramaic), was the site of the Crucifixion. "Is that Calvary and Golgotha becoming a building of pity and compassion?" (*J* 12:28). "Such the Holy Gospel of Mount Olivet & Calvary" (*J* 16:69). Satan prophesies to Jehovah: "Thou shalt Thyself be Sacrificed to Me, thy God, on Calvary" (*GhA* 46). Tyburn Street, which led to the gallows, is called "Calvary's foot" (*Mil* 4:21).

CALVIN (John, 1509–64) was one of the two great leaders of the Protestant Reformation.

"Remember how Calvin and Luther in fury premature sow'd War and stern division between Papists & Protestants" (*Mil* 23:47).

The CAM is the river on which Cambridge University is situated.

"The banks of Cam, cold learning's streams" lament (*Mil* 19:39). Cam withers to a little stream (*J* 5:9).

CAMBEL is placed twelfth and last in the original list of the Daughters of Albion (*FZ* ii:62), but is placed first of all in the

Jerusalem lists. She and the next four are united into Tirzah (*J* 5:41). She is the "bright beaming Counterpart" of Hand (*J* 80:58).

Her name seems to have been derived from Kambreda, one of the thirty daughters of King Ebrauc, who were sent to Italy, where they married among the Trojan nobility (*Geof* II, viii). "Kambreda" suggests Kamber (Cambria, or Wales); but although once she sends her consort Hand over Wales (*J* 80:63), their position is South, as Hand is Reason; and their counties are on the southern coast.

On Plate 81 of *Jerusalem*, she is depicted in the modest posture of the Medicean Venus, the "Venus pudica," which is appropriate to Tirzah. Once she is identified with Boadicea (*J* 71:23), whose name was dropped from the original list of Daughters; and as Boadicea, invoking a British god, declared war on the Romans, Cambel would then be the Warring Female.

She is usually paired with Gwendolen, second of the Daughters, who was also leader of an army. Together they weave the webs of War and Religion, to involve all Albion's Sons (*J* 7:44)—here Cambel replaces Conwenna, who with Gwendolen wove the same garment earlier (*Mil* 23:16). Battersea and Chelsea (the place of wounded soldiers) mourn for the pair (*J* 21:32). Gwendolen casts the shuttle of war while Cambel returns the beam (*J* 66:62). They rise between Hand and Hyle (*J* 71:23). They dance and sing before the captains (*J* 80:39). Los melts the pair with Gwineverra into precious metals and stones (*J* 9:22).

But the greatest collaboration of the two occurs when they conspire to enslave their consorts and mold them into forms of love. Gwendolen as usual takes the lead (*J* 80: 57–85:4).

Hand sleeps on Mount Skiddaw, divided from Cambel, who drinks his sighs; meanwhile Hyle sleeps on East Moor in Derbyshire, and Gwendolen weaves him a physical form of Moral Virtue. Gwendolen calls to Cambel, asking how to keep these awful

forms in their soft bands, for unless they do, they themselves shall be annihilated; and she attempts to lure her sisters to Babylon, by a falsehood which she hides in her left hand. But Hyle does not become the infant she wants, and is revealed as a Worm; she screams and flees.

Cambel is jealous. Los draws her into his seventh Furnace to diminish her envy. There she labors to form Hand according to her will, and he also becomes an infant Worm. Gwendolen repents, and tries to mold her Worm into a form of love.

Los approves the work of Cambel and her sisters, though in creating the embryo senses they are making the Mundane Shell, which varies according to the observer, an outside shadowy surface superadded to the real and unchangeable surface.

Then the Daughters of Albion take Gwendolen's falsehood; it grows into the allegory of earthly marriage (Canaan), into which Los leads the wandering Reuben, where he finds at last his satisfactory dwelling place (*J* 80:57–85:4).

CAMBERWELL was a pleasant village in Surrey, near Lambeth; it is now included in the south of London.

Weaving the Loom of Death, Tirzah's courts are on Camberwell (*Mil* 35:8). From Camberwell to Highgate, Luvah breaks forth in war (*J* 47:2). From the hills of Camberwell and other places, Jerusalem's pillars fall (*J* 68:43). "O lovely Hills of Camberwell, we shall behold you no more in glory & pride, for Jerusalem lies in ruins" (*J* 84:5). "The Tree of Good & Evil sprang from the Rocky Circle & Snake of the Druid, along the Valley of Rephaim from Camberwell to Golgotha, and framed the Mundane Shell" (*J* 92:25).

CAMBRIDGE is one of England's great universities.

Leutha dwells in Palamabron's tent "in Cambridge & in Oxford, places of Thought" (*Mil* 13:42). When Albion rises, his bosom is girt in gold, and "on the front are Bath, Oxford, Cambridge, and Norwich" (*Mil*

39:44). "Cambridge & Oxford & London are driven among the starry Wheels" (*J* 5:3). "Worcester & Hereford, Oxford & Cambridge reel & stagger" (*J* 66:66). The Four ungenerated Sons of Los have the Four Provinces of Ireland, the Four Universities of Scotland, and "Oxford, Cambridge, & Winchester" (*J* 71:53). The Daughters of Albion listen to Gwendolen and Cambel "on Cambridge & Oxford beaming soft," uniting with Rahab's cloud (*J* 82:11).

CAMBRIDGESHIRE is an eastern inland county of England. With the adjoining counties of Bedford and Huntingdon, it is assigned to Zebulun (*J* 16:48), and with seven other counties, it is assigned to Scofield (*J* 71:38).

In Cambridgeshire is the Gate of Los, where Los encounters Albion fleeing towards Eternal Death; here Los has "his eternal station; he is the twenty-eighth & is four-fold" (*J* 39:8–13). As the "twenty-eighth," Los is the climax of the spiritual activities of the Cathedral Cities. The Cathedral City of Cambridgeshire is Ely; and Ely is identified with Milton. (See ELY.) Elsewhere, however, Ely is only the twelfth in the list of the Twenty-four (*J* 46:6), while Sodor is the last (*J* 46:19).

CANAAN was the land which the Lord promised his chosen. It symbolizes the ideal home or (more often) that state which the Individual thinks is ideal.

He may be mistaken. Thus, when Satan is quarrelling furiously with Palamabron, he hardens his heart and reverts to the ancient errors of Rome, Babylon, and Tyre (*Mil* 9:51). Though it is "a World of Deeper Ulro" (*Mil* 9:34), "the Space is named Canaan" (*Mil* 10:4), for it seems to be the perfect basis for civilization. His Spectre (reason) enters this space raging; "And Satan vibrated in the immensity of the Space, Limited to those without, but Infinite to those within: it fell down and became Canaan, closing Los from Eternity in Albion's Cliffs" (*Mil* 10:8).

One cannot force an Individual to dwell in what oneself considers to be Canaan. Los makes effort after effort to drive Reuben, the average sensual man, into the Chosen Land. Four times Reuben crosses the Jordan, but each time he returns (*J* 34:43–54; 36:1–20). His official allotment of land is on the other side of the river. Therefore, after the Daughters of Albion have created the Mundane Shell around his predestined Canaan (*J* 64:1), Gwendolen's falsehood "grew & grew till it became a Space & an Allegory [conventional marriage] around the Winding Worm. [The Daughters of Albion] nam'd it Canaan & built for it a tender Moon. Los smil'd with joy, thinking on Enitharmon, & he brought Reuben from his twelvefold wand'rings & led him into it" (*J* 84:31–85:4). For the Canaan of the women, see CANAANITES.

Albion is in love with the true Canaan; but when war broke it, his Canaan rose into heaven: "Canaan roll'd apart from Albion . . . And all the Land of Canaan suspended over the Valley of Cheviot" (*J* 63:41). The Treddles of Ragan's loom drop "crimson gore with the Loves of Albion and Canaan" (*J* 64:37). The heavenly Canaan is always overhead, above all its earthly perversions. "And above Albion's land was seen the Heavenly Canaan as the Substance is to the Shadow" (*J* 71:1). The three stages of life, Creation, Redemption, and Judgment, are "display'd in the Emanative Visions of Canaan" (*J* 92:21). The twelve kingdoms of the unconquered land are "call'd after the Names of Israel, as they are in Eden" (*Mil* 40:25).

When Luvah is crucified, his mocking INRI is "Behold the King of Canaan, whose are seven hundred chariots of iron!" (*J* 66:25). Thus Blake combined an *Ecce Homo* with a reference to the tyrant Jabin, king of Canaan, whose chariots of iron, however, numbered nine hundred (*Judges* iv:2–3).

Before Canaan is conquered, it symbolizes the unregenerated heart.

The CANAANITES, who inhabited Palestine before the Israelites conquered it, were a variety of tribes: the Canaanites themselves (descendants of the evil Ham), and among others the Hittites (*J* 34:48) and the Jebusites (*J* 68:23). They were ruled by the Twelve Kings of Canaan (*J* 68:61), that is, "the Seven [Kings] of Canaan & Five Baalim [lords] of Philistea" (*Mil* 40:24), who dwell in the devouring Stomach of the Covering Cherub (*J* 89:46).

The men of Canaan were great shipbuilders and merchants. Jesus "scourg'd the Merchant Canaanite from out the Temple of his Mind" (*EG* b:48). In the waste outside Golgonooza, Los sees "Pits of bitumen ever burning, artificial Riches of the Canaanite, like Lakes of liquid lead" (*J* 43:62). This explains why "Albion was call'd the Canaanite & all his Giant Sons" (*J* 74:39)—perhaps a reply to Napoleon's gibe about the nation of shopkeepers. It also explains why Reuben "enroots his brethren in the narrow Canaanite" (*J* 15:25), and why Canaan is the portico of Urizen's temple (*J* 58:33).

Twice Los sees a quaternary of "the Amalekite, the Canaanite, the Moabite, the Egyptian" (*J* 13:58; 43:66), who are "by Demonstrations the cruel Sons of Quality & Negation, driven on the Void in incoherent despair into Non Entity" (*J* 43:67). Presumably these represent the false Head (the Amalekite), the false Heart (the Canaanite), the false Loins (the Moabite), and the false Spirit (the Egyptian).

Canaan and the other pagan countries practised child-sacrifice. Canaan is one of the six countries surrounding Israel which receive Jerusalem's little ones for sacrifice (*J* 5:14). Los cries out: "O when shall Jehovah give us Victims from his Flocks & Herds instead of Human Victims by the Daughters of Albion & Canaan?" (*J* 63:30). The women are responsible for this perversion of the maternal instinct: among their victims they "examine the Infant's limbs in cruelties of holiness" (*J* 68:58).

For the Canaanites still belong to that primitive religion which Blake called Druidism. The Spectre constricts into "Druid

Rocks round Canaan, Agag & Aram & Phar[a]oh" (*J* 54:26). "The Serpent Temples thro' the Earth, from the wide Plain of Salisbury [Stonehenge], resound with cries of Victims . . . to Amalek, Canaan and Moab" (*J* 80:48). Milton's family ranges round him "as the rocks of Horeb round the land of Canaan" (*Mil* 17:12). Hand becomes "a Polypus of Roots, of Reasoning, Doubt, Despair & Death, going forth & returning from Albion's Rocks to Canaan, devouring Jerusalem from every Nation of the Earth" (*J* 69:3).

But already the barriers of the races have been broken by those very intermarriages which the Jews condemned, and the original races have been swallowed up and disappeared. When mankind becomes amalgamated, Los sees the female Canaanite "united with the fugitive Hebrew, whom she divided into Twelve [Tribes] & sold into Egypt, then scatter'd the Egyptian & Hebrew to the four Winds" (*J* 92:3). Thus the Brotherhood of Man is accomplished.

CANADA, the northernmost country in North America, is the twenty-fifth of the Thirty-two Nations which shall guard liberty and rule the world (*J* 72:41).

Orc folds round the Shadowy Female on the Canadian wilds (*Am* 1:17). She sees him as a Serpent in Canada courting her to his love (*Am* 2:12).

CANTERBURY, the ecclesiastical metropolis of England, symbolizes the Established Church.

Blake, believing that the Church had gone materialistic and was spiritually in ruins (*Mil* 39:41), veiled his criticism by identifying Canterbury with the ruined Roman city of Verulam (*J* 38:45), and only under that name does it appear in the list of Cathedral Cities. See VERULAM. It is South, under Urizen. The cathedral is described as a Druid structure where the senses are closed, a serpent temple of Nature; "image of infinite shut up in finite revolutions, and man became an Angel, Heaven a mighty circle turning, God a tyrant crown'd"

(*Eur* 10:4–23). It is the head of the Polypus, which corrupts the other Cathedral Cities (*J* 67:35).

Los was thinking of it in its uncorrupted state when he called it "Verulam! Canterbury! venerable parent of men, generous immortal Guardian, golden clad!" (*J* 38: 45), gold being the metal of Urizen.

At the progress of the Worm, London and Canterbury tremble (*J* 33:12). Bath's Spectre attempts to "cast Jerusalem forth upon the wilds to Poplar & Bow, to Malden & Canterbury, in the delights of cruelty" (*J* 41:5). The voices of Bath, Canterbury, York, and Edinburgh cry over the Plow of Nations (*J* 57:1). At Gwendolen's laugh, London and Canterbury groan in pain (*J* 63:35). Los bids his Spectre: "Go thou to Skofield: ask him if he is Bath or if he is Canterbury" (*J* 17:59). The Spectre Sons of Albion bid the warring Vala descend into the sepulcher of Canterbury (*J* 65: 39). When Albion finally rises, his right heel rests on Canterbury's ruins (*Mil* 39: 41).

In *Milton* 39:35, where we expect the name Canterbury, "Legions" is substituted; but *Jerusalem* 41:1 identifies Legions with Bath.

CAPANEUS was one of the seven kings who besieged Thebes. When he said that even the fire of Jupiter should not prevent his scaling the walls, Jupiter struck him down with his lightning. Dante used him as a type of the blasphemer (*Inferno* xiv: 39–69); Blake depicted him in his twenty-seventh illustration of the *Divine Comedy*. He sits, proud and unmoving, on a bed of flames which lick his legs and groin; other flames rise from his body and form a halo; while several lightning bolts smite him. "The Grandest characters [are] Wicked, Very Satan—Capanius, Othello a murderer, Prometheus, Jupiter, Jehovah, Jesus a wine bibber" (On Boyd, *K* 412).

The **CARBUNCLE** was one of the twelve precious stones on the high priest's breastplate: it represented Judah. It was also one of the precious stones which formed a cov-

ering for the prince of Tyre (*Ezek* xxviii: 13).

When Orc broke loose as a serpent, "A crest of fire rose on his forehead, red as the carbuncle" (*FZ* viii:69).

CARDIGANSHIRE is a county in South Wales. It is the Gate of Simeon (*J* 16:36).

CARLISLE is the eleventh of the Twenty-four Cathedral Cities. It is under Urthona and Edinburgh.

It is particularly associated with William Paley (1743–1805), who is buried there. He refuted the Deists, and proclaimed that "the divine right of kings is no more than the divine right of constables."

When Albion rises, his bosom girt with gold involves York, Edinburgh, Durham, and Carlisle (*Mil* 39:43). Lincoln, Durham, and Carlisle are counsellors of Los (*J* 46: 5).

CARMARTHENSHIRE is a county of South Wales. It is the Gate of Reuben (*J* 16:38).

CARMEL is the mountain in the territory of Asher, where Elijah defeated the prophets of Baal.

Rahab, standing on Carmel, beholds the strife of Milton and Urizen (*Mil* 19:28).

CARNARVONSHIRE is a county in North Wales. It is the Gate of Asher (*J* 16:39).

CAROLINA was given by Charles II to eight of his favorites, who employed John Locke to draw up an ideal constitution; this attempt to establish a feudal system failed and was formally abandoned in 1693. In 1700, Carolina was divided into two states, North and South Carolina, which became two of the original Thirteen States.

In the list of the Thirty-two Nations, which shall protect liberty and rule the world, the twenty-seventh is Carolina, sole representative of the nation which Blake's friend Paine had named the United States of America (*J* 72:41).

THE
CATHEDRAL
CITIES

URTHONA
(NORTH)

EDINBURGH

CARLISLE

DURHAM

SODOR

THARMAS
(WEST)

YORK

LUVAH
(EAST)

BANGOR

ASAPH

CHESTER

LINCOLN

LITCHFIELD

NORWICH

PETERBORO

ST. DAVID'S

WORCESTER

ELY

HEREFORD

GLOUCESTER

OXFORD

VERULAM

LANDAFF

BRISTOL

BATH

LONDON

ROCHESTER

CANTERB

SALISBURY

WINCHESTER

CHICHESTER

EXETER

SELSEY

URIZEN
(SOUTH)

The CATHEDRAL CITIES of Great Britain represent the Church of England. They are the reflection and manifestation on earth of the Communion of Saints. (See DIVINE FAMILY.) They are an organization of spiritual forces; but they are irregular, imperfect, and fallible, as compared with their divine original.

In Blake's day the Cities numbered twenty-seven; but he brought the list up to a number divisible by four by including Sodor, which together with the Isle of Man was a bishopric, although the cathedral there had long since fallen in ruin.

There are four chief Cities: Verulam (i.e., Canterbury: see VERULAM), Edinburgh, London, and York (J 46:24; 74: 3–4). They correspond to the Four Zoas: Urizen (south), Urthona (north), Luvah (east), and Tharmas (west).

In these four, the remaining twenty-four appear fourfold (Mil 42:18; J 46:23). Blake grouped them in sixes; they have geographical allocations, although they do not necessarily accord with strict geography.

The first six (J 40:50–61) are South, under Urizen; they are Chichester (the scene of Blake's trial), Winchester, Gloucester, Exeter, Salisbury, and Bristol. They all lie loosely along the southern part of England. The third six (J 46:17) are East, under Luvah. They are Oxford, Norwich, Peterboro, Rochester, Chester, and Worcester. The list begins with Oxford, midpoint of the line, which zigzags in an easterly direction from Chester to Norwich. The fourth six, under Tharmas, are West. They are Lichfield, St. David's, Llandaff, Asaph, Bangor, and Sodor. Lichfield is in west central England, and the next four are all in Wales; their line points north to Sodor in the Western Isles. But the second six, being North under Urthona (Bath, Hereford, Lincoln, Durham, Carlisle, and Ely, J 46: 1–6) are scattered all over the map, for genius may spring up anywhere. This, the most important list, zigzags downward from Edinburgh in the north to the prominent figure of Bath (pacifism).

SOUTH	NORTH
Urizen	*Urthona*
Verulam	Edinburgh
[Canterbury]	
Chichester (Selsey)	Bath
Winchester	Hereford
Gloucester	Lincoln
Exeter	Durham
Salisbury	Carlisle
Bristol	Ely
EAST	WEST
Luvah	*Tharmas*
London	York
Oxford	Lichfield
Norwich	St. David's
Peterboro	Llandaff
Rochester	Asaph
Chester	Bangor
Worcester	Sodor

The Communion of Saints, seen close to, consists of Individuals; so consequently do the Cathedral Cities. Blake characterized some of these Cities, and the scholar needs to follow his clues and try to identify them. For Blake they are the most distinguished persons associated with their respective cathedrals; to him they are spiritual forces operative in his day.

On this theory, some of the Cities are instantly identifiable: Bristol is Chatterton, Lichfield is Dr. Johnson; Carlisle is its archdeacon Paley, the classic apologist of eighteenth-century Anglicanism.

Sometimes there are subtleties. Ely is the Cathedral City of Cambridgeshire; its university, where the clergy were trained, is Cambridge; and the greatest man produced by Cambridge was the anticlerical Milton, "Scribe of Los, whose pen no other hand dare touch" (J 46:6). With parallel irony, Blake (in my opinion there is no alternative) identified Oxford with the poet expelled from Oxford for his atheism, the anticlerical Shelley, "immortal Bard; with eloquence divine he wept over Albion, speaking the words of God in mild perswasion, bringing leaves of the Tree of Life"

(*J* 46:7). See BARD OF OXFORD, under OX-
FORD.

Selsey and Chichester head Blake's list.
Selsey, the original cathedral site, is now a
mile out to sea. When it was submerged,
the bishopric was transferred to Chichester.
According to Blake, Selsey was "devour'd
by the waves of Despair"; but its Emanation, Chichester, "rose above the flood,"
and "her lambs bleat to the sea-fowls' cry,
lamenting still for Albion" (*J* 40:48–51).
Blake himself was the most important person associated with Chichester, where he
was tried for high treason. Selsey can be
regarded as Blake in his despair before his
acquittal, and Chichester is Blake afterwards, when the trial became the inspiration (Emanation) for *Jerusalem.*

The third in Blake's list is Winchester,
the cathedral nearest Chichester; I identify
it as Blake's neighbor Hayley ("Hyle dwelt
in Winchester," *J* 71:20), who, although a
country squire, let himself be known as a
poet and patron of poets. "Submitting to
be call'd the son of Los . . . Winchester
stood devoting himself for Albion, his tents
outspread with abundant riches" (*J* 40:
52). "And at his own door the bless'd Her-
mit does stand, | Dispensing Unceasing to
all the whole Land" (To Mrs. Flaxman, 14
Sept 1800).

The bishopric of Bath and Wells after
the Reformation possessed not only the
original cathedral at Wells but also the
great abbey church at Bath, which Blake
preferred as the representative city of the
diocese. He probably did so because he was
deeply impressed by the courage of Richard Warner of Bath (identified by Erdman),
who defiantly preached, published, and republished his sermon *War Inconsistent
with Christianity* in the midst of the war
fever of the Napoleonic era. "Benevolent
Bath" (*J* 40:61) is "the Seventh" (*J* 41:1)
in the list of the Twenty-four; he therefore
heads the list of the six under Urthona. His
"Spectre [reason] first assimilated with
Luvah [love] in Albion's mountains [places
of high thought]" (*J* 41:3).

The eighth in the list is Hereford, "an-

cient Guardian of Wales, whose hands
builded the mountain palaces of Eden" (*J*
46:3); he would seem to be Inigo Jones, the
architect of Welsh descent, builder of famous palaces, including the Queen's House
at Greenwich and the Banqueting House
at Whitehall; he also built the Lincoln's
Inn Chapel and reconstructed St. Paul's
Cathedral.

The next three are linked together as
"Councillors of Los" (*J* 46:5); while not
poets themselves, they furnished ideas for
poetry. Lincoln suggests at once its famous
bishop Robert Grosseteste, recognized in
Blake's time as an opponent of both king
and pope. Durham is Thomas Sutton,
whom Blake had already praised in a poem
(*IslM*); he had made his fortune in the Durham coal fields and founded the Charterhouse School. Carlisle is William Paley,
who is buried there; he attacked Deism
and also the Divine Right of Kings.

Therefore the high points, the greatest
spiritual forces of the Cathedral Cities, we
may identify as follows:

Selsey and Chichester: Blake before and
 after his trial
Winchester: William Hayley
Bath: Richard Warner
Oxford: Shelley
Hereford: Inigo Jones
Lincoln: Robert Grosseteste
Durham: Thomas Sutton
Carlisle: William Paley
Ely: Milton
Bristol: Chatterton
Lichfield: Dr. Johnson

Despite Blake's continuous attacks on
established churches, he recognized from
the beginning that "the Gothic Artists
who Built the Cathedrals" (*K* 604) were
true Christians; and that, in spite of all
errors and corruptions, the central ideal of
the churches was their fundamental and
eternal reality; and that this reality, in
crucial times, was bound to manifest.

He first mentioned the Cathedral Cities
near the end of *Milton*, where some of them
appear as jewels on the rising Albion.

"London & Bath & Legions & Edinburgh [not yet London, York, Verulam, and Edinburgh] are the four pillars of his Throne" (*Mil* 39:35). At the very end, "I beheld the Twenty-four Cities of Albion arise upon their Thrones to Judge the Nations of the Earth; and the Immortal Four in whom the Twenty-four appear Fourfold arose around Albion's Body" (*Mil* 42:16). These Four blow the trumpets of the Last Judgment.

The history of the Churches in this world is told at length in *Jerusalem*. They are fundamentally sound, always well-meaning; but they err, they fail, they are corrupted, and finally resign their imaginative function to their friend Los. Yet at the end they rise from their slumbers and do their part in the slaying of the Covering Cherub. They are "the Friends of Albion" (*J* 40:3; 48:27). In the persecutions following Albion's worship of his own Shadow, "the Twenty-eight Cities of Albion stretch their hands" to the Saviour, seeking his face (*J* 30:26), but without apparent results, probably because they have not yet learned the uselessness of calling on God for help, instead of on "ourselves, in whom God dwells" (*J* 43:13), as Los later reminds them.

When Albion flees towards Eternal Death, Los summons these Friends. The Four with their Emanations appear first; they shudder before the porch of sixteen pillars (the Bible—see *J* 48:7) and weeping fall on their knees, "swearing the Oath of God." The Twenty-four hear; they come also, "trembling on wat'ry chariots [the Church in this world] borne by the Living Creatures of the third procession of Human Majesty [Luvah]." The Divine Family [Brotherhood] appears in the Twenty-four, and they are One in Him (*J* 40:3–9, 21–23, 45).

The Twenty-eight trembling kneel around Albion's death-couch "in deep humiliation and tortures of self condemnation, while their Spectres rag'd within" (*J* 41:24). Hand and Hyle seize "the Twenty-four rebellious ingratitudes" (*J* 42:48).

The Spectres of the Cities, wishing to build Babylon, cry out: "Depart, ye twenty-four, into the deeps" (*J* 42:65). Meanwhile the "Human majestic Forms" of the Cities sit up on their death-couches; "they curb their Spectres as with iron curbs; they enquire after Jerusalem," and long for the morning (*J* 42:66–74). They see their Zoas plotting against Albion; America is closed out and Tharmas is sacrificed in Mexico (*J* 43:1–7).

Los, raging against the demoralized universe, asks why they are not calling on themselves, in whom God is, to save man. "Bristol & Bath, listen to my words; & ye Seventeen [the rest of the Cities after Bath], give ear!" (*J* 43:55). But he sees that they are infected with Albion's disease of Sin and Repentance (*J* 43:75), and "with kindest violence . . . against his will" they try to force Albion back to Eden, his native home (*J* 44:1–5). Such is Blake's estimate of the period of religious persecutions. But they fail; and feeling the damps of death, their Emanations lost, their Spectres raging, they delegate all their powers to Los, naming him Elijah, the Spirit of Prophecy (*J* 44:28–31). "The Slumbers of Death came over them around the Couch of Death" (*J* 44:35).

Yet Bath from the house of death is able to call on Oxford to heal Albion, and "the Seventeen conjoining with Bath, the Seventh: in whom the other Ten [the six before Bath plus the Four chief Cities] shone manifest a Divine Vision, assimilated and embrac'd Eternal Death for Albion's sake" (*J* 45:37). But Albion turns away from the words of Oxford, who faints (*J* 46:16). The separated Emanations of the Cities concenter in the form of Eno, who opens the moment and the atom, which become gates to Eden and Beulah; she also peruses Albion's tomb of the Scriptures (*J* 48:27–41).

War breaks out (*J* 47:4) and the Cities are helpless. London's brain and Edinburgh's heart are cut around; York and Lincoln hide among the flocks; Worcester and Hereford, Oxford and Cambridge reel and stagger (*J* 66:64). The Churches become materialized; "In Verulam the Polypus's Head" winds its bulk through Rochester, Chichester, Exeter, Salisbury, and Bristol; "his Heart beat strong on Salisbury Plain, shooting out Fibres round the Earth" (*J* 67:35). Bath stands upon the Severn, holding the cup of Rahab (*J* 75:2).

As the end of the poem approaches, Los glimpses Albion who, "stretch'd on Albion's rocks, reposes amidst his Twenty-eight Cities, where Beulah lovely terminates in the hills & valleys of Albion, Cities not yet embodied in Time and Space" (*J* 85:25) — not yet realized in their ideal form. But when Albion sacrifices himself for Jesus, "all the Cities of Albion rose from their Slumbers" (*J* 96:38); and when he seizes his bow, he "Clothed himself in Bow & Arrows, in awful state, Fourfold, in the midst of his Twenty-eight Cities, each with his Bow breathing. Then each an Arrow flaming from his Quiver fitted carefully; they drew fourfold the unreprovable String" (*J* 97:16–98:2), and annihilate the Druid Spectre. The twenty-eight weapons constitute the four weapons of the Zoas, which in turn constitute the single weapon of Albion.

CATHEDRON is the body of woman, particularly the womb. Here Enitharmon weaves bodies of vegetation (living flesh) for the spectres, and her daughters weave the ovarium and the integument in soft silk drawn from their own bowels in lascivious delight (*FZ* viii:38, 210).

Cathedron is situated in Luban's Gate of Golgonooza (*FZ* viii:36; *J* 13:25; 73:52). This is the North Gate, in the West of the North, towards Beulah (*J* 59:23). Luban is in the center of Golgonooza, and a moat of fire surrounds Luban, Los's Palace, and Cathedron (*J* 13:25; see GOLGONOOZA, diagram).

The main feature of Cathedron is its looms, on which the bodies are woven of the wires drawn by Los's demons from the terrific passions and affections of the "dead" spectres (*FZ* viii:208). The looms are of gold (Urizen's metal), as is the whole build-

ing, with its dome, halls, courts, towers, and pinnacles (*Mil* 26:36; *J* 13:25; 59:25).

Every generated body is inwardly a house of pleasure and a garden of delight, built by the Sons and Daughters of Los in Bowlahoola and in Cathedron. The Sons build the house and garden in Bowlahoola and Allamanda; the Daughters weave the herbs, flowers, furniture, beds, and chambers in Cathedron (*Mil* 26:31–36; *J* 73:50). From the higher point of view, however, the looms "weave only death" from Eternity (*Mil* 24:35). This "Body of Death," a Female Tabernacle (Mary), is woven around the Lamb himself (*Mil* 13:25). Los makes every revolution of space permanent in Bowlahoola and Cathedron (*J* 75:9).

When Reuben slept, the Daughters of Albion sent him over Europe in streams of gore, out of Cathedron's looms (*J* 74:37). Cambel sends Hand over Wales into the loom of Cathedron (*J* 80:63). Her envy runs through Cathedron's looms into the heart of Jerusalem (*J* 82:53). Enitharmon joys in weaving the web of life for Jerusalem in Cathedron (*J* 83:72); she separates in milky fibres of love with sweet visions for the wandering Jerusalem (*J* 86:40).

CATHERLO[G]H is the Irish name for Carlow, a county in Leinster, under Judah, Issachar, and Zebulun (*J* 72:20).

CATHNES. See CAITHNESS.

The CATTERPILLER (the modern spelling is a corruption adopted by Dr. Johnson) is always for Blake, as in the Bible and Shakespeare, a "piller" or pillager, the chief enemy of the Rose. "I never heard | Of any true affection, but 'twas nipt | With care, that, like the caterpillar, eats | The leaves off the spring's sweetest book, the rose. | Love bred on earth, is often nurs'd in hell; | By rote it reads woe, ere it learn to spell" (Thomas Middleton, *Blurt, Master-Constable*, iii:1).

"As the caterpillar chooses the fairest leaves to lay her eggs on, so the priest lays his curse on the fairest joys" (*MHH* 9:16).

"The Catterpiller on the Leaf | Repeats to thee thy Mother's grief" (*Aug* 37, *K* 432; *GoP*, "The Keys" and frontis.). In the first proof of *Jerusalem* 28, the catterpiller appears on a petal of the Lilly of honeymoon love (see Illustrations). "The Catterpiller and Fly" feed on the leaves of the Tree of Mystery (*SoE*, "The Human Abstract" 15). Elsewhere it symbolizes the political parasite "who creeps into State Government like a catterpiller to destroy" (*Mil* 41:11). The Daughters of Los create the catterpiller with the silkworm and the spider "to assist in their most grievous work of pity & compassion" (*J* 59:47).

CAVAN was a county in Ulster, Ireland, before 1920; it is under Dan, Asher, and Naphtali (*J* 72:27).

The CAVE or Cavern is the Platonic symbol of the body in which man is confined. "For man has closed himself up, till he sees all things thro' narrow chinks [the four senses] of his cavern" (*MHH* 14; see also the third and fourth Memorable Fancies, *MHH* 15–20). On Plate 11 in one copy, the "chink" through which the world of nature is perceived is actually painted as the eye-hole of a skull. "Reuben slept in the Cave of Adam" (*J* 36:5). The Cave is situated in the vegetative universe, outside Golgonooza (*J* 13:38; 43:60).

In another sense, the Caves are the obscurer parts of the psyche. The fallen Albion's bosom contains "caves of despair & death . . . of solitude & dark despair" (*J* 31:4). Orc is chained in caves (*FZ* vii:5); Tharmas struggles with Enion in his caves (*FZ* i:136, 179). In Bromion's caves the adulterate pair are bound back to back (*VDA* 2:5). Here is the place of the erotic dream (*Eur* 14:6; *Mil* 25:53). See also *Milton* 9:2; 25:20; 37:58.

By extension, the Mundane Shell is full of caverns (*Mil* 20:42; 23:22; 35:39; 37:56).

Into the caves of the subconscious retire those who have died on earth. Such is the case of "The Little Girl Lost" (*SoI*) and her

parents. Cf. "grot & cave beneath the Moon, dim region of death" (*J* 34:11).

The CENTER is the heart, or moon, in Man's present state. It is one of the "Four Points"; the other three are the Circumference, Zenith, and Nadir. When Man fell and assumed his present physical form, the West [Tharmas] went outward and became the Circumference, or body; the South [Urizen] ascended and took dominion as the Zenith, or head; the North [Urthona] sank out of sight and became the Nadir, or subconscious; while the East [Luvah] turned inward and became "the Center, unapproachable for ever," or the heart. When they were thus materialized, the Four established communication with the outer world by the Four Senses: "the Eyes are the South, and the Nostrils are the East, and the Tongue is the West, and the Ear is the North" (*J* 12:54–60).

"When Luvah assum'd the World of Urizen to the South and Albion was slain upon his mountains & in his tent, all fell towards the Center in dire ruin sinking down" (*Mil* 19:20; *J* 59:17). "When the moon shot forth in that dread night when Urizen call'd the stars round his feet; then burst the center from its orb, and found a place beneath" (*Am* b:4). "Albion's Circumference was clos'd: his Center began dark'ning into the Night of Beulah, and the Moon of Beulah rose clouded with storms" (*J* 19:36).

The Center, or heart, becomes selfish. "Without is formed the Selfish Center . . . and the Center has Eternal States" (*J* 71:7–9), which are the Sons of Albion. When Enitharmon misuses Los's affection, "she scatter'd his love on the wind Eastward into her own Center, creating the Female Womb in mild Jerusalem around the Lamb of God" (*J* 88:52). Satan, the Great Selfhood, has "a white Dot call'd a Center, from which branches out a Circle in continual gyrations: this became a Heart from which sprang numerous branches" (*J* 33:19)—the Polypus.

The earth is not corrupted: "The Vegetative Universe opens like a flower from the Earth's center, in which is Eternity" (*J* 13: 34). But Man needs special aid. Eno takes an Atom of Space (the grain of sand), "with dire pain opening it a Center into Beulah" (*J* 48:38). Jesus corrects "the disobedient Female" by removing from her inner sanctuary the "False Holiness hid within the Center" (*J* 69:40). He also opens man's closed heart so that it may grow beyond its selfishness: "Wonder siez'd all in Eternity, to behold the Divine Vision open the Center into an Expanse, & the Center rolled out into an Expanse" (*J* 57:17).

The CHAIN OF JEALOUSY keeps Orc from manifesting prematurely. It is the natural reaction against an unripe and revolutionary idea.

In a remarkable anticipation of Freud's Oedipus theory, Blake describes the jealousy of the father (Los) and of the son (Orc) in their rivalry for the mother (Enitharmon). Each day, a girdle grows round Los's bosom; his sobbings burst it; but another girdle succeeds, "These falling down on the rock into an iron Chain in each other link by link lock'd" (*Ur* 20:9–20). The jealousy is clarified later: "Los beheld the ruddy boy embracing his bright mother, & beheld malignant fires in his young eyes, discerning plain that Orc plotted his death" (*FZ* v:80–90). So the parents take their child to an iron mountain top (Mount Atlas, where Prometheus was bound, *SoL* 3:21) and bind him down "beneath Urizen's deathful shadow" (*Ur* 20:25). The Spectre holds the boy while Los with the hammer of Urthona nails him down (*FZ* v:92–104).

Enitharmon's tears cause Los to repent, "tho' terrible his dread of that infernal chain . . . & to compensate for her tears even if his own death resulted" (*FZ* v:146–54). But he cannot release Orc now, for the Chain has vegetated round the rock, the cave, and the boy, and has taken root "beneath the Earth even to the Center, wrapping round the Center; & the limbs of Orc entering with fibres become one with him" (*FZ* v:155–70). Vala sees "the infernal

roots of the chain of Jealousy, & felt the rendings of fierce howling Orc" (*FZ* v:181).

There is a slight discrepancy concerning the age at which Orc is bound: according to *The Book of Urizen* 20, he is apparently still an infant; but according to *The Four Zoas* v:79 he is fourteen. However, he is fourteen when, after being fed by the fallen Vala, "the Shadowy Female," he breaks his bonds and embraces her (*Am* 1:2; 2:2).

In *Milton*, it is the spirit of Milton, acting through Blake, who shall break the Chain. "The beautiful Amalekites behold the fires of youth bound with the Chain of Jealousy by Los & Enitharmon" (*Mil* 19:37). But there is an old prophecy recorded in Eden "that Milton of the land of Albion should up ascend forwards from Ulro from the Vale of Felpham, and set free Orc from his Chain of Jealousy" (*Mil* 20:59), "& break the Chain of Jealousy from all its roots" (*Mil* 23:37).

CHALDEA was a kingdom hostile to the Israelites.

Abraham, at the command of God, left Chaldea for Canaan. "Abram fled in fires from Chaldea" (*SoL* 3:16). "Abraham flees from Chaldea shaking his goary locks" (*J* 15:28).

Albion complains that his children are taken "in solemn pomp into Chaldea across the bredths of Europe" (*J* 21:43)—perhaps a reference to the departure of the British soldiers for the Napoleonic wars. The voice of an innocent explains, "The Chaldean took me from my Cradle" (*J* 61:40). Hutton, Skofeld, and Kox, fleeing from Reuben, "fled over Chaldea in terror" (*J* 36: 18). Long ago, the skiey tent of Man reached over Asia, "even to Great Chaldea & Tesshina" (*J* 60:20).

CHAOS is commonly understood to be that confused mass of matter, the *prima materia*, out of which God, by his Divine Word, created this world, beginning all things. He did this by dividing opposites and imposing order.

Blake, however, believed that the Bible

began *in medias res*, and that the creation described in *Genesis* was really a series of falls, breaking up the original Unity. "Many suppose that before the Creation All was Solitude & Chaos. This is the most pernicious Idea that can enter the Mind, as it takes away all sublimity from the Bible & Limits All Existence to Creation & to Chaos, To the Time & Space fixed by the Corporeal Vegetative Eye, & leaves the Man who entertains such an Idea the habitation of Unbelieving demons. Eternity Exists, and All things in Eternity, Independent of Creation, which was an act of Mercy" (*LJ*, *K* 614). Albion, or Man, is our Ancestor, "whose History Preceded that of the Hebrews & in whose Sleep, or Chaos, Creation began" (*LJ*, *K* 609). Blake's Chaos is then a disintegration from Eternity, and not the "First Matter." Parallels between Urizen's acts in "the petrific, abominable chaos" (*Ur* 3:26) and the Creator in *Genesis* are traced in *The Book of Urizen* (20:33–41; 25:39–42) and *The Four Zoas* (*passim*).

The Chaos is the confused mind of the man without Vision. It is based chiefly on his Memory, his "Unformed Memory" (*J* 33:2), "the Memory between Man & Man" (*J* 54:8), "the Shadows of Remembrance . . . the Chaos of the Spectre" (*J* 92:22). It is his Spectre, his rational power, the Great Selfhood Satan, who preaches materialism (*J* 33:1–24), and proclaims himself God (*J* 54:6–24).

Many people to this day believe that God dwells in physical space beyond the stars, and will point to heaven upwards instead of inwards. Milton's God, in spite of Galileo, reigns high above the stars, unapproachable, dark with excessive bright. But Blake insisted that only chaos exists beyond the stars (*Mil* 20:42; 23:21). They seek "thro' Chaos . . . for delight, & in spaces remote . . . the Eternal which is always present to the wise" (*FZ* ix:170). Albion names his Tree of Mystery "Moral Virtue and the Law of God who dwells in Chaos hidden from the human sight" (*J* 28:15). His children "call the Rocks Parents of Men & adore the frowning Chaos" (*J* 67:15). But it is really "the

Chaos of Satan" (*J* 15:31). "Seek not thy heavenly father then beyond the Skies; there Chaos dwells & ancient Night & Og & Anak old" (*Mil* 20:33).

Chaos is often paired with Ancient Night (*Mil* 12:21; 17:24; 20:33; 39:29) because Milton made the two consorts (*PL* ii: 894–96, 959–63). When Blake's Satan finally reveals himself, "Beneath sat Chaos: Sin on his right hand, Death on his left; and Ancient Night spread over all the heav'n his Mantle of Laws" (*Mil* 39:29). The quaternary is obvious. Chaos replaces the Imagination in the North; Sin, the Heart in the East; Night, with "his" laws, the Head in the South; and Death, the Body in the West.

SATAN'S EVIL QUATERNARY

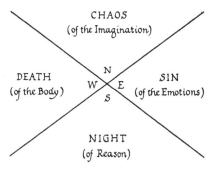

CHAOS
(of the Imagination)

DEATH
(of the Body)

SIN
(of the Emotions)

N
W   E
S

NIGHT
(of Reason)

Paradise Lost ii : 894-96, 959-63   *Milton* 39:29

Chaos is within the Mundane Shell (*Mil* 17:24; 20:42). A comet travels into Chaos (*Mil* 17:24). The black storm comes out of Chaos beyond the stars; it issues through the dark and intricate caves of the Mundane Shell, passing the planets and the firmament; the sun rolls into Chaos and the stars into deserts; and then the storm becomes visible, audible, and terrible, covering the light of day and rolling down upon the mountains (*Mil* 23:21–28).

Los's egg-shaped world stretches from zenith to nadir "in midst of Chaos" (*Mil* 34:34). Milton falls through Albion's heart, "travelling outside of Humanity, beyond the Stars in Chaos in Caverns of the Mundane Shell" (*Mil* 20:42). Ololon and her children follow Milton, travelling a long and dark journey through Chaos; here, in these Chaoses, in caverns of the Mundane Shell, her sons take their abode (*Mil* 34:22, 40). Finally, all things shall remain "in the Shadows of Remembrance & in the Chaos of the Spectre" (*J* 92:22), when it "brighten'd beneath, above, around" (*J* 98:14).

CHARLEMAINE (Charlemagne, A.D. 742–814) was one of the great warring kings; his realm was the beginning of the Holy Roman Empire. He represents War and Dominion.

He is the thirty-sixth son of Los and Enitharmon, standing between Constantine and Luther (*FZ* viii:362). He is the third of the Four Churches into which the Covering Cherub divided: Paul, the missionary; Constantine, who made Christianity the official religion of his empire; Charlemaine, whose Holy Roman Empire divided from the Greek Church; and Luther, who divided the Papists and the Protestants (*Mil* 24:32). Charlemaine is the twenty-sixth of the Twenty-seven Churches, the sixth in the third group, who are "the Male-Females, the Dragon Forms, Religion hid in War, a Dragon red & hidden Harlot" (*Mil* 37:41; *J* 75:16).

The lyric "I saw a Monk of Charlemaine" (*J* 52) describes the persecution of the pacifist. The original working copy is in the Rossetti Manuscript (*K* 418–20). Blake eventually deleted so many good stanzas that he salvaged them as *The Grey Monk*, a fair copy in the Pickering Manuscript (*K* 430).

"CHARLES [I] calls on Milton for Atonement. Cromwell is ready" (*Mil* 5:39). According to David Erdman, he is one of the evil monarchs listed in the deleted line of *Jerusalem* 73:36.

CHATTERTON (Thomas, 1752–70) was a young poet of Bristol, who rediscovered the beauty of Elizabethan verse. Writing in an archaic English of his own contriving, he pretended that the real authors were Thomas Rowley, a monk of the fifteenth century, and other ancients. His suicide at the age of seventeen was one of the tragedies of English literature. His poems were collected in 1777; Blake owned a copy but did not annotate it. The long controversy over the authenticity of the poems was finally settled by Professor W. W. Skeat (1871). Meanwhile, Chatterton's notoriety as a forger quite overshadowed the literary value of his works.

Blake's first revolutionary poem, "Gwin, King of Norway" (*PS*), was obviously influenced by Chatterton's "Godred Crovan," which had appeared in the *Town & Country Magazine* (Aug. 1769) and was collected in Chatterton's *Miscellanies* (1778). Blake refers to Chatterton several times in *An Island in the Moon* (Chaps. iii, v, vii). Quid, loudly denouncing Homer, Shakespeare, and Milton, according to highbrow standards, continues: "Chatterton never writ those poems! A parcel of fools, going to Bristol! If I was to go, I'd find it out in a minute, but I've found it out already" (Chap. vii).

Towards the end of his life, Blake asserted his faith in the genuineness of the poems: "I believe both Macpherson & Chatterton, that what they say is Ancient Is so. I own myself an admirer of Ossian equally with any other Poet whatever, Rowley & Chatterton also" (On Wordsworth, *K* 783).

CHAUCER, in Blake's opinion, was one of the three greatest English poets. He was "the great poetical observer of men" (*K* 569). "Chaucer's characters live age after age. Every age is a Canterbury Pilgrimage" (*K* 570). With Milton and Shakespeare, he appears in the terminal apotheosis of *Jerusalem* (98:9).

Blake's engraving of the Canterbury Pilgrims is well known, also his criticism of Chaucer in the *Descriptive Catalogue*, which Lamb praised so highly.

Dryden, in the preface to his *Fables*, asserted that Chaucer had assembled "the various manners and humours (as we now call them) of the whole English nation, in his age. Not a single character has escaped him." Furthermore, "their general characters are still remaining in mankind, and even in England, though they are called by other names than those of Monks, and Friars, and Canons, and Lady Abbesses, and Nuns; for mankind is ever the same, and nothing lost out of Nature, though everything is altered." From Dryden's hint, Blake went the whole way:

"The characters of Chaucer's Pilgrims are the characters which compose all ages and nations: as one age falls, another rises, different to mortal sight, but to immortals only the same; for we see the same characters repeated again and again, in animals, vegetables, minerals, and in men; nothing new occurs in identical existence; Accident ever varies, Substance can never suffer change nor decay.

"Of Chaucer's characters, as described in his Canterbury Tales, some of the names or titles are altered by time, but the characters themselves for ever remain unaltered, and consequently they are the physiognomies or lineaments of universal human life, beyond which Nature never steps. Names alter, things never alter. I have known multitudes of those who would have been monks in the age of monkery, who in this deistical age are deists. As Newton numbered the stars, and as Linneus numbered the plants, so Chaucer numbered the classes of men" (K 567).

With this thought in mind, Blake organized his picture; even "the Horses [are] varied to accord to their Riders," proving that English Blake knew his horseflesh. The upper classes lead the way, the lower classes follow, and democratic Harry Bailly unites them.

The good Parson is balanced by the evil Pardoner; the Knight, by Chaucer himself. It will be noted that each of the two groups has a woman at its center: the Prioress (Tirzah the Prude) and the Wife of Bath, who holds the cup of Rahab. "The characters of Women Chaucer has divided into two classes, the Lady Prioress and the Wife of Bath." These two are "leaders of the ages of men. The lady prioress in some ages [as that of Victoria] predominates; and in some the wife of Bath [as that of Charles II]." Blake never approved of dominant females; he calls both "a scourge and a blight" (K 572). Both, moreover, are childless. So Blake added the woman whom Chaucer failed to include: the mother with her children. She stands apart from the social pageant; but lest the observer suppose that she is meaningless, a sage behind her particularly points her out to us.

"Chaucer has been misunderstood in his sublime work. Shakespeare's Fairies . . . are the rulers of the vegetable world [the regents of sex], and so are Chaucer's [in *The Marchantes Tale*]; let them be so considered, and then the poet will be understood, and not else" (K 569–70).

Chaucer introduced Dante to the English world by paraphrasing, in *The Monkes Tale*, the story "De Hugelino, Comite de Pize." This record of priestly cruelty greatly impressed Blake. See DANTE.

CHEBAR was the river in Babylon where Ezekiel during the Captivity had his vision of the "four living creatures."

"Ezekiel saw [the Four Zoas] by Chebar's flood" (J 12:58).

CHELSEA, in Blake's day a very large and populous village two miles from London, of which it is now a borough, is almost opposite Battersea across the Thames. It contained Ranelagh Gardens and the Chelsea Hospital, an old soldiers' home, said to have been founded by Charles II at the suggestion of Nell Gwyn.

"Indignant self-righteousness . . . rose up against [Los] . . . from the Brook of Albion's River, from Ranelagh & Strumbolo, from Cromwell's gardens & Chelsea, the place of wounded Soldiers" (J 7:73–8:3). Battersea and Chelsea mourn for Cambel and Gwendolen (J 21:32). At the sight of the Worm, Battersea and Chelsea mourn (J 33:12).

CHEMOSH was the national deity of Moab; his worship, which closely resembled that of Molech, included the burning alive of children.

Blake calls them two "Generalizing Gods" (*J* 89:31), that is, laws of conduct drawn up by the priests to apply to mankind generally, but which sacrifice the happiness of the individual.

Chemosh is third of the Twelve Gods of Asia (*Mil* 37:20). As in Blake's day the chief sacrifice of children was sending them into the army, Chemosh is invoked by the Warriors (*J* 68:18). Hand combines into the Double Molech and Chemosh (*J* 84: 21). In the bosom of the Covering Cherub appear the two "Generalizing Gods" who hold Israel in bondage (*J* 89:31).

The CHERUBIM are Ideas. Being newborn, they are often symbolized as baby heads. They are usually the second angelic order, that of Wisdom, which is surpassed only by the Seraphim, the order of Love. These two orders surround God (*Mil* 39: 28), but Satan, when imitating God, has only Cherubim (*Mil* 39:25).

Two Cherubim of gold (see GOLD) spread their wings over the Mercy Seat on the Ark of the Covenant (*Exod* xxv:18–20; *LJ, K* 613); they signify the understanding which sustains the divine presence. The Nordic war-gods contend with Jehovah "among the Cherubim" of the Mercy Seat itself (*J* 63:10). Cherubim were embroidered on the Veil of the Temple (*Exod* xxvi:31); the Daughters of Albion weave an imitation Veil, "the Web of Ages & Generations, folding & unfolding it like a Veil of Cherubim" (*J* 64:2). Jerusalem asks: "Why should Punishment Weave the Veil with Iron Wheels of War, when Forgiveness might it Weave with Wings of Cherubim?" (*J* 22:35). She has her own "Cherubims of Tender-mercy" (*Mil* 35:10; *J* 24:21; 79: 54; 84:10). By a characteristic extension, they become the labia of the female genitals (*J* 21:21; 30:35; 63:14, 24).

The Cherubim of God are the spirits of understanding which are Forgiveness. The Cherubim of Man are the Four Zoas, the "four living creatures" of Ezekiel (*J* 63:2). The Cherubim of the heathen are human qualities personified. "The Artist . . . in vision . . . has seen those wonderful originals called in the Sacred Scriptures the Cherubim . . . being originals from which the Greeks and Hetrurians copied Hercules Farnese, Venus of Medicis, Apollo Belvidere, and all the grand works of ancient art" (*DesC* II, *K* 565). "Visions of these eternal principles or characters of human life appear to poets, in all ages; the Grecian gods were the ancient Cherubim of Phoenicia . . . These gods are visions of the eternal attributes, or divine names, which, when erected into gods, become destructive to humanity" (*DesC* III, *K* 571).

"The Gods of Priam are the Cherubim of Moses & Solomon, The Hosts of Heaven" (*Laoc, K* 777). The gods who defended Troy were the material Apollo, the amorous Venus, and the belligerent Mars. (See PRIAM.) Blake accuses Moses and Solomon of worshipping these false gods. They still dominate mankind.

The Cherubim may become forms of prohibition. Such were the Cherubim with the flaming sword which kept fallen man from the Tree of Life (*Gen* iii:24). "The cherub with his flaming sword is hereby commanded to leave his guard at [the] tree of life; and when he does, the whole creation will be consumed and appear infinite and holy, whereas it now appears finite & corrupt" (*MHH* 14; *J* 14:2). The closed Western Gate is guarded by four Cherubim (*J* 13:6). The Twenty-seven Heavens which shut Man from Eternity constitute "the Cherub" (*Mil* 37:44, 60). See COVERING CHERUB.

Once Blake (possibly thinking of Reynolds' celebrated picture) called the offspring of a loveless marriage "the abhorred birth of cherubs in the human form" (*VDA* 5:28).

CHESELDEN (i.e., Chisledon) is in Wilts, due west from London.

"The Sun forgets his course like a drunken man; he hesitates upon the Cheselden hills, thinking to sleep on the Severn" (*J* 66:74).

CHESHIRE is an English county assigned to Benjamin (*J* 16:49) and Peachey (*J* 71: 30). When Bowen and Conwenna cut the fibres of Benjamin from Chester's River, "Cheshire & Lancashire & Westmoreland groan in anguish" (*J* 90:18).

"CHESTER awful" is the seventeenth Cathedral City; it is under Luvah and London (*J* 46:18). Perhaps Blake called it "awful" because for four centuries it was the headquarters for the famous Roman Twentieth Legion.

CHESTER'S RIVER is the River Dee. Chester is in Cheshire, which is assigned to Benjamin (*J* 16:49); consequently, the river is associated with him (*J* 63:12; 90:18).

The CHEVIOT Hills, culminating in The Cheviot (2,676 ft.), form a natural barrier between eastern England and Scotland.

Blake associated Cheviot with cruelty and warfare. Albion declares, "the Malvern & the Cheviot, the Wolds, Plinlimmon & Snowdon are mine" (*J* 4:30). "The Peak, Malvern & Cheviot Reason in Cruelty" (*J* 21:34). "Such the appearance in Cheviot, in the Divisions of Reuben" (*J* 63:23). When war breaks out, "all the Land of Canaan" is "suspended over the Valley of Cheviot" (*J* 63:42). Rintrah and Palamabron, in pride of dominion, risk divorce from their Emanations "upon East Moor in Devonshire & along the Valleys of Cheviot" (*J* 93:6).

CHICHESTER is a city in the maritime county of Sussex, near Felpham. "Chichester is a very handsom City, Seven miles from us; we can get most Conveniences there" (To Butts, 2 Oct 1800). The see was originally at Selsey, but was removed to Chichester in 1075; the site of the original cathedral is now a mile out to sea. Blake listed Selsey-Chichester first of the

Twenty-four Cathedral Cities, and placed it under Urizen and Verulam (Canterbury). His desperation before his trial for high treason at Chichester on January 11, 1804, and his relief at his acquittal, are reflected in his account of the Cathedral Cities which assemble round Albion's death-bed at the summons of Los. "Selsey, true friend! who afterwards submitted to be devour'd by the waves of Despair, whose Emanation rose above the flood and was nam'd Chichester, lovely mild & gentle! Lo! her lambs bleat to the sea-fowls' cry, lamenting still for Albion" (*J* 40:48). The South Downs nearby produce a famous breed of sheep.

The Polypus starts in Verulam and reaches through various Cathedral Cities, including Chichester (*J* 67:36).

CHILDREN are the State of Innocence, still close to the Eternity from which they came "trailing clouds of glory" (to quote Wordsworth's *Ode* which delighted Blake so), and as yet uncorrupted by Experience. "Little children always behold the Face of the Heavenly Father" (On Berkeley, *K* 774). "That is Heaven," said Blake to Palmer, indicating a group of children playing outside (*Gil* I, 345), "for of such is the kingdom of heaven" (*Matt* xix:14).

Childless himself, he adored children, and not only the Linnell children adored him in return. His first published book, *Songs of Innocence*, was addressed to them, also the first issue of his *Gates of Paradise*. He wrote to Trusler (23 Aug 1799) about his designs: "Particularly they have been Elucidated by Children, who have taken a greater delight in contemplating my Pictures than I ever hoped."

A man's children are not only his offspring but everything he produces: his works, his ideas, even his joys. They are the male's "secret loves & Graces" (*FZ* i: 164), his "infant Loves & Graces" (*J* 8:44; 20:27), his "infant thoughts & desires" (*J* 9:2). The god who demands their sacrifice is Molech. Children symbolize the fecundity of the imagination, the "Eternal Creation flowing from the Divine Humanity

in Jesus" (To Ozias Humphry, *K* 444).
"Jesus is surrounded by Beams of Glory in
which are seen all around him Infants emanating from him; these represent the Eternal Births of Intellect from the divine Humanity" (*LJ*, *K* 613). The "Church Universal" appears as the Woman crowned with
stars, with the moon under her feet; she is
"Surrounded by Infants" (*LJ*, *K* 609–10).
"Multitudes of Men in Harmony appear
like a single Infant, sometimes in the Arms
of a Female; this represented the Church"
(*LJ*, *K* 607). (See Illustrations, "LJ" Nos.
6, 64, 73.) Charity, in the eighty-eighth illustration of Dante, is surrounded by five
infants.

CHINA is usually mentioned with Japan,
to indicate the eastern end of the earth, in
Blake's sweeps across the map (*FZ* ii:59;
Mil 6:23; 14:7; *J* 24:47; 67:40; 82:28). In
Urizen's Temple, China, India, and Siberia are his temples for entertainment (*J*
58:39).
Once Jerusalem covered China, with all
other lands (*J* 24:47), but the Polypus has
reached there (*J* 67:40). Eventually it will
be the thirteenth of the Thirty-two Nations,
guardians of liberty and rulers of the rest of
the world (*J* 72:39).

CHRIST was a term that Blake used only
five times in his poetry, outside *The Everlasting Gospel*, as he preferred the personal
name "Jesus." See JESUS.
"Christ took on Sin in the Virgin's Womb
& put it off on the Cross" (*Mil* 5:3). "A
Vegetated Christ & a Virgin Eve are the
Hermaphroditic Blasphemy" (*J* 90:34).
The other three references are "believe
Christ & his Apostles" (*Mil*, Pref.); "that
One Man we call Jesus the Christ" (*J* 38:
19); "cast out devils in Christ's name" (*J*
77:24).

The CHURCH Universal (*LJ*, *K* 609) was
the only church that Blake recognized. Its
doctrine is the Everlasting Gospel, its con-
gregation the Brotherhood of Man, its symbol the Woman in the Wilderness, its ar-

chitecture Gothic. (See Illustrations, "LJ"
No. 64.)
All other churches Blake rejected with
the Dissenter's loathing. For the Church
and the State (palace), the priest and the
king, are the two evil powers which rule
society. *An ancient Proverb* (*K* 176) begins:
"Remove away that black'ning church."
In the *Songs of Experience*, the parents of
the little chimney sweep have "gone up
to the church to pray. . . . to praise God
& his Priest & King, who make up a
heaven of our misery." His cry "every
black'ning church appalls" ("London" 10).
The Little Vagabond complains that the
Church is cold, whereas the Ale-house is
healthy and warm. In "A Little Boy Lost,"
the priest burns the boy alive for his innocent remarks. Preaching materialism, the
Church is the Serpent Temple of the Druids
(*Eur* 10:21; 12:11). Preaching error, it is
the church, or synagogue, of Satan (*Mil*
38:37; 39:62). The ruling spirit is Mystery,
the Whore of Babylon; her seven-headed
beast is the double organization of Church
and State.

The CHURCH OF ROME, as every good Protestant knew, was "Mystery, Babylon
the Great," popularly called "The Whore
of Babylon." Was she not "that great city
which reigneth over the kings of the earth"?
Did she not sit upon "seven mountains"?
(*Rev* xvii:5, 9, 18). And did not this church
rely on "mysteries"—doctrines which cannot be explained and must not be challenged? See MYSTERY.
Blake, naming her "Rahab," made her
an important character in *The Four Zoas*,
Milton, and *Jerusalem*, where she is the
false Church, which tries to destroy Jerusalem and does crucify Jesus.
"Wilt thou make Rome thy Patriarch
Druid & the Kings of Europe his Horsemen?" (*J* 61:50). In two pictures Blake
emphasized Rome's political power. His
title page to Night viii of Young's *Night
Thoughts* shows "Mystery" in full detail
riding on her seven-headed Beast. The
Beast symbolizes the combination of Church

and State. The Pope is the key figure. Above him his hierarchy ascends up the left margin, culminating in the simple curate, who alone has no horns; along the lower margin are the emperor, the king, the judge, and the warrior. In the illustration to Dante's *Purgatorio* (xxxii:146), which is also based on *Revelation* xvii, the Whore (the corrupted Church) kisses a Giant (the Emperor), who has on a leash the first head of the Beast, a hornless monkey's head crowned with the papal tiara.

The Whore is the secret and central motivation of war: "Religion hidden in War . . . a Dragon red & hidden Harlot" (*Mil* 40:20–22; *J* 75:20). In a water color of 1809 (British Museum), she wears a castellated (civic) headdress: she is Rome, the instigator of war. From her cup rise heavy fumes containing female figures with the trumpets of fame and the wine-cups of intoxication; they descend to a warrior riding to battle; and the Beast gobbles up the victims.

Blake as a Liberty Boy detested authoritarianism in all its forms; the Pope claimed to be the supreme authority. One sees him in *Europe* (11): bat-winged and crowned with the tiara, he sits on a (usurped) Gothic throne with an open book in his lap; and two angels sink their wands submissively before him. According to the text, this is Urizen with his brazen book "that Kings & Priests had copied on Earth" (11:4).

The papal tiara is also worn by the King of Babylon in Hell (a water color in the Boston Museum of Fine Arts). An angel leads him by his manacled hands and points sternly forward; but he stares backward at a man entwined with a serpent and falling head downward, while the ghosts of kings and warriors rise before "the king."

By insisting on literal interpretations, Rome killed the spiritual meanings. "The letter killeth, but the spirit giveth life" (*II Cor* iii:6; *Illustr Job* 1). Thus, in spite of St. Paul's statement that the material body dies, whereas the spiritual body is raised (*I Cor* xv:44; *SoE*, "To Tirzah"), Rome by insisting on the resurrection of the material body committed a basic error. The literal interpretation of the resurrection of Lazarus became part of the false doctrine, the "Covering Cherub," which infected all the churches (*Mil* 24:26–33). The same thing, with worse results, happened over the resurrection of Jesus. Rahab weaves her web of religion times after times around the sepulcher where she had placed "the body which she had taken from the Divine Lamb" (*FZ* viii:586). Thus Rome came to worship death instead of life. "He took on Sin in the Virgin's Womb, | And put it off on the Cross & Tomb, | To be Worship'd by the Church of Rome" (*EG* b:57). To worship "A Vegetated Christ . . . [is] The Hermaphroditic Blasphemy" (*J* 90:34); but here Blake may have been attacking Transubstantiation.

The most harmful error of Rome lay in its debasement of sex, an error which had lasted for eighteen hundred years (*Eur* 9:2). Blake's works are full of declarations that the act is holy. Jesus forgave the adulteress: "her sins, which are many, are forgiven; for she loved much" (*Luke* vii:47; cf. *EG* e:59–80). Monasticism is bad. "The human race began to wither, for the healthy built secluded places, fearing the joys of Love" (*SoL* 3:25). In the fifth illustration to *L'Allegro*, the youth led astray by the will-o-the-wisp "is seen following the Friar's Lantern towards the Convent" (*K* 618).

Blake renounced completely any worship of the Virgin. He scoffed at Mary's virginity, which, with the Vegetated Christ, was "the Hermaphroditic Blasphemy" (*J* 90:34). She was not the Mother of God but only of the mortal part of Jesus; and he rejected her: "Woman, what have I to do with thee?" (*John* ii:4; *SoE*, "To Tirzah" 4, 16). Any doctrine based on the idea of Mary's supposed virginity is the result of "the Spectrous Uncircumcized Vegetation," which in dreadful pain forms "a Sexual Machine, an Aged Virgin Form, in Erin's Land [the realm of the body] toward the north, joint after joint, & burning in love & jealousy immingled, & calling it Religion" (*J* 44:24). "Thus God himself become[s] a Male subservient to the Female" (*J* 88:21). Blake's last drawing for the *Divine Comedy* represents the intoxicating Rose of Heaven (99), which he turned into an attack on mariolatry. (See *Roe* 193.)

Blake also challenged and rejected the whole complex of sin and its punishment, which sprang from Rome but was accepted by all Christendom. "Every thing is good in God's eyes" (*CR* 256); the Divine Mercy forgives everybody. Sin is only an error, a state through which one passes: "To be an Error & to be Cast out is a part of God's Design" (*LJ*, *K* 613). The error springs from the false and artificial division of Good and Evil. "Satan thinks that Sin is displeasing to God; he ought to know that Nothing is displeasing to God but Unbelief & Eating of the Tree of Knowledge of Good & Evil" (*LJ*, *K* 615). The Atonement "is a horrible doctrine. If another man pay your debt, I do not forgive it" (*CR* 271; cf. *J* 61:17). Guilt is a lack of faith, a spiritual disease (*J* 21:3); whereas the passions are positive goods. "Men are admitted into Heaven not because they have curbed & govern'd their Passions or have No Passions, but because they have Cultivated their Understandings. The Treasures of Heaven are not Negations of Passion, but Realities of Intellect, from which all the Passions Emanate Uncurbed in their Eternal Glory. The Fool shall not enter into Heaven let him be ever so Holy. Holiness is not The Price of Enterance [*sic*] into Heaven. Those who are cast out are All Those who, having no Passions of their own because No Intellect, Have spent their lives in Curbing & Governing other People's by the Various arts of Poverty & Cruelty of all kinds" (*LJ*, *K* 615).

Blake did not accept the creation *ex nihilo*; like Milton and various others before him, he believed that all things originated in the divine substance. It followed therefore that souls existed before the conception of the body, nor could any suffer everlasting punishment in a posthumous hell. He could never accept an abstract God or a personal Devil. He detested all ritual: "The outward Ceremony is Antichrist" (*Laoc*, *K* 776). Such matters he considered the petrifactions of uninspired logic, the outgrowths and excrescences which ruined the symbolism of the fundamental truths. Blake agreed with these fundamentals, but disagreed with their traditional interpretations. He would accept the symbol but understood it otherwise.

It is not surprising then that Satan reposes "on the seven mou[n]tains of Rome [cf. *Rev* xvii:9], in the whole place of the Covering Cherub [cf. *J* 89:39], Rome, Babylon & Tyre" (*Mil* 9:50), and that in the Rosenwald "Last Judgment," the papal tiara of dominion and the rosary of vain repetitions fall into annihilation, along with the Cross itself, on which is nailed the Serpent of Nature (*EG b*:53). (See Illustrations, "LJ" Nos. 28, 29.)

Nevertheless, as has been made obvious elsewhere, Blake's most sweeping condemnations are never total. In his "Last Judgment," the falling cross does not signify a rejection of the Crucifixion: it signifies a rejection of cruciolatry, the worship of death, and of the materialism which is essential to that belief. Blake was attacking the errors of Rome, not the Church Triumphant.

Therefore Blake had a way of defending Rome which to his orthodox auditors seemed whimsically perverse. "One day, rather in an opposing mood, I think, he declared that the Romish Church was the only one which taught the forgiveness of sins.... The English Church, as he thought, too little inculcated it. He had a sentimental liking for the Romish Church, and, among other paradoxes, would often try to make out that priestly despotism was better than kingly. He believed that no subjects of monarchies were so happy as the Pope's. ... I fancy this was one of his *wilful* sayings, and meant that he believed priests to be more favourable to liberty than kings: which he certainly did" (*Gil* 1863, I, 330—this passage is not in the second edition, 1880, I, 373).

Blake's regard for Rome was more than

whimsy: it was really a counter-attack against those who automatically rejected everything that smacked of popery. Error itself is prophetic of Truth. Anything possible to be believed is an expression, however misinterpreted, of something real in the psyche. Aquinas and Blake deal with the same fundamentals; they are not so far apart as they might seem.

The SEVEN CHURCHES are the seven churches of Asia addressed by John the Divine at the beginning of *Revelation*. Blake believed that their Christianity was already subverted. They are the "seven houses of brick" which he saw in the fourth "Memorable Fancy" (*MHH* 19), populated by monkeys, chained round the middle yet preying on each other. In *Europe* (14:20) they are "the seven churches of Leutha" (sin).

The TWENTY-SEVEN CHURCHES, or Heavens, represent dogmatic Christianity in its successive aspects. They are to man's spiritual life what the Mundane Shell (which contains them) is to his physical being: an enclosure which shuts him from Eternity. They are "Satan & Adam . . . States Created into Twenty-seven Churches" (*Mil* 32:25). They are described in *Milton* 37:35-43 (after the analysis of paganism as the Twelve Gods of Asia) and in *Jerusalem* 75:10-26. The Twenty-seven are divided into three series. The first runs from Adam to Lamech, according to *Genesis* v; the second from Noah to Terah, according to *Genesis* xi:10-26 (but with the addition of Cainan the Second, from *Luke* iii:36); while the third begins with Abraham, abandons genealogy for historical names, and ends with Luther. "And where Luther ends Adam begins again in Eternal Circle" (*J* 75:24).

The first series (Adam, Seth, Enos, Cainan, Mahalaleel, Jared, Enoch, Methuselah, and Lamech) are "Giants mighty"—the giants before the flood—and "Hermaphroditic" or self-contradictory. Adam is the Natural Man, devoid of imagination (*Laoc, K* 776), the limit of Contraction, also the division between man and man (*J* 73:28);

and as Scofield is identified with him (*J* 7:42), he is the Accuser of Sin. He is a Druid (*DesC* V, *K* 578), and therefore believes in human sacrifice. The spirit of his church is that of Abel's Ghost (blood for blood). "Abel kneels on a bloody cloud descriptive of those Churches before the flood, that they were fill'd with blood & fire & vapour of smoke; even till Abraham's time the vapor & heat was not extinguish'd" (*LJ, K* 606). Adam's line, however, passes through Seth, who is "Male & Female in a higher state of Happiness & wisdom than Noah, being nearer the State of Innocence . . . The figures of Seth & his wife comprehends the Fathers before the flood & their Generations" (*LJ, K* 611).

The second series (Noah, Shem, Arphaxad, Cainan the Second, Salah, Heber, Peleg, Reu, Serug, Nahor, and Terah) consists of "the Female Males, a Male within a Female hid as in an Ark & Curtains." They continue the ideal of Vengeance for Sin. Noah is also a Druid (*DesC* V, *K* 578; *J* 27), who punishes the offending Ham in his children called Canaan; Shem, Heber, and (originally) Abraham were also Druids (*J* 27). But the Flood of Matter has come; men are drowned in their limited senses. Only Noah and his family escaped, in the Moon-Ark of Love (see ARK OF NOAH; BRYANT). Noah can still communicate with Eternity; he symbolizes Poetry, his sons Shem and Japhet, Painting and Music, "the three Powers in Man of conversing with Paradise, which the flood did not Sweep away" (*LJ, K* 609). Heber (so Blake spells "Eber") was the eponymous ancestor of the Hebrews. In the days of Peleg ("division"), the earth was divided amongst the tribes.

The third series (Abraham, Moses, Solomon, Paul, Constantine, Charlemaine, and Luther) brings the list to modern times. These are "the Male Females, the Dragon Forms . . . Religion hid in War, a Dragon red & hidden Harlot."

When Abraham substituted a ram for the son he expected to sacrifice, he foreshadowed the Vicarious Atonement, and marked the beginning of the end of Druidism.

"Abraham was called to succeed the Druidical age, which began to turn allegoric and mental signification into corporeal command, whereby human sacrifice would have depopulated the earth" (*DesC* V, *K* 578). The other names represent the growth of the Church Militant: Moses, the promulgator of the Ten Commandments; Solomon, the great king and judge; Paul, the great missionary; Constantine, who established Christianity as the official religion of his empire; Charlemaine, great warrior and founder of the Holy Roman Empire; and Luther, the revolutionist, who divided Papists and Protestants. As Moses, Constantine, and Charlemaine resorted to the force of arms, and as Luther provoked it, Blake felt justified in calling the whole movement "religion hid in War" culminating in the revelation of Rahab herself, "Mystery, Babylon the Great, the Abomination of Desolation." "And where Luther ends, Adam begins again in Eternal Circle" (*J* 75:19, 24): the warring revolutionist merely reduces man back to the Natural Man.

At first Blake thought of the Churches "ever consuming & ever building" as caused by "the Spectres of all the inhabitants of Earth wailing to be Created" (*J* 13:62). But on second thought, he realized that they were all products of the imagination, which therefore Los creates, though within the Mundane Shell, "to awake the Prisoners of Death, to bring Albion again with Luvah into light eternal in his eternal day"; because when Rahab is revealed in her full horror, Jesus, "breaking thro' the Central Zones of Death & Hell, Opens Eternity in Time & Space, triumphant in Mercy" (*J* 75:21–26).

The circle of Churches is penetrable from this side also. "The Lark is Los's Messenger thro' the Twenty-seven Churches, that the Seven Eyes of God, who walk even to Satan's Seat thro' all the Twenty-seven Heavens, may not slumber nor sleep" (*Mil* 35:63).

CICERO (106–43 B.C.), the Roman orator, was the the author of several philosophical and moral books, including *De natura deorum*, *De divinatione*, and *De officiis*. "The Stolen and Perverted Writings of Homer & Ovid, of Plato & Cicero, which all men ought to contemn, are set up by artifice against the Sublime of the Bible" (*Mil* 1:2).

The CIRCLE OF DESTINY is the revolving world of matter with its system of cause and effect.

When Enion separated from Tharmas, he groaned weeping, "then bending from his Clouds, he stoop'd his innocent head, and stretching out his holy hand in the vast deep sublime, turn'd round the circle of Destiny with tears & bitter sighs, and said: 'Return, O wanderer, when the day of Clouds is o'er' " (*FZ* i:72). Enion labored nine days, "but on the tenth trembling morn, the Circle of Destiny [was] complete" (*FZ* i:87). Then the Daughters of Beulah, "creating spaces, lest they fall into Eternal Death, the Circle of Destiny complete, they gave to it a space, and nam'd the space Ulro" (*FZ* i:100).

It is probably not pertinent; but when Urizen casts out Ahania, "The bounds of Destiny were broken" (*FZ* iii:135), and Urizen himself fell.

"The CIRCLE OF LIFE" is a tentative title given to a recently discovered painting by Blake (see Illustrations). There have been various interpretations of it; but certainly it is a study of Neo-Platonic philosophy, as indicated by the classical temple in the mid-background, also by the absence of Los, or true inspiration. The painting depicts the descent of a soul into the material world.

On the top left of the picture, Urizen, drunken on the wine of the Almighty (*FZ* v:234–37), falls asleep in his sun-chariot, which comes to a halt. Four maidens, with comb and towel, rush forward to groom the horses, stopping them in their clockwise progress. Urizen's sinking scepter touches blindly one head in a group of nymphs with musical instruments. In a kind of explosion, the nymph reappears below, breast-deep in the Sea of Time and Space, drawn floating in wild career by four horses.

Red-robed Luvah, in his role of Love the incarnator, sits on a rock of the shore, extending his arms as though charming the waves. Close behind him, Vala in her veil points with her left hand to Urizen's horses above.

Beneath them, in a slab-roofed cave, shell-crowned Tharmas, floating on his back, extends his left hand to a culvert from which water flows, and the other to a phallic twist of rope. Pressing close above him are the Three Fates of classical mythology. Clotho, who presides over birth, draws a rope from the twist, her face expressing pain. Lachesis, who presides over life, passes the rope on over her head, while she stares at Tharmas with a look of rage. Atropos, who presides over death, cuts the rope with her shears; her expression is benign.

The water flows counterclockwise along the base of the picture; it comes from the Sea of Time and Space, emerging from the culvert which Tharmas grasps, and disappears into another culvert on the right, which represents death, as indicated by the body of a woman lying across it.

George W. Digby, with whom I frequently disagree, correctly identifies this current as the River of Generation, variously known as Storge, Arnon, and Pison (*Symbol and Image in William Blake*, Oxford, 1957, p. 83).

The right third of the picture is framed in two pairs of trees. It represents the world of women, the water carriers, who weave the material body and perpetuate the generations by the umbilical cord. From the river of Tharmas ascends the fallen soul, her wild hair now neatly coifed, carrying a scaly bucket.

She must pass between two women. On her left is the woman who represents Motherhood; her left hand passes the umbilical cord to her young daughter, who winds it into a hank, preparing for maturity. The ascending soul confronts Motherhood with a gesture of alarm. She ignores

the other woman, who represents Marriage; this woman trails the cord from her right hand, and from her left a net, in which her daughter feeds her cord to a group of three women above. These three are weaving furiously at the loom of generation, against a background of flames.

In the upper right corner are a group of idealized women with angel wings. Arched over by vegetation they walk (counterclockwise) to the left, each bearing a waterbucket on her head.

The CIRCUMFERENCE is the outward body, or Tharmas (*J* 12:55), the Zenith being the Head (Urizen), the Nadir the depths within (Urthona), and the Center the Heart (Luvah). Albion's Circumference is closed (*J* 19:36). His last words are uttered from the Circumference into Eternity (*J* 23:28). "The Sanctuary of Eden is in . . . the Circumference" (*J* 69:42). "What is Above is Within . . . the Circumference is Within, Without is formed the Selfish Center, and the Circumference still expands going forward to Eternity" (*J* 71:6), "Rejoicing in Unity in the Four Senses, in the Outline, the Circumference & Form" (*J* 98:21).

CLAKMANAN (i.e., Clackmannan) is a Scottish county which, with Bute and Caitnes (Caithness), is assigned to Dan (*J* 16:55). As part of Scotland, it is also assigned to Bowen (*J* 71:46).

CLARE is an Irish county in Munster; with the other five counties of Munster it is assigned to Reuben, Simeon, and Levi (*J* 72:22).

Three CLASSES of men are accepted in Milton's three great poems: the Elect, the Redeemed, and the Reprobate. The Elect are the saints, those persons divinely chosen before the foundation of the world to do God's work (*Eph* i:4), and are predestined to salvation. They are above the law; for though they might break every Commandment, they would do so because of their deeper insight into the will of God.

No man can tell certainly that he or anybody else is of the Elect; yet the Congregational churches in their early days limited their membership to those who could show visible signs of God's favor—usually a New Birth. The Redeemed are the repentant sinners who are saved by the Christ. The Reprobate or the Transgressors are those who go their own way to damnation.

Milton's Jesus and Samson are examples of the Elect, his Adam and Eve of the Redeemed, and his Satan and Dalila of the Reprobate.

Blake deftly inverted the classification. His Reprobate and Transgressors are (like the devils in *The Marriage of Heaven and Hell*) the original geniuses, whether in religion, art, or science. They break all the rules and transgress the laws because they act from immediate inspiration, the direct perception of the truth. They are reprobated by the conventional angels as lawbreakers.

So Blake's Jesus is numbered amongst the Transgressors, according to Isaiah's prophecy (*Isaiah* liii:12; also *Mark* xv:28 and *Luke* xxii:37). "He died as a Reprobate, he was Punish'd as a Transgressor" (*Mil* 13:27). All the Reprobate are "form'd to destruction from the mother's womb" (*Mil* 7:3). After accusing Palamabron of the seven deadly sins, Satan rages: "transgressors I will rend off for ever" (*Mil* 9:28). Jerusalem is to be destroyed as a harlot and her sons as Reprobates (*Mil* 22:47). Even Swedenborg showed the Transgressors in Hell (*Mil* 22:51). As is well known from such cases as Socrates, society frequently martyrs its saviors. Not till the end shall things be understood clearly; then the Elect and the Redeemed shall be "astonish'd at the Transgressor, in him beholding the Saviour" (*Mil* 13:31).

As for the Elect, Blake had his own opinion of such Visible Saints, whom he considered Pharisees. Satan represents this class (*Mil* 7:6; 11:21). But the angels do not recognize him as such: it is a proverb of Eden that "Satan is among the Reprobate" (*Mil* 9:12).

When Los is preparing for the final harvest, he bids his laborers bind the sheaves, not by nations or families, but according to the Three Classes, whom he describes: "under pretence to benevolence the Elect Subdu'd All from the Foundation of the World. The Elect is one Class: You shall bind them separate: they cannot Believe in Eternal Life except by Miracle & a New Birth. The other two Classes, the Reprobate who never cease to Believe, and the Redeem'd who live in doubts & fears perpetually tormented by the Elect, these you shall bind in a twin-bundle for the Consummation: but the Elect must be saved [from] fires of Eternal Death, to be formed into the Churches of Beulah that they destroy not the Earth" (*Mil* 25:31).

The Classes are "the Two Contraries & the Reasoning Negative [the Elect]" (*Mil* 5:14). They are not eternal, being only threefold (*Mil* 4:4-5). "When Albion was slain upon his Mountains," Los and Enitharmon created them (*Mil* 3:1; 6:35) within the Mundane Shell (*Mil* 4:3); specifically in London (*Mil* 6:31, 32). These three Classes run through all creation: "in every Nation & every Family . . . and in every Species of Earth, Metal, Tree, Fish, Bird & Beast" (*Mil* 25:40). The Class of Satan is called the Elect; of Rintrah, the Reprobate; of Palamabron, the Redeemed (*Mil* 11:21). The purpose is almost that of the Vicarious Atonement: the innocent must be condemned for the guilty; because if the guilty were condemned, "he must be an Eternal Death, and one must die for another throughout all Eternity" (*Mil* 11:17). Ololon understands this when she calls on her companions to descend and give themselves to death in Ulro among the Transgressors (*Mil* 21:46).

CLAY is the living substance with which the creator works (*Mil* 28:14). Our bodies are "mortal clay" (*J* 27:59). "Adam" means "red clay" (*MHH* 2:13). See ADAMAH. Milton takes "the red clay of Succoth" to model a human form on Urizen's bones (*Mil* 19:10). Before Los gives him form, Urizen is "a clod of clay" (*Ur* 6:14).

The self-sacrificing clod of clay is contrasted with the hard and selfish pebble (*SoE*, "The Clod & the Pebble"). In *Thel* (4:6; 5:14), the Clod of Clay is the mother. When Thel in imagination enters the matron Clay's house, she is foreseeing her own future when her senses wake; and she flees, terrified. Gwendolen becomes a Clod of Clay, and Merlin a worm or baby (*J* 56: 28). The southern and western gates of Golgonooza opening towards Ulro are made of clay (*J* 13:4, 10). Oothoon speaks of "the red earth of our immortal river" (*VDA* 3:19).

The CLOUD, in *The Book of Thel* (2:13–3:31), is the male principle, the fructifier. In *Europe* (14:15–20), he is named "the youthful Antamon, prince of the pearly dew . . . [a] crystal form, floating upon the bosom'd air with lineaments of gratified desire." His consort is Leutha (sin).

Earlier, the cloud is our body, which conceals Eternity from us (*SoI*, "The Little Black Boy"). The crying baby is like "a fiend hid in a cloud" (*SoE*, "Infant Sorrow" 4).

Elsewhere, the cloud may be anything that obscures the mind: "clouds of reason" (*SoI*, "The Voice of the Ancient Bard" 4); "clouds of learning" (*J* 52:7); "clouds of War" ("I saw a Monk of Charlemaine" 17, *K* 420); "Why dost thou hide thyself in clouds" (*To Nobodaddy* 3, *K* 171).

COBAN (Koban) was presumably somebody connected with Blake's trial for treason. His name is a variant of Coburn or Cockburn.

He is the third Son of Albion (*J* 5:25; 19:18; 32:10). His Emanation is Ignoge, who adjoined with Guantok's children and produced Cordella, the Emanation of Guantok. The ideal Coban dwells in the Cathedral City of Bath. He is assigned the English counties of Somerset (in which Bath is situated), Wiltshire (also assigned to Kox), and Gloucestershire (*J* 71:26–29) — three adjoining counties on the east side of the Severn; they are also assigned to Judah (*J* 16:45).

Six times Coban appears in a triad with the first two Sons. As Hand is the head and Hyle the heart, Coban must be the loins. Hand is a rock; Hyle and Coban are Sinai and Horeb (*Mil* 19:58). The three surround Milton as a girdle (*Mil* 23:15). The three, with Skofeld, Kox, and Kotope, labor mightily in the wars of Babel and Shinar (*J* 8:41). Los heats his spiritual sword in the flames of the three (*J* 9:21). Hand absorbs the twelve Sons; a polypus vegetates from his bosom; and Hyle and Coban are "his two chosen ones for Emissaries in War" (*J* 18:41). The three flee from Reuben and become what they behold (*J* 36:15).

In Urizen's temple, "Hand & Koban arch'd over the Sun" at noon; "Hyle & Skofeld arch'd over the Moon at midnight, & Los Fix'd them there" (*J* 58:29).

Coban's son is Nimrod, the first king, the builder of Babel and its Tower, and the hunter of men (*J* 7:19).

COLCHESTER, the largest town in Essex, is a port on the river Colne. Like Maldon, it was probably a port of embarkation for the soldiers leaving for the Continent. "Malden & Colchester Demonstrate" (*J* 21:37). The Atlantic weeps over his children "in Stone-henge, in Malden & Colchester" (*J* 57:6).

The Ten COMMANDMENTS (*Exod* xx:2–17) were promulgated at Mount Sinai to the Jews in their forty-year trek through the wilderness. The finger of God wrote the Commandments on two tables (tablets) of stone, which he gave to Moses (*Exod* xxxi: 18). In his wrath at the apostasy of his people, Moses broke them (*Exod* xxxii:19); but later, at the command of God he himself hewed two more tables, on which he inscribed the words of the Lord (*Exod* xxxiv:1, 10–27).

According to tradition, this event was the beginning of writing. "God . . . | Who in mysterious Sinai's awful cave, | To Man the wondrous art of writing gave" (*J* 3:2).

The tables were kept in the sacred Ark, beneath the Mercy Seat. What eventually became of them is not known.

Blake detested the basic idea of the Ten Commandments as absolute law. They were negative generalizations drawn up regardless of the individual. They were Justice without Mercy. Blake was emphatic that human happiness should never be sacrificed to the traditional rules; the individual should always be considered first. "One Law for the Lion & Ox is Oppression" (*Tir* viii: 10; *MHH* 20).

Furthermore, the Commandments are impossible to keep, even though literally obeyed. "Thought is Act" (On Bacon, *K* 400). Hatred *is* murder (*I John* iii:15). Illegal lust, though unconsummated, *is* adultery (*Matt* v:28). Urizen curses his children because "no flesh nor spirit could keep his iron laws one moment" (*Ur* 23:25). The Divine Voice says: "No individual can keep these Laws, for they are death to every energy of man and forbid the springs of life" (*J* 35: 11). The inspired Devil in the climactic "Memorable Fancy" (*MHH* 23) says that Jesus, in spirit, broke them all. "I tell you, no virtue can exist without breaking these ten commandments. Jesus was all virtue, and acted from impulse, not from rules."

Urizen was the inventor of the Commandments. "Leading his starry hosts thro' the waste wilderness, he promulgates his ten commands" (*MHH* 27). Orc attacks them: "The fiery joy, that Urizen perverted to ten commands, what night he led the starry hosts thro' the wide wilderness, that stony law I stamp to dust" (*Am* 8:3). In *The Book of Ahania* (3:45), the poisoned rock with which Urizen smote his rebellious son Fuzon "fell upon the Earth, Mount Sinai in Arabia." The prophets themselves promulgated Urizen's laws: "They saw Urizen give his Laws to the Nations by the hands of the children of Los" (*SoL* 3:8). "Thus the terrible race of Los & Enitharmon gave Laws & Religions to the sons of Har, binding them more and more to Earth, closing and restraining, till a Philosophy of Five Senses

was complete" (*SoL* 4:13). Thus the Commandments end in complete materialism.

In the "Last Judgment," the two tables constitute the Book of Death, by which sinners are condemned. They "utter lightnings" (To Ozias Humphry, *K* 443), and are crowned with the turgid flames of wrath.

God himself repented of his authorship. "Jehovah's Finger Wrote the Law: | Then Wept! then rose in Zeal & Awe, | And in the midst of Sinai's heat | Hid it beneath his Mercy Seat. | O Christians, Christians! tell me Why | You rear it on your Altars high" (*GoP*, Prologue). But see YOD.

For Mercy, even in the very act of thwarting Justice, is based on it: when fairness is ignored, Mercy becomes a blind, corrupting indulgence. The Old Dispensation must precede the New. By the time Blake came to write *Jerusalem*, he had concluded that the Law is an essential stage in the development of Man. The second chapter, which starts the rise of the fallen man, is dedicated to the Jews: their primitive religion corresponds to Man's childhood.

But even though the Elohim are Justice, Jehovah is Mercy: the two, hyphenated, are the supreme God. Meanwhile Blake searched the Old Testament for examples of divine Mercy, and found plenty, beginning with Cain.

The Commandments are often called the Decalogue. Blake uses that term only once, and then to designate all the five books of Moses, of which they are the core (*J* 48:9).

COMMERCE was all-important to England. The second scene of *King Edward the Third* (*PS*) is devoted to its praise. In *Jerusalem* (24:42) Albion recalls the days of peace when "in the Exchanges of London every Nation walk'd," demonstrating the true spirit of Brotherhood. This ideal Commerce Blake compared to the nervous system. See ALLAMANDA. When Bacon argued that "the increase of any state must be upon the foreigner," Blake corrected the fallacy: "The Increase of a State as of a Man is from Internal Improvement or Intellectual Acquirement. Man is not

Improved by the hurt of another. States are not Improved at the Expense of Foreigners" (On Bacon, K 402).

But his attitude towards Commerce altered radically about 1780, when he realized that the pretenders to art were hogging the market, and became explicit after the failure of his exhibition in 1809. "The Life's Labour of Ignorant Journeymen [is] Suited to the Purposes of Commerce no doubt, for Commerce Cannot endure Individual Merit; its insatiable Maw must be fed by What all can do Equally well; at least it is so in England, as I have found to my Cost these Forty Years. Commerce is so far from being beneficial to Arts, or to Empires, that it is destructive of both, as all their History shews, for the above Reason of Individual Merit being its Great hatred. Empires flourish till they become Commercial, & then they are scatter'd abroad to the four winds" (PubA, K 593–94). "The wretched State of the Arts in this Country & in Europe, originating in the wretched State of Political Science, which is the Science of Sciences, Demands a firm & determinate conduct on the part of Artists to Resist the Contemptible Counter Arts Establish'd by such contemptible Politicians as Louis XIV & originally set on foot by Venetian Picture traders, Music traders, & Rhime traders, to the destruction of all true art as it is this Day" (PubA, K 600). "In a Commercial Nation Impostors are abroad in all Professions; these are the greatest Enemies of Genius" (PubA, K 601).

"Where any view of Money exists, Art cannot be carried on, but War only" (Laoc, K 776). In a fragment, Blake refers to Brittannia's Isle "Round which the Fiends of Commerce [roar del.] smile" (K 557).

See CANAANITES.

The COMPASS (compasses, dividers) was used by the Creator even before the creation of light. "He set a compass upon the face of the depth" (Prov viii:27). Milton built an elaborate paragraph on this passage: "The King of Glory, in his powerful Word and Spirit . . . took the golden compasses, prepared in God's eternal store, to circumscribe this Universe and all created things . . ." (PL vii:208, 225–27). Voltaire, in Candide, Chapter xxv, ridiculed Milton's use of the compass. Blake replied with one of his greatest designs, the frontispiece to Europe.

But his Creator is not Milton's Trinity: it is Urizen, who "formed golden compasses and began to explore the Abyss" (Ur 20:39; FZ ii:142). His universe is geometrical, like Plato's, and Plato's Jupiter also holds the compasses (3rd illustr. to Il Penseroso; see Illustrations). So does Newton also in the color print (see NEWTON).

CONGO, in Africa, is one of the Thirty-two Nations which shall guard liberty and rule the rest of the world (J 72:41).

CONNAUT (i.e., Connaught, now Connacht), the western province of Ireland, is Joseph's Gate (J 72:3).

CONSTANTINE the Great (A.D. 280?–337) warred until he became emperor of the entire Roman world, and established Christianity as the official religion of his empire.

For Blake, he was a promoter of religious war. He is named as the thirty-fifth son of Los and Enitharmon (FZ viii:362). When Lazarus was raised, he entered the Covering Cherub, who divided into the four churches of Paul, Constantine, Charlemaine, and Luther, which now extend over Europe and Asia (Mil 24:32). Constantine is the twenty-fifth of the Twenty-seven Churches, the fifth of the third series, which are "the Male-Females, the Dragon Forms, Religion hid in War, a Dragon red & hidden Harlot" (Mil 37:42; J 75:17). In "I saw a Monk of Charlemaine," Titus, Constantine, and Charlemaine are assured that their warfare against the Lord is vain (J 52:21).

CONWAY'S VALE. The river Conway in North Wales was the scene of Gray's "Bard." The ambassadors from Beulah kneel before the Divine Presence in Conway's Vale (FZ i:483). Blake originally wrote "Beth-Peor," then substituted the Welsh valley.

CONWENNA, according to Geoffrey of Monmouth, was the wife of King Dunwallo, the first of the British kings to wear a crown of gold. After his death, their two sons Belin and Brennius fought over their inheritances until Conwenna intervened and persuaded them to join forces against the Continent.

In the original list of the Daughters of Albion (FZ ii:62), Conwenna was eighth, but took third place in Jerusalem; there she is one of the five who united into Tirzah (J 5:41). Her consort is Bowen; their position is North (J 71:47).

Gwendolen and Conwenna surround Milton as a garment woven of War and Religion (Mil 23:16), but later Cambel replaced her in weaving the same garment (J 7:44).

When Albion, disillusioned with the idea of children's purity, sees Conwenna, he cries out at her "cradled innocence" as "most piteous" (J 21:23). Later, Bowen and Conwenna stand on Mount Skiddaw cutting the fibres of Benjamin from Chester's River. He sears the fibres and fixes them into Bones of chalk and rock. She sits above; with solemn cadences she draws Fibres of life out from the Bones into her golden loom (J 90:19–21).

In their eternal state, Bowen has all Scotland. His Emanation, Conwenna, "shines a triple form over the north with pearly beams gorgeous and terrible" (J 71:49).

CORDELLA (Geoffrey and Milton spell her name "Cordeilla," and Shakespeare "Cordelia") was the faithful daughter of King Leir. After her father repudiated her, she married Aganippus, king of the Franks; to her Leir fled when expelled from his kingdom; but Aganippus regained the kingdom for his father-in-law. After Leir's death, Cordeilla became queen of Britain. Then the two sons of her two sisters, incensed to see Britain ruled by a woman, deposed her. She killed herself in her prison.

In the original list of the Daughters of Albion (FZ ii:61) she is the sixth; but in Jerusalem she is the fourth, one of the first five, who unite into Tirzah (J 5:41). Her consort is Guantok, who forgave and took her as Emanation, when Ignoge "adjoin'd with Gwantoke's children; soon lovely Cordella arose" (J 71:28). Kox's Estrild, "join'd with Cordella . . . shines southward over the Atlantic" (J 71:43).

When Albion discovers the secret impulses behind the purity of girlhood, he exclaims: "Cordella! I behold thee whom I thought pure as the heavens in innocence & fear, thy Tabernacle taken down, thy secret Cherubim disclosed. Art thou broken?" (J 21:19).

CORK is an Irish county, which with the other five counties of Munster is assigned to Reuben, Simeon, and Levi (J 72:22).

CORNWALL is an English county on the south coast. The cape "Land's End" is the westernmost point of England. Its mines extend under the Atlantic.

Cornwall, with Devon and Dorset, is assigned to Dan (J 16:46), and with Hants, Dorset, and Devon to Hand (J 71:20). Albion on rising moves his right foot to Cornwall (Mil 39:49). The ancient world of Urizen was created from the valley of Middlesex by London's River, from Stonehenge and from London Stone, from Cornwall to Caithness, which is the northernmost point of Britain (J 58:46). Brittannia lies upon Albion's bosom "as deadly damps of the Mines of Cornwall & Derbyshire" (J 94:7).

The COUNCIL OF GOD is the Communion of Saints. See DIVINE FAMILY.

The COUNTIES of the British Isles were "fix'd down" by Los (J 28–29): Wales (J 16:35–41), England (J 16:44–50), Scotland (J 16:53–58), and Ireland (J 16:29). The Irish counties are treated separately from the others (J 72:1–4, 17–27); see IRELAND.

All the counties are distributed among

the Sons of Israel. Each Son is assigned one of the twelve counties of Wales and three of the thirty-six of Scotland. Each Son also has three of the forty counties of England, the extra four (the four northernmost) being assigned respectively to Reuben, Judah, Dan, and Joseph (*J* 16:50–51). These four Sons are the same to whom the four provinces of Ireland are assigned (*J* 72:3–4). The counties within each province are then assigned to groups of three Sons each.

The counties of Great Britain are also assigned to the twelve Sons of Albion (*J* 71:10–49). There is, or should be, correspondence between the two lists: "as the Soul is to the Body, so Jerusalem's are to the Sons of Albion" (*J* 71:1–5).

But there are difficulties. By what seems to be a slip of the pen, Blake omitted Lancashire, though we can conjecture that his Son is Slade, as Stafford is assigned later to Slade as well as Kotope. But Wiltshire is also assigned to both Coban and Kox, and Warwick to Hutton and Kox. Guantok has all of South Wales; Peachey has all of North Wales and the Isle of Man; and Bowen all Scotland and the Isles. Scofield has all three of Reuben's counties but also four others; Hand has all three of Levi's but also Sussex; Hyle has the three of Dan's but also Hampshire.

The discrepancies are best seen in the following Table.

SONS OF ISRAEL	ENGLISH COUNTIES	SONS OF ALBION
Reuben:	Norfolk	Scofield
	Suffolk	Scofield
	Essex	Scofield
Simeon:	Lincoln	Slade
	York	Brereton
	Lancashire	[Slade?]
Levi:	Middlesex	Hand
	Kent	Hand
	Surrey	Hand
Judah:	Somerset	Coban
	Gloucester	Coban
	Wiltshire	Coban & Kox

Dan:	Cornwall	Hyle
	Devon	Hyle
	Dorset	Hyle
Naphtali:	Warwick	Hutton & Kox
	Leicester	Hutton
	Worcester	Kotope
Gad:	Oxford	Kox
	Bucks	Hutton
	Hertfordshire	Scofield
Asher:	Sussex	Hand
	Hampshire	Hyle
	Berkshire	Hutton
Issachar:	Northampton	Hutton
	Rutland	Scofield
	Nottingham	Slade
Zebulun:	Bedford	Hutton
	Huntingdon	Scofield
	Cambridge	Scofield
Joseph:	Stafford	Kotope & Slade
	Shropshire	Peachey
	Hereford	Kotope
Benjamin:	Derby	Slade
	Cheshire	Peachey
	Monmouth	Peachey
Reuben, Judah, Dan, and Joseph:	Cumberland	Bowen
	Northumberland	Bowen
	Westmoreland	Brereton
	Durham	Brereton

The COVERING CHERUB is the final error, the last enemy to be slain. The term comes from *Ezekiel* xxviii:16: "I will destroy thee, O covering cherub, from the midst of the stones of fire," a denunciation of the prince of Tyre, which was interpreted by Tertullian and subsequent Church Fathers as meaning Satan himself. For Blake, however, Satan sums up the pagan religions; whereas the Covering Cherub sums up the Twenty-seven Christian heavens (*Mil* 37:60), which shut man out from eternity.

The ultimate meaning of the Covering Cherub is the Selfhood (*J* 89:10; 96:8), that self-seeking which is the root of all the Christian errors. But error is prophetic: it preserves concealed the very thing it denies. The truth becomes petrified into dogma and relegated to ritual; yet these are but the graveclothes, to be cast off when the truth is resurrected. Jerusalem is hidden within the Covering Cherub "as in a Tabernacle of threefold workmanship, in allegoric delusion & woe" (*J* 89:44).

The Covering Cherub represents the false dogmas of the Church Militant. When Jesus raised Lazarus, the risen man entered the Covering Cherub as the mistaken belief in a literal resurrection of the mortal flesh. The Cherub then divided into the four warring Churches of Paul, Constantine, Charlemaine, and Luther (*Mil* 24:26–33); and Milton accepted and embodied the whole error (*Mil* 23:14; 37:8, 44).

When the Covering Cherub is finally revealed, he contains the whole organization of Satan's Synagogue. He is the "majestic image of Selfhood," "the Antichrist accursed," "a Human Dragon terrible." His head encloses "a reflexion of Eden all perverted" (*J* 89:9–15); then follows a full analysis of all false churches and states; whereupon Rahab appears and is absorbed in him (*J* 89:51–63).

When at last Albion wakes and finds Jesus standing by him, the Covering Cherub (Albion's Selfhood) overshadows and divides them; but Albion sacrifices himself and is transfigured; then the fourfold bows of his Zoas and Cities annihilate "the Druid Spectre" (*J* 96–98:7).

There are various other references. Satan reposes on the seven mountains of Rome, in the whole place of the Covering Cherub, Rome, Babylon, and Tyre (*Mil* 9:51). Orc tells the Shadowy Female that Milton's garment should be Jerusalem "& not thy Covering Cherub" (*Mil* 18:37). "The Covering Cherub advances from the East"; how long beneath him shall we "give our Emanations?" (*Mil* 23:10, 12). Seven of Albion's Daughters enter into Rahab in the Covering Cherub on the Euphrates (*J* 5: 42).

The two Cherubs on the Ark, whose wings "covered" the Mercy Seat, symbolize the wisdom which is understanding, and therefore support the Divine Mercy; but Vala's two Covering Cherubs are named Voltaire and Rousseau (*J* 66:12).

CREATION is not the beginning of existence, for all things are eternal: it is a consequence of the fall towards "Eternal Death" (separation from Eternity). Urizen, and later Los, but first and last Jesus, is the Creator, whether cruelly forcing law and matter upon existence; or giving to the Fallen a protective covering or shell while it is in the realm of Ulro; or mercifully giving Error a form, that it may be recognized and cast out. Thus the Creation is "an act of Mercy" (*LJ*, *K* 614).

Creation is Error. "Error is Created. Truth is Eternal. Error, or Creation, will be Burned up, & then, & not till Then, Truth or Eternity will appear. It is Burnt up the Moment men cease to behold it" (*LJ*, *K* 617). But as everything is eternal in essence, not "one hair nor particle of dust, not one can pass away" (*J* 14:1). "Man Brings All that he has or can have Into the World with him. Man is Born Like a Garden ready Planted & Sown. This World is too poor to produce one Seed" (On Reynolds, *K* 471).

The process of Creation is one of dividing up the original Unity. Beginning with the separation of light from darkness, it proceeds through the six Days of Creation, culminating in the separation of man from God. After that, the sexes are divided, in the creation of Eve; Good and Evil, in the eating of the fruit; man and happiness, in the expulsion from the Garden; soul and body, in the first murder; man from his brother, in the confusion of tongues at Babel.

To reattain Eternity, all these divisions must eventually be reunited. Blake set about the task in *The Marriage of Heaven and Hell*. The Second Coming is the ultimate revelation of Truth; the Mystical Marriage finally reunites Man and God.

CROMWELL (Oliver, 1599–1658) was the

great Puritan general in the Puritan Revolution; he became Lord Protector of England. "Charles calls on Milton for Atonement. Cromwell is ready" (*Mil* 5:39).

CROMWELL'S GARDENS was a pleasure garden at Brompton, where tea, music, and equestrian performances entertained the rank and fashion of Kensington. About 1780, its name was changed to the "Florida Tea Gardens."

Whirlwinds of indignant self-righteousness rise up against Los "from the Brook of Albion's River, from Ranelagh & Strumbolo, from Cromwell's gardens & Chelsea" (*J* 8:1).

The CROSS, as the symbol of the great sacrifice of Jesus, appears above his head in the Petworth "Last Judgment." However, in the Rosenwald "Last Judgment" (see Illustrations), it is cast out prominently among the other errors. To it is nailed the Serpent of Materialism ("LJ" No. 29).

Blake had decided that the Cross is an instrument of execution, of the Vengeance for Sin, and therefore should not symbolize the true religion of Forgiveness. The death of Jesus was the triumph over the Cross, which thereby was cast out. It should have been the last crucifixion, although Blake knew that "Christ's Crucifixion shall be made an Excuse for Executing Criminals" (jotted at the end of *FZ* iv, *K* 380).

Furthermore, the Cross signifies Death, causing the false church of Rahab to worship the mortal death of Jesus instead of the living eternal Jesus.

The Church of This World is commonly represented by a dome surmounted by the cross. No cross appears on the altar in Blake's picture "Hervey's *Meditations*" (see Illustrations). In *Jerusalem* 76, Jesus is crucified upon a tree bearing apples.

The CRYSTAL CABINET (*K* 429) symbolizes the delusions of love. It may be the record of some casual affair in Surrey, which ended unhappily. A maiden locks the poet in her crystal cabinet; in its Moony Night, he sees another England, including "another pleasant Surrey Bower" and "another Maiden like herself." But when he strives to seize "the inmost Form," he bursts the cabinet and becomes "a Weeping Babe," while she is a "Weeping Woman."

Enitharmon's dwelling is a "crystal house" where she greets her sons and daughters (*Eur* 3:6). Her son Antamon, the male sexual impulse, has a "crystal form" (*Eur* 14:17).

CUMBERLAND is one of the four northernmost counties of England; its position among the four is West.

Cumberland, Northumberland, Westmoreland, and Durham are divided in the Gates of Reuben, Judah, Dan, and Joseph (*J* 16:50). Bowen is assigned all Scotland, the Isles, Northumberland, and Cumberland (*J* 71:46).

CUSH was a son of Ham and the father of Nimrod (*Gen* x:8). Blake, however, in his two references calls him Nimrod's son.

"Coban's son is Nimrod: his son Cush is adjoin'd to Aram" (*J* 7:19). Vala was nailed to the gates by Albion's Sons, until "Skofield's Nimrod . . . came with Cush his Son" and released her (*J* 22:4).

D

DAGON, half man, half fish, was the national god of the Philistines. His temple at Gaza was destroyed by Samson. When the Ark was carried into his temple at Ashdod, his idol fell twice and was broken, and the Philistines were smitten with emerods. Milton calls him "Sea Monster, upward Man and downward Fish."

Dalila prays to "Dagon furious" (*PS*, "Samson" 42).

"Dagon, Sea Monster" is fifth of the Twelve Gods of Asia. He is worshipped in Palestine and over the sea (*Mil* 37:25).

DAMASCUS is the capital of Syria. It contained a famous temple of Rimmon.

Rimmon is worshipped "in Damascus curtain'd" (*Mil* 37:26). At the sight of Reuben, Gwantock and Peachy hid in Damascus beneath Mount Lebanon (*J* 36:16). In the Covering Cherub's left breast is "Philistea, in Druid Temples over the whole Earth with Victim's sacrifice, from Gaza to Damascus, Tyre & Sidon" (*J* 89:31).

DAN was Jacob's fifth son and founder of the northernmost Tribe; hence the saying "From Dan to Beersheba."

With his brothers, he was a Son of Los who fled (*FZ* viii:360, 376). Jerusalem remembers the days of innocence of him and various brothers (*J* 79:30). The Daughters of Albion drink up Dan and Gad (*J* 67:22). He is one of the six brothers who roll apart into Non Entity (*J* 74:50).

Blake ignores the fact that Dan is some-how omitted from the list of Tribes in *Revelation*; instead, he makes him one of the four who have special Gates. Of the English counties, the four northernmost, Cumberland, Northumberland, Westmoreland, and Durham, are "divided in the Gates of Reuben, Judah, Dan & Joseph" (*J* 16:51). Likewise, the four provinces of Ireland are divided: "Munster South in Reuben's Gate, Connaut West in Joseph's Gate, Ulster North in Dan's Gate, Leinster East in Judah's Gate" (*J* 72:4).

Dan's Gate in Wales is Flintshire; his English counties are Cornwall, Devon, and Dorset; his Scottish counties are Bute, Caithness, and Clackmannan; with Asher and Naphtali he shares the Irish counties of Donnegal, Antrim, Tyrone, Fermanagh, Armagh, Londonderry, Down, Managhan, and Cavan (*J* 16:37, 46, 55; 72:25).

DANTE (1265-1321) was one of the greatest poets; Blake ranked him with Shakespeare (*MHH* 23). In spite of his errors, Dante was inspired by the Holy Ghost and is now with God (*CR* 274). Blake in his old age began a vast project of illustrating the entire *Divine Comedy*; at his death he left 102 water colors, mostly uncompleted, and had started engraving seven of them.

As always, Blake was the severest critic of those he admired most. Dante was "an 'Atheist,' a mere politician busied about this world as Milton was, till in his old age he returned back to God whom he had had in his childhood" (*CR* 262). In the great conflict between Emperor and Pope, Dante sided with the Empire. "Dante gives too much Caesar: he is not a Republican. Dante was an Emperor's, a Caesar's man" (On Boyd, *K* 413). "Every thing in Dante's *Comedia* shews That for Tyrannical Purposes he has made This World the Foundation of All, & the Goddess Nature . . . is his Inspirer & not [Imagination] the Holy Ghost. . . . Homer [who idealized war] is the Center of All—I mean the Poetry of the Heathen, Stolen & Perverted from the Bible . . . It seems as if Dante's supreme Good was something Superior to the Father or Jesus; for if he gives his rain to the Evil & the Good, & his Sun to the Just & the Unjust, He could never have Built Dante's Hell, nor the Hell of the Bible neither, in the way our Parsons explain it—It must have been originally Formed by the devil Himself; & So I understand it to have been" (*K* 785). "Dante saw Devils where I see none" (*CR* 260).

The episode of Ugolino (*Inferno* xxxiii: 29–91) particularly caught the imagination of the English poets and painters, as an example of the cruelty of the Roman ecclesiastics. Count Ugolino della Gherardesca (1220?–89) was imprisoned and starved to death with his two sons and two grandsons by the Archbishop of Pisa. The first paraphrase of Dante in English was Chaucer's "De Hugolino, Comite de Pize" (*Monk's Tale*). Gray turned the tale into blank verse (1737–40). The first painting from Dante by an Englishman was Reynolds' "Count Hugolino" (1773), which caused a sensation. In 1782, Hayley published the first attempt to translate Dante in *terza rima*, his proper stanza (*Essay on Epic Poetry*), but he got no further than the first three books. In 1793 Flaxman published at Rome his *Compositions for the Divine Comedy*. Blake had assisted him so much that he believed his help deserved acknowledgment: "how much of his Homer & Dante he will allow to be mine, I do not know, as he went far enough off to Publish them, even to Italy, but the Public will know & Posterity will know" (*PubA*, *K* 592). In 1806, Fuseli's picture "Count Ugolino" met with such severe criticism

that Blake defended it in a letter to the *Monthly Magazine* (1 July 1806) : "Fuseli's Count Ugolino is a man of wonder and admiration, of resentment against man and devil, and of humiliation before God; prayer and parental affection fill the figure from head to foot" (*K* 864).

Blake made several designs of the fate of Ugolino. The twelfth plate of *The Gates of Paradise* (1793) is inscribed: "Does thy God, O Priest, take such vengeance as this?" (*K* 768). The sixteenth plate of *The Marriage of Heaven and Hell* repeats and improves the design; and Ugolino's hair no longer bristles in horror. Other versions are described by Albert S. Roe. The sketch for this last scene (No. 68) includes hovering angels, which appear in another painting. Blake used the same episode as a supporting subject in his portrait of Dante made for Hayley's library, necessarily a different composition (*Roe* 103).

Blake owned Boyd's translation of the *Inferno* (Dublin, 1785) in which he annotated only the Introduction. At the end of his life he started to illustrate the entire *Commedia*. He procured Sessi Velutello's text, learning Italian to read it, but also used Henry Cary's translation of 1814 (*Symons* 347). The 102 designs have been reproduced by Roe, with a valuable commentary. Naturally, Blake introduced his own ideas, to correct Dante's errors. "The Mission of Virgil" (3) shows the figure of monarchy worshipping "The Angry God of this World." "The Circle of the Lustful" (10) sweeps the lovers along in a whirlwind above the Sea of Time and Space; one man dominated by lust (upside down, in the cruciform position) crashes upon the rocky bank; but beyond him the rapturous lovers are carried on, to escape upward, presumably from Hell. "The Symbolic Figure of the Course of Human History Described by Virgil" (28) represents the form of Empire shedding fruitless tears; from the waist down he is scaled. "Ugolino Relating his Death" (47) includes a cardinal's hat laid over his cave.

"The Queen of Heaven in Glory" (99) is an attack on mariolatry.

Blake believed that Dante, like Milton, saw clearly, but he did not always understand what he saw.

The DANUBE and the Rhine were always associated by Blake with the battlegrounds of the Napoleonic wars.

"The Rhine was red with human blood, | The Danube roll'd a purple tide" (*J* 27:45). "Loud the cries of War on the Rhine & Danube with Albion's Sons" (*J* 47:9). "Till Canaan roll'd apart from Albion across the Rhine, along the Danube" (*J* 63:41). "Jerusalem's Pillars fall in the rendings of fierce War over France & Germany" (*J* 68:45).

The DARGLE flows east through Wicklow into the Irish Sea. "Stand ye upon the Dargle from Wicklow to Drogheda" (*J* 49:5).

DARWIN (Erasmus, 1731–1802) was a scientist-poet, who expounded the origin of species, the struggle for survival, and other theories which his famous grandson Charles was to prove. His fame as a poet rests on *The Botanic Garden* (1791) : Part I, "The Economy of Vegetation" and Part II, "The Loves of the Plants." This second part (published anonymously in 1789) is based on the system of Linnaeus. Unfortunately, the closed heroic couplet was exhausted by the time Darwin used it; his verses are compact but stiff and frigid. Worse yet, his fancy led him to personify his plants as classical gods and goddesses, also as Pope's Rosicrucian Elementals (nymphs, gnomes, and sylphs) ; but these characters remain only puzzles, which require long scientific footnotes to explain what Darwin was talking about. This intellectual trick actually prevents our appreciating his ideas. But though his science is outdated and his verse unreadable today, he impressed Coleridge and inspired Shelley, who translated his petty allegories into living symbols.

Blake used Darwin's Elementals, though he may have got them from Pope. He may have had in mind Darwin's account of the moon's origin—"earth's huge sphere exploding burst in twain" ("Econ. Veg." ii:76) —when he wrote a similar account in *America b*:6–7. He engraved Fuseli's "Fertilization of Egypt" for the first edition of *The Botanic Garden* (1791) and Fuseli's "Tornado" for the third edition (1795).

DAVID was the second king of Israel, succeeding Saul, whose unbalanced suspicions led him to seek the life of his erstwhile favorite. "Adam, who is Peleg & Joktan, & Esau & Jacob, & Saul & David" (*J* 73:28).

He was a "great poet," who understood that the "Poetic Genius" was "the first principle" and that all other gods "would at last be proved to originate in [our God] & to be the tributaries of the Poetic Genius; it was this that our great poet, King David, desired so fervently & invokes so pathetic'ly, saying by this he [God] conquers enemies & governs kingdoms" (*MHH* 12–13), probably referring to *Psalms* lxvii and lxviii.

"Jesus, as also Abraham & David, consider'd God as a Man in the Spiritual or Imaginative Vision" (On Berkeley, *K* 774).

He is the thirty-second in the list of the Sons of Los and Enitharmon, standing between Benjamin and Solomon (*FZ* viii: 361).

David was the royal ancestor of Jesus, but Blake never claimed him as such, possibly because the irreconcilable genealogies in *Matthew* i:1–16 and *Luke* iii:23–28 both trace the line to Joseph.

"Cruel sacrifices had brought Humanity into a Feminine Tabernacle in the loins of Abraham & David" (*J* 27). "Planting the Seeds of the Twelve Tribes & Moses & David" (*J* 85:5).

Los declares that no Individual should model himself upon various sacred persons, beginning with David (*J* 90:30).

The DEAD are those who have lost touch with Eternity. They sleep in Beulah; and when they burst the bottoms of their tombs, they descend into the world of matter. "Then myriads of the dead burst thro' the bottoms of their tombs, descending on the shadowy female's clouds in Spectrous terror, beyond the Limit of Translucence on the Lake of Udan Adan. These they nam'd Satans, & in the Aggregate they nam'd them Satan" (*FZ* vii *b*:298).

The DEAD SEA in Palestine is the lowest sheet of water in the world. The Jordan pours into it on the north, and the Arnon through a magnificent gorge on the east. It has no outlet, and as the result of ages of evaporation, the water is so salty that no fish can live in it. The ruins of Sodom and Gomorrah are said to lie under the waters in the southeast.

Blake utilized it as typifying this world of matter ("Which is too poor to produce one Seed," On Reynolds, *K* 471) into which we are born. The Arnon represents the genital tract of the female.

"Songs of amorous delight . . . lure the Sleepers of Beulah down the River Storge (which is Arnon) into the Dead Sea" (*Mil* 34:28). The Covering Cherub's bosom reflects Moab and Ammon on the River Pison, since called Arnon, and the fish-pools of Heshbon, whose currents flow into the Dead Sea by Sodom and Gomorrah (*J* 89:27).

DEATH of the physical body is the shedding of the shell which the soul, or spiritual body, has grown for protection in this world. It is the return of the soul to Eternity. It is an episode in life, a state through which one passes, awakening to Eternal life (*J* 4:1–2). "I cannot consider death as anything but a removing from one room to another," Blake told Crabb Robinson shortly before his own death (*CR* 270).

In spite of all reasoning or even desire, it seems impossible to convince oneself of one's own annihilation. The inner being knows nothing of death. Blake accepted this intuition. "Fear & Hope are— Vision," he wrote under the scene of a

deathbed (*GoP* 13, *K* 768). When his brother Robert died, he saw the released spirit ascend "clapping its hands for joy"; and the two never lost touch. "Thirteen years ago I lost a brother & with his spirit I converse daily & hourly in the Spirit & See him in my remembrance in the regions of my Imagination. I hear his advice & even now write from his Dictate," he wrote in a letter of consolation to Hayley (6 May 1800).

As the inner being knows nothing of death, death exists only in the conscious mind and the world of matter. It is learned only by Experience (*SoE*, t.p.). Milton's Adam does not learn of death until he has eaten of the apple. The children in Blair's *Grave* (illustr. 2) advance smiling and fearless into the Vale. In the *Songs of Innocence*, little Lyca does not fear the lion, who is the Angel of Death, but her parents do, until they see his real form. To the chimney sweeper Tom Dacre, death is a dream-angel who unlocks coffins and sets the boys free. Thel becomes aware of death as she approaches Experience, but learns that all life is change, and death is no more than that; it is a giving of oneself for others. Even the corpse benefits the worm.

Only man fears death. The flowers ask to be picked; the cut worm forgives the plow and dies in peace (*K* 183); the grasshopper folds his slender bones without a murmur (*FZ* ix:761). But man's fears are augmented by the religion of Satan: "Thy purpose & the purpose of thy Priests & of thy Churches is to impress on men the fear of death, to teach trembling & fear, terror, constriction: abject selfishness. Mine is to teach Men to despise death" (*Mil* 38:37). In *The Gates of Paradise* "The Traveller hasteth in the Evening" (14) to enter death's door. The illustrations to Blair's *Grave* were intended to contradict the charnel horrors of the text, "to spread a familiar and domestic atmosphere round the most important of all subjects," as Fuseli put it. Only "the strong and wicked man," who has perished in his Selfhood, shows any terror.

"When the man gently fades away in his immortality, when the mortal disappears in improved knowledge, cast away the former things, so shall the Mortal gently fade away and so become invisible to those who still remain" (*FZ* viii:551). However, when Jesus separates the spirits of Los and Enitharmon from their bodies, they are "Terrified at Non Existence, for such they deem'd the death of the body"; then Los with his vegetable hands tears down the sun and moon, "cracking the heavens across from immense to immense"; and the Last Judgment begins (*FZ* ix:4–10).

Death is only an illusion of Leutha (sin): "In dreams she bore the Shadowy Spectre of Sleep & nam'd him Death" (*Mil* 13:40). Otherwise, Eve is the mortal mother of Death: when she was separated from Adam and ate the fatal fruit, then Generation and Death appeared in this world. It is an interesting coincidence that the modern biologists say that death does not appear in nature until the sexes are separated.

Not Eve alone but every woman is the Mother of Death when she creates the mortal body. The looms of Cathedron weave only death (*Mil* 24:35). "To Tirzah" (*SoE*) renounces the mother, who betrayed the poet to mortal life; but the marginal comment reads, "It is Raised a Spiritual Body" (*I Cor* xv:44).

Spiritual Death is sacrificing oneself for another; greater love hath no man (*John* xv:13). The Crucifixion is the supreme example. "Every thing that lives lives not alone nor for itself" (*Thel* 3:26). "Such are the Laws of Eternity, that each shall mutually annihilate himself for others' good" (*Mil* 38:35). "Every kindness to another is a little Death in the Divine Image, nor can Man exist but by Brotherhood" (*J* 96:27).

DECALOGUE is the Greek word for the Ten Commandments. Blake used the word only once, and then to designate the first five books of the Bible, the Pentateuch ascribed to Moses, of which the Commandments are the focal point. It occurs in

Blake's list of the inspired books of the Bible (*J* 48:9). See COMMANDMENTS.

DEISM, or Natural Religion, the fashionable philosophy of the Age of Reason, attempted to make religion intellectually respectable by the application of common sense. The reaction against the fanaticism which had caused the bloodiest of wars; the rise of the sciences on the principles of Bacon, Newton, and Locke; the appearance of scholarly historians like Gibbon and Hume; and the beginnings of higher criticism trumpeted so defiantly by Thomas Paine, all tended to produce the Age of Reason, as they all attacked tradition, and inspired such scoffers and free thinkers as Voltaire and Rousseau.

Deism was a religion made by historians, sociologists, and economists, not by the religious, the metaphysicians, or mystics. It was based on the facts of nature, and was not evolved by logic from metaphysical premises. It believed in the progress of man towards a Golden Age just ahead.

The great earthquake of November 1, 1755, which destroyed Lisbon and some fifteen thousand of its inhabitants, strengthened the position of the Deists, for they took it as proof of their theory that the Creator did not interfere with the workings of his creation. Meanwhile the theologians who taught Divine Justice and the Optimists who followed Leibnitz in believing that this is the best of possible worlds were quite at a loss.

The Deists accepted God the Creator; but once his creation was established according to his principles, there was no reason for him to interfere with it again. All miracles and revelations therefore were delusion and superstition. Man was created naturally good, and the moral systems of all religions were derived from his laws of conduct, as found in human nature. All religions were basically one, and a religion based on Reason, like Deism, should be universally acceptable.

Deism infiltrated the upper classes and became exceedingly influential. Pope uncritically accepted Bolingbroke's outline of ideas for the *Essay on Man*; then the Catholic poet was much embarrassed to discover what ideas he had endorsed so brilliantly. Thomas Paine, fighting French atheism, wrote *The Age of Reason*, which has caused him to be denounced as an atheist to this day.

All his life, Blake fought Deism. His first illuminated printing was *There is No Natural Religion*; and in his last poem, *Jerusalem*, the third chapter is directed against the Deists.

The Eighth Night of *The Four Zoas* ends as the Synagogue of Satan changes the form, but not the substance, of Rahab; "they call'd it Deism and Natural Religion; as of old so now anew began Babylon again in Infancy, call'd Natural Religion" (*FZ* viii:618). It is attacked throughout *Milton*. When Tirzah triumphs, she and Rahab command: "In Natural Religion, in experiments on Men, let [Jerusalem] be Offer'd up to Holiness!" for the images in the constricting skull are "born for War, for Sacrifice to Tirzah, to Natural Religion" (*Mil* 19:47, 53). Blake is commissioned "to display Nature's cruel holiness, the deceits of Natural Religion" (*Mil* 36:25). Milton himself comes to reveal "the Self righteousness in all its Hypocritic turpitude, opening to every eye these wonders of Satan's holiness, shewing to the Earth the Idol Virtues of the Natural Heart, & Satan's Seat explore in all its Selfish Natural Virtue" (*Mil* 38:43). Ololon asks: "how is this thing, this Newtonian Phantasm, this Voltaire & Rousseau, this Hume & Gibbon & Bolingbroke, this Natural Religion, this impossible absurdity?" (*Mil* 40:11). In *Jerusalem*, Blake describes the Deists as "Denying in private, mocking God & Eternal Life, & in Public Collusion calling themselves Deists, Worshipping the Maternal Humanity, calling it Nature and Natural Religion" (*J* 90:64).

Blake objected to the deist God, remote, impassive, and inaccessible, as he believed that God exists actively in our own bosoms.

He objected to the deistic nature worship, with its idea that the world of three dimensions is all, and that it operates by mechanical causes and effects. The Deists were blind to the deeper life. All effects are the result of spiritual causes: consider the animals, who live by the instincts which Locke denied. Blake objected to the deist ethics, as he denied that man was naturally good, and that the ethics derived from his laws of conduct were true: it was only a system of the artificial values of Good and Evil, of Justice with its single standards which disregarded the individual, and therefore was inhuman, subjecting people to the cruel laws of punishment for sin. It was actually the instigator of wars. All pagan moral systems, including Aristotle's, overlooked and omitted the supreme Christian virtues of humanitarianism, love, and the forgiveness of sins. Blake objected to deistic psychology, which taught that reason is man's supreme faculty, when the creative imagination is the true fount of our being.

But Blake never launched a frontal attack on anything he did not respect; his denunciations are not so sweeping as they seem. He shared the Deists' hostility to priests and kings, as enslavers of the minds of man. Voltaire was "commissioned" to expose the "natural sense" (the literal interpretation) of the Bible. Blake agreed that the true God could never have ordered the massacres of the heathen in the Old Testament. He endorsed Paine's theory that the prophets were only poets, but with a great difference: they were therefore the voice of genuine inspiration. Likewise he endorsed the deistic argument that physical miracles never happened, but added that spiritual miracles did, using the effect of Paine's own pamphlets as an example. The curious should read Blake's indignant annotations in Bishop Watson's poqular attack on Paine, the *Apology for the Bible*: Blake proves to his own satisfaction that Paine is the real Christian and the bishop is not. And from the position of Chapter iii in *Jerusalem*, it would seem that Blake regarded Deism as a stage in man's mental development.

DELUGE. See FLOOD OF NOAH.

DEMOCRITUS, a Greek philosopher of the late fifth and early fourth centuries B.C., believed that the basis of reality is the Atom.

"The Atoms of Democritus | And Newton's Particles of light | Are sands upon the Red sea shore, | Where Israel's tents do shine so bright" ("Mock on, Mock on" 9, K 418).

DENBIGHSHIRE, a county of North Wales, is the Gate of Joseph (*J* 16:41).

DENMARK is a temple among the pillars of Urizen's ancient world (*J* 58:41).

DERBY (Derbyshire) is a north Midland county of England. It is remarkably picturesque, with mountains, underground caverns, medicinal springs, rivers that disappear into the "Swallows," East Moor, which extends for miles, and other wonders. It has a variety of mines.

With Cheshire and Monmouth it is assigned to Benjamin (*J* 16:49); with Lincoln, Stafford, and Nottingham, it is assigned to Slade (*J* 71:34). Derbyshire, with five other counties, labors in the furnaces (*J* 16:18). Albion's last words relapse from caverns of Derbyshire, Wales, and Scotland (*J* 23:27). Hyle on East Moor in rocky Derbyshire raves to the moon (*J* 80:66). Rintrah and Palamabron risk divorce from their Emanations on East Moor in Derbyshire and other places (*J* 93:6). Blake refers to the deadly damps of the mines of Cornwall and Derbyshire (*J* 94:8).

Derbyshire is particularly associated with Gwendolen. See GWENDOLEN.

DERBY PEAK is the highest mountain in England (2,088 ft.). The seven *Wonders of the Peake* were celebrated in a long poem (1681) by Charles Cotton. They are

Poole's Hole, a subterranean cavern; St. Anne's Well, which runs hot and cold; the Wedding Well or Tides Well, which ebbs and rises unexpectedly; Eldon Hole, described in Cary's Atlas (1787) as "a horrible chasm in the side of a mountain, which with a line of 884 yards could not be fathomed"; the perpendicular Mam Tor; the Devil's Arse, another subterranean cavern; and Chatsworth, the seat of the Duke of Derbyshire.

"The Great Voice of the Atlantic howled over the Druid Altars, weeping over his Children in Stone-henge, in Malden & Colchester, round the Rocky Peak of Derbyshire, London Stone & Rosamond's Bower" (*J* 57:5). "Derby Peak yawn'd a horrid Chasm at the Cries of Gwendolen & at the stamping feet of Ragan" (*J* 64:35).

A DESCRIPTIVE CATALOGUE *of pictures, poetical and historical inventions, painted by William Blake in water colours, being the ancient method of fresco painting restored: and drawings, for public inspection, and for sale by private contract*, London ...1809.

From May to September, 1809, Blake exhibited his pictures in his brother James's hosiery shop, Broad Street, Golden Square. The price of admission (2s. 6d.) included the catalogue. Lamb told Crabb Robinson that it contained "the finest criticism he had ever read of Chaucer's poem," and bound up his copy. Robert Hunt, in the *Examiner*, however, reviewed the exhibition and catalogue with an extravagant malicious attack on the artist and his works. The exhibition failed.

The *Catalogue* is fascinating reading. It contains descriptions of the sixteen pictures on exhibition (six of which are now lost); an explanation of Blake's aesthetic principles, with high praise for Michelangelo and Raphael, and attacks on Rembrandt, Rubens, Titian, and Correggio (wherein Blake was wrong, but sometimes for the right reasons); a defense of his own character, with blasts at his defamers; a brief account of the poem to be called

Jerusalem; the splendid criticism of Chaucer's masterpiece, mixed with scoldings about Stothard's rival picture (the idea for which had been stolen from Blake); and much defiantly visionary material, which gives valuable clues to Blake's symbolism.

In spite of the failure of his exhibition, Blake planned another for 1810: scribblings in the Rossetti manuscript contain notes for a *Public Address* (concerning the "Canterbury Pilgrims," now engraved) and the "Vision of the Last Judgment" to be added to the original catalogue. But these never were printed until modern times, and the second exhibition was never held.

DEUS is the Latin for God. The Deists worship "the Deus of the Heathen, The God of This World, & the Goddess Nature, Mystery, Babylon the Great, The Druid Dragon & hidden Harlot" (*J* 93:23).

DEVILS for Blake are usually evil spirits, probably Accusers of Sin (*diabolus* means "accuser"); but in *The Marriage of Heaven and Hell*, for once they are the original geniuses, those who are familiars in the "Hell" of the subconscious, which is the source of all "energy." They are contrasted to the Angels, the restricting spirits of conventionality. On a pencil drawing of nine grotesque heads, Blake noted: "All Genius varies Thus. Devils are various. Angels are all alike" (*K* 773). Milton was a true poet, and of the devil's party, though without knowing it; so was Blake, knowingly; and so also (he more than implies) was Jesus.

DEVON is a maritime county of England, lying on the south coast between Cornwall and Dorset.

With Cornwall and Dorset, it is assigned to Dan (*J*1 6:46); with Hants, Dorset, and Cornwall, it is assigned to Hyle (*J* 71:20). Hants, Devon, and Wilts are "surrounded with masses of stone in order'd forms" (*J* 83:9).

DHINAS-BRAN (Dinas Bran) is a hill a mile from Llangollen, in Denbighshire, North Wales. It is topped by the ruins of the Castell Dinas Bran, an ancient camp.

"Penmaenmawr & Dhinas-bran Demonstrate in Unbelief" (*J* 21:35). Blake might really have had in mind Dinas Penmaen, an ancient British fort which could hold twenty thousand men. It was on the summit of Mount Penmaenmawr.

The **DIAMOND**, representing Gad, was the sixth stone in the high priest's breastplate. It is also one of the gems worn by the Covering Cherub (*Ezek* xxviii:13).

"The poor indigent is like the diamond which, tho' cloth'd in rugged covering in the mine, is open all within, and in his hallow'd center holds the heavens of bright eternity" (*Mil* 28:36). Jerusalem dismisses her sons with "blessings of gold and pearl & diamond" (*J* 24:39).

"Also On the right hand of Noah A Female descends to meet her Lover or Husband, representative of that Love, call'd Friendship, which Looks for no other heaven than their Beloved, & in him sees all reflected as in a Glass of Eternal Diamond" (*LJ, K* 610; see Illustrations, "LJ" No. 77).

The **DIMENSIONS** in Eternity are fourfold: "the North is Breadth, the South is Heighth & Depth, the East is Inwards, & the West is Outwards every way" (*J* 14:29). "[Urizen] knew that weakness stretches out in breadth & length, he knew that wisdom reaches high & deep" (*FZ* vii:161).

But when "The Visions of Eternity, by reason of narrowed perceptions, are become weak Visions of Time & Space" (*J* 49:21), the dimensions become threefold, "Satan's Mathematic Holiness, Length, Bredth & Highth" (*Mil* 32:18). "Accident & Chance were found hidden in Length, Bredth & Highth" (*J* 36:35). But when the Divine Mercy redeems man, "Length, Bredth, Highth again Obey the Divine Vision" (*J* 36:56).

DINAH was a daughter of Jacob and Leah. Shechem, son of Prince Hamor of the Hivites, fell in love with her, lay with her, and honorably sought her in marriage. But Dinah's brothers, Simeon and Levi, pretending to agree to Hamor's treaty of friendship, treacherously slaughtered Hamor, Shechem, and all the Hivite males, seizing their women, children, and property. Jacob reproved them, fearing reprisals (*Gen* xxxiv).

Blake, sympathetic to this tragedy of true love, and perhaps also remembering the rape of Ireland, gives Dinah's name to Erin (*J* 74:54).

DIRALADA is another spelling of the name of Thiralatha (*SoL* 3:31). See THIRALATHA.

DISEASE is another word for Sin; Jesus is the great healer.

The Seven Deadly Sins, according to tradition, were Pride, Envy, Wrath, Lust, Gluttony, Sloth, and Avarice; Milton identified them with Satan, Beelzebub, Chemos, the Baalim and Ashtaroth, the brutish Egyptian gods, Belial, and Mammon (*PL* i:81, 391–490, 678).

In the early fragment "Then she bore Pale desire," Blake attempted to outline the spiritual decay of mankind in the course of history. Amongst the personifications, or "Gods," the Deadly Sins appear unsystematically and unnumbered. The most prominent are Pride and her consort Shame. Thereafter, Blake never sank again into allegory. While he kept the number Seven, he never listed the Sins, with whom he included Shame (*K* 40; *J* 10:34; 18:13; 21:3; 28:27).

Originally they were pure spiritual energies; Eno recalls the Golden Age, when Covet, Envy, Wrath, and Wantonness (and presumably the others) were unbanned and good (*BoL* 3:10–26). But when Urizen opened his Book of Brass, they became the "Seven deadly Sins of the soul" (*Ur* 4:30, 48).

Blake mentioned the Seven first in *The*

French Revolution (35): "In the den nam'd Religion, a loathsome sick woman bound down to a bed of straw; the seven diseases of the earth, like birds of prey, stood on the couch and fed on the body." The Prester Serpent (the Priest at war) orders: "Take thou the Seven Diseases of Man; store them for times to come in store houses, in secret places that I will tell thee of, to be my great & awful curses at the time appointed" (*FZ* vii *b*:118). The Eastern Gate of Golgonooza is fourfold: "that toward Beulah, stone, the seven diseases of the earth are carved terrible" (*J* 13:16). "The seven diseases of the Soul settled around Albion" (*J* 19:26). Jerusalem complains: "my incense is a cloudy pestilence of seven diseases" (*J* 79:56).

Jesus is the healer. "None but the Lamb of God can heal this dread disease, none but Jesus" (*J* 45:15). "All Mental Powers by Diseases we bind, | But he heals the deaf & the Dumb & the Blind. | Whom God [Satan] has afflicted for Secret Ends | He comforts & Heals & calls them Friends" (*EG e*:87). Satan "created Seven deadly Sins, drawing out his infernal scroll of Moral Laws and cruel punishments" (*Mil* 9:21). "Is God a smiter with disease?" (*EG b*:30). "Go therefore, cast out devils in Christ's name, heal thou the sick of spiritual disease, pity the evil" (*J* 77:24).

DIVINE ANALOGY is the symbolism by which the Bible should be read.

"Building the Body of Moses in the Valley of Peor, the Body of Divine Analogy" (*J* 49:57). Los calls the allegory of earthly marriage "Divine Analogy" (*J* 85:7).

The DIVINE BODY is the Human Imagination itself (*J* 5:59; 24:23; 60:57; 74:13), which is Jesus. "The Eternal Body of Man is The Imagination, that is, God himself, The Divine Body, Jesus: we are his Members" (*Laoc, K* 776). "All Things are comprehended in their Eternal

Forms in the divine body of the Saviour, the True Vine of Eternity, The Human Imagination" (*LJ, K* 605–6). "The Spirit of Jesus is continual forgiveness of Sin: he who waits to be righteous before he enters into the Saviour's kingdom, the Divine Body, will never enter there" (*J* 3).

The DIVINE FAMILY, or Council of God, is the Communion of Saints, that aggregate of Christian thought, the Body of Christ, consisting of all the Elect, dead or alive. Blake, however, never called them by their conventional name.

"Mutual in one another's love and wrath all renewing we live as One Man; for contracting our infinite senses we behold multitude, or expanding, we behold as one, as One Man all the Universal Family, and that One Man we call Jesus the Christ; and he in us, and we in him live in perfect harmony in Eden, the land of life, giving, recieving, and forgiving each other's trespasses" (*J* 38:16). (Some of these phrases are paraphrased from *John* xvii:21–23, which concerns the unity of the Father, the Son, and the believers; Blake gives the location of this passage, also *John* i:14— "And the Word was made flesh"—as a marginal reference to the opening lines of *The Four Zoas*.)

As they live in Eden, the garden of God, they are sometimes called the "Sons of Eden" and once "all Eden" (*Mil* 9:1). Their Zoas are perfectly balanced (*FZ* i:9). Jesus walks among them, beheld in every face (*Mil* 30:17). Seen close to, they are multitudes of individuals; seen from afar, they are one man, who is Jesus himself (*FZ* i:470; viii:1).

Their "two Sources of Life" are "Hunting and War" (*Mil* 35:2; *J* 43:31), "the great Wars of Eternity, in fury of Poetic Inspiration, to build the Universe stupendous, Mental forms Creating" (*Mil* 30:19), dealing "Giant blows in the sports of intellect" (*J* 48:15). "For the Soldier who fights for Truth calls his enemy his brother; they fight & contend for life & not for eternal death" (*J* 43:41). When

they are weary, they descend into Beulah to rest (*Mil* 30:13).

They follow events below with great interest, and at times confer in the "Council of God," where they may argue, but always act as one, as Jesus (*FZ* i:198, 469; viii:1; *Mil* 21:58; *J* 40:45), and appear like the sun (*Mil* 21:40; *J* 29:27; 62:34).

In *The Four Zoas* they meet as One Man, hovering over Gilead and Hermon (i:199) or over Snowdon (i:475). On hearing the disasters reported by the messengers from Beulah, they draw up the Universal Tent (our sky) and elect the seven Eyes of God to follow wandering Man (i:553). Later, they meet upon Gilead and Hermon to create the fallen man (viii:2).

In *Milton*, Palamabron summons "all Eden" into his tent, to judge his quarrel with Satan (9:1), and their judgment falls upon Rintrah. Later, at Ololon's prayer, "all the Family Divine collected as Four Suns in the Four Points of heaven, East, West & North & South, enlarging and enlarging till their Disks approach'd each other, and when they touch'd, closed together Southward in One Sun over Ololon; and as One Man who weeps over his brother in a dark tomb, so all the Family Divine wept over Ololon" (21:37). They bid her watch over this world below and renew it to Eternal Life; they unite with her; and the appearance is of One Man, Jesus, "coming in the Clouds of Ololon" (21:53–60).

In *Jerusalem*, after Albion has announced his defection from the eternal order, Jesus appears as a mild sun, promising that Albion shall rise again, and encloses the Human Family (29:27). Los and Enitharmon escape from Albion's darkening locks and report the disaster, then trembling join the Divine Family (29:83). Many of the Eternals laugh at the sexual perplexities of the fallen man, while others comment on the dangers of illusion (36:43–56). Los then stands forth from the Divine Family to warn Albion (37:1–9). Jesus follows, "displaying the

Eternal Vision, the Divine Similitude, in loves and tears of brothers, sisters, sons, fathers and friends, which if Man ceases to behold, he ceases to exist, saying, 'Albion! Our wars are wars of life, & wounds of love with intellectual spears, & long-winged arrows of thought'" (38:11). The words of Jesus are the words of the Divine Family (38:27) as they follow Albion. They appear in the Twenty-four Cathedral Cities, who are One in Jesus (40:45). After the Cities fail to force Albion back into Eden, the Divine Family hovers around him (44:20). At the end, Los announces: "He who would see the Divinity must see him in his Children, one first, in friendship & love, then a Divine Family, & in the midst Jesus will appear" (91:19).

Mostly the members of the Family are not named; but Milton is one, and Albion, "mildest Son of Eden," is another (45:3). The Zoas belong to another category; but Los once stands forth from the Divine Family, to speak to Albion (37:1), and the Sons of Eden praise Urthona's Spectre in songs because he kept the Divine Vision in time of trouble (30:14; 95:19).

The DIVINE HAND is an act of Providence, transcending both human knowledge and the human will (FZ vi:176, 282). It is the power behind poetic inspiration (FZ viii:40; J 42:56; 47:17).

The Daughters of Beulah, in a time of disaster, keep on hoping although "They saw not yet the Hand Divine, for it was not yet reveal'd" (FZ i:230). The wandering Urizen is led unknowingly by the Divine Hand (FZ vi:176). Los in a creative mood loves the Spectres, "for the Divine hand was upon him" (FZ viii:40). Life Eternal depends alone upon "the Universal Hand" (FZ viii:198).

The Divine Hand finds the two Limits: Opacity or Satan and Contraction or Adam (Mil 13:20; J 35:1).

"The Divine Hand went forth on Albion in the mid Winter" (J 15:32). When Los's Spectre and Emanation flee back to their Humanity, "the Divine hand was upon them" (J 30:12). "All things are so constructed and builded by the Divine hand that the sinner shall always escape" (J 31:30). The Divine Hand strengthens Los at his furnaces (J 42:56). Blake is bidden: "Shudder not, but Write, & the hand of God will assist you" (J 47:17).

The DIVINE HUMANITY is God. He is identified thrice with Mercy (Mil 32:14; J 28:26; 61:43) and once with the Poetic Genius (Mil 15:2). Cherubim and Seraphim surround him (Mil 39:27). He plants his paradise in the human brain (Mil 2:8). He gives forth fountains of Living Water (J 96:37).

He is "all protecting" (Mil 14:2). He is opposed by the Twenty-seven Churches, which are "Swell'd & bloated General Forms, repugnant to the Divine-Humanity, who is the Only General and Universal Form, to which all Lineaments tend & seek with love & sympathy. All broad & general principles belong to benevolence, who protects minute particulars, every one in their own identity" (J 43:19).

Abstract Philosophy seeks to destroy him (J 70:19). The "rocky form" of the exterior world is hardened against him (J 19:35); and the Sons of Albion erect "a Strong Fortification" against him (J 28:26).

The DOME (a female symbol) surmounted by a cross represents worldly religion. Obviously Blake had in mind the classical St. Paul's Cathedral, which as a boy he contrasted with the gothic Westminster Abbey. The contrast is used thrice in Jerusalem: 32, which represents Vala and Jerusalem; 57, where London stands above the fallen Jerusalem; and 84, where the child leads the blind man. In the Blair "Last Judgment," the dome, though with a broken cross, may be discerned behind the condemned.

Urizen's palace has three domes named

for his daughters (*FZ* ii:174, 178). Cathedron, where our mortal bodies are woven, has a golden dome (*Mil* 26:36).

DONNEGAL was part of Ulster until 1920. It is one of the nine counties of Ulster, all of which are assigned to Dan, Asher, and Naphtali (*J* 72:26).

DORSET, Devon, and Cornwall are three adjacent counties along the southwest coast of England, which are assigned to Dan (*J* 16:42). The same three, with the addition of the adjacent Hants, are assigned to Hyle (*J* 71:20).

The DOVE is a conventional symbol for love. It is one of a quaternary (*J* 98:47): Eagle (north), Dove (east), Fly (south), and Worm (west).

DOVEDALE, famous for its lovely scenery, is a narrow limestone valley, with fantastic rocks and woods, three miles north of Ashbourne, Derbyshire.

Gwendolen draws aside her veil, north to south, from Mam-Tor (her breasts) to Dovedale (her pudenda) (*J* 82:45).

DOVER, on a small bay in Kent, is famous for its lofty cliffs of white chalk.

Blake indicates the entire south coast of England by associating Dover, in the east, with Lizard Point in Cornwall, the southernmost point of England. When he associates these two with Caithness, the northernmost county of Scotland, he is covering the entire island.

Enitharmon's looms operate "from Caithness in the north, to Lizard-point & Dover in the south" (*Mil* 6:7; *J* 83:71). "There are Two Gates thro' which all Souls descend, One Southward from Dover Cliff to Lizard Point, the other towards the North, Caithness . . . " (*Mil* 26:13). "Deepest night of Ulro roll'd round [Albion's] skirts from Dover to Cornwall" (*J* 42:17). When Albion wakes, "his right foot stretches to the sea on Dover cliffs" (*Mil* 39:40).

DOWN is one of the nine Irish counties of Ulster, which are all assigned to Dan, Asher, and Naphtali (*J* 72:27).

The DRAGON symbolizes War. Albion's wrathful Prince appears as "a dragon form" (*Am* 3:15). "The dragons of the North put on their armour" (*FZ* vii *b*:150). Nature (Vala) becomes hostile when Luvah materializes her: "When I call'd forth the Earth-worm . . . she grew a scaled Serpent, yet I fed her tho' she hated me . . . I brought her thro' the Wilderness . . . till she became a Dragon, winged, bright & poisonous" (*FZ* ii:83-89). When Brittannia is divided from Albion, she resists him like a serpent "with Dragon wings" (*J* 54:30). As Druidism promotes war, its temples and altars are dragon-shaped (*J* 23:21; 25:4; 47:6), and the Dragon himself is once called "Druid" (*J* 93:25).

Spiritual warfare, however, is the necessary initial step for creative work. In the first chamber of the printing-house in Hell is "a Dragon-Man, clearing away the rubbish from a cave's mouth; within, a number of Dragons were hollowing the cave" (*MHH* 15). See CAVE.

In its full meaning, the Dragon is the combined Church and State Militant. To this subhuman form, Urizen (like Milton's Satan) finally sinks (*FZ* viii:420-28; *J* 14:3). Jerusalem is compelled to worship him thus (*FZ* viii:599), and Vala forces Jerusalem's children to weave her a body "according to her [Vala's] will, a Dragon form on Zion Hill's most ancient promontory" (*J* 80:36).

According to *Revelation* xvii, the Whore of Babylon rides on a beast with seven heads and ten horns; Blake identified the beast with the Dragon. A water color in the British Museum depicts her; the fumes from her cup drive the men to war; as they fight, the Dragon eats them. In Young's *Night Thoughts*, the title page of Night viii repeats the scene without the warriors; this time the heads of the beast wear the headgear of Church and State.

The Whore and her Dragon represent

the last group of the Twenty-seven Heavens or Churches, the line from Abraham to Luther, "the Male-Females, the Dragon Forms, Religion hid in War, a Dragon red & hidden Harlot" (*Mil* 37:42; *J* 75:17–20; 89:53; 93:25), "which John in Patmos saw" (*Mil* 40:22). It is the Antichrist (*J* 89:10–11).

Orc is never called a dragon, though Albion's Angel asks him if he is not the "serpent-form'd" waiting to devour Enitharmon's children (*Am* 7:3) —a reference to *Revelation* xii:4, where the Dragon waits to devour the child of the Woman in the Wilderness. Another reference to this myth is Leutha's envy of Elynittria: "O wherefore doth a Dragon-Form forth issue from my limbs to sieze her new born son?" (*Mil* 12:2).

DRANTHON is mentioned twice by Blake. After Los and Enitharmon, having failed to release Orc, return to Golgonooza, "Enitharmon on the road of Dranthon felt the inmost gate of her bright heart burst open & again close with a deadly pain" (*FZ* v:177). Later, when Enitharmon inspires Los to create, his hand inspired began "to hew the cavern'd rocks of Dranthon into forms of beauty" (*FZ* vii:457); but Blake deleted the line.

DROGHEDA, county Louth in Leinster, Ireland, is a port on the Boyne. It lies north of Wicklow.

Erin, bidding the Daughters of Beulah lament, says, "Stand ye upon the Dargle from Wicklow to Drogheda" (*J* 49:5).

The DRUIDS were the priests and judges of Gaul before it was Romanized and of Britain before it was Christianized. Caesar, whose account is the most important, found their religion much like the Roman one; he says they worshipped Dis, Mercury, Apollo, Mars, Jupiter, and Minerva (under other names, of course), but differed in preaching transmigration. They offered human sacrifice, burning their victims in wicker cages. They held the oak sacred, and worshipped in oak groves, cutting the rare mistletoe with a golden knife.

By Blake's time, the Druids had become thoroughly romanticized. They were confused with the bards, as in Gray's ode. They were supposed to have erected Stonehenge, the temple at Avebury, and all other prehistoric remains, which were actually much earlier. The mythagogues speculated wildly where the British and their priests had come from. Of course they had to be descendants of Noah. William Stukeley considered them Phoenicians who had preserved the religion of Abraham uncorrupted. Edward Davies put them still earlier: they were descendants of Ashkenaz, eldest son of Gomer and great-grandson of Noah. Richard Brothers believed they were of the ten Lost Tribes. The climax came when the unfortunate Francis Wilford actually placed the Biblical patriarchs in Britain, and apparently was about to reveal that Britain itself was the original seat of Biblical history, when in 1805, he was obliged to reveal the forgeries of his Hindu assistants, who had provided for him what they thought he wanted.

Blake seized upon Wilford's theory with patriotic zeal, and gave it full expression. "All things begin & end in Albion's ancient Druid rocky shore" (*Mil* 6:25; *J* 32:15). Adam, Noah, and the others were Druids, and Britain was "the Primitive Seat of the Patriarchal Religion" as the Druid Temples and Oak Groves "over the whole Earth witness to this day" (*J* 27; 70:16; 79:66; 89:23; 98:50). For this belief Blake had classical authority. Richard of Cirencester wrote (and Holinshed quoted him): "The doctrine of the druids is said to have been first invented in Britain, and from thence carried into Gaul; on which account Pliny says (in his thirtieth book), 'But why should I commemorate these things with regard to an art which has passed over the sea, and reached the bounds of nature? Britain even at this time celebrates it with so many wonderful ceremonies, that she seems to have taught it to the Persians.'" Julius

Caesar affirms much the same in his *Commentaries*.

Wilfred's retraction of 1805 did not deter Blake from using his theory: is not poetry truer than history? Blake was an enthusiast but no fool; and his claim of the British origin of everything is to be taken in precisely the same spirit which led him to put Gothic churches as well as druidic ruins in the land of Uz during the days of Job, and to assert that the Lamb of God in ancient times lived in England's pleasant pastures, and that Jerusalem was built there among the mills.

But to Blake, Druidism, far from being the pure faith of Abraham, symbolized Deism, the religion of the Natural Man, the savage, which was originally universal, and which (however modified) still exists. It is the Covering Cherub itself, the "Druid Spectre" which is the last enemy to be overcome. It is the whole system of Good and Evil, of the Accuser of Sin and human sacrifice for sin, the invention of "Albion's Spectre, the Patriarch Druid" (*J* 98:46–50). It was the religion of the patriarchs from Adam, until Abraham shrank from sacrificing his first born, substituting the ram. It overspread the earth "in patriarchal pomp & cruel pride" (*J* 79:67). Blake describes the building of Stonehenge "of Reasonings, of unhewn Demonstrations in labyrinthine arches (Mighty Urizen the Architect) thro' which the Heavens might revolve & Eternity be bound in their chain. Labour unparallell'd! a wondrous rocky World of cruel destiny, rocks piled on rocks reaching the stars, stretching from pole to pole. The Building is Natural Religion & its Altars Natural Morality, a building of eternal death, whose proportions are eternal despair" (*J* 66:3).

Stukeley (1740) believed that the temples were erected for serpent worship and that the sanctuary at Avebury was actually laid out in the form of a snake. To Blake, the serpent was the symbol of Nature. So he described the imaginary temple at Verulam as "serpent-form'd," with "oak-surrounded pillars"; it was made of "massy stones, uncut with tool . . . plac'd in order of the stars." It was built when the senses had been closed. Then "Thought chang'd the infinite to a serpent, that which pitieth to a devouring flame"; consequently the serpent temple was "image of infinite shut up in finite revolutions, and man became an Angel, Heaven a mighty circle turning, God a tyrant crown'd" (*Eur* 10:1–23).

Elsewhere Blake refers to the "Serpent Temples" (*J* 42:76; 80:48) and even calls them "Dragon Temples" (*J* 25:4; 47:6), because Deism promotes war. He represented the Avebury temple as a serpent on the last plate of *Jerusalem*, but with simple coils in place of head and tail.

Human sacrifice, for Blake, was the keynote of Druidism. Twice he referred to the wicker idol in which human beings, innocent as well as guilty, were burned alive (*Mil* 37:11; *J* 43:65); but his attention was centered on the altar, the "slaughter stone" of Stonehenge (*J* 66:13, 19), on which the victims were presumably sacrificed (*Mil* 12:8; *J* 27:30–32; 63:39; 65:63; 78:29; 83:12; 94:25; 98:48).

Blake credits the Druids with inventing "Female chastity" (*J* 17:14; 63:25), so that they become slaughterers of men. (It is quite possible that the mythagogues had developed some theory of vestal virgins, of the type of Bellini's Norma.)

The enormous rocks of these temples are their most impressive feature, and Blake constantly connects rocks and stones with the Druids, meaning that their religion is a petrifaction of human feelings. He uses their architecture symbolically, as in the illustrations to *Job*. There is a magnificent trilithon, far huger than anything actually erected, on Plate 70 of *Jerusalem*; others appear in *Milton*, Plates 4 and 6.

There are many prehistoric stone circles in Britain. "The Druids rear'd their Rocky Circles to make permanent Remembrance of Sin, & the Tree of Good & Evil sprang from the Rocky Circle & Snake of the Druid" (*J* 92:24). Blake refers to circles in Malden, Strathness, and Dura (*J* 90:62), and refers again to Hants, Devon, and

Wilts, "surrounded with masses of stone in order'd forms" (*J* 83:10).

Rocking Stones were also supposed to have been erected by the Druids. Blake refers to them once (*J* 90:59) and depicts one in *Milton*, Plate 6.

He also refers to the sacred mistletoe as a parasite. "As the Mistletoe grows on the Oak, so Albion's Tree on Eternity" (*J* 66:55).

The various pillars which the patriarchs erected were druidic (*J* 27:40). Greek philosophy was "a remnant of Druidism" (*J* 52)—possibly a reminiscence of the mythagogues' theory that Pythagoras learned of transmigration from the Druids. Jerusalem, fainting at the cross, hears a voice: "Wilt thou make Rome thy Patriarch Druid & the Kings of Europe his Horsemen?" (*J* 61:50). Druid architecture is seen in the head of the Covering Cherub (*J* 89:22). But "the whole Druid Law [Jesus] removes away" (*J* 69:39).

DRYDEN (John, 1631–1700), master of contempt, was the dominant literary figure of the Restoration period. He established Waller's closed heroic couplets as the standard verse-form for the next century. "I do not condemn Pope or Dryden because they did not understand Imagination, but because they did not understand Verse" (*PubA*, *K* 602). Dryden also did much to establish modern prose by disencumbering it of its Latinate complexities. He stands with Swift and Pope as one of the greatest satirists. He was also a prominent playwright. "While the Works of Pope & Dryden are look'd upon as the same Art with those of Milton & Shakespeare ... there can be no Art in a Nation but such as is Subservient to the interest of the Monopolizing Trader" (*PubA*, *K* 595).

Dryden, however, was greatest as a critic. His criticism of the forgotten Chaucer was a rediscovery of one of England's greatest poets; and Blake expanded Dryden's ideas into his own famous criticism. Dryden praised the undervalued Shakespeare at every opportunity. He was among the very

first to proclaim the greatness of *Paradise Lost* by the still unmentionable Milton.

However, not content to discover and praise these great writers, he felt it necessary to prove his points by adapting them to contemporary taste. His paraphrases of Chaucer are negligible. His reduction of *Antony and Cleopatra* to the Aristotelean unities, though the best of the rewritings of Shakespeare, is only an interesting curiosity. And his operatic libretto based on *Paradise Lost* never even found a composer.

Dryden saw splendid opportunities for the stage mechanist to contrive magnificent transformation scenes; and he found many marvelous lines which needed only rhyme to set them off. He asked the aging Milton for permission, who replied "Aye, you may tag my lines if you will." But Milton prefixed to the next edition (1674) a laudatory poem by the disgusted Marvell, who scoffed at "the Town Bayes" ("Bayes" was Buckingham's satiric name for Dryden, which the other satirists took up) and his tagging. But Dryden also had his admirers; when his *State of Innocence, and the Fall of Man, an Opera, written in Heroick Verse* was published in the same year, he prefixed a commendatory poem by his collaborator Nat Lee, "To Mr. Dryden, on his Poem of Paradise":

> To the dead Bard your Fame a little owes,
> For Milton did the wealthy Mine disclose,
> And rudely cast what you cou'd well dispose.

> He roughly drew, on an old-fashion'd Ground,
> A Chaos, for no perfect World was found,
> Till through the Heap your mighty Genius shin'd;
> He was the Golden Ore which you refin'd.

Blake commented: "An Example of these Contrary Arts is given us in the Characters of Milton & Dryden as they are written in a Poem signed with the name of Nat Lee, which perhaps he never wrote & perhaps he wrote in a paroxysm of insanity, In which it is said that Milton's Poem is a rough Unfinish'd Piece & Dryden has finish'd it. Now let Dryden's Fall & Milton's Paradise be read, & I will assert that every Body of Understanding must cry out Shame on such Niggling & Poco-Pen as Dryden has degraded Milton with. But at the same time I will allow that Stupidity will Prefer Dryden, because it is in Rhyme & Monotonous Sing Song, Sing Song from beginning to end" (*PubA*, *K* 600).

This passage accounts for Blake's line: "Dryden in Rhyme cries: 'Milton only Plann'd' " (*K* 554, 555, 595).

DUBLIN is one of the twelve Irish counties of Leinster, which are all assigned to Judah, Issachar, and Zebulun (*J* 72:19).

DUMBARTON is a Scottish county which, with Selkirk and Glasgow, is assigned to Issachar (*J* 16:57). All Scotland is assigned to Bowen (*J* 71:46).

DUMFRIES is a Scottish county which, with Aberdeen and Berwick, is assigned to Judah (*J* 16:54). All Scotland is assigned to Bowen (*J* 71:46).

DURA is the site of a druidic circle of stones, mentioned by Blake along with Malden and Strathness (*J* 90:62); but I have been unable to locate it in any atlas, gazetteer, guidebook, or map. The nearest guess would seem to be Duror, a village in Argyllshire on Linnhe Loch.

DURHAM is tenth in the list of Cathedral Cities, and is under Urthona and Edinburgh. Durham, like Lincoln and Carlisle, is a Councellor of Los (*J* 46:5). Blake obviously had in mind Thomas Sutton (1532–1611), to whom he addressed a laudatory poem, "To be, or not to be," in *An Island in the Moon*, Chapter ix. Sutton, from his dealings in the coal fields of Durham, became the richest commoner in England; a philanthropist, he founded the Charterhouse school and hospital in London.

Durham county stands east in the group of the four northernmost counties of England. The four are "divided in the Gates of Reuben, Judah, Dan & Joseph" (*J* 16:51). With Yorkshire and Westmoreland, Durham is assigned to Brereton (*J* 71:32).

DURNESS, county Sutherland, is a coastal town in the extreme north of Scotland. The northern Gate through which souls descend is "toward the North, Caithness & rocky Durness, Pentland & John Groat's House" —the whole northern coast (*Mil* 26:14).

E

The EAGLE, which was reputed to be able to gaze unblinded on the sun, is the symbol of genius. Its position is North in the quaternary of Eagle (north), Dove (east), Fly (south), and Worm (west) — (*J* 98:43). "When thou seest an Eagle, thou seest a portion of Genius: lift up thy head" (*MHH* 9:15). In the infernal printing house, the third chamber is inhabited by an Eagle, who causes the inside of the Cave to be infinite; and the decoration of this plate shows a soaring Eagle uplifting the serpent of Nature (*MHH* 15). (This device had already appeared in the *Iliad* xii:200; the *Choephoroi* of Aeschylus, 247; the *Aeneid* xi:751; the *Metamorphoses* iv:362; and the *Faerie Queene* I.v.8. Shelley was to use it in *The Revolt of Islam*, and Mexico was to adopt it as the emblem on its national banner.) The manacled Orc compares his free spirit to an Eagle, and his consort sees "in Mexico an Eagle" (*Am* 1:13; 2:13); furthermore, the eagles hide their young in Orc's hair (*FZ* v:129).

"The Eagle returns from nightly prey and lifts his golden beak to the pure east, shaking the dust from his immortal pinions to awake the sun that sleeps too long" (*VDA* 2:25). "Ask ... the wing'd eagle why he loves the sun ... Does not the eagle scorn the earth & despise the treasures beneath?" (*VDA* 3:12; 5:39). Thrice Blake mentions the cliffs where the eagles hide their young (*VDA* 5:37; *MHH* 15; *FZ* v:129).

Blake found great inspiration in sex. The thirty-fifth plate of *Milton* shows the Eagle hovering with outspread wings above a pair of lovers; the woman looks at the man, while the man gazes upward at the Eagle. Even though the love is only physical, Manathu-Varcyon, consort of Ethinthus, is accompanied by eagles as well as "flames of soft delusion" (*Eur* 14:8).

When Urizen orders the creation of the Mundane Shell, his eagles fly "far into the vast unknown," hanging "the universal curtains" and spreading out "from Sun to Sun the vehicles of light" (*FZ* ii:150–55). These eagles are depicted in the fifteenth illustration to *Job*.

But when the Eagle of Genius is starved, he becomes (as in the Bible) an eater of carrion, an unclean bird. When Albion sinks into his deadly sleep, the Eagle is there, waiting. "And the strong Eagle, now with numming cold blighted of feathers, once like the pride of the sun, now flagging on cold night, hovers with blasted wings aloft, watching with Eager Eye till Man shall leave a corruptible body" (*FZ* viii:521; cf. *FR* 97, 103; *J* 94:15). With the vultures the eagles cry over the battle-field (*FZ* vii *b*:44). When the trumpet summons the dead to rise, the Eagle calls on the Vulture, but disappointed they fly away (*FZ* ix:59). Theotormon's Eagles are substituted for Prometheus' vultures when Oothoon summons them to rend away her defiled bosom (*VDA* 2:13, 17).

When the universe explodes at the Last Judgment, all spirits are released from their bodies, including the Eagle (*FZ* ix:231); and they humanize in the forgiveness of sins (*J* 98:43).

The EAR is the fourth of the four special senses, in their counterclockwise creation, beginning with the "parent sense," the Tongue (west). Its compass-point is north (*J* 12:60; 98:18); its Zoa is Urthona-Los (*FZ* i:14–18); its art is Poetry. The "Auricular Nerves of Human Life" are "the Earth of Eden" itself (*FZ* i:18). Here Los creates the sun by day and the moon by night (*Mil* 29:40). In its normal state, the Ear is "a whirlpool fierce to draw creations in" (*Thel* 6:17). Ears can hear the "music of the spheres" (*Eur* iii:2). They are "the ever-varying spiral ascents to the heavens of heavens" (*Eur* 10:13); "a golden ascent winding round to the heavens of heavens" (*FZ* vi:250)— like the Jacob's Ladder in Blake's famous design. "Even from the depths of Hell [God's] voice I hear | Within the un-fathom'd caverns of my Ear" (*J* 3:7).

But after the senses shrink in the Fall, the "labyrinthine Ear" (*J* 83:36; 98:18) is merely "a little shell, in small volutions shutting out all melodies & comprehending only Discord and Harmony" (*Mil* 5:23), a line which Blake amended to "shutting out True Harmonies & comprehending great as very small" (*J* 49:36). "Can such an Ear, fill'd with the vapours of the yawning pit, judge of the pure melodious harp struck by a hand divine?" (*Mil* 5:30).

The EARTH is the body, or the subconscious, from which all Energy comes (*MHH* 4), "where the fibrous roots of every heart on earth infixes deep its restless twists" (*Thel* 6:3). It is fourth (or west) in a quarternary: the Sun (imagination), the Moon (love), the Stars (intellect), and the Earth (generation).

In the first two poems of the *Songs of Experience*, the "Holy Word," calling on "the lapsed Soul" to return, addresses her as "O Earth."

"In that dread night when Urizen call'd the stars round his feet, then burst the center from its orb, and found a place beneath; and Earth conglob'd, in narrow room, roll'd round its sulphur Sun" (*Am* b:5).

The EAST is the third of the four compass-points. Its Zoa is Luvah (*Mil* 19:17; 34:37; *J* 59:12; 97:9); its sense organ is the Nostrils (*J* 98:16); its art is Music. As the heart is the seat of the emotions, the East is inwards (*J* 14:30); it is "the Center, unapproachable for ever" (*J* 12:56), from which "the Vegetative Universe opens like a flower" (*J* 13:34). All outward nature is the projection of man's emotions; or, to put it in Blake's words, Vala is the Emanation of Luvah. When the heart becomes selfish, its Center is outwards (*J* 71:7). When the Zoas change places, Urizen assumes the East (*J* 36:29), which becomes a Void (*Mil* 19:22; *J* 59:18).

The East is particularly important because Jesus, descending from the North, is incarnated in the East—dons "Luvah's robes of blood." *Ex oriente lux.* Jerusalem is constantly associated with the East (*J* 5:48; 14:31; 31:24; 82:55). When Albion rises at last "his face is toward the east, toward Jerusalem's Gates" (*Mil* 39:33). Los strives toward the East (*Mil* 26:18; *J* 85:12).

It follows that the enemies of Jesus and Jerusalem war against them in the East. The Wine-press of Los is eastward (*Mil* 27:1). The Covering Cherub advances from the East (*Mil* 23:10); Satan (*Mil* 9:40; 39:24) and Rahab (*Mil* 40:18) manifest there. "The clouds of Albion's Druid Temples rage in the eastern heaven" (*J* 60:1). And to the east lay France: "the strife of Albion & Luvah is great in the east" (*J* 31:55).

EASTMEATH is an Irish county in Leinster which, with the eleven others of that province, is assigned to Judah, Issachar, and Zebulun (*J* 72:19).

EBAL, in Manasseh's land (Samaria), was known as the "Mount of Cursing" because there Joshua announced the curses which would follow infractions of the Law.

The daughters of Zelophehad bind Manasseh down on "Ebal, mount of cursing" (*FZ* viii:315; *J* 68:3).

The EDEN of *Genesis* was the land in the east of which God planted a garden ("Paradise") for the dwelling-place of the newly created Adam. It contained every tree that was beautiful or good for food, including the Tree of Life (immortality) and the forbidden Tree of the Knowledge of Good and Evil (traditionally an apple tree). After Adam and Eve were expelled, cherubim with a flaming sword were set to prevent their return, lest they eat of the Tree of Life. According to *Revelation* ii:7, the Tree of Life now grows "in the midst of the Paradise of God," which is in the afterworld.

Urizen created this earthly Eden (*Ur* 20:41). After he promulgated his laws, Adam withered to a skeleton there (*SoL* 3:6; 7:20). Then "all the Garden of God was caught up with the Sun in one day of fury and war" (*J* 49:15).

But the spiritual Eden is the dwelling-place, or state of mind, of the Divine Family: those who have achieved the Brotherhood of Man. Its position is North (*J* 12:60). It is "the garden of God" (*J* 38:25), "the land of life" (*FZ* i:474). The "Auricular Nerves" are "the Earth of Eden" (*FZ* i:17). It contains "golden mountains" (*J* 28:2) and "mountain palaces" built by Hereford (*J* 46:4) where the evening feasts are held. Stonehenge was built of its previously unhewn stones (*Eur* 10:7; *J* 66:1). There are looms on which garments of immortality are woven (*J* 38:53). There are wheels (perhaps suggested by Behmen's seven wheels with one hub)—"Wheel within Wheel [which] in freedom revolve in harmony & peace" as contrasted to the wheels of science, "wheel without wheel, with cogs tyrannic moving by compulsion each other" (*J* 15:18–20).

Blake mentions twice the four rivers of Eden, for which see below. There is also the sweet river of milk and liquid pearl

which is Ololon (*Mil* 21:15). There is also a stream, one of the two springing beside the rock of crystal under the wild thyme, which flows through Golgonooza and Beulah into Eden (*Mil* 35:49–51). Beulah surrounds Eden on all sides (*Mil* 30:9).

Golgonooza has four Gates, the northern one facing Eden; but each gate also opens into Eden, Generation, Beulah, and Ulro (*J* 12:48–50). The north, south, and western gates into Eden are formed of the four symbolic metals, but the eastern gate is "eternal ice frozen in seven folds of forms of death" (*J* 13:1, 5, 10), and they are all "walled up till time of renovation" (*J* 12:52). Other entrances to Eden are open, however. Poetry, Painting, and Music are "the three Powers in Man of conversing with Paradise, which the flood did not Sweep away" (*LJ*, *K* 609). The Wild Thyme is Los's messenger to Eden (*Mil* 35:54). When Eno stretches a Moment of time into seven thousand years, every year has windows into Eden (*FZ* i:224); but in *Jerusalem* (48:37) her Moment is extended to eight thousand five hundred years, and every two hundred years has its door into Eden. The Sanctuary of Eden is "in the Camp, in the Outline, in the Circumference, & every Minute Particular is Holy" (*J* 69:41).

Eden partakes of Eternity, but differs from it in that it also partakes of this world. It has seasons; the males labor at their agriculture during the winter, as in the Holy Lands. There is marriage; the Emanations labor at their looms, and join their consorts at the evening feasts. Their social life would be impossible in the Mystical Ecstasy.

The FOUR RIVERS OF EDEN. According to *Genesis*, a river went out of Eden and divided into four: (1) Pison, which encompassed the land of Havilah, (2) Gihon, which encompassed Ethiopia, (3) Hiddekel, which went towards the east of Assyria, and (4) the Euphrates. Ancient scholars tried in vain to locate the single source of these rivers; Milton concluded that Noah's Flood had altered the original topography past recognition. The Euphrates was the modern Euphrates; the Hiddekel was obviously the Tigris; the Gihon was surely the Nile (as in *J* 89:15); but the Pison remained a puzzle.

For Blake, the source was the River of Life; its four branches were the four Zoas: "The Four Living Creatures, Chariots of Humanity Divine Incomprehensible, in beautiful Paradises expand. These are the Four Rivers of Paradise and the Four Faces of Humanity, fronting the Four Cardinal Points of Heaven" (*J* 98:24). Much earlier (*FR* 183) he had mentioned "the soul whose brain and heart cast their rivers in equal tides thro' the great Paradise."

Blake identified the Pison with the Arnon (*J* 89:26), which is "the River Storge," the parental urge for offspring (*Mil* 34:30); it corresponds to the female genital tract (*FZ* viii:215). The compass-points therefore are as follows: Gihon (the Nile), south; Pison, west; Hiddekel (the Tigris, which lies east of the Euphrates), east; and by elimination, Euphrates, north. These points are reversed in the Covering Cherub, whose brain "incloses a reflexion of Eden all perverted": Gihon is in his head, Pison and Hiddekel in his bosom, and Euphrates in his loins (*J* 89:14, 25, 35, 38).

Urizen, of course, debased them in his creation. "His Brain in a rock & his Heart in a fleshy slough formed four rivers obscuring the immense Orb" of the sun (*BoL* 5:52); they are the limited Senses. The River of Life becomes the River of Death—that is, of material generation. His three daughters tend it; the youngest, Ona (the loins), divides the source into four currents (*FZ* vi:18).

The early Gnostic sect of Naasenes (Ophites) strikingly anticipated Blake's symbolism. According to Hippolytus (*Refutation of All Heresies* V, iv), they taught that Eden is in the brain, and that its four rivers are the Four Senses. Only in assigning Hiddekel to the Nostrils, however, did they coincide with Blake's assignments; the others are Pison, the Eyes; Gihon, the Ears; and Euphrates, the Mouth. As Hippolytus' second-century manuscript was not recovered until 1842, Blake could not have known of these parallels.

EDINBURGH, London, York, and Verulam (Canterbury) are the four leading Cathedral Cities, in which the other Twenty-four appear (*J* 46:24). They are "the English names" of the Four Zoas (*J* 59:14). Edinburgh (north) is under Urthona and Rintrah (*J* 74:1–4). The six of the Twenty-four which are delegated to Edinburgh are Bath, Hereford, Lincoln, Durham, Carlisle, and Ely (*J* 46:1–6).

Elsewhere, Blake seems to have had other possible quaternaries in mind. London, Bath, Legions, and Edinburgh are the four pillars of the waking Albion's throne (*Mil* 39:35). "His bosom girt with gold involves York, Edinburgh, Durham & Carlisle" (*Mil* 39:42). Jerusalem's children are piteous "from Lincoln & Norwich, from Edinburgh & Monmouth" (*J* 21:39). Bath, Canterbury, York, and Edinburgh cry out over the Plow of Nations (*J* 57:1). "From London to York & Edinburgh the Furnaces rage terrible" (*J* 73:53).

Edinburgh is "cloth'd with Fortitude" as with an immortal garment of martyrdoms (*J* 38:51). At the outbreak of war, his heart is circumscribed (*J* 66:64).

Edinburgh, Roxboro, and Ross are Scottish counties assigned to Levi (*J* 16:54). All Scotland is assigned to Bowen (*J* 71:46).

EDOM is another name for Esau (*Gen* xxxvi:1), who first was deprived of his birthright and later of his father's blessing by the craft of his brother Jacob. Thus disinherited, Esau departed for the wilderness, where he prospered and established his tribe, the Edomites. Esau and Jacob thus became types of fraternal hatred (*J* 73:28).

Actually Esau forgave Jacob handsomely (*Gen* xxxiii:1–15). But Esau's descendants forbade Moses and his people to pass through their land on the way to Canaan; and the hatred between the two tribes continued unabated. Even today, to call somebody a "son of Esau" is an insult.

But, proclaiming the advent of the new heaven, Blake announced the return of Esau to the inheritance of which he had been unjustly deprived. "Now is the dominion of Edom, & the return of Adam into Paradise; see Isaiah xxxiv & xxxv Chap." (*MHH* 3). The hypocritical villain, the "sneaking serpent," is about to be expelled by the just man's rage (*MHH* 2:14–20); evidently this refers to Jacob. *Isaiah* xxxv prophesies the flourishing of God's kingdom, when "the desert shall rejoice, and blossom as the rose," and the blind, the deaf, and the lame shall be cured. The preceding chapter, however, prophesies the complete slaughter of the Edomites and the destruction of their cities.

Edom is also the name for the land inhabited by Esau and his descendants. It lay south of the Dead Sea, and was bounded on the north by Judah and Moab. Blake refers to it several times in company with the other hostile lands surrounding Palestine (*Mil* 17:20; *J* 49:43; 92:23; 96:9). "Schofield is Adam who was New-created in Edom" (*J* 7:25).

EGYPT signifies Slavery, because of the bondage of Israel.

It is one of the surrounding hostile countries that receives Jerusalem's little ones for sacrifice and the delights of cruelty (*J* 5:14). They are dashed upon Egypt's iron floors and the marble pavements of Assyria (*J* 79:2). They labor at the looms, mills, prisons, and workhouses of the hostile nations (*J* 13:58). Joseph is sold there (*Mil* 24:20) "for Negation, a Veil the Saviour born & dying rends" (*J* 55:16). "The Canaanite [female] united with the fugitive Hebrew, whom she divided into Twelve [tribes] & sold into Egypt,

then scatter'd the Egyptian & Hebrew to the four Winds" (*J* 92:3).

In Egypt is worshipped the trinity of Osiris, Isis, and Orus, counted as the eighth of the Twelve Gods of Asia (*Mil* 37:27). The pagan nations in general are "by Demonstrations the cruel Sons of Quality & Negation" (*J* 43:67).

The thirty cities of Africa, created by Urizen, were originally called Egypt (*Ur* 28:10); when Fuzon summons the still ungenerated children of Urizen to leave the pendulous earth, "they call'd it Egypt" (*Ur* 28:22). Fuzon's fiery beam is a pillar of fire to Egypt (*Ahan* 2:45).

Egypt is eight steps within Urizen's world (*J* 58:35). Brereton and Slade flee from Reuben into Egypt (*J* 36:17). The fallen Sons of Albion take root in Egypt and other pagan nations (*J* 49:43). The Daughters of Albion, however, find it "as the Garden of Eden" (*J* 82:30), and get spies from Egypt to make the kings of Canaan jealous (*J* 68:60). The Double Molech and Chemosh marches through Egypt in his fury (*J* 84:21). In the head of the Covering Cherub is "Egypt on the Gihon . . . Minute Particulars in slavery . . . among the brick-kilns disorganiz'd; & there is Pharoh in his iron Court and the Dragon of the River & the Furnaces of iron" (*J* 89:15–19).

Nevertheless, Egypt and Assyria appear before the feet of the transfigured Jerusalem (*J* 86:31); "Egypt and Lybia" hear the sacred songs in her court, and their sons inquire about her from the Lamb (*J* 79:50). Eventually, Egypt shall be the sixteenth of the Thirty-two Nations guarding liberty and ruling the rest of the world (*J* 72:40), while whatever evil the hostile nations represented will exist only in the Shadows of Remembrance (*J* 92:23).

When Blake engraved Fuseli's "Fertilization of Egypt" for Darwin's *Botanic Garden* (1791), he interpreted an Egyptian god as the blind cry of the flesh, the prayer of the animal which is in us all. The dog-headed Anubis faces inward; his uplifted hands pierce the cloud-barrier as he appeals to Sirius, the dim, six-pointed Dog Star. But all stars are Urizen's, and it is Urizen who answers the prayer with lightnings and storm-floods of water (matter). Blake added a musical instrument, a systrum, lying neglected on a bank; hinting that a means of invoking true deity (as in the last plate of *Job*) was being overlooked.

The "EIGHTH Image Divine" (*Mil* 15:5) is the Individual, without whom God is incomplete. He is the Eighth, being added to the seven Eyes of God (the Seven Angels of the Presence); but he is elusive: when summoned, "he hid in Albion's Forests" (*J* 55:33).

Milton's sleeping body is his Eighth. He walks with the Seven Angels (*Mil* 15:5). They guard his couch (*Mil* 20:47); they are drawn down into Ulro (*Mil* 34:4); they rejoice when Ololon descends (*Mil* 35:34).

The form of the Eighth is visible in Job's Whirlwind (*Illustr Job* 13). See EYES OF GOD.

ELECT. See CLASSES.

The ELEMENTS are the traditional four: Water (west), Air (south), Fire (east), and Earth (north). Blake mentions them first in "To the Muses" (*PS*); the poet wonders where the muses are to be found, whether in Greece or the Holy Land (the two great sources of our culture), or in the four Elements, "Heaven" being substituted for Fire. They became a convenience to indicate anything that is all pervasive in effect, as in *The Four Zoas* vii:49–53 (flood, rock, fire, and whirlwind) and ix:812 (thunders, earthquakes, fires, water floods).

They are personified for the first time as the sons of Urizen: Thiriel (air), Utha (water), Grodna (earth), and Fuzon (fire), "first begotten, last born" (*Ur* 23:11–18), but Blake later abandoned these names. They are a consequence of the Fall. Urizen cannot control their warfare, "because himself was subject" (*FZ* vi:145). Their creation is explained further (*J*

36:27–40). When the Zoas, "who are the Four Eternal Senses of Man," change places, they become "Four Elements separating from the Limbs of Albion." Then the three Dimensions "divided into Four ravening deathlike forms, Fairies [air] & Genii [fire] & Nymphs [water] & Gnomes [earth] of the Elements: These are States Permanently Fixed by the Divine Power"; and the Flood of Matter ensues (see FLOOD OF NOAH). "All are the work of Fairy hands of the Four Elements" (*Mil* 28:60). When at last Albion rises, he speaks his Words of Eternity "thro' the Four Elements on all sides surrounding his awful Members" (*J* 95:10).

Thus the Four Elements are the inexorable forces of Matter in the unending strife of Nature. "These in the aggregate are named Satan and Rahab: they know not of Regeneration, but only of Generation: the Fairies, Nymphs, Gnomes & Genii of the Four Elements, unforgiving & unalterable; these cannot be regenerated but must be Created, for they know only of Generation. These are the Gods of the Kingdoms of the Earth, in contrarious and cruel opposition, Element against Element, opposed in War not Mental, as the Wars of Eternity, but a Corporeal Strife in Los's Halls, continual labouring in the Furnaces of Golgonooza" (*Mil* 31:18).

Men in their power must "War on, slaves to the eternal Elements" (*SoL* 3:14). Yet it is also stated that Los can renew the "ruin'd souls of Men thro' Earth, Sea, Air & Fire" (*FZ* iv:30). For the Elements, when servants, have their valuable functions. The Gnomes, for example, tend Palamabron's horses in *Milton*. And sixty-four thousand of each Element guard the respective gates of Golgonooza; and here Blake records their compass-points (*J* 13:26–29). They are pictured in the illustration to *Il Penseroso* where young Milton is studying the philosophy of Plato; it is the Fairies (south—reason) who play about his head (see Illustrations).

The ELEPHANT, the largest land creature, appears as a noble beast in the quaternary of the thirty-fourth Proverb of Hell (*MHH* 8) : Lion (east), Tyger (north), Horse (south), and Elephant (west). The same quaternary reappears in *Jerusalem* (98:43). He is included in a list of animals (*FZ* viii:446). He falls in the downfall of Urizen (*MHH* 26:15). This fall is pictured in the 508th illustration to Young's *Night Thoughts* (ix:1851). But in the illustrations to *Job*, he is replaced by Behemoth.

ELETH is the eldest of the three Daughters of Urizen; she represents the Head in the division of Man into Head, Heart, and Loins (*FZ* vii:95). She fills her iron pail, or urn, with water and pours it forth, as her part in making the bread of Orc (*FZ* vi:10). See URIZEN'S DAUGHTERS, under URIZEN.

ELGIN is a Scottish county which, with Lanerk and Kinross, is assigned to Joseph (*J* 16:58) and also to Bowen, to whom is assigned all Scotland (*J* 71:46).

ELIAKIM, the son of Hilkiah, King Hezekiah's steward, was a prominent man in the court. He was one of the three who treated with Sennacherib's general; he was a messenger between the king and Isaiah, who prophesied his elevation to viceregal power: "And the key of the house of David will I lay upon his shoulder; so he shall open, and none shall shut; and he shall shut, and none shall open" (*Isaiah* xxii:22).

Blake depicted him as "a Mighty fiend with a Book in his hand, which is Shut; he represents the person nam'd in Isaiah, xxii c. & 20 v., Eliakim, the Son of Hilkiah: he drags Satan down headlong: he is crown'd with oak" (*LJ*, *K* 607; see Illustrations, "LJ" No. 31).

ELIAS is the name for Elijah in the Greek Testament. "[Los] is the Spirit of Prophecy, the ever apparent Elias" (*Mil* 24:71). See ELIJAH.

ELIJAH, the prophet who communicated directly with God, and who never died but was carried to heaven in a fiery chariot, was confidently expected to return as herald for the Messiah. He appeared in the Transfiguration, when Jesus was suspended between the Law (Moses) and the Prophet.

Elijah "comprehends all the Prophetic Characters" (*LJ*, *K* 611). His poetical equivalent is Los, "the Spirit of Prophecy, the ever apparent Elias" (*Mil* 24:71). When the stricken Cathedral Cities are unable to help Man further, they give their power to Los, "naming him the Spirit of Prophecy, calling him Elijah" (*J* 44: 31).

In *The Ghost of Abel*, Blake addresses Lord Byron with the words of Jehovah, "What doest thou here, Elijah?" (*I Kings* xix:9, 13), thus hailing Byron as a true poet while correcting his ideas.

At the marriage of the cloud-Angel and the fire-Devil in the last "Memorable Fancy" of *The Marriage of Heaven and Hell* (24), the Angel finally embraced the flame of fire "& was consumed and arose as Elijah."

The chariot of fire—which Blake summons in his famous hymn "And did those feet" (*Mil* 1)—he defined as "Contemplative Thought" (*LJ*, *K* 611), probably recollecting Milton's "Cherub Contemplation" (*Il Penseroso* 54). Blake's picture of Elijah in his chariot is well known. On Plate 46 of *Jerusalem* is another picture: the sage and his Emanation sit in the flaming chariot formed by the Serpent of Nature and drawn by the Bulls of Luvah (with faces of bearded men, whose single horns are coiling serpents with hands for heads, pointing forward and backward) on whom ride two winged gnomes carrying pens.

ELLAYOL is mentioned just once by Blake, as the eleventh son of Los and Enitharmon (*FZ* viii:359). Apparently he has no connection with the eleventh daughter, who is Ada, one of the two wives of Lamech.

ELOHIM ("judges") is the name of God
generally used from Adam through Noah
to Abraham (as in *Gen* xxxiii:20) ; it was
followed by El Shaddai, used from Abraham
to Moses (in *Gen* xxxvii, it is translated
"God Almighty"); and finally by Jehovah
(Yahveh), revealed to Moses at Horeb
(*Exod* iii:14).

Elohim (an honorific plural) is the Creator in *Genesis* i. It represents God in his
aspect of Justice, as contrasted with Jehovah, the aspect of Mercy. Sometimes the
word should have been translated simply
"judges," as in *Psalm* lxxxii:1; also in
Exodus xxi:6 and xxii:28; and according to
some commentators, including Moses
Maimonides, in *Genesis* iii:5 ("ye shall be
as gods [judges], knowing good and evil").
Blake would have embraced this reading, as
it would clarify the nature of the primal
sin: that of dividing all human realities into
good and evil, thus setting oneself up as
judge—an error corrected by the "Judge
not" of Jesus (*Matt* vii:1).

Blake uses the Elohim as the Creator and
the Judge, and places him as the third of
the seven Eyes of God.

"The Creator of this World is a very
Cruel Being" (*LJ, K* 617). Blake's col-
or print, "The Elohim Creating Adam,"
shows a monstrous, bearded angel extended over the agonized form of Adam,
who is wreathed in a serpent, while a blood-
colored sun sets. In a conversation with
Crabb Robinson, Blake referred to Nature
as the work of the Devil; and when the
diarist objected that according to *Genesis*
it was God who created the world, Blake
replied triumphantly "that this God was
not Jehovah but Elohim; and the doctrine
of the Gnostics was repeated with sufficient
consistency to silence one so unlearned as
myself" (*CR* 298). "Nature is a Vision of
the Science of the Elohim" (*Mil* 29:65).
" . . . in [Albion's] Chaotic State of Sleep,
Satan & Adam & the whole World was
Created by the Elohim" (*J* 27).

As judges, the Elohim swear "Vengeance
for Sin," and thus become the gods of the
Heathen (*GhA* 50). As judges also they

take their place as the third of the seven
Eyes of God, that path through error
which leads man from Lucifer to Jesus. It
was after Molech (the executioner, or second Eye) became impatient that the Elohim
created Adam, then "wearied, fainted"
(*FZ* viii:401; *Mil* 13:22; *J* 55:32). In
the *Milton* reference, Blake calls the
Elohim "triple," referring to their limited
threefold power; Blake obviously could not
have meant the Trinity itself.

God contains all things, including those
we call evil; and the aspect named Elohim
may be mistaken for the basic God. Blake
often speaks of the Divine Name's being
ascribed wrongly, and once (*LJ, K* 610)
mentions particularly that the Angel of the
Divine Presence (*Exod* xiv:19) is "frequently call'd by the Name of Jehovah
Elohim, The 'I Am' of the Oaks of Albion."

When Jehovah, God of Mercies (*GhA*
25), appears, the Elohim perceive that their
oath of vengeance is eternal torment, and
roll apart, "trembling over The Mercy
Seat, each in his station fixt in the Firmament by Peace, Brotherhood and Love"
(*GhA* 53). Jehovah and Elohim are necessary to each other: sin cannot be forgiven
unless it first is judged to be sin. Therefore
the two names are paired in the vision of the
forgiveness of Mary (*J* 61:1–2), also in
The Ghost of Abel (51), and in *A Vision of
the Last Judgment* (*K* 610). Once the Lamb
is seen hovering "in clouds of Jehovah &
winds of Elohim" (*Mil* 14:26).

Los is "of the Elohim" (*J* 73:24), being
a creator, though never a judge.

ELY, in Cambridgeshire, is the twelfth of
the Twenty-four Cathedral Cities (*J*
46:6). It is North, under Urthona and
Edinburgh, and is assigned to Scofield (*J*
71:38). In the confusion at the beginning
of *Jerusalem* (5:9), Ely is "almost swallow'd up" while Cam is shrunk to a little
stream.

Blake naturally associated Ely with
Cambridge University (on the Cam) in the
same county. Cambridge and Oxford were
still fundamentally religious institutions:

the bulk of the students were candidates for the ministry. The Cathedral City was therefore the soul of the university.

The supreme product of Cambridge was Milton; hence Ely is the "Scribe of Los, whose pen no other hand dare touch" (*J* 46:6). It would seem to be a paradox that Milton, who attacked the bishops so severely, should be identified with a Cathedral City; but after all, he was inspired by the true spirit of Christianity.

Blake repeated this intellectual feat when he identified the Cathedral City of Oxford with Shelley, who was ejected from the college for his atheism.

ELYNITTRIA, the second daughter of Los and Enitharmon (*FZ* viii:363), is the Emanation of Palamabron, the second son. Their position is East; their planet is the Moon. She represents the tolerant wife. Her attribute is a silver bow and arrows (*Eur* 8:4; *Mil* 5:43; 10:17; 11:38; 13:37).

Elynittria plays a part only in the Bard's Song at the beginning of *Milton*. This song, which concerns all our salvations, obviously sprang from the Blake-Hayley quarrel; but the ideas involved developed far beyond a mere recounting of the events at Felpham under altered names. To interpret it so would end in ridiculous absurdities: such as Mrs. Blake's bearing a son there, the poet's father reproving her for new-fangled jealousy, Hayley's ousting a mistress because he was infatuated with Catherine, and Catherine's leading her to William's bed. No: these are accounts of Emanations, studies in psychology, and not local scandals about people long dead.

Satan faints beneath Elynittria's arrows (*Mil* 5:43). Los reproves her for jealousy: her arrows, "bound up in the horns of Jealousy to a deadly fading Moon," darken every internal light (*Mil* 10:14–23). However, Leutha complains that Elynittria's arrows repel her when she approaches Palamabron's tent (*Mil* 11:38); jealously she feels a dragon-form issue from her limbs to seize Elynittria's newborn son (*Mil* 12:2–3). At noon, she tries to un-

harness Palamabron's horses, as Elynittria was wont to do, but she only maddens them (*Mil* 12:10–13). But in the evening, Elynittria with all her singing women welcomes Satan with such powerful wine that he drives Leutha out (*Mil* 12:42–43). Then Elynittria, laying aside her arrows, brings Leutha to Palamabron's bed (*Mil* 13:36–38).

In *Europe* (8:3), Enitharmon, summoning her children, bids Rintrah "bring Palamabron, horned priest, skipping upon the mountains, and silent Elynittria, the silver bowed queen." In *Jerusalem* (93:1–5), Enitharmon warns Rintrah and Palamabron that they "seek a Love of the pride of dominion that will Divorce Ocalythron & Elynittria upon East Moor in Derbyshire & along the Valleys of Cheviot."

ELYTHIRIA is mentioned only once, as the fifth daughter of Los and Enitharmon (*FZ* viii:364). Her position in the list probably identifies her as the Emanation of Antamon, the Cloud; and the aerial sound of her name strengthens the supposition.

The EMANATION is the feminine portion, or "counterpart," of the fundamentally bisexual male. In Eternity, where the Individual is complete again, there is neither marrying nor giving in marriage (*Matt* xxii:30; *J* 34:15), as the sexual division no longer exists there (*J* 92:13). Not that the Emanation is annihilated: she is absorbed into the Individual, of whom she is still an active part, though without a separate will. "In Eternity Woman is the Emanation of Man; she has No Will of her own. There is no such thing in Eternity as a Female Will" (*LJ*, *K* 613). But without her, the Brotherhood of Man would be impossible. "When in Eternity Man converses with Man, they enter into each other's Bosom (which are Universes of delight) in mutual interchange, and first their Emanations meet surrounded by their Children; if they embrace & comingle, the Human Fourfold Forms mingle also in thunders of Intellect; but if the Emanations mingle not, with storms & agitations of earthquakes & consuming fires they roll apart in fear; for Man cannot unite with Man but by their Emanations, which stand both Male & Female at the Gates of each Humanity" (*J* 88:3).

The Emanation is necessary for the union with God as well as Man. "Man is adjoin'd to Man by his Emanative portion, who is Jerusalem in every individual Man" (*J* 44:38), and Jerusalem is the Bride of the Lamb. This is "the Mystic Union of the Emanation in the Lord" (*J* 53:24).

It will be noted that the Emanations, when they achieve a separate existence (and get names of their own, which the Spectres never do), exhibit all the characteristics of the *personae* of the split personality which modern science has discovered. They seek for domination, can be dangerously destructive, and fight reintegration (which seems to them like annihilation); but the moment they are reabsorbed, their voices cease at once.

In Eden, however, which is the ideal life on this earth, the male and female, when reconciled, cooperate. The male labors in the fields while the female works at her loom; but at the noon-rest and again in the evening, the Emanation unlooses the horses and refreshes the male (*FZ* iii:126; *Mil* 12:8–12; *J* 34:12). The Emanation bears children, which are the male's "secret loves & Graces" (*FZ* i:164), his "infant Loves & Graces" (*J* 8:49; 20:27), his "infant thoughts & desires" (*J* 9:2). These expressions of the constant play of his imagination are also called Emanations.

At times, the Emanations withdraw into the night of Beulah, where they sleep. According to *The Four Zoas* they retire periodically each winter, returning in the spring (*FZ* i:64; iii:115; ix:210–19); but in *Milton* and *Jerusalem*, they descend whenever the intellectual warfare in Eternity exhausts and terrifies them. See BEULAH.

But the division of the Emanation from the Individual is a split in the personality, a stage in the Fall of Man, symbolized in

Genesis by the extraction of Eve from the side of the sleeping Adam. The division of Enitharmon from Los is described in *The Book of Urizen* and of Ahania from Urizen in *The Book of Ahania*; both events are detailed in *The Four Zoas*.

The separated Emanation takes the female form, an event which horrifies the Eternals (*Ur* 18:7; *FZ* ix:622). Man is left "a dark Spectre" (*J* 53:25), or perhaps only in his Spectre's power. Worse yet, the Emanation acquires a will of her own (*FZ* ii:206), which by definition is turned against her consort.

Through the Divine Mercy, the separated Emanation descends into the world of Generation (*J* 53:27), where the error is limited to Time and Space. Here she becomes her consort's wife (*J* 14:14). In the case of Milton, she is sixfold, consisting of his three wives and three daughters (*Mil* 2:19; 17:1). In this world, the wife should be the husband's "concentering vision" (*FZ* vii:402), his comforter and co-worker; but her separate will produces all "the torments of love & jealousy." "My Spectre around me" (*K* 415) describes this warfare of the sexes; it is elaborated in the nuptial troubles of Los, and elsewhere. See also the pathetic analysis of the unhappy marriage in *Milton* (33:2–10).

The Emanation's self-centered pride seeks dominion over the male. She is jealous of all his activities, and seeks to stop them by denying her husband his freedom (Jerusalem). She drives all females away from him, invents the theory of sin and the sense of guilt, and curbs him with the laws of chastity. She denies herself to him, fleeing his embraces. She murders all his innocent pleasures, not knowing that she herself is the mother of these "Emanations" (*FZ* i:165). She is even jealous of her husband's labors, which take his attention from her; so she prevents his working.

Meanwhile the male is left a selfish and ravening Spectre. His rational power, unchecked by his lost Emanation, dominates him. He denounces all delights as sin (*FZ* i:54; *J* 28:6), and condemns Jerusalem as the mother of sin. His only remaining pleasure is "what he imbibes from decieving a Victim" (*J* 65:59).

To save the marriage, the Emanation must renounce her thirst for dominion and sacrifice her selfishness; just as the male must also kill his Selfhood and sacrifice himself, to be absorbed in the Brotherhood which is Jesus.

The marital troubles of Los and Enitharmon continue until her heart is broken (*FZ* vii:323, 413) and she becomes Los's co-worker (*FZ* vii:467). When Brittannia wakes at last, she denounces herself as "the Jealous Wife" (*J* 94:26).

All living things have their Emanations, even nations (Jerusalem is the Emanation of England, and Shiloh of France), except the unborn and wandering Spectres (*FZ* vii:329, 400); therefore "counterparts" must be created for them (*FZ* vii:408). When Satan is born from the Hermaphrodite of War, he also lacks an Emanation (*FZ* viii:253). However, his Emanations are mentioned once (*Mil* 38:20), and Leutha seems to act that part for him.

The EMIM were that branch of the giant Anakim who lived in Moab (*Deut* ii:11). Blake mentions them among the giants dwelling in the Covering Cherub's stomach (*J* 89:47).

ENANTO is mentioned once, as the sixth daughter of Los and Enitharmon (*FZ* viii:364). From her position and from the similarity of names, it is probable that she is the Emanation of the sixth son, Ananton.

ENGLAND's position among the four British nations is East. Blake always uses the name to mean the literal land of his birth, except once (*J* 54:27), when he uses it to mean Brittannia, his symbolic name for England. See BRITTANNIA.

ENGLISH. In "When Klopstock England defied" (6) the poet calls himself "English Blake" (*K* 187).

"O when shall the Saxon return with the English, his redeemed brother?" (*J* 83:14). Just before the final apotheosis, Los beholds "The Briton, Saxon, Roman, Norman amalgamating in my Furnaces into One Nation, the English, & taking refuge in the Loins of Albion" (*J* 92:1)—that is, becoming one man again.

ENION is the Emanation of Tharmas. Their position is West, and their element Water. He represents the Body, that portion of us perceived by the five senses; she represents the Generative Instinct, or Lust. Their two names, as suggested by David Erdman (*Erd* 275, n. 27) and accepted by Margoliouth (*Marg Vala* 159), are taken from ENItharmON.

The Four Zoas opens with the coming of puberty, the difficult passage from Innocence to Experience, or the separation of Tharmas and Enion. Their struggles are the struggles of the growing lad when he discovers for the first time the power of his awakening sex, which he tries in agonized despair to suppress or control. As morality forbids the expression of his instincts, he discovers sin and guilt. Compulsions and repulsions develop, the world of the mind is explored, the world of matter is revealed, and the poetic powers are born.

When the epic opens, Enion, who is naturally coy (*FZ* ix:526, 543, 549), has already been seeking dominion (iii:78; *J* 29:60), and the new sense of guilt is operating. She has been killing Tharmas' Emanations, his "secret loves & Graces," not recognizing them as her own children (*FZ* i:25, 164). She is jealous of Enitharmon, though only through pity had Tharmas let her take refuge in his bosom (i:31); yet Enion murders her and hides her embalmed corse in her own bosom (i:525). She also takes Jerusalem (freedom) from his inmost soul (i:29), and concealing herself from Tharmas, weaves a hiding place for her (i:69).

When Enion is lost to him, Tharmas sinks into the sea (i:76 ff.); he flows among the woof of Enion's weaving, which animates with a life of its own and becomes the world of matter (Ulro). On her shining loom of Vegetation she draws the Spectre of Tharmas from his feet; it is the phallus, glorying in its strength and beauty, and completely selfish and cruel. As a result of their fierce struggles, she bears two children, Los and Enitharmon (the poetic faculty); then the rocks vegetate into the beauties of nature. (Later we learn that when Urthona fell, his Spectre, scorning the frail body, was born from Enion's brain through her nostrils—i:530; iv:105; vii: 277–95—while Los and Enitharmon were drawn down into her womb.)

The children flee from her; she follows weeping, blind, and age-bent. She utters the first of her magnificent laments, this one about the cruelty in the world of nature (i:445–60).

Henceforth, until the end of the epic, the aged Enion wanders in the void, hungry, wailing, while Tharmas seeks her in vain.

The dying Albion hears her voice, and resigning his scepter to Urizen, asks him what the voice is. Urizen, now lord, investigates and is terrified when he beholds the abyss where Enion laments (ii:4–18).

Los and Enitharmon plot to divide Urizen and Ahania, by letting her hear Enion's voice. Enion laments her errors and the cruelty of life in general. Ahania hears her; before dawn she is drawn to the margin of Non Entity, where she sees Enion, and thenceforth cannot rest (ii: 290, 420).

After Ahania is cast out, Tharmas rises from his ocean, taking human form, and seeking Enion, "ah, too near to cunning, too far off and yet too near"; he begins to hate her now, while she withers away to Entuthon Benython (the physical frame), "a world of deep darkness, where all things in horrors are rooted." Again she laments, begging Tharmas to leave her a little life. With mixed emotions, Tharmas bids her return, but she is now "only a voice eternal wailing in the Elements." Ahania also now wanders in the abyss (iii:169–211).

Tharmas remains in despair at her loss (iv:7; vi:273), but eventually begins to hope (vii:486) because of his meeting the Shadowy Female, whom he momentarily mistakes for Enion (vii b:228), and to whom he describes his original bliss in the garden of delight; but even there Enion turned away from him (vii b:228–35).

When Ahania is wailing, Enion replies to her from the caverns of the grave, but this time with hope. She herself has heard the midnight voice heralding the bridegroom; she foresees the coming of the Lamb, and the time when Man, now scattered through Nature, will reassume his ancient bliss (viii:534–83).

In the first day of the final apocalypse, the rejuvenated Vala while bathing sees into the world of waters. There Tharmas calls on Enion to return, "for Lo, I have calm'd my seas"; but her light fades, nor does she answer Vala's call. Then, when Vala returns to her house, she finds the two as children, whom she tends. Enion revives Tharmas by night, but in the daytime she still turns from him, and his loins fade. At Vala's direction, he leads Enion into Vala's garden, where "in infant sorrow & joy alternate" they play. "They are the shadows of Tharmas & of Enion in Vala's world" (ix:483–556).

This, however, is only a vision of what sex should be in the world of nature. The eternal Enion rises in the dawn of the third day, in a whirlwind, a shriek, and a rattling of bones reminiscent of the formation of Tharmas in the third Night. But she is like a gentle light; she casts off her death-clothes, for the winter is gone; and all nature is rejuvenated. Tharmas embraces her and raises her through the heavens, sounding his trumpet to awake the dead. Albion welcomes them to the feast (ix:590–620). At the end of the fifth day, the four Emanations rise from the feast, "in joy ascending to their Golden Looms" (ix: 779).

In the other two epics, Enion is mentioned only in casual references to her tale in *The Four Zoas*. She wanders "like a weeping inarticulate voice" (*Mil* 19:42). The four Emanations are named, and Enion is one of the three who are "evanescent shades" (*J* 14:10, 12). Albion hears her voice and repeats his question: "can love seek for dominion?" (*J* 29:59). Los protests against being born of Enion (*J* 83:5); nevertheless, Enitharmon and he are born as two infants wandering from Enion, "blind & age-bent, into the fourfold desarts" (*J* 86:63–87:1).

ENITHARMON is Spiritual Beauty, the twin, consort, and inspiration of the poet Los. Her name has been derived from the Greek *anarithmon* ("numberless") or from (*z*)*enith* plus (*h*)*armon*(*y*). From her name were derived the names of her earthly parents, as Margoliouth (*Marg Vala* 159) points out: ENItharmON. Her emblem is the Moon; her outstanding emotion is Pity.

Unlike the other three Emanations of the Zoas, Enitharmon is not an "evanescent shade": she is "a vegetated mortal Wife of Los, his Emanation, yet his Wife till the sleep of Death is past" (*J* 14:13). Her model on earth was Catherine Blake herself. "Here is Enitharmon's bower," Blake wrote to Butts (22 Nov 1802) from Surrey. In *The Four Zoas* (vii:469) she colors Los's designs.

Their position is North, for they were originally one as the Zoa Urthona. But when Los had given a form to Urizen, his "gentle passions" (*FZ* vii:279) or "pity" (*Ur* 19:1) grew away from him as a Globe of Blood, which developed into the first female form (*Ur* 13:51–59; 18:1–8; *FZ* iv:279; *Mil* 3:30; *J* 17:51; 86:50–54). At the horrible sight, Urthona fell from his anvil "even to the place of seed" (*FZ* vii:287), entering the womb of Enion as the two sexes. But scorning the frail body, his masculine spirit issued from Enion's brain through her nostrils, then returned to form a counterpart for the female; and in due time Los and Enitharmon were born of Enion (*FZ* vii:277–95; iv:84–106).

THE REPRESSION OF SEX UNDER ENITHARMON

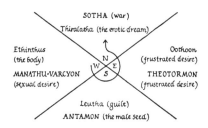

The movement is counterclockwise. Males are indicated by capital letters. When the sexual impulse is reduced to a mere dream (Thiralatha), the male (SOTHA) takes precedence again and explodes into War. (*Eur* 13:9 – 14:28)

Thus the birth of the poetic instinct is the result of the sexual struggles at the period of puberty (*FZ* i:181). "Two Wills they had, Two Intellects, & not as in times of old" (*J* 86:61). Los gives her her name (*FZ* i:249). At once Enitharmon declares her independence (*FZ* i:251) and announces that this is Woman's World: "Let Man's delight be Love, but Woman's delight be Pride. In Eden our loves were the same; here they are opposite. . . . This is Woman's World . . . I will Create secret places . . . A triple Female Tabernacle for Moral Law I weave, that he who loves Jesus may loathe, terrified, Female love, till God himself become a Male subservient to the Female" (*J* 87:16; 88:16–21). They are married "in discontent & scorn" while the demons of the deep sing the nuptial song of war (*FZ* i:376–441).

The first fruit of their union is Orc (revolution), for all true artists are revolutionists in one way or another. Los is jealous of his son; he chains him down on a mountain top (*Ur* 20:3–25; *FZ* v:79–103). Enitharmon's tears persuade Los to try and release Orc, but it cannot be done (*FZ* v:143–72). Afterwards Enitharmon "bore an enormous race" (*Ur* 20:45). "First Orc was Born, then the Shadowy Female: then All Los's Family. At last Enitharmon brought forth Satan, Refusing Form in vain" (*Mil* 3:40). In the long list of thirty-eight sons and eighteen daughters, "and myriads more" (*FZ* viii:357–67), which culminates in Milton and Mary, the name of Satan is only the fifteenth.

However, Enitharmon generally remains independent of Los. In *Europe* he appears at the beginning and the end, but the bulk of the book is devoted to "the night of Enitharmon's joy" (5:1), when she establishes her Woman's World with its false religion of chastity and vengeance— a religion of eighteen hundred years, which is the error of official Christianity. In *The Four Zoas* she plays the part of Eve in eating the apple and persuading Los to do likewise (vii:386–400) ; but soon she appreciates her husband's work and aids him at it (vii:446–75); and at the end Urthona is "no longer now divided from Enitharmon, no longer the Spectre Los" (ix:849). Throughout *Jerusalem* Enitharmon is separate from Los until the end, when she realizes that she must vanish: "The Poet's Song draws to its period, & Enitharmon is no more" (92:8), and her last words are a lament over the disobedience of her children (93:1–16).

By herself, Enitharmon is "the Eternal Female" (*MHH* 25:1), the Great Mother. She is the Moon of love to Los's Sun. She stamps with solid form the vigorous progeny of fires (*Eur* 2:8). At her looms in Cathedron she weaves the three Classes of men (*Mil* 2:26–3:1), and there her daughters weave beautiful bodies for the Spectres about to be born (*FZ* viii:209–17).

This creation of bodies is the creation of space. "Los is by mortals nam'd Time, Enitharmon is nam'd Space" (*Mil* 24:68). Spaces are protective: they are havens from justice and other woes. Thus she "form'd a Space for Satan & Michael & for the poor infected. Trembling she wept over the Space & clos'd it with a tender Moon" (*Mil* 8:43). Practically speaking, she forms a home, where the oppressed man finds a refuge from the Angry God of this World, as in the third illustration to Dante. For Enitharmon's Looking Glass, see LOOKING GLASS.

ENO (whose name is obviously an ana-gram of "eon") is the ability of seeing the eternity in all things. She perceives the world in the grain of sand and the spiritual meaning of the inspired Scriptures. She is thus the mother of all poetry. Her lament opens *The Book of Los*, and *The Four Zoas* is her song (*FZ* i:1–2).

In *The Book of Los* (3:1–26) she is called the "aged Mother, who the chariot of Leutha guides since the day of thunders in old time, sitting beneath the eternal Oak [of weeping]." She trembles and shakes the steadfast earth as she recollects the age of Innocence when the vices were the exuberance of virtues.

In *The Four Zoas* (i:222–26) she is a daughter of Beulah. When Los and Enitharmon were born, she drew out a Moment of Time into "seven thousand years with much care & affliction and many tears, & in every year made windows into Eden. She also took an atom of space & opened its centre into Infinitude & ornamented it with wondrous art." Los and Enitharmon delight in her moony spaces.

She reappears in *Jerusalem* (48:27–45), though there she is not named. She is now the concentration of all the Emanations of the Cathedral Cities, "an Aged pensive Woman." While the Daughters of Beulah watch, she draws out the Moment of Time into "a Rainbow of jewels and gold, a mild Reflection from Albion's dread Tomb." (The pillars of his couch are the inspired books of the Bible.) The rainbow is extended into eight thousand five hundred years, every two hundred years having a door into Eden. She also opens an Atom of Space "with dire pain opening it a Center into Beulah." The Daughters dry her tears; "she ardent embrac'd her sorrows, occupied in labours of sublime mercy." She sits, perusing Albion's Tomb; she walks among the ornaments, "solemn mourning." Los then sees her in his seventh Furnace, which is touched by the finger of God.

ENOCH, the son of Jared and seventh in

Adam's line, was both prophet and patriarch (*Gen* v:18; *Jude* 14). "And Enoch walked with God: and he was not; for God took him" (*Gen* v:24). This cryptic statement was interpreted to mean that God took Enoch still alive into heaven. "By faith Enoch was translated that he should not see death; and was not found, because God had translated him: for before his translation he had this testimony, that he pleased God" (*Heb* xi:5).

Enoch's translation was the first Biblical evidence for immortality, a point on which the writers of the Old Testament were obscure. Job, for example, believed that the grave was his final home: "I have said to corruption, Thou art my father: to the worm, Thou art my mother and my sister" (xvii:14), although he came to believe that after the destruction of his body, "in my flesh shall I see God" (xix:26). Blake depicted Job's state of mind in his lithograph (*ca.* 1807) "Job in Prosperity." Flooded with heavenly light, the sage ponders the problem, while holding on his lap an open book labelled (in Hebrew) "Enoch." On his right two floating figures hold a page with the Hebrew of the crucial text of *Genesis* v:24.

Enoch, holding the scroll of prophecy, follows the figures of Cain and Abel in the painting "Meditations Among the Tombs" (see Illustrations). Blake also made some unfinished sketches to illustrate the Apocryphal *Book of Enoch* (first translated in 1821), which describes the loves of the sons of God for the daughters of man.

Enoch is the seventh in the first group of the Twenty-seven Churches, the "Giants mighty, Hermaphroditic" (*Mil* 37:36; *J* 75:11). Hutton once is called "the Father of the Seven from Enoch to Adam" (*J* 7:25).

ENOS was the grandson of Adam and the son of Seth.

Blake names him as the third in the first group of the Twenty-seven Churches, the "Giants mighty, Hermaphroditic" (*Mil* 37:36; *J* 75:11).

ENTUTHON BENYTHON (or simply "Entuthon") is the physical frame of the generated man, "a world of deep darkness, where all things in horrors are rooted" (*FZ* iii:181). The Sons of Albion dwell here (*J* 5:12, 24). It belongs to Urizen (*J* 88:48).

It is a land of forests, deep vales, gloom (*FZ* iii:181; v:149; viii:269; *Mil* 19:35; 26:25; 27:43; *J* 5:24, 56; 14:34). It stands east of Golgonooza and contains the Lake of Udan-Adan (*FZ* viii:225; *Mil* 26:25), though elsewhere its forests are described as surrounding Golgonooza, but separated from it by the cultivated land of Allamanda (*Mil* 27:43; *J* 78:17). As a place of deep valleys it is described as "beneath" Golgonooza (*J* 14:34).

Into Bowlahoola, Allamanda, and Entuthon Benython, all uncreated souls descend to Los (*Mil* 37:59); here under the governorship of Rintrah and Palamabron, Orc and the uncreated souls wail (*Mil* 29:28). In Golgonooza, Enitharmon weaves for them the Web of Life, which descends into Entuthon's vales (*J* 83:74). But in Entuthon itself, Tirzah and her sisters weave the Web of Death (*Mil* 29:55).

In Entuthon Benython, the Lamb of God is judged and condemned (*FZ* viii:269). Here also Los sees Jerusalem (*J* 14:34), but here too the Sons of Albion give Vala power (*J* 78:17). In Golgonooza, Udan-Adan, and Entuthon, Los divides the Space of Love (*J* 88:47–48). After binding Orc, the repentant Los and Enitharmon travel for nine days through its gloom (*FZ* v:149). And here the Hermaphrodite stands glowing before Milton (*Mil* 19:35). Fearful warriors are there (*J* 5:12). When Albion falls, "all within is open'd into the deeps of Entuthon Benython, a dark and unknown night, indefinite, unmeasurable, without end, Abstract Philosophy warring in enmity against Imagination . . . And there Jerusalem wanders with Vala" (*J* 5:56–60); that is, Albion's interior opens outward into a physical form.

"Abstract Philosophy" is not an actual definition, but rather an extension of meaning, just as "Commerce" is not a definition of Allamanda.

EON is a contraction of "Emanation," thrice applied to Jerusalem (*Mil* 11:1; *J* 19:16; 40:41). It was probably suggested by the Gnostic term "aeon," an emanation from the Supreme Being.

EPHRAIM was the second son of Joseph and the younger brother of Manasseh. As the two were only grandsons of Jacob, they do not appear in the list of the Sons proper; but when Joseph's holdings were divided between them, they were named among the Tribes.

Ephraim and six other children of Israel left Los (prophetic inspiration) to wander with Tirzah (the laws of purity), and were generated (*Mil* 24:3). Ephraim and Menassheh (*sic*) gathered the Sons of Los together in the sands of Midian (*Mil* 24:20). Ephram (so the name is popularly pronounced) and six other Tribes are remembered by Jerusalem in their days of innocence (*J* 79:30). To Ephraim, Manasseh, and Benjamin are assigned the seven counties of Connaught, Ireland (*J* 72:23).

The land assigned to Ephraim lay in the center of Canaan, south of Manasseh's, from which it was separated by the river Kanah. It consisted of hill country, the valley of the Jordan, and the plain of Sharon.

To Tirzah and her ilk, the lands of these two brothers were a place of love. "Ephraim was a wilderness of joy where all my wild beasts ran. The river Kanah wander'd by my sweet Manasseh's side" (*FZ* viii:309; *J* 67:56). "Come thou to Ephraim! . . . Come then to Ephraim & Manasseh, O beloved-one!" (*Mil* 19:36; 20:3).

But to Jerusalem, the land of Ephraim contained "Mount Ephraim" (really a low hill) on which was Shiloh ("peace"), the sacred first site of the Tabernacle. "I walk to Ephraim. I seek for Shiloh" (*J* 79:10).

"O Shiloh of Mount Ephraim" (*J* 85:22). Mount Ephraim calls to Mount Zion (*FZ* i:386).

The hills of Ephraim are mentioned (*J* 68:22), also its valleys (*J* 68:35).

EPHRATAH is another name for Bethlehem, the birthplace of Jesus. When David was seeking a place for the Ark, the habitation for the mighty God of Jacob, "Lo, we heard of it at Ephratah: we found it in the fields of the wood" (*Psalm* cxxxii:6).

"The City of the Woods in the Forest of Ephratah is taken" (*J* 29:18).

EPICURUS (342?–270 B.C.) taught that pleasure is the only good and is the purpose of all morality. This tenet caused his philosophy to be denounced, especially by those who overlooked his corollary that true pleasure depends on a life of justice, prudence, and honor. His philosophy was essentially egocentric, however, and dealt only with life in this world, finding no need for a God or an Eternity.

When Lavater (366) wrote: "The purest religion is the most refined Epicurism. He, who in the smallest given time can *enjoy* most of what he never shall repent, and what furnishes enjoyments, still more unexhausted, still less changeable—is the most religious and the most voluptuous of men," Blake commented: "True Christian philosophy" (*K* 75). But later he altered his opinion. In his annotations on Bacon, he wrote: "Every Body Knows that this is Epicurus and Lucretius & Yet Every Body says, that it is Christian Philosophy; how is this Possible?" (*K* 397). "Bacon was a Contemplative Atheist. Evidently an Epicurean" (*K* 403). His annotations on Reynolds repeat his charges: "Bacon's Philosophy has Ruin'd England. Bacon is only Epicurus over again" (*K* 456). "Here is a Plain Confession that [Reynolds] Thinks Mind & Imagination not to be above the Mortal & Perishing Nature. Such is the End of Epicurean or Newtonian Philosophy; it is Atheism" (*K* 475).

"Denying Eternity by the Atheistical Epicurean Philosophy of Albion's Tree" (J 67:12).

Suction the Epicurean is one of the three philosophers in *An Island in the Moon* (K 44). He denounces mathematics and philosophy. "I hate reasoning. I do everything by my feelings" (K 50). He calls early for rum and water; and later proposes that they all get drunk.

ERIN (the ancient name of Ireland) is the Western nation of the British Isles. It is separated from the other three nations of Britain by the Atlantic, just as America is separated from the other three continents.

Erin symbolizes Blake's belief in the holiness of the body and its instincts. (Usually he distinguishes Erin, his philosophy of love, from Ireland, the place.) She is the first product of Los's furnaces (J 9:34; 11:8–12). Her spaces reach from the starry height to the starry depth (J 12:23).

The selfish materialized Spectre creates a substitute parody, "a Sexual Machine, an Aged Virgin Form in Erin's Land toward the north," and calls it Religion (J 44:25).

When Jerusalem bursts from Albion's bosom, the Daughters of Beulah receive and weep over her in "the Spaces of Erin, in the Ends of Beulah" (J 48:51). Erin then addresses them (J 48:53–50:18). Her rainbow (the spiritualized body, promise of immortality) encloses the wheels of Albion's Sons (J 50:23). The Daughters of Beulah respond by calling upon the Lamb to take away the remembrance of Sin (forgiving and forgetting), and in a deeper sense the feeling of Guilt (J 50:24–30).

Blake sees Dinah, the youthful form of Erin, beautiful but terrible, arise from the Four Zoas (J 74:54). The Emanations weave the looms of Beulah for Jerusalem and Shiloh, "concentering in the majestic form of Erin" (J 86:45). The "little lovely Allegoric Night of Albion's Daughters" (ordinary marriage) expands through all the world of Erin (J 88:31). Erin watches at the Tomb of Albion (J 94:13). Albion's Sons surround the forty-two gates of Erin in their war against Jerusalem and the Lamb. Jerusalem's twelve gates are thrown down and filled with blood from Japan to Erin's continent (J 78:12, 27).

When Albion awakes, "his right elbow leans on the Rocks of Erin's Land, Ireland, ancient nation" (Mil 39:44).

The ERYTHREAN (or Red) Sea, according to Jacob Bryant (*New System*, 3rd ed., 1807; see BRYANT), was not the Red Sea around the peninsula of Sinai, which the Israelites crossed (IV, 236), but is the Indian Ocean (IV, 290; V, 228) from which the sun rises (V, 84). He also calls it "the great Southern Sea" (IV, 238).

Blake, who calls it "the Great South Sea" (Mil 29:63) and "the Red Sea," places it beyond Japan, where it "terminates the World of Generation & Death" (J 89:49). Here, men's "Uncircumcision in Heart & Loins" shall be lost forever when "they shall arise from Self by Self Annihilation" (J 49:44). All other references are to Blake's customary sweep across the eastern hemisphere, from the Atlantic to the Erythrean (Mil 29:63; J 24:46, 63; 83:22; 89:49).

ESAU was the older brother of Jacob, who cheated him of his birthright and his father's blessing. His land was the wilderness of Edom, and his descendants the Edomites. See EDOM.

Blake refers to Esau once as an example of the strife between brothers (J 73:28).

ESHER was a village in Surrey, near Walton upon Thames, fourteen and a half miles southwest of London.

"From the Valleys of Walton & Esher . . . Jerusalem's Pillars fall" (J 68:44).

ESOP. "The wisest of the Ancients consider'd what is not too Explicit as the fittest for Instruction, because it rouzes the faculties to act. I name Moses, Solomon, Esop, Homer, Plato" (To Trusler, 23 Aug 1799).

ESSEX is a maritime county in the southeast of England.

With the adjoining counties of Norfolk and Suffolk, it is assigned to Reuben (*J* 16:44). These three counties, with four others, are assigned to Skofeld (*J* 71:38).

ESTRILD (Estrildis) was the first love of King Locrine. When he married Guendoloena for reasons of state, he kept Estrildis in secret; their child was Sabre (Sabrina). After his father-in-law's death, he divorced his first wife, and made Estrildis his queen. But the enraged Guendoloena raised an army, slew her husband in battle, and drowned Estrildis with her daughter in the Severn (*Geof* II, 1–6).

In the original list of the Daughters of Albion, Estrild is the ninth (*FZ* ii:62); but in the revised list she is the tenth, one of the seven who unite in Rahab (*J* 5:44). She is the Emanation of Kox. "Join'd with Cordella she shines southward over the Atlantic" (*J* 71:43).

"Hackney and Holloway sicken for Estrild & Ignoge" (*J* 21:33).

ETERNAL PROPHET. See LOS.

ETERNALS. See DIVINE FAMILY.

ETERNITY is what always is, the reality underlying all temporal phenomena, the *nunc stans* of St. Thomas Aquinas. It is vulgarly supposed to be an endless prolongation of Time, to begin in the future; it is instead the annihilation of Time, which is limited to this temporal world; in short, Eternity is the real Now.

"Eternity Exists, and All Things in Eternity" (*LJ*, *K* 614). Whatever was, is, and shall be is there. "Every thing exists & not one sigh nor smile nor tear, one hair nor particle of dust, not one can pass away" (*J* 13:66–14:1). Nothing real can have a literal beginning. Man "pre-existed" before his creation in Eden, which was only his materializing, an episode of his Fall.

Eternity is Truth. "Error is Created. Truth is Eternal. Error, or Creation, will be Burned up, & then, & not till Then, Truth or Eternity will appear" (*LJ*, *K* 617). "Whatever can be Created can be Annihilated: Forms cannot: the Oak is cut down by the Ax, the Lamb falls by the Knife, but their Forms Eternal Exist Forever" (*Mil* 32:36).

The Arts discover and record Eternal Truth. "In Eternity, the Four Arts . . . are the Four Faces of Man" (*Mil* 27:55). The poet (or prophet) who penetrates to the human fundamentals sees past, present, and future simultaneously (*J* 15:8). For example, Chaucer's characters are "the characters which compose all ages and nations: as one age falls, another rises, different to mortal sight, but to immortals only the same . . . Accident ever varies, Substance can never suffer change nor decay. . . . they are the physiognomies or lineaments of universal human life" (*DesC* III, *K* 567).

Eternity lies behind Nature also. Nature is a projection of Man; all its Forms are human. The rising constellations, the dancing flies, the mountain trees, the thunderstorm are "the Sons of Los: These the Visions of Eternity; but we see only as it were the hem of their garments when with our vegetable eyes we view these wondrous Visions" (*Mil* 26:10). "The Visions of Eternity, by reason of narrowed perceptions, are become weak Visions of Time & Space" (*J* 49:21). "The Vegetative Universe opens like a flower from the Earth's center in which is Eternity. It expands in Stars to the Mundane Shell and there it meets Eternity again, both within and without" (*J* 13:34).

The Divine Substance is the substance of everything. "Eternal Things . . . All Springing from the Divine Humanity. All beams from him" (*LJ*, *K* 612). "This world of Imagination is the world of Eternity; it is the divine bosom into which we shall all go after the death of the Vegetated body. . . . There Exist in that Eternal World the Permanent Realities of Every Thing which we see reflected in this Vegetable Glass of Nature. All Things are comprehended in their Eternal Forms in the divine body of the Saviour . . . The Human Imagination" (*LJ*, *K* 605). "Our own Imaginations [are] those Worlds of Eternity in which we shall live for ever in Jesus our Lord" (*Mil* 1).

Each Individual is immortal. "Each Identity is Eternal . . . it retains its own Individuality" (*LJ*, *K* 607). "In Great Eternity every particular Form gives forth or Emanates its own peculiar Light, & the Form is the Divine Vision and the Light is his Garment. This is Jerusalem in every Man . . . And Jerusalem is called Liberty" (*J* 54:1). "Every thing in Eternity shines by its own Internal light" (*Mil* 10: 16).

Eternity is a place of great activity. Man is "a traveller thro' Eternity" (*Mil* 15:22, 35). Man passes through the States like a traveller (*LJ*, *K* 606). "Every Man . . . went still going forward thro' the Bosom of the Father in Eternity on Eternity" (*Mil* 31:4).

"The Treasures of Heaven are not Negations of Passion, but Realities of Intellect, from which all the Passions Emanate Uncurbed in their Eternal Glory" (*LJ*, *K* 615). The sexes do not exist there, as each Individual has already absorbed and synthesized his feminine portion (*J* 30:33; 34:15; 92:13). The great activity therefore consists in the hunting of Ideas and the mental warfare between them (*Mil* 35:2), "the great Wars of Eternity, in fury of Poetic Inspiration" (*Mil* 30:19). But they are not wars of hatred. "For the Soldier who fights for Truth calls his enemy his brother: they fight & contend for life & not for eternal death" (*J* 43:41). "Our wars are wars of life, & wounds of love with intellectual spears, & long winged arrows of thought. Mutual in one another's love and wrath all renewing we live as One Man" (*J* 38:14). "One must die for another throughout all Eternity" (*Mil* 11:18). "Such are the Laws of Eternity, that each shall mutually Annihilate himself for others' good" (*Mil* 38:35).

Blake's great task therefore was "to open the Eternal Worlds, to open the immortal Eyes of Man inwards into the Worlds of Thought, into Eternity ever expanding in the Bosom of God, the Human Imagination" (*J* 5:18).

ETHINTHUS is the first of the eight children summoned by Enitharmon after her sleep of eighteen hundred years. They represent the progressive frustration of sex under the domination of the female. The cycle runs counterclockwise, from Ethinthus in the West to Thiralatha in the North, for the restriction of sex is against nature. It will be noted that in the listing, the female takes precedence of the male. See ENITHARMON, diagram.

Ethinthus (west) is the mortal flesh; her attributes are the grave-worm and water; she is love reduced to the physical act. Her consort Manathu-Varcyon is the flesh's "flames of soft delusion." The next pair (south) are Leutha and Antamon (the rainbow and the cloud): Leutha, "sweet, smiling pestilence," is sex under the domination of Reason (that is, Sin), while Antamon, "prince of the pearly dew," is the male seed. The third pair (east) are the hapless lovers Oothoon and Theotormon, suffering the tortures of separation. In the last pair (north), the male recovers his precedence: he is Sotha, or war, the physical outbreak of frustrated sex; she is Thiralatha, the erotic dream, the last effort of the starved imagination (*Eur* 13:16–14:28).

Ethinthus is eighth in the list of the Daughters of Los and Enitharmon (*FZ* viii:364), but the name of her consort, apparently by a slip of the pen, precedes her as the seventh daughter. It would seem that Blake, associating the names, wrote them both down, possibly as a reminder to insert the male in the list of the Sons when he revised the passage.

Ethinthus is mentioned once in *Jerusalem*: "where was the burying-place of soft Ethinthus? near Tyburn's fatal Tree?" (12: 25). The builders of Golgonooza would resurrect the flesh that has been punished as a criminal and buried near the gallows.

ETHIOPIA, in Africa, is the eighteenth of the Thirty-two Nations which shall defend liberty and rule the rest of the world (*J* 72:40). Jerusalem beholds the liberation of the Negroes: "The swarthy sons of Ethiopia stood round the Lamb of God enquiring for Jerusalem; he led them up my steps to my altar" (*J* 79:51). Ethiopia supports the pillars of Urizen's temple (*J* 58:35). It is included in the brain of the Covering Cherub (*J* 89:16).

ETRUSCAN COLUMN the Antiquarian is a character in Chapter i of *An Island in the Moon*, where he provokes a quarrel over Voltaire, denouncing him as "an errant blockhead." Harper (p. 40) cleverly conjectures that he might be the Rev. John Brand (1744–1806), a friend of Flaxman's. He had come to London in 1784 as rector of the combined parishes of St. Mary-at-Hill and St. Mary Hubbard. In the same year he was appointed secretary of the Society of Antiquaries and was re-elected annually until his death. His best-known publication was *Observations on Popular Antiquities* (1777).

The EUPHRATES was the fourth river flowing (north) out of Eden, on which Babylon, the worldly city of warfare and lust, was founded. See EDEN.

The references to warfare are as follows. "On the Euphrates Satan stood | And over Asia stretch'd his pride" (*J* 27:47). Jerusalem weeps upon Euphrates' banks (*J* 78:27). "Tell me . . . why Euphrates is red with blood" (*J* 79:68). Vala complains that Jerusalem is shaking her towers on Euphrates (*J* 31:59). Vala's laments are heard from Arnon and Jordan to Euphrates (*J* 80:9).

The Daughters of Albion are particularly attracted to Babylon. Gwendolen "took a Fals[e]hood & hid it in her left hand to entice her sisters away to Babylon

on Euphrates" (*J* 82:17). Los watches the Sons of Albion "that a place be prepar'd on Euphrates" (*J* 83:63). The Daughters build Babylon on Euphrates (*J* 84:8) and ask Los: "let thy voice be heard upon Euphrates" (*J* 84:28).

The looms of the daughters of Zelophehad cover "the whole Earth . . . Europe to Euphrates & Hindu to Nile" (*Mil* 35:14, 16). Seven of the Daughters of Albion are united into Rahab in the Covering Cherub on Euphrates (*J* 5:42). His loins "inclose Babylon on Euphrates beautiful" (*J* 89:38).

The Euphrates runs under the arches of Urizen's temple (*J* 58:24). The repentant Mary is like a river "Emanating into gardens & palaces upon Euphrates" (*J* 61:30).

EUROPE is one of the four continents. As its position is North, it represents the realm of the Imagination. In the cycle of continents indicated by *The Song of Los*, it stands third, being preceded by America and followed by Asia. It is cut off from America (the body) by the Atlantic. It looks anxiously towards America on occasion; but it is connected with Asia. As Blake believed that whatever happens in Europe affects Asia, they are frequently mentioned together.

EUROPE[,] A PROPHECY[.] *Lambeth*[,] *Printed by Will: Blake: 1794* is a handsome book, when complete consisting of eighteen plates. Twelve copies are known. It is a sequel to, and sometimes bound up with, *America, a Prophecy*. The other two continents appear in *The Song of Los*, which Blake intended to be a title for all four, the song sung to "four harps" (*SoL* 3:2). "Africa" precedes *America*, while "Asia" continues *Europe*.

The "Preludium" of *Europe* continues the myth of Orc from the "Preludium" of *America*; it consists chiefly of the lament of the Shadowy Female over the incessant fertility and cruelty of Nature, but it ends with a comforting prevision of the Nativity of him who shall bring salvation to all, including the world of matter.

The Prophecy then opens with the birth of Jesus and the world peace at that time (quoting from Milton's "Hymn to the Nativity"). Two themes are then developed, both of them errors of official Christianity.

The first of these is the triumph of the Female Will over the male by means of the false doctrine that sex is sin. For Urizen has escaped from his fetters into the North; and Los, having announced that now strong Urthona (himself) takes his rest, unobtrusively disappears, leaving Enitharmon free to establish her will.

She begins by entering the red light of Orc (becoming aggressively independent); she then announces that "Woman's love is Sin" (5:5) and bids her sons Rintrah and Palamabron, with their now jealous Emanations, to proclaim it to the human race. She then falls into a "female dream" for eighteen hundred years—a round number, covering the Christian era to Blake's time. Presently she laughs in her sleep to see every man bound and "Thou Shalt Not" written over the doors. When at last she wakes, she evokes four pairs of her children, who represent the unnatural debasement and starvation of sex, in a cycle running backwards, or counterclockwise, from west to north. The first pair consists of Ethinthus, "queen of waters," and her consort Manathu-Varcyon with his "flames of soft delusion"; then follow Leutha, "sweet smiling pestilence," and Antamon, "prince of the pearly dew" (the male seed); Oothoon and Theotormon, the baffled lovers; and finally Sotha and Thiralatha. Thiralatha is the sexual dream, the last effort of the starved imagination, while Sotha is the spirit of violence (war) into which frustrated sex is transformed. See ENITHARMON, diagram.

The other error of official Christianity is its materialism, which also begins with Enitharmon. Having closed the chief gate (sex) into Eternity, she relegates Eternity and its bliss to a future time and place which do not exist, the supposed heaven after death. Her words are: "an Eternal life awaits the worms of sixty winters in an allegorical [false] abode where existence hath never come" (5:6).

Eventually Europe is divided between revolution and counter-revolution (the American Revolution specifically, but with the Reformation and the Puritan Revolution behind it). The council house of Albion collapses, and the new materialistic philosophy of Bacon is constructed, the serpent-temple at Verulam. Urizen opens his brazen book, which organizes society under "One King, One God, One Law." Religion becomes tyrannous, debased, canting. Albion's Guardian tries in vain to bring all to judgment, until Newton finally blows the Trumpet—i.e., completes the three-dimensional philosophy of materialism.

Then the revolution reaches France, and Los, reappearing, calls all his sons to the "strife of blood."

About 1795 Blake added as preface the charming poem "Five windows light the cavern'd Man." A fairy, sitting on a streaked tulip (which reminds one of Dr. Johnson's tulip, whose streaks he disdained to count), sings of the five senses through which Eternity may be perceived. The cavern, of course, is Plato's, which Blake identified with the skull. The fifth sense is Touch (sex): "Thro' one himself pass out what time he please; but he will not, for stolen joys are sweet & bread eaten in secret pleasant." Man can actually enter Eternity through the union of true love; but he prefers secret dalliance with the foolish woman of *Proverbs* (ix:13–18): "Whoso is simple, let him turn in hither: and as for him that wanteth understanding, she saith to him, Stolen waters are sweet, and bread eaten in secret pleasant. But he knoweth not that the dead are there; and that her guests are in the depths of hell."

Blake then asks the fairy: "what is the material world, and is it dead?" The fairy replies with a vision of Nature which is flatly opposed to that of the Shadowy Female: it is the vision of the artist, as contrasted with that of the materialist. The fairy tells the poet that this world is all alive, and "every particle of dust breathes forth its joy." He also shows Blake the eternal forms of the wild flowers he plucks. So Blake takes him home where, sitting on the parlor table, the fairy dictates *Europe*. (He who knows the eternal joys is the more aware of the miseries of this world.)

The illustrations to *Europe* are chiefly concerned with the woes of the fallen world. The famous frontispiece depicts Urizen striking its bounds with his brazen compasses. The title page is decorated with the coiling serpent of Nature. There are full-page illustrations of Famine and the Plague; others represent Treachery, Cruelty, War, the Blighted Harvest, and Imprisonment.

EVE, the first woman, was extracted from Adam's side while he slept. It was the Divine Mercy, and not Urizen, who created woman; Jesus did it "That Himself may in process of time be born Man to redeem" (*J* 42:34). This division of the sexes, however, introduced Generation and Death.

In *The Ghost of Abel*, Eve acts as Adam's Emanation. It is she who recognizes that the Ghost is not the true Abel; and when Jehovah is manifest, it is she who with her mind's eye sees that Abel is living, and knows that it is better to believe Vision, though they are fallen and lost.

In *The Four Zoas* (viii), Los and Enitharmon play the roles of Adam and Eve in plucking the fatal fruit. Between Adam and Eve, Satan puts the veil of morality which the Saviour rends (*J* 55:11).

"A Vegetated Christ & a Virgin Eve are the Hermaphroditic Blasphemy" (*J* 90:34). "Eve" is here a cautious substitute for "Mary."

"Since Eve first chose her hellfire spark" ("When Klopstock England defied" 24, *K* 187) treats her first encounter with the Serpent as a flirtation.

Los forbids any individual to try to copy any other person, including Eve (*J* 90: 30).

The EVERLASTING GOSPEL is an unfinished poem (1818 or later), whose fragments are scattered through the *Note-Book*. The meter is hudibrastic iambic tetrameter, treated with extreme freedom. It contains some of Blake's most telling couplets.

"Everlasting Gospel" signified to Blake the essential ethics of man, which always existed but was first formulated by Jesus. Its basis is the Forgiveness of Sins; its opposite is the conventional system of moral virtues, which are based on the Punishment of Sins.

The body of the poem is devoted to proving that Jesus was not "meek and mild" but rather a heroic rebel against established religion. It is an extension of the theory found in the last "Memorable Fancy" of *The Marriage of Heaven and Hell* that Jesus in one way or another broke all of the Ten Commandments. "Jesus was all virtue, and acted from impulse, not from rules"; he did not honor his parents; he declared that humility, even to God, was wrong; and in saving the adulterous woman from execution he exalted unchastity.

"EVERY THING THAT LIVES IS HOLY" proclaims the sanctity of all life. It is the final line of the "Song of Liberty" (*MHH* 25) and is repeated in *Visions of the Daughters of Albion* (8:10) and *America* (8:13). When annotating Lavater (about 1788), Blake had written in capitals by the 309th aphorism, "ALL LIFE IS HOLY" (*K* 74).

EVIL is not an absolute: it is an error, a delusion, a quality springing from the mistaken division of Good and Evil.

"Every thing possible to be believ'd is an image of truth" (*MHH* 8:18), as every belief is a reflection of something in the human mind. But it is an image only.

"What seems to Be, Is, To those to whom it seems to Be, & is productive of the most dreadful Consequences to those to whom it seems to Be, even of Torments, Despair, Eternal Death" (*J* 36:51).

EXETER is the fourth of the Twenty-four Cathedral Cities (*J* 40:61). It is under Urizen and Verulam. The Polypus' head is in Verulam and extends through Rochester, Chichester, Exeter, and Salisbury to Bristol (*J* 67:36).

EXPERIENCE. See INNOCENCE.

The EYE is the second of the four special senses in their counterclockwise creation from the "parent sense" the Tongue (west) to the Ear (north). Its compass-point is south (*J* 12:59; 98:16); its Zoa is Urizen; its art is architecture.

Originally, like the three other senses, Sight was universally diffused through the whole being (as Touch still is), but in the Fall it became localized and turned outward. "Then turn'd the fluxile eyes into two stationary orbs, concentrating all things" (*Eur* 10:11). Sight is "a little narrow orb, clos'd up & dark, scarcely beholding the great light, conversing with the Void" (*Mil* 5:21) or "with the ground" (*J* 49:34). Lids have been made to grow over the eyes "like veils of tears" (*J* 66:31).

However, one need not be limited to "the Vegetated Mortal Eye's perverted & single vision" (*J* 53:11), if one looks "not with but through the eye," a phrase which Blake may have taken from Plato's *Theaetetus*. This ability consists in that spontaneous translating of the visible into human qualities, the process now called "empathy." All the arts are based on this power. The poem in Blake's letter to Butts (22 Nov 1802) describes how Blake's outward eye saw a thistle, while his inward eye beheld it as a cross old man. " 'What,' it will be Question'd, 'When the Sun rises, do you not see a round disk of fire somewhat like a Guinea?' O no, no, I see an Innumerable company of the Heavenly host crying, 'Holy, Holy, Holy is the Lord God Almighty.' I question not my Corporeal or Vegetative Eye any more than I would Question a Window concerning a Sight. I look thro' it & not with it" (*LJ*, *K* 617).

The EYES OF GOD are seven, according to *Zechariah* (iv:10) : "those seven . . . are the eyes of the Lord, which run to and fro through the whole earth." In *Revelation* (v:6) they are the seven eyes of the Lamb, "which are the seven Spirits of God sent forth into all the earth." In popular thought, they are the seven archangels, and Blake identified them with the seven Angels of the Presence, who watch and guard mankind (*Mil* 20:46; 24:7).

These seven Eyes are the whole course of human thought in its search for an ideal by which to live; they are also the path of Experience fixed for the Individual by the Divine Mercy, so that proceeding through his errors he must eventually reach the true God. They are established by the Eternals. The immediate object is to find one who will sacrifice himself for Satan.

The first Eye is Lucifer, the complete egotist (such as we all are born) ; he "refus'd to die for Satan & in pride he forsook his charge" (*FZ* viii:399). The next three represent the infernal system of Justice, inverted in the order of its discovery: (2) Molech, the Executioner, who would solve problems by annihilating all opposition, fails through impatience; (3) Elohim, the Judge (definer of guilt), who creates Satan and Adam, then faints, wearied; (4) Shaddai, the Accuser, who fails through anger. The result is (5) Pahad (Pachad), the state of bewildered terror at the results of Justice. Next is the attempt at order: (6) Jehovah, the law-giver, who becomes leprous, seeking to grasp Eternity. Finally (7) Jesus, who abrogates the whole system with the Forgiveness of Sins, and is sacrificed to Satan.

Blake listed the Eyes thrice (*FZ* viii:398–406; *Mil* 13:17–27; *J* 55:31). In *Milton* and *Jerusalem*, a mysterious Eighth is added to the list: he is the Individual himself, whose "Sleeping Body . . . now arose and walk'd with them in Eden, as an Eighth Image Divine tho' darken'd and tho' walking as one walks in sleep, and the Seven comforted and supported him" (*Mil* 15:4). God would be incomplete without the Individual. "They nam'd the Eighth: he came not, he hid in Albion's Forests" (J 55:33).

"The Lark [the inspiration which comes at dawn] is Los's Messenger thro' the Twenty-seven Churches, that the Seven Eyes of God, who walk even to Satan's Seat thro' all the Twenty-seven Heavens, may not slumber nor sleep" (Mil 35:63). The twenty-eight Larks "all night consult with Angels of Providence & with the Eyes of God all night in slumbers inspired" (Mil 36:4).

The seven Eyes of God are represented on the title page of the Illustrations of the Book of Job, and are the structure of the fundamental idea: Lucifer, Plates 1–2; Molech, 3–4; Elohim, 5–6; Shaddai, 7–8; Pahad, 9–10; Jehovah, 11–12; Jesus, 13–14. Then the system is reversed: Jehovah, 15; Jesus, 16; Pahad, 17; Shaddai, 18; Elohim, 19; Molech, 20; and Lucifer, 21. In the Whirlwind (13), the form of the Eighth can be just discerned.

EZEKIEL was the most imaginative of the major prophets. During his Babylonian captivity, he beheld his visions on the bank of the river Chebar.

His vision of the Four Living Creatures became the Four Beasts of Revelation and the Four Zoas of Blake (J 12:58). His magnificent denunciation of the prince of Tyre was applied by the Church Fathers to Satan, and gave Blake his Covering Cherub. His vision of the four-square city on the River of Life and the return of the Twelve Tribes underlies much of Jerusalem. Blake names him as one of the seven prophets and patriarchs whom Los creates to offset the evil kings (J 73:40). He quotes Ezekiel (iii:9) in a letter to Butts (6 July 1803) and refers to it again (xxxviii:8) in A Vision of the Last Judgment (K 609).

In the third "Memorable Fancy" of The Marriage of Heaven and Hell (Plates 12–13), Isaiah and Ezekiel dine with Blake. Ezekiel explains his denunciations of neighboring kingdoms as denunciations of their false gods, and his lying so long on one side and the other, and his eating of dung, as prompted by "the desire of raising other men into a perception of the infinite."

Blake made pictures of the Four Living Creatures appearing to Ezekiel, the Valley of Dry Bones, and the death of Ezekiel's wife.

EZRA wrote the fifteenth book of the Old Testament. He was the priest who played a prominent part in the return from Babylon and the rebuilding of the Temple at Jerusalem; he also strove to dissolve the mixed marriages of the faithful.

In a letter to Flaxman (12 Sept 1800), which contains a poem concerning his mental development, Blake mentions him as an early influence: "Ezra came with Isaiah."

F

FAIRIES, in the lyrics "A fairy leapt upon my knee" (*K* 188), "Motto to the Songs of Innocence and Experience" (*K* 183), *Long John Brown* (*K* 434), and *William Bond* (*K* 434), are spirits of sexual delight—"rulers of the vegetable world" like those of Chaucer and Shakespeare (*DesC* III, *K* 570). The fairy who dictates *Europe* tells of the eternal joys discovered by opening the senses, especially Touch (sex). In the illustrations to *Il Penseroso*, fairies circle about young Milton's head in his dream of repressed sex (see Illustrations). ("I will tell you what Joseph of Arimathea" is apparently a fragment: we never learn what he said to Blake's fairy.)

Fairies are mentioned only once in *The Four Zoas* (i:19), in a late interpolation, where the Emanations of Los are called "Fairies of Albion, afterwards Gods of the Heathen." This might put them in the North. But in *Milton* and *Jerusalem* they are placed South (*J* 13:29) in the quaternary of the Four Elements: Fairies, Nymphs, Gnomes, and Genii (*Mil* 31:20; *J* 13:26–29; 36:37), the spirits animating the world of matter. When the Zoas fell, they divided into these "Four ravening deathlike Forms" (*J* 36:36). They are "unforgiving & unalterable . . . the Gods of the Kingdoms of the Earth in contrarious and cruel opposition, Element against Element, opposed in War . . . a Corporeal Strife"; "in the aggregate" they are Satan and Rahab (*Mil* 31:18–25). Time is "the work of Fairy hands of the Four Elements" (*Mil* 28:60). Sixty-four thousand Fairies guard the southern gate of Golgonooza (*J* 13:29).

One evening at Felpham, Blake saw a fairy funeral. "I was walking alone in my garden, there was great stillness among the branches and flowers and more than common sweetness in the air; I heard a low and pleasant sound, and I knew not whence it came. At last I saw the broad leaf of a flower move, and underneath I saw a procession of creatures of the size and colour of green and gray grasshoppers, bearing a body laid out on a rose leaf, which they buried with songs, and then disappeared. It was a fairy funeral" (Allan Cunningham, "Life of Blake," 1830, in *Symons*, p. 409).

FAYETTE. See LAFAYETTE.

FELPHAM is a village on the south coast of West Sussex, too unimportant to be mentioned in my old copy of Baedeker. It is sixty-odd miles from London. In *Milton*, Blake calls it a "Vale" ten times. Here Blake hired a thatched cottage from one Grinder, host of the Fox Inn, for three years at £20 a year. It was about a hundred yards from "The Turret," the "marine villa" where dwelt his new patron, the poet and connoisseur William Hayley. The Blakes lived in the cottage from September 18, 1800 to September 1803, although it was very damp and afflicted Catherine with rheumatism and ague. But they had "a fine view of the sea" a few furlongs away. There was a beach where Blake's wife and sister liked to bathe, and where he had his "first Vision of Light" (To Butts, 2 Oct 1800). In front of the cottage was a small vegetable garden enclosed by a low flint wall. Here one night

Blake beheld a fairy funeral (see FAIR-IES), and one dawn had the stupendous mystical experience recorded in *Milton*. It was also from this garden that he ejected the drunken soldier Scholfield, who caused him to be tried for high treason.

There were wheat fields stretching to the sea; and Blake mentions riding every morning with Hayley "over the fields of corn" (*Epig* 3:23, *K* 537), Blake bestriding the pony Bruno. There were gentle hills of flocks and herds (*J* 71:12; 79:18); the "lambs bleat to the sea-fowls' cry" (*J* 40:51) —the famous South Down breed. A mile away to the east, behind a tongue of land, lay Bognor, just being built up as a fashionable watering place. To the west the bay was terminated by Selsey Hill, seven miles south of the cathedral city of Chichester.

"For when Los join'd with me he took me in his fi'ry whirlwind: my Vegetated portion was hurried from Lambeth's shades, he set me down in Felpham's Vale & prepar'd a beautiful Cottage for me, that in three years I might write all these Visions" (*Mil* 36:21). "In Felpham I heard and saw the Visions of Albion" (*J* 38:41).

These visions are forecast in a repeated prophecy that Milton "should up ascend forwards from Ulro from the Vale of Felpham" (*Mil* 20:59; 23:37). They begin with the descent of Ololon (*Mil* 36:26), an event pictured on Plate 36; Alexander Gilchrist remarks that the sketch of the cottage "bears no accurate resemblance to the real place," although Blake labelled it as such. The visions then continue to the end, when Jesus enters Albion's bosom. Blake falls unconscious for a moment on the garden path, recovering to find his wife standing by him.

One of Blake's rare landscapes is a pencil and water-color sketch, now at the Tate Gallery, which shows Hayley's "Turret" and a cottage, probably Blake's.

FEMALE, SHADOWY. See SHAD-OWY FEMALE.

FEMALE WILL. See WILL.

FÉNELON (François de Salignac de La Mothe, 1651–1715), archbishop, author, and the leading liberal of his time, became an advocate of the mystical quietism practised by Madame Guyon and others. This was an attempt to rise above all dogmas, sacraments, and ceremonies by emptying the soul of all will, thought, and feeling (the *via negationis*), until the Mystical Union was achieved. Fénelon's *Maximes des Saintes sur la vie intérieure* studied the practice. But this bypassing of all the elaborate machinery of the Church roused the wrath of Bossuet. Fénelon's book was part cause of his fall from the royal favor, although when the Pope condemned the book, he submitted.

Fénelon was the first to foresee the coming ruin of France. Preaching the Brotherhood of Man, he attacked autocracy, nationalism, wars, trade barriers, and the like.

"Fenelon, Guion, Teresa, Whitefield & Hervey . . . with all the gentle Souls who guide the great Wine-press of Love" guard Los's southern gate towards Beulah (*J* 72:50).

FERMANAGH is one of the nine counties of Ulster, which province is under Dan, Asher, and Naphtali (*J* 72:26).

FIFESHIRE, a maritime county in the east of Scotland, was oddly omitted from Blake's list of the Scottish counties. All Scotland, however, is assigned to Bowen (*J* 71:46).

FINCHLEY, county Middlesex, seven miles north of London, was a village in Blake's day. It is the northern member of the quaternary of Finchley (north), Blackheath (east), Norwood (south), and Hounslow (west), which probably represent the extent of Blake's usual rambles about London. They constitute "the spiritual Four-fold London" (*Mil* 6:1); the center of the quaternary is London Stone.

Albion's four forests overspread all the earth from London Stone to Blackheath, Hounslow, Finchley, and Norwood (*Mil*

6:1–5). Finchley is one of five places which rage loud before Bromion's tongs and poker (*J* 16:1). Albion bids Hand and Hyle seize Los and bring him to judgment at London Stone in the midst of the quaternary (*J* 42:51). Los builds the Mundane Shell "in the Four Regions of Humanity" until the quaternary covers the whole earth (*J* 42:78).

The FINGER OF GOD was probably suggested by Michelangelo's picture on the Sistine ceiling, where the Deity extends his life-giving finger to touch the finger of the newly created Adam. In Blake's symbolism, however, the Finger touches Los's seventh Furnace, these furnaces corresponding to the seven Eyes of God, the last being Jesus. It is the moment when Divinity gives life to the creative work of the poet.

This episode occurs first in *The Four Zoas* (iv:277), and involves the creation of Adam. Los has just bound Urizen. The Daughters of Beulah lament the death of Albion and appeal to Jesus, who promises his resurrection. He then fixes the two limits of Opacity and Contraction (Satan and Adam), thus limiting Eternal Death. The Starry Wheels feel the divine hand. Los also feels the limit and sees the "Finger of God touch the Seventh furnace." He is terrified; drops his hammer; and on beholding the shapes which enslaved humanity puts on, he becomes what he beholds (identifies himself with the sufferings of mankind).

In *Jerusalem* (12:5–14) Albion is dead when the terrified Los sees "the finger of God go forth upon my Furnaces from within the Wheels of Albion's Sons, fixing their Systems permanent, by mathematic power giving a body to Fals[e]hood that it may be cast off for ever, with Demonstrative Science piercing Apollyon with his own bow." Later (48:45), after Eno has opened the Moment and the Atom, Los sees her "in his seventh Furnace," and also sees terrified "the finger of God go forth" upon it.

The Finger of God is also credited with

writing the Ten Commandments (*Exod* xxxi:18; *Deut* ix:10). In the picture of that event (National Gallery, Edinburgh) the writer has inscribed in the top center of the right-hand table the Hebrew letter Yod, the first letter—but the first letter only—of the Divine Name. Apparently this identifies him with the Angel of the Divine Presence. Therefore the true God can command: "Cease, finger of God, to write!" (*EG* e:23). See YOD.

FIRE is one in the quaternary of Elements: Water (west), Air (south), Fire (east), and Earth (north). Being East, it is the creative spirit of Love.

"For the Lord thy God is a consuming fire" (*Deut* iv:24; *Heb* xii:29) was a text often quoted to prove the existence of Hell. But according to Blake, it is Jesus who is "the God of Fire and Lord of Love" (*J* 3). "The Jehovah of the Bible [is] no other than he who dwells in flaming fire. Know that after Christ's death, he became Jehovah" (*MHH* 6).

In *The Marriage of Heaven and Hell*, fire is identified with the forces of the subconscious, the sources of inspiration. " . . . I was walking among the fires of hell, delighted with the enjoyments of Genius, which to Angels look like torment and insanity" (*MHH* 6). In the final "Memorable Fancy" (*MHH* 22–24), a Devil in a flame of fire converts an Angel on a cloud; the Angel then embraces the flame of fire " & he was consumed and arose as Elijah." This union is depicted on the title page, where it is placed beneath the surface of the earth, in the mind.

Spiritual fire consumes nothing but errors. "The ancient tradition that the world will be consumed in fire at the end of six thousand years is true"; for when the cherub of prohibition leaves guarding the Tree of Life, "the whole creation will be consumed and appear infinite and holy, whereas it now appears finite & corrupt" (*MHH* 14). "Error, or Creation, will be Burned up; & then, & not till Then, Truth or Eternity will appear. It is Burnt up the Moment Men cease to behold it" (*LJ*, *K* 617). The dread lake of fire and brimstone which shall receive death and hell, with all other falsities and cruelties (*Rev* xx:14), destroys them: it is the Lake of Los. See LAKE. Revolution, which clears away ancient errors, is a conflagration, whether the flames of Orc or the Tyger burning in the forests of the night.

When Urizen creates his universe, the fallen Elements are born as his sons. Fire is named Fuzon, "first begotten, last born," who rebels against his father with sad results (*Ur* 23:17). When the Elements are materialized, the spirits of Fire are the Genii (*J* 36:37). See ELEMENTS.

As a state of mind in the fallen man, Fire is blind warfare, "Two Horn'd Reasoning, Cloven Fiction, | In Doubt, which is Self contradiction" (*GoP*, "Of the Gates" 11, *K* 770). Black flames are traditionally those of the conventional Hell: they give heat (torture) but no light (insight), as in *Illustrations of the Book of Job* 11. (See also *Am* 4:11 and *Ur* 5:17).

FLINTSHIRE is a northern county of Wales, bordering on the North Sea and the River Dee. It is the Gate of Dan (*J* 16:37). As part of North Wales, it is under Peachey, along with Shropshire, Cheshire, Monmouth, and the Isle of Man (*J* 71:30).

The FLOOD OF NOAH, or the Deluge, was the greatest catastrophe which ever overtook man, as it killed everybody except Noah and his family, who began a new epoch. As water symbolizes Matter, to Blake the Flood was the overwhelming of man in a physical body, with its limited five senses and the three dimensions—the Sea of Time and Space.

The earliest reference occurs in *Europe* (10:10-20), "when the five senses whelm'd in deluge o'er the earth-born man . . . circles of space, that like an ocean rush'd and overwhelmed all except this finite wall of flesh" within which spiritual life continued. Noah and his family survived by

taking refuge in the moon Ark of Love. See NOAH.

The Flood is one of the themes running through *Jerusalem*. Its chief effect is to submerge the Atlantic Continent, and thus to separate America from Britain. It begins when "In all the dark Atlantic vale down from the hills of Surrey a black water accumulates" (4:9). When Los bends the senses of Reuben, "The Atlantic Continent sunk round Albion's cliffy shore, and the Sea poured in amain upon the Giants of Albion" (36:39). Then "The narrow Sea between Albion & the Atlantic Continent . . . became a boundless Ocean bottomless" (44:14). While Albion operates the Plow of Nations, "the deep black rethundering Waters of the Atlantic . . . poured in, impetuous, loud, loud, louder & louder" (57:3). During the war, the dove and the raven, with the serpent, eagle, and lion, are sent forth but return not (66:70). America is beheld no more (79:53).

Kox is once called the Noah of the Flood of Udan-Adan (7:24).

The FLY in Blake's writings is a butterfly. It appears in a quaternary (*J* 98:43): Eagle (north), Dove (east), Fly (south), and Worm (west). "The Fly" (*SoE*) originally had "gilded, painted pride" (*K* 182); the poet equates himself with the gay thoughtless insect. But being the product of the Catterpiller, for once it is destructive, when it feeds on the Tree of Mystery (*SoE*, "The Human Abstract" 15).

However, when the city man removed to Felpham, the fly returned to its aspect of the joy of essential life. "Seest thou the little winged fly, smaller than a grain of sand? It has a heart like thee, a brain open to heaven & hell, withinside wondrous & expansive; its gates are not clos'd: I hope thine are not: hence it clothes itself in rich array: hence thou are cloth'd with human beauty, O thou mortal man" (*Mil* 20:27). And again, flies are children of Los, dancing a country-dance ("contra-"): "Thou seest the gorgeous clothed Flies that dance & sport in summer upon the sunny brooks & meadows: every one the dance knows in its intricate mazes of delight artful to weave: each one to sound his instruments of music in the dance, to touch each other & recede, to cross & change & return: these are the Children of Los" (*Mil* 26:2).

Blake also used the butterfly as the Greek symbol for the resurrection of the soul. Above his illustration of Christ healing a youth (Young's *Night Thoughts* iv:687) he added a butterfly risen from a corpse. In "Albion's Dance," he used it to symbolize the spiritual rebirth.

The FOOT is the lowest part of the body, and generally represents its physical aspects. Thus the Spectre of the pubescent Tharmas issues from his feet (*FZ* i:78); Vala, separated from Luvah, can see only his feet (*FZ* ii:229); and Job's wife, separated from him by his afflictions, still supports his feet (*Illustr Job* 6). In the "Last Judgment" appear "two figures, a Male & Female, chain'd together by the feet; they represent those who perish'd by the flood" (*K* 607), which was caused by the lust of the fallen angels for the human women. (See Illustrations, "LJ" No. 38)

The Tree of Mystery springs up under Urizen's heel (*Ahan* 3:62), though later it springs up under the heel of Albion (*J* 28:14). See TREE OF MYSTERY, under TREE.

The basic symbolism of right and the sinister left was discovered and brilliantly applied by Joseph Wicksteed in his study of the *Job* illustrations, the hands and feet indicating spiritual or materialistic attitudes; his conclusions have been universally accepted. They apply often in other pictures. Thus in "I Want!" (*GoP* 9) the youngster starts to climb the ladder to the moon with his left foot, and falls into the Sea of Time and Space.

Dr. Merrill Patterson, however, once suggested to me that the hands and feet might fall into the fourfold system, the right hand being North; the left hand, East; the left foot, South; and the right foot, West. This theory explains the descent of Milton into Blake's left foot, which is under Urizen (*Mil* 15:49, etc.).

Blake was influenced more by Milton's ideas than even his subject matter, his epical sweep, and his poetic style. *Milton* was written to correct that poet's ideas. Thus it is that Milton enters Blake through the foot ascribed to Urizen; and it also should be noted that Milton's chief antagonist in Blake's poem is Urizen. Therefore Blake's emphasis on his left foot is a statement that Milton became part of Blake primarily through his ideas.

Besides correcting Milton's conception of sex, Blake discovered that Milton's Elect were only the Pharisees, and that the Transgressors were the real saviours (*Mil* 13:31). Thereupon, the Vegetable World appears as a sandal for Blake's left foot, on which he walks into Eternity (21:12). Rintrah and Palamabron, however, are terrified at the sight of Blake's "fibrous left Foot black," and fear the revolutionary release of energy which this implies (22:35), but Los protects him.

Los, by the way, had earlier put his left sandal on his head, in token of mourning (8:11).

FOOTE (Samuel, 1720–77) was known as "the English Aristophanes" because he satirized or burlesqued particular persons in his farces. Among them was the great evangelist George Whitefield, who appeared as "Dr. Squintum" in *The Minor* (1750). This caricature raised such vehement protests that the published text was much modified. Blake remarked: "Foote in calling Whitefield, Hypocrite, was himself one; for Whitefield pretended not to be holier than others, but confessed his Sins before all the World" (*J* 52).

The FOREST OF GOD was on the heights of the Atlantic Continent; here Ariston, king of beauty, built his archetypal palace for his stolen bride (*Am* 10:9).

FORESTS are traditionally a place where

the way is lost and the light obscured. *The Divine Comedy*, *The Faerie Queene*, and *Comus* all begin with somebody lost in a forest.

Blake's forests are composed of dead trees, symbolizing the complicated rooted errors either of the social order or of the dogmatic mind. Eliphaz preaches amid dead trees, which later are blown flat by the whirlwind (*Illustr Job* 9, 13). The American Revolution also blows them flat (*Am* 6).

The parson surrounds the farmer with "cold floods of abstraction and with forests of solitude," where he builds castles and churches (*VDA* 5:19). Under the rule of Reason, man hides in "forests of night"; then "all the eternal forests" divide into "earths rolling in circles of space" (*Eur* 10:18)—the stars of Urizen's heaven, the laws of the material universe. The Tyger of wrath (revolution) blazes in the forests of the night (*SoE*, "Tyger" 2, 22); tygers roam in the forests of affliction (*FZ* vii:9). The "ancient forests of France" are shaken by the Revolution (*FR* 101, 300). Orc rouses his lions from his "forests black" (*FZ* vii *b*:141; ix:60).

The FORESTS OF ALBION are the fourfold Oak Groves of the Druids (*J* 89:23). They overspread all the earth from London Stone (*Mil* 6:3; *J* 80:43; 89:23). In Albion's fall, they flee (*J* 21:8). Albion's Reactor has possessed himself of them, and lurks there hidden (*J* 29:17). See OAK.

The FORESTS OF ENTUTHON surround the cultivated land Allamanda, in which is situated the city of Golgonooza or Art (*Mil* 27:43). Sociologically, Entuthon is "Abstract Philosophy," and Allamanda, "Commerce." For the individual, Entuthon is man's physical body, and Allamanda the nervous system by which we communicate.

FORFAR is a county on the east coast of Scotland. With Kincardine and Haddington, it is assigned to Reuben (*J* 16:53).

As part of Scotland, it is assigned to Bowen (*J* 71:46).

The FORGIVENESS OF SINS was the particular teaching of Jesus, a doctrine unknown to Aristotle and the other classical writers. In proclaiming it, Jesus initiated a spiritual revolution, for it abrogated the whole system of justice and punishment: it was the repealing of the Ten Commandments, the annulling of the standards of Good and Evil, the prohibition of "vengeance for sin," the neutralizing of the apple in Eden. "Judge not" (*Matt* vii:1) reverses the serpent's "Ye shall be as gods [judges], knowing good and evil" (*Gen* iii:5). "Every thing is good in God's eyes" (*CR* 256, 288). Our heavenly Father does not judge: he gives his sun and rain impartially to the good and evil; we should imitate him (*Matt* v:45–48; On Dante, *K* 785).

In short, we should take people for what they really are, distinguishing the individual from the state he may be in. "Learn ... to distinguish the Eternal Human ... from those States or Worlds in which the Spirit travels. This is the only means to Forgiveness of Enemies" (*J* 49:72–75).

The Forgiveness of Sins is the fundamental assumption for all that is best in our lives. The Brotherhood of Man is based on it; and without Brotherhood we cannot exist (*J* 96:28), as we are becoming fearfully aware. All science is based on it: the physician seeking the cause and cure of cancer is not concerned whether his patients are good people or bad. All great art is based on it: Shakespeare, for example, in drawing Macbeth, was tracing the causes and consequences of murder—he did not waste time explaining that he disapproved of his hero; "the grandest Poetry is Immoral, the Grandest characters Wicked ... Poetry is to excuse Vice & shew its reason & necessary purgation" (On Boyd, *K* 412).

The outstanding example of the doctrine of Jesus was his forgiveness of the woman taken in adultery. The law of Moses com-

manded that she be stoned to death, but
Jesus saved her (*John* viii:3–11; *EG e*).
There are many other cases in the Bible.
The mark on Cain's brow which forbade
anybody to kill him was, in Blake's tran-
script of *Genesis*, the kiss of "the Forgiveness of Sins written upon the Murderer's
Forehead." In his account of Joseph's forgiving Mary (see *Matt* i:18–25), Blake went
far beyond the traditional "Hate the sin
but love the sinner." "Doth Jehovah Forgive a Debt only on condition that it shall
be Payed? Doth he Forgive Pollution only
on conditions of Purity? That Debt is not
Forgiven! That Pollution is not Forgiven!
Such is the Forgiveness of the Gods, the
Moral Virtues of the Heathen whose tender
Mercies are Cruelty. But Jehovah's Salvation is without Money & without Price, in
the Continual Forgiveness of Sins, in the
Perpetual Mutual Sacrifice in Great Eternity; for behold, there is none that liveth &
Sinneth not! And this is the Covenant of
Jehovah: If you Forgive one-another, so
shall Jehovah Forgive You, that He Him-
self may Dwell among You" (*J* 61:17).
See MERCY.

The FOUR ZOAS, *the Torments of Love &
Jealousy in the Death and Judgement of
Albion, the Ancient Man*, was the final title
of Blake's longest poem, originally named
*Vala, or the Death and Judgement of the
Ancient Man. A Dream of Nine Nights.*
Blake never finished it; the manuscript is
in the British Museum. It has been repro-
duced in facsimile by G. E. Bentley, Jr.
(*Vala ; or, The Four Zoas*, New York,
1963).

The *Four Zoas* is a magnificent attempt
to incorporate all Blake's myths into a
single narrative. It is a symbolic poem, the
"Song of the Aged Mother," who is Eno;
it is she who perceives the eternity in all
things (see ENO). According to the title,
the basic plot is the fall and resurrection of
Albion, who symbolizes all mankind. But
Albion is a passive character: he soon sinks
into a deadly sleep; and the actual story is
that of the warfare between his members,

the four Zoas and their Emanations. To
complete the quaternary, Tharmas (with
his Emanation Enion) is added to Urthona-
Los, Luvah, and Urizen. The champion of
Albion is Los, the real hero of the poem;
his great opponent is Urizen. Albion's
saviour is Jesus, who now takes an active
part in the narrative; seconding him is the
Divine Family (the whole body of true or
Christian thought—the Communion of
Saints). The opponent of Jesus is Rahab,
the false church of this world. Satan also
appears for the first time.

For a proper epical setting, Blake has
now organized a fourfold universe (psychological, not Ptolemaic or Copernican),
dividing it into sunny Eden (the Eternity
of the Zoas), moony Beulah (the subconscious), Urizen's starry realm (law), and
Ulro (the earthy world of generation).

The epic is all-inclusive: it attempts to
establish the complete formula of Man.
This attempt puts Blake in the company of
Homer, Dante, Spenser, and Milton,
whether or not we think he was a worthy
companion. Needless to say, his poem goes
far beyond Fletcher's *Purple Island*, Prior's
Alma, Pope's *Essay on Man*, and Young's
Night Thoughts, which were inspired by the
same ambition.

Like this last poem, which Blake had
been busy illustrating, *The Four Zoas* is
divided into nine "Nights." But the poem
with which *The Four Zoas* really challenges
comparison is *Paradise Lost*, of which, in
the realm of ideas, it may be considered a
rewriting or a running commentary, although it is superficially as different from
Milton's poem as *The Book of Thel* is from
Comus.

Blake's epic starts *in medias res.* Man's
fall has begun: his Zoas are splitting already. The first episode concerns the outbreak of adolescence (the Fall into Experience); the tale then continues (sweeping
through the previous Prophetic books,
except the earliest) to Man's death, resurrection, and assumption. Milton's epic has
the same theme: the fall and salvation of
man. His setting is also cosmic. It begins

with the fall of Satan into Experience; and although it ends with the expulsion from Paradise, all the events until man's final salvation are rehearsed on the prophetic Hill of Vision. The parallels between Milton's Satan and Blake's Urizen were noted long ago by P. Berger. Urizen also seeks dominion over everything; he too explores his self-made hell and the chaos outside; he too sinks through his obduracy into the subhuman form of the Dragon. But the moment he renounces his ambition, he is saved and returns to his original glory; whereas Milton's Satan persists in his damnation until he is past all hope.

Perhaps Blake's greatest contribution to literary methods occurs in this poem: his invention of the dream technique. It was also the cause of the greatest confusion among his earlier critics. This technique destroys the effect of a continuous and logical narrative. It permits the tangling of many threads, abrupt changes of subject, recurrent repetitions, obscure cross references, sudden intrusions, even out-and-out contradictions. Crucial scenes are omitted; others are expanded out of all seeming proportion. But this technique is closest to our deeper mental processes, and it was Blake's ideal—complete freedom of the imagination. It permits the correlation of actions on different levels: thus in Night ix, the horrors on earth are a great harvest and vintage in Eternity.

Nothing like it had been done in English, to the best of my recollection, since Chaucer's *Boke of the Duchesse*, or was to be attempted again until Lewis Carroll wrote *Sylvie and Bruno*. It is much to Blake's credit that he never reduces his dreamworld to the special contents of a single individual's mind—a fault committed by his imitator, James Joyce, in *Finnegans Wake*.

However, beneath all the superficial confusion, Blake's structure is firm. It was discovered by Max Plowman.

Night i. The Division of the Loins (Tharmas)
    ii. The Division of the Heart (Luvah)
    iii. The Division of the Head (Urizen)
    iv. The Division of the Spirit (Urthona)
    v. Revolution (Orc)
    vi. Intellect versus Spirit
    vii. The Division of Good and Evil (Adam and Eve)
    viii. The Culmination of Errors (the Crucifixion)
    ix. The Last Judgment

Blake dated his title page 1797. The last of the Lambeth books had been published two years earlier, and probably he was then thinking of combining them into a bigger poem. The year 1796 was occupied with illustrating Young's *Night Thoughts*, but work in one medium can stimulate work in another. In 1797, he began a fair copy of what he had written; but the latest evidence indicates the probability that in that period of depression he wrote only a couple of "Nights" or so. However, when he went to Felpham in 1800, the gates of inspiration were opened; and in spite of Hayley's commissions and general pestering, and Blake's own moral compunctions about wasting his time on non-profitable work, he wrote, sometimes furiously. On April 25, 1803, he sent to Butts what is surely an account of this poem:

But none can know the Spiritual Acts of my three years' Slumber on the banks of the Ocean, unless he has seen them in the Spirit, or unless he should read My long Poem descriptive of those Acts; for I have in these three years composed an immense number of verses on One Grand Theme, Similar to Homer's Iliad or Milton's Paradise Lost, the Persons & Machinery intirely new to the Inhabitants of Earth (some of the Persons Excepted). I have written this Poem from immediate Dictation, twelve or sometimes twenty or thirty lines at a time, without Premeditation & even against my Will; the Time it has taken in writing was thus render'd Non Existent, & an immense Poem Exists which seems to be the Labour of a long Life, all produc'd without Labour or Study.

The original version was called *Vala* after the Emanation of Luvah; but the idea expanded and became a study of all four Zoas. A new "Night" was written to open the poem properly. Blake erased and rewrote, adding new passages. Fresh ideas were developed and fairly thrust in. After his return to London, he continued to insert new material: the quarrel with Hayley, the Daughters of Albion, the wartime conditions of London in 1804 (which David Erdman noted).

Eventually the poem became so overwritten that the first version had almost sunk out of sight. The result had become too unwieldy to finish. Some of the material really belonged in new poems, *Milton* and *Jerusalem*, to which he devoted himself in 1804.

But more important: some of his concepts had become outdated; the poem was no longer an adequate expression of his reconsidered ideas. The new wine had burst the old bottles. His Eden was not Eternity after all: it had seasons, and the Emanations never were absorbed into their counterparts. Albion must fall through his own errors, and not because Luvah once seized Urizen's chariot. Los should be the friend and avowed champion of Albion. Jesus must do more than appear at the Last Judgment and then must vanish without condemning the obdurate sinners—an act which would have been contrary to his character and teachings. The activities of the Female Will in torturing men had not been developed at all. It was easier to write new poems than to struggle longer with *The Four Zoas*.

The first printings of the complete text were very bad (1893, 1906). Edwin J. Ellis and William Butler Yeats did not order the pages correctly, and they seemed incapable of reading Blake's writing. Worse yet, they "improved" passages constantly according to their own notions of what Blake intended. Geoffrey Keynes (1925) first pub-lished the text correctly; D. J. Sloss and J. P. R. Wallis (1926) re-edited it. There will always remain the problems of Blake's punctuation and syntax. H. M. Margoliouth has recently (1956) made an illuminating attempt to reconstruct the original *Vala* from Blake's confusing manuscript, with many brilliant explanations and conjectures. G. E. Bentley, Jr.'s edition (1963) endeavors to indicate all Blake's additions and corrections, page by page. For a critique of this edition and an indication of further necessary work on the text, see Erdman in *The Library*, Vol. XIX, 1964.

FRANCE was the great rival of England, from the time of the Plantagenets to the fall of Napoleon. Blake's *King Edward the Third* was his unfinished attempt at a historical play in the style of Shakespeare. Although the scene is laid in France, and the battle of "Cressy" is impending, there is no criticism or even characterization of France or the French whatsoever.

"The American War began. All its dark horrors passed before my face across the Atlantic to France. Then the French Revolution commenc'd in thick clouds" (To Flaxman, 12 Sept 1800). The liberals exulted in expectation of the freeing of all mankind; Blake is said to have sported the red liberty cap in the streets of London.

He blamed France's feudalism for the breakdown. The scepter was "too heavy for mortal grasp" (*FR* 4). French repressive measures were typified by the Bastille, where the supposed enemies of Church and State were confined (*FR* 19–51). "France, rend down thy dungeon!" (*MHH* 25). In "Fayette," Blake blamed the king for the famine and the "beautiful Queen of France" for the general immorality. Lafayette had been a hero of the American Revolution, but in France his ambivalent attitude led him to kiss the queen's hand in public. Blake blames him for pitying the royal couple and thus (as with Burke) clouding his judgment as to the basic principles of the situation (*K* 186, 892).

From the beginning Blake knew that though the ideas from America were the cause of the French Revolution (*FR* 89–90; *Am* 16:15; *Eur* 15:1), its means were material and therefore not ultimately effective. The horrors of the September massacres strengthened the cause of the terrified conservatives; the counter-revolutionary reaction was a period of severe repression in which many were jailed, including Blake's friend and publisher Johnson. Paine just managed to escape. Johnson had started to print Blake's *French Revolution*, but only the first of the seven Books was set up, and the project was abandoned. "To defend the Bible in this year 1798 would cost a man his life" (On Watson, *K* 383). As late as 1804 Blake believed that his trial for treason was the result of a governmental trap to catch the former liberal.

But he disbelieved in Napoleon's attempt to spread culture by military power: that could be done only by the cult of the Humanities. "Let us teach Buonaparte, & whomsoever else it may concern, That it is not Arts that follow & attend upon Empire, but Empire that attends upon & follows The Arts" (*PubA*, *K* 597). Blake even felt that the divine purpose in having him born was to offset Napoleon's attempt to "subdue the World in Arms"; Blake was to "renew the Arts on Britain's Shore"; then "France shall fall down & adore" ("Now Art has lost its mental Charms," *K* 557).

For all his horror at the slaughter on the Continent, Blake never fell into the vulgar error of supposing that the war sprang from a fundamental hostility. France's real ideal (his Emanation) is Shiloh ("peace"), corresponding to Albion's Jerusalem ("city of peace"); both places were sites of the Tabernacle. But now, "Shiloh is in ruins, our brother is sick: Albion, He whom thou lovest, is sick" (*FZ* i:477). His Emanation has become masculine (*J* 49:47) — aggressive and cruel, like that of the Wicked Strong Man in Blair's *Grave*. His Luvah, the Zoa of love, has been transformed into the war of hate—the war which lies behind

much of *The Four Zoas* and *Jerusalem*. Then, after the fall of Napoleon, the Allies took their vengeance, which Blake deplored as the crucifixion of France. "Albion brought [Luvah] to Justice in his own City of Paris" (*J* 63:5). "They vote the death of Luvah & they nail'd him to the tree, they pierc'd him with a spear & laid him in a sepulcher to die a death of Six thousand years, bound round with desolation" (*FZ* vii *b*:166; *J* 65:8). "Luvah is France, the Victim of the Spectres of Albion" (*J* 66:15).

But the time shall come when France will be the first in the brotherhood of the Thirty-two Nations, devoted to preserving liberty and ruling the rest of the world (*J* 72:38).

FRANKLIN (Benjamin, 1706–90), one of the greatest of Americans, was a leading figure in the American Revolution. He meets with Washington and other patriots "on the coast glowing with blood" (*Am* 3:4) after the Boston Massacre, in a non-historical conference on the approaching enslavement of the colonies. He is also among those who watch the coming of Albion's hosts (*Am* 14:2).

Albion's Angel calls Orc a Viper; this symbol may well have been derived from the first American newspaper cartoon, Franklin's "Join, or Die" (1754), which was widely circulated again at the time of the Revolution. It was used as a masthead for Revere's *Massachusetts Spy*, where the snake's opposing dragon at first sight resembles very closely Blake's dragon depicted at the top of *America* 4.

The **FRENCH REVOLUTION**, *A Poem in Seven Books* (1791) was Blake's daring attempt to make contemporary history into a poem. He intended to analyze impartially the causes and the course of the world-altering events across the Channel, which his countrymen regarded with such blind horror. Jos. Johnson, printer for the radicals, agreed to publish it; but either the government pressure was too great or the events which Blake foretold did not take place: for all that remains is the page proofs of Book the First. The six remaining Books had been written, but are lost. Book the First was not published until 1913, in Dr. John Sampson's Oxford edition of Blake's poems.

Book the First deals with the events from May to mid-July, 1789. It mixes fact, surmise, and symbol; the characters are historical or invented. However, Blake used no names from his own special mythology, although there are anticipations of some later ideas. The Bastille is the dominant image as the obvious symbol of French oppression. Each of its seven towers contains a non-historical person representing some victim of authoritarianism. They are the prophet, the prisoner of state, the schismatic, the pure woman, the preacher of truth, the good man turned parasite, and the patriot.

France is sick; the scepter, "too heavy for mortal grasp"; the king, frankly incompetent. The tensions and oppositions caused by the National Assembly are personified. Blake invented "the ancientest Peer, Duke of Burgundy" to speak for the proud spirit of feudalism in protesting the spread of the American idea of democracy. The Archbishop of Paris, "in the rushing of scales" (the warring prelate), prophesies the decay of the Church and calls for military force against the Assembly. When the Abbé de Sieyès recommends the removal of the troops from the city, Burgundy disdainfully bids him first to order the Bastille itself to remove. However, Lafayette gives the order; the troops depart as a new day dawns.

The next Book must have dealt with the fall of the Bastille.

The French Revolution is written in the rare, probably unique, meter of anapestic-iambic septenary. Blake never used it again.

FRIGA is the goddess of love and beauty, the Scandinavian equivalent of Venus, the mistress of Mars. She symbolizes the sexual intoxication which accompanies war. She dances the dance of death with Thor (*J* 63:9, 14; 68:17). "Woden and Thor and Friga wholly consume my Saxons on their enormous Altars built in the terrible North" (*J* 83:19).

In naming her, Blake confused Freya, the goddess of love, with Frigga, the Scandinavian Juno.

FURNACES are "furnaces of affliction" (*FZ* ii:72; *Mil* 38:20; *J* 9:34; 55:59; 73:25; 82:79; 86:49; 96:35). They represent the suffering which human beings must endure as part of their Experience, or education. They are even called furnaces of death (*J* 8:10; 10:1; 42:5). Jesus, the Good Shepherd, works in them, protecting Jerusalem's children (*J* 35:3–16; 60:5–9; 62:35).

Anybody may have furnaces. Hand has one (*J* 7:71; 90:23), also Bowen (*J* 90:20) and by implication the other brothers. The Satan of *Milton* has his own (*Mil* 38:20). Tirzah's soul is seven furnaces (*J* 67:50–52). There are Molech's furnaces of iron, where children are sacrificed (*Mil* 37:21; *J* 89:19). The potter's furnace is referred to (*J* 28:22; 53:28).

In *The Four Zoas*, Urizen orders furnaces erected, to build his palace, the Mundane Shell, or material world (ii:30). As a result, Jerusalem falls (ii:45). Luvah is cast into the furnaces, and Vala feeds the fire, until he is melted and she becomes a heap of ashes (ii:72–116). The furnaces are then unsealed; the molten metal runs out and is forged by Urizen's lions (ii:117, 135). Urizen then builds his palace, the material universe (ii:166–200, 240–48, 266–86). His furnaces are then ruined, but Tharmas compels Los to rebuild them (iv:149–52, 165–69). Los then binds Urizen (iv:199–246), after which the furnaces go out (v:17).

But the most important are the furnaces of Los.

The FURNACES OF LOS were at first merely a necessary "prop" for his blacksmithing.

They are barely mentioned in the binding of Urizen (*Ur* 10:29) and again in the forging of the material sun (*BoL* 5:21). In *The Four Zoas* ii (which Margoliouth accepts as part of the original *Vala*), Blake shows a knowledge of casting, but may not have seen it done, if we take lines 66–69, 117–18, 136–40 to be a poetic re-creation of the process.

Then, some time shortly before he wrote *Milton* 6 (an insert), he seems to have been enormously impressed by the actual sight of casting mills in operation. The glare and roar of the fires, the clatter of hammers and blowing of bellows, the clinkers, the rattling chains, the ladles carrying molten ore, the "dark gleam" of the ashes still burning before the iron doors, are all suddenly detailed in *Milton* 6; and in *Jerusalem* 5, he made use of the columns of smoke billowing up to the stars and overspreading the skies.

This new vividness of the "minute particulars" came simultaneously with a symbolizing of the whole process. The breaking up of the ore, the smelting in the furnaces, the release of the molten metal, and the casting into new form, while the slag is discarded, represented to Blake the poetic process itself.

This is basic to the total being. The psychological process has its physiological correspondence in the alimentary system, where similarly the food is broken up and digested, the good part being incorporated into the human form, while the useless is discarded. "The Bellows are the Animal Lungs: the Hammers the Animal Heart: the Furnaces the Stomach for digestion . . . Bowlahoola is the Stomach in every individual man" (*Mil* 24:58–62, 68; *J* 53:12). When the Sons of Albion are divided into sexes, "The Male is a Furnace of beryll; the Female is a golden Loom" (*J* 5:34; 90:27). "Translucent the Furnaces, of Beryll & Emerald immortal and Seven-fold each within other" (*J* 53:9).

Los's seven furnaces represent the path of Experience to the point of creation. They evidently correspond to the seven Eyes of God, as the seventh Eye is Jesus, and it is the seventh Furnace which is touched by the Finger of God. They are "of Golgonooza" (*Mil* 31:26); they are also situated in Bowlahoola (*Mil* 24:51), which is no hindrance to their generally being in London; and Primrose Hill, where Blake saw the spiritual sun, "is the mouth of the Furnace & the Iron Door" (*J* 73:54).

Los's labors represent the development of Blake's thought. In *Milton*, Urizen is bound (3:6–27)—Blake's great triumph over Reason, the god of the eighteenth century, which he accomplished by reducing it to human limitations and fixing its just place in the universe. Then Los forges the three Classes of men (2:26; 6:35), also "the Plow & Harrow to pass over the Nations" (6:13), the instruments for revolution. Rintrah and Palamabron, fearing this revolution, beg Los to throw Blake into the furnaces (22:32), but Los refuses.

But the most significant sequence occurs in *Jerusalem*. Los is now the avowed champion of Man, and his furnaces are at work almost up to the end of the epic. The sequence begins when Los forces his hostile Spectre (Reason) to labor with him (7–10). Los already has forged out of "sighs & tears & bitter groans . . . the spiritual sword that lays open the hidden heart" (9:17)—his poetic purpose as exemplified in the *Songs of Experience*. He correlates justice and mercy now: "The blow of his Hammer is Justice, the swing of his Hammer Mercy, the force of Los's Hammer is eternal Forgiveness" (88:49). He is now perfecting his theory of the holiness of free love (Erin), as in the *Visions of the Daughters of Albion*. He is also laboring to make the children of Jerusalem his own children (10:3). Erin emerges from the furnaces with the Daughters of Beulah—the new inspiration his theory has released—and the children of Los (11:7–15). His four chief sons, Rintrah (wrath), Palamabron (pity), Theotormon (desire), and Bromion (reason) then labor with him (16:2–11; 73:5). All this is part of the process of building Golgonooza (art).

When Vala ejects Jerusalem as a harlot, the furnaces are ruined (32:6); however, they are in order again when Los opens them before Vala (34:19), and again when Los, trying to force Reuben (the common man) across the Jordan, limits his four senses (34:43–54; 36:1–13). Los builds for him the ark-Moon of Ulro (earthly love), "plank by plank & rib by rib" (36:4). While this is going on, Jesus announces from the furnaces his divine purpose of saving individuals (35:3–17) — an event which suggests *Daniel* iii:25.

Los also opens the furnaces before Albion (42:2), who sickens at the sight and denounces him. London is in the furnaces (38:37), and so is Oxford (42:58). When Oxford faints—i.e., when Shelley dies—Los's furnaces rage again (46:17–22). Eno appears in them, and the Finger of God touches the seventh Furnace (48:45), with the result that Jerusalem breaks out.

When the war spirit is spreading over Europe, the Divine Voice again speaks from the furnaces to Jerusalem, recalling her days of innocence and comforting her for her bondage in Babylon (60:10–67; 61:1–27). The sight of Jesus among the flames gives Los new hope (62:35–36).

When Gwendolen invents her falsehood, Cambel is jealous; the seventh Furnace is blighted; but Los draws her into his Furnace, where she labors, trying vainly to mold Hand according to her will. Then the other sisters soften towards London and begin to give their souls away in the furnaces of affliction (82:51–78). Los sings his Watch Song, working and walking from furnace to furnace (83:75; 85:14–32; 86:1–33). Enitharmon at last appears to him, and the wound in his loins closes (86:39–41, 53–61); but they have two wills now. When his Spectre builds his "stupendous works," Los shatters him and them with one blow of his hammer, thus altering "every Ratio of his Reason" (91:33–53).

But that is the last of his troubles. "The Briton, Saxon, Roman, and Norman"

amalgamate in his furnaces to one nation, the English (92:1–6), thus implying that all nations are becoming one. When the awakened Albion throws himself into the furnaces of affliction, they become fountains of living water (96:35–37).

FUZON, "first begotten, last born" of the Sons of Urizen (*Ur* 23:18), represents fire in the quaternary of Elements, the other three being Thiriel (air), Utha (water), and Grodna (earth). After the degeneration of man under Urizen's laws, "Fuzon call'd all together the remaining children of Urizen, and they left the pendulous earth" (*Ur* 28:19), which they named Egypt (bondage).

Fuzon then molds his wrath into a vast globe, which he flings against his despised father; it lengthens to a hungry beam, which pierces Urizen's shield and divides his loins (*Ahan* 2:1–29). As a result, Ahania becomes a separate being, whom Urizen names Sin and conceals. Fuzon's "fiery beam" becomes a pillar of fire to Egypt, until Los forges it into the body of the sun (*Ahan* 2:44–48).

In retaliation, Urizen forms a black bow of the ribs of a serpent he has killed; and with a poisoned rock (moral law), he shoots Fuzon just as he proclaims "I am God! eldest of things." The rock falls to earth on Mount Sinai (*Ahan* 3:1–46).

Urizen then crucifies the "dead corse" of Fuzon on the topmost stem of the Tree of Mystery (*Ahan* 3:52–4:8). For forty years (the period of the wanderings in the wilderness), the arrows of pestilence fly round "the pale living Corse on the tree"; and Fuzon groans (*Ahan* 4:9–44).

This myth looks back to Saturn's castration of his father Uranus, and anticipates Freud's Oedipus complex. But Fuzon never reappears in the later books. Blake doubtless realized that Passion is not the child of Reason; therefore, in *The Four Zoas*, Urizen's antagonist is Luvah; furthermore, it is Jesus who is crucified on the Tree.

G

GAD was Jacob's seventh son and the founder of a Tribe.

With his brothers, he is listed as a Son of Los who fled (*FZ* viii:361, 376). Jerusalem recalls him and some of his brothers in their days of innocence (*J* 79:30). They fled, to wander with Tirzah, and were generated (*Mil* 24:2). Los fears that Rintrah and Palamabron might also depart, even as Reuben and Gad (*Mil* 20:53). The Daughters of Albion drink up Dan and Gad (*J* 67:22). Gad and five of his brothers roll apart into Non Entity (*J* 74:50). Gad and four brothers are closed up in narrow vales of Cabul (*J* 79:64).

In Wales, Gad is assigned the county of Pembrokeshire; in England, Oxford, Bucks, and Harford (Hertfordshire); in Scotland, Peebles, Perth, and Renfru (*J* 16:38, 47, 56). He is omitted without explanation from those assigned to the Irish counties, being replaced by Levi.

GALWAY is a western county of Connaught, Ireland. With the other counties of "Connaut," it is assigned to Ephraim, Manasseh, and Benjamin (*J* 72:24). Connaut itself is assigned to Joseph (*J* 72:3).

GATES (Horatio, 1728?–1806) was the American general who received Burgoyne's sword at the surrender of the British army at Saratoga (1777).

He is one of the American patriots who meet on the Atlantic coast after the Boston Massacre (*Am* 3:4). They watch the approach of the armies of Albion's Angel (*Am* 14:2).

The GATES OF PARADISE (1793) was Blake's first attempt to convey his message primarily by a series of pictures. The foretitle was "For Children." About 1818 he reissued the book with the foretitle "For the Sexes," adding explanatory verses.

The plates depict the life of man in this world, from the embryo to the grave. The frontispiece shows the embryo as a cocoon on an oak leaf, while a "catterpiller" feeds on another leaf. (1) Birth. The mother pulls the baby like a mandrake from the ground beneath a weeping willow. (2–5) The difficulties of childhood are symbolized by passage through the four elements—water, earth, air, fire—suggesting the initiation in *The Golden Ass*, which was also used by Keats in *Endymion*. (6) The child asserts his personality, emerging from an eggshell. (7) The boy heartlessly pursues the girls. (8) He revolts against his father. (9) He tries to climb to the moon of love. (10) He falls into the Sea of Time and Space. (11) As Aged Ignorance he clips the wings of his own joys. (12) He starves in the dungeon of religion, as Ugolino. (13—the number of death) At the deathbed of his father he beholds the spirit rising and pointing to heaven. (14) As a traveller, he hastens toward his journey's end. (15) The old man, blown by the wind, enters death's door. (16) Tirzah, representing the mystery of the flesh, sits with a wand and a worm beneath the roots of a tree. The motto is quoted from *Job* xvii:14: "I have said . . . to the worm, Thou art my mother, and my sister."

The versified "Keys" relate this tale to Blake's cosmic myth. When Albion was "set in Repose, | The Female from his darkness rose"; and hid the infant in the veil of Vala. The false education in moral values results in doubt, melancholy, shame, and division of the intellect. Vala's veil becomes the Mundane Shell; the lad rends the veil and discovers sex. He mistreats women, revolts against his father, seeks the moon of love, falls into Time's ocean. He clips the wings of the imagination, and imprisons both father and sons. Then he perceives that man is immortal, and hastens to death's door. Here he contemplates the mystery of the Worm—the mortal body, given by the mother ("And me to mortal life betray"—*SoE*, "To Tirzah" 14) with the problems of sex and the entire web of physical life.

The Epilogue is addressed "To the Accuser [diabolos] who is The God of This World [*II Cor* iv:4]," and begins with a line paraphrased from the last line of the eighth "Night" of Young's *Night Thoughts*. Satan is a dunce because he cannot distinguish the outer from the incorruptible inner man, and believes he can change one individual into another. Though the worldly worship him as the true God, he is only the Son of Morn (Lucifer), the star announcing the coming of day; and a dream of the lost traveller.

For the influence of Young's *Night Thoughts*, see YOUNG.

GAUL was the ancient name of France.

The heart of the Polypus on Salisbury Plain shoots out fibres through Gaul, Italy, Greece, Judea, India, China, and Japan (*J* 67:38).

GAZA was an important city in southern Philistia, chiefly remembered as the place of Samson's captivity and death. Blake followed current belief in identifying the Philistines with the Amalekites.

The Druid religion spread from England over the earth, "from Troy to Gaza of the Amalekite" (*J* 63:43). In Satan's bosom, the Druid temples spread over the whole earth, including Gaza (*J* 89:33).

GENERATION is the act of true love. It is the simplest way into Eternity (*Eur* iii:5). It is the image of Regeneration; it is the birthplace of the Lamb (*J* 7:65). But "false and Generating Love [is] a pretence of love to destroy love" (*J* 17:25); then it may "swallow up Regeneration" (*J* 90:37).

"The World of Generation" is the state of the Darwinian struggle for life, "devouring & devoured" (*Eur* 2:5), "the Generation of decay & death" (*FZ* i:22), where "Life lives upon death & by devouring appetite all things subsist on one another" (*FZ* vii:390). This "vegetative" world (*FZ* ix:625; *Mil* 14:5) is in Ulro and was seemingly identified with it until *Jerusalem*, where Ulro is South (*J* 12:51) and Generation is West. Each of the fourfold Gates of Golgonooza has openings respectively into Eden, Beulah, Generation, and Ulro. "The North Gate of Golgonooza, toward Generation has four sculptur'd Bulls, terrible, before the Gate of Iron, and iron the Bulls" (*J* 12:61); the golden Gate of the South has four iron Lions (*J* 13:2); the closed Western Gate has four living Cherubim of iron "like Men hermaphroditic, each winged with eight wings," the work of elemental hands (*J* 13:8); the Eastern Gate, ornamented with Wheels, has "toward Generation, seven generative forms" (*J* 13:19).

When the Contraries, Rational Philosophy and Mathematic Demonstration, war against each other, "Los fixes them on his Anvil . . . to Create a World of Generation from the World of Death [Ulro], dividing the Masculine & Feminine, for the comingling of Albion's & Luvah's Spectres was Hermaphroditic" (*J* 58:15–20), "a World of Generation continually Creating out of the Hermaphroditic Satanic World of rocky destiny, and formed into Four precious stones for enterance from Beulah" (*J* 58:50–59:1).

The last twelve of the sixteen Sons of Los left him in pursuit of Tirzah, were generated, and became tribes. "Nor can any consummate bliss without being Generated on Earth" (*J* 86:42) .

The World of Generation is essential to the scheme of Providence; otherwise, the Incarnation would be impossible. Eventually, however, Generation destroys itself. "Two Beings each with three heads [representing] Vegetative Existence" strip and burn the harlot Mystery in "the Eternal Consummation of Vegetable Life & Death with its Lusts. The wreathed Torches in their hands represents Eternal Fire which is the fire of Generation or Vegetation; it is an Eternal Consummation" (*LJ*, *K* 609) .

GENESIS, the first book of the Bible, particularly challenged Blake's powers of symbolic interpretation. Its story does not start with the actual beginnings of things, for there cannot be any beginning for things eternal. "Many suppose that before the Creation All was Solitude & Chaos. This is the most pernicious Idea that can enter the Mind, as it takes away all sublimity from the Bible & Limits All Existence to Creation & to Chaos, To the Time & Space fixed by the Corporeal Vegetative Eye" (*LJ*, *K* 614). Man's "History Preceded that of the Hebrews & in [his] Sleep, or Chaos, Creation began" (*LJ*, *K* 609) . Man had already lost the divine vision before the first chapter of *Genesis*. What follows is a series of splittings of the original unity. Light is divided from darkness; earth is divided from heaven; the waters are divided from the dry land; vegetation arises from the earth; the sun and moon (now separated from man) divide day and night; fish and fowl arise from the waters; and on the sixth day, man is materialized and thus divided from the spirit. Man is still an androgyne (*Gen* i:27); the division of the sexes occurs later (*Gen* ii:22) . Then good and evil are divided when the two eat of the Tree, and are manifest in their first two children, Cain and Abel; and life and death are finally divided in the murder of Abel.

All these divisions must be reunited if Eternity is to be achieved; and the six days of the Last Judgment (*FZ* ix) reverse the six days of Creation.

Towards the end of his life, Blake began an illuminated text of *Genesis*, extending only to eight uncompleted pages. He sketched two different title pages; both depict the Trinity as Creator.

In the more elaborate sketch, the Father and Son appear according to tradition, while the Holy Ghost is a nude youth. On the left is Christ with arms extended in the cruciform position, but he is not suffering. From his left hand a scroll descends, which reaches to the uplifted right hand of the Holy Ghost. On the right, counterbalancing the Son, is the Father, who stands on a black cloud and points upward to another; behind his glory, black flames are just peeping out.

In a row beneath sit the Four Zoas, represented as the traditional four beasts (see Illustrations). On the far left is Luvah, as Orc turning into the Serpent. Crowned with gems, snake-tongued, laughing, he uplifts his left hand towards the apple tree above him. He is the only active Zoa; the three others apparently have their hands folded in prayer. The second is Urthona-Los as an eagle with a crown; he inclines towards Luvah-Orc but turns his head away. Urizen as a lion draws away from the eagle. Last is Tharmas as a horned ox; above him is the fruit-laden Tree of Life.

In the second sketch for a title page, the Holy Ghost is given more prominence; Christ, emerging from a sphere, points to the Father, who uplifts the bow of spiritual warfare. The Zoas and the two trees are replaced by the twelve apostles, who float in ecstasy, crested with the Pentecostal flames.

Chapter i, "The Creation of the Natural Man": the Father, supported by two angels, reaches down with his left hand and blesses his work with his right. At the end of the chapter, Adam stands in amazement and praise before the Trinity, who extend their right hands. Chapter ii, "The Natural Man divided into Male and Female and of the Tree of Life and of the Tree of Good and Evil": at the end of the chapter, Adam sleeps with a girdle about his chest; above him Eve hovers horizontally beneath the Trinity, the nearest being the Father. Chapter iii, "Of the Sexual Nature and the Fall into Generation and Death": above the heading, Adam and Eve kneel by the Tree and its Serpent. Eve repeats the gesture of the "Venus pudica." At the chapter end, the Son kisses the kneeling Cain on the forehead. Chapter iv, "How Generation and Death took Possession of the Natural Man and of the Forgiveness of Sins written upon the Murderer's Forehead": on the left, Adam supports Eve over Abel's body, whose ghost floats in mid-air, while Cain flees away to the right.

Interpretations of events in *Genesis* are to be traced particularly in *The Book of Urizen* (Chap. vii), *The Book of Los*, and *The Four Zoas*.

A manuscript poem in Blake's handwriting, *Genesis, the Seven Days of the Created World*, has been identified as the opening lines of Tasso's *Le Sette Giornale del Mondo Creato*. Probably Hayley, translating at sight, dictated these lines to Blake, his amanuensis.

The GENII represent Fire in the quaternary of the Four Elements (*Mil* 31:20; *J* 36:37). Their position is East: sixty-four thousand Genii guard the eastern gate of Golgonooza (*J* 13:26). Los addresses them as "Ye Genii of the Mills" (*Mil* 8:16). See ELEMENTS.

GEOFFREY OF MONMOUTH (1100?–1154) based his *Historia Britonum* (*ca.* 1147) on manuscript sources and legends, inventing freely whenever necessary. The result was perhaps the most influential of all British histories.

The biggest gap occurred before Caesar's landing; Geoffrey filled it with a romance beginning with the flight of Aeneas from Troy; continuing with the adventures of his great-grandson Brutus (Brut), who

eventually invaded Britain and slew most of the giant inhabitants except their champion Goemagot (Gogmagog), who was killed in a wrestling match; and concluding this portion with the stories of his regal descendants—tales which Shakespeare and Milton, among others, drew upon. Geoffrey expanded the scant records of King Arthur remarkably, much to the advantage of all posterity. Holinshed and Camden drew on this material with increasing skepticism; but in his *History of Britain*, Milton repeated the dubious material for the benefit of future poets.

Blake utilized the material freely for his own symbolic purposes. He recounted the tale of Trojan Brutus' invasion in the minstrel's song at the end of *King Edward the Third* (*PS*), and named his Daughters of Albion from women mentioned by Geoffrey, "names anciently remember'd, but now contemn'd as fictions, although in every bosom they controll our Vegetative powers" (*J* 5:38).

GEORGE III (1738–1820) is not named in *America*; he is usually "the Guardian Prince of Albion," though once he is called "the King of England" (4:12). He "burns in his nightly tent" (3:1). The American leaders meet on their coast, which is "glowing with blood from Albion's fiery Prince" (3:5)—an obvious reference to the Boston Massacre. The Americans behold him standing on his cliffs in dragon form (war) (3:15). He trembles at the appearance of Orc (4:12). He sees the thirteen colonies renounce their allegiance (12:2). In the reaction, pestilence begins by smiting him with streaks of red (15:1), and he writhes in torment (15:6).

George is actually named, however, in the cancelled plates of *America* (*b*:9); and though he was only thirty-eight in 1776, Blake represents him as an aged apparition with a snowy beard extending over his chest. The text of Plate *a* is identical with *America* 3, then everything is different. George's glowing eyes "reveal the dragon thro' the human" (*b*:1), but in the "close hall of counsel . . . his Angel form renews" (*b*:2). All rise before him (*b*:15), then an earthquake shatters the roofs, which fall on "th' Angelic seats" (*b*:24). Then the king is armed in gold: Albion's Angel brings his shield, London's Guardian his helm, and the "wise spirit of London's river" his spear (*c*:1–5). Standing on the stone of Truth, he smites his shield with his scepter (*c*:11). Another earthquake follows this declaration of war, and the stone sinks (*c*:12). His fifty-two armies gather around their Prince from the four cliffs of Albion (*c*:16). He had wept, Urizen-wise, in the council hall (*b*:17); now he weeps again when the Angels of Albion hang over him, a "frowning shadow like an aged King in arms of gold, who wept over a den, in which his only son outstretch'd by rebels' hands was slain; his white beard wav'd in the wild wind" (*c*:25).

Line 1 of *America* 3 is repeated as the last line of "Africa" (*SoL*), thus acting as a connective.

GERMANY, Poland, and the North once wooed Jerusalem's footsteps (*J* 79:45), but in the Napoleonic wars, Jerusalem's pillars fell in France and Germany (*J* 68:45). Germany and five other European nations are temples among the pillars of Urizen's great temple (*J* 58:41). When Ololon descends, all the nations weep, Germany towards France and Italy (*Mil* 31:13). Eventually Germany will be one of the Thirty-two Nations which shall guard liberty and rule the rest of the world (*J* 72:38).

The GHOST OF ABEL[,] *A Revelation In the Visions of Jehovah*[,] *Seen by William Blake* [1822].

In December 1821, when Byron's *Cain, a Mystery* appeared, the religious world was profoundly shocked. Byron had analyzed the story in *Genesis*, with results which were Gnostic and practically Manichaean. His Creator is a tyrant rejoicing in cruelty, the sole author of sin, death, and Hell. Lucifer, the friend of Man, endures the

tyranny with quiet scorn and silent resistance. The Tree of the Knowledge of Good and Evil is the Tree of Truth, not evil at all, but necessary for human advancement. Adam and Eve are models of stupid piety, kissing the rod that scourges them. At the beginning, Cain is already critical of God's justice, thereby winning his displeasure; the colloquy with Lucifer enlarges his knowledge and confirms his attitude. He insists that he is innocent. He will not admit that he inherited the primal sin, and even rejects the Vicarious Atonement: "By sacrificing the harmless for the guilty? What atonement were there? Why, *we* are innocent" (III.i).

The climax comes when he kills Abel accidentally in a scuffle: it is unintentional homicide, not murder. But Adam banishes Cain; Eve curses him thoroughly; the Angel of the Lord (substituted for his master in person) declares that the voice of Abel's blood cries out to the Lord and therefore Cain shall be a vagabond and the earth shall not yield its strength when he plants. His forehead is marked, not out of mercy to Cain, but simply to prevent more murders. Cain longs for death, and would give his own life if Abel might live again. He believes that Abel would forgive him, but that neither God nor his own soul can ever do so. But his penitence is unavailing; he and his sister-wife Adah depart from Eden.

Blake's reply, *The Ghost of Abel*, a two-page leaflet, appeared the next year, 1822. It is dedicated "To Lord Byron in the Wilderness" of the forests of the night; but Blake adds, "What doest thou here, Elijah?"—the words of the Lord to Elijah when he fled for his life into the wilderness of Horeb (*I Kings* xix:9, 13). To Blake, Elijah was the perfect type of prophet; therefore Blake is hailing Byron as a genuine poet—and he was the only contemporary poet whom Blake named in his publications. Everything Byron had written was true as far as it went, but he had not gone far enough. To be specific, he had reached only the eleventh illustration of *Job*, where the God of This World is revealed in his full horror. The whirlwind, which would prostrate the forests, had not come yet.

So Byron's blasphemies did not shock Blake in the least; on the contrary, they were a necessary stage in Byron's spiritual development; and they were directed solely against the Elohim (whom Blake earlier would have named "Urizen" or "Nobodaddy"). Byron had not perceived that Jehovah, "Father of Mercies," was at work; nor did he guess that the mark on Cain's forehead was the kiss of Forgiveness (so Blake depicted it in his illuminated copy of *Genesis*).

Blake therefore rewrote the last scene of Byron's play, with two important changes. Eve, whom Byron made curse Cain so thoroughly, is changed completely into a distressed wife and mother, and consequently plays the part of Emanation: it is she who perceives instantly that the Ghost is not the person of Abel at all.

This Ghost is the voice of Abel's blood, mentioned so casually by Byron's Angel but now given the titular role. For he is the result of the first murder, the *lex talionis*, "the Accuser & Avenger of Blood," demanding "Life for life!" He is the seed of Satan, who is the Druid system of human sacrifice, and the great opponent of the God of Mercy.

When Blake's playlet opens, Cain has fled, leaving Abel's body by the grave he was digging. Adam and Eve, stunned with grief, refuse to listen further to Jehovah's voice. The Ghost of Abel enters, crying for vengeance, but neither parent can kill their remaining child. Jehovah, "Father of Mercies," then appears visibly to them, and they adore him. Yet the Ghost, still crying out for vengeance, sinks into the grave, whence Satan rises, crowned and armed; he proclaims that to him Jehovah himself shall be sacrificed on Calvary. Then Jehovah decrees that Satan shall go to Eternal Death until, self-subdued, he put off Satan into the bottomless Abyss.

A final chorus of angels sings how "The Elohim of the Heathen Swore Vengeance

for Sin"; but when Elohim Jehovah (God in both aspects of justice and mercy) stood forth all clothed in his "Covenant of the Forgiveness of Sins," the Elohim saw that their oath was eternal torment, and rolled apart "trembling over The Mercy Seat, each in his station fixt in the Firmament by Peace, Brotherhood and Love."

The Ghost of Abel is dated in the colophon, where this note is appended: "Blake's Original Stereotype was 1788," meaning that thirty-four years had passed since his first relief-etching.

GHOSTS seldom appear in Blake's writings. ". . . He was wont to say they did not appear much to imaginative men, but only to common minds, who did not see the finer spirits. A ghost was a thing seen by the gross bodily eye; a vision, by the mental." He saw a ghost only once—a horrible grim figure, "scaly, speckled, very awful," which stalked downstairs towards him at Lambeth, and frightened him into running out of the house (*Gil* I, 125).

Blake's simplest statement on his method of communicating with the dead occurs in his letter of condolence to Hayley (6 May 1800):

I know that our deceased friends are more really with us than when they were apparent to our mortal part. Thirteen years ago I lost a brother & with his spirit I converse daily & hourly in the Spirit & See him in my remembrance in the regions of my Imagination. I hear his advice & even now write from his Dictate.

The "Visionary" portraits which Blake drew for John Varley (*Symons* 352–54, 420–23) were obviously the product of memory and imagination, although Varley (in spite of Blake) was positive they were drawn from external ghosts. The "Ghost of a Flea" is the spirit of blood-lust, given form by the symbolizing imagination.

In the *Poetical Sketches*, the ghosts are merely literary conventions. "Fair Elenor" imagines she sees "pale sickly ghosts gliding" (16). In "Gwin, King of Norway," the "tall ghost of Barraton" is mentioned as a simile (53), and as a result of the battle, "Ghosts glut the throat of hell" (96) and "accusing groan" (100). The "War Song to Englishmen" depicts "ghosts over the well-fought field" (14). Over another battlefield, "the Giants & the Witches & the Ghosts of Albion dance with Thor & Friga" (J 63:13). The "Ghost of Abel" is not Abel at all, but the voice of his blood demanding vengeance.

When illustrating the works of others, Blake depicted ghosts according to the texts: the ghost of Hamlet's father (a hallucination of the corpse reanimated), the jolly ghosts in L'Allegro, and the graveyard ghosts (not spirits of the dead at all) who terrify Blair's schoolboy.

GIANTS symbolize the great primeval powers within us, though mostly hidden within our bodies of flesh; also, the great thinkers, those individuals who have overcome these earthly limitations and realized their powers. When separated from humanity, they become its fiercest enemies.

The Biblical giants consisted of the Antediluvians and the Postdiluvians.

The Antediluvians were the offspring of the angelic sons of Elohim and human women; they were "mighty men which were of old, men of renown" (Gen vi:1–4). The loves of their parents were described in the Book of Enoch, for which Blake began sketching illustrations, depicting the power of sex. These giants were so wicked that God sent Noah's Flood to destroy them.

Blake mentions them first as "Giants of Mighty arm, before the flood" in the early fragment "Then she bore Pale desire" (K 41). In the "Vision of the Last Judgment" (see Illustrations) they are represented beneath the cloud of Moses as "two figures, a Male & Female, chain'd together by the feet" (K 607), their union being of the lowest possible kind. However, another pair "with numerous Children . . . represent those who were not in the Line of the Church & yet were Saved from among the Antediluvians who Perished" (K 611), a statement which seems to mean that all the Antediluvians were not wicked but that some were saved. (See "LJ" Nos. 38, 66).

The line of the churches begins with Adam and his lineal descendants through Lamech, "Giants mighty, Hermaphroditic" (Mil 37:37; J 75:12).

As only errors, states, and the like can be annihilated, the Antediluvians still survive, though sunk beneath the Sea of Time and Space. Blake identified them with the five senses in the sixtieth illustration to the Inferno. Facing inward, the five giants are sunk to the hips beneath a raging storm of rain and lightning. "The Giants who formed this world into its sensual existence, and now seem to live in it in chains, are in truth the causes of its life & the sources of all activity . . . Messiah or Satan or Tempter was formerly thought to be one of the Antediluvians who are our Energies" (MHH 16, 17). The Tempter, it is implied, is the fifth sense, Touch—the salvation through Sex.

The Postdiluvian giants were the original inhabitants of Palestine, who were conquered by the invading Israelites. They are placed in the stomach of the Covering Cherub: "There the Seven Kings of Canaan & Five Baalim of Philistea, Sihon & Og, the Anakim & Emim, Nephilim & Gibborim" (J 89:46).

These are inhibiting forces, preventing man from passing the gates in head, heart, and loins. Sihon, king of the Amorites, and Og, king of Bashan, together constitute the Mundane Shell. Anak, ancestor of the gigantic Anakim, dwells with Og in Chaos. These three with Satan form an infernal quaternary.

The Biblical giants are psychological forces; the British, sociological. Thus, in the revolutionary "Gwin, King of Norway" (PS) the giant Gordred, who represents the masses, wakes from his sleep and slays the tyrant.

The British giants were the primordial inhabitants of the island, named "Albion" after their leader. They were nearly all slaughtered in a great battle when the

Trojans arrived, led by King Brutus, who named the island "Britain" after himself. In *King Edward the Third* (*PS*), the minstrel sings of this victory. But never again did Blake refer to this triumph of classicism over the primeval, and evidently altered his interpretation of the tale; for the giants (being living) could not be annihilated, but still are potent forces.

The giant Albion himself symbolizes Man (or, more narrowly, England). He is sunk in the deadly sleep of materialism. His giant sons have torn loose from his limbs and (being thus separated) have turned against humanity, on whom they prey, grinding the bones of the English in their mills, to make them bread—a reminiscence of the nursery tale of "Jack the Giant-Killer" (*J* 43:47).

Originally the British giants "dwelt in Intellect" on the Atlantic Mountains (*J* 50:1). But when Los bended the senses of Reuben, the Flood of Time and Space took place, and "the Atlantic Continent sunk round Albion's cliffy shore, and the Sea poured in amain upon the Giants of Albion" (*J* 36:39). Thus Albion became separated from the other nations. "Come & mourn over Albion, the White Cliff of the Atlantic, the Mountain of Giants: all the Giants of Albion are become weak, wither'd, darken'd, & Jerusalem is cast forth from Albion. They deny that they ever knew Jerusalem, or ever dwelt in Shiloh" (*J* 49:6).

When war breaks out, "the Giants & the Witches & the Ghosts of Albion dance with Thor & Friga" (*J* 63:13). But when Los speaks, "the Giants of Albion, terrified & ashamed . . . began to build trembling rocking Stones" which sometimes come to rest in the circles of druidic temples, still "plotting to devour Albion & Los" in their Natural Religion (*J* 90:58–66); and the Starry Wheels of their mills revolve round the sleeping Albion (*J* 94:11). Eventually they are reabsorbed into Albion.

The Giants built their causeway "into the Sea of Rephaim, but the Sea o'erwhelm'd them all" (*J* 89:51). The "Triple Headed Gog-Magog Giant of Albion Taxed the Nations into Desolation" (*J* 98:52). Jehovah placed Og and Anak, Giants of Albion, to guard Albion's tomb (*J* 49:56). Merlin was like Rintrah among the Giants of Albion (*J* 93:13). Mount Zion is once called "the Hill of Giants" (*J* 78:22).

The GIANT'S CAUSEWAY is a spectacular geological formation of some forty thousand basaltic columns on the north coast of Antrim, Ireland, which once crossed over to Scotland. Traditionally it was built by Finn MacCool, so that a Scottish giant could come over and fight him. The first account of this natural wonder was published in Dr. William Hamilton's *Letters Concerning the Northern Coast of Antrim* (1786).

Blake, however, took it to be the westernmost part of the Europeo-Asiatic land-mass. The Covering Cherub's wings spread "from Japan, where the Red Sea terminates the World of Generation & Death, to Ireland's farthest rocks, where the Giants builded their Causeway, into the Sea of Rephaim, but the Sea o'erwhelm'd them all" (*J* 89:48; see also *J* 78:26).

Modern geologists say that such a land bridge did once actually extend from western Ireland to Newfoundland.

GIBBON (Edward, 1737–94) published his great *Decline and Fall of the Roman Empire* from 1776 to 1788. The fifteenth chapter, which counted Christianity as one of the causes of the fall of the ideal empire, caused a great controversy, but his scholarship proved impeccable. Unperturbed, he continued to include church history and its miracles with an expert touch of amused skepticism, until he found "the triumph of barbarism and religion" complete in the sixteenth century, and ended his book.

Blake paid Gibbon his characteristic compliment of assailing him as one of the leading skeptics, along with Voltaire, Rousseau, Hume, and the Deists (*Mil* 40:12; *J* 52). He particularly deplored Gibbon's lack of any feeling for genuine religious experience: "Voltaire, Rousseau,

Gibbon, Hume, charge the Spiritually Religious with Hypocrisy; but how a Monk, or a Methodist either, can be a Hypocrite, I cannot concieve" (*J* 52). In the poem on the same plate, "I saw a Monk of Charlemaine," he mentions Gibbon's "lash of steel" and links the apologist for empire with the militant emperors as well as the skeptics: "Titus! Constantine! Charlemaine! | O Voltaire! Rousseau! Gibbon! Vain | Your Grecian Mocks & Roman Sword | Against this image of his Lord!"

The GIBBORIM were the Antediluvians, the progeny of the sons of Elohim and human women. The word does not appear in the King James Bible, being translated "mighty men" (*Gen* vi:4) and, in the singular, "giant" (*Job* xvi:14).

Blake places them with other giants in the stomach of the Covering Cherub (*J* 89:47).

GIHON, the second of the four rivers of Eden, ran south and encompassed "The whole land of Ethiopia" (*Gen* ii:13); it was consequently identified with the Nile.

In the head of the Covering Cherub is seen "Egypt on the Gihon, many tongued and many mouth'd" (*J* 89:15). Mary, when forgiven by Joseph, rejoices like the four rivers (*J* 61:32).

GILEAD, in Palestine east of the Jordan, was bounded on the north by Bashan (across the Yarmuk), on the east by the desert, on the south by Moab and Ammon, on the west by the Jordan. The balm of Gilead was famous. King Sihon ruled here until the Israelites slaughtered him and all his people.

Erin bids Sihon and Og return to Bashan and Gilead (*J* 48:64). Jerusalem complains that she seeks vainly in Gilead for a physician and comforter (*J* 79:11–12), recollecting Jeremiah's words (viii:22): "Is there no balm in Gilead; is there no physician there? why then is not the health of the daughter of my people recovered?"

Mount Gilead is mentioned in *Genesis*

xxxi:25 and *Judges* vii:3. The site is uncertain, but it may be the peak seven miles north of the Jabbok.

The Council of God meets, hovering over Gilead and Hermon (*FZ* i:199; viii:2). Elsewhere it hovers over Gilead alone, where it draws up the Universal Tent (*FZ* i:475, 552); in these two passages Blake substituted the name "Snowdon."

Tirzah complains that if her schemes do not succeed, mercy and truth will flee from Shechem and Mount Gilead (*FZ* viii:320; *J* 68:8). Five Daughters of Albion unite into Tirzah and her sisters on Mount Gilead (*J* 5:40). Reuben stands on Mount Gilead, looking toward Gilgal (*J* 36:12).

GILGAL was the place where Joshua and the Israelites encamped after crossing the Jordan, which had parted its waters at the presence of the holy Ark (*Josh* iv).

Reuben, unable to stay across the Jordan, stood on Mount Gilead, looking toward Gilgal (*J* 36:12).

GLAMORGANSHIRE is a maritime county in southern Wales. It is the Gate of Benjamin (*J* 16:41), and is under Guantok (*J* 71:29).

GLASGO[W] is a Scottish county which, with Selkirk and Dumbarton, is assigned to Issachar (*J* 16:57). All Scotland is assigned to Bowen (*J* 71:46).

The GLOBE OF BLOOD separated from Los when, after the binding of Urizen, he began to feel pity; and "pity divides the soul" (*Ur* 13:53; *Mil* 8:19). This division became the Globe of Blood, which developed into Enitharmon, the first separate female (*Ur* 13:51, 58; 18:1–8; 19:1; *Mil* 3:30; *J* 86:50–54). This episode was to be inserted into *The Four Zoas*, after v:287. See ENITHARMON.

GLOUCESTER is third in the list of the Cathedral Cities (*J* 40:61). It is under Urizen and Verulam.

Gloucestershire is an English county on

the Severn. With the adjoining counties of Somerset and Wiltshire, it is assigned to Judah (*J* 16:45), and is under the rule of Coban (*J* 71:26).

GLYCON was the sculptor of the Farnese Hercules. "That mankind are in a less distinguished Situation with regard to mind than they were in the time of Homer, Socrates, Phidias, Glycon, Aristotle, etc., let all their works witness" (On Watson, *K* 388). Blake's father gave his son a cast of the Hercules (*Gil* I, 9).

The GNOMES are the element of Earth in the list of the Four Elements (*Mil* 31:20; *J* 36:37). Their compass-point is north: "sixty-four thousand Gnomes guard the Northern Gate" of Golgonooza (*J* 13:27).

Their subliminal activities in the work of poetic creation are described in *Milton* 7 and 12, and resemble the work of R. L. Stevenson's brownies. They are the friends of Palamabron and servants of his harrow. When Satan interferes, they are his accusers. The horses bite many of the strongest. Satan then compels them to curb the horses and throw up sandbanks around the flaming harrow. They curse Satan, but labor, then refuse to labor more. When Leutha springs from Satan's head, "back the Gnomes recoil'd and called me Sin and for a sign portentous held me" (*Mil* 12:38) —a direct quotation from *Paradise Lost* ii:760–61, where Sin is born similarly from Satan's head, and the Host of Heaven recoils and names her.

The Gnomes are depicted holding pens and riding the horses of Elijah's chariot (*J* 47).

Blake may have known that a "gnome" also means a wise but cryptic saying.

"GOD is Jesus" (*Laoc*, *K* 777). But in defining Deity as the Second Person of the Trinity, Blake was not eliminating the other Persons, for they are aspects of Jesus. While still on earth, Jesus claimed to be one with the Father (*John* x:30); and after his death, he "became Jehovah," the merci-

ful God (*MHH* 6; cf. *CR* 255). So thoroughly have the two been identified, I cannot recall throughout the Christian world any festival or church devoted solely to the Father. As for the Holy Ghost, he is the efflux of Jesus, the intellectual fountain proceeding from Jesus to man. Blake began a prayer: "Jesus, our Father, who art in thy heaven call'd by thy Name the Holy Ghost" (On Thornton, *K* 788). In his illuminated *Genesis*, however, Blake depicted all three Persons distinct but working together (see Illustrations).

Jesus is the Human God. "Human Nature is the image of God" (On Lavater 554, *K* 83), because we were made in his image (*Gen* i:27). "[Jesus] is the only God. . . . And so am I and so are you" (*CR* 255). "We are all co-existent with God—members of the Divine body. We are all partakers of the Divine nature" (*CR* 255). Whatever individuality or genius we have is the divine within us. "Thou art a Man, God is no more [than Man], | Thy own humanity learn to adore, | For that is my Spirit of Life" (*EG* d:75). Lavater wrote (549): "He who hates the wisest and best of men hates the Father of men; for, where is the Father of men to be seen but in the most perfect of his children?" Blake altered "hates" to "loves," underlined the last clause, and commented: "This is true worship" (*K* 82). "The worship of God is: Honouring his gifts in other men, each according to his genius, and loving the greatest men best: those who envy or calumniate great men hate God; for there is no other God" (*MHH* 22). In *Jerusalem* (91:8), Blake expanded this: "The Worship of God is honouring his gifts in other men: & loving the greatest men best, each according to his Genius, which is the Holy Ghost in Man; there is no other God than that God who is the intellectual fountain of Humanity. He who envies or calumniates, which is murder & cruelty, murders the Holy-one." "He who despises & mocks a Mental Gift in another, calling it pride & selfishness & sin, mocks Jesus the giver of every Mental Gift, which always appear to the ignorance-loving Hypocrite as Sins; but that which is a Sin in the sight of cruel Man is not so in the sight of our kind God" (*J* 77).

God and Man are inseparable. "God is Man & exists in us & we in him" (On Berkeley, *K* 775; cf. *John* xvii:21–23).

Jesus is the source of everything. "Around the Throne Heaven is open'd & the Nature of Eternal Things Display'd, All Springing from the Divine Humanity. All beams from him" (*LJ*, *K* 612). "Jesus is surrounded by Beams of Glory in which are seen all around him Infants emanating from him; these represent the Eternal Births of Intellect from the Divine Humanity" (*LJ*, *K* 613; see Illustrations, "LJ" No. 6).

"Every thing is good in God's eyes" (*CR* 256). Impartially "he gives his rain to the Evil & the Good, & his Sun to the Just & the Unjust" (On Dante, *K* 785, paraphrasing *Matt* v:45). "Nothing is displeasing to God but Unbelief & Eating of the Tree of Knowledge of Good & Evil" (*LJ*, *K* 615).

Jesus is the Imagination, the creative power which is the core of man's being. "All Things are comprehended in their Eternal Forms in the divine body of the Saviour, the True Vine of Eternity, the Human Imagination" (*LJ*, *K* 605–6). See MINUTE PARTICULARS. He is the Creator. "All things were made by him" (*John* i:3); "by him were all things created" (*Col* i:16). In his Mercy he creates the worlds of each of us, setting limits to the Fall, like Los giving form to Error that it may be cast out. "Creation is God descending according to the weakness of man, for our Lord is the word of God & every thing on earth is the word of God & in its essence is God" (On Lavater 630, *K* 87).

As the Truth (*John* xiv:6) he appears like Light "To those poor Souls who dwell in Night, | But does a Human Form Display | To those who Dwell in Realms of day" (*Aug* 130, *K* 434). As Truth, he is the great healer of mental diseases, tracing them to their source (*EG b*:36), for "the truth shall make you free" (*John* viii:32).

See DISEASE. As the Truth, he sits enthroned at the Last Judgment, casting out all Errors and thus saving all those who were in error. See LAST JUDGMENT.

Jesus descended from heaven and took on a mortal body to save fallen Man. "And the Word was made flesh" (*John* i:14). Thus the Creator became the Redeemer, the Saviour.

To Blake, this was an eternal and never-ending process. "God becomes as we are, that we may be as he is" (*NNR* ii, *Application*). Every heart is the Stable. As the Imagination, Jesus comes from the North; when Luvah (love) fails on earth, Jesus descends into the East and assumes Luvah's robes of blood, "lest the state call'd Luvah should cease; & the Divine Vision walked in robes of blood till he who slept [Albion] should awake" (*FZ* ii:263–65).

Jesus is the seventh of the seven Eyes of God, which represent the spiritual progress of man from Lucifer, through the stages of revelation, to the true God. There is a "shadowy Eighth," the Individual himself. See EYES OF GOD.

Blake did not distinguish between the two natures of Jesus as defined in the Prayer Book: the Divine and the Human were identical in him; *because* he is Human, he is Divine. Blake did distinguish, however, between the Eternal and the Mortal. In this body Jesus could and did err. See JESUS.

The ABSTRACT GOD of the Anglican Prayer Book, "without passion or parts," was for Blake a mere logical abstraction without significance.

Lavater wrote (552): "He, who adores an impersonal God, has none; and, without guide or rudder, launches on an immense abyss that first absorbs his powers, and next himself." Blake commented: "Most superlatively beautiful & most affectionately Holy & pure; would to God that all men would consider it" (*K* 82). This Abstract God is the invention of the Spectre: "He is Righteous, he is not a Being of Pity & Compassion, he cannot feel Distress, he feeds on Sacrifice & Offering, delighting in cries & tears & clothed in holiness & solitude" (*J* 10:47). "[Plato and Aristotle] considered God as abstracted or distinct from the Imaginative World; but Jesus . . . consider'd God as a Man in the Spiritual or Imaginative Vision" (On Berkeley, *K* 774). The Abstract God is "a Shadow from [Albion's] wearied intellect of living gold, pure, perfect, holy" (*FZ* iii:50; *J* 29:37). He is Bildad's God: "the stars are not pure in his sight" (*Job* xxv:5), or the sinister Angel of the Divine Presence: "Tho' thou wast so pure & bright | That Heaven was Impure in thy Sight" (*EG* e:35).

Milton's Father accepts the sacrifice of the Son without apparent emotion except satisfaction (*PL* iii:274-343), but Blake, illustrating this scene, represents the Father as sunk in deepest grief and love, "for God so loved the world, that he gave his only begotten Son" (*John* iii:16).

The ANGRY GOD is the jealous God of the Old Testament. He dwells, not within us, but high above. (To this day, most people, asked to point to heaven, point upwards, in spite of Galileo.) He is the giver of law and the punisher of sin. He is the contrary of the Loving Father.

His wrath (or Justice) at Adam and Eve's trespass could be satisfied only by diverting and exhausting it upon the crucified Saviour. This "Vicarious Atonement," according to Blake, "is a horrible doctrine. If another man pay your debt, I do not forgive it" (*CR* 271; cf. *J* 61:17). He ridiculed the doctrine: "First God Almighty comes with a Thump on the Head. Then Jesus Christ comes with a balm to heal it" (*LJ*, *K* 617).

Blake renamed the Angry God "Nobodaddy." "Why art thou silent & invisible, Father of Jealousy? Why dost thou hide thyself in clouds from every searching Eye? Why darkness & obscurity in all thy words & laws?" (*To Nobodaddy*, *K* 171).

The Angry God is the invention of the falling Albion. "God in the dreary Void dwells from Eternity, wide separated from

the Human Soul. . . . May God, who dwells in this dark Ulro & voidness, vengeance take" (*J* 23:29, 38). Albion names his Tree "Moral Virtue and the Law of God who dwells in Chaos hidden from the human sight" (*J* 28:15). "Seek not thy heavenly father then beyond the skies: there Chaos dwells & ancient Night & Og & Anak old" (*Mil* 20:32).

Nonetheless, wrath is a human emotion and therefore exists in Deity. "The Fall of Man" (1807) depicts the Father shaking with rage while the Saviour conducts Adam and Eve from Eden. On a title page of *Genesis*, he is shown with black clouds and flames (see Illustrations). As Urizen he creates the Tyger of wrath; elsewhere he is called "Elohim." See ANGEL OF THE DIVINE PRESENCE, under ANGEL.

The GOD OF THIS WORLD (so named by St. Paul, *II Cor* iv:4) is Satan. "To the Accuser who is The God of This World. Truly, My Satan . . ." (*GoP*, Epilogue). "Satan . . . who is God of This World, the Accuser. Let his Judgment be Forgiveness that he may be consumed [? "cursed"—*K*] on his own throne [? "in his own Shame"—Erdman]" (On Thornton, *K* 788).

According to the Christian legend (repeated in *Paradise Lost*), after man ate the fruit of the Tree of Moral Values, Satan took possession of the world, thus becoming "the prince of the power of the air" (*Eph* ii:2). "The Bible says that God formed Nature perfect, but that Man perverted the order of Nature, since which time the Elements are fill'd with the Prince of Evil, who has the power of the air" (On Watson, *K* 388).

The God of This World is the god mistakenly worshipped by the worldly under the names of the real God. "Tho' thou art Worship'd by the Names Divine of Jesus & Jehovah . . ." (*GoP*, Epilogue 5). "There is a God of this World, A God Worship'd in this World as God & set above all that is call'd God" (On Watson, *K* 394).

The religion of Satan the Accuser (*diabolos*) is that of punishment ("vengeance") for sin. "Loud howl'd | The God of this World" at the triumphal progress of Jesus' fire-chariot (*EG b*:43) .

He is identical with the Angry God. In the third illustration to Dante, Blake depicted "The Angry God of This World" as a Urizenic old man with a cloven left foot, turgid flames spiralling down from his hands. Before him kneels Empire swinging a censer.

The GODS are various human faculties deified by the heathen. "All deities reside in the human breast" (*MHH* 11) . But to elevate one to the supreme position is to distort the harmony of life, resulting in disaster. "These gods are visions of the eternal attributes, or divine names, which, when erected into gods, become destructive to humanity. They ought to be the servants, and not the masters, of man, or of society. They ought to be made to sacrifice to Man, and not man compelled to sacrifice to them" (*DesC* III, *K* 571) . They are "the Moral Virtues of the Heathen," whose Forgiveness and "tender mercies are Cruelty" (*J* 61:20) .

In *The Four Zoas*, each of three of the Zoas in turn comes to believe that he is God, and each fails. "Attempting to be more than Man We become less," says Luvah (*FZ* ix:709) . Urizen also has learned his lesson: "If Gods combine against Man, setting their dominion above the Human form Divine, Thrown down from their high station in the Eternal heavens of Human Imagination, buried beneath in dark Oblivion, with incessant pangs, ages on ages, in enmity & war first weaken'd, then in stern repentance they must renew their brightness, & their disorganiz'd functions again reorganize, till they resume the image of the human, co-operating in the bliss of Man, obeying his Will, servants to the infinite & Eternal of the Human form" (*FZ* ix:366) .

Their source is the Imagination, the "Poetic Genius." "The Religions of all Nations are derived from each Nation's different reception of the Poetic Genius" (*AllR* 5) . "The philosophy of the east taught the first principles of human perception: some nations held one principle for the origin, & some another: we of Israel taught that the Poetic Genius (as you now call it) was the first principle and all others merely derivative, which was the cause of our despising the Priests & Philosophers of other countries, and prophecying that all Gods would at last be proved to originate in ours & to be the tributaries of the Poetic Genius" (*MHH* 12) .

Blake's first attempt to describe the gods occurs in an early fragment, "Then she bore Pale desire," an allegory of the deadly sins (*K* 40) . Later he listed them as the Twelve Gods of Asia (*Mil* 37:20–34) .

The GODS OF ASIA are "twelve monstrous dishumaniz'd terrors, Synagogues of Satan . . . the Twelve Spectre Sons of the Druid Albion" (*Mil* 37:17, 34) .

In the yet unredeemed Milton, Blake beheld all the religious errors of the past, "the Monstrous Churches of Beulah [religions based on sex], the Gods of Ulro dark [religions based on materialism]" (*Mil* 37:16) . They are "a Double Twelve & Thrice Nine," the double twelve being the pagan gods and goddesses, with their Emanations or Spectres, the thrice nine being the Twenty-seven "Christian" Churches.

The pagan gods are Baal, Ashtaroth, Chemosh, Molech, Dagon, Thammuz, Rimmon, the Egyptian trinity (Osiris, Isis, and Orus [Horus]) , Belial, Saturn, Jove, and Rhea (*Mil* 37:16–34) . The list is copied from *Paradise Lost* i:391–513; but where Milton placed Baalim and Ashtaroth ("those male, these feminine") as third and fourth in his grouping according to the Deadly Sins, Blake put Baal and Ashtaroth (mistaking the plural for the singular "Ashtareth") at the head of the list.

The once unspoiled Atlantic Mountains are now given over to "the Twelve Gods of Asia, the Spectres of those who Sleep, sway'd by a Providence oppos'd to the Divine Lord Jesus" (*J* 50:1–4)—a Darwinian world, where all creatures prey on each other and live by devouring Death. But these gods are "deceased" when the clouds of Revolution roll round them (*SoL* 4:19).

The Sons and Daughters of Albion become "the Twelve Gods of Asia, Opposing the Divine Vision" (*J* 74:22). In Eden, however, they are called after the names of the Twelve Tribes of Israel (*Mil* 40:25).

GOG of the land of Magog (probably Scythia) was a predatory conqueror whose eventual destruction was prophesied by Ezekiel (xxxviii–xxxix). In *Revelation* (xx: 8–9), Gog and Magog are forerunners of the Last Judgment. At the close of the millennium, Satan is to be released temporarily, when he shall deceive "the nations which are in the four quarters of the earth, Gog and Magog, to gather them together to battle." After they surround the camp of the saints and the beloved city, fire from God shall consume them.

Blake, however, declared that these nations shall themselves bind the Great Red Dragon. "He is bound in chains by Two strong demons; they are Gog & Magog, who have been compell'd to subdue their Master (Ezekiel, xxxviii c. 8 v.) with their Hammer & Tongs, about to new-Create the Seven-Headed Kingdoms" (*LJ*, *K* 609).

Hyle, who is "the Affections rent asunder & opposed to Thought" (*J* 74:28), is called Gog because he tries "to draw Jerusalem's Sons into the Vortex of his Wheels . . . age after age drawing them away towards Babylon, the Rational Morality" (*J* 74:29).

GOGMAGOG, according to Camden's *Britannia* (London, 1695, p. v), was the greatest of the British giants whom Brutus conquered in 1108 B.C. He is called "Goemagot" by Geoffrey of Monmouth (Chap. xvi), who says that Brutus spared him for a wrestling match with his comrade-in-arms Corineus. Corineus flung him into the sea at the "Haw," near Plymouth.

Brutus is said to have had the two chained as porters at the gate of the palace he built where the Guildhall now stands.

Their wooden statues, destroyed by German bombs in the late war, were popularly renamed Gog and Magog; they were supposed to have been brothers of the slain Albion.

There are Gog Magog Hills in Cambridgeshire.

"Where are the Kingdoms of the World & all their glory that grew on Desolation, the Fruit of Albion's Poverty Tree, when the Triple Headed Gogmagog Giant of Albion Taxed the Nations into Desolation & then gave the Spectrous Oath?" (*J* 98:52).

GOLD (south) is one of the four symbolic metals, the others being silver (east), iron (north), and brass (west). It is appropriately assigned to the sun-god Urizen (*J* 97:8). His compasses are of gold (*Ur* 20:39; *FZ* ii:29). His chariot (*FZ* v:235), his horses (*FZ* vii *b*:201), his hall (*FZ* ii:179) are all golden; and so forth.

Although Blake often used "gold" to describe anything beautiful or precious, his general meaning is "intellectual." Such are the keys of Paradise, the poet's bow, the string which he gives us as clue to his meaning. Among the bad things are the Abstract God which is the product of man's "wearied intellect" (*FZ* iii:50), matrimony's cage, the chapel in the Garden of Love, and the serpent adorned with gems and gold.

GOLGONOOZA is Los's city of "Art & Manufacture" (*Mil* 24:50). It contains, or consists of, the physical bodies of man and woman. The city is foursquare, like the New Jerusalem. It has "mighty Spires & Domes [male and female] of ivory & gold" (*Mil* 35:25). In the South—the intellect— is Los's palace (*J* 13:25), and in the center is his forge with its furnaces (*J* 59:23), called Bowlahoola, being the organs of the animal man (*Mil* 24:49–59). "In the North Gate, in the West of the North, toward

GOLGONOOZA

Jerusalem 12:45–13:29

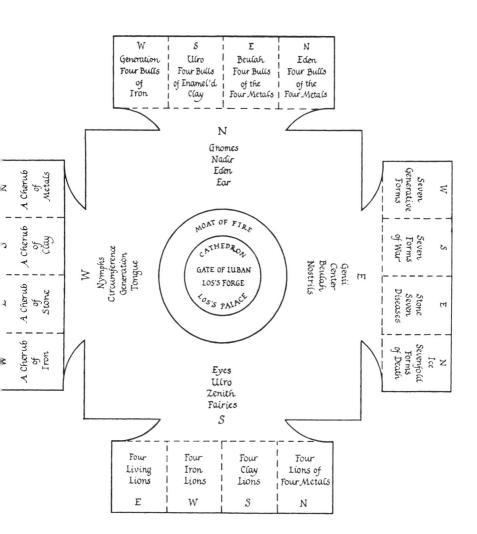

W	S	E	N
Generation	Ulro	Beulah	Eden
Four Bulls	Four Bulls	Four Bulls	Four Bulls
of	of Enamel'd	of the	of the
Iron	Clay	Four Metals	Four Metals

N
Gnomes
Nadir
Eden
Ear

MOAT OF FIRE

CATHEDRON

GATE OF LUBAN

LOS'S FORGE

LOS'S PALACE

W
Nymphs
Circumference
Generation
Tongue

E
Genii
Center
Beulah
Nostrils

A Cherub of Metals — N
A Cherub of Clay — S
A Cherub of Stone — E
A Cherub of Iron — W

W
Seven Generative Forms
Seven Forms of War
Stone Seven Diseases
Ice Sevenfold Forms of Death

S
Eyes
Ulro
Zenith
Fairies

Four	Four	Four	Four
Living	Iron	Clay	Lions of
Lions	Lions	Lions	Four Metals
E	W	S	N

NOTE: Golgonooza, being four-dimensional, cannot be reduced to a chart of two dimensions. Each of the four gates not only opens into each of the other gates but does so "each within other toward the Four points." (J 12:48)

Beulah," is the golden hall of Cathedron, with courts, towers, and pinnacles (*J* 59:22–25); it contains Enitharmon's looms (the womb), where the physical body of man is woven. In the middle of the city is the Gate of Luban (the vagina); a moat of fire surrounds Luban, Los's palace, and the looms of Cathedron (*J* 13:24–28). The whole city is walled against the wars of Satan (*FZ* viii:109).

Besides Luban, Golgonooza has four gates, one towards each compass-point; they are described elaborately in *Jerusalem* 12–13. Every gate has four openings, "each within other," to the four regions of Eden, Generation, Beulah, and Ulro. Thus the imagination opens into all phases of existence, except for the western gate, which is closed until "the last day."

At the eastern gate is a rock of crystal, odorous with wild thyme; here is the Lark's nest. (See LARK.) A fountain there divides into two streams: "one flows thro' Golgonooza and thro' Beulah to Eden, beneath Los's western Wall; the other flows through the Aerial Void & all the Churches." They meet again in Golgonooza (*Mil* 35:49–53).

Los stands in London on the banks of the Thames, building Golgonooza (*J* 10:17; 53:15). It covers the whole of Britain (*Mil* 6:1–7). From it extends the spiritual fourfold London, in the creative loins of Albion (*Mil* 20:40). All the counties of Great Britain center in London and Golgonooza (*J* 72:28).

Around the city is the cultivated land of Allamanda, in the forests of Entuthon Benython (*Mil* 27:43). To the east is the Lake of Udan Adan, the indefinite, upon the Limit of Translucence, or Satan (*FZ* v:76; viii:224). Eastward is also Los's Wine-press, or war, before the Seat of Satan, which is this world (*Mil* 27:1). Beneath Golgonooza lie the deep vales of Entuthon Benython (*J* 14:34). In general, the city is surrounded by "the land of death eternal" (*J* 13:30), a hell elaborated from Milton's description, inside the "Concave Earth," which is the inner side of the

Mundane Shell (*J* 13:38–54). Nevertheless, Golgonooza is continuous from Urthona's realm (*FZ* vii:382). "For travellers from Eternity pass outward to Satan's seat, but travellers to Eternity pass inward to Golgonooza" (*Mil* 17:29).

The great work of Golgonooza is to give forms to all uncreated things, particularly threefold man. Blake believed that all life is eternal; that all causation is mental; and that the imagination is the prenatal power which shapes the human body.

Golgonooza appears first in *The Four Zoas*. It starts as the development of the individual poet-painter, but expands into the cosmic. Los begins building Golgonooza around Enitharmon after the birth of Orc (*FZ* v:76)—the beginning of revolt starts the poetic instinct's creation. It is the re-creation of the fallen man, opening new heavens and a new earth through head, heart, and loins, "but yet having a Limit Twofold named Satan & Adam" (*FZ* vii:378–83). After the fruit of the forbidden Tree is eaten, Urthona's Spectre, terrified at the Spectres of the Dead, suggests that they should be given created bodies (*FZ* vii:401–9). Los agrees. These "piteous victims of battle" in the wars of Satan, which seek refuge in Enitharmon's bosom, "feed upon our life; we are their victims. Stern desire I feel to fabricate embodied semblances in which the dead may live before us in our palaces" (*FZ* vii:436–41). Los draws the outline; Enitharmon tinctures it "with beams of blushing love" (*FZ* vii:468). The artist's sympathetic understanding of his enemies draws them from their wars, and Los wonders to find that now he loves them, instead of hating them.

In the next "Night," however, the aesthetic "semblances" become material actualities, real bodies of flesh. Enitharmon erects her looms to give the Spectres "Bodies of Vegetation" (viii:36–38) — threefold material bodies. The eventual result is the Incarnation: Jesus appears in their midst (viii:44); the Divine Family of the brotherhood combines into Jerusalem, in whose bosom is the Divine Vision (viii:187–93). Thus the poetic imagination creates both the human body and the ideal society.

In *Milton*, the process is localized in Britain. The souls descend to the body through the southern gate, which extends the length of the southern coast of England, while those delivered from the body descend through the northern gate along the northern coast of Scotland (*Mil* 26:13–17). Los's forge is identified with the organs of the human body: "The Bellows are the Animal Lungs; the Hammers the Animal Heart; the Furnaces the Stomach for digestion" (*Mil* 24:58). "Energy is from the body"; man's entire physiology takes part in the creative process.

The yet unbodied and unborn Spectres are still mere "piteous Passions & Desires with neither lineament nor form, but like to wat'ry clouds" (*Mil* 26:26), drifting, wailing incessant, and sometimes fighting if they are "Doubts & fears unform'd" (*Mil* 28:11). The myriad Sons of Los now take active part in catching and housing them. They create "form & beauty around the dark regions of sorrow, giving to airy nothing a name and a habitation delightful, with bounds to the Infinite putting off the Indefinite into most holy forms of Thought; such is the power of inspiration" (*Mil* 28:2). These lines refer to the speech of Theseus (*Midsummer Night's Dream*, V.i. 11–17): "The poet's eye, in a fine frenzy rolling, doth glance from heaven to earth, from earth to heaven; and as imagination bodies forth the forms of things unknown, the poet's pen turns them to shapes, and gives to airy nothing a local habitation and a name." Gilchrist records, however, that Blake objected to the word "nothing" (*Gil* I, 363).

Antamon (the semen) draws the indelible outline of the sweet form, which the Spectre admiring puts on (*Mil* 28:13–18). If a cruel Spectre refuses, Theotormon and Sotha (both balked desire) terrify it into their nets of kindness, to be born a weeping terror. The sons of Ozoth control the sense of sight: they give delights unknown, opening "the heavens of bright eternity" within the poor indigent (*Mil* 28:38). It was in the optic vegetable nerves that Satan once transformed Sleep into Death (*Mil* 29:32). In the Nostrils, the Saviour formed the "Opake and Indefinite" into Satan (opake) and Adam (solid) — (*Mil* 29:35–39). In the Ear, Los creates the sun and moon, "Death to delude" (*Mil* 29:40–43). The nerves of the Tongue, however, are closed. Other Sons create Time from the Four Elements; Rintrah and Palamabron govern the day and night (*Mil* 29:27).

After all this is done, Los conducts the spirits into Golgonooza to be actually "vegetated" (*Mil* 29:47). At his forge, or Bowlahoola, the three "Classes of Men are all mark'd out determinate in Bowlahoola, & as the Spectres choose their affinities, so they are born on Earth" (*Mil* 26:37). But first Enitharmon and her Daughters take them in charge and "give them to their lovely heavens till the Great Judgment Day" (*Mil* 29:52).

Jerusalem (12–13) adds the elaborate description of the four gates, each leading to the four worlds of Eden, Generation, Beulah, and Ulro.

It is significant that Los and Enitharmon leave Golgonooza (sympathetic understanding) to bind Orc, but repent on returning (*FZ* v:98, 143). Rintrah and Palamabron cut Satan-Hayley off from Golgonooza (*FZ* viii:370, 394). The same two meet Los and Blake at "the Gate" of Golgonooza to protest against permitting the dangers of Blake's revolutionary thought (*Mil* 22:27).

GOLGOTHA (Aramaic), or Calvary (Latin), was the site of the Crucifixion. Blake uses both names: "is that Calvary and Golgotha becoming a building of pity and compassion?" (*J* 12:28). It is the place of the execution of martyrs: "spiritual deaths of mighty men who give themselves in Golgotha, Victims to Justice" (*J* 38:54). It is related to Tyburn (*J* 63:33). Druidism spread "from Camberwell to Golgotha" (*J* 92:26).

GOMORRHA and Sodom were the chief of the cities of the plain on the Dead Sea, which were destroyed by divine wrath presumably because of their addiction to homosexuality. But see SODOM.

"Belial of Sodom & Gomorrha, obscure Demon of Bribes and secret Assassinations, not worship'd nor ador'd, but with the finger on the lips & the back turn'd to the light" (*Mil* 37:30). The heart of the Polypus sends out fibres round the earth, including Sodom and Gomorrha (*J* 67:37–40). The two are seen in the bosom of the Covering Cherub (*J* 89:27).

GON is the thirteenth son of Los and Enitharmon (*FZ* viii:359).

GONORILL, or "Gonorilla" (*Geof* II, xi), was the eldest daughter of King Leir, and the leader in cruelty to her father. She married Maglaunus, duke of Albania, to whom Leir had given half his kingdom as a dowry. Regan and she drove her father from the kingdom, but with the aid of Cordeilla and her husband, he got it back. Milton spelled her name as Blake did; Shakespeare dropped the second *l*.

In the original list of the Daughters of Albion, Gonorill is the fourth (*FZ* ii:61); but later she became the eighth, and is one of the seven who unite under Rahab (*J* 5:43). Ragan, the Emanation of Brereton, "adjoin'd to Slade, & produced Gonorill far beaming." Slade's "lovely Emanation" is Gonorill, who "rejoices over hills & rocks & woods & rivers" (*J* 71:32–35).

GOSHEN was "the best of the land" in Egypt; here Joseph settled his father Jacob and his brothers (*Gen* xlvii:6, 11).

"Goshen hath follow'd Philistea. Gilead hath join'd with Og" (*J* 79:13).

"GRAMMATEIS" is translated "scribes" in the King James Bible. They were the archivists and authorities on the Law, who played a conspicuous part in the Crucifixion.

They appear with the "Pharisaion" and others in the Covering Cherub, covering the eastern heaven (*J* 89:6).

GRASSHOPPERS were one of the pests which afflicted the Israelites. They came in such huge swarms that the encroaching Midianites and Amalekites were compared to them: they "destroyed the increase of the earth" and "left no sustenance for Israel, neither sheep, nor ox, nor ass. . . . they came as grasshoppers for multitude . . . and they entered into the land to destroy it" (*Judges* vi:4–5; also *Amos* vii:2). "The grasshopper shall be a burden" (*Ecclesiastes* xii:5) and therefore appears in the margin of *Illustrations of the Book of Job*, Plate 6. They are bred among the other vermin round the Wine-press of War (*FZ* ix:760; *Mil* 29:19).

GREAT GEORGE STREET runs from Parliament Square to St. James's Park.

In the counter-revolutionary uproar, the "Guardian of the secret codes" is driven by the flames of Orc to forsake his ancient mansion in Westminster; "he fled groveling along Great George Street thro' the Park gate" (*Eur* 12:15–19).

Erdman identifies the Guardian as Lord Thurlow, the Lord High Chancellor and Keeper of the Seal and Guardian of the King's Conscience. He was, surprisingly, the first victim of the anti-Jacobin ban, Pitt having persuaded the king to dismiss him (1792). Thurlow therefore doffed his judicial robes and great wig (which Blake represents as growing to him), left the Westminster government buildings, and went to St. James's Palace to surrender the Seal (*Erd* 199–201).

GREAT QUEEN STREET, near Blake's birthplace on the corner of Broad Street and his residence at 28 Poland Street, was a pleasant promenade to the open space of Lincoln's Inn Fields, on which is situated Lincoln's Inn, one of the Inns of Court.

On this street was the shop of the engraver James Basire, to whom young Blake was apprenticed on August 4, 1772. Blake's earliest surviving signature, on the flyleaf of a book, reads "William Blake[,] Lincolns Inn" (*K Studies* 47). William Hayley lived at No. 5, Great Queen Street, from 1769 to 1774; he must have dropped in at Basire's print shop, where he might have encountered the young apprentice.

"The Corner of Broad Street weeps; Poland Street languishes; to Great Queen Street & Lincoln's Inn all is distress & woe" (*J* 84:15).

GREECE (Grecia) and the Holy Lands are the two historic sources of our culture. Blake recognized them as such in his early "To The Muses" (*PS*): "Whether on Ida's shady brow, | Or in the chambers of the East . . ." The Greek cult of ideal nudes, with their firm outlines, appealed strongly to Blake, as well as to his friends Cumberland and Flaxman. He also read eagerly Taylor's translations of the philosophers. On August 16, 1799, he wrote to Trusler of "the purpose for which alone I live, which is, in conjunction with such men as my friend Cumberland, to renew the lost Art of the Greeks"; and on July 2, 1800, to Cumberland, of "the immense flood of Grecian light & glory which is coming on Europe."

Blake, however, reversed his attitude completely; the date is indicated in a letter to Hayley, October 23, 1804: "For now! O Glory! and O Delight! I have entirely reduced that spectrous Fiend to his station, whose annoyance has been the ruin of my labours for the last passed [*sic*] twenty years of my life. He is the enemy of conjugal love and is the Jupiter of the Greeks, an iron-hearted tyrant, the ruiner of ancient Greece." This revelation came on the day after visiting the Truchsessian gallery of pictures, and left him "really drunk with intellectual vision."

In short, Blake had escaped from neoclassicism and proceeded to attack it in *Milton* and *Jerusalem*. "We do not want either Greek or Roman Models if we are but just & true to our own Imaginations" (*Mil* 1).

Blake's prime objection to the Greeks was their glorification of war. Homer, the center of Greek culture, therefore carries a sword in the seventh and eighth illustrations to Dante. Virgil was even worse: he not only glorified war, but empire as well; so Blake often blamed the Trojans as well as the Greeks for the cult of war. It has overshadowed the world ever since. "Shakespeare & Milton were both curb'd by the general malady & infection from the silly Greek & Latin slaves of the Sword" (*Mil* 1). "The Americans will consider Washington as their god. This is only Grecian, or rather Trojan, worship" (To Hayley, 28 May 1804). It is "Laws from Plato & his Greeks" which "renew the Trojan Gods in Albion" (*Mil* 22:53). "The Classics! it is the Classics, & not Goths nor Monks, that Desolate Europe with Wars" (*On Homer's Poetry, K* 778).

Blake also blamed homosexuality on pagan militarism: " 'Twas the Greeks' love of war | Turn'd Love into a Boy, | And Woman into a Statue of Stone— | And away flew every Joy" ("Why was Cupid a Boy," *K* 552).

Blake even denied the originality of all classic art by reviving the old theory that the Hebraic culture was necessarily the original. He never tired of insisting that the Greek muses were the daughters of Memory (Mnemosyne) and not the daughters of Inspiration. He sensed correctly, somehow, that practically all the famous statues were only "justly admired copies" of "some stupendous originals now lost." So also with Homer's or Ovid's mythology (*DesC* II, *K* 565).

"A Warlike State can never produce Art," he stated: it can only steal works already created, as Napoleon then was doing. "Rome & Greece swept Art into their Maw & destroy'd it . . . Grecian is Mathematic Form: Gothic is Living Form" (*On Virgil, K* 778). Even the writings of Homer, Ovid, Plato, and Cicero are "Stolen and Perverted" (*Mil* 1). Greek philosophy is "a remnant of Druidism" (*J* 52).

Blake attributed to the Greeks a gift of

destructive satire, probably because of Aristophanes' brilliant misrepresentation of Socrates. In "I saw a Monk" (*J* 52), he refers to "Grecian Mocks," and stated in a deleted stanza, "A Grecian Scoff is a wracking wheel" (*K* 420).

Once the Greeks had loved liberty; in their primeval state they belonged to Jerusalem (*J* 60:13–20). Then they tuned their instruments in thanksgivings to the Lamb (*J* 79:48–50). But now they are in the Covering Cherub's bosom (*J* 89:34).

However, in *A Vision of the Last Judgment*, Blake represented among the saved "the Greek Learned & Wise," symbolized as a mother meeting "her numerous Family in the Arms of their Father" (*K* 610; see Illustrations, "LJ" No. 76).

The GREEN MAN was an inn on the New Road from Paddington to Islington (*Erd* 437); it was some two miles from Golden Square. Blake mentions it as one of the places where he used to ramble as a boy (*J* 27:13). Paul Miner reproduced a picture of it; the sign reads "The Old Farthing Pye-House Green Man." It still stands on its original site, but its modern address is No. 383 Euston Road between Cleveland and Bolsover Streets.

The Green Man, or the wild man of the woods, was a traditional figure in heraldry, pageantry, and the like. He was clad entirely in green leaves and bore a club.

There was another Green Man Inn at Blackheath, and there may well have been others.

GREEN[E] (General Nathanael, 1742–86) succeeded Gates as commander of the Southern Department of the Continental Army. His astute maneuvering drove Lord Cornwallis out of Georgia and the Carolinas to Yorktown, where the British surrender ended the fighting in the American Revolution.

"Green" is one of the American leaders who meet on the Atlantic coast after the Boston Massacre (*Am* 3:4).

GREENLAND is the twenty-sixth of the Thirty-two Nations which shall guard liberty and rule the rest of the world (*J* 72:41).

GRODNA, the element of Earth, is the third son of Urizen to be born. He "rent the deep earth howling amaz'd: his heavens immense cracks like the ground parch'd with heat" (*Ur* 23:15).

GROVES of oak were the meeting-places of the Druids. Blake mentions them frequently as a symbol of error.

GUANTOK (Gwantock, Gwantoke, Kwantok) is the fourth of the twelve Sons of Albion (*J* 5:25; 19:18; 32:11). He is assigned to South Wales (*J* 71:29). His Emanation is Cordella (*J* 71:28). He was named for John Guantock, M.P., a judge at Blake's trial; he signed Lieut. George Hulton's recognizance for the appearance of the two accusing soldiers (*Notes & Queries*, ccii, 484, Nov. 1957).

At the appearance of Reuben, Gwantok and Peachy hide in Damascus (*J* 36:16). When Coban's Emanation Ignoge "adjoin'd with Gwantoke's Children . . . lovely Cordella arose; Gwantoke forgave & joy'd over South Wales & all its Mountains" (*J* 71:28).

GUINEA is the nineteenth of the Thirty-two Nations which shall guard liberty and rule over the rest of the earth (*J* 72:40).

GUION. Mme Jeanne Marie Bouvier de la Motte-Guyon (1648–1717) was the Quietist who interested Fénelon in the practice of self-annihilation as a means of attaining the mystical union. Bossuet had her imprisoned (1695) and later banished from Paris to Blois.

"Fenelon, Guion, Teresa, Whitefield & Hervey . . . with all the gentle Souls who guide the great Wine-press of Love" guard Los's southern gate towards Beulah (*J* 72:50). See FÉNELON.

GWANTOCK, GWANTOKE. See GUAN-TOK.

GWENDOLEN was originally the first of the twelve Daughters of Albion (*FZ* ii:61), but in *Jerusalem* she is usually listed second, after Cambel. When these two work together, Gwendolen usually takes the lead.

She is named for Guendoloena, the daughter of Brutus' comrade Corineus (*Geof* II, ii–v). Locrin, Brutus' eldest son, married her only under pressure, because after their betrothal he fell in love with Estrildis, who became secretly his mistress and bore him a daughter, Sabre. Eventually Locrin divorced Guendoloena and made Estrildis his queen. The furious Guendoloena raised an army; defeated Locrin, who was killed in the battle; assumed the throne; and ordered Estrildis and Sabre to be drowned in the river, which she renamed "Sabren" or "Sabrina" (the Severn) after her husband's illegitimate daughter, to perpetuate his infamy.

Blake does not refer to her story but uses only her name. She is the Female Will rampant. As the Emanation of Hyle, the bad artist, (*J* 80:67), she is the perverted and selfish Imagination, and therefore takes the lead over Cambel (perverted Reason) in initiating schemes for the conquest of man.

To achieve this end, they refuse sexual satisfaction. (Cambel and Gwendolen are two of the five who unite into Tirzah and her sisters—*J* 5:40.) This refusal provokes the men to make war. "If you dare rend their Veil with your Spear, you are healed of Love" (*J* 68:42); but "I must rush again to War, for the Virgin has frown'd & refus'd" (*J* 68:63). Blake here anticipated the theory of Freud that war is the result of repressed sex.

It is Gwendolen who first dances naked and drunk to the timbrel of war (*J* 58:2); it is she who laughs in triumph at the idea of chastity (*J* 63:32); and it is she who casts the shuttle of war as Cambel returns the beam (*J* 66:62). But Cambel is named first when the two weave webs of War and

Religion which involve all Albion's Sons (*J* 7:44).

In the chapter addressed "To the Christians" (*J* Chap. iv) Cambel and Gwendolen conspire to mold man to their wishes. Cambel compels Hand "to weave Jerusalem a Body repugnant to the Lamb" (*J* 80:65), and Gwendolen limits Hyle to "a shape of Moral Virtue against the Lamb" (*J* 80:71). Then she asks Cambel, "what shall we do to keep these awful forms in our soft bands?" (*J* 80:84). She fears annihilation: "I gather our eternal fate. Outcasts from life and love, unless we find a way to bind these awful Forms to our embrace, we shall perish annihilate; discover'd our Delusions" (*J* 82:2).

To entice her sisters to Babylon, Gwendolen hides a Falsehood in her left hand behind her back, then utters her deceit. She says that Enitharmon told Los to forget Albion and scatter his daughters and to hide America (liberty) for a curse.

(In the illustration of this scene, *J* 81, Gwendolen points to a couplet in reversed writing: "In Heaven the only Art of Living | Is Forgetting & Forgiving," continuing "Especially to the Female," and with a detached corollary: "But if you on Earth Forgive | You shall not find where to Live." As she points with her right hand, while her left remains clenched and hidden, the lines cannot be, as usually supposed, her Falsehood—the more so, as they bear little if any relation to the Falsehood as given in the text.)

Gwendolen continues to address her sisters, praising the lands of heathen love. "See how the fires of our loins point eastward to Babylon" (*J* 82:36). They should plant the Tree of Mystery before Jerusalem, "to judge the Friend of Sinners to death without the Veil, to cut her off from America, to close up her secret Ark and the fury of Man exhaust in War, Women permanent remain" (*J* 82:32–35).

She boasts that Hyle is now an infant love on her bosom, but shrieks on discovering that he is only a Worm. Cambel is envious; she reduces Hand to an infant

Worm, and strives "to form the Worm into a form of love" (*J* 82:76). Los has intervened, trying to make the best of a bad situation. He permits Cambel and her sisters to form the Mundane Shell according to their will (*J* 83:33).

But terrified at the Sons, the Daughters of Albion take Gwendolen's Falsehood, which grows into "an Allegory around the Winding Worm" (*J* 85:1). This is the establishment of conventional marriage. They name it "Canaan" and build for it "a tender Moon" (*J* 85:2). Here Reuben (the sensual man) at last finds rest from his wanderings; and the "little lovely Allegoric Night" stretches abroad "thro' all the World of Erin & of Los & all their Children" (*J* 88:31–34).

Gwendolen is particularly associated with mountainous Derbyshire. "Derby Peak yawn'd a horrid Chasm at the Cries of Gwendolen" (*J* 64:35). "Hyle on East Moor in rocky Derbyshire rav'd to the Moon for Gwendolen" (*J* 80:66). When Gwendolen uncovered her torso, "she drew aside her Veil, from Mam-Tor [the breasts] to Dovedale [the genitals]" (*J* 82:45).

"GWIN, KING OF NORWAY" (*PS*) was Blake's first poem of Revolution. It is addressed to the kings, who are blamed in the twenty-fifth stanza. The ballad form came from Percy's *Reliques*, the substance from Chatterton's "Godred Crovan" (1769), the imagery from Ossian.

Blake's Gordred is one of the surviving British giants driven to dwell in caves after the invasion of the Trojans. He symbolizes the power of the people. At the cry of the poor, whom the nobles have reduced to starvation, he rouses himself from sleep and leads his "num'rous sons of blood" against the tyrant Gwin, who also assembles

his forces. In the battle, Gordred with a single blow kills Gwin, whose forces then flee.

GWINEFRED is the most elusive of the twelve Daughters of Albion. Her name does not appear in Geoffrey's *History*, nor in Milton's; neither is it to be found in the Arthurian romances. As she is under Rahab (*J* 5:43), she cannot be St. Winifred, the virgin martyr, whose well was one of the Seven Wonders of Wales.

She is tenth in the first list of Daughters (*FZ* ii:62); then she becomes the seventh (*J* 5:43). "Gwinefred beautiful" is the Emanation of Hutton (*J* 71:37).

GWINIVERRA was King Arthur's faithless wife. In Geoffrey (IX, ix) she is Guanhumara, the most beautiful woman in Britain. During her husband Arthur's conquest of Rome, she wickedly married Arthur's nephew Modred (X, xiii). After Arthur defeated Modred, she fled from York to Legions, where she became a nun. (Geoffrey makes no mention of Lancelot.) Milton calls her "Gueniver," and dismissing Geoffrey's "trash," quotes Caradoc to the effect that King Melvas of Somerset detained her a year, then restored her. Blake uses none of these tales.

She was not included in the first list of the twelve Daughters of Albion (*FZ* ii:61), but replaces Boadicea in *Jerusalem* 5:43, where she is the sixth in the list and the first of those who unite into Rahab.

She is the Emanation of Skofeld; "Gwinevera . . . beams towards the east, all kinds of precious stones and pearl, with instruments of music in holy Jerusalem" (*J* 71:39). Los melts Gwendolen and Cambel and Gwineverra into precious metals and stones (*J* 9:22).

H

HACKNEY, now a city borough in London County, was in Blake's day a large and wealthy village of Middlesex, on the northeast side of London.

"Hackney and Holloway sicken for Estrild & Ignoge" (*J* 21:33). Los "came down from Highgate thro' Hackney & Holloway towards London" (*J* 31:14). "Awake, Highgate's heights & Hampstead's, to Poplar, Hackney, & Bow" (*J* 84:1).

HADDNTN (i.e., Haddington) is a county of Scotland, which with Kincardine and Forfar is assigned to Reuben (*J* 16:53). It is also under Bowen (*J* 71:46).

HADES was the classical Hell.

Albion, worshipping his own Shadow, cries: "If thou withdraw thy breath, I die & vanish into Hades" (*FZ* iii:61; *J* 29:48).

HAGAR was an Egyptian slave of Sarah, who, having been childless for ten years, gave her as a concubine to Abraham. When Hagar conceived, the jealous Sarah, with her husband's acquiescence, treated her so harshly that Hagar ran away; but the angel of the Lord bade her return, and she gave birth to Ishmael (*Gen* xvi). After Sarah gave birth to her own son, Isaac, she bade Abraham drive Hagar and Ishmael out. They were near death in the wilderness, but the angel of the Lord directed Hagar to a well, which saved their lives. They then flourished in the wilderness of Paran, and Hagar got her son a wife from Egypt (*Gen* xxi:9–21).

"On the Right, Beneath the Cloud on which Abel Kneels, is Abraham with Sarah & Isaac, also Hagar & Ishmael" (*LJ*, *K* 606; see Illustrations, "LJ" Nos. 70, 71). Sarah and Isaac rise beneath his right arm, while on the left are Hagar and Ishmael.

HAM was the second son of Noah, "the father of Canaan" (*Gen* ix:22) and the supposed ancestor of the Negroes.

Kox, as the Noah of the Flood of Udan-Adan, is the father of Shem, Ham, and Japheth (*J* 7:23). The skiey tent of primitive innocence "reach'd over Asia to Nimrod's Tower, to Ham & Canaan" (*J* 60:17).

HAMATH was a city on the northern border of Israel, notable for its abundant water and extensive irrigation (*Numb* xiii:21).

"O Virgin of terrible eyes, who dwellest by Valleys of springs beneath the Mountains of Lebanon in the City of Rehob in Hamath" (*J* 68:54).

HAMPSHIRE (Hants) is a southern county in England. It is assigned, with Sussex and Berkshire, to Asher (*J* 16:47), and also to Hyle: "Hyle dwelt in Winchester, comprehending Hants, Dorset, Devon, Cornwall" (*J* 71:20). "Hants, Devon, & Wilts" are "surrounded with masses of stone in order'd forms" (*J* 83:9).

HAMPSTEAD was a pleasant village on a hill in Middlesex, about four miles to the northwest of London. It was on the edge of the Heath, and near the sister hill of

Highgate; it had an extensive view of London as far as Shooter's Hill, and of the surrounding counties. It was famous for its healthful air, which did not agree with Blake (To Linnell, 1 Feb 1826).

Hampstead was a literary center. Leigh Hunt's extensive circle there, before he left for Italy in 1821, included practically all the young liberal writers: Shelley, Keats (who lived there 1817–20), Wordsworth, Coleridge (at nearby Highgate), Lamb, Southey, Hazlitt, and many others. Blake, however, would not have visited Hunt, who had attacked Blake so outrageously in *The Examiner.*

The Flaxmans were there for a time; the Blakes visited them just before the departure to Felpham in 1800. The Linnells started going there in 1822, but settled permanently in 1824, at Collins' Farm, North End. Blake often visited them, though towards the end his ill health interfered, his last visit being in the summer of 1826.

Los's forge is heard "before London to Hampstead's breadths & Highgate's heights" (*Mil* 6:9). "Milcah's Pillars shine from Harrow to Hampstead, where Hoglah on Highgate's heights magnificent Weaves over trembling Thames to Shooters' Hill, and thence to Blackheath" (*Mil* 35:11). Hampstead, Highgate, and three other places rage loud with the furnaces of Los (*J* 16:1). "Awake, Highgate's heights & Hampstead's" (*J* 84:1).

HANCOCK (John, 1737–93), American statesman, was a leading figure in the Boston disturbances which preluded the American Revolution. Among many other things, he was the first signer of the Declaration of Independence.

He is one of the patriots who "meet on the coast glowing with blood from Albion's fiery Prince" (*Am* 3:4) after the Boston Massacre.

HAND is the eldest of the twelve Sons of Albion (*J* 34:22). Like his brothers, he is a giant (*J* 43:50). His Emanation is Cam-

bel (*J* 80:58). His Israelite correlative is Reuben (*J* 34:36), whose fibres he cruelly cuts (*J* 90:25). In his unfallen state, he dwells in Selsey (the first in Blake's list of the Twenty-four Cathedral Cities), and has Sussex, Surrey, Kent, and Middlesex (*J* 71:11).

When Hand and his brothers separate from Albion's bosom, and from each other, he becomes the Reasoning Spectre (*J* 36:23), and thus is the source of the whole materialistic system of society. When he absorbs all the other Sons (*J* 8:43), from his bosom grows the Polypus (*J* 18:40), which overspreads the earth. He is responsible for war (*J* 9:3–5) and for the Satanic Mill of the Industrial Revolution (*J* 19:19; 43:50; 60:43). As Molech, he would destroy all innocent joys (*J* 84:21). He opposes love with cruelty (*J* 21:28; 67:62) and drives lovers into hiding (*J* 83:30). He would exile Jerusalem, and enslaves her in his mills (*J* 18:16; 60:43). With his brothers he would devour both Los and Albion (*J* 90:63). He would destroy even the Saviour (*J* 18:37).

The first three Sons constitute an evil trinity: Hand (the heartless Head), Hyle (the headless Heart), and Coban (presumably the selfish Loins). When we first see Hand, he is "become a rock: Sinai & Horeb is Hyle & Coban" (*Mil* 19:58). The three surround Milton as with a girdle (*Mil* 23:15). "Hand has peopled Babel & Nineveh: Hyle, Ashur & Aram: Coban's son is Nimrod" (*J* 7:18). With three other Sons, they "labour mightily in the Wars of Babel & Shinar" (*J* 8:41). To combat their warfare, Los heats his spiritual sword in the flames of the three (*J* 9:21). When Hand absorbs all his brothers, Hyle and Coban are "his two chosen . . . Emissaries in War" (*J* 18:41). When they behold the materializing Reuben, the three flee: "they became what they beheld" (*J* 36:15). Eventually the three assume one three-headed body, "the form of mighty Hand . . . Three Brains, in contradictory council brooding incessantly, neither daring to put in act its councils, fearing each-other, therefore rejecting Ideas as nothing & holding all Wisdom to consist in the agreements & disagree[me]nts of Ideas, plotting to devour Albion's Body of Humanity & Love" (*J* 70:1–9). Occasionally its chest opens to release the other Sons, who then combine into Bacon, Newton, and Locke (*J* 70:11–15).

This event is pictured on Plate 50 of *Jerusalem.* Hand sits on the rocky isle surrounded by the black Sea of Time and Space. His three heads are crowned. From his chest issues in a flame a figure with two heads facing opposite ways; from its chest in turn issues a one-headed figure, from whom issues yet another, who looks backward and points forward. On the left is a planet and an eyed lightning bolt striking below; on the right is a crescent moon, towards which a huge comet rushes, while below a sun begins to rise (or set?) above the black horizon.

In this Selfhood, the three "appropriate the Divine Names" (set up as God), "seeking to Vegetate the Divine Vision" (materialize religion) "in a corporeal & ever dying Vegetation & Corruption; mingling with Luvah in One, they become One Great Satan" (*J* 90:40).

Hand is often associated with Hyle alone. The two are rooted into Jerusalem by a fibre of strong revenge (*J* 15:1). They accept Nature (Vala) as their mother (*J* 18:30) and cry out to destroy the Saviour (*J* 18:36). Hyle sees in fear the sins of infant love, which Hand lashes in fury through the streets of Babylon (*J* 21:28–30). Albion bids the two seize Los, "the abhorred friend" (*J* 42:47). Hand and Coban arch over the sun, while Hyle and Scofield arch over the moon (*J* 58:29). Tirzah complains that the pair are cruel to her (*J* 67:62). When Judah is divided, he takes root "in Hebron, in the Land of Hand & Hyle" (*J* 74:49).

In a longish episode, Hand and Hyle fall into the power of their separated Emanations (*J* 80:57–82:76). Hand sleeps on Mount Skiddaw; Cambel, inspired by the Tree of Moral Virtue, sends him over Wales into the looms of Cathedron; his tender fibres of nerves run across Europe "to Jerusalem's Shade, to weave Jerusalem a Body repugnant to the Lamb" (*J* 80:62). Meanwhile Gwendolen limits Hyle's form; raving, he is "compell'd into a shape of Moral Virtue against the Lamb" (*J* 80:77). Then follows the conspiracy of Gwendolen and Cambel to keep the two under their domination. They reduce their consorts, not to the babies they intend, but to winding worms. Los intervenes. Cambel then labors in the furnace "to form the mighty form of Hand according to her will" (*J* 82:63). Gwendolen also labors to form her worm "into a form of love by tears & pain" (*J* 82:76).

Hand and Hyle flee away, followed by Jerusalem (*J* 83:86). Hand, now in his strength again, combines into the double Molech and Chemosh (to whom children were sacrificed), marching through Egypt in his fury (*J* 84:21). Hand and Hyle, after assuming the Divine Names, "condense the Little-ones & erect them into a mighty Temple even to the stars; but they Vegetate beneath Los's Hammer, that Life may not be blotted out" (*J* 90:49).

At the very end, Hand and the other children of Albion awake from their slumbers (*J* 96:39).

Hand is depicted on the frontispiece to Chapter ii (*J* 26). With outspread arms, he walks forward haloed in flames, advancing his left foot. He looks backward at Jerusalem, who follows him fearfully.

The HAND is frequently mentioned in Blake's writings, but seldom with special meaning. It is the means of accomplishment: Vala's hand, for example, is "a Court of Justice" (*J* 64:9). In "The Tyger" (*SoE*) it is differentiated from the creative vision: "What immortal hand or eye . . . ?"

In the *Job* engravings and many other pictures, the right hand signifies a spiritual act and the left (sinister) a materialistic act. Thus when Job shares his last loaf with a beggar, because the Law prescribes charity, and not because Job loves the beggar as a fellow man, the bread is given, and taken, with the left hand.

The left-right symbolism is seldom employed in the poems. When he falls, Urizen seizes Luvah in his left hand (*FZ* v:225). Gwendolen hides her Falsehood in her left hand (*J* 82:17-19; 84:32).

Sometimes both hands are specified. The dying Los's right hand tears down the sun, his left the moon (*FZ* ix:7). "The Souls descending to the Body wail on the right hand of Los, & those delivered from the Body on the left hand" (*Mil* 26:16). When Albion rises, "his right hand covers lofty Wales, his left Scotland" (*Mil* 39:41).

HANTS. See HAMPSHIRE.

HAR ("mountain"), when he first appears, in the early and discarded *Tiriel*, is apparently the father of all mankind, for his wife is Heva ("Eve"). He has three sons: Tiriel (the tyrant), Zazel (the rebel), and Ijim (the people). Har is a foreshadowing of Los, just as Tiriel is a foreshadowing of Urizen. But Har has not the strength to be a Prophet, for ultimately he is Self-love.

Yet Har has the spirit of Christianity. His God is Love, his Heaven is Joy (*Tir* viii:9); he is "holy & forgiving, fill'd with loving mercy, forgetting the offences of [his] most rebellious children" (vi:26). But by the end of the Age of Reason, official religion had sunk into the imbecility of second childhood. Har has been too weak to cope with his lawless sons (viii:7), who long ago revolted and left him (vi:28), and of course he has not slain them with the power of the paternal curse. He who was a mountain now lives in a vale, cut off from mankind.

Har also represents the decadent poetry of Blake's day. The aged but vigorous Mnetha, the spirit of neoclassicism, whom Har and Heva mistakenly call "mother" (ii:23), nurses them. "But they were as the shadow of Har & as the years forgotten. Playing with flowers & running after birds they spent the day, and in the night like infants slept, delighted with infant dreams" (ii:7). Har's great accomplishment is to "sing in

the great cage" (iii:23) of the closed heroic couplet.

Later references confirm and explain Har's weakness, his inability to deal with the problems of mankind. In the genealogy of the Sons of Los, Har is no longer the father of all mankind, but only the sixteenth in the list. His immediate father is Satan (self-love); his children are Ochim and Ijim, that is, "doleful creatures" and "satyrs" (*Isaiah* xiii:21). Like Job's children, they could not stand the piety of their father; they were "compell'd to pray repugnant & to humble the immortal spirit" (*Tir* viii:36); therefore they rebelled and abandoned him.

Har and Heva then "fled because their brethren & sisters liv'd in War & Lust; and as they fled they shrunk into two narrow doleful forms creeping in reptile flesh upon the bosom of the ground; and all the vast of Nature shrunk before their shrunken eyes" (*SoL* 4:5), becoming serpents of materialism. Meanwhile the prophets "gave Laws & Religions to the sons of Har, binding them more and more to Earth, closing and restraining, till a Philosophy of Five Senses was complete" (*SoL* 4:13).

At the end of his life, blind Tiriel at last returns to his parents, but only to denounce them with his dying breath: "O weak mistaken father of a lawless race, thy laws, O Har, & Tiriel's wisdom, end together in a curse" (*Tir* viii:7).

In *The Book of Thel*, Har's domain is a place of primal innocence. The self-centered, nubile Thel is "mistress of the vales of Har" (2:1), the "beauty of the vales of Har" (4:10); and when she is terrified at the voices issuing from her grave-plot, she flees back unhindered to the vales of Har (6:22).

HARFORD. See HERTFORDSHIRE.

HARHATH is the fourteenth son of Los and Enitharmon, standing between Gon and Satan (*FZ* viii:359).

HARROW, the site of the famous school,

is a town fifteen miles northwest of London. Situated on the highest hill in Middlesex, it is visible from Hampstead. "Milcah's Pillars shine from Harrow to Hampstead" (*Mil* 35:11).

The HARROW follows the Plow, breaking the clods and covering the seeded furrows.

In *The Four Zoas*, the Harrow is always mentioned after the Plow; they symbolize the political upheavals in Europe, preparatory (as Blake believed) for the New Age. The Plow is of iron (ii:70), while the Harrow is of gold: "howling & drunk with fury, the plow of ages & the golden harrow wade thro' fields of goary blood; the immortal seed is nourish'd for the slaughter" (vii:13). After the rejuvenated Urizen plows the universe and sows the human seed for the Great Harvest, "Then follows the golden harrow in the midst of Mental fires. To ravishing melody of flutes & harps & softest voice the seed is harrow'd in, while flames heat the black mould & cause the human harvest to begin" (ix:335).

In *Milton*, the opening song of the Bard deals with the disasters of interfering with a poet's proper work; this episode, inspired by Blake's quarrel with Hayley, also follows in part the revolt and fall of Satan and the birth of Sin, according to *Paradise Lost*. Los is now the farmer; the plow is assigned to his eldest son, Rintrah (wrath), and the "Harrow of the Almighty" (4:1) to Palamabron (pity). Preparation for the New Age must begin with wrath at the present state of affairs, and should be followed by pity for the sufferings of humanity.

Pity is from the merciful Almighty, and the Bard's song describes the attempt of Satan-Hayley to run Palamabron-Blake's Harrow. Los refuses the request of the essentially heartless Satan: "Anger me not! thou canst not drive the Harrow in pity's paths" (4:16). When Palamabron returns with his "fiery Harrow," Satan faints "beneath the artillery" (5:1–2). Palamabron also refuses Satan, but Los finally yields to Satan's importunities, and gives him "the Harrow of the Almighty" (7:10–12). The

next morning the horses of the Harrow are maddened; the Gnomes, who serve the Harrow, accuse Satan (7:19–21). Los is perplexed, for Satan really believes he is not guilty of the confusion. Meanwhile Palamabron has replaced Satan at his Mills (the easier task), with the result that the servants there stage a bacchanal, drinking, dancing, and singing Palamabron's songs (8:4–10). Los blames himself for his mistaken decision: "Mine is the fault! I should have remember'd that pity divides the soul and man unmans" (8:19); and he bids each henceforth to keep his own station (7:43). The very heavens are troubled: the abundant rain of Jehovah (mercy) contends with the thunder and lightning of Molech (sacrifice of innocent joy), above the plowing. Rintrah's indignation bursts out; and when Palamabron calls an assembly of all Eden to judge, the judgment falls on Rintrah's rage (9:10).

The revolt and fall of Satan now ensue. Also influenced by Rintrah "in a feminine delusion of false pride self-deciev'd" (11:26), he sets himself up as God, proclaims the moral law, and denounces transgressors (9:19–29), closing Los from Eternity in Albion's bosom and becoming a mighty fiend against the Divine Humanity (10:10–11).

Leutha then appears, taking the blame for Satan's sin. She loved Palamabron, and jealous of his Emanation Elynittria, sought to replace her in unloosing the horses, but the horses rebelled. Satan then made the Gnomes curb the horses and throw sandbanks around the flaming Harrow; but the flames "orb'd us round in concave fires, a Hell of our own making" (12:22). Hell being thus created, Satan continues his revolt: "Jehovah thunder'd above. Satan in pride of heart drove the fierce Harrow among the constellations of Jehovah, drawing a third part in the fires as stubble north & south to devour Albion and Jerusalem" (12:24; cf. *Rev* xii:4). A dragon had issued from Leutha's limbs to seize Elynittria's newborn son (12:2–3; cf. *Rev* xii:3–4); and now "with our dark fires which now gird round us (O eternal torment!) I form'd the Serpent" (12:28). Then she is born as Sin: "I came forth from the head of Satan: back the Gnomes recoil'd and called me Sin, and for a sign portentous held me" (12:38; cf. *PL* ii:758–60). Elynittria generously takes her to Palamabron's bed, where "In dreams she bore the shadowy Spectre of Sleep & nam'd him Death" (13:40; cf. *PL* ii:785–87), and also in dreams bore Rahab (13:41).

The Twelve Sons of Israel "successive fled away in that thousand years of sorrow of Palamabron's Harrow & of Rintrah's wrath & fury" (23:62–24:1).

At the end of *Milton*, all is preparing for the Great Harvest and Vintage, when "the Plow has pass'd over the Nations, and the Harrow & heavy thundering Roller upon the mountains" (25:10). "The Plow goes forth in tempests & lightnings, & the Harrow cruel in blights of the east; the heavy Roller follows in howlings of woe" (27:47).

The whole episode is anticipated in an intruded passage of *The Four Zoas* (viii: 368): "But Satan accus'd Palamabron before his brethren, also he madden'd the horses of Palamabron's harrow, wherefore Rintrah & Palamabron cut him off from Golgonooza." In *Jerusalem*, Albion is bid wait "till the Plow of Jehovah and the Harrow of Shaddai have passed over the Dead to awake the Dead to Judgment" (46:14).

HARTFORD. See HERTFORDSHIRE.

The HARVEST and Vintage are briefly mentioned in *Revelation* xiv:14–20; xix:15; on these hints Blake built his great vision of the making of the Eternal Bread and Wine, during the six Days before the Millennium, reversing the six Days of Creation (*FZ* ix, "The Last Judgment"). The agricultural pursuits of Eden, however, are apocalyptic woes and disasters on this earth. In *The Four Zoas*, the whole process takes place immediately after death; in *Milton*, the woes are the contemporary wars

in Europe and are the preparation for the New Age in this world.

HAVILAH was a land rich in gold, bdellium, and onyx; it was encompassed by the Pison, the first of the four branches of the river of Eden (*Gen* ii:11–12).

To Blake, Havilah signified the basic purity and freedom of love, which is now forbidden. The unfallen Vala (east) is "the Lilly of Havilah" (*J* 19:42). To the east of the Garden of Eden, the cherubim were placed with the flaming sword, to keep man from the Tree of Life (*Gen* iii:24); "In Havilah . . . the Cherub roll'd his redounding flame" (*J* 55:22). "The golden Gate of Havilah and all the Garden of God was caught up with the Sun in one day of fury and war" (*J* 49:15), at the same time that the Atlantic Continent became part of the distant moon. "Molech rejoices thro' the Land from Havilah to Shur" (*J* 68:38).

HAYLEY (William, 1745–1820), poet, biographer, connoisseur, and patron, is remembered today chiefly as the man who persuaded Blake to live near him at Felpham (1800–1803); and Blake's stinging epigrams have done much to ruin his would-be friend's reputation. Indeed, it is difficult not to poke fun at so fatuous a personality, but Morchard Bishop's *Blake's Hayley* (London, 1951) has rectified considerably our estimate of that really estimable gentleman.

In 1774 Hayley retired from London to a rural life in Sussex, where he devoted himself in quiet to his literary pursuits. In 1777 his first success appeared: *The Epistle on Painting, Addressed to George Romney*, which was intended as an encouragement to that very neurotic painter, whom Hayley was to support for years at Eartham and Felpham. After other poetical Epistles and Essays, he wrote a best-seller, *The Triumphs of Temper* (1780). In 1769 he had married an unbalanced lady, whose extravagances curbed his natural generosity until her sudden death in 1797. To console him, however, he had a brilliant son, the illegitimate Thomas Alphonso Hayley (1780–1800), a lad of great talents from whom the proud father expected much. Meanwhile he had been corresponding with the unbalanced poet William Cowper; they met; and after Hayley had seen Cowper in a state of collapse, he devoted himself to procuring a pension for the poet and to saving his sanity. After incessant efforts, he succeeded in winning the pension, but too late: Cowper had become hopelessly insane, and died April 25, 1800. Exactly a week later, Thomas Alphonso Hayley died, after a long siege of infantile paralysis.

The bereaved father then set about publishing his versified *Essay on Sculpture* (1800) dedicated to Flaxman, through whom he probably had met Blake some time before. He commissioned Blake to engrave three plates for the new book; one was a design by the unfortunate Thomas Alphonso, and another a profile of the poor lad. Presently Hayley persuaded the temperamental Blake to leave London and reside at Felpham, near Hayley's new home "The Turret." Blake needed a patron; Hayley seemed to be the very man; and the Blakes arrived on September 18, 1800.

Hayley immediately set about procuring employment for the impecunious engraver. Four days after his arrival, Hayley wrote *Little Tom the Sailor*, for the benefit of the Widow Spicer, which Blake decorated and printed as a broadside on his own press. Hayley then commissioned Blake to do for his library a series of heads of the poets, from Homer to Cowper and Thomas Alphonso. Although he was working hard on his biography of Cowper, Hayley turned out some juvenile ballads about animals, for the advantage of Blake, who designed twelve and engraved fourteen illustrations. *The Triumphs of Temper* was due for a twelfth edition; Blake engraved six plates for it, after designs by Maria Flaxman. Hayley introduced Blake to the distinguished people in the vicinity, from whom he procured commissions; he got Blake to painting miniatures; he started to teach him Greek; he had Blake help with the

Cowper manuscript, for which Blake engraved six plates; at the news of Klopstock's death, he dictated to Blake a translation from that poet's *Messiah*. Meanwhile Blake could not finish *The Four Zoas*, which he had started before he left London. The inevitable explosion occurred at last. Blake returned to London, where he did some work collecting material for Hayley's *Life of Romney*, for which he engraved one plate.

For Blake's trial for high treason, at which Hayley figured handsomely, see FELPHAM.

This quarrel with Hayley was so important that we must examine it more closely. To Blake it was a cosmic tragedy, not just because it happened to him, but because it happened at all, and shall repeat itself whenever a genius is under the domination of a pretender to his art.

The event became the Satan-Palamabron quarrel which opens *Milton*. Translating it into temporal terms, it becomes evident that Hayley had quite disrupted Blake's great work; that Blake astonished Hayley with accusations; Hayley wept, blamed Blake's temper, mentioned ingratitude, and finally lost his own temper. In the awful silence that ensued, Mrs. Blake intervened; and the two men agreed to part as friends.

The obtuse Hayley was astounded. He had always won friends, even the devotion of such difficult persons as Cowper and Romney; and proud of his benevolence, the lonely man never dreamed that his friendship with Blake had been too demanding. After all, who was Blake? An unsuccessful engraver, whose work was not always satisfactory: Hayley only tolerated his profile of Thomas Alphonso; he rejected his portrait of Romney; and he even hired the very inferior Caroline Watson to do over Blake's work for the 1805 edition of the *Life of Cowper*. As for Blake's poetry and painting, those were the negligible eccentricity of a visionary.

Meanwhile Blake was of two minds about Hayley. One side recognized his unusual generosity (which had kept the Blakes from starving), his support of the arts, and his great capacity for friendship. I think that Blake's letters of gratitude were perfectly sincere, although the other side of him despised himself for writing them (On H the Pick thank, K 549).

Yet there was no mistaking the fact that Hayley was a domineering ass. "O God, protect me from my friends, that they have not power over me" (Mil 9:5). Hayley was only a "corporeal friend," which is a spiritual enemy. "I have tried to make friends by corporeal gifts, but have only made enemies. I never made friends but by spiritual gifts, by severe contentions of friendship & the burning fire of thought" (J 91:16). Blake was actually relieved when he recognized the unconscious enmity of Hayley (K 538, Nos. 4, 5). "Thy Friendship oft has made my heart to ake: | Do be my Enemy for Friendship's sake" (K 545).

There could be no interchange of spiritual gifts with Hayley: he was too blandly self-assured of his own ideas. If his conversation was like his prose, it was voluble, inflated, affected, incessant, and empty. As for his verse, his ideal was the worn-out closed heroic couplet. "Hayley on his Toilette seeing the sope, | Cries 'Homer is very much improved by Pope' " (K 555, 556). When he read his poems, Blake kept quiet, although "my heart knock'd against the root of my tongue" (To Butts, 22 Nov 1802). But then, Hayley did not praise Blake's verse either: "My title as a Genius thus is prov'd: not Prais'd by Hayley . . ." (K 546).

Blake's squibs were obviously the petulant outbursts of exasperation, never intended for the public; and they can be quite unfair. He even seems to have supposed for one moment that Hayley, after failing to persuade Catherine to get her husband to work for a proper living, set Scholfield on him: "when he could not act upon my wife, | Hired a Villain to bereave my Life" (K 544); but if this interpretation be right (and I know no other), Blake quickly altered his mind.

But there was certainly something odd about "the Hermit" who was deserted by both of his wives, and who could never keep a female friend permanently. Blake put his finger on the spot: "his Mother on his Father him begot" (K 539). In the grand language of symbolism, Hayley had never found his Emanation. In psychological terms, Hayley was unconsciously a homosexual.

This flaw in his psyche is symbolized by Leutha. "I loved Palamabron [Blake] & I sought to approach his Tent, but beautiful Elynittria with her silver arrows repell'd me . . . I fade before her immortal beauty" (Mil 11:37–12:1). Jealously she wants to destroy the fruit of Blake's inspiration, with which Elynittria is pregnant.

"This to prevent, entering the doors of Satan's brain night after night like sweet perfumes, I stupified the masculine perceptions and kept only the feminine awake: hence rose his soft delusory love to Palamabron, admiration join'd with envy" (Mil 12:4). Hayley's subconscious falls into deep disorder; as Satan he rebels and sinks into a hell of their own making (Mil 12:23). Eventually Leutha (springing from his head) becomes visible to him. She is recognized instantly as Sin, and he rejects her. "He drove me from his inmost Brain & the doors clos'd with thunder's sound" (Mil 12:47).

Thus the person of Hayley grew into the figure of Satan, the epitome of all errors. In Milton and Jerusalem, Hayley also appears as Hyle, the bad artist. But Blake's final estimate of Hayley is a kindly one, to be found under the name of Winchester, where he is praised for his generous hospitality; and though he could never be a poet, yet he was willing at least to be known as one. "Submitting to be call'd the son of Los, the terrible vision, Winchester stood devoting himself for Albion, his tents outspread with abundant riches, and his Emanations [his verses] submitting to be call'd Enitharmon's daughters and be born in vegetable mould, created by the Hammer and Loom in Bowlahoola & Allamanda where the Dead wail night & day" (J 40:52).

HAZAEL was sent by Ben-hadad, the king of Syria, to Elisha, to inquire if he would recover from an illness. Elisha replied that the king would recover, but that he should also die, adding meaningfully that Hazael himself would become king. On this hint, Hazael murdered Ben-hadad, and became king in his place (*II Kings* viii:7–15). Then, as Elisha foresaw, he became a persecutor of Israel.

"On the rock & above the Gate, a fiend with wings urges the wicked onwards with fiery darts; he is Hazael the Syrian, who drives abroad all those who rebell against their Saviour" (*LJ, K* 608; see Illustrations, "LJ" No. 39).

HAZOR was a city of north Galilee destroyed by Joshua (*Josh* xi:1–14); it was later in the lot given to Naphtali (*Josh* xix:36).

Rahab-Tirzah invites Milton to become king of Canaan "and reign in Hazor where the Twelve Tribes meet" (*Mil* 20:6).

HEBER (i.e., Eber) was the son of Shem (*Gen* x:21) and the eponymous ancestor of the Hebrews.

He is the fifteenth in the line from Adam to Luther, the sixth in the line from Noah to Terah, "the Female-Males" (*Mil* 37:39; *J* 75:14). Addressing the Jews, Blake wrote: "Your Ancestors derived their origin from Abraham, Heber, Shem and Noah, who were Druids" (*J* 27). Elsewhere he refers to "the pyramids of Heber & Terah," built of human souls (*J* 31:12).

HEBRON was a city nineteen miles southwest of Jerusalem, near the center of Judah's land. It was deeply associated with Abraham, and David was crowned there.

"They have divided Judah: he hath took Root in Hebron, in the Land of Hand & Hyle" (*J* 74:48).

HELA is the youngest of the five daughters of Tiriel (*Tir* v:24). Her name is that of the Scandinavian goddess of Hell. She symbolizes Sex under the curse. "What are the Pains of Hell but ... Bodily Lust ... ?" (*J* 77).

After Tiriel's second curse, his five daughters run to him weeping (v:18), but by morning four of them are dead of pestilence (v:31). Hela is spared, to guide her blind father to the Vales of Har. Far from being grateful, she denounces him, and he replies with a curse which maddens her and turns her hair to snakes. However, she continues to lead him through the woods to the mountains of Har, and finally to the tent of Har.

This episode is the first of Blake's many references to the death of the four senses and the corruption of the fifth (touch, or sex). Her Medusan locks are the torturing thoughts of suppressed lust.

HELL, as a place where sinners are punished after death with unending tortures because they offended God, does not exist. "I do not believe there is such a thing litterally" (On Lavater 309, *K* 74). If God "gives his rain to the Evil & the Good, & his Sun to the Just & the Unjust, He could never have Built Dante's Hell, nor the Hell of the Bible neither, in the way our Parsons explain it—It must have been originally Formed by the devil Himself; & So I understand it to have been" (On Dante, *K* 785). Although "all Bibles or sacred codes" have taught "That God will torment Man in Eternity for following his Energies," the contrary is true: "Energy is Eternal Delight" (*MHH* 4). Even Swedenborg, "strongest of men," was misled by the churches when he showed "the Transgressors in Hell, the proud Warriors in Heaven, Heaven as a Punisher, & Hell as One under Punishment" (*Mil* 22:50–52). Such a belief contradicts flatly the concept that God is Love and the Forgiveness of Sins, his basic ethics. "O, God, thou art Not an Avenger" (*J* 46:28). His Mercy is infinite and unconditional, requiring not even the Atonement. "It is a horrible doctrine. If another man pay your debt, I do not forgive it" (*CR* 271). "Doth Jehovah Forgive a Debt only on condition that it shall be Payed? Doth he forgive Pollution only on conditions of Purity? That Debt is not Forgiven! That Pollution is not Forgiven!" (*J* 61:17).

The real Hell is not a place but a state; and states of mind are something through which the Individual passes. "Hell is the being shut up in the possession of corporeal desires which shortly weary the man, for ALL LIFE IS HOLY" (On Lavater 309, *K* 74). "What are the Pains of Hell but Ignorance, Bodily Lust, Idleness & devastation of the things of the Spirit?" (*J* 77). "In Hell all is Self Righteousness; there is no such thing there as Forgiveness of Sin; he who does Forgive Sin is Crucified as an Abettor of Criminals, & he who performs Works of Mercy in Any shape whatever is punish'd &, if possible, destroy'd, not thro' envy or Hatred or Malice, but thro' Self Righteousness that thinks it does God service, which God is Satan. They do not Envy one another: They contemn & despise one another: Forgiveness of Sin is only at the Judgment Seat of Jesus the Saviour, where the Accuser is cast out, not because he Sins, but because he torments the Just & makes them do what he condemns as Sin & what he knows is opposite to their own Identity" (*LJ*, *K* 616).

It is a result of turning the back on the Divine Vision. It is "The Negation of the Poetic Genius," which is God (On Swed *DL*, *K* 90). It is "Eternal Death"—the being cut off from Eternity; but this cutting off is not everlasting, because of the Divine Mercy. The Hell depicted by Blake in his paintings of the Last Judgment is the Lake of Fire into which Errors (but not Individuals) are cast and annihilated. "It ought to be understood that the Persons . . . are not here meant, but the States Signified by those Names" (*LJ*, *K* 607).

In *The Marriage of Heaven and Hell*, Blake, having discarded the arbitrary standards of good and evil, revaluated the psyche, with the conclusion that Energy (usually called "evil") rises from the subconscious ("hell") and is restricted by Reason ("good"), the product of the superego

("heaven"). The fires of this hell are the flames of inspiration, and Blake implies that they may be the means of salvation.

But many believe in the conventional Hell, and "Every thing possible to be believ'd is an image of truth" (*MHH* 8:18) — an image only, and only of one aspect of psychological truth. "What seems to Be, Is, To those to whom it seems to Be, & is productive of the most dreadful consequences to those to whom it seems to Be, even of Torments, Despair, Eternal Death"; but "the Divine Mercy steps beyond and Redeems Man in the Body of Jesus" (*J* 36:51).

The reasonable but shortsighted Bromion believes in the conventional Hell: "And is there not eternal fire and eternal chains to bind the phantoms of existence from eternal life?" (*VDA* 4:23). Urizen sees his victims as "The horrid shapes & sights of torment in burning dungeons & in fetters of red hot iron; some with crowns of serpents & some with monsters girding round their bosoms; some lying on beds of sulphur, on racks & wheels" (*FZ* vi:103) — cursed in head, heart, and loins. Enitharmon fears that the coming Lamb "will give us to Eternal Death, fit punishment for such hideous offenders: Uttermost extinction in eternal pain: an ever dying life of stifling & obstruction: shut out of existence to be a sign & terror to all who behold, lest any should in futurity do as we have done in heaven" (*FZ* vii:426). But the Daughters of Beulah see further: "they saw the Divine Vision surrounding them on all sides beyond sin & death & hell" (*FZ* viii:50). The human grapes in Luvah's Wine-press (war) are in the Miltonic Hell: "they howl & writhe in shoals of torment, in fierce flames consuming, in chains of iron & in dungeons circled with ceaseless fires, in pits & dens & shades of death, in shapes of torment & woe" (*FZ* ix:749; *Mil* 27:31—cf. *PL* ii:621).

In *Milton*, Leutha (Sin), telling of the fall of Satan, ascribes the flames of the "Hell of our own making" to the uncontrollable fires of Palamabron's misused Harrow (12:23). "Death and Hell & the Grave" are "States that are not, but ah! Seem to be" (32:29).

In *Jerusalem*, Hell is "the land of death eternal" which lies around Golgonooza, "a Land of pain and misery and despair and ever brooding melancholy" (13:30). Blake mingles Miltonic and classical symbols to describe it (13:48–54; 43:60–65); it is "self-righteousnesses conglomerating against the Divine Vision" (13:52). The Spectre (Reason separated from humanity) is born from Hell (*FZ* i:157), and Los tells his Spectre that "if any enter into thee, thou shalt be an Unquenchable Fire, and he shall be a never dying Worm, mutually tormented by those that thou tormentest: a Hell & Despair for ever & ever" (*J* 17:45). The Divine Mercy alone prevents Albion from releasing his Spectre, when "a nether-world must have reciev'd the foul enormous spirit under pretence of Moral Virtue, fill'd with Revenge and Law, there to eternity chain'd down," tortured and cursing heaven (40:31–43). Erin bids the Daughters of Beulah "Remove from Albion, far remove these terrible surfaces: they are beginning to form Heavens & Hells in immense circles, the Hells for food to the Heavens, food of torment, food of despair" (49:60).

HELLE is Greece, the land of the Hellenes. "Let the Looms of Enitharmon & the Furnaces of Los create Jerusalem & Babylon" and eight other places, including Helle and extending to China and Japan (*J* 82:26–28).

HENDON was a Middlesex village eight miles northeast of St. Paul's, London. "Hampstead, Highgate, Finchley, Hendon, Muswell [all north of London] rage loud before Bromion's iron Tongs" (*J* 16:1).

HERCULES (Heracles) early chose Duty instead of Pleasure, according to Prodicus' celebrated apologue. "The Asylum given to Hercules, who labour[s] in Tirzah's Looms for bread" (*Mil* 25:49) has been identified (*Erd* 266) as the Royal Asylum for Female Orphans, built on the site of the old Hercules Tavern in Lambeth, near the Blakes' residence at 13 Hercules Building; there Pleasure is set against Duty (*Mil* 25:51).

HEREFORD (Heref) is an English county, assigned with Stafford and Shropshire to Joseph (*J* 16:49), and with Stafford and Worcester to Kotope (*J* 71:44). Its cathedral city, near the Welsh border, is the eighth of the Twenty-four Cathedral Cities; it is under Urthona and Edinburgh. "Hereford, ancient Guardian of Wales, whose hands builded the mountain palaces of Eden, stupendous works" (*J* 46:3). Hereford would seem to be Inigo Jones (1573–1651), called "the English Palladio," who built royal palaces in Denmark and England, also the Gothic chapel of Lincoln's Inn.

When war breaks out, "Worcester & Hereford, Oxford & Cambridge reel & stagger, overwearied with howling" (*J* 66:66).

A HERMAPHRODITE is a being with the organs of both sexes. To Blake it symbolized a sterile state of unreconciled and warring opposites. "In Doubt, which is Self contradiction, | A dark Hermaphrodite I stood" (*GoP*, "Of the Gates" 12, *K* 770). He applied the term to war, to rational philosophy, to Nature herself ("I, Nature, Hermaphroditic Priest & King," On Thornton, *K* 789), and unadjusted sex.

In *The Four Zoas*, the yet unformed Satan (war in the aggregate) is "a Shadowy hermaphrodite, black & opake . . . Hermaphroditic it at length became, hiding the Male within as in a Tabernacle, Abominable, Deadly" (viii:103–6). Later, "a Vast Hermaphroditic form heav'd like an Earthquake, lab'ring with convulsive groans intolerable; at length an awful wonder burst from the Hermaphroditic bosom, Satan he was nam'd . . . a male without a female counterpart . . . yet hiding the shadowy female Vala as in an ark & Curtains" (viii:248-55).

Milton in heaven, still divided from his Emanation (his attitude towards sex still unresolved), descends to the verge of Beulah (marriage), when he enters the Shadow of his suppressed desires, "a mournful form double, hermaphroditic, male & female in one wonderful body" (*Mil* 14:36-38). He then encounters the temptations of sex: the daughters of Rahab and Tirzah assume "The Twofold form Hermaphroditic and the Double-sexed, the Female-male & the Male-female, self-dividing stood before him in their beauty & in cruelties of holiness" (19:32).

The first nine of the Twenty-seven Heavens (the line from Adam up to Noah) are "giants mighty, Hermaphroditic" (*Mil* 37:37; *J* 75:12).

In *Jerusalem*, the four cherubim who guard the closed western gate of Golgonooza are "like Men hermaphroditic" (13:8). When Albion's Emanation appears separate, she reflects back to Albion "in Sexual Reasoning Hermaphroditic" (33:28). When the Daughters of Albion torture the Sons, "the Hermaphroditic Condensations are divided by the Knife" (58:11); and Los divides the sexes, "for the comingling of Albion's & Luvah's Spectres was Hermaphroditic" (58:19). When the Spectre draws Vala into his bosom, they become "a dark Hermaphrodite" (64:31). The Wine-presses of love and wrath are "double, Hermaphroditic" (88:58; 89:4). "A Vegetated Christ & a Virgin Eve are the Hermaphroditic Blasphemy" (90:34). Self-deified individuals are "Hermaphroditic worshippers of a God of cruelty & law" (90:55).

The opposite of the Hermaphrodite is the Androgyne, in which man's bisexual nature is perfectly harmonized. This was his original state. Blake found the theory in Ovid (*CR* 263), in Plato's *Symposium*, in Spenser's *Faerie Queene*, and also in

Genesis i:27 and v:2: "So God created man in his own image, in the image of God created he him; male and female created he them." Later, Eve was divided from Adam; this was a stage in the Fall, which brought death into the world.

HERMES TRISMEGISTUS was a legendary Egyptian sage, identified by Cicero (*De natura deorum* iii:5) with the god Thoth. He was the reputed author of various mystical works, such as the *Divine Pymander*. Lactantius (*De irae dei*) believed that he was far older than Pythagoras and the Seven Sages, a belief accepted by Blake: "To Trismegistus, Palamabron gave an abstract Law: to Pythagoras, Socrates & Plato" (*SoL* 3:18). Actually, the "hermetic books" are Neo-Platonic, show a good knowledge of the Old Testament, and refer to the New. In Christian thought, he was ranked with the sibyls. Il Penseroso in his midnight tower studied "thrice great *Hermes*."

Many alchemical and other occult writings were freely ascribed to Trismegistus. Most important was the "Smaragdine (or Emerald) Table," reputed to have been found in the hands of his corpse in a cave near Hebron, by a woman, or else by Alexander the Great. It became the basic text of alchemy.

The Greek original has never been recovered. The earliest known text is Arabic, in a book by Geber (eighth century), who ascribed it to "Balinas" (Apollonius of Tyana). It reached Latin Europe by the thirteenth century, but was not printed until 1541 at Amsterdam. (For details, see A. J. Holmyard, "The Emerald Table," *Nature*, cxii, 6 Oct 1923.) The text follows:

True without error, certain, and most true. What is below is like that which is above, and what is above is like that which is below, to perform the miracle of the one thing. And as all things were from one thing, by the mediation of one, so all things were produced from this one thing by adaptation. Its father is the sun, its mother the moon, the wind carried it in its belly, its nurse is the earth. This is the father of all perfection of the whole world.

Its power is perfect if it be changed into earth. Separate the earth from the fire, the subtle from the gross, gently, with great art. It ascends from the earth to heaven and again descends to earth, and receives the power of things superior and inferior.

Thus you have the glory of the whole world, and all obscurity flies from you. This is the strength of all strengths, because it conquers every subtle thing and penetrates every solid. Thus the world was created. Thence are marvelous adaptations, performed in this way.

Therefore I am called Hermes Trismegistus, having the three parts of the philosophy of the entire world. I have told everything about the operation of the sun.

Blake rejected this document, and with it all occultism. It was the magician trying to be the mystic; it was a material experiment instead of spiritual experience; it imposed the will on the four elements; it was the invention of the Spectre. "The Spectre builded stupendous Works, taking the Starry Heavens like to a curtain & folding them according to his will, repeating the Smaragdine Table of Hermes to draw Los down into the Indefinite, refusing to believe without demonstration" (*J* 91:33).

Mount HERMON, the highest mountain in Palestine, is a snow-crowned peak marking the northern limit.

The Council of God hovers over Gilead and Hermon (*FZ* i:199; viii:2). Hermon is one of the six mountains surrounding Palestine which are equated with Milton's Sixfold Emanation, his three wives and three daughters (*Mil* 17:16). At Los's Watch Song, Hermon and Lebanon bow their crowned heads (*J* 85:17).

HEROD Antipas, the tetrarch, was the son of Herod the Great who had ordered the massacre of the innocents at Bethlehem. The tetrarch ordered the execution of John the Baptist and was one of the authorities involved in the execution of Jesus.

In *The Everlasting Gospel*, Satan tempts Jesus with promise of the kingdoms of the world if he will only be obedient to the authorities. "John for disobedience bled . . . | If Caiaphas you will obey, | If Herod you with bloody Prey | Feed with the sacrifice, & be | Obedient . . . " (*EG* b:17, 21). Elsewhere Blake refers to Herod twice, in connection with Caiaphas and Pilate (On Bacon, *K* 407; On Thornton, *K* 786).

HERTFORDSHIRE (Harford, Hartford) is an inland southeastern county of England. It is assigned with Oxford and Bucks to Gad (*J* 16:47) and with seven others to Skofeld (*J* 71:39). When Los's furnaces are at work, "Hertfordshire glows with fierce Vegetation" (*J* 16:3). Vala casts her dark threads "from the hills of Hertfordshire to the hills of Surrey across Middlesex" (*J* 31:68).

HERVEY (James, 1714–58) was a popular devotional writer, in the line of Young and Blair. Although he had been a member of the Oxford group of Methodists, with Whitefield and Wesley, he remained a Calvinist. Calvinism, which derived from St. Augustine, was probably the grimmest of the Christian sects; yet Blake listed Hervey with Fenelon, Guion, Teresa, Whitefield, and "all the gentle Souls who guide the great Wine-press of Love," as a guardian of Los's fourfold Gate towards Beulah (*J* 72:52). He also painted one of his more extraordinary and complicated pictures to illustrate Hervey's popular *Meditations Among the Tombs* (1746; see Illustrations).

Death is the supreme terror of mankind; Death was the subject of Hervey's book; Death accordingly was the subject of

Blake's picture. But although Hervey repeated the customary horrors, his real emphasis lay on the pathos of the separations caused by premature deaths; and to this tenderness Blake responded. But with this difference: Blake depicted no tombs. The two sides of his picture are filled with groups named or suggested by Hervey; they are labelled, to ensure identification; and they ascend and unite in perfect bliss. Sophronia who died in childbed suckles her babe; the bride who died on her wedding day embraces her husband; those who died for love embrace passionately; angels succor the orphans, the fatherless. Hervey's tragic anecdotes have become ecstasies. Yet Hervey anticipated something of this bliss. "And O! with what cordial congratulations, what transporting endearment, do the soul and body, those affectionate companions, re-unite" may well have inspired the celebrated "Reunion of the Soul and Body" in Blake's illustration to Blair's *Grave*.

God, who sits at the top of the picture with a scroll open on his lap, is of course the Calvinist God. On his right (our left) is Mercy; on his left is Wrath. On this side Blake wrote "God out of Christ is a Consuming Fire," a text commonly quoted by Calvinists to prove the existence of Hell; but the text is not Biblical. However, the only evidence of his Wrath (unless it be the existence of Death itself, which is punishment for the sin of Adam) is a dim angel in the upper right corner, who pursues a fleeing sinner. Otherwise, the examples of Mercy completely overflow the side of the picture devoted to Wrath.

From the lower right corner (on the side of God's Wrath) a spiral stair (Jacob's ladder?) winds upward to God. At its foot, a widow sits desolate amidst the bodies of her husband and children. But the Angels of Death are there, taking charge of the children and beckoning the husband (now young again, in his spiritual body), referring them to "Mother," a radiant woman haloed with stars (the true

church). A Virgin regards her intently, her hands clasped in prayer.

The descent of this stair from God to this world is a brief résumé of sacred history. It begins with the first death; Adam looks up to God while Eve faints across his lap. Abel (or his ghost) and Cain both flee from the Serpent. Enoch with a scroll of prophecy (the first intimation of immortality) stands slightly below them. Noah beneath his rainbow rises dripping above the Sea of Time and Space. Next, the mother of Rebecca, in a rose-colored dress, ascends the stair, frowningly taking precedence of her niece, the mother of Leah and Rachel, in a pale green dress. This example of family pride (on the wrong side of God) goes against the descending current. Next is Abraham, who embraces Isaac, letting the sacrificial knife fall from his left hand. This episode is labelled "Abraham Believed God." Then comes Aaron with his censer; David, who faces inward as he plays his harp; and Solomon. Sacred history reaches its climax in the Transfiguration: Jesus floats between Moses, who turns his back on his Tables, and Elijah with his fiery chariot.

Death is not the only approach to God. Hervey himself illustrates the Mystic Way. He stands facing inward before the Communion table on which is the bread and wine. There is no cross on the table. Beside him is the overflowing fountain of baptism. An Angel of Providence points with both hands to the Transfiguration (the illumination while in the body) which stands in the place of an altarpiece. Continuing upward on the central axis of the picture, Hervey sees the sparing of Isaac (love overcoming the law), the ascension of Noah (the resurrection of the spiritual body), and the woe which causes Adam to look upward to God.

Blake first referred to Hervey in *An Island in the Moon* (Chap. viii), where the gloomy Steelyard is making extracts from the *Meditations*. Steelyard also refers (erroneously as it happens) to Hervey's *Theron and Aspasio* (1755), a series of theological dialogues and letters particularly designed to defend the unpopular doctrine of Imputed Righteousness.

HESHBON was an ancient hill-town in the kingdom of Jordan, twenty miles east of the entrance of the Jordan river to the Dead Sea. It lay southwest of Rabbath-ammon, and midway between the Arnon and the Jabbok rivers. Its excellent spring was highly prized. "Thine eyes like the fishpools in Heshbon, by the gate of Bathrabbim" (*Song of Sol* vii:4).

After Reuben has come back from being sent across the Jordan for the third time, he returns to Heshbon (*J* 36:10). Jerusalem laments: "I melt my soul in reasonings among the towers of Heshbon" (*J* 79:3). Gwendolen says of Hyle, "I have nail'd his hands on Beth Rabbim & his hands [feet?] on Heshbon's Wall" (*J* 82:43). In the bosom of the Covering Cherub, "there is Heshbon beautiful, the Rocks of Rabbath on the Arnon & the Fish-pools of Heshbon whose currents flow into the Dead Sea by Sodom & Gomorra" (*J* 89:25).

HESPERIA is Italy. Jerusalem once "cover'd the Atlantic Mountains & the Erythrean from bright Japan & China to Hesperia, France & England" (*J* 24:46). In the age of Innocence, they walked "with solemn songs to Grecia and sweet Hesperia, even to Great Chaldea . . . " (*J* 60:19). "Let the Looms of Enitharmon & the Furnaces of Los create Jerusalem & Babylon" and eight other places, including Hesperia (*J* 82:26–28). The Loins of the Covering Cherub include Babylon "and Rome in sweet Hesperia" (*J* 89:39).

HETH, descended from Noah through Ham and Canaan, was the supposed ancestor of the Hittites. "Bathsheba of the daughters of Heth" (*J* 62:11).

HEUXOS was the most prominent of the sons of Tiriel, and probably the eldest. He calls a son of Zazel to dig his mother's grave (*Tir* i:35). Ijim, on returning with Tiriel, summons Heuxos (iv:43), who kneels to Ijim, saying that Tiriel desires the death of all his sons and that they submit to their fate. Tiriel's curse then kills with pestilence all but thirty of his sons.

HEVA (Eve) is the consort of Har. See HAR.

HIDDEKEL (the river Tigris) was the third branch of the river of Eden; "that is it which goeth toward the east of Assyria" (*Gen* ii:14).

When Joseph forgives Mary, her tears of joy flow like the four rivers of Eden (*J* 61:32). The left breast of the Covering Cherub includes Hiddekel, which "pursues his course among the rocks" (*J* 89:35).

HIGHGATE, now absorbed by London, was a picturesque village five-and-a-half miles northwest of St. Paul's. Highgate and Hampstead were on sister hills, with extensive views. Coleridge made his permanent residence there, with the family of James Gillman, in 1816; it may have been here that Blake met him.

Los's forge in London is heard "to Hampstead's breadths & Highgate's heights . . . " (*Mil* 6:9). When the daughters of Zelophehad weave the Woof of Death, "Hoglah on Highgate's heights magnificent Weaves over trembling Thames to Shooters' Hill and thence to Blackheath, the dark Woof" (*Mil* 35:11). The risen Albion's left instep reaches "from Windsor to Primrose Hill, stretching to Highgate & Holloway" (*Mil* 39:37). Hampstead, Highgate, and three other northern villages "rage loud before Bromion's iron Tongs & glowing Poker" (*J* 16:1). When Los "walk'd difficult, he came down from Highgate thro' Hackney & Holloway towards London" (*J* 31:13). "From Camberwell to Highgate . . . where Los's Furnaces stand" (*J* 47:2). Enitharmon appears to Los like a faint rainbow "in the awful gloom of London City on the Thames, from Surrey

Hills to Highgate" (*J* 83:67). Albion's Daughters cry out: "Awake, Highgate's heights & Hampstead's . . . " (*J* 83: 87–84:1). "Hand had his Furnace on Highgate's heights & it reach'd to Brockley Hills across the Thames" (*J* 90: 23).

HILLEL is Blake's spelling of Hêlēl, the Hebrew for Lucifer, or the morning star (*Isaiah* xiv:12): "Hillel, who is Lucifer" (*Mil* 32:8), the first of the Eyes of God.

HINDOSTAN (Hindu) is the twelfth of the Thirty-two Nations which shall guard Jerusalem and rule the rest of the world (*J* 72:39). "Albion trembled to Italy . . . Hindostan . . . " (*Mil* 14:6). The dark Woof of Death is let down over the whole earth, " . . . on Europe to Euphrates & Hindu to Nile" (*Mil* 35:16). It is one of the ten nations to be created by Los and Enitharmon (*J* 82:28).

HINNOM Valley contained a high place, Tophet, where as late as Isaiah and Jeremiah, children were sacrificed to Molech. "And they have built the high places of Tophet, which is in the valley of the son of Hinnom, to burn their sons and their daughters in the fire" (*Jeremiah* vii:31). To stop the practice, the place was polluted and made a place for the burning of trash. It thus became a symbol of Hell. The New Testament "Gehenna" is a corruption of "Ge-Hinnom."

"Albion sat in Eternal Death among the Furnaces of Los in the Valley of the Son of Hinnom" (*J* 15:33). Man's Emanation "is made receptive of Generation thro' mercy, in the Potter's Furnace among the Funeral Urns of Beulah, from Surrey hills thro' Italy and Greece to Hinnom's vale" (*J* 53:27).

The HITTITES encountered by the Israelites were evidently colonists from what we now know to have been the great Hittite Empire. Their land, which the Lord gave to Joshua, reached from the Mediterranean to the Euphrates (*Josh* i:4).

When Los first sent Reuben "over Jordan to the Land of the Hittite," Reuben could not stay there (*J* 34:48).

HOGLAH was the third of the five daughters of Zelophehad (*Numb* xxvi:33); being brotherless, they were allowed to inherit their father's possessions.

Tirzah, the youngest, bidding her sisters torture mankind, calls Hoglah from Mount Sinai (*FZ* viii:316; *J* 68:4). The sonless Milton's wives and daughters are named for Rahab and the five daughters (*Mil* 17:11). These six weave the Woof of Death; Hoglah "on Highgate's heights magnificent Weaves over trembling Thames to Shooters' Hill and thence to Blackheath, the dark Woof" (*Mil* 35:11).

HOLINESS is a word which Blake often used in a pejorative sense, as the virtue of the Pharisees, the state of the "Fiends of Righteousness" who enact and execute cruel laws. It is opposed to Mercy (*Mil* 39:2). "The Fool shall not enter into Heaven let him be ever so Holy. Holiness is not The Price of Enterance into Heaven" (*LJ*, *K* 615).

HOLLAND is one of the six European nations which are temples among the pillars of Urizen's Temple (*J* 58:41).

HOLLOWAY, once a rural town, is now a northern district of London.

When Albion rises, his left instep reaches "from Windsor to Primrose Hill, stretching to Highgate & Holloway" (*Mil* 39:37). "Hackney and Holloway sicken for Estrild & Ignoge" (*J* 21:33). Los "came down from Highgate thro' Hackney & Holloway towards London" (*J* 31:14).

The HOLY GHOST is the inspiration in each individual. He is the influx from the Divine Imagination. "Imagination, Art & Science & all Intellectual Gifts" are "the Gifts of the Holy Ghost" (*LJ*, *K* 604). "Is the Holy Ghost any other than an Intellectual Fountain?" (*J* 77). "What are all the Gifts of the Spirit but Mental Gifts?" (*LJ*, *K* 613). "If God is anything, he is Understanding. He is the Influx from that into the Will" (On Swed *DL*, *K* 89). He comes from Jesus, for he is "the Comforter . . . the Spirit of Truth," whom Jesus promised (*John* xiv:16–17, 26): "the comforter, or Desire, that Reason may have Ideas to build on" (*MHH* 6). Ultimately he is identical with Jesus, because the Trinity is One: "Jesus, our Father, who art in thy heaven call'd by thy Name the Holy Ghost" (On Thornton, *K* 788).

The Holy Ghost is the divine in man. "What? know ye not that your body is the temple of the Holy Ghost?" (*I Cor* vi:19). Blake claimed that Newton denied this "Indwelling of the Holy Ghost" (*EG d*: 45). But this is the only manifestation of the divine in this world. "God only Acts, & Is, in existing beings or Men" (*MHH* 16).

The Holy Ghost is the Genius of each Individual (*J* 91:10). It follows therefore that "the Worship of God is honouring his gifts in other men: & loving the greatest men best, each according to his Genius: which is the Holy Ghost in Man; there is no other God than that God who is the intellectual fountain of Humanity. He who envies or calumniates, which is murder & cruelty, murders the Holy-one" (*J* 91:8; cf. *MHH* 22).

The Holy Ghost is the inspiration of all true artists, such as Bezaleel and Aholiab (*Exod* xxxi:3; *K* 543). Blake invoked him (*J* 74:14). Milton invoked him as inspiration for his epic (*PL* i:17), yet omitted him as a visible character, so that Blake complained he had made him a "Vacuum" (*MHH* 6). "The human mind cannot go beyond the gift of God, the Holy Spirit" (*DesC* V, *K* 579). It was the Holy Ghost who inspired Mary to fulfill the deep purpose of her existence, the conceiving of the child Jesus; and Joseph, learning this in his dream (*Matt* i:20), forgave her self-acknowledged adultery (*J* 61).

Blake implies that all Transgressors, however shortsighted or misled, are inspired by the Holy Ghost. And the only unforgivable sin is that against the Holy Ghost (*Matt* xii:31). For example, while defending Paine the Deist against Bishop Watson's attacks, Blake wrote: "Let the Bishop prove that he has not spoken against the Holy Ghost, who in Paine strives with Christendom as in Christ he strove with the Jews" (On Watson, *K* 387). Again: Blake lashed the great skeptic Voltaire as fervently as Voltaire himself lashed others. But the spirit of Voltaire told Blake (quoting *Matt* xii:32): "I blasphemed the Son of Man, and it shall be forgiven me. But they (the enemies of Voltaire) blasphemed the Holy Ghost in me, and it shall not be forgiven them" (*CR* 267).

Criticizing Dante's ideas, Blake said that Nature was his inspirer, " & not [Imagination], the Holy Ghost" (On Dante, *K* 785).

In the Rosenwald "Last Judgment" (see Illustrations, "LJ" No. 1), the Holy Ghost as a dove replaced the cross above the head of Jesus. On the title page of the illuminated *Genesis*, the Holy Ghost, as a phallic youth, holds the central position. (See Illustrations.)

HOLY THURSDAY in the Anglican calendar is not the Thursday of Holy Week, but the day of the Ascension. On that date, the orphans of London were assembled in St. Paul's for a special service. King George III particularly delighted in it; Haydn was deeply impressed.

Blake's two poems with that title (*SoI* and *SoE*) present contrary views, the first being a naïve delight at the charitable spectacle of the children, the second being indignation at their misery. "Fed with cold and usurous hand" anticipated Oliver Twist.

HOMER was one of the greatest poets. Blake ranked him with Milton, Virgil, Ovid, Shakespeare, and Dante (To Trusler, 23 Aug 1799; To Butts, 22 Nov 1802; 25 Apr 1803; *On Virgil*, *K* 778; *Mil* 1; On Boyd, *K* 411) and even with the Bible (To

Trusler, K 794). When he himself attempted an epic, it was "similar to Homer's Iliad or Milton's Paradise Lost" (To Butts, 25 Apr 1803).

Blake read Homer as a symbolist. "The wisest of the Ancients consider'd what is not too Explicit as the fittest for Instruction, because it rouzes the faculties to act. I name Moses, Solomon, Esop, Homer, Plato. . . . What is it sets Homer, Virgil & Milton in so high a rank of Art? . . . Is it not because they are addressed to the Imagination, which is Spiritual Sensation, & but mediately to the Understanding or Reason?" (To Trusler, 23 Aug 1799).

Blake strongly resented Henry Boyd's moralizing attacks on the *Iliad*. "Nobody considers these things when they read Homer or Shakespear or Dante. . . . If Homer's merit was only in these Historical combinations & Moral sentiments he would be no better than |Richardson's highly moral| Clarissa. . . . the grandest Poetry is Immoral, the Grandest characters Wicked" (On Boyd, K 411–12). Twenty years later he repeated the idea in his essay *On Homer's Poetry*. He considers first the structure of the *Iliad*.

Every Poem must necessarily be a perfect Unity, but why Homer's is peculiarly so, I cannot tell; he has told the story of Bellerophon & omitted the Judgment of Paris, which is not only a part, but a principal part, of Homer's subject.

But when a Work has Unity, it is as much in a Part as in the Whole: the Torso is as much a Unity as the Laocoon.

As Unity is the cloke of folly, so Goodness is the cloke of knavery. Those who will have Unity exclusively in Homer come out with a Moral like a sting in the tail. Aristotle says Characters are either Good or Bad; now Goodness or Badness has nothing to do with Character . . .

It is the same with the Moral of a whole Poem as with the Moral Goodness of its parts. Unity & Morality are

secondary considerations, & belong to Philosophy & not to Poetry . . .

However, after Blake broke with neoclassicism, Homer, without losing his grandeur, went from Good to Bad; indeed, his very greatness made him the Worst.

The historians of the world (and Milton) had agreed that as the Hebrew mythology came first, any resemblances in the classical mythology were weakened and distorted memories of their great original. The Greek Muses, as Blake never tired of pointing out, were the daughters of Memory, and not of Inspiration. "No man can believe that either Homer's mythology, or Ovid's, were the production of Greece or of Latium" (*DesC* II, K 565). "The Poetry of the Heathen" was "Stolen & Perverted from the Bible, not by Chance but by design, by the Kings of Persia & their Generals, The Greek Heroes, & lastly by the Romans" (On Dante, K 785). "The Stolen and Perverted Writings of Homer & Ovid, of Plato & Cicero, which all Men ought to contemn, are set up by artifice against the Sublime of the Bible" (*Mil* 1).

Homer had glorified the Greek love of war, and this ideal still operated. "The Classics! it is the Classics, & not Goths nor Monks, that Desolate Europe with Wars" (*On Homer's Poetry*, K 778). "Homer is the Center of All" (On Dante, K 785); therefore Blake placed him in Satan's place, at the core of the Inferno (illustr. 7 to Dante); in fact, as Dr. Roe points out (*Roe* 57), Blake labelled him "Satan" and then partially erased the name. Homer is crowned with laurel and bears a sword. He is attended by six classical poets: some are bearded; one bears a lyre and another a thin book of song. In the next illustration, Homer with his sword stands beneath a thick oak grove. He is attended by four poets; one holds a closed book, another a scroll, yet another a lyre. Through the heavy foliage they cannot see the floating forms of mothers with their babes. Above them, a heavy layer of black cloud shuts them out from the light of heaven.

When Blake painted the head of Homer for Hayley's library, he chose the supporting figures not from the two epics but (in ridicule of Homer's heroics) a frog and a mouse, from the pseudo-Homeric burlesque *Batrachomyomachia*.

HOR was the mountain where Aaron died (*Numb* xx:28). It is one of the six mountains "in the Desarts of Midian" to which Milton's three wives and three daughters are compared (*Mil* 17:15–17).

HOREB was "the mountain of God" at the back side of the desert near Midian (*Exod* iii:1). Here Moses saw the burning bush and heard God proclaim himself to be "I am that I am." During the Exodus, when the Israelites were desperate with thirst, Moses procured water by smiting "the rock in Horeb" (*Exod* xvii:6). Here the Israelites made and worshipped the golden calf (*Psalm* cvi:19). Here also Elijah took refuge from the wrath of Jezebel and heard the voice of God (*I Kings* xix:8).

Horeb and Sinai are often identified, but Blake distinguished between them as stages of the Mosaic revelation. He particularly associated Horeb with rocks, perhaps because the Old Testament God is "the Rock" (*Deut* xxxii:4), and seemingly referred it to the body. "Sinai & Horeb is Hyle [heart] & Coban [loins]" (*Mil* 19:58). Milton's wives and daughters "sat rang'd round him as the rocks of Horeb round the land of Canaan" (*Mil* 17:12). Milton's Shadow journeys "in that Region call'd Midian among the Rocks of Horeb" (*Mil* 17:28). Tirzah's shadowy sisters, when materializing the body, "form the bones, even the bones of Horeb around the marrow" (*Mil* 19:51). When Milton is developing his Urizenic philosophy, "his Mortal part sat frozen in the rock of Horeb" (*Mil* 20:10), and his Spectrous body "brooded over his Body in Horeb against the Resurrection" (*Mil* 20:22). In the Vale of Surrey, "Horeb terminates in Rephaim" (*Mil* 29:57).

The sculptures (ideas) in Los's halls record "all that can happen to Man in his pilgrimage of seventy years. Such is the Divine Written Law of Horeb & Sinai, and such the Holy Gospel of Mount Olivet & Calvary" (*J* 16:67). The daughters of Tirzah "Weave their Work in loud cries over the Rock of Horeb" (*J* 67:26). The warriors cry "The Feminine & Masculine Shadows, soft, mild & ever varying in beauty, are Shadows now no more, but Rocks in Horeb" (*J* 68:69). The Dragon of war, with the hidden Harlot within, is "a Warlike Mighty-one of dreadful power sitting upon Horeb" (*J* 89:54).

HORSES represent Reason. "The tygers of wrath are wiser than the horses of instruction" (*MHH* 9:5): the deep impulse of wrath has more wisdom than what we have merely learned with our brains. Blake often associates tigers and horses (*MHH* 8:14; *FZ* i:402; ii:35; vii:6; viii:445; *J* 98:43). They are two of a quaternary: Lion (north), Tyger (east), Horse (south), and Elephant (west) — (*MHH* 8:14; *J* 98:43).

Horses are animals of Urizen; therefore they are "golden" (*FZ* vii *b*:201; *J* 65:47). They are "horses of light" (*FZ* iv:113; ix:94). As such they pull the sun chariot of the redeemed Urizen (the Greek Apollo) in the fourteenth illustration to *Job*.

The function of Urizen's horses is to draw his Plow of Nations: the preparations for the New Age must be drawn by Reason. Unfortunately, Urizen made the fatal error of giving his horses to Luvah, a disaster often referred to. We glimpse the horses raging in the cave of Orc, "bound to the chariot of Love" (*FZ* vii *b*:201; *J* 65:47). However, in the apocalypse, Urizen recovers his "Eternal horses" (cf. *MHH*, "A Song of Liberty" 20, where Orc releases them) and plows the universe for the final harvest (*FZ* ix:308).

In *Milton*, it is Satan who tries to drive the Harrow of Palamabron, with the result that the horses are maddened, and Palamabron's work is disrupted (*Mil* 7; 8; 12).

HOUNSLOW, once a Middlesex village (since absorbed by the metropolis), was thirteen miles west of London proper. It is one of a quaternary surrounding the city.

Albion's four forests "overspread all the Earth from London Stone to Blackheath east: to Hounslow west: to Finchley north: to Norwood south" (*Mil* 6:3). "Los against the east his force continually bends along the Valleys of Middlesex from Hounslow to Blackheath" (*Mil* 26:18). Albion bids Hand and Hyle seize Los: "Bring him to justice before heaven here upon London stone, between Blackheath & Hounslow, between Norwood & Finchley" (*J* 42:50). "Los built the Mundane Shell in the Four Regions of Humanity, East & West & North & South, till Norwood & Finchley & Blackheath & Hounslow cover'd the whole Earth" (*J* 42:78).

The HUMANITY is man's innermost part, the image of God in which he was created. "Thou art a Man, God is no more [than Man], | Thy own humanity learn to adore, | For that is my Spirit of Life" (*EG* d:75). He corresponds to Urthona. His joy is in the hunting of ideas and the making of friends. "When Souls mingle & join thro' all the Fibres of Brotherhood, can there be any secret joy on Earth greater than this?" (*J* 88:14). "When in Eternity Man converses with Man, they enter into each other's Bosom (which are Universes of delight) in mutual interchange, and first their Emanations meet surrounded by their Children; if they embrace & comingle, the Human Four-fold Forms mingle also in thunders of Intellect; but if the Emanations mingle not, with storms & agitations of earthquakes & consuming fires they roll apart in fear; for Man cannot unite with Man but by their Emanations, which stand both Male & Female at the Gates of each Humanity" (*J* 88:3).

Such is the proper role of the Emanation in the undivided or reintegrated Man. As the two are now one, he is above sex (*J* 30:33; 79:73); in heaven there can be no

marrying (*Mark* xii:25), as marriage presupposes a division.

When Man falls, he is divided. "I see the Four-fold Man: The Humanity [north] in deadly sleep, and its fallen Emanation [east], The Spectre [south], & its cruel Shadow [west]" (*J* 15:6).

The process of reuniting is analyzed most clearly in *Milton*. Milton, though in heaven, is unhappy because he is still divided. His Emanation is lost to him, his Shadow is separate, his Spectre has become Satan. So Milton determines to leave heaven and reintegrate himself.

His Humanity falls into a dreamful sleep: this "real and immortal Self" remains in heaven "as One sleeping on a couch of gold" (*Mil* 15:11). While his other aspects are on their journeys, "His real Human walk'd above in power and majesty, tho' darken'd, and the Seven Angels of the Presence attended him" (20:13). At other times he sits up on his couch and converses "in vision & dreams beatific" with them (32:1).

Meanwhile the person of Milton has entered his Shadow of unsatisfied desire. When he descends, he comes upon Albion, also sleeping "in solemn death" (15:39). Milton bends over his bosom (15:41), and falls through Albion's heart, "travelling outside of Humanity" (20:41), and reaches Satan, his Spectre.

When Ololon (the true form of his Emanation) descends to find Milton, his Shadow collects himself, is revealed as the Covering Cherub (37:7), and descends into Blake's garden. Error is now defined and is cast out. Milton confronts and denounces Satan, who disappears when Milton wakes Albion. Ololon recognizes her own mistake (Rahab) and divides, her error fleeing with a shriek into Milton's Shadow. Milton is now reintegrated completely, and for a mystical moment Blake beholds Jesus enter Albion's bosom (42: 20).

The Humanity within us can be reached. When it wakens, one can cast out the Spectre (*J* 41). Los, denouncing the

"Fiends of Righteousness," sends them word to "obey their Humanities & not pretend Holiness when they are murderers" (*J* 91:6). After a certain disaster, Los's Spectre and Emanation return "back safe to their Humanity ... & Los put forth his hand & took them in" (*J* 30:13,16).

Jesus, when he was conceived, entered the world of Nature, taking on the erroneous "Maternal Humanity," which the Deists worship, but which must be put off eternally (*J* 90:36, 65).

The DIVINE HUMANITY is God (*Mil* 2:8; 30:15; 39:27; *J* 19:35; 28:26; 49:30; 96:5). He is Mercy (*J* 61:43) and Pity (*Mil* 23:19). He is "the Only General and Universal Form, to which all Lineaments tend & seek with love & sympathy" (*J* 43:20). When compulsory cruel Sacrifices bring him "into a Feminine Tabernacle," he is born as Jesus (*J* 27, *K* 652). In the apocalypse, he is an "intellectual fountain" or the Holy Ghost (*J* 91:11); "Fountains of Living Waters" flow from him (*J* 96:37).

Unlike the Humanity of man, who was made in his image, the Divine Humanity never falls (though he descends for the Incarnation) and never is divided. Otherwise, the two resemble each other so closely that the adjectives "human" and "divine" are virtually interchangeable.

The HUMBER River, the estuary of the Ouse and the Trent, is on the east coast of England; it separates the counties of Lincoln and York.

"Humber & Trent roll dreadful before the Seventh Furnace" (*J* 16:16). "The Humber & the Severn are drunk with the blood of the slain" (*J* 66:63).

HUME (David, 1711–76), philosopher and historian, was famous for his skepticism ("Humism"). He restricted human knowledge to impressions and ideas, their fainter copies, and denied we could ever prove their existence or truth. We cannot prove that a physical cause produces a physical effect, as when one billiard ball hits another.

Blake attacked him along with the other Deists. "How is this thing, this Newtonian Phantasm . . . this Hume & Gibbon & Bolingbroke . . . ?" (*Mil* 40:12). "The reasoning historian, turner and twister of causes and consequences, such as Hume, Gibbon, and Voltaire . . . " (*DesC* V, *K* 579). "Voltaire, Rousseau, Gibbon, Hume, charge the Spiritually Religious with Hypocrisy" (*J* 52, *K* 682).

HUMILITY is considered a great virtue in all authoritarian religions, as it means submission to the authorities. Blake hated it, because it means the sacrifice of the God within man, the sin against the Holy Ghost. Forced humility is spiritual murder. Individuals should never be subjected to Urizen's "One Law for the Lion & Ox" (*MHH* 24). Humility is "the trick of the ancient Elf" (*EG* d:66). It is the teaching of the Spectre (*J* 54:17). Tiriel when a lad was obliged to "humble" his immortal spirit, and thus became a hypocritical serpent (*Tir* viii:37). "Now the sneaking serpent walks in mild humility" (*MHH* 2), having driven the just man into the wilds. But Job refused to sacrifice his personality: "Though he slay me, yet will I trust in him; but I will maintain mine own ways before him" (*Job* xiii:15).

"Humility is only doubt, | And does the Sun & Moon blot out" (*EG* d:99). It takes root under Cruelty's foot (*SoE*, "Human Abstract" 11) and grows into the Tree of Mystery. The "humble" sheep was originally "coward" (*SoE*, "The Lilly" 2, *K* 171).

"Was Jesus Humble?" (*EG* d:1). No: his "honest triumphant Pride" brought him to his death, because he would not humble himself to Caiaphas. "God wants not Man to Humble himself" (*EG* d:65), not even to God: "If thou humblest thyself, thou humblest me" (*EG* d:73). However, in *The Ghost of Abel*, when Jehovah becomes visible, Adam and Eve kneel before his feet.

Only in one picture, as far as I can recollect, does Blake depict man kneeling before God: this is the Humphry (Petworth) version of the "Last Judgment," where Adam and Eve, representing the entire human race, kneel in humiliation before the Throne (*K* 443); but Blake later changed his mind: in the Rosenwald version, they are standing (see Illustrations, "LJ" Nos. 24, 25). Job and his wife (*Illustr Job* 13, 17) face God sitting on their heels; they are not kneeling nor do they show any trace of humility. In a painting, Moses crouches abjectly before God who is writing the Ten Commandments; but Moses was in error, and this was not the true God.

Real humility is modesty at the revelation of one's own good deeds (On Lavater 573, *K* 83). In the Blair "Last Judgment," a single redeemed soul bows humbly before the opened Book of Life, where its deeds are recorded; in the Petworth version, four souls bow before the same book; in the Rosenwald version, only three. (See Illustrations, "LJ" No. 19.)

HUNTINGDON (Huntgn) is a county of Midland England, bounded by the counties of Northampton, Cambridge, and Bedford.

With Bedford and Cambridge it is assigned to Zebulun (*J* 16:48). With Cambridge and six others, it is assigned to Skofeld (*J* 71:38).

HUTTON (Hutn, Huttn) was probably Lt. George Hulton, "who entered into recognizancies for the soldiers to appear at [Blake's] trial" in Chichester (*K* 919).

Hutton is the eighth of the giant Sons of Albion, and is usually paired with Slade, the seventh Son (*J* 5:25; 19:18; 32:11). His Emanation is Gwinefred; he is assigned to Warwick, Northampton, Bedford, Buckingham, Leicester, and Berkshire (*J* 71:36). He is "the Father of the Seven from Enoch to Adam" (*J* 7:24), Adam being identified with Schofield, the ninth Son. When the Sons flee at the sight of Reuben, "Hutton & Skofeld & Kox

fled over Chaldea in terror, in pains in every nerve" (*J* 36:17).

HYDE PARK is a large fashionable park in the center of London. Just outside, to the east, where the Marble Arch now stands, was the Tyburn gallows with its brook.

Here is the invisible gate of death: "Bending across the road of Oxford Street, it from Hyde Park to Tyburn's deathful shades admits the wandering souls of multitudes who die from Earth" (*J* 38:57).

It is also a place of birth. Beulah terminates "in Hyde Park on Tyburn's awful brook" (*Mil* 11:5). "Such is the nature of the Ulro, that whatever enters becomes Sexual & is Created and Vegetated and Born. From Hyde Park spread their vegetating roots beneath Albion" (*J* 44:21).

Los works here: "he heaves the iron cliffs in his rattling chains from Hyde Park [west] to the Alms-houses [east] of Mile-end & old Bow" (*Mil* 6:30). And here he hides Enitharmon from the sight of the Satan-Palamabron quarrel (*Mil* 11:2).

HYLE is the second of the giant Sons of Albion (*J* 5:25; 8:41; 19:18; 32:10). His position is East. He represents "the Affections rent asunder & opposed to Thought" (*J* 74:28). He is associated with the Heart (*J* 80:66), lovers (*J* 80:82), and the Moon (*J* 58:30; 80:66). His Emanation is Gwendolen (*J* 80:67). He dwells in the Cathedral City of Winchester, "comprehending Hants, Dorset, Devon, Cornwall" (*J* 71:20).

The first three Sons, Hand, Hyle, and Coban, form an evil trinity of the heartless Head, the headless Heart, and the selfish Loins. For a full account of the three, and also of the pair Hand and Hyle, see HAND.

When Cambel, inspired by Albion's Tree of moral virtue, tries to subject Hand, Gwendolen similarly tries to subject Hyle. She hides his open heart in ribs, conceals his tongue with teeth, forms his kidneys, and "looking on Albion's Tree" weaves and hides his testicles "of self interest & selfish natural virtue," thus compelling him "into a shape of Moral Virtue against the Lamb" (*J* 80:66–80). Gwendolen thinks thus to reduce him to a baby on her bosom, but he is now only a Worm (*J* 82:37–51). Then, under the influence of Los, she strives bitterly "to form the Worm into a form of love" (*J* 82:72–76).

Hyle is depicted in the frontispiece to Chapter iii of *Jerusalem* (51). He sits on the ground, his head sunk below his knees. On either side are Vala and Scofield.

Although "Hyle" is Greek for "matter," the name seems rather to be derived from that of Hayley, the brainless sentimentalist. See WINCHESTER.

I

IDENTITY is a word Blake used carelessly, but generally it meant for him the type, the eternal Form, or Platonic ideal. "The Oak is cut down by the Ax, the Lamb falls by the Knife, but their Forms Eternal Exist For-ever" (*Mil* 32:37). "Each Identity is Eternal . . . A Man can never become Ass nor Horse" (*LJ, K* 607). "Individual Identities never change nor cease" (*Mil* 32:23).

But Identity is not to be confused with Individuality, which differentiates each person from every other person. See INDIVIDUAL.

Before Blake had established his vocabulary, his terms were confused in his annotations on Swedenborg's *Divine Love*: "Essence is not Identity, but from Essence proceeds Identity & from one Essence may proceed many Identities, as from one Affection may proceed many thoughts. . . . If the Essence was the same as the Identity, there could be but one Identity, which is false. Heaven would upon this plan be but a Clock; but one & the same Essence is therefore Essence & not Identity" (*K* 91).

The IEREUS, or priest, is one of the six religious figures who compose "a terrible indefinite Hermaphroditic form," the Antichrist and Covering Cherub (*J* 89:7).

IGNOGE is the third Daughter of Albion (*J* 5:41), although originally she was listed as the eleventh (*FZ* ii:62). She is the Emanation of Coban (*J* 71:27), the selfish loins. "She adjoin'd with Gwantoke's Children; soon lovely Cordella arose; Gwantoke forgave & joy'd" (*J* 71:28). When cruelty impends, "Sabrina & Ignoge begin to sharpen their beamy spears of light and love; their little children stand with arrows of gold" (*J* 11:19). "Hackney and Holloway sicken for Estrild & Ignoge" (*J* 21:33).

Ignoge's name is that of the daughter of King Pandrasus of Greece. When Pandrasus was captured by the Trojan Brutus, he won his freedom by giving Brutus his daughter in marriage. In Britain, she became the mother of Locrine, Albanact, and Humber (*Geof* I, xi). Milton spelled her name "Innogen."

IJIM is the eighteenth "son" of Los (*FZ* viii:360). In this genealogy, Ochim and Ijim were inserted later between Har and Adam (*Bentley*, Pl. 115), probably because Ijim, a brother of Tiriel (*Tir* iv:11, 21), was already established as a son of Har. As Northrop Frye discovered (*Frye* 243), Ijim's name means "satyrs" (*Isaiah* xiii:21). Blake, however, used the Hebrew plural as a singular noun.

As a satyr, Ijim dwells in woods (*Tir* iv: 4, 90), the forests of error. His religion is as animistic as that of Browning's Caliban. The forces of nature are to him the protean forms of a hostile fiend; for the Self-love (Har) of whom he is a son interprets anything in his way as an enemy. In Swedenborg's *True Christian Religion* (where, as Frye notes, Blake found his name) self-love "causes its lusts to appear at a distance like various wild beasts; some are like . . . wolves and tigers, and some like crocodiles and venemous serpents." Ijim encounters a lion, a tiger, a river torrent, a thunder-cloud, a serpent; "then like a toad or like a newt would whisper in my ears" (*Tir* iv:59—one recalls Satan as a toad whisper-ing in the ear of Eve), a rock, a poisonous shrub, and finally Tiriel himself.

Ijim symbolizes the power of the people. He is invincible: his strength is "terrible"; no weapon can wound him (iv:70); his voice is "as the voice of Fate" (iv:27). Yet he has an inherent nobility. Though he mistakes Tiriel for the fiend, he scorns to smite a blind and aged man (iv:18), and offers to guide him. When Tiriel becomes exhausted, he carries him back to Tiriel's palace (iv:39). When he learns that this is indeed Tiriel and that his sons have cast him out, he can scarcely believe it, yet will not lift his hand against them, but departs to his "secret forests," where he wanders all night "in desolate ways" (iv:90).

ILIUM. See TROY.

The IMAGINATION in the Age of Reason was considered a degenerative malady of the intellect. Dr. Johnson could write: "All power of fancy over reason is a degree of in-sanity" (*Rasselas*, Chap. xliv, "The Dan-gerous Prevalence of Imagination"). And to this day, the word "imagination" is sometimes a polite substitute for "false-hood."

To Blake, however, the Imagination was the central faculty of both God and Man; indeed, here the two become indistinguish-able. "The Eternal Body of Man is The Imagination, that is, God himself, The Divine Body, Jesus: we are his Members" (*Laoc, K* 776). "Man is All Imagination. God is Man & exists in us & we in him" (On Berkeley, *K* 775). Imagination is "the Divine-Humanity" (*J* 70:19); it is "the Divine Body of the Lord Jesus" (*Mil* 3:3; *J* 5:58; 24:23; 60:57; 74:13; *Laoc, K* 776). It is the gift of the Holy Ghost (*LJ, K* 604); it is the Holy Ghost himself (On Dante, *K* 785).

It is existence. "All Things Exist in the Human Imagination" (*J* 69:25). "All Animals & Vegetations, the Earth & Heaven [are] contain'd in the All Glorious Imagination" (*J* 49:13). "In your own Bosom you bear your Heaven and Earth & all you behold; tho' it appears Without, it is Within, in your Imagination, of which this World of Mortality is but a Shadow" (*J* 71:17). "All that we See is Vision . . . Permanent in The Imagination" (*Laoc, K* 776). It is "the real & eternal World of which this Vegetable Universe is but a faint shadow, & in which we shall live in our Eternal or Imaginative Bodies when these Vegetable Mortal Bodies are no more" (*J* 77).

It is the basis of all art. "One Power alone makes a Poet: Imagination, The Divine Vision" (On Wordsworth, *K* 782). "Na-ture has no Outline, but Imagination has. Nature has no Tune, but Imagination has. Nature has no Supernatural & dissolves: Imagination is Eternity" (*GhA* 1:3). In the creative act, it is the completest liberty of the spirit. "Imagination is surrounded by the daughters of Inspiration, who in the aggregate are call'd Jerusalem" (*LJ, K* 604). "I know of no other Christianity and of no other Gospel than the liberty both of body & mind to exercise the Divine Arts of Imagination" (*J* 77). It is the exploring "inwards into the Worlds of Thought, into Eternity ever expanding in the Bosom of God, the Human Imagination" (*J* 5:19).

Its enemy is "Abstract Philosophy" (*J* 5:58; 70:19; 74:26) or the Reasoning Spectre (*J* 36:24; 74:7, 11). The Daugh-ters of Memory (tradition) are often con-trasted with the Daughters of Inspiration: "Imagination has nothing to do with mem-ory" (*CR* 301).

Blake's theory may have originated with Paracelsus. See PARACELSUS.

INCEST was the outstanding vice in romantic literature. In Walpole's *Mys-terious Mother* (1768) it was merely a dramatic device. But Chateaubriand's *René* was a personal confession. Byron adver-tized his torturing complex in various works, especially *Manfred* (1817) and *Cain* (1821). For Shelley, it was an example of arbitrary law: he used it in *Laon and Cythna* (1818), omitted it in the expurgated version, *The Revolt of Islam*, then used it again in *The Cenci* (1819). Thereafter, incest was to be found broadcast in minor authors' works, usually as a dramatic device which collapsed when the hero and heroine were discovered not to be kin at all. The subject was continued by the next generation, producing Poe's perfect symbol, *The Fall of the House of Usher* (1839), Melville's extraordinary analysis, *Pierre* (1852), and Hawthorne's *Marble Faun* (1860), where the author was interested not so much in Miriam's secret sin as in its effect on conscience. To ensure racial purity, Wagner made Siegfried's parents brother and sister (*Die Walküre*, 1856).

Blake shared Shelley's belief in its innocence, and indeed considered it the very root of marriage. The Emanation is always a sister as well as a consort. Los and Enitharmon, for example, are twin children of Enion. Vala is Luvah's daughter as well as consort. None of them are troubled by the taboo. Albion, to be sure, denounces incest as a sin (*J* 28:7), but he is in a state of error, and he has no influence on his Sons and Daughters, for whose marital entanglements see *Jerusalem* 71.

INDIA, in Blake's day, was composed of a number of separate states.

When all nations wept in affliction at the sight of the Lord's coming, "India rose up from his golden bed as one awaken'd in the night" (*Mil* 31:14). "China & India & Siberia" are "temples for entertainment" in Urizen's temple (*J* 58:39). The Daughters of Albion rage through all the nations of Europe "to Lebanon & Persia & India" (*J* 80:47). When Hand marches through Egypt in his fury, "the East is pale at his course, the Nations of India" (*J* 84:22).

The INDIVIDUAL is unique, eternal, and therefore uncreate and indestructible. It is the *esse* of each person, and differs from that of every other person.

Each Individual is sacred: his special Genius is "the Holy Ghost in Man" (*J* 91:10). If he humbles himself, he humbles his God (*EG* c:39). He has his own particular duty to perform in this world. Jesus was sent "to abolish the Jewish Imposture" (On Watson, *K* 387); Voltaire was sent to expose the literal sense of the Bible (*CR* 267); Blake himself was sent to "renew the Arts on Britain's Shore" and thus overcome militaristic France spiritually ("Now Art has lost its mental Charms," *K* 557).

The Individual's duty is to be himself, to develop all his potentialities, and within his own limitations to perform the functions for which he was designed. His ideal is Liberty: Jerusalem is "the Divine Vision" in every individual (*J* 54:2). He is not to model himself on any other Individual, however sacred or profane. Particularly is it blasphemous to assume the Universal Attributes of the Lord (*J* 90:30). "When the Individual appropriates Universality he divides into Male & Female, & when the Male & Female appropriate Individuality, they become an Eternal Death, Hermaphroditic worshippers of a God of cruelty & law! Your Slaves & Captives, you compell to worship a God of Mercy" (*J* 90:52).

Other Individuals must be estimated for what they are. "The Worship of God is honouring his gifts in other men; & loving the greatest men best, each according to his Genius: which is the Holy Ghost in Man" (*J* 91:8; cf. *MHH* 22). "In Great Eternity every particular Form gives forth or Emanates its own peculiar Light & the Form is the Divine Vision and the Light is his Garment. This is Jerusalem in every Man, a Tent & Tabernacle of Mutual Forgiveness, Male & Female Clothings" (*J* 54:1).

"Every Man's Wisdom is peculiar to his own Individuality" (*Mil* 4:8). Any failings may be imputed not to the Individual but to the State he is in (*FZ* viii:380; *Mil* 32:22; *J* 25:16). As "Individual Identities never change nor cease" (*Mil* 32:23), it is impossible to correct matters by trying to alter a person's character. Satan is a dunce when he tries to "change Kate into Nan" (*GoP*, Epilogue 4). As we are all different, "One Law for the Lion & Ox is Oppression" (*MHH* 24).

The Individual is inviolable. What can happen when it is assaulted is told in *The Crystal Cabinet* (*K* 429), a poem describing a love affair in Surrey. The poet becomes enamored of a maiden who returns his threefold kiss. But when he strives to seize her "inmost Form," the whole illusion is shattered.

INFLAMMABLE GASS, the Wind-finder, represents experimental science (*An Island in the Moon*, Chaps. i, iii, iv, x, xi). He is married to Gibble Gabble.

A reference to "flogiston" (phlogiston) indicates that Joseph Priestley (1733–1804) was the inspiration for Inflammable Gass. He was a religious and political radical and a prominent chemist. He experimented on "different kinds of air" (1767); discovered oxygen, which he called "dephlogisticated air"; and adhered to the phlogistic theory of combustion. When his house and effects at Birmingham were burned by an anti-revolutionary mob, he removed to Pennsylvania, where he continued his experiments and publications.

For details, see Erdman (*Erd* 96–99).

INNOCENCE and Experience, as the full title of *Songs of Innocence and of Experience* indicates, are the "Two Contrary States of the Human Soul," ecstasy and misery, or heaven and hell.

"Innocence" was the standard term for man before his Fall; Blake extended the meaning to the state of childhood, into which we are all born, a state of free imagination and spontaneous joy.

"Experience" is Blake's term for the contrary of Innocence; it is man's state when disaster has destroyed the initial bliss. The Fall made Adam aware of death for the first time; on the title page of *Songs of Experi-*

ence, initial bliss is destroyed by the death of the parents.

A further state, a synthesis of the two, is indicated in the "Introduction" to *Songs of Innocence,* when the piper's tune makes the poet laugh, then weep, and the third time weep "with joy." This third state is again indicated in "To Tirzah," the last poem of *Songs of Experience,* when the death of Jesus frees the poet from his parents and his mortality.

The INTELLECT is to be distinguished from Reason. Intellect is the source of ideas, reason is merely the process of logic. In the painting "The Ancient Britons" (*DesC* V), "the Ugly Man [Urizen] represents the human reason" (*K* 578), which is also "the incapability of intellect" (*K* 580). The difference is that between the fountain and the mill, the Holy Ghost and Urizen.

The hunting of Ideas and their intellectual warfare are the great sports of Eternity, "the Two Fountains of the River of Life" (*Mil* 35:2; *J* 43:32).

"There is no other God than that God who is the intellectual fountain of Humanity" (*J* 91:10). Blake's task was "To open the immortal Eyes of Man inwards into the Worlds of Thought, into Eternity ever expanding in the Bosom of God, the Human Imagination" (*J* 5:18).

"Men are admitted into Heaven not because they have curbed & govern'd their Passions or have No Passions, but because they have Cultivated their Understandings. The Treasures of Heaven are not Negations of Passion, but Realities of Intellect, from which all the Passions Emanate Uncurbed in their Eternal Glory. The Fool shall not enter into Heaven let him be ever so Holy" (*LJ, K* 615).

INVERNES[S] is a Scottish county, assigned with Nairn and Linlithgo to Naphtali (*J* 16:55).

IRELAND, in the quaternary of British nations, lies west, and like America (west in the quaternary of continents) it is separated from the others by the Atlantic.

Blake sometimes calls Ireland "Erin," but usually reserves that name for his doctrine of the purity of sex and the beauty of the body. He generally thinks of Ireland as the westernmost part of Europe; when he wishes to describe a world-wide movement, it goes from Ireland to Japan (*Mil* 6:22; *J* 34:42; 63:34; 67:7; 83:21; 89:50). In doing this, he erroneously placed the Giant's Causeway at Ireland's farthest point west (*J* 89:50); actually, it is in the northeast county of Antrim.

The Four Provinces of Ireland are each assigned to a son of Israel: Munster (south) to Reuben; "Connaut" (west) to Joseph; Ulster (north) to Dan; and Leinster (east) to Judah (*J* 72:3–4). The thirty-two counties (Blake miscounted them as thirty-four in *J* 16:29, but corrected himself later) are assigned according to their provinces: the six of Munster to Reuben, Simeon, and Levi; the five of Connaught to Ephraim, Manasseh, and Benjamin; the nine of Ulster to Dan, Asher, and "Napthali"; and the twelve of Leinster to Judah, Issachar, and Zebulun (*J* 72:18–27).

When the diseases of Albion's Angel are driven back on Great Britain, the Guardians of Ireland, Scotland, and Wales become spotted with plagues and forsake their frontiers (*Am* 15:13). When Albion rises, "his right elbow leans on the Rocks of Erin's Land, Ireland, ancient nation" (*Mil* 39:44). When the British counties flee out of Jerusalem's gates, Los fixes them down (*J* 16:29). When Jerusalem is taken, Ireland is "her holy place" (29:20); and the Daughters of Beulah lament for Og and Sihon upon the Lakes of Ireland (49:4). The four ungenerated Sons of Los "dwell over the Four Provinces of Ireland in heavenly light" (71:52); they remain to guard the walls of Jerusalem, whose foundations remain in the British counties (72:14). The wings of the Covering Cherub spread from Japan "to Ireland's farthest rocks, where Giants builded their

Causeway, into the Sea of Rephaim, but the Sea o'erwhelm'd them all" (89:50). See ERIN.

The IRISH SEA is the body of water which lies between Ireland and England.

Chester's River (the Dee), the Mersey, and the Ribble "thunder into the Irish sea" (*J* 90:16).

IRON is one of the four symbolic metals, standing north in a quaternary with Gold (south), Silver (east), and Brass (west). It is the metal with which Los works. His forge and furnace and all his instruments are of iron; he has an iron mace; and Urthona's bow is of iron.

However, Blake also associates Iron with all forms of cruelty: war (which comes from the North), with its weapons, armor, and the captains' whips (*J* 65:35); also Urizen's Book of Iron (*Ahan* 3:64), and his Plow of the Nations (*FZ* ii:70); Vala's spindle of destruction (*J* 66:10); and imprisonment, with its chains and fetters, including the bonds of selfish love. Fuzon's chariot (*Ahan* 2:1), Los's Chain of Jealousy (*Ur* 20:19, 24), the vessels of the Shadowy Female (*Am* 1:3) and of Urizen's daughters (*FZ* vii:96), and the trumpet of the Last Judgment (*Eur* 13:2) are all of iron.

"Some Sons of Los surround the Passions with porches of iron & silver" (*Mil* 28:1); that is, in the writing of comedy, the poets use Iron (wit-combat) and Silver (love).

ISAIAH was the greatest of the Hebrew prophets. Blake admired him early: "Ezra came with Isaiah the Prophet" (To Flaxman, 12 Sept 1800). In *The Marriage of Heaven and Hell* (12), Blake asserted:

The Prophets Isaiah and Ezekiel dined with me, and I asked them how they dared so roundly to assert that God spoke to them; and whether they did not think at the time that they would be misunderstood, & so be the cause of imposition.

Isaiah answer'd: "I saw no God, nor heard any, in a finite organical perception; but my senses discover'd the infinite in every thing, and as I was then perswaded, & remain confirm'd, that the voice of honest indignation is the voice of God, I cared not for consequences, but wrote.

ISHMAEL was the son of Abraham and his concubine Hagar (see HAGAR). Before his birth, Hagar fled from the harshness of the jealous Sarah into the wilderness, but the angel of the Lord bade her return, prophesying that her son's descendants would be numberless past counting. "Behold, thou art with child, and shalt bear a son, and shalt call his name Ishmael; because the Lord hath heard thy affliction. And he will be a wild man; his hand will be against every man, and every man's hand against him" (Gen xvi:11–12). Therefore the hero of Melville's *Moby Dick* assumed his name: "Call me Ishmael."

When he was thirteen, he was circumcised the same day as his father (Gen xvii:25–26), and the Lord prophesied: "Behold, I have blessed him, and will make him fruitful, and will multiply him exceedingly; twelve princes shall he beget, and I will make him a great nation" (Gen xvii:20). The twelve are named and listed (Gen xxv:12–16).

Although Abraham loved his eldest son, he yielded to the jealous Sarah and expelled him and his mother. They nearly died of thirst in the wilderness, but again the angel of the Lord appeared to her, assuring her that God had heard the boy's voice and repeating the prophecy that he would father a great nation (Gen xxi:17–18). Then God opened her eyes so that she saw a well, and the water saved their lives. "And God was with the lad; and he grew, and dwelt in the wilderness, and became an archer. And he dwelt in the wilderness of Paran: and his mother took him a wife out of the land of Egypt" (Gen xxi:20–21). He died at the age of "an hundred and thirty and seven years" (Gen xxv:17).

Mahomet claimed Ishmael as his ancestor. "[Beneath] Ishmael is Mahomed" (*LJ, K* 607; see Illustrations, "LJ" Nos. 71, 80). He is a sage with wings and a halo.

ISIS was the sister-wife of Osiris and mother of Horus (Orus). These three, worshipped in Egypt, constitute a trinity which Blake names as the eighth of the Twelve Gods of Asia (*Mil* 37:27).

An ISLAND IN THE MOON is an unfinished prose satire which lacks at least one leaf before the last page. The manuscript is in the Fitzwilliam Museum at Cambridge University. David Erdman has pointed out that many references to women's styles and such matters make it likely that it was written 1784–85; but the final pages must have been added later, about 1787–88, as they contain references to Blake's illuminated printing and working copies of three of the *Songs of Innocence.* Blake himself may have destroyed the missing leaf, to preserve the secret of his method of printing.

The identification of the characters has caused much speculation. Quid the Cynic has always been recognized as Blake himself, though in a very contrary mood. Inflammable Gass is obviously Joseph Priestley; and his wife Gibble Gabble must be Mary Priestley. Jack Tearguts is the famous surgeon Dr. John Hunter, whose name Blake wrote, then crossed out.

The identification of Sipsop the Pythagorean as Thomas Taylor the Platonist is "probable" according to Keynes (*K* 884), but "does not hold water" according to Erdman (*Erd* 93). Erdman, however, produces excellent evidence that Steelyard the Lawgiver is John Flaxman (100) and Mr. Jacko is Richard Cosway, the miniaturist (88). He also surmises that Suction the Epicurean may be Robert Blake (92); Obtuse Angle, James Parker (89); Aradobo, Joseph Johnson the bookseller (96); and Mrs. Nannicantipot, Mrs. Barbauld (99). But George Mills Harper, after carefully reconsidering Erdman's proofs and conjectures, identified Sipsop as the son of the Rev. A. S. Mathew, who was "the late John Hunter's favourite pupil" (*Harper* 39), and suggested convincingly that Obtuse Angle was Thomas Taylor the Platonist; and Etruscan Column, the Rev. John Brand, author of the well-known *Observations on Popular Antiquities* (1777). But whoever they were, they certainly were friends and acquaintances of Blake who were familiars in the Mathew circle.

The tale opens with promise of an analysis of contemporary thought, personified by Suction the Epicurean (the philosophy of the senses), Sipsop the Pythagorean (science), and Quid the Cynic (the doubter of all). "I call them by the names of those sects, tho' the sects are not ever mention'd there, as being quite out of date; however, the things still remain, and the vanities are the same" (*K* 44). Already Blake had learned that "Names alter, things never alter" (*DesC* III, *K* 567), as he wrote in proving that Chaucer's characters are an analysis of all human society in every epoch.

But the grand scheme degenerates immediately into nonsensical and ignorant chatter about Voltaire, Chatterton, Locke, and other subjects of highbrow conversation in Blake's day. There is no apparent structure; that is, no basic and controlling idea. It is a lively, coarse burlesque of the kind of thing that went on in Blake's shop. Yet every now and then, underlying the inconsequences, may be traced Blake's ideas. In Inflammable Gass's dangerous experiments, Blake hints his fears that Science may yet destroy us all. When the talk runs on Phoebus and Pharaoh, Quid exclaims, "Hang them both!"—thus cursing both God and Emperor (*Erd* 99).

Then, in the last chapter, something happens. As usual, the characters sing, but the first three songs are real poems— they are, in fact, first drafts of three of the *Songs of Innocence*. After Obtuse Angle sings "Holy Thursday," "they all sat silent for a quarter of an hour, & Mrs. Nannicantipot said, 'It puts me in Mind of my mother's song.' " This is the "Nurse's Song." Quid follows it with "The Little Boy Lost." "Here nobody could sing any longer, till Tilly Lally pluck'd up a spirit," and made them laugh with a coarse song of his own.

Could this not mark the awe that came over Blake when he felt a new spirit of poetic creation, something wholly his own, and not the adolescent imitations of the *Poetical Sketches*? And with it came the discovery of an original method for publishing them: "—thus Illuminating the Manuscript" begins the last leaf. Quid is talking with some woman, who might be Catherine Blake, only that Quid apparently has no wife; or possibly the talented Miss Gittipin, who sings "like a harpsichord," and therefore could well be envied by all the other women for her "abilities." Quid, having got her to agree that his face is very like a goat's, says that hers is "like that noble beast the Tyger," and plans with her to make a scene at a party. "I'll hollow and stamp, & frighten all the People there, & show them what truth is."

Thus Blake made fun of his own undoubtable propensity for pushing arguments too hotly in social gatherings, and in a measure excused them.

The ISLE OF LEUTHA'S DOGS is the Isle of Dogs, formed by a bend of the Thames, opposite Greenwich; it is the place of the West India Docks.

Los, walking through London, comes to the Isle of Leutha's Dogs, which he doubtless so named because of the prostitutes who swarmed about the shipping (*J* 31:16). See LEUTHA.

The ISLE OF MAN is in the Irish Sea. See SODOR.

"Peachey had North Wales, Shropshire, Cheshire & the Isle of Man" (*J* 71:30).

The ISLES are the Hebrides and the Orkney Islands, lying northwest and north of Scotland.

"Bowen had all Scotland, the Isles, Northumberland & Cumberland" (*J* 71:46).

ISLINGTON, a large village in Middlesex, is now part of the metropolis. It lies two and a half miles north of St. Paul's. It is one of the places where Blake roamed as a boy and learned the principles of freedom. "The fields from Islington to Marybone, | To Primrose Hill and Saint John's Wood, | Were builded over with pillars of gold, | And there Jerusalem's pillars stood" (*J* 27). "The Shuttles of death sing in the sky to Islington & Pancrass, round Marybone to Tyburn's River" (41:7). "Awake, Highgate's heights & Hampstead's, to Poplar, Hackney & Bow, to Islington & Paddington & the Brook of Albion's River" (83:87).

ISRAEL was the name given to Jacob (*Gen* xxxii:28; xxxv:10). As he is the ancestor of all the Jews proper, through his twelve sons, his name commonly signifies all God's chosen people. Blake always uses his name in this generic sense ("Mock On," *K* 418; *Mil* 40:26; *J* 27; 86:17, 26; 89:30, 39).

The SONS OF ISRAEL were twelve: Reuben, Simeon, Levi, Judah, Dan, Naphtali, Gad, Asher, Issachar, Zebulun, Joseph, and Benjamin. Each was the founder of a Tribe, and to each was assigned a tract of land, except Levi the priest, who was given instead forty-eight "cities of refuge" scattered through the other allotments. Hence the names of the Twelve Tribes on the map do not correspond precisely to the list of the Sons: Levi is omitted; but the number is kept to Twelve by omitting Joseph also, and substituting the names of his two sons Manasseh and Ephraim.

Blake commonly used the original list (*FZ* viii:360, 375; *J* 16:35–41, 44–49, 53–58; 74:42–56). But at other times he includes Manasseh and Ephraim, excluding Joseph, though always including Levi.

Thus, in referring to the flight of the twelve Sons, he names seven of them: "Reuben & Manazzoth & Gad & Simeon & Levi, and Ephraim & Judah" (*Mil* 24:2). When assigning the provinces and counties of Ireland, he gives Joseph the Gate of the province of "Connaut," but drops his name in favor of his two sons when assigning the counties; he also drops the name of Gad, substituting Levi (*J* 72:3, 18–25). When Jerusalem recalls their days of innocence she names seven: "Levi and Judah & Issachar, Ephra[i]m, Manasseh, Gad, and Dan" (*J* 79:30).

After the Babylonian captivity, only two tribes returned, those of Judah and Benjamin. What became of the ten Lost Tribes has caused much speculation. They could not have died out, as Ezekiel, in the great vision of the Temple which ends his prophecy, assigned a gate to each of the Sons, and also land to each of the Tribes. The return of the Lost Tribes is confirmed by *Revelation* vii, where the Tribes are named for the Sons, except that Dan is omitted without explanation, his place being taken by Manasseh.

Blake put the list of the twelve Sons between Adam and David as the twentieth to thirty-first of the thirty-eight Sons of Los (*FZ* viii:360), a genealogy later discarded. In *Milton* and *Jerusalem*, they are listed after Rintrah, Palamabron, Theotormon, and Bromion, as the last of Los's sixteen Sons. The first four remained constant to Los, and never were generated; the remaining twelve, however, fled from him successively in "that thousand years of sorrow, of Palamabron's Harrow & of Rintrah's wrath & fury," and were "Generated [materialized] . . . wandering with Tirzah" (*Mil* 23:62–24:4); that is, they abandoned true inspiration for the restrictive laws on sex. Urizen tempted them to do this (*FZ* viii:374). Before that, they had lived as innocent shepherds (*J* 79:30). Now "they became Nations . . . beneath the hands of Tirzah" (*Mil* 24:16). They rolled apart and enrooted: Reuben in Bashan (which Blake apparently supposed was part of his inheritance); Simeon in Philistia; Levi in forty-eight roots all over Canaan—the forty-eight cities of refuge; Judah in Hebron (which is near the center of his land) ; and Joseph and Benjamin in Cabul (actually in Asher's land). The remaining six Sons dissipated into Non Entity—became Lost Tribes (J 74:42–51, 56, 57) .

This dispersal and enrooting represents the nationalizings of mankind. When Rahab is finally revealed, "all beneath, the Nations innumerable of Ulro appear'd: the Seven Kingdoms of Canaan & Five Baalim of Philistea into Twelve divided, call'd after the Names of Israel, as they are in Eden" (Mil 40:23) .

But before that, the Sons become the victims of the Daughters of Albion, who sacrifice them for their own lovers. They "drink up" Reuben and Benjamin, who, being the oldest and youngest, represent all Twelve (J 90:46) . They drink up Dan and Gad "to feed with milk Skofeld & Kotope. They strip off Joseph's Coat & dip it in the blood of battle" (J 67:22) . Tirzah gives the coat to Scofield (J 68:1) , while Gwendolen strips off Joseph's "beautiful integument" for her beloved Hyle (J 81:11). This involves cutting the Sons' fibres (uprooting them from their homes): Bowen and Conwenna cut Benjamin's, while Hand and Boadicea cut Reuben's (J 90:15, 25). The younger generation, Manasseh and Ephraim, are tortured for their own sakes by Tirzah (FZ viii:309–10; J 67:56–57).

The return of the redeemed Sons and Tribes is indicated by Blake's assigning them Gates and counties in the four kingdoms of the British Isles; confusedly in the first assignment (J 16:28–58), but in the Irish counties roughly according to Moses' arrangement of tribes (J 72:1–27). Blake's assignments were inspired by Ezekiel's vision of the New Jerusalem, and are to be understood in the same way: a New Jerusalem is in preparation above, for each of the kingdoms. The Heavenly Canaan and the Twelve Sons are suspended

above Albion, and Blake indicates that the relation of the Sons of Israel to the Sons of Albion is as the Soul to the Body (J 71:1–5). Presumably, these New Jerusalems will descend eventually, as did the sacred city in *Revelation* xxi:2.

Blake was interested in only two of the Sons: Reuben, who represents the average sensual man, and Joseph, the victim of fraternal rivalry. Joseph's coat, however, is stripped off by the women, with reference to Potiphar's wife.

ISSACHAR was Israel's ninth son. With his brothers, he is listed as a Son of Los who fled (FZ viii:361, 376). With five of his brothers, he rolls apart into Non Entity (J 74:50). Jerusalem remembers him and some of his brothers in their time of innocence (J 79:30).

In Wales he is assigned the county of Brecknockshire; in England, Northampton, Rutland, and Nottingham; in Scotland, Selkirk, Dumbarton, and Glasgow (J 16:37, 48, 57); in Ireland, with Judah and Zebulun, he is assigned the twelve counties of Leinster (J 72:18).

ITALY, in her days of primal innocence, beheld Jerusalem "in sublime astonishment" (J 79:39); but after the fall, she sank under the control of organized religion. France, Spain, and Italy, the three chief Catholic nations, consequently behold with terror the effects of the American Revolution. "They slow advance to shut the five gates of their law-built heaven," but the fires of Orc consume the gates (Am 16:16–21). "France & Spain & Italy & Denmark & Holland & Germany" are temples among the pillars of Urizen's temple (J 58:41). At the awakening song of the Bard, Albion trembles "to Italy, Greece, & Egypt" and through the rest of the world (Mil 14:6). The social system of the Polypus shoots its fibres round the earth, "thro' Gaul & Italy" and other places (J 67:38). The Daughters of Albion "rage thro' all the Nations of Europe, thro' Italy & Grecia" and other nations (J 80:46).

The lost Emanation is mercifully "made receptive of Generation . . . from Surrey hills thro' Italy and Greece to Hinnom's vale" (*J* 53:27–29). On foreseeing the coming of the Lord, all the nations lament in affliction; Germany, the center of the Reformation, "wept towards France & Italy" (*Mil* 31:13). And eventually Italy shall be one of the Thirty-two Nations which shall guard liberty and rule the rest of the world (*J* 72:38).

IVORY was highly prized in the Scriptures. It is the material for Ahania's bed (*Ahan* 5:4) and Urizen's pavilions (*FZ* v:202). But the fact that ivory, unlike the metals, was once living substance had meaning for Blake; when it is used, it adds a human element. Jerusalem's pillars are of ivory and gold (*J* 24:18); so are the mighty spires and domes of Golgonooza (*Mil* 35:25). The harness of Urizen's horses is of gold (thought), silver (affection), and ivory (*FZ* ii:28). When making the Wine of Ages, the Sons of Tharmas and Urthona form "heavens of sweetest woods, of gold & silver & ivory, of glass & precious stones" (*FZ* ix:792).

In *Milton* (28:1–20), the elements of Comedy are silver (love) and iron (combat), while the elements of Tragedy are gold (thought) and ivory (human woes, perhaps traditional tales).

In *Jerusalem*, the third gate in every house in Golgonooza is described as being "clos'd as with a threefold curtain of ivory & fine linen & ermine" (*J* 13:23).

J

JACHIN AND BOAZ were the twin free pillars flanking the steps of Solomon's temple. Their significance remains obscure, though they are generally supposed to represent the Pillars of Cloud and of Fire. At the Last Judgment, Jesus is "seated between the Two Pillars, Jachin & Boaz, with the Word of divine Revelation on his knees" (*LJ*, *K* 606; see Illustrations, "LJ" No. 22).

JACOB, the third of the Hebrew patriarchs, was a grandson of Abraham, a son of Isaac, and the younger brother of Esau (Edom), whom he defrauded of his birthright and his father's blessing (*Gen* xxv:29–34; xxvii:1–29). Blake implies that he is the "villain" who "drove the just man into barren climes," and prophesies Esau's return and "the dominion of Edom" (*MHH* 2:14–16; 3:4). Later, Blake cites Esau and Jacob as examples of fraternal rivalry (*J* 73:28).

But after Jacob's mystical experiences at Bethel and Peniel (the ladder and the wrestling), he became a different man, changed his name to Israel, and was reconciled to Esau. His twelve sons founded the Twelve Tribes. See ISRAEL.

JAMES, Duke of York, later James II (1633–1701), was as immoral as his brother Charles. He was the center of the Jesuit intrigues to convert England to Roman Catholicism. The Catholics were supposed to have started the Great Fire of London (1666). Blake accepted the popular belief, since discredited. "James calls for fires in Golgonooza, for heaps of smoking ruins in the night of prosperity and wantonness which he himself Created among the Daughters of Albion, among the Rocks of the Druids" (*Mil* 5:40).

JAPAN is always used by Blake to indicate the eastern termination of some worldwide event. Ireland (less often America) is the western termination. Thus the wings of the Covering Cherub "spread from Japan, where the Red Sea terminates the World of Generation & Death, to Ireland's farthest rocks" (*J* 89:48).

JAPHETH was the third son of Noah. In Blake's *Vision of the Last Judgment*, "Noah is seen . . . Canopied by a Rainbow, on his right hand Shem & on his Left Japhet: these three Persons represent Poetry, Painting, & Music, the three Powers in Man of conversing with Paradise, which the flood did not Sweep away" (*K* 609, "LJ" 68).

"Kox is the Father of Shem & Ham & Japheth; he is the Noah of the Flood of Udan-Adan" (*J* 7:23).

JARED was the son of Mahalaleel (*Gen* v:15), the sixth in the line from Adam to Lamech (*Mil* 37:36; *J* 75:11), and thus one of the "Giants mighty, Hermaphroditic" who constitute the first division of the cycle of the Twenty-seven Churches.

JAVAN was the fourth son of Japheth (*Gen* x:2). His name is identical with the Greek "Ion," ancestor of the Ionians or Greeks. His sons took over "the isles of the

Gentiles" (*Gen* x:5). "The Isles of Javan" (*J* 86:32) are therefore the isles of Greece; "the Gods of Javan thro' the Isles of Grecia" (*J* 89:34) were the Greek gods.

JEALOUSY was an attribute of the tyrant author of the Ten Commandments, who proclaimed himself "a jealous God, visiting the iniquity of the fathers upon the children unto the third and fourth generation of them that hate me" (*Exod* xx:5). Blake would not accept this god as the true God. "Starry Jealousy" (*SoE*, "Earth's Answer" 7) is Urizen, and jealousy is one of his outstanding characteristics. See URIZEN. Blake also applied the term to Nobodaddy (*K* 171).

In love, jealousy is a form of selfishness and involves fear; it is the enemy of true love, and makes a bondage of marriage. Oothoon, denouncing the "Father of Jealousy" (*VDA* 7:12), offers to bring Theotormon all the girls he wants; "Oothoon shall view his dear delight, nor e'er with jealous cloud come in the heaven of generous love" (*VDA* 7:28). The second title of Blake's first epic reads: *The Four Zoas, The torments of Love & Jealousy in The Death and Judgement of Albion the Ancient Man.*

Orc is bound in the Chain of Jealousy (*Ur* 20:24; *SoL* 3:21). This chain was created by the paternal jealousy of the father, when Orc began to embrace his mother; but in *Milton*, this Oedipean emotion has become the root of all jealousy. An old prophecy has predicted that Milton, in purging his errors through Blake, will rise and "set free Orc from his Chain of Jealousy" (20:60) and break it "from all its roots" (23:38).

Previously, Los has reproved Palamabron's Emanation for this artificial emotion: "Elynittria! whence is this Jealousy running along the mountains? British Women were not Jealous when Greek & Roman were Jealous. Every thing in Eternity shines by its own Internal light, but thou darkenest every Internal light with the arrows of thy quiver, bound up in the horns of Jealousy to a deadly fading Moon, and Ocalythron binds the Sun into a Jealous Globe, that every thing is fix'd Opake without Internal light" (10:14). Elynittria reforms, and leads Leutha to Palamabron's bed (13:38).

The JEBUSITES originally dwelled on the heights where Jerusalem later was located. Blake describes the pagan warfare as extending "across the hills of Ephraim & down Mount Olivet to the Valley of the Jebusite" (*J* 68:22). The Bible does not associate the Jebusites with any valley, but it was undoubtedly the sinister Valley of Kidron, which lies between the Mount of Olives and Temple Hill. Being a burial place, it was noted for its impurity.

JEHOVAH is the name of God revealed to Moses at Horeb (*Exod* iii:14; vi:2–3).

Many deeds, evil in our sight, were ascribed to him. He destroyed Sodom and Gomorrah (*Gen* xix:24); he slew Er and Onan (*Gen* xxxviii:7, 10); he hardened Pharaoh's heart so that the plagues might continue (*Exod* ix:12, etc.); he sent a lying spirit to lure Ahab to his death (*I Kings* xxii:22). He was the author of the Ten Commandments and of good and evil. "Out of the mouth of the most High proceedeth not evil and good?" (*Lam* iii:38). "I make peace and create evil" (*Isaiah* xlv:7). "Shall there be evil in a city and the Lord hath not done it?" (*Amos* iii:6).

Consequently, Jesus' description of him as the loving Father of all was a revolutionary concept. He was no longer the God of vengeful Justice but the God of Mercy. Blake therefore assigned the evil deeds of the original Jehovah to an inferior deity: Urizen or even Satan, "That Angel of the Divine Presence," who "is frequently call'd by the Name of Jehovah Elohim" (*LJ, K* 610). Nevertheless, it is the historical Jehovah who, as the sixth Eye of God, precedes the coming of Jesus. "Jehovah was leprous; loud he call'd, stretching his hand to Eternity, for then the Body of Death was perfected in hypocritic holiness around the Lamb" (*Mil* 13:24; *FZ* viii:405). See ANGEL OF THE DIVINE PRESENCE, under ANGEL, and EYES OF GOD.

In *The Marriage of Heaven and Hell*, however, Jehovah is the God of inspiration and mercy, "the Jehovah of the Bible being no other than he who dwells in flaming fire. Know that after Christ's death, he became Jehovah" (*MHH* 6). It had been Jehovah who saved Isaac from being sacrificed by substituting the ram for the child. "O when shall Jehovah give us Victims from his Flocks & Herds instead of Human Victims . . . ?" (*J* 63:30; cf. "All the atonements of Jehovah spurn'd, | And Criminals to Sacrifices Turn'd"—"If it is True" 14, *K* 543).

Therefore, in *Milton*, Jehovah's rain, which he gives to the just and unjust alike, contends with the thick fires of Molech, to whom the innocent are sacrificed (8:27). He is still surrounded by the clouds of Sinai when Satan creates "Seven deadly Sins, drawing out his infernal scroll of Moral laws and cruel punishments upon the clouds of Jehovah" (9:21), clouds which Los disperses (23:31).

But in *Jerusalem*, the clouds are cleared away. The Covenant of Jehovah, "If you Forgive one-another, so shall [I] Forgive You" (61:25), is the greatest of virtues: "Forgiveness of Sins which is Self Annihilation; it is the Covenant of Jehovah" (98:23).

According to the rabbinical tradition, Elohim represents justice and Jehovah mercy. The two combined are the perfect synthesis. The forgiveness of Mary is a vision of Elohim Jehovah (*J* 61:1). *The Ghost of Abel*, which affirms the triumph of forgiveness, is another such vision. "The Elohim of the Heathen Swore Vengeance for Sin! Then Thou stood'st forth, O Elohim Jehovah! in the midst of the darkness of the Oath, All Clothed in Thy Covenant of the Forgiveness of Sins: Death, O Holy! Is this Brotherhood" (*K* 781).

The name "Jehovah Elohim" first occurs

in *Genesis* ii:4, after the Sabbath of the seventh day, when the Creator rested.

JERUSALEM is Liberty (*J* 26:3; 54:5). As the Emanation of Albion, she is the inspiration of all mankind. She is the Divine Vision in every individual (*J* 54:3). She is also the Holy City of Peace, which is the perfect society. As the Bride of the Lamb (*Rev* xxi:2), she is communion with God, "the Mystic Union of the Emanation in the Lord" (*J* 53:24).

The marriage of the Lamb and Jerusalem is conventionally interpreted as the union of Christ and his church. Blake expanded the meaning of "church" to signify all mankind and (as Nature is a projection of man) all Nature as well, united in the mystical ecstasy (*J* 99:1–5).

The name Jerusalem means "City of Peace" and is paralleled with Shiloh ("peace"); both were places where the Ark of the Covenant rested. As Jerusalem is the Emanation of Albion (England), so Shiloh is the Emanation of France (*J* 55:29): the deepest desire of both warring nations was peace.

Blake specifically defines Jerusalem as Liberty. Liberty was early taken as a gift of God. From *Leviticus* xxv:10 on (the inscription on the American Liberty Bell), the idea grew from political to spiritual significance, as a glance at the Concordance will prove. *Isaiah* lxi:1 was the text on which Jesus preached at Nazareth, for which he was expelled from the local synagogue (*Luke* iv:18, 29). Thus he himself became the Liberator, an idea which was a favorite of Paul's: "the glorious liberty of the children of God" (*Romans* viii:21); "our liberty which we have in Christ" (*Galatains* ii:4); and "Christ hath made us free" (*Galatians* v:1) are some of his phrases.

Blake went still further. Liberty was more than a special privilege of the Elect: it was a requisite of all society. "What is Liberty without Universal Toleration?" (On Dante, *K* 413). The spirit of Christ (for which "Toleration" is a weak word) and the liberty of the individual are essential to each other. Thus Blake translated the Biblical symbolism of the mystical Marriage into sound sociology.

Jerusalem as Liberty appears on the first pages of *The Four Zoas* (i:27, 29), when Tharmas and Enion, at the onset of puberty, have hidden her. Urizen conspires with Luvah to enslave her (i:497). In the strife of nations she becomes a ruin (i:545). The Daughters of Albion bind her children in the dungeons of Babylon (ii:63). Later, Enitharmon beholds the Lamb within Jerusalem's Veil (viii:190–93). Jerusalem attends the Crucifixion (viii: 331) and the entombment (viii:338) and weeps over the sepulcher two thousand years—until Blake's day (viii:598; ix:1). Then, at the Last Judgment, Jesus descends from the New Jerusalem (ix:273).

In *Milton*, Jerusalem is Liberty, without mystical implications. She is now Albion's Emanation (2:15). Blake laid her foundations in Lambeth (6:15; 25:48, 54; 35:10), but she is now in ruins, and has been forced to become a harlot (22:47; 33:21). She is also bound in the dens of Babylon (38:27). Her children are condemned as Reprobates (22:47). Her enemies are Satan (11:1; 12:27), Rahab and Tirzah (22:47), and the doubters (41:21). But the time is coming when Jerusalem shall return and overspread all nations (6:18; 25:55). The rising Albion faces towards the east, towards Jerusalem's Gates (39:34). And Blake himself, in the introductory poem, arms himself to build Jerusalem in England's green and pleasant land.

In *Jerusalem*, Jerusalem is not only Albion's Emanation but the wife of the Lamb as well. Albion in jealousy hides her in his bosom, thus turning his back on the Divine Vision. As a result, he embraces Vala, whom the Lamb then gives him for his wife (4:16–17, 33; 20:36–40). In confusion and guilt, Albion flees "inward" into his bosom, where he finds Jerusalem and Vala in Beulah, as yet in a state of harmony; but his fall drives them apart. A colloquy between Man, Freedom, and Nature ensues. Jerusalem laments the loss

of the state of innocence. When Vala accuses her of sin, she replies that sin is "but a little error & fault that is soon forgiven." Though she has tried, she cannot put off the human form (cease to be humane). She begs Albion not to analyze his sins, and asks why he has hidden her "remote from the divine Vision, my Lord and Saviour." But though he will not annihilate Jerusalem, as he intended, he denounces and rejects her; recoiling "outward," he gives himself to Vala and sinks down dying (19:39–23:26).

Jerusalem, rejected, divides into two aspects. Her "form" or central identity remains in Beulah, "shut within [Albion's] bosom" (19:29), and takes refuge with Beulah's Daughters (5:49, 55; 14:33; 60:40), who hide her (41:14). Outwardly, she is reduced to an inoperative theory, "scatter'd abroad like a cloud of smoke thro' non-entity" (5:13). This pillar of smoke, or "folding cloud" (81:14), rises from Los's furnaces (5:50). In it she is drawn eastward (5:48; 14:31) by maternal anguish (5:47; 14:32; 48:18) for the fate of her children (5:65) and revolves towards the Starry Wheels of Abstract Philosophy, which is Entuthon Benython (5:52–58; 12:43; 14:34). Vala is with her in the cloud, weeping and wandering upon the mountains (5:48, 60) of abstract thought. So Los beholds Jerusalem early in the poem; so also Blake, for she took refuge at Lambeth (41:11), where Albion fell (20:1).

After the entombment of Albion, Jerusalem's maternal love wakes her in Beulah, and she leaves it with solemn mourning (48:18–25). She bursts from the tomb, "struggling to put off the Human form," but the weeping Daughters of Beulah receive her "among the Spaces of Erin in the Ends of Beulah, where the Dead wail night & day" (48:49–52). That is: Blake's theory of Liberty is implicit in his doctrine of the holiness of the body and the purity of sex. But Erin warns the Daughters that if Jerusalem remains there, she will become "an Avenger of Sin, a Self-righteousness, the proud Virgin-Harlot! Mother of War!" (50:14–16).

A curious fact now comes to light. Albion's Brittannia is the unit which divided into Jerusalem and Vala during the dislocation of the Zoas (36:28). When Albion now tries to draw Brittannia (England) into his bosom, she resists him, and in her dragon wings Jerusalem and Vala appear, beneath the dimmed Divine Vision (54: 27–32).

A touching colloquy between Jesus and Jerusalem follows. Though her form sleeps in Beulah, she is seemingly at work in the mills of Babylon. Jesus reminds her of her days of innocence; why does she now sacrifice to idols? Often she sees and hears him; she affirms her faith in him, but wonders how he can take such a sinner as she for his bride. To demonstrate the Forgiveness of Sins, he comforts her with a vision of the scene between Joseph and Mary, when Joseph decides not to renounce her. Jerusalem replies, showing that the female ancestors of Jesus, as far as known, were all sinners or outlanders. He assures her that he is always with her, and will save her and her children (60:10–62:29).

But the necessary war, which Jesus predicted, breaks out (62:20–21, 30); the Sons of Albion beleaguer the Gates of Erin, raging against the Lamb and Jerusalem (78:13). Her city is laid in ruins, and she and her children are carried into captivity (78:21). She laments, recalling her days of prosperity (78:31–80:5). Trembling, she follows her children (80:9–10), but they become involved in the materialism of Vala. "The Children of Jerusalem, the Souls of those who sleep, were caught into the flax of [Vala's] Distaff & in her Cloud to weave Jerusalem a body according to [Vala's] will, a Dragon form [of war] on Zion Hill's most ancient promontory" (80:33). Cambel, inspired by the Tree of Moral Virtue, sends Hand "to weave Jerusalem a Body repugnant to the Lamb" (80:65). At the sight of Hyle as a worm, Cambel's envy "ran thro' Cathedron's Looms into the Heart of mild Jerusalem to

destroy the Lamb of God. Jerusalem languish'd upon Mount Olivet, East of mild Zion's Hill" (82:53).

Meanwhile Enitharmon weaves "the Web of life for Jerusalem; the Web of life, down flowing into Entuthon's Vales, glistens with soft affections" (83:73). And Los, singing his Watch Song, describes a vision of Jerusalem in her ideal form, with Albion's land in her head, and the Twelve Tribes in her bosom, while in her reins are Israel in her tents, with the Pillars of Cloud and Fire, and the gentile lands (86:1–32).

This vision is depicted on Plate 14. Arched over with a rainbow, Jerusalem in the night of Beulah hovers above the sleeping Albion.

When the "all perverted" Covering Cherub appears, Jerusalem is hidden within his "devouring Stomach . . . as in a Tabernacle of threefold workmanship, in allegoric delusion & woe" (89:43).

But the risen Albion calls on Jerusalem to "Awake and overspread all Nations as in Ancient Time" (97:2). And in the final mystical union of all human forms, the name of their Emanations is Jerusalem (99:5).

JERUSALEM *The Emanation of The Giant Albion* | *1804* | *Printed by W. Blake Sth Molton S^{t}* was Blake's largest published work. It contains exactly one hundred plates. Eight complete copies are known, three of them printed posthumously. Only one colored copy exists, though there are colored examples of several plates. It was once supposed that Ruskin owned and cut up a second colored copy, a theory since disproved by Kerrison Preston.

The date 1804 is evidently that of the year when Blake started work on it, "after my three years slumber on the banks of the Ocean" at Felpham (*J* 3). But he did not really settle down to it until he had finished *Milton*, about 1810. In 1809, in his *Descriptive Catalogue* (V, "The Ancient Britons"), he gave an account of the poem: "The Strong Man represents

JERUSALEM ❖ 209

the human sublime [Urthona]. The Beautiful Man represents the human pathetic [Luvah], which was in the wars of Eden divided into male [Luvah] and female [Vala]. The Ugly Man represents the human reason [Urizen]. They were originally one man [Albion], who was fourfold; he was self-divided and his real humanity slain on the stems of generation, and the form of the fourth was like the Son of God [Los]. How he became divided is a subject of great sublimity and pathos. The Artist has written it under inspiration, and will, if God please, publish it; it is voluminous and contains the ancient history of Britain, and the world of Satan and of Adam" (K 578). Fifteen years and more were to pass before the book appeared.

On July 14, 1811, Southey called on Blake, who showed him "a perfectly mad poem called Jerusalem" (K Census 112—this passage is not printed in Symons). As an example of its supposed insanity, Southey told Crabb Robinson that "Oxford Street is in Jerusalem." But Southey read hastily or remembered wrongly: Blake's sole reference to Oxford Street (J 38:57) places it near Hyde Park in London.

On June 9, 1818, Blake sent Dawson Turner a list of his works for sale; it did not include Jerusalem. A year and a half later, on December 30, 1819, Blake sold John Linnell a copy of Chapter ii, possibly a second installment.

Certainly a year later, the manuscript was nearing completion. Blake's admirer, Thomas Griffiths Wainwright, inserted a squib in The London Magazine for September 1820: "Talking of articles, my learned friend Dr. Tobias Ruddicombe, M.D. [Blake's hair was red] is, at my earnest entreaty, casting a tremendous piece of ordnance, an eighty-eight pounder! which he proposeth to fire off in your next. It is an account of an ancient, newly discovered illuminated manuscript, which has to name 'Jerusalem the Emanation of the Giant Albion' ! ! ! It contains a good deal anent one 'Los,' who, it appears, is

now, and hath been from the Creation, the sole and four-fold dominator of the celebrated city of Golgonooza! The doctor assures me that the redemption of mankind hangs on the universal diffusion of the doctrines broached in this M.S." Unfortunately, the promised article, Blake's own account of his epic, never appeared.

Then Shelley died in 1822; and if my conjectures be right (see BARD OF OXFORD, under OXFORD), Blake inserted some plates which included a eulogy.

The watermarks in five of the copies issued by Blake run from 1818 to 1820; but these watermarks prove only that the book could not have been published before those dates. The colored copy (E) is watermarked 1820; but four months before Blake's death he wrote to George Cumberland (12 April 1827), giving our only reference to any completed copy: "The Last Work I produced is a Poem Entitled Jerusalem the Emanation of the Giant Albion, but find that to Print it will Cost my Time the amount of Twenty Guineas. One I have Finish'd. It contains 100 plates but it is not likely that I shall get a Customer for it." He never sold this "Finish'd" or colored copy; after Mrs. Blake's death it passed into the possession of Frederick Tatham.

Blake worked long and hard on the text of Jerusalem, which shows evidence of many deletions, insertions, and rearrangements. Words and even lines were scratched out, or inked or painted over; or new words and lines might be added by incision on a dark background. Single words might even be cunningly altered; thus "pale" became "blue" (37:10). When inspiration struck, new pages were etched and inserted, such as Joseph's forgiveness of Mary (Pl. 61). In such cases, a plausible continuity had to be managed.

Sometimes these added plates are distinguishable by a larger lettering, which contrasts with the earlier somewhat cramped style. The entire episode of Los's trying to force the unstable Reuben to settle across the Jordan in the Holy Lands is such an addition (33–36); furthermore, Plate 35, which interrupts that narrative, is a still later insertion. Plates 56, 61, 72–73, 81, and 85–88 are all insertions in this larger lettering; they contain some of Blake's most splendid poetry. The catchword "To" on Plate 9 leads to Plate 11; therefore Plate 10 is another interpolation.

The death of Shelley in 1822, I believe, inspired an elegy which eventually involved no fewer than three plates (41, 45, 46), each of which was once intended to follow Plate 40. On Plate 40 began the list of the Cathedral Cities, ending on "benevolent Bath." Plate 41 begins "Bath who is Legions," but the subject is changed until the end of Plate 44, when "at length was heard the voice of Bath . . . " Plate 45 begins "Bath, healing City!" and gives his speech, in which he calls on Oxford to heal Albion with leaves from the Tree of Life. The last line is an addition not in the trial proof, needed for the continuity: "And these the names of the Eighteen combining with those Ten"; whereupon Plate 46, beginning "Bath, mild Physician of Eternity," concludes the list of Cities begun on Plate 40, and contains the fainting of Oxford (the death of Shelley). Then Plate 47 abruptly changes the subject: it deals with the outbreak of war.

My conjecture is that originally the sequence ran 40, 41, 42, 47; that 43 (where there is no textual continuity from 42) and 44 were insertions, for the sake of Los's splendid tirade "Why stand we here trembling" and the futile attempt of the Churches to force Albion back into Eden; that Shelley's death inspired the writing of 46; and that in turn inspired 45, the tribute to Richard Warner. See BATH.

Plates already etched were sometimes moved from their original positions. Plate 14 was intended to end Chapter i; and Plate 28, which begins the text proper of Chapter ii, once was numbered 16—indicating that when they were etched, Blake had not yet decided to have four chapters of twenty-five pages each. (David Erdman has restored, almost miraculously, most of the deleted passages. Among other things, he claims to have deciphered "In XXVIII Chapters" on the title page. See "The Suppressed and Altered Passages in Blake's *Jerusalem*," *Studies in Bibliography*, XVII, 1, 1964.) Plate 75, the last of Chapter iii, was once numbered 77. The Gate of precious stones and gold (38:55) is conceivably the Gate guarded by the mystics (72:51), which apparently was once followed by Plate 59. But the biggest shift came in Chapter ii, where Plates 43–46 were put before 29–32, the resulting order being 26–28, 33–41, 43–46, 42, 29–32, 47–50. Blake's intent is clear: he wanted the Spectre to appear immediately after Albion proclaimed Moral Law and set himself up as the punisher and judge.

The dream-plot of *Jerusalem* is so complex, so interrupted by laments, colloquies, repetitions, and seemingly unrelated episodes, that the basic structure was not discovered until Dr. Karl Kiralis analyzed it in a brilliant study (*ELH*, Vol. XXIII, June 1956).

The tale proceeds not by action but by the sequence of ideas. Chapter i describes the Fall of Man into "the Sleep of Ulro"; the remaining three chapters describe his "passage through Eternal Death! and . . . the awaking to Eternal Life" (*J* 4:1). These three are addressed respectively to the Jews, the Deists, and the Christians; they analyze man's progress through Experience until he reaches the Truth. They correspond to Blake's threefold division into "the Three Regions immense of Childhood, Manhood, & Old Age [maturity]" (14:25; 98:33). The Jewish religion is that of Moral Law and the Angry God; it pertains to the childhood of the human race and of the individual as well. The Deist religion, that of young manhood, retains the Moral Law, but substitutes Nature for God. The Christian religion, that of maturity, is particularly plagued by the errors of sex—the false ideal of chastity, which produces the spiritual dominion of woman. Eventually all these errors are worked out, and the final truth is obtained in the recovery to man of his perfect balance of faculties and the fullness of power, and in his eternal union with God.

"Jerusalem" is both the first and the last word of the poem, indicating that Blake was concerned, first and last, with Liberty. It is the ideal for the individual and also for society, for on Liberty is based the Brotherhood of Man, without which Man cannot exist. It is "the Divine Appearance" (33:52); it is the true religion (57:10); without it, "Man Is Not" (96:16).

Chapter i opens as Albion rejects Jesus, in jealousy hiding Jerusalem, his Emanation, who should be the Bride of the Lamb. Albion exteriorizes his affections, which manifest as his Sons, raging against Jerusalem. Albion flees inward, where he encounters Jerusalem and Vala (nature); once they were friends, but now they become opposed. In revulsion, Albion casts Moral Law (Vala's veil) into the Atlantic, "to catch the Souls of the Dead" (23:23); but even at the moment when he believes he is dying, and utters his last words, he beholds the Slain Lamb.

Meanwhile Los, ever the champion of Man, is affected. He divides into Spectre and Emanation. He forces the threatening Spectre to help him in his work; his first creation is Erin (the purity and holiness of the body); he also creates Golgonooza (the City of Art) and assigns the British counties to the Sons of Israel. His separated Emanation in the meantime has become a Globe of Blood (Pity, which divides the soul).

At the end of the chapter, the Daughters of Beulah, protesting against Vengeance (punishment of sin), beg the Lamb to create States, and thus deliver Individuals evermore. These States are the path of Experience, detailed in the following chapters.

Chapter ii is the triumph of Moral Law. Albion, discovering himself in a world of sin, proclaims himself "the punisher & judge" (28:4). The Spectre appears im-

mediately (33), preaching materialism, and Vala (nature) asserts her superiority. Los, who is now able to intervene, deplores this creation of the Female Will, and in vain tries to force the unstable Reuben (the ordinary man) to cross the Jordan into the Promised Land, but Reuben cannot settle there. When the falling Albion flees to the threshold of Eternal Death, Los expostulates with him, and in despair calls upon the Cathedral Cities (religion) to save him, but they cannot do so against his will. Meanwhile Los's Spectre and Emanation report to the Saviour about the false god risen from Albion's wearied intellect (29).

Albion's Sons issue from his bosom and bear him to a Druid temple. War breaks out (47); Albion then utters again his last words, "Hope is banish'd from me" (47:1, 19); but the Saviour reposes him on the Rock of Ages where he builds for him a protecting tabernacle (the inspired books of the Bible). After Erin laments over Man and his fallen universe, the Daughters of Beulah reply by imploring the Lamb of God to take away "the remembrance of Sin," which is the sense of guilt.

Chapter iii is the triumph of Reason, against a confused background of war. The Spectre (reason) proclaims himself God; reacting against him the Eternals elect the seven Eyes of God. The plowing of the Nations begins; when Albion himself falls into the furrow and is plowed under, his Spectre then drives the plow. Los labors to create "a World of Generation from the World of Death" (58:18); Urizen directs the building which becomes his temple. Jerusalem (liberty) is degraded and enslaved. Luvah (France) is conquered and crucified (63:5; 65:8).

The children of Albion now rage at will. Gwendolen dances naked to the timbrel of war, leading her sisters in inciting the warriors. The females unite into Vala, who proclaims her contempt for the males, "Woman-born and Woman-nourish'd & Woman-educated & Woman-scorn'd"

(64:16). She becomes one with the plowing Spectre as the Hermaphrodite. The Sons rejoice about the victim in Salisbury, where they build Stonehenge. The Daughters unite in Rahab and Tirzah; the Sons become united as Hand. Finally Rahab and her cycle of Twenty-seven Heavens and their Churches are revealed.

Chapter iv contains the triumph of the Female Will, the climaxing of all errors, the self-sacrifice of Albion, and the final reunion of all things.

The great error of official Christianity was its exaltation of "chastity," which gave dominance to the Female. Consequently, this problem occupies much of this chapter in the tale of the conspiracy of Gwendolen and Cambel to dominate the male. The Daughters of Albion develop Gwendolen's falsehood into the "allegory" of marriage (85:1), which spreads over Erin (88:31); in marriage Reuben finally finds his abiding place (85:4).

Meanwhile Enitharmon, who had become a Globe of Blood much earlier (17:51), separates completely from Los (86:50) and develops a will of her own. They wander from Enion (FZ i:264); his love becomes desire; Enitharmon repels him and proclaims, "This is Woman's World" (88:16); and the Spectre, who has caused their "divisions & shrinkings," declares that "The Man who respects Woman shall be despised by Woman" (88:37).

Blake's Fourfold Correspondences in *Jerusalem*

NORTH	EAST	SOUTH	WEST	
Urthona (Los)	Luvah	Urizen	Tharmas	The Four Zoas
Blacksmith	Weaver	Plowman	Shepherd	Their callings
Imagination	Emotions	Reason	Senses (Body)	Their meanings
Poetry	Music	Architecture	Painting	Their Arts
Friendship	Love	Hunger	Lust	Their Desires
Nadir	Center	Zenith	Circumference	Their places
Breadth	Inward	Height & Depth	Outward	Directions
Iron	Silver	Gold	Brass	Their Metals
Enitharmon	Vala	Ahania	Enion	Their Emanations
Spiritual	Natural	Pleasure (Sin)	Generative In-	Their meanings
Beauty (In-	Beauty		stinct (the	
spiration)	(Nature)		Earth Mother)	
Rintrah	Theotormon	Bromion	Palamabron	The Four Sons of Los
Wrath	Desire	Reason	Pity	Their meanings
Ocalythron	Oothoon	Leutha	Elynittria	Their Emanations
Jealousy	Free Love (The Magdalen)	Condemnation	Toleration	Their meanings
Eternity (or Eden)	Beulah	Ulro	Generation	The Four Worlds
Sun	Moon	Stars	Earth	Their symbols
Gods	Men	Matter	Vegetation	States
Earth	Fire	Air	Water	Elements
Gnomes	Genii	Fairies	Nymphs	Elementals
Humanity	Emanation	Spectre	Shadow	Divided Man
Head	Heart	Stomach (Bowels)	Loins	The Body
Ears	Nostrils	Eyes	Tongue	The Senses
Europe	Asia	Africa	America	Continents
Scotland	England	Wales	Ireland	British Isles
Edinburgh	London	Verulam	York	Cities
Euphrates	Hiddekel	Gihon	Pison	Rivers of Eden

The Covering Cherub is then revealed, and in his tabernacle is disclosed Rahab. But Los, contending with the Spectre, proclaims truth after truth, until his song draws to a close. Brittannia wakes and repents; Albion wakes and rises; Jesus appears; and Albion sacrifices himself. He finds himself in Eternity, seizes his fourfold bow, and slays the last enemy, the Covering Cherub. Then Eternity is reestablished, and all becomes one in the Divine Vision.

JESUS the man, according to Blake, was the son of an unidentified human father; he was begotten out of wedlock; thus from the beginning he was an offense against the Law. The girl Mary was "innocently gay & thoughtless" (*LJ, K* 610); her illicit act was one of free love in obedience to the Holy Ghost within her; it was the fulfillment of the purpose of her existence. (In the picture "The Assumption of the Virgin," she flies upward, not towards the Trinity, but towards the Babe.) Joseph understood this, and his forgiveness of his adulterous betrothed was one of the great examples of the Forgiveness of Sins (*J* 61). See MARY THE VIRGIN.

Blake traced her descent back to Cain's sister-wife; the line included many of the worst women in the Old Testament. See MATERNAL LINE.

He followed Swedenborg in believing that Mary gave her son nothing but his mortal body. "Christ took on Sin in the Virgin's Womb & put it off on the Cross" (*Mil* 5:3; *EG b*:55).

His illegitimacy was kept a secret: it was not known to the neighbors in Nazareth (*Matt* xiii:55; *Luke* iv:22), or to those who hailed him as a descendant of David (*Matt* xxi:9; xxii:42, etc.), or to the compilers of the genealogies in *Matthew* and *Luke*, both of whom agree (and agree only) in tracing his descent from David through Joseph.

The picture showing the boy learning carpentry from Joseph is entitled "The Humility of the Saviour"; but when he was twelve, he defied his mother and renounced Joseph in the temple: to Mary's reproof, "Behold, thy father and I have sought thee sorrowing," he replied, "Wist ye not that I must be about my Father's business?" (*Luke* ii:49). At Cana, he snubbed his mother again: "Woman, what have I to do with thee?" (*John* ii:4), and yet again (*Luke* xi:28). He renounced his whole family (*Matt* xii:47–50), and taught that his disciples must also hate their families (*Luke* xiv:26). "A man's worst enemies are those of his own house & family" (*J* 27:81).

Blake agreed with the Deists that Christ never performed any miracles which violate the laws of physical nature. "The manner of a miracle being performed is in modern times considered as an arbitrary command of the agent upon the patient, but this is an impossibility, not a miracle, neither did Jesus ever do such a miracle. . . . I cannot do a miracle thro' experiment & to domineer over & prove to others my superior power, as neither could Christ. . . . Christ & his Prophets & Apostles were not Ambitious miracle mongers" (On Watson, *K* 391–92).

The Triumphal Entry into Jerusalem was a mistaken attempt to fulfill Daniel's prophecy (*Dan* vii:13–14) by overthrowing the Roman government and establishing himself on the temporal throne of David as the king of the Jews. Jesus had prepared for this revolution by sending out his seventy disciples (*Luke* x:1) "against Religion & Government" (*EG i*:37), and ordering all his followers to obtain swords (*Luke* xxii:36). When he foresaw that his attempt was doomed to fail, he prayed in Gethsemane for "a Bodily Pardon" (*EG d*:90), which he could have obtained easily by submission to the authorities (*EG d*:30–36). "He was wrong in suffering Himself to be crucified. He should not have attacked the Government. He had no business with such matters" (*CR* 255). "There was his turning the money changers out of the Temple. He had no right to do that" (*CR* 271). So he was quite correctly

numbered with the transgressors and executed "as an Unbeliever" (On Watson, *K*
387).

The resurrection of his physical body
was also a myth. Los and Enitharmon see
"the Crucified body . . . still in the Sepulcher" when "Jesus stood beside them in
the spirit" (*FZ* ix:2–4). "It is raised a
spiritual body" (*I Cor* xv:44).

But whatever the mistakes of the mortal
man, spiritually they were right, because
"Jesus was all virtue and acted from impulse, not from rules" (*MHH* 23). Thus
the Crucifixion, politically an error, is one
of the greatest of symbols; and so with all
his acts.

He called himself the "Son of Man," a
phrase which Ezekiel used constantly to
describe himself when directly inspired by
God; Daniel also used it once in his vision
of Him who shall have everlasting dominion
(*Dan* vii:13–14). Believing in his mission,
Jesus considered himself the chosen Mes-
siah, but he did not consider himself the
Son of God in any special sense. When the
Jews accused him of setting himself up as
God (*John* x:33), he replied by quoting
Psalm lxxxii:6: "Ye are gods, and all of
you are children of the most high."

"Thought is Act. Christ's Acts were
Nothing to Caesar's if this is not so" (On
Bacon, *K* 400).

A transgressor from the womb, he offended the Law both in his begetting and
in his death. He was a born revolutionist in
the spiritual world, and broke, at least by
implication, every one of the Commandments (*MHH* 24). "Wherefore did Christ
come? Was it not to abolish the Jewish Imposture? Was not Christ marter'd because
he taught that God loved all Men & was
their father & forbad all contention for
Worldly prosperity, in opposition to the
Jewish Scriptures . . . Christ died as an Unbeliever" (On Watson, *K* 387).

The universal paternity of the all-loving
Father signifies the Brotherhood of Man,
the only basis for a peaceful society. But
this must rest upon the freedom and development of the Individual, for "What

is Liberty without Universal Toleration?"
(On Boyd, *K* 413). And "Toleration" is a
weak word for the Forgiveness of Sins, the
greatest of Christ's spiritual discoveries,
which had been completely overlooked by
the pagan philosophers.

This revolutionary doctrine, which made
Mercy the outstanding attribute of the
Father, abolished the standards of Good
and Evil and abrogated the whole system of
Justice, which is based on the Ten Commandments. See FORGIVENESS OF
SINS. The clearest example of this
doctrine was the forgiveness of the woman
taken in adultery (*EG e*). It was inspired
by Jesus' perception of the woes of lovers.
When the frustrated Oothoon "hover'd
over Judah & Jerusalem . . . Jesus heard
her voice (a man of sorrows) [and] reciev'd a Gospel from wretched Theotormon" (*SoL* 3:22).

"Plato did not bring Life & Immortality
to Light. Jesus only did this" (On Berkeley, *K* 774).

Crabb Robinson understood Blake to
say that "Christ took much after his
mother (the law), and in that respect was
one of the worst of men" (*CR* 271). The
first great schism in the Christian church
came over the question whether Jesus
taught the fulfillment of the Law or its
abrogation. Blake believed that Jesus was
of the line of prophets, who were always
against "religion"; he too denounced the
priests and kings, and was "the image of
the Invisible God" (*Mil* 2:12), with whom
he became so identified that "after Christ's
death, he became Jehovah" (*MHH* 6);
and until he became the Father, he was still
liable to errors (*CR* 255).

For Jesus as God, see GOD.

The JEWS held a high though ambivalent
position in Blake's thought. Practically all
the Old Testament was inspired (On Watson, *K* 390, 392). "The Five books of the
Decalogue, the books of Joshua & Judges,
Samuel a double book, & Kings a double
book, the Psalms & Prophets" were all
"Spiritual Verse" (*J* 48:8–10). But as they

were poetry, they were not to be understood literally, being "canopied with emblems" (*J* 48:7). St. Paul had interpreted the story of Sarah and Hagar as "allegory" (*Gal* iv:22–31), and the later mystical writers made much of "the veil of Moses" (*Exod* xxxiv:33–35), which concealed from the people the spiritual meaning behind the literal.

Blake rejected the literal meaning as unreliable history (On Watson, *K* 391–92) and as gross immorality. "God never makes one man murder another, nor one nation" (On Watson, *K* 388) . Like Amos and other prophets, he despised the laws and rituals which had been involved. "Wherefore did Christ come? Was it not to abolish the Jewish Imposture?" (On Watson, *K* 387) . With characteristic vehemence, Blake attacked even the Ten Commandments as the product of a false God, inventors of sin, and negators of life. See MOSES.

Nevertheless, Blake came to accept Judaism as an essential step in the spiritual development of man. In *Jerusalem* 26–50, it is the state of the childhood of the nations and of every individual as well. It is followed by the Deism of the youth who rejects the Angry God but preserves the morality, and carries on through the errors of official Christianity to the Truth.

This change, or development, may be accounted for by Blake's study of Hebrew. In 1797 he had copied some Hebrew words on his design for the last page of the third of the *Night Thoughts*. Young's text is a eulogy of Death, whom Blake represented as a benign sage holding an open scroll, on which are nine lines of Hebrew. But Blake as yet did not know the Hebrew alphabet, and the letters are so erroneous that it seems impossible to identify or translate them. Six years later, however, he wrote from Felpham to his brother James (30 Jan 1803): "am now learning my Hebrew [ABC's]. . . . If the Hebrew Bible is as well translated [as the Greek testament], which I do not doubt it is, we need not doubt of its having been translated as well as written by the Holy Ghost."

We do not know who Blake's teachers were. He left Felpham for London on September 18, 1803, where he continued his studies, probably with some local rabbi, who must have been a remarkable person, as the information he gave Blake was a tremendous stimulus. Blake of course used this information after his own fashion.

He learned the letters and tried to sketch them as human forms. He learned the names of God which were not to be found in the King James translation, and organized them as the seven Eyes of God mentioned by Zechariah (iv:10) . See EYES OF GOD. He learned that Elohim-Jehovah represented the perfect synthesis of the Contraries, Justice and Truth. He learned of the Angel of the Divine Presence, to whom he attributed evil deeds usually ascribed to God (*LJ*, *K* 610) . He learned of Adam Kadmon, who "anciently contain'd in his mighty limbs all things in Heaven & Earth" and transferred the tradition to Albion; "But now the Starry Heavens are fled from the mighty limbs of Albion" (*J* 27) . He learned of Naamah, the wife of Noah, and of Lilith.

He either learned or invented for himself the heresy that the Messiah should encompass all sin by having the worst of ancestry. "If he intended to take on Sin | The Mother should an Harlot been, | Just such a one as Magdalen | With seven devils in her Pen" (*EG* i:3) . See MATERNAL LINE.

He disapproved when he learned that the Jews never pronounce aloud the name of God, the Tetragrammaton, because the true God could never be feared. "And all the Spectres of the Dead, calling themselves Sons of God, in his Synagogues worship Satan under the Unutterable Name" (*Mil* 11:13) .

Apparently Blake took nothing directly from the Kabbalah, if he knew of it, although Denis Saurat (*Blake and Modern Thought*, London, 1929) points out various parallels.

Unfortunately, Blake disliked the London Jews. His unusual interpretation of Jesus' miracle with the Gadarene swine struck at the Jews' abhorrence of pork, which Blake said made them look like the very thing they detested. "He turn'd the devils into Swine | That he might tempt the Jews to dine; | Since which, a Pig has got a look | That for a Jew may be mistook" (*EG* i:17–30). "I always thought that Jesus Christ was a Snubby or I should not have worship'd him, if I had thought he had been one of those long spindle nosed rascals" (*K* 555).

The JEW'S-HARP-HOUSE was a fashionable tea-garden with a bowling green situated out in the country, under a mile and a half north of Golden Square. A landmark on the maps, it stood on Love Lane, just off the New-road from Paddington to Islington (*Erd* 437). Paul Miner reproduced a picture of it (*Bull. N. Y. Public Lib.*, November 1958).

It was one of the places which Blake knew in the freedom of his boyhood; it shone "in Jerusalem's pleasant sight" (*J* 27:13). A quarter of a mile away was Willan's Farm, and half a mile to the south was the Green Man.

JOB, one of the inspired books of the Old Testament, was written to dispute the theory that material misfortunes are punishment for sin.

Job is perfect and upright. He has prospered until he is the greatest of all the men of the east. His seven sons feast every night with their three sisters; Job sacrifices for them lest they have sinned.

Satan, however, claims to the Lord that Job's piety depends on his prosperity, so the Lord gives him permission to test Job by destroying that prosperity. Marauders carry off his flocks, and all his sons are killed when the house where they are feasting collapses upon them. Job still blesses the Lord, so Satan is permitted to afflict him a second time, striking him with leprosy; but though Job's wife bids him curse God and die, he refuses.

Then Job's three friends come to comfort him. And Job curses the day he was born, "for the thing which I greatly feared is come upon me." The threefold speeches of the three friends consist in trying to persuade him that as God is just, Job must have sinned; but Job persists in his innocence: "Though he slay me, yet will I trust in him; but I will maintain mine own ways before him." The friends are finally silenced; a young man, Elihu, however, is wrathful because Job justifies himself instead of God, and because the friends have found no answer to Job yet have condemned him. But Elihu, extolling the magnitude and mystery of God's particular care for man, reaffirms the justice of God.

Then the Lord answers Job out of a whirlwind (a mystical experience). As they converse, the glory of the whole universe is manifest; God's omnipotence is revealed in the beasts Behemoth and Leviathan. Job, having seen God, repents. The Lord's wrath is kindled against the three friends for having misrepresented him. When Job prays for them, God turns "the captivity of Job." Job's neighbors comfort him and give him money. The Lord doubles his former possessions and also gives him seven more sons and three daughters. He lives to an old age in happiness and prosperity.

Blake's earliest indication of an interest in *Job* occurs in a drawing (*ca.* 1785) of Job protesting his innocence. It was thoroughly reconceived as a sepia painting (*ca.* 1792), which was engraved in 1793, with the inscription "What is Man That Thou shouldest Try him Every Moment?" In the same year he quoted from *Job* (xvii:14) "I have said to the Worm: Thou art my mother & my sister" on the concluding plate of *The Gates of Paradise*. About the same time, in *The Marriage of Heaven and Hell* (5), Blake claimed that the story of *Job* is the same as that of *Paradise Lost* but Milton had so misinterpreted it that his Messiah is Job's Satan. About 1800 he painted a water color of the Whirlwind, which differs from the final engraving completely, although the Whirlwind now consists of the seven Eyes of God. He also did a tempera of Satan smiting Job with boils, which is close to the final engraving. In *The Four Zoas* (iii:82) and again in *Jerusalem* (29:64), Albion is smitten with Job's boils, "the terrible smitings of Luvah," which are no mere skin disease. In 1807 Blake produced his only lithograph, called "Job in his Prosperity" (which sometimes is erroneously named "Enoch"). It represents a crucial moment in Job's spiritual life, when he first considers the possibility of immortality. See ENOCH.

Towards the end of his life, Blake completed his conception of the meaning of the whole book and about 1820 made a set of twenty-one water colors illustrating it for Thomas Butts. Linnell in 1821 ordered a set for himself. Then Albin Martin, a pupil of Linnell's, ordered a reduced copy, which is now in New Zealand. In 1823 Linnell commissioned Blake to engrave the set, which he did, adding a title page and margins. *Illustrations of the Book of Job* was published officially on March 8, 1825, although the plates were not approved until early the next year.

In 1935 the Pierpont Morgan Library issued a magnificent reproduction of *Illustrations of the Book of Job*, containing all the water colors, designs, pencil drawings, and engravings. It included also elaborate descriptions of the pictures with all their variants, their histories and symbolism, the stage version, a bibliography, and an introduction by Laurence Binyon and Geoffrey Keynes.

Illustrations of the Book of Job was Blake's last completed prophetic book. Like *The Gates of Paradise* and *Blair's Grave*, it was planned without text, although the margins of the engravings are filled with important Biblical quotations. It was produced while Blake was still working on *Jerusalem*, his most obscure book; yet the *Illustrations* are Blake's most lucid; and they are the supreme example of his reading the Bible in its spiritual sense. The meaning of his book was not discovered until Joseph Wicksteed published *Blake's Visions*

of the Book of Job in 1910; a much expanded second edition appeared in 1924. In interpreting Blake's engravings, Wicksteed taught us how to read all of Blake's designs. Particularly important was his discovery of the significance of right and left, a symbolism which is deep within all of us.

Blake's problem was to justify the ways of God, to explain his providence. If Job was truly innocent, how account for his calamities? Blake found Job's tragic flaw in that very innocence. Supported by his material prosperity, he has never grown up spiritually, has never trod the path of Experience. Instead, he has kept himself "perfect" by obeying all the laws of conduct laid down so elaborately in the Old Testament. He is, in short, a Pharisee. And to avoid "sin," one must disapprove of it; thus Satan the Accuser dwells in his own brain. And this Satan is to usurp for a time the place of the true God.

The title page shows the path of Experience which Job must tread, symbolized as the seven Eyes of God, seven angels descending and reascending clockwise. They are the path of Job's sun, which sinks into the underworld but rises again at the end. The turning point is Shaddai, the State of Accusation, who looks backward. Once he is passed, the Eyes ascend again, ending with Jesus, who turns his face inward, toward the spiritual life.

1. Job in his Innocence, surrounded by his family and flocks. Innocence is in touch with the true God; in the background is a Gothic church, the true faith. But Job and his wife hold books of the Law open on their laps, while the musical instruments of spontaneous praise hang silent on the tree above them, and their sun is setting.

2. This picture reveals the state of Job's soul. Though outwardly he is serene in his prosperity, this "perfect" man has serious faults. He fears God—sure proof that he does not know him as a friend. He regulates his conduct according to the Law, mistaking it for the way of life; but the Law is only a negation. He eschews

evil, thereby accepting the fallacious standards of Good and Evil. The mere choice is a judgment; he knows only half of life and thus has stopped his spiritual development: in fact, he has admitted Satan the Accuser into his heaven. Consequently he suspects that his high-living children may be sinners. Finally, he knows well enough that his great wealth is only material, and can be destroyed. When that disaster comes, he cries out: "For the thing which I greatly feared is come upon me . . . I was not in safety, neither had I rest, neither was I quiet; yet trouble came" (*Job* iii:25–26).

Therefore, when his mind is opened to us, Satan the Accuser is before the Throne; and his first words are those of doubt: "Doth Job fear God for nought?" (i:9). Beneath his arms are the dim faces of Job and his wife, representing their yet undefined errors.

God (whom Job has made in his own image) sits securely on his throne, his book of Law open on his lap. Angels defending Job against the Accuser cast before the throne the evidences of his innocence. Only one of them shows a book, and that is not wide open; the others exhibit scrolls, Job's good deeds done instinctively, although God himself has no scroll, and does not value them. Two more angels with scrolls visit Job and his wife; but the pair cling to their books; Job only half sees the angels, and his wife ignores them. All but one of the children bear books, proof that Job is bringing up his children properly.

But the eldest son has reacted against his father's strict piety. He holds a scroll, not a book: he is living his life according to his own instincts. With him is his mistress (none of the sons is married) and their baby.

In the margins are symbols of Innocence, and the vegetation extends upward into Gothic arches. But angels mourn over the Pillars of Cloud and Fire which lead the Elect in the wilderness to Mount Sinai and the Ten Commandments; one sees also the peacock of vanity and the parrot of vain repetitions.

3. The destruction of Job's sons. The younger sons have followed their eldest brother's example and have also taken mistresses. Job's wrath bursts forth. The Accuser in his own brain brings about their destruction. Lightnings and black (infernal) fire destroy their (classical) palace of delight. The eldest son, rising on his left foot, tries in vain to save his child. Another son falls in the position of the Crucifixion upside down (the loins above heart and head); beneath him is the immediate cause of their destruction: their father's wealth, represented by a heap of massy plate, which includes a wine goblet. The seven women are their concubines. One has fallen supine with a timbrel degraded beneath her feet.

As we are warned on the first illustration that the story is not to be taken literally, we may understand that the sons are not actually killed, nor are any shown dead. Job has denounced them; henceforth they are dead to their father—until the last illustration, when the family is reunited in harmony. The Bible does not say that the daughters were killed; they also reappear later.

In the margins, flames are breaking out behind the clouds, and the coils of the Serpent of materialism begin to appear.

4. Three messengers bring tidings of the disasters to Job and his wife, who sit beneath two stone crosses, signifying their errors. The Gothic church is still in the background. Above, in the margin, Satan, armed with a sword in his left hand, faces inward, entering Job's soul. In another margin, a lightning bolt strikes.

5. Job's charity. Job halves his last loaf with a blind beggar; but he does so only because it is commanded; therefore the bread is given and taken with the left hand. The architecture in the background is now druidic, yet angels still attend Job. In the heavens above, God with a dimmed halo is sinking downward from his throne, but holds his position by clinging to his

book. He does not notice the scroll which now appears in his left hand. Satan, who has now been given permission to try Job again, is concentrating his flames on Job's head, while the angels, who have caught fire, shrink away. In the margin, the Serpent is fully revealed.

6. The smiting with boils. Job, sick nearly to death, swoons. Satan stands on his body, pouring the leprosy on Job's head. These boils are "the terrible smitings of Luvah," the regent of love (*J* 29:64). Satan the Accuser (his genitals scaled over) infects Job with the feeling of guilt over sex. "The disease of Shame covers me from head to feet. I have no hope. Every boil upon my body is a separate & deadly Sin. Doubt first assail'd me, then Shame took possession of me" (*J* 21:3).

The death of four of Job's senses (sight, hearing, taste, and smell) is indicated by the four arrows beneath Satan's right hand. The fifth, touch, which in its highest form is sex, man's easiest way into Eternity, is now corrupted. The sun is disappearing, not to be seen again until it rises in the last illustration.

Job's wife is now separated from her husband; nevertheless she still ministers to his lowest needs (his feet).

In the margin below is the broken sheephook of Innocence, with symbols from the despairing last chapter of *Ecclesiastes*. The grasshopper is dying desire. The pitcher is broken at the fountain, which now is choked with rubbish and identifiable only by the frog still dwelling there. Bat-winged angels lower poisonous spiders.

7. Job's friends arrive, left foot first. They are the last trial, for corporeal friends are spiritual enemies. Job and his wife sit beneath the two crosses. The barren landscape is covered with druidic ruins. The sun has set.

This seventh illustration ends the first cycle, passing from Innocence (1–2) into Experience (3–7).

8. Job curses the day he was ever born. His anger is the beginning of a new cycle. No longer does he accept his afflictions

passively; his spirit is roused at last to protest, however blindly. The State of Experience has become the State of Revolution. Although the way ahead is still long, the stone cross appears above him no longer.

9. The God of Eliphaz. Into this illustration are condensed the long arguments of Job's friends that as God is just, Job is being punished for sin. This God is a nightmare. His arms are bound because by his very nature he is obliged to punish. In the margins are the sterile forests of error.

10. The friends unite in accusing Job of sin. Even his wife doubts him momentarily, and the cross stands above her. But Job persists in protesting his innocence, and appeals to his God for justification. The result, in the next illustration, is a terrible revelation.

In the lower margin, the cuckoo of slander, the owl of false wisdom, and the adder of hate mock the scrolls of true inspiration. Even thus, Blake's own works were assailed by his critics.

11. At last Job beholds the false God he has ignorantly been worshipping. The right hand of this God points to the Ten Commandments, from which spring the lightnings of damnation, and his left to the Hell to which his Law condemns Job. The Serpent of materialism entwines him. He is identical with the God of Eliphaz. But for the first time Job sees this God's cloven hoof: the God of Justice is only Satan, masquerading as an angel of light.

This revelation leads to another, indicated in the lower margin. Job had always supposed that death is the end of everything; now he is convinced that his Redeemer lives and that after death he shall see God (xix:25-27). "Tho' consumed be my wrought Image," which Blake added to emphasize his belief in the spiritual body, may be a free translation of "though my reins be consumed within me" (xix:27).

12. When Job and his friends are both silenced, neither having convinced the other, young Elihu bursts forth. He re-

proves Job for justifying himself instead of God, and the friends for condemning him without answering him. The friends now sit beneath the crosses.

Elihu's arguments for the greatness of God are based on the astronomical universe; nevertheless certain phrases of his (copied in the margins) plunge Job into deep thought. Job has complained that his God has remained silent; Elihu says that "God speaketh once, yea twice, & Man perceiveth it not." Had Job been missing the divine instruction? "In a Dream, in a Vision of the Night . . . Then he openeth the ears of Men & sealeth their instruction." Had Job not understood the meaning of his nightmare? "That he may withdraw Man from his purpose & hide Pride from Man." Had Job had the wrong purpose, and had he not been proud? "Then he is gracious unto him & saith Deliver him from going down to the Pit. I have found a Ransom." The Redeemer?

In the lower margin is Job's sleeping Humanity, with streams of soaring angels who urge him to wake. Hidden under his head is a text which suggests that the true God is not the God of Morality but one who is unconcerned about the petty faults or virtues of his children: "If thou sinnest what doest thou against him or if thou be righteous what givest thou unto him?"

13. The Whirlwind. At last in the whirlwind of the mystical ecstasy, the true God appears. He is in the cruciform position and he shows his right foot. He descends below the cloud-barriers which normally separate the worlds. Although the force of the wind raises Job's hair, he and his wife face God with serene joy. Meanwhile the friends cannot see him because the blast blows them flat, like the Forest of Error in the margin below.

The Lord's answer to Job is not a reasoned reply to his plaints but is instead a typically mystical and fundamentally ineffable vision of God's divine power in his greatness, the glory and the harmony of his creation the universe. Job's pride is

crushed at last; his life is made straight; his faith is confirmed.

Thirteen is the number of Death (as also in *The Gates of Paradise*); it is therefore the number of the New Birth.

The upper margin continues the circular motion of the Whirlwind. The figures are the Eyes in their rotation; inevitably they have reached the seventh, who is Jesus, although his likeness is that of Job. Behind Job's head is the suggestion of an eighth Eye: this is Job's own Individuality, "an Eighth Image Divine, tho' darken'd and tho' walking as one walks in sleep, and the Seven comforted and supported him" (*Mil* 15:5).

14. The mystical ecstasy is a state of knowledge as well as emotion. This vision of the universe is an aspect of Job's experience with the Whirlwind.

This universe is the fourfold soul of man: the flesh, the brain, the heart, and the spirit. Lowest is the world of flesh, wherein Job sits with his wife and friends; they are shut in by the thickest of the cloud-barriers. Above them to the left is the Greek god Apollo, who represents the intellect. The radiant sun-god, drawn by the horses of instruction, endeavors perpetually to push back the clouds enclosing his world, thus enlarging it. Balancing him on the right is the moon-goddess Diana. Her purity directs the dragons of passion in the night of Beulah. Highest of all is the realm of spirit, enclosed by the thinnest of the cloud-barriers. Binding all together is the central figure of God, the Divine Imagination. He is in the cruciform position of self-sacrifice. His arms protect the brain and the heart, and only through him can the realm of spirit be entered.

In his poems, Blake named the realms "the Four Zoas": Tharmas, the flesh; Urizen, the intellect; Luvah, the emotions; and Los, the spirit of poetry.

In the side margins are the six days of the creation, which are but a framework for this, the seventh and last creation, the Sabbath and Millennium, the spiritual rebirth of man. The lower margin continues the cloud-barrier of the realm of the flesh with the body of the Leviathan of Nature in the Sea of Time and Space. Below him is the worm of death, coiled round a grave or shrouded corpse. In the upper corners are the constellations of the Pleiades and Orion.

15. Job's illumination continues. God explains the mystery of the incessant warfare in the human world. He reaches down through the cloud-barrier with his left hand, like Urizen in the frontispiece to *Europe*, and the stars further identify the two. He indicates Behemoth and Leviathan, with whose long description he ends his speech to Job.

These two exist in man himself. "Behold now Behemoth which I made with thee." The cloud-barrier of Job's world includes the separate sphere in which they exist. It is a picture of the subconscious, the unredeemed portion of the psyche, which the bulrushes identify as Egypt. These are the terrible forces within man, against which he seems helpless, "the War by Sea enormous & the War by Land astounding, erecting pillars in the deepest Hell to reach the heavenly arches" (*J* 91:40). They function as a means of God's providence. Behemoth is "the chief of the ways of God": warfare of the spirit is one of the chief joys of Eternity, though when materialized on earth it is rendered deadly (*Mil* 34:50–52; 35:2–3). Leviathan is "King over the children of Pride"—pride, the primal sin which caused Lucifer to fall and become Satan. Here as elsewhere, Leviathan (whose name means "coiled") is depicted as having a huge spiral, representing the everlasting repetitions in the round of nature.

At the upper corners, recording angels write the laws of the universe; at the lower corners are the eagles which Urizen sends forth in his work of creation (*FZ* ii:150). Below are the emptied shells of the mortal bodies grown by man then abandoned on the margin of the Sea of Time and Space.

This illustration begins the last and third cycle, which reverses the errors of the first two cycles.

16. "Whenever any Individual Rejects Error & Embraces Truth, a Last Judgment passes upon that Individual" (*LJ, K* 613). Satan the Accuser is cast out of Job's heaven, and with him fall the errors of Job and his wife, now given full form. (In the second illustration they were only dim faces beneath Satan's arms.) They fall into the flames of annihilation—not of everlasting torture, for such a hell Blake did not admit—since Error recognized is Error destroyed.

God is again firm upon his throne: he still holds the book of his justice, but his halo now contains figures of love and pity.

In the margins, flames consume the material creation.

17. In the Whirlwind God descended below the clouds into this world; now he has returned and brought man with him. This is clearly indicated by the clouds on which the Deity stands.

The last four lines of the *Auguries of Innocence* (*K* 434) explain this picture: "God Appears & God is Light | To those poor Souls who dwell in Night, | But does a Human Form Display | To those who Dwell in Realms of day." The friends are still in the night, and the light to them is intolerable; but Job and his wife face God and know him for a comrade, in whose image they were made. "We know that when he shall appear we shall be like him for we shall see him as He Is."

The angel in the margin below is the Comforter, who is the Spirit of Truth. Her texts (all from the Gospel of John) assert the identity of the Son with the Father, who loves all his children equally, irrespective of their virtues or vices.

18. Though the mystical ecstasy is temporary, it affects the entire afterlife of man. God has now withdrawn from his complete manifestation as Man to the likeness of a great sun in the heavens. Meanwhile Job finds that in prayer the great mystical descent (typified by the angels in the margin) is mildly repeated.

Rebuked by the Lord, the friends ask Job to pray for them. He does so; it is the

Forgiveness of Sins. Thereupon the Lord accepts Job and releases him from his captivity under Satan the Accuser.

This Forgiveness is self-sacrifice (represented by his cruciform attitude), an inward act (since he faces inward). And the flame of his sacrifice pierces the clouds which separate the worlds and reaches to the heart of God. The wheat in the margin signifies that Forgiveness is the Daily Bread of the soul. The Wine, the other aspect of the Eucharist, appears two pages later.

In Plato's *Timaeus* Blake would have found the cube representing the earth and the pyramidal flame symbolizing the spirit; he combined the two.

In the lower margin is the text for Forgiveness, also the scrolls of Blake's poems, his palette, and his graver: the arts are also forms of prayer.

19. As Job lost virtue by giving to a beggar, so now he gains it by receiving from his neighbors and friends. This is the true charity springing from personal sympathy, which was missing in the fifth illustration. One woman even offers him her gold earring.

At last the heavy cross over Job's head is broken. Prosperity is shown by the fruiting fig-tree and the standing wheat. Angels crowd round the corners of the design with the palms of victory, for Job now has conquered his pride; and below are the roses and lilies of material and spiritual beauty.

"The thankful reciever bears a plentiful harvest" (*MHH* 9).

As Mr. Wicksteed points out, the picture is a "tender and delicate acknowledgement" of Blake's indebtedness to the Linnells.

20. Job is recounting his experiences to his three daughters, the three arts which had vanished during Job's trials. In the Butts painting they hold the attributes of their respective arts.

Job is in the cruciform position, for he is giving himself. Immediately above him is a panel depicting the Whirlwind, as aesthetic creation is a reflection of the mystical ecstasy. In his prayer he had faced inward; now he faces outward, as he is addressing mankind. The two texts from *Psalm* cxxxix in the margin state that inspiration comes from God and is to be found everywhere.

The floor consists of a great circle tessellated with many smaller interlacing circles. This represents the communion of the heaven of art; the smaller circles represent the individuals entering each other's bosoms (the inscribed portions being significantly four-sided), all of them being contained in the one great circle, who is the One Man, Jesus himself.

Art is the sacrificial wine of the Eucharist. In the margins are fruiting grapevines and instruments of music. The little angels who embrace on the corners repeat this communing of delight.

21. And here the story of Job ends. His manhood, purged of all error, is now complete. His sons are restored to him and his wealth is doubled. The books of Law have disappeared and are replaced by scrolls of song. The musical instruments no longer hang silent on the tree. The family is now reunited in harmony. The marginal texts indicate the burden of their song; they praise the truth and justice of the marvelous works of the Almighty. This is the song of Moses and the Lamb (*Rev* xv:3), the synthesis of both Testaments.

The long night is over and the sun rises.

The angels on the title page indicate that Job is to pass along the path of Experience; the seven angels are the seven Eyes of God. In the first two cycles, the Eyes progress in pairs. The first two plates represent the state of Lucifer, Job contented in his Selfhood; the next two (Molech, the executioner) deal with the destruction of the children; the next two (Elohim, the judge) include the false legal charity; the next two (Shaddai, the accuser) are concerned with the arrival of Job's friends and his curse; the next two (Pahad, or terror), with the God of Eliphaz and the mocking; the next two (Jehovah of the Commandments), with the revelation of the Devil; but Jesus (the seventh) brings the Whirlwind and the discovery of the human universe. The circle is now reversed, with one Eye for each illustration. Jehovah reveals Behemoth and Leviathan; Jesus causes the Last Judgment; Pahad is reversed in the visible appearance of the loving God; Shaddai the accuser, in Job's forgiveness; Elohim, the true charity; Molech, in the reappearance of the daughters; and finally Lucifer, in Job now freed of his Selfhood.

In 1911 a "rectified" edition of the tarot cards was published by Arthur Edward Waite, who supervised the new designs made by Pamela Colman Smith. In his book *The Pictorial Key to the Tarot* (London, 1911), Mr. Waite failed to mention that the trumps major were obviously adapted to parallel the twenty-two plates of Blake's *Illustrations of the Book of Job*.

JOHN GROAT'S HOUSE (John o'Groat's House) is in the extreme north of Scotland, county Caithness. It is a measuring point of Great Britain, the southern point being Land's End, Cornwall.

The northern of the two gates through which souls descend is "Caithness & rocky Durness, Pentland & John Groat's House" (*Mil* 26:15).

JOHN THE BAPTIST was a cousin of Jesus and his immediate forerunner. His ministry centered in the wilderness of Judea, especially on the Jordan, where he baptized Jesus. His denunciation of the incestuous marriage of Herod Antipas led to his imprisonment and beheading.

"John from the Wilderness loud cried . . . John for disobedience bled" (*EG* b:13, 17).

JOHN THE "DIVINE" (i.e., the theologian) wrote *Revelation*, the final book of the Bible, on the penal island of Patmos. His visions, especially those of the Last Judgment, had a great influence on Blake's writings.

"John saw these things Reveal'd in Heaven on Patmos Isle" (*FZ* viii:600). "A Dragon red & hidden Harlot which John in Patmos saw" (*Mil* 40:22).

The complications of the visions were also a challenge to Blake's visualizing. George Goyder lists eleven illustrations (*Goyder* 160–70), to which we may add the title page for the eighth of Young's *Night Thoughts*. Here Mystery, holding her cup, rides on the seven-headed Beast, these heads being the authorities in Church and State: the Judge, the Warrior, the King, the Pope, the Cardinal (but crowned, without his flat hat), the Bishop, and the Curate. The ten horns are ingeniously distributed, the curate having none.

JOKTAN ("who is made small") and Peleg ("to divide") were the two sons of Eber. In their time "was the earth divided" (*Gen* x:25). Blake mentions them as examples of fraternal strife (*J* 73:28).

The JORDAN, the sacred river of Palestine, flows southward from the Lebanons through the Sea of Galilee into the Dead Sea. The early Israelites regarded it as a dread barrier to be crossed. It was the scene of the baptism of Jesus.

Blake used the Jordan once to symbolize the deadening effect of the Hebraic traditions on Milton. "With cold hand Urizen stoop'd down and took up water from the river Jordan, pouring on to Milton's brain the icy fluid from his broad cold palm" (*Mil* 19:7).

In his attempts to get Reuben, the average man, into the Promised Land, Los sends him across the Jordan four times, but in vain, as Reuben's lot lay on the eastern side of the river (*J* 34:48, 54; 36:6, 13).

In Urizen's Temple, the Jordan springs from the threshold, and is a fountain in his porch (*J* 58:23, 33).

In the Age of Innocence, "Thames reciev'd the heavenly Jordan" (*J* 79:35).

JOSEPH is the type of Innocence Be-

trayed, and a great exemplar of the Forgiveness of Sins. He was Israel's eleventh
son, and the founder of a Tribe. Later, his
two sons, Manasseh and Ephraim, replaced
him in the official list, each becoming the
head of a Tribe.

Joseph and his brothers are listed as
Sons of Los who fled (*FZ* viii:361, 377).
Joseph and Benjamin rolled apart in vain
and became fixed into Cabul (*J* 74:56).
With four other brothers he is closed up in
narrow vales of "the dark land of Cabul"
(*J* 79:64).

Blake was particularly impressed with the
episode of Joseph's betrayal by his
brothers. Their father had favored Joseph
and made him a coat of many colors. The
envious brothers, further irritated by
Joseph's dreams of his superiority, planned
at first to kill him, but instead sold him to
some Midianites, who sold him to Potiphar
in Egypt. Meanwhile the brothers dipped
Joseph's coat in goat's blood, as proof that
he had been killed by some wild beast.
Later, he forgave them in a dramatic scene.

Thus Joseph, the victim of fraternal
hatred, became a symbol of the Sacrifice
of the Innocent and (in paintings now in
the Fitzwilliam Museum at Cambridge University) of the Forgiveness of Sins. The
many-colored coat itself symbolizes the
flesh. The Princes of the Dead teach their
votaries "to make One Family of Contraries, that Joseph may be sold into
Egypt for Negation, a Veil the Saviour
born & dying rends"—this veil being that
"which Satan puts between Eve & Adam"
(*J* 55:11, 15–16).

However, the coat is usually stripped off
by women—perhaps in reminiscence of
Potiphar's wife—to benefit their lovers.
The Daughters of Albion strip it off and
"dip it in the blood of battle" (*J* 67:23).
Tirzah gives both Joseph and his coat to
Scofield "to make you One, to weave you
both in the same mantle of skin" (*J* 68:1).
Gwendolen strips off Joseph's "beautiful
integument" for her Beloved (*J* 81:11).

Blake gives another account of the kid-
napping of Joseph, for which I have found

no source. In this account, Joseph, an infant wrapped in needlework of emblematic
texture, was stolen from his nurse's
cradle and sold to the Amalekite, who
carried him down to Egypt (*Mil* 24:17).

Los names Joseph as one of those whose
characteristics are not to be appropriated
(*J* 90:31).

In the assignment of counties, Joseph is
one of the four who are given special Gates.
The four northernmost English counties
of Cumberland, Northumberland, Westmoreland, and Durham are divided between Reuben, Judah, Dan, and Joseph
(*J* 16:50–51). The four counties of
northern Ireland are divided similarly:
"Munster South in Reuben's Gate, Connaut West in Joseph's Gate, Ulster North
in Dan's Gate, Leinster East in Judah's
Gate" (*J* 72:3). However, Joseph is not
assigned any counties in southern Ireland,
being replaced by his sons. In Wales, he is
given Denbighshire; in England, Stafford,
Shropshire, and Hereford; in Scotland,
Elgin, Lanark, and Kinross (*J* 16:41,
49, 58).

JOSEPH OF ARIMATHEA was a secret
disciple of Jesus. Though a member of the
Sanhedrin, he was evidently absent when it
unanimously condemned Jesus to death.
After the execution, he buried the body in
a new tomb which he had hewn for himself out of a rock.

According to British legend, Joseph, to
escape persecution, then fled to England,
taking the Holy Grail with him. His
planted staff sprouted into the Glastonbury Thorn, which blossomed every year
on Christmas day. He founded the Glastonbury Abbey, the first Christian church in
England, where he was finally entombed.

When Blake was an apprentice of sixteen,
he engraved a figure from Michelangelo's
"Crucifixion of St. Peter." On the unique
impression of the first state, he wrote:
"Engraved when I was a beginner at
Basire's, from a drawing of Salviati after
Michael Angelo" (*K Studies* 46; Plate 14).
About 1810, he almost completely re-en-

graved it, with the inscription: "Joseph of Arimathea among The Rocks of Albion. This is One of the Gothic Artists who Built the Cathedrals in what we call the Dark Ages, Wandering about in sheep skins & goat skins, of whom the World was not worthy; such were the Christians in all Ages. Michael Angelo Pinxit. Engraved by W. Blake 1773 from an old Italian Drawing" (*K* 604).

Thus Joseph of Arimathea became a symbol of the true Christian and the true artist (for the Abbey was Gothic), solitary in an unappreciative England. Blake applied to him St. Paul's description of the early martyrs: "they wandered about in sheepskins and goatskins; being destitute, afflicted, tormented; (of whom the world was not worthy:) they wandered in deserts, and in mountains, and in dens and caves of the earth" (*Heb* xi:37–38).

In *The Four Zoas* (viii:339) Joseph is equated with Los; for Jesus is entombed in "the Sepulcher which Los had hewn in the rock of Eternity for himself: he hew'd it despairing of Life Eternal."

Joseph is also mentioned in an enigmatic trifle, in which Pliny and Trajan come to hear what Joseph said to Blake's Fairy: "Listen patient, & when Joseph has done | 'Twill make a fool laugh & a Fairy Fun" (*K* 552).

There is a colored relief-etching by Blake, tentatively entitled "Joseph of Arimathea Preaching to the Inhabitants of Britain," but I believe this title is wrong. A sage, with a staff in his left hand, stands beneath a tree, stretching out his right hand to a group of young couples, who betray consternation and guilt. The preaching of the true Gospel could never have any such effect. The tree overshadowing the sage seems to be a leafless oak. The sage's staff is not flowering. Instead of Gothic architecture, there is a high fence in the left background. And no such title occurs in Blake's list of subjects for "The History of Britain" (*K* 208).

JOSEPH OF NAZARETH, the husband of Mary, was an outstanding example of the Forgiveness of Sins.

According to *Matthew* i:18–25, he discovered that his betrothed Mary was already with child. He was tempted to "put her away privily," but dreamed that the angel of the Lord told him to marry her, because she was pregnant "of the Holy Ghost." He did as the angel bade him, and her first-born child was Jesus.

Matthew's account differs from Luke's, where the Annunciation was made to Mary. Blake followed Matthew's account. In his retelling, Mary does not deny her guilt, but justifies herself: "If I were pure, never could I taste the sweets of the Forgive[ne]ss of Sins," and Joseph forgives her. "There is none that liveth & Sinneth not! And this is the Covenant of Jehovah: If you forgive one-another, so shall Jehovah Forgive You, that He Himself may Dwell among You. Fear not then to take to thee Mary thy Wife, for she is with Child by the Holy Ghost" (*J* 61:3–33).

JOSHUA was the brilliant general chosen by Moses. His name is also spelled "Oshea" (*Numb* xiii:8). Of the twelve spies sent into Canaan, only Joshua and Caleb advocated its conquest; and these two were the only Israelites, of all those who originally left Egypt, to enter the Promised Land (*Numb* xxvi:64–65).

In describing the general confusion of mankind, Los remarks that even "Oshea and Caleb fight; they contend in the valleys of Peor, in the terrible Family Contentions of those who love each other. The Armies of Balaam weep—no women come to the field" (*J* 43:37). Later, Erin has a vision of reconciliation, in which "Og & Sihon in the tears of Balaam, the Son of Beor, have given their power to Joshua & Caleb" (*J* 49:58).

See BALAAM.

JOSHUA is one of the inspired books of the Bible, written in "Spiritual Verse," and is one of the sixteen pillars of Albion's tomb (*J* 48:9).

JOVE was the conventional poetic substitute for "God"; Blake so uses it in his early "Imitation of Spencer" 23, 45 (*PS*). He uses it once for Jupiter (*Mil* 37:33).
See JUPITER.

JUDAH was the fourth son of Israel, and the founder of a Tribe. He was an ancestor of David, and hence of Jesus. His dying father, passing over his three elder brothers, gave him his blessing; he compared him to a lion and prophesied that he would rule "until Shiloh come; and unto him shall the gathering of the people be" (*Gen* xlix:8–12). His Tribe and Benjamin's were the only ones to return after the Babylonish exile. Judah's Tribe acquired most of southern Palestine, and became the Southern Kingdom.

With his brothers he is listed as one of the Sons of Los who fled (*FZ* viii:360, 375). He and six of his brothers (implying them all) were generated because they left Los, to wander with Tirzah (*Mil* 24:3). Enitharmon, appreciating his magnanimous spirit, compares him to the merciful Palamabron (*J* 93:14). Jerusalem remembers him and his brothers in their days of innocence (*J* 79:30). Later, with Reuben, Gad, Joseph, and Levi, he is closed up in the narrow vales of the dark land of Cabul (*J* 79:64). Los names him in the list of those whose characteristics are not to be appropriated (*J* 90:31).

He is one of the four to whom special Gates are assigned. The four northernmost counties of England are divided between Reuben, Judah, Dan, and Joseph (*J* 16:51). The four provinces of Ireland are assigned to the same four, Judah's Gate being Leinster (*J* 72:4). In Wales, he is assigned the county of Merionethshire (*J* 16:37); in England, Somerset, Gloucester, and Wiltshire (*J* 16:45); in Scotland, Aberdeen, Berwick, and Dumfries (*J* 16:54) ; and in Ireland, with Issachar and Zebulun he shares all the counties of Leinster (*J* 72:18).

JUDEA was the Southern Kingdom of Palestine, as distinguished from Samaria and Galilee. Its name is sometimes given as "Judah." It contained Jerusalem, but nearly half was wilderness.

Oothoon hovered over Judah and Jerusalem and was heard by Jesus (*SoL* 3:22). Urizen "stood over Judea and stay'd in his ancient place, and stretch'd his clouds over Jerusalem" (*SoL* 7:17). The Polypus' heart sends out fibres "round the Earth," including Judea (*J* 67:39). Jerusalem laments: "The hills of Judea are fallen with me into the deepest hell" (*J* 79:8). The Selfhood marches against Jesus "from Sinai & from Edom into the Wilderness of Judah" (*J* 96:10).

JUDGES is one of the inspired books of the Bible, written in "Spiritual Verse." It is one of the sixteen pillars of Albion's tomb (*J* 48:9).

JUDGMENT DAY. See LAST JUDGMENT.

JUPITER (Jove) was the Latin name for Zeus, the ruler of heaven and the chief god of the classical pantheon. He was the son of Saturn and Rhea. His dethronement of his father ended the Golden Age and began the Iron Age. His many amours caused the notorious jealousy of his wife Juno. Among his children were the Muses, whose mother was Mnemosyne. According to Milton, the cult of the classical gods spread westward, even to "the utmost Isles" (*PL* i:510–21).

Blake, writing to Hayley (23 Oct 1804) of the revival of his creative powers, said: "For now! O Glory! and O Delight! I have entirely reduced that spectrous Fiend to his station, whose annoyance has been the ruin of my labours for the last passed twenty years of my life. He is the enemy of conjugal love and is the Jupiter of the Greeks, an iron-hearted tyrant, the ruiner of ancient Greece." In rejecting him, Blake rejected all classicism.

"The [Ancients are right?] when they Assert that Jupiter usurped the Throne of his father, Saturn, & brought on an Iron Age & Begat on Mnemosyne, or Memory, The Greek Muses, which are not Inspiration as the Bible is" (*LJ*, *K* 605).

Blake lists "Saturn, Jove & Rhea of the Isles of the Sea remote" as the last of the twelve pagan gods, "the Twelve Spectre Sons of the Druid Albion" (*Mil* 37:33).

Jupiter is depicted in the third illustration to *Il Penseroso*, where "the Spirit of Plato unfolds his Worlds to Milton." There are three worlds, those of Venus, Mars, and Jupiter, each surmounted by one of the Fates. Jupiter sits with his left foot lower than his right. In his right hand he bears the scepter of sovereignty, in his left the compasses of Urizen. Before him is Hermes, pointing downward to the Great Bear, which indicates the center of the astronomical universe. Behind Jupiter, a youth trundles away a shield. (See Illustrations.)

JUSTICE, the punishment of (or vengeance for) sin, as Blake originally conceived it, was the Contrary of Mercy, the forgiveness of sin. It was the Old Dispensation of Moses, annulled by the New Dispensation of Jesus.

In the rabbinical tradition, the two were correlated as Elohim Jehovah; Blake used these combined names in *Jerusalem* and *The Ghost of Abel* to signify the combination of Justice and Mercy. Each is essential to the other. Mercy must be based on Justice, for the forgiveness of sin depends on the awareness of sin. The child who is brought up in continual forgiveness without this awareness is simply a spoiled child. In the Arts, Mercy without Justice is bathetic sentimentalism.

Therefore, when Los is at work, "The blow of his Hammer is Justice, the swing of his Hammer Mercy, the force of Los's Hammer is eternal Forgiveness" (*J* 88:49).

The KANAH RIVER was the boundary between Ephraim and Manasseh. "Ephraim was a wilderness of joy where all my wild beasts ran. The river Kanah wander'd by my sweet Manasseh's side" (*FZ* viii:309; *J* 67:57).

The KENSINGTON GARDENS lie west of Hyde Park, with a sunken fence between. They were near the gallows. The bellows of Los is heard "before London to Hampstead's breadths & Highgate's heights, To Stratford & old Bow & across to the Gardens of Kensington on Tyburn's Brook" (*Mil* 6:9). "Then the Divine Vision like a silent Sun appear'd above Albion's dark rocks, setting behind the Gardens of Kensington on Tyburn's River" (*J* 29:1).

KENT is a maritime county of England, lying between the Thames and the Strait of Dover. With Middlesex, Surrey, and Sussex, it forms the southeast corner of England.

With Middlesex and Surrey, it is assigned to Levi (*J* 16:45). With Sussex, Surrey, and Middlesex, it is assigned to Hand (*J* 71:12).

The "stern Bard" of the "Preludium" to *America* smashes his harp and wanders "down the vales of Kent in sick & drear lamentings" (2:21), possibly considering emigrating to France. When Albion falls, Sussex and Kent are the scattered garments of Jerusalem (*J* 29:20).

KENTISH-TOWN is a district to the north of London. It is one of the places where Blake in the freedom of his boyhood used to roam. "Pancrass & Kentish-town repose | Among her [Jerusalem's] golden pillars high" (*J* 27:9).

KERRY is an Irish county in Munster, which with the other counties of Munster is assigned to Reuben, Simeon, and Levi (*J* 72:22).

KILDARE is an Irish county in Leinster, which with the other counties of Leinster is assigned to Judah, Issachar, and Zebulun (*J* 72:19).

KILKENNY is an Irish county in Leinster, which with the other counties of Leinster is assigned to Judah, Issachar, and Zebulun (*J* 72:20).

KINCARD[INE] is a Scottish county which, with Forfar and Haddington, is assigned to Reuben (*J* 16:53). As part of Scotland, it is assigned to Bowen (*J* 71:46).

KING EDWARD THE THIRD (*PS*) is an unfinished attempt to write a historical play in the style of Shakespeare. It shows no sense of dramatic construction, the only action being the preparations for the battle of "Cressy" (Crécy, 1346). There is no estimate of the French opponents. The most interesting character is William, the wise simpleton, whose discussion of Ambition with his master is amusingly naïve, yet expresses William Blake's own moral shrewdness. David Erdman (*Erd* 60–80) traces Blake's irony throughout the play.

The play is an expression of the uncritical patriotism of the young Englishman aware of the impending war with France (1778). Liberty is praised at the very beginning by the king and at the end by the Minstrel. There are passages exulting in England's sovereignty over the ocean. The Duke of Clarence and a bishop emphasize the importance of commerce, and recommend that the merchants defend themselves against the French attacks on English shipping.

The Minstrel's song, which terminates the fragment, indicates that Blake was already making use of the mythical history of Britain. The English are the "Sons of Trojan Brutus." After defeating the giants, Brutus prophesies the future glory of England.

As an apprentice, Blake drew and engraved the effigy of Edward in Westminster Abbey which was signed by Basire. It is reproduced in Keynes's *Blake Studies*, Plate 13.

Later, Blake changed his mind about Edward: he questioned his spirit about "the butcheries of which he was guilty in the flesh," and received the "detestable" reply that the carnage was "a trifle unworthy of notice," and that "destroying five thousand men" was "merely removing them from one state of existence to another" (*Erd* 64).

KINGS, "a double book," is one of the inspired books of the Bible, and is one of the sixteen pillars of Albion's tomb (*J* 48:10).

KING'S COUNTY is an Irish county in Leinster. With the other counties of Leinster it is assigned to Judah, Issachar, and Zebulun (*J* 72:19).

KINROS[S] is a Scottish county which, with Elgin and Lanerk, is assigned to Joseph (*J* 16:58). Being part of Scotland, it is also assigned to Bowen (*J* 71:46).

KIRKUBRIHT (i.e., Kirkcudbright) is a Scottish county which, with Kromarty (Cromarty) and Murra (Moray, also called Elgin), is assigned to Benjamin (*J* 16:58). As part of Scotland, it is also assigned to Bowen (*J* 71:46).

The KISHON is a river of northern Palestine, made famous by the song of Deborah (*Judges* v:21). In the days of Innocence, "Medway mingled with Kishon" (*J* 79:35).

KLOPSTOCK (Friedrich Gottlieb, 1724–1803) spent much of his life writing his epic *Messias* (1748–73), which caused him to be called "the German Milton." However, the poem lacks unity of conception, plastic force, and precision of style.

Blake read it in translation while at Lambeth; and believing that Klopstock's God was Nobodaddy, rendered that God helpless by a brief ritual of scatologic magic, which he recorded in an indecent fragment, "When Klopstock England defied" (*K*186).

In March 1803, Hayley learned of Klopstock's death, and "read Klopstock into English to Blake," (*Gil* I, 183), who evidently withheld his opinion.

KOBAN. See COBAN.

KOCK. See KOX.

KOTOPE is the eleventh of the Sons of Albion (*J* 5:27; 19:19; 32:11). He has "Hereford, Stafford, Worcester, & his Emanation is Sabrina; join'd with Mehetabel she shines west over America" (*J* 71:44). His name may be an alteration of "Courthope."

The last four of the Sons of Albion constitute a quaternary. They revolve against the furnaces of Los (*J* 5:27), and become one in Scofield (*J* 7:48). "Hand & Hyle & Koban, Skofeld, Kox, & Kotope labour mightily in the Wars of Babel & Shinar" (*J* 8:41). When the Sons flee at the sight of Reuben, Kotope and Bowen become what they behold, fleeing over the Earth (*J* 36:19). The Daughters of Albion, united in Rahab and Tirzah, "drink up Dan & Gad to feed with milk Skofeld & Kotope" (*J* 67:22).

KOX (Kock) was Private Cock, the seconder of Scofield in his accusations against Blake.

He is the tenth of the Sons of Albion (*J* 5:27; 19:19; 32:11). He has "Oxford. Warwick, Wilts: his Emanation is Estrild; join'd with Cordella she shines southward over the Atlantic" (*J* 71:42). Kox is "the Father of Shem & Ham & Japheth, he is the Noah of the Flood of Udan-Adan" (*J* 7:23). The last four of the Sons of Albion constitute a quaternary. They revolve against the furnaces of Los (*J* 5:27), and become one in Scofield, "a Fourfold Wonder," which involves the other eight (*J* 7:48). "Hand & Hyle & Koban, Skofeld, Kox & Kotope labour mightily in the Wars of Babel & Shinar" (*J* 8:41). When the Sons fled at the sight of Reuben, "Hutton & Skofeld & Kox fled over Chaldea in terror" (*J* 36:17). Los cries out: "Scofeld & Kox are let loose upon my Saxons! they accumulate a World in which Man is by his Nature the Enemy of Man, in pride of Selfhood unwieldy stretching out into Non Entity, generalizing Art & Science till Art & Science is lost" (*J* 43:51).

KROMARTY (i.e., Cromarty) is a (former) Scottish county (now part of Ross and Cromarty) which, with Murra (Moray) and Kirkubriht (Kirkcudbright), is assigned to Benjamin (*J* 16:58). As part of Scotland, it is assigned to Bowen (*J* 71:46).

KWANTOK. See GUANTOK.

L

LABAN the Syrian was a friend of Abraham; the brother of Rebecca, who married Isaac; and the father of Rachel and Leah, both of whom he gave to Jacob in marriage. His craftiness in obtaining the service of Jacob for twenty years made him a type of the good man who nevertheless would fleece his own family. And though he worshipped the true God, he also revered his family gods (teraphim), which Rachel stole.

"On the right hand of Noah, a Woman with Children Represents the State Call'd Laban the Syrian; it is the Remains of Civilization in the State from whence Abraham was taken" (*LJ*, *K* 610; see Illustrations, "LJ" No. 74).

The LACEDAEMONIANS, or Spartans, used to get their slaves drunk and then exhibit them in the public messes, so that their young men might learn how degrading drunkenness was (Plutarch, *Demetrius*). Blake's couplet *Lacedemonian Instruction* speaks for itself: " 'Come hither, my boy, tell me what thou seest there.' | 'A fool tangled in a religious snare' " (*K* 180).

LAFAYETTE (1757–1834), the champion of liberty and the intimate friend of Washington, was idolized when he returned to France, where he became an outstanding figure in the French Revolution. The marquis tried to be the conservative liberal and the peaceful mediator. But though considered incorruptible, he was suspected of being used as a tool by the Royalists. His kissing of the queen's hand when the women invaded Versailles (1789), his firing on the mob in the Champ de Mars (1791), and finally his attacking the Jacobins instead of Austria (1792) led to his being denounced as a traitor. He fled (1792), and spent five years in an Austrian dungeon as a prisoner of state.

In Blake's *French Revolution* (1791), "Fayette" responds "sudden as the bullet wrapp'd in his fire" to the call of the Nation's Assembly for the "General of the Nation," and carries out their vote to remove the troops ten miles from Paris, thus ending Book I.

In his unfinished "Fayette" (*K* 185, 891), Blake considered the position of this great humanitarian caught in the toils of a revolution he could not control. Blake blames the king for the famine and the queen for the immorality; Lafayette sees their guilt, but pities them and guards them when they are "in tears & iron bound." He has been "bought & sold." His compassion for the royal couple has overridden his libertarian principles, and the result is tragedy. He has exchanged his tears of pity for "the tears of sorrow"—for "the links of a dungeon floor."

LAKE. The LAKE OF FIRE, according to *Matthew* particularly, was a furnace of everlasting fire prepared for the devil and his angels and all the iniquitous (*Matt* xiii:42; xxv: 41; etc.). In *Revelation* (xix:20; xx:10, 14, 15; xxi:8), it is a lake of fire into which are cast the beast, the false prophet, the devil, and even death and Hell; this is the second death.

Blake identified this Lake of Fire (*MHH*

passim) with Hell, or the subconscious. It is the Furnace of Los where not Individuals but States—all the falsities and errors and cruelties—are cast. There the dross is burned away and the true metal purified and melted for new creations. "Awake, Albion awake! reclaim thy Reasoning Spectre. Subdue him to the Divine Mercy. Cast him down into the Lake of Los that ever burneth with fire ever & ever, Amen!" (*Mil* 39:10).

LAKE OF UDAN-ADAN. See UDAN-ADAN.

The LAKE OF URIZEN is the amnion. See URIZEN.

The "LAMB OF GOD" was an epithet applied by John the Baptist to Jesus; in *Revelation* it is a symbol of the Christ.

The central idea of persecuted innocence, vicarious suffering, and deliverance, as in the Paschal Lamb of Passover, had been common in the Old Testament.

Blake used the Lamb as a symbol of Innocence (*SoI*, "The Lamb"), and of God's love, as contrasted with his wrath (*SoE*, "The Tyger"). The Lamb of God appears frequently in the last three prophetic books; his mystical marriage to Jerusalem, "A City, yet a Woman" (*FZ* ix:221; *Rev* xxi:2), indicates that the ideal state of society is the combination of forgiveness and peace. "What is Liberty without Universal Toleration?" (On Boyd, *K* 413).

LAMBETH (in Surrey) is a district of London, across from Chelsea, on the southern side of the Thames. One reaches it by the Westminster Bridge. Immediately four roads fan out: Barley Street, New Road, York Place, and Hercules Road. The location attracted pleasure gardens; there were the Temple of Flora, the Apollo Gardens, the Flora Tea Gardens, and half a mile down York Place, Vauxhall. These gardens kept the district a place of open spaces and shady trees (Blake refers twice to Lambeth's "shades," in *Mil* 36:22 and *J* 38:40)—a grateful contrast to the cramped buildings of Broad and Poland Streets.

But all was not ideal. The gardens had lost their fashionable clientele, and had become the resort of "democratic shopmen . . . railing against King and Church" (war with France broke out in 1793), and of disorderly roughs and loose women. Worse yet, to Blake's mind, was the Royal Asylum for Female Orphans, a workhouse built on the site of the old Hercules Tavern. "Lambeth, ruin'd and given to the detestable Gods of Priam, to Apollo, and at the Asylum given to Hercules, who labour in Tirzah's Looms for bread" (*Mil* 25:48). For a detailed account of Lambeth, see David Erdman's "Lambeth and Bethlehem in Blake's Jerusalem" (*Modern Philology*, XLVIII, 184–92, 1951).

The Blakes lived at 13 (now 23) Hercules Buildings from 1791 to 1800. There was a small garden behind, with a grapevine which Blake would not allow to be pruned (*Gil* I, 98); its tendrils run all through *America*. Here Mr. Butts once caught the Blakes taking a sun bath. There were poplar trees also, under which the poet lost his temper on reading Klopstock. Here Blake spent some of his happiest and most productive years. Five of his prophetic books (*America* through *Ahania*) bear "Lambeth" in the imprint; and the sunrise glory of the *America* undoubtedly reflects Blake's exultation at his escape from what his wife called "the terrible desart of London" (To Mrs. Flaxman, 14 Sept 1800). At Lambeth he also completed and evidently issued *Songs of Innocence and of Experience, Visions of the Daughters of Albion*, and *The Marriage of Heaven and Hell*, as well as *The Gates of Paradise* and *The History of England*, a book advertised in October 1793, but now lost, if it ever was finished.

America, the first to bear the Lambeth imprint, was Blake's first analysis of the problems of liberty. He practically identified Jerusalem (who is liberty) with Lambeth. "Lambeth's Vale, where Jerusalem's foundations began" (*Mil* 6:14). "Lambeth! the Bride, the Lamb's Wife, loveth thee. Thou art one with her" (*J* 12:41). Half of his references to Lambeth involve Jerusalem.

As "Beth" is the Hebrew for "house," Lambeth is the house of the Lamb. It is "Jerusalem's Inner Court" (*Mil* 25:48). There the furniture and curtains of Jerusalem's secret chamber are made (*J* 12:38); there "we began our Foundations" of Jerusalem's city and temple (*J* 84:3).

But in the European turmoil, Blake's ideal of freedom was temporarily ruined. "Jerusalem came down in a dire ruin over all the Earth, she fell cold from Lambeth's Vales in groans & dewy death" (*FZ* ii:45). "Lambeth's Vale, where Jerusalem's foundations began, where they were laid in ruins" (*Mil* 6:14), "ruin'd and given to the detestable Gods of Priam" (*Mil* 25:48). When France is crucified, "they give the oath of blood in Lambeth" (*J* 65:7). Blake's prophetic books were getting progressively pessimistic.

Yet for him, Lambeth was a place of inspiration. When Los appears to Blake, "trembling I stood exceedingly with fear & terror, standing in the Vale of Lambeth" (*Mil* 22:9). Here "the Cherubs of Jerusalem spread to Lambeth's Vale" (*Mil* 35:10). Here Enitharmon utters her last words before sinking herself in Los (*J* 92:7).

Blake hints that his freedom in Lambeth included a clandestine love affair, described in *The Crystal Cabinet* (*K* 429). "There is a Grain of Sand in Lambeth that Satan cannot find, nor can his Watch Fiends find it; 'tis translucent & has many Angles, but he who finds it will find Oothoon's palace; for within opening into Beulah, every angle is a lovely heaven. But should the Watch Fiends find it, they would call it Sin and lay its Heavens & their inhabitants in blood of punishment. Here Jerusalem & Vala were hid in soft slumberous repose" (*J* 41:15). "Remember all thy [Vala's] feigned terrors on the secret couch of Lambeth's Vale" (*J* 65:42). There Oothoon pants, "weeping o'er her Human Harvest" (*Mil* 42:33).There Leutha (who is Sin) is admitted by Elynittria to Palamabron's bed, where she dreams she is the mother of Death, also of Rahab, "the mother of Tirzah & her sisters" (*Mil* 13:41). But the harmony between wife and mistress could not last; that situation underlies the colloquy between Albion, Jerusalem, and Vala (*J* 19:42; 20:1).

See SURREY.

LAMECH was either the sixth generation from Cain (*Gen* iv:17–18) or the eighth from Seth (*Gen* v:25). He was the first polygamist, the husband of Adah and Zillah. He killed a young man, and told his wives: "If Cain shall be avenged sevenfold, truly Lamech seventy and sevenfold" (*Gen* iv:24).

According to rabbinical tradition, Lamech killed Cain accidentally, and hoped that, as the vengeance on Cain had been deferred for seven generations of mankind, the punishment for his own misdeed might be deferred for seventy-seven generations.

Blake followed the fifth chapter of *Genesis* in making Lamech a descendant of Cain, the son of Methuselah, and the father of Noah. In the cycle of the Twenty-seven Churches, Lamech is the ninth, the last of the first group, the "Giants Mighty, Hermaphroditic" (*Mil* 37:37; *J* 75:12). However, the two wives were descended from Cain and were ancestresses of the Virgin Mary (*FZ* viii:365; *J* 62:9).

In a picture, Blake represented Lamech clutching his head in horror as he looks at the dead youth, while his wives clasp each other in terror.

"LAMIA" (Margoliouth's version) is the most likely reading of the eighth word in *The Four Zoas* viii:446; it has also been read as "llama" and "Larma." During Urizen's agony as the Dragon, Lamia is among the various animals called forth by the deserts.

The Lamia was a vampire who lured and then killed young men by sucking their blood. The story in Philostratus was retold by Robert Burton and again by Keats (1820), who altered Lamia into a serpent-woman.

The LAMPS burning before the throne in heaven are the seven Spirits of God (*Rev* iv:5). Blake identified them with the seven Eyes of God (*FZ* i:554).

LANCASHIRE is a northern county of

England which, with the adjoining counties of Lincoln and York, is assigned to Simeon (*J* 16:44). Probably through carelessness, Blake did not assign it to any of the Sons of Albion. He seems to have intended Lancashire instead of Stafford for Slade (*J* 71:34), as Stafford is later assigned to Kotope (*J* 71:44); but there are overlappings in other assignments.

"Cheshire & Lancashire & Westmoreland groan in anguish" when the Sons of Albion "cut the fibres from the rivers" (*J* 90:18).

LANDAFF (i.e., Llandaff), in Glamorganshire, South Wales, is the nineteenth of the Twenty-four Cathedral Cities (*J* 46:19). It is West, under Tharmas and York.

LANERK (i.e., Lanarkshire) is a Scottish county which, with Elgin and Kinros[s], is assigned to Joseph (*J* 16:58). With the rest of Scotland, it is assigned to Bowen (*J* 71:46).

LAOCOÖN was the priest of Poseidon who warned his countrymen against the Trojan Horse. While he was preparing to sacrifice to Poseidon (who was hostile to Troy), two serpents from the sea killed Laocoön and his two sons (Virgil, *Aeneid* ii, 199).

Pliny described the famous statue of the event, and said it was the work of three Rhodians, Agesander, Polydorus, and Athenodorus. It was rediscovered in A.D. 1506. The concept, however, was not original.

Blake made a drawing from a cast in 1815, and engraved it for Abraham Rees's *Cyclopaedia*. About 1820 he re-engraved it on a larger scale and crowded the background with symbolic epigrams. The central figure is "King Jehovah," or the Angel of the Divine Presence, with his two sons Satan and Adam; the two serpents are labelled "Evil" and "Good." "Good & Evil are Riches & Poverty, a Tree of Misery, propagating Generation & Death" (*Laoc*, *K* 776). The statue was "copied from the Cherubim of Solomon's Temple, by three Rhodians, & applied to Natural Fact or History of Ilium" (*Laoc*, *K* 775). Laocoön is also identified with the constellation Ophiuchus. Beneath the "Good" serpent is written the name of Lilith, Adam's first wife.

The LARK is the new idea which comes as inspiration in the dawn. Blake depicted him as a naked boy singing in ecstasy as he flies upward into the yet starry sky. He startles the dull night and wakes the earth beneath (*K* 618). "His little throat labours with inspiration; every feather on throat & breast & wings vibrates with the effluence Divine" (*Mil* 31:34). "The Lark is a mighty Angel" (*Mil* 36:12), "an Angel on the Wing" (*K* 618). An Angel is by definition a messenger, and the Lark is Los's messenger (*Mil* 35:67). His nest is at Los's eastern gate of Golgonooza, above a fount by a "Rock of odours" covered with the purple flowers of the wild thyme (*Mil* 35:58). Here the Mundane Shell ends (*Mil* 17:27).

The new idea must undergo a considerable period of incubation before it comes clear. This subliminal activity is symbolized as a series of twenty-eight Larks. Each Lark passes through one of the Twenty-seven Heavens, beginning with Luther, the latest. When the first Lark has reached "the highest lift of his light pinions," he meets the second Lark, and they return to earth "& there all night consult with Angels of Providence & with the Eyes of God all night in slumbers inspired, & at the dawn of day send out another Lark into another Heaven to carry news upon his wings" (*Mil* 36:1–7). Thus "the Seven Eyes of God, who walk even to Satan's Seat thro' all the Twenty-seven Heavens, may not slumber nor sleep" (*Mil* 35:64). Finally the twenty-eighth Lark, after his predecessors have gone through all the orthodox systems of thought, is able to fly clear, in unsullied inspiration.

The importance of the Lark in *Milton* is clear: he is the new idea which inspires the entire poem. He meets Ololon as she descends (36:10); and when Blake recovers from his swoon, the Lark immediately rises to hail the dawn of a new day (42:29).

The LAST JUDGMENT, according to orthodox Christianity, will not occur until the end of the world; then Jesus shall return and judge all mankind, living and dead, separating the good sheep from the evil goats. The saved shall be rewarded with everlasting bliss, while the damned shall be punished with everlasting torture.

Such a concept was utterly opposed to Blake's belief in the character and teachings of Jesus. It contradicted both infinite Mercy and the Forgiveness of Sins. But Blake reconciled his belief and the words of the Bible by means of an idea which he developed from Swedenborg. A Last Judgment occurs whenever an error is recognized and cast out. It may occur at any time for the individual (as with Job, *Illustr Job* 16), and it also occurs on a world-wide basis at great moments of historical upheavals (as in *Am* 16). Swedenborg said that such a Judgment had occurred in 1757, when his New Church, or New Jerusalem, was established; but as 1757 was also the date of Blake's birth, he applied it to himself, and proclaimed his new concept of man and the universe in *The Marriage of Heaven and Hell* (3).

Jesus is Truth, and his appearance puts an end to all errors, which are cast out and consumed in the Lake of Fire. Nothing that really exists can be destroyed, only the unrealities of moral judgments, cruel laws, the church of this world, kingships, and the "States" through which individuals pass. In a comment on one of his pictures of the Last Judgment, Blake is specific: the figures he drew are given the names of familiar characters, yet they are not the actual persons "but the States Signified by those Names" (*LJ*, *K* 607).

Blake made several pictures of the Last Judgment. Of these, the simplest and most orthodox is that in Blair's *Grave* (1808). Jesus sadly turns his face from the self-justifying Pharisees; beneath them various figures fall, among whom are Satan entwined with his serpent, the Whore of Babylon, and her Beast.

In the same year Blake painted for the Countess of Egremont a Last Judgment, which still hangs in Petworth Hall. Blake thanked the countess for the commission in a poem, "The Caverns of the Grave I've seen" (*K* 558). Though it is only 19⅞ by 15¾ inches, it contains hundreds of symbolic figures. Blake explained the chief of these figures in a letter to Ozias Humphry (*K* 442). Above the figure of Christ the Veil of the Temple is opened, revealing the Cross in place of the Ark.

In 1810 he made the ink drawing of the Last Judgment now in the Rosenwald Collection (see Illustrations). A preliminary pencil sketch was reproduced by Keynes in the first Nonesuch edition of Blake's works (1925, III, 148). The Rosenwald picture, though a trifle smaller than that at Petworth, contains even more figures, which Blake explained in a series of long notes intended as an addition to his *Descriptive Catalogue* for 1810 (*LJ*, *K* 604–17). The Dove of the Holy Ghost replaced the Cross, which, being an instrument of execution, of vengeance for sin, is now cast down on the left hand, along with the papal tiara and the royal crown (spiritual and physical despotism) and the rosary of vain repetitions. (See CROSS.) Albert S. Roe, in the *Huntington Library Quarterly* for November 1957, has a long and detailed description of this drawing, which he dates between 1820 and 1825. He points out that Christ extends his arms, with open hands, to all, and does not damn those on his left; furthermore, the Virgin does not appear as intercessor.

Those on his left are separated from the glories of Christ by a row of three figures with crossing hands: a youth with a spade and a vessel pouring water, an old man with a similar vessel and an axe, and a third man with an axe. These are three of the plagues poured from the vials of Wrath; they represent Labor, Materialism, and Hate (see Illustrations, "LJ" No. 26).

"My Picture is a History of Art & Science, the Foundation of Society, Which is Humanity itself" (*LJ*, *K* 613).

At the end of his life, Blake did yet another picture, a fresco, this time 7 feet by 5, estimated to contain over a thousand figures. Blake worked long at it, and priced it at twenty-five guineas, but found no buyer; he intended to exhibit it at the Academy but died too soon. William Rossetti described it (*Gil* I, 402; II, 223); it has since disappeared.

The last of the nine "Nights" of *The Four Zoas* is entitled "The Last Judgment," but as it is concerned with the tremendous readjustments of the Zoas in the mind of Man, it does not correspond particularly to the pictures, except when both refer to the events of *Revelation*.

The trumpets waking the dead sound immediately after the moment of death; in the General Resurrection, all the oppressed wreak their vengeance on the oppressors for all unexpiated injustices and cruelties, an idea which Blake found in the Koran (see George Sale, *Preliminary Discourse* IV, 1734—London, 1825 ed., p. 119). Albion wakes; he blames Urizen, who on renouncing all idea of dominion instantly regains his pristine youth. The Son of Man descends from Jerusalem and sits upon his throne; but there is work to be done before Albion can enter the consummation.

This work takes six days, to reverse and undo the six days of Creation. It consists of the great Harvest and Vintage, for making the Bread and Wine of Eternity. On the earth, however, these rural activities are the disasters described in *Revelation*. Eventually the Zoas find their Emanations; Los becomes Urthona again; and the epic ends with the sunrise of the Seventh Day, the Sabbath of the Millennium: "The war of swords departed now, the dark Religions are departed & sweet Science reigns."

LAVATER (Johann Kaspar, 1745–1801) was a Swiss poet, dramatist, mystic, physiognomist, and spiritual adviser to thousands of Protestants, among them Goethe, who recorded his impressions of Lavater in *Dichtung und Wahrheit* (particularly in the fourteenth, eighteenth, and nineteenth books).

Lavater's successful exposure of a corrupt official caused him to flee with his colleague and university friend Fuseli to England, where Fuseli remained. On Lavater's return to Zurich, he wrote his *Aphorisms on Man,* which he dedicated to Fuseli, who made an English translation and had it printed by Joseph Johnson (London, 1788).

Blake, who engraved the frontispiece for Fuseli's translation, was fascinated by the book and annotated it elaborately. The very first aphorisms inspired Blake's first illustrated publication *All Religions Are One* (1788), and others suggested some of Blake's fundamental theories: the finding of God only in other men, humanity as the image of Christ, and the Incarnation as God's descent into nature to restore man to his original perfection.

LAZARUS was the brother of Mary and Martha whom Jesus raised from the dead after he had been four days in the tomb. This, the most astounding of the miracles, is not mentioned by Matthew, Mark, or Luke, but only by John (xi).

Blake interpreted the miracle symbolically. Lazarus represents the physical bodies of all mankind ("the Vehicular Body of Albion the Redeem'd"). Understood literally by man's reason ("the Spectre of Albion") as the resurrection of the physical (not spiritual) body, the miracle became part of the false doctrine of the church ("the Covering Cherub"), who divided into the four churches of Paul, Constantine, Charlemaine, and Luther (*Mil* 24:26–32).

LEAH, the daughter of Laban and sister of Rachel, was married by trickery to Jacob, who had served seven years for Rachel. After another seven years, he married Rachel. Their rivalry for the attentions of Jacob was intense. When they finally fled from Laban, Rachel stole Laban's teraphim, or images of his family gods (*Gen* xxix–xxxi).

Blake speaks of the "Deadly Hate between Leah & Rachel, Daughters of Deceit & Fraud bearing the Images of various Species of Contention and Jealousy & Abhorrence & Revenge & deadly Murder" (*J* 69:11).

LEBANON consists of a double mountain range marking the northern limit of the Promised Land. On the Lebanon range rises the snow-crowned peak of Mount Lebanon; its twin, Mount Hermon, rises on the Anti-Lebanon range, which curves northeast past Damascus. The beauty of the scenery (including the famous cedars), the fertility of the valley between the ranges, and the numerous watercourses are celebrated in the *Song of Solomon* and elsewhere.

Blake associates the erotic Daughters of Albion with Lebanon. Thammuz is worshipped there (*Mil* 37:26). Tirzah bids Malah come from Lebanon (*FZ* viii:316; *J* 68:4; cf. *Song of Sol* iv:8). Gwendolen dwells by valleys of springs beneath the mountains of Lebanon (*J* 68:55; cf. *Song of Sol* iv:15). At the sight of Reuben, Guantok and Peachy hide in Damascus beneath Mount Lebanon (*J* 36:16). The Daughters of Albion rage through all the nations of Europe, to Lebanon, Persia, and India (*J* 80:47). Hermon and Lebanon bow their crowned heads at Los's Watch Song (*J* 85:17). Lebanon is one of the places he sees in Jerusalem's reins (*J* 86:32).

Lebanon is one of the six mountains around Palestine which are equated with Milton's three wives and three daughters (*Mil* 17:16). The clouds of the coming Revolution roll on the Alps, also on the mountains of Lebanon round the deceased Gods (*SoL* 4:19).

LEE ("Light Horse" Harry, 1756–1818) was a cavalry commander in the American Revolution, whose brilliant covering of Greene's retreat was particularly admired. His eulogy of Washington contained the famous words: "First in war, first in peace, first in the hearts of his countrymen." He is one of the seven commanders who watch the approach of Albion's plague-armed hosts (*Am* 14:2).

LEE (Nat, 1653?–92) was the last great representative of the Tragedy of Blood and the poetry of enthusiasm. His *Rival Queens* (1677), which restored blank verse to the writing of tragedy, held the stage for a century and a half and was still being produced in Blake's day. It contains the famous line "When Greeks join'd Greeks, then was the tug of war." Eventually Lee lost his mind and was in Bedlam for five years.

He was Dryden's chief collaborator; for Lee's fulsome panegyric *To Mr. Dryden, on his Poem of Paradise*, which praised Dryden at the expense of Milton, see DRYDEN. Blake's indignation was expressed in his Public Address (*K* 600), and also in the squib "Dryden in Rhyme cries: 'Milton only Plann'd' " (*K* 554, 555, 595).

After Lee's death, Dryden, in his *Parallel of Poetry and Painting*, wrote of Lee's "great genius for tragedy," but said all his characters were "stark staring mad," so that his plays were "a mere hurricane from the beginning to the end." This criticism condemns all the Tragedy of Blood; and Lee's works are still underestimated.

The LEFT is usually the "sinister" side. As applied to hands and feet, it signifies the material or the reasonable side. See HAND and FOOT.

LEGIONS was a city mentioned by Geoffrey of Monmouth (III, x; V, v; IX, xii); Holinshed identified it with Caerlheon.

It was built by King Belinus on the Usk in Glamorganshire, and was first called Caerosc, but the name was changed to "the City of Legions" when the Roman invaders used it for winter quarters. It became one of the three noblest cities of Britain, the others being London and York. Under King Lucius, the first Christian king, these three cities were made archbishoprics. Julius and Aaron from this city were among the first British martyrs. Later, because of its wealth and magnificence, King Arthur was crowned and established his court there.

The four pillars of Albion's throne are London, Bath, Legions, and Edinburgh (*Mil* 39:35). But later Bath is identified with Legions (*J* 41:1).

LEICESTER[SHIRE] is a Midland county

of England which, with the adjoining counties of Warwick and Worcester, is assigned to Naphtali (*J* 16:46). With Warwick and four others it is assigned to Hutton (*J* 71:37). It is one of the seven counties that "labour within the Furnaces" of Los (*J* 16:18).

LEINSTER is the eastern province of Ireland. Judah's Gate is in Leinster (*J* 72:4); its counties are assigned to Judah, Issachar, and Zebulun (*J* 72:18–20).

LEITRIM is a county of the western province of Connaught, Ireland. The province contains Joseph's Gate; but all its counties are assigned to Ephraim, Manasseh, and Benjamin (*J* 72:3, 24).

LEUTHA symbolizes sex under law, and hence may most easily be understood as the sense of sin, or guilt. Her compass-point is south, as she is the Emanation of Bromion (*FZ* viii:363); and it should not be confusing that she is also paired with the male seed, Antamon (*Eur* 14:15; *SoL* 3:28), with Satan (*Mil* 11:28), and even with Palamabron (*Mil* 13:38). Her attributes are the Valley of Delight (the female genitals), the flower (whose plucking is a sexual act), and the rainbow of expectation. She also has a chariot, which the aged mother Eno now guides (*BoL* 3:2).

Oothoon hides in Leutha's Vale, seeks flowers there, and plucks the fatal Marygold (*VDA* iii:4; 1:4–12). An imperfect erotic dream vanishes to "obscured traces in the Vale of Leutha" (*Am* frag., "As when a dream" 3). When Milton is tempted, Orc (revolt), Oothoon (desire), and Leutha (guilt) hover over Milton's couch of fire (*Mil* 18:39).

When Enitharmon is degrading sex by the domination of her Female Will, she summons Leutha from the South, calling her "silent love," "my lureing bird of Eden," "soft soul of flowers," "sweet smiling pestilence," and "silken queen," also referring to her "many colour'd bow" (*Eur* 14:9–14). Antamon is summoned immediately after, and is told that the "seven

churches of Leutha" seek his love—the seven houses of chained monkeys (*MHH* 20), which are the seven churches of Asia (*Rev* i:4).

In the Bard's Song (*Mil* 11:28–13:44), Leutha is identified as Sin itself, for here Blake paraphrases and enlarges Milton's account of the birth and offspring of Sin (*PL* ii:766–87), which itself is an elaboration of *James* i:15: "Then when lust hath conceived, it bringeth forth sin: and sin, when it is finished, bringeth forth death." Milton's development is as follows: in the assembly of angels discussing the conspiracy against God, suddenly Sin sprang, Minerva-like, from Satan's head. The heavenly host recoiled and called her Sin, "and for a Sign Portentous held me"; but soon she became Satan's paramour; and while the devils were falling from heaven, she gave birth to Death.

Blake mingled *Paradise Lost* and *Revelation* with his own mythology to analyze his quarrel with Hayley and describe the degeneration of Hayley's character. Leutha's part is as follows:

When Leutha, a daughter of Beulah, beholds Satan's condemnation, she descends to the great Assembly and offers herself as a ransom for her father Satan's sin, for which she blames herself. Immortal, heart-piercing, she glows with varying colors (the rainbow, which is actually painted across the text of Plate 10 [i.e., 12] in the Huntington copy of *Milton*, and across Plate 9 [i.e., 11] in the New York copy).

She is now the personification of Hayley's unconscious homosexuality. She confesses that she loved Palamabron (Blake), but his Emanation Elynittria repelled her. A Dragon-form issues from her limbs to seize Elynittria's yet unborn son (cf. *Rev* xii:1–6); to prevent this birth, she entered Satan's brain, "night after night, like sweet perfumes"; thus she "stupified the masculine perceptions and kept only the feminine awake: hence rose his soft delusory love to Palamabron, admiration join'd with envy" (*Mil* 12:4).

When the horses of Palamabron's Harrow are to rest at noon, she tries to unloose them, but they rage against her. The servants of the Harrow see her only as a bow of varying colors. The Harrow bursts into flames; Satan compels the gnomes to throw up sand-banks against the fire, "a Hell of our own making" (*Mil* 12:23); and he drives the Harrow among the constellations of Jehovah, drawing a third part to devour Jerusalem and Albion (cf. *Rev* xii:4—this "third part" is the number of angels who fell with Satan). Then, surrounded by "dark fires" (of Hell), she forms the Serpent. The gnomes retaliate; she hides in Satan's brain. When the gnomes refuse to labor more, she reveals herself with sweet blandishments; "back the Gnomes recoil'd and called me Sin and for a sign portentous held me" (*Mil* 12:38).

At sundown, Elynittria and her singing women meet Satan and give him wine; his former life becomes a dream; he is clothed in the Serpent's folds and demands purity; then he drives Leutha from his inmost brain.

Leutha repents before the Divine Vision, but the sleepless Satan will not. "We are the Spectre of Luvah, the murderer of Albion" (*Mil* 13:8). Enitharmon creates a new Space to save Satan from punishment; Leutha hides in Enitharmon's tent. After the seven Eyes of God are appointed, Elynittria soothes Leutha and brings her to Palamabron's bed. Here in dreams she gives birth to Death, and to Rahab, the mother of Tirzah and her sisters. While Leutha lives with Palamabron, Oothoon is her charming guard.

The DOGS OF LEUTHA are those baser passions (like those of Actaeon) which destroy their masters.

Blake associated them with the Isle of Dogs, a cape-shaped projection into the Thames, occupied by the East India docks and other wharves, where the prostitutes swarmed.

Los, searching Albion's bosom, comes to Stepney and the Isle of Leutha's Dogs (*J* 31:16). Los, on his watch, is accompanied by the Dogs of Leutha; "at his feet they lap the water of the trembling Thames, then follow swift" (*J* 83:82).

LEVI was the third son of Jacob and the founder of a Tribe. Because of the priestly character of the Levites, they were not assigned a separate tract of land, but were given forty-eight cities of refuge scattered through the lands of the others. See LEVITES.

With his brothers, Levi is listed as one of the Sons of Los who fled (*FZ* viii:360, 375). He and six of his brothers were generated because they left Los to wander with Tirzah (*Mil* 24:2). Jerusalem recalls him and his brothers in their days of innocence (*J* 79:30) and laments that they fled (*J* 93:14). The Daughters of Albion divide him; he shoots out forty-eight roots (the cities of refuge) over the land of Canaan (*J* 74:47). Levi is one of the brothers closed up in narrow vales of the dark land of Cabul (*J* 79:64). Elsewhere, he sleeps on Snowdon while Reuben sleeps on Penmaenmawr, where their senses roll outward (*FZ* ii:53). He is one of those whose characteristics are not to be appropriated (*J* 90:31).

In Wales, Levi's Gate is the county of Montgomeryshire (*J* 16:36); in England he is assigned the adjoining counties of Middlesex, Kent, and Surrey (*J* 16:45); in Scotland, Edinburgh, Roxbro (Roxburgh), and Ross (*J* 16:54); and in Ireland he shares with Reuben and Simeon the counties of the southern province of Munster (*J* 72:21).

LEVIATHAN was a huge sea-dragon symbolic of evil, mentioned in *Job* xli; *Psalm* lxxiv:14; *Psalm* civ:26; and *Isaiah* xxvii:1. The long description in *Job* is preceded by that of Behemoth. Isaiah calls Leviathan a "crooked serpent"; Blake always pictures it in a coil like that of his Serpent of Nature.

Thomas Hobbes (1588–1679) was an astute and cynical materialist who insisted (before Locke) that our knowledge originates in what we learn through the senses, and that imagination "is nothing but *decay-*

ing sense" (Hobbes, *Leviathan*, 1651, pp. 3, 5). He used the Leviathan to symbolize "a Commonwealth or State" (p. 1), which he depicted as a giant composed of human bodies. The giant wears the crown of absolute authority; his hands hold the sword of secular power and the crozier of religious power. This social order, Hobbes says, originated not in any divine ordinance, as commonly supposed, but only in a human social contract, caused by the fearful need of men for self-protection in their natural state of war.

Hobbes's Leviathan appears in the fourth "Memorable Fancy" of *The Marriage of Heaven and Hell*. He is the logical outcome of the Angel's arguments from good and evil (the black and white spiders); he is the wrathful (tygerish) and repetitious system of Natural Morality. But he is only an illusion: "All that we saw was owing to your metaphysics" (*K* 156).

In Blake's tempera, "The spiritual form of Nelson guiding Leviathan, in whose wreathings are infolded the Nations of the Earth" (*DesC* I), the monster represents naval warfare, as distinguished from Behemoth, "the War by Sea enormous & the War by Land astounding" (*J* 91:40). Nelson is a naked youth (with both arms and both eyes) who calmly guides the dragon; from his left hand a cord reaches to the monster's head (*Job* xli:1). In the companion picture, Pitt guides Behemoth.

The two monsters appear again in the fifteenth plate of the *Illustrations of the Book of Job*. God, pointing down with his left hand, explains to Job the terrible forms which symbolize the tremendous powers in the subconscious. The cloud-barriers indicate that they are part of Job's world; the left hand, the Egyptian bulrushes, and the books in which two angels record history indicate that they are Urizenic.

But Creation is now a work of Mercy. The Creator is the benevolent Jehovah-Elohim and not the evil demiurge. The two beasts are "erecting pillars in the deepest Hell to reach the heavenly arches" (*J* 91:41). Leviathan, as Blake notes in a marginal quotation from *Job* xli:34, is "King over all the Children of Pride." Another marginal quotation (*Job* xxxvii:11) promises that the cloud-barriers shall be scattered; and the emptied shells of the Sea of Time and Space symbolize the deliverance from this material body.

The LEVITES, or descendants of Levi, constituted the priestly caste. See LEVI. Their forty-eight cities of refuge are equated with the forty-eight constellations of the Mundane Shell, also the heads of the Great Polypus (*Mil* 38:1–2).

LIBYA. See LYBIA.

LICHFIELD. See LITCHFIELD.

LILITH was the name given to Adam's first wife, whose existence is implied in *Genesis* i:28, as Eve was not created until the next chapter. According to rabbinical tradition, Lilith became the mother of demons, so Eve was created to replace her. In *Isaiah* xxxiv:14, the King James version translated "Lilith" as "screech owl" and (in the margin) "night monster."

On the Laocoön plate (*K* 775), Blake inscribed Lilith's name in Hebrew characters below the "good" serpent entangling young Adam.

The LILLY (lily) is the flower of Innocence. As the humble Lilly of the Valley, she symbolizes Thel's virginity, and is the food of the Lamb (*Thel* 1:15–2:17). In "The Lilly" (*SoE*), however, she represents the freedom of pure love, and is contrasted with the "modest" (originally "lustful") Rose with its thorn. The unfallen Vala is called "the Lilly of Havilah," symbolizing the same thing (*J* 19:42). Blake often associated lilies with roses to indicate an ideal state; and in the illustration on *Jerusalem* 18, Vala is crowned with lilies and Jerusalem with roses.

The heading for Chapter ii of *Jerusalem* (Plate 28; see Illustrations) is a picture of two figures passionately embracing in the intoxicating perfume of a water-lily heart. The symbolism of the water lily is ancient: it is rooted in the invisible mud (subconscious) and rises to beauty in the conscious. Blake's picture signifies the ecstasy of newly-married love. The leaves of the plant are lily pads, floating on the Sea of Time and Space. Blake, however, gave the blossom only six petals (could he have intended a lotus?), thus making room for the lovers. It uplifts them temporarily above the cares of material life. The young husband with Apollonian locks sits in the rear, his strong right arm passed around his wife's waist, while his left hand rests on her head. She faces him; their lips meet. Her delicate right hand rests on his right hip, the other hand on his head. Her hair, however, is shorter than his. Neither of them notes the Golden Net (marriage) draped over him. In a trial proof, a caterpillar prophesies the woes of gestation and childbirth.

LIMERICK is a county of the province of Munster, Ireland. With the other counties of Munster, it is assigned to Reuben, Simeon, and Levi (J 72:22).

The LIMITS of Opacity and Contraction (or Satan and Adam) were fixed as an act of mercy by the Saviour, to put bounds to error.

He made them in Albion's bosom "While yet those beings were not born nor knew of good or Evil" (FZ iv:271–74). They limit Los's threefold creation (FZ vii:383). When the Limit of Contraction is fixed, Albion begins to awake (FZ viii:16).

In *Milton*, the two Limits are fixed after the election of Molech, the second of the seven Eyes (13:20). "In the Nerves of the Nostrils [east], Accident . . . became Opake & Indefinite, but the Divine Saviour formed it into a Solid by Los's Mathematic power. He nam'd the Opake, Satan: he nam'd the Solid, Adam" (29:35–39).

In *Jerusalem*, after Los has materialized two of the senses of Reuben, the nostrils (east) and eyes (south), the Divine Hand finds the two Limits in Albion's bosom (35:

1), after which Los materializes Reuben's other two senses. Every individual contains these two Limits; "but when Man sleeps in Beulah, the Saviour in Mercy takes Contraction's Limit [Adam], and of the Limit he forms Woman [Eve], That Himself may in process of time be born, Man to redeem. But there is no Limit of Expansion; there is no Limit of Translucence" (42:29–35).

Los is once named the fixer of the Limits (J 73:27).

LINCOLN is the ninth in the list of the Twenty-four Cathedral Cities. It is under Urthona and Edinburgh. The minster is said to be the earliest purely Gothic building in Europe.

Lincoln is one of the three "Councellors of Los" (J 46:5); they are persons who, though not poets, furthered the cause of spiritual liberty. For Lincoln, Blake obviously had in mind its famous bishop Robert Grosseteste (ca. 1175–1253), one of the most distinguished of all English medieval prelates. He was a rooter-out of abuses, fighting the unjust demands of his archbishop, the king, and even the pope, for which he was excommunicated various times.

At the beginning of *Jerusalem*, "Lincoln & Norwich stand trembling on the brink of Udan-Adan!" (5:10). At the coming of war, "York & Lincoln hide among the flocks because of the griding Knife" (66:65).

LINCOLN'S INN is one of the four Inns of Court. The Gothic chapel, with brilliantly painted windows, was built by Inigo Jones, who also laid out Lincoln's Inn Fields, the largest square in London, and one of the most beautiful. Into it runs Great Queen Street, where lived the engraver James Basire, and also young Blake when he was apprenticed to him. Blake's earliest known signature gives his address as simply "Lincolns Inn" (K Studies 47). "To Great Queen Street & Lincoln's Inn, all is distress & woe" (J 84:16).

LINCOLNSHIRE is a maritime county of

England. With the adjoining counties of York and Lancashire, it is assigned to Simeon (*J* 16:44). With the adjoining counties of Stafford, Derby, and Nottingham, it is assigned to Slade (*J* 71:34). It is one of the seven counties which labor among the furnaces of Los (*J* 16:18).

"The LINEAMENTS of Gratified Desire" are what men and women require of each other (*The Question Answer'd, K* 180); see also "In a wife I would desire" (*K* 178). Enitharmon perceives Antamon "floating . . . with lineaments of gratified desire" (*Eur* 14:18–19). Tharmas complains to Enion, "Deform'd I see these lineaments of ungratified desire" (*FZ* iv:24).

LINLITHGO[W] is a Scottish county which, with Nairn and Inverness, is assigned to Naphtali (*J* 16:55). As part of Scotland it is also assigned to Bowen (*J* 71:46).

The LION is a "noble" beast, typifying Judah (*Gen* xlix:9) and Jesus (*Rev* v:5). One of the four heads of each of the "living creatures" of *Ezekiel* (i:10) has the face of a lion; whereas in *Revelation* (iv:7) the first of the four beasts (*zoa*) has a lion's head. (This lion was eventually identified with St. Mark.) A common misquotation of *Isaiah* xi:6 prophesies that the lion shall lie down with the lamb (*SoI*, "Night" 42).

The Lion's compass-point is north, as in the quaternary Lion (north), Tyger (east), Horse (south), and Elephant (west)— (*MHH* 8:14; *J* 98:43).

The Lion is commonly known as the protector of the Lamb. Una's Lion, in Spenser's *Faerie Queene* (I), is a familiar example. In Blake's poems, the Lion's wrath is particularly directed against the wolves, who prey on the flocks. "Empire is no more! and now the lion & wolf shall cease" (*MHH* 27). In "Night" (*SoI*), the Lion defends the flocks against the wolves and the tygers; but the innocents are actually killed: it is in Eternity that the Lion lies down with the Lamb. In "The Little Girl Lost" and "The Little

Girl Found," the Lion himself is the Angel of Death, who carries little Lyca to his den, or palace, and then (appearing in his true form as "a Spirit arm'd in gold") conveys her parents there, where they dwell together in happiness.

The Lion is often associated with the Tyger, for they both are forms of wrath: the Lion is spiritual wrath, inspired by pity ("the wrath of the Lamb," *Rev* vi:16), while the Tyger's blind wrath is purely emotional. The one rages in flames, the other in redounding smoke (*FZ* vii:9; vii *b*:111). See TYGER.

Urthona's Lions (*FZ* ix:841) are of course those of Los; his sons Theotormon and Sotha create them "in compassionate thunderings" to force the wandering Spectres to "take refuge in Human lineaments" (*Mil* 28:27–28; cf. *J* 73:17). Urizen has Lions, who forge the geometrical shapes which underlie the material universe (*FZ* ii:135); in his fall, they become "dishumaniz'd men" (*FZ* vi:116). Luvah as Orc also has his Lions (*FZ* vii:8); but apparently Tharmas has none.

The Lion is contrasted with the castrated Ox. "Why is one law given to the lion & the patient Ox?" (*Tir* viii:10). "One Law for the Lion & Ox is Oppression" (*MHH* 24).

The golden southern gate of Golgonooza "has four Lions terrible, living" (*J* 13:2).

LITCHFIELD (i.e., Lichfield) is the nineteenth in the list of the Twenty-four Cathedral Cities (*J* 46:19). It is the first in the last group of six, which are under Tharmas and York. Lichfield is in west central England; the rest form a roughly perpendicular line in the far west. Lichfield was doubtless included because it was the birthplace of Dr. Johnson, whom Blake disliked.

LIVERPOOL is a principal seaport of England. "Manchester & Liverpool are in tortures of Doubt & Despair" (*J* 21:36).

LIZARD POINT, in Cornwall, is the southernmost point of Great Britain.

"The weights of Enitharmon's Loom play lulling cadences on the winds of Albion, from Caithness in the north to Lizardpoint & Dover in the south" (*Mil* 6:5; *J* 83:71). Of the two gates through which souls descend, "One Southward from Dover Cliff to Lizard Point, the other toward the North" (*Mil* 26:13).

LLANDAFF. See LANDAFF.

LLEWELLYN. Llewelyn ab Gruffydd, the last prince of Wales, reigned from A.D. 1254 to 1282.

> He was an able and magnanimous prince, who would have conferred happiness on his country had its destinies permitted; but the insatiable ambition of Edward the first, king of England, to reduce the whole island to his sway, could not be resisted by the mutilated power of Llywelyn; he therefore fell, and with him perished the name of the Cymry as an independent nation upon the face of the earth.
> —William Owen, *Cambrian Biography*, London, 1803, p. 224.

"Place the Tribes of Llewellyn in America for a hiding place, till sweet Jerusalem emanates again into Eternity" (*J* 83:59). There seems to be no tradition that the defeated Welsh fled to America; probably Blake had in mind the supposed discovery of America by the Welsh prince Madoc in A.D. 1170, concerning which Southey wrote his long narrative *Madoc* (1805). Reports of Welsh-speaking Indians were still current in Blake's time.

LOCKE (John, 1632–1704), the great Whig philosopher, in his *Essay Concerning Human Understanding* (1690), denied any innate knowledge, or instinct. A newborn baby's brain is a blank leaf; he learns only through his five senses and through the use of reason. Blake read and annotated this book "when very young," along with Burke's *On the Sublime* and Bacon's *Advancement of Learning*. "I felt the Same Contempt & Abhorrence then that I do

now. They mock Inspiration & Vision" (On Reynolds, *K* 477). The book is mentioned flippantly in *An Island in the Moon* (Chap. viii).

"Blake was the first great artist to reject Locke's theory" (*Harper* 63). "Innate Ideas are in Every Man, Born with him; they are truly Himself" (On Reynolds, *K* 459). In the *Visions of the Daughters of Albion* (3:2–13) he attacked at length Locke's "philosophy of the five senses": "With what sense is it that the chicken shuns the ravenous hawk? . . ."

Locke became the third of the Satanic trinity, Bacon, Newton, and Locke, the teachers of the atheism of unbelief and materialism, or Natural Religion. When the philosophy of the five senses was complete, "Urizen wept & gave it into the hands of Newton & Locke" (*SoL* 4:16–17). Satan is "Newton's Pantocrator, weaving the Woof of Locke" (*Mil* 4:11). The redeemed Milton is determined "to cast off Bacon, Locke & Newton from Albion's covering" (*Mil* 41:5).

In *Jerusalem*, Blake sees in the universities of Europe "the Loom of Locke, whose Woof rages dire, wash'd by the Waterwheels of Newton: black the cloth in heavy wreathes folds over every Nation" (15:15). "Is this the Female Will, O ye lovely Daughters of Albion, To Converse concerning Weight & Distance in the Wilds of Newton & Locke?" (34:39). The Spectre claims to be "Bacon & Newton & Locke who teach Humility to Man, who teach Doubt & Experiment" (54:17). In the temple of Natural Religion is "the feminine Tabernacle of Bacon, Newton, & Locke" (66:14). Hand divides and combines into "Three Forms named Bacon & Newton & Locke in the Oak Groves of Albion which overspread all the Earth" (70:15).

But Los sees the completion of their philosophy as the necessary prelude to the revelation of truth. "If Bacon, Newton, Locke deny a Conscience in Man & the Communion of Saints & Angels, contemning the Divine Vision & Fruition, Worshiping the Deus of the Heathen, The God of This World, & the Goddess Nature, Mystery, Babylon the Great, The Druid Dragon & hidden Harlot, is it not that Signal of the Morning which was told us in the Beginning?" (93:21). But in the final apotheosis, the three are revealed in their essential genius as the three great scientists counterbalancing the three great poets Milton, Shakespeare, and Chaucer (98:9).

The LOINS form a trinity with the Head and the Heart in the threefold materialized body. The vegetated bodies woven by Enitharmon open "within their hearts & in their loins & in their brain" into Beulah, although some are woven only single- or twofold, "& some threefold in Head or Heart or Reins, according to the fittest order of most merciful pity & compassion to the spectrous dead" (FZ viii:55–60). In man, the three gates open to Golgonooza (Mil 20:38); the third gate is in the region called Al-Ulro (Mil 34:15). But the gates of the Daughters of Los all open into the vegetative world (J 14:19). (In the additional lines [560 ff.] to FZ i, which were never fitted in, and perhaps discarded, the three gates of Enitharmon originally opened into Eternity, but this was altered to Beulah, l. 563.)

The Loins are the source of the material body; they are symbolized as Ona, youngest of the three daughters of Urizen (FZ vi:9; vii:101). "From Albion's loins fled all Peoples and Nations of the Earth" (FZ ii:43). Eventually they will amalgamate and return, "taking refuge in the Loins of Albion" (J 92:3).

When frustrated, the Loins are the cause of war (J 27:37; 47:4). See SOTHA.

Gwendolen hides her Falsehood behind her loins (J 82:21). The Covering Cherub's Loins enclose Babylon and Rome and the Israelites in captivity (J 89:38–42). But when man begins to examine the errors concerning sex (his most pressing problem), he begins the process of casting out all errors. "Albion hath enter'd the Loins, the place of the Last Judgment" (J 30:38).

When the Loins are depicted as scaly (as in Illustr Job 6), the sexual instinct has been corrupted.

LONDON is the metropolis of England. Here Blake lived all his life, except for the three years at Felpham, 1800–1803. He loved London, but at the same time was intensely depressed by its darkness (J 5:36; 16:9; 83:67), the pillars of smoke from the mills, and the degradation of its inhabitants: the beggars, the crowds of ragamuffins, the swarms of prostitutes. When he got out of the city—to Lambeth in 1793 and to Felpham in 1800—his relief found expression in tremendous creative activity.

"London" (SoE) is a record of his depression. The blackening of the churches was literal: all visitors noticed it; but the real blot on the Church was its complacence at the misery of those most unfortunate children, the chimneysweeps. The bloodstain on the palace is only symbolic: the State was guilty of the slaughter of its soldiers. Worst of all was the condition of the youthful harlots, who killed married love and infected mother and child with diseases (notably gonorrhea) which blinded the newborn babies. Another dismal account of London occurs in Jerusalem when Los walks round through London, from Highgate (north) to the Tower (east), to Bethlehem, or Bedlam (south), and to Westminster and Marybone (west). Everywhere he sees "every Minute Particular of Albion degraded & murder'd . . . the jewels [children] of Albion running down the kennels of the streets & lanes as if they were abhorr'd" (J 31:2–43). He beholds Babylon in the London streets (J 74:16), "London, blind & age-bent, begging thro' the Streets of Babylon, led by a child; his tears run down his beard" (J 84:11). Milton ends when Los's angry thundercloud is roused by the "Cry of the Poor Man" (Mil 42:34).

The coming of war made everything worse. When the plagues sent against America recoil upon England, London is smitten with leprosy (Am 15:3). English liberties are lost in the war-fever: Jerusalem falls, and London is a stone of her ruins (J 29:

19). Gwendolen dances, "reeling up the Street[s] of London" (*J* 58:3). The reluctant recruits "were carried away in thousands from London" (*J* 65:33).

Official religion was no help. "London's Guardian" (Canterbury) sickens (*Am* 15:9), and gives the helmet of prejudice to the king, to protect him against any new thoughts in the intellectual war (*Am c*:4). A fog envelops the city, "& aged ignorance preaches, canting, on a vast rock, perciev'd by those senses that are clos'd from thought: bleak, dark, abrupt, it stands & overshadows London city" (*Eur* 12:7). The chief Cathedral Cities are in deadly opposition to each other (*J* 74:5). Jerusalem is driven "far away from London's spires" (*J* 43:70).

It was not so always. Blake recalled the days of peace when "In the Exchanges of London every Nation walk'd, and London walk'd in every Nation, mutual in love & harmony. Albion cover'd the whole Earth, England encompass'd the Nations, mutual each within other's bosom in Visions of Regeneration" (*J* 24:42; cf. 79:22).

And it should be so again. For the foulness and misery which Blake saw around him was not the true, essential London. Therefore it was the poet's task, not only to rebuild Jerusalem in England, but also to build "the spiritual fourfold London" (*Mil* 6:1; 20:40; *J* 59:14).

Blake had had the idea in Lambeth and again in Felpham, but it came upon him most strongly when he returned from the country to the city and took lodgings in South Molton Street (*J* 38:40–43). "I behold London, a Human awful wonder of God! He says: 'Return, Albion, return! I give myself for thee. My Streets are my Ideas of Imagination. Awake Albion, awake! and let us awake up together. My Houses are Thoughts, my Inhabitants, Affections, the children of my thoughts walking within my blood-vessels, shut from my nervous form which sleeps upon the verge of Beulah' " (*J* 38:29).

"Found ye London!" Los cries to the Daughters of Beulah (*J* 83:23), and Enitharmon's rainbow appears to him "in the awful gloom" of the city (*J* 83:68). But already he has set up his furnaces, which are heard from "Hampstead's breadths & Highgate's heights, To Stratford & old Bow & across to the Gardens of Kensington on Tyburn's Brook" (*Mil* 6:9). His seventh Furnace is on the Tower of London (*J* 82:57). "Primrose Hill is the mouth of the Furnace & the Iron Door" (*J* 73:54). The new London is continuous from Golgonooza (*Mil* 6:1); indeed, Golgonooza "is the spiritual fourfold London in the loins of Albion" (*Mil* 20:40; *J* 53:18), "continually building & continually decaying desolate" (*J* 53:19)—"Continually Building, Continually Decaying, because of Love & Jealousy" (*J* 72, illustr.).

When Albion rises, "his left foot near London covers the shades of Tyburn . . . London is between his knees, its basements fourfold . . . his head bends over London" (*Mil* 39:36–46).

London has a special role as a Cathedral City. It is one of the Four (Verulam, London, York, Edinburgh) in which the other Twenty-four appear (*J* 46:24). They are identified with the Four Zoas, London being Luvah (*J* 74:3–4). In *Milton* (39:35), the quaternary was given as "London & Bath & Legions & Edinburgh," the four pillars of Albion's throne.

London & Canterbury tremble as the Spectre prophesies their disappearance (*J* 33:12). The Four mourn towards one another (*J* 46:24). At Gwendolen's laughter, "London and Canterbury groan in pain" (*J* 63:35). In the war, "London feels his brain cut round: Edinburgh's heart is circumscribed" (*J* 66:64). Los's furnaces "rage terrible" "from London to York & Edinburgh" (*J* 73:53). When they forsake Imagination for Reason, the Four are in deadly opposition; they become Spectres, while their Human Bodies sleep in Beulah (*J* 74:5–9).

LONDON STONE is a Roman milestone, now set against the south wall of St. Swithin's, Cannon Street, London. Camden believed it was the central miliarium, from which the

British high roads radiated and the distance on them was reckoned.

It was a place of druid execution; thus, with its central position, it summarized the whole system of Justice, the heart of the Polypus (*J* 67:37). Albion's forests "overspread all the Earth from London Stone" (*Mil* 6:3). Albion bids Hand and Hyle bring Los to justice, "here upon London stone" (*J* 42:50). After studying the condition of London, Los ponders it, sitting on London Stone (*J* 31:43). Standing on it, he forces his Spectre to kneel to him (*J* 8:27).

As a place of execution, Blake associated it with Stonehenge. The victims of the Druids "groan'd aloud on London Stone, | They groan'd aloud on Tyburn's Brook" (*J* 27:34). The Atlantic weeps over his children in Stonehenge and on London Stone (*J* 57:7). Urizen's ancient world is created from Stonehenge and London Stone (*J* 58: 46). Stonehenge has "chains of rocks round London Stone, of Reasonings" (*J* 66:2). Fallen men "look forth from Stone-henge: from the Cove round London Stone" (*J* 66:57). Reuben sleeps on London Stone (*J* 74:34). Brittannia in her sleep slays Albion with the knife of the Druid "in Stonehenge & on London Stone" (*J* 94:24).

LONDON'S GUARDIAN is the personification of orthodoxy. Therefore I believe he is not the Bishop of London, but the Archbishop of Canterbury (whose palace was in Lambeth), especially as he is given precedence over York.

When the plagues sent upon America recoil upon England, "Sick'ning lay London's Guardian, and the ancient miterd York" (*Am* 15:9). It is he who gives the king the helmet of prejudice, to protect his brain against generous thoughts in the intellectual warfare (*Am* c:4).

LONDON'S RIVER. See THAMES.

The TOWER OF LONDON is a gloomy state prison, in the east of the city, on the Thames. The square White Tower rises in the center; around it are eleven other towers.

"London's dark frowning Towers" lament over Ahania and Enion (*Mil* 19:39).

Los walks "To where the Tower of London frown'd dreadful over Jerusalem, a building of Luvah, builded in Jerusalem's eastern gate, to be his secluded Court" (*J* 31:23). Los sees "the envious blight" of Cambel "above his Seventh Furnace on London's Tower on the Thames" (*J* 82:56). But eventually "London's towers | Recieve the Lamb of God to dwell | In England's green & pleasant bowers" (*J* 77:10).

LONDONDERRY is a county in Ulster, the northern province of Ireland. With the other counties of Ulster, it is assigned to Dan, Asher, and Naphtali (*J* 72:26).

LONGFORD is a county in Leinster, the eastern province of Ireland. With the other counties of Leinster, it is assigned to Judah, Issachar, and Zebulun (*J* 72:18).

The LOOKING GLASS of Nature (a familiar Platonic symbol) mirrors the realities of Eternity on the material plane. "There Exist in that Eternal World the Permanent Realities of Every Thing which we see reflected in this Vegetable Glass of Nature" (*LJ*, *K* 605). When all things become "Unhumanized," there is "No Human Form but Sexual, & a little weeping Infant pale reflected Multitudinous in the Looking Glass of Enitharmon" (*J* 63:18–21; see also l. 38).

In Blake's ninety-ninth illustration to Dante, the Queen of Heaven holds the scepter of female dominion and the looking glass of materialism.

The LORD'S SUPPER and baptism are the two sacraments of the Protestant churches. The Supper is a service commemorating Jesus and his Last Supper: for Blake, the sharing of the bread and the wine symbolizes the Brotherhood of Man.

See SACRAMENTS.

LOS is Poetry, the expression in this world of the Creative Imagination. He is the manifestation in time and space of Urthona, the deepest Zoa, who is the center of each Individual. On the verge of "the billows of Eternal Death [this world]," Urthona takes the name of Los (J 39:8), who is henceforth "the Vehicular Form of strong Urthona" (J 53:1), until the very end, when Los is reabsorbed into Urthona.

His position is North; he works as a blacksmith; his sense is the Ear; his element is Earth; his elementals are the Gnomes; his Emanation is Enitharmon; his planet is the (spiritual) sun; and he creates the material sun. It is reasonable to suppose that his name is an anagram of "Sol."

Los is the last faculty of man to start functioning; therefore, counting anti-clockwise from Tharmas, the "parent power," he is the fourth Zoa (FZ i:14–18; Mil 24:8; J 39:7). As both the creator and the great champion of Man, he resembles Jesus (J 96:22), who constantly supports him. It is he who sustains Shadrach, Meshach, and Abed-nego in the fiery furnace of Nebuchadnezzar; "and the form of the fourth [was] like the Son of God" (Dan iii:25); he also sustains the Strong Man, the Beautiful Man, and the Ugly Man in the last battle of King Arthur, "and the form of the fourth was like the Son of God" ($DesC$ V, K 578).

As the poet, Los is "the Prophet of Eternity," who reveals the basic truths. He is once equated with the ideal prophet Elijah (J 44:30). He directly inspires Blake himself (Mil 22:4; 36:21). He creates the line of poet-prophets who destroy the kings (J 73:40). He is the spiritual revolutionist, whose son Orc is outward revolution. At the end of $Europe$, when the French Revolution begins, Los wakes in the dawn and calls all his sons to the strife of blood (15:9). In $Milton$, it is Los (no longer Urizen) who operates "the Plow . . . to pass over the Nations" (6:13; 7:5; 8:20) in preparation for the New Age. (In $Jerusalem$, Albion operates the Plow.) Los also runs the Winepress of war. The poem ends with his preparing for "the Great Harvest & Vintage" (Mil 43:1).

Los, the expression of the Imagination, is the creator of all that we see. "All Things Exist in the Human Imagination" (J 69:25).

See IMAGINATION. Like his original, Urthona, Los is a blacksmith, smelting the crude ore, consuming the slag, and casting the molten iron into new forms. "The blow of his Hammer is Justice, the swing of his Hammer Mercy, the force of Los's Hammer is eternal Forgiveness" (J 88:49). He has seven furnaces, evidently corresponding to the seven Eyes of God; at the climax of creation the Divine Finger touches the seventh Furnace.

Los creates Golgonooza, the city of art (FZ v:76, etc.); he creates Jerusalem, the idea of liberty (FZ viii:190); he creates Erin, the belief that all living things, especially the body and its impulses, are holy (J 11:8).

He also gives "a body to Falsehood that it may be cast off for ever" (J 12:13). Only thus can an error be limited, recognized, and annihilated. His first great feat is forging a body for Urizen (Ur 10:35–13:19, etc.). In doing this, he creates Time (Ur 10:18; FZ iv:179); indeed, he is Time itself (Mil 24:68), which mercifully prevents error from being eternal. He creates the material sun, which he binds to the spine of Urizen (BoL 5:34–47). Urizen thus becomes its regent, the equivalent of the Greek Apollo. Los recreates this sun for us every morning (Mil 29:23, 41); he also creates the material Moon (J 36:4). In fact, he creates the whole universe (FZ iv:27; vii:380), including the Mundane Shell (Mil 34:31; J 42:78) and the Twenty-seven Heavens and their Churches (J 75:6). He himself is the twenty-eighth (J 39:13), thus again being related to Jesus, who breaks the cycle.

Los is also the conductor of the human souls at birth and at death. "Los conducts the Spirits to be Vegetated into great Golgonooza" (Mil 29:47), where Enitharmon weaves their bodies. "The Souls descending to the Body wail on the right hand [south] of Los, & those deliver'd from the Body on the left hand [north]. For Los against the east his force continually bends" (Mil 26:16). He also fixes the three Classes of men on this earth (Mil 2:26; 25:26).

Los appears first in $Europe$ (3:7), but

only to retire as "strong Urthona," for the night has come. Enitharmon is thus left free to establish her female dominion over mankind. When dawn comes at the end of the poem, the French Revolution is breaking out. "Then Los arose . . . and with a cry that shook all nature to the utmost pole, call'd all his sons to the strife of blood" (15:9).

In *The Book of Urizen*, Los is the prenatal force shaping the embryo. Urizen, who has been rent from his side (6:4), is attempting to set himself up as tyrant; Los therefore binds him into a temporal form. Los pities; pity divides the soul; and Enitharmon becomes a separate being. On her he begets Orc, baptizes him in the "springs of sorrow" (20:4), and binds him down with the Chain of Jealousy.

The Book of Los retells the binding of Urizen, ending when Los creates the material sun and fastens it to Urizen's spine; then "a Form was completed, a Human Illusion in darkness and deep clouds involv'd" (5:55).

In *The Book of Ahania*, Los beats the fiery beam of Fuzon into a mass with the sun (2:47).

The Song of Los, which he sings to the four harps which are the continents, outlines the religious life of man from Adam to the Last Judgment. In "Africa," the children of Los (the prophets) give Urizen's laws and religions to the nations (Blake had anticipated Shelley's theory—in *Defence of Poetry*—that "poets are the unacknowledged legislators of the world"); mankind becomes more and more spiritually debased, until Materialism is complete under Newton and Locke. In *America* and *Europe*, revolution breaks out; *The Song of Los* ("Asia") ends with the general resurrection, while the grave triumphs.

Although *The Four Zoas* deals with "The Death and Judgement of Albion the Ancient Man," Albion sleeps through most of the epic; the active hero is Los. "Daughter of Beulah, Sing [Los's] fall into Division & his Resurrection to Unity: his fall into the Generation of decay & death, & his Regenera-

tion by the Resurrection from the dead" (i:20).

The tale begins with the division of Tharmas and Enion at the onset of puberty; the result is the birth of their children, Los and Enitharmon (i:192). These two have already fallen; the events leading up to their birth in the material world are described later.

Urthona was working at his forge when Urizen and Luvah began warring; as a result, Enitharmon (pity) became separated from Urthona. "Dividing from his aking bosom fled a portion of his life [Enitharmon]; shrieking upon the wind she fled, and Tharmas took her in, pitying. Then Enion in jealous fear murder'd her & hid her in her bosom . . . Urthona stood in terror, but not long; his spectre [Los] fled to Enion & his body fell" (i:523–31).

Los, as the Spectre, gives a fuller account.

All my [Urthona's] sons fled from my side; then pangs smote me unknown before. I saw my loins begin to break forth into veiny pipes & writhe before me in the wind englobing; trembling with strong vibrations, the bloody mass [the Globe of Blood] began to animate. I, bending over, wept bitter tears incessant. Still beholding how the piteous form dividing & dividing from my loins, a weak & piteous soft cloud of snow, a female pale & weak, I soft embrac'd my counter part & call'd it Love. I nam'd her Enitharmon, but found myself & her together issuing down the tide which now our rivers were become, delving thro' caverns huge of goary blood, strugg[l]ing to be deliver'd from our bonds. She strove in vain; not so Urthona strove, for breaking forth, a shadow blue, obscure & dismal, from the breathing Nostrils of Enion I issued into the air, divided from Enitharmon.   (iv:92)

Later, he tells Enitharmon about it, with a few more details.

One dread morn of gory blood, the manhood was divided, for the gentle passions, making way thro' the infinite labyrinths of the heart & thro' the nostrils issuing in odorous stupefaction, stood before the Eyes of Man a female bright. . . . sudden down I sunk with cries of blood issuing downward in the veins which now my rivers were become, rolling in tubelike forms shut up within themselves descending down. I sunk along the goary tide even to the place of seed . . . I was divided in darkness & oblivion; thou an infant woe and I an infant terror in the womb of Enion. My masculine spirit, scorning the frail body, issued forth from Enion's brain In this deformed form, leaving thee there till times pass'd over thee; but still my spirit returning hover'd and form'd a Male, to be a counterpart to thee, O Love Darken'd & Lost! In due time issuing forth from Enion's womb thou & that demon Los were born. (vii:278–95) Enitharmon remembers little of it all. When Beulah fell as a result of the conspiracy of Urizen and Luvah, "Los was born & Enitharmon, but how, I know not; then forgetfulness quite wrap'd me up a period, nor do I more remember till I stood beside Los in the Cavern dark, enslav'd to vegetative forms according to the Will of Luvah" (vii:259).

After their birth, Los and Enitharmon rapidly drain the strength from the aging Enion, and wander away from her. For nine years they delight in the revelations of Eno (who opens the moment and the atom of space) and the visions of Beulah. Their embryo passions begin: Los feels alternate love and hate; she, scorn and jealousy; "they kiss'd not nor embrac'd for shame & fear" (i:238). Los announces the purpose of their existence: man is sunk into a deadly sleep, "But we, immortal in our own strength, survive by stern debate till we have drawn the Lamb of God into a mortal form" (i: 293). Enitharmon retorts by invoking Urizen instead, who descends and announces himself as God. Los defies him, and feeling love arise, embraces the reluctant Enithar-

mon. They sit at their nuptial feast in discontent and scorn while the demons of the deep sing the song of war. She flees from him until he dies, then she revives him with a love song and leads him into shadows. They rejoice at the torments of Luvah and Vala (ii:213) and mischievously cause Ahania to hear the laments of the fading Enion, thus ensuring Ahania's separation from Urizen (ii:239).

When Urizen has finished his world, it is chaos, and his furnaces are ruined. Tharmas orders Los to "Rebuild this Universe beneath my indignant power, a Universe of Death & Decay" (iv:27). Los is reluctant; therefore Tharmas manifests his power by tearing Enitharmon away, then returning her. Los rebuilds the furnaces (iv:165), binding Urizen into a definite form. The Saviour fixes the limits of Satan and Adam, thus limiting Eternal Death, and his finger touches Los's seventh Furnace (iv:277). Enitharmon separates into the Globe of Blood, and the two shrink into fixed space (v:12). Los builds Golgonooza (v:76). Orc is born; when he reaches the age of fourteen, Los binds him down on a mountain top, and gives the Spectre charge over him, "concenter'd into Love of Parent, Storgous Appetite, Craving" (v:113). But when Los repents, he cannot release Orc (v:155), and the couple returns to Golgonooza.

In Night vii, Los reaches his lowest point, then recovers. He is still distinct from the Spectre of Urthona, but Enitharmon has become only a Shadow. Beneath the fatal Tree of Mystery, the Spectre tempts her; as a result, she gives birth to the Shadowy Female (vii:317); then many of the dead burst the bottoms of their tombs and are released into dreams of Ulro, "male forms without female counterparts" (vii:329). The Spectre then tempts Los, but Los embraces both the Spectre and Enitharmon (vii:370), and builds Golgonooza, opening the threefold world (vii:380). Enitharmon eats of the fruit of the Tree, and persuades Los to eat also (vii:395).

The Spectre, terrified at the sight of the spectres, repents and takes the blame on himself, and suggests that Los and he give them counterparts, "for without a Created body the Spectre is Eternal Death" (vii: 410). Both Los and Enitharmon see the Lamb of God descending, clothed in Luvah's robes of blood (vii:414, 424). Los feels the creative urge, and Enitharmon, in whose bosom the spectres take refuge, urges Los to give them sublime forms, so that "they shall be ransoms for our Souls that we may live" (vii:455). So Los begins the creation of art: "first he drew a line upon the walls of shining heaven, and Enitharmon tinc- tur'd it with beams of blushing love. It re- main'd permanent, a lovely form, inspir'd, divinely human" (vii:467); and the weep- ing spectres assimilate to the forms.

The aesthetic approach divides the ranks of war. Rintrah and Palamabron return to infant innocence; Orc rejoices and becomes a father to his brethren; Urthona's Spectre is comforted; Tharmas has a new hope of Enion's return. Los draws Urizen's Shadow from the war, "leaving his Spectrous form, which could not be drawn away. Then he divided Thiriel, the Eldest of Urizen's sons: Urizen became Rintrah, Thiriel became Palamabron. Thus dividing the powers of Every Warrior, startled was Los; he found his Enemy Urizen now in his hands; he wonder'd that he felt love & not hate" (vii: 492).

In Night viii, Los and Enitharmon both see the Lamb of God descending (viii:20). Los conducts the wandering spectres to Enitharmon, who weaves them bodies of vegetation (viii:38). Urizen, terrified at the sight of the Lamb in Luvah's robes, declares war; Los builds the walls of Golgonooza against the battle (viii:109). With his sons he forms "a vast family," which, uniting, becomes Jerusalem (viii:190). From her the Lamb of God is born (viii:260) and is cruci- fied (viii:325). Los takes the body from the cross and lays it in the sepulcher "which Los had hewn in the rock of Eternity for himself: he hew'd it despairing of Life Eter- nal" (viii:339).

When Rahab, the false religion, who had caused the Crucifixion, confronts Los (viii:

345), he declares himself and names his children; the last of his sons is Milton, the last of his daughters Mary. The succeeding tale of the enmity of Satan is an anticipation of the Hayley quarrel described in *Milton*, and concludes with the appointment of the Seven Eyes and the self-sacrifice of Jesus, the seventh.

When Urizen forgets his wisdom "in forms of priesthood, in the dark delusions of repentance" (viii:464), Los is among those who feel "the stony stupor, & his head roll'd down beneath into the Abysses of his bosom; the vessels of his blood dart forth upon the wind in pipes, writhing about in the Abyss" (viii:471), while Eni- tharmon vegetates. Tharmas and Urthona, however, give their strength to Los.

The Last Judgment (Night ix) begins at the moment of death.

And Los & Enitharmon builded Jeru- salem, weeping over the Sepulcher & over the Crucified body which, to their Phantom Eyes, appear'd still in the Sepulcher; but Jesus stood beside them in the spirit, separating their spirit from their body. Terrified at Non Ex- istence, for such they deem'd the death of the body, Los his vegetable hands outstretch'd; his right hand, branch- ing out in fibrous strength, siez'd the Sun; His left hand, like dark roots, cover'd the Moon, and tore them down, cracking the heavens across from immense to immense. Then fell the fires of Eternity with loud & shrill sound of Loud Trumpet thundering along from heaven to heaven. (ix:1)

Thereafter, Los has nothing to do in his own person, for Man has waked and his Zoas take their original form. On the Sixth Day, Urthona manifests. "Then Los, who is Urthona, rose in all his regenerate power" (ix:801), and the sea gives up its dead. Ur- thona then makes the Bread of Eternity. "Urthona is arisen in his strength, no long- er now divided from Enitharmon, no longer the Spectre Los. Where is the Spectre of Prophecy? where the delusive Phantom? Departed: & Urthona rises from the ruinous Walls in all his ancient strength to form the golden armour of science for intellectual War" (ix:849).

Milton opens with the Bard's Song, which analyzes the quarrel of Satan and Palamabron (2:24). The preliminaries are sketched in very briefly, in inserted plates. Los binds Urizen and himself divides: Enitharmon separates as the Globe of Blood, while his Spectre separates from his back. Golgonooza is built; Orc and the Shadowy Female are born; "At last Enitharmon brought forth Satan, Refusing Form in vain" (3:41). Los is working in London, forging the Plow and Harrow of Revolution, to pass over the nations (6:13); his initial working is distinguishing the three Classes of men (2:26).

The quarrel of Palamabron-Blake and Satan-Hayley is then described in detail. Satan is the corporeal friend, interfering with the poet's creative work. Los errs in permitting Satan to run the Harrow (7:12); confusion ensues. For the details of the quarrel, see HAYLEY. It ends by Los's identifying Satan as Urizen.

The Bard's Song rouses Milton to descend. Enitharmon fears him: "Surely to unloose my bond is this Man come! Satan shall be unloos'd upon Albion!" (17:32); and Los in terror opposes his descent, until he recalls the ancient prophecy that Milton shall "set free Orc from his Chain of Jealousy" (20:60).

Los also descends and becomes one with Blake (22:12). Rintrah and Palamabron fear Blake's revolutionary tendencies (22:29), and recall the errors of Christianity; but Los silences them by repeating the prophecy (23:32), and affirming that the reappearance of Milton is "the Signal that the Last Vintage now approaches" (24:42). Into the Wine-press of Luvah, Los puts "the Oppressor & the Opressed together" (25:6). "This Wine-press is call'd War on Earth: it is the Printing-Press [history] of Los" (27:8). He conducts the spirits to be vegetated into Great Golgonooza, where Enitharmon takes charge (29:47). His sons build the bodies (26:33), surrounding the Passions with porches (28:1); others build

the divisions of time (28:44) and the sky (29:4). Los himself creates the sun every morning (29:41). Thus the egocentric world in which each individual lives is the creation of his imagination; "Such is the World of Los, the labour of six thousand years" (29:64).

Los takes no part in the final apocalypse, but at the very end, he and Enitharmon rise over the hills of Surrey (42:31); in anger he listens to the cry of the poor man, and all things are prepared for "the Great Harvest & Vintage of the Nations" (43:1).

In *Jerusalem*, although Blake once sees Los at work (15:21), Los may be taken as Blake himself, the poet developing his own philosophy and warring against the spiritual evils that afflict his nation. His great task is "To open the Eternal Worlds, to open the immortal Eyes of Man inwards into the Worlds of Thought, into Eternity ever expanding in the Bosom of God, the Human Imagination" (5:18). Los takes his Globe of Fire to search Albion's bosom (31:3).

Enitharmon corresponds to Catherine Blake; she is "a vegetated mortal Wife of Los, his Emanation, yet his Wife till the Sleep of Death is past" (14:13). She begins to divide eastward from Los (pity divides the soul) when he hears the lamentations of the lost Jerusalem over her children (5:67). She continues to divide (12:7) and becomes the Globe of Blood (17:51). Although Los takes her and her guard, the Spectre, into his bosom (30:16), she continues to divide from him (53:6), until she becomes entirely separate and appears to him as a lovely female weeping (86:57), and they are born from Enion. Los then feels love for her (87:2), but she proclaims her independence (87:12) and the domination of woman (88:16). Obdurate to the last, she fears annihilation as the poet's song draws to a close (92:8); Los replies that in Eternity the sexes must vanish and cease (92:13); and in his final speech he affirms they shall not die but shall be united in Jesus (93:19).

The Spectre is Los's chief enemy. Dividing westward from Los's back, he preaches despair (7:6), but Los compels him to assist at his furnaces (8:15) "till he should bring the Sons & Daughters of Jerusalem to be the Sons & Daughters of Los" (10:3). The first product of the furnaces is Erin (11:8); she is the holiness of all living things, particularly the innocence of the body and its impulses—the beginning of Blake's philosophy.

The Spectre reappears near the end of the poem, rejoicing at the division of Los and Enitharmon, which he has caused (88:35). He proclaims that "While you are under the dominion of a jealous Female . . . you shall want all the Minute Particulars of Life" (88:41–43). Los defies him and his philosophy, then smites him with his hammer (91:45), breaking him into shivers, as he had threatened (8:10). "Thus Los alter'd his Spectre, & every Ratio of his Reason he alter'd time after time with dire pain & many tears, till he had completely divided him into a separate space" (91:51).

But Los's real concern is the salvation of Albion, who has turned his back on the Divine Vision (4:13, 22). In the first confusion of the fall, Los builds Golgonooza in London (10:17), and walks round the walls night and day (13:55) as Albion's guard (19:38). He fixes down the counties of the British Isles (16:28).

At the beginning of Chapter ii, Albion sets himself up as punisher and judge (28:4); the dread Tree of Moral Virtue and the Law shoots up beneath his heel (28:15). Los then takes his globe of fire to search Albion's bosom (31:3), and walks through the degraded city of London (31:14). He sits on London Stone (the place of judgment), "but the interiors of Albion's fibres & nerves were hidden from Los; astonish'd he beheld only the petrified surfaces and saw his Furnaces in ruins" (32:4). At the contentions of Vala, he opens his furnaces before her (34:19), and cries: "O Albion, why wilt thou Create a Female Will?" (34:31). He tries to send Reuben into the Promised Land by closing his four senses (34:47, 53; 36:5, 13), but Reuben always returns. Albion flees to Los's Gate of Death,

where Los confronts him (39:11), and summons the Cathedral Cities (religion) to aid him (40:3). Albion tries to destroy their Emanations; but when Los opens his furnaces before him, he sees that "the accursed things were his own affections and his own beloveds" (42:3). Furious, he orders his two oldest sons to bring Los to judgment on London Stone (42:50), but the Divine Hand protects him. Los builds the Mundane Shell (42:78); then he denounces the state of the world (43:12). The Cathedral Cities, failing to force Albion back to Eden (44:3), transfer their power to Los (44:30).

When war breaks out (47:4), Albion utters his last words, "Hope is banish'd from me" (47:18), and sinks into the arms of the Saviour, who reposes him on the Rock of Ages, then erects over him a tomb of the inspired books of the Bible. When Eno (interpretation) peruses it (48:40), Los sees the finger of God touch his seventh Furnace (48:45).

In Chapter iii, Los fights Natural Religion and the horrors of war. He weeps over Albion, "and the roots of Albion's Tree enter'd the Soul of Los" (53:4). He builds Golgonooza, the Spiritual Fourfold London (53:18). He sings his cradle song, for "This World is all a Cradle for the erred wandering Phantom" (56:8), and the Daughters of Albion begin to reply to him. He fixes the two Contraries, "to Create a World of Generation from the World of Death" (58:18). He fixes Hand and Koban over the sun and Hyle and Skofield over the moon (58:29); he also forms gates in the Veil of Vala (59:5). In the midst of the war, he beholds the Divine Vision among the flames of his furnaces (62:35). He denounces female chastity, at which Gwendolen laughs (63:32). He sees with horror the druid temple of Natural Religion (66:8). He demolishes the kings (73:31), and creates the prophets to oppose them (73:40). He drives the Sons and Daughters of Albion from their ancient mountains; they become the Twelve Gods of Asia (74:21). He fixes the Twenty-seven Heavens of Rahab (75:6); he himself is the twenty-eighth (39:13).

In Chapter iv, Los is chiefly concerned with opposing the domination of the Female Will, caused by the outstanding error of Christianity in exalting chastity. With his iron mace he protects Albion against the attacks of Albion's Sons (78:3). He tries in vain to send the Daughters elsewhere (80: 42). He attacks Cambel (82:57). The pangs of love draw him down into his loins, which become a fountain of veiny pipes (82:83), and Enitharmon appears to him like a faint rainbow (83:67). The Daughters of Albion call upon Los for aid (84:25); and when on Gwendolen's lie they build their allegory of mundane marriage, Los smiles (for it is a Divine Analogy) and leads the wandering Reuben into it (85:3). Los sings his Watch Song and has a vision of the perfect Jerusalem (85:22).

His quarrel with the now completely separated Enitharmon follows (87:3–88:43). He demolishes the Spectre, who has caused the trouble (91:43). At last the races amalgamate, forming the English (92:1).

When Albion wakes, he compels the Zoas to their places and proper tasks; "Urthona he beheld, mighty labouring at his Anvil, in the Great Spectre Los unwearied labouring & weeping: therefore the Sons of Eden praise Urthona's Spectre in songs, because he kept the Divine Vision in time of trouble" (95:17). Albion then sees Jesus in "the likeness & similitude of Los" (96:7, 22). "Self was lost in the contemplation of faith and wonder at the Divine Mercy & at Los's sublime honour" (96:31). Thenceforth, Los is Urthona, and with the other Zoas rises into Albion's bosom (96:41).

The CHILDREN OF LOS. Los and Enitharmon may be said to have had only one child, Orc, or Revolution, for every real poet is in some measure a revolutionist. But when Los lists his many sons (FZ viii:357–62), Orc is not included, because these other sons are all aspects of Orc.

The first two sons, Rintrah (just wrath) and Palamabron (pity), are the beginnings of revolution. Their number is made four

by the addition of Theotormon (frustrate desire) and Bromion (frustrate thought). These four never become generated (Mil 24:10), but remain with their father Los. The number is then brought up to sixteen by the addition of the twelve sons of Israel; but these wander away in pursuit of Tirzah (the ideal of female chastity).

But in The Four Zoas list (viii:358) Blake inserted sixteen names between Bromion and Reuben, seven of which are not to be found elsewhere. They are Antamon (the male seed), Ananton, Ozoth (the optic nerve), Ohana, Sotha (frustrate sex, which becomes war), Mydon, Ellayol, Natho, Gon, Harhath, and Satan (error); then Har (man in the state of self-love), Ochim (sorrows), Ijim (aimless lust), and Adam (man in the flesh). After the sons of Israel follow the poet-kings David and Solomon; then comes the quaternary of Paul (founder of the Church Militant), Constantine (establisher of the Church Militant and persecutor), Charlemaine (founder of the Holy Roman Empire), and Luther (reform). The list of sons concludes with Milton.

The Daughters are then listed. First are the four Emanations of the first Four Sons: Ocalythron, Elynittria, Oothoon, and Leutha. Elythiria and Enanto are obviously the Emanations of Antamon and Ananton. Manathu Vorcyon seems to be included by error, as he is the male counterpart of Ethinthus (fleshly love), whose name follows his. Moab and Midian represent the outlandish women who tempt the sons of Israel; Adah and Zillah are the polygamous wives of Lamech; Caina is Blake's name for the sister-wife of Cain; Naamah is the wife of Noah; Tamar seduced her father-in-law Judah. These evil women are followed by Rahab (harlotry) and Tirzah (prudery); and the list concludes with Mary the mother of Jesus. The latter part of this list was revised as the Maternal Line (J 62).

But Los and Enitharmon had "myriads more" of children not listed (FZ viii:366; Ur 20:45). Among them are all the false religions: "Every one is a fallen Son of the

Spirit of Prophecy" (*Mil* 24:75). The children of Los (the prophets) gave Urizen's laws to the nations (*SoL* 3:9).

LOTHO is one of Tiriel's sons (*Tir* iv:45, 73).

LOT'S WIFE, on looking back at the burning of Sodom, was changed to a pillar of salt (*Gen* xix:26). "Lot's Wife being Changed into [a] Pillar of Salt alludes to the Mortal Body being render'd a Permanent Statue [i.e., State], but not Changed or Transformed into Another Identity while it retains its own Individuality" (*LJ*, *K* 607).

LOWTH is a county of Leinster, the eastern province of Ireland. With the other counties of Leinster, it is assigned to Judah, Issachar, and Zebulun (*J* 72:18).

LUBAN is the vagina, the Gate of Golgonooza which opens into this world. It is "the North Gate, in the West of the North, toward Beulah [marriage]" (*J* 59:22). Los built it "Upon the Limit of Translucence [Satan] . . . Tharmas laid the Foundation & Los finish'd it in howling woe" (*FZ* v:77). There "he had erected many porches where branched the Mysterious Tree, where the Spectrous dead wail" (*FZ* vii:434). Tharmas also founded Bowlahoola outside the Gate, because of Satan (*Mil* 24:49).

In Luban, Enitharmon erected her looms (*FZ* viii:36). See CATHEDRON.

The Sons of Los labor in Luban, also in Allamanda and Golgonooza, and around Udan-Adan, snaring the bodiless Spectres and giving them physical bodies (*Mil* 26:24). Theotormon and Sotha work particularly in the Gate, driving the Spectres into Human Lineaments (*Mil* 28:21).

LUCIFER ("the light-bearer") is the morning star. Under this name, Isaiah celebrated the death of the King of Babylon: "How art thou fallen from heaven, O Lucifer, son of the morning!" (*Isaiah* xiv:12). Origen was the first to apply this passage to Satan, an interpretation generally accepted. "Lucifer" thus became the name of Satan before his fall.

In *The Gates of Paradise*, Blake calls Satan "The Son of Morn in weary Night's decline" (Epilogue 7).

Blake chose Lucifer to be the first of the seven Eyes of God (*J* 55:32); i.e., the initial step away from God on the path of Experience. Lucifer was proverbially proud; his blind selfishness inspired him to try to make himself the center of the universe. (Nothing is more self-centered than the newborn baby.)

As an Eye of God, however, Lucifer is not Satan; neither is he adequate for the salvation of man. "Lucifer refus'd to die for Satan & in pride he forsook his charge" (*FZ* viii:399; *Mil* 13:18). In *Milton* 32:8–10, "Hillel, who is Lucifer," as the first of the seven Angels of the Presence, tells Milton that they are "not Individuals but States," through which man must pass.

A water color entitled "Satan in his Original Glory" shows the crowned Lucifer extending the globe and scepter. The scepter of temporal power lies heavy upon a scroll which two figures are endeavoring to unroll. A recording angel sits above three angels trumpeting downward; beneath them, a figure descends with a book of laws for the starry world below. Beside the cross-surmounted globe of spiritual authority, a female intervenes between a figure reading a book and two fleeing babes. Beneath the globe a figure points to a hint of flames behind Lucifer's robe. There are several figures of woe, including a youth attempting to embrace a maiden, who points upward, in warning against Lucifer.

LUTHER (Martin, 1483–1546) was the founder of the Reformation in Germany, and the most influential in the forming of the Anglican Church.

Paul, Constantine, Charlemaine, and Luther constitute a quaternary, representing the four great Christian orthodox churches. They are numbers thirty-four through thirty-seven of the thirty-eight Sons of Los, the last being Milton (*FZ* viii:362).

In the list of the Twenty-seven Heavens

or Churches, they complete the cycle, being the last four of the Seven who begin with Abraham (*Mil* 37:42; *J* 13:32; 75:17). "And where Luther ends, Adam begins again in Eternal Circle" (*J* 75:24).

These last Seven represent the Church Militant, which uses force to promulgate its doctrines, whereas Blake believed that Thought is more powerful than armies. Therefore, the Seven are "the Male-Females, the Dragon Forms, Religion hid in War, a Dragon red & hidden Harlot" (*Mil* 37:42; *J* 75:17). Blake blamed Luther because he "left the Priest & join'd the Soldier" (On Boyd, *K* 413). "Remember how Calvin and Luther in fury premature sow'd War and stern division between Papists & Protestants. Let it not be so now! O go not forth in Martyrdoms & Wars!" (*Mil* 23:47).

A chief source of the errors of the quaternary was its emphasis on the physical resurrection of Lazarus; and they are "stretch'd over Europe and Asia" (*Mil* 24:33). Blake also told Crabb Robinson that Calvin's "house" was "better than . . . Luther's"; "In *Luther's* there were *harlots*" (*CR* 260, 291).

To reverse their errors and reach the Truth, one must go in reverse through all these religions; therefore "the enterance of the First Heaven" is "named Luther" (*Mil* 35:62).

LUVAH is the third of the four Zoas. He is the Prince of Love (*FZ* i:325; ii:104; iv:142; v:42; ix:700); his name might be derived from "lover." Love is the greatest of the emotions, and Luvah includes all of them, especially its contrary, Hate (*FZ* v:42). Therefore the Tower of London is "a building of Luvah" (*J* 31:24). His place in man is the Heart (*FZ* i:262; ii:143; iii:95) or the Center, "unapproachable for ever" (*J* 12: 56). However, at the final consummation, when Albion puts the reformed Urizen in charge of Luvah, Urizen announces: "Luvah & Vala, henceforth you are Servants; obey & live. You shall forget your former state; return, & Love in peace, into your place, the place of seed, not in brain or

heart" (*FZ* ix:363). Apparently, Reason insists that love should express itself only through creation.

Luvah is a weaver (*J* 95:17), though we never see him at his loom. His compass-point is east (*FZ* vi:280; *Mil* 19:17; *J* 98: 16). His realm is Beulah (*FZ* ix:383, 558). His sense is smell (*J* 98:17); his metal is silver (*J* 97:9); his element is fire, and his elementals the Genii (*J* 13:26); his art is music (*FZ* ix:711); his Cathedral City is London (*J* 74:4); and his Emanation is Vala (natural beauty).

Luvah is closely associated with Jesus. When Luvah is perverted into Hate, he causes the Incarnation; "for when Luvah sunk down, [Jesus] himself put on [Luvah's] robes of blood [the flesh] lest the state call'd Luvah should cease; & the Divine Vision walked in robes of blood till he who slept [Albion] should awake" (*FZ* ii:263). Jesus is Love in the human form. He bears all Luvah's afflictions (*FZ* i:364). "The Lamb of God descended thro' the twelve portions of Luvah, bearing his sorrows & recieving all his cruel wounds" (*FZ* viii: 323). "As the Sons of Albion have done to Luvah, so they have in him done to the Divine Lord & Saviour" (*J* 25:6). Luvah also wears the crown of thorns (*FZ* ix:711); he too is crucified (*FZ* vii *b*:166; *J* 65:8); and Jesus is closed in Luvah's Sepulcher (*J* 24: 51).

Luvah is mentioned first in *The Book of Thel*; the Cloud asks her: "O virgin, know'st thou not our steeds drink of the golden springs where Luvah doth renew his horses?" (3:7). Thus early Blake had the Zoas in mind; but Luvah does not reappear in his writings until *The Four Zoas*, where his animals are Bulls. See BULLS.

Originally, Luvah and Vala enjoyed a Golden Age of innocence and youth in Vala's garden of shadows (*FZ* i:286; ii:79; ix:376, 798). See VALA'S GARDEN, under VALA. They became separated when Vala, pregnant by Albion, "brought forth Urizen, Prince of Light, first born of Generation. Then behold a wonder to the Eyes of the now fallen Man; a double form Vala appear'd, a Male and female; shudd'ring pale the Fallen Man recoil'd from the Enormity & call'd them Luvah & Vala" (*FZ* vii:244). Feeling guilt for her embrace, Vala took refuge in her garden, weeping for her lost Luvah (*FZ* i:286).

Meanwhile Urizen conspires with Luvah to establish their empire over Man. Urizen would control man's imagination, allowing Luvah to dominate man's reason. "Deep in the North I place my lot; thou in the South . . . thou, siezing the chariots of the morning, Go, outfleeting ride afar into the Zenith high, bending thy furious course Southward" (*FZ* i:491). They are both activated by "foul ambition" (*FZ* iv:141); and Luvah has intoxicated Urizen on "the wine of the Almighty [desire for omnipotence?]" (*FZ* v:234).

Luvah refuses to cooperate in Urizen's scheme; nevertheless, he seizes Urizen's chariot of light, drawn by the horses of instruction (*FZ* i:264; iii:31; iv:113; v:208; ix:94). "How rag'd the golden horses of Urizen, bound to the chariot of Love" (*FZ* vii *b*:201).

The consequences of that fatal act are such as to make the event forever memorable. Luvah and Urizen war about the holy tent of Albion (*FZ* i:480, 517). Urthona falls and is divided. Suddenly Urizen and his armies withdraw to his coveted North, "leaving the rage of Luvah to pour its fury on himself & on the Eternal Man" (*FZ* i: 539). Luvah and Vala ride triumphant in the bloody sky (*FZ* i:409), until Tharmas, reddening with rage, smites with his sheephook (*FZ* i:413). Suddenly they all fall together into an unknown space (Ulro).

The dying Albion then resigns his scepter to Urizen. "Thy brother Luvah hath smitten me, but pity thou his youth" (*FZ* ii:7). But preparing to build the Mundane Shell, Urizen casts Luvah into his Furnaces of affliction, and Vala, forgetting that he was her Luvah, feeds the furnaces in cruel delight (*FZ* ii:72; *J* 7:30). Here "wretched Luvah is howling in the Furnaces, in flames among Albion's Spectres, to prepare the Spectre of Albion to reign over thee, O Los,

forming the Spectres of Albion according to his rage: to prepare the Spectre Sons of Adam" (*J* 7:38). Luvah recalls his metamorphoses of Vala, first as earth-worm, then serpent, then dragon, and finally as beloved infant. "O when will you return, Vala the Wanderer?" (*FZ* ii:81–110).

When he is completely melted, the furnaces are unsealed, and the Lions of Urizen use the molten metal to create the astronomical universe, which is Emotion solidified by Reason (*FZ* ii:117).

The suppressed Luvah becomes a cloud (*FZ* iii:48) like Antamon, and torments Albion. When the darkening Man makes a god of his Shadow of suppressed desire (*FZ* iii:50; *J* 29:37), Luvah descends from his cloud, strives to gain dominion over Albion (*FZ* iii:79; *J* 29:61), and infects him with boils, "the terrible smitings of Luvah" (*FZ* iii:82; *J* 29:64). Albion rejects Luvah, whose senses become closed (*FZ* iii:86; *J* 29:67). Then the Serpent of Nature rolls between Luvah and Vala; she shrinks, "and from her bosom Luvah fell far as the east and west" (*FZ* iii:100; *J* 29:79), "hidden in the Elemental forms of Life & Death" (*FZ* iv:130).

He cannot remain suppressed. Vala becomes a worm in Enitharmon's womb, and "Luvah in the loins of Los a dark & furious death" (*FZ* iii:22). Luvah is born of Enitharmon as Orc (*FZ* v:42, 240); Love suppressed has turned to hate. "Luvah, King of Love, thou art the King of rage & death" (*FZ* v:42). His is the Wine-press which is war on earth; "Luvah laid the foundation & Urizen finish'd it in howling woe" (*Mil* 27:2).

This war becomes specifically the conflict with Napoleon. "Luvah tore forth from Albion's Loins, in fibrous veins, in rivers of blood over Europe: a Vegetating Root, in grinding pain, animating the Dragon Temples, soon to become that Holy Fiend, the Wicker Man of Scandinavia" (*J* 47:4); he is now Albion's Spectre (*J* 60:2). "Luvah is France" (*J* 66:15). The treatment of France after Napoleon's defeat is the crucifixion of Luvah (*FZ* vii *b*:166; *J* 63:5; 65:8), and he is laid in a sepulcher (*FZ* vii *b*:167).

"The Lamb of God . . . is clos'd in Luvah's Sepulcher" (J 24:50–51). The spiritual forms of Gwendolen and Ragan "without a Veil wither in Luvah's Sepulcher" (J 21:15). Luvah "in his dark Spectre [ravens] from his open Sepulcher" (J 36:30). Hand commingles "with Luvah & with the Sepulcher of Luvah" (J 90:26). Luvah sleeps in death beside the fount above the Lark's nest in Golgonooza, "& here is Luvah's empty Tomb" (Mil 35:59).

But dead or alive, Luvah continues to rage in the form of Orc. "When Urizen saw the Lamb of God clothed in Luvah's robes, perplex'd & terrifi'd he stood, tho' well he knew that Orc was Luvah. But he now beheld a new Luvah, Or One [sic] who assum'd Luvah's form & stood before him opposite" (FZ viii:61). "When Luvah in Orc became a Serpent, he descended into that State call'd Satan" (FZ viii:382).

When at last Albion wakes, he orders Urizen to "Let Luvah rage in the dark deep, even to Consummation; for if thou feedest not his rage, it will subside in peace" (FZ ix:142). Luvah-Orc soon burns himself out; Albion gives "the flaming Demon & Demoness of smoke" to Urizen, who commands them to return to the place of seed (FZ ix:361–65).

They enter Vala's Garden, the dreams of Beulah. A charming pastoral follows (FZ ix:375–553). Luvah in his cloud remains as invisible as Apuleius' Cupid; but he speaks to Vala, and builds her a palace while she sleeps, and she sees him in her dreams.

This is but dreaming, however, for at the evening feasts, "the wine of Eternity [is] serv'd round by the flames of Luvah" (FZ ix:588, 619).

On the fifth Day, Albion orders Luvah to the Vintage, " 'Attempting to be more than Man We become less,' said Luvah as he arose from the bright feast, drunk with the wine of ages. His crown of thorns fell from his head, he hung his living Lyre behind the seat of the Eternal Man & took his way sounding the Song of Los, descending to the Vineyards bright" (FZ ix:709). He and Vala work at the Vintage (which on earth is

the last war) until they finally fall asleep on the floor; and the sons of Tharmas and Urthona put him for dung upon the ground (FZ ix:791). Nevertheless, Luvah and Vala wake with their children; weeping they reascend to Albion, who casts them wailing into the world of shadows until winter is over (FZ ix:795).

When that time comes, Albion orders Luvah to his loom (J 95:17); with the other Zoas he ascends into Albion's bosom (J 96: 41), and draws his silver bow (J 97:9) to assist in the slaying of the Covering Cherub.

In Jerusalem, the warring Sons of Albion "assimilate with Luvah, bound in the bonds of spiritual Hate, from which springs Sexual Love as iron chains" (54:11). It is Los who makes this possible: in creating the World of Generation from the World of Death, he divides the Masculine and Feminine, "for the comingling of Albion's & Luvah's Spectres was Hermaphroditic" (58:19). "The Twelve Sons of Albion drank & imbibed the Life & eternal Form of Luvah" (90:16). "Mingling with Luvah in One, they became One Great Satan" (90:43).

When Albion dismissed Luvah after the smiting with boils, it was the equivalent of killing him. The event was complicated, however; indeed, a trifle confused. Luvah commanded Vala, at once his daughter and lover, to murder Albion, who instead conquered Luvah and slew both of them. But she "revived them to life in my warm bosom. [Albion] saw them issue from my bosom dark in Jealousy. He burn'd before me. Luvah fram'd the Knife & Luvah gave the Knife into his daughter's hand . . . But I, Vala, Luvah's daughter, keep [Albion's] body embalm'd in moral laws . . . lest he arise to life & slay my Luvah" (80:16–29).

In Jerusalem we also learn that Jesus permitted the war, as the buried hate must find expression if it is to be expiated. "Luvah must be Created and Vala, for I cannot leave them in the gnawing Grave, but will prepare a way for my banished-ones to return" (62:20). The war follows.

See also VALA.

LYBIA (i.e., Libya) is an African country on the coast to the west of Egypt. It is the seventeenth in the list of the Thirty-two Nations which shall protect liberty and rule the rest of the world (*J* 72:40). Once, Egypt and Lybia heard the thanksgivings to Jerusalem (*J* 79:50); but now, Lybia and the Lands unknown are the ascent outside into Urizen's Temple (*J* 58:36), and the head of the Covering Cherub contains Egypt, Ethiopia, and Lybia (*J* 89:16).

LYCA is the seven-year-old child of "The Little Girl Lost" and "The Little Girl Found" (*SoI*, later transferred to *SoE*). Following the birds' songs, she loses herself in a desert and goes to sleep beneath a tree. The beasts of prey spare her; the lion (the angel of death) weeps over her while his lioness removes "her slender dress," and they convey her, still sleeping, "to caves." Her parents seek her in woe for seven days; then the lion encounters them, bears them to the ground, and licks their hands. At last they perceive his real form as a crowned spirit armed in gold. He assures them that their daughter is asleep in his palace. They follow him, and "to this day" live in a lonely dell, safe from the wild beasts.

The decoration of the first of the two poems, however, represents the embrace of a youth and a maiden. She points upward to a bird ("the joy as it flies," *Eternity, K* 179) while even the serpent averts his head. This design is evidently an illustration to another poem, "A Little Girl Lost" (*SoE*).

"Lyca" was the name originally given (*K* 63) to Susan in the "Laughing Song" (*SoI*). Blake evidently did not know that "Lyca" was Greek for "wolf."

The LYRE is a musical instrument strung with cords. The daughter of Job who plays on it in the lithograph "Job in his Prosperity" symbolizes music; and the lyre is the instrument of Luvah (*FZ* ix:711), whose art is music.

Sometimes the lyre is used to contrast the lighter song with the grander music of the harp. In the water color "The Sacrifice of Jephthah's Daughter," the innocent girl kneels praying on a Doric altar, between a timbrel and a lyre. Both harp and lyre hang on the willow tree in the water color "By the Waters of Babylon." In the last illustration to *Job*, he plays a harp while a daughter plays a lyre.

But the lyre was also the attribute of Erato, muse of lyrical poetry; Blake therefore sometimes used it as a symbol of pagan poetry.

When Urizen builds his universe, "many a corded lyre" is formed "outspread over the immense" to trap the listeners (*FZ* ii: 161). The "sweet inspiring lyres" of "all the elements," says Tharmas, will encourage Los when he rebuilds Urizen's furnaces (*FZ* iv:154). The daughters of Rahab and Tirzah tempt Milton to "Come, bring with thee Jerusalem with songs on the Grecian Lyre!" (*Mil* 19:46).

M

MACHPELAH was a double-chambered cave in western Hebron, which Abraham bought for a family burial place.

Ragan's web of war drops "with crimson gore with the Loves of Albion & Canaan, opening along the Valley of Rephaim, weaving over the Caves of Machpelah" (*J* 64:37).

MACPHERSON. See OSSIAN.

MADRID is one of the cities of the nations in which the voice of the wandering Reuben is heard (*J* 84:14).

MAGDALEN. See MARY MAGDALENE.

MAGGOTS were supposed to generate spontaneously in rotting flesh; therefore "the tender maggot" is an "emblem of Immortality" (*FZ* ix:759; *Mil* 27:16).

MAGOG. See GOG.

MAHALALEEL was the fifth in the line of Adam; he is one of the nine "Giants mighty, Hermaphroditic" who constitute the first section of the Twenty-seven Heavens (*Mil* 37:36; *J* 75:11).

MAHANAIM was east of the Jordan, about eighty miles north of the Arnon. Here Milton met Urizen, where they strove "among the streams of Arnon, even to Mahanaim" (*Mil* 19:6).

MAHOMET (570–632) was the founder of the Moslem religion and the author of the Koran. As he was traditionally descended from Ishmael, Blake placed "Mahomed" just beneath Ishmael in his picture of the Last Judgment (*K* 607; see Illustrations, "LJ" No. 80).

George Sale, in his *Preliminary Discourse* (1734), noted "the opinion of some learned Arabians, who would have the Koran so named, because it is a collection of the loose chapters or sheets which compose it" (London, 1825 ed., p. 79). As Christians were shocked at the inclusion of sex among the joys of Paradise, Sale carefully refuted the error that there were no spiritual pleasures as well (133–35). Blake believed that Mahomet's attitude was a reaction against the Christian ideal of celibacy, which threatened the continuance of the human race: "Antamon [the male seed] call'd up Leutha [sex as sin] from her valleys of delight, and to Mahomet a loose Bible gave" (*SoL* 3:28).

According to the Koran, the General Resurrection shall be followed immediately by a period of "mutual retaliation," when "every creature will take vengeance one of another, or have satisfaction made them for the injuries which they have suffered" (Sale, 119). Blake incorporated this idea into *The Four Zoas* (ix:19–23, 146–77).

In the Koran also is to be found the original of the tale in Thomas Parnell's *The Hermit*, to which Blake referred on December 10, 1825: "Who shall say what God thinks evil? That is a wise tale of the Mahometans —of the Angel of the Lord that murdered the infant. . . . Is not every infant that dies of disease in effect murdered by an angel?" (*CR* 260, 291).

MAKUTH was a son of Tiriel, named in a deleted line (*Tir* iv:73).

MALAH ("disease") was the oldest of the five daughters of Zelophehad, who left no son; consequently his daughters were allowed to inherit, by special legislation, thus marking a date in the emancipation of women.

To Blake, therefore, the daughters were manifestations of the Female Will. Rahab and the five daughters are equated with Milton's three wives and three daughters (*Mil* 17:11). Tirzah, singing of the triumphs of the female sex, bids Malah "come forth from Lebanon" (*FZ* viii:316; *J* 68:4). When the five daughters weave the woof of death over London, Malah is situated on Blackheath (*Mil* 35:9).

MALDEN (i.e., Maldon) is a small port on the Blackwater River in Essex; it is seventeen miles southwest of Colchester and forty-four miles northeast of London. It contains some prehistoric ruins, although no rocking stones or druidic circle.

The passage at the opening of *Jerusalem*, "Malden & Colchester Demonstrate" (*J* 21:37), suggests that these ports were connected in Blake's mind with naval or military disturbances.

Blake particularly associated Malden with the fall of Jerusalem and the establishment of Druidism. Jerusalem fell "from Lambeth's Vale | Down thro' Poplar & Old Bow, | Thro' Malden & acros[s] the Sea" (*J* 27:41). Bath seeks to "cast Jerusalem forth upon the wilds to Poplar & Bow, to Malden & Canterbury in the delights of cruelty" (*J* 41:5). The Atlantic weeps over his children "in Stone-henge, in Malden & Colchester" and other places (*J* 57:6). Also with other places, "from Stone-henge & from Malden's Cove, Jerusalem's Pillars fall in the rendings of fierce War" (*J* 68:44). At the sound of Los's voice, the Giants of Albion erect "trembling rocking Stones," which sometimes come to rest "in a Circle in Malden or in Strathness or Dura" (*J* 90: 59–62). When Brittannia wakes, she laments that she has murdered Albion "In Stone-henge & on London Stone & in the Oak Groves of Malden" (*J* 94:24). "O mel-

ancholy Magdalen, behold the morning over Malden break" (*J* 65:38).

The MALVERN Hills run north and south along the border of Herefordshire and Worcestershire, reaching their highest point in the Worcester Beacon, which rises 1,395 feet. In these hills William Langland had his vision of Piers Plowman.

Mountains always mean the high places of thought; therefore when Albion says: "The Malvern and the Cheviot, the Wolds, Plinlimmon & Snowdon are mine" (*J* 4:30), he is establishing thought-control. As a result, "the Peak, Malvern, & Cheviot Reason in Cruelty" (*J* 21:34).

MAMMON. The "mammon of unrighteousness," denounced by Jesus as incompatible with service to God (*Matt* vi:24; *Luke* xvi: 9–13), has always been understood as the deification of money. In "I rose up at the dawn of day" (*K* 558), Blake renounced the pursuit of money.

MAM-TOR (altitude 1,710 feet) is one of the "Seven Wonders of the Peake" in Derbyshire (see DERBY PEAK). With Mam-Win, it is a double peak, named for the female breasts. Gwendolen draws aside her Veil "from Mam-Tor to Dovedale," exposing her perfect torso, and revealing Hyle as a worm (*J* 82:45). When Los addresses Hand and the other Sons of Albion, lamenting the creation of the Female Will, he stands "on Mam-Tor, looking over Europe & Asia. The Graves thunder beneath his feet from Ireland to Japan" (*J* 34:41). Later, Los and Enitharmon "converse upon Mam-Tor; the Graves thunder under their feet" (*J* 93: 27).

MANAGHAN (i.e., Monaghan) was in Blake's day a county of Ulster, North Ireland. With the other counties of Ulster, it is assigned to Dan, Asher, and "Napthali" (*J* 72:27).

MANASSEH ("to make forget") was the elder son of Joseph; Ephraim ("double fruitfulness") was the younger. The dying Jacob gave the greater blessing to Ephraim (*Gen* xlviii), prophesying his greater future. In the allotment of land, as Levi was omitted, these two sons of Joseph replaced their father, thus keeping the number of Tribes up to twelve. Blake usually gives Ephraim the precedence.

Manasseh's line was established through his concubine "the Aramitess" or Syrian (*I Chron* vii:14); he thus became the great-great-grandfather of Zelophehad. Blake therefore used the two brothers to demonstrate the lure of outlandish women.

Tirzah, summoning the daughters of Zelophehad, says: "The River Kanah wander'd by my sweet Manasseh's side to see the boy spring into heavens sounding from my sight! Go, Noah, fetch the girdle of strong brass, heat it red-hot, press it around the loins of this ever expanding cruelty" (*J* 67:57; *FZ* viii:310). Rahab and Tirzah tempt Milton: "Come then to Ephraim & Manasseh, O beloved-one!" (*Mil* 20:3).

As in Hebrew script only the consonants were written, Blake took advantage of the possibility of using other vowels in transliterating Manasseh's name. When the Sons flee, "Reuben & Manazzoth ['struggle" or "strife"] & Gad & Simeon & Levi and Ephraim & Judah were Generated because they left me, wandering with Tirzah" (*Mil* 24:2). "We call'd him Menassheh ["forgetfulness of God"] because of the Generations of Tirzah, because of Satan" (*Mil* 24:6); and again: "Egypt, where Ephraim & Menassheh gather'd my Sons together in the Sands of Midian" (*Mil* 24:20).

Ephraim, Manasseh, and Benjamin are assigned the counties of the western Irish province of Connaught (*J* 72:23). The western Gate of Connau[gh]t, however, is assigned to their father, Joseph (*J* 72:3).

Jerusalem recalls how, in the days of innocence, Ephraim, Manasseh, and five other tribes (doubtless meaning all) kept their flocks and herds, and the Lamb of God appeared to them (*J* 79:30).

MANATHU-VARCYON is the male con-

sort of Ethinthus. Their position is West. This couple is the first in the counterclockwise circuit of the repression of sex under Enitharmon's ideal of chastity. Ethinthus represents the mortal flesh; Manathu-Varcyon is its "flames of soft delusion." He also has golden wings and "lovely eagles"—his aspirations, or possibly the eagles of conscience which tortured Oothoon (*Eur* 14: 6–8).

However, in the list of the sons and daughters of Los and Enitharmon (*FZ* viii:364), "Manathu Vorcyon" appears oddly as the seventh daughter, preceding Ethinthus. It would seem as though Blake recollected the association of the pair, and having accidentally omitted Manathu-Varcyon from the list of sons, jotted his name down here, as a reminder to reinsert it in its proper place when he revised the list.

MANAZZOTH. See MANASSEH.

MANCHESTER is one of the chief industrial towns of England. It lies thirty-one miles east of Liverpool.

In the opening confusion of *Jerusalem*, "Manchester & Liverpool are in tortures of Doubt & Despair" (*J* 21:36).

The MANDRAKE is a plant with a forked root, whose resemblance to the human form caused much magical speculation. Amongst other things, it was supposed to shriek horribly when pulled from the earth.

Blake used it as a symbol of birth. The second plate (numbered 1) of *The Gates of Paradise* shows a woman pulling a mandrake-baby from the earth. "And She found me beneath a Tree, | A Mandrake, & in her Veil hid me" (*K* 770). In many other pictures, Blake showed babies rising from the earth, though without a leafy head.

The mandrake was supposed to be an aphrodisiac and a promoter of fertility. Therefore, in the contest for Jacob's affections, Reuben gave mandrakes to his mother Leah, thus rousing Rachel's jealousy (*Gen* xxx:14–16). "As Reuben found Mandrakes in the field & gave them to his Mother, Pride meets with Pride upon the Mountains in the stormy day, in that terrible Day of Rintrah's Plow & of Satan's driving the Team" (*J* 93:8).

The MARRIAGE OF HEAVEN AND HELL has nothing but the title on the title page— no author, no place, no date. The place was Lambeth, whither Blake had moved in 1791. The date is 1793, when Blake advertised the book for sale. He had been working on it for some time; in one copy he wrote 1790 on Plate 3, to confirm the year which the text hinted at. But the omission of the author's name would seem almost an act of impudence. Convinced of the importance of his book, he challenged the public to seek him out.

It contains twenty-seven plates, the last three being devoted to the terminal lyric "A Song of Liberty." Nine complete copies have been located; a tenth has not been traced; and there are three fragments.

This book is Blake's *Principia*, in which he announced a new concept of the universe, thus quietly equating himself with Ptolemy and Copernicus (cf. *J* 83:40). Mind, not matter, is the basic substance. This universe is psychological; it is the universe in which we really live. It is egocentric, and differs with each individual, yet is essentially the same. See UNIVERSE.

In analyzing this universe of man's mind, which contains heaven and hell and nature, Blake anticipated the theories of Freud, for Blake's "Energy" is the libido, the Id, and his "Reason" is the censor, the Superego. As these contraries are essential to each other in the psychic structure, Blake reduced "Good" and "Evil" to mere technical terms, denoting arbitrary and artificial qualities devoid of any real moral significance.

Heaven and its angels, the "Good," are simply the unthinking orthodox. But Hell and its devils, the "Evil," required revaluation. The forces of the Id are the fountain of life; its "devils" are the original thinkers, essentially revolutionists, who are always disturbing to orthodoxy.

This universe is a unity. All those things long since separated by Reason—God and man, man and nature, body and soul, good and evil, all religious differences—are accounted for and reconciled. The contraries are essential to each other; they work together; and Blake's universe is therefore dynamic.

The manifesto of this universe began a New Age. Blake audaciously dated it from his own birth: Swedenborg himself had written that in 1757 a general Last Judgment had passed over the earth, when all things were reduced into order, "the spiritual equilibrium between good and evil, or between heaven and hell being thence restored" (Swedenborg, *Last Judgment*, par. 45). Now Adam returns to Paradise; Esau (Edom) returns to his inheritance from which the crafty Jacob had ousted him; and Isaiah's prophecy of the Golden Age (*Isaiah* xxxv) is being fulfilled.

In the excitement of his discovery, Blake challenged every great thinker before him. "All Bibles or sacred codes have been the causes of the following Errors. . . . But the following Contraries to these are True" (*MHH* 4). Isaiah and Ezekiel were wrong in implying that their visions appeared to their material eyes. Milton mistook Satan for the Messiah. With superb insolence, Blake parodied Swedenborg to whom he owed so much, and could even state: "Swedenborg has not written one new truth. . . . he has written all the old falshoods" (*MHH* 21). He sneered at Behmen and Paracelsus. He spared only Dante and Shakespeare.

But to be attacked by Blake was a supreme compliment, as he attacked only the greatest thinkers. Precisely because they were the greatest, their errors were the more dangerous and must be exposed. Just as Newton discovered gravity, which organized his material universe, by studying all the speculations of the astronomers and discarding their errors, so Blake studied all the explorers of the mental universe, and discovered the non-moral universe of the psyche. He seems to have taken cognizance of all the contradictory theories afloat in his time. Did

Berkeley promulgate idealism and Paine skepticism, Blake took note of them both and combined what he found true. Lavater wrote: "He, who hates the wisest and best of men, hates the Father of men; for, where is the Father of men to be seen but in the most perfect of his children?" (*K* 82). Blake changed "hates" to "loves," underlined the last clause, and commented: "This is true worship." He then expanded the thought in his last "Memorable Fancy": "The worship of God is: Honouring his gifts in other men, each according to his genius, and loving the greatest men best: those who envy or calumniate great men hate God; for there is no other God" (*K* 158).

Every one of those he attacked had contributed something to his concepts. Behmen had come the nearest to abolishing Justice as the supreme universal power; but Milton and Swedenborg were both victims of this error. Behmen had discovered the Contraries; Paracelsus, the supremacy of the Imagination; Milton, the organization of the mental universe; Swedenborg, the concepts of God and Judgment—all these were incorporated into Blake's discovery, which is basic to our own modern view of life.

The structure of the book was first discovered by Max Plowman. In his Everyman edition of Blake's works (1927, p. xxiii), he wrote: "It consists of a poem as prologue, a prose argument composed in six chapters, and a song as epilogue. Blake indicates the beginning and end of these chapters by the use of designs for chapter headings and designs as colophons. Each chapter consists of a series of dogmatic statements, followed by a fanciful dithyramb which illustrates the foregoing statements, much as a parson's sermon illustrates his text." In the facsimile edition of the *Marriage*, issued the same year, he amplified his analysis. Chapter i states the principles; Chapter ii applies them to the Fall; Chapter iii describes the origin of the gods; Chapter iv deals with regeneration; Chapter v defines the two types of man: "the Prolific" (the purposeful, the creative) and "the Devourer" (who seeks

only for pleasure); and Chapter vi concludes with Christ as diabolist.

The terminal "Song of Liberty" describes the ensuing revolution, but without naming the characters involved. "The Eternal Female" (Enitharmon) groans in childbirth. Her son is "the new born terror" (Orc), who stands before "the starry king" (Urizen). Urizen hurls Orc into the western sea, then himself falls in ruins on Urthona's dens (the subconscious). Like the fallen Satan, Urizen rouses himself to reorganize his forces: "leading his starry hosts thro' the waste wilderness, he promulgates his ten commands" (the Decalogue). But Orc appears as the dawn in the east, and "stamps the stony law to dust," crying "Empire is no more! and now the Lion [protector of the flock] & Wolf [predator of the flock] shall cease.... For every thing that lives is Holy."

MARS was the classical god of war and also the red fifth planet of the Ptolemaic astronomy. In the ninety-seventh illustration to Dante, it is represented by a crucified sphere, attended by the armed heads of warriors, whom Albert S. Roe identified as the "Virtues" of the heavenly hierarchy (*Roe* 188). Mars is also one of the three heavens of Plato (see Illustrations, "Milton and the Spirit of Plato").

For symbolic reasons, to indicate that warfare was the original state of the natural man, Blake constructed his own astronomy in *America* (5:2-5). Orc is likened to "the planet red that once enclos'd the terrible wandering comets in its sphere. Then, Mars, thou wast our center, & the planets three [the Moon, Mercury, and Venus] flew round thy crimson disk: so e'er the Sun was rent from thy red sphere."

MARY MAGDALENE (Magdalen) became one of Jesus' most devoted followers after he delivered her from seven devils. She attended the Crucifixion (*J* 56:42) and the burial, and was the first to find the tomb empty and the first to see the risen Jesus.

According to tradition, she had been a harlot (*EG* i:4-7). She was also supposed to be the woman taken in adultery, whom Jesus saved from being stoned to death according to the law of Moses. To Blake, this episode was the most clear-cut example of Jesus' repudiation of the Mosaic law. In *The Everlasting Gospel* (*e*) he wrote up this episode very movingly. Mary was an adulteress, but her real sin was in concealing her true nature, her

> dark pretence to Chastity,
> Blaspheming Love, blaspheming thee.
> Thence Rose Secret Adulteries,
> And thence did Covet also rise.
> My sin thou hast forgiven me,
> Canst thou forgive my Blasphemy?
> Canst thou return to this dark Hell,
> And in my burning bosom dwell? (71)

Jerusalem says: "but I, thy Magdalen, behold thy Spiritual Risen Body" (*J* 62: 14). Vala is addressed: "O Melancholy Magdalen" (*FZ* vii *b*:192; *J* 65:38).

MARY THE VIRGIN was the mother of Jesus and the wife of Joseph. According to Matthew (in whose account the annunciation is made to Joseph), Joseph, on discovering that Mary his betrothed was already with child, "was minded to put her away privily"; but after a dream, in which the angel of the Lord announced that she was with child by the Holy Ghost, he married her.

Blake did not believe in the supernatural conception of Jesus. He ridiculed the idea in an epigram *On the Virginity of the Virgin Mary & Johanna Southcott* (*K* 418), and detested the mariolatry which was based on it (Dante, illustr. 99, and *Roe* 193–96). Mary was simply one of those who are "innocently gay & thoughtless . . . in the midst of a corrupted Age" and therefore not to be condemned (*LJ*, *K* 610).

It is not only that the sexual urge is essentially pure, and "can never be defiled" (*MHH* 9; *Am* 8:13); the matter goes deeper than that. The Holy Ghost is the genius of each individual; the fundamental purpose of Mary's existence was to conceive the Holy Child; therefore (and in this sense only) when she was impregnated, she was obey-

ing the Holy Ghost within her. In Blake's water color of the Assumption, Mary rises from the tomb, not towards the conventional Trinity, but towards the Babe.

Matthew's story, as Blake interpreted it, thus became an outstanding example of the Forgiveness of Sins. Mary is the *felix culpa*. When Joseph calls her an adulteress, she does not deny it (*J* 61:6), but replies: "If I were pure, never could I taste the sweets of the Forgiveness of Sins." In his dream, Joseph has learned that the Forgiveness of Sins is unconditional: "doth Jehovah . . . Forgive Pollution only on conditions of Purity? . . . That Pollution is not Forgiven! . . . for behold, there is none that liveth & Sinneth not! And this is the Covenant of Jehovah: If you Forgive one-another, so shall Jehovah Forgive You" (*J* 61:17–25; *Matt* vi: 14). Thus Joseph has come to understand that Mary is "with Child by the Holy Ghost" (*J* 61:27).

Mary is one of the Transgressors, and therefore the appropriate mother of the greatest Transgressor of all, who also forgave an adulteress. Her female ancestry included some of the worst women in the Old Testament. See MATERNAL LINE. Here Blake adapted, or reinvented, a Jewish heresy of the seventeenth century: that the Messiah, to penetrate to the very heart of evil, must have the worst possible ancestry (information from Dr. Gershom Scholem).

Blake followed Swedenborg in believing that Mary could give the pre-existent Jesus only his mortal body, which is the equivalent of sin. "Assume the dark Satanic body in the Virgin's womb, O Lamb Divine!" (*FZ* viii:241). "Christ took on Sin in the Virgin's Womb & put it off on the Cross" (*Mil* 5:3). "He took on Sin in the Virgin's Womb, | And put it off on the Cross & Tomb, | To be Worship'd by the Church of Rome" (*EG* *b*:57). Blake told Crabb Robinson: "Christ took much after his mother (the law), and in that respect was one of the worst of men" (*CR* 271, 304).

Blake was always distressed by Rome's literal interpretation of the miracles, which seemed to him mere materialism. Thus the resurrection of Lazarus, understood as that of the physical body, became the basis of serious errors in the official church (*Mil* 24:26–33). Similarly, Rome emphasized the mortal death of the immortal Jesus (*FZ* ix: 1–5). "The Pope supposes Nature & the Virgin Mary to be the same allegorical personages, but the Protestant considers Nature as incapable of bearing a Child" (On Cennini, *K* 779).

But spiritual matters must not be taken literally. "A Vegetated Christ & a Virgin Eve [a tactful slip of the pen for "Mary"] are the Hermaphroditic Blasphemy; by his Maternal Birth he is that Evil-One and his Maternal Humanity must be put off Eternally, lest the Sexual Generation swallow up Regeneration. Come Lord Jesus, take on thee the Satanic Body of Holiness!" (*J* 90: 34).

In Blake's pictures of the Last Judgment, Mary does not appear as intercessor with the all-forgiving God. She is to be found with her family (see Illustrations, "LJ" No. 13).

MARYBONE (so "Marylebone" is usually pronounced) is a district of London, northwest of the city and immediately north of Westminster. In Blake's boyhood it consisted mainly of pasture lands, where Willan's Farm was to be found. One section was marked out to be a park; in 1811 this became Regent's Park, which reaches to Primrose Hill.

"The fields from Islington to Marybone, | To Primrose Hill and Saint John's Wood, | Were builded over with pillars of gold, | And there Jerusalem's pillars stood" (*J* 27: 1). Los concludes his clockwise walk about the city: "and he beheld Jerusalem in Westminster & Marybone among the ruins of the Temple" (*J* 31:40). "The Shuttles of death sing in the sky to Islington & Pancrass, round Marybone to Tyburn's River" (*J* 41:7). The recruits for war "were carried away in thousands from London & in tens of thousands from Westminster & Marybone, in ships clos'd up" (*J* 65:33).

The MARYGOLD (marigold) symbolizes

the first experiment with sex. Blake chose it for its name, "Mary's gold," which doubly indicates its purity.

Oothoon, on the verge of Experience, fearfully hides her love for Theotormon; she longs for freedom (America) and seeks flowers in Leutha's Vale (her genitals) to comfort her. At last she dares to pluck the Marygold from its dewy bed, then flies free towards Theotormon, only to be raped by Bromion (*VDA* iii:1).

The plucking of a flower is an ancient symbol for sexual experience. But Oothoon's act is only the first tentative exploration of the powers awakening within her; it is undertaken in solitude; and not till then does she seek for her lover.

Neo-Platonism is evident in the symbolism. Oothoon's plucking of the flower strongly suggests the similar fatal act of Persephone. Oothoon sees the flower as a nymph. Nymphs were Elementals of water (matter), and according to Thomas Taylor's translation of Porphyry's *On the Cave of the Nymphs* (sec. 4), "this term is commonly applied to souls descending into generation." See NYMPHS.

The MATERNAL LINE consists of the traceable female ancestry of Mary, and hence of Jesus. As the genealogies given by Matthew and Luke both trace his ancestry (surprisingly) through Joseph, Blake accepted the Roman theory that Mary was Joseph's cousin; and as he believed that all she gave her son was this mortal and sinful body, it seemed appropriate to him that her female ancestry included some of the worst characters in the Old Testament. Matthew himself named the harlot Rahab as an ancestor. Blake, forced to choose between the two irreconcilable genealogies, preferred Matthew's.

There is a preliminary sketch of the Maternal Line in *The Four Zoas* (viii:363–65). The list of the Daughters of Los and Enitharmon begins with the jealous Ocalythron, and continues with Elynittria, Oothoon, Leutha, Elythiria, Enanto, Manathu Vorcyon, to Ethinthus (the body), after which follow, without regard for chronology, Moab [Ruth?], Midian [Zipporah, wife of Moses?], Adah, Zillah, Caina, Naamah, Tamar, Rahab, Tirzah, and Mary.

In *Jerusalem* (62:8–13), the list was revised and expanded. When the fallen Jerusalem marvels that Jesus shall be born of Nature (Vala), she calls the Maternal Line "the Daughters of Vala, Mother of the Body of death." Their names are as follows:

Cainah, Blake's name for Cain's sister-wife.

Adah and Zillah, the Cainite polygamous wives of Lamech (*Gen* iv:19).

Naamah, wife of Noah, a very evil woman according to rabbinical tradition.

Shuah's daughter, a Canaanite wife or concubine of Judah (*Gen* xxxviii:2).

Tamar, a Canaanite, who tricked her father-in-law Judah into begetting her twins, of whom Pharez continued the royal line (*Gen* xxxviii:13–30).

Rahab, the Canaanite harlot, who betrayed her city of Jericho (*Josh* ii:1–24); she married Salmon and became the mother of Boaz (*Matt* i:5).

Ruth, a Moabite, who married Boaz (*Ruth* iii; *Matt* i:5).

Bathsheba, of the daughters of Heth (i.e., a Hittite), who committed adultery with David, and later married him, becoming the mother of Solomon (*II Sam* xi–xii; *Matt* i:6).

Naamah the Ammonite, the Cainite concubine of Solomon; she was mother of the evil king Rehoboam (*I Kings* xiv: 21; *Matt* i:6).

Zibeah the Philistine, who was the domineering mother of the weak king Joash (*II Kings* xii:1).

Mary.

As Duncan Sloss and J. P. R. Wallis note (*The Prophetic Writings of William Blake*, Oxford, 1926, I, 560), Blake emphasizes the "outlandish" origin of most of the women, obviously to prove that the Chosen Race, far from being pure, was a mixture of bloods. To Blake, who stressed the mixture of bloods which had produced the English

(*J* 92:1–2), this miscegenation was a virtue, an expression of the Brotherhood of Man. That most of the women were also Transgressors against conventional morality struck him as particularly significant in the ancestry of the two Transgressors, Mary and Jesus.

It is to be noted that Blake followed *Genesis* iv in tracing the ancestry to Cain instead of Seth (*Gen* v). It would seem as though Blake knew of the seventeenth-century Jewish heresy which taught that the ancestry of the Messiah must consist of the worst stock if he is to plumb the depths of sin. "If he intended to take on Sin | The Mother should an Harlot been, | Just such a one as Magdalen | With seven devils in her Pen" (*EG* i:3).

MATHA, a term apparently of Blake's invention, suggests "matter." Ijim calls Tiriel's house "as false as Matha & as dark as vacant Orcus" (*Tir* iv:87). In Ossian's *Fingal* (I), the father of Colmar is named Matha, but we know nothing more of him, certainly nothing to show he was ever false.

MATTER is a delusion, a thin coating of unreality, which is mistaken for reality by those whose vision is single only, like Newton's. It is the veil of Vala.

MAYO is a county of Connaught, the western province of Ireland. With the other counties of Connaught, it is assigned to Manasseh, Ephraim, and Benjamin (*J* 72:24).

MEDIA lay south of the Caspian Sea and north of Persia. In Urizen's temple, "Persia & Media are his halls" (*J* 58:38).

The MEDWAY rises in Sussex, passes through Kent, and empties into the Thames estuary. Some time in 1780–82, Blake went on a boating and sketching expedition up the Medway with Stothard and a Mr. Ogleby. Some soldiers detained them on suspicion of being French spies; and having contrived a tent of their oars and sails, they remained camping until members of the Royal Academy could identify them. Stothard's etching of the episode is reproduced in Mrs. Bray's *Life of Thomas Stothard* (London, 1851, p. 20).

The marriage of the Thames and Medway occupies most of the eleventh canto of Spenser's *Faerie Queene*, Book IV. Consequently, for Blake the two rivers symbolize married love.

Albion, in jealous fears, hides his Emanation "upon the Thames and Medway, rivers of Beulah" (*J* 4:34). Gwendolen's "Lions & Tygers & Wolves sport before Los on the Thames & Medway" (*J* 63:34). In the days of innocence, "Medway mingled with Kishon; Thames reciev'd the heavenly Jordan" (*J* 79:35).

MEHETABEL is the eleventh Daughter of Albion, although originally she was named the fifth (*FZ* ii:61). She is one of the seven Daughters who unite into Rahab (*J* 5:44). She is the Emanation of Peachey; she is "terrible & lovely upon the mountains" of North Wales (*J* 71:31). She joins with Kotope's Emanation, Sabrina, who then "shines west over America" (*J* 71:45).

Her name was apparently derived from "Methahel," one of King Ebrauc's thirty daughters, who were sent to Rome, where they married into the Trojan nobility (*Geof* II, viii). But Blake gives her the spelling of the wife of Hadar, king of Edom (*Gen* xxxvi: 39); "Mehetabel" signifies "God makes happy."

MEMORY and Imagination are two entirely different things, according to Blake. "Imagination is the divine vision not of the world, nor of man, nor from man as he is a natural man, but only as he is a spiritual man. Imagination has nothing to do with memory" (*CR* 301). Swedenborg, in his *Divine Love*, had already distinguished between true wisdom, which is from "the Affection of Truth," and the "Thought from the Memory by the Sight of the natural Mind" (*K* 95); Blake underlined this passage, with the comment "Note this." Milton had made the

same distinction: "A work of Genius is a Work 'Not to be obtain'd by the Invocation of Memory & her Syren Daughters, but by Devout prayer to that Eternal Spirit, who can enrich with all utterance & knowledge & sends out his Seraphim with the hallowed fire of his Altar to touch & purify the lips of whom he pleases' " (On Reynolds, *K* 457). See MUSES.

Blake identified Memory with the formless Chaos, which is the Spectre, not perceived until Man turns his back on the Divine Vision (*FZ* vii:347; *J* 33:8). "But Albion fell down . . . hurl'd by his own Spectre, who is the Reasoning Power in every Man, into his own Chaos, which is the Memory between Man & Man" (*J* 54:6). "The Memory is a State always" (*Mil* 32: 34). Urizen's book is "The Book of my Remembrance," which when opened reveals only indefinite blotches (*K* 262).

Blake had invoked both Memory and the Muses in his *Poetical Sketches* (*K* 8, 10); but as neoclassicism spread and stifled the artistic output of his time, he reversed his attitude towards the Greeks. It was commonly supposed that all pagan culture was necessarily derived from the aboriginal Hebrew culture; mythologies were imperfect recollections of the Biblical stories; indeed, the Greeks themselves admitted that Jupiter begat the Muses on Mnemosyne, or Memory (*LJ*, *K* 605). Blake therefore argued that the Muses, who were never to be confused with the Daughters of Inspiration, were the goddesses governing all secondhand, imitative art.

Blake's exasperation became personal when he realized that the second-raters, the merely talented, were in control everywhere. Original geniuses, who perceive the truth, are always few; but the talented are many. They learn their professions not from discovering truths but by studying their predecessors, and flourish on the memory of what has been done already. Reynolds was the obvious example: he tried to reduce art to a science, generalizing from the great painters of the past. Thus academic styles are established; "schools" come into existence. The classical Muses therefore can be called "tradition."

Unfortunately, the second-rater is politically minded. He is adept at becoming the head of the academy, the conservatory, the museum, the art school, the critical column. He cultivates pupils, not painters. In his position of power, he instinctively condemns anything new, because it would imperil his prestige. Thus the custodians of art become actually the bitter enemies of their profession, "whose pretence to knowledge is envy ... who pretend to Poetry that they may destroy Imagination by imitation of Nature's Images drawn from Remembrance" (*Mil* 41:16, 23). "There is a class of artists, whose whole art and science is fabricated for the purpose of destroying art" (*DesC* III, *K* 573). They are as fiercely destructive today as when Blake lived.

It has been noted that Blake borrowed more freely from other works than any of his contemporaries did. Anthony Blunt (*The Art of William Blake*, New York, 1959) has traced a surprising number of sources and parallels. But Blake did not copy what he took: he *used* it for his own very different purposes, and therefore the results are as fresh as though entirely original.

There was more Memory in Blake's Visions than he admitted. But in the act of creation, the threshold of consciousness vibrates so strongly that it is impossible to decide whether or not he knew what he was doing. Certainly his years of studying paintings and prints stored up an enormous number of impressions. This was the place, I believe, where the artist was "taken in vision" to see "those wonderful originals called in the Sacred Scriptures the Cherubim" (*DesC* II, *K* 565). These were "the bright Sculptures of Los's Halls" (*J* 16: 61). Here is the cosmic memory where "every thing exists & not one sigh nor smile nor tear, one hair nor particle of dust, not one can pass away" (*J* 13:66).

MENASSHEH (*Mil* 24:6, 20). See MANASSEH.

The MENTAL TRAVELLER (*K* 424) is the

formula of the history of the idea of Liberty, showing how it is born, how it triumphs, how in its age its opposite is born, how it is cast out, how it then rejuvenates, until it becomes a babe again, and the cycle recurs.

The idea of Liberty was begotten in woe, then born in joy. But at once his Contrary, Society (the "Woman Old"), crucifies him; yet insensibly she is rejuvenated as he matures, until he can break loose and embrace her. (So far, this is the story of Orc.)

She becomes his dwelling place and fruitful garden. His earthly cot is filled with spiritual gems (cf. *Riches*, *K* 181), which are also meat and drink; and his door is always open to travellers and the poor. Yet he has already aged to a mere shadow of his mature state.

Therefore, from his own hospitality (the fire on his hearth) can be born his Negative, the Female Babe. She is the false church, Mystery or Babylon, whom Blake elsewhere named Rahab. The Negation of Liberty is Intolerance. ("This is a free country, and we won't allow—.") Blake does not name her consort, but in *Revelation* (xvii:2) he is "the kings of the earth" (power politics). They soon drive out the original idea, who thus becomes an aged beggar.

However, he finds his Contrary again, who is now a young maiden. For a time, the earth is materialized; but her embraces rejuvenate him again, though she flees from him in fear. Then their courtship gradually restores the beauty of the earth. At the end, he is the Babe again, and she the Woman Old, "and all is done as I have told."

There have been various interpretations of this extraordinary poem, the latest of which is Morton D. Paley's "The Female Babe and 'The Mental Traveller' " (Boston Univ., *Studies in Romanticism*, Vol. I, No. 2, Winter 1962, p. 97). In Joyce Cary's *The Horse's Mouth*, Gulley Jimson, the painter, who considers Blake the "greatest Englishman who ever lived," quotes copiously from *The Mental Traveller* to illustrate his own difficulties (Chaps. xi, xii, xiii, xiv).

MERCURY (Mercurius) was the herald of Jupiter; for the pagans, Mercury was "the angelic word of God" (Justin Martyr, *Apology* xxii).

As herald, Mercury was the god of eloquence. Therefore Blake invoked him in "An Imitation of Spenser," stanzas 3–5 (*PS*). Mercury enters the halls where "Jove weighs the counsel of futurity; | Then, laden with eternal fate, dost go | Down, like a falling star." If he alights where none but "envious hissing adders dwell," his golden caduceus charms them to harmony and establishes a social order. "Such is sweet Eloquence, that does dispel | Envy and Hate." Then the poet calls on him to "assist my lab'ring sense," which aspires to fly "round the circle of the world," like the eagle.

In the third illustration to *Il Penseroso* (see Illustrations, "Milton and the Spirit of Plato"), Mercury stands before Jupiter, his caduceus and left hand pointing downward to the North Star, the pivot of the astronomical universe.

Mercury also conducted souls to the lower world, but Blake assigned that function to Los.

MERCY is the first attribute of God, for it is the Forgiveness of Sins. Jesus is "mercy's Lord" (*J* 52:20). "Glory to the Merciful One, for he is of tender mercies!" (*J* 40:43). "O Mercy, O Divine Humanity! O Forgiveness & Pity & Compassion!" (*J* 61:43). "For Mercy, Pity, Peace and Love | Is God, our father dear" (*SoI*, "The Divine Image" 5). "The Divine Mercy . . . Redeems Man in the Body of Jesus" (*J* 36:54).

When Albion fell into his deadly sleep, "the merciful Saviour in his arms reciev'd him, in the arms of tender mercy" (*J* 48:1); and when he wakes, he is still there, "in the Saviour's arms, in the arms of tender mercy & loving kindness" (*FZ* viii:19). This fall might have been death, "but Mercy chang'd Death into Sleep" (*SoE*, "To Tirzah" 7). "Time is the mercy of Eternity" (*Mil* 24:72). This sleep is the cause of the Incarnation: "when Man sleeps in Beulah, the Saviour in Mercy takes Contraction's Limit [the mortal form]" (*J* 42:32). The creation itself was "an act of Mercy" (*LJ*, *K* 614); thus Jesus set limits to man's fall, and gave

error a form, that it might be cast out. Yet, to note a seeming contradiction, he who made the Lamb did not make the Tyger: that was the work of Urizen, who as "the Creator of this World is a very Cruel Being" (*LJ*, *K* 617).

Mercy and Justice are sometimes opposed (as in *J* 65:1), but the real opposite of Mercy is Cruelty, its negation. "Mercy has a human heart" (*SoI*, "The Divine Image" 9), but in the contrasting poem, "Cruelty has a Human Heart" (*SoE*, "A Divine Image" 1). The second of these poems (and note the contrasted articles) describes the God of This World. His sentiments are expressed in "The Human Abstract" (*SoE*): "Mercy no more could be | If all were as happy as we"; and a cynical devil, provoked by an angel's song, curses: "Mercy could be no more | If there was nobody poor" and "Miseries' increase | Is Mercy, Pity, Peace" ("I heard an Angel singing" 11, 30, *K* 164) — all too factual in this world where "pity is become a trade, and generosity a science that men get rich by" (*Am* 11:10).

Cruelty is the Negation of Mercy, but Mercy and Justice are Contraries, which ultimately are synthesized, for each is essential to the other. In the rabbinical tradition, the two are combined as Elohim Jehovah. See JUSTICE.

Los combines the two. "The blow of his Hammer is Justice, the swing of his Hammer Mercy, the force of Los's Hammer is eternal Forgiveness" (*J* 88:49). Albion reproaches Los for worshipping Mercy; Los replies: "Righteousness & justice I give thee in return for thy righteousness, but I add mercy also and bind thee from destroying these little ones; am I to be only merciful to thee and cruel to all that thou hatest?" (*J* 42:19).

Mercy is also Blake's inspiration. "Sweet Mercy leads me on" (*Morning* 4, *K* 421). Palamabron, whose name Blake assumed in *Milton*, is the pity which is constantly associated with Mercy.

MERIBAH KADESH was Kadesh, or Kadesh-barnea (*Deut* i:19), a place in the land of the Amalekites, on the border of Edom. Here Moses encamped, preparing for the conquest of Canaan, and sent out the spies, who reported back to Kadesh (*Numb* xiii: 26). To relieve the extreme drought, Moses (a second time?) got water by smiting a rock; but the Lord was angered, and said, "This is the water of Meribah ['division'],'' proclaiming that of the Israelites there, only Joshua and Caleb should reach the Promised Land (*Numb* xx:12–13; *Deut* i:35–38).

Blake disapproved of the conquest of Canaan. "To me, who believe the Bible & profess myself a Christian, a defence of the Wickedness of the Israelites in murdering so many thousands under pretence of a command from God is altogether Abominable & Blasphemous. . . . God never makes one man murder another, nor one nation" (On Watson, *K* 387–88). In *Jerusalem* (68: 59) it is Gwendolen who is taught "to bring the Spies from Egypt, to raise jealousy in the bosoms of the Twelve Kings of Canaan, then to let the Spies depart to Meribah Kadesh, to the place of the Amalekite."

MERIONETHSHIRE is a maritime county in North Wales. It is the Gate of Judah (*J* 16:37) and is also assigned to Peachey (*J* 71:30).

MERLIN was the prophet and wizard at the court of King Arthur. There are many tales of his miraculous birth, his magical feats, and mysterious disappearance. His mistress was Vivien (or "Nimue," probably a misreading of "Vivien"), the Lady of the Lake, who was an enchantress. She learned from him all his lore, and finally turned it against him: to rid herself of his importunities, she entrapped him by magic under a rock or in a tree, whence he could never escape. Thus he died an ignoble death, which he foresaw in vain. According to some accounts, he could never die, and his voice is heard occasionally.

Merlin symbolizes the immortal Imagination of the Vegetative Man (*J* 36:23), "exploring the Three States of Ulro: Creation, Redemption, & Judgment" (*J* 36:42). Ac-

cording to Enitharmon, he was like Rintrah (prophetic wrath) "among the Giants of Albion" (*J* 93:13). But, like Arthur, he was eventually ruined by woman. Enitharmon exclaims: "This is Woman's World . . . I will Create secret places, and the masculine names of the places, Merlin & Arthur" (*J* 88:16). Gwendolen rejects him: "I have refused to give love to Merlin the piteous. He brings to me the Images of his Love & I reject in chastity and turn them out into the streets for Harlots, to be food to the stern Warrior" (*J* 81:2). As a result, "Gwendolen is become a Clod of Clay! Merlin is a Worm of the Valley!" (*J* 56:27). "O Merlin! Unknown among the Dead where never before Existence came, is this the Female Will...?" (*J* 34:37).

When the Cathedral Cities degenerated, "Bath stood upon the Severn with Merlin [spirit] & Bladud [body] & Arthur [heart], the Cup of Rahab in his hand" (*J* 75:2).

Blake ascribed to him one of his own revolutionary prophecies (*K* 177).

The MERSEY, like the Dee ("Chester's River") and the Ribble, empties into the Irish Sea, into which they thunder when Bowen and Conwenna cut the fibres of Benjamin (*J* 90:15).

The MESSIAH (Hebrew) is the Christ (Greek), the promised deliverer of mankind.

In *The Marriage of Heaven and Hell*, when Blake was reversing and revaluating Good and Evil, and exalting the Subconscious (or Hell), he played with the gnostic idea that the real Messiah is not the Miltonic Reason but its opponent, Desire, who was indeed cast out but formed a heaven of what he stole from the Abyss. Something was erased where the text now reads "the Jehovah of the Bible being no other than he who dwells in flaming fire" (6); I suspect that it might read ". . . [t]he [Devil] who dwells . . ." Later, the Messiah is actually called "Satan or Tempter" (17).

METALS. The four symbolic metals are

Gold (south), Silver (east), Iron (north), and Brass (west). These four are commonly grouped together in the Old Testament (*Josh* xxii:8; *I Chron* xxii:14; *II Chron* ii:7; *Job* xxviii:1–2; *Isaiah* lx:17; *Daniel* ii:32–33).

Blake assigned them to his four Zoas (*J* 97:7–11) with their compass-points. He first mentioned the quaternary in a cancelled plate of *America* (*c* 15), where four winged heralds blow their trumpets of the four metals. In the final version of this prophecy, the risen man has feet like brass, knees and thighs like silver, and a head like gold (*Am* 8:16), a vision obviously inspired by Nebuchadnezzar's dream of empire (*Dan* ii:32–33), but the freed American has no vulnerable feet of clay and brittle iron.

Although each Zoa has his special metal, he may use any or all of the others. Thus Los employs all in his work (*FZ* v:73; *J* 73:10). Urizen makes instruments of all four to measure the Immense (*FZ* vi:229), and writes four books, each of one of the metals (*FZ* viii:140). His four sons who lead the squadrons of Urthona are armed in the four metals (*FZ* vi:315).

Before *The Four Zoas*, references to the metals are usually poetic rather than symbolic; yet even so, every now and then, there are unmistakable signs that Blake had symbolism in mind. Thus, in Thel's motto, "Can Wisdom be put in a silver [love] rod [phallus]? | Or Love in a golden [reason] bowl [brain-pan]?" (*Thel* i:3–4; also earlier in *Tir* viii:18).

METHODISM originated in the spectacular revival of John and Charles Wesley and George Whitefield, which reached the masses as the official church did not do. Methodism taught an inner religion, the direct influence of the Holy Ghost upon the believer, the love of God for all mankind, and consequently salvation offered freely to all, although man's Free Will could reject it. The abuses and persecutions which followed were a matter of history. (In 1763, six students were actually expelled from Oxford for their Methodism.)

Blake admired Methodism for its emphasis on God as Love, his direct communication with the individual, and his offer of universal salvation, which contradicted official Predestination. Blake defended the Methodists against the trite accusation of hypocrisy (*J* 52, *K* 682), and praised Whitefield and Wesley (*Mil* 22:55–62), equating them with the martyred Witnesses of *Revelation* xi:7–12. "Can you have greater Miracles than these? Men who devote their life's whole comfort to intire scorn & injury & death?" (*Mil* 23:1). He named Whitefield as one of the guardians of the Gate to Beulah and a guide of the "great Wine-press of Love" (*J* 72:51).

METHUSELAH, eighth in Adam's line, is the eighth of the Twenty-seven Heavens; he is one of the first group, which are "Giants mighty, Hermaphroditic" (*Mil* 37:37; *J* 75:12).

MEXICO horrified the invading Spaniards by the sacrifice of enormous numbers of captives on the altars of pyramidic temples of stone. After an abortive attempt to achieve independence in 1810, Mexico finally threw off the Spanish yoke in 1821, adopting as the national flag the ancient Aztec emblem of an eagle flying upward with a serpent.

After Jerusalem's fall, Druid temples "were rear'd from Ireland to Mexico & Peru west" (*Mil* 6:22). The Cathedral Cities see "America clos'd out . . . and Tharmas dash'd on the Rocks of the Altars of Victims in Mexico" (*J* 43:6). But when Orc is ready to break loose, the Shadowy Female sees an Eagle in Mexico, who courts her to his love (*Am* 2:3). And Mexico is named as the twenty-eighth of the Thirty-two Nations which shall guard liberty and rule the rest of the world (*J* 72:41).

Plate 15 of *The Marriage of Heaven and Hell* depicts an eagle soaring with a serpent in its talons; Blake's design anticipates Shelley's *Revolt of Islam* I (1818) and the adoption of the Mexican flag (1821).

MICHAEL is one of the seven archangels.

He contended with the devil over the body of Moses (*Jude* 9), and is to bind Satan the Dragon in the last days (*Rev* xii:7). Blake painted water colors of both these scenes. In *A Vision of the Last Judgment* (*K* 612) Michael defeats Apollyon (*Rev* ix:11; see Illustrations, "LJ" Nos. 16, 17).

Milton used Michael in *Paradise Lost* to symbolize God's Justice. As the leader of the celestial armies, he wounds Satan in the battle of the virtues and vices, which however is drawn until the appearance of the Son. It is Michael who reveals to Adam the course of history up to the Incarnation, and then ejects the sinful pair from Paradise.

In Blake's *Milton* there is an episode probably suggested by the inconclusive battle in *Paradise Lost* vi. During the quarrel between Satan and Palamabron over the plowing, "Michael contended against Satan in the rolling thunder"; Rintrah's flames, however, caused Michael to sit down in the furrows "weary, dissolv'd in tears"; then Satan, having slain Thulloh, "stood terrible over Michael, urging him to arise"; but Enitharmon "kissed Satan, she wept over Michael: she form'd a Space for Satan & Michael . . . & clos'd it with a tender Moon" (*Mil* 8:32–44).

MICHELANGELO was to Blake's painting what Milton was to Blake's poetry.

As soon as the boy had pocket money, he collected prints by the then underestimated Michelangelo and Raphael. The first evidence of the former's influence was the engraving "Joseph of Arimathea" (1773); thereafter the influence was patent everywhere in his work.

Blake's remark to Crabb Robinson that "Michelangelo could not have done better" than the illustrations in the Law edition of Behmen (*CR* 259) was obviously a philosophical and not aesthetic judgment. It suggests that Blake had understood the symbolism of the paintings in the Sistine Chapel. Michelangelo's system starts at the entrance to the chapel with the drunkenness of Noah —man sunk in the intoxicated sleep of materialism, condemned to labor and the shame

of his own body. It continues (reversing the story of *Genesis*) towards the revelation of deity above the altar. The prophets begin with Zechariah, who is merely reading a book, and (zigzagging across the ceiling), reveal the increasing of inspiration and knowledge till it reaches Jonah (prototype of Christ), who actually beholds the deity above him. The sybils represent the corresponding decline of pagan inspiration. The whole system culminates in the Last Judgment.

MIDDLESEX is a county of England on the north bank of the Thames. Before the formation of the county of London in 1888, Middlesex contained the city. As the county is mostly flat, Blake refers to it often as a valley or valleys.

With the adjacent counties of Surrey and Kent, it is assigned to Levi (*J* 16:45); and with Sussex, Surrey, and Kent, it is also assigned to Hand (*J* 71:12).

In the disruption of England, "the little Villages of Middlesex & Surrey hunger & thirst" (*J* 30:25). When Vala casts her dark threads over the Thames "from the hills of Hertfordshire to the hills of Surrey across Middlesex" (*J* 31:68), Los combats her influence by establishing his forge in the valleys of Middlesex (*Mil* 26:19; *J* 32: 9; 34:18; 56:1; 90:39).

The ancient world of Urizen is "Created from the Valley of Middlesex by London's River" (*J* 58:45).

MIDIAN ("strife") was a son of Abraham and Keturah (*Gen* xxv:1–2). The Midianites, however, were vaguely identified with the Ishmaelites (*Gen* xxxvii:27–28). Originally they were friendly to the Israelites; Zipporah, who was married to Moses, was a Midianite; perhaps this is why "Midian" is listed in the ancestry of Mary (*FZ* viii:364), although it should be noted that the women of Midian and those of Moab were a sore temptation to the lads of Israel (*Numb* xxv: 1, 6, 18; xxxi:16). Merchants of Midian bought Joseph. Eventually the Midianites turned hostile, and for seven years occupied land claimed by the Israelites, until Gideon defeated them (*Judges* vi:1).

The Midianites inhabited the deserts across from the Sinai peninsula and south of Moab. Here the Israelites prepared for the conquest of Canaan. Joseph was carried off "into Egypt, where Ephraim & Menassheh gather'd my Sons together in the Sands of Midian" (*Mil* 24:20). Rahab appears "sitting upon Horeb, pondering dire and mighty preparations, mustering multitudes innumerable of warlike sons among the sands of Midian & Aram" (*J* 89:55).

This event is paralleled in the development of Milton's thought, when he was still involved in Old Testament morality. Rahab and the six wives and daughters surround him like "seven rocky masses terrible in the Desarts of Midian" (*Mil* 17:17). The lands of "Edom & Aram & Moab & Midian & Amalek," which engirdle the Promised Land, are the Mundane Shell, where Milton's Shadow travels (*Mil* 17:20); "here Milton journeyed in that Region call'd Midian among the Rocks of Horeb" (*Mil* 17:27).

MILCAH was the fourth daughter of Zelophehad. When man is being subjugated, Milcah is allotted the task of fastening his ear into the rock (*FZ* viii:317; *J* 68:6). The daughters are equated with Milton's wives and daughters (*Mil* 17:11). When they erect the Loom of Death in London, "Milcah's Pillars shine from Harrow to Hampstead" (*Mil* 35:11).

MILE-END, so called from its being a mile from Aldgate, is near Stepney, on the road to Bow. Here was once a hospital of lepers, to whom Edward VI granted letters patent, allowing them to beg for their support.

Los at his labors heaves iron cliffs "from Hyde Park to the Alms-houses of Mile-end & old Bow" (*Mil* 6:31).

The MILL has a function inferior to the creative Plow: it is Reason working on the ideas furnished by the Imagination. Thus it

symbolizes Aristotelean logic, the basis of dogmatism.

In the fourth "Memorable Fancy" (*MHH*), the dogmatic "angel" takes Blake down through a stable (where the horses of instruction are tethered), through a church (established dogma), into the church vault (the emphasis on death), to a mill (Aristotle's *Analytics*), and so to the Cave. When the outcome of this descent reveals the dread Leviathan, the angel retreats to the mill, but Blake refuses to argue longer with one "whose works are only Analytics."

One would expect this process to be Urizen's; but in *The Four Zoas*, when the human grain is ready, it is ground in the mills of "Dark Urthona" (who also has his logic), powered by the disastrous whirlwind of Tharmas. "Nature in darkness groans and Men are bound to sullen contemplations in the night: restless they turn on beds of sorrow; in their inmost brain feeling the crushing Wheels, they rise, they write the bitter words of Stern Philosophy & knead the bread of knowledge with tears & groans" (*FZ* ix: 816).

In *Milton*, the mills are Satan's, whose inferior work is contrasted with the creative agriculture of Palamabron. When Satan undertakes the harrowing so disastrously, Palamabron shifts to Satan's mills ("the easier task"); but under his influence the servants of the mills get intoxicated, and Los stops the grinding (8:4–23). The "dark Satanic Mills" of the opening hymn (1:8) visualize as the enormous mills of the Industrial Revolution, but signify the philosophy under which all England was suffering.

Theotormon also has his mills; they are in Allamanda, "on the verge of the Lake of Udan-Adan. These are the starry voids of night & the depths & caverns of earth. These Mills are oceans, clouds & waters ungovernable in their fury: here are the stars created & the seeds of all things planted, and here the Sun & Moon recieve their fixed destinations" (27:50).

In *Jerusalem*, the mills are simply places where slaves (like Samson) are forced to work. They are situated in the hell outside

Golgonooza (13:49; 39:3), and belong to the enemies of Israel (13:57). In winter time, the captive groans in the mill of the stranger, "sold for scanty hire" (20:16). Here the English are ground to make bread for the giants Hand and Scofield (43:49). Here Jerusalem labors, while "the Wheel of Hand incessant" turns day and night without rest (60:41); yet even here she sees her Saviour and knows that she is deluded by "the turning mills" (60:59).

The entire astronomical universe is a Mill. "O Satan . . . art thou not Prince of the Starry Hosts [Urizen] and of the Wheels of Heaven, to turn the Mills day & night? . . . To Mortals thy Mills seem every thing . . . Thy Work is Eternal Death with Mills & Ovens & Cauldrons" (*Mil* 4:9–17). But it is not so for the man of Vision. "If it were not for the Poetic or Prophetic character the Philosophic & Experimental would soon be at the ratio of all things, & stand still, unable to do other than repeat the same dull round over again" (*NNR* 1st ser., Concl.). "The bounded is loathed by its possessor. The same dull round, even of a universe, would soon become a mill with complicated wheels" (*NNR* 2nd ser., IV).

MILTON (John, 1608–74), in Blake's opinion, was England's greatest poet. He is the latest and greatest of the Sons of Los (*FZ* viii:362; *J* 73:42 *del*); and in the final revelation in *Jerusalem* (98:9), Milton takes precedence of Shakespeare and Chaucer.

In a literature dominated by realism, the symbolic line was sustained by Spenser (Milton's "original"), Milton, and Blake, his poetic son. For Milton was to Blake's poetry what Michelangelo was to his painting. The influence began early: "Milton lov'd me in childhood & shew'd me his face" (To Flaxman, 12 Sept 1800); and it continued for the rest of his life. But Blake never borrowed and copied; he took and used, for his own purposes; therefore he was no plagiarist.

The parallels between the lives as well as the works of the two men were striking.

Milton's father was disinherited for turning Protestant; Blake's father was a Dissenter. Milton's first poetic period was a great one; so was Blake's. Milton considered himself divorced from his first wife, who abandoned him, but he did not take a second wife when his first returned; Blake, unhappy with Catherine, considered taking a second woman into his home, but was dissuaded by Catherine's tears, according to Swinburne. When Milton abandoned poetry for politics, Blake condemned him as an atheist, "till in his old age he returned back to God whom he had had in childhood" (*CR* 262). But in his dishonored retirement, Milton wrote his three greatest poems; and Blake, after returning from Felpham into obscurity, wrote his three greatest poems.

Milton was one of the greatest versifiers; and Blake, the first to catch the freedom of Milton's cadences, also became one of the greatest versifiers. Milton had been the first to write a non-dramatic great poem in blank verse; Blake's first book, *Poetical Sketches*, opens with experiments in Miltonic verse (now first used for lyrics), and ends with a long poem on a Miltonic subject. Blake then applied Milton's principles to the septenary, and attacked him (quoting his own words) for not being freer (*J* 3).

Hitherto the public had read *Paradise Lost* as a versified account of past history or as an Aristotelean epic; Blake was the first to understand that Milton was trying to say something—to record "things unattempted yet in Prose or Rhime" (*PL* i:16). The challenge of Milton's ideas inspired Blake over and over.

For example, *L'Allegro* and *Il Penseroso* constitute together a circular poem, expressing innocent cheerfulness and thoughtfulness, the alternating moods of the Puritan gentleman. Each begins when the other leaves off. The poems are bound together by extensive contrasts: day—night, the lark—the nightingale, and so forth. Blake expanded the idea to the "Two Contrary States of the Human Soul," the extremes of ecstasy and despair, and bound the *Songs of Innocence* to the *Songs of Experience* by pairing contrasted lyrics, so that each complements the other.

Comus describes a young girl on the verge of Experience, who evades the evil snare of dissipation. *The Book of Thel* is a study of the same situation, but Blake's approach is biological, not moralistic, and he makes much of the strange voices which Milton's Lady silenced so easily.

Visions of the Daughters of Albion corresponds to Milton's courageous divorce pamphlets. Both attack the unhappy marriage; but where Milton is content to advocate divorce for incompatibility, Blake demands the complete freedom of love, regardless of ceremony.

America corresponds to Milton's political works. Both attack the policies of their kings and hail the revolution against them; but Blake achieves the formula of all revolutions.

In *The Marriage of Heaven and Hell*, Blake for the first time disagreed with his idol. His book may be compared to *The Christian Doctrine*; but where Milton consolidated the old system, with important alterations, Blake demolished it entirely, and proclaimed a totally new view of the universe, incidentally suggesting broadly that Milton's Messiah is really Satan, and hinting that the real Messiah, the tempter, is what Milton considered the Devil. But Milton "was a true Poet and of the Devil's party without knowing it" (*MHH* 5).

In *Europe*, Blake attacked one of Milton's favorite ideals, Chastity, asserting that it was a product of the Female Will, for which he blamed conventional Christianity, quoting from the *Hymn on the Nativity* to fix the date of its beginning.

The Four Zoas is Blake's rewriting of *Paradise Lost*. Both are epics beginning *in medias res*; both deal with the fall and salvation of man; both demonstrate the justice (or mercy) of God; both use the whole universe for setting. There are necessary parallel episodes, but acted by different characters. Urizen and Luvah conspire at midnight to seize the supreme power; Urizen creates the universe with his compasses; Orc becomes

the Serpent; Los and Enitharmon eat of the fruit of the fatal Tree. Milton's chief interest —and hence the chief interest of the poem —lay in his analysis of the progressive damnation of Satan, who sinks lower and lower until he loses all human form and becomes the Dragon; while Urizen, whom Blake identified with Satan, sinks steadily until he is also the Dragon. However, once he renounces his desire for dominion, he instantly recovers his "radiant youth."

Milton, a Poem in 2 Books is a study of Milton's spiritual development, an analysis of his errors, and an account of his relationship to Blake. See MILTON, A POEM, below.

Jerusalem corresponds to the *History of Britain*. "Believing with Milton the ancient British History" (*DesC* V, *K* 578), Blake expanded the myths into the fall and resurrection of Albion, the history of all mankind. His daughters are named for characters in the *History*. At the end, Milton appears in the heavens with Shakespeare and Chaucer.

Blake also illustrated all of Milton's chief poems, except *Samson Agonistes*. No other illustrator was ever so precise in following the text, even through the more complicated metaphors, and no other illustrator ever included interpretations of his own.

See ELY.

MILTON, A POEM | *in 2 Books* | *The Author* | *& Printer W Blake* | *1804.* | *To Justify the Ways of God to Men*. Originally the title page seems to have read "in 12 Books," indicating that in 1804 Blake may have intended a much longer poem; indeed, writing to Butts (25 April 1803) of his quarrel with Hayley at Felpham, he spoke of his poem as containing "an immense number of verses on One Grand Theme, similar to Homer's Iliad or Milton's Paradise Lost . . . I have written this Poem from immediate Dictation, twelve or sometimes twenty or thirty lines at a time, without Premeditation & even against my Will . . . & an immense Poem Exists which seems to be the Labour of a long Life, all produc'd without Labour or Study. . . ." In his next letter to Butts (6 July 1803) he wrote further of it: "Thus I hope that all our three years' trouble Ends in Good Luck at last & shall be forgot by my affections & only remember'd by my Understanding; to be a Memento in time to come, & to speak to future generations by a Sublime Allegory, which is now perfectly completed into a Grand Poem. I may praise it, since I dare not pretend to be any other than the Secretary; the Authors are in Eternity. I consider it as the Grandest Poem that this World Contains. . . . [Mr. Hayley] knows that I have writ it, for I have shewn it to him, & he has read Part by his own desire, & has looked with sufficient contempt to inhance my opinion of it." R. L. Smith, in his *Nativity of Mr. Blake* (not published until 1825), stated: "He has now by him a long poem nearly finished, which he affirms was recited to him by the spirit of Milton" (*Symons* 340). On January 6, 1826, Crabb Robinson (who did not always understand just what Blake meant) recorded: "The oddest thing he said was that he had been commanded . . . to write about Milton, and that he was applauded for refusing—he struggled with the Angels and was victor" (*CR* 265). Blake indeed had written "against his will" at times.

The poem was partly written at Felpham; it was continued in London; the title page was etched in 1804; but it was not until around 1810 that Blake wrote in his *Public Address* about "a Poem concerning my Three years' Herculean Labours at Felpham, which I will soon Publish" (*K* 592).

But after it was published, Blake continued to work on it. Four copies are known. The first two have forty-five leaves each; the third omits the preface and adds five new leaves; the fourth is like the third, but adds yet another leaf. This last copy is watermarked 1815, and may have been the copy offered for sale to Dawson Turner in 1818.

The leading purpose of the poem was avowedly to correct Milton's errors. On December 17, 1825, Crabb Robinson understood Blake to say: "I saw Milton in imagination, and he told me to beware of being misled by his Paradise Lost. In particular

he wished me to show the falsehood of his doctrine that the pleasures of *sex* arose from the fall. The fall could not produce any pleasure" (*CR* 263). Of course Robinson misunderstood: Milton had made sex one of the joys of Paradise; Blake doubtless was referring to the untimely outburst of lust after the eating of the apple. But when Robinson rewrote this episode (*CR* 295), he deepened his error: Blake said that Milton "came lately as an old man . . . he came to ask a favour of me. He said he had committed an error in his Paradise Lost, which he wanted me to correct, in a poem or picture; but I declined. I said I had my own duties to perform. . . . He wished me to expose the falsehood of his doctrine, taught in the Paradise Lost, that sexual intercourse arose out of the Fall. Now that cannot be, for no good can spring out of evil."

While Blake agreed heartily with Milton on the holiness of sex, he did not agree that love "hath his seat in Reason" (*PL* viii: 590); for Milton was a traditionalist in accepting Reason as man's supreme faculty, "Fansie" coming only second (*PL* v:102). Here evidently lay Milton's flaw: sensitive to sex, he yet feared its irrational power. It is only a relief, not an inspiration. Adam, who as the image of God is Reason, is warned particularly against allowing Eve to influence him; and when she does, man falls. Eve should be simply his "help," assisting in cultivating the garden, providing lunches for unexpected guests, and sharing the nuptial couch. Milton, in short, undervalued women; hence perhaps his honeymoon difficulties with Mary Powell; hence also his difficulties with his daughters.

In elevating Reason, Milton had mistaken Urizen for God. His Father is "Destiny" (*MHH* 6); "what I will is Fate" (*PL* vii: 173). He is enthroned inaccessible and invisible in the highest heaven. The Son, whom Blake calls "a ratio of the five senses" (*MHH* 6), is a materialist of the school of Locke. Blake equates him with the accusing Satan in *Job* (*MHH* 6); and indeed, the chief action of the Son is that of driving the revolted angels out of heaven. The real Messiah is Milton's "Satan or Tempter" (*MHH*

17). Milton's Holy Ghost is "Vacuum" (*MHH* 6). He does nothing visibly in *Paradise Lost*; but then he could not become visible until the Pentecost. (It might be argued, however, that Satan's temptations to relent and spare were due to the Ghost working invisible and unrecognized.)

We can trace much of this in "Milton's Dream," the penultimate illustration of *Il Penseroso* (see Illustrations). The lad sleeps on the bank of a brook in a grove of oaks. His hands are crossed over his lap, suggesting repression rather than protection; while behind a heavy fold in his dream, two hidden lovers embrace. In the sky, Urizen is attended by wailing souls; he partially obscures the Father seated behind him. The "strange mysterious dream" hovers above Milton, drawing from the brook figures caught in nets and webs, while six fairies play musical instruments around the poet.

These points should clarify Blake's poem, which concerns Milton's coming to Blake so that his errors could be corrected. It is a criticism of Milton's ideas and of their effect on Blake. It is also the autobiography of the poem itself, a study of the psychology of creation; like Joyce's *Ulysses*, it is a book whose subject is its own composition.

Milton (d. 1674) has been a century in Eternity, "unhappy tho' in heaven" because he is still separated from his Sixfold Emanation (his three wives and three daughters), which is "scatter'd thro' the deep in torment." Therefore "a Bard's prophetic Song" moves him to descend into the deep to redeem her, though it means that he himself shall perish (*Mil* 2:16–24).

The Bard's song recounts the quarrel of Satan (Hayley) and Palamabron (Blake). It involves the revolt and fall of Satan, the creation of Hell, and the birth of Sin and Death. A brief prelude tells of the preliminaries: Albion is slain; Los forges a form for Urizen; and Enitharmon, having become separate, gives birth to Orc, the Shadowy Female, and all her other children, last of whom ("Refusing Form in vain") is Satan.

Satan-Hayley is one of the Elect (*Mil* 7: 6). See CLASSES. He is a Pharisee, absolutely sure of himself, the corporeal friend who is a spiritual enemy, "seeming a brother, being a tyrant, even thinking himself a brother while he is murdering the just" (7:24). He persists in taking over the harrow of Palamabron-Blake, and throws everything into confusion. Rintrah (Blake's wrath) flames up. Palamabron calls an assembly of Eternals; they lay the blame on Rintrah, for "If the Guilty should be condemn'd he must be an Eternal Death, and one must die for another throughout all Eternity" (11:17). Meanwhile Satan has also flamed up, proclaiming himself God; "his bosom grew opake against the Divine Vision" and in his bosom was revealed "a World of deeper Ulro" (9:31–35).

At this point, Leutha (Hayley's feminine side) takes the blame on herself (11:35). Because she loved Palamabron, she "stupified [Satan's] masculine perceptions and kept only the feminine awake" (12:5). "Satan astonish'd and with power above his own controll compell'd the Gnomes to curb the horses & to throw banks of sand around the fiery flaming Harrow" (12:16). The revolt of the angels ensued: "Chaos & ancient night fled"; the flames "orb'd us round in concave fires, a Hell of our own making . . . Satan in pride of heart drove the fierce Harrow among the constellations of Jehovah, drawing a third part in the fires" (12:21–26; cf. *Rev* xii:4); and finally Leutha sprang from Satan's head, and is recognized as Sin (12:38; cf. *PL* ii:760). At this revelation, Satan "drove [her] from his inmost Brain & the doors clos'd with thunder's sound" (12:48).

Leutha hides in Enitharmon's tent (13: 14); Elynittria brings her to Palamabron's bed "in moments new created for delusion . . . In dreams she bore the shadowy Spectre of Sleep & nam'd him Death [cf. *PL* ii:787]; in dreams she bore Rahab, the mother of Tirzah & her sisters . . . and Oothoon was her charming guard" (13:39–44).

Here the Bard ends his song. Terrified at its earth-shaking consequences, he takes refuge in Milton's bosom.

Then Milton rises, announcing his return to earth. "I will go down to self annihilation and eternal death, lest the Last Judgment come & find me unannihilate and I be siez'd & giv'n into the hands of my own Selfhood. . . . What do I here before the Judgment? without my Emanation? . . . I in my Selfhood am that Satan: I am that Evil One! He is my Spectre!" (14:22–31).

Descent is division. As Spectre he enters his Shadow of unfulfilled desire, while his "real and immortal Self" (15:11) reposes on a golden couch in Beulah, sleepwalking with the seven Angels of the Presence, of whom he is the Eighth (15:5). This descent in his Shadow re-enacts his mental development. First he sees Albion in his sleep of death (15:36), and falls through his bosom into the Sea of Time and Space (15:42). Then he perceives his distant wives and daughters, whom he recognizes as human, though in this world ("Death's Vale") he was in conflict with them (17:1–8), and to them he dictates "the cruelties of Ulro . . . and his body was the Rock Sinai" (17:9–17). Then he continues journeying in the heathen lands surrounding Palestine (17:18) on his way to Golgonooza.

Los and Enitharmon, fearing his errors, oppose him (17:31). The Shadowy Female laments what must be the results of his doctrine, which would set her up as God (18:19); Orc begs her not to take "the Human Form" (which is God's), for Jerusalem is man's Garment, "& not thy Covering Cherub" (18:37).

Urizen then opposes Milton's progress. They struggle. Urizen baptizes Milton with the icy waters of the Jordan (conventional dogma), while Milton molds for Urizen a human form of the living red clay of Succoth. See SUCCOTH. Rahab and Tirzah also oppose him, sending forth their daughters to mislead him with the allures of sex. But Milton does not heed them: he is busy giving Urizen a human (divine) form; he is establishing him as God. Milton's "Mortal part," which is of the Elect, is "frozen in the rock of Horeb," the morality of the Old Testament; his "Redeem'd portion" gives form to Urizen; while within, his "real Human," though darkened, walks above with the Seven Angels.

Blake was particularly challenged by Milton's errors, though he did not know it for some time, "for man cannot know what passes in his members till periods of Space & Time reveal the secrets of Eternity" (21:8). He had first seen the descending Milton in the Zenith (south) as he dropped like a falling star into the Sea of Time and Space (15:47); then "that portion nam'd the Elect, the Spectrous body of Milton" (20:20) entered Blake's left foot (south). Blake depicted this event on Plate 29, adding another, showing on Plate 33 the same thing happening to his brother Robert, his constant collaborator, though there the falling star enters Robert's right foot.

Blake, sensing the inspiration, prepares to work. "All this Vegetable World appear'd on my left Foot as a bright sandal form'd immortal of precious stones & gold. I stooped down & bound it on to walk forward thro' Eternity" (21:12). Los appears behind him in a terrible sun and helps bind his sandals, kisses him, and enters his soul, so they become one man (22:4–13). But Rintrah and Palamabron try to persuade Los not to admit Blake, with his "fibrous left Foot black" (22:35), to Golgonooza because of the dangers of his revolutionary thought. They blame Milton's religion as the cause of the world chaos; they assert that he has entered the Covering Cherub and will utterly consume them (23:13). Los replies that he has become one with "the falling Death" (23:33); that there is an old prophecy that Milton shall "up ascend forward from Felpham's Vale & break the Chain of Jealousy from all its roots" (23:37); and "as to this Elected Form who is return'd again, he is the Signal that the Last Vintage now approaches" (24:41).

Los's Wine-press at the Vintage is the war in Europe. "The Wine-press on the Rhine groans loud, but all its central beams act more terrific in the central Cities of the Nations where Human Thought is crush'd beneath the iron hand of Power" (25:3). Los directs his workers to sort all men into the three Classes (25:26); and his reapers for the Great Harvest are to start at Lambeth (25:48).

Meanwhile Ololon is drawn to the falling

Milton. Though he does not know her, she is his basic sexual ideal, the eternal form of the Sixfold Emanation. Therefore it was she who drove Milton down to redeem the Sixfold Emanation (21:31; 34:3), for which she feels penitent (21:50). As yet she has no fixed form; she is a river (21:15), a fiery circle (34:3), clouds which contain the Saviour (21:50); she is "multitudes" (35:47). She proposes: "Let us descend also, and let us give ourselves to death in Ulro among the Transgressors" (21:45); but though the Divine Family warns her "you cannot renew Milton: he goes to Eternal Death" (21:57), "all Ololon" descends into Beulah (31:8), lamenting over Milton. When the multitudes find Milton's death-couch, "they thunderous utter'd all a universal groan, falling down prostrate before the Starry Eight asking with tears forgiveness, confessing their crime with humiliation and sorrow" (35:31). But their descent has opened a wide road back into Eternity (35: 35-36).

Already Milton has been learning something of his mistakes; he has often sat up on his death-couch and "conversed in vision & dream beatific" with the Seven Angels. He admits that he has not faced "these Heavens builded on cruelty"; therefore "my Spectre still wandering thro' them follows my Emanation" (32:3). But Lucifer the morning star instructs him to avoid blaming individuals, by distinguishing them from the States through which they are passing (32:8–38). Then the Divine Voice describes Milton's unhappy marriage, saying that the hostile wife will change.

Behold Milton descended to Redeem the Female Shade from Death Eternal ... When the Sixfold Female percieves that Milton annihilates himself, that seeing all his loves by her cut off, he leaves her also, intirely abstracting himself from Female loves, she shall relent in fear of death; She shall begin to give her maidens to her husband, delighting in his delight. And then & then alone begins the happy Female joy as it is done in Beulah.

(33:11–20)

All these events now culminate in the great moment of inspiration. It takes place in Blake's garden at Felpham, in the earliest dawn, when the scent of the wild thyme impregnates the air and the larks are just beginning to soar. See LARK. One lark meets Ololon as she descends into the garden (36:10). At last she has taken a definite form, that of "a Virgin of twelve years" (36:17), who has just reached the point of fertility. She asks Blake: "Knowest thou of Milton who descended driven from Eternity? him I seek, terrified at my Act in Great Eternity which thou knowest: I come him to seek" (37:1).

Her question precipitates the ensuing revelations. Milton's Shadow shows himself as the Covering Cherub (37:8), who is the Twenty-seven Churches of conventional Christianity (37:35, 60); within him is Satan, who sums up the Twelve Gods of paganism (37:20, 60). But the Human Form of Milton, "clothed in black, severe & silent," descends into Blake's garden (37:14; 38:8). He is now able to confront his Spectre or Satan, who stands upon the ocean, thundering against him (38:9). Milton denounces him and his Natural Religion (38: 29); Satan replies that he himself is "God the judge of all" (38:51). He imitates "the Eternal Great Humanity Divine" surrounded by Cherubim, though without Seraphim (39:26; cf. "God-like imitated State," PL ii:511). But "Beneath sat Chaos: Sin on his right hand, Death on his left, and Ancient Night spread over all the heav'n his Mantle of Laws" (39:29). See CHAOS.

Already the Starry Seven have blown the trumpets of Judgment, calling on Albion to awake (39:10). He had begun to turn on his couch when Milton descended (20:25); he now rises up (39:32), but his strength fails him and he sinks back (39:50). Urizen, who is still striving with Milton's spirit, faints (39:53). Ololon sees him and tells Milton; she says he also strives with the fallen Zoas, and condemns his Natural Religion (40:4). Rahab then manifests, "glorious as the midday Sun in Satan's bosom glowing ... Religion hidden in War" (40: 19) — the historical Milton had endorsed religious war—and beneath her are the divided Nations.

The inspired Milton now addresses Ololon, denouncing "the Spectre, the Reasoning Power in Man" (40:34), also all the pretenders to art and science, for "These are the destroyers of Jerusalem, these are the murderers of Jesus . . . These are the Sexual Garments, the Abomination of Desolation, hiding the Human Lineaments as with an Ark & Curtains, which Jesus rent & now shall wholly purge away with Fire, till Generation is swallow'd up in Regeneration" (41:21–28).

To Ololon, the absorption of the Female in the Male, when the sexes are united in Eternity, seems to be nothing less than annihilation. "Is this our Femin[in]e Portion, the Six-fold Miltonic Female? . . . Altho' our Human Power can sustain the severe contentions of Friendship, our Sexual cannot, but flies into the Ulro. Hence arose all our terrors in Eternity; & now remembrance returns upon us; are we Contraries, O Milton, Thou & I?" (41:30–35).

The question answers itself. The error is faced; the false is cast out. The Sixfold Emanation divides from Ololon and flees into the depths of Milton's Shadow, as a Dove upon a stormy sea (42:8)—the erring wife repents and finds refuge in her husband's love.

Then, like "a Moony Ark" (42:7)—the love which bears man over the Sea of Time and Space—the purified Ololon descends "into the Fires of Intellect that rejoic'd in Felpham's Vale around the Starry Eight; with one accord the Starry Eight became One Man, Jesus the Saviour, wonderful! round his limbs the Clouds of Ololon folded as a garment dipped in blood [the wedding garment of the Word at his marriage to Jerusalem, Rev xix:13], written within & without in [symbolic] woven letters, & the Writing is the Divine Revelation in the Litteral expression, a Garment of [spiritual] War," which is the basic history of all time (42:9).

The rejuvenated Twenty-four Cathedral Cities resume their thrones to judge the nations, while their dominant Four arise round

Albion's body (42:16). Then Jesus enters Albion's bosom, "the bosom of death"—God and man are reunited in the mystical ecstasy.

Terror-struck, Blake falls unconscious on his garden path, and recovers, to find Catherine, "my sweet Shadow of Delight" (42:28), beside him.

Immediately the lark mounts, greeting the new day with his song. For everything is prepared and waiting for "the Great Harvest & Vintage of the Nations" (43:1).

The act of the poem is one, but the causes are so complex that Blake had to invent an original structure, to suggest the simultaneousness of all the material. He introduced material without any preparation, abruptly changing the subject over and over. Thus the lark, who is the idea of the poem, and whose song marks the mystical ecstasy (42:29), first is mentioned in 17:27; he sings in 31:29; his nest is located in 35:58; he is a messenger in 35:63–67; and (with material about the other larks) he meets Ololon (36:10). The universe of Los, which is the setting for the poem, is thus introduced at considerable length, while the astronomical universe is described and related to man.

Had Blake taken time to introduce his material in logical sequence, he would have ruined the effect of culminating immediacy.

MINUTE PARTICULARS are the outward expression in this world of the eternal individualities of all things. God, "the Divine-Humanity," is ultimately "the Only General and Universal Form" (J 43:20); he contains all things, including the various Universal Forms, the sources of the Particulars (LJ, K 605). The Minute Particulars of God are men (J 91:31); of men, they are their children (J 55:51); of life, the joys of living (J 31:7), especially the embraces of love (J 69:42); of ethics, forgiveness instead of judgment (J 43:61); of art, the vision and the finished product; of science, the basic facts (J 55:62). In short, they are reality as we encounter it. They are not negligible aberrations from a Platonic norm, but are highly organized and direct expressions of their eternal and individual existences. "Every Minute Particular is Holy" (*J* 69: 42).

"The Oak dies as well as the Lettuce, but Its Eternal Image & Individuality never dies, but renews by its seed . . . There Exist in [the] Eternal World the Permanent Realities of Every Thing which we see reflected in this Vegetable Glass of Nature. All Things are comprehended in their Eternal Forms in the divine body of the Saviour" (*LJ*, *K* 605–6).

As the body is the source of energy (*MHH* 4), so the Minute Particulars are the source of vitality. "General Forms have their vitality in Particulars, & every Particular is a Man, a Divine Member of the Divine Jesus" (*J* 91:30).

Blake was reacting against the neoclassical attempt to get at the principles of things by discarding the details; these very details, he insisted, were the key to perception, whatever the subject. "Sacrifice the Parts, What becomes of the Whole?" (On Reynolds, *K* 462). "Minute Discrimination is Not Accidental. All Sublimity is founded on Minute Discrimination" (On Reynolds, *K* 453). "What is General Nature? is there Such a Thing? what is General Knowledge? is there such a Thing? Strictly Speaking, All Knowledge is Particular" (On Reynolds, *K* 459).

"Art & Science cannot exist but in minutely organized Particulars" (*J* 55:62). In poetry, "Every word and every letter" must be studied (*J* 3); in painting, every line and stroke. "He who wishes to see a Vision, a perfect Whole, must see it in its Minute Particulars, Organized" (*J* 91:21). "He who does not imagine in stronger and better lineaments, and in stronger and better light than his perishing and mortal eye can see, does not imagine at all. The painter of this work asserts that all his imaginations appear to him infinitely more perfect and more minutely organized than any thing seen by his mortal eye" (*DesC* IV, *K* 576).

In love, "every Minute Particular is Holy: Embraces are Cominglings from the Head even to the Feet, and not a pompous High Priest entering by a Secret Place" (*J* 69: 42). But if you are "under the dominion of a jealous Female . . . you shall want all the Minute Particulars of Life" (*J* 88:41–43).

The degradation of the poor in London and the attempts of the benevolent to ameliorate it with their asylums and workhouses and other charities provoked Blake's horror and scorn, because Moral Virtue had replaced and petrified the immediate perceptions and reactions.

The poet, in his walk through the city, "saw every Minute Particular of Albion degraded & murder'd . . . every minute particular, the jewels of Albion, running down the kennels of the streets & lanes as if they were abhorr'd. Every Universal Form was become barren mountains of Moral Virtue, and every Minute Particular harden'd into grains of sand" (*J* 31:7–20). In true charity, "All broad & general principles belong to benevolence, who protects minute particulars, every one in their own identity" (*J* 43:22). "Labour well the Minute Particulars, attend to the Little-ones, and those who are in misery cannot remain so long, if we do but our duty" (*J* 55:51). "He who would do good to another must do it in Minute Particulars: General Good is the plea of the scoundrel, hypocrite, & flatterer" (*J* 55:60). But alas! "Instead of the Mutual Forgivenesses, the Minute Particulars, I see Pits of bitumen" (*J* 43:61). In the head of the Covering Cherub, "Minute Particulars in slavery I behold among the brick-kilns disorganiz'd" (*J* 89: 17). The poet addresses the Fiend of Righteousness: "You smile with pomp & rigor, you talk of benevolence & virtue . . . You accumulate Particulars & murder by analyzing, that you may take the aggregate, & you call the aggregate Moral Law, and you call that swell'd & bloated Form a Minute Particular" (*J* 91:25–29).

MIRACLES which violate the laws of nature never have occurred. "The manner of a miracle being performed is in modern times considered as an arbitrary command of the agent upon the patient, but this is an impossibility, not a miracle, neither did Jesus ever do such a miracle" (On Watson, *K* 391). Blake of course interpreted the miracles ascribed to Christ as spiritual events.

The real miracle takes place in the mental realm, not the physical. "Thought is Act. Christ's Acts were Nothing to Caesar's if this is not so" (On Bacon, *K* 400). Thomas Paine was such a thinker.

Is it a greater miracle to feed five thousand men with five loaves than to overthrow all the armies of Europe with a small pamphlet? Look over the events of your own life & if you do not find that you have both done such miracles & lived by such you do not see as I do. True, I cannot do a miracle thro' experiment & to domineer over & prove to others my superior power, as neither could Christ. But I can & do work such as both astonish & comfort me & mine. How can Paine, the worker of miracles, ever doubt Christ's in the above sense of the word miracle? But how can Watson ever believe the above sense of a miracle, who considers it as an arbitrary act of the agent upon an unbelieving patient, whereas the Gospel says that Christ could not do a miracle because of Unbelief? If Christ could not do miracles because of Unbelief, the reason alledged by Priests for miracles is false; for those who believe want not to be confounded by miracles. Christ & his Prophets & Apostles were not Ambitious miracle mongers.

(On Watson, *K* 391)

However, physical miracles were commonly taken to be proofs of the genuineness of the prophet. Pharaoh demanded them (*Exod* vii:9); the mockers at the Crucifixion demanded them. "Shew us Miracles!" the skeptics demanded of Whitefield and Wesley (*Mil* 22:62). Blake replied: "Can you have greater Miracles than these? Men who devote their life's whole comfort to intire scorn & injury & death?" (*Mil* 23:1).

The MIRTLE (myrtle) tree (*Myrtus communis*) was sacred to Venus and thus a symbol of sex. In the long first draft of "Infant

Sorrow" (*SoE*; *K* 167, 890), the shady mirtle tree symbolizes the bondage of marriage. The father (or priest) binds the growing lad in a "mirtle shade"; but when he perceives that the hypocritical father embraces the blossoms, the lad smites him, "& his gore | Stain'd the roots my mirtle bore." In warfare, there is no "shadow of a mirtle tree" (*J* 65:50).

MIZRAIM, a son of Ham and grandson of Noah, was the traditional ancestor of the Africans. In the days of Innocence, man walked "with Mizraim upon the Egyptian Nile" (*J* 60:18).

MNE SERAPHIM is a parent of Thel and her sisters (*Thel* 1:1). The name means nothing, and seems to be Blake's alteration of "Bne Seraphim" ("the sons of the Seraphim"). This latter name is to be found in Agrippa's *Occult Philosophy* (II, xxii), in which book Blake also found the names of Tiriel and Zazel. According to Agrippa, the Bne Seraphim are "the Intelligences of Venus."

MNETHA, a character in *Tiriel*, is the guardian of Har and Heva. Her name is virtually an anagram of "Athena." She represents neoclassical criticism, which protects decadent poetry and painting. Har (poetry) mistakenly supposes she is his mother (*Tir* ii:26).

Though she is "now aged" (*Tir* ii:6) she is thoroughly active. She provides her charges with a tent, food, and clothing. When she thinks they are threatened, she arms herself with bow and arrows. She pities the blind and starving Tiriel, and offers to take care of him the rest of his life. He is able to deceive her as to his identity, and frightens her with his frowns when he insists on leaving.

MOAB was one of the heathen nations surrounding Palestine.

Moab was the son of Lot by his older daughter (*Gen* xix:37). His descendants occupied land on the eastern shore of the

Dead Sea. To the south lay Midian; to the north, across the Arnon, lay Sihon and Ammon. The Moabites worshipped Chemosh (*Mil* 37:20).

Ruth the Moabite was an ancestress of David and the Messiah (*Matt* i:5; *J* 62:11). "Moab" is the tenth daughter of Los and Enitharmon and an ancestress of Mary, in the Maternal Line as given in *The Four Zoas* viii:365.

Moab generally signifies whoredom: the heathen women were a great temptation to the sons of Israel (as in *Numb* xxv:1, 6). Babylon is their chief desire, Moab their bath in summer (*J* 82:31). They torture their victims, and try to lure Milton from his path (*Mil* 19:36–20:6). Vala once is called a "beautiful daughter of Moab" (*J* 20:28).

Amalek, Canaan, and Moab form an evil trinity, probably representing the loins, heart, and head, or vice versa. Tirzah's "various divisions are call'd the daughters of Amalek, Canaan & Moab, binding on the stones their victims, & with knives wounding them" (*FZ* viii:294). The Daughters of Albion are divided in three and named Amalek, Canaan, and Moab (*J* 82:24). When the tribes fled, the three also fled "into that abhorred Void; they became Nations in our sight beneath the hands of Tirzah" (*Mil* 24:15). Their victims' cries resound to the three lands (*J* 80:50).

Los and Enitharmon flee from Albion's valleys eastward from the three (*J* 29:31). He calls in vain to the three (*J* 83:16–17). With Ammon, Egypt, and Aram, the three "recieve" (enslave) Jerusalem's children (*J* 5:14). The tribes take root in Moab and four others (*J* 49:43). In Jerusalem's reins the poet beholds "Moab & Ammon & Amalek" (*J* 86:28). Moab and others are in the bosom of the Covering Cherub (*J* 82:24), also in his chaos (*J* 92:23).

MODESTY was not a virtue, according to Blake: it was instead a concealment of natural desire, a cowardice, an acquired hypocrisy, and a trap for the male. The honest Oothoon praises the frankness of virgin

bliss, then asks the other women: "Who taught thee modesty, subtil modesty? . . . Then com'st thou forth a modest virgin, knowing to dissemble, with nets found under thy night pillow . . . And does my Theotormon seek this hypocrite modesty, this knowing, artful, secret, fearful, cautious, trembling hypocrite?" (*VDA* 6:7–17).

It is the "modest" (or "lustful") rose which puts forth the defensive thorn, in contrast to the genuine innocence of the lily (*SoE*, "The Lilly"). Fearful modesty drives away the true lover, until the girl is an old maid (*SoE*, "The Angel"). This "dark pretence to Chastity" led the Magdalen into secret adulteries (*EG* e:70–73).

Men also can be hypocrites. When Stothard was praised for his "reserve & modesty," Blake replied: "The Fox, the Owl, the Beetle & the Bat | By sweet reserve & modesty get Fat" (*K* 545).

It should be noted that Shame was the first sign of the Fall of Man.

The MOLE is the explorer of the subconscious. "Does the Eagle know what is in the pit? | Or wilt thou go ask the Mole?" (*Thel* i:1).

MOLECH was the god for whom children (especially first sons) were burned alive. Blake depicted him as a furnace in human form, sceptered and crowned with iron, in the third illustration to Milton's *Hymn on the Nativity*.

The practice of sacrificing children was anciently widespread in the Near East. Molech was originally an Ammonite deity; his duplicate, Chemosh (*J* 84:21), was worshipped in Moab (*I Kings* xi:7; *Mil* 37:21). Children were also sacrificed in Canaan (Tyre) and in its colony, Carthage.

The Lord himself ordered Abraham to sacrifice Isaac; and though the tragedy was averted, he later accepted the sacrifice of Jephthah's daughter. "The firstborn of thy sons" were among the first fruits which he demanded as his (*Exod* xxii:29). Although the sacrifice had been forbidden in *Leviticus* (xviii:21; xx:2), Solomon erected the sacrificial altar at Topheth in the Hinnom Valley of Jerusalem (*I Kings* xi:7); here King Manasseh sacrificed his son (*II Kings* xxi:6). Josiah tried to stop the practice by defiling Topheth (*II Kings* xxiii:10); yet Isaiah, attacking the Assyrians, praised the practice as anciently and divinely ordained: "the breath of the Lord, like a stream of brimstone, doth kindle it" (*Isaiah* xxx:33). The other prophets, however, denounced the practice (*Jeremiah* vii:31; *Ezek* xx:26; *Amos* v:22, 26; *Micah* vi:7), and the chroniclers described it as a reversion to idolatry.

It is not so startling then that Blake (anticipating the modern scholars) should have included Molech in the seven Eyes of God. These Eyes represent man's spiritual development from the completely self-centered Lucifer to Jesus. Molech, to whom others are sacrificed, follows Lucifer as the second Eye (*FZ* viii:400; *Mil* 13:19; *J* 55:32). He is the Executioner, but proves too impatient to hold his post.

When Satan interferes with Palamabron's creative work, they quarrel beneath a thunderstorm, in which Jehovah's rain (inspiration) contends with the destructive "thick fires" of Molech (*Mil* 8:27).

In *Paradise Lost*, Molech symbolizes blind wrath and the spirit of war. Blake saw that nowhere else are sons sacrificed more extensively than on the battlefield; and he also was aware of the connection between suppressed sex and warfare. Therefore Molech, the fourth of the Twelve Gods of Asia, has his pale priestesses "infolded in Veils of Pestilence border'd with War, Woven in Looms of Tyre & Sidon by beautiful Ashtaroth" (*Mil* 37:23). Molech presides over the saturnalia of the warriors and the Daughters of Albion. The warriors invoke him (*J* 68:17). He rejoices to see the Daughters torturing their victims (for in the sexual war, such "love" is really hate). His spirit rushes into the kings, who seek the Daughters' love in vain; they refuse, and demand "your first born of seven years old, be they Males or Females" (*J* 68:31). "Molech rejoices thro' the Land from Havilah to Shur: he rejoices in moral law & its severe penalties" (*J* 68:38).

For Molech and Chemosh are the "Generalizing Gods" who (ignoring that "One Law for the Lion & Ox is Oppression") devise laws of conduct from the general behavior of mankind and then punish individuals for not obeying their laws. Thus they are seen in the bosom of the Covering Cherub, holding Israel in bondage (*J* 89:31). Hand, at the height of his power, combines into "the Double Molech & Chemosh" (*J* 84:21).

The MOMENT of Inspiration is the time when "the Poet's Work is Done, and all the Great Events of Time start forth & are conciev'd in such a Period, within a Moment, a Pulsation of the Artery" (*Mil* 29:1). "Every Time less than a pulsation of the artery is equal in its period & value to Six Thousand Years" (*Mil* 28:62), that is, to all preceding time. For "to create a little flower is the labour of ages" (*MHH* 9), and all preceding history is the preparation for the creative inspiration. The entire book of *Milton* is an analysis of the causes of Blake's moment in his Felpham garden.

As Los is Time, his Sons build all Moments and the other periods of time. But all Moments are not creative. "And every Moment has a Couch of gold for soft repose . . . and between every two Moments stands a Daughter of Beulah to feed the Sleepers on their Couches with maternal care" (*Mil* 28:46–49). Each period of time has its guard, and "All are the work of Fairy hands of the Four Elements" (*Mil* 28:59–60).

There is a Moment in each Day that Satan cannot find, nor can his Watch Fiends find it; but the Industrious find this Moment & it multiply, & when it once is found, it renovates every Moment of the Day if rightly placed. In this Moment Ololon [the real inspiration of Milton] descended to Los & Enitharmon [the poetic powers] unseen beyond the Mundane Shell [this world of matter], Southward [the realm of thought] in Milton's track.

(*Mil* 35:42)

MONA was the Roman name for the Isle of

Anglesea, a county of North Wales. It is unique among the counties of North Wales in that it is not mountainous, its highest point being Holyhead Hill (703 feet). Notable druidic ruins are to be found here.

When the Daughters of Albion triumph among the Druid Temples, "the Moon is leprous as snow, trembling & descending down, seeking to rest on high Mona, scattering her leprous snows in flakes of disease over Albion" (*J* 66:78).

See ANGLESEA.

A MONK could not conceivably be a hypocrite, according to Blake, nor were "the poor Monks & Religious" the causes of war, as Voltaire and the other skeptics believed (*J* 52, *K* 682–83).

The "Monk of Charlemaine" is a pacifist who is crucified in his cell because of the accusations of Gibbon, Voltaire, and "the Schools" (*J* 52). The first draft of this poem is to be found in the Note-Book (*K* 418–20). A fair copy, *The Grey Monk*, in the Pickering Manuscript (*K* 430), contains stanzas not used in *Jerusalem*.

MONMOUTH is a maritime county in the west of England. With Derby and Cheshire it is assigned to Benjamin (*J* 16:49). Apparently through an oversight it is not assigned to any Son of Albion.

Albion sees his children (soldiers) scourged along the roads "from Lincoln & Norwich, from Edinburgh & Monmouth" (*J* 21:39).

MONTGOMERYSHIRE, an inland county of North Wales, is "the Gate of Levi" (*J* 16:36). As part of North Wales, it is assigned to Peachey (*J* 71:30).

The MOON symbolizes Love. Thus in *The Gates of Paradise* (9), "I want! I want!" represents the adolescent's craving for love— physical love, because he starts to ascend the ladder with his left foot. *The Crystal Cabinet*, into which the maiden locks the poet, contains "a little lovely Moony Night" (*K* 429)—a phrase usually applied to Beulah.

The Moon is second in the quaternary of the Sun (imagination—Eternity), the Moon (love—Beulah), the Stars (reason—the Mundane Shell), and the Earth (generation). Their respective points are north (Urthona), east (Luvah), south (Urizen), and west (Tharmas).

The Sun and Moon are often mentioned together as the two luminaries which guide man onward. "The Sun shall go before you in Day, the Moon shall go before you in Night" (*J* 49:51). "The Sun & Moon lead forward the Visions of Heaven & Earth" (*J* 95:21; 96:1). When Los dies, he tears them both down (*FZ* ix:8).

The original place for the Moon was in Man's heart, or center (*Am* b:6; *J* 19:37; 48:24), but when Man was divided, the Moon became separated. "The moon shot forth in that dread night when Urizen call'd the stars round his feet; then burst the center from its orb and found a place beneath, and Earth, conglob'd in narrow room, roll'd round its sulphur sun" (*Am* b:4). "In one night the Atlantic Continent was caught up with the Moon and became an Opake Globe far distant, clad with moony beams" (*J* 49: 19). "Albion's Circumference was clos'd: his Center began dark'ning into the Night of Beulah, and the Moon of Beulah rose clouded with storms" (*J* 19:36). At Albion's death groan, "aloft the Moon fled with a cry" (*FZ* ii:42).

When Man started falling, love became debased to sex. The Moon "found a place beneath" (*Am* b:6). "The Sun fled from the Briton's forehead, the Moon from his mighty loins" (*J* 24:10). Albion recognizes that the Sun and Moon were "driv'n forth by my disease" (*J* 21:10).

As a result of the fall, the luminaries become darkened and meaningless, and the Moon is corrupted. "The moon anguish'd circles the earth" (*Ahan* 2:40). The Sun and Moon are trapped in Urizen's temple, the former being dominated by Hand and Koban, the latter by Hyle and Skofield (*J* 58:27–31). When war breaks out, "the Fairies lead the Moon along the Valley of Cherubim, bleeding in torrents from Mountain to Mountain, a lovely Victim" (*J* 63:14). "The Moon is leprous as snow, trembling & descending down, seeking to rest on high Mona [west], scattering her leprous snows in flakes of disease over Albion" (*J* 66:78).

In order to give form to the error, Los creates the material moon, or love in this world. When Reuben is vainly seeking his place, Los builds the Moon of Ulro, "plank by plank & rib by rib" (*J* 36:4). Los does this "in the Nerves of the Ear [poetry] . . . Death to delude, who all in terror . . . leaves his prey" (*Mil* 29:40–44) —i.e., love conquers death. Here in Ulro "the Sun & Moon recieve their fixed destinations" (*Mil* 27:54).

It is the function of the female to provide a moony space of refuge and rest for the male (*J* 69:16–24). Such a space is pictured in the third illustration to Dante: beneath an overarching vine, the female sits in her home at the spinning wheel, unperceived by the God of This World and his adoring monarch. In the Palamabron-Satan quarrel, the latter is cut off from Golgonooza, "But Enitharmon in tears wept over him, Created him a Space clos'd with a tender moon" (*FZ* viii:370, 394). In *Milton*, this quarrel involved a contest between Satan and Michael, and the pitying Enitharmon "form'd a Space" for them, "& clos'd it with a tender Moon" (8:43). In *Jerusalem*, Jerusalem and Vala created such a space in Lambeth for the falling Albion (19:44). See BEULAH.

Blake represented Noah's Ark as a crescent moon, because love saves man from the Sea of Time and Space. See NOAH.

MORN, an obvious symbol, is the "Image of truth new born" (*SoI*, "Voice of the Ancient Bard" 3).

MOROCCO, in Africa, is the twenty-second of the Thirty-two Nations which shall rule the rest of the world and protect liberty (*J* 72:40).

MOSES was the great lawgiver, who led the Israelites from their Egyptian captivity to the Promised Land of Canaan. Blake paint-ed pictures of the chief events of his life. The Keynes catalogue *William Blake's Illustrations to the Bible* reproduces eight of them. As a baby he is set afloat on the Nile (34); Pharaoh's daughter finds him (35); he encounters the Burning Bush (36); he rages at the golden calf (42); he produces water by striking the rock (44); he erects the brazen serpent, himself involved in its folds (45); he crouches, hiding his head, while God ("Yod") writes the Commandments (46); and he is buried by angels (47).

Blake considered Moses one of the great prophets, yet denied his teachings, because Moses did not evaluate rightly what he recorded. In the picture of the Burning Bush (see Illustrations), his sheephook and flock represent his care for his people; but his scroll of prophecy lies unregarded at his feet, and he only half-sees the bush, which is a miniature oak tree (of error), burning with a dark flame. Similarly, when God writes the Ten Commandments, Moses does not watch but crouches, hiding his head. Perhaps that is the basic reason why he could never enter the Promised Land.

Yet his books are inspired (*J* 48:9). They are to be read exclusively as symbols (To Trusler, 23 Aug 1799). As literal history, they are appalling, especially the massacres of the nations which Moses conquered. "God never makes one man murder another, nor one nation" (On Watson, *K* 388). "To me, who believe the Bible & profess myself a Christian, a defence of the Wickedness of the Israelites in murdering so many thousands under pretence of a command from God is altogether Abominable & Blasphemous" (*K* 387). But are these books history at all? Moses could not have written the account of his own death and secret burial; yet the author makes Moses refer to himself as "I." "If Moses did not write the history of his acts, it takes away the authority altogether; it ceases to be history & becomes a Poem of probable impossibilities, fabricated for pleasure, as moderns say, but I say by Inspiration" (*K* 390). Indeed, it is not history at all, but poetry, "& that poetry inspired," like *Paradise Lost* (*K* 392).

Thus Blake turned one of the chief objections to the Pentateuch into a vindication.

Moses was most pernicious as the lawmaker. "The laws of the Jews were (both ceremonial & real) the basest & most oppressive of human codes, & being like all other codes given under pretence of divine command were what Christ pronounced them, The Abomination that maketh desolate, i.e., State Religion, which is the source of all Cruelty" (K 393).

The Decalogue was the core of the great error. "Moses beheld upon Mount Sinai forms of dark delusion" (SoL 3:17). Urizen, and not the Divine Humanity, was the real author. "With thunder and fire, leading his starry hosts thro' the waste wilderness, he promulgates his ten commands" (MHH, "A Song of Liberty" 18). He perverted "the fiery joy" of life "to ten commands" (Am 8:3).

In doing this, Urizen's ideal was an absolute morality: "one command, one joy, one desire, one curse, one weight, one measure, one King, one God, one Law" (Ur 4:34–40); but though his intent was the best, "no flesh nor spirit could keep his iron laws one moment" (Ur 23:25). Jesus, who was "all virtue, and acted from impulse, not from rules," violated in spirit every one of the Commandments. "I tell you, no virtue can exist without breaking these ten commandments" (MHH 23).

Jesus was "sent" to replace the Old Dispensation by his New. Against the law with its catalogue of sins and punishments he taught "Judge not" and the Forgiveness of Sins. The clearest example is the case of the woman taken in adultery.

Moses commands she be stoned to death.
What was the sound of Jesus' breath?
He laid His hand on Moses' Law:
The Ancient Heavens, in Silent Awe
Writ with Curses from Pole to Pole,
All away began to roll:
The Earth trembling & Naked lay
In secret bed of Mortal Clay,
On Sinai felt the hand divine
Putting back the bloody shrine,
And she heard the breath of God

As she heard by Eden's flood:
"Good & Evil are no more!
"Sinai's trumpets, cease to roar!
"Cease, finger of God, to write!
"The Heavens are not clean in thy Sight.
"Thou art Good, & thou Alone;
"Nor may the sinner cast one stone. . . .
"Still the breath Divine does move
"And the breath Divine is Love. . . ."
(EG e:9–42)

See DECALOGUE.

In the cycle of the Twenty-seven Heavens, Moses stands second in the last series of Abraham to Luther, "the Male-Females, the Dragon Forms, Religion hid in War, a Dragon red & hidden Harlot" (Mil 37:42; J 75:16). These are they whose inspiration is the Whore of Babylon, the promoters of wars—they who believe in spreading religion by violence. "The Gods of Priam [war] are the Cherubim of Moses & Solomon, The Hosts of Heaven" (Laoc, K 777).

Moses is oddly omitted from the list of the Sons of Los (FZ viii:361), but is included in the list of prophets whom Los created to offset the kings and nobles created by Rahab and Tirzah (J 73:41).

In the letter to Humphry describing a lost Last Judgment, Moses kneels beneath Eve, to the left of Jesus; "from the Cloud on which Eve kneels & beneath Moses & from the Tables of Stone which utter lightnings is seen Satan . . . falling headlong" (K 443). In the prose Vision of the Last Judgment, "on the left, beneath the falling figure of Cain is Moses casting his tables of stone into the deeps. It ought to be understood that the Persons, Moses & Abraham, are not here meant, but the States Signified by those Names" (K 607). This description identifies him in the Rosenwald drawing (see Illustrations, "LJ" No. 37).

Blake's final estimate of Moses is revealed in his picture of Moses' burial, according to Jude 9. Angels lay him to rest, while Good and Evil combat for his soul; but Michael, pointing heavenward, rebukes and baffles Satan. It is a "Divine Analogy" (J 49:57).

The MUNDANE EGG is this three-dimensional world of time and space, in which fallen Man incubates until he hatches and re-enters Eternity. Man's consciousness has shrunk: the greater part of the four Zoas remain outside his ken. The Egg stretches "from Zenith to Nadir in midst of Chaos" (*Mil* 34:34). The lower half of the Egg (mostly in Urizen) is the Limit of Opacity, or Satan, whose flames ascend beyond his sphere towards the upper half of the Egg (mostly in Urthona), which is the Limit of Contraction, or Adam (*Mil* 19:15; *J* 59:10).

Los creates the Egg as a protection. "We form the Mundane Egg, that [for] Spectres [the unborn] coming by fury or amity, all is the same, & every one remains in his own energy" (*Mil* 25:42).

THE MUNDANE EGG

Milton 33

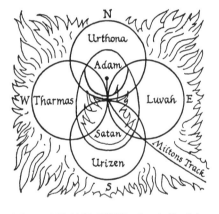

The MUNDANE SHELL, the shell of the Mundane Egg, is the visible sky. As the crust of Matter which encloses us, it is the Veil of Vala (*J* 59:2–7; *GoP*, "Of the Gates" 17, *K* 770). Like all Nature, it is a projection of Man.

"Whatever is visible in the Vegetable Earth, the same is visible in the Mundane Shell revers'd" (*J* 72:46).

The Mundane Shell is a vast Concave Earth, an immense harden'd shadow of all things upon our Vegetated Earth, enlarg'd into dimension & deform'd

into indefinite space, in Twenty-seven Heavens and all their Hells, with Chaos and Ancient Night & Purgatory. It is a cavernous Earth of labyrinthine intricacy, twenty-seven-folds of opakeness, and finishes where the lark mounts [inspiration]. (*Mil* 17:21)

By day, it is "the lovely blue & shining heavenly Shell," the sky (*Mil* 31:33; 21:30).

The black storm, coming out of Chaos beyond the stars [for all things have a spiritual cause] . . . issues thro' the dark & intricate caves of the Mundane Shell, passing the planetary visions & the well adorned Firmament. The Sun rolls into Chaos & the stars into the Desarts, and then the storms become visible, audible & terrible, covering the light of day, & rolling down upon the mountains, deluge all the country round. (*Mil* 23:21)

By night, the forty-eight constellations are visible: twenty-seven in the northern hemisphere and twenty-one in the southern. The dominant northern constellation is Orion (Og), or Justice; the southern is Ophiuchus (Sihon), the man entangled with the serpent.

For the Chaotic Voids outside of the Stars are measured by the Stars, which are the boundaries of Kingdoms, Provinces and Empires of Chaos invisible to the Vegetable Man. The Kingdom of Og is in Orion: Sihon is in Ophiucus. Og has Twenty-seven Districts: Sihon's Districts Twenty-one. From Star to Star, Mountains & Valleys, terrible dimension stretch'd out, compose the Mundane Shell, a mighty Incrustation of Forty-eight deformed Human Wonders of the Almighty, with Caverns whose remotest bottoms meet again beyond the Mundane Shell in Golgonooza. (*Mil* 37:47)

The Shell contains all the errors of man: the gods of the heathen and the Twenty-seven false churches of the Christians (*Mil* 37:19–43). Mortals can never enter Eternity through this sky, but must pass through the flesh, because "the Fires of Los rage in the remotest bottoms of the Caves, that none can pass into Eternity that way, but all descend to Los, to Bowlahoola & Allamanda & to Entuthon Benython" (*Mil* 37:56).

Immortals, however, can enter the Shell. The erring Milton leaves Eternity and journeys "above the rocky masses of The Mundane Shell, in the Lands of Edom & Aram & Moab & Midian & Amalek" (*Mil* 17:18). He falls through Albion's heart, "travelling outside of Humanity, beyond the Stars in Chaos, in Caverns of the Mundane Shell" (*Mil* 20:41). But his descent breaches the Chasms to the south and east, which are then occupied by the sons of Ololon (*Mil* 34:41; 35:39). She follows Milton and enters the Mundane Shell (*Mil* 36:13); and the two appear to Blake in his Felpham garden.

MUNSTER is the southern of the four Irish provinces. It is the Gate of Reuben (*J* 72:2).

MURDER is a spiritual deed, whether or not it results in a killing, for "Thought is Act" (On Bacon, *K* 400). "Whosoever hateth his brother is a murderer" (*I John* iii: 15). The ego of "A Poison Tree" (*SoE*) is a murderer, though he committed no overt act.

Blake told Crabb Robinson "that he had committed many murders" (*CR* 270, 304). He called Bishop Watson a "Presumptuous Murderer" for wishing that Thomas Paine had died before publishing, adding, "Dost thou, O Priest, wish thy brother's death when God has preserved him?" (On Watson, *K* 384); and again, when Watson defended the Jewish massacres of the Canaanites, "Horrible! The Bishop is an Inquisitor. God never makes one man murder another, nor one nation" (On Watson, *K* 388).

As for literal murder, it does not have the virtue of a positive act. "To hinder another is not an act; it is the contrary; it is a restraint on action both in ourselves & in the person hinder'd, for he who hinders another omits his own duty at the same time. Murder is Hindering Another" (On Lavater, *K* 88).

MURRA (i.e., Moray) is a county in the north of Scotland. With Kromarty and Kirkubriht, it is assigned to Benjamin (*J* 16:58). Being a part of Scotland, it is also assigned to Bowen (*J* 71:46).

The MUSES were the nine Greek goddesses who presided over the arts and sciences. Blake accepted them as such in his early "To the Muses" (*PS*). Later, he altered his attitude, because their mother was Mnemosyne, or Memory; therefore classical art was not truly inspired.

"A work of Genius is a Work 'Not to be obtain'd by the Invocation of [dame] Memory & her Syren Daughters but by Devout prayer to that Eternal Spirit, who can enrich with all utterance & knowledge & sends out his Seraphim with the hallowed fire of his Altar to touch & purify the lips of whom he pleases.' MILTON [*The Reason of Church Government*, Bk. II, pref.]" (On Reynolds, *K* 457).

Several times, Blake contrasts the Greek Muses with true inspiration (On Reynolds, *K* 452; *Mil* pref.; 14:29; *DesC* II, *K* 565; *LJ*, *K* 604, 605).

See MEMORY.

MUSIC, Poetry, and Painting are "the three Powers in Man of conversing with Paradise, which the flood did not Sweep away" (*LJ*, *K* 609). Music is invisible and intangible; it does not think or visualize; it is the immediate expression of pure Emotion; and therefore it belongs to the eastern Zoa Luvah, whose attribute is his "living Lyre" (*FZ* ix:711).

Music is the most direct communication with Eternity, as it does not utilize the intervention of words or images. Therefore while poetry and painting are prayer, the Bread of life (*Illustr Job* 18, margin), music is the Wine (*Illustr Job* 20, margin). In the lithograph "Job in his Prosperity," music is represented by a daughter, while two sons represent the other arts. Job's spiritual defect is indicated by the silent musical instruments at the beginning (*Illustr Job* 1), whereas in the final plate (21), his whole family composes an orchestra greeting the rising sun.

The arts are the sources of all human activity.

In Eternity the Four Arts, Poetry, Painting, Music, and Architecture, which is Science, are the Four Faces of Man. Not so in Time & Space: there Three are shut out, and only Science remains thro' Mercy, & by means of Science the Three become apparent in Time & Space in the Three Professions, Poetry in Religion: Music, Law: Painting in Physic & Surgery: that Man may live upon Earth till the time of his awaking. And from these Three, Science derives every Occupation of Men. (*Mil* 27:55)

As on this earth music is governed by the complicated laws of harmony and orchestration, it becomes the body of laws which govern mankind.

Blake disliked harmony as a sophistication of the inspired melody. "Music as it exists in old tunes or melodies . . . is Inspiration and cannot be surpassed" (*DesC* V, *K* 579). "Nature has no Tune, but Imagination has" (*GhA* 1:3). But "Demonstration, Similitude & Harmony are Objects of Reasoning. Invention, Identity & Melody are Objects of Intuition" (On Reynolds, *K* 474). Blake despised "the tame high finisher of . . . paltry Harmonies" (*Mil* 41:9). The Sons of Albion are responsible for "Harmonies of Concords & Discords, opposed to Melody" (*J* 74:25).

Yet we know that Blake enjoyed orchestral music, from his comparison of the workings of physiology to the playing of an orchestra. "[The] softly lilling flutes . . . make sweet melody" (*Mil* 24:56). There are also (*Mil* 24:61-66) stringed instruments; "the long sounding clarion"; "the double drum" (kettledrums); "the shrill fife"; and "the crooked horn mellows the hoarse raving serpent, terrible but harmonious." (The serpent was a bass instrument, now obsolete.) To be sure it is "the dance of death" (*Mil* 24:62). But not so the *contredanse* performed by "the gorgeous clothed Flies" in

summer; "every one the dance knows in its intricate mazes of delight artful to weave: each one to sound his instruments of music in the dance, to touch each other & recede, to cross & change & return" (*Mil* 26:2).

When he was a young man, Blake composed melodies for his own poems. "These he would occasionally sing to his friends; and though, according to his confession, he was entirely unacquainted with the science of music, his ear was so good, that his tunes were sometimes most singularly beautiful, and were noted down by musical professors" (J. T. Smith, *Symons* 360). Towards the end of his life, he was still doing this. "He was very fond of hearing Mrs. Linnell sing Scottish songs, and would sit by the pianoforte, tears falling from his eyes, while he listened to the Border Melody to which the song is set commencing—

O Nancy's hair is yellow as gowd,
And her een as the lift are blue.

"To simple national melodies Blake was very impressionable, though not so to music of a more complicated structure. He himself still sang, sometimes his own songs, to melodies of his own" (*Gil* I, 339).

He never lost his gift. "On the day of his death, August 12, 1827, he composed and uttered songs to his Maker so sweetly to the ear of his Catherine, that when she stood to hear him, he, looking upon her most affectionately, said, 'My beloved, they are not mine—no—they are not mine'" (J. T. Smith, *Symons* 386).

MUSWELL HILL, in Middlesex, is an elevation overlooking London from the north. With Hampstead, Highgate, Finchley, and Hendon, it rages loud while Bromion works at Los's forge (*J* 16:1).

MY SPECTRE (*K* 415), one of Blake's most powerful poems, was unfortunately never finished. It describes the unhappy marriage. The poet finds the solution in giving up love.

Blake quoted it in *Milton* (32:4); on the next plate, he finds the solution when the selfish wife, on losing his love, relents and reforms.

MYDON is the tenth son of Los and Enitharmon (*FZ* viii:359). He is not mentioned elsewhere.

MYRATANA, "once the Queen of all the western plains," is the spouse and inspiration of Tiriel. At the opening of the book, Tiriel bears her dying form before his palace, where he summons his rebellious sons. They show no sympathy. He curses them as the cause of her death, and starts to dig her grave with his own hands. But Heuxos calls a son of Zazel to dig it, and Tiriel wanders away, while his sons attend to the burial (*Tir* i).

MYRTLE. See MIRTLE.

"MYSTERY" is the word written on the forehead of the false religion, the Whore of Babylon (*Rev* xvii:5; *FZ* viii:330, 603; *Mil* 22:48; 38:23).

"Jesus supposes every Thing to be Evident to the Child & to the Poor & Unlearned. Such is the Gospel" (On Berkeley, *K* 774). But in "A Little Boy Lost" (*SoE*), the priest burns alive the little child "who sets reason up for judge of our most holy Mystery." See RAHAB.

Blake commonly symbolizes the false religion as Urizen's Tree of Mystery, as in "The Human Abstract" (*SoE*). It bears the fruit of the knowledge of Good and Evil, which Enitharmon and Los eat (*FZ* vii:210–395). On the same tree Jesus is crucified (*FZ* viii:326).

MYSTICISM has been recognized and studied too long to need exposition here. The Ecstasy, which has been taken to be the supreme experience of man and is the basis of most religions, occurs regardless of creed, race, age, sex, or state of culture. It may strike young Prince Siddhartha in the midst of his luxury, or Job on his dunghill, or Saul riding to extirpate the Christians, or the pagan Plotinus and his master Plato, or the nun Teresa in her convent, or the shoemaker apprentice Behmen, or Blake himself sitting by the seaside or walking at dawn in his Felpham garden.

Blake has long been recognized as one of the great mystics. His life followed the pattern laid out by Evelyn Underhill: the Innocence of childhood, the Experience of adolescence, the New Birth of his revolutionary young manhood, the Dark Night of obscurity after his return from Felpham, and finally the Attainment of his last years.

Blake took his mystical experiences as a normal part of life. Single vision was the abnormality of blindness. A double vision was always with him (To Butts, 22 Nov 1802): then he saw a heaven in a wild flower or a frowning old man in a thistle. Threefold vision occurred "in soft Beulah's night"; and " 'Tis fourfold in my supreme delight," when the entire world became man, and man became joined to God.

Although the fourfold vision underlies all his work—even its omission is significant—he seldom took the trouble to describe his own experiences, as they were personal and as such were no authority for others. One such experience he described in a letter to Butts (2 Oct 1800), when the whole world was revealed as human, and he found himself in the arms of the Good Shepherd. Still more important is his epic *Milton*: the entire poem is an analysis of the events leading up to the supreme vision. Such a vision is the turning point of *Job* and the climax of *Jerusalem*.

With such spiritual aptitude, Blake had no need of cultivating the experience by the classical *Via Negativa*, the official practice of both the Orientals and the Christians. Indeed, his own practice was the very reverse: the opening instead of closing the senses, the exploration and not the dismissing of emotional and intellectual states. Therefore with his two arts he was able to record his visions of Truth and Love, which for others are usually ineffable.

He was particularly interested in the events which led up to his mystical experiences. However unexpected they might be, they were not fortuitous but were preceded by a complex of causes. On the path of Experience, six Eyes of God must precede the revelation of the seventh: the whole process is analyzed in the *Illustrations of the Book of Job*. The seventh Furnace is the one touched by the Divine Finger.

In *Milton*, twenty-seven Larks must pass through the Twenty-seven Heavens before the twenty-eighth Lark can fly free. They symbolize the successive disclosures (and hence destruction) of errors which must precede the revelation of the truths which lead to the climax. In *Jerusalem*, the Emanation must sacrifice herself before Albion can do so and destroy his Selfhood. But the Individual himself is not and never can be destroyed.

NAAMAH was the wife of Noah (*J* 62:9). His wife is not named in the Bible, but Blake could have found her in the *Midrash Rabba, Genesis* xxiii:3, or in the *Book of Jasher* v:16. (This latter is not Jacob Ilive's forgery of 1751.)

Naamah is one of the daughters of Los and Enitharmon. Blake placed her between Caina and Tamar as the fourteenth in the Maternal Line from Ocalythron to Mary (*FZ* viii:365), and the fourth, between Zillah and Shuah's daughter, in his revised list from Cainah to Mary (*J* 62:9).

The Biblical Naamah was the daughter of Lamech and Zilla, and was descended from Cain (*Gen* iv:17–22). If the Lamechs of *Genesis* iv and v were the same person, Noah married his own sister, a fact compatible with *Tobit* iv:12, which says that Noah's wife was "of his own kindred." But the genealogies are confused. The second Lamech was of the line of Seth (*Gen* v:3, 19); and the *Book of Jasher* (v:16) says that Naamah was the daughter of Enoch; in which case Noah married his own grandmother, who was eighty-two years older than he.

According to rabbinical tradition, Naamah the Cainite was utterly evil. Among other things she was foremost in seeking the love of the angels, and gave birth to the devil Asmodeus. The reputation of this second mother of mankind would doubtless have appealed to Blake, who therefore would have included her in his Maternal Line; but it is only fair to add that the evil Naamah is never mentioned in connection with Noah, whose wife, according to the *Midrash Rabba*, was very pious.

NAAMAH THE AMMONITE is named tenth in the revised Maternal Line from Cainah to Mary (*J* 62:12). She was a wife or concubine of Solomon and the mother of the weak king Rehoboam (*I Kings* xiv:21).

The NADIR is the lowest point directly beneath each individual. It symbolizes the subconscious. Its opposite is the Zenith.

When Man fell, he became inverted: the South rose to the Zenith (Urizen's place is in the brain), while the North sank to the Nadir (Urthona's place is in the subconscious). "North, the Nadir . . . the Ear [imagination] is the North" (*J* 12:55–60). Completing the quaternary of the Zoas, the East (the heart) contracted to the Center, while the West (the body) expanded to the Circumference.

When Los shrank from Urizen's furnaces, he left an immense space "As far as highest Zenith from the lowest Nadir" (*FZ* v:14); but later, his "Egg form'd World," the Mundane Egg, stretched "from Zenith to Nadir in midst of Chaos" (*Mil* 34:33).

NAHOR (the first) was the son of Serug, the father of Terah, the grandfather of Abraham (*Gen* xi:26), and the great-great-grandfather of Rebecca.

Nahor is the nineteenth of the Twenty-seven Heavens; he is of the second group, "the Female-Males, A Male within a Female hid as in an Ark & Curtains" (*Mil* 37:39; *J* 75:14).

NAIRN is a county of Scotland. With Inverness and Linlithgo, it is assigned to

Naphtali (*J* 16:55). Being part of Scotland, it is also assigned to Bowen (*J* 71:46).

NAPHTALI (Napthali) was Jacob's sixth son, and the founder of a Tribe.

With his brothers, he is listed as a Son of Los who fled (*FZ* viii:361, 376). With five of his brothers, he rolled apart and dissipated into Non Entity (*J* 74:50), thus becoming one of the Lost Tribes.

In Wales the county of Radnor is assigned as his Gate (*J* 16:38); in England, he is given the counties of Warwick, Leicester, and Worcester (*J* 16:46); in Scotland, Nairn, Inverness, and Linlithgo (*J* 16:55); and in Ireland, he shares with Dan and Asher all the counties of Ulster (*J* 72:25).

NATHO is listed as the twelfth son of Los and Enitharmon, in the line from Rintrah to Milton (*FZ* viii:359). He is not mentioned elsewhere.

NATIONS in themselves are good, being manifestations of the infinite variety of mankind. Once they flourished under liberty, and shall do so again (*Mil* 6:18; 25:55; *J* 72:35; 97:2). Before the great war, "England encompass'd the Nations, and all the Nations of the Earth were seen in the Cities of Albion" (*J* 79:22).

But when they got separated and turned hostile, they became the Negation of the Brotherhood of Man. The primal fault was that of Urizen, "whose labours vast order the nations, separating [the dynasties] family by family" (*FZ* ix:176). "Is this thy soft Family-Love, | Thy cruel Patriarchal pride, | Planting thy Family alone, | Destroying all the World beside?" (*J* 27:77). Rahab and Tirzah also separate the Nations (*Mil* 24:16; 25:29). Under Urizen, "They become Nations [*sic*] far remote, in a little & dark Land" (*FZ* ii:56).

Apparently they all originated in the Thirty-two Counties of Ireland (the body), which now center in London and Golgonooza (*J* 72:28), and they are to become the Thirty-two Nations. At first there were "the Seven Kingdoms of Canaan & Five Baalim

[rulers] of Philistea, into Twelve divided, call'd after the Names of Israel, as they are in Eden" (*Mil* 40:24). It was the seven nations of Canaan that fled at the sight of Reuben (*J* 36:14).

Now the Nations "follow after the detestable Gods of Priam [war]" (*Mil* 14:15). The Spectre of Albion frowns over the Nations "in glory & war" (*Mil* 6:24; *J* 27:37, 73). All of them seek to destroy Liberty (*J* 69:5; 80:46). "Albion is shut out from every Nation under Heaven" (*J* 79:80; 94:14).

However, all the warfare is the preparation for a new age. It is "the Great Harvest & Vintage of the Nations" (*Mil* 43:1). Urizen's Plow is passing over the Nations; and Los's Wine-press is crushing the human grapes. See PLOW.

"Nations are Destroy'd or Flourish in proportion as Their Poetry, Painting and Music are Destroy'd or Flourish!" (*J* 3). Blake prophesied that eventually there shall be a fraternity of thirty-two independent nations which shall preserve liberty and rule the rest of the world. He also saw mankind amalgamating into "One Nation, the English" (*J* 92:2). But in *The Four Zoas* (ix: 653, 656) he expected the flail of Urizen to thresh out all the Nations, and the winnowing fan of Tharmas to toss the Nations "like chaff into the seas of Tharmas."

The THIRTY-TWO NATIONS are a prophetic view of a brotherhood of the great nations, which shall protect liberty ("dwell in Jerusalem's Gates") and rule the rest of the world (*J* 72:32; 98:55). Blake calls them "islands" because of their mutual independence.

To insure a perfect balance, he assigned eight nations to each of the four continents. The European nations are France, Spain, Italy, Germany, Poland, Russia, Sweden, and Turkey. The Asian nations are Arabia, Palestine, Persia, Hindostan, China, Tartary, Siberia—and Egypt, because culturally it belongs to Asia. So the eight African nations are Lybia, Ethiopia, Guinea, Caffraria [Kaffraria], Negroland, Morocco, Congo, and Zaara [Sahara?]. And finally, the eight

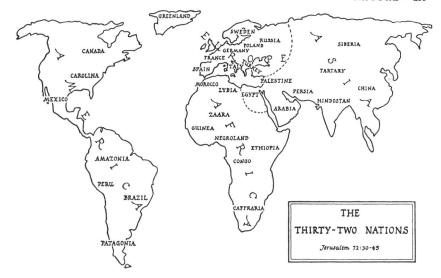

THE
THIRTY-TWO NATIONS
Jerusalem 72:30-45

American nations are Canada, Greenland, Carolina, Mexico (independent 1810), Peru (1821), Patagonia, Amazonia, and Brazil (1822).

As though to indicate that the scheme was tentative as to details, Blake modestly omitted the nations of the British Isles, while the United States is represented only by "Carolina," of which there are two. More surprising is the omission of Greece, whose heroic struggle for independence from Turkey, begun in 1821, was being made famous by Byron and Shelley.

NATURAL RELIGION. See DEISM.

NATURE is part of man—that part which, including the physical body, is perceived by the senses. According to Jewish tradition man originally "contain'd in his mighty limbs all things in Heaven & Earth." "But now the Starry Heavens are fled from the mighty limbs of Albion" (*J* 27). (I have not been able to trace this Jewish tradition to a definite source; but as Adam was originally the microcosm, it is constantly implied in the Jewish writings). Or, as the Hinayana Buddhists teach, "Thou art That."

But when Man fell, his senses turned outward: "they behold what is within now seen without" (*FZ* ii:54); and Nature appeared to be separate from Man. That is a delusion: "in your own Bosom you bear your Heaven and Earth & all you behold; tho' it appears Without, it is Within" (*J* 71:17).

Nature is an external visualizing of the Individual's emotions. Vala (who is Nature) is the Emanation of Luvah (the emotions). But Vala is now covered with her Veil of matter, which (in another symbol) is the shell of the Mundane Egg, the starry heavens.

To accept this world of matter as real is "atheism"—wherefore Wordsworth was an atheist; it is "Single vision & Newton's sleep" (To Butts, 2nd letter, 22 Nov 1802). Its religion is Deism; its science is the materialism of Newton. The laws of cause and effect are false in themselves: "every Natural Effect has a Spiritual Cause, and Not a Natural; for a Natural Cause only seems: it is a Delusion of Ulro & a ratio of the perishing Vegetable Memory" (*Mil* 26:44). "Meer Nature" is "Hell" (On Swed *DL*, *K* 93). Blake anticipated the cruel world of Darwin: Nature is "A Creation that groans, living on Death, where Fish & Bird & Beast & Man & Tree & Metal & Stone live by Devouring, going into Eternal Death continually" (*J* 50:5; cf. *Rom* viii:22).

"But to the Eyes of the Man of Imagination, Nature is Imagination itself" (To Trusler, 23 Aug 1799). In Blake's egocentric universe, everybody sees everything differently. "The Sun's Light, when he unfolds it, | Depends on the Organ that beholds it" (*GoP*, frontis.). The visionary sees it as "an Innumerable company of the Heavenly host crying 'Holy, Holy, Holy is the Lord God Almighty' " (*LJ, K* 617). "A fool sees not the same tree that a wise man sees" (*MHH* 7). "The tree which moves some to tears of joy is in the Eyes of others only a Green thing that stands in the way" (To Trusler, 23 Aug 1799). The poet, seeing not with but through the eye, beholds the eternity which is in everything: "the real & eternal World of which this Vegetable Universe is but a faint shadow" (*J* 77). He sees "a World in a Grain of Sand | And a Heaven in a Wild Flower" (*Aug* 1, *K* 431). In the golden age of Innocence, "A Rock, a Cloud, a Mountain" are "Vocal as in Climes of happy Eternity, where the lamb replies to the infant voice, & the lion to the man of years, giving them sweet instructions; where the Cloud, the River & the Field Talk with the husbandman & shepherd" (*FZ* vi:134–38).

This Eternity which the poet perceives is the human significance, for Nature is only a projection of ourselves. The Swedenborgian calls this "correspondence"; the psychologist, "empathy"; the writer, "symbolism." It is personal: no two artists can possibly paint the same picture of the same landscape, for they are really painting their own separate states of mind.

Therefore, from the grain of sand up, all things are "Men Seen Afar" (To Butts, 2 Oct 1800). The thistle, for example, is "the indignant Thistle whose bitterness is bred in his milk, and who lives on contempt of his neighbour" (*FZ* ix:763; *Mil* 27:26). Blake, out walking one gloomy day, found one in his path. "With my inward Eye, 'tis an old Man grey," who preaches discouragement; but when Blake kicks him away, the sun comes out and Los appears: "in my double sight | 'Twas outward a Sun: inward Los in his might" (To Butts, 2nd letter, 22 Nov 1802). "For all are Men in Eternity, Rivers, Mountains, Cities, Villages, All are Human, & when you enter into their Bosoms you walk in Heavens & Earths, as in your own Bosom you bear your Heaven and Earth & all you behold; tho' it appears Without, it is Within, in your Imagination, of which this World of Mortality is but a Shadow" (*J* 71:15).

Double Vision reveals a universe which is entirely different from that of Single Vision. The one is imaginative, the other materialistic. Blake contrasts the two in the introductory "Five Windows" and "Preludium" of *Europe*. In the former poem, Blake asks the fairy, "What is the material world, and is it dead?" The fairy replies, "I will ... shew you all alive the world, where every particle of dust breathes forth its joy" (*Eur* iii:13–17). Yet this same fairy, with his innocent knowledge of the ecstasy of the material world, dictates the contrasting view, the world of experience. Here the Shadowy Female (the fallen Vala) complains of the agony of incessant births and the struggle for life, where all is "devouring & devoured" (*Eur* 2:5). However, one should note that her roots are "in the heavens" (*Eur* 1:8), for every material effect has its spiritual cause.

"Every thing that lives is Holy" (*MHH* 27, etc.). Nature, being human, was created from the divine substance. If all things are of and from God, it follows that all must eventually return to him. This is "the restitution of all things" (*Acts* iii:21), when God shall be "all in all" (*I Cor* xv:28). Not only are "all men to be saved" (*I Tim* ii:4), but Nature as well.

This doctrine of the apocatastasis was first promulgated by Origen; it was accepted by many, including Erigena, until Rome pronounced against it (creation being *ex nihilo*, from nothing, and Hell being everlasting). But the doctrine was revived during the Reformation. Milton (*Christian Doctrine*), Thomas Vaughan, Ruysbroeck, Tauler, and many others accepted it; and so did Blake.

When the Last Judgment approaches, "Man looks out in tree & herb & fish & bird & beast, collecting up the scatter'd portions of his immortal body into the Elemental forms of every thing that grows" (*FZ* viii: 561). And in the final reunion of God and Man, "All Human Forms [are] identified, even Tree, Metal, Earth & Stone: all Human Forms identified, living, going forth & returning wearied into the Planetary lives of Years, Months, Days & Hours; reposing, and then Awaking into his Bosom in the Life of Immortality" (*J* 99:1).

NAZARETH, in lower Galilee, was the home town of Joseph the carpenter and his family (*J* 61:3).

A NAZARITE was a person specially dedicated to God. Samson, Samuel, and John the Baptist were Nazarites, although Samson is the only one who was actually so called. Before his conception, an angel announced to Samson's mother that her son would be "a Nazarite unto God from the womb" (*Judges* xiii:5; cf. *PS*, "Samson," *K* 39–40).

Samson was specially ordered never to cut his hair; Blake depicted Delilah shearing his locks, the secret of his strength.

NEBUCHADNEZZAR, the most powerful of the Babylonian kings, captured Jerusalem thrice, finally destroying it and deporting the inhabitants. On the first of these conquests (607 B.C.), he brought to Babylon the prophet Daniel, also Shadrach, Meshach, and Abed-nego. When the last three refused to worship his golden idol, he had them cast into a fiery furnace; but they were released when he saw them walking unharmed in the fire with a fourth person; "and the form of the fourth is like the Son of God" (*Dan* iii:25).

In "The Ancient Britons," the only survivors of King Arthur's last battle were "the Strongest Man, the Beautifullest Man, and the Ugliest Man . . . They were originally one man, who was fourfold . . . and the form

of the fourth was like the Son of God" (*DesC* V, *K* 577–78).

In the height of his glory, Nebuchadnezzar went insane: "he was driven from men, and did eat grass as oxen, and his body was wet with the dew of heaven, till his hairs were grown like eagles' feathers, and his nails like birds' claws" (*Dan* iv:33).

Blake considered this to signify the madness of the materialist with single vision: he becomes bestial in seeking his sustenance in material things only. Plate 24 of *The Marriage of Heaven and Hell* depicts him crowned and naked, crawling terrified on his hands and knees, in the gloom of the crossed trunks of two huge sterile trees. Blake also made a magnificent color print of the same subject, in which the Biblical details are emphasized. Another version is an illustration to Young's *Night Thoughts* (vii: 27).

According to *Daniel* (iv:32), Nebuchadnezzar's insanity lasted until "seven times" had passed over him. "Nebuchadnezzar had seven times passed over him; I have had twenty; thank God I was not altogether a beast as he was" (To Hayley, 23 Oct 1804).

NEGROLAND, in Africa, is the twenty-first in the list of the Thirty-two Nations which shall guard liberty and rule the rest of the world (*J* 72:40).

The NEPHILIM were the giant progeny of the sons of Elohim and the daughters of men; they were "mighty men which were of old, men of renown," whose wickedness caused the Lord to destroy them all in Noah's Flood (*Gen* vi:1–8).

They appear with others of their ilk in the stomach of the Covering Cherub (*J* 89: 47).

The NET symbolizes the snares of sex, "these nets of beauty & delusion" (*J* 79: 78). It appears as early as Blake's juvenile "How sweet I roam'd" (*PS*); the prince of love catches the poet in his silken net and shuts him in his golden cage of marriage. *The Golden Net* (*K* 424) lists the entanglements: the flames of desire, the iron wire of bondage, and the tears of suffering. The Net (colored gold) is draped behind the entwined lovers in the water lily (*J* 28; see Illustrations), though they do not notice it. In "Milton's Dream," the fifth illustration to *Il Penseroso*, "Spirits in the Air & in the Brook" unfold "Scrolls & Nets & Webs" (see Illustrations).

The Veil of Vala is a Net (*J* 20:30; 42:81; 80:1).

"NEVER PAIN TO TELL THY LOVE"

(*K* 161) is a brief sketch for a poem describing woman's sexual fear. She rejects the poet's love; then a traveller (death) takes her. "O, was no deny"—she offers no resistance to death.

This sketch is the basis of Tennessee Williams' tragedy *Summer and Smoke* (1948); it is read—or misread—in Act I, scene iii. John Buchanan, the doctor's son, tells his desires to Alma ("soul"), daughter of the minister. She flees "trembling, cold, in ghastly fears." Later, when she changes her mind, she learns that he is now secretly engaged to another girl; in despair, she gives herself to a "traveller," a travelling salesman.

NEW YORK

is frightened by the threat of Albion's plagues; its citizens "close their books & lock their chests" (*Am* 14:13).

NEWTON

(Sir Isaac, 1642–1727) was known as "the greatest of natural philosophers." His supreme feat was the defining of the modern astronomical universe. Sweeping away the confusions and contradictions of Christian dogma, Pythagorean geometry, and Platonic metaphysics, he selected the true and rejected the false from the theories of Kepler, Galileo, and others, and by an extraordinary feat of the imagination, synthesized them with his own discovery, the natural force of universal gravity.

The universe which he conceived was a neat, compact, self-sufficient, three-dimensional, and impersonal machine. It was simple and yet accounted for everything. It was completely material. Even light was a stream of particles (a theory since revived by Einstein); Blake equated these particles with the atoms of Democritus ("Mock on" 9–10, *K* 418; *FZ* ii:154).

Because this universe involved no spiritual "intelligences" or other supernatural forces, it appealed to the anti-magical trend of advanced thought, and was accepted everywhere. It was England's boast and the marvel of the world.

Blake recognized Newton's genius, and therefore attacked his error, which was the triumph of materialism. Newton, and Bacon, the inventor of experimentalism, and Locke, the author of the philosophy of the five senses, constitute an infernal trinity (*Mil* 41:5; *J* 54:17; 66:14; 70:15; 93:21). Newton is particularly associated with Locke (*IslM* 9, *K* 57; *SoL* 4:17; *Mil* 4:11; *J* 15:16; 34:40), because the mechanistic universe of the one and the mechanistic psychology of the other fitted together perfectly.

According to Blake, the trouble with Newton's universe was that it left out God, man, life, and all the values which make life worth living. The songs of the swallow and sparrow are enough to confute it ("You don't believe," *K* 536). It is "Single vision & Newton's sleep" (To Butts, 2nd letter, 22 Nov 1802). It is the invention of Urizen (*SoL* 4:17), or better, of the Spectre, who is "Newton's Pantocrator" or creator (*Mil* 4: 11). "Am I not Bacon & Newton & Locke, who teach Humility to Man, who teach Doubt & Experiment?" (*J* 54:17). These three "Deny a Conscience in Man & the Communion of Saints & Angels, Contemning the Divine Vision & Fruition, Worshiping the Deus of the Heathen, The God of This World, & the Goddess Nature, Mystery, Babylon the Great, The Druid Dragon & hidden Harlot" (*J* 93:22). Blake commented on Sir Isaac's Unitarian writings:

Poor Spiritual Knowledge is not worth
  a button!
. . . .
For thus the Gospel Sir Isaac confutes:

"God can only be known by his Attri-
butes;
"And as for the Indwelling of the Holy
Ghost
"Or of Christ & his Father, it's all a
boast
"And Pride & Vanity of the imagina-
tion,
"That disdains to follow this World's
Fashion."   (*EG d*:40–48)
The cruel philosophy of materialism has
spread from England over the world. "I
turn my eyes to the Schools & Universities
of Europe and there behold the Loom of
Locke, whose Woof rages dire, wash'd by
the Water-wheels of Newton: black the
cloth in heavy wreathes folds over every
Nation" (*J* 15:14). It is Natural Religion,
Rahab, which promotes war, "The Druid
Dragon & hidden Harlot" (*J* 93:25). Vol-
taire and Rousseau, precursors of the French
Revolution, are "Frozen Sons of the femi-
nine Tabernacle of Bacon, Newton & Locke"
(*J* 66:14). It is the issue of Hand, the united
Twelve Sons of Albion, who "combine into
Three Forms named Bacon & Newton &
Locke in the Oak Groves of Albion which
overspread all the Earth" (*J* 70:15).

But when an error culminates, its overthrow is near. "Is it not that Signal of the
Morning which was told us in the Beginning?" (*J* 93:26). Indeed, it is the "mighty
Spirit . . . from the land of Albion, nam'd
Newton" who alone has the power to blow
"the Trump of the last doom" and "awake
the dead to Judgment" (*Eur* 13:2–5). And
in the final apocalypse, Bacon and Newton
and Locke, who first and last were seekers
of the truth, whatever their errors, appear
in the heavens as the greatest representatives of Science, among the chariots of the
Almighty, counterbalancing Milton and
Shakespeare and Chaucer, the greatest representatives of Art (*J* 98:9).

Blake's color print "Newton" depicts a
nude youth beneath the ocean, seated on a
rock covered with marine growths. On the
sea-floor beside him is a Polypus. He leans
forward, looking down, while his left hand
draws a geometrical design with the com-

passes. But he draws it, not on a stone tablet or in a book, but on the scroll which always signifies imaginative creation.

NIGHT needs no explanation. It is the winter of Time (*FZ* ix:824). When night comes,
Los ("strong Urthona") disappears to take
his rest, leaving Enitharmon free to work
her will; he reappears at dawn (*Eur* 3:10;
15:9).

"Ancient Night," however, is a character
in *Paradise Lost*. She is the "eldest of
things," and the consort of Chaos (*PL* ii:894,
963, 970, 986).

The pair appear in *Milton*. They flee from
beneath the fiery Harrow (12:21); the Mundane Shell contains them (17:25; 20:33).
When Satan manifests, imitating God, "Beneath sat Chaos: Sin on his right hand,
Death on his left, and Ancient Night spread
over all the heav'n his Mantle of Laws"
(39:29). See CHAOS.

The change of Night's sex is due to association or identification with Urizen. The
four constitute the infernal quaternary: Chaos of the Imagination (north), Sin of the
Emotions (east), Night of Reason (south),
and Death of the Body (west).

NIMROD was a son of Cush and a grandson of the evil Ham (*Gen* x:8). He was the
first king, the founder of the Babylonian
empire, and the traditional builder of the
Tower of Babel. He was "a mighty hunter
before the Lord" (*Gen* x:9), a phrase which
is commonly interpreted as "a mighty hunter of men" (that is, a mighty conqueror)
without regard for the Lord.

Blake calls him "the mighty Huntsman
[of] Jehovah" (*J* 22:3). "Of" seems required both by sense and meter; it would
be an objective genitive, signifying that
Nimrod, in hunting down men, was hunting down divinity.

The twelve Daughters of Albion "play
before the Armies, before the hounds of
Nimrod" (*FZ* ii:64). "Great is the cry of the
Hounds of Nimrod along the Valley of Vision; they scent the odor of War in the Valley of Vision" (*J* 22:8). "Nimrod's Tower"

of Babel is mentioned twice (*J* 60:18; To Butts, 6 July 1803).

In the list of evil kings (*J* 73:35), Nimrod is the fourth, being preceded by Satan, Cain (the first murderer), and Tubal (the artificer of iron and brass, and hence of weapons).

When equating the Sons of Albion with these Biblical characters, Blake says, "Coban's son is Nimrod," and refers oddly to Nimrod's "son Cush" (*J* 7:19).

Nimrod is depicted in the sixty-first illustration to the *Inferno*. Wearing the spiky crown of the tyrant, with his hunting horn hanging on his breast, the giant kneels howling. "He ought to be reckon'd of the Giant brood" (To Butts, 6 July 1803). Jagged rocks of the roof of a cave impend over him. Behind him is a wall of masonry—probably, as Albert S. Roe conjectures (*Roe* 122), the dungeons of Babylon. To the left is the unfinished Tower of Babel, in the entrance of which sits the figure of Empire, with spiky crown, orb, and scepter, for the attempt to reach heaven is the ultimate and Satanic ambition of the conqueror.

Nimrod is also depicted in the thirty-second engraving for Young's *Night Thoughts* (iv:96), illustrating the line "Till *Death*, that mighty Hunter, earths them all." Wearing his spiky crown, he brandishes his spear in furious exultation as one of his dogs springs at the throat of a helpless man.

NINEVEH was the capital city of Assyria. It was founded by Asshur (*Gen* x:11; but Nimrod may have been meant), and was part of Nimrod's empire.

In equating the Sons of Albion with characters in *Genesis*, the Spectre states: "Hand has peopled Babel & Nineveh" (*J* 7:18).

Nineveh was the city to which the Lord sent Jonah to prophesy its destruction in forty days for its wickedness. But the king and all his people repented, "and God repented of the evil, that he said he would do unto them; and he did it not" (*Jonah* iii: 10). Crabb Robinson understood Blake to say that the Supreme Being is liable to error. "Did he not repent him that he had made Nineveh?" (*CR* 257, 289). "Jonah

was no prophet in the modern sense, for his prophecy of Nineveh failed" (On Watson, *K* 392).

NOAH, tenth in the line of Adam, was the hero of the Flood and the inventor of wine. He is the man of imagination who survives the Flood of time and space by building an Ark of love for himself and his family.

The Flood, which destroyed all mankind except Noah and his family, was the greatest disaster of all time. When the waters receded, a new period of history began. The four seasons were instituted (*Gen* viii:22; cf. *LJ*, *K* 611). Men were no longer giants, and their life-span decreased from hundreds of years to what it is today.

Blake indicates the position of Noah in the new era by making him the first in the second series of the Twenty-seven Heavens (Churches)—the tenth from the beginning of the list. The first series were giants; the second, which runs from Noah to the father of Abraham, are "Female-Males, A Male within a Female hid as in an Ark & Curtains" (*Mil* 37:38–40; *J* 75:13–15).

As all forms of water signify Matter, the Flood was the overwhelming of mankind with Matter, which separated them from Eternity. This is the Sea of Time and Space, in which we are all submerged. Blake was particularly concerned with the Flood as separating America (the body) from England and the rest of the world.

The Ark, which preserved Noah and his family, symbolizes Love: consequently Blake depicted it as a crescent moon. As early as 1776, he used this pictorial idea as a tailpiece for Jacob Bryant's *New System . . . of Ancient Mythology* (III, 601; discovered and reproduced by Ruthven Todd as Plate 12 of *Tracks in the Snow*, New York, 1947). Blake repeated his symbol in the illustrations to *Jerusalem* 24 and 44[39].

The rainbow, God's covenant with man, symbolizes the spiritual body, in which we shall be raised; hence, it is the promise of immortality. Blake agreed with St. Paul that the physical body would not be raised: "flesh and blood cannot inherit the kingdom of God" (*I Cor* xv:50); but "It is sown a natural body; it is raised a spiritual body" (*I Cor* xv:44; Blake quoted the last clause on the plate of "To Tirzah," *SoE*). The rainbow, as a form of water sublimated and transfigured, is the perfect symbol for the spiritual body.

Noah is second in the list of those whom Los created to offset the monarchical Satan-Cain line (*J* 73:41).

Noah and his sons Shem and Japhet "represent Poetry, Painting & Music, the three Powers in Man of conversing with Paradise, which the flood did not Sweep away" (*LJ, K* 609).

In *The Song of Los*, Noah, the man of vision, preserved by God (he is on Ararat, where the Ark grounded), is paired with Adam, the Natural Man (still in Eden), to show the evil effects of Urizen's laws upon them both. Noah faded, "shrunk beneath the waters" of his flood, and eventually is seen "white as snow" (leprous?) (*SoL* 3:6–10, 15; 7:22).

In other references, Kox is called "the Noah of the Flood of Udan-Adan" (*J* 7:23); "Reuben enroots his brethren in the narrow Canaanite from the Limit Noah to the Limit Abram"—i.e., in the second group of the Twenty-seven Churches (*J* 15:25); Noah, with other patriarchs, is called a Druid (*J* 27).

See also ARK OF NOAH and FLOOD OF NOAH.

For Noah's wife, see NAAMAH.

NOAH (female) was the second of the five daughters of Zelophehad, who won the right to inherit when they had no brother (*Numb* xxvii:1–11). As representatives of the Female Will, they torture the men. Noah is bid "fetch the girdle of strong brass, heat it red hot, press it around the loins of this expanding cruelty" (*FZ* viii:312; *J* 67:59).

Milton had no son; Rahab and the five daughters are equated with his three wives and three daughters and with the mountains surrounding Palestine (*Mil* 17:11, 17). Noah would seem to be the second daughter and Mount Lebanon.

"Rahab & Noah dwell on Windsor's heights" (*Mil* 35:9).

NOBODADDY ("nobody's daddy") was Blake's name for the false God of this World. *To Nobodaddy* (*K* 171) questions this "Father of Jealousy" about the reasons for his secrecy and obscurity. In "Let the Brothels of Paris be opened" (*K* 185), Nobodaddy coarsely approves the fatal actions of the French king and queen. Lines from this poem are repeated in "When Klopstock England defied" (*K* 186), where Nobodaddy is baffled by Blake's contempt for the "German Milton."

NORFOLK is a maritime county in the east of England; it is bounded north and east by the North Sea, south by Suffolk, and west by Cambridgeshire.

With Suffolk and Essex, it is assigned to Reuben (*J* 16:44); with five more, it is assigned to Skofeld (*J* 71:38). Various counties "from Oxfordshire to Norfolk on the Lake of Udan Adan labour within the Furnaces" of Los (*J* 16:19).

The "NORMAN Conqueror" is included in the list of bad kings (*J* 73:36); but the amalgamation of the British, Saxon, Roman, and Norman into one nation, the English (*J* 92:1) is a symbol of the Brotherhood of Man and a preparation for the final apocalypse.

The NORTH symbolizes the Imagination. It is the compass-point of Urthona-Los, and is counterbalanced by the South, which is Reason. Jesus came from the North (Galilee); and in the North, Satan assembled his armies for the great war in heaven (*PL* v: 726, 755; cf. *Isaiah* xiv:13).

Tiriel hypocritically pretends to come from the North (*Tir* ii:51). Thel enters the vision of her future through the "northern bar" (*Thel* 6:1).

As the North is the place of spiritual warfare, war on earth is the result of the perverted imagination. When Enitharmon suppresses sex, it is reduced to the erotic dream in the North, where it is transmuted into war. See SOTHA. Here Sotha gives a code of war to Odin (*SoL* 3:30). In "I saw a Monk of Charlemaine," Charlemaine "& his clouds of War | Muster around the Polar Star" (*K* 420), and "Thy father drew his sword in the north" (*K* 419). It is "th' attractive north, that [when fallen] round the feet, a raging whirlpool, draws the dizzy enquirer to his grave" (*Eur* 10:30). Compare "the northern drum" (*Am* b:18; *FZ* vii b:148).

Urizen always wants to usurp the North. When the "Eternals spurn'd back his religion," they mistakenly gave him a place in the North (*Ur* 2:2). When Urthona takes his rest, "Urizen, unloos'd from chains, glows like a meteor in the distant north" (*Eur* 3:11). In *The Four Zoas* (vi:290–317), however, Urthona's Spectre prevents him from getting there.

NORTHAMPTON is a Midland county of England, bounded by Leicestershire, Rutlandshire, Lincolnshire, Cambridgeshire, Huntingdonshire, Bedfordshire, Buckinghamshire, Oxfordshire, and Warwickshire.

With Rutland and Nottingham, it is assigned to Issachar (*J* 16:48); with Warwick, Bedford, Buckingham, Leicester, and Berkshire, it is assigned to Hutton (*J* 71:36).

NORTHUMBERLAND is the northernmost county of England. With the adjoining group of Cumberland, Westmoreland, and Durham, it is "divided in the Gates of Reuben, Judah, Dan, & Joseph" (*J* 16:50–51); with Scotland, the Isles, and Cumberland, it is assigned to Bowen (*J* 71:46).

NORWICH is the fifteenth in the list of the twenty-four Cathedral Cities (*J* 46:18). It is under Luvah and London.

"Lincoln & Norwich stand trembling on the brink of Udan-Adan" (*J* 5:10). Albion sees the piteous faces of his children gleam out "from Lincoln & Norwich, from Edinburgh & Monmouth" (*J* 21:39). Oxford faints in the arms of Norwich and ten other Cathedral Cities (*J* 46:18). With Bath, Oxford, and Cambridge, it is on the front of the bosom of the rising Albion (*Mil* 39:44).

NORWOOD is a London suburb. It is the southern member of the quaternary including Blackheath (east), Hounslow (west), and Finchley (north), which probably represent the usual extent of Blake's ramblings. The London Stone of justice is the center; thence Albion's four Forests of error overspread all the earth (*Mil* 6:5). Albion bids Hand and Hyle seize Los and bring him here to justice (*J* 42:51); and here Los builds the Mundane Shell, till the four suburbs cover the whole earth (*J* 42:80).

The NOSTRILS are one of the four features, organs of the four Senses. Their position is East (*J* 12:59; 98:17); they represent the Emotions, and are particularly important to Love. Their element is obviously Air (*MHH* 9:9; *VDA* 3:9; *FZ* viii:422), although the Genii, or Fire, are East (*J* 13:26), and Orc's nostrils breathe fire (*FZ* v:127).

In Eternity, the Nostrils are "in Rivers of bliss" (*J* 98:16). They expand "with delight in morning skies" (*FZ* viii:303). They "tell of autumn fruits when grapes & figs burst their covering to the joyful air" (*Mil* 5:32).

But like the other Senses they have become limited and materialized. Their "golden gates" are "shut, turn'd outward, barr'd and petrify'd against the infinite" (*Eur* 10:14). They are "clos'd up" (*SoL* 7:6; *FZ* vi:125; *Mil* 5:32; *J* 49:38; 66:37). Then "Odours cannot them expand [nor] joy on them exult" (*J* 49:39). It is Tirzah who bends the Nostrils downward (*FZ* iii:86; viii:303; *J* 67:49). The Daughters of Albion "weave . . . the little Nostrils" in the embryo (*J* 83:35) and in the man "pour cold water on his brain in front to cause . . . caverns to freeze over his nostrils" (*J* 66:30).

Los, however, also does his part. In the fifth Age, he creates Urizen's nostrils, which are then "bent down to the deep" (*Ur* 13:1; *FZ* iv:237; *Mil* 3:20). When Los creates Reuben's nostrils, Reuben cannot find Tirzah because "his Nostrils scented the ground" (*J* 36:2).

Los and Enitharmon are born into the

lower world "from the breathing Nostrils of Enion" (*FZ* iv:105), that is, from her brain (*FZ* vii:291). This would seem to be the reason why "in the Nerves of the Nostrils, Accident being formed into Substance & Principle by the cruelties of Demonstration, it became Opake & Indefinite, but the Divine Saviour form'd it into a Solid by Los's Mathematic power. He named the Opake, Satan: he named the Solid, Adam" (*Mil* 29:35).

NOTTINGHAM is an inland county of England. With Northampton and Rutland it is assigned to Issachar (*J* 16:48); with the adjoining Lincoln, Stafford, and Derby, it is assigned to Slade (*J* 71:34). Nottingham, with the adjoining group of Lincolnshire, Derbyshire, and Leicestershire, "from Oxfordshire to Norfolk on the Lake of Udan Adan, labour within the Furnaces" of Los (*J* 16:18–20).

NUDITY was a word Blake never used and probably despised as an invention of the blushing Tirzah. God created us in his own image (*Gen* i:27); therefore our bodies are "the Human form Divine" (*FZ* ix:367), and "the human form divine" is Love (*SoI*, "The Divine Image" 11). "The Naked Human form divine" is "Love's temple that God dwelleth in" (*EG* e:66, 64). "The nakedness of woman is the work of God" (*MHH* 8:5), and "the genitals [are] Beauty" (*MHH* 10: 1). Modesty is not a virtue; shame is a disease (*J* 21:3), the result of the Curse; and Blake depicted the celibate Satan being bitten by his own snake while watching the bridal bower of Adam and Eve.

Blake carried to its logical conclusion the trend of the Puritan poets before him. Spenser described the beauty of Scudamore and Amoret embracing on their bridal bed. Milton dwelt on the "naked Majestie" and the "looks Divine" of Adam and Eve, and took occasion to denounce "dishonest shame" as a sin against "spotless innocence" (*PL* iv: 290, 312).

Blake practised what he preached, at least to the extent of sunbathing in his garden, where Butts happened upon him and his wife as they were reciting *Paradise Lost.* " 'Come in,' cried Blake; 'it's only Adam and Eve, you know!' " (*Gil* I, 112). The ancient Britons went healthily naked. "The flush of health in flesh exposed to the open air, nourished by the spirits of forests and floods in that ancient happy period, which history has recorded, cannot be like the sickly daubs of Titian or Rubens. Where will the copier of nature, as it now is, find a civilized man who has been accustomed to go naked? ... As to a modern Man, stripped from his load of cloathing, he is like a dead corpse" (*DesC* V, *K* 580–81).

Blake's own nudes are probably the first in English art which are completely devoid of any suggestion of sensuality. They exist in a world where clothing was never dreamed of. Blake was also the first English painter who really understood that the nude is the basis of all art. "Art can never exist without Naked Beauty displayed" (*Laoc*, *K* 776) of course has much wider implications.

"NUMBER, WEIGHT & MEASURE" is a phrase which Blake found in the apocryphal *Wisdom of Solomon* xi:20: "Thou hast ordered all things in measure and number and weight." When the Sons of Urizen are creating the stars, they are "outmeasur'd by proportions of number, weight and measure" (*FZ* ii:273). "Bring out number, weight & measure in a year of dearth" (*MHH* 7:14). Compare "To converse concerning Weight & Distance in the Wilds of Newton & Locke" (*J* 34:40).

NYMPHS, in the Neo-Platonic tradition, were spirits of generation, because water signified the world of matter.

The Marygold of Leutha's vale, which Oothoon plucks, is "a Golden nymph" (*VDA* 1:5–11); the plucking symbolizes the sexual act.

In the quaternary of the Four Elements, the Nymphs are the western element, Water (*Mil* 31:20; *J* 36:37). Sixty-four thousand nymphs guard the western gate of Golgonooza (*J* 13:28).

In "Milton and the Spirit of Plato," the third illustration of *Il Penseroso* (see Illustrations), behind Milton's chair is a bat-winged nymph with a net hovering above an inverted male. In the fifth illustration, "Milton's Dream," spirits in the air and brook unfold nets and webs (see Illustrations). In *Jerusalem* 40, a nymph in a rain cloud flees from a vegetating man. In the painting called "The Circle of Life" (see Illustrations), which is an exposition of the Neo-Platonic philosophy, a group of nymphs (one with a musical pipe) cluster behind the stopped chariot of the sleeping Urizen; his scepter blindly touches the head of one spirit; and she descends, in a kind of explosion, to ride behind four horses through the Sea of Time and Space.

The OAK, reputed the toughest and most long-lived of trees, was almost a symbol of England. An oak tree stood in the center of many a village green; there were oak forests where the Druids had once held their mysterious ceremonies; the warships were built of oak; and "Hearts of Oak" was a popular patriotic song.

The Oak appears first in Blake as the protector of innocence. Old John sits beneath an oak, laughing while the children play (*SoI*, "The Ecchoing Green" 13). Job's family is gathered beneath an oak. Then "laughter sat beneath the Oaks, & innocence sported" (*FZ* vi:214). But the Sons of Albion proclaim an end to these "sinful delights of age and youth and boy and girl ...beneath the Oak & Palm" (*J* 18:16–19).

The Oak next appears as a stubborn, rooted Error. Har and Heva sit beneath an oak (*Tir* ii:5). The margin of the second "Holy Thursday" (*SoE*) contains oak leaves, in one of which is cradled a dead baby. The Angel of the fourth "Memorable Fancy" (*MHH*) sits in the twisted root of an oak while he propounds his theory of the afterlife. The punishing demons of Albion "cannot bring the stubbed oak to overgrow the hills" of America (*Am* 9:8). Urizen sits on his "dark rooted Oak" (*Ahan* 3:16).

Eno sits beneath "the eternal Oak" (*BoL* 3:4). Probably this is the "Oak of Weeping" which, with the Palm of Suffering, overshadows the Rock of Ages on the verge of Beulah, where the Saviour lays Albion to sleep (*FZ* i:464; *J* 23:24; 59:5).

The Groves of Oak are most terrible, for they were sanctuaries of the diabolic druid religion, which practised "Human Sacrifice[s] for Sin in War & in the Druid Temples of the Accuser of Sin beneath the Oak Groves of Albion, that cover'd the whole Earth beneath his Spectre" (*J* 98:48; see also *Mil* 6:16; *J* 16:4; 25:4, 27; 43:9, 11, 81; 44:37; 65:51; 66:55; 70:16; 71:61; 89: ∼3; 94:24).

OBTUSE ANGLE. See TAYLOR.

OCALYTHRON, the first of the daughters of Los and Enitharmon (*FZ* viii:363), is the Emanation of Rintrah (wrath), first offspring of the poetic function. Their position is North.

Twice she is called "jealous" (*Eur* 8:7; *Mil* 10:19); being of the North, she is jealous of her consort's ideas. When Enitharmon is summoning her children, she asks: "Rintrah, where hast thou hid thy bride? Weeps she in desart shades? Alas! my Rintrah, bring the lovely jealous Ocalythron" (*Eur* 8:5). Twice she is associated with Elynittria, Emanation of Palamabron (pity, the second poetic function); and Elynittria is jealous of her consort's affections. While Elynittria is "bound up in the horns of Jealousy to a deadly fading Moon," Ocalythron "binds the Sun into a Jealous Globe, that every thing is fix'd Opake without Internal light" (*Mil* 10:18). Together, they represent the consort's opposition to the husband's work.

However, as Emanations they can be and should be inspirations. Enitharmon warns Rintrah and Palamabron against seeking a "pride of dominion that will Divorce Ocalythron & Elynittria" (J 93:5). Elynittria is cured of her jealousy in *Milton*, and unselfishly ministers to her husband's affections; presumably, Ocalythron can do the same, encouraging her husband's ideas.

OCHIM is the seventeenth son of Los and Enitharmon; the line runs: "Rintrah . . . Satan, Har, Ochim, Ijim . . ." (FZ viii:357–60). Blake found the name in Swedenborg (*True Christian Religion*, spotted by Northrop Frye, *Frye* 243), who in turn had found it in *Isaiah* xiii:21, where it is translated "doleful creatures." "Ochim" signifies the sorrows that follow self-love (Har). See IJIM.

ODIN, chief god of the Scandinavian pantheon, was the god of war. "In the North, to Odin, Sotha [frustrated sex] gave a Code of War, because of Diralada, thinking to reclaim his joy" (SoL 3:30). It was "the Thor & cruel Odin who first rear'd the Polar Caves" (Mil 25:53). These caves are the dwelling-place of Sotha and his love, the erotic dream, where suppressed lust is transformed into war (Eur 14:26). See SOTHA and WODEN.

OG, a giant of the remnants of the Rephaim, was king of Bashan. After the Israelites had conquered Sihon, he attacked them, only to be defeated at his capital Edrei, where all his people were slaughtered. His iron bedstead nine cubits long was preserved for many years at Rabbath-ammon.

Og symbolizes Justice. He is depicted as "scaled with iron scales from head to feet, precipitating himself into the Abyss with the Sword & Balances" (LJ, K 606; see Illustrations, "LJ" No. 35). "Cruel Og | With Moral & Self-righteous Law | [crucifies] in Satan's Synagogue" (J 27:22). Satan, Og, and Sihon build mills which unwind the clothing woven in Cathedron for the Spectres, leaving them naked to the accusing heavens (FZ viii:217). Molech's furnaces rage among the wheels of Og (Mil 37:22).

Og, Sihon, Anak, and Satan constitute an evil quaternary (FZ i:508; viii:217; Mil 22:33), whose function is to oppose Man's progress towards Eternity.

Og and Anak dwell beyond the skies with chaos and night, in the seat of Satan; they are set there as guards to prevent Man from passing through the Gates in brain and heart and loins, which open into Golgonooza (Mil 20:32–40); these are the doors of eternity (Mil 31:49). These two "Giants of Albion" were placed there by Jehovah (J 49:56). They are also responsible for the looms, mills, prisons, and workhouses which prevent Man from leading a spiritual life (J 13:57).

Og and Sihon together constitute the Mundane Shell. Og's kingdom, centered in Orion, consists of the twenty-seven northern constellations; Sihon's kingdom, centered in Ophiuchus, consists of the twenty-one southern constellations. Orion is the giant slain by Artemis, the virgin goddess, representative of the Female Will; Ophiuchus represents Man entangled with the serpent Nature—in the Laocoön plate, the twin serpents of Good and Evil (Mil 37:50–51). The Four Sons of Los peruse Albion's tomb in the starry characters of Og and Anak [Sihon?] (J 73:16).

Luvah says erroneously that the quaternary are Jerusalem's sons (FZ i:508). The two Sons of Los fear that Milton will loose the four upon Albion (Mil 22:33). Erin bids Sihon and Og remove to their own lands and "leave the secret coverts of Albion & the hidden places of America"; she also bids the Daughters of Beulah to lament for the two (J 48:63–49:3). Og and Sihon "in the tears of Balaam . . . have given their power to Joshua & Caleb" (J 49:58). Jerusalem laments that Gilead has joined with Og (J 79:13). In the stomach of the Covering Cherub are seen the enemies of Jerusalem, including Og and Sihon (J 89:42–47).

OHANA is the eighth son of Los and Enitharmon (FZ viii:358). He follows Ozoth and is followed by Sotha.

OLD BOW. See BOW.

OLIVET (the Mount of Olives) is the most conspicuous landmark of Jerusalem. It was the mount of the Ascension (*Acts* i:11–12). On its lower reaches is the Garden of Gethsemane, the scene of the Agony and the Betrayal.

In "the bright Sculptures of Los's Halls" is recorded "All that can happen to Man in his pilgrimage of seventy years. Such is the Divine Written Law of Horeb & Sinai, and such the Holy Gospel of Mount Olivet & Calvary" (*J* 16:61–69). In other words, the two Testaments are the true and complete records of man's spiritual existence.

In the Golden Age of Innocence, "the Mount of Olives was beheld over the whole Earth" (*J* 24:49). But in the present state of war, a "curtain of blood is let down from Heaven across the hills of Ephraim, & down Mount Olivet to the Valley of the Jebusite" (*J* 68:21); and Jerusalem languishes "upon Mount Olivet, East of mild Zion's Hill" (*J* 82:55).

OLOLON appears only in the poem *Milton*. Although she does not know it, she is the spiritual form of Milton's Sixfold Emanation; she is the truth underlying his errors about woman.

Milton had never discovered Ololon—had never really understood the other sex. His honeymoon difficulties with his first wife had inspired his great tome on divorce; he loved his second wife at least to the extent of a great sonnet; his third wife was merely a housekeeper. It is well known how his three daughters mistreated their great father. (The three wives and the three daughters constitute his Sixfold Emanation.) Milton's Eve is only a helpmate; Adam fears the inspiration she might give. And Milton's Dalila is a marvelous analysis of the Satanic Female Will.

Therefore Milton is unhappy though in heaven, and descends to earth to recover his lost Emanation. The immediate cause of his descent is the song of a bard; the unrecognized and fundamental cause is his very real love of woman, or Ololon (*Mil* 21:31; 34:3; 37:2).

She has not yet taken a definite form. In Eden she is "a sweet River of milk & liquid pearl" (21:15). She is "multitudes" (35:37), for she has many sons and daughters (30:4); they are a "Fiery Circle" (34:3); and her clouds contain the coming Saviour (21:60; 31:10; 31:15; 35:41).

She feels guilty at having driven Milton from heaven (35:31; 37:1). Therefore, in the full spirit of self-sacrifice, she proposes: "Let us descend also, and let us give ourselves to death in Ulro among the Transgressors" (21:45); but though the Divine Family warns her "you cannot renew Milton: he goes to Eternal Death" (21:57), "all Ololon" descends into Beulah (31:8). Thence she descends into Ulro, seeking out even the lowest state of sleeping Humanity, Or-Ulro, which consists of "the Stomach & Intestines terrible, deadly, unutterable" (34:16)—the final abasement of self-sacrifice. She is horrified to see in Ulro a universe of "decay & death," and the mortal warfare of men on earth (34:49–35:6). When she finds the death couch of Milton, "they thunderous utter'd all a universal groan, falling down prostrate before the Starry Eight [Milton's Humanity and his seven guardian Angels], asking with tears forgiveness, confessing their crime with humiliation and sorrow" (35:31). But the Starry Eight rejoice, because her descent to Los and Enitharmon, who lie on their death couches beside Milton (35:27), has opened a wide road back to Eternity (35:35).

The great moment comes when Ololon meets the twenty-eighth Lark (of pure inspiration—see LARK), enters the Polypus (see POLYPUS), and descends into Blake's garden (36:9–13). At last she reveals her "Eternal Form" (40:1), which is that of "a Virgin of twelve years" (36:17), who has just reached the point of fecundity.

She asks Blake about Milton, whose Shadow instantly appears in all his errors (37:1). But in his real and human form, Milton confronts Satan. He then sees Ololon, who questions him about Natural Religion (40:1), whereupon Rahab manifests (40:17). Milton then addresses Ololon:

"All that can be annihilated must be annihilated" (40:30), referring to the errors of the separated Emanation. She despairs (41:30), as this seems to mean the annihilation of herself. But the Sixfold Emanation divides from Ololon and like the repentant wife seeks refuge in Milton's bosom. Then "as a Moony Ark Ololon descended . . . into the Fires of Intellect" (42:7–9): love and wisdom are combined. The Starry Eight become Jesus; Ololon's clouds are his wedding garment; and Jesus becomes one with mankind (42:19). The mystical union has been achieved, and Blake falls fainting on his garden path.

ON HOMER'S POETRY [&] *On Virgil* is a single plate, etched about 1820. It is basically a denunciation of Homer's praise of war and Virgil's praise of empire. "The Classics! it is the Classics, & not Goths nor Monks, that desolate Europe with Wars." Other illuminating remarks concern unity, aesthetic form, morality in art, and the Scriptures.

ONA is one of the three daughters of Urizen (*FZ* vii:95) who make the bread of Orc. She is the "youngest Woman, clad in shining green," who divides the River of Generation into four currents (*FZ* vi:17), even as the river of Eden was divided into four. She carries a sieve (*FZ* vii:101). She represents the Loins; her sisters Uveth and Eleth represent the Heart and the Head.

"Ona" is also the name given to "A Little Girl Lost" (*SoE*).

"ONE LAW for the Lion & Ox is Oppression" is the final line of *The Marriage of Heaven and Hell* 24. The individual should be judged by his own nature and not by some generality. Tiriel, approaching the wisdom of his end, asks: "Why is one law given to the lion & the patient Ox? Dost thou not see that men cannot be formed all alike?" (*Tir* viii:10). The bewildered Bromion asks: "And is there not one law for both the lion and the ox?" (*VDA* 4:22).

Urizen's mistaken ideal includes "One King, one God, one Law" (*Ur* 4:40).

ONYX is the eleventh stone in the Hebrew high priest's breastplate; it represents Manasseh (*Exod* xxviii:20–21). Seven of these twelve stones (including onyx) appear on the back and bosom of the serpent Orc (*FZ* viii:74).

OOTHOON, the central figure of *Visions of the Daughters of Albion*, represents thwarted love. She is the third daughter of Los and Enitharmon (*FZ* viii:363), and the Emanation of Theotormon. As "the soft soul of America" she is the ideal of physical freedom (*VDA* 1:3).

Oothoon plucks "the bright Marygold of Leutha's vale" (*VDA* 1:5) and is winging her way towards her beloved Theotormon when she is raped by Bromion, to whom she is "bound back to back" (*VDA* 2:5). The rest of the poem is a series of lamentations of the soul torn between desire and duty. Oothoon insists on the essential purity of love and the holiness of sex. She denounces the bondage of marriage, modesty, jealousy, secrecy, selfishness, religious prohibitions, and the self-abuse of the solitary. She blames the whole situation on Urizen, "Creator of men! mistaken Demon of heaven! . . . Father of Jealousy, be thou accursed from the earth!" (*VDA* 5:3; 7:12).

In *Europe*, Enitharmon asks Oothoon: "Why wilt thou give up woman's secrecy, my melancholy child?"; she also sees the weeping Theotormon "robb'd of joy" (14:21–24). In *The Song of Los*, Oothoon hovers over Judah and Jerusalem; "and Jesus heard her voice (a man of sorrows) he reciev'd a Gospel from wretched Theotormon" (3:22–24). Oothoon "pants in the Vales of Lambeth, weeping o'er her Human Harvest" (*Mil* 42:33).

As a practical matter, Oothoon is obliged to give up her ideal of frankness, and resort to secrecy. She is the "charming guard" who watches over the affair of Leutha and Palamabron (*Mil* 13:44). In Lambeth is a Grain of Sand which Satan cannot find; his watch fiends would call it Sin and destroy it. But he who does find it will find within it Oothoon's palace, which opens into Beulah (*J* 41:17). Antamon hides Oothoon in Oxford, "In graceful hidings of error, in merciful deceit, lest Hand the terrible destroy his Affection" (*J* 83:29).

Oothoon's name and tale may have been suggested by Ossian's Oithona. See OSSIAN.

OPACITY is imperviousness to the divine light. Opacity (Satan) and Contraction (Adam) are the two limits to the Fall, established by the Saviour. See LIMITS.

OPHIUC[H]US (the man with the serpent) was selected by Blake as the dominant constellation of the twenty-one in the southern hemisphere. It symbolizes Man in the coils of Morality or Nature. It is counterbalanced by Orion in the northern hemisphere. "The Kingdom of Og is in Orion: Sihon is in Ophiucus. Og has Twenty-seven Districts: Sihon's Districts Twenty-one." Together they compose the Mundane Shell, "a mighty Incrustation of Forty-eight deformed Human Wonders of the Almighty" (*Mil* 37:50–54).

In a plate engraved about 1820, Laocoön is labelled in Greek "Ophiuchus" and the two serpents "Evil" and "Good."

OPTIC NERVE. See OZOTH.

OR-ULRO is the fourth state of humanity in repose; it is situated in "the Stomach & Intestines, terrible, deadly, unutterable" (*Mil* 34:16). The other three states are Beulah (head), Alla (heart), and Al-Ulro (loins).

Or-Ulro is the lowest and most abject state of self-sacrifice; therefore Ololon seeks it in her descent to save Milton (*Mil* 34:19).

It is not to be confused with the bowels (compassion) or Bowlahoola. See STOMACH.

ORC is Revolution in the material world. He is a lower form of Luvah, the emotions (*FZ* v:42; vii:151; viii:382; *Mil* 29:34), because repressed love turns to war. Orc's consort is the Shadowy Female, who is this material world—a lower form of Luvah's Emanation, Vala.

He is the first-born of Los and Enitharmon (*Eur* 3:25, 28, etc.). Sometimes Rintrah is the eldest (*Eur* 8:1); indeed, Orc is completely omitted from the list of the sons (*FZ* viii:357), where Rintrah heads the list. The paradox is explained when we understand that Rintrah (just wrath), Palamabron (pity), Theotormon (frustrate desire), and Bromion (logic) are an analysis of Orc. The true poet, being a prophet, is always a revolutionary in one way or another; and the four are his motivations.

Orc's name is an anagram of *cor*, because he is born from Enitharmon's heart (*FZ* v: 37). However, it might also come from *orca*, "whale," as in one of his forms he is a whale in the South Seas (*Am* 1:14; 2:14).

The tale of Orc is a revolutionist's analysis of the contemporary American and French revolutions; Blake shows their cause, outburst, initial success, and eventual failure, thus establishing the formula for all revolutions. The story is told chiefly in "A Song of Liberty" (*MHH*), *America*, *Europe*, *The Book of Urizen* (19–25, Chaps. vi–viii), and *The Four Zoas* (v–ix).

The begetting of Orc is the result of the separation of Los and Enitharmon. His gestation proceeds from a worm to a serpent, with "many forms of fish, bird, & beast" (*Ur* 19:34)—a striking anticipation of the modern theory of phylogeny. His birth is terrible (*MHH* 25; *Ur* 19:40–46; *FZ* v:35). Enormous Demons howl: "Luvah, King of Love, thou art the King of rage & death" (*FZ* v:42).

As Orc grows up, Los becomes jealous of the boy's affection for his mother (*Ur* 20: 9–24), and when Orc reaches puberty, he hates his father (*FZ* v:79–91)—the situation is that later named by Freud as the "Oedipus complex." Los therefore binds Orc down on a mountain top (Mount Atlas, suggesting Prometheus; *SoL* 3:21) with the Chain of Jealousy (*Ur* 20:21–24; *FZ* v:97). When the parents relent, it is too late; they cannot release him, because his limbs have become enrooted in the rock, and strong fibres from the Chain of Jealousy have woven themselves around the rock and the cave, and over the boy (*FZ* v:155).

Though Orc's body is bound on a mountain top, his imagination rages in a cave of fire, deep in the south (*FZ* vi:265; *J* 14:3). This situation is explained by the picture on *America* 1, where Orc lies manacled on a rock beneath a sterile tree; but below its roots he appears again in a sullen rage. The south is Urizen's proper realm, but now he has abandoned it, and beneath his seat the flames of revolt are incubating. Orc's imagination reaches everywhere (*FZ* v:114–42); it permeates everything. "The dead heard the voice of the child and began to awake from sleep; all things heard the voice of the child and began to awake to life" (*Ur* 20: 26).

It particularly rouses Urizen. Long since, Urizen had known that Orc would be his enemy (*FZ* iii:14). In "A Song of Liberty" (*MHH*) he instantly hurls the newborn Orc into the night, and himself falls. But in *The Four Zoas*, he only trembles at the child's voice, and explores the dens, to "find that deep pulsation that shakes my caverns with strong shudders" (v:238). He descends and confronts Orc in his cave (viii:5); as a result of Urizen's hypocrisy, Orc finds freedom from his fetters by reverting to the Worm, and grows again into the Serpent, which Urizen forces to climb the Tree of Mystery (vii:162).

As the Serpent in Eden, he is the Tempter. The impulses of suppressed desire become "Messiah or Satan or Tempter [who] was formerly thought to be one of the Antediluvians who are our Energies" (*MHH* 17). "When Luvah in Orc became a Serpent, he descended into that State call'd Satan" (*FZ* viii:382).

Thus the corruption of the revolutionary ideal began. Like Prometheus, Orc stole Urizen's fire. " 'I well remember how I stole thy light & it became fire consuming.' . . . And Orc began to organize a Serpent body, despising Urizen's light & turning it into

flaming fire, recieving as a poison'd cup Recieves the heavenly wine, and turning affection into fury, & thought into abstraction, a Self consuming dark devourer rising into the heavens" (*FZ* vii:147–56; cf. iii:15).

In the "Preludium" to *America*, Orc, having reached the age of potency, breaks loose and unites with the Shadowy Female—war enters the material world. In the later version, however, it is she who embraces Orc, "that he might lose his rage and with it lose himself in meekness" (*FZ* vii *b*:124–28); but war follows immediately, and Orc, now completely the Serpent, has lost any trace of his human form (*FZ* vii *b*:215). Continuing to eat the bitter bread of Urizen's daughters, he augments in fury; his scaly armor bears seven of the gems on the high priest's breastplate (viii:69, 74); but six of them were also worn by the Covering Cherub (*Ezek* xxviii:13). Although the enemy of religion, he has become a religion of his own, "in forms of priesthood, in the dark delusions of repentance" (*FZ* viii:461); the cup of Rahab holds the "food of Orc & Satan, press'd from the fruit of Mystery" (*FZ* viii: 603).

But eventually Orc burns himself out (*FZ* ix:34, 69), especially when Urizen stops trying to control him; and he becomes Luvah again (*FZ* ix:358–62).

Orc's role in *America* is that of the impact of the American idea on Europe. When Albion's Prince threatens the colonies, Orc appears on the Atlantic, and proclaims, in poetical paraphrase, life, liberty, and the pursuit of happiness. Albion's Angel accuses him of being "Orc, who serpentform'd stands at the gate of Enitharmon to devour her children" (7:4), a reference to the dragon Satan waiting to devour the child of the woman in the wilderness (*Rev* xii:4). He replies: "I am Orc, wreath'd round the accursed tree" (8:1). The Angel also calls him the "Eternal Viper" (9:15), the viper being fabled to destroy his mother in the act of birth. The apparition of Orc terrifies the royal governors and their troops. Orc retorts Albion's plagues on England, corrupting the church and everything else, until at last the source of the whole trouble is revealed: leprous Urizen. But after twelve years, "France reciev'd the Demon's light" (16:15); then France, Spain, and Italy try to "shut the five gates of their law-built heaven...But the five gates were consum'd" in Orc's fires (16:19–22).

In *Europe*, history is overshadowed by the tale of Enitharmon's repression of sex in order to establish the domination of woman. Urthona-Los disappears, to take his rest, whereupon Enitharmon summons Orc from his deep dens (3:24–29), and descends into his red light (revolts against Los's dominion); then she summons Rintrah and Palamabron, and establishes her own domination by proclaiming that "Woman's love is Sin" (5:5). While she sleeps for eighteen hundred years (the Christian era), Orc's flames torment Albion's Angel and others in England (12:12–22). When she wakes, terrible Orc reaches the "vineyards of red France" (15:2), and Los reappears in the dawn.

The relationship of Urizen and Orc, or convention and revolt, is that of the Contraries, without which progression is impossible. Their warfare goes back to the original antagonism of Urizen and Luvah. Urizen, by suppressing Luvah, only forces him into the lower form of physical revolt, a state of error; and Urizen himself is also debased. "Satan is Urizen drawn down by Orc & the Shadowy Female into Generation" (*Mil* 10:1); "Satan is the Spectre of Orc, & Orc is the generate Luvah" (*Mil* 29:34). Orc is only a stage, and no immediate answer to the problem: revolution in the material world degenerates, till in its fury it loses all of its original meaning. The illustrations to *America* show this progressive descent, ending in the agony of Nature herself.

But the very triumph of error is prophetic of its ending. The real solution is Jesus, whose garments are Luvah's robes of blood. When Urizen sees Orc and Jesus simultaneously, all his reason cannot reconcile the Prince of Peace with the King of War (*FZ* viii:62). In the "Preludium" to *Europe*, Je-

sus is the "secret child," the Saviour of all, even Nature herself (*Eur* 2:13; 3:2).

ORCUS was the classical Hades. Ijim, refusing to believe that Tiriel's own sons have turned him out, says: "It is as false as Matha & as dark as vacant Orcus" (*Tir* iv: 87).

ORION, a young hunter, was beloved by Diana, who slew him unintentionally through a trick of Apollo's. In her anguish she placed him in the heavens as a constellation. Blake selected him as the dominant constellation of the northern hemisphere; he is counterbalanced by Ophiuchus (the man entangled with the serpent) in the southern.

Orion symbolizes justice. "The Kingdom of Og [justice] is in Orion" (*Mil* 37:50). In the last illustration to *Il Penseroso*, "Milton's Old Age," the poet particularly studies Orion, who soars, brandishing his sword, between Taurus and Gemini (where he always rises).

Albion's limbs once contained all the starry heavens (*J* 27). *Jerusalem* 25 shows Orion on Albion's torso (Betelgeuse on his shoulder, the Belt around his waist), the sun upon his right thigh, the moon and Pleiades on his left.

ORKNEY is an insular county in the north of Scotland. With Shetland and Skye, it is assigned to Zebulun (*J* 16:57), and with the rest of Scotland to Bowen (*J* 71:46).

ORUS (i.e., Horus) was the child of Osiris and Isis, and a member of that Egyptian trinity which Blake names as the eighth of the Twelve Gods of Asia (*Mil* 37:27).

OSHEA. See JOSHUA.

OSIRIS was the sun-god of Egypt. Osiris, Isis (his sister-wife), and their child Horus ("Orus" in Blake) were the Holy Family of Egypt.

Blake treats this trinity as one, the eighth of the Twelve Gods of Asia. Their dark tabernacles float nightly on the Nile and the

Egyptian lakes until morning comes and Osiris appears in the sky (*Mil* 37:27).

OSSIAN was a semi-mythical Scottish bard of the third century, whom James Macpherson (1736–96) made famous by ascribing to him certain alleged translations from the Gaelic. *Fragments of Ancient Poetry Collected in the Highlands of Scotland* (1760) initiated the Revolutionary period of English poetry; the epics *Fingal* (1762) and *Temora* (1763) followed.

These poems, which conflicted on all points with neoclassical theory, caused an international sensation. Ossian was hailed as a Gaelic Homer who had lived far to the north in a desolate landscape of fogs and bleak winds and ghosts. Blind with age, he dwelt in a cave, tended by Malvina, the widow of his son Oscar. All others had perished. He sang to his harp the tales of old, of the great feats of his father Fingal, his son Oscar, and himself; of his courtship of Everallen; of the battles and tragic loves of others.

Goethe admired the poems; Napoleon kept a copy of them under his pillow; the German composers set them to music; Whitman and Melville spoke in their praise. But there were those who denied their authenticity. Dr. Johnson, who affected a hatred of anything Scottish, attacked them outrageously, denied flatly that there were any manuscript sources, and even threatened Macpherson with a cudgelling.

Blake insisted throughout his life that the poems were genuine. He listed "the Songs of Fingal" with the Eddas and Homer (On Watson, *K* 389). Nearing his end, he wrote: "I believe both Macpherson & Chatterton, that what they say is Ancient Is so. I own myself an admirer of Ossian equally with any other Poet whatever" (On Wordsworth, *K* 783). Evidently he sensed the genuine folk material in these poems. The tales did exist as traditions in Ireland as well as Scotland; and there were also manuscript collections which Macpherson consulted. But believing that they actually were the surviving fragments of disintegrated epics,

he built the epics himself, adding, altering, and subtracting as he saw fit. When the great controversy over their authenticity began, he tried to publish the original manuscripts, but could get no subscribers; however, he persevered, leaving three volumes which finally appeared in 1807.

Macpherson did not suffer from the accusations of forgery. Among other things, he was surveyor-general of the Floridas from 1764 to 1766; in 1780, he was elected to Parliament; in 1784 he was re-elected, and kept his seat for the rest of his life. In 1785 he was considered for the laureateship, and finally was buried in Westminster Abbey.

Like many another young poet (such as Byron and Shelley), Blake was influenced in his early work by Ossian's wild and primitive imagery, notably in the ballad "Gwin, King of Norway" (*PS*), and again in *The French Revolution*, and up through the discarded plates of *America*.

Although "Ossian's" poems were printed as prose, they were really written in rough septenaries and alexandrines, with a great variety of unaccented syllables; but though the accents and caesuras are strong, the lines are insensitive, short-breathed, and monotonous. Blake's free septenaries in the Prophetic Books were evidently derived from Ossian's; but Blake's rhythms vary according to the sense, from *Tiriel* and the limpid *Thel* to the choral thunders of *Jerusalem* (see *J* 3).

Although Blake used none of Ossian's narrative material and none of his characters, he did like the general sound of the names, and adopted their primitive flavor in choosing names for his own characters. As a result, resemblances have been taken for sources, but actually there is no connection. "U-thorna" and "Lutha" sound like "Urthona" and "Leutha," but the former are only place names, with no significance beyond the geographical. The father of Colmar is "Matha," but we know nothing more of him, certainly nothing to explain "false as Matha" (*Tir* iv:87). Theotormon's name resembles that of Tonthormod, king of Sardronlo, who fell in love with Ossian's daughter Oina-morul. On being refused because of family enmities, he came with his army to seize her; Ossian captured him, then relented, and united the lovers. There is nothing here that throws light on Theotormon. Perhaps the closest to Blake is the tale of Oithona, who has been suggested as the original of Oothoon (*Erd* 218). She loved Gaul, but Dunromath carried her off and raped her. Disguised as a soldier, she was killed in the battle in which Gaul slew Dunromath.

OVID'S *Metamorphoses* was the great source book in England for knowledge of the classical myths. Ovid gathered them together in a very loose framework and retold them in a style of easy elegance. It was he who furnished the English authors with the classical references which had become so monotonous by Blake's time. However, the Roman poet was quite insensitive to the deeper, human significance of the Greek material, which now furnishes a vocabulary for the psychoanalysts.

Blake "delighted in Ovid, and, as a labour of love, had executed a finished picture from the *Metamorphoses*, after Giulio Romano. This design hung in his room," wrote Samuel Palmer to Alexander Gilchrist in 1855. Through Ovid's paraphrases, Blake felt clearly the original significance of the myths. "The Greek Fables originated in Spiritual Mystery & Real Visions, which are lost & clouded in Fable & Allegory . . . Apuleius's Golden Ass & Ovid's Metamorphosis & others of the like kind are Fable; yet they contain Vision in a sublime degree, being derived from real Vision in More ancient Writings" (*LJ*, *K* 605, 607).

But when Blake was fighting neoclassicism, he naturally selected Ovid as one of the enemy. "The Stolen and Perverted Writings of Homer & Ovid, of Plato & Cicero, which all Men ought to contemn, are set up by artifice against the Sublime of the Bible" (*Mil* 1). Indeed, Ovid's account of the Creation and the Flood resembles the account in *Genesis* so closely that it might well seem "Stolen and Perverted." Greece

and Rome, Blake went so far as to write, "were destroyers of all Art. Homer, Virgil & Ovid confirm this opinion & make us reverence The Word of God, the only light of antiquity that remains unperverted by War" (*On Virgil*, *K* 778). It was the classical cult of war that made Blake call these great pagan writers "the silly Greek & Latin slaves of the Sword" (*Mil* 1).

The OWL, the bird of Minerva, was proverbially wise. To Blake, its ominous nocturnal hoot suggested instead False Wisdom.

"The Owl that calls upon the Night | Speaks the Unbeliever's Fright" (*Aug* 27, *K* 431). When misfortune strikes and friends are tried, "the Eagle is known from the Owl" ("Motto" 8, *K* 183). When Brittannia laments her murder of Albion, the Owl is among the evil witnesses of her deed (*J* 94: 27). The Owl appears in the color print "Hecate" and in the margin at the mocking of Job (*Illustr Job* 10).

The OX is a castrated bull, who drags the plow (*FZ* vii *b*:202; *J* 65:48), and is slaughtered for meat (*FZ* ii:409; *J* 58:9). He is docile and patient, although there are "moping terrors" in his brain (*FZ* ix:236). "He who the Ox to wrath has mov'd | Shall never be by Woman lov'd" (*Aug* 31, *K* 431); it would require an excess of cruelty to rouse the wrath of such a gentle creature or his human equivalent. He is contrasted with the lion: "One Law for the Lion & Ox is Oppression" (*MHH* 24).

In the first version of the title page of his illuminated *Genesis*, Blake assigned Tharmas the head of the Ox, as a beast of the Apocalypse (see Illustrations). Tharmas also is patient, though he can be roused to wrath.

OXFORD is the thirteenth of the Twenty-four Cathedral Cities (*J* 46:17). It is under Luvah and London. It is also the site of Oxford University, and as such is frequently associated with Cambridge.

Warfare and materialism disorganize it.

"Cambridge & Oxford & London are driven among the starry Wheels" (*J* 5:3). "London is a stone of [Jerusalem's] ruins, Oxford is the dust of her walls" (*J* 29:19). "Oxford groans in his iron furnace" (*J* 42:58). "Worcester & Hereford, Oxford & Cambridge reel & stagger" (*J* 66:66). But the first Four Sons of Los (*FZ* viii:357) "dwell over the Four Provinces of Ireland in heavenly light, the Four Universities of Scotland, & in Oxford & Cambridge & Winchester" (*J* 71:52, where they are called the sons of Jerusalem). And when Albion rises, "his bosom girt with gold involves York, Edinburgh, Durham & Carlisle & on the front Bath, Oxford, Cambridge, Norwich" (*Mil* 39:42).

Blake associated the universities with secret loves, perhaps having student amours in mind. The Daughters of Albion listened to Gwendolen's teachings "in secret shades, on Cambridge and Oxford beaming soft, uniting with Rahab's cloud" (*J* 82:10). "Oothoon! Where hides my child? in Oxford hidest thou with Antamon? In graceful hidings of error, in merciful deceit, lest Hand the terrible destroy his Affection, thou hidest her, in chaste appearances for sweet deceits of love & modesty immingled, interwoven, glistening to the sickening sight" (*J* 83:27). When Leutha has her affair with Palamabron, "in dreams she bore Rahab, the mother of Tirzah & her sisters in Lambeth's vales, in Cambridge & in Oxford, places of Thought, intricate labyrinths of Times and Spaces unknown, that Leutha lived in Palamabron's Tent, and Oothoon was her charming guard" (*Mil* 13:41).

The BARD OF OXFORD. Oxford, the Cathedral City, is also "an immortal bard," whose divine eloquence fails to cure Albion. This episode is evidently a tribute to Shelley. Of all the contemporary poets, none was closer to Blake in revolutionary fervor, poetic rapture, intense visualizing, and daring thought. He denounced the tyrant God, and called himself an atheist, although only Blake surpassed him in religious feeling and insight. Shelley not only preached free love but

practised it, yet without being a libertine. He attacked the oppressors of the poor, the corruption in government. He was an overt, fighting Reprobate.

Blake never seems to have mentioned him, but he must have known of the son-in-law of his friends William Godwin and Mary Wollstonecraft. It was characteristic of Blake to have chosen Shelley, who was expelled from Oxford for his atheism, to represent the Cathedral City; for the Reprobate is of the true church.

The episode is brief. Albion lies diseased; the Cathedral Cities assemble, but cannot help him; then Bath, "healing City" (*J* 45:1), suggests: "Oxford, take thou these leaves of the Tree of Life; with eloquence that thy immortal tongue inspires, present them to Albion; perhaps he may recieve them, offer'd from thy loved hands" (*J* 45:30). In the City of God, the Tree of Life bears leaves "for the healing of the nations" (*Rev* xxii:2); but Blake also must have had in mind the role of the leaves in Shelley's "Ode to the West Wind" ("Drive my dead thoughts over the universe like withered leaves to quicken a new birth"), for Shelley was also much concerned about the healing of the nations. "Oxford, immortal Bard, with eloquence divine he wept over Albion, speaking the words of God in mild perswasion, bringing leaves of the Tree of Life" (*J* 46:7). He tells Albion that he is in error, that one error not removed will destroy a human soul; and bids him repose in Beulah till the error is removed, and rest on the bosom of the Cathedral Cities "Till the Plow of Jehovah and the Harrow of Shaddai have passed over the Dead to awake the Dead to Judgment" (*J* 46:10–15) —that is, until the New Age has come. But Albion turns away, refusing comfort, and the trembling Oxford faints in the arms of the other cities.

This fainting would seem to be Shelley's death; if so, this plate was not written until the latter part of 1822.

However, the identification with Shelley is not positive, because Blake, in a fulsome letter to Hayley (27 Jan 1804), mentions "my much admired & respected Edward the Bard of Oxford whose verses still sound upon my Ear like the distant approach of things mighty & magnificent; like the sound of harps which I hear before the Sun's rising." This reference was to Edward Garrard Marsh of Oriel College, Oxford, who arrived at Felpham September 1, 1803. He was about twenty at the time. He read aloud Hayley's poems to Hayley and Blake (*Gil* I, 203). Eventually he became a clergyman and in 1837 published a volume of hymns, which included seventy of his own. They are not impressive. Certainly this forgotten poet hardly deserved the tribute in *Jerusalem*; whereas all the references in that poem fit Shelley.

The RIVER OF OXFORD is the Isis. "Groans ran along Tyburn's brook and along the River of Oxford among the Druid Temples" (*FZ* ii: 39).

OXFORD STREET (or Tyburn Road) is one of the principal thoroughfares of London. It extends from the northeast corner of Hyde Park to Holborn.

The Gate of Los, through which pass the souls of the martyrs to Justice and the other dead, bends "across the road of Oxford Street . . . from Hyde Park to Tyburn's deathful shades" (*J* 38:57).

In the summer of 1811, Southey called on Blake, who showed him "a perfectly mad poem" called *Jerusalem*. As an example of its supposed insanity, Southey told Crabb Robinson erroneously: "Oxford Street is in Jerusalem" (Crabb Robinson's Diary, 24 July 1811).

OXFORDSHIRE is an inland county of England. With the adjoining Bucks and Harford, it is assigned to Gad (*J* 16:47); with the adjoining Warwick and Wilts, it is assigned to Kox (*J* 71:42).

Lincolnshire, Derbyshire, Nottinghamshire, and Leicestershire labor within the furnaces of Los "from Oxfordshire to Norfolk on the Lake of Udan Adan" (*J* 16:19).

OZOTH is the seventh son of Los and Enitharmon (*FZ* viii:358). His eight million and eight sons stand in the Optic Nerve, closing the eyes of the rich to the glories of nature, but giving delight to the poor indigent who is open within to eternity. Here Ozoth builds rock walls against the surging Sea of Time and Space, and iron-cramped timbers to protect the joys of life from destruction by the Spectre. "He Creates the speckled Newt, the Spider & Beetle, the Rat & Mouse, the Badger & Fox: they worship before his feet in trembling fear" (*Mil* 28:29–43). "But in the Optic vegetative Nerves, Sleep was transformed to Death in old time by Satan the father of Sin & Death" (*Mil* 29:32). It is the mortal eye of Reason which mistakes our last sleep for literal death.

P

"PACHAD" is a competent transliteration of one of the Hebrew names for God. Blake used it once (*FZ* viii:404) but thereafter preferred "Pahad." See PAHAD.

PADDINGTON was one of the slum districts of London, a waste of wretched huts occupied by squatters; but in 1811, the expansion of the city caused new houses to be built there (*Erd* 438). "What are those golden builders doing? . . . is that mild Zion's hill's most ancient promontory, near mournful ever weeping Paddington?" (*J* 12:25). "What are those golden Builders doing | Near mournful ever-weeping Paddington, | Standing above that mighty Ruin | Where Satan the first victory won?" (*J* 27:25). Albion's Daughters exhort various sections of London to awake, "to Islington & Paddington & the Brook of Albion's River" (*J* 84:2).

PAHAD (Pachad) is a name of God, which first appears in *Genesis* xxxi:42: "Except the God [Elohim] of my father, the God [Elohim] of Abraham, and the fear [Pahad] of Isaac had been with me . . ."; and also eleven verses later: "And Jacob sware by the fear [Pahad] of his father Isaac." This name is never found in the King James Bible, where it is always translated as "terror," "trembling," or the like; indeed, it is not always clear just when the Deity is intended.

Blake used Pahad as the fifth of the seven Eyes of God. After Shaddai failed through anger, Pahad fails through terror, and is succeeded by the leprous Jehovah (*FZ* viii: 404; *Mil* 13:23; *J* 55:32).

In the *Illustrations of the Book of Job*, Pahad manifests in the ninth and tenth illustrations, representing the God of Eliphaz and the Mocking of Job. In *Job* iv:14, Eliphaz used the name of Pahad: "Fear came upon me, and trembling, which made all my bones to shake"; and the quotations in the margins of Plate 9 all come from the same speech of Eliphaz. The seventeenth illustration, which reverses Pahad, shows God as the friend, faced without fear.

PAINE (Thomas, 1737–1809) was the outstanding propagandist of the American Revolution and the first to discover America's mission. A failure in England, when he was thirty-eight he left for Philadelphia at Franklin's urging and at once became a prominent journalist. When the country was hesitating as to its future course, his pamphlet *Common Sense* (10 Jan 1776) was the catalyst which crystallized the American determination to become independent. After the war had begun and its success was very dubious, the first number of his *Crisis* (Dec. 1776) restored the American morale miraculously. Washington ordered it read to his troops. Following the war, Paine returned to England to spread the American idea. In 1791, his *Rights of Man*, an answer to Burke's sentimental *Reflections on the Revolution in France*, made a sensation, calling on the English to abolish their monarchy and establish a republic. Too late, the government tried to suppress it.

In September 1791, according to Alexander Gilchrist (*Gil* I, 94), "Paine was giving at [the printer] Johnson's an idea of the inflammatory eloquence he had poured forth at a public meeting of the previous night. . . . On Paine's rising to leave, Blake laid his hands on the orator's shoulder, saying, 'You must not go home, or you are a dead man!' and hurried him off on his way to France." Paine sailed from Dover only twenty minutes before the pursuing officers arrived. (A few have doubted this anecdote; see *Erd* 140). Then, on December 18, 1792, Paine was convicted *in absentia* of high treason.

The famous apostle of liberty was hailed in France, but being of the moderate Gironde type, he escaped the guillotine only by the happy accident of a chalk mark on the wrong side of his cell door. Just before his arrest, he smuggled out the manuscript of *The Age of Reason*, Part I, which began: "I believe in one God, and no more; and I hope for happiness beyond this life." Horrified by the spread of French atheism, the Quaker-bred Deist endeavored to save religion by applying common sense. He wanted to salvage it from the superstitions of centuries. He rejected all miracles and revelations; he refused to believe that God could have ordered the atrocities recorded in the Old Testament; and he treated such things as the Virgin Birth and the Resurrection with a vulgar jocosity aimed at destroying the brain-paralyzing awe with which those doctrines were usually approached. Sometimes devastatingly brilliant, sometimes petulantly trifling, the book delighted the few but shocked the many. Yet it contained little that is not today a commonplace of critical scholarship.

But his reputation was ruined. So powerful was his book that all the orthodox of all the sects rejected it with horror, and his works are still on the Roman Index. All manner of slanders were invented and eagerly believed. To this day, the religious thwart with a burst of anger any attempt to defend him.

Paine returned to America in 1802, only to find himself anathema. He lived out his remaining seven years on his farm at New Rochelle, New York, suffering poverty, declining health, social ostracism, and the most vicious slanders. He died at New York City in 1809.

Paine wrote many sentences that have proved unforgettable. " 'The United States of America' will sound as pompously in the world or in history as 'The Kingdom of Great Britain' " he prophesied, thus inventing the name of the nation he served so well. The opening lines of his first *Crisis* were repeated by the second Roosevelt in a later time of national peril: "These are the times that try men's souls. The summer soldier and the sunshine patriot will, in this crisis, shrink from the service of their country; but he that stands now deserves the love and thanks of man and woman. Tyranny, like hell, is not easily conquered; yet we have this consolation with us, that the harder the conflict, the more glorious the triumph." Garrison took for the motto of his *Liberator* Paine's "My country is the world, and my religion is to do good." It was Paine also who wrote: "Government is for the living and not for the dead." "Man is not the enemy of man but through the medium of a false system of government." "Society is produced by our wants and government by our wickedness." "The ragged relic and the antiquated precedent, the monk and the monarch, will molder together." "All religions are in their nature mild and benign." "Where liberty is *not*, there is my country."

Blake names Paine four times in *America*. He meets with six other great Americans (3:4). Orc sees him with Washington and Warren (9:11). The Thirteen Angels stand by the same trio (12:7). Paine is one of the seven American leaders who view the approach of Albion's hosts (14:2).

The most effective answer to Paine's *Age of Reason* was Bishop R. Watson's *An Apology for the Bible* (1797), which was a best seller. The title is typical. The margins of Blake's copy are filled with furious notes. Blake detested Deism, but now he is defending Paine's truths instead of attacking his errors. Like Voltaire, Paine was a "sent" man. He had not attacked Christianity but only the perversions of the Bible. "Wherefore did Christ come? Was it not to abolish the Jewish Imposture? . . . Christ died as an Unbeliever & if the Bishops had their will so would Paine: see page 1: but he who speaks a word against the Son of man shall be forgiven. Let the Bishop prove that he has not spoken against the Holy Ghost, who in Paine strives with Christendom as in Christ he strove with the Jews" (*K* 387). Blake was applying to Paine, as he also did to Voltaire, the text: "And whosoever speaketh a word against the Son of man, it shall be forgiven him: but whosoever speaketh against the Holy Ghost, it shall not be forgiven him, neither in this world, neither in the world to come" (*Matt* xii:32; *Mark* iii:29; *Luke* xii:10). Thus Blake consigned Watson to eternal damnation; and his other comments on the bishop would sustain his opinion. "Dost thou, O Priest, wish thy brother's death when God has preserved him?" (On Watson, *K* 384). Paine had attacked the miracles; Blake replied that Paine himself was a "worker of miracles." "Is it a greater miracle to feed five thousand men with five loaves than to overthrow all the armies of Europe with a small pamphlet?" (*K* 391). But although "The Bishop never saw the Everlasting Gospel any more than Tom Paine" (*K* 394), yet "It appears to me Now that Tom Paine is a better Christian than the Bishop" (*K* 396).

Blake associated Paine with Voltaire when they claimed personal freedom. "You may do so in Spirit, but not in the Mortal Body as you pretend, till after the Last Judgment" (*LJ*, *K* 616).

PAINTING, poetry, and music are "the three Powers in Man of conversing with Paradise, which [Noah's] flood did not sweep away" (*LJ*, *K* 609). "In Eternity the Four Arts, Poetry, Painting, Music and Architecture, which is Science, are the Four Faces of Man. Not so in Time & Space: there Three are shut out, and only Science remains thro' Mercy: & by means of Sci-

ence the Three become apparent in Time & Space in the Three Professions: Poetry in Religion: Music, Law: Painting in Physic & Surgery" (*Mil* 27:55). That is, religion is petrified poetry; law corresponds to the most mathematical art, music; while painting, which deals with the human form in the outer world, becomes the medical profession.

The source of Blake's painting was "Vision" or Imagination. He had an astounding power of visualizing, which went far beyond the power of seeing with the mind's eye what Robert Bruce or Corinna or Milton must have looked like—those visionary heads which he amused himself by drawing for John Varley. The flattest banalities of Young would take literal yet startling form, for Blake saw past the cliché to its original inspiration. Did Shakespeare write a complicated mixed metaphor, it would organize itself into a splendid picture, like "Pity." No illustrator was ever more precise in following the text, yet Blake could add details of his own, which might change the meaning of the picture entirely. Blake's picturizations of the visions of Ezekiel and John the Divine are the most convincing and least grotesque ever made.

"A Spirit and a Vision are not, as the modern philosophy supposes, a cloudy vapour, or a nothing: they are organized and minutely articulated beyond all that the mortal and perishing nature can produce. He who does not imagine in stronger and better lineaments, and in stronger and better light than his perishing and mortal eye can see, does not imagine at all. The painter of this work asserts that all his imaginations appear to him infinitely more perfect and more minutely organized than any thing seen by his mortal eye" (*DesC* IV, *K* 576). "Vision is Determinate & Perfect & [the artist] Copies That without Fatigue" (On Reynolds, *K* 457).

Such visions carried Blake into the realm of archetypes. "The Artist having been taken in vision into the ancient republics, monarchies, and patriarchates of Asia, has seen those wonderful originals called in the

Sacred Scriptures the Cherubim . . . being the originals from which the Greeks and Hetrurians copied Hercules Farnese, Venus of Medicis, Apollo Belvidere, and all the grand works of ancient art" (*DesC* II, *K* 565). "These gods are visions of the eternal attributes, or divine names, which, when erected into gods, become destructive to humanity" (*DesC* III, *K* 571).

His visions, thus charged with the fullest human significance, utilize ideas. "Painting . . . exists and exults in immortal thoughts" (*DesC* IV, *K* 576). It can and should include wisdom. Just as one reads a picture of Hogarth's detail by detail to get the story, so one reads a picture of Blake's symbol by symbol to get the idea.

Tiriel and *The Book of Thel* were merely illustrated; *Songs of Innocence* was decorated; but thereafter the pictures became more and more independent of the immediate text, serving as commentaries on the fundamental idea of the poem. *The Gates of Paradise* and the *Illustrations of the Book of Job* use the sparsest of texts as commentaries on the intellectual sequence of the pictures. The plates for Blair's *Grave* are specifically intended to be studied independent of the poem and arranged to form a "poem" by themselves. Blake could summarize the philosophy of Plato or of young Milton in a single small picture. "The Last Judgment" has the complexity of a cathedral: it is "a History of Art & Science, the Foundation of Society, Which is Humanity itself" (*LJ*, *K* 613; see Illustrations).

The minuteness of detail in Blake's visions led naturally to his stressing the "Minute Particulars" in his painting. Every detail is the outgrowth of the central reality. They are all packed with meaning. "I intreat, then, that the Spectator will attend to the Hands & Feet, to the Lineaments of the Countenances; they are all descriptive of Character, & not a line is drawn without intention, & that most discriminate & particular. . . . Painting admits not a Grain of Sand or a Blade of Grass Insignificant . . ." (*LJ*, *K* 611).

Blake's insistence on firm outlines was also a result of his philosophy. "The great and golden rule of art, as well as of life, is this: That the more distinct, sharp, and wirey the bounding line, the more perfect the work of art . . . The want of this determinate and bounding form evidences the want of idea in the artist's mind . . . How do we distinguish the oak from the beech, the horse from the ox, but by the bounding outline? . . . What is it that distinguishes honesty from knavery, but the hard and wirey line of rectitude and certainty in the actions and intentions? Leave out this line, and you leave out life itself; all is chaos again, and the line of the almighty must be drawn out upon it before man or beast can exist. . . ." (*DesC* XV, *K* 585). "Every Line is the Line of Beauty" (*PubA*, *K* 603).

The Creator began his work by drawing a circle with his golden compasses; Los begins his recovery by drawing "a line upon the walls of shining heaven" (*FZ* vii:467). "Nature has no Outline, but Imagination has" (*GhA* 1:2).

With these convictions in mind, one can understand Blake's furious assaults on Rembrandt, Rubens, and others for unimaginative, vulgar subjects and blurring techniques —remembering always that Blake attacked only those he thought worth attacking, that the very fury of the assault is a measure of his admiration. "To recover Art has been the business of my life to the Florentine Original & if possible to go beyond that Original" (*PubA*, *K* 600). He also despised those who merely copied nature, the painters of portraits and landscapes; and when the Linnell group concentrated on landscapes, he taught them to emphasize the human moods to be found there. The Pre-Raphaelites, who rediscovered Blake, followed his precepts: the Florentine original, the imaginative subject, the sensitive outline, and the precision of details.

"To learn the Language of Art, 'Copy for Ever' is My Rule" (On Reynolds, *K* 446); "Copying Correctly . . . is the only School to the Language of Art" (*K* 448). "No one can ever Design till he has learn'd the Language of Art by making many Finish'd Copies both of Nature & Art & of whatever comes in his way from Earliest Childhood" (*K* 455). In so doing, the student learns and absorbs the techniques of others, until at last he is free to express himself and develop his own style. "No man can Embrace True Art till he has Explor'd & cast out False Art" (*LJ*, *K* 613). "The Great Style is always Novel or New in all its Operations" (On Reynolds, *K* 468). "Ridiculous it is to see One Man Striving to Imitate Another" (*K* 470).

Scattered through Blake's writings are many aphorisms; the following are taken from his annotations to Reynolds:

The Arts & Sciences are the Destruction of Tyrannies or Bad Governments (*K* 445).

Execution is the Chariot of Genius (*K* 454).

Every Eye Sees differently (*K* 456).

Innate Ideas are in Every Man, Born with him; they are truly Himself (*K* 459).

Passion & Expression is Beauty Itself (*K* 466).

If Art was Progressive We should have had Mich. Angelos & Rafaels to Succeed & to Improve upon each other. But it is not so. Genius dies with its Possessor & comes not again till Another is Born with It (*K* 470).

Obscurity is Neither the Source of the Sublime nor of any Thing Else (*K* 473).

Opinions differ, often violently, as to Blake's achievement as a painter. Gulley Jimson, the painter-genius in Joyce Cary's *Horse's Mouth*, believed that Blake was "the greatest artist who ever lived" (Chap. i). At the other extreme is Maurice Grosser, a painter of fine merit and a hearty admirer of Blake's poetry. In his *Painter's Eye* (New York, 1951, pp. 46–48), he affirms that Blake "as a painter is only a minor illustrator in the ornamental style," whose works reveal a "titillating and incompatible mixture . . . of English stained glass, Gothic Revival, Michelangelo, and Directoire." He "landed in a morass of singularity, limita-

tion, and mannerism. In fact, he landed not in painting at all but squarely in the arts and crafts."

It is true that Grosser's trained eye detected Blake's indebtedness to many sources. Blake himself remarked that "the Bad Artist Seems to Copy a Great deal. The Good one Really Does Copy a Great Deal" (On Reynolds, *K* 456). But the full extent of Blake's indebtednesses is revealed in Anthony Blunt's excellent *Art of William Blake* (New York, 1959), which traces sources, influences, and parallels exhaustively. "Blake, who was by far the most original English artist of his time, borrowed more extensively and more systematically from the works of other artists than did any of his contemporaries" (32). "What appears to be a startlingly original and independent style is in fact built up on material derived from a wide range of sources, European and Oriental. Just as Blake's thought was enriched by his reading of the Neo-Platonists, of the Christian mystics of all ages, whether orthodox or heretical, and of Oriental writers on religion, so his art was broadened and deepened by his study of everything that had gone before him" (43).

In short, Blake was no more a plagiarist than Milton. Sources are no proof of stealing. Whatever Blake took he did not copy passively, but *used* actively for his own purposes. So did Shakespeare.

The PALACE, a royal residence, is a symbol of State, when paired with the Church (or Temple), as in "London" (*SoE*): "How the Chimney-sweeper's cry | Every black'ning Church appalls; | And the hapless Soldier's sigh | Runs in blood down Palace walls."

"These were the Churches [north], Hospitals [west], Castles [south], Palaces [east], like nets & gins & traps to catch the joys of Eternity" (*SoL* 4:1). When there is threat of revolution, "most the polish'd Palaces, dark, silent, bow with dread, hiding their books & pictures underneath the dens of Earth" (*FZ* i:396).

Urizen's palace is modeled upon his

twelve sons and three daughters; he places his Emanation, Ahania, in the western side (*FZ* ii:174–200).

PALAMABRON symbolizes the poet's Pity for the oppressed, and in *Milton* plays the role of Blake himself in his quarrel with Satan-Hayley. Enitharmon compares him to the greathearted Judah, ancestor of Jesus (*J* 93:14). Though he is "the strongest of Demons" (*Mil* 7:47), he is "mild & piteous" and "good natur'd" (*Mil* 24:11; *FZ* viii:391). His position is East; he is under Luvah and London (*J* 74:3); but when the Zoas shift, he is found in the West (*J* 54, design).

As the second son of Los and Enitharmon (*FZ* viii:357), he is one of a quaternary: "Rintrah fierce, and Palamabron mild & piteous, Theotormon fill'd with care, Bromion loving science" (*Mil* 24:11). These four are an analysis of the revolutionary forces (see ORC), and thus constitute the prime factors of the poet's work. They were never generated but remained with their father Los, laboring at his furnaces (*J* 73:5), when the others fled (*J* 71:51; 72:11). With Los they guard the Western Wall of Golgonooza and the four walls of Jerusalem (*J* 72:13). "They dwell over the Four Provinces of Ireland in heavenly light, the Four Universities of Scotland, & in Oxford & Cambridge & Winchester" (*J* 71:51).

Palamabron is usually paired with Rintrah because Rintrah's wrath at a bad situation works with Palamabron's sympathy for the oppressed. Rintrah is the Reprobate and Palamabron the Redeemed (*Mil* 11:22); Rintrah drives the Plow, while Palamabron follows with the Harrow (*Mil* 4:1); Rintrah wields the hammer and Palamabron plies the bellows (*J* 16:9). They are the first two whom Los draws from out the ranks of war (*FZ* vii:476); and when Urizen becomes Rintrah, his eldest son Thiriel (air) becomes Palamabron (*FZ* vii:494). When Rintrah raises up the thundering Whitefield, Palamabron raises the gentler Wesley (*Mil* 22:55). The two cut Satan off from Golgo-

nooza (*FZ* viii:370); Rintrah defends Palamabron in the quarrel with Satan (*FZ* viii: 390); together they protest against Blake's entrance into Golgonooza (*Mil* 22:27); they descend with Los to the Wine-presses (*Mil* 25:2); they govern day and night in Allamanda and Entuthon Benython (*Mil* 29: 27); they guide the souls clear from the Rock of Death (*Mil* 29:44); they view together the human harvest (*Mil* 42:36).

Palamabron is first mentioned in *Europe* (5:4). When Enitharmon revolts against the dominion of the sleeping Los, she immediately summons him and Rintrah to preach the sin of sex and the futurity of eternal life, and to forbid all joy. Palamabron is the "horned priest, skipping upon the mountains" and his spouse is "silent Elynittria, the silver bowed queen" (8:3, 4). They suggest Bacchus and Diana. Orc rejoices at the confusion of the counter-revolution in England, "but Palamabron shot his lightnings, trenching down his wide back; and Rintrah hung with all his legions in the nether deep" (12:23).

In *The Song of Los*, after Rintrah "gave Abstract Philosophy to Brama in the East" (3:11), "To Trismegistus, Palamabron gave an abstract Law: to Pythagoras, Socrates & Plato" (3:18).

In *Milton*, it is Palamabron who (in the position of Blake) quarrels with Satan (Hayley). Satan persuades Los to let him drive Palamabron's Harrow, while Palamabron takes the easier task, that of Satan at his mills. The result is confusion. Palamabron calls an assembly to justify himself; Rintrah defends him; but the judgment falls against Rintrah. Then Leutha (who is Sin in *Paradise Lost*) takes the blame on herself, for she has fallen in love with Palamabron. So Elynittria, the once jealous but now tolerant wife, lays aside her bow and arrows and leads her to Palamabron's tent. There in dreams Leutha gives birth to death, Rahab, Tirzah, and her sisters. All this tale is sung by a bard; it causes Milton to leave heaven in search of his lost Emanation (*Mil* 4–13). An earlier incomplete version of this tale is inserted into *The Four Zoas* (viii:388–96).

PALESTINE is the tenth of the Thirty-two Nations which shall guard liberty and rule the rest of the world (*J* 72:39).

The PALM of Suffering and the Oak of Weeping stand over the Rock of Ages on the edge of Beulah; here the Saviour lays Albion in his deathly sleep (*FZ* i:464; *J* 23: 24; 59:6).

PANCRASS (i.e., St. Pancras) was a small hamlet in Middlesex, on the northwest side of London, in the road to Kentish-town. Its church was a plain old Gothic structure, with a square tower but without a spire, reputed to be older than St. Paul's.

It was one of the places where Blake wandered as a boy (*J* 27:9).

"The Shuttles of death sing in the sky to Islington & Pancrass" (*J* 41:7).

The PANTOCRATOR is the supreme God, ruler of all.

"O Satan . . . Art thou not Newton's Pantocrator . . . ?" (*Mil* 4:9–11).

PARACELSUS (Philippus Aureolus) was the pen name of Theophrastus Bombastus von Hohenheim (1493?–1541), "the Luther of medicine," who revolutionized medical theory and practice. Insisting on observation and experiment, he attacked the antique theories of physiology and healing, even (it is said) burning the works of Galen and Avicenna before his pupils. His pen name boasted that he was "the equal of Celsus."

He wrote, or had ascribed to him, numerous alchemical and philosophical treatises, from which Behmen borrowed the alchemical vocabulary to express his own mystical ideas.

Before the American Revolution, Paracelsus and Behmen "appear'd" to Blake (To Flaxman, 12 Sept 1800); he recorded this event as important in his own intellectual development, later paying them both the compliment of a sneer in *The Marriage of Heaven and Hell* (22), which was really an acknowledgment of indebtedness.

Blake had evidently studied thoroughly Paracelsus' *Three Books of Philosophy* (London, 1657) addressed to "the Athenians," or followers of Aristotle. Here Blake found a preliminary sketch of his own universe. Creation was a series of divisions from the original unity, the "Mysterium Magnum." These divisions were caused by an inferior god, Blake's Urizen. The first division was fourfold, into the non-material "elements," Blake's Zoas. The final division is to be the Last Judgment, where all falsities and illusions shall be destroyed, leaving every thing in its fundamental, indestructible, eternal form.

The imagination—and here was Paracelsus' great discovery—is the central function of man and the source of all his activities. As a physician, Paracelsus had noted its influence on disease and sex, and thus was an important precursor of psychiatry. The imagination operates through man's spiritual body, which dominates his physical body. In *Paracelsus his Archidoxies* (London, 1661), Blake read: "The imagination is . . . the sun of man. . . . It irradiates the earth, which is man. . . . The whole heaven, indeed, is nothing but an imagination. . . . Even as [man] imagines himself to be, such he is, and he is also that which he imagines."

Blake made this unobtrusive dethronement of reason a central fact in his own system.

PARADISE was the original state of bliss into which man was created. It was a garden which God planted eastward in Eden for the home of Adam and Eve (*Gen* ii:8). It was watered by a river which divided into four (*Gen* ii:10).

Blake twice placed Paradise in the Human Heart (*FZ* iii:95; *J* 29:74). He also placed it in his own brain where "the Eternal Great Humanity Divine planted his Paradise" (*Mil* 2:8). The Four Zoas correspond to the rivers: "The Four Living Creatures . . . in beautiful Paradises expand. These are the Four Rivers of Paradise" (*J* 98:24). See FOUR RIVERS OF EDEN, under EDEN.

PARIS is the capital city of France. Much as Blake deplored the excesses of the French Revolution and the conquests of Napoleon, he was deeply distressed at the plight of the nation itself when the conquering Allies occupied Paris in 1814 and 1815 and attempted to crucify France (*Erd* 431). "Luvah slew Tharmas, the Angel of the Tongue; & Albion brought him to Justice in his own City of Paris" (*J* 63:5). "They vote the death of Luvah & they nail'd him to Albion's Tree" (*J* 65:8). "For Luvah is France, the Victim of the Spectres of Albion" (*J* 66:15).

PARK GATE in St. James's Park leads to Great George Street and Westminster. Through this gate the Guardian of the secret codes fled groveling (*Eur* 12:19). See GREAT GEORGE STREET.

PARTICULARS. See MINUTE PARTICULARS.

PATAGONIA is the thirtieth of the Thirty-two Nations which shall protect liberty and rule the rest of the world (*J* 72:42).

PATMOS is an Aegean island in the Greek archipelago. Here the banished John the Divine wrote *Revelation* (*Rev* i:9). "John saw these things Reveal'd in Heaven on Patmos Isle" (*FZ* viii:600). "A Dragon red & hidden Harlot which John in Patmos saw" (*Mil* 40:22).

PAUL (Latin), or Saul (Hebrew), of Tarsus, a hellenized Jew, was a zealous persecutor of the first Christians, until on the road to Damascus, Jesus appeared to him in a blinding light, saying "Saul, Saul, why persecutest thou me?" (*Acts* ix:4), words which Blake quoted at the head of his fourth chapter of *Jerusalem*, "To the Christians" (*J* 77).

The vision converted Paul completely; he devoted the rest of his life to proclaiming Christianity. He became the great missionary apostle, introducing Christianity to Europe. By abolishing the necessity of circum-

cision and other legal restrictions, he opened the new religion to the gentiles. Though he thus created the first schism in the Church, he made it possible for Christianity to become a universal religion. Faith alone was the essential. The great Atonement had already been made; one needed only to accept it.

As he himself had personally perceived the risen and living Christ, he put his main emphasis on the Resurrection. Jesus, in breaking the bonds of death, broke them for us all. But Paul taught the resurrection of the spiritual and not the physical body: Blake quoted "It is raised a spiritual body" (*I Cor* xv:44) on the decoration of "To Tirzah" (*SoE*). The Church, however, doubtless with Lazarus in mind, altered the doctrine to the raising of the physical body itself, and thus promulgated another serious error. "When Jesus rais'd Lazarus from the Grave, I stood & saw Lazarus . . . arise into the Covering Cherub . . . I saw the Covering Cherub divide Four-fold into Four Churches when Lazarus arose: Paul, Constantine, Charlemaine, Luther: behold, they stand before us stretch'd over Europe & Asia" (*Mil* 24:26-33).

Paul's statement of his ideals, "For we wrestle not against flesh and blood, but against principalities, against powers, against the rulers of the darkness of this world, against spiritual wickedness in high places" (*Eph* vi:12), Blake used as an epigraph for *The Four Zoas*; he too defended the flesh against dominion, authority, and the corruptions of worldly and spiritual rulers. Paul's phrase "the god of this world" Blake echoed several times, identifying this false god with the Accuser and Satan (*GoP*, Epilogue, *K* 771).

For Paul, the Crucifixion had bought forgiveness and wiped out the sins of the faithful. Mutual forgiveness of each other's sins followed as a corollary (*Eph* iv:32) and is implied in his praise of "charity" (*I Cor* xiii); but Paul never emphasized this doctrine as Blake did.

In Blake's opinion, Paul's chief error was his hostile attitude towards sex. "It is good for a man not to touch a woman. . . . But if they cannot contain, let them marry, for it is better to marry than to burn" (*I Cor* vii: 1, 9). This reduction of love to a mere physical need, better foregone, leads to the dominion of the Female Will. "Look back into the Church Paul! Look! Three Women around the Cross! O Albion, why didst thou a Female Will Create?" (*J* 56:42). The three women are the virgin mother, the whore, and the wife.

The Church Paul (*Mil* 24:31–32) is the first of the four which outline historical Christianity: Paul, founder of the church militant (his attribute is the spiritual sword); Constantine, who forbade all other religions; Charlemaine, founder of the Holy Roman Empire; and Luther, the spirit of reform. These four, with Milton, end the list of the sons of Los and Enitharmon (*FZ* viii:362).

These four also end the list of the Twenty-seven Heavens or Churches. They conclude a septenary representing the aggressive church: "Abraham, Moses, Solomon, Paul, Constantine, Charlemaine, Luther; these seven are the Male-Females, the Dragon Forms, Religion hid in War, a Dragon red & hidden Harlot" (*Mil* 37:41; *J* 75:16). The harlot is the false Whore of Babylon; only she could inspire the attempt to spread religion by warfare or any other aggressive means.

Blake's estimate of the saint is expressed in a water color, "Paul Preaching" (Museum of Art, R. I. School of Design). He is inspired, but the rays thrilling from him are cold blue and black; he stands as though obscuring the light behind him. Children listen devoutly, for he teaches charity. An old man, still holding a book of law (which he need not renounce), is enraptured to learn that his immortality depends on faith, not law. But on the right, a maiden with a book in her lap is terrified, while the youth behind her sinks his head in guilty shame.

The PAVED WORK of precious stones on which the erring Milton, Satan, and Rahab appear (*Mil* 38:6; 39:24; 40:18) is Satan's. When Moses and others beheld the God of Israel, "there was under his feet as it were a paved work of a sapphire stone" (*Exod* xxiv:10). Satan is always the Ape of God; he is imitating God (*Mil* 39:26).

PEACHEY is the fifth of the twelve Sons of Albion (*J* 5:25). His name is that of John Peachey, J.P., one of the judges at Blake's trial. "Peachey had North Wales, Shropshire, Cheshire & the Isle of Man. His Emanation is Mehetabel, terrible & lovely upon the Mountains" (*J* 71:30). Mehetabel, joined with Kotope's Sabrina, "shines west over America" (*J* 71:45). "Gwantock [another of Blake's judges] & Peachy hid in Damascus beneath Mount Lebanon" (*J* 36: 16) when the twelve Sons fled at the sight of Reuben. At all other times, Peachey acts in concert with the other Sons of Albion.

The PEAK (Kinder Scout), in Derbyshire, is the highest hill in England, rising 2,088 feet. "Because the Peak, Malvern & Cheviot Reason in Cruelty, Penmaenmawr & Dhinas-bran Demonstrate in Unbelief" (*J* 21: 34).

The PEARL symbolizes love, and is frequently paired with the Ruby (wisdom), as in "The rubies & pearls of a loving eye" (*Riches* 2, *K* 181; also *The Mental Traveller* 34, *K* 425). The pavement in "I saw a chapel all of gold" is "set with pearls & rubies bright" (*K* 163); and the entrance was originally a "pearly door." *The Crystal Cabinet* is "form'd of Gold and Pearl & Crystal" (*K* 429). The shapes watching over Albion form an arch of "precious stones & pearl" (*FZ* viii:14). Ololon is "a sweet river of milk & liquid pearl" (*Mil* 21:15). The narrow sea between Albion and the Atlantic Continent originally had "waves of pearl" (*J* 44: 15). Gwineverra "beams towards the east [with] all kinds of precious stones and pearl" (*J* 71:40), while Conwenna shines over the north "with pearly beams gorgeous & terrible" (*J* 71:48).

The pearl is particularly associated with Jerusalem. Her walls are "of pearl and gold" (*J* 24:19). She brings "blessings of gold and pearl & diamond" (*J* 24:39). Her sandals are of "gold & pearl" (*J* 86:31). Her forehead has "Gates of pearl" (*J* 86:4; cf. *Rev* xxi:21).

When Orc becomes a serpent, he has "scales of pearl" (*FZ* viii:70). This seems to be the only example when the Pearl is not reasonably connected with love, but may be accounted for by the moral confusion involved in Orc's transformation.

PECKHAM RYE (by Dulwich Hill) was a village in Surrey, on the south side of Peckham. Here Blake, while still quite a child, had his first vision, "a tree filled with angels, bright angelic wings bespangling every bough like stars" (*Gil* I, 7).

PEEBLES is an inland county of Scotland. With Perth and Renfrew it is assigned to Gad (*J* 16:56); and being part of Scotland, it is also assigned to Bowen (*J* 71:46).

PELEG was a descendant of Noah and an ancestor of Abraham. He was the elder son of Eber, and had a brother, Joktan. He was named Peleg "for in his days was the earth divided" (*Gen* x:25).

In the list of the Twenty-seven Heavens, Peleg is the seventh, in the line from Noah to Terah. "These are the Female-Males, a Male within a Female hid as in an Ark & Curtains" (*Mil* 37:39; *J* 75:14). Adam is "Peleg & Joktan, & Esau & Jacob, & Saul & David" (*J* 73:28).

PEMBROKESHIRE is a county of South Wales. It is "the Gate of Gad" (*J* 16:38). It is also assigned to Gwantoke (*J* 71:29).

PENMAENMAWR is the northern terminating point of the Snowdon range in Wales. "Reuben slept on Penmaenmawr & Levi slept on Snowdon," where their four senses rolled outward (*FZ* ii:53). "Penmaenmawr & Dhinas-bran Demonstrate in Unbelief" (*J* 21:35).

PEN[N]SYLVANIA was the central colony of North America. When Albion's plagues threaten, "the scribe of Pensylvania casts his pen upon the earth" (*Am* 14:15).

PENTLAND Firth lies between Scotland and the Orkneys. Of the Gates through which all souls descend, the one to the north consists of "Caithness & rocky Durness, Pentland & John Groat's House"—all along the northern coast of Scotland (*Mil* 26:13–15).

PEOR is a mountain in Moab, south Jordan; on this peak Balaam blessed Israel instead of cursing it. It is one of six mountains around Palestine which are equated with Milton's three wives and three daughters (*Mil* 17:16).

The VALLEY OF PEOR is a Moabite valley, also known as Beth-Peor; here was the secret burial place of Moses.

Here Milton forms Urizen (*Mil* 19:14). Here Oshea and Caleb fight, until only death remains (*J* 43:37, 45). Here Jehovah builds the body of Moses, the body of Divine Analogy (*J* 49:57). Here originally the ambassadors from Beulah knelt in the Divine Presence, but Blake altered "Beth Peor" to "Conway's Vale" (*FZ* i:483).

PERSIA is the eleventh of the Thirty-two Nations which shall protect liberty and rule the rest of the world (*J* 72:39). The Daughters of Albion rage against Jerusalem "thro' all the Nations of Europe, thro' Italy & Grecia to Lebanon & Persia & India" (*J* 80:46). The altars of the northern war-gods are built "from Ireland's rocks to Scandinavia, Persia and Tartary" (*J* 83:21).

PERTH, a central county of Scotland, is assigned with Peebles and Renfrew to Gad (*J* 16:56).

PERU lies along the western coast of South America. It achieved its independence from Spain in 1821–24. It is one of the Thirty-two Nations which shall protect liberty and rule the rest of the world (*J* 72:42).

The Shadowy Female sees there a Lion

"who courts me to his love" (*Am* 2:12). Druid Temples spread from Lambeth throughout the whole earth, "to Mexico & Peru west, & east to China & Japan" (*Mil* 6:23).

PETERBORO[UGH], fifteenth of the Twenty-four Cathedral Cities (*J* 46:18), is East, under Luvah and London.

PHARAOH (often "Pharoh") was the title of the rulers of ancient Egypt, the enslavers of the Israelites. "So spoke the hard cold constrictive Spectre: he is named Arthur, constricting into Druid Rocks round Canaan, Agag & Aram & Pharoh" (*J* 54:25). Pharaoh is fifth in the list of kings created by Rahab, standing between Nimrod and Priam (*J* 73:35). In the head of the Covering Cherub is "Pharoh in his iron Court" (*J* 89:18).

PHARISAION is the sect of Pharisees, whom Blake treated as one of the seven sects of the Covering Cherub, "double, Hermaphroditic, twelvefold in Allegoric pomp, in selfish holiness . . . double each withoutside of the other, covering eastern heaven" (*J* 89:4–8).

The PHARISEES constituted one of the three philosophical sects of Judaism, zealous students of the Law and overscrupulous enforcers of its rules. Jesus accused them of being pious show-offs, holier-than-thous, hypocrites, blind guides, and whited sepulchres. They were very active in procuring his execution.

Blake condemned them as an early manifestation of Deism. "Deism is the Worship of the God of this World by the means of what you call Natural Religion and Natural Philosophy, and of Natural Morality or Self-Righteousness, the Selfish Virtues of the Natural Heart. This was the Religion of the Pharisees who murder'd Jesus. . . . Voltaire! Rousseau! You cannot escape my charge that you are Pharisees & Hypocrites, for you are constantly talking of the Virtues of the Human Heart and particularly of

your own, that you may accuse others, & especially the Religious, whose errors you, by this display of pretended Virtue, chiefly design to expose" (*J* 52). "Pity the evil, for thou art not sent | To smite with terror & with punishments | Those that are sick, like to the Pharisees | Crucifying & encompassing sea & land | For proselytes to tyranny & wrath" (*J* 77:26). Blake also accused them of hypocrisy (*EG b*:37) and denounced their "Virtuous Rules" (*EG d*:28). "To be Good only, is to be | A God [Devil *in pencil*] or else a Pharisee" (*EG e*:27). At the Last Judgment, they "appear on the left hand, pleading their own righteousness" (To Ozias Humphry, *K* 443).

PHILISTIA (Philistea) was a nation on the southwest Mediterranean coast, a great religious and military rival of Israel. It was ruled not by a king but by five masters, or Baalim (*Mil* 40:25). Blake places it in the left breast of the Covering Cherub (*J* 89:31), where he associates it with Druid Temples (also in *J* 78:30). It is one of the heathen nations that attracted the straying children of Israel (*J* 49:43; 79:13); Simeon is particularly named (*J* 74:46). Eventually, with the other heathen nations, it shall be preserved only "in the Shadows of Remembrance & in the Chaos of the Spectre" (*J* 92:22).

PILATE (Pontius) was the Roman governor of Judea when Jesus was executed. Although he believed in the innocence of Jesus, he yielded to Jewish pressure and pronounced the death sentence, at the same time publicly washing his hands of responsibility.

Pilate and Caiaphas represented to Blake the twin evils of State and Church. Founded upon morality, their principles were contrary to those of Jesus (On Bacon, *K* 397, 407). "If Moral Virtue was Christianity, | Christ's Pretensions were all Vanity, | And Caiaphas & Pilate Men | Praise Worthy" (*EG* 1:1). Therefore, when Jesus pronounced the Forgiveness of Sins, "Loud Pilate Howl'd, loud Caiaphas yell'd" (*EG* 2:

19). In *A Vision of the Last Judgment* (K 608), "Two persons, one in Purple, the other in Scarlet, are descending down the steps into the Pit; these are Caiphas & Pilate—Two States where all those reside who Calumniate & Murder under Pretence of Holiness & Justice. Caiphas has a Blue Flame like a Miter on his head. Pilate has bloody hands that never can be cleansed." (See Illustrations, "LJ" Nos. 41, 42.)

The PISON (west) was the first of the four rivers of Paradise. It encompassed the land of Havilah, which to Blake symbolized the original purity and freedom of love. Blake identified it with the river Arnon, the female genital tract that empties into the Dead Sea (*J* 89:25). See DEAD SEA. When Joseph forgives Mary, her tears of joy overflow into all four rivers, including "Pison & Arnon & Jordan" (*J* 61:33).

PITY is one of the Divine attributes. "For Mercy, Pity, Peace, and Love | Is God" and also Man (*SoI*, "The Divine Image"). God is "the ever pitying one who seeth all things" (*FZ* vi:157; cf. *Mil* 18:20). "Am I pure thro' his Mercy and Pity? . . . O Mercy, O Divine Humanity! O Forgiveness & Pity & Compassion!" (*J* 61:36, 43).

Pity reunites the divided. "Pity must join together those whom wrath has torn in sunder" (*J* 7:57, 62). When obdurate Los finally feels pity, he embraces the Spectre, first as a brother, then as another self; and thus the great reconciliation of all things is begun (*FZ* vii:338). Wrath and Pity, when they work together, as Rintrah and Palamabron, are the most effective agents of Los, being his first two sons. See PALAMABRON.

Pity cannot reunite unless there has been a previous division. "Pity began" when Los had finally bound Urizen (*Ur* 13:51). Pity divides Los, for "pity divides the soul" (*Ur* 13:53; *Mil* 8:19); and his separated half develops into a "round globe of blood" (*Ur* 13:58), which grows into a female form, Enitharmon. "All Eternity shudder'd at sight of the first female now separate. . . .

They call'd her Pity, and fled." Los pities her, and begets Orc (*Ur* 14:51–19:10). But pity separate is not the real thing. Los "felt that Love and Pity are the same, a soft repose, inward complacency of Soul" (*J* 23:14).

This false pity is hypocritical: it "would be no more | If we did not make somebody Poor" (*SoE*, "The Human Abstract" 1). Boston's Angel complains that "pity is become a trade," no doubt with charitable organizations in mind; "What pitying Angel lusts for tears and fans himself with sighs?" (*Am* 11:13). But there is worse. We all profess sorrow for those whom we punish; and these are the hypocritical tears of Urizen for his victims: "he wept & he called it Pity" (*Ur* 25:3).

PLATO was the Greek philosopher who most interested Blake. The third illustration to *Il Penseroso* is Blake's summary of the Platonic philosophy. Plato, a benevolent sage clad in white, points with his right hand to the sphere of Venus, while his left hand points to an open tome, over which young Milton sits pondering (see Illustrations).

At the very top are the Three Fates, weaving the thread of mortal life (counterclockwise); they are seated on the three heavens of Jupiter, Mars, and Venus. Plato's concept of the ruling divinity is represented by Jupiter, in the right-hand heaven. He sits on a throne, his left foot depressed; his left hand holds the scepter of sovereignty, his right the compasses of geometry. Before Jupiter stands Mercury, his caduceus and left hand both pointing downward to the Great Bear, the pivot of the astronomical universe. The central heaven, that of Mars, who holds a spear in his left hand and is attended by a bat, represents the Greek love of war. In his utopia, Plato accepted war as a normal function of the perfect state. The third heaven, of Venus, is on the left. She emerges from a tree trunk (vegetative or fleshly love), looking upward and pressing in vain with her left hand against the sphere that encloses her. She ignores the unhappy marriage of a man and woman bound back to back by two entwining snakes, and also the youth who rejects a weeping female.

The rest of the picture is occupied by the Four Elements. The genius (fire) symbolizes Plato's theory of immortality. The flame of dissolution rises from three corpses; in it a male genius points upward with both hands while he hovers above two ascending souls. Five fairies (air) circle round young Milton's head. Behind his chair a bat-winged nymph (water) hovers triumphant above a man, who sinks head down, entangled in network. Beneath Milton's feet are the elementals of earth. A mother, holding a child who plays with a crown, watches another emerge from the ground in a leaf; a second woman with rooting feet points upwards to flowers; and a third reclines in vegetation beside another figure.

Blake listed Plato among those who "consider'd what is not too Explicit as fittest for Instruction because it rouzes the faculties to act" (To Trusler, 23 Aug 1799); and claimed that Plato's definition of the most sublime poetry was somewhat like his own: "Allegory address'd to the Intellectual powers, while it is altogether hidden from the Corporeal Understanding" (To Butts, 6 July 1803). "The Ancients did not mean to Impose when they affirm'd their belief in Vision & Revelation. Plato was in Earnest; Milton was in Earnest. They believ'd that God did Visit Man Really & Truly" (On Reynolds, K 473).

Yet "Plato has made Socrates say that Poets & Prophets do not know or Understand what they write or Utter; this is a most Pernicious Falshood. If they do not, pray is an inferior kind to be call'd Knowing? Plato confutes himself" (LJ, K 605). And Moral Precepts "belong to Plato & Seneca & Nero" (On Watson, K 395). "There is not one Moral Virtue that Jesus Inculcated but Plato & Cicero did Inculcate before him; what then did Christ Inculcate? Forgiveness of Sins" (EG, K 757). "Plato did not bring Life & Immortality to Light. Jesus only did this" (On Berkeley,

K 774). "The Whole Bible is fill'd with Imagination & Visions from End to End & not with Moral Virtues; that is the baseness [business?] of Plato & the Greeks & all Warriors" (On Berkeley, K 774). Plato "knew of nothing but of the virtues and vices and good and evil. There is nothing in all that. Every thing is good in God's eyes" (CR 256). "The Stolen and Perverted Writings of Homer & Ovid, of Plato & Cicero, which all Men ought to contemn, are set up by artifice against the Sublime of the Bible" (Mil 1). "What Jesus came to Remove was the Heathen or Platonic Philosophy, which blinds the Eye of Imagination, The Real Man" (On Berkeley, K 775).

As usual, Blake was attacking most severely those whom he admired most. When Thomas Taylor was publishing his translations, Blake was stimulated deeply; then he reversed his attitude completely in or about 1803, repudiating his former idol. The whole story is detailed in George Mills Harper's excellent The Neoplatonism of William Blake. Nevertheless, in the Last Judgment the Greek learned and wise are among the saved who shall meet the Lord in the air (K 610).

Thus it is that although Plato banished poets from his republic, made God a geometrician, preached morality, was a fatalist when he accepted the Three Fates, debased love to homosexuality, admitted war to his ideal state, and considered Art an imitation of Nature (hence second-rate), Blake was indebted to him. He accepted Plato's Ideal Form: "Whatever can be Created can be Annihilated: Forms cannot: the Oak is cut down by the Ax, the Lamb falls by the Knife, but their Forms Eternal Exist Forever" (Mil 32:36). The Book of Ahania was undoubtedly suggested by the first part of the Philebus. The Timaeus stimulated Blake's own concept of the universe. Many other parallels will suggest themselves.

"The Gods of Greece & Egypt were Mathematical Diagrams—See Plato's Works" (Laoc, K 776). "To Trismegistus, Palamabron gave an abstract Law: to Pythagoras, Socrates & Plato" (SoL 3:18).

PLINLIMMON is a mountain in central Wales on the border between Cardiganshire and Montgomeryshire. Albion declares: "My mountains are my own, and I will keep them to myself: the Malvern and the Cheviot, the Wolds, Plinlimmon & Snowdon are mine: here will I build my Laws of Moral Virtue" (*J* 4:29). At the threat of war, "Plinlimmon shrunk away, Snowdon trembled" (*J* 66:59).

PLINY was the author of the *Historia Naturalis*. He is quoted in *An Island in the Moon* (Chap. i) concerning the flight of swallows. His name also appears in an enigmatic trifle, "I will tell you" (*K* 552), where Pliny and Trajan are invited to listen to Joseph of Arimathea.

The PLOW cuts the furrows for the fresh seed; the Harrow follows, breaking and spreading the clods; and finally the Roller packs down the soil.

Blake used the Plow as a sexual symbol in "Earth's Answer" (*SoE*); and used it differently in three of the "Proverbs of Hell": "Drive your cart and your plow over the bones of the dead" (*MHH* 7:2), which means that the dead past is not to be respected if it hinders your work; "The cut worm forgives the plow" (*MHH* 7:6), which signifies that in Nature there is no instinct of revenge; and "As the plow follows words, so God rewards prayers" (*MHH* 9:4), meaning that God helps only those who help themselves.

But when the Londoner went to Felpham, agriculture took on a new significance. "I met a plow on my first going out at my gate the first morning after my arrival, & the Plowboy said to the Plowman, 'Father, The Gate is Open.'" (To Butts, 23 Sept 1800). Henceforth, plowing symbolized the preparation for a New Age. So Blake interpreted the confusion in Europe. Napoleon was still spreading the principles of the French Revolution, dethroning kings and abolishing the inquisitions; he did not disappoint the libertarians until he made himself Emperor in December 1804.

Blake must have had in mind the famous prophecy of Micah: "Therefore shall Zion for your sake be plowed as a field, and Jerusalem shall become heaps, and the mountain of the house as the high places of the forest" (*Micah* iii:12); Jeremiah quoted it (*Jeremiah* xxvi:18); and it was fulfilled literally.

Urizen is the Plowman (*J* 95:16). In *The Four Zoas* his "plow of ages" (vii:14; ix:312), drawn by the bulls of Luvah (ii:120), is the Revolutionary idea powered by Revolutionary ardor. It is made by Urizen's sons (ii:27). It is of iron and operates dreadfully in Ulro (ii:70). The sons abandon it for the implements of war (vii *b*:170). But when Urizen is rejuvenated in the Last Judgment, his sons cleanse the Plow from the rust of ages (ix:291), and he plows over the entire universe (ix:311). (In Young's account of the Last Judgment, "Final Ruin fiercely drives Her Ploughshare o'er Creation," *Night Thoughts* ix:167.) Urizen then lays the plow aside, "in the northern corner of the wide Universal field" (ix:319), after which he sows the seed of the human harvest, to make the Bread of Eternity.

Reason, however, can originate nothing: it is the Imagination which provides the ideas for the New Age. Therefore in *Milton*, the Plow "to pass over the Nations" (6:13; 25:10) is Los's (8:20), although more specifically it is Rintrah's (4:1), who is the poet's wrath at the present state of affairs. The Plow is forged by all four of Los's eldest sons (6:13). In the confusion, the plowing takes place during a storm of Jehovah's merciful rain and the murderous lightning of Molech (8:27). "Twelve Sons successive fled away in that thousand years of sorrow of Palamabron's Harrow & of Rintrah's wrath & fury" (23:62–24:1). Later, Enitharmon recalls "that terrible Day of Rintrah's Plow & of Satan's driving the Team" (*J* 93:10). Eventually, in preparation for the final harvest, "The Plow goes forth in tempests & lightnings, & the Harrow cruel in blights of the east; the heavy Roller follows in howlings of woe" (*Mil* 27:47).

In *Jerusalem*, Blake had come to the conclusion that the revolutionary ideas which had inspired America and France were English in origin, and that England was the dominant power; therefore Albion becomes the Plowman, and the four Zoas his team (63:2–4).

At first, Albion deplores the "implements of War . . . the Plow to go over the Nations" (34:13). Oxford in vain bids him repose on the bosoms of the Cathedral Cities "Till the Plow of Jehovah and the Harrow of Shaddai have passed over the Dead to awake the Dead to Judgment" (46: 13–15). But he essays the plowing, and the four chief Cities "Cry over the Plow of Nations in the strong hand of Albion, thundering along among the Fires of the Druid & the deep black rethundering Waters of the Atlantic, which poured in impetuous" (57:1).

But Albion cannot control the situation, and becomes its victim. "Albion fled from the Divine Vision; with the Plow of Nations enflaming, the Living Creatures madden'd, and Albion fell into the Furrow; and the Plow went over him & the Living was Plowed in among the Dead. But his Spectre rose over the starry Plow. Albion fled beneath the Plow till he came to the Rock of Ages, & he took his Seat upon the Rock" (57:12). There is an apparition of Jehovah. "Jehovah stood among the Druids in the Valley of Annandale when the Four Zoas of Albion, the Four Living Creatures, the Cherubim of Albion tremble before the Spectre in the starry Harness of the Plow of Nations" (63:1). But the Plow of Nations continues "thund'ring in the hand of Albion's Spectre" (64:30).

The "POETIC GENIUS" was a phrase used by Blake when he discovered the central importance of the Imagination. He applied it first to the Lord, from whom love descends (On Swed *DL, K* 90), but he soon transferred it to the essential Man, especially those in whom it manifests, the poets or prophets.

"The Poetic Genius is the true Man, and . . . the body or outward form of Man is de-

rived from the Poetic Genius. . . . all are alike in the Poetic Genius. . . . all sects of Philosophy are from the Poetic Genius, adapted to the weaknesses of every individual. . . . an universal Poetic Genius exists. . . . The Religions of all Nations are derived from each Nation's different reception of the Poetic Genius, which is every where call'd the Spirit of Prophecy. . . . The Jewish & Christian Testaments are An original derivation from the Poetic Genius . . . all Religions . . . have one source. The true Man is the source, he being the Poetic Genius" (*AllR*).

In *The Marriage of Heaven and Hell* (11–13) Blake expanded his theory of the origins of religions. Ezekiel states that "we of Israel taught that the Poetic Genius (as you now call it) was the first principle and all others merely derivative, which was the cause of our despising the Priests & Philosophers of other countries, and prophecying that all Gods would at last be proved to originate in ours & to be the tributaries of the Poetic Genius."

POETICAL SKETCHES. *By W.B. London: Printed in the Year MDCCLXXXIII.* This slim volume was printed for Blake by his two admirers, Rev. Anthony Stephen Mathew and John Flaxman. Mathew contributed an apologetic preface (which is not in Blake's personal copy) from which we learn that they were "the production of untutored youth, commenced in his twelfth and occasionally resumed by the author till his twentieth year" (1769–77), and that he had been "deprived of the leisure requisite to such a revisal of these sheets, as might have rendered them less unfit to meet the public eye"—that is, Blake had excused himself from "correcting" them. In fact, he did not even read the proofs: there are glaring misprints. And the book was never published. Blake kept the entire edition, occasionally giving copies to friends. Only twenty-two copies have been located.

He probably felt that he had been overpersuaded into letting his juvenilia be printed, so he gave no assistance to the production, being embarrassed, not by "the irregularities and defects to be found in almost every page," but by the immaturity of the whole. Sources are obvious. He had not yet found himself.

It is a book of the Revolutionary period, a time of seeking for non-neoclassical inspiration, a preparation for the Romantic period. It was initiated by the first poems of Macpherson's Ossian (1760) and of Chatterton (1764), by the first Gothic romance, Walpole's *Castle of Otranto* (1764), and by Percy's *Reliques of Ancient English Poetry* (1765), which rediscovered the ballad. All of these influenced the *Poetical Sketches*. Blake had also been reading the Elizabethans: Spenser (for whom one still apologized), Shakespeare (not yet supposed to be a poet), Jonson, and Fletcher. Of the poets in his own century, Thomson and Gray had their influence; but there is no trace of Dryden's and Pope's closed heroic couplet, which had been the style for three generations. And of course, first and last, there was the influence of Milton.

Nevertheless, for all the derivative material, the book is a work of genius in its daring figures, its metrical experiments, its musical tone. "Speak silence with thy glimmering eyes, and wash the dusk with silver" ("To the Evening Star" 9), which would have been flat nonsense to Dr. Johnson, was pure Romanticism way ahead of time. "Fair Elenor" has the real Gothic thrill which Walpole never achieved. The "Mad Song" marks a new period of metrics. "How Sweet I Roam'd," Blake's first symbolic poem, a protest against marriage, was written, according to Benjamin Heath Malkin, when Blake was fourteen. His first fourfold system appears in the first four lyrics, to the Seasons, which move from morning, through noon, and afternoon, to darkness; also through the four compass points: east, south, west, and north. "To the Muses" is so musical that few have noticed how compact and deep is its meaning. The poet gives Greece and the Holy Lands as the sources of our poetry, and fails in his day to find the muses in the fire of heaven, the earth, the air, or the sea—the four elements. The last selections in the book are printed as prose, but are metrical even to the point of free verse.

See KING EDWARD THE THIRD.

POETRY is the expression of human experience in the most efficient language. Blake was one of the greatest English poets. He conceived the role of the poet to be that of the prophet: the great prophets were poets, and great poetry is prophecy, for the terms are interchangeable.

His "great task" was to explore and record the mysteries of the human psyche, "To open the Eternal Worlds, to open the immortal Eyes of Man inwards into the Worlds of Thought" (J 5:18); and thought, animated by passion, is the substance of his verse. Not until man understands the workings of his mind can peace and liberty be accomplished. Thus Blake became one of the great psychologists, anticipating many of the discoveries of later scientists.

He was not interested in illustrating moral precepts but in the analysis and cure of evil, which are very different matters. "Poetry is to excuse Vice & shew its reason & necessary purgation. . . . the grandest Poetry is Immoral, the Grandest characters Wicked, Very Satan—Capanius, Othello a murderer, Prometheus, Jupiter, Jehovah, Jesus a wine bibber. Cunning & Morality are not Poetry but Philosophy; the Poet is Independent & Wicked; the Philosopher is Dependent & Good" (On Boyd, K 412).

Los, the Spirit of Prophecy, is the inspirer of Blake, the great champion of man, and the friend of Jesus, whom he resembles. His sons create both comedy and tragedy from the sufferings of mankind. Comedy is based on the real woes of lovers, as in *A Midsummer Night's Dream*, from which Blake quotes (V.i.16). "Some Sons of Los surround the Passions with porches of iron [combats of wit] & silver [love], creating form & beauty around the dark regions of sorrow, giving to airy nothing a name and a habitation delightful, with bounds to the Infinite putting off the Indefinite into most holy forms of Thought" (*Mil* 28:1). Other Sons "Cabinets richly fabricate of gold & ivory for Doubts & fears unform'd & wretched & melancholy. The little weeping Spectre stands on the threshold of Death eternal, and sometimes two Spectres like lamps quivering, and often malignant they combat; heart-breaking sorrowful & piteous . . . The soft hands of Antamon draw the indelible line, form immortal with golden pen, such as the Spectre admiring puts on the sweet form" (*Mil* 28:8–18).

Historically Blake belongs—or began—in the Revolutionary generation, when the closed heroic couplet was exhausted, and new subjects and new rhythms were being sought out. The cadences of the Bible, the misunderstood Milton, and the poetic Shakespeare with his fellow Elizabethans were Blake's staples from the first; to them we must add the wildness of Ossian, the music of Chatterton, the balladry of Percy's *Reliques*, and the Gothicism of Walpole. All the principles of Romanticism are to be found in Blake's first book, the juvenile *Poetical Sketches*; by the time the Romantic poets were flourishing, he had already passed beyond them.

In metrics, Blake was a daring experimentalist from the first, especially in free verse, the free septenary, the unrhymed trimeter. But he was always using traditional forms for new effects.

"Passion & Expression is Beauty Itself" (On Reynolds, *K* 466). "Obscurity is Neither the Source of the Sublime nor of any Thing Else" (*K* 473). He despised the poetasters "who pretend to Poetry that they may destroy Imagination by imitation of Nature's Images drawn from Remembrance" (*Mil* 41:23), "the tame high finisher[s] of . . . paltry Rhymes" (*Mil* 41:9). His own ideal was "to cast aside from Poetry all that is not Inspiration" (*Mil* 41:7).

POLAND is the fifth of the Thirty-two Nations which shall protect liberty and rule the rest of the world (*J* 72:38). In Urizen's temple, "Poland & Russia & Sweden [are] his soft retired chambers" (*J* 58:40). In the

Golden Age, "Germany, Poland, & the North wooed [Jerusalem's] footsteps, they found my gates in all their mountains & my curtains in all their vales" (*J* 79:45).

POLAND STREET is next to Broad Street. Blake lived at 28 Poland Street from 1785 to 1791. (For the dates, see *Miner*.) "The Corner of Broad Street weeps: Poland Street languishes" (*J* 84:15).

The POLAR region is the originating point of war. The North belongs to the imagination, and it is here that thwarted sex finally is transmuted to war and thus can break out.

The Scandinavian war-gods, "the Thor & cruel Odin . . . first rear'd the Polar Caves" (*Mil* 25:53). The age of chivalry was a period when war was the normal state of society. "Arthur was a name for the constellation Arcturus, or Boötes, the keeper of the North Pole" (*DesC* V, *K* 577). "Charlemaine & his clouds of War | Muster around the Polar Star" ("I saw a Monk" 17, *K* 420).

See NORTH and SOTHA.

POLITICS is "the Science of Sciences," but is in a wretched state (*PubA*, *K* 600). "Are not Religion & Politics the Same Thing? Brotherhood is Religion" (*J* 57:10).

For Blake's interest in contemporary politics, see David Erdman's *Blake, Prophet Against Empire*.

The POLYPUS is an aquatic animal with tentacles. There are various kinds; some are "colonial" organisms of individuals. Blake's first reference seems to be to a jellyfish, when he describes Los's lungs as "dim & glutinous as the white Polypus driv'n by waves & englob'd on the tide" (*BoL* 4:57). Next, it could be a sea anemone, when Vala is "Ajoin'd to Beulah as the Polypus to the Rock" (*FZ* vii *b*:289). In the color print "Newton" and on *Jerusalem* 28, it is depicted as a squid.

However, when Blake progressed from simile to symbol, he chose the "colonial" organism to symbolize human society in this world and its religion.

Its source is the "dead" Albion. "As a Polypus that vegetates beneath the Sea, the limbs of Man vegetated in monstrous forms of Death, a Human polypus of Death" (*FZ* iv:266). "The Twelve Sons of Albion enrooted into every Nation, a mighty Polypus growing from Albion over the whole Earth" (*J* 15:3); and, after Hand has devoured his brothers, it grows "Out from his bosom, a mighty Polypus vegetating in darkness" (*J* 18:40).

This worldly society is the antithesis of the Brotherhood of Man. "By Invisible Hatreds adjoin'd, they seem remote and separate from each other, and yet are a Mighty Polypus in the Deep" (*J* 66:53). "Every Man born is joined within into One mighty Polypus, and this Polypus is Orc" (*Mil* 29:30)—Orc being the hatred men bear each other. "Then all the Males conjoined into One Male, & every one became a ravening eating Cancer growing in the Female, a Polypus of Roots, of Reasoning, Doubt, Despair & Death, going forth & returning from Albion's Rocks to Canaan, Devouring Jerusalem from every Nation of the Earth" (*J* 69:1). The attempt to enter the Promised Land and the inability to remain there is particularly characteristic of Reuben. The "ravening eating Cancer" suggests that Blake also had in mind the tumorous growth (particularly in the nose) called a polypus because its ramifications resemble tentacles.

The false worldly religion which organizes and motivates the Polypus is materialistic and corresponds to the Twenty-seven Churches. "They see the Ulro, a vast Polypus of living fibres down into the Sea of Time & Space growing, a self-devouring monstrous Human Death Twenty seven fold." Within it sit the five daughters of Zelophehad and the fallen Vala ("the nameless Shadowy Mother") luring the sleeping souls down into Generation. "Around this Polypus Los continual builds the Mundane Shell" (*Mil* 34:24–31). The Daughters of Albion then alter the Human Form and dissipate its perceptions "into the Indefinite,

Becoming a mighty Polypus nam'd Albion's Tree" (*J* 66:47). This is the Tree of Mystery, the druidic religion. "O Polypus of Death! O Spectre over Europe and Asia, withering the Human Form by Laws of Sacrifice for Sin!" (*J* 49:24). This "Great Polypus of Generation" covers the whole earth. Its head is in Verulam, or Reason; its heart is on Salisbury Plain, or Stonehenge (*J* 67:34–40).

In *Milton*, the Polypus springs from Milton's Shadow of suppressed desires. When the immortal poet sinks into mortal slumber, his Shadow vegetates beneath his Couch of Death "Like as a Polypus that vegetates beneath the deep" (*Mil* 15:8). His error expands into the entire universe. "The [Christian] Heavens are the [Covering] Cherub; the Twelve Gods [of paganism] are Satan; and the Forty-eight Starry Regions [the constellations] are Cities of the Levites, the Heads of the Great Polypus, Four-fold twelve enormity, in mighty & mysterious comingling, enemy with enemy, woven by Urizen into Sexes from his mantle of years" (*Mil* 37:60–38:4).

Were it not for Bowlahoola (assimilation) and Allamanda (communication), the Web of Death (this body) would be "No Human Form; but only a Fibrous Vegetation, a Polypus of soft affections without Thought or Vision, must tremble in the Heavens & Earths thro' all the Ulro space" (*Mil* 24:37).

Human society must be taken into account before the creation of art is possible; or, as Blake puts it, "Golgonooza cannot be seen till having pass'd the Polypus, it is viewed on all sides round by a Four-fold Vision, or till you become Mortal & Vegetable in Sexuality" (*Mil* 35:22). Therefore Ololon, descending to find Milton, must enter "the Polypus within the Mundane Shell . . . [the] Vegetable Worlds" (*Mil* 36:13).

POPE (Alexander, 1680–1744), master of rage, was one of the great English satirists. He perfected the closed heroic couplet, which Dryden had established. Blake condemned the two "because they did not understand Verse" (*PubA*, *K* 602), their rhymes being a "Monotonous Sing Song, Sing Song from beginning to end" (*PubA*, *K* 600).

In doing Pope's portrait for Hayley's library, Blake (or Hayley) selected for supporters the *Elegy on an Unfortunate Lady* and *Eloisa to Abelard* as his best poems. Neither is a satire.

POPLAR is a London district which contains the great docks. This was one of the ports where the soldiers embarked for the Continent. "Jerusalem fell from Lambeth's Vale | Down thro' Poplar & Old Bow, | Thro' Malden & acros[s] the Sea, | In War & howling, death & woe" (*J* 27:41). "To cast Jerusalem forth upon the wilds to Poplar & Bow, to Malden & Canterbury in the delights of cruelty" (*J* 41:5). "Awake, Highgate's heights & Hampstead's, to Poplar, Hackney & Bow" (*J* 83:87–84:1).

PRAYER is the prelude to action; it is the invoking of the God within us for inspiration and strength to perform something we must do. It is not calling upon an exterior God to give us something independently of our own efforts. Blake may have had in mind Aesop's fable of Hercules and the carter: Hercules gives the strength, but the carter supplies the muscle to get his cart out of the mud. "God helps those who help themselves" was a commonplace.

"As the plow follows words, so God rewards prayer" (*MHH* 9:4). "Why stand we here trembling around calling on God for help and not ourselves in whom God dwells?" (*J* 43:12). Gilchrist (I, 343) tells us that when George Richmond, the young portrait painter, lost his inspiration, he told Blake about his distress. "To his astonishment, Blake turned to his wife suddenly and said: 'It is just so with us, is it not, for weeks together, when the visions forsake us? What do we do then, Kate?' 'We kneel down and pray, Mr. Blake.'" George's son was the painter Sir William Blake Richmond.

The PRESBUTERION [*sic*] is the Presby-

tery in the religious organization of the Covering Cherub (*J* 89:6).

The PRESTER SERPENT, a snake with a cowl-like head, is the priest who, on the authority of his God, gives the warriors religious sanction to commit the horrors of war, including "the Seven Diseases of Man" (*FZ* vii *b*:118). Blake depicted him in the lower margin of page 98 of the manuscript.

PRIAM, king of Troy, is chiefly remembered as a tragic victim in the fall of his city. Blake, however, lists him as sixth of the evil kings created by Rahab and Tirzah (*J* 73:35), and calls his gods "detestable." The gods who fought for Troy were Mars, Venus, and Apollo. Apollo, with his sun-chariot, was the equivalent of Urizen-Satan; the other two speak for themselves.

"The Nations still follow after the detestable Gods of Priam in pomp of warlike selfhood" (*Mil* 14:14). "Lambeth, ruin'd and given to the detestable Gods of Priam, to Apollo . . ." (*Mil* 25:48). "The Greeks, and since them the Moderns, have neglected to subdue the gods of Priam" (*DesC* III, *K* 571). "Where is the Covenant of Priam, the Moral Virtues of the Heathen?" (*J* 98:46).

"The Gods of Priam are the Cherubim of Moses & Solomon, The Hosts of Heaven" (*Laoc*, *K* 777). For the pagan gods are "Visions of the eternal principles or characters of human life . . . which, when erected into gods, become destructive of humanity" (*DesC* III, *K* 571).

PRIMROSE HILL rises northwest of Regent's Park in London. It has an extensive view. In Blake's day, one looked across fields with their hedgerows and occasional trees toward the low-lying line of houses. Above the roofs rose the dome of St. Paul's and the spires of the churches. Behind the city ran a low line of hills.

This is one of the places where Blake roamed as a boy. "The fields from Islington to Marybone, | To Primrose Hill and Saint John's Wood, | Were builded over with pillars of gold, | And there Jerusalem's pillars stood" (*J* 27:1). When Albion rises, the instep of his left foot extends "from Windsor to Primrose Hill, stretching to Highgate & Holloway" (*Mil* 39:37).

Here Blake had the vision which he recounted to Crabb Robinson: " '*You* never saw the spiritual Sun. I have. I saw him on Primrose Hill.' He said, 'Do you take me for the Greek Apollo?' 'No!' I said. '*That* (pointing to the sky) that is the Greek Apollo. He is Satan' " (*CR* 291). "Primrose Hill is the mouth of [Los's] Furnace & the Iron Door" (*J* 73:54).

"PRINCE OF LIGHT" is an epithet frequently applied to Urizen.

The PRINTING PRESS of Los is war on earth; "here he lays his words in order above the mortal brain, as cogs are form'd in a wheel to turn the cogs of the adverse wheel" (*Mil* 27:8–10). It is identical with Los's Wine-press.

The PROPHET OF ETERNITY is Los (*Mil* 7:38). "His vigorous voice was prophecy" (*FZ* i:239). "He is the Spirit of Prophecy, the ever apparent Elias" (*Mil* 24:71). When in the apocalypse Los is reunited with Enitharmon, he becomes Urthona. "Where is the Spectre of Prophecy? where the delusive Phantom? Departed: & Urthona rises . . ." (*FZ* ix:851).

PROPHETS are not foretellers of future facts; they are revealers of eternal truths. As Paine and others had pointed out, the Biblical prophets were poets, corresponding to the Latin *vates*. When Bacon sneered at heathen religion because "the chief doctors and fathers of their church were the poets," Blake underlined the last word and added "prophets" (On Bacon, *K* 399).

"Prophets, in the modern sense of the word, have never existed. Jonah was no prophet, in the modern sense, for his prophesy of Nineveh failed. Every honest man is a Prophet; he utters his opinion both of private & public matters. Thus: If you go on So, the result is So. He never says, such a

thing shall happen let you do what you will. A Prophet is a Seer, not an Arbitrary Dictator" (On Watson, *K* 392).

Isaiah told Blake: "I saw no God, nor heard any, in a finite organical perception; but . . . as I was then perswaded & remain confirm'd, that the voice of honest indignation is the voice of God, I cared not for consequences, but wrote" (*MHH* 12). Blake underlined Lavater's words, "every genius, every hero, is a prophet" (*K* 77).

The prophets, generally speaking, were anti-"religious," as in the case of Amos (*Amos* v:21–23), who proclaimed that God hated the Jewish feasts and burnt offerings. The prophets therefore suffered as Transgressors. Jesus, denouncing the Scribes and the Pharisees, said their fathers were guilty of the blood of the prophets, and that they themselves would be guilty, concluding "O Jerusalem, Jerusalem, thou that killest the prophets" (*Matt* xxiii:29–37). He himself was numbered with the Transgressors (*Mark* xv:28; *Luke* xxii:37; *FZ* viii:274; *Mil* 13:27) and was executed as a criminal.

It is comprehensible then that in the very first tower of the Bastille before its fall a man was confined for "a writing prophetic" (*FR* 29). Blake's own two books with the subtitle "A Prophecy" were not prophecies in the conventional sense, as they were written after the facts; but they are prophecies in the poetic sense because they record the eternal formula for all revolutions.

PROVIDENCE is the over-all guidance of the Son, usually not apparent to its subject. Thus "he that leadeth all led [Tiriel] to the vales of Har" (*Tir* ii:4), and also guided the aimlessly wandering Urizen (*FZ* vi:176) to the world of Urthona (*FZ* vi:282). Providence, however, does not operate against the will of the Individual, "for the Will cannot be violated" (*FZ* vi:283) "but in the day of Divine Power" (*J* 44:18). Blake objected to Swedenborg's concept of Providence as mere Predestination (*K* 131–33).

The general plan of the Divine Providence for Man "was Subverted at the Fall of

Adam & . . . was not restored till Christ" (On Watson, *K* 390). It is "oppos'd to, & distinct from, divine vengeance" (*LJ, K* 611).

It is fatal for anybody to try to assume the Divine Providence: "O my Children, I have educated you in the crucifying cruelties of Demonstration till you have assum'd the Providence of God & slain your Father" (*J* 24:54).

The whole Darwinian world is "sway'd by a Providence oppos'd to the Divine Lord Jesus: a murderous Providence! A Creation that groans, living on Death, where Fish & Bird & Beast & Man & Tree & Metal & Stone live by Devouring" (*J* 50:4).

See DIVINE HAND.

PYTHAGORAS was the early Greek philosopher whose mathematical studies became the basis of Platonic geometry.

"To Trismegistus, Palamabron gave an abstract Law: to Pythagoras, Socrates & Plato" (*SoL* 3:18).

Q

QUEEN'S COUNTY (now Laoighis or Leix) is in the eastern province of Leinster, Ireland. With the other counties of Leinster, it is assigned to Judah, Issachar, and Zebulun (*J* 72:20).

QUID THE CYNIC, in *An Island in the Moon*, is a lusty caricature of Blake himself. He is the second of the three philosophers, the others being Suction the Epicurean and Sipsop the Pythagorean. He is a poet who characteristically runs down those he admires most: "I think that Homer is bombast, & Shakespeare is too wild, & Milton has no feelings: they might be easily outdone. Chatterton never writ those poems! A parcel of fools, going to Bristol! If I was to go, I'd find it out in a minute, but I've found it out already" (Chap. vii). He is also a singer, who sings five of the songs: "Little Phebus," a satire on sex; the modest "Honour & Genius is all I ask"; "When old corruption," a satire on surgery; "Hail Matrimony," a satire on marriage; and "O father, father," which was to become the "Nurse's Song" in the *Songs of Innocence*. He also furnishes an extra stanza to a song very insulting to Dr. Johnson and his predilection for the classics. He boasts of his abilities. He makes scenes at parties, as Miss Gittipin complains, and he does it deliberately, to impress people. And he has a scheme for "illuminating" and publishing his books.

R

RABBATH was an Ammonite city northeast of Heshbon. Blake erroneously located it on the Arnon. "The Rocks of Rabbath on the Arnon & the Fish-pools of Heshbon" (*J* 89:26).

RACHEL was the second wife of Jacob, her father Laban having tricked Jacob into marrying her older sister Leah first. When Jacob and his family fled from Laban, Rachel stole the teraphim, the images of her family's gods. The rivalry of the two sisters in conceiving the sons of Jacob was intense. (See *Gen* xxix–xxx.)

Blake speaks of the "Deadly Hate between Leah & Rachel, Daughters of Deceit & Fraud, bearing the Images of various Species of Contention and Jealousy & Abhorrence & Revenge & deadly Murder" (*J* 69:11).

RADNORSHIRE is in South Wales. It is the Gate of Naphtali (*J* 16:38); it is also assigned to Guantok (*J* 71:29).

RAGAN was the second daughter of King Leir, the legendary prototype of Shakespeare's King Lear. Geoffrey spelled her name "Regau"; Shakespeare and Milton, "Regan."

Ragan is second in the first list of Albion's Daughters (*FZ* ii:61), but is twelfth in *Jerusalem* (5:44), where she is under Rahab. However, she is the Emanation of the sixth son, Brereton. "She adjoin'd to Slade [the seventh Son] & produced Gonorill" (*J* 71:33).

When Albion is distressed at the immorality of his little daughters, he wants Gwendolen and Ragan (the first and last, thus meaning all of them) covered "with costly Robes of Natural Virtue, for their Spiritual forms without a Veil wither in Luvah's Sepulcher" (*J* 21:14).

"Ragan is wholly cruel" (*J* 11:21). Like her sisters, she is a weaver at the loom of war (*J* 64:36).

RAHAB, in the Old Testament, was the harlot of Jericho who concealed Joshua's two spies from the authorities; in return, they bade her identify her house with a scarlet thread in the window, so she and her family would be spared in the ensuing massacre (*Josh* ii). In the New Testament she is listed as an ancestress of Jesus: she became the wife of Salmon and the mother of Boaz and great-grandmother of Jesse, the father of David (*Matt* i:5–6). Blake lists her as an ancestress of Mary (*FZ* viii:365; *J* 62:10).

Blake applied the name Rahab to the Whore of Babylon, "Mystery, Babylon the Great, the mother of harlots and abominations of the earth" (*Rev* xvii:5; *FZ* viii:330; *Mil* 40:17; *J* 75:1, 18). She symbolizes the false church of this world, the opponent of Jerusalem, and the crucifier of Jesus (*FZ* viii:406).

The Synagogue of Satan (*Rev* ii:9) created her from "Fruit of Urizen's tree," and hid "the false Female" in Satan's bosom. At the trial she appears, beaming triumphant, "a False Feminine Counterpart, of Lovely Delusive Beauty, Dividing & Unit-

ing at will in the Cruelties of Holiness."
They clothe her in scarlet and gems, "and
on her forehead was her name written in
blood, 'Mystery'" (*FZ* viii:277–82). It is
she who kills Jesus, cutting off "the Mantle
of Luvah from the Lamb of God" (*FZ* viii:
341), thus revealing her own turpitude.

She then stands before Los in her pride,
questioning him; but he does not condemn
her. "O Rahab, I behold thee. I was once
like thee, a Son of Pride, and I also have
pierc'd the Lamb of God in pride & wrath"
(*FZ* viii:347–55). He bids her repent and
free Jerusalem. "Rahab, burning with pride
& revenge" (*FZ* viii:410), leaves him for
Urizen, whereupon Urizen sinks to dragon
form. "Rahab triumphs over all; she took
Jerusalem Captive, a Willing Captive, by
delusive arts impell'd to worship Urizen's
Dragon form, to offer her own Children upon the bloody Altar" (*FZ* viii:597)—that is,
to worship war and send her own children
to be slain. But when Rahab sees the weeping Ahania and hears Enion's voice, she repents. The Synagogue then burns her; but
"Rahab is an Eternal State" (*J* 52), and
her animating ashes become Natural Religion.

In *Milton* we have another account of her
creation. When Leutha (Sin) has her affair
with Palamabron, "In dreams she bore the
shadowy Spectre of Sleep & nam'd him
Death: in dreams she bore Rahab, the
mother of Tirzah & her sisters" (*Mil* 13:40).
Rahab is Natural Religion. She is "Vala,
drawn down into a Vegetated body" (*FZ*
viii:280), the temporal form of the eternal
Vala (*J* 70:31). The aggregate of the Four
Elements is named Satan and Rahab; "these
are the Gods of the Kingdoms of the Earth
... opposed in ... Corporeal Strife" (*Mil*
31:18–25). Rahab is the system of Moral
Virtue (*J* 39:10). She imputes Sin and
Righteousness to individuals (*J* 70:18), although Los tells her to distinguish between
States and the Individuals in them (*FZ* viii:
379). Albion's twelve Sons crown their
mother Vala, name her Rahab, and give her
power over the Earth, "exalting her Throne,
to build beyond the Throne of God and the

Lamb, to destroy the Lamb & usurp the
Throne of God" (*J* 78:15–19).

Rahab, as Natural Religion, is the seduc-
tive harlot. She insinuates herself into
Hand, usurping the throne within him,
which should be God's, and becoming his
Goddess, his central, unquestioned motivation: "Imputing Sin & Righteousness to
Individuals, Rahab sat, deep within him
hid, his Feminine Power unreveal'd, brooding Abstract Philosophy to destroy Imagination, the Divine-Humanity: A Threefold Wonder, feminine, most beautiful,
Three-fold each within other. On her white
marble & even Neck, her Heart, inorb'd
and bonified, with locks of shadowing modesty, shining over her beautiful Female features soft flourishing in beauty, beams mild,
all love and all perfection, that when the
lips recieve a kiss from Gods or Men, a
threefold kiss returns from the press'd
loveliness; so her whole immortal form
three-fold, three-fold embrace returns, consuming lives of Gods & Men, in fires of
beauty melting them as gold & silver in the
furnace. Her Brain enlabyrinths the whole
heaven of her bosom & loins to put in act
what her Heart wills. O who can withstand
her power! Her name is Vala in Eternity:
in Time her name is Rahab" (*J* 70:17).

Rahab as the Female Will seeks dominion
by means of sex: "All the Jealousies become
Murderous, uniting together in Rahab a
Religion of Chastity, forming a Commerce
to sell Loves, with Moral Law an Equal Balance not going down with decision. Therefore the Male severe & cruel, fill'd with
stern Revenge, mutual Hate returns & mutual Deceit & mutual Fear. Hence the Infernal Veil grows in the disobedient Female,
which Jesus rends & the whole Druid Law
removes away from the Inner Sanctuary, a
False Holiness hid within the Center" (*J*
69:32).

Rahab is the mother of Tirzah: the Harlot is mother of the Prude (*FZ* viii:294, 365;
Mil 13:41; 19:54). They work together constantly (*Mil* 19:27; *J* 34:52; 59:43; 67:34;
89:2). They weave the Natural Body, as
opposed to the Spiritual Body (*FZ* viii:201,

220), "till the Great Polypus of Generation covered the Earth" (*J* 67:34). They divide the twelve Daughters of Albion amongst themselves (*J* 5:42); and Gwendolen does the same for the two (*J* 34:52); then the twelve unite into the two, "a Double Female" (*J* 67:3); and again they unite in Rahab's Cloud (*J* 82:11; 84:30). They created the kings in Ulro (*J* 73:39). In preparing for the French Revolution, "Rahab created Voltaire, Tirzah created Rousseau" (*Mil* 22:41). They weave men by war into nations (*Mil* 25:29).

Rahab remains secret, refusing definite form, a cloud (*J* 80:40, 51). Hers are the Twenty-seven Heavens (*J* 75:4). But she herself is still hidden until finally she is exposed, complete in error. In *The Four Zoas* (viii) this occurs at the trial and execution of Jesus; in *Milton* (40) in a Last Judgment, when Ololon denounces Natural Religion; in *Jerusalem* (89) at the revelation of the Covering Cherub, within whom are Satan and Rahab (*Mil* 37:9). Then, being a definite form, she can be cast out. In the Last Judgment, Mystery is burned up (*Rev* xvii; *FZ* ix:67; *LJ*, *K* 609); but what is consumed are only her errors. "Sin, Even Rahab, is redeem'd in blood & fury & jealousy—that line of blood that stretch'd across the windows of the morning—redeem'd from Error's power" (*FZ* ix:159).

In another version (abandoned and deleted), Rahab herself hewed the Sepulcher and placed in it "the body which she had taken from the divine Lamb," over which she weeps, "weaving her web of Religion around the Sepulcher times after times, beside Jerusalem's Gate" (*FZ* viii:585–88). Obviously this is not Natural Religion at all, but an attack on the orthodoxy which builds its faith on the death of Jesus, mistaking the corpse for the immortal spiritual body. "But as she wove, behold! the bottom of the Sepulcher rent & a door was open'd thro' the bottom of the Sepulcher into Eternity. And as she wove, she heard a Voice behind her calling her. She turn'd & saw the Divine Vision . . ." (*FZ* viii:589). At this point, Blake, realizing the contradic-

tions and inconsistencies, stopped writing and deleted the whole episode.

The Female Babe in *The Mental Traveller* (44, *K* 424) is Rahab.

The RAINBOW is commonly accepted as a symbol of hope, and so Blake uses it.

When Enitharmon flees from Los, "delusive hopes kindling, she led him into shadows & thence fled outstretch'd upon the immense like a bright rainbow, weeping & smiling & fading" (*FZ* ii:380; see also *J* 83: 67; 86:50).

Leutha's rainbow is akin to Enitharmon's. Leutha (Sin) is making advances to Palamabron, but he does not know it yet, as Elynittria has been acting as his Freudian censor. His gnomes therefore see Leutha only "as a bow of varying colours on the hills" (*Mil* 12:14), although the horses are raging. Blake emphasized Leutha's rainbow by painting it across the page in the Huntington copy (where page 12 is numbered 10) and on the previous page in the New York copy (where page 11 is numbered 9).

But hopes need not be delusions. When Eno, who has prophetic insight, draws out a moment of time "into a Rainbow of jewels and gold," she is perceiving in time a prevision of eternity (*J* 48:35). After Erin has expounded the Forgiveness of Sins and invoked Jesus, her "lovely Bow enclos'd the Wheels of Albion's Sons" with the hope of his coming (*J* 50:22).

Noah's rainbow is the hope and promise of immortality, as it symbolizes the spiritual body. See NOAH.

On *Jerusalem* 14, the vision of Jerusalem is overarched by a rainbow, for she is the hope of a perfect society.

A rainbow sweeps across the title page of *Visions of the Daughters of Albion*. It is the only sign of hope in the whole book. It signifies that in spite of the storm, the sun is shining; and that there is hope for the solution of Oothoon's problems, though perhaps only in the spiritual body.

The RAM, the guardian of the flock, is the protector of Innocence.

In the mystical vision described in a letter to Butts (2 Oct 1800), the Good Shepherd twice calls Blake "O thou Ram horn'd with gold" (62, 70). Gold is the southern metal; Blake defends innocence with his ideas.

RANELAGH was a famous pleasure garden in Chelsea; it was demolished in 1803. Los asserts that "indignant self-righteousness . . . rose up against me thundering, from the Brook of Albion's River, from Ranelagh & Strumbolo" (*J* 7:73–8:2). In *An Island in the Moon* (viii), Miss Gittipin jealously remarks: "There they go in Postchaises & Stages to Vauxhall & Ranelagh" (*K* 53).

RATHLIN is an island of County Antrim, Ireland. "Lament . . . from Rathlin to Baltimore" (*J* 49:3) means from the north to the south of Ireland.

A RATIO is a limited system founded on what facts are available, and organized by Reason. Locke's materialistic universe based on his philosophy of the five senses is such a ratio. It is an "ideology."
"If it were not for the Poetic or Prophetic character, the Philosophic & Experimental would soon be at the ratio of all things & stand still, unable to do other than repeat the same dull round over again" (*NNR* 1st ser.). "Reason, or the ratio of all we have already known, is not the same that it shall be when we know more" (*NNR* 2nd ser.; cf. On Reynolds, *K* 475). "He who sees the Infinite in all things, sees God. He who sees the Ratio only, sees himself only" (*NNR* 2nd ser.).
Blake described Milton's Christ as "a Ratio of the five senses" (*MHH* 5). The "Vegetable Ratio" is all that the fallen senses can perceive (*Mil* 5:35). "A Natural Cause only seems: it is a Delusion of Ulro & a ratio of the perishing Vegetable Memory" (*Mil* 26:45). "The Reason is a State Created to be Annihilated & a new Ratio Created" (*Mil* 32:34). "The Spectre is the Reasoning Power in Man, & when separat-

ed from Imagination and closing itself as in steel in a Ratio of the Things of Memory, It thence frames Laws & Moralities to destroy Imagination, the Divine Body, by Martyrdoms & Wars" (*J* 74:10). "Thus Los alter'd his Spectre, & every Ratio of his Reason he alter'd time after time" (*J* 91:51).

The RAVEN symbolizes the fear of death, which orthodox religion emphasizes. The Raven makes his nest in the thickest shade of the Tree of Mystery (*SoE*, "The Human Abstract" 19). Compare "The purpose of thy Priests & of thy Churches is to impress on men the fear of death; to teach trembling & fear, terror, constriction: abject selfishness" (*Mil* 38:37). Death, however, is really the dawn of the new day. "Let the Priests of the Raven of dawn, no longer in deadly black, with hoarse note curse the sons of joy" (*MHH* 27). "When fleeing from the battle, thou fleeting like the raven of dawn" (*FZ* iv:86).

The REACTOR is Satan the adversary, not yet named because still unrevealed.
In *Paradise Lost*, when the Son was proclaimed and appointed lord of all the angels, Satan became envious (v:662); this was the beginning of his fall. In *Jerusalem*, when Albion is declared father of all the Sons of God, the Reactor "hid himself thro' envy. . . . you cannot behold him till he be reveal'd in his System. . . . Hidden in Albion's Forests he lurks: he admits of no Reply from Albion, but hath founded his Reaction into a Law of Action, for Obedience to destroy the Contraries of Man. He hath compell'd Albion to become a Punisher" (*J* 29:9–16).

REASON is the function of Urizen, and should be counterbalanced by the Imagination. It becomes evil either when it tries to dominate the other functions, or when the Individual is divided from his Emanation; then it becomes his Spectre. The eighteenth century proudly called itself the Age of Reason; Blake's antagonism to reason arose from his awareness of its shortcomings.

The RED SEA is the Pacific Ocean. "Japan, where the Red Sea terminates the World of Generation & Death" (*J* 89:48). See ERYTHREAN SEA.

The REDEEMED, in Milton's poems, are the sinners who have atoned for their guilt, such as Adam and Eve. The other two classes are the Elect, or saints, such as Jesus and Samson; and the Reprobate, or damned, such as Satan and Dalila. Blake inverted this system: his Elect are the Pharisees and his Reprobate the true believers; the Redeemed, in between, "live in doubts & fears perpetually tormented by the Elect" (*Mil* 25:35).

REHOB was a northern city of Palestine, explored by Joshua's spies before the conquest of Canaan. "So they went up, and searched the land from the wilderness of Zin unto Rehob, as men come to Hamath" (*Numb* xiii:21). The warriors address the daughter of Albion: "O Virgin of terrible eyes who dwellest by Valleys of springs beneath the Mountains of Lebanon in the City of Rehob in Hamath" (*J* 68:54).

The REINS (kidneys) are a Biblical symbol for a seat of the affections. Jeremiah associates them four times with the heart (xi:20; xii:2; xvii:10; xx:12).

Blake used them in the threefold division of Head, Heart, and Reins. The Dead from Ulro are woven "some threefold in head or heart or reins, according to the fittest order of most merciful pity & compassion" (*FZ* viii:59–60; frag. 6:27). The Daughters of Albion are "threefold in Head & Heart & Reins" (*Mil* 5:6). Jerusalem is "lovely Three-fold in Head & Heart & Reins, three Universes of love & beauty" (*J* 86:2; see also 86:22–32). Blake situates the Reins in the loins (*FZ* viii:55; *Mil* 5:8); but it is to be noted that the Covering Cherub has loins but no Reins (*J* 89:38).

In his eleventh illustration to *Job*, Blake, quoting *Job* xix:27, altered "though my reins be consumed within me" to "tho'

consumed be my wrought Image," a possible translation.

RELIGION, so Blake believed, was the basic problem of mankind. Early in his life he conceived the idea of a fundamental and universal religion that he developed throughout his life.

He was born in the third—Revolutionary —generation of the eighteenth century. The orthodox Anglican Church had become devoted to place-hunting and was spiritually dead. The Dissenters considered themselves members of this church, but kept apart. Deism had captured the intellectual world and established the "Age of Reason" by denying all miracles and revelations. Generally the public was hostile to all religious controversies, which had been responsible for some of the bloodiest pages in history. "Enthusiasm" was a term of contempt.

Nevertheless—or consequently—things were stirring beyond the bounds of orthodoxy and "common sense." The Friends (Quakers) long since had swept away all ritual, and depended solely on the Voice of the Spirit addressed to the individual. The Methodists, also preaching the immediate experience of God, had opened the inner life of man and reintroduced emotion into religion. Then there was the small sect of Behmenists, who studied his obscure metaphysics in the handsome "Law edition." Thomas Taylor was preaching Platonism as the true religion and publishing translations of the mystical works of the classical philosophers. But most provocative were the revelations of the famous scientist Swedenborg, who claimed the ability to travel in the spiritual worlds of heaven and hell.

Blake read and pondered all these things, and more. "No man can think, write, or speak from his heart, but he must intend truth" (*AllR* 3). There was some truth in all of them, and those truths he wanted. He was following the advice of St. Paul: "Prove all things: hold fast that which is good" (*I Thess* v:21). "Whatsoever things are true . . . honest . . . just . . . pure . . . lovely . . .

think on these things" (*Phil* iv:8). But Blake never accepted anything that was not a psychological fact.

He knew his Bible thoroughly, reading it symbolically, "for the letter killeth, but the spirit giveth life" (*II Cor* iii:6). He knew his Milton by heart—he apparently was the first man to understand what Milton was writing about—and in spite of his great admiration, disagreed with some of Milton's conclusions. If he read the Church Fathers, it was chiefly to learn about the heresies they attacked. But he read everything else that he could find in English, with a thoroughness which probably had not been paralleled since Milton. Although at first ignorant of other languages, he covered an extraordinary range of material, particularly seeking out those uncanonical writings which the authorities had ignored or "answered" and condemned.

Somewhere he found the repudiated doctrines of the ancient Gnostics and in 1793 adopted their evil creator, the Demiurge, for his own Urizen. He studied Plato and dismissed Aristotle. From Bryant or Stukeley or Davies, he accepted the idea that Druidism began in Britain and spread over the rest of the world, being the origin of Greek and all other pagan philosophies; it was responsible for the universal practice of human sacrifice. He read and was much impressed by the Bhagavad-Gita. He borrowed a couple of ideas from the Koran. He found Lilith in the rabbinical tradition. He studied the materialists Bacon, Newton, and Locke; admired their genius but condemned their ideas, especially as they prepared the way for the Deists. On the other hand, he read the mystics St. Teresa, Fénelon, Mme Guyon, and particularly Lavater, in whose aphorisms he found great stimulus. He also read the mystical alchemists Paracelsus and Behmen, and was particularly indebted to Swedenborg. He helped himself silently to their best ideas and scolded them thoroughly for their errors.

The extraordinary thing is that Blake reconciled all these warring philosophers so that they fitted, or at least were accounted for, in his own philosophy. He was devoted to the Bible, yet he agreed with Paine in his strictures. The only trouble with Paine was that he did not go far enough to see the limitations of those strictures. Nor did Blake ever disagree so completely with anyone as might be supposed. He attacked most fiercely those whose genius he genuinely admired: just because they were great, their errors were the most dangerous. Even the scoffer Voltaire had his role in the divine providence; the Holy Ghost had inspired him to expose the literal sense of the Bible, thus clearing the way for the truth. "He who is out of the Church & opposes it is no less an Agent of Religion than he who is in it; to be an Error & to be Cast out is a part of God's design" (*LJ*, *K* 613). Furthermore, "those who contemn Religion & seek to annihilate it become in their Femin[in]e portions the causes & promoters of these Religions" (*Mil* 40:9). Blake's infernal trinity of Bacon, Newton, and Locke at the end are exalted in heaven as the greatest scientists (*J* 98:9). Contraries are equally true and are essential to each other.

Blake's religion was planned to be all-inclusive. To be exclusive would be incomplete. Therefore, instead of weighing the respective credibilities of contradictory dogmas or the preferability of various rituals, he evaded the wrangling of the sects and struck straight to the heart of the matter, which he found in the human soul.

From his two tractates of 1788, we learn that he had already dethroned reason from its ancient place as the supreme faculty of man, replacing it with the Imagination. Therefore he attacked the Deists: "There is No Natural Religion." The Imagination he called the Poetic Genius, which is the "true man," creator of the outward body. All men are alike in this genius, however various they may be as individuals; all religions and philosophies are derived from it; therefore "All Religions are One."

Earlier, Blake had identified the Poetic Genius with God (On Swed *DL*, *K* 90), and while there is a distinction, there is no contradiction, for man was made in the image of God. This point comes out more clearly in "The Divine Image" (*SoI*): "Mercy, Pity, Peace, and Love | Is God, our father dear . . . Then every man of every clime, | That prays in his distress, | Prays to the human form divine, | Love, Mercy, Pity, Peace."

The worldly religions were all derived from Nature. The Deists drew their conclusions by logic from the material world, but before that, the poets had drawn theirs by imaginative insight. "The ancient Poets animated all sensible objects with Gods or Geniuses . . . And particularly they studied the genius of each city & country, placing it under its mental deity; till a system was formed, which some took advantage of, & enslav'd the vulgar by attempting to realize or abstract the mental deities from their objects: thus began Priesthood . . . Thus men forgot that All deities reside in the human breast" (*MHH* 11).

Blake's religion became really all-inclusive when he decided that "every thing that lives is holy." This was a natural conclusion from the ancient belief that all things were created from the divine substance. Nature is a projection of man, and therefore "Tree, Metal, Earth & Stone" are admitted to the divine bosom in their "Human Forms" (*J* 99:1). See NATURE. The human body is also a projection of the inner man; its beauty and its instincts are all holy; even its worst vices spring from staminal virtues and are "the highest sublimities in the spiritual world" (*CR* 262). Man's body is also the temple of the Holy Ghost, who inspires each individual according to his special potentialities. One should obey this Divine Voice within, carrying out its behests—doing the work one was born to do. Thus and thus only does God manifest in this world. And only thus can the individual achieve happiness. To this end, Liberty is essential; and Liberty (Jerusalem) is the central inspiration of all mankind.

But one must also recognize the Divine Voice in others. "The worship of God is: Honouring his gifts in other men, each according to his genius, and loving the greatest men best: those who envy or calumniate

great men hate God: for there is no other God" (*MHH* 22). See GOD. One's liberty is limited only by the liberties of others. "All Act [from Individual propensity *inserted and deleted*] is Virtue. To hinder another is not an act; it is the contrary; it is a restraint on action both in ourselves & in the person hinder'd, for he who hinders another omits his own duty at the same time. Murder is Hindering Another. Theft is Hindering Another. Backbiting, Undermining, Circumventing & whatever is Negative is Vice" (On Lavater, *K* 88).

"Brotherhood is Religion" (*J* 57:10). The Brotherhood of Man, which is the only solution to our personal and international problems, is made possible by the great discovery of Jesus, the mutual forgiveness of sins, which differentiates Christianity from all other religions. One must learn to distinguish the essentially good individual from the state of error through which he is travelling. Blake searched the Scriptures and found examples, from the forgiveness of Cain through the forgiveness of Mary.

For the true religion is eternal, and was manifesting long before Jesus revealed it. "All had originally one language and one religion: this was the religion of Jesus, the everlasting Gospel. Antiquity preaches the Gospel of Jesus" (*DesC* V, *K* 579).

Blake's religion was one of joy. From the play of childhood to the supreme ecstasy, life should be joy. The happiness of man *is* the glory of God, and Blake took it for granted there was no other. That is heaven. "Men are admitted into Heaven not because they have curbed & govern'd their Passions or have No Passions, but because they have Cultivated their Understandings. The Treasures of Heaven are not Negations of Passion, but Realities of Intellect, from which all the Passions Emanate Uncurbed in their Eternal Glory. The Fool shall not enter into Heaven let him be ever so Holy. Holiness is not The Price of Enterance into Heaven" (*LJ*, *K* 615).

Opposed to the true religion is the false religion of this world, whose God is Satan. "Man must & will have Some Religion: if he has not the Religion of Jesus, he will have the Religion of Satan & will erect the Synagogue of Satan, calling the Prince of this World, God, and destroying all who do not worship Satan under the Name of God. Will any one say 'Where are those who worship Satan under the Name of God?' Where are they? Listen! Every Religion that Preaches Vengeance for Sin is the Religion of the Enemy & Avenger and not of the Forgiver of Sin, and their God is Satan, Named by the Divine Name" (*J* 52). "Vengeance" was Blake's subtle and precise substitution for "punishment."

The error began with the primal sin, when Adam and Eve, by eating the apple, invented the false values of Good and Evil, and set themselves up as judges over all others. They were pre-empting God's place and arrogating his function. The error reached a climax in the promulgation of the Ten Commandments, which subjected Individuals to general laws and restricted their energies by negations. So the system of Justice was formed, with its infernal trinity of Accuser, Judge, and Executioner. Jesus came to abrogate this system, under which he was crucified. But it revived as Deism, which has corrupted all the churches.

The false religion is perfectly logical; in fact, it is the product of Urizen (*FZ* ix:150). As he wandered, lost in his sorrows, "a cold shadow follow'd behind him, like a spider's web . . . and all call'd it The Net of Religion" (*Ur* 25:5–22). Beneath it the senses are limited; man materializes and shrinks; and the creation according to *Genesis* ensues (*Ur* 25:23–47). The tale is repeated in *The Four Zoas* (vi:243–59), with the conclusion that the Net becomes saturated with tears and falls, entangling Urizen in his own Net (*FZ* viii:176–81). A picture of this event ends *The Book of Urizen* (28); it had already appeared in "The Human Abstract" (*SoE*).

The worldly religion is also likened to a fiery wheel, the cherub's revolving sword of flame which bars man from re-entering Paradise (*J* 77; *Gen* iii:24). This wheel turns against the current of creation, limiting sun and moon and shrinking man into "a little root a fathom long." "Jesus died because he strove against the current of this Wheel; its Name is Caiaphas, the dark Preacher of Death, of sin, of sorrow & of punishment: opposing Nature! It is Natural Religion; but Jesus is the bright Preacher of Life . . ." (*J* 77:1–21).

Another symbol for the worldly religion is Urizen's Tree of Mystery, the tree of Moral Values. See TREE OF MYSTERY, under TREE. Among other things, this has produced the cruel religion of sex (or "generation"). Urizen's temple of sex, "builded . . . in the image of the human heart," with its "Secret place, reversing all the order of delight . . . the hidden wonders, allegoric of the Generations of secret lust," and its priests and priestesses "cloth'd in disguises beastial, inspiring secrecy," is described in *The Four Zoas* vii *b*:18–38. (See also *J* 30:11.) See RAHAB.

All members of this worldly church are barred from heaven. "Those who are cast out are All Those who, having no Passions of their own because No Intellect, Have spent their lives in Curbing & Governing other People's by the Various arts of Poverty & Cruelty of all kinds. Wo, Wo, Wo to you Hypocrites" (*LJ*, *K* 615).

It can be understood why Blake often used "religion" as a smear word. The Orc in him would "scatter religion abroad to the four winds as a torn book, & none shall gather the leaves" (*Am* 8:5). The Los in him declared: "their God I will not worship in their Churches, nor King in their Theatres" (*Mil* 10:12); he would "overthrow their cup, their bread, their altar-table, their incense & their oath, their marriage & their baptism, their burial & consecration" (*J* 91:13), for their rituals have lost all meaning and are Antichrist (*Laoc*, *K* 776).

Eventually Blake admitted the original and hence fundamental goodness of the churches (Cathedral Cities), but thought that they had become corrupted almost past hope. Only the Divine Imagination, operating through the poet, could save them.

As individuals, men are separate from

each other; but they are united by their Humanities. Therefore Los orders: "Go to these Fiends of Righteousness, tell them to obey their Humanities & not pretend Holiness when they are murderers" (J 91:5). "Thy [Satan's] purpose & the purpose of thy Priests & of thy Churches is to impress on men the fear of death; to teach Trembling & fear, terror, constriction: abject selfishness. Mine is to teach Men to despise death & to go on in fearless majesty, annihilating Self, Laughing to scorn thy Laws & terrors, shaking down thy Synagogues as webs. I come to discover before Heav'n & Hell the Self righteousness in all its Hypocritic turpitude, opening to every eye these wonders of Satan's holiness, shewing to the Earth the Idol Virtues of the Natural Heart, & Satan's Seat explore in all its Selfish Natural Virtue, & put off in Self annihilation all that is not of God alone, to put off Self & all I have, ever & ever. Amen" (Mil 38:37).

The Self seems to be the Individual but is not. It is the Selfhood, the false front put up to fool oneself and protect oneself from the world; it is Selfishness, the cruel pride which made Lucifer fall; it is the last enemy, and must be sacrificed. " 'Cannot Man exist without Mysterious Offering of Self for Another? is this Friendship & Brotherhood?' ... 'Wouldest thou love one who never died for thee, or ever die for one who had not died for thee? And if God dieth not for Man & giveth not himself Eternally for Man, Man could not exist; for Man is Love as God is Love; every kindness to another is a little Death in the Divine Image, nor can Man exist but by Brotherhood' " (J 96: 20–28).

RENFRU (i.e., Renfrew) is a maritime county in southwest Scotland. With Peebles and Perth, it is assigned to Gad (J 16: 56); with all the rest of Scotland, it is assigned to Bowen (J 71:46).

The REPHAIM ("ghosts") were the original inhabitants of Canaan, Edom, Moab, and Ammon. The invading Israelites called them giants. Og, King of Bashan, was the last survivor. Blake, however, used "Rephaim" simply as a place name.

The SEA OF REPHAIM was Blake's invention. He probably meant it to signify a Miltonic limbo of amorphous and decaying superstitions.

Its location is variable. It would seem to be the Atlantic Ocean (J 48:33), for here the giants built their Causeway, but were drowned (J 89:51). It also seems to lie between Greece and Judea, as the heart of the Polypus shoots out its fibres "round the Earth thro' Gaul & Italy and Greece & along the Sea of Rephaim into Judea" (J 67:39). It is contained in the head of the Covering Cherub: "Ethiopia, Lybia, the Sea of Rephaim" (J 89:16).

The VALE OF REPHAIM runs from Jerusalem to Bethlehem. According to the Jewish mythology, it was the final dwelling-place of the ghosts of the wicked giants, the Rephaim. The place therefore was a Tartarus.

To Blake, the Vale was the place of dead but still operative traditions, the repository of ancient errors, the source of superstition. Once he identifies it with the Atlantic Vale, the gulf opened between Great Britain and America (J 48:33), but it is to be found in various other places. Cam and London, because of the fall of Enion and Ahania, "lament upon the winds of Europe in Rephaim's Vale" (Mil 19:40). Horeb terminates there (Mil 29:57), as do the Surrey Hills (J 41:12). It seems also to be in Derbyshire and Yorkshire (J 64:38). It runs from Camberwell to Golgotha (J 92:26). Reuben and Benjamin hide there (J 68:47), taking refuge in the errors of the past. When Eno opens the Moment of Time, she draws it out into a rainbow, "across the Atlantic Vale, which is the Vale of Rephaim"; she also opens the Atom of Space into Beulah, "occupied in labours of sublime mercy in Rephaim's Vale" (J 48:30–41).

REPRESSION OF SEX. See ENITHARMON.

REPROBATE. See TRANSGRESSORS.

REU, the son of Peleg and father of Serug, is the seventeenth of the Twenty-seven Heavens. He is the eighth in the second group (Noah to Terah), "the Female-Males, a Male within a Female hid as in an Ark & Curtains" (*Mil* 37:39; *J* 75:14).

REUBEN was the oldest son of Jacob, and the founder of a Tribe. He lost his birthright because he lay with his father's concubine Bilhah ("pleasure"). Jacob called him "unstable as water." Reuben found some mandrakes (supposed to promote fertility) and gave them to his mother, Leah, who traded them to the favorite, Rachel, in exchange for a night with her husband (*Gen* xxx:14–16)—one episode in that unhappy rivalry. Blake called the event a meeting of two Prides (*J* 93:8).

In the allotment of lands by Moses, Reuben's portion lay across the Jordan, on the east side of the Dead Sea upward from the river Arnon; but Blake, for symbolic reasons, assigned Bashan as well to Reuben, though it was actually given to Manasseh.

To Blake, Reuben symbolized the average sensual man. (Louis Ginzberg, in his *Legends of the Jews* I, 362, translates his name as "See the normal man.") He is the "vegetative man" (*J* 36:23). As he enroots in Bashan (*J* 74:43), once ruled by Og (justice), he is Man under Law. He is once described as man's "Immortal Imagination" exploring Creation, Redemption, and Judgment, the three states of Ulro, this world of matter (*J* 36:24, 41).

Reuben is the twentieth in the long line of the Sons of Los (*FZ* viii:360), but later this genealogy was discarded. In *Milton* and *Jerusalem*, he is the fifth of the sixteen Sons of Los, and the first of the twelve brothers to flee and become generated, wandering with Tirzah (*Mil* 20:53; 23:62–24:2)—they abandon inspiration for the laws of Moral Virtue. The dispersal of the brothers also represents the division of man into separate nations. When Reuben, the oldest, is named with Benjamin, the youngest (*J* 63:12; 68:

47; 90:46), the two are inclusive, representing all materialized men.

There are three accounts of the flight of the twelve brothers: (1) Satan uses the arts of Urizen to tempt them to flee (*FZ* viii: 375). (2) The Sons flee successively in "that thousand years of sorrow of Palamabron's Harrow & of Rintrah's wrath & fury"; and because they leave Los to wander with Tirzah (Moral Virtue), they become generated (*Mil* 23:62–24:4). (3) While Reuben sleeps on London Stone, the Daughters of Albion admire his awful beauty; they then divide him upon the Thames to send him over Europe in streams of gore; and when they cut his fibres, he rolls apart and takes root in Bashan. Then the Daughters act similarly with the other Sons, who also disperse and enroot, or else are lost (*J* 74:33).

Los tries to rouse Reuben from his sleep and make him transcend the limits imposed by Moses, but in vain. Four times he sends him across the Jordan, but Reuben returns each time. Unaware of the Holy City, he develops instead his sexual theory of Moral Virtue. The process is somewhat complicated. Each time, Los first limits one of Reuben's four senses—nostrils, eyes, tongue, and ears. Each time, all who see him (eventually the Seven Nations and the Sons of Albion) flee from his horrible form, and become what they behold. The development of Reuben's sexual ideals meanwhile is symbolized in three stages: (1) the Daughters of Albion divide Luvah into three bodies; (2) Gwendolen divides Rahab and Tirzah in twelve portions; and (3) when Reuben returns, vainly seeking Tirzah, Los in sixty winters builds the Moon of Ulro (earthly love); whereupon Reuben, still seeking Tirzah, complains: "Doubt is my food day & night" (*J* 34:43–54; 36:1–14).

The geography of these travels of Reuben presents some difficulties, which are simplified if we suppose that he was assigned all Transjordan, of which Bashan is the northern part. First he sleeps in Bashan between Succoth and Zaretan on the eastern bank of the Jordan—"the clay ground between Succoth and Zarthan" (*I Kings* vii:

46), where the ornaments for Solomon's Temple were made. Reuben is evidently dead to the possibilities of the divine work to be done. Here also Blake places the Stone of Bohan, on which Reuben sleeps; this stone was erected by "a son of Reuben," but was actually on the other side of the river, marking the boundary between Judah and Benjamin. Reuben crosses the Jordan into the Land of the Hittite (which contained Bethel and Luz, north of Jerusalem, and was assigned to Ephraim). He then returns "to his place," seeking Tirzah in vain. This time he sleeps in the Cave of Adam (probably the skull, although Blake may have had in mind "the city Adam that is beside Zaretan," near where the Ark was carried across the Jordan, *Josh* iii:16). Sent across again, he returns to Heshbon ("reason") in his own land, which he rebuilt after its capture from the Amorites; it was made a Levitical city of refuge. He then walks through Moab ("of the father"), south of his land, and stands before the Furnaces of Los on Mount Gilead, and looks towards Gilgal (just across the Jordan, the first camp of the Israelites after they crossed the river).

Reuben then flees before the Daughters of Albion. He flees head downward (the loins dominating heart and head) among the Caverns of the Mundane Shell (*J* 63:44). He and Benjamin flee, hiding in the Valley of Rephaim (*J* 68:47), the valley of the giant ghosts, a border of Judah. The Daughters of Albion drink Reuben and Benjamin (*J* 90:46). He wanders (*J* 69:45; 72:36); his voice is heard in the streets of all the nations (*J* 84:13). Gwendolen destroys him because he strove to bind her will (*J* 81:10). Eventually Los brings him from his twelvefold wanderings and leads him into the allegory built around the Worm (ordinary marriage) which developed from Gwendolen's falsehood; here at last is Reuben's Canaan, or Promised Land (*J* 85:4), where the seeds of the Twelve Tribes are to be planted. Finally it is prophesied that Reuben shall take refuge in Abram's loins, thus reversing the creation and separation (*J* 15:26).

Reuben is also seen sleeping on Mount Penmaenmawr (unbelief, *J* 21:35) while Levi sleeps on Mount Snowdon (*FZ* ii:53) —both in Carmarthenshire, which is Reuben's Welsh Gate (*J* 16:35). Scofield is bound in iron armor before Reuben's Gate, like a mandrake in the earth (*Mil* 19:59; *J* 11:22; 15:2). Reuben enroots his brothers (*J* 15:25). He is equated with Hand enrooting in Bashan (*J* 34:36). He and Benjamin are divided, the latter bleeding from Chester's River (*J* 63:12); this division occurs in the cruelty (*J* 21:34) of Cheviot (*J* 63:23). With four of his brothers, he is closed up in the vales of dark Cabul (*J* 79:64). Hand and Boadicea cut him apart from the hills of Surrey (*J* 90:25). No individual should appropriate any of the characteristics of Reuben, among others (*J* 90:31).

Ezekiel prophesied the final return of the Twelve Sons and assigned them Gates in the New Jerusalem. Blake similarly assigns them Gates in the Heavenly Canaan which hovers above Great Britain. In England, to Reuben's Gate are assigned Norfolk, Suffolk, and Essex (*J* 16:44), but the northern counties, Cumberland, Northumberland, Westmoreland, and Durham, are divided between the Gates of Reuben, Judah, Dan, and Joseph (*J* 16:50). In Scotland, Reuben's Gate is assigned Kincardine, Haddington, and Forfar (*J* 16:53). In Wales, the Gate of Reuben is fixed in Carmarthenshire (*J* 16:35). The counties of Northern Ireland are assigned as follows: "Munster South in Reuben's Gate, Connaut West in Joseph's Gate, Ulster North in Dan's Gate, Leinster East in Judah's Gate" (*J* 72:3). In Southern Ireland, Waterford, Tipperary, Cork, Limerick, Kerry, and Clare are under Reuben, Simeon, and Levi (*J* 72:21).

REVOLUTION is the third stage in the life of man. He begins with the joys of Innocence, then encounters the woes of Experience. When these woes become intolerable, he revolts.

Rebellion against the established order is the first necessity for progress. Every advance in civilization has begun with dissatisfaction and action against the *status quo*. But revolution is no end in itself. The Tyger burns up the forests of the night, but that is all which physical violence can accomplish. The high hopes of the original ideals vanish in the blood-bath. For an analysis of the initial success and subsequent failure of Revolution, see ORC.

In the cycle of the continents (*SoL*), Revolution (being physical) breaks out in the West and spreads to the North. In world history, Jesus was the spiritual Revolutionist. In the eighteenth century, the American Revolution followed the formula. In the history of the individual, Job's blind curse was the beginning of his salvation.

RHADAMANTHUS, a son of Jupiter, was so noted for his justice that he was appointed a judge in Hades. Virgil placed him at the gate of Dis, the infernal city of unending torture (*Aeneid* vi:566): "Here the Gnosian Rhadamanthus holds the harshest of reigns. He punishes first, then listens afterwards to the miserable" (*castigatque, auditque dolos*). After he forces confession of all secret and unexpiated crimes, the avenging Furies drive his victims into Dis.

"For what is Antichrist but those | Who against Sinners Heaven close | With Iron bars, in Virtuous State, | And Rhadamanthus at the Gate?" (*EG* i:11).

RHEA. According to Roman mythology, Rhea, the earth-goddess, was married to Saturn, and became the mother of Jove, among others, who dethroned his father. Milton spreads the worship of these three westward to "the utmost Isles" (*PL* i:521).

Rhea is the twelfth of the Twelve Gods of Asia. Blake says they were worshipped in "the Isles of the Sea remote" (*Mil* 37:33).

The RHINE and the Danube were battle fronts during the Napoleonic wars. "The Wine-press on the Rhine groans loud, but all its central beams act more terrific in the central Cities of the Nations, where Human Thought is crush'd beneath the iron hand of Power" (*Mil* 25:3). "The Rhine was red with human blood, | The Danube roll'd a

purple tide" (*J* 27:45). "Loud the cries of War on the Rhine & Danube" (*J* 47:9). Los "saw in Vala's hand the Druid Knife of Revenge & the Poison Cup of Jealousy, and thought it a Poetic Vision of the Atmospheres till Canaan roll'd apart from Albion across the Rhine, along the Danube" (*J* 63:39). "Jerusalem's Pillars fall in the rendings of fierce War, over France & Germany, upon the Rhine & Danube" (*J* 68:46).

The RIBBLE, the Dee ("Chester's River"), and the Mersey all empty into the Irish Sea (*J* 90:16).

RICHARD Coeur de Lion is the twelfth in the list of evil kings (*J* 73:36). However, "Lion Heart" had been mentioned admiringly in "A War Song to Englishmen" (28, *PS*).

RIMMON was the thunder-god of Syria. His temple at Damascus contained an altar raised to the God of Israel by Naaman, after Elisha cured him of leprosy.

Rimmon, seventh of the Twelve Gods of Asia, is worshipped in "Damascus curtain'd" (*Mil* 37:26).

RINTRAH is Wrath; he is the just wrath of the Prophet, except once, when he flames high in Satan (*Mil* 9:11, 19). There is a seeming discrepancy in that he is usually called the first of the sons of Los and Enitharmon (as in *FZ* viii:357), whereas Orc is also the first born—a discrepancy which Blake emphasized (*Eur* 3:25; 8:1); but Rintrah and his three brothers are actually the analysis of Orc's motivation. These four are also called the Four Sons of Jerusalem (*J* 71:51; 72:11).

These first four of Los's sons stood by him and thus were never generated (*J* 71:51; 72:11). They are "Rintrah fierce and Palamabron mild & piteous, Theotormon fill'd with care, Bromion loving Science" (*Mil* 24:11). They correspond respectively to Urthona and Edinburgh, Luvah and London, Tharmas and York, Urizen and Verulam (*J* 74:2-4). They work at Los's forge (*Mil* 6:12; *J* 73:5), where Rintrah wields the hammer (*J* 16:11).

Rintrah's compass-point is north; however, when the Zoas shift, his position is east (*J* 54, design). His Emanation is the jealous Ocalythron (*Eur* 8:7; *Mil* 10:19; *J* 93:5). He roars, presaging Revolution (*MHH* 2:1, 21). He is a lion in black forests (*Eur* 8:2); he is king of fire and prince of the sun (*Eur* 8:8–9). He is of the Reprobate (*Mil* 8:34; 11:22). Merlin, the immortal imagination, was like him (*J* 93:13). "Rintrah gave Abstract [inhuman] Philosophy to Brama in the East" (*SoL* 3:11). In one odd passage, Urizen becomes Rintrah (*FZ* vii:494).

Rintrah usually collaborates with Palamabron: just wrath at oppression and pity for the victims are united in the poet's mind. For this constant collaboration, see PALAMABRON.

ROCHESTER is the eighteenth of the Twenty-four Cathedral Cities (*J* 46:18). It is under Luvah and London. "In Verulam the Polypus's Head [winds] around his bulk thro' Rochester and Chichester & Exeter & Salisbury to Bristol" (*J* 67:35).

The ROCK OF AGES (also the Rock of Albion) is the place where Jesus lays the sleeping Albion (*FZ* i:468; *J* 48:4). It is on the verge of Beulah and is overshadowed by the Palm of Suffering and the Oak of Weeping (*FZ* i:464; *J* 23:24; 59:6). Against it the Sea of Time and Space rages (*Mil* 15:39). It is "a Horrible rock far in the South; it was forsaken when Urizen gave the horses of Light into the hands of Luvah" (*FZ* ix:93). Here, according to the erroneous Burgundy, "the eternal lion and eagle remain to devour" (*FR* 97).

Over the sleeping Albion, the Saviour builds a tomb, which consists of prototypes of the inspired Scriptures (*J* 48:5–11). It overshadows the whole earth (*Mil* 11:9).

When Albion loses control of the Plow and himself is plowed under, he flees beneath the Plow till he comes to the Rock of Ages and takes his seat there (*J* 57:16).

The Rock is once called "white" (*J* 94:7), thus being identified with Albion's rocky isle.

The ROCK OF ETERNITY (except in *FR* 97) is to be distinguished from the Rock of Ages. When Urizen first appears to the Eternals, they see "his hand on the rock of eternity unclasping the Book of brass" (*Ur* 4:42). When Urthona is dividing, "he laid his gloomy head down on the Rock of Eternity" (*FZ* v:54). Los finds himself "frozen amidst the vast rock of eternity" (*BoL* 4:11) until he shatters it.

"ROME & Greece swept Art into their maw & destroy'd it." When Blake wrote this, he had accepted the common theory that all things were derived from Hebraic originals. "Sacred Truth has pronounced that Greece & Rome, as Babylon & Egypt, so far from being the parents of Arts & Sciences as they pretend, were destroyers of all Art.... Virgil in the Eneid, Book VI, line 848, says 'Let others study Art: Rome has somewhat better to do, namely War & Dominion'" (*On Virgil*, K 778). And their influence on the neoclassical arts was bad. "We do not want either Greek or Roman Models if we are but just & true to our own Imaginations" (*Mil* 1). However, the Romans are one of the four races which amalgamate to form the English (*J* 92:1).

See also CHURCH OF ROME, under CHURCH.

ROSAMOND'S BOWER symbolizes secret, illicit love. Henry II is said to have built the bower at Woodstock (Oxfordshire) for his mistress, the "Fair Rosamond" Clifford. For her better protection, it was set in the midst of a labyrinth, but the jealous Queen Eleanor penetrated it and killed her rival.

The Atlantic weeps over his children "in Stone-henge [human sacrifice], in Malden & Colchester [ports of the departing soldiers], round the Rocky Peak of Derbyshire [the sexual allurements of Gwendolen], London Stone [justice], & Rosamond's

Bower [secret love]" (*J* 57:6). Blake may have had the bower in mind when he referred to the "intricate labyrinths of Times and Spaces unknown that Leutha lived in Palamabron's Tent" (*Mil* 13:43).

ROSCOMMON is an Irish county in the western province of Connaught. With the other counties of Connaught it is assigned to Ephraim, Manasseh, and Benjamin (*J* 72:24).

The ROSE is the traditional symbol of love. When associated with the Lily of Innocence, it is ideal. But in the state of Experience, "The modest [originally "lustful"—*K* 171] Rose puts forth a thorn" (*SoE*, "The Lilly"). It is sickened by the "dark secret love" of "The invisible worm" (*SoE*, "The Sick Rose"). "My Pretty Rose Tree" (*SoE*) is the jealous wife.

ROSS is a Scottish county which, with Edinburgh and Roxburgh (Roxbro), is assigned to Levi (*J* 16:54). With the rest of Scotland, it is assigned to Bowen (*J* 71:46).

ROUSSEAU (Jean Jacques, 1712–78) was one of the great prophets of Revolution. His *Discours sur les arts et sciences* (1750) argued that man uncorrupted by civilization was naturally good; thus Rousseau invented the concept of the Noble Savage. His *Nouvelle Héloïse* (1760) demonstrated that the impulses of the heart are superior to the rules of morality. His *Contrat social* (1762), the profoundest of his works, placed the rightful and ultimate sovereignty in the general will of the common man. Therefore Rousseau has been called "the Father of the American Revolution," as the Colonies put his principles into practice by sweeping away the official State and Church, and drawing up their own laws and constitutions. *Emile* (1762), although suppressed as anti-monarchical, laid the basis for elementary education lasting to this day. His protest against the neglect of children persuaded the women of France again to suckle their babies. ("While the mother idle plays

with her dog on her couch, the young bosom is cold for lack of mother's nourishment, & milk is cut off from the weeping mouth," *Tir* viii:26.) His *Confessions* (1782–88) startled his readers by his admissions of shortcomings which need never have been known, and by his unconvincing explanations of his quarrels with Diderot, Hume, and others who had tried to befriend him.

Blake always associated Rousseau and Voltaire as the mainsprings of the French Revolution. He attacked their Deism and particularly disbelieved in Rousseau's virtuous Natural Man, the height of perfection until corrupted by civilization. Blake's equivalent figure was Adam, the limit of contraction set to the falling Man.

The "fiery cloud of Voltaire and thund'rous rocks of Rousseau" drive the religious from their abbeys (*FR* 276). The soul of Voltaire shines fiery over Lafayette's head, while Rousseau unfolds his white cloud over the army (*FR* 282). Presaging the Revolution, "Clouds roll heavy upon the Alps round Rousseau & Voltaire" (*SoL* 4:18). They continue the materialism which Bacon started. Albion's Spectre announces: "I am God . . . Am I not Bacon & Newton & Locke . . . & my two Wings, Voltaire, Rousseau?" (*J* 54:16). They are Vala's "Two Covering Cherubs, afterwards named Voltaire & Rousseau, two frowning Rocks on each side of the Cove & Stone of Torture, frozen Sons of the feminine Tabernacle of Bacon, Newton & Locke" (*J* 66:12). When the churches were about to die out, "Rahab created Voltaire, Tirzah created Rousseau, asserting the Self-righteousness against the Universal Saviour, mocking the Confessors & Martyrs, claiming Self-righteousness, with cruel Virtue making War upon the Lamb's Redeemed to perpetuate War & Glory, to perpetuate the Laws of Sin" (*Mil* 22:41). Naturally, Ololon rejects them (*Mil* 40:12).

"Voltaire, Rousseau, Gibbon, Hume, charge the Spiritually Religious with Hypocrisy; but how a Monk, or a Methodist either, can be a Hypocrite I cannot conceive. . . . Voltaire! Rousseau! You cannot escape my charge that you are Pharisees & Hypocrites, for you are constantly talking of the Virtues of the Human Heart and particularly of your own, that you may accuse others, & especially the Religious, whose errors you, by this display of pretended Virtue, chiefly design to expose. Rousseau thought Men Good by Nature: he found them Evil & found no friend. Friendship cannot exist without Forgiveness of Sins continually. The Book written by Rousseau call'd his Confessions, is an apology & cloke for his sin & not a confession" (*J* 52).

ROXBRO (i.e., Roxburgh) is an inland county of Scotland. With Edinburgh and Ross, it is assigned to Levi (*J* 16:54). With all the rest of Scotland, it is assigned to Bowen (*J* 71:46).

The RUBY for Blake symbolizes Wisdom (see *Job* xxviii:18; *Prov* iii:15; viii:11), but particularly wisdom of the heart. It is associated with the Pearl (love), as in "The rubies & pearls of a love-sick eye" (*The Mental Traveller* 34, *K* 425; cf. *Riches* 2, *K* 181).

The pavement in "I saw a chapel all of gold" is "Set with pearls & rubies bright" (*K* 163). Los's daughters have "a gate of rubies & all sorts of precious stones in their translucent hearts, which opens into the vegetative world" (*J* 14:21). Jerusalem's wings are "feather'd with soft crimson of the ruby" (*J* 86:8).

RUSSIA is the sixth of the Thirty-two Nations which shall guard liberty and rule the rest of the world (*J* 72:38). In Urizen's temple, "Poland & Russia & Sweden" are "his soft retired chambers" (*J* 58:40).

RUTH the Moabite was the great-grandmother of David (*Ruth* iv:13–17). Matthew therefore includes her in his genealogy of Jesus (*Matt* i:5). Blake includes "Ruth the Moabite" in the ancestry of Mary (*J* 62:11).

RUTLAND is a county of England which, with Northampton and Nottingham, is assigned to Issachar (*J* 16:48). With seven others, it is assigned to Scofield (*J* 71:38).

S

SABRINA was originally Sabre, the illegitimate daughter of King Locrin and his mistress Estrildis. When Locrin finally divorced his wife Guendoloena in favor of Estrildis, Guendoloena raised an army; Locrin was killed in battle, whereupon Guendoloena had Estrildis and Sabre "thrown into the river now called the Severn, and published an edict through all Britain, that the river should bear the damsel's name, hoping by this to perpetuate her memory, and by that the infamy of her husband. So that to this day the river is called in the British tongue Sabren, which by the corruption of the name is in another language Sabrina" (*Geof* II, v).

Milton used the legend in *Comus*, but softened it. Sabrina is the legitimate daughter of Locrine; Guendolen is her stepmother, whose "mad pursuit" causes Sabrina to commend her innocence to the river that bars her way. The nymphs bear her to Nereus, who makes her the goddess of the Severn.

Sabrina is third in Blake's first list of Albion's daughters (*FZ* ii:61); she is ninth in the second list (*J* 5:43), where she is one of the seven united into Rahab in the Covering Cherub on the Euphrates; she is the eleventh in the final list (*J* 71:45), where she is the Emanation of Kotope; "join'd with Mehetabel she shines west over America." After the appearance of Erin, "Sabrina & Ignoge begin to sharpen their beamy spears of light and love; their little children stand with arrows of gold" (*J* 11:19). When Albion discovers that his little daughters were not so innocent as he had supposed,

he cries out: "Ah me, Sabrina, running by my side, in childhood what wert thou?" (*J* 21:22).

The SACRAMENTS of the Protestant churches are two: baptism, which by symbolically washing away sin admits to the church; and the commemorative Lord's Supper, or Communion, which symbolizes the brotherhood of man in the mystical body of Christ. Blake understood the two as complementary: the casting away of error and the acceptance of truth.

Jesus himself "is the Bread & the Wine; he is the Water of Life; accordingly on Each Side of the opening Heaven appears an Apostle: that on the Right Represents Baptism, that on the Left Represents the Lord's Supper. All Life consists of these Two, Throwing off Error & Knaves from our company continually & Recieving Truth or Wise Men into our Company continually. ... On the Side next Baptism are seen those call'd in the Bible Nursing Fathers & Nursing Mothers; they represent Education. On the Side next the Lord's Supper, The Holy Family, consisting of Mary, Joseph, John the Baptist, Zacharias & Elizabeth, recieving the Bread & Wine, among other Spirits of the Just made perfect" (*LJ*, *K* 612-14; see Illustrations, "LJ" Nos. 8, 13).

The meaning is all. When the sacraments are reduced to repetitious rituals, they kill their original meanings. "The outward Ceremony is Antichrist" (*Laoc*, *K* 776). Therefore Los bids his Spectre destroy all the rituals: "overthrow their cup, their bread, their altar-table, their incense & their oath, their marriage & their baptism, their burial & consecration" (J 91:13).

SADDUSAION is a word apparently invented by Blake to indicate the Sadducees, whom he supposed to be an organized body. The Saddusaion is one of the six groups "Twelvefold in Allegoric Pomp in selfish holiness" whose appearance reveals the Covering Cherub (J 89:7).

SAINT DAVID'S is the twentieth of the Twenty-four Cathedral Cities (J 46:19). It is under Tharmas and York.

SAINT JOHN'S WOOD is a district of London, to the northwest of Golden Square, where Blake roamed as a boy. "The fields from Islington to Marybone, | To Primrose Hill and Saint John's Wood, | Were builded over with pillars of gold, | And there Jerusalem's pillars stood" (J 27).

SALAH was the son of Arphaxad (Gen xi: 12) or the grandson of Arphaxad and the son of Cainan (Luke iii:35–36); in either case, he was the father of Eber. Blake followed Luke in drawing up his list of the Twenty-seven Heavens. Salah is the fourteenth, the fifth in the second group, "the Female-Males, A Male within a Female hid as in an Ark & Curtains" (Mil 37:38; J 75: 13).

Los curiously begs his sons for patience "till the Last Vintage is over, till we have quench'd the Sun of Salah in the Lake of Udan-Adan" (Mil 23:59). It would seem that this is the material sun, and has nothing to do with the Biblical character.

The SALAMANDRINE MEN, who live in a state of continual wrath, have their cities in the land of death eternal, around Golgonooza (J 13:43).

SALISBURY is the fifth of the Twenty-four Cathedral Cities (J 40:61). It is under Urizen and Verulam: "In Verulam the Polypus's Head, winding around his bulk thro'

Rochester and Chichester & Exeter & Salisbury to Bristol" (J 67:35).

SALISBURY PLAIN, in Wiltshire, contains the Druid circle of Stonehenge. The daughters of Albion play before the armies, "while the Prince of Light on Salisbury Plain [reigns?] among the Druid Stones" (FZ ii:65). There the Spectre Sons of Albion mock and deride the writhings of their victim Luvah (J 65:57). There they erect the stupendous building of Natural Religion (J 66:2). There the heart of the Polypus beats strong (J 67:37). "The Serpent Temples thro' the Earth, from the wide Plain of Salisbury, resound with cries of Victims" (J 80:48).

The "SALT LAKE" is probably the Dead Sea, and could not refer to the yet undiscovered Great Salt Lake of Utah. "As the stars rise from the salt lake," Albion's Angels rise from the ruins of their council house (Eur 9:15).

SAMSON, the strongest man in the Bible, was betrayed to his enemies by his Philistine wife, who cut off his hair, in which lay the secret of his strength. Blake's unfinished prose poem "Samson" is in the Poetical Sketches. Blake called Swedenborg "strongest of men, the Samson shorn by the Churches" (Mil 22:50), meaning that Swedenborg was betrayed, or shorn, by the churches when he accepted their system of morality.

SAMUEL, the prophet, was one of those created by Los to offset the kings created by Rahab and Tirzah (J 73:41). The two books of Samuel are among the inspired books of the Bible (J 48:10).

The left SANDAL is emphasized in Milton. If the right hand symbolizes Urthona, its opposite, the left foot, symbolizes Urizen. Thus, in the confusion that followed Satan's pre-empting of Palamabron's harrow, "Los took off his left sandal, placing it on his head, signal of solemn mourning" (Mil 8:

11); that is, he gave up working for a time to reason things out.

When Milton entered Blake's left foot (through the realm of ideas), "all this Vegetable World appear'd on my left Foot as a bright sandal form'd immortal of precious stones & gold. I stooped down & bound it on to walk forward thro' Eternity" (*Mil* 21: 12): the whole system of Milton's universe became an intellectual means of progress. But mere intellect is not enough. Los then appeared and helped him: "he also stoop'd down and bound my sandals on in Udan-Adan . . . and I became One Man with him" (*Mil* 22:9–12).

The SANHEDRIM (i.e., Sanhedrin) was the supreme court of the Jews.

Urizen secretly communes with Orc "and with the Synagogue of Satan in dark Sanhedrim" to undermine the world of Los (*FZ* viii:97). Urizen also "call'd together the Synagogue of Satan in dire Sanhedrim to judge the Lamb of God to Death" (*FZ* viii: 272). It burns Mystery, from whose ashes rises Deism (*FZ* viii:615).

The SAPPHIRE was the middle stone in the second row of the high priest's breastplate (*Exod* xxxix:11). It represented Naphtali. It is one of the six stones (also on the breastplate) which adorn Orc as a serpent (*FZ* viii:74). Vala has sapphire shoes (*FZ* vii *b*:191; *J* 65:37).

SATAN is Error. He "Seems but Is Not" (*J* 93:20). "What seems to Be, Is, To those to whom it seems to Be, & is productive of the most dreadful consequences to those to whom it seems to Be" (*J* 36:51). "One Error not remov'd will destroy a human Soul" (*J* 46:11).

Satan is not a person: he is "the State of Death & not a Human existence" (*J* 49: 67). This "death" is Eternal Death, the inability to receive the divine light. To prevent Man from falling further, the Saviour set two Limits: "he found the Limit of Opacity & nam'd it Satan, in Albion's bosom, for in every human bosom these limits stand;

and next he found the Limit of Contraction & nam'd it Adam, while yet those beings were not born nor knew of good or Evil" (*FZ* iv:271). Thus "Limit was put to Eternal Death" (*FZ* iv:276). Opacity is resistance to the Light, whereas "there is no Limit of Translucence" (*J* 42:35). See LIMITS.

Elsewhere not Jesus but Los, his spiritual representative, is credited with this creation: giving form to Error is an essential poetic function. Satan is the youngest son of Los (*Mil* 4:9)—although in the earlier list of his sons, Satan is only the fifteenth (*FZ* viii:359)—and of Enitharmon: "At last Enitharmon brought forth Satan, Refusing Form in vain" (*Mil* 3:41; *FZ* i:507). But there is another possibility of parentage: "in [Albion's] Chaotic State of Sleep, Satan & Adam & the whole World was Created by the Elohim" (*J* 27).

Satan is a State (*FZ* viii:285; *Mil* 11:21; 32:25; *J* 35:13; 49:67). "There is a State nam'd Satan; learn distinct to know, O Rahab! the difference between States & Individuals of those States" (*FZ* viii:379). "Learn therefore, O Sisters, to distinguish the Eternal Human . . . from those States or Worlds in which the Spirit travels. This is the only means to Forgiveness of Enemies" (*J* 49:72–75). Satan is the State of Death (*J* 49:67), given form "that Men may be deliver'd time after time evermore" (*J* 49: 70) and "put off Satan Eternally" (*FZ* viii: 286), "that Albion may arise again" (*J* 35: 14). See STATES.

Satan is the "prince of this world" (*John* xii:31; xiv:30; xvi:11), but Blake preferred St. Paul's term "god of this world" (*II Cor* iv:4; *EG b*:31, 44; suppl. 2:13; *GoP*, Epilogue), the "adversary" (for such his name means) of Jesus, whose kingdom is "not of this world" (*John* xviii:36). Satan asserts: "I am God alone: there is no other!" (*Mil* 9:25); "being call'd God, setting himself above all that is called God" (*Mil* 11:12; also *Mil* 32:13; 38:51, 56). He is "Worship'd as God by the Mighty Ones of the Earth" (*J* 33:18), "Worship'd by the Names Divine of Jesus & Jehovah" (*GoP*,

Epilogue 5). He even claims superiority to the true God: "I am God of Men: Thou Human, O Jehovah! . . . Thou shalt Thyself be Sacrificed to Me, thy God, on Calvary" (*GhA* 2:18–21).

His religion is that of Morality (*Mil* 9: 26), "the Idol Virtues of the Natural Heart . . . Selfish Natural Virtue" (*Mil* 38:46). "Every Religion that Preaches Vengeance for Sin is the Religion of the Enemy & Avenger and not of the Forgiver of Sin, and their God is Satan, Named by the Divine Name. Your Religion, O Deists! Deism is the Worship of the God of this World by the means of what you call Natural Religion and Natural Philosophy, and of Natural Morality, or Self-Righteousness, the Selfish Virtues of the Natural Heart. This was the Religion of the Pharisees who murder'd Jesus" (*J* 52).

"Moral Virtues all begin | In the Accusations of Sin" (*EG* suppl. 2:34). Satan is the Accuser, or *diabolos* (*J* 98:49; *EG* suppl. 2: 13; *GoP*, Prologue 3 and Epilogue). In *Job*, he is the angel who plants doubt and the suspicion of sin in the mind of the patriarch.

His church is the "Synagogue of Satan" (*Rev* ii:9; iii:9). "And all the Spectres of the Dead, calling themselves Sons of God, in his Synagogues worship Satan under the Unutterable Name [the tetragrammaton]" (*Mil* 11:13). Here Jesus is condemned as a criminal (*FZ* viii:272, 325). "When Satan first the black bow bent | And the Moral Law from the Gospel rent, | He forg'd the Law into a Sword | And spill'd the blood of mercy's Lord" (*J* 52:17).

"Satan [error] & Adam [the natural man] are States Created into Twenty-seven Churches" (*Mil* 32:25). The Twelve Gods of paganism, being utterly false, are especially Satan's (*Mil* 37:60); whereas the Twenty-seven Churches at least sprang from the seed of Truth, though they have been perverted into the official Christianity which culminates in war (*Mil* 37:35–43).

"Satan the Accuser" is the "Father of Hell," which "must have been originally Formed by the devil Himself" (On Dante, *K* 785). When Satan and Sin fell, they fell

into "a Hell of [their] own making" (*Mil* 12:23).

In the Individual, Satan is the principle of selfishness (the Selfhood) and the function of rationalizing (the Spectre). "Man is born a Spectre or Satan & is altogether an Evil, & requires a New Selfhood continually, & must continually be changed into his direct Contrary" (*J* 52). The Spectre is "the Great Selfhood, Satan . . . having a white Dot call'd a Center, from which branches out a Circle in continual gyrations: this became a Heart from which sprang numerous branches varying their motions, producing many heads, three or seven or ten, & hands & feet innumerable at will of the unfortunate contemplator who becomes his food: such is the way of the Devouring Power" (*J* 33:17).

The supreme manifestation of Satan in this world is war. When liberty is generally under attack, "a Vast Hermaphroditic form" takes hideous shape; "at length an awful wonder burst from the Hermaphroditic bosom: Satan he was nam'd . . . a male without a female counterpart . . . yet holding the shadowy female Vala as in an ark & Curtains . . . being multitudes of tyrant Men in union blasphemous against the Divine image, Congregated assemblies of wicked men" (*FZ* viii:248–58). War springs from suppressed sex. "Albion's Spectre from his Loins | Tore forth in all the pomp of War: | Satan his name . . ." (*J* 27:37). The reality within this error is Luvah (love) perverted to Orc (hate). "Luvah tore forth from Albion's Loins" (*J* 47:4). "But when Luvah in Orc became a Serpent, he descended into that State call'd Satan" (*FZ* viii:382). "Luvah is named Satan because he has enter'd that State: a World where Man is by Nature the enemy of Man" (*J* 49: 68). "Satan is the Spectre of Orc, & Orc is the generate Luvah" (*Mil* 29:34).

Everybody is born into the state of Satan; one escapes only by recognizing and rejecting the Selfhood, as Milton does, in the poem named for him. But all do not escape; and the character named Satan in the same poem is an example, for he is William Hayley, who acts out the part of the Miltonic Satan in *Paradise Lost*.

The myth of Satan is not biblical: the early Fathers contrived and constructed it from various unrelated passages, particularly Isaiah's denunciation of the king of Babylon (*Isaiah* xiv), Ezekiel's denunciation of the king of Tyre (*Ezek* xxviii), the serpent of *Genesis* (iii), the dragon of *Revelation* (xii, xx), and the tempting agent of the Lord in *Job*. The supreme summation of the myth is to be found in *Paradise Lost*.

Lucifer ("the morning star") was the first of the angels. His pride was offended and his jealousy roused when the Father proclaimed the Son. Lucifer's ambition led him to conspire against the Father; at that moment, Sin was born from his head; coupling incestuously with her, he begat Death. He seduced a third of the angelic host into trying to seize the Throne for him. After inconclusive battling, the Son drove them out of Heaven; they fell into Hell. Thereafter, Lucifer's name was Satan ("the adversary"). Realizing now that any frontal attack was doomed to failure, Satan resolved to revenge himself indirectly by ruining God's latest creation, Man. He insinuated himself into Paradise where in the guise of a serpent he persuaded Eve to eat of the forbidden Tree of the Knowledge of Good and Evil; she persuaded Adam to do likewise; and they were expelled from the Garden, though with the foreknowledge of ultimate salvation. Meanwhile, when Satan announced his triumph to his devils, they were debased into the serpent-form which he had assumed, while he became the great Dragon.

Milton's chief interest lay in analyzing the process of damnation, which Satan exemplifies. It is a continuous process, the persistence in sin. At the beginning he is still the archangel though blasted; but bit by bit his character degenerates. He is constantly tempted to pity, to repent, but he always hardens his heart. He loses his sense of truth, and becomes deceived by his own lies. At the end, he has lost all semblance of the human form.

Blake's first criticism of Milton's poem (*MHH* 5–6) was based on his thesis that Hell and Heaven are what Freud called the subconscious and the superego. Milton's Son is "the Governor or Reason," while Satan, "the original Archangel, or possessor of the command of the heavenly host," is Desire. "It indeed appear'd to Reason as if Desire was cast out; but the Devil's account is that the Messiah [himself] fell, & form'd a heaven of what he stole from the Abyss."

In *Milton*, however, Hayley when quarreling with Blake acts out, though obscurely, the official Miltonic damnation. He wants to be what he is not, a poet, for his true calling is at the Mill, not the Harrow. (See MILL.) As the Accuser, he blames Palamabron for things he himself has done (7:36; 8:1; 9:20), and Michael contends with him as inconclusively as in *Paradise Lost* vi. In the Assembly, when Satan formally accuses Palamabron, he sets himself up as God: "I am God alone: there is no other! let all obey my principles of moral individuality. I have brought them from the uppermost innermost recesses of my Eternal Mind: transgressors I will rend off for ever" (9:25); whereupon his bosom grows "opake against the Divine Vision" (9:31) and he falls into an unfathomable Abyss.

At this point, Hayley's feminine side, Leutha (who is Milton's "Sin"), takes the blame on herself. "The Harrow cast thick flames & orb'd us round in concave fires, a Hell of our own making . . . Jehovah thunder'd above; Satan in pride of heart drove the fierce Harrow among the constellations of Jehovah, drawing a third part in the fires" (12:20). (In *Rev* xii:4, the dragon's tail "drew the third part of the stars of heaven, and did cast them to the earth"; these were interpreted to mean a third part of the angelic host whom Satan seduced.) " 'Twas then . . . I form'd the Serpent" (12:28). "I weeping hid in Satan's inmost brain. . . . I came forth from the head of Satan: back the Gnomes recoil'd and called me Sin and for a sign portentous held me" (12:36–39, quoting from *PL* ii:760). Thus Sin became manifest. "In dreams she bore the shadowy spectre of Sleep & nam'd him Death" (13:40).

When at last Satan is wholly revealed, he appears "by Cherubim surrounded, so permitted (lest he should fall apart in his Eternal Death) to imitate the Eternal Great Humanity Divine" (39:25)—the "Godlike imitated State" of Milton (PL ii:511). "Beneath sat Chaos: Sin on his right hand, Death on his left, and Ancient Night spread over all the heav'n his Mantle of Laws" (39:29; see CHAOS, diagram).

Satan sometimes performs deeds ascribed to Jehovah. See ANGEL OF THE DIVINE PRESENCE, under ANGEL.

Being the State of Error, there is no possible salvation for Satan: at the revelation of truth, he is cast into the fires of annihilation and is burned up. "The State nam'd Satan never can be redeem'd in all Eternity" (FZ viii:381). "Be permanent, O State! and be thou for ever accurs'd, that Albion may arise again" (J 35:13): "permanent" in the sense that the State is given form that it may be cast off. "The Evil is Created into a State, that Men may be deliver'd time after time evermore" (J 49:70).

"Christ comes . . . to deliver Man, the Accused, & not Satan, the Accuser. We do not find any where that Satan is Accused of Sin: he is only accused of Unbelief & thereby drawing Man into Sin that he may accuse him. Such is the Last Judgment—a deliverance from Satan's Accusation. Satan thinks that Sin is displeasing to God: he ought to know that Nothing is displeasing to God but Unbelief & Eating of the Tree of Knowledge of Good & Evil" (LJ, K 615).

Yet a possibility of salvation of a person in the State of Satan seems indicated by Jehovah's address to Satan: "Such is My Will that Thou Thyself go to Eternal Death in Self Annihilation, even till Satan, Self-subdu'd, Put off Satan into the Bottomless Abyss, whose torment arises for ever & ever" (GhA 2:21), thus reverting to his original condition as the unfallen Lucifer.

Edward Young ended the eighth of his Night Thoughts with the line: "Satan, thy Master, I dare call a Dunce." From this sprang the Epilogue to Blake's Gates of Paradise: "Truly, My Satan, thou art but a Dunce." He is "The Accuser who is The God of This World. . . . Worship'd by the Names Divine of Jesus & Jehovah." He is stupid not to distinguish "the Garment from the Man," and therefore tries to change one individual into another. Yet he is Lucifer, the Morning Star, "the Son of Morn in weary Night's decline," heralding a new day when "the lost Traveller's Dream" will have vanished.

"The Little Vagabond" (SoE) has a touching decoration depicting Satan as the Prodigal Son returned to his Father.

SATURN, son of Uranus, castrated and deposed his father; later he dethroned his brother Titan. His wife was Rhea; the chief of their sons was Jove, who in turn dethroned Saturn. Saturn with others fled to Italy "and o'er the Celtic roam'd the utmost Isles" (PL i:510–21). Thus Milton described the cult of the classical gods spreading westward through Europe.

Saturn is tenth of the Twelve Gods of Asia. Blake states that the three, Saturn, Jove, and Rhea, were worshipped in "the Isles of the Sea remote" (Mil 37:33).

The reign of Saturn was remembered as "the Golden Age," which ended when Jupiter ascended the throne. "The [Ancients are right?] when they Assert that Jupiter usurped the Throne of his Father, Saturn, & brought on an Iron Age & Begat on Mnemosyne, or Memory, The Greek Muses . . . Reality was Forgot & the Vanities of Time & Space only Remember'd & call'd Reality" (LJ, K 605).

SATURN the planet, in the Ptolemaic system, was the outermost of the seven planets; beyond it lay the sphere of the fixed stars. "The void between saturn & the fixed stars" is the miserable lot of the Angel in the fourth "Memorable Fancy" (MHH 19).

If Blake knew that Herschel in 1781 had found another planet, Uranus, beyond Saturn, he ignored the discovery, preferring to use the Ptolemaic system, which Milton had also used in spite of Galileo.

SAUL, first king of Israel, had a moody and suspicious temperament which led him to quarrel even with his son-in-law David. Blake's Adam contains the possibilities of relative-hating: he is "Peleg & Joktan, & Esau & Jacob, & Saul & David" (*J* 73:28).

SAUL OF TARSUS. See PAUL.

SAVIOUR. See JESUS.

The SAXONS were one of the four races which amalgamated to produce the English (*J* 92:1). Los cries: "Scofeld & Kox are let loose upon my Saxons!" (*J* 43:51). "O when shall the Saxon return with the English, his redeemed brother?" (*J* 83:14). "Woden and Thor and Friga wholly consume my Saxons on their enormous Altars built in the terrible north" (*J* 83:19).

"SCANDINAVIA fled with all his mountains fill'd with groans" when shame smote the naked Briton (*J* 24:11). The northern war-gods build enormous altars for human sacrifice "from Ireland's rocks, to Scandinavia, Persia and Tartary" (*J* 83:21). See WICKER MAN.

SCHOFIELD, SCHOLFIELD. See SCOFIELD.

"SCIENCE" apparently had two contrary meanings for Blake. Certainly the "sweet Science" which is to reign when the "dark Religions" have departed (*FZ* ix:855) is not Science "the Antichrist . . . the Tree of Death," which is the contrary of the Tree of Life (*Laoc*, *K* 777). Yet the two, the good and the bad, must basically be one, because Bacon, Newton, and Locke, the infernal trinity of the great scientists responsible for modern materialism, finally appear in heaven, counterbalancing the three great poets (*J* 98:9). The paradox is easily explained. True Science is eternal and essential, but it turns bad when it cuts loose from Humanity

and runs wild, abstracting, generalizing, and domineering.

"Science" means knowledge; complete knowledge is the understanding which is love and forgiveness. In the Golden Age, "liberty was justice & eternal science was mercy" (*FZ* iii:40). "Imagination, Art & Science, & all Intellectual Gifts [are] all the Gifts of the Holy Ghost" (*LJ*, *K* 604). "The Primeval State of Man was Wisdom, Art, and Science" (*J* 3). Then the sower Urizen cast on the human soul "the seed of eternal science" (*Ahan* 5:34). And Tharmas, sunk to the status of a God, remembers that time when he laments: "far rather would I be a Man, to know sweet Science" (*FZ* iv:146). And even now, "Political Science . . . is the Science of Sciences" (*PubA*, *K* 600). "Are not Religion & Politics the Same Thing? Brotherhood is Religion" (*J* 57:10).

Blake often paired Art and Science. "What is the Life of Man but Art & Science?" (*J* 77). His picture of the Last Judgment is "a History of Art & Science, the Foundation of Society, Which is Humanity itself" (*LJ*, *K* 613). "The Arts & Sciences are the Destruction of Tyrannies or Bad Governments. . . . The Foundation of [spiritual] Empire is Art & Science. Remove them or Degrade them, & the Empire is No More. Empire follows Art & Not Vice Versa as Englishmen suppose" (On Reynolds, *K* 445). They must be completely truthful: "Art & Science cannot exist but by Naked Beauty display'd" (*J* 36:49). They must be specific in the smallest details: "Art & Science cannot exist but in minutely organized Particulars, and not in generalizing Demonstrations of the Rational Power" (*J* 55:62). Scofield and Kox are "Generalizing Art & Science till Art & Science is lost" (*J* 43:54).

The Sciences in this world are derived from the Arts. "In Eternity the Four Arts, Poetry, Painting, Music, and Architecture, which is Science, are the Four Faces of Man. Not so in Time & Space: there Three are shut out, and only Science remains thro' Mercy, & by means of Science the Three become apparent in Time & Space in the Three Professions, Poetry in Religion: Music,

Law: Painting, in Physic & Surgery: that Man may live upon Earth till the time of his awaking. And from these Three, Science derives every Occupation of Men, and Science is divided into Bowlahoola [assimilation] & Allamanda [communication]" (*Mil* 27:55). Science can assimilate its material and communicate it, but cannot create. "Study Sciences till you are blind, Study Intellectuals till you are cold, Yet science cannot teach intellect. Much less can intellect teach Affection" (On Swed *DL*, *K* 93).

"The Philosophy of Causes & Consequences" is false. It misled Lavater and "all his Cotemporaries. Each thing is its own cause & its own effect" (On Lavater, *K* 88). "There is no Such Thing as a Second Cause nor as a Natural Cause for any Thing in any Way" (On Bacon, *K* 403). "Every Natural Effect has a Spiritual Cause, and Not a Natural; for a Natural Cause only seems: it is a Delusion of Ulro & a ratio of the perishing Vegetable Memory" (*Mil* 26:44). "Every thing is conducted by Spirits, no less than Digestion or Sleep" (*J* 3).

In *The Book of Urizen*, the Eternals themselves weave the tent called Science, to conceal the sight of the horrors below (*Ur* 19:9); but Urizen is already obsessed with his idea of One Law, and presently has his instruments (including the compasses) to explore the Abyss, where he plants his "garden of fruits" (*Ur* 20:33-42). In the next and much expanded version, it is Urizen himself who establishes the astronomical universe on the basis of the geometrical solids so dear to Pythagoras and all astronomers before Newton (*FZ* ii:135-44; 150-55; 266-86).

As a matter of fact, any astronomical system which appeals to the imagination may be taken as true: "sometimes the Earth shall roll in the Abyss [the Copernican system] & sometimes stand in the Center [Ptolemaic], & sometimes stretch flat in the Expanse [Blakean]" (*J* 83:40).

After establishing his universe, Urizen tries to found the immense into another world better suited to obey his will, where he shall be King of All; he creates "many a

Vortex" and fixes "many a Science in the deep . . . [that] all futurity be bound in his vast chain. And the Sciences were fix'd & the Vortexes began to operate on all the sons of men" (*FZ* vi:187, 233). The result is dreadful. The Shadowy Female absorbs "the enormous Sciences of Urizen" (*FZ* viii:144); his net of religion falls and entangles him; and when, "forgetful of his own Laws," he embraces the Female, he sinks to the form of a dragon (*FZ* viii:415-31). Los threatens him: "Thy self-destroying, beast form'd Science shall be thy eternal lot" (*FZ* ix:150), whereupon Urizen repents and renounces his attempted dominion, and is redeemed.

After describing the world of Los, Blake concludes the "First Book" of *Milton* with: "Thus Nature is a Vision of the Science of the Elohim" (*Mil* 29:65). The Elohim were the creators of the whole world (*J* 27), and Los "is of the Elohim" (*J* 73:24).

SCOFIELD (whose name Blake contemptuously misspelled also as Schofield, Scofeld, Skofeld, and Skofield) was John Scholfield, a private in Captain Leathe's troop of First Royal Dragoons; he was formerly a sergeant but had been demoted for drunkenness. On August 12, 1803, Blake found him drunk in the Felpham garden and ordered him out; and when he refused to go, ran him back to his quarters at the Fox Inn. The humiliated Scholfield, seconded by his friend Private Cock (whose name Blake preferred to misspell as Kock and Kox), retaliated by accusing Blake and his wife of treasonable utterances, a dangerous accusation when England was in something of a panic at the dangers of invasion by the French. Blake's account of the affair is to be read in his *Memorandum* (*K* 437). He was tried and acquitted of high treason at Chichester on January 10, 1804. The speech of Blake's counsel, Samuel Rose, and the report of the trial in the *Sussex Advertizer*, January 16, 1804, are included in Herbert Ives's "The Trial of William Blake" (*Nineteenth Century*, 1910, LXVII, 849-61).

Naturally Blake was thoroughly perturbed by the event. At one time he conjectured that Scholfield was a provocative agent sent against him by the government because earlier he had been a pro-revolutionist. Another time, he jotted down lines in which he seems to believe that Hayley, having failed to seduce Mrs. Blake, hired Scholfield to get him executed (*K* 544; cf. *PS*, "Fair Elenor" 67). Whatever the cause, the whole system of justice threatened him; and in *Jerusalem* the names of those involved against him (as far as they have been identified) are the names of the Sons of Albion. Scofield the Accuser is one of the most prominent; and on Plate 51, he is pictured naked, in flames, and dragging his chains.

Scofield is the ninth of Albion's Sons (*J* 5:27; 7:42, 47). His Emanation is Gwinevera; their position is East. He is assigned the Cathedral City of Ely, and a group of eastern counties—Rutland, Cambridge, Huntingdon, Norfolk, Suffolk, Hertford, and Essex (*J* 71:38–40).

Scofield is the Accuser activated by the emotions (hate—east). He involves Kox, Kotope, and Bowen, the last three Sons, thus making a fourfold Accuser, who utilizes all four compass-points, "to separate a Law of Sin to punish thee [Blake] in thy members" (*J* 7:47–50). These four "revolve most mightily upon the Furnaces of Los; before the eastern gate bending their fury, they war to destroy the Furnaces, to desolate Golgonooza, and to devour the Sleeping Humanity of Albion in rage & hunger" (*J* 5:27).

Scofield is identified with Adam, the man without imagination (*J* 7:42; 60:16). As such he is "the father of all his brethren in the Shadowy Generation" (*J* 7:43); that is, all men on earth are born accusers. Nimrod, the hunter of men, is Scofield's (*J* 22:3); and Joseph is his victim (*J* 68:1). Scofield is "Adam New-created in Edom" (*J* 7:25); that is, cheated of his birthright and therefore underprivileged. As a soldier protecting the average sensual man, he is "bound in iron armour before Reuben's Gate" (*Mil* 19:59). See REUBEN for his various Gates.

To be set before a gate is to guard it; to become enrooted is to be fixed there blindly. He "Vegetated by Reuben's Gate in every Nation of the Earth, till the Twelve Sons of Albion enrooted into every Nation, a mighty Polypus growing from Albion over the whole Earth" (*J* 15:2). He is "bound in iron armour; he is like a mandrake in the earth before Reuben's gate; he shoots beneath Jerusalem's walls to undermine her foundations" (*J* 11:21).

Scofield and his companion accuser Kox "are let loose upon my Saxons! they accumulate a World in which Man is by his Nature the Enemy of Man, in pride of Selfhood unwieldy stretching out into Non Entity, generalizing Art & Science till Art & Science is lost" (*J* 43:51). "In Selfhood, Hand & Hyle & Bowen & Skofeld appropriate the Divine Names, seeking to Vegetate the Divine Vision in a corporeal & ever dying Vegetation & Corruption; mingling with Luvah [now War] in One, they become One Great Satan" (*J* 90:40).

"Hand & Hyle & Koban, Skofeld, Kox & Kotope labour mightily in the Wars of Babel & Shinar; all their Emanations were Condens'd" (*J* 8:41). When the Sons scatter at the sight of Reuben, "Hutton & Skofeld & Kox fled over Chaldea in terror, in pains in every nerve" (*J* 36:17). Hand and Scofield are called Giants (*J* 43:50). In Urizen's temple, "Hand & Koban arch'd over the Sun in the hot noon as he travel'd thro' his journey; Hyle [east] & Skofield [east] arch'd over the Moon [east] at midnight; & Los Fix'd them there" (*J* 58:29). The Daughters of Albion "drink up Dan & Gad to feed with milk Skofeld & Kotope" (*J* 67:22). When Los is struggling with his Spectre, he orders him: "Go thou to Skofield: ask him if he is Bath or if he is Canterbury [demand of the Accuser if he be the healer of things physical or spiritual]. Tell him to be no more dubious: demand explicit words. Tell him I will dash him into shivers where & at what time I please; tell Hand & Skofield they are my ministers of evil to those I hate, for I can hate also as well as they!" (*J* 17:59).

SCOPPRELL, a character in *An Island in the Moon* (Chaps. ii, v, viii–xi), is small in stature, and retiring and taciturn by nature, but an admirer of the ladies, particularly Miss Gittipin. He is first really moved to speak when Steelyard, interrupted by Miss Gittipin's chatter when he is meditating the profundities of Young and Hervey, snubs her; then Scopprell defends ladies' discourses as more improving than any book, and soon compliments her on her song. Again he is shocked into protest by Quid's satire on marriage; and when Quid calls him a skipping flea and threatens to dash him through his chair, Miss Gittipin rebukes Quid. Later, after a modest refusal, Scopprell is persuaded to sing; his "There's Dr. Clash" is a satire on concerts.

SCOTLAND is North in the quaternary of British nations. It is assigned to Bowen (*J* 71:46), and its counties are divided among the twelve Sons of Israel (*J* 16:52–58). It is particularly associated with Wales, as soul and body. "Wales and Scotland shrink themselves to the west and to the north" (*J* 5:11). Albion's last words relapse "from caverns of Derbyshire & Wales and Scotland" (*J* 23:27). "The murder'd bodies of [Jerusalem's] little ones are Scotland and Wales" (*J* 29:21). "The mountains of Wales & Scotland behold the descending War" (*J* 66:60). "Wales & Scotland alone sustain the fight" (*J* 66:67).

When Albion's plagues recoil from America, they are driven over the Guardians of Ireland and Scotland and Wales, who forsake their frontiers (*Am* 15:13). The rising Albion's left hand covers Scotland, while his right covers Wales (*Mil* 39:42). The four ungenerated Sons of Los dwell over the four provinces of Ireland, "the Four Universities of Scotland, & in Oxford & Cambridge & Winchester" (*J* 71:53). Jerusalem's foundations remain in the counties of Ireland, Wales, England, and Scotland (*J* 72:16).

The SCULL (skull) is the Platonic cavern in which man is now confined; "for man has closed himself up, till he sees all things thro' narrow chinks of his cavern" (*MHH* 14). Oothoon complains: "they inclos'd my infinite brain into a narrow circle" (*VDA* 2:32). It is the "image of that sweet south once open to the heavens and elevated on the human neck, now overgrown with hair and cover'd with a stony roof" (*Eur* 10:27). When Los binds Urizen, the first Age fixes the skeleton, and "a roof, shaggy wild, inclos'd in an orb his fountain of thought" (*Ur* 10:33). Later, the sisters of Tirzah are the ones who form the bones "and the orbed scull around the brain" (*Mil* 19:51–52). At the harvest and vintage of men, the inhabitants of Albion "feel their Brain . . . Bonifying into a Scull" (*J* 58:7).

The SCULPTURES of Los's Halls in Golgonooza are the ideal forms of "all that can happen to Man in his pilgrimage of seventy years" in every conceivable combination. They are the reservoir of inspiration for all artists. Such also are the Old and New Testaments, "the Divine Written Law of Horeb & Sinai and . . . the Holy Gospel of Mount Olivet & Calvary" (*J* 16:61–69). Los's sculptures are the "wonderful originals called in the Sacred Scriptures the Cherubim" (*DesC* II, *K* 565).

When Blake saw something that was perfect, he had the sensation of its becoming fixed, permanent, like sculpture. Such was his vision of lambs, which he described to a lady at one of Mr. Aders' parties. " 'The other evening . . . taking a walk, I came to a meadow and, at the farther corner of it, I saw a fold of lambs. Coming nearer, the ground blushed with flowers; and the wattled cote and its wooly tenants were of an exquisite pastoral beauty. But I looked again, and it proved to be no living flock, but beautiful sculpture.' The lady . . . eagerly interposed, 'I beg your pardon, Mr. Blake, but *may* I ask *where* you saw this?' '*Here*, madam,' answered Blake, touching his forehead" (*Gil* I, 362–63).

The SEA OF TIME AND SPACE is the material world in which we are all submerged. It is the result of Noah's Flood. Its tides and storms beat against the Rock of Eternity, where Albion sleeps. Although it is not named until *The Four Zoas* iv:265, it is pictured earlier in *Visions of the Daughters of Albion* and *America*.

SEA SHELLS are symbols of the mortal body, which is grown by the soul for self-protection, and then discarded and left empty on the shores of the Sea of Time and Space. They belong in the realm of Tharmas (*FZ* iii:167; iv:135; ix:489), who wears a helmet of shell in the picture called "The Circle of Life" (see Illustrations). Sea shells appear in the margin of the fifteenth of the *Illustrations of the Book of Job*, also on *America* 13 and *Jerusalem* 28.

The SECRET CHILD is Jesus, whose birth is promise of the end of the agony of Nature, the Shadowy Female (*Eur* 2:13; 3:2).

SELAH is a word frequently used in the Psalms. It signifies "amen" or "hallelujah." "Amen! Huzza! Selah!" (*J* 27).

The SELF or SELFHOOD is the innate selfishness with which we are born; yet it is not the central Humanity, but is opposed to it. As it develops, it becomes the Spectre (*J* 33:17) and as such is one's Satan (*Mil* 14:30). The Spectre is "the Great Selfhood Satan, Worship'd as God by the Mighty Ones of the Earth, having a white Dot call'd a Center, from which branches out a Circle in continual gyrations: this became a Heart . . . producing many heads, three or seven or ten, & hands & feet innumerable at will of the unfortunate contemplator who becomes his food: such is the way of the Devouring Power" (*J* 33:17–24). "O Polypus of Death! O Spectre over Europe and Asia, withering the Human Form by Laws of Sacrifice for Sin! By Laws of Chastity & Abhorrence I [Erin] am wither'd up; striving to Create a Heaven in which all shall be pure & holy in their Own Selfhoods: in Natural Selfish Chastity to banish Pity and

dear Mutual Forgiveness, & to become One Great Satan inslav'd to the most powerful Selfhood: to murder the Divine Humanity" (*J* 49:24).

The Selfhood is furious in Pride (*J* 43:53; 58:48). It assumes the universal Attributes and appropriates the divine Names (*J* 90:33). It becomes the Covering Cherub and the Antichrist (*J* 89:10).

Unless we can annihilate it, we shall be given into its hands at the Last Judgment (*Mil* 14:24). At the beginning of *Jerusalem*, Blake prays to the Saviour: "Annihilate the Selfhood in me: be thou all my life!" (5:22) "In Selfhood we are nothing" (45:13). Only by giving up Selfhood can Milton resume his separated Sixfold Emanation (*Mil* 17:3). Only by arising from Self into Self Annihilation can one enter Jerusalem's courts (*J* 49:45). Blake pictured the process (*Mil* 16): "To Annihilate the Self-hood of Deceit & False Forgiveness." The youthful Humanity tears down Urizen, who with his tables of Law bars the way to the celestial rejoicings above.

Self-annihilation is not easy. Los speaks of its terrors (*J* 7:61). The Selfhood is the last enemy. "O Lord, what can I do? my Selfhood cruel marches against thee deceitful . . . to meet thee in his pride" (*J* 96:8). But when, for Jesus' sake, Albion gives himself to death in the furnaces of affliction, he achieves eternity instantly, and the Zoas with their fourfold bow shoot the Druid Spectre (*J* 96–98).

SELKIRK is a county of Scotland which, with Dumbarton and Glasgow, is assigned to Issachar (*J* 16:57). With the rest of Scotland, it is assigned to Bowen (*J* 71:46).

SELSEY is the first in Blake's list of the Twenty-four Cathedral Cities. Because of the encroachments of the ocean, the see was removed to Chichester in 1075; the site of the original cathedral is now a mile out to sea.

"Selsey, true friend! who afterwards submitted to be devour'd by the waves of Despair, whose Emanation rose above the flood and was nam'd Chichester, lovely, mild & gentle! Lo! her lambs bleat to the sea-fowls' cry, lamenting still for Albion" (*J* 40:48).

Selsey is under Urizen and Verulam. The redeemed Hand dwells there (*J* 71:11).

SENECA (54 B.C.–A.D. 39) was the most eminent rhetorician of the Silver Age of Latin literature. He was the tutor and later the collaborator of Nero. His style was marked by a profusion of moral aphorisms and *sententiae*. Roger L'Estrange endeavored "to digest and Common-Place" them in his *Seneca's Morals* (1678), which went through many editions.

"The Gospel is Forgiveness of Sins & has No Moral Precepts; these belong to Plato & Seneca & Nero" (On Watson, *K* 395).

The SENSES originally were "all flexible" and could be expanded or contracted at will (*Ur* 3:38; *FZ* ii:296; v:120). They were not limited to special organs, but were diffused all over the being, as Milton's angels were and as the sense of Touch still is. There may well be more senses than the five we know (*MHH* 7; *VDA* 4:15).

However, the Senses became limited in the Fall. Man has "closed himself up, till he sees all things thro' narrow chinks of his cavern" (*MHH* 14). Urizen's Net of Religion caused them to rush inward (*Ur* 25: 29), though later they are described as turning outward.

This limiting of the Senses is a closing out of life; once it is identified with Noah's Flood, "when the five senses whelm'd in deluge o'er the earth-born man" (*Eur* 10: 10). "Beyond the bounds of their own self their senses cannot penetrate" (*FZ* vi:94). Finally, Locke's "Philosophy of Five Senses was complete" (*SoL* 4:16), against which Oothoon protested. "They told me that I had five senses to inclose me up" (*VDA* 2: 31); and she asks how, if not by instinct, the various animals live such different lives: "Is it because of eye, ear, mouth, or skin, or breathing nostrils?" (*VDA* 3:8).

Yet the five Senses remain "the chief inlets of Soul in this age" (*MHH* 4), nor need we be satisfied with their limitations. It does not require the fires of Revolution to consume "the five gates of their law-built heaven" (*Am* 16:19). The ancient poets perceived through "their enlarged & numerous senses" (*MHH* 11), and so can we if we learn to see not with but through the eye. "Five windows light the cavern'd Man," through which he can perceive "small portions of the eternal world that ever groweth; thro' one himself pass out what time he please" (*Eur* iii:1–5). This fifth Sense is Touch, which, according to Milton and Swedenborg, is Sex; then "the whole creation will be consumed and appear infinite and holy" (*MHH* 14).

For Sex differs from the other Senses in still being spread over the entire body, and capable of rousing the deepest ecstasy, even though stunted and "diseased." This differentiation runs through Blake's works: from the death of four daughters of Tiriel, while the fifth, Hela, is left alive, although her hair is turned to snakes (*Tir* v:24–32), to the sixth of the *Illustrations of the Book of Job*, where four arrows descend from Satan's right hand, while his left pours vial of boils upon Job's head.

Consequently, Blake often treated the Four special Senses apart from the fifth.

"The FOUR SENSES are the Four Faces of Man & the Four Rivers of the Water of Life" (On Berkeley, *K* 773). "Each Four Faces had . . . according to the Human Nerves of Sensation, the Four Rivers of the Water of Life. South stood the Nerves of the Eye; East, in Rivers of bliss, the Nerves of the Expansive Nostrils; West flow'd the Parent Sense, the Tongue; North stood the labyrinthine Ear" (*J* 98:12–18). Such are the Four Senses in Eternity; but here on earth they are turned outward or bent down. When the fallen Albion ejects Luvah, he announces that he will so degrade the Senses (*FZ* iii:86; *J* 29:67). The males at the Furnaces lament over their faded Senses (*Mil* 5:21–36); later, this lament is uttered by Erin (*J* 49:34–41). Cambel and her sisters limit the Senses when they weave the embryo (*J* 83:36). When the women torture the males, they repress their Senses (*FZ* viii:301–18; *J* 67:47–68:6).

However, limiting the Senses may be giving a form to error that it may be cast out. Thus Los creates the four Senses of Urizen (*Ur* 11:10–13:11; *FZ* iv:227–40; *Mil* 3:15–23). Later, trying in vain to get Reuben into the Promised Land, he limits his Senses, thus developing his sexual instincts (*J* 34:47–54; 36:5–13).

The SERAPHIM are Affections, the spirits of love whose symbol is fire. They are associated with the Cherubim, spirits of wisdom, whose usual symbol is the heads of children.

The reins of Jerusalem "reveal the flames of holiness, which like a robe covers & like a Veil of Seraphim in flaming fire unceasing burns from Eternity to Eternity" (*J* 86:23). Jerusalem laments: "And thou, America! I once beheld thee, but now behold no more thy golden mountains where my Cherubim & Seraphim rejoic'd together among my little-ones" (*J* 79:53). When Satan appears, he imitates "the Eternal Great Humanity Divine surrounded by his Cherubim & Seraphim in ever happy Eternity"; but Satan has only Cherubim and no Seraphim (*Mil* 39:27).

Thel is the youngest daughter of Mne Seraphim. See MNE SERAPHIM.

The SERPENT has been a symbol of evil ever since it seduced Eve into eating of the fruit of the Tree of the Knowledge of Good and Evil. Blake gives the serpent a number of overlapping meanings, all related.

The first is Hypocrisy. The young Tiriel was "compell'd to pray repugnant & to humble the immortal spirit, till [he was] subtil as a serpent in a paradise, consuming all, both flowers & fruits, insects & warbling birds" (*Tir* viii:36). Hypocrisy is the result of external pressure, and ruins the subject. The self-centered Har and Heva thus lose their human form and become reptiles (*SoL*

4:9). The longest analysis of this process is Blake's study of the degeneration of Revolution. Orc is compelled by Urizen to assume the serpent form and to climb the Tree of Mystery (*FZ* vii:137–63). He has lost all semblance of his original humanity (*FZ* vii *b*:214) and has descended into "that State call'd Satan" (*FZ* viii:383). He encircles Man (*FZ* viii:509) with the twenty-seven folds of the false heavens or churches (*FZ* ix:69) "in forms of priesthood" (*FZ* viii:461). Thus Orc, originally the avowed enemy of religion (*Am* 8:5), becomes his own opposite.

The Priest is serpentine. The Archbishop of Paris arises "in the rushing of scales and hissing of flames and rolling of sulphurous smoke . . . his voice issued harsh grating; instead of words, harsh hissings" (*FR* 127, 177). "Now the sneaking serpent walks in mild humility and the just man rages in the wilds" (*MHH* 2:17). In the first draft of "Infant Sorrow," the priests like serpents embrace the myrtle tree (*K* 167). When Revolution opens the doors of marriage, "the Priests in rustling scales rush into reptile coverts, hiding from the fires of Orc" (*Am* 15:19). Blake, describing the casuistic prose of Bishop Watson, wrote: "The sting of the serpent is in every Sentence as well as the glittering Dissimulation" (On Watson, *K* 384). The Prester Serpent exhorts the warriors to commit the horrors of war: "Listen to the Priest of God, ye warriors: this Cowl upon my head he plac'd in times of Everlasting, and said, 'Go forth & guide my battles . . . Take thou the Seven Diseases of Man . . . to be my great & awful curses at the time appointed' " (*FZ* vii *b*:114).

The Serpent also symbolizes the worship of Nature. Coiled and threatening, he occupies the title page of *Europe*. His church is serpent-shaped. It belongs to Urizen; it was formed "in the order of the stars, when the five senses whelm'd in deluge o'er the earth-born man . . . Thought chang'd the infinite to a serpent, that which pitieth to a devouring flame . . . Then was the serpent temple form'd, image of infinite shut up in finite revolutions, and man became an Angel, Heaven a mighty circle turning, God a tyrant crown'd" (*Eur* 10:2-21). The druid Serpent Temples are found all over the earth (*J* 42:76; 80:48; 100, illustr.). In *America* (14), Vala is depicted beneath a barren tree preaching the doctrines of her serpent to a youth, who turns backward to pray to her, his elbow resting on a couple of books. "Reasonings like vast Serpents infold around my limbs, bruising my minute articulations" (*J* 15:12). There are many pictures of falling men entwined with serpents (as in *Am* 5 and *Ur* 5); on the Laocoön plate, these serpents are labelled "Evil" and "Good."

Finally, the Serpent is Nature herself. Its coils (*MHH* 20; *Eur* t.p.) represent its dull rounds and repetitions. "The Vast form of Nature" is "like a Serpent" (*FZ* iii:97, 101; *J* 29:76, 80). As Nature offers us the seduction of material wealth, the Serpent is often described as of precious stones and gold. "The wild snake [takes] the pestilence to adorn him with gems & gold" (*VDA* 8:7). The degenerating Orc is clad "in scales that shine with gold & rubies" (*FZ* vii:136); eventually he is covered with a variety of precious stones, seven of which are to be found on the high priest's breastplate (*FZ* viii:69-74), while six are worn by the Covering Cherub (*Ezek* xxviii:13). In *Milton* it is Leutha who "form'd the Serpent of precious stones & gold, turn'd poisons on the sultry wastes" (12:29). Among the many pests that flourish round Los's Wine-press is "the Serpent cloth'd in gems & gold" (*Mil* 27:22). "The Princes of the Dead enslave their Votaries, teaching them to form the Serpent of precious stones & gold" (*J* 55:12). When the Covering Cherub finally marches against Jesus, Albion beholds "the Visions of my deadly Sleep . . . dazling around thy skirts like a Serpent of precious stones & gold. I know it is my Self" (*J* 96:11). And finally he sees all things, including "the all wondrous Serpent clothed in gems & rich array, Humanize" (*J* 98:44).

Sometimes it is tempting to interpret the Serpent as a sexual symbol, and that indeed might seem to be its meaning in Blake's design of the infants playing with the serpent (*Thel* 6; *Am* 11), for Blake was well aware of the sexual activities of children. "I saw a chapel all of gold" (*K* 163) is based on the thesis that a forced and unwanted act of sex (the Serpent) is a pollution of the sacrament of real love.

SERUG is the eighteenth of the Twenty-seven Heavens, and the ninth in the second group, the "Female-Males, A Male within a Female hid as in an Ark & Curtains" (*Mil* 37:39; *J* 75:14).

SETH was the third son of Adam, the father of Enos, and an ancestor of Jesus. He is second of the Twenty-seven Heavens, and second in the first group, the "Giants mighty, Hermaphroditic" (*Mil* 37:37; *J* 75:11).

"This State call'd Seth is Male & Female in a higher state of Happiness & wisdom than Noah, being nearer the State of Innocence; beneath the feet of Seth two figures represent the two Seasons of Spring & Autumn, while beneath the feet of Noah Four Seasons represent the Changed State made by the flood. By the side of Seth is Elijah; he comprehends all the Prophetic Characters . . . in like manner The figures of Seth & his wife comprehend the Fathers before the flood & their Generations; when seen remote they appear as One Man; a little below Seth on his right are Two Figures, a Male & Female, with numerous Children; these represent those who were not in the Line of the Church & yet were Saved from among the Antediluvians who Perished; between Seth & these a female figure represents the Solitary State of those who, previous to the Flood, walked with God" (*LJ*, *K* 611; see Illustrations, "LJ" Nos. 62, 63, 69, 60, 66, 67).

SEVEN ANGELS. See ANGELS OF THE PRESENCE, under ANGEL.

SEVEN DISEASES. See DISEASE.

SEVEN EYES. See EYES OF GOD.

The SEVERN is one of England's three chief rivers, the other two being the Thames and the Tweed (Humber). The Severn is in the west, dividing South Wales from Cornwall and emptying into the Bristol Channel. It was named for Sabrina. See SABRINA.

For some reason, Blake associated the Severn with bloodshed. "The brother & the brother bathe in blood upon the Severn" (*FZ* ii:49). "The Humber & the Severn are drunk with the blood of the slain" (*J* 66: 63). "The Sun forgets his course like a drunken man; he hesitates upon the Cheselden hills, thinking to sleep on the Severn. In vain: he is hurried afar . . . He bleeds in torrents of blood" (*J* 66:74).

"Bath stood upon the Severn with Merlin & Bladud & Arthur, the Cup of Rahab in his hand" (*J* 75:2). "Outwoven from Thames & Tweed & Severn, awful streams, twelve ridges of Stone frown over all the Earth in tyrant pride, frown over each River, stupendous Works of Albion's Druid Sons" (*J* 89:20).

SEX, according to Blake, is our most immediate and all-pervading problem. He exalted the act as few Christians have done, extolling its holiness and purity, and preaching the right of free love. Sex, the fifth sense, is the highest and least corrupt. "O holy Generation, Image of regeneration! O point of mutual forgiveness between Enemies! Birthplace of the Lamb of God incomprehensible!" (*J* 7:65). It is the easiest door into Eternity (*Eur* iii:5); it is the paradisal Tree of Life, which Urizen's Cherub prohibits (*MHH* 14).

In Eternity, sexes do not exist, because there the Humanity is completely one with his Emanation. "In Eternity they neither marry nor are given in marriage" (*J* 34:15; cf. *Matt* xxii:30). "Sexes must vanish & cease to be when Albion arises from his dread repose" (*J* 92:13). "Humanity is far above Sexual organization & the Visions of the Night of Beulah, where Sexes wander in dreams of bliss among the Emanations" (*J* 79:73).

Below the sunlight of Eternity is this moonlit night of Beulah. Here the Humanity is divided from his Emanation, but is joined in the perfect marriage. "In Beulah the Female lets down her beautiful Tabernacle, which the Male enters magnificent between her Cherubim and becomes One with her" (*J* 30:34). Here "every Female delights to give her maiden to her husband: the Female searches sea & land for gratifications to the Male Genius, who in return clothes her in gems & gold and feeds her with the food of Eden; hence all her beauty beams" (*J* 69:15). Seen from above, Beulah is a descent into division and dreams; but seen from below, it is an ascent into an ideal, which opens the way into Eternity.

Below Beulah is this material world, the dark realm of Ulro. Here the Female has a will of her own, and the divided sexes war upon each other. By refusing herself, the Female dominates the Male, who then is tormented by love and jealousy. Such a marriage is described in *Milton*: "When I first Married you, I gave you all my whole Soul. I thought that you would love my loves & joy in my delights . . . Then thou wast lovely, mild & gentle; now thou art terrible in jealousy . . . thou hast cruelly cut off my loves in fury till I have no love left for thee" (33:2–7).

But if the husband domineers, the result is equally unhappy. "She who burns with youth . . . is bound in spells of law to one she loathes. And must she drag the chain of life in weary lust? must chilling, murderous thoughts obscure the clear heaven of her eternal spring; to bear the wintry rage of a harsh terror, driv'n to madness, bound to hold a rod over her shrinking shoulders all the day, & all the night to turn the wheel of false desire . . . ?" (*VDA* 5:21).

In either case, sexual repression becomes a religion, intoxicating but bestial at heart. (See Urizen's Temple of the Heart, *FZ* vii *b*:18–38.) Man takes it for granted that "Woman's Love is Sin" (On Lavater, *K* 88), a doctrine zealously promoted by Enitharmon (*Eur* 5:5) as the foundation of her domination. Man comes to believe that "All is Eternal Death unless you can weave a chaste Body over an unchaste Mind" (*J* 21: 11). He contracts the spiritual diseases of Shame and Guilt. "Pale religious letchery [calls] that virginity that wishes but acts not" (*MHH* 27). Marriage is now a bondage of two souls bound back to back, based on "spiritual Hate, from which springs Sexual Love as iron chains" (*J* 54:12). The ecstasy is degraded to the routine of localized false desire, of weary lust (*VDA* 5:23, 27), whereas embraces should be "Cominglings from the Head even to the Feet, and not a pompous High Priest entering by a Secret Place" (*J* 69:43). The Eternals laugh at us when "a Man dare hardly to embrace his own Wife for the terrors of Chastity that they call by the name of Morality" (*J* 36:45). Blake believed that the outstanding fault of historic Christianity was this cult of Chastity (*Eur, passim*).

"He who desires but acts not, breeds pestilence" (*MHH* 7:5). Our sanitariums are crowded with the victims of suppressed desires. Blake anticipated Freud by declaring that the greatest of social evils, war, is a product of this same repression. Anybody who has been frustrated knows how instantly desire can turn to rage. "I must rush again to War, for the Virgin has frown'd & refus'd" (*J* 68:63). See SOTHA and LOINS.

To achieve true happiness, one must be reunited with one's Emanation. Milton, though in heaven, was unhappy until he descended to find his lost Emanation and become one with her. But the process is not esoteric. "For the cherub [inhibition] with his flaming sword is hereby commanded to leave his guard at tree of life; and when he does, the whole creation will be consumed and appear infinite and holy, whereas it now appears finite & corrupt. This will come to pass by an improvement of sensual enjoyment. But first the notion that man has a body distinct from his soul is to be expunged" (*MHH* 14).

SHADDAI is a name of God usually translated "the Almighty." Generally speaking, it was used from Abraham (*Gen* xvii:1) to Moses (*Exod* iii:14). It was preceded by "Elohim" and followed by "Jehovah." Shaddai tormented Job with the belief in his justice (*Job* v:17; vi:4; viii:3; xxiii:17; xxvi:2).

Blake gave Shaddai the role of the Accuser. He is the fourth of the seven Eyes of God, and fails through anger (*FZ* viii:404; *Mil* 13:23; *J* 55:32). Looking backward, he is the lowest point in the flight of angels on the title page of the *Illustrations of the Book of Job*.

However, Shaddai is also paralleled with the pitying Palamabron. Satan is to go to his own place "beneath the Plow of Rintrah & the Harrow of the Almighty in the hands of Palamabron" (*Mil* 4:1), and only a few lines later, "the Harrow of Shaddai" seems to mortals "a Scheme of Human conduct invisible & incomprehensible" (*Mil* 4: 12). Albion is bid repose on the bosoms of the Cathedral Cities "till the Plow of Jehovah and the Harrow of Shaddai have passed over the Dead to awake the Dead to Judgment" (*J* 46:14). "Loud Shaddai & Jehovah thunder above" when they see the victims of the Daughters of Albion (*J* 68: 39). Is this storm a conflict between the wrathful Jehovah-Rintrah and the pitying Shaddai-Palamabron?

Bunyan, to preserve the tone of his marvelous allegory *The Holy War*, wrote "Shaddai" instead of "God" throughout his book.

The SHADOW is a member of the quaternary of the divided Man, the others being the Humanity, the Emanation, and the Spectre (*J* 15:7). The Shadow is the residue of one's suppressed desires. "Being restrain'd, it by degrees becomes passive, till it is only the shadow of desire" (*MHH* 5). When Ahania is cast out, she becomes a Shadow, the mother of pestilence (*Ahan* 2: 38, 41; *FZ* ii:204); and so does Enion (*FZ* i:40; iii:185). When Man worships his own Shadow, Luvah smites him with boils (*FZ* iii:50; *J* 29:37). When Milton sets out to find his lost Emanation, he appropriately enters his Shadow, "a mournful form double, hermaphroditic, male & female in one wonderful body; and he enter'd into it in direful pain, for the dread shadow twenty-seven fold reach'd to the depths of direst Hell & thence to Albion's land, which is this earth of vegetation" (*Mil* 14:37).

In a secondary meaning, the Shadow is a reflection or projection of something else. This "vegetable earth" is a Shadow of the eternal world (*Mil* 29:22; *J* 71:19; 77). The Mundane Shell is a "harden'd shadow of all things upon our Vegetated Earth" (*Mil* 17:22). Vala is a Shadow of Jerusalem, "builded by the Reasoning power in Man" (*J* 11:24; 12:19; 31:41; 44:40). Jerusalem in turn is a Shadow of Albion (*J* 23:1; 60: 36; 85:29); and of course so is England, who contains Jerusalem (*J* 94:7). Woman is the Shadow of Man, and Catherine Blake is the poet's "sweet Shadow of Delight" (*Mil* 36:31; 42:28), although Vala would have it contrariwise: "The Human Divine is Woman's Shadow" (*J* 64:14); indeed the Female Will would "hide the most evident God in a hidden covert, even in the shadows of a Woman" (*J* 34:32).

Thus the Shadow becomes a term for delusion. Los erroneously calls Urthona "but my shadow" (*FZ* iv:43). Albion rejects Jesus as only a "shadow of immortality" (*J* 4: 24), and Jerusalem as "The Shadow of delusions" (*J* 18:11).

The SHADOWY FEMALE is this material world, a fallen form of Vala (*FZ* vii *b*:137, 229). She is a daughter of Urthona (*Am* 1: 1), because Urthona, as Los, daily creates our world, and of Enitharmon (*Eur* 1:4). The birth bursts Enitharmon's heart open forever, but presages war. The Spectre then gives the Shadowy Female charge over the manacled Orc (*FZ* vii:317–32).

Naked except for the cloud about her loins, and unable to speak (make meaning), she keeps Orc alive with food and drink from iron utensils until he reaches the age of fourteen, breaks loose, and embraces her (i.e., Revolution enters the material world). She speaks at last, hailing him as her lover. (*Am* 2:6). The sequel (*Eur* 1:10; 2:4) consists of her agonized cry at her incessant

fertility. She is the voice of the Darwinian world, the struggle for life, "Consumed and consuming . . . howling terrors . . . devouring & devoured." But in the vision of the birth of Jesus, she sees her future salvation, the apocatastasis. See NATURE.

Her story is retold, much expanded, in *The Four Zoas* (vii *b*–viii). "The nameless shadowy Vortex" embraces Orc's fire that he may lose his rage and become meek. He is "jealous that she was Vala, now become Urizen's harlot and the Harlot of Los & the deluded harlot of the Kings of the Earth." He breaks loose, "rending the nameless shadow," and the song of war immediately begins. She varies the war in her delight, "making Lamentations to decieve Tharmas in his rage, to soothe his furious soul," and tells him she is Vala. Her "sweet delusive cruelty" draws the dead from Beulah into Urizen's temple (viii:25). She continues to feed the ravenous Orc; compelled by Urizen's three daughters, she spreads herself through all the branches of the mysterious Tree (viii:80); there her incessant tears saturate the Web of Religion until it sways heavy and falls, entangling Urizen "in his own net, in sorrow, lust, repentance" (viii: 171–81). "Forgetful of his own Laws, pitying he began to embrace the shadowy Female" and sinks to become the Dragon, while his human form petrifies to a mere stone (viii:415–31). The "stony stupor" spreads through all. "Thus in a living death the nameless shadow all things bound: all mortal things made permanent that they may be put off time after time by the Divine Lamb who died for all, and all in him died, & he put off all mortality" (viii:467–84). Thus Nature's initial vision of her salvation in the Nativity is fulfilled in the Crucifixion.

The "Woman Old" of *The Mental Traveller* (*K* 424) plays in part the role of the Shadowy Female. See VALA.

SHAKESPEARE (whose name Blake also spelled three other ways) was one of the three greatest English poets, rated by Blake second only to Milton, the third being Chaucer (*J* 98:9).

Benjamin Heath Malkin recorded that "Venus and Adonis, Tarquin and Lucrece, and his Sonnets . . . now little read, were favourite studies of Mr. Blake's early days" (*Symons* 322); and indeed the influence of Shakespeare's lyrics is obvious in the *Poetical Sketches*. Blake appreciated him much as young Milton did in the last illustration to *L'Allegro*, where the sleeping lad reaches up towards the faintly haloed Shakespeare, who holds the Panpipes of his "native Wood-notes wilde."

When Quid says: "I think that Homer is bombast & Shakespeare is too wild, & Milton has no feelings" (*IslM*, Chap. vii), he is merely repeating the conventional chatter of the critics, which was the exact opposite of what Blake actually thought; but it should be noted that he places the dramatist with Homer and Milton.

Blake did not really begin to appreciate Shakespeare until later. "Shakespeare in riper years gave me his hand" (To Flaxman, 12 Sept 1800).

In *The Marriage of Heaven and Hell* (22), Blake paired Dante and Shakespeare as the sources of infinite inspirations, placing them far above Paracelsus, Behmen, and Swedenborg. In his annotations on Boyd (*K* 411), he placed him with Homer and Dante.

Shakespeare's supernatural beings particularly fascinated Blake, as he understood rightly their psychological significance. "By way of illustration, I instance Shakspeare's Witches in Macbeth. Those who dress them for the stage consider them as wretched old women, and not as Shakspeare intended, the Goddesses of Destiny . . . Shakspeare's Fairies also are the rulers of the vegetable world . . . let them be so considered, and then the poet will be understood, and not else" (*DesC* III, *K* 569). Indeed, when the fairies in *A Midsummer Night's Dream* are understood as the spirits of sex—obvious enough once Blake has said it—the play becomes a brilliant unit.

In the portraits of the poets which Blake executed for Hayley, Shakespeare's supporters are Hamlet with the ghost and Mac-

beth with the witches. He also finished or sketched pictures of Richard III with the ghosts of his victims, Brutus with the ghost of Caesar, Hamlet with the ghost of his father, Macbeth with the ghost of Banquo; also two charming water colors of Oberon and Titania; and a very fine painting of Queen Katherine's vision. The dying queen in the dazzle of her fading eyes perceives a double vortex of angels drawing her heavenward.

Most remarkable is the color print "Pity," which is based on a complicated metaphor in *Macbeth* (I.vii.20) but has nothing to do with the play; also "A Spirit vaulting from a cloud to turn and wind a fiery Pegasus" (*DesC* VI, *K* 581), based on *Henry IV* (IV.i. 109). Again, this has nothing to do with Prince Hal, according to Blake's description: "The Horse of Intellect is leaping from the cliffs of Memory and Reasoning; it is a barren Rock: it is also called the Barren Waste of Locke and Newton." The color print "Hecate" may be intended for "the close contriver of all harms" (*Macbeth* III. v.7), but is otherwise independent of that play.

Besides the obvious imitations in the *Poetical Sketches*, there are two or three verbal echoes from Shakespeare: "The Prince of darkness is a Gentleman" (On Bacon, *K* 399; *King Lear* III.iv.140), and "my Mind's Eye" (*GhA* 1:35; *Hamlet* I.ii.184). Of real interest, however, is "Giving to airy nothing a name and a habitation" (*Mil* 28:3), which is deliberately quoted from *A Midsummer Night's Dream* (V.i.16), where Theseus, the man of reason, lumps together the lunatic, the lover, and the poet as negligible victims of the imagination (thus blaspheming against his own creator). Blake, insisting that "the things imagination saw were as much realities as were gross and tangible facts," objected to Theseus' word "nothing" (*Gil* I, 364).

SHAME was the first sign of the Fall of Man. It did not exist in Paradise until Adam and Eve discovered they were naked (*Gen* iii:7) and hid from God. Early missionaries to the New World were troubled in their theology on learning that the natives apparently had not inherited Adam's shame. "Dishonest shame of natures works, honor dishonorable, sin-bred, how have ye troubl'd all mankind with shews instead, mere shews of seeming pure, and banisht from mans life his happiest life, simplicitie and spotless innocence," wrote Milton (*PL* iv:313), the first English poet to praise nakedness, although Spenser had admired it frankly.

Blake depicted not God but the Angel of the Presence clothing Adam and Eve in skins. He treated Shame as a disease consequent to Albion's Fall (*J* 10:34; 21:3).

SHECHEM, son of Hamor, prince of the Hivites, was the lover of Jacob's daughter Dinah, whom he sought in marriage. Jacob's sons insisted that the Hivites be circumcised first; then, while they were still sore, treacherously slaughtered them all (*Gen* xxxiv).

What to Jacob seemed a mistake in policy seemed to Blake a tragedy of true love. "I see a Feminine Form arise from the Four terrible Zoas, beautiful but terrible, struggling to take a form of beauty, rooted in Shechem: this is Dinah, the youthful form of Erin" (*J* 74:52). See ERIN.

Shechem was also the name of a plain and of a large town in Ephraim's territory. "Mercy & truth are fled away from Shechem & Mount Gilead" (*FZ* viii:320; *J* 68:8).

SHELL, MUNDANE. See MUNDANE SHELL.

SHELLEY. See BARD OF OXFORD, under OXFORD.

SHELLS. See SEA SHELLS.

SHEM was one of the three sons of Noah, and eponym of the Semites. He is the eleventh of the Twenty-seven Heavens, and second in the second group, "the Female-Males, a Male within a Female hid as in an Ark & Curtains" (*Mil* 37:38; *J* 75:13).

"Kox is the Father of Shem & Ham & Japheth, he is the Noah of the Flood of Udan-Adan" (*J* 7:23). "To the Jews ... Your Ancestors derived their origin from Abraham, Heber, Shem and Noah, who were Druids" (*J* 27). "Noah ... on his right hand Shem & on his Left Japhet; these three Persons represent Poetry, Painting & Music, the three Powers in Man of conversing with Paradise, which the flood did not Sweep away" (*LJ*, *K* 609; see Illustrations, "LJ" No. 68).

SHETLAND is an insular county of Scotland. With Orkney and Skye it is assigned to Zebulun (*J* 16:57), and with the rest of Scotland and its isles, to Bowen (*J* 71:46).

SHILOH ("peace") was the sacred first site of the Ark of the Covenant, a sanctuary town in the land assigned to Ephraim. The dying Jacob prophesied: "The sceptre shall not depart from Judah, nor a lawgiver from between his feet, until Shiloh come; and unto him shall the gathering of the people be" (*Gen* xlix:10). The Christians applied this prophecy to Jesus.

Blake identified Shiloh with France (*J* 49:48; 55:29). Although at war, the ideal of both nations was really peace, as the names of both Jerusalem and Shiloh signify.

"Shiloh is in ruins, our brother is sick; Albion, He whom thou lovest is sick; he wanders from his house of Eternity" (*FZ* i: 477). "Destroy these oppressors of Jerusalem & those who ruin Shiloh" (*FZ* i:549). The Giants of Albion "deny that they ever knew Jerusalem, or ever dwelt in Shiloh" (*J* 49:9). "Then they shall arise from Self by Self Annihilation into Jerusalem's Courts & into Shiloh, Shiloh, the Masculine Emanation among the Flowers of Beulah. Lo, Shiloh dwells over France, as Jerusalem over Albion" (*J* 49:45). "The Stars in their courses fought, the Sun, Moon, Heaven, Earth, contending for Albion & for Jerusalem his Emanation, and for Shiloh the Emanation of France, & for lovely Vala" (*J* 55:27). Jerusalem seeks for Shiloh (*J* 79:10). "O lovely mild Jerusalem! O Shiloh of Mount Ephraim!" (*J* 85:22). "Nor can any consummate bliss without being Generated on Earth, of those whose Emanations weave the loves of Beulah for Jerusalem & Shiloh in immortal Golgonooza" (*J* 86:42). All evils shall be "display'd in the Emanative Visions of Canaan, in Jerusalem & in Shiloh" (*J* 92:21).

SHINAR was the Assyrian plain where the city and the tower of Babel were built (*Gen* xi:1–10). Amraphel king of Shinar was one of the combatants in the War of the Four and the Five Kings (*Gen* xiv:1).

Blake wrote as though Babel and Shinar were rival warring cities, perhaps because Jacob Bryant (*Bryant* VI, 336) said that Shinar was a city between Nineveh and Babylon.

"Behold what cruelties are practised in Babel & Shinar, & have approach'd to Zion's Hill. . . . the Spectre saw to Babel & Shinar . . . Kox & Kotope labour mightily in the Wars of Babel & Shinar" (*J* 8:19, 23, 42). During Los's Watch Song, "Babel & Shinar look toward the Western Gate; they sit down silent at his voice; they view the red Globe of fire in Los's hand as he walks from Furnace to Furnace" (*J* 85:18).

SHOOTER'S HILL, a district of London, lies south of the Thames and of Woolwich Common; it is "a conspicuous eminence commanding an extensive and charming view of the richly-wooded plains of Kent" (Baedeker, *London*, 1892, p. 312). "Hoglah on Highgate's heights magnificent Weaves, over trembling Thames to Shooters' Hill and thence to Blackheath, the dark Woof" (*Mil* 35:11).

SHROPSHIRE (Shrops) is a western county of England. With the adjoining counties of Stafford and Hereford, it is assigned to Joseph (*J* 16:49); with the adjoining counties of North Wales, Cheshire, and the Isle of Man, it is assigned to Peachey (*J* 71:30).

SHUAH'S DAUGHTER, a Canaanite, was wife or concubine to Judah, and the mother of Er, Onan, and Shelah (*Gen* xxxviii:2–5).

Blake names her fifth in the Maternal Line from Cainah to Mary (*J* 62:10).

SHUR was a wilderness near Egypt. "Molech rejoices thro' the Land from Havilah to Shur" (*J* 68:38) simply means "from north to south."

SIBERIA is the fifteenth in the list of the Thirty-two Nations who shall guard liberty and rule the rest of the world (*J* 72:39). In Urizen's Temple, "China & India & Siberia are his temples for entertainment" (*J* 58:39).

SIDON and Tyre were sister cities of ancient Phoenicia.

"In Tyre & Sidon I saw Baal & Ashtaroth . . . Veils of Pestilence border'd with War, Woven in Looms of Tyre & Sidon by beautiful Ashtaroth" (*Mil* 37:20, 23). "Druid Temples over the whole Earth with Victims' Sacrifice from Gaza to Damascus, Tyre & Sidon" (*J* 89:32).

SIHON was king of the Amorites. His kingdom lay east of the Jordan, bounded on the north by Gilead (from which it was separated by the Jabbok); on the west by the Dead Sea and the Jordan; on the south by Moab (from which it was separated by the Arnon); and on the east by Ammon. Its capital city was Heshbon.

Sihon refused to let the Israelites pass through his land, and sent his army against them; but at Jahaz he was defeated overwhelmingly in the first great victory of the Israelites. Sihon and all his people were slaughtered and his land occupied (*Numb* xxi:21–31; *Deut* ii:24–36). Reuben and Gad were given the territory.

Sihon, Og, Anak, and Satan constitute an evil quaternary (*FZ* i:508; viii:217; *Mil* 22:33; 37:50), whose function is to oppose Man's progress towards Eternity.

Sihon and Og together constitute the Mundane Shell. Og's kingdom, centered in Orion, consists of the twenty-seven northern constellations; Sihon's kingdom, centered in Ophiuchus, consists of the twenty-one southern constellations. Orion was the giant slain by Artemis, the virgin goddess, representative of the Female Will; Ophiuchus represents Man entangled with the serpent Nature—in the Laocoön plate, the twin serpents of Good and Evil (*Mil* 37: 50–51).

Satan, Og, and Sihon build the mills which unwind the clothing made in Cathedron for the spectres, leaving them naked to the accusing heavens (*FZ* viii:217).

Luvah says erroneously that the quaternary are Jerusalem's sons (*FZ* i:508). The two Sons of Los fear that Milton will loose the four upon Albion (*Mil* 22:33). Erin bids Sihon and Og to remove to their own lands and leave the secret coverts of Albion and the hidden places of America; she also bids the Daughters of Beulah to lament for the two (*J* 48:63–49:3). Og and Sihon in the tears of Balaam have given their power to Joshua and Caleb (*J* 49:58). In the Stomach of the Covering Cherub are seen the enemies of Israel, including Sihon and Og (*J* 89:47).

SILVER is one of the quaternary of symbolic metals, the other three being Gold (south), Iron (north), and Brass (west). Silver stands East (*J* 97:9), and therefore pertains to the affections.

It is frequently associated with Gold, suggesting a combination of love and wisdom, as in the walls and wings of Jerusalem (*J* 85:23; 86:20). Or they may be contrasted: "Can Wisdom be put in a silver rod [the phallus]? Or Love in a golden bowl [the brain]?" (*Thel* i:3). Writers of comedy use Iron (north—intellectual war, i.e., satire) and Silver (love); whereas the writers of tragedy use Gold (wisdom) and Ivory (human woes) to give shape to our "Doubts & fears unform'd" (*Mil* 28:1–9).

Particularly notable is the emphasis on Silver in the "Woes of Urizen" (*FZ* v:189–220). His metal is Gold, but in his Age of Innocence he had plenty of Silver too. His creator gave him a golden crown (to rule with wisdom) and a silver sceptre (to operate with love). He fed his horses of instruc-

tion in silver pastures. Sweet dreams hovered round him when he slept in his silver bed. But now his mountains, where the sons of wisdom dwelt, are no longer silver, but rocks of desolation.

However, Blake seldom tied himself down completely to any dictionary meaning of his symbols, and he was particularly free with the Metals whenever his poetic instinct or painter's eye was operating. For example, Oothoon's "girls of mild silver or of furious gold" (*VDA* 7:24) are merely contrasts in maidenly temperaments.

SIMEON was the second son of Jacob and the eponymous founder of a Tribe.

With his brothers he is listed as a Son of Los who fled (*FZ* viii:360, 375). With six of his brothers, he left Los, to wander with Tirzah, and was generated (*Mil* 24:2). Jerusalem laments his flight (*J* 93:14). When the Daughters of Albion divided him, he "roll'd apart in blood over the Nations, till he took Root beneath the shining Looms of Albion's Daughters in Philistea by the side of Amalek" (*J* 74:44).

In Wales, Los assigns him the county of Cardiganshire; in England, the counties of Lincoln, York, and Lancashire; in Scotland, Ayr, Argyll, and Banff; in Ireland, he shares with Reuben and Levi the six counties of Munster (*J* 16:35, 44, 53; 72:21).

SIN, so-called, is usually some infraction of the artificial code of Morality. "We do not find any where that Satan is Accused of Sin; he is only accused of Unbelief & thereby drawing Man into Sin that he may accuse him. Such is the Last Judgment—a deliverance from Satan's Accusation. Satan thinks that Sin is displeasing to God; he ought to know that Nothing is displeasing to God but Unbelief & Eating of the Tree of Knowledge of Good & Evil" (*LJ*, *K* 615). Eventually Blake came to consider Sin a spiritual disease, cured by the Great Healer's Forgiveness of Sins. "Go therefore, cast out devils in Christ's name; | Heal thou the sick of spiritual disease; | Pity the evil, for thou art not sent | To smite with terror &

with punishments | Those that are sick, like to the Pharisees" (*J* 77:24). See DIS-EASE.

SINAI was the mountain on which Moses received the Decalogue. The first set of Tables was "written by the finger of God" (*Exod* xxxi:18); but it was broken by Moses, who himself wrote the second set. Thus, according to popular belief, God instituted the art of writing: he "Who in mysterious Sinai's awful cave | To Man the wondrous art of writing gave" (*J* 3:3). Sinai is sometimes identified with Horeb.

Although Blake eventually came to believe that "the Divine Written Law of Horeb & Sinai" (*J* 16:68) was a necessary stage in man's history, originally he took it as a work of diabolism. "Moses beheld upon Mount Sinai forms of dark delusion" (*SoL* 3:17). The poisoned rock with which Urizen smote Fuzon "fell upon the Earth, Mount Sinai in Arabia" (*Ahan* 3:45). See COMMANDMENTS.

Sinai thus signifies the stony Law. Milton's body is Mount Sinai (*Mil* 17:14); Sinai and Horeb are Hyle and Coban (*Mil* 19:58); the Selfhood marches from Sinai and Edom against Jesus (*J* 96:9). The torturing Hoglah comes from Mount Sinai (*FZ* viii:316; *J* 68:4). But when the adulteress was brought before Jesus, he laid his hand on Moses' Law, and the earth

On Sinai felt the hand divine
Putting back the bloody shrine,
And she heard the breath of God
As she heard by Eden's flood:
"Good & Evil are no more!
Sinai's trumpets, cease to roar!
Cease, finger of God, to write!"
(*EG* e:11–23)

Blake was not the first to denounce the Old Dispensation in favor of the New. St. Paul (*Heb* xii:18), recalling all the terrors of the original account—the untouchable mountain burning with fire, the blackness and the tempest, the supernatural trumpet, and finally the voice—had contrasted Sinai with Sion, the habitation of angels. Bunyan's Christian was advised by Mr. Worldly Wiseman to go live in the City of Morality; but the pilgrim was so terrified by the burning mountain and the avalanching rocks that he wisely fled for his life.

SION. See ZION.

SIPSOP THE PYTHAGOREAN is the third of the three philosophers with whom *An Island in the Moon* opens. The other two are Suction the Epicurean and Quid the Cynic. "I call them by the names of those sects, tho' the sects are not ever mention'd there, as being quite out of date; however, the things still remain, and the vanities are the same." This remark anticipates Blake's comments on the characters of Chaucer, who seem to differ as the ages pass but are to immortals "only the same . . . Names alter, things never alter" (*DesC* III, *K* 567). But if Blake's three philosophers indicate the beginning of a system, nothing came of it.

Suction is the all-absorbing atheist who lives entirely for his feelings and sensations; Quid is the lively and conceited skeptic who tests all things; but why Sipsop is a Pythagorean is not clear. Pythagoras was a mathematician, but Obtuse Angle is "the Mathematician." Sipsop is a student of surgery; and if Blake read Diogenes Laertius (viii, 12, 14, 32), he may have learned that medicine was among the innumerable subjects which Pythagoras studied. David Erdman (*Erd* 93) ingeniously conjectures that Pythagoras' vegetarianism might account for Sipsop's squeamishness in the operating room. But certainly Sipsop does not symbolize science, as that part is played by Inflammable Gass, the practical experimentalist, at whom Sipsop laughs.

Sipsop is apprenticed to Jack Tearguts, the famous surgeon. "When I think of Surgery—I don't know. I do it because I like it. My father does what he likes, & so do I. I think, somehow, I'll leave it off. There was a woman having her cancer cut, & she shriek'd so that I was quite sick." But except for the brutalities of operations before anesthesia, Sipsop is a gay soul. He plays with a cat, he joins in the singing, he interrupts a silly argument with "Pho! nonsense! hang Pharoh & all his host . . . Sing away, Quid. . . . Hang names!" When Miss Gittipin sings the nursery classic, "This frog he would a-wooing ride," Sipsop cries out: "Hang your serious songs!" and obliges with a song of nonsense syllables which Quid mistakes for Italian. Sipsop was originally intended to be the singer of the satire on the progress of surgery, "When old corruption first begun" (*K* 50), but Blake liked it so well, he assigned it to Quid, and Ellis and Yeats (I, 194) commented: "It may be called Blake's first true symbolic book."

Some of the characters in *An Island in the Moon* have been identified. Blake himself is Quid; Inflammable Gass is as unmistakably Dr. Priestley; and Jack Tearguts is John Hunter, the founder of modern surgery, whose name Blake wrote down and then changed to "Tearguts." George Mills Harper (*Harper* 39) has established that the son of Blake's great admirer, Dr. A. S. Mathew, was Hunter's favorite pupil: "Young Mathew seems to me the best candidate for Sipsop the Pythagorean, who was a surgeon's apprentice with a father of a different profession."

SKIDDAW is the third highest mountain in Britain. It rises 3,053 feet in Cumberland, northwest England.

Here Hand sleeps, dreaming of his Emanation Cambel; drinking his sighs she visits Albion's tree at night, returning to Skiddaw in the morning (*J* 80:57–62). Meanwhile Gwendolen materializes Hyle on East Moor, weaving his "two vessels of seed, beautiful as Skiddaw's snow" (*J* 80:74). Gwendolen utters her falsehood to the Daughters of Albion "standing on Skiddaw's top" (*J* 82:16). Later Bowen and Conwenna stand on Skiddaw, cutting Benjamin's fibres (*J* 90:14).

SKOFELD, SKOFIELD. See SCOFIELD.

SKULL. See SCULL.

SKYE, in Scotland, is the largest island of the Hebrides. Blake called it a county and with Orkney and Shetland assigned it to Zebulun (*J* 16:57). As part of Scotland it is also assigned to Bowen (*J* 71:46).

SLADE (Slaid, Slayd) has not yet been identified; he was presumably connected with Blake's trial. He is the seventh Son of Albion (*J* 5:25). When the Sons flee at the sight of Reuben, Brereton and Slade hide in Egypt (*J* 36:17). In his redeemed state, he dwells in the Cathedral City of Lincoln and is assigned the counties of Stafford, Derby, and Nottingham: "& his lovely Emanation, Gonorill, rejoices over hills & rocks & woods & rivers" (*J* 71:35).

Blake probably intended to assign Lancashire instead of Stafford to Slade, as Stafford is also assigned to Kotope (*J* 71:44), whereas Lancashire is not assigned to any of Albion's Sons.

SLIGO is a county of Ireland, in the western province of Connaught (which was assigned to Joseph). Sligo, with the other counties of Connaught, is assigned to Ephraim, Manasseh, and Benjamin (*J* 72:24).

SMARAGDINE TABLE. See HERMES TRISMEGISTUS.

SNOWDON ("Hill of Snow") is in Carnavon, Wales; it is the highest peak (3,560 feet) in either Wales or England. It is snow-capped for five months every year. Gray used it as the setting of "The Bard." Blake asserted that the three British survivors of the last battle of Arthur (the strongest man, the beautifullest, and the ugliest) still live there: "they are there now, Gray saw them in the person of his bard on Snowdon; there they dwell in naked simplicity; happy is he who can see and converse with them above the shadows of generation and death" (*DesC* V, *K* 578).

Blake considered Snowdon the British equivalent of Mount Gilead. The Universal Family consults "as One Man above [Mount Gilead, *del*] the Mountain of Snowdon Sublime" (*FZ* i:475); and it draws up "the Universal Tent above [Mount Gilead, *del*] High Snowdon" (*FZ* i:552).

"Reuben slept on Penmaenmawr & Levi slept on Snowdon" (*FZ* ii:53). Albion declares: "The Malvern and the Cheviot, the Wolds, Plinlimmon & Snowdon are mine" (*J* 4:30). When war is descending, "Plinlimmon shrunk away: Snowdon trembled" (*J* 66:59).

SOCRATES was the wisest of the Greek philosophers; Blake included his name among those of the great pagans when rebutting Bishop Watson's claim that Christianity had advanced civilization (On Watson, *K* 388). Socrates fell a judicial victim to the accusers Anytus, Meletus, and Lycon. "Socrates taught what Meletus | Loath'd as a Nation's bitterest Curse" (*EG* a:9). "Anytus, Meletus & Lycon thought Socrates a Very Pernicious Man. So Caiphas thought Jesus" (*J* 93).

The gentle Palamabron inspired the Greek philosophers, but the result was "an abstract Law" (*SoL* 3:18). "If Morality was Christianity, Socrates was the Saviour" (*Laoc*, *K* 775; On Thornton, *K* 786). "Plato has made Socrates say that Poets & Prophets do not know or Understand what they write or Utter; this is a most Pernicious Falshood" (*LJ*, *K* 605).

Blake felt very close to Socrates. His countenance, as Crabb Robinson noted, was "Socratic" (*CR* 253), a fact Blake himself was well aware of; indeed, they were both "snubbies."

And it was on this first day that, in answer to a question from me, he said, "*The Spirits told me.*" This led me to say: "Socrates used pretty much the same language. He spoke of his Genius. Now, what affinity or resemblance do you suppose there was between the *Genius* which inspired Socrates and your *Spirits?*" He smiled, and for once it seemed to me as if he had a feeling of vanity gratified. "The same is in our countenances." He paused and said, "I was Socrates"—and then as if he

had gone too far in that—"or a sort of brother. I must have had conversations with him. So I had with Jesus Christ. I have an obscure recollection of having been with both of them."
(*CR* 287, 254)

SODOM and Gomorrah were the two cities of the plain on the Dead Sea which the Lord (Jehovah) destroyed with fire and brimstone, after the men of Sodom had tried to rape Lot's angelic visitors (*Gen* xix). Milton assigned the devil Belial (sloth) as their God (*PL* i:490–505); so Blake also: "Belial of Sodom & Gomorrha, obscure Demon of Bribes and secret Assassinations, not worship'd nor ador'd, but with the finger on the lips & the back turn'd to the light" (*Mil* 37:30).

Because of the attack on the angels, homosexuality is known as "sodomy." Blake did not condemn the practice as such. "What are called the vices in the natural world are the highest sublimities in the spiritual world" (*CR* 262). "It does not signify what the laws of Kings & Priests have call'd Vice; we who are philosophers ought not to call the Staminal Virtues of Humanity by the same name that we call the omissions of intellect springing from poverty" (On Lavater, *K* 88). Only when Albion sets up as "punisher & judge" does he condemn "friendships horrid to think of when enquired deeply into" (*J* 28:3, 7). The real sin of Sodom was not sex but the sloth symbolized by Milton's Belial. "Pride, fullness of bread, & *abundance of Idleness* was the sin of Sodom. See Ezekiel, Ch. xvi, 49 ver" (On Lavater, *K* 79).

However, Blake deplored not the impulse itself but its perversion; not the active expression but the negative inhibition involved. " 'Twas the Greeks' love of war | Turn'd Love into a Boy, | And Woman into a Statue of Stone— | And away fled every Joy" ("Why was Cupid a Boy" 17, *K* 552). The raging warriors invoke the "Double God of Generation" as well as Bacchus and Venus (*J* 68:18). In Plato's sphere of Venus (illustr. 3 to *Il Penseroso*), a youth rejects a weeping female, and Blake's sympathy is obviously with the woman (see Illustrations). Official Christianity can do the same thing with its moral law: "That he who loves Jesus may loathe, terrified, Female love" (*J* 88:20). Blake probably had Cowper in mind.

SODOR and Man is a bishopric on the Isle of Man and the adjacent islands. The cathedral, at Peel, long since fell to ruins. Blake added it to the list of the Twenty-four Cathedral Cities (*J* 46:19). It is under Tharmas and York. The Gate of Zebulun is in Anglesea and Sodor (*J* 16:40).

SOLOMON, the third king of Israel, ruled over Israel's widest extent of territory and brought it to its greatest prosperity. He is supposed to have written the Biblical *Proverbs*, *Ecclesiastes*, and *The Song of Songs*. Blake listed him among "The wisest of the Ancients [who] consider'd what is not too Explicit as the fittest for Instruction, because it rouzes the faculties to act" (To Trusler, 23 Aug 1799). After building the magnificent Temple, Solomon married Pharaoh's daughter (*I Kings* iii:1), and eventually took many wives and concubines of other religions, whose gods he honored in Jerusalem, thereby corrupting his own religion. "Solomon, when he Married Pharoh's daughter & became a Convert to the Heathen Mythology, Talked exactly in this way of Jehovah as a Very inferior object of Man's Contemplation; he also passed him by unalarm'd & was permitted. Jehovah dropped a tear & follow'd him by his Spirit into the Abstract Void; it is called the Divine Mercy" (On Wordsworth, *K* 784).

Solomon is the twenty-third of the Twenty-seven Heavens, and although his reign was notably one of peace, Blake listed him as third in the third group, "the Male-Females, the Dragon Forms, Religion hid in War, a Dragon red & hidden Harlot" (*Mil* 37:42; *J* 75:16). Blake also listed him as the thirty-third son of Los and Enitharmon, placing him between David and Paul (*FZ* viii:361).

SOMERSET is an English county which contains the city of Bath.

With Gloucester and Wiltshire Somerset is assigned to Judah (*J* 16:45); the same three are also assigned to Coban, who dwells in Bath (*J* 71:26).

"A SONG OF LIBERTY" is an appendage to *The Marriage of Heaven and Hell* (25–27). It contains the first telling of the birth of Orc; his rejection by Urizen; the consequent fall of Urizen; his promulgation of the Ten Commandments; and Orc's proclamation of revolution. None of these characters is named, however.

The SONG OF LOS, *Lambeth, printed by W Blake, 1795*, contains eight color-printed plates. Five copies are known.

The Song of Los completes the cycle of the four continents; these are the "four harps" to which Los sang it at the feast of Eternity. *America* and *Europe* had already been published; the *Song* contains the first and the last of the cycle, *Africa* and *Asia*. *The Book of Los* may be read as a prelude.

The complete work tells the story of mankind from Adam in Eden to the Last Judgment, the triumph of death, and the general resurrection caused by the revolution. *Africa* (the land of slavery) begins the tale with man's enslavement under the various religions until the time of Newton and Locke. The last line (4:31) is repeated as the first line of the main text of *America* (3:1), which continues the story with the outbreak of Orc.

Europe belongs in third place in the cycle, ending as the revolution reaches France. The howl in Europe rouses *Asia* into counter-revolution, but the flames of Orc are a pillar of fire; the dead awake to the new thought, while the grave rejoices.

Blake leaves the story there. The cycle stops with the end of *Asia*; *Africa* does not take up the tale again. But the implication is obvious that the millennium is to follow the resurrection, and the triumph of the grave is its fecundating for the generation of the New Age.

SONGS OF INNOCENCE AND OF EX-
PERIENCE. *Songs of Innocence, 1789, the
Author & Printer W. Blake* contains thirty-
one plates. Twenty-two copies of this separate issue are known. The complete work
of fifty-four plates was published in 1794
with the title *Songs of Innocence and of Experience Shewing the Two Contrary States of
the Human Soul.* Twenty-eight copies are
known, plus sixteen issued posthumously.

"Innocence" was the technical word for
the state of the unfallen man; "Experience"
was used by Blake to indicate man's state
after the Fall. The idea of a single work of
two contrasting parts was doubtless suggested by Milton's *L'Allegro* and *Il Penseroso,* which together form a single cyclical
work: where either ends, the other begins.
But where Milton contrasted gaiety and
thoughtfulness, Blake contrasted ecstasy
and despair; and he anticipated not repeti-
tion but progress to a third state.

Blake's obvious parallels are limited to
comparatively few of the poems: the two
"Chimney Sweepers," the two "Nurse's
Songs," the two "Holy Thursdays"; there
are also contrasting titles: "Infant Joy" and
"Infant Sorrow," "The Divine Image" and
"A Divine Image." Some parallel titles are
not real contrasts, but different subjects:
thus "The Little Girl Lost" deals with the
death of a child, while "A Little Girl Lost"
describes her first love affair; and "The Little Boy Lost" describes the child's agony at
being misled, while the second poem with
a similar title tells of his martyrdom for
having his own ideas.

Other poems are contrasted only by subject. Thus "The Lamb" (God's love) is to
be paired with "The Tyger" (God's wrath);
"The Blossom" with "The Sick Rose"; and
probably "The Ecchoing Green" with "The
Garden of Love," and "The Shepherd"
with "London." Beyond this, the reader
may make his own conjectures, because
Blake was not mechanically systematic.

The first poem in the book, the "Introduction" to the *Songs of Innocence,* indicates
the two Contrary States when the piper
plays his tune twice: the first time, the child

laughs, and the second time, he weeps.
But at the third performance (this time
with words) the child weeps with joy—the
third stage where the contraries are synthesized. The last poem of the book, "To Tirzah" (added about 1795), is a fitting conclusion, as it expresses the third stage—
revolution. The lad becomes himself by rejecting the maternal authority, using Jesus'
own words to Mary: "Woman, what have I
to do with thee?" (*John* ii:4). But the sense
goes deeper; for in rejecting the mother,
the lad also rejects what his mother gave
him: his mortal body, with its closed senses
and the misery of sex. When that is tran-
scended, "it is Raised a Spiritual Body"
(*I Cor* xv:44).

SOTHA symbolizes the outbreak of war in
this world. He is the ninth son of Los and
Enitharmon (*FZ* viii:359), but his Emanation Thiralatha (or Diralada) does not appear among the daughters, the ninth being
Moab. Sotha's position is North (*Am* b:21;
SoL 3:30). The North is the place of Los's
spiritual warfare; Sotha is its reduction to
physical conflict.

In *Europe* (14:26), Sotha and Thiralatha
are the fourth and last of the pairs of Enitharmon's children whom she summons to
operate her ideal of Female Chastity. This
unnatural, counterclockwise cycle begins
with Ethinthus (the mortal flesh) and her
consort Manathu-Varcyon in the West,
proceeding through Leutha and Antamon
(south), and the starved lovers Oothoon
and Theotormon (east), to Sotha and Thiralatha (the erotic dream) in the North, "secret dwellers of dreamful caves," their other
attributes being the golden-hoofed thunders
and black horses. They are bidden to please
Orc with their songs. (See ENITHAR-
MON, diagram.)

Thiralatha, or Diralada (*SoL* 3:31), the
dream, is the last overt expression of thwarted sex. Hitherto, in this cycle, the female
has preceded the male; but when they
reach the North, the male, Sotha, reasserts
his priority. His repressed energy breaks
out, perverted into physical war. When sex

is refused, man is set in a rage. War is "energy Enslav'd" (*FZ* ix:152). The warriors cry out: "I must rush again to War, for the Virgin has frown'd & refus'd" (*J* 68:63). "But in the North, to Odin, Sotha gave a Code of War, because of Diralada, thinking to reclaim his joy" (*SoL* 3:30). Thus it was that "the Thor & cruel Odin . . . first rear'd the Polar Caves" (*Mil* 25:53). It was Sotha who seized the northern helm (of the imagination) when "the solemn globe" was launched to the "unknown shore" of war, "till to that void it came & fell" (*Am* b:20).

However, Los puts Sotha and the frustrated Theotormon to good use: they "stand in the Gate of Luban anxious" fabricating soothing forms to net the unborn Spectres (*Mil* 28:21). And in the apocalypse, the released slaves sing a new song of rejoicing, "composed by an African Black from the little Earth of Sotha" (*FZ* ix:686), "earth" being the northern Element.

The SOUTH is the compass-point assigned to Urizen. Its continent is Africa, its British nation is Wales, its river of Eden is Gihon, its Cathedral City is Verulam.

When man falls into his threefold material form, the South rises to the top and becomes the head, "now overgrown with hair and cover'd with a stony roof" (*Eur* 10:29). Thus Reason becomes man's zenith (*J* 12:55), the heaven beyond which he cannot see.

When Urizen, ambitious to conquer the North, bids Luvah soar into the zenith (*FZ* i:495), he is abandoning his proper realm to the Emotions. "When Luvah assum'd the World of Urizen to the South . . . all fell towards the Center in dire ruin sinking down. And in the South remains a burning fire [of Luvah]" (*Mil* 19:19–22).

SOUTH MOLTON STREET is in the West End of London. The open fields to the north were being built over in Blake's time. He lived at 17 South Molton Street after his return from Felpham in the middle of September 1803, until 1821. The title pages of both *Milton* and *Jerusalem* bear this address.

"I write in South Molton Street what I both see and hear in regions of Humanity, in London's opening streets" (*J* 38:42).

The site of the old Tyburn gallows was at the intersection of South Molton Street and Stratford Place, where Tyburn Brook crossed Oxford Street and plunged underground. "Between South Molton Street & Stratford Place, Calvary's foot" (*Mil* 4:21). "The Wound I see in South Molton St[r]eet & Stratford Place" (*J* 74:55).

The SOUTH SEA was that part of the Pacific where the American whalers sought their prey. Edmund Burke paid them a handsome compliment in his *Speech on Conciliation.*

The Shadowy Female cries: "I see a Whale in the South-sea, drinking my soul away" (*Am* 2:14).

SOUTHCOTT (Joanna, 1750–1814), a religious fanatic, declared herself to be the woman of *Revelation* xii. At the age of sixty-four she claimed to be pregnant of the second messiah "Shiloh" by the Holy Ghost; after her death, her supposed pregnancy was proved to be dropsy. Her followers at one time are said to have numbered a hundred thousand.

William Sharp, the engraver, "became a warm partizan of Joanna Southcott. He endeavoured to make a convert of Blake the engraver, but as Fl[axman] judiciously observed, such men as B[lake] are not fond of playing the 2nd. fiddle" (Crabb Robinson's Diary, 30 Jan 1815). Blake's real motive, however, is expressed in his satirical quatrain *On the Virginity of the Virgin Mary & Johanna Southcott* (*K* 418), where he complains of the latter's vacuity.

SPACE and Time at root are one; but in this world they are twin manifestations of Eternity. "Los is by mortals nam'd Time, Enitharmon is nam'd Space" (*Mil* 24:68); but actually Los is the creator of man's span of

Six Thousand Years. "Both Time & Space obey [his] will" (*Mil* 22:17), though only when Enitharmon is obedient.

Enitharmon creates and controls Spaces (*FZ* i:241). Time is Mercy (*Mil* 24:72); she, the feminine half, is Pity (*Ur* 19:1), and her Spaces are always protective. She makes a home for the Male: "She Creates at her will a little moony night & silence with Spaces of sweet gardens & a tent of elegant beauty, closed in by a sandy desart & a night of stars shining and a little tender moon & hovering angels on the wing; and the Male gives a Time & Revolution to her Space till the time of love is passed in ever varying delights" (*J* 69:19). Such a Space is depicted in the third illustration to Dante. Beneath a fruiting grapevine, the female sits by her loom, completely hidden from Empire and the Angry God of This World.

Enitharmon's function is analyzed in the Hayley-Blake quarrel. When Satan and Michael contend, "She wept, she trembled, she kissed Satan, she wept over Michael: she form'd a Space for Satan & Michael & for the poor infected. Trembling she wept over the Space & clos'd it with a tender Moon" (*Mil* 8:42). "Oft Enitharmon enter'd weeping into the Space, there appearing an aged Woman raving along the Streets . . . The nature of a Female Space is this: it shrinks the Organs of Life till they become Finite & Itself seems Infinite. And Satan vibrated in the immensity of the Space, Limited to those without, but Infinite to those within" (*Mil* 10:3–9). She had created this Space "to protect Satan from punishment" (*Mil* 13:13).

The material world itself is a dream, a Space: "The daughters of Beulah follow sleepers in all their Dreams, creating spaces lest they fall into Eternal Death. The Circle of Destiny complete, they gave to it a space and nam'd the space Ulro" (*FZ* i:99). "The Ulro space" (*Mil* 24:39) is also called "Los's Mundane space" (*Mil* 20:21). "Every Space that a Man views . . . such Space is his Universe" (*Mil* 29:5–7).

"The Satanic Space is delusion" (*Mil* 36:20). All crimes and the like "appear only in

the Outward Spheres of Visionary Space and Time" (*J* 92:17). Yet it can be a gate to higher things. Eno "took an atom of space & opened its center into Infinitude & ornamented it with wondrous art" (*FZ* i:225), "with dire pain opening it a Center into Beulah" (*J* 48:38).

See TIME.

SPAIN is the second of the Thirty-two Nations which shall guard liberty and rule the rest of the world (*J* 72:38). Because the conquest of America made Spain the wealthiest of nations, Blake twice called it "golden." France, Spain, and Italy view in terror the effects of the Revolution upon England (*Am* 16:16). "Golden Spain, burst the barriers of old Rome!" (*MHH* 25:4). "France & Spain & Italy [Catholic nations] & Denmark & Holland & Germany [Protestant] are the temples among [the] pillars" of Urizen's temple (*J* 58:41).

In the Golden Age, the Lord gave Jerusalem "Sheep-walks upon the Spanish Mountains" (*J* 60:12). Recalling St. Teresa, Jerusalem says: "Spain was my heavenly couch, I slept in his golden hills; the Lamb of God met me there; there we walked as in our secret chamber among our little ones; they looked upon our loves with joy, they beheld our secret joys with holy raptures of adoration, rap'd sublime in the Visions of God" (*J* 79:40).

SPARROW. Enion laments: "Why fall the Sparrow & the Robin in the foodless winter?" (*FZ* i:446). But Blake had *Matthew* x:29 in mind: "For not one sparrow can suffer & the whole Universe not suffer also in all its Regions, & its Father & Saviour not pity and weep" (*J* 25:8).

In "The Blossom" (*SoI*) the Sparrow is a phallic symbol.

The SPECTRE is the rational power of the divided man (*Mil* 39:10; 40:34; *J* 10:13; 33:5; 36:23; 54:7–16; 64:5; 74:8–10; 91:51). He is one of a quaternary: "I see the Four-fold Man: The Humanity in deadly sleep and its fallen Emanation, The Spectre

& its cruel Shadow" (*J* 15:7). Being separated from its Emanation, the Spectre is completely unable to sympathize with any other person (*J* 53:25; 88:10), and therefore becomes the self-centered Selfhood. See SELF.

This identification with the Selfhood reveals the Spectre's true nature. For the Selfhood is that selfish "superiority complex" which is determined to be the God of the universe. Its "reason" is not the detached, impersonal thing it claims to be; it is not common sense at all; it is "rationalizing," the false reasonings which are invented to justify its selfish desires. The Spectre is ruthless in getting its way, and cares nothing for the Individual it obsesses: it will drive him into unhappiness, disaster, and even suicide. "Each Man is in his Spectre's power | Untill the arrival of that hour | When his Humanity awake | And cast his Spectre into the Lake" (*J* 41, illustr.). This Lake is "the Lake of Los that ever burneth with fire ever & ever, Amen!" (*Mil* 39:11), in which all errors are consumed and annihilated.

"The Negation is the Spectre, the Reasoning Power in Man: this is a false Body, an Incrustation over my Immortal Spirit, a Selfhood which must be put off & annihilated alway" (*Mil* 40:34). "And this is the manner of the Sons of Albion in their strength: they take the Two Contraries which are call'd Qualities, with which Every Substance is clothed: they name them Good & Evil; from them they make an Abstract, which is a Negation, not only of the Substance from which it is derived, a murderer of its own Body, but also a murderer of every Divine Member: it is the Reasoning Power, an Abstract objecting power that Negatives every thing. This is the Spectre of Man, the Holy Reasoning Power, and in its Holiness is closed the Abomination of Desolation" (*J* 10:7). "The Spectre is the Reasoning Power in Man, & when separated from Imagination and closing itself as in steel in a Ratio of the Things of Memory, It thence frames Laws & Moralities to destroy Imagination, the Divine Body, by Martyr-

doms & Wars" (*J* 74:10). It dwells in the Chaos of Memory (*J* 33:1–5; 54:7; 92:22).

The Spectre Selfhood is Satan (*Mil* 38:29; *J* 27:76; 33:18). "The Almighty hath made me his Contrary, to be all evil, all reversed & for ever dead: knowing and seeing life, yet living not" (*J* 10:56). He sets himself up as God; "he is the Great Selfhood, Satan, Worship'd as God by the Mighty Ones of the Earth" (*J* 33:17). "I am God, O Sons of Men! I am your Rational Power" (*J* 54:16).

But although the Spectre is the Rational Power, he is anything but reasonable: rather, he is a machine which has lost its controls and is running wild. "Thou knowest that the Spectre is in Every Man insane, brutish, deform'd, that I [the Spectre] am thus a ravening devouring lust continually craving & devouring" (*FZ* vii:304; also *FZ* i:103; *J* 37:4). His craving is for the lost Emanation. "I have turned my back upon these Heavens builded on cruelty; my Spectre still wandering thro' them follows my Emanation, he hunts her footsteps thro' the snow & the wintry hail & rain" (*Mil* 32:3). "My Spectre around me night & day" (*K* 415) is a poem analyzing an unhappy marriage. "These Spectres have no [Counterparts], therefore they ravin without the food of life" (*FZ* vii:408). "For a Spectre has no Emanation but what it imbibes from decieving a Victim; Then he becomes her Priest & she his Tabernacle" (*J* 65:59).

In *The Four Zoas* (vii:211–397), the Spectre finally encounters Enitharmon; as a result, the Shadowy Female is born, and Los and Enitharmon eat of the fruit of the Tree. The situation does not begin to ameliorate until Los embraces the Spectre (vii:370). At the very end, when Urthona is his complete self once more, "the Spectre Los" himself vanishes (ix:850).

In *Jerusalem*, Los keeps the Spectre and the Emanation apart, lest his negating reason destroy his inspiration. His Emanation divides eastward, while his Spectre divides westward from his back (5:66–6:4). He hungers to devour Los's Humanity, but cannot because "he saw that Los was living"

(6:13–7:1). In spite of the Spectre's discouragements, Los compels him to work with him at the forge, "that Enitharmon may not be lost, & lest he should devour Enitharmon" (17:16–18). He hides the Spectre from Enitharmon, who then acquires a separate will (86:54); the Spectre smiles, "knowing himself the author of their divisions & shrinkings," and debases their love (88:34–44). But Los smites him to fragments on his anvil, and then sends him forth, altering "his Spectre & every Ratio of his Reason . . . time after time . . . till he had completely divided him into a separate space" (91:3–53), and the apocalypse is near.

Anything in which reason and heart are separated has its Spectre. The Cathedral Cities, in their attempt to save man, are obliged to curb their Spectres, the Sons of Albion (*J* 42:67). All four Zoas have Spectres, even Urizen (*FZ* v:173; vii:490). However, we must not expect to understand them always as "reason" but rather as their compulsive machinery. Thus the Spectre of Tharmas (*FZ* i:103–220) is the sexual potency of the male, which awakes and is divided at puberty, when the attraction and repulsion between the sexes begins. Luvah's Spectre is War, the "murderer of Albion" (*Mil* 13:8), but Albion's Spectre is also War.

The SPECTRE OF ALBION appears when Albion is separated from his Emanation, Jerusalem (liberty), and sets himself up as Judge: "Turning his back to the Divine Vision, his Spectrous Chaos before his face appear'd, an Unformed Memory" (*J* 33:1; in the revised version, Blake shifted this plate to follow 28, where Albion becomes the judge); "he is the Great Selfhood, Satan" (*J* 33:17). He is "the Patriarch Druid," author of "Human Sacrifices for Sin in War & in the Druid Temples of the Accuser of Sin, beneath the Oak Groves of Albion that cover'd the whole Earth beneath his Spectre" (*J* 98:48). He is the "destroyer of Definite Form" who dwells in "Non-Entity's dark wild" (*J* 56:17,16), which is the

Chaos of Memory (*J* 33:1). He tears forth from Albion's loins "in all the pomp of War, Satan his name" (*J* 27:37, 73; also *Mil* 29:34; 32:12). As War, he becomes identified with Luvah, or France (*J* 22:31; 41:3; 47:13; 58:20; 60:2; 66:15). When Albion loses control of the Plow of Nations, his Spectre runs it, plowing Albion under (*J* 57:15; 63:3; 64:30). As Satan, were he loosed completely, the traditional Hell would be created (*J* 40:31–42). Instead, he becomes the Covering Cherub (*Mil* 24:28; 37:45).

The SPECTRE OF URTHONA is Los when divided from Enitharmon (*FZ* iv:43, 63; *J* 10:32), although at times they act as separate personalities (as in *FZ* vii:403). He aids in the binding of Urizen (*FZ* iv:194) and Orc (*FZ* v:100). He thwarts Urizen's attempt to enter the North (*FZ* vi:295–313); armed with a club and scaled with iron, he suggests Spenser's Talus, "Made of iron mould, immoveable, resistlesse, without end, who in his hand an yron flale did houlde, with which he thresht out falshood, and did Truth unfould" (*FQ* V.i.12). "Therefore the Sons of Eden praise Urthona's Spectre in Songs, because he kept the Divine Vision in time of trouble" (*J* 30:14; 95:19).

The SPECTRES OF THE DEAD are those wandering fragments of spirit, "the terrific Passions & Affections" (*FZ* viii:208) which have not yet been incarnated, "each male form'd without a counterpart, without a concentering vision" (*FZ* vii:402). They "ravin without the food of life" (*FZ* vii:408). To be saved, they must be incarnated, "for without a Created body the Spectre is Eternal Death" (*FZ* vii:410). They wail around the Tree of Mystery (*FZ* vii:435). "The Spectres of all the inhabitants of Earth, wailing to be Created" are "ever consuming & ever building" the Twenty-seven Heavens or Churches (*J* 13:62). They have come from Beulah. "And now the Spectres of the Dead awake in Beulah; all the Jealousies become Murderous, uniting together in Rahab a Religion of Chastity, forming a Commerce to sell Loves, with Moral Law an Equal Balance not going down with decision. Therefore the Male severe & cruel, fill'd with stern Revenge, mutual Hate returns & mutual Deceit & mutual Fear" (*J* 69:32).

Los and Enitharmon agree to create their bodies. "Weeping, the Spectres view'd the immortal works of Los, Assimilating to those forms, Embodied & Lovely in youth & beauty, in the arms of Enitharmon mild reposing" (*FZ* vii:473). She erects the looms of Cathedron; "in these Looms she wove the Spectres Bodies of Vegetation, singing lulling Cadences to drive away despair from the poor wondering spectres" (*FZ* viii:37); these bodies open "within their hearts & in their loins & in their brain to Beulah . . . and some were woven single, & some twofold, and some threefold" (*FZ* viii:55–58). They become a vast family, also the single female, Jerusalem (*FZ* viii:182–190). The Sons of Eden sing of the process, which makes the incarnation of Jesus possible; and "Astonish'd, stupified with delight, the terrors put on their sweet clothing on the banks of Arnon, whence they plunge into the river of space for a period, till the dread Sleep of Ulro is past" (*FZ* viii:214).

In *Milton*, the process is described at greater length, and the outcome is not so joyous. The types of Spectres are differentiated: the piteous sufferer, the fearful doubter, the seeker for cruelty. The Sons and Daughters of Los conduct the operation: Antamon (instead of Los himself) "draw[s] the indelible line" and the Daughters weave the form. Meanwhile Theotormon and Sotha terrify the cruel Spectre into their net; "howling the Spectres flee: they take refuge in Human lineaments" and are "born a weeping terror" (*Mil* 28:10–28); "Like a fiend hid in a cloud" (*SoE*, "Infant Sorrow" 4). In Bowlahoola they choose their affinities, thus marking out their various Classes (*Mil* 26:38).

But at birth the Spectres do not change their natures. (What is more self-centered than a baby?) "Man is born a Spectre or

Satan & is altogether an Evil, & requires a New Selfhood continually & must continually be changed into his direct Contrary" (*J* 52). "The Veil of Vala is composed of the Spectres of the Dead" (*J* 47:12); it becomes "the beautiful Mundane Shell, the Habitation of the Spectres of the Dead, & the Place of Redemption & of awaking again into Eternity" (*J* 59:7). "The Spectres of the Dead howl round the porches of Los in the terrible Family feuds of Albion's cities & villages, to devour the Body of Albion, hung'ring & thirsting & rav'ning. The Sons of Los clothe them & feed" (*J* 73:46).

SPENSER (Edmund, 1552?–99) was Milton's "original," and Milton in turn became Blake's original, thus establishing the symbolic line in English literature. "An Imitation of Spencer" (*PS*) proves that Blake admired him early. The six stanzas are all different and all wrong; but this seeming carelessness was quite in the tradition of the followers of Spenser, who usually tried to "improve" his famous stanza: from Barnfield (1595) to Shenstone (1742) practically no correct Spenserians are to be found; nor was Blake ever the man to aspire to pedantic conformity.

The Faerie Queene is an allegory, of which Blake disapproved, and furthermore is based (not too precisely) on the Aristotelian virtues and vices; nevertheless Blake evidently found the epic to be "full of vision," like *Pilgrim's Progress* (*LJ*, *K* 604).

Blake's criticism of Spenser is to be found in his painting "Spenser's *Faerie Queene*" (*ca.* 1815; see Illustrations). It was obviously planned as a companion piece to "Chaucer's Canterbury Pilgrims" (1809): each depicts a cavalcade of characters, but the two groups move in contrary directions. In order to make the pictures balance, there is some correspondence between the two sets of characters. Redcrosse, like Chaucer's Knight, leads the cavalcade; Una, next to him, balances the Prioresse; Sir Guyon looks backward, just as does the Pardoner; then with extended arms Amoret holds the center of the picture, like Harry Bailey. But these parallels are aesthetic only; for the deeper significance, we must study the symbols in the skies above them.

Spenser's characters are progressing from Babylon to the New Jerusalem. On the far right Babylon, identified by Nimrod's Tower and other pagan architecture, is dominated by the red-rayed Molech, who commands the sacrifice of the baby of the two parents standing at the flaming altar. Next (to the left) is Justice with her even scales; haloed against a background of stars, she is canopied by a thick cloud. Between her and the central figure of the God of This World is a symbol of the beginning of art: under a rainbow a seated youth, with his left elbow on a book, draws on a sketching pad while his winged inspiration turns inward. The God of This World (the globe floating before him) blindly extends a sword in his left hand. His red star-pointed halo is overarched by a heavy cloud through which black rays pierce. His closed eyes do not see (to the left) the gateway to the Bower of Bliss and the temple of the bisexual Venus, represented by a dome extended into a spire. Next to the God is Mercy, who counterbalances Justice. Mercy is the true church, the woman of *Revelation* x with the moon under her feet; she is surrounded by crowds of babies. She soars upward with arms extended above the New Jerusalem, an irradiant Gothic cathedral.

The characters of the poem are aligned in Spenser's own order, as follows. Book I, "Holinesse": the procession is led by Redcrosse and Una, who rides on the ass with the open Bible in her lap. A haloed boy leads her lion by a thread; the expiring dragon is just behind them. Book II, "Temperance": the Palmer, holding Amavia's babe, stands before Sir Guyon. Blake did not endorse what he considered Sir Guyon's prudery. The knight stares backward at his ideal (Amoret), completely overlooking his own animal nature, a powerful hairy male (naked except for drawers and a sword), who grins up obscenely at him, while he holds Amoret's bridle. Sir Guyon's spear is

pointed blindly upward at the Bower of Bliss, which he is to destroy. Books III and IV, "Chastity" and "Friendship": Amoret sits sidesaddle with arms extended in the cruciform position (like Mercy above and Harry Bailey). She is "th' ensample of true loue alone, and Lodestarre of all chaste affections" (*FQ* III.vi.50); as such she properly holds the center of the picture, whereas her warlike twin, the armed Britomart, does not appear at all. Blake did not approve of amazons. Above Amoret, in the middle distance, Sir Scudamore in a cave looks down the path to Busyrane's palace where a double-pointed flame burns directly in front of the entrance. In the heavens, the empty and relaxed hand of the God of This World dangles over Amoret's head. Book V, "Justice": Sir Arthegall, wearing a crown, points with his left hand to the figure of Justice above him. His uplifted left hand almost touches the sword-point of the God of This World. Beneath his rearing horse is a thistle. Behind him stands the iron-colored, spiky-haired Talus with his flail and spear. Prince Arthur comes next, in his magnificent helmet, but without his diamond shield. His left hand points upward to the child-sacrifice of Molech, calling attention to its horrors, while his right hand points forward. Book VI, "Courtesy": Sir Calydore, riding behind, points with his spear to the child-sacrifice. He looks backward at two bound Babylonian captives, a young woman and an old man, between whom is the Blatant Beast. The rear hooves of Sir Calydore's horse trample a heap of stones from which emerge the head and hands of a man caught in the pit. A small spirit drags the Beast by a chain; another sits on its muzzle, binding the flame-belching jaws with thread; a third perches on the shoulder of the male captive, and a fourth on the head of the female.

On the extreme left, in the middle distance, just before the head of Redcrosse's horse is Spenser himself, symbolized as a sage crouching in a cave. He studies an open tome on the ground but points upward; a youth bending over him, also reading, presses with both hands against the roof of the cave.

It is needless to remark that many important characters besides Britomart (and how many there are in *The Faerie Queene*!) are omitted. The painting itself is filled with minute figures which have become blurred with age and neglect, so that it would be easy to overlook significant details.

Spenser's influence on Blake is evident from the first. "An Imitation of Spencer" (*PS*) attempts to utilize the pagan gods in Spenser's manner. Blake invokes Apollo, the god of poetry, and rejects Pan, the god of superficial verse. He then invokes Mercury, the eloquent messenger direct from heaven, and asks the warrior maid Minerva if she ever feels pity. "For soule is forme, and doth the bodie make" (*Hymn to Beauty* 132) is an obvious precursor of "the body or outward form of Man is derived from the Poetic Genius" (*AllR* 1). The jealous Theotormon, paralyzed on the threshold of Bromion's cave (*VDA* 2:6), strongly resembles Spenser's jealous Malbecco (*FQ* III.x.60) petrifying in his cave. The Spectre of Urthona (*FZ* vi:295) suggests Talus (*FQ* V.i.12). Vala's shadowy garden (*FZ* ix:376) is the garden around the temple of Spenser's Venus (*FQ* IV.x.23–27). Spenser described Verulam at length (*Ruines of Time*), but erroneously located it on the Thames, a mistake repeated by Blake (*Eur* 10:5). Spenser married the Thames and the Medway (*FQ* IV.xi); Blake called them "rivers of Beulah" (*J* 4:34). He would also have noted Spenser's use of Albion (*FQ* II.x.11; IV.xi.16).

The SPIDER was observed by Blake with the precise eye of the painter and the sympathy of the poet. "The Spider sits in his labour'd Web, eager watching for the Fly. Presently comes a famish'd Bird & takes away the Spider. His Web is left all desolate that his little anxious heart so careful wove & spread it out with sighs and weariness" (*FZ* i:457). This is not symbolism, but only an example of the cruelties in nature.

However, when Blake wrote "The ambi-tious Spider in his sullen web," he was seeing not with but through the eye. The Spider is then among the vermin which spring up in wartime, around the Wine-press of Luvah (*Mil* 27:13–17; also *FZ* ix:758, where this line had not yet been added). It is even a cause of war: when the demons sing the wedding song of Los and Enitharmon, they call on the Spider to spread his web, to humanize, and summon his hosts (*FZ* i:404).

When the Sons of Urizen are building the material universe, "all the time, in Caverns shut, the golden Looms erected first spun, then wove the Atmospheres; there the Spider & Worm plied the wing'd shuttle, piping shrill thro' all the list'ning threads" (*FZ* ii:145). When Ozoth is protecting the joys of life from the Spectre, he creates the Spider and other vermin; "they worship before his feet in trembling fear" (*Mil* 28:43); but later it is the Daughters of Los who "create the Silk-worm & the Spider & the Catterpiller to assist in their most grievous work of pity & compassion" (*J* 59:46). In the Last Judgment, the spider and bat, "the Furious forms of Tharmas humanizing," burst from the hardened slime, crying out to one another in wonder (*FZ* ix:608, 613).

STAFFORD is a Midland English county which is assigned, with the adjoining Shropshire and Hereford, to Joseph (*J* 16:49). Apparently by error it is also assigned to two different Sons of Albion: to Slade (*J* 71:34) and to Kotope (*J* 71:44). As Joseph and Kotope are both eleventh sons, the assignment of Stafford to Kotope is probably right. Slade therefore would have Lancashire instead, which (by another oversight) is not assigned to any Son of Albion.

The STARRY HOSTS are the Israelites, who follow Urizen through the Wilderness, where he promulgates the Ten Commandments (*MHH* 26:18; *Am* 8:4).

The STARRY SEVEN (*Mil* 22:1, etc.), or the seven Angels of the Presence (*Mil* 14:42, etc.), are the seven Eyes of God, the series of States, which revolve as inevitably as the stars. See EYES OF GOD.

The STARS symbolize Reason. (Their dim light is equated with Reason in the opening lines of Dryden's *Religio Laici*.) They are a member of a quaternary: Sun (imagination), Moon (love), Stars (reason), and Earth (the senses). They are assigned to Urizen.

They are the visible machinery of the astronomical universe, and may be considered as Fate. Originally they were part of Man, "but now the Starry Heavens are fled from the mighty limbs of Albion" (*J* 27; 34:20; 70:32; 75:27). They are created in "the Mills of Theotormon on the verge of the Lake of Udan-Adan" (*Mil* 27:49). They are "the boundaries of Kingdoms, Provinces, and Empires of Chaos, invisible to the Vegetable Man" (*Mil* 37:48), and constitute the Mundane Shell, "a mighty Incrustation of Forty-eight deformed Human Wonders of the Almighty" (*Mil* 37:53), the Forty-eight being the forty-eight constellations, and the Almighty being Shaddai. See ORION and OPHIUC[H]US.

"In that dread night when Urizen call'd the stars round his feet," the whole universe was disorganized and took its present form (*Am* b:5). Elsewhere Urizen recalls how he disobeyed the divine Fiat of *Genesis* i:3; rather than guide Man, who was wandering on the ocean, "I hid myself in black clouds of my wrath; I call'd the stars around my feet in the night of councils dark; the stars threw down their spears & fled naked away" (*FZ* v:222). This reference definitely places the creation of the Tyger (*SoE*) later than that of the Lamb, and would seem to make Urizen the Tyger's creator.

As I read the "Introduction" of the *Songs of Experience*, the lapsed soul "might controll | The starry pole | And fallen, fallen light renew." But the soul persists in turning away from Jesus, the Holy Word, and therefore is given mercifully "The starry floor, | The wat'ry shore" until the true day breaks.

STATE RELIGIONS, or established churches, are "codes given under pretence of divine command, [which] were what Christ pronounced them, The Abomination that maketh desolate, i.e., State Religion, which is the source of all Cruelty" (On Watson, *K* 393). "The English Crusade against [atheist] France. Is it not . . . State Religion?" (On Watson, *K* 385).

STATES are stages of error, which the Divine Mercy creates (or defines) so that the State and not the Individual in it shall be blamed. Each period of life has its own peculiar errors; as one grows out of one period into another, one is maturing. "Man Passes on, but States remain for Ever; he passes thro' them like a traveller" (*LJ, K* 606).

Blake first mentions a state, "the State called Satan," in *The Four Zoas* (viii:285). "There is a State nam'd Satan; learn distinct to know, O Rahab! the difference between States & Individuals of those States" (viii:379). "The Evil is Created into a State, that Men may be deliver'd time after time evermore. Amen. Learn therefore . . . to distinguish the Eternal Human . . . from those States or Worlds in which the Spirit travels. This is the only means to Forgiveness of Enemies" (*J* 49:70–75).

The seven Eyes of God are the stages of Experience, successive attempts to find that State which will die for Satan, that is, sacrifice himself to redeem Error. The first Eye, Lucifer (the morning star) explains: "We are not Individuals but States, Combinations of Individuals. . . . Distinguish therefore States from Individuals in those States. States Change, but Individual Identities never change nor cease. . . . Satan & Adam are States Created into Twenty-seven Churches, and thou, O Milton, art a State about to be Created, called Eternal Annihilation [self-sacrifice] . . . Death and Hell & the Grave [are] States that are not, but ah! Seem to be. . . . The Imagination is not a State: it is the Human Existence itself. . . . The Memory is a State always, & the Reason is a State Created to be Annihilated & a new Ratio Created" (*Mil* 32:8–35).

Chapter i of *Jerusalem* ends with the plea of the Daughters of Beulah: "Descend, O

Lamb of God, & take away the imputation of Sin by the Creation of States & the deliverance of Individuals Evermore" (*J* 25: 12). The succeeding chapters represent the passage of Albion through these States to his Redemption. "And the Center has Eternal States; these States we now explore" (*J* 71:9), and these states of the heart are a list of the Sons and Daughters of Albion.

In *A Vision of the Last Judgment*, the characters depicted are not the individuals named, "but the States Signified by those Names . . . these various States I have seen in my Imagination; when distant they appear as One Man, but as you approach they appear Multitudes of Nations" (*LJ, K* 607).

STEPNEY was a very ancient village east of London. Los, when perambulating London, passes through old Stratford and Stepney, to the Isle of Dogs (*J* 31:15).

STERLING (i.e., Stirling) is a county of Scotland which, with Sutherland and Wigtoun, is assigned to Asher (*J* 16:56). Being a part of Scotland, it is also assigned to Bowen (*J* 71:46).

The STOMACH is Bowlahoola in every individual man (*Mil* 24:67). It corresponds to Los's Furnaces, "terrible their fury" (*Mil* 24:59; *J* 53:13). It is the fourth stage of fallen Humanity; it is "dreadful, it is named Or-Ulro. . . . terrible, deadly, unutterable" (*Mil* 34:8–16). Yet it is a Gate, which the descending Ololon, apparently in an act of supreme self-sacrifice, seeks out (*Mil* 34: 19). Vala "vegetated into a hungry Stomach & a devouring Tongue" (*J* 64:8). The devouring stomach of the Covering Cherub contains Jerusalem "in allegoric delusion & woe," also the seven kings of Canaan, the five Baalim of Philistea, and the giants (*J* 89:43–46).

STONE, LONDON: See LONDON STONE, under LONDON.

STONE OF BOHAN. See BOHAN.

The STONE OF NIGHT is the druidic doctrine of revenge. When Orc first appears, "Albion's Angel wrathful burnt beside the Stone of Night" (*Am* 7:1). King George takes his stand "on the vast stone whose name is Truth" (*Am c*:10), but "truth" in name only. The Stone is enclosed within a coil of the Serpent Temple by the southern porch, in a heavily wooded vale. "Oblique it stood, o'erhung with purple flowers and berries red [deadly nightshade], image of that sweet south once open to the heavens, and elevated on the human neck, now overgrown with hair and cover'd with a stony roof." But fallen man is now upside down and in a state of war. "Downward 'Tis sunk beneath th'attractive north, that round the feet, a raging whirlpool, draws the dizzy enquirer to his grave. Albion's Angel rose upon the Stone of Night" (*Eur* 10:26–11:1); "& aged ignorance preaches, canting, on a vast rock, perciev'd by those senses that are clos'd from thought" (*Eur* 12:7). Although situated in Verulam (*Eur* 10:5), it overshadows London city with "the Serpent temple lifted above, shadowing the Island white" (*Eur* 12:9, 11).

STONEHENGE is a fane of enormous standing stones on Salisbury Plain, Wiltshire, dating from the Bronze Age. Inigo Jones thought it was a Roman temple. John Aubrey (1626–97) was the first to conjecture that it was Druid; William Stukeley (1742) elaborated the theory, which is still popularly believed, though the fane is much earlier. It seems to have been built for sunworship, and was also used as a burial place. One slab is known as "the slaughter stone."

Blake accepted the common belief and used Stonehenge as a symbol of the evil Druid religion and its human sacrifices. It was built by the warriors, and is Natural Religion (*J* 66:2, 8). Here the Daughters of Albion torture their victims (*J* 66:20); here Brittannia murdered Albion "with the Knife of the Druid" (*J* 94:25). It is associated with London Stone and the Oak Groves of Malden's Cove (*J* 58:46; 68:44; 94:24). See SALISBURY PLAIN.

Stonehenge was sometimes called "The Dance of the Giants." Blake referred to this dance in describing the disruption of the universe consequent upon the establishment of Natural Religion. "We reared mighty Stones, we danced naked around them, thinking to bring Love into light of day, to Jerusalem's shame displaying our Giant limbs to all the winds of heaven. Sudden Shame siez'd us, we could not look on one-another for abhorrence: the Blue of our immortal Veins & all their Hosts fled from our Limbs and wander'd distant in a dismal Night clouded & dark. The Sun fled from the Briton's forehead, the Moon from his mighty loins, Scandinavia fled with all his mountains fill'd with groans" (J 24:4).

Although there were many more stones, Blake specified only twelve "Stones of Power" (J 68:41; 80:45; 89:21), like the twelve pillars of the Serpent Temple "plac'd in the order of the stars" (Eur 10:10). He was particularly impressed by the trilithons, which appear in his pictures, especially the magnificent one on Jerusalem 70. See also Milton 4, 6 and Illustrations of the Book of Job 6, 7.

STONES. FOUR PRECIOUS STONES constitute the southern Gate of Los, which leads into Beulah. It is guarded by Fenelon, Guion, Teresa, Whitefield, and Hervey, "with all the gentle Souls who guide the great Winepress of Love" (J 72:49–52). This Gate is mentioned earlier: "A World of Generation continually Creating out of the Hermaphroditic Satanic World of rocky destiny, and formed into Four precious stones for enterance from Beulah" (J 58:50–59:1) — a confused statement which suggests that Plate 59 has been moved from its original position.

ROCKING STONES are huge boulders poised on a narrow base so nicely that a little pressure makes them rock without dislodging them. To a generation ignorant of the Ice Ages, they seemed to be the work of giants. "So Los spoke. And the Giants of Albion, terrified & ashamed with Los's thunderous

Words, began to build trembling rocking Stones, for his Words roll in thunders & lightnings among the Temples; terrified rocking to & fro upon the earth, & sometimes resting in a Circle in Malden or in Strathness or Dura" (J 90:58). There is a picture of a rocking stone on Milton 6.

The STONES OF FIRE are to be found in Ezekiel's denunciation of the prince of Tyre (Ezek xxviii:13–16): "Thou hast been in Eden, the garden of God . . . Thou art the anointed cherub that covereth . . . Thou hast walked up and down in the midst of the stones of fire. Thou wast perfect in thy ways from the day that thou wast created, till iniquity was found in thee. . . . I will destroy thee, O covering cherub, from the midst of the stones of fire."

This placing of the prince in the garden of Eden has caused him to be given a deeper identity than that of a single political figure. In The Gates of Paradise (Prologue 4) it is the Accuser "who walk'd among the Stones of Fire," but in Jerusalem (49:72) it is man himself who has fallen: "Learn therefore, O Sisters, to distinguish the Eternal Human that walks about among the stones of fire in bliss & woe."

"STORGE" is the Greek word for parental affection, which Blake would have found in Swedenborg's Conjugial Love 395.

The Five Females (daughters of Zelophehad) and the Shadowy Mother (Vala), sitting in the Ulro, weave the physical bodies with songs of amorous delight, "that lure the Sleepers in Beulah down the River Storge (which is Arnon) into the Dead Sea" (Mil 34:30), i.e., through the female genital tract down into the Sea of Time and Space. See ARNON.

When Orc is bound, Los gives the Spectre "sternest charge over the howling fiend, concenter'd into Love of Parent, Storgous Appetite, Craving" (FZ v:112).

STRATFORD, or Stratford-le-Bow, is a London district in the borough of Poplar. Los's forge is heard "to Stratford & old

Bow & across to the Gardens of Kensington on Tyburn's Brook" (*Mil* 6:9). Los, when perambulating London, walks "to old Stratford & thence to Stepney" (*J* 31:15). See BOW.

STRATFORD PLACE intersects South Molton Street; there Tyburn Brook crossed Oxford Street and plunged underground. "Between South Molton Street & Stratford Place, Calvary's foot" (*Mil* 4:21). "The Wound I see in South Molton St[r]eet & Stratford place" (*J* 74:55).

STRATHNESS (which, with Dura, I cannot find in any atlas, gazetteer, or guidebook) is probably the valley (strath) of the river Ness, in Inverness, Scotland. According to Blake, it contains a circle of "druid" stones (*J* 90:62).

STRUMBOLO, or Strumbolo House, was a pleasure garden, which featured fireworks. Hand's indignation "rose up against [Los] thundering, from the Brook of Albion's River, from Ranelagh & Strumbolo, from Cromwell's gardens & Chelsea" (*J* 8:1).

According to Paul Miner, Strumbolo House in the eighteenth century was actually in the parish of St. George's, Hanover Square, although it is usually located in Chelsea. It is now 77–79 Pimlico Road, and carries the original stone tablet reading "STRUMBOLO, HOUSE AND GARDENS. 1765." In 1958–59 the upper floors were converted into flats and the premises were also converted into flats, partly rebuilt.

SUCCOTH was a highland city north of the Jabbok, on the eastern bank of the Jordan. "The clay ground between Succoth and Zarthan [Zaretan]" furnished the materials for the casting of the metal ornaments to adorn Solomon's Temple (*I Kings* vii:46).

In the strife between Urizen and Milton, the latter takes "the red clay of Succoth" to model a human form on Urizen's bones (*Mil* 19:10). Reuben sleeps on a valley of Bashan, "cut off from Albion's mountains & from all the Earth's summits between Succoth & Zaretan" (*J* 34:45).

SUCTION THE EPICUREAN is the first-named of the three philosophers in *An Island in the Moon* (Chaps. i–iii; v–vii; ix). He is of course an atheist like Epicurus (*J* 67:12) and lives the life of the senses, despising everything else. "I hate reasoning. I do everything by my feelings" (*K* 50). "Hang Philosophy! I would not give a farthing for it! Do all by your feelings, and never think at all about it" (*K* 51). He is a painter. "If I don't knock them all up next year in the Exhibition, I'll be hang'd . . . I'm hang'd if I don't get up to-morrow morning by four o'clock & work Sir Joshua" (*K* 51). He likes his liquor. "Let's have some rum & water, & hang the mathematics" (*K* 49). "I say, this evening we'll all get drunk" (*K* 54).

He calls Voltaire a fool (*K* 45); believes he can paint better than Reynolds (*K* 51); invents an insulting song against Dr. Johnson's classical aspirations (*K* 54); and takes a slap at Dryden's *Parallel of Poetry and Painting* (which Reynolds admired) when he propounds the absurd question "if Pindar was not a better Poet than Ghiotto was a Painter" (*K* 49), a question which nobody tackles.

As he lives with Quid, Erdman identifies him with Robert Blake (*Erd* 90).

SUFFOLK is a county on the east coast of England. With Norfolk and Essex it is assigned to Reuben (*J* 16:44); with these and four others, it is assigned to Scofield (*J* 71:39).

SULPHUR, when burning, emits a powerful mephitic odor which is traditionally associated with hell-fire. "The Archbishop of Paris arose in the rushing of scales and hissing of flames and rolling of sulphurous smoke" (*FR* 126). "Some lying on beds of sulphur" (*FZ* vi:105).

The "sulphur sun" (*Am* b:7; *FZ* ii:128; *Mil* 21:20) is the material sun, as contrasted with the spiritual sun. See SUN.

SUMMER. See WINTER.

The SUN is the symbol of the imagination, and is one in a quaternary: Sun (imagination), Moon (love), Stars (reason), and Earth (the senses). It is associated with the Divine Vision and the Divine Family (*Mil* 21:40; *J* 29:1; 62:34), with Los (*Mil* 22:6), and with the forehead (*J* 24:10).

Swedenborg distinguished the spiritual sun (love) from the material sun (heat); so did Blake. "The dead Sun is only a phantasy of evil Man" (On Swed *DL*, *K* 92). But Blake identified them instead with the imagination and reason (or the material world). On Primrose Hill, the spiritual sun told Blake that he was not the material sun, who was the Greek Apollo or Satan. See PRIMROSE HILL. Blake depicted Urizen as Apollo driving his chariot of light in *Illustrations of the Book of Job* 14.

The "sulphur sun" (*Am b*:7; *FZ* ii:128; *Mil* 21:20) is the material sun. When man was divided, this sun was rent from Mars (*Am* 5:5)—spiritual warfare being a prime activity of Eternity—and became materialized. It was rent from the Briton's forehead (*J* 24:10). "The golden Gate of Havilah and all the Garden of God was caught up with the Sun in one day of fury and war" (*J* 49:15).

Los gave it form: he created and launched it after the binding of Urizen; he then bound Urizen's vast spine "to the glowing illusion" (*BoL* 5:27–47). Los beat the fiery beam of Fuzon "in a mass with the body of the sun" (*Ahan* 2:47). Later, Blake decided that Los creates the sulphur sun every morning (*Mil* 29:23, 41).

For the Sun of Salah, see SALAH.

The SUNFLOWER, rooted in the earth yet keeping its blossom turned towards the sun, is a symbol of man's spiritual aspirations, which cannot be attained while he is still rooted in the flesh.

"Ah! Sun-flower" (*SoE*) is one of Blake's most beautiful lyrics. The flower ends its day facing the sunset in the west, where lies America, the land of liberty, but also the place of death, "Where the traveller's journey is done." To this place those overburdened with the flesh aspire. The Sunflower thus becomes the death wish, though not the wish of annihilation.

Blake depicted the flower in the right margin (left margin in the original painting) of the eighty-seventh illustration to Young's *Night Thoughts* (iii:117–23). The poet sustains the dying Narcissa and gazes appealingly to the chariot of the indifferent Apollo, who drives into blackening clouds. The Sunflower rises behind Young; a female form emerges from the blossom, stretching her hands vainly toward the sun.

On *Jerusalem* 23, the Sunflower, rising from the Sea of Time and Space, is the throne of Vala, who wears the papal tiara. Her wings contain the moon, the stars, and the world, but not the sun. Her church is based on the yearning to escape the flesh into a future immortality.

Albert S. Roe (*Roe* 195) has identified the Rose of Heaven (99th illustr. to Dante), on which the Virgin kneels in glory, as the Sunflower.

SUPERSTITION, being honest belief, was defended by Blake against the Age of Reason. However, he distinguished it sharply from the false and dishonest beliefs promulgated by the religious. Then "honesty [is] bound in the dens of superstition" (*FR* 228), and the will-o'-the-wisp "Friar's Lantern" leads the bewildered youth "to the Convent" (illustr. 5 to *L'Allegro*, *K* 618).

"No man was ever truly superstitious who was not truly religious as far as he knew. True superstition is ignorant honesty & this is beloved of god and man. I do not allow that there is such a thing as superstition taken in the strict sense of the word. A man must first decieve himself before he is thus Superstitious and so he is a hypocrite. Hipocrisy is as distant from superstition as the wolf from the lamb" (On Lavater 342, *K* 75). "Superstition has been long a bugbear by reason of its being united with hypocrisy; but let them be fairly seperated & then superstition will be honest feeling, & God, who loves all honest men, will lead the poor enthusiast in the paths of holiness" (On Lavater 605, *K* 85). "Chaucer . . . was very devout, and paid respect to true enthusiastic superstition" (*DesC* III, *K* 575).

The color print "Hecate," "the close contriver of all harms" (*Macbeth* III.v.7), represents superstition in a deeper sense. She is triple, according to mythology: a girl and a boy hide their heads behind her back. Her left hand lies on a book of magic; her left foot is extended. She is attended by a thistle-eating ass, the mournful owl of false wisdom, the head of a crocodile (blood-thirsty hypocrisy), and a cat-headed bat.

See REPHAIM.

SURGERY and Physic are the temporal expressions of Painting (*Mil* 27:60). The art of Painting deals with the outward man and his world; the medical profession deals with the physical man. For a satire on Surgery, see "When old corruption first begun" (*IslM*, Chap. vi).

SURREY is a southeastern county of England which lies between Middlesex (to the north, across the Thames), Kent (to the east), and Sussex (to the south). These four counties constitute the southeast corner of Great Britain; they are assigned to Hand (*J* 71:11). Without Sussex, the remaining three are assigned to Levi (*J* 16:45).

In Surrey was Blake's beloved Lambeth (which is now in the new county of London); therefore Surrey was a place of great inspiration. Here was Los's forge: "The Surrey hills glow like the clinkers of the furnace; Lambeth's Vale . . . dark gleams before the Furnace-mouth, a heap of burning ashes" (*Mil* 6:14–17). "Surrey and Sussex are Enitharmon's Chamber" (*J* 83:25). "Los & Enitharmon rose over the Hills of Surrey" (*Mil* 42:31). Jerusalem "fled to Lambeth's mild Vale and hid herself beneath the Surrey Hills" (*J* 41:11). The Emanation "is made receptive of Generation thro' mercy

in the Potter's Furnace among the Funeral Urns of Beulah, from Surrey hills thro' Italy and Greece to Hinnom's vale" (*J* 53:27). See HINNOM.

One special cause of inspiration was the secret and over-fervent love affair of *The Crystal Cabinet* (*K* 429), which took place in a "pleasant Surrey bower." "Remember all thy feigned terrors on the secret couch of Lambeth's Vale" (*J* 65:42). For more details, see LAMBETH.

But materialism and the wars threatened the inspiration. Vala cast her dark threads "over the trembling River and over the valleys from the hills of Hertfordshire to the hills of Surrey across Middlesex" (*J* 31:67). "In all the dark Atlantic vale down from the hills of Surrey a black water accumulates" (*J* 4:9). "The little villages of Middlesex & Surrey hunger & thirst" (*J* 30:25). "The plains of Sussex & Surrey . . . no more seek to Jerusalem" (*J* 79:18). Hand and the double Boadicea "in cruel pride cut Reuben apart from the Hills of Surrey" (*J* 90:25). Enitharmon, reduced to a faint rainbow, "waved before [Los] in the awful gloom of London City on the Thames from Surrey Hills to Highgate" (*J* 83:67).

Surrey is twice associated with Rephaim. "Tirzah & her sisters weave the black Woof of Death upon Entuthon Benython, in the Vale of Surrey, where Horeb terminates in Rephaim" (*Mil* 29:55), that is, in the Indefinite, where the Law terminates in superstition. Jerusalem "fled to Lambeth's mild Vale and hid herself beneath the Surrey Hills where Rephaim terminates" (*J* 41:11). See REPHAIM.

SUSSEX is a county on the south coast of England. With the adjoining counties of Hampshire and Berkshire, it is assigned to Asher (*J* 16:47). With the adjoining counties of Surrey, Kent, and Middlesex, it is assigned to Hand (*J* 71:11). Felpham, the village where Blake lived for three years under the patronage of Hayley, is in Sussex; consequently it was a place of inspiration. "Surrey and Sussex are Enitharmon's Chamber" (*J* 83:25). Chichester, the cathedral city where Blake was tried for treason, is also in Sussex.

The war had a sinister effect on the various counties. "Sussex & Kent are [Jerusalem's] scatter'd garments" (*J* 29:20). "The plains of Sussex & Surrey ... no more seek to Jerusalem" (*J* 79:18). "Sussex shuts up her Villages" (*J* 83:9). After Enitharmon has declared in scorn and jealousy that "This is Woman's World ... she sat down on Sussex shore, singing lulling cadences & playing in sweet intoxication among the glistening Fibres of Los" (*J* 88:16–25).

Blake's letter to Butts (22 Sept 1800), in raptures on his arrival, is in contrast to his petulant epigram against William Haines (*K* 538): "The Sussex Men are Noted Fools."

SUTHERLAN[D], a county of northern Scotland, is assigned with Stirling and Wigtoun to Asher (*J* 16:56). Being part of Scotland, it is also assigned to Bowen (*J* 71:46).

SWEDEN is the seventh of the Thirty-two Nations which shall guard liberty and rule the rest of the world (*J* 72:38). Poland and Russia and Sweden are the "soft retired chambers" in Urizen's temple (*J* 58:40).

SWEDENBORG (Emanuel, 1688–1772) was one of the leading scientists of his generation when at the age of fifty-seven his spiritual eyes were opened. For years he explored Heaven and Hell and conversed with their inhabitants under the divine command to teach the new doctrines. He resigned all his posts, to write about his visions and his interpretation of the Scriptures. In 1757 he witnessed the Last Judgment, when the Second Coming of Jesus (the final revelation of truth) inaugurated his New Church (which, however, he never considered to be a separate sect). In 1771 he went to London, where a Swedenborgian group was being organized; he had a shock on Christmas Eve, and died in London, March 29, 1772, aged eighty-five. His works were not translated into English until after his death.

Swedenborg's writings belong very definitely in the Revolutionary period (1760–98), when radical ideas were also germinating in literature, politics, and economics. His books represent the revolutionary spirit in religion: the reintroduction of the imagination, the psychological explorations for new thoughts, and the revaluation of the old.

Swedenborg had an amazing power of visualizing thoughts into symbols; these visualizings were characterized by the "minute particulars" which Blake accepted as the proofs of true vision. For example: "When the satan had heard this, his countenance, from being bright at first, turned ghastly, and then black, and speaking from his own mouth he said, 'You have uttered paradoxes on paradoxes' " (*True Christian Religion*, par. 71; parodied by Blake, as noted in *Gleckner* 309).

The legend that Blake was born into a Swedenborgian household has been completely demolished by David Erdman ("Blake's Early Swedenborgianism," *Comp. Lit.* 1953, V, 247–57). Blake could scarcely have known his writings until they were translated into English; and the first of these was *Heaven and Hell*, published in 1778 when the poet was twenty-one. The Theosophical Society, founded to translate the works of the Swedish sage, began publishing in 1788. The New Church in England was founded on January 27, 1788. On April 13, 1789, Blake and his wife signed the attendance sheet at the open Conference; he then procured and annotated the *Divine Love*, and the next year the *Divine Providence*. But he resisted all efforts to persuade him to join the Church.

Besides these two books, we know that he read the *Heaven and Hell* (which he parodied), *Conjugial Love* ("his sexual system is dangerous," *CR* 260), *True Christian Religion* (which inspired a picture), and also apparently the *Apocalypse Revealed*, as well as others. Nor did Blake hesitate to give Swedenborg great praise. "The works of this visionary are well worthy the attention of Painters and Poets; they are foundations for grand things; the reason they have not been more attended to is because corporeal demons have gained a predominance" (*DesC* VIII, *K* 581). Even in *The Marriage of Heaven and Hell*, Swedenborg is the Angel of the Resurrection, and his books are the guidebooks for travelling in eternity. In *Milton* (22:50) he is hailed "O Swedenborg! strongest of men." Blake told Crabb Robinson, on December 10, 1825: "He was a divine teacher—he has done much good, and will do much good—he has corrected many errors of Popery and also of Luther and Calvin . . . Swedenborg was wrong in endeavouring to explain to the rational faculty what the reason cannot comprehend" (*CR* 257). Apparently Blake considered Swedenborg's visions as the same as Dante's, though Dante was the greater poet.

Blake adopted, or adapted, many of Swedenborg's ideas. Both accepted Jesus as the only God, who contains the two other members of the Trinity as aspects but not as persons: "Jesus, our Father, who art in thy heaven call'd by thy Name the Holy Ghost" (On Thornton, *K* 788). He descended to save man, getting nothing from Mary but his mortal body and human nature, which he put off completely by living the truth: "He took on Sin in the Virgin's Womb, and put it off on the Cross & Tomb" (*EG* b:57). His Second Coming was the final revelation of truth; it took place in 1757 (the year of Blake's birth), when the New Church was inaugurated by the revelation. This was the Last Judgment of the entire world, when all things were reduced into order, and the spiritual equilibrium between good and evil, or Heaven and Hell, was restored. "As a new heaven is begun, and it is now thirty-three years since its advent, the Eternal Hell revives. And lo! Swedenborg is the Angel sitting at the tomb"(*MHH* 3).

Jesus created all things from the divine substance of love and wisdom. The "Grand Man" (Blake's Albion) is heaven, or the human form of society, and is the image of God. (See "The Divine Image," *SoI.*) The man and woman of a perfect marriage become a single "angel" in eternity. The physical world is merely a symbol of the spiritual world (Blake's "vegetable looking-glass"). Swedenborg called these symbols "correspondences"; when Blake saw not with but through the eye, he saw the spiritual meaning of things; but he interpreted them according to his own poetic insight, and not according to the Swedenborgian dictionary of correspondences. Like Swedenborg, Blake distinguished between the spiritual and material suns.

Swedenborg selected certain books of the Bible—the Law, the prophets, the *Psalms*, the four Gospels, and *Revelation*—as inspired, and to be understood symbolically; Blake accepted them also as such, and listed them in *Jerusalem* (48:9–11).

There are many other indications that Blake read Swedenborg thoroughly. He probably found the word "storge" in *Conjugial Love* (395), and the explanation of the *ijim* and *ochim* in *True Christian Religion* (par. 45). But so much in Swedenborg is paralleled in Behmen, not to mention Holy Writ, that it is not always possible to say which was Blake's source.

But he did not accept Swedenborg's doctrines blindly; and as was his practice, he attacked Swedenborg's errors the more fiercely for the very reason that he admired him so much. The greater the seer, the more dangerous his errors. In the annotations to *Divine Love*, Blake is already translating Swedenborg's ideas into his own terms; the mystic is expanding the doctrines of the philosopher. "Good & Evil are here both Good & the two contraries Married" (*K* 91) is a point of departure; also the final annotation, "Heaven & Hell are born together" (*K* 96). But in the annotations to *Divine Providence*, Blake disagrees flatly with Swedenborg's idea of predestination.

Swedenborg's greatest error, according to Blake, lay in his not understanding the real nature of "evil," and therefore accepting conventional morality. "He conversed with Angels . . . & conversed not with Devils . . ." (*MHH* 21). Consequently, everything is classified as Good or Evil, and Swedenborg's universe, in its final state, is no universe, being irreparably split in two: the heaven of the Good above and the hell of the Evil below. "O Swedenborg! strongest of men, the Samson shorn by the Churches, shewing the Transgressors in Hell, the proud Warriors in Heaven, Heaven as a Punisher, & Hell as One under Punishment" (*Mil* 22:50). On the other hand, Blake had made his own universe a unit by identifying Heaven and Hell not with states of a future life, but with powers eternally within every individual—with what we now call the superego and the id. They are essential to each other; they are the contraries which work together. To label them as "good" and "evil" is meaningless. The dreadful dichotomy of official Christianity, which Swedenborg had accepted, was healed; the universe was one again; and a new period of human thought was inaugurated.

The Marriage of Heaven and Hell (1790–93) was the proclamation of this new age. It is the first manifesto of modern psychology. It is also a book which the Swedenborgians will probably never forgive, for in the exuberance of his great discovery Blake not only renounced his former teacher but ridiculed him. The title points straight to Swedenborg's error. He is indeed the Angel of the Resurrection, but "his writings are the linen clothes folded up," which preserved the divine form in the time of death, but are now cast off as useless. The "Memorable Fancies" parody Swedenborg's "Memorable Relations." Sex is no longer divided into the good "conjugial" marriage and the evil "scortatory" affairs: it is the very Tree of Life, to be forbidden only at one's peril. The angels are the conventional persons, complacent and unintelligent, whereas the devils are the original thinkers, delighting in the flames of creation ("which to Angels look like torment and insanity"); and Blake more than hints that the tempting Devil is the real Messiah.

Blake's final attack is reserved for the text just before the last "Memorable Fancy." "Swedenborg boasts that what he writes is new; tho' it is only the Contents or Index of already publish'd books. . . . he shews the folly of churches, & exposes hypocrites, till he imagines that all are religious, & himself the single one on earth that ever broke a net. Now hear a plain fact: Swedenborg has not written one new truth. Now hear another: he has written all the old falsehoods. . . . Thus Swedenborg's writings are a recapitulation of all superficial opinions, and an analysis of the more sublime—but no further. Have now another plain fact. Any man of mechanical talents may, from the writings of Paracelsus or Jacob Behmen, produce ten thousand volumes of equal value with Swedenborg's, and from those of Dante or Shakespear an infinite number" (*MHH* 21).

One feels as though Newton were denouncing Galileo. But it must be remembered that Blake is characteristically overstating his case; and these denunciations are to be read in the light of his several later affirmations that Swedenborg was "a divine teacher."

The SYNAGOGUE OF SATAN (*Rev* ii:9; iii:9) is the worldly church. When Satan sets himself up as God, "all the Spectres of the Dead, calling themselves Sons of God, in his Synagogues worship Satan under the Unutterable Name" (*Mil* 11:13). The Synagogue consists of the twelve pagan gods and the Twenty-seven Churches of Beulah, "a Double Twelve & Thrice Nine" (*Mil* 37:18). Blake sees them in Milton, but when Milton faces Satan, he shakes down the Synagogues as webs (*Mil* 38:42).

The Synagogue is Urizen's temple (*FZ* viii:30). He calls it together "in dire Sanhedrim to judge the Lamb of God to Death." It meets "twelvefold in Amalek, twelve rocky unshap'd forms, terrific forms of torture & woe." When Vala appears in it, they clothe her in scarlet robes and gems as Mystery the Whore of Babylon (*FZ* viii:272–94). After the Crucifixion, Vala is divided in her mind; sometimes she is repentant and communes with Orc in secret; sometimes she returns to the Synagogue in pride. The Synagogue then unites against her, and burns her to death; but her ashes animate and become Natural Religion (*FZ* viii:606–20).

.

T

A TABERNACLE is the shrine for a god. "Osiris, Isis, Orus in Egypt, dark their Tabernacles on Nile" (*Mil* 37:27). It is the holy place for an ideal. The starry warriors make a religion of their dead heroes, "with blood weaving the deaths of the Mighty into a Tabernacle for Rahab & Tirzah" (*J* 67:33). It may be a protective hiding place for an ideal; thus the falling Enion weaves a tabernacle for Jerusalem (*FZ* i:70); and the Eight, when they flee, close up Albion's death-couch as a tabernacle (*Mil* 20:48).

Specifically, the Tabernacle was the portable shrine carried by the Israelites through the Wilderness. It was heavily curtained; behind the Veil was the Holy of Holies, which contained the Ark (see ARK OF THE COVENANT), where dwelt the invisible God. It was the result of the corruption of love into the eternal torment of love and jealousy on this earth: "stolen by secret amorous theft [from Beulah] till they have had Punishment enough to make them commit Crimes. Hence rose the Tabernacle in the Wilderness & all its Offerings, from Male & Female Loves in Beulah & their Jealousies" (*J* 69:26).

In the religion of sex, the female genitals constitute her Tabernacle (*J* 21:21; 30:34; 68:15, 49; 80:26). Enitharmon, proclaiming the supremacy of Woman, weaves "a triple Female Tabernacle for Moral Law" (*J* 88:19). But the females also weave the mortal body as a tabernacle to protect the Lamb (*Mil* 13:26; *J* 56:40).

Liberty is every man's ideal: Jerusalem is "in every man, a Tent & Tabernacle of Mutual Forgiveness" (*J* 54:4). Though re-

duced and perverted, she is even "hidden within the Covering Cherub, as in a Tabernacle of threefold workmanship, in allegoric delusion & woe" (*J* 89:44). But when Albion turns from his ideal towards nature worship, he begs Vala to hide him in her Scarlet Tabernacle (*J* 22:30), but himself becomes "the Tabernacle of Vala & her Temple, and not the Tabernacle & Temple of the Most High" (*J* 34:29).

The god hidden and invisible within the tabernacle is the fixed idea operating as subconscious motivation, irresistible because it is unacknowledged. Thus Vala, the goddess of Natural Religion, becomes the "hidden Harlot" who motivates the dragon War (*Mil* 37:43; *J* 89:52).

Most curious: our victim becomes our own Emanation, dwelling hidden in our Tabernacle. When Luvah (France) is being tortured to death on the druid Stone of Trial, the spectre Sons of Albion drink in his Emanation, "for a Spectre has no Emanation but what he imbibes from decieving a Victim: Then he becomes her Priest & she his Tabernacle" (*J* 65:59); as a result, "their iron necks bend unwilling towards Luvah . . . they become like what they behold" (*J* 65:77). Meanwhile the Daughters of Albion suddenly behold Vala, "the Emanation of their murder'd Enemy, become their Emanation and their Temple and Tabernacle" (*J* 65:69). When Milton finally faces Satan, he says: "Satan! my Spectre! I know my power thee to annihilate and be a greater in thy place & be thy Tabernacle, a covering for thee to do thy will, till one greater comes and smites me as I smote thee & becomes my covering" (*Mil* 38:29). But Milton, instead of founding a new religion on the destruction of the old (which would then operate unseen), practises instead Self-Annihilation.

TAMAR, a Canaanite woman, is sixth in Blake's list of the Maternal Line from Cainah to Mary (*J* 62:10). Tamar married successively Er and Onan, sons of Judah, both of whom were slain by the Lord. Being still childless, she disguised herself as a harlot and lay with her father-in-law, Judah, who begot on her the twins Pharez and Zarah (*Gen* xxxviii). Pharez was an ancestor of Jesus (*Matt* i:3).

TARTARY was a huge undefined waste sparsely inhabited by nomadic Tartars. The Asian portion, which once reached to Siberia, was "Great Tartary."

Tartary is the fourteenth of the Thirty-two Nations which shall guard liberty and rule the rest of the world (*J* 72:39). Great Tartary is the inmost hall in Urizen's Temple (*J* 58:38).

At the finish of the harper's song, "Albion trembled [eastward] to Italy . . . to Tartary . . . & to Great America" (*Mil* 14:6). At the approach of Hand, "the Wild Tartar that never knew Man starts from his lofty places & casts down his tents & flees away" (*J* 84:23). When the warrior is smitten by sex, "his spear and sword faint in his hand from Albion across Great Tartary" (*J* 68:51). The Scandinavian gods erect their altars "from Ireland's rocks to Scandinavia, Persia, and Tartary" (*J* 83:21). Those who "consummate bliss" and are generated view "the Winding Worm on the Desarts of Great Tartary" (*J* 86:42, 46).

TAXES had increased heavily because of the wars. Blake, referring to *Luke* ii:2, identified Empire with Tax (*Laoc*, *K* 777). Vala's weaving "turn'd fierce with the Lives of Men . . . Taxing the Nations" (*J* 64:33). Elsewhere it is "the Triple Headed Gog-Magog Giant" that "Taxed the Nations into Desolation" (*J* 98:52).

TAYLOR (Thomas, 1758–1835) was commonly called "the Platonist" because of his translations of Plato and the Neo-Platonists, and because of his rejection of Christianity in favor of Greek theology and mythology.

The cause of his steadfast devotion to paganism was his own mystical experiences, which he attained apparently through studying the mathematics of Proclus, for whom he named his youngest son. At least once he experienced what he called the conjunction of "the phantasy" with divinity; and a single event of this sort is quite enough to account for his lifetime devotion to expounding his occult philosophy.

Taylor, a modest man, apparently never told anyone of his ecstasies, so that his biographers have not known of them. But the evidence lies in his own annotated copy of his *The Philosophical and Mathematical Commentaries of Proclus*, London, 1788 (now in the Houghton Library, Harvard University), as Dr. Ronald Levinson informed me. Included in the second volume is his "History of the Restoration of the Platonic Theology," in which he described the process of intellectual illumination which culminates in the mystical ecstasy. On page 277 he underlined a couple of significant phrases: "We may add too, as a symbol of this exalted purgation, that a perpetual serenity, unceasing delight, and *occasional rapture will be produced in the soul*. . . . Such too will be the temperament of the soul in this case, that *she will spontaneously utter musical sounds, as indications of the harmony within; and as echoes of the perpetual felicity she enjoys*." This second sentence is marked "N.B." with the marginal note: "I wrote this from my own experience at the time. T. T."

Bound in with this volume is Taylor's unpublished manuscript "Medicina mentis, A specimen of Theological Arithmetic. By Thomas Taylor. Far ye profane, far off!"

In 1784 (or less probably 1785) Taylor broke loose from his "thraldom" at the bank where he worked, and wrote twelve lectures on the Platonic philosophy, which he delivered in the largest room of Flax-

man's house. The lectures were well attended by the intellectuals, and it would be
straining credulity too far to suppose that
Blake was not there, and did not make Taylor's acquaintance.

For in *An Island in the Moon* (1784), Taylor, as Obtuse Angle (*Harper* 40), is a familiar figure. He is "the Mathematician"
and a friend of Steelyard (Flaxman). He has
a very exalted estimate of Phoebus, to
whom he ascribes practically all the arts
and sciences. Taylor had said that Newton
was "no philosopher"; Obtuse Angle says
the same of Voltaire (Chap. i, *K* 45). He is a
great arguer, to the point of being a bore.
Blake preserved other characteristics which
we cannot verify today. "Obtuse Angle, entering the room, having made a gentle bow,
proceeded to empty his pockets of a vast
number of papers, turned about & sat
down, wiped his face with his pocket hand-
kerchief & shutting his eyes, began to
scratch his head." He says he always understands better when he shuts his eyes
(*K* 45). He fixes his eyes on a corner of the
ceiling when he sings "To be, or not to be."
His head-scratching and face-wiping are
also referred to again. Blake liked him, as
he assigned him the innocent "Holy Thursday" for his other song. The manuscript
stops with " 'Oh I am glad you are come,'
said Quid" (Chap. xi, *K* 63).

Taylor's influence on Blake was immediate. Blake adopted eagerly Taylor's insistence that the ancients wrote obscurely, veil-
ing their deeper meanings in symbols. *All
Religions are One* (1788) anticipated Taylor's *The Spirit of All Religion* (1790—a title
which I have found only in *Webster's Bio-
graphical Dictionary*; but Taylor's bibliography is so uncertain and obscure that this
is not wholly surprising). Blake's *The Book
of Thel* (1789) anticipated Taylor's *Dissertation on the Eleusinian Mysteries* (1790). In
Visions of the Daughters of Albion, Oothoon
plucks Persephone's flower. But it is needless to go into details. Professor Harper has
done an excellent job in tracing parallels
which prove that Blake was wholly sympathetic to this new world of non-Christian

thought (*Harper*). Inevitably, as was his
custom, he helped himself to whatever he
wished and transformed it into his own. Most
surprisingly, he liked his fellow mystic so
well that he never attacked him. Not until
he turned against all classicism, as a result
of his visit to the Truchsessian Gallery in
October 1804 (To Hayley, 22 Oct 1804), did
he even suggest that he disapproved of Taylor's mathematical approach to God, and
then only in a couple of obscure grumbles:
"God forbid that Truth should be Confined
to Mathematical Demonstration!" (On
Reynolds, *K* 474), and "The Gods of
Greece & Egypt were Mathematical Diagrams—See Plato's Works" (*Laoc, K* 776).

A TENT, as a temporary and protective
dwelling place, represents a man's philosophy. Associated with the Tabernacle, it is
every man's inmost ideal: "This is Jerusalem in every Man, a Tent & Tabernacle of
Mutual Forgiveness" (*J* 54:3). Luvah and
Urizen battle around the "holy tent" in
which Albion sleeps (*FZ* i:480–514), while
"half the tents of men [are] inclos'd in
clouds of Tharmas & Urthona" (*FZ* i:496).

The Universal Tent is the sky. When
Enitharmon became separate from Los, the
Eternals built it ("and called it Science") to
shut out the horrible sight; they completed
it after the birth of Orc, and "No more Los
beheld Eternity" (*Ur* 19:2–20:2).

At the news of the warfare of the Zoas,
"the Family Divine drew up the Universal
tent above High Snowdon" (*FZ* i:551). It is
"the wing-like [or protecting] tent of the
Universe, beautiful, surrounding all, or
drawn up or let down at the will of the immortal man" (*FZ* vi:254). "The Sky is an
immortal Tent built by the Sons of Los"
(*Mil* 29:4). In Blake's egocentric universe,
it is the sky above each individual. "In every bosom a Universe expands, as wings let
down at will around & call'd the Universal
Tent" (*J* 38:49).

TERAH was the father of Abraham. He is
the twentieth of the Twenty-seven Heavens, and the last of the second group which

began with Noah, "the Female-Males, a Male within a Female hid as in an Ark & Curtains" (*Mil* 37:39; *J* 75:14). "Souls are bak'd in bricks to build the pyramids of Heber & Terah" (*J* 31:11).

TERESA (St. Teresa, or Theresa of Avila, 1515–82) was a Spanish mystic famous for her visions. Blake was fond of her works, "and often quoted them with other writers on the interior life" (*Gil* I, 346). She is one of the mystics who guard the gate into Beulah, "with all the gentle Souls who guide the great Wine-press of Love" (*J* 72:51). Blake obviously had in mind her "transverberation" (see Bernini's sculpture in St. Peter's) when Jerusalem says: "Spain was my heavenly couch, I slept in his golden hills; the Lamb of God met me there. There we walked as in our secret chamber among our little ones. They looked upon our loves with joy, they beheld our secret joys with holy raptures of adoration, rap'd sublime in the Visions of God" (*J* 79:40).

TESSHINA is a place name apparently known only to Blake. He tells us that in the days of Man's primal innocence, his "skiey tent" reached "even to Great Chaldea & Tesshina" (*J* 60:17, 20).

The THAMES is the most important river of Great Britain. For Blake, it was the river of London, its "soft, mild parent stream" (*J* 53:3). In a petulant manuscript poem, "Why should I care?" (*K* 166), he referred to himself as "born on the cheating banks of Thames"; and in the pessimistic "London" (*SoE*), he called the river "chartered." But in the age of Innocence, the Thames was fed by "the heavenly Jordan" (*J* 79:35); now its "currents spring from the rivers of Beulah" (*J* 53:2); and its shores are "infinite" (*Eur* 10:5).

It is naturally a focus of activities. The forge of Los and his sons is on the Thames (*Mil* 6:11; *J* 16:14; 47:2; 82:57), and here he builds Golgonooza (*J* 53:15). Here he determines the forms of Vala and Luvah, where the Druid's victim howls (*J* 83:11), for the Druid Temple, which frowns over

the whole earth, is "Outwoven from Thames & Tweed & Severn, awful streams" (*J* 89:20). Hand also has his furnace on the Thames (*J* 90:24). When the Spectre unites with Vala, they stand "A dark Hermaphrodite . . . frowning upon London's River" (*J* 64:31). Hoglah weaves the dark woof of war "over trembling Thames" (*Mil* 35:12); "Thames is drunk with blood" as Gwendolen and Cambel cast the shuttle (*J* 66:61).

One tiny tributary of the Thames was Tyburn Brook, which passed the gallows before plunging underground. Blake mentions it several times in connection with the Thames (*Mil* 6:11; 11:5; 13:35; *J* 90:48). See TYBURN.

The Medway enters the mouth of the Thames; Spenser celebrated at length the marriage of the two rivers (*FQ* IV.xi). The two are therefore "rivers of Beulah" (*J* 4:34) and are associated elsewhere (*J* 63:35; 79:35). See MEDWAY. Beulah, however, terminates in Hyde Park; here Los hides Enitharmon from the sight of the destructive Satan (*Mil* 11:2–5). Albion also hides his Emanation "upon the Thames and Medway, rivers of Beulah" (*J* 4:34). Gwendolen's wild beasts sport on the two rivers (*J* 63:35). The Daughters of Albion divide Reuben "in love upon the Thames" (*J* 74:36). Here the Emanations weave bowers of delight (*J* 83:50), and Enitharmon's rainbow appears in "the awful gloom of London City on the Thames" (*J* 83:67).

THAMMUZ was the god
> Whose annual wound in Lebanon allur'd
> The Syrian Damsels to lament his fate
> In amorous dittyes all a Summer's day,
> While smooth Adonis from his native Rock
> Ran purple to the Sea, suppos'd with blood
> Of Thammuz yearly wounded: the Lovetale
> Infected Sions daughters with like heat.
> (*PL* i:446–53)

Thammuz, sixth of the Twelve Gods of Asia, is worshipped in Lebanon (*Mil* 37:26).

THARMAS, the last of the Zoas to be named (*FZ* i:24), is the first in their counterclockwise numeration, Los being the fourth and last (*FZ* i:14). Tharmas represents the Senses, and hence the physical body, "for that call'd Body is a portion of Soul discern'd by the five Senses" (*MHH* 4). As "Energy is the only life, and is from the Body" (*MHH* 4), Tharmas is the "Parent power" (*FZ* i:24) and "the Mighty Father" (*FZ* i:413). His place is in the Loins; his Emanation is Enion, the sexual urge. He is a shepherd; his attribute is a sheephook (*FZ* i:414; ix:776); he has flocks and a sheepfold (*J* 95:16).

As an aspect or reflection of Deity, he is the first Person of the Trinity, the ever pitying Father, but also the Good Shepherd. His metal is brass, which is the metal of social organization. See BRASS.

His compass-point is west (*FZ* i:24; *Mil* 19:17; 34:37; *J* 59:12; 97:10). When Man falls, Tharmas goes outward and becomes the Circumference (*J* 12:55). Although his world is described once as the Platonic "cavern'd rock" (*FZ* i:534), his real Element is water, the Sea of Time and Space: "the World of Tharmas where in ceaseless torrents his billows roll, where monsters wander in the foamy paths" (*FZ* ii:256, etc.). He is the "Demon of the Waters" (*FZ* iv:37; vii *b*:72).

His Art is Painting, which chooses its forms from the outward world; when it degenerates to a Profession, it becomes Physic and Surgery, the cure of the outward body (*Mil* 27:55–60).

His special sense is the Tongue, called "the Parent Sense" (*J* 98:17) because it is the first to operate in a baby. It is also the organ of self-expression. When Tharmas quarrels with Enion, the Daughters of Beulah close "the Gate of the Tongue in trembling fear" (*FZ* i:108). In revolutionary times, public emotion kills the free press: "Luvah slew Tharmas, the Angel of the Tongue" (*J* 63:5). When Tharmas falls, his doctrine becomes the false doctrine of materialism: "Tharmas the Vegetated Tongue, even the Devouring Tongue, a threefold region, a false brain, a false heart and false bowels, altogether composing the False Tongue, beneath Beulah, as a wat'ry flame revolving every way [cf. *Gen* iii:24], and as dark roots and stems, a Forest of affliction, growing in seas of sorrow" (*J* 14:4). See TONGUE.

The story of Tharmas is told in *The Four Zoas*. The epic begins *in medias res* with the onset of puberty, the division of the Loins. As a result of the warfare of Luvah and Urizen, Man has already fallen and his Zoas have become separated. Originally Tharmas was "the mildest son of heaven" (*FZ* iv:81), when he and Enion wandered with his flocks and slept together at night (iv:138). But when the warfare broke out, "redd'ning with rage, the Mighty Father siez'd his bright sheephook studded with gems & gold; he swung it round his head, shrill sounding in the sky; down rush'd the Sun with noise of war; the Mountains fled away . . . Tharmas endur'd not; he fled howling; then, a barren waste, sunk down conglobing in the dark confusion" (i:413–20). In his fall, he outstretched "an expanse where ne'er expanse had been" and drew "all the Sons of Beulah into [his] dread vortex, following [his] Eddying spirit down the hills of Beulah" (iv:87).

Then "Night the First" begins with the torture of awakening sex and the consequent division and opposition between the boy and his forbidden sexual instincts. Thus Enion, separated from Tharmas, reduces him to a Spectre, who is Eternal Death (i:107). In furious conflict, Tharmas begets on Enion the poetic instinct, the infants Los and Enitharmon (i:192), who sulk and wander away from their mother; she stumbles after them without ever reaching them. Tharmas also seeks Enion in vain, hearing her lamentations but not seeing her until the final "Night."

In his struggles he becomes a man—he manages to achieve the human form (iii:153–76); then "The bounds of Destiny were broken, & hatred now began instead of love to Enion" (iii:177). Although his basic emotion is Pity, he suffers from the rage of thwarted sex: he has become "a Rage, a terror to all living things" (iv:81).

Pitying Los and Enitharmon, he bids them rebuild the universe though fallen: "a Universe of Death & Decay. Let Enitharmon's hands weave soft delusive forms of Man above my wat'ry world" (iv:28). When Los refuses, Tharmas establishes his authority—"my will shall be my Law" (iv:55) —and shows his power by separating the two, thus reducing Los to a Spectre. But in pity he reunites them and proclaims reluctantly that he is God, though he would far rather be a man (iv:132, 146); and after bidding Los again to rebuild the universe, he departs. But when Los builds Golgonooza, Tharmas lays the foundations for Luban, its gate into this world, "& Los finish'd it in howling woe" (v:78). Furthermore, "Bowlahoola is nam'd Law by mortals; Tharmas founded it because of Satan, before Luban in the City of Golgonooza" (*Mil* 24:48).

Tharmas does not confront Urizen until he hears the screams of the expelled children and comes riding, but his waters freeze; and threatening to starve Urizen, he flees (*FZ* vi:274). He takes his stand by the Spectre of Urthona, or Los (vi:302), but is forced to flee again (vii:1). However, still God, he promises to support Los (vii *b*:49–72). Although Urizen slowly petrifies them, Tharmas still gives his power to Los (viii: 477). Meanwhile, mistaking Vala (the Shadowy Female) for Enion, he recalls the times of his happiness, and tells Vala that she is "our Curse" (vii *b*:257).

Urizen finally relinquishes his attempts to curb Tharmas' rage, and immediately rises in his original Apollonian form (ix: 187). When on the First Day of the Last Judgment Vala is redeemed to Innocence, her eyes are opened to "the world of waters," and she perceives "the shadows of Tharmas & of Enion in Vala's world." They are two children; she is their nurse. Enion is "modest"; she avoids Tharmas by daylight, then at night he shares her couch, where he drinks new life; "But in the morning she arises to avoid my Eyes . . . Thus in

Eternal Childhood, straying among Vala's flocks, in infant sorrow & joy alternate, Enion & Tharmas play'd round Vala" (ix: 484–556). Such is the vision of the ideal sexual life in this world; the two are yet to be united in Eternity.

On the Third Day, Enion rises in a whirlwind, resumes her true form, and is reunited to Tharmas. "Joy thrill'd thro' all the Furious form of Tharmas humanizing. Mild he Embrac'd her whom he sought; he rais'd her thro' the heavens. Sounding his trumpet to awake the dead, on high he soar'd over the ruin'd worlds, the smoking tomb of the Eternal Prophet. The Eternal Man arose. He welcom'd them to the Feast" (*FZ* ix:613). On the Fourth Day, Tharmas plies the fan at the winnowing: "the winnowing wind furious above veer'd round by the violent whirlwind, driven west & south, tossed the Nations like chaff into the seas of Tharmas"; and he rejoices at the destruction of Mystery and the releasing of all slaves (ix: 654–84). On the Fifth Day, at the vintage, he and his sons separate the lees from the wine (ix:790). On the Sixth Day, his winds drive the wheels of the Mill, and he sifts the corn for the Bread of Ages (ix:809–21). On the Seventh Day, the Sabbath, he is feeding his flocks upon the hills (ix:838).

As Tharmas was a late comer to Blake's mythology, there are not many pictures of him. Most of them are sketches in the manuscript of *The Four Zoas*. One of them (fol. 3 recto, reproduced in *Marg Vala*; also *Bentley*, Pl. 5) shows him as a winged youth reclining on the verge of the Sea of Time and Space; his curly head is sunk in despair on his cupped hands. On *Jerusalem* 87, as a vague, bearded nude, he presses his hands outward against the circumference of his sphere, while Enion stumbles away in pursuit of the infants Los and Enitharmon. In the so-called "Circle of Life," he is young and beardless. (See Illustrations.) Helmeted with shell and half sunk in the waters, he faces inward and extends his arms. His right hand rests on a phallic hank of rope, the line of material life, which the Three Fates (crowding closely down upon him) grasp, Atropos cutting it with her shears. In the first title page of Blake's illuminated *Genesis* (see Illustrations), Tharmas has the head of the patient ox. See GENESIS.

The names of Tharmas and Enion, as Erdman suggested (*Erd* 275, n.27) and Margoliouth points out (*Marg Vala* 159), are back formations from the name of Enitharmon, their daughter.

THEL is the heroine of *The Book of Thel*. She is the innocent girl on the verge of Experience, and is frightened at the thought of some day becoming a mother. The youngest and most beautiful daughter of Mne Seraphim, she tends her flocks by the river of Adona, in the vales of Har. But Har is the state of Self-love. See HAR. Therefore, as Robert F. Gleckner has noted (*Gleckner* 163), Thel is still self-centered, and has yet to learn the greater life of self-sacrifice, though the Cloud tells her: "Every thing that lives lives not alone nor for itself" (3: 26).

Her life seems meaningless; her spring is fading; she fears death. In her disquietude, she questions successively the Lily of the Valley (her own Innocence), the Cloud (the fertilizing male), and the Clod of Clay with its Worm (the mother with her baby), learning that life, taken as it comes without questioning, is wonderful, and that all things have a deeper, unperceived purpose. Death is but change; all change is death to what we were; and Thel herself shall be blessed in becoming the food of worms (becoming a mother). Through the Imagination (the Northern Gate), she enters this future land of death, and from her own grave-plot hears a voice lamenting the power of the five senses, especially the voice of awakening sex. Thel is terrified, and "the Virgin" flees back to her vales of Har.

This interpretation of the poem seems to me quite obvious, especially when we compare it to *Comus*, which inspired it. But Thel's flight at the end is puzzling. It could be simply the girl's natural revulsion from the impulses of her maturing flesh. However, on the strength of that passage, the poem is usually interpreted as the refusal of a yet unbodied soul to descend into this mortal world of "dolours & lamentations" (*Thel* 6:6). Such a theory is perfectly possible on the macrocosmic plane, and there is a reference in *Jerusalem* (56:13–16) which would support it. There the Daughters of Albion weave the mortal body on the golden Loom of Love, "a Garment and Cradle . . . for the infantine Terror, for fear at entering the gate into our World of cruel Lamentation, it flee back & hide in Non-Entity's dark wild." This is evidently a miscarriage. One speculates: might not Catherine have given birth to a stillborn girl? Perhaps *The Book of Thel*, with its strange ending, was an elegy to the Blakes' dead daughter, their only offspring.

Thel never reappears in any other of Blake's writings: she was far too nice a girl to fit in amongst Blake's furious elementals. *Visions of the Daughters of Albion* is intellectually a sequel to *The Book of Thel*, but there the woman in Experience is renamed Oothoon. The Cloud reappears in *Europe* and elsewhere, under the name of Antamon. Har and Luvah (now first named) also appear elsewhere.

See BOOK OF THEL.

THEOTORMON is Desire; when suppressed, he becomes Jealousy. His correspondent Zoa is Luvah; his Cathedral City is London (*J* 74:2). His eternal position is East, but in the shiftings consequent upon the Fall, he is forced to move into the South (*J* 54, illustr.), when he becomes thwarted desire "fill'd with care" (*Mil* 24:12). His name might be a combination of *theo* (god) and *torah* (law), signifying the divine in man under the law. His Contrary is Bromion (reason).

He is the third of the first four (and ungenerated) sons of Los (*FZ* viii:358; *Mil* 24:12; *J* 73:5; 74:2) or of Jerusalem (*J* 71: 51). These Four labor at Los's smithy "to forge the instruments of Harvest, the Plow & Harrow to pass over the Nations" (*Mil* 6:12). They labor "with the innumerable multitudes of Golgonooza round the Anvils of Death! But how they came forth from the Furnaces, & how long, vast & severe the anguish e'er they knew their Father, were long to tell" (*J* 73:6). Their forging takes place beneath Theotormon's storms, caused by the woes of mankind (*J* 16:8).

The Four Sons as spirits of freedom (Jerusalem) "dwell over the Four Provinces of Ireland in heavenly light, the Four Universities of Scotland, & in Oxford & Cambridge & Winchester" (*J* 71:52).

The story of Theotormon is told in *Visions of the Daughters of Albion*. Oothoon loves and seeks him, but Bromion intercepts and rapes her. "Then storms rent Theotormon's limbs: he roll'd his waves around and folded his black jealous waters round the adulterate pair"; he sits at the entrance of Bromion's caves, "wearing the threshold hard with secret tears," hearing the voices of all the enslaved (2:3–10). At Oothoon's call, his Eagles descend to rend away her defiled bosom, and he smiles severely (2:18). But henceforth he will have nothing to do with her: he will not hear her call (2:37) nor "turn his loved eyes" upon her (3:15). In his envy he laments his lost joys (3:21–4:11). Oothoon denounces Urizen as the cause of Theotormon's prudery (6:19; 7:13). Rejecting her ideal of free and true love, Theotormon "sits upon the margin'd ocean conversing with shadows dire" (8:11), recalling the paralysis of Spenser's jealous Malbecco in his cave (*FQ* III.x.58–60).

Theotormon's refusal of Oothoon is symbolized in the illustrations of the poem. On the frontispiece, he crouches at the entrance of Bromion's cave, with his arms wrapped round his head, so that he can see and hear nothing. On page 4, he sits with his head sunk on his knees, while Oothoon, chained in the flame of her passion, hovers over him. On page 6, he scourges himself while Oothoon passes by him weeping.

In *Europe* (14:24), Enitharmon addresses her son: "O Theotormon! robb'd of joy, I see thy salt tears flow down the steps of my crystal house." Jesus hears Oothoon's voice; "(a man of sorrows) he reciev'd a Gospel from wretched Theotormon" (*SoL*

3:23), for Theotormon's woes have revealed to him the woes of all sufferers (*VDA* 2:3–10). In the Satan-Palamabron quarrel, Theotormon and Bromion contend on the side of Satan, "pitying his youth and beauty, trembling at eternal death" (*Mil* 8:30–31). The Daughters of Los "in deceit . . . weave a new Religion from new Jealousy of Theotormon" (*Mil* 22:37). "Theotormon & Sotha stand in the Gate of Luban anxious. Their numbers are seven million & seven thousand & seven hundred." There in their kindness they scare the unborn Spectres into taking refuge in Human lineaments (*Mil* 28:21–28).

THERE IS NO NATURAL RELIGION

and *All Religions are One* (*ca.* 1788) are two philosophical tractates, Blake's first trials of his illuminated printing. *There is No Natural Religion*, two series of aphorisms in the style of Lavater, attacks Deism. The First Series states Locke's philosophy of the five senses until it becomes self-evidently absurd. The Conclusion is: "If it were not for the Poetic or Prophetic character, the Philosophic & Experimental would soon be at the ratio of all things, & stand still, unable to do other than repeat the same dull round over again." The function of the Imagination having been thus affirmed, the Second Series opens with flat contradictions of the aphorisms of the First Series, and concludes: "He who sees the Infinite in all things, sees God. He who sees the Ratio only, sees himself only. Therefore God becomes as we are, that we may be as he is."

This last sentence, which describes the Incarnation, is surprisingly close to Athanasius: "He indeed assumed humanity that we might become God" (*On the Incarnation* 54; cf. Irenaeus, *Against the Heresies* III. xviii.1; and Calvin, *Institutes* IV.xvii.2). But where the theologians all use the past tense, as of a historical event, Blake uses the present tense, for the act is eternal and is always going on.

THIRALATHA, or Diralada, is the erotic

dream. "As when a dream of Thiralatha

flies the midnight hour: in vain the dreamer grasps the joyful images, they fly seen in obscured traces in the Vale of Leutha" (*Am*, frag. 1–3).

Thiralatha is the final stage in Enitharmon's repression of sex, its reduction to the last, futile effort of the imagination. The counterclockwise cycle, which she concludes, runs: Ethinthus (the body—west), Leutha (sin—south), Oothoon (frustration —east), and Thiralatha (the dream— north). But here in the north, the male takes precedence again: Sotha, her consort, translates the dream into war. "Sotha & Thiralatha! secret dwellers of dreamful caves, arise and please the horrent fiend [Orc] with your melodious songs; still all your thunders, golden-hoof'd, & bind your horses black" (*Eur* 14:26). Thiralatha's name is given as Diralada in *The Song of Los*: "But in the North, to Odin, Sotha gave a Code of War, because of Diralada, thinking to reclaim his joy" (3:30).

Thiralatha is not included in the list of the Daughters of Los and Enitharmon, although Sotha is the ninth Son (*FZ* viii: 359). The ninth Daughter is Moab (364).

THIRIEL is the oldest of the four Sons of Urizen. In the quaternary of the four elements, Thiriel represents Air. "First Thiriel appear'd, astonish'd at his own existence, like a man from a cloud born" (*Ur* 23:11). When Los learns how to conquer his enemies by his art, he divides them: "First his immortal spirit drew Urizen['s] Shadow [sic] away from out the ranks of war, separating him in sunder, leaving his Spectrous form, which could not be drawn away. Then he divided Thiriel, the Eldest of Urizen's sons: Urizen became Rintrah, Thiriel became Palamabron" (*FZ* vii:490).

The THISTLE is an excellent example of Blake's seeing not with but through the eye —that is, perceiving the human attitudes expressed in the outer world. "The indignant Thistle whose bitterness is bred in his milk, who feeds on contempt of his neighbour" (*Mil* 27:26; *FZ* ix:763) is the frowning Thistle which attempted to discourage

Blake on his walk from Felpham to Lavant (To Butts, 22 Nov 1802, 2nd letter). "With my inward Eye, 'tis an old Man grey; | With my outward, a Thistle across my way" (29). It threatens him with failure: "Poverty, Envy, old age & fear | Shall bring thy Wife upon a bier; | And Butts shall give what Fuseli gave, | A dark black rock & a gloomy Cave" (37). But Blake kicks the Thistle from its root, thus banishing his fears. "So I spoke & struck in my wrath | The old man weltering upon my path" (53); whereupon Los appears in the sun.

THOR and Odin (Woden) were the war-gods of Scandinavia. "Strife: the Thor & cruel Odin, who first rear'd to the Polar Caves [of Sotha]" (*Mil* 25:52). Thor's consort was Friga, the goddess of love; they are the northern equivalent of Mars and Venus. "Thor & Friga dance the dance of death, contending with Jehovah among the Cherubim. . . . The Giants & the Witches & the Ghosts of Albion dance with Thor & Friga" (*J* 63:9, 13). "The hearts of their Warriors glow hot before Thor & Friga" (*J* 68:16). "Woden and Thor and Friga wholly consume my Saxons" (*J* 83:19).

THREE CLASSES OF MEN. See CLASSES.

THULLOH represents the natural affection between Blake and Hayley. In the Satan-Palamabron quarrel, "Thulloh the friend of Satan" and Michael reproved him faintly; but Rintrah "smote Thulloh & slew him, & he stood terrible over Michael." Then "Los hid Thulloh from [Enitharmon's] sight, lest she should die of grief"; and "Los secret buried Thulloh, weeping disconsolate over the moony Space" (*Mil* 8:33, 39, 41, 45).

THYME (the wild thyme, *Thymus serpyllum*) is a creeping weed with purple flowers, common in Britain. Its strong aroma had its part in the mystical moment when Blake perceived Ololon in his Felpham garden at dawn. "First the Wild Thyme and Meadow-sweet, downy & soft waving among the reeds, light springing on the air, lead the sweet Dance [of precious odours]" (*Mil* 31:51). "Just in this Moment, when the morning odours rise abroad, and first from the Wild Thyme, stands a Fountain in a rock" (*Mil* 35:48). "The Wild Thyme is Los's Messenger to Eden, a mighty Demon; terrible, deadly & poisonous his presence in Ulro dark; therefore he appears only a small Root creeping in grass, covering over the Rock of Odours his bright purple mantle beside the Fount above the Lark's nest in Golgonooza" (*Mil* 35:54). When Blake recovered from the vision, "Immediately the Lark mounted with a loud trill from Felpham's Vale, and the Wild Thyme from Wimbleton's green & impurpled Hills" (*Mil* 42:29).

TIME and Space have no absolute existence: they are twin aspects of Eternity, as perceived by our limited senses in this world of matter. Together they constitute the Sea of Time and Space which as Noah's Flood swept over creation. "The Visions of Eternity, by reason of narrowed perceptions, are become weak Visions of Time & Space" (*J* 49:21).

Los, who creates the sun "to measure Time and Space to mortal Men every morning" (*Mil* 29:23), is Time; his sister-spouse Enitharmon is Space. "Los is by mortals nam'd Time, Enitharmon is nam'd Space: but they depict him bald & aged who is in eternal youth all powerful and his locks flourish like the brows of morning: he is the Spirit of Prophecy, the ever apparent Elias" (*Mil* 24:68). "The Greeks represent Chronos or Time as a very Aged Man; this is Fable, but the Real Vision of Time is in Eternal Youth." In comparison to moral virtues, which are "Allegories and dissimulations . . . Time & Space are Real Beings, a Male & a Female. Time is a Man, Space is a Woman, & Her Masculine Portion is Death" (*LJ*, *K* 614).

"Time is the mercy of Eternity; without Time's swiftness, which is the swiftest of all things, all were eternal torment" (*Mil* 24: 72). All the woes of earth are limited to

"the Outward Spheres of Visionary Space and Time" (*J* 92:17). Nevertheless, everything that happens is preserved: "not one Moment of Time is lost, nor one Event of Space unpermanent, but all remain . . . The generations of men run on in the tide of Time, but leave their destin'd lineaments permanent for ever & ever" (*Mil* 22:18–25). "Los in Six Thousand Years walks up & down continually, that not one Moment of Time be lost, & every revolution of Space he makes permanent in Bowlahoola & Cathedron" (*J* 75:7), that is, in the body as well as in the imagination.

Both Time and Space are compressible or extensible. (One thinks of Rosalind's fantasy, in *As You Like It* III.ii.) Los proclaims: "both Time & Space obey my will" (*Mil* 22:17). "We raise ourselves upon the chariots of the morning, Contracting or Expanding Time" (*J* 55:44). Eno, who perceives the eternal in all things, extends a moment of Time into "seven thousand years" (*FZ* i:223—but Blake originally wrote only "twenty years") or into "Eight thousand and five hundred years" (*J* 48:36); she also opens an atom of space into Beulah (*FZ* i:225; *J* 48:38).

The divisions of Time, from the Moments to the Periods, are created by Sons of Los; and "All are the work of Fairy hands of the Four Elements" (*Mil* 28:44–60). "Every Time less than a pulsation of the artery is equal in its period & value to Six Thousand Years, for in this Period the Poet's Work is Done, and all the Great Events of Time start forth & are conciev'd in such a Period, within a Moment, a Pulsation of the Artery" (*Mil* 28:62–29:3). It is Jesus who, "breaking thro' the Central Zones of Death & Hell, opens Eternity in Time & Space, triumphant in Mercy" (*J* 75:21).

The relation of Time and Space is that of lovers. The Female "Creates at her will a little moony night & silence with Spaces of sweet gardens & a tent of elegant beauty, closed in by a sandy desert & a night of stars shining and a little tender moon & hovering angels on the wing; and the Male gives a Time & Revolution to her Space till the time of love is passed in ever varying delights" (*J* 69:19). When the Daughters of Albion invent marriage, Los "gave a Time & Revolution to the Space, Six Thousand Years. He call'd it Divine Analogy, for in Beulah the Feminine Emanations Create Space, the Masculine Create Time & plant the Seeds of beauty in the Space" (*J* 85:6).

Time has an end, as prophesied in *Revelation* x:6; then the sea (of Time and Space) shall give up its dead (*Rev* xx:13). The Six Days of the Last Judgment are a reversal of the six thousand years of Creation. On the First Day, Urizen had sowed the human seed; at the dawn of the Second Day, he cries "Times are Ended!" (*FZ* ix:568) and goes forth for the reaping. In *Jerusalem* (94:18), "Time was Finished!" when Brittannia awoke on Albion's bosom. But this is not the end, for there can be no end. In Eternity, the Four Zoas continue their visionary work, "Creating Space, Creating Time, according to the wonders Divine of Human Imagination throughout all the Three Regions immense of Childhood, Manhood & Old Age . . . such was the variation of Time & Space, which vary according as the Organs of Perception vary" (*J* 98:31, 37).

See SPACE.

TIPPERARY is an Irish county in the (southern) province of Munster, which is Reuben's Gate (*J* 72:3). With the other counties of Munster, it is under Reuben, Simeon, and Levi (*J* 72:22).

TIRIEL, the first of Blake's prophetic books, was written about 1789, shortly before *The Book of Thel*. It is his first poem in free septenaries. Dissatisfied with it, he did not engrave it; it remained unpublished until W. M. Rossetti's edition of 1874. The manuscript has no decorations; however, Blake made twelve sepia drawings, which are straight illustrations, with a few symbolic details.

Tiriel is king of the West (ii:18, 20; viii:4); therefore he is of the Body. The poem is an analysis of the decay and failure of Ma-

terialism at the end of the Age of Reason. Although it is Blake's best organized (conventional) plot, the commentators have often been baffled: a great deal has happened before the poem begins, but these important events are referred to so casually in passing that they are easy to overlook.

Har is the father of Tiriel, Ijim, and Zazel, and apparently of all mankind, for his wife's name is Heva (Eve), and Mnetha is surprised at the thought that there might be other human beings than Har's descendants (*Tir* ii:55). Har is the traditional spirit of Christianity, "holy & forgiving, fill'd with loving mercy, forgetting the offenses of [his] most rebellious children" (vi:26). He is also Poetry, and his wife could be Painting. But from the beginning there was something wrong with Har. He was self-centered (the son of Satan, *FZ* viii:360); he brought up his children to be hypocrites, as Tiriel complains at the end; he was too "weak" (*Tir* viii:7) to cope with the wars and lusts of mankind (*SoL* 4:6), and fled. Now Har and Heva have sunk into senility; Har the poet is inspired only with the trivial delights of second childhood, and he loves to sing in a cage. Mnetha, their nurse, is the spirit of neoclassicism; they suppose her to be their mother. See HAR.

Long ago, Har's sons revolted (*Tir* vi:27), but he did not kill them with his curse, as he might have done. Tiriel set himself up as a tyrant in the West (i:3; ii:18, 20; viii:4). He chained his brother Zazel and enslaved his sons (i:41; vii:9); his other brother Ijim he drove into the wilderness (iv:10). He made slaves of his own sons until they rebelled (i:17). Heuxos was the oldest (i:25; iv:43, 83); others were Yuva (i:25) and Lotho (iv:45). Clithyma and Makuth are also named, in a deleted line (iv:73). Altogether, there seem to have been a hundred and thirty sons (v:29, 34). Tiriel also had five daughters (v:18), the youngest of whom was Hela (v:24).

After the triumph of his sons, Tiriel refused to stay with them, "chusing to wander like a Son of Zazel in the rocks" (i:39). He cursed them and "dwelt with Myratana five years in the desolate rock, and all that time we waited for the fire to fall from heaven" on his rebellious children (vi:8).

But no fire fell, and the poem begins when he returns with his failing spouse to his palace. He is blind, and his wife (his inspiration: "O Soul! O Spirit! O fire!" i:30) is dying. He summons his sons to be present at their mother's death. In the illustration, the three sons are crowned respectively with the bays, the vine, and a golden circlet. In the background is a pyramid (Egypt—slavery). (See Kathleen Raine, "Some Sources of Tiriel," *Huntington Library Quarterly*, XXL, Nov. 1957, 13.) Tiriel begins to dig Myratana's grave with his own hands, but Heuxos calls a son of Zazel to bury her. Tiriel then wanders away, "till he that leadeth all led him to the vales of Har" (ii:4).

Har and Heva are childishly afraid of him at first. He names himself, but their nurse Mnetha cannot believe him (ii:17); and thereafter he dissembles his identity, even when the pitying Har recognizes him (iii: 6). They feed him with milk and fruits, and beg him to stay and hear Har sing in his cage (iii:14, 23); but Tiriel is compelled to wander.

He then encounters his brother Ijim, who identifies him with all the hostilities in nature. Like the giant Gordred ("Gwin, King of Norway," *PS*), Ijim symbolizes the people, superstitious and all-powerful. He carries Tiriel back to his palace, and summons the sons to expose the hypocrite. When the terrified sons submit to their fate, though it means their death, the disillusioned Ijim, shocked at this treachery in the high places, departs.

Tiriel then summons the thunder, earthquake, and pestilence; one hundred sons, four daughters, and all their children are killed. Thirty sons (cf. the thirty cities of Africa) remain "to wither in the palace" (v: 34). Hela (touch—sex), the youngest of the daughters, is spared, to lead her father to Har. She obeys, but denounces Tiriel so bitterly that he turns her hair to snakes (the curse on sex).

On the way, at eventide they come to the caves where Old Zazel (who still wears his chains) and his sons dwell. They mock and pelt Tiriel. (Zazel symbolizes the chained and outcast genius. He calls himself "foolish," probably because he allowed himself to be subjected by his brother.)

The next noon, the two reach the tents of Har and Heva. Tiriel gives his true name and falls at Har's feet. "O weak mistaken father of a lawless race, thy laws, O Har, & Tiriel's wisdom end together in a curse" (viii:7). Tiriel laments the state of mankind, which he blames on the restricted way in which children are brought up. "Such was Tiriel, [hypocrisy, the idiot's wisdom & the wise man's folly, *del*] compell'd to pray repugnant & to humble the immortal spirit, till I am subtil as a serpent in a paradise, consuming all, both flowers & fruits, insects & warbling birds. And now my paradise is fall'n, & a drear sandy plain returns my thirsty hissings in a curse on thee, O Har. Mistaken father of a lawless race, my voice is past" (viii:34). So he dies, cursing to the end, at the feet of his parents.

The names of Tiriel and Zazel were taken from Agrippa's *Occult Philosophy* (II, xxii). Blake probably found Ijim (*Isaiah* xiii:21, where it is translated as "satyrs") in Swedenborg's *Universal Theology* (45), but he used the Hebrew plural as a singular proper name. Rousseau probably inspired the lines about the birth and early miseducation of the child (viii:25–34). Erdman proves, I think, that the madness of George III (though not yet blind and bearded) over the loss of his American colonies suggested some of the actions of Tiriel; but the poem is not a political allegory.

The death of Tiriel's four daughters and the corruption of the fifth is Blake's first use of his recurrent symbol of the death of the four senses and the corruption of the fifth (touch, or sex). The compass-points are now first used symbolically. "Can wisdom be put in a silver rod, or love in a golden bowl?" (viii:18) is repeated in the "Motto" for *The Book of Thel*. "Why is one law given to the lion & the patient Ox?" (viii:10) reappears as "One Law for the Lion & Ox is Oppression" (*MHH* 24). Only Har, Heva, and Ijim are mentioned in later books. Tiriel, however, is a foreshadowing of Urizen. He too revolted, set himself up as a tyrant, became a hypocrite, ruined his children by his curse, and finally collapsed.

TIRZAH was the fifth, last, and most important of the daughters of Zelophehad (*Mil* 17:11, etc.). As the fifth, she represents sex. See ZELOPHEHAD. Blake also had in mind a passage from *The Song of Solomon* (vi:4): "Thou art beautiful, O my love, as Tirzah, comely as Jerusalem, terrible as an army with banners."

Tirzah is the creator of the physical body, the "Mother of my Mortal part" (*SoE*, "To Tirzah" 9), and thus the mother of death. "She numbers with her fingers every fibre ere it grow.... She ties the knot of nervous fibres into a white brain! She ties the knot of bloody veins into a red hot heart!... She ties the knot of milky seed into two lovely Heavens, two yet but one, each in the other sweet reflected" (*Mil* 19:49, 55, 60). Meanwhile "Her shadowy Sisters form the bones, even the bones of Horeb around the marrow, and the orbed scull around the brain" (*Mil* 19:51). The three—head, heart, and loins—"are our Three Heavens beneath the shades of Beulah" (*Mil* 20:2), "the Three Heavens of Ulro where Tirzah & her Sisters weave the black Woof of Death upon Entuthon Benython, in the Vale of Surrey where Horeb terminates in Rephaim" (*Mil* 29:55).

Tirzah is the daughter of Rahab (*FZ* viii: 294; *Mil* 13:41). Rahab is the Whore; Tirzah is the Prude, the "pure woman," the false ideal which leads men astray. Rahab squanders her lust; but Tirzah, though her soul is "seven furnaces" (*FZ* viii:305; *J* 67: 52), withholds her lust, to use it as a weapon against man. She is his temptress (*FZ* viii:294–99; *Mil* 19:31; 24:4). She tortures him (*FZ* viii:299–310; *J* 67:45–55), and directs her sisters in the torturing (*FZ* viii: 312–20; *J* 67:59–68:7). Reuben, the average sensual man, cannot stay in the Prom-

ised Land because "in vain he sought beautiful Tirzah ... In the love of Tirzah he said: 'Doubt is my food day & night'" (*J* 36:1, 7). The Twelve Tribes abandoned their father Los to wander with Tirzah (*Mil* 24:4); she generated them (*Mil* 24:6; 25: 58) and then separated them into Nations (*Mil* 24:16), with the assistance of her mother Rahab (*Mil* 25:29), and together they created "all the Kings & Nobles of the Earth & all their Glories" (*J* 73:38).

Rahab and Tirzah constantly work together. They spin (*FZ* viii:201, 220); they conspire against Milton (*Mil* 19:28); they separate the Nations (*Mil* 25:29); they pervert the influences of Enitharmon and her daughters (*Mil* 29:53). Each one becomes Natural Religion (*FZ* viii:620, etc.; *Mil* 19: 47, 54). In the time of revolution, "Rahab created Voltaire; Tirzah created Rousseau" (*Mil* 22:41). They divide the Daughters of Albion between them, Tirzah and her sisters on Mount Gilead taking the first five, while Rahab in the Covering Cherub on the Euphrates takes the remaining seven (*J* 5: 40–44). The Twelve unite into the two, "a Double Female" (*J* 67:2). Gwendolen divides into Rahab and Tirzah in "Twelve Portions" or tribes (*J* 34:52). Finally, early in the Last Judgment, "Rahab & Tirzah wail aloud in the wild flames; they give up themselves to Consummation" (*FZ* ix:32).

"To Tirzah" was added as the terminal lyric for the *Songs of Experience* about 1795 (*K Census* 55, copies E, F). It is a declaration of individuality, and hence of independence from the mother and the whole material system which she represents. In renouncing Tirzah, the "Mother of my Mortal part," who so cruelly molded his heart, limited his senses, and betrayed him to mortal life, the poet twice uses the words of Jesus to Mary: "Woman, what have I to do with thee?" (*John* ii:4). The lad who does not cast off the mother-image is not yet a man. Thus this act of Revolution is a fitting end to Experience.

In "The Canterbury Pilgrims," the Prioress represents Tirzah, and is contrasted with the Wife of Bath, who represents Rahab. Blake remarks that they are equally "a scourge and a blight" (*DesC* III, *K* 572).

TITUS was an emperor of Rome (A.D. 79–81), who is particularly remembered as the conqueror of Jerusalem, in celebration of which his triumphal arch was erected. Blake lists him with the emperors Constantine and Charlemaine as an enemy of Jesus in "I saw a Monk of Charlemaine" (*J* 52: 21; also *K* 420).

The TONGUE is the first of the Four special Senses, "the Parent Sense" (*J* 98:17) —the first because it is the first to become active. Its position is West (*J* 12:60; 98: 17); its Zoa is Tharmas (*J* 14:4; 63:5); its element is Water ("the mouth of water" *MHH* 9; *J* 14:7; 49:40). Besides being an organ of assimilation (*J* 64:8), it is also the organ of speech (*Mil* 20:15; *J* 45:31; 98: 29). See THARMAS.

When man falls, he becomes inarticulate: the Gate of the Tongue is closed (*FZ* i:108, 479; *Mil* 29:40; *J* 14:26)—in fact, the entire West is cut off by the Sea of Time and Space. Speech becomes Babel (*J* 64:11). The Tongue is hidden behind the "deadly" teeth (*J* 43:24; 80:69).

Thus the Tongue becomes the False Tongue, the doctrine of materialism, "vegetated beneath [Beulah's] land of shadows," responsible for "its sacrifices and its offerings: even till Jesus . . . became its prey, a curse . . . and an atonement for Death Eternal" (*Mil* 2:10). "The Sons of Los labour against Death Eternal, through all the Twenty-seven Heavens of Beulah in Ulro, Seat of Satan, which is the False Tongue beneath Beulah: it is the Sense of Touch" (*Mil* 27:44). See TOUCH. "Tharmas, the Vegetated Tongue, even the Devouring Tongue, a threefold region, a false brain, a false heart and false bowels, altogether composing the False Tongue, beneath Beulah a wat'ry flame revolving every way [cf. *Gen* iii: 24], and as dark roots and stems, a Forest of affliction, growing in seas of sorrow" (*J* 14: 4).

When Los is closing Reuben's four Senses, he "folded his Tongue between Lips of mire & clay" (*J* 36:5). When Tirzah is torturing men, she bids Milcah (or Malah) to "circumscribe this tongue of sweets" (*FZ* viii:317; *J* 68:5). In revolutionary France, "Luvah slew Tharmas, the Angel of the Tongue" (*J* 63:5), meaning that the emotions of the public killed free speech and thus ensured a conviction.

TOUCH is the fifth of the five Senses; but being still diffused over the entire body (unlike the other four Senses, which have been limited to local organs), it has no specific Zoa or compass-point. However, it is identified once with the False Tongue, the doctrine of materialism (*Mil* 27:46), which is of the fallen Tharmas. It is identified with Sex, as Milton (*PL* viii:530) and Swedenborg (*Conjugial Love*, 201) had done already. It is capable of rousing the greatest ecstasy, which admits man into Eternity; therefore it is not "dead," like the other senses, but only cursed.

The symbol of the death of the four Senses and the cursing of the fifth runs through Blake's works from *Tiriel* to the *Illustrations of the Book of Job*. Tiriel kills four of his daughters and curses the fifth, Hela, with snaky hair. It is the voice of the fifth which terrifies Thel. In "Five windows light the cavern'd Man" (*Eur* iii:1–6), the joys of the four are listed; then, "thro' one himself pass out what time he please." Tirzah, the fifth and most powerful of the daughters of Zelophehad, symbolizes repressed Sex. The sixth illustration to *Job* shows four arrows of death descending from Satan's right hand, while his left empties the vial of boils upon Job.

TRAJAN, Roman emperor (A.D. 98–117), is best remembered for the column celebrating his conquest of Dacia. "Pliny and Trajan! what are you here?" is a line in Blake's cryptic trifle, "I will tell you what Joseph of Arimathea" (*K* 552).

The TRANSFIGURATION is the subject of a Blake painting once owned by Butts. Moses and Elijah, without their attributes, their hair bristling as with electricity, kneel with hands clasped in prayer, on either side of the floating Christ. Behind each of the two saints is a bearded cherub. In the foreground are the three apostles. John, in the center, sleeps, while the other two peer upward.

The Transfiguration also appears as the altarpiece in Blake's painting epitomizing Hervey's *Meditations*, Blake's idealization of Calvinism (see Illustrations). There is no cross on the altar, the Transfiguration, as it were, replacing it. It is the climax of the unfolding of sacred history. Jesus hovers between Moses (Law) and Elijah (Prophecy). Behind Moses are the tables of the Commandments; beneath Elijah are the wheels of his fiery chariot. The thinnest of cloudbarriers surrounds the scene, indicating that this is a mystical experience, the illumination while in the body. It is the first step upward towards God. See HERVEY.

The TRANSGRESSORS are the lawbreakers and therefore presumably sinners. Isaiah (liii:12) prophesied: "he hath poured out his soul unto death: and he was numbered with the transgressors; and he bare the sin of many, and made intercession for the transgressors." Jesus announced that this prophecy should be fulfilled in himself (*Luke* xxii:37); and Mark saw its fulfillment when Jesus was crucified with the two thieves (*Mark* xv:28). Blake also quoted Isaiah (*FZ* viii:274); but it was no tragic injustice, because Jesus was actually the greatest of Transgressors. As a bastard, he violated the Law in his birth; his whole life was passed in fighting the Law; and in his death he triumphed over it.

The Reprobates, whom Blake identified with the Transgressors (*Mil* 13:27), were those who rejected the "truth" and therefore were presumably rejected of God, according to Paul (*Romans* i:28; *II Timothy* iii:8). Paul affirmed that Jesus was in all men except the reprobates (*II Cor* xiii:5) — an exception which Blake would not have endorsed.

For to him the Transgressors and Reprobates were really the saviours of mankind: the original geniuses who are always cruci-

fied, being devoted to that fate from the mother's womb (*Isaiah* xlviii:8; *FZ* i:297; *Mil* 7:3). They are the "devils" with ways "which to Angels look like torment and insanity" (*MHH* 6).

Milton's three great poems are based on a threefold division of mankind: (1) the Elect, or sinless saints, whom God chose for salvation before the foundation of the world; (2) the Redeemed, who have sinned and repented; and (3) the Reprobate, or the damned. Blake, in his poem *Milton*, accepted the threefold division but changed the meanings of the terms.

His Elect are the self-righteous Pharisees, the moralists, the "Reasoning Negative" to "the Two Contraries" (*Mil* 5:13). "Under pretence to benevolence, the Elect Subdu'd All from the Foundation of the World. . . . they cannot Believe in Eternal Life except by Miracle & a New Birth" (25:31). Although it is an erroneous proverb in Eden that "Satan is among the Reprobate" (9:12), he is actually the prime example of the Elect (7:6; 11:21). So also was Milton (23:56) until he confessed he was Satan (14:30) and returned to correct his errors before the Last Judgment. Satan would rend off Transgressors forever (9:28). Through him, Rahab and Tirzah would "destroy Jerusalem as a Harlot & her Sons as Reprobates" (22:47); while Hand and Hyle, inciting the war against Jerusalem, would stop Transgressors from "meeting in brotherhood around the table or in the porch or garden" (*J* 18:15). "The Elect cannot be Redeem'd, but Created continually by Offering & Atonement in the crue[l]ties of Moral Law" (*Mil* 5:11; 11:20). "The Elect must be saved [from] fires of Eternal Death, to be formed into the Churches of Beulah that they destroy not the Earth" (25:38). But at the Last Judgment they shall be "astonish'd at the Transgressor, in him beholding their Saviour" (13:31), and shall confess to the Redeemed, "our Virtues & Cruel Goodnesses have deserv'd Eternal Death" (13:34).

The second class, the Redeemed, are under Palamabron, the spirit of pity and understanding, who is "redeem'd from Satan's

Law" (11:23). They "live in doubts & fears perpetually tormented by the Elect" (25:36); to them the Elect shall finally confess their errors (13:32).

The third class, the Reprobate, far from rejecting the truth, "never cease to Believe" (25:35), and therefore are "form'd to destruction from the mother's womb" (7:3; 8:34). They are of the class of Rintrah, or poetic wrath at the state of the world, for which they are condemned by the Elect (9:10). The greatest of the Transgressors was Jesus (*FZ* i:297; viii:274; *Mil* 13:27), whose example, as Ololon knew, we should follow (*Mil* 21:46).

See CLASSES.

"The TREE which moves some to tears of joy is in the Eyes of others only a Green thing that stands in the way" (To Trusler, 23 Aug 1799). "A fool sees not the same tree that a wise man sees" (*MHH* 7). Trees become manifest immediately after the birth of the poetic instinct at puberty. "Enion brooded o'er the rocks; the rough rocks groaning vegetate. Such power was given to the Solitary wanderer: the barked Oak, the long limb'd Beech, the Chestnut tree, the Pine, the Pear tree mild, the frowning Walnut, the sharp Crab, & Apple sweet" (*FZ* i:202).

However, the Tree, like the Sunflower, though it aspires upward, is rooted in this world. In one of the earliest of Blake's songs, "Love and harmony combine" (*PS*), it symbolizes the physical body: the lovers are two trees whose branches and roots embrace.

Later, the tree signifies error. The Oak, as symbol of a stubborn error, appears first in the fourth "Memorable Fancy" (*MHH* 18). See OAK. The Mirtle Tree is a symbol of marriage. See MIRTLE. Forests are accumulations of error, where the light is gone and the way is lost. See FORESTS.

"A Poison Tree" (*SoE*) is the growth of a man's concealed hatred for his foe, by which he traps him to his death. Dostoyevsky could have written a full novel on the idea in this poem. Elsewhere, Blake refers to "the Trees of Malice" (*J* 13:42).

In the final apocatastasis, the Trees, with the rest of the universe, will become merged in the union of God and Man (*J* 99:1).

The TREE OF LIFE, together with the forbidden Tree of the Knowledge of Good and Evil, was planted in the midst of the Garden of Eden (*Gen* ii:9). After the Fall, God drove Adam out of the Garden lest he eat of the fruit of the Tree of Life and live forever; and to prevent his return, he posted cherubim with a flaming sword at the gate (*Gen* iii:22–24). Blake interpreted the Tree of Life to be the phallus. "For the cherub with his flaming sword is hereby commanded to leave his guard at tree of life; and when he does, the whole creation will be consumed and appear infinite and holy, whereas it now appears finite & corrupt. This will come to pass by an improvement of sensual enjoyment" (*MHH* 14), because sex is man's chief gateway into eternity. But Blake later saw the cherub still there (*J* 14:2).

The Tree was removed to the New Jerusalem, where it flourished by the River of Life, "and the leaves of the tree were for the healing of the nations" (*Rev* xxii:2). Blake saw it there (*J* 86:18). Bath gives Oxford leaves from the Tree of Life, hoping he will cure Albion (*J* 45:30), but Albion turns away (*J* 46:9, 16).

The TREE OF MYSTERY is the contrary of the Tree of Life. It is the Tree of Death, the forbidden Tree of the Knowledge of Good and Evil, whose fatal fruit brings spiritual death, causing man to set himself up as a god (Elohim—judges). It is the system of Morality, the false church of Mystery, the Whore of Babylon. On this Tree Jesus was crucified.

It is described first in "The Human Abstract" (*SoE*). When selfishness increases, Cruelty (Urizen) knits a snare; he waters the ground with his hypocritical tears; "Then Humility takes its root | Underneath his foot. | Soon spreads the dismal shade | Of Mystery over his head . . . | And it bears the fruit of Deceit"; and here the Raven of death makes his nest.

Its growth is described again in *The Book*

of *Ahania* (3:55–4:4). Shrunk away from the Eternals, Urizen sits on a rock of his own petrifying, where he sheds his tears. "Soon shot the pained root of Mystery under his heel: it grew a thick tree . . . till the horrid plant bending its boughs grew to roots when it felt the earth, and again sprung to many a tree." With difficulty Urizen escaped from the labyrinth. On this Tree of Mystery he crucified Fuzon, his rebellious son of fire (4:5–8). For forty years the arrows of pestilence flew round the living corpse (4:9, 36), while the invisible Ahania, hovering around it, lamented (4:45).

In *The Four Zoas*, the Tree springs up beneath Urizen's heel while he is trying to curb the fires of the manacled Orc; it becomes a labyrinth from which Urizen escapes with difficulty (vii:30–39). His hypocrisy divides Orc's spirit; endeavoring to escape, Orc becomes the Serpent in Paradise and is forced to climb the Tree (vii: 135, 151, 163; cf. *Am* 8:1). Los and Enitharmon, reduced to Spectre and Shadow, eat of its fruit (vii:233, 385, 395). The Shadowy Female feeds Orc on the fruit (viii:84); she laments to Urizen that her lost Luvah (Orc) was the "source of every joy that this mysterious tree unfolds in Allegoric fruit" (viii:168). She spreads herself "thro' all the branches in the power of Orc" (viii:174) until the web of religion falls of its own weight and entangles Urizen (viii:181). Later, the Synagogue of Satan creates Rahab-Mystery "from Fruit of Urizen's tree" (viii: 287); and Jesus is crucified on the Tree (viii:326).

In *Jerusalem*, the Tree has become Albion's, Urizen being only an aspect of Albion. When he became a Spectre and set himself up by Tyburn's brook as punisher and judge, "underneath his heel shot up a deadly Tree: he nam'd it Moral Virtue and the Law of God who dwells in Chaos hidden from the human sight. The Tree spread over him its cold shadows (Albion groan'd); they bent down, they felt the earth, and again enrooting shot into many a Tree, an endless labyrinth of woe" (28:14). It is "deadly and poisonous, unimaginative" (43:60); it is "the Atheistical Epicurean Philosophy" (67:13). As a social system it becomes "a mighty Polypus" (66:48) and "Albion's Poverty Tree" (98:52). It is the delight and resort of Albion's Daughters (80:61, 73; 82:32, 40). Luvah is crucified on "Albion's Tree in Bath" (65:8). Its roots enter the soul of Los (53:4); it encompasses Jerusalem (80:1). But in Eternity it vanishes: "Where is the Tree of Good & Evil that rooted beneath the cruel heel of Albion's Spectre, the Patriarch Druid?" (98:47).

The Tree of Mystery was copied from the deadly upas of Java (*Antiaris toxicaria*), described in Erasmus Darwin's *The Loves of the Plants* (III, 237–54): "Fierce in dead silence on the blasted heath | Fell Upas sits, the Hydra-Tree of death. | Lo! from one root, the envenom'd soil below, | A thousand vegetative serpents grow; | In shining rays the scaly monster spreads | O'er ten square leagues his far-diverging heads. . . ."

Blake, in his unfinished "Let the Brothels of Paris be opened" (*K* 185), contrasted the pestilential Marie Antoinette (as Rahab) with the virtuous Queen Charlotte (as Tirzah), whom he thought equally poisonous: "But our good Queen quite grows to the ground, | [There is just such a tree at Java found, *del*] | And a great many suckers grow all around." However, Blake felt it more significant to have his Tree of Mystery spread by layering, not by suckering: one error begets another, though of course they all refer back to the first root.

The TRENT is the third largest river in England. "Humber & Trent roll dreadful before the Seventh Furnace" (*J* 16:16).

TRISMEGISTUS. See HERMES TRISMEGISTUS.

TROY (Ilium) was the city captured and destroyed by the Greeks, according to Homer and Virgil. British mythology claimed that the British were descendants of the scattered Trojans. See BRUTUS.

Blake blamed the Trojans for the war, as their gods were Mars, Venus, and Apollo.

See PRIAM. Hero worship "is only Grecian, or rather Trojan, worship" (To Hayley, 28 May 1804). The Laocoön symbolizes "Natural Fact or History of Ilium" (*Laoc*, *K* 775).

The TRUCHSESSIAN GALLERY was a huge collection of pictures brought to England by Joseph, Count Truchsess, and exhibited in August 1803. The count claimed to have lost a fortune in the French Revolution, and hoped to sell his pictures as the nucleus of a permanent gallery (*Wilson* 174).

According to Richard Phillips' *The Picture of London for 1805* (London, 1805, pp. 255–56), the Gallery was in the New Road, opposite Portland-place. "Some idea of the worth of this capital collection of pictures may be formed, when it is stated, that the duties charged upon them, *ad valorem*, at the Customhouse, amounted to more than 4000*l*. which, added to the expense of bringing them from Vienna to London, and erecting the building in which they are now exhibiting, brings the whole amount of their removal from Germany to this metropolis, to upwards of twelve thousand guineas. . . . there are eight different rooms appropriated to more than 900 most capital pictures, of the German, Flemish, Dutch, Spanish, Italian, and French masters, arranged according to their respective schools. . . . The two first rooms . . . are devoted to the German school."

Phillips' book did not have space to notice more than a few of these pictures; nevertheless (255–57) it listed some fifty names, among which are three Holbeins (two portraits and a Descent from the Cross), seven Van Dycks, three Hals, eight Rembrandts, five Rubens, six Ruysdaels, five Teniers, one Correggio, three Guido Renis, one Callot, two Lorrains, and two Watteaus.

If the ascriptions were correct, the collection would indeed have formed a valuable nucleus for a larger gallery. But the German and the Dutch schools were not to the public taste. Lawrence reported that "there was scarcely an original picture of a *Great Master* among them." He did not think the

whole were worth £2,000, whereas the Count valued them at £60,000 (*Wilson* 174).

Yet a visit to this gallery was a turning point in Blake's life. He wrote to Hayley (23 Oct 1804): "Suddenly, on the day after visiting the Truchsessian Gallery of pictures, I was again enlightened with the light I enjoyed in my youth, and which has for exactly twenty years been closed from me as by a door and by window-shutters. . . . Dear Sir, excuse my enthusiasm or rather madness, for I am really drunk with intellectual vision whenever I take a pencil or graver into my hand, even as I used to be in my youth, and as I have not been for twenty dark, but very profitable years."

What could have caused this illumination? Was it the "very correct" Madonna and Child by Dürer, "of whom Hogarth asserts that *he never deviates into grace*" (Phillips 257)? Was it the "8 curious pieces of antiquity, painted in 1436, about the time when painting in oil was first invented" (255)? Or was it not the total effect of the big exhibition in unpopular subjects and styles?

But we know that the effect was Blake's escape from all classicism, which he personified as the head of the Greek pantheon. "For now! O Glory! and O Delight! I have entirely reduced that spectrous Fiend to his station, whose annoyance has been the ruin of my labours for the last passed twenty years of my life. He is the enemy of conjugal love and is the Jupiter of the Greeks, an ironhearted tyrant, the ruiner of ancient Greece" (*K* 851).

And thereafter Blake had not a good word to say for pagan culture.

TUBAL, or Tubal-cain, sixth in descent from Cain, was the son of Lamech and Zillah (*Gen* iv:22). He was the first blacksmith, and doubtless made weapons of war. His sister was Naamah. Blake lists him as the third king: "Satan, Cain, Tubal, Nimrod . . ." (*J* 73:35).

TURKEY is the eighth of the Thirty-two

Nations which shall guard liberty and rule the rest of the world (*J* 72:38). In the days of Innocence, "Turkey & Grecia saw [Jerusalem's] instr[u]ments of music; they arose; they siez'd the harp, the flute, the mellow horn of Jerusalem's joy; they sounded thanksgivings in my courts" (*J* 79:48). In "The Divine Image" (*SoI*), the Turk is among those who love the human God.

The TWEED is a river in northern England, which runs partly along the boundary of Scotland and England. "Tweed & Tyne anxious give up their Souls for Albion's sake" (*J* 16:17). "Thames & Tweed & Severn, awful streams," are overshadowed by druid temples (*J* 89:20).

TWELVE GODS OF ASIA. See GODS OF ASIA, under GODS.

TWELVE TRIBES. See ISRAEL.

TWENTY-SEVEN HEAVENS. See the CHURCHES OR HEAVENS OF BEULAH, under BEULAH.

TYBURN was the site of the famous gallows in London. It was situated about the lower corner of Edgeware Road, just to the north of Hyde Park, which was adjoined by Kensington Gardens. As the name indicates, Tyburn was near a brook, which crossed Oxford Street a little to the east of the present Marble Arch, and flowed through St. James's Park, then plunged underground at the intersection of Stratford Place and South Molton Street, which is "Calvary's foot" (*Mil* 4:21). Elsewhere, Blake thrice associated Tyburn and Golgotha (*J* 12:28; 38:54; 63:33).

Here Albion made himself the judge, and the deadly Tree of Mystery sprang up beneath his heel (*J* 28:14). Here the Divine Vision set as a sun in clouds of blood (*J* 29:3; 62:34). Here Beulah terminates (*Mil* 11:5). Here is Los's Gate of Death: "bending across the road of Oxford Street it from Hyde Park to Tyburn's deathful shades admits the wandering souls of multitudes who

die from Earth" (*J* 38:57). Here Albion utters his loud death groan (*FZ* ii:39–41). Here the repentant Elect weep (*Mil* 13:35). When Albion rises, "his left foot near London covers the shades of Tyburn" (*Mil* 39:37).

The TYGER is Wrath (*MHH* 9:5; *FZ* ii:35). He is the Wrath of the Heart, for his position is East. He is one of a quaternary (*MHH* 8:14; *J* 98:43): Lion (north), Tyger (east), Horse (south), and Elephant (west). He is the fallen Luvah, when Love has turned to Hate; he is Orc (revolution).

"Wrath is a fire," wrote Spenser (*FQ* II. iv.35), utilizing a common symbol; and fire in Blake is often associated with the Tyger. But though at least once he is "burning bright" (*SoE*, "The Tyger" 1), his flames are largely a blinding smoke, as in Dante's *Purgatorio* xvi. "[Urizen's] tygers roam in the redounding smoke in forests of affliction" (*FZ* vii:9–10; also *FZ* vii *b*:111; i:418; ix:361). Orc is "a Human fire"; yet his flames emit "heat but not light" (*Am* 4:8–11).

When the Wrath breaks forth, it is Revolution (*Eur* 15:7; *Ahan* 3:36; *FZ* iii:37; v:128; *Mil* 42:38), consuming with its flames the forests of the night, and thus is part of the divine scheme. "The tygers of wrath are wiser than the horses of instruction" (*MHH* 9:5; cf. *FZ* ii:35; vii:6, 9). But "the wild furies from the tyger's brain" (*FZ* ix:236) cannot perceive the Human because he is blinded by the redounding smoke (*FZ* vii:9; vii *b*:111). "The Tyger fierce laughs at the Human form" (*FZ* i:402). He is "dishumaniz'd" (*FZ* vi:116). In battle, "the monsters of the Elements, Lions or Tygers or Wolves . . . terrific men they seem to one another, laughing terrible among the banners. And when, the revolution of their day of battles over, relapsing in dire torment they return to forms of woe" (*FZ* viii:120). But in Eternity the beasts all "Humanize in the Forgiveness of Sins" (*J* 98:44).

Even as Rintrah (north) and Palamabron (east) constantly work together, so do the Lion (north) and the Tyger (east) (*FZ* iii:

37; v:128; vi:116; vii:9; vii *b*:111; viii:120, 445; ix:39, 236, 301; *Mil* 42:38; *J* 63:34; 98:43). See LION.

"The Tyger" (*SoE*) is probably Blake's best-known poem. Charles Lamb called it "glorious" (To Bernard Barton, 15 May 1824). It was written about 1793, when just across the Channel the French Revolution was consuming those "forests of the night," Church and State. In the *Songs of Innocence and Experience*, it counterbalances "The Lamb." The Lamb symbolizes the Loving God; the Tyger, the Angry God. "God out of Christ is a consuming fire" (see HERVEY).

The poem describes the forging of the Tyger, which is glimpsed, as it were, in sudden flashes through the chaos; meanwhile Blake iterates the question "who"— or rather, "what"—is the creator. At last, when the Tyger's form is completed, the stars throw down their spears in terror and water heaven with their pitying tears; then Blake reaches his climax in the question "Did he who made the lamb make thee?"

Blake knew the answer, but he wanted to force his reader to find that answer himself. The whole poem is an extended query. Could the all-loving Father be responsible for these horrors without Mercy or even Justice? Of course not. The Tyger is not the contrary of the Lamb but its negation.

As Kathleen Raine has demonstrated ("Who Made the Tyger?" *Encounter*, June 1954), the Tyger was created by Urizen. The event took place at the very first Fiat of Creation, and was the result of Urizen's primal disobedience. Urizen, "first born of Generation" (*FZ* vii:245), "heard the mild & holy voice saying, 'O light, spring up & shine' [*Gen* i:3], & I sprang up from the deep. . . . [He] said, 'Go forth & guide my Son [Albion] who wanders on the ocean.' I went not forth: I hid myself in black clouds of my wrath; I call'd the stars around my feet in the night of councils dark; the stars threw down their spears & fled naked away" (*FZ* v:218–24).

Thus Wrath came into being. It is Urizen's, not the benign Creator's. Urizen's satanic Pride was affronted when he was

appointed to serve Man. That his Wrath was the creation of the Tyger is confirmed by the action of Urizen's stars, who fling down their spears in terror.

It was a crucial event for the whole universe. "The moon shot forth in that dread night when Urizen call'd the stars round his feet; then burst the center from its orb, and found a place beneath; and Earth, conglob'd in narrow room, roll'd round its sulphur Sun" (*Am b*:4).

Urizen is not invariably the creator of the Tyger. Theotormon and Sotha "create the Lion & Tyger in compassionate thunderings" to frighten the unbodied Spectres into human lineaments (*Mil* 28:27). The Four Sons of Los, in war time, "Create the lion & wolf, the bear, the tyger & ounce" (*J* 73:17).

Blake was dissatisfied with line 12, "What dread hand? & what dread feet?" In one copy of the *Songs of Experience* (watermarked 1802) he altered it to "What dread hand Formd thy dread feet?" In 1806, Benjamin Malkin, who obviously got his material from Blake himself, printed a still better version: "What dread hand forged thy dread feet?" (*Malkin* xxxix).

The TYNE is a river in northern England, which opens into an important harbor. "Tweed & Tyne anxious give up their Souls for Albion's sake" (*J* 16:17). There is also a smaller river with the same name in Scotland.

TYRE, "daughter of Sidon," was a great port of Phoenicia, "the crowning city, whose merchants are princes, whose traffickers are the honourable of the earth" (*Isaiah* xxiii:12, 8). Its prosperity was not due to military conquests but to its shipbuilding and sea trade, particularly in lumber and the famous Tyrian purple. Ezekiel celebrated its glory and prophesied its downfall; according to him, the king of Tyre was the Covering Cherub (*Ezek* xxviii: 14, 16).

Satan sleeps "in the whole place of the Covering Cherub: Rome, Babylon & Tyre"

(*Mil* 9:51). In the left breast of the Covering Cherub are "Druid Temples over the whole Earth with Victims' Sacrifice from Gaza to Damascus, Tyre & Sidon" (*J* 89: 33). "In Tyre & Sidon I saw Baal & Ashtaroth ... [Molech's] pale ... Priestesses infolded in Veils of Pestilence border'd with War, Woven in Looms of Tyre & Sidon by beautiful Ashtaroth" (*Mil* 37:20–24).

TYRONE is an Irish county in the northern province of Ulster. With the other counties of Ulster it is under Dan, Asher, and Naphtali (*J* 72:26).

U

UDAN-ADAN is the condition of formlessness, of the indefinite (*J* 7:22). Los, the maker of form, therefore builds Golgonooza on its verge (*FZ* v:76).

Udan-Adan is first mentioned as the place of the unborn. "Myriads of the dead [the sleepers in Beulah] burst thro' the bottoms of their tombs, descending on the shadowy female's clouds [of matter] in Spectrous terror, beyond the Limit of Translucence on the Lake of Udan Adan" (*FZ* vii *b*:298). There, "Souls incessant wail, being piteous Passions & Desires, with neither lineament nor form" (*Mil* 26:26).

Udan-Adan is "a Lake not of Waters but of Spaces, perturb'd, black & deadly . . . this Lake is form'd from the tears & sighs & death sweat of the Victims of Urizen's laws, to irrigate the roots of the tree of Mystery" (*FZ* viii:224–29). It is situated eastward of Golgonooza (*FZ* viii:224), in the forest of the physical body, Entuthon Benython (*FZ* viii:225; *Mil* 26:25). It is within the Mundane Shell (*J* 13:35).

On its islands and margins are the Mills of Satan and Beelzeboul, round the roots of Urizen's Tree (*FZ* viii:227). Satan has his couch here (*Mil* 21:2). The Sons of Albion "put forth their spectrous cloudy sails, which drive their immense constellations over the deadly deeps of indefinite Udan-Adan. Kox . . . is the Noah of the Flood of Udan-Adan" (*J* 7:21). Los descends and binds on Blake's sandals in Udan-Adan (*Mil* 21:1; 22:9). Los divides "the Space of Love with brazen Compasses in Golgonooza & in Udan-Adan & in Entuthon of Urizen" (*J* 88:47). Various English counties labor in the furnaces of Golgonooza on the Lake of Udan-Adan (*J* 16:19). Lincoln and Norwich "stand trembling on the brink" of the Lake (*J* 5:10).

After the Last Vintage, Los and his Sons will quench "the Sun of Salah in the Lake of Udan-Adan" (*Mil* 23:60).

UGOLINO. See DANTE.

ULRO is this material world. It is a space (*FZ* i:102; *Mil* 24:39); its position is South. It is Error (*J* 46:10), "deepest night" (*J* 42:17), Voidness (*J* 78:20), the "Seat of Satan" (*Mil* 27:45). It is a "dread Sleep" (*FZ* viii:217; *J* 4:1), a place of "unreal forms" (*FZ* ii:112), of "dreams . . . dark delusive" (*FZ* vii:331; *Mil* 26:45; 29:16; *J* 42:62). It is "the Grave" (*FZ* viii:223), the world of Death, not merely because all things die here, but because they are spectres "dead" to Eternity (*FZ* ii:71; viii:56, 189; *Mil* 14:12; 21:46; *J* 4:2).

The Ulro is beneath Beulah (*FZ* ii:71; *Mil* 21:7). "Such is the nature of the Ulro that whatever enters becomes Sexual & is Created and Vegetated and Born" (*J* 44:21; cf. *Mil* 41:33). It has a Moon for the "poor mortal vegetations" (*Mil* 24:24), a feeble imitation of the real Moon. Los builded it "plank by plank & rib by rib" in his attempts to save Reuben (*J* 36:4). Nevertheless the inhabitants of Ulro are plagued by "the terrors of Chastity that they call by the name of Morality" (*J* 36:46; 55:38).

The heavens of Ulro are the thrice nine revolving Twenty-seven Heavens of Beulah, "a mighty circle turning" (*Eur* 10:23), "the

Monstrous Churches of Beulah, the Gods of Ulro dark" (*Mil* 37:16). See CHURCHES OR HEAVENS OF BEULAH, under BEULAH. These are the successive systems of "Christian" thought without Christ, the Synagogues of Satan. Underneath these heavens, the undying "double Twelve" pagan deities are also worshipped; they are the "Twelve Spectre Sons of the Druid Albion" (*Mil* 37:20–34).

This system is "the Circle of Destiny," which the falling Tharmas established and set in motion (*FZ* i:71–87). The Daughters of Beulah "gave to it a space, and nam'd the space Ulro, & brooded over it in care & love" (*FZ* i:101). Later, the seven Eyes of God are its watchers (*Mil* 20:50; 22:1). The Circle has three States: "Creation, Redemption & Judgment," which Merlin as Reuben explores (*J* 36:42).

The inhabitants of Ulro "wail Night & Day" (*FZ* ii:71) in "the unreal forms of Ulro's night" (*FZ* ii:112). "What seems to Be, Is, To those to whom it seems to Be, & is productive of the most dreadful Consequences to those to whom it seems to Be, even of Torments, Despair, Eternal Death" (*J* 36:51). The sleepers doubt and despair, and impute "Sin & Righteousness to Individuals & not to States" (*J* 25:15). It is a place of "cruelties" (*Mil* 17:9). "In the dreams of Ulro they repent of their human kindness" (*J* 42:62). Here the Plow of Ages cuts "dreadful furrows" (*FZ* ii:70). Here Tirzah and her sisters "weave the black Woof of Death" (*Mil* 29:56).

Our social system is one of the delusions. "Ulro is the space of the terrible starry wheels of Albion's sons" (*J* 12:51). It becomes "a vast Polypus of living fibres, down into the Sea of Time & Space growing" (*Mil* 34:24). Here are "the Nations innumerable" (*Mil* 40:23); here Rahab and Tirzah create "all the Kings & Nobles of the Earth & all their Glories" (*J* 73:38).

Another delusion is material science. The law of Cause and Effect is an error: "a Natural Cause only seems: it is a Delusion of Ulro & a ratio of the perishing Vegetable Memory" (*Mil* 26:45). "There is no Such Thing as a Second Cause nor as a Natural Cause for any Thing in any Way" (On Bacon, *K* 403). So is the astronomical universe, "that false appearance which appears to the reasoner as of a Globe rolling thro' Voidness, it is a delusion of Ulro" (*Mil* 29:15).

The descents of Milton and Ololon from heaven into Ulro are described at length in *Milton*. Each of the four fourfold Gates of Golgonooza has an entrance into Ulro. The North Gate's entrance has four Bulls "clay bak'd & enamel'd" (*J* 12:64); the South Gate's, four "clay bak'd" Lions (*J* 13:4); the Western Gate's, four Cherubim of clay (*J* 13:6); the Eastern Gate's, "forms of war, seven enormities" (*J* 13:18). Before the description of these Gates, Blake had treated Ulro and the World of Generation as the same. Ulro is now South and Generation is West. See GENERATION; GOLGONOOZA, diagram.

The Saviour "awakes sleepers in Ulro" (*FZ* viii:237). And it is once said that the "Universal female form" of Jerusalem is created "from those who were dead in Ulro, from the spectres of the dead" (*FZ* viii:188). "Let the Human Organs be kept in their perfect Integrity . . . Then as the moss upon the tree, or dust upon the plow, or as the sweat upon the labouring shoulder, or as the chaff of the wheat-floor, or as the dregs of the sweet wine-press, such are these Ulro Visions" (*J* 55:36–42).

ULSTER is the northern of the four provinces of Ireland. "Ulster North" is "in Dan's Gate" (*J* 72:4).

The UNIVERSE of William Blake is in flat contradiction to the universe of the astronomers. See ULRO. It is one of immediate sensuous and imaginative perception, not of geometrical logic; psychological, not material.

It is egocentric. Each individual is the center of his own universe. "Every Space that a Man views around his dwelling-place, standing on his own roof or in his garden on a mount of twenty-five cubits in height, such space is his Universe: and on its verge the Sun rises & sets, the Clouds bow to meet the flat Earth & the Sea in such an order'd Space: the Starry heavens reach no further, but here bend and set on all sides, & the two Poles turn on their valves of gold; and if he move his dwelling-place, his heavens also move where'er he goes" (*Mil* 29:5). "Thus is the earth one infinite plane" (*Mil* 15:32).

Everything the individual sees is a projection of his own personality. Outermost is the sky with its forty-eight constellations: "the Mundane Shell, a mighty Incrustation of Forty-eight deformed Human Wonders of the Almighty" (*Mil* 37:53), which concenter in Orion, the giant slain by the goddess of chastity, and Ophiuchus, the man entangled with the serpent. See MUNDANE SHELL. Every living thing within it is deformed and materialized: "the Beasts & Birds & Fishes & Plants & Minerals [are] here fix'd into a frozen bulk subject to decay & death" (*Mil* 34:53).

But looking within, man's enlarged senses perceive the eternal, human originals. "For all are Men in Eternity . . . in your own Bosom you bear your Heaven and Earth & all you behold; tho' it appears Without, it is Within, in your Imagination, of which this World of Mortality is but a Shadow" (*J* 71:15–19). Man's body is "a garden of delight & a building of magnificence," with "herbs & flowers & furniture & beds & chambers continually woven" (*Mil* 26:32–35); or it is the very smithy of Los, which operates to the playing of an orchestra (*Mil* 24:51–67). He sees the unborn souls descending into the body in the South, and the released souls ascending in the North, on either side of Los (*Mil* 26:13–22).

Looking deeper within himself, man perceives his four Zoas, now chaotic: "in the South [Urizen's place] remains a burning fire [of Orc]; in the East [Luvah's place], a void; in the West [Tharmas' place], a World of raging waters [matter]; in the North [Urthona's place], a solid, unfathomable, without end. But in the midst of these is built eternally the Universe of Los and Enithar-

mon" (*Mil* 19:15–25). In this fallen world, Urizen has risen to the Zenith (the head), Luvah has sunk to the Center (the heart), Tharmas has gone outward, to the Circumference (the body), and Urthona has disappeared into the Nadir (the subconscious) (*J* 12:54–60).

But in Eternity, the Zoas take their original places: Urthona, the Sun of the Imagination, in the North, or Eden; Luvah, the Moon of the Emotions, in the East, or Beulah; Urizen, the Stars of Reason, in the South; and Tharmas, the Earth, or the world of the Senses, in the West. Thus, in the well-balanced man, the Imagination and Reason are cooperating contraries; so are Love and Lust.

Blake's idea is the unifying of the universe, which had been divided by the Elohim in the six days of creation, the separation of the sexes, the separation of good from evil, of body and soul in the sentence of death, and man from man in the confusion of tongues at Babel, ending in the dreadful and irreconcilable dichotomy of Heaven and Hell. Blake reunited man and God, who are inseparable; man and man in the Brotherhood which is the Divine Family; man and nature, which is his projection; man and woman, who together constitute the Individual; soul and body; good and evil; life and death. The basic, ultimate reality is the union of God and man in the mystical ecstasy.

Nevertheless, what seems to be, is, however erroneous. Ptolemy and Copernicus were both right, according to their lights. "Sometimes the Earth shall roll in the Abyss [Copernicus] & sometimes stand in the Center [Ptolemy] & sometimes stretch flat in the Expanse [Blake]" (*J* 83:40). Thus Blake modestly took his place with the great astronomers. But actually these theories (even Blake's?) are the work of Cambel and her sisters (*J* 83:33): "these Females shall fold & unfold, according to their will, the outside surface of the Earth, an outside shadowy Surface superadded to the real Surface, which is unchangeable for ever & ever" (*J* 83:45).

URIZEN is the southern Zoa, who symbolizes Reason. But he is much more than what we commonly understand by "reason": he is the limiter of Energy, the lawmaker, and the avenging conscience. He is a plowman, a builder, and driver of the sunchariot. His art is architecture, his sense is Sight, his metal is Gold, his element is Air. His Emanation is Ahania (pleasure); his Contrary, in the north, is Urthona (the Imagination). His name has been translated as "Your Reason," a derivation quite characteristic of Blake, who continually used semi-conscious puns; but Kathleen Raine and others prefer to derive it from the Greek οὑριζειν ("to limit"), which is the root of the English "horizon." However, it is not certain that Blake knew Greek as early as 1793, when he first used Urizen's name.

Man, the image of God, is fourfold; God therefore must also be fourfold. As the Trinity is reflected in the other three Zoas (Tharmas, the Father; Luvah, the Son; and Urthona, the Holy Ghost), Urizen must be (as Kerrison Preston has suggested) that aspect of deity which, when fallen, becomes Satan (FZ v:217). All things, even the Devil, are of the divine substance.

Urizen's tale begins with the *fiat lux* on the first day of Creation (*Gen* i:3). "I heard the mild & holy voice saying 'O light, spring up & shine,' & I sprang up from the deep. He gave to me a silver scepter [of love], & crown'd me with a golden crown [of reason], & said 'Go forth & guide my Son [Albion] who wanders on the ocean' " (FZ v:218). He was the "first born Son of Light" (FZ ii:108). He was a naked "bright beaming" youth (*J* 97:7), who is depicted as Apollo on the fourteenth illustration to *Job*. He was "Faith & certainty" before he became Doubt (FZ ii:105). He dwelt in the "glorious World" of the South (*Mil* 34:36), where his expanding throne was founded on mountains of silver (love) (FZ v:192). Here he was surrounded by his children, the sons of wisdom and the singing virgins; his palace, with its fountains and gardens, was situated in "those sweet fields

of bliss where liberty was justice & eternal science was mercy" (FZ iii:39).

In the lower world, Urizen is the son of Albion and Vala. "Vala was pregnant & brought forth Urizen, Prince of Light" (FZ vii:244), and he "grew up in the plains of Beulah" (FZ vii:251). The Eternal One appointed him "leader of his hosts" (FZ iii:27); thus Urizen became the charioteer of the material sun. (The spiritual sun belongs to Los; the material sun, which Los forged, is the chief of the Stars, which are Urizen's proper sphere.) Harps sound at his daily riding forth (FZ v:195, 199; vii *b*:198; ix:126; *J* 65:44—cf. "the sound of harps which I hear before the Sun's rising," To Hayley, 27 Jan 1804).

The cause of Urizen's downfall into the state of Satan or error (*Mil* 10:1) was that of the traditional Satan: the desire for dominion, which he does not renounce until the Last Judgment (FZ ix:180-87). He is "the King of Pride" (FZ viii:453; i:342; v:235), motivated by "foul ambition" (FZ iv:141; ii:109), and incurs the Satanic "self deci[e]t" (FZ viii:86) with its resultant hypocrisy, which leads him constantly to weep over his own victims. He is jealous, not of the Son, as in *Paradise Lost*, but of Man.

When he was called forth to guide Albion, "I went not forth: I hid myself in black clouds of my wrath; I call'd the stars around my feet in the night of councils dark; the stars threw down their spears & fled naked away. We fell" (FZ v:222).

The result was the creation of this world. "The moon shot forth in that dread night when Urizen call'd the stars round his feet; then burst the center from its orb and found a place beneath; and Earth, conglob'd in narrow room, roll'd round its sulphur Sun" (*Am b*:4). Thus simultaneously, because of Urizen's jealousy of man, which caused his disobedience to the divine command, Wrath and Justice (the "councils dark") began with the creation. This was the creation of the Tyger. (See TYGER.) Man was left sleeping on "a Horrible rock far in the South" (FZ ix:93).

"The Steeds of Urizen . . . were kept back from my Lord & from his chariot of mercies. . . . O I refus'd the lord of day the horses of his prince" (*FZ* v:208–11). Urizen lost his steeds in an episode often referred to but never described. He aspired to be throned in the North (Reason would rule the Imagination), while Luvah occupied the South and stole the horses of instruction (the Emotions ruled Reason). On a "dread morn" (*FZ* iii:31) or in "deadly night" (*FZ* iv:112), Urizen gave his chariot to Luvah, who persuaded him to the act by getting him drunk on stolen wine of the Almighty (*FZ* v:234–37; see, in Illustrations, the so-called "Circle of Life," where Urizen falls asleep in his chariot). "Deep in the North I place my lot, thou in the South; listen attentive. In silent of this night I will infold the Eternal tent in clouds opake, while thou, siezing the chariots of the morning, Go, outfleeting ride afar into the Zenith high, bending thy furious course Southward" (*FZ* i:491). "Vala slumber'd, and Luvah siez'd the Horses of Light & rose into the Chariot of Day" (*FZ* i:263). No longer were the horses of instruction obedient to Urizen's will; he was compelled "to forge the curbs of iron & brass, to build the iron mangers, to feed them with intoxication from the wine presses [war] of Luvah" (*FZ* iii:33). When Luvah has become Orc, Urizen sees the horses in Orc's cave; "here bound to fiery mangers . . . [they] dash their golden hoofs, striking fierce sparkles from their brazen fetters" (*FZ* vii:7). "How rag'd the golden horses of Urizen, bound to the chariot of Love!" (*FZ* vii *b*:201). When Orc gets free, he uses them for his revolutionary propaganda, "loosing the eternal horses from the dens of night, crying Empire is no more!" (*MHH* 27:20). However, at the Last Judgment, Urizen gets his horses back for his Plowing (*FZ* ix:308).

Nevertheless, Urizen has become the God of This World, the "jealous god" of the Old Testament (*Exod* xx:5; *MHH* 25:9–10; 26:15; *SoE*, "Earth's Answer" 7; *VDA* 7:12; *Ahan* 2:33,37; 5:41; *To Nobodaddy* 2, *K* 171). He created this world, using the traditional

compasses (*Eur*, frontis.; *Ur* 20:33–49; *FZ* ii:25–248), and planted the Garden of Eden (*Ur* 20:41) with its fatal Tree (see TREE OF MYSTERY, under TREE). He was the "Creator of men; mistaken Demon of heaven" (*VDA* 5:3; *SoE*, "Earth's Answer" 10–12; *Ur* 25:39–42; *BoL* 5:55); he led them in the wilderness (*MHH* 27:18; *Am* 8:4) and was the author of the Ten Commandments (*MHH* 27:18; *Am* 8:7; *Ahan* 3:45).

Urizen is the plowman (*FZ* ii:119; *J* 95:16). In the Last Judgment, after the Son of Man (the Human Truth) is revealed, Urizen drives the Plow of Ages over the entire universe; this, the dreadful logic of history, is the preparation for the New Age (*FZ* ix:311). See PLOW. Urizen then sows the human seed (*FZ* ix:321). Now that he has returned to his true vocation, Ahania, also rejuvenated, rejoins him at the evening feast (*FZ* ix:344–53). On the Second Day, Urizen and his sons reap the human crop and store it in the barns (*FZ* ix:579). On the Fourth Day, he flails out the chaff, threshing the Nations and the Stars (*FZ* ix:650), for Urthona's use in making the Bread of Life (*FZ* ix:806).

As architect (*FZ* ii:166; *J* 66:4) Urizen builds the Mundane Shell (*FZ* ii:25–248) on the geometrical solids which were dear to Pythagoras and subsequent astronomers, and which persisted down to Kepler's five "perfect solids." He also builds his own palace (*FZ* ii:166), the temple of the religion of suppressed sex (*FZ* vii *b*:19–38), the temple of materialism (*J* 58:21–43), and the druidic temple of Natural Religion (*J* 66:1–9).

The story of Urizen is told at length in *The Four Zoas*. It begins *in medias res*, when Enitharmon, angry at Los, summons Urizen, who descends, proclaiming "Now I am God from Eternity to Eternity" (i:319), a pretension he repeats elsewhere (i:336, 338; iii:106; vii:93; vii *b*:9). Los defies Urizen's claim (i:333); so does Luvah (i:504), who fights with him over the sleeping Albion (i:488–518). But Urizen suddenly abandons the battle, to invade the North, "leaving the rage of Luvah to pour its fury on himself & on the Eternal Man" (i:539), with the result that "sudden down they fell all together into an unknown Space . . . separated from Beulah" (i:541).

On his death-couch, Albion yields the mastery to Urizen (ii:5), who then builds the Mundane Shell, also his own palace, where Ahania is already a separate being (ii:204). She asks him: "Why wilt thou look upon futurity, dark'ning present joy?" (iii:11); he replies that the "Boy [Orc] is born of the dark Ocean, whom Urizen doth serve, with Light replenishing his darkness. . . . & that Prophetic boy must grow up to command his Prince" (iii:14–19). Indignant at her visions, he casts her out (iii: 131) and himself falls "into the Caverns of the Grave & places of Human Seed" with all his hosts (iii:141–52), where he lies "in a stoned stupor" (iv:170).

Although Los now accepts Urizen as his only God (iv:38), Tharmas declares regretfully that he himself is now God, for Urizen has fallen (iv:129), and orders Los to rebuild Urizen's ruined furnaces (iv:149); Los does so, and in seven ages forges a limiting human form for Urizen (iv:199–245; *Ur* 10:35–13:19; *Mil* 3:6–27).

When Orc is born, his voice rouses Urizen (*FZ* v:185), who then plans to "find that deep pulsation that shakes my caverns with strong shudders; perhaps this is the night of Prophecy, & Luvah hath burst his way from Enitharmon [the birth of Orc]" (v:238).

Exploring his worlds, he first encounters his three daughters, whom he curses with his sons (vi:5–46). He beholds the infernal tortures of his fallen children (vi:87–130), but his repentance cannot remove his curse (vi:141–46). Passing the South, he flings himself "into the Eastern vacuity, the empty world of Luvah" (vi:156), where he falls into a sleep, waking to write his books and explore the chaos further, but in vain. Therefore he determines to make "another world better suited to obey his will, where none should dare to oppose his will, himself being King of All, & all futurity be bound in his vast chain" (vi:231); and wherever he

travels, the spider web of religion follows him (vi:243; *Ur* 25:9–22). He fails, however, to penetrate the world of Urthona (vi:317).

Urizen then descends into the caves of Orc (vii:5). The Tree of Mystery springs up under his heel (vii:31—see TREE OF MYSTERY, under TREE), and becomes a labyrinth from which he escapes with difficulty, losing his Book of Iron (vii:39—see URIZEN'S BOOKS, below). When the crucified Orc defies him, Urizen summons his daughters to make Orc's bitter bread (vii:95–107). But when he reads from his Book of Brass (social philosophy), Orc curses his hypocrisy, and divides, becoming the Serpent in Eden (vii:152); Urizen forces him to climb into the Tree (vii:163).

Meanwhile Los has begun to create Art; he discovers that when he analyzes the real motives of his enemies (dividing them), his hate turns to love. "First his immortal spirit drew Urizen['s] Shadow [*sic*] away from out the ranks of war, separating him in sunder, leaving his Spectrous form, which could not be drawn away. Then he divided Thiriel, the Eldest of Urizen's sons; Urizen became Rintrah, Thiriel became Palamabron, thus dividing the powers of Every Warrior. Startled was Los; he found his Enemy Urizen now in his hands; he wonder'd that he felt love & not hate. His whole soul loved him; he beheld him an infant lovely, breath'd from Enitharmon" (vii:490).

But Los's discovery has no effect on Urizen's career. He proclaims himself "a God & not a Man, a Conqueror in triumphant glory" (vii *b*:9). He institutes Empire and the traffic in slaves, both white and black (vii *b*:12–17); then he builds the heart-shaped temple of the sexual religion (vii *b*:19–38). Both Los (spirit) and Tharmas (body) revolt; Orc breaks loose (vii *b*:140). Jesus also descends, and Urizen is confounded to see that the Prince of Peace and the Spirit of Revolution are both forms of the same thing. He declares war on the Lamb (viii:61), but the conflict gets beyond his control (viii: 102). When he consecrates his books in the temple of sex (viii:140), his web of Religion falls of its own weight and entangles him (viii:176–81; cf. illustrations to *SoE*, "The Human Abstract" and *Ur*, last plate). He assembles the Synagogue of Satan to condemn Jesus as a Transgressor (viii:272) and the Crucifixion follows. In Rahab he beholds his secret holiness revealed before the face of heaven (viii:413); he becomes stupefied; and "Forgetful of his own Laws, pitying he began to embrace the shadowy Female" (viii:420). Then, bitterly regretting his loss of the human form, he becomes the Dragon, "abominable to the eyes of mortals who explore his books" (viii:430).

In the Last Judgment, Albion summons him: "Come forth from slumbers of thy cold abstraction!" and when the Dragon cannot answer, Albion threatens him (ix: 129–61). The repentant Urizen at last gives up his fear of futurity and his attempts to curb Orc and Tharmas (ix:180–87). Instantly he is restored to his pristine youth; the lost Ahania returns, only to die of joy (ix:188–200). When the Son of Man appears, Albion and Urizen advance to meet him (ix:285–90), but first there is much to be done. On the First Day, Urizen plows and sows; then Ahania is restored to him. On the Second Day he reaps; on the Fourth Day he flails the grain and fills his barns; on the Sixth Day, his sons aid at the vintage (ix:694). Then Urizen's work is done in preparing for a New Age, his labors not to be repeated until winter comes again (ix: 214).

It will be noted that the grand outline of Urizen's career parallels that of Milton's Satan. He creates Sin when he rejects Ahania (*Ahan* 2:34). He conspires in the night with his comrade against man (*FZ* i:487); he explores his chaotic world, in which the ruined spirits suffer the tortures of the traditional Hell (*FZ* vi:100–130); eventually he sinks until he loses his human form and becomes the Dragon (*FZ* viii:422). But whereas Milton's Satan symbolizes the persistence in sin which is damnation, Urizen learns by experience; he repents (*FZ* viii: 463), and on giving up his determination to dominate, instantly recovers his original glorious form (*FZ* ix:184–88).

Urizen first appears, though without being named, in "A Song of Liberty," 1793 (*MHH* 25–27). "The starry king" hurls the newborn Orc into the night; when he falls, "the jealous king" with all his cohorts also falls "on Urthona's dens." Then leading "his starry hosts thro' the waste wilderness, he promulgates his ten commands"; but the fiery Orc, "Spurning the clouds written with curses, stamps the stony law to dust."

To Nobodaddy addresses him as the "Father of Jealousy" (*K* 171). Oothoon is the first to name him (*VDA* 5:3); she denounces him as the author of her slavery. He is depicted on the title page. At the end of *America* (16:2–15) he emerges as the evil God of the Age of Reason, "who sat above all heavens, in thunders wrap'd, emerg'd his leprous head from out his holy shrine, his tears in deluge piteous falling into the deep sublime; flag'd with grey-brow'd snows and thunderous visages"; then he pours forth his weapons of "stored snows . . . and his icy magazines." (It should be noted that Urizen's weapons are always forms of water: thunderclouds, snows, fogs, rain, ice, and hail.) He is able to hide Orc in clouds and cold mists for twelve years, "when France reciev'd the Demon's light."

In the *Songs of Experience* (1794) he is never named; but Earth denounces him ("Earth's Answer"); he creates the Tyger; his Tree springs up in "The Human Abstract" (in the lower margin of which he is pictured entangled in his net); and his psychology is described in "A [*not* The] Divine Image."

At the beginning of *Europe* (1794), Los announces: "Again the night is come that strong Urthona takes his rest; and Urizen, unloos'd from chains, glows like a meteor in the distant north" (3:10). When the revolution breaks out in America, Urizen appears on the Atlantic (11:2) and opens his Book of Brass (12:4), which "Kings & Priests had copied on Earth" (11:4).

The Book of Urizen (1794) begins with an analysis of the spiritual conflicts which create the physical body, tracing the development of the embryo to the foetus. The primitive Urizen, "self-clos'd, all-repelling" (3:

3), contracts into a separate being, struggles and divides, then manifests, proclaiming the laws he has invented. Eternity is split; its inhabitants pour fires on Urizen's armies; he creates the womb for self-protection (5:29). Los (the imagination) is now separated from Urizen, who was rent from his side (6:4), and begins to forge a human form for the demon. First the amnion (lake) appears (10:22); then in seven ages are created the skull, spine, and other bones; the heart and its circulatory system; the nervous system and the eyes; the ears, nostrils, and alimentary system; and lastly the limbs (10:31–13:19; *FZ* iv:215–46; *Mil* 3:6–27). Urizen, however, remains in his "deadly sleep" (13:27) until the voice of the chained Orc awakens him (20:30). He creates this world, with the Garden of Eden (20:41), explores his dens, curses his children, and creates the net of Religion, under which the inhabitants of earth wither, as described in *The Four Zoas* vi.

The Book of Ahania is the sequel to *The Book of Urizen*. His son, the fiery Fuzon, revolts against him, castrating him even as Cronus castrated Uranus. This division of the loins separates Ahania from Urizen, who names her Sin and casts her out; he then crushes Fuzon with the rock of the Ten Commandments and crucifies him on the Tree of Mystery.

The Book of Los (1795) retells the tale of *The Book of Urizen* from the standpoint of Los. When Light begins (5:10), Urizen's spine appears. In nine ages Los forges the material sun, which he binds to Urizen's spine, and eventually the illusory human form is completed (5:56).

The Song of Los (1795) continues the tale from Adam to a Last Judgment. The prophets, children of Los, give Urizen's laws to the nations; Adam (the natural man) shudders (3:10) and is reduced to a skeleton (7:20), while Noah (the man of imagination) fades (3:10), shrinks beneath the waters (3:15), and becomes leprous (7:22). When Urizen's thought reaches its ultimate in the Philosophy of Five Senses, he weeps and gives it to Newton and Locke (4:17). In the counter-revolution, Urizen flies over Europe, spreading despair, while his books melt; he finally stops over Judea, stretching his clouds above Jerusalem (7:19). At this obscuring of Liberty, Orc appears; the dead rise; the grave is impregnated. "The Song of Los is ended. Urizen Wept" (7:41).

Milton had placed Reason as the chief of man's faculties (*PL* v:102); therefore in Blake's *Milton*, Urizen is the basis of Milton's philosophy and his outstanding difficulty. Milton's descent to this earth is the formation of his thought. Urizen freezes to marble the clay in which Milton walks (*Mil* 19:1–4) and strives with him on the shores of Arnon (19:6). He baptizes Milton with the icy water of Jordan, pouring it on Milton's brain; "But Milton took of the red clay of Succoth" (19:10) and beginning with Urizen's feet molds for him "a Human form in the Valley of Beth Peor" (19:14). Urizen opposes his progress towards the universe of Los (19:26). "The Man and Demon strove many periods" (19:27); and while Milton's "Mortal part sat frozen in the rock of Horeb . . . his Redeemed portion thus form'd the Clay of Urizen" (20:10). Finally "Urizen faints in terror striving among the Brooks of Arnon with Milton's Spirit" (39:53). Thus Milton gave new form and life to the ancient error.

In "Milton's Dream" (5th illustr. to *Il Penseroso*), Urizen, clutching two figures of despair, holds the central place in the poet's heaven, but not quite hiding the true God behind him (see Illustrations).

In *Jerusalem*, Urizen's role consists chiefly of references to activities already outlined. When Los forges the World of Generation out of the World of Death, Urizen directs the work, "delivering Form out of confusion" (58:22); the result is a temple, "the Ancient World of Urizen in the Satanic Void" (58:44). He is also the architect of Stonehenge, which is Natural Religion (66:4–7). When Albion wakes at last, he compels Urizen to his furrow, and the other Zoas to their proper tasks (95:16). At the great moment of Albion's self-sacrifice, the four Zoas arise into his bosom (96:41). When the Covering Cherub is to be slain, "bright beaming Urizen lay'd his hand on the South & took a breathing Bow of carved Gold" (97:7); it is his part of Albion's fourfold bow.

URIZEN'S BOOKS contain his laws governing the four departments of life. Each is made of one of the four metals: Gold (science), Silver (love), Iron (war), and Brass (sociology). He wrote them "alone . . . by fightings and conflicts dire with terrible monsters Sin-bred, which the bosoms of all inhabit, Seven deadly Sins of the soul"; and in them are "the secrets of wisdom, the secrets of dark contemplation" (Ur 4:24–30). When he dies, he hides them in his death clothes; when he revives, the clothes have rotted but the books remain (FZ vi: 167–75). He continually works on them, regulating them (FZ vi:180) and interleaving them "with brass & iron & gold" (FZ vi:172). Even when confronting Orc, he writes in them (FZ vii:81), "in horrible fear of the future" (FZ vii:86); and when Orc is climbing the Tree, Urizen still "trac'd his Verses" (FZ vii:169). He consecrates and reads them aloud in his Sun Temple (FZ viii:140). At the Last Judgment, they "unroll with dreadful noise" (FZ ix:33) and presumably are burned in the flames that consume Orc.

The most important is the Book of Brass, or sociology. It contains Urizen's laws for establishing an ideal society, seeking for "a joy without pain, for a solid without fluctuation" (Ur 4:10), "laws of peace, of love, of unity, of pity, compassion, forgiveness . . . one command, one joy, one desire, one curse, one weight, one measure, one King, one God, one Law" (Ur 4:34–40). Unfortunately, laws cannot establish love and the rest; the Eternals are furious; and the Seven Deadly Sins, which Urizen had planned to prevent, appear immediately (Ur 4:49). On earth, the kings and priests copy the book (Eur 11:4), and the youth of England curse the canting (Eur 12:5). Urizen reads a long extract to his daughters: "Listen to the Words of Wisdom, so shall [you] govern over all; let Moral Duty tune your tongue, but be your hearts harder than the nether millstone. . . . Compell the poor to live upon a Crust of bread, by soft mild arts. . . ." (FZ vii:109–34).

The Book of Iron is the book of war. Urizen works on it while the Tree of Mystery grows into a labyrinth around him; he barely escapes, leaving the Book of Iron (Ahan 3:64–4:1; FZ vii:29–39). It may be noted that Urizen can start a war, but it soon runs out of his control (FZ viii:102). His three daughters place the Book above on clouds of death and sing its words while they knead the bread of Orc (FZ vii:97–104).

The Book of Silver (love) is remarkable only for not being included in the melting of the books over Europe (SoL 7:14), or in the interleaving with the other three metals (FZ vi:172). The Book of Gold (Urizen's own metal) also is not mentioned separately.

URIZEN'S DAUGHTERS were originally "the ever changing Daughters of the Light" who surrounded their sun-father in his glory (FZ iii:9), and would seem to have been the planets or the stars. Urizen describes them as "those whom I loved best, on whom I pour'd the beauties of my light, adorning them with jewels & precious ornament labour'd with art divine, vests of the radiant colours of heaven & crowns of golden fire. I gave sweet lillies to their breasts & roses to their hair, I taught them songs of sweet delight, I gave their tender voices into the blue expanse, & I invented with laborious art sweet instruments of sound; in pride encompassing my knees they pour'd their radiance above all; the daughters of Luvah envied at their exceeding brightness, & the sons of eternity sent them gifts" (FZ vi:25–34).

When Urizen falls, they become materialized, emerging "from green herbs & cattle, from monsters & worms of the pit" (Ur 23:20); and he curses them, "for he saw that no flesh nor spirit could keep his iron laws one moment" (Ur 23:24).

His daughters, like his sons, are innumerable (as in FZ vi:106), but three are particularly named: Eleth, Uveth, and Ona

(*FZ* vii:95). They symbolize the division into head, heart, and loins. (See ELETH; UVETH; ONA.) In Urizen's palace, "three Central Domes after the Names of his three daughters were encompass'd by the twelve bright halls [of his sons]" (*FZ* ii:174).

When exploring his dens, Urizen encounters the three on a river bank, where they are directing and dividing the waters of Generation; they scream and flee, and he curses them (*FZ* vi:5–46). When he confronts Orc, he summons them to knead the Bread of Sorrow on which to feed Orc; they do it, singing war-songs from the Book of Iron, then beg for rest (*FZ* vii:92–107). Urizen then reads to them from his Book of Brass (sociology); "so shall [you] govern over all" (*FZ* vii:111). Later they compel the Shadowy Female to feed Orc on their bread (*FZ* viii:83). In the Last Judgment, they "guard Ahania's death couch; rising from the confusion in tears & howlings & despair, calling upon their father's Name upon their Rivers dark" (*FZ* ix:201). Then they are presumably restored to their original forms, for at the Sowing, they "stand with Cups & measures of foaming wine, immense upon the heavens with bread & delicate repasts" (*FZ* ix:333).

URIZEN'S SONS were originally identified as materialized men (*VDA* 5:3). The first four emerge from the four Elements: Thiriel (air), Utha (water), Grodna (earth), and Fuzon (fire), then "all his eternal sons in like manner" (*Ur* 23:10–19). He curses his children, "for he saw that no flesh nor spirit could keep his iron laws one moment" (*Ur* 23:23–26). Beneath the spider web of his religion, they reptilize. "Six days they shrunk up from existence, and on the seventh day they rested, and they bless'd the seventh day in sick hope and forgot their eternal life" (*Ur* 25:39). Degenerating, they inhabit thirty cities in Egypt. Fuzon calls together "the remaining children of Urizen" and they abandon "the pendulous earth" (*Ur* 28:20). *The Book of Ahania* continues the tale with the Oedipean revolt of Fuzon against his father. Fuzon's globe of wrath divides Urizen's loins; Urizen's Emanation Ahania becomes separated from him and is named Sin; then Urizen retaliates with the poisonous rock of the Ten Commandments, and crucifies the smitten Fuzon on the Tree of Mystery. (See FUZON; BOOK OF AHANIA.)

Blake abandoned this myth, however. In *The Four Zoas* the Sons are "the sons of wisdom" who dwelt on the silver mountains of Urizen (v:192, 199) and fulfilled his commands. They gathered round his knees (vi: 209) and round his ample table (ix:127). They are musicians, singing and playing "the instruments of harmony" (ix:302), and are followed by the harpers of the sunrise (v:199).

They are the signs of the Zodiac, for although they are innumerable, Blake twice numbers them as twelve, after whose names Urizen built the twelve halls of his palace (ii:173) and erected the altar with twelve steps (ii:199). They build the Mundane Shell (ii:26–248). "They weigh'd & order'd all" (ii:259), dividing the deep with compasses and weighing the cubes in scales (ii:142). They create the stars of heaven "like a golden chain to bind the Body of Man to heaven from falling into the Abyss. Each took his station & his course began with sorrow & care" (ii:266). "The morning stars [are Urizen's] obedient Sons" (iii:5). With the Daughters they rule the astronomical heavens and the seasons (ii:269–86).

When Luvah assumed Urizen's world to the South, the Sons fell with their father to the Center (*FZ* i:538; *Mil* 19:19; 34:38; *J* 59:15); and when Urizen casts out Ahania, they flee from his throne to the four quarters (*FZ* iii:133). In his ruined world, Urizen curses his children (*FZ* vi:46); then, on seeing them in the tortures of Hell, he repents but is helpless, as they are cursed beyond his curse (*FZ* vi:142). He fixes the sciences, thus gaining a new dominion over his children (*FZ* vi:237). However, when he approaches the North, four of his mighty sons, armed in the four metals, lead Urthona's armies against their father (*FZ* vi:314).

At his command, they build the temple of sexual religion, and drag down the sun to illuminate it (*FZ* vii *b*:18–38). When the hostilities break out, they forge the weapons of war and the machinery of the Industrial Revolution (*FZ* vii *b*:170–86; *J* 65:12). They are warriors, can man ten thousand chariots (*FZ* i:344), and could teach warfare to Orc (*FZ* vii:91).

However, at the end they are rejuvenated with their father. On the First Day of the Last Judgment, they fling away their weapons, singing and playing musical instruments while they prepare Urizen's plow; then they bring him the seed for the sowing, finally feasting and resting (*FZ* ix:291–341). On the Second Day, they reap the harvest, bind it in sheaves, and store it in the barns (*FZ* ix:583). On the Fourth Day, they gather the grapes for the vintage (*FZ* ix:694).

In *Jerusalem*, the Sons presumably build Urizen's druid temple under his direction (*J* 58:21–51).

URTHONA ("earth owner") is the northern Zoa, the creative Imagination of the Individual. (Jesus is the universal Imagination.) In the Trinity, Urthona corresponds to the Holy Ghost. His southern contrary is Reason (Urizen). In the counterclockwise numeration, which begins with Tharmas (the body), he is the fourth (*FZ* i:14–16; *J* 39:7), or the last to be perceived. His position is North (*FZ* vi:268; *Mil* 19:16; *J* 59:11); his Element is Earth (*FZ* i:18); his Metal is Iron (*J* 97–11). He is a blacksmith (*FZ* i:519; *J* 95:17), constantly occupied with creating forms. He makes the "spades & coulters" of peace (*FZ* i:520) and "the golden armour of science for intellectual War" (*FZ* ix:853). His forge is in the deep dens or caves of the subconscious (*MHH* 26; *FZ* v:189; vii *b*:133; ix:840). His Sense is the Ear (*J* 12:60; *FZ* i:17); his Art is Poetry, which when it degenerates becomes Religion (*Mil* 27:60). He is "keeper of the gates of heaven" (*FZ* iv:42; *J* 82:81), where he is assisted by Luvah (*FZ* v:232).

Urthona is the deepest and most mysteri-

ous of the Zoas. He is called "dark" thirteen times (*FZ* i:519–ix:821). He never manifests in his own person. Unlike the other Zoas, he has no Emanation, although Enitharmon once sits as his unnamed "wife" beside him at the feast (*FZ* ix:778); but she is really the Emanation of Los, who is the manifestation of Urthona.

He fell during the warfare of Urizen and Luvah over Man. In the tumult, Urthona's sons fled from him; Enitharmon and his Spectre (Los) were divided from him; his body fell like a raging serpent; and he was driven "into the world of Tharmas, into a cavern'd rock" (*FZ* i:519–34). Later, Urizen blames himself for dragging down Urthona and Luvah (*FZ* vi:225). Urthona sank out of sight into the Nadir, or subconscious mind. See NADIR. Thereafter, he sits there "doubting & despairing" (*J* 43:3). His world has become impenetrable. "North stood Urthona's stedfast throne, a World of Solid darkness, shut up in stifling obstruction, rooted in dumb despair" (*FZ* vi:269); it is "solid Darkness, unfathomable, without end" (*J* 59:19; *Mil* 19:23).

However, in this world, Urthona is divided fourfold, and his separated faculties are active. Los is his Humanity (*J* 30:13, 16); Los's Emanation is Enitharmon (*J* 30:3–4); he also has a Spectre (*J* 30:4) and a Shadow (*J* 30:6). Los himself is "the Vehicular Form of strong Urthona" (*J* 53:1). He takes his name where "Mortality begins to roll the billows of Eternal Death before the Gate of Los" (*J* 39:8). The theme of *The Four Zoas* is "his fall into Division & his Resurrection to Unity: his fall into the Generation of decay & death, & his Regeneration by the Resurrection from the dead" (*FZ* i:21).

However, when at the moment of death, Los destroys the sun and moon, (*FZ* ix:6–9), he disappears, flashing forth momentarily as the regenerate Urthona (*FZ* ix:801), then vanishing completely (*FZ* ix:851). Meanwhile, when on the Fifth Day Albion summons Urthona, the latter is already sitting at the Feast. Tharmas and he rise, "satiated with Mirth & Joy," and for a moment he is equated with Vulcan: "Urthona, limping from his fall, on Tharmas lean'd, in his right hand his hammer" (*FZ* ix:774). On the Sixth Day, he grinds the wheat; men sorrowing at night "write the bitter words of Stern Philosophy & knead the Bread of Knowledge with tears & groans" (*FZ* ix:819); then Urthona bakes "the Bread of Ages," and takes his repose "in Winter, in the night of Time" (*FZ* ix: 824). Thus the experience of one age becomes the food of the next.

Then on the Seventh Day, he is heard at work in his "deep caves beneath" (*FZ* ix: 841). "Urthona is arisen in his strength, no longer now divided from Enitharmon, no longer the Spectre Los. . . . Urthona rises from the ruinous Walls in all his ancient strength to form the golden armour of science for intellectual War" (*FZ* ix:849–51).

In *Europe* (3:9), Los announces: "Again the night is come that strong Urthona takes his rest, and Urizen, unloos'd from chains, glows like a meteor in the distant north." Los then disappears until the end of the poem, leaving the world in the dominion of Enitharmon, the Female Will.

Urthona is mentioned first in "A Song of Liberty" (*MHH* 26), when the fallen Urizen is "buried in the ruins on Urthona's dens." The Shadowy Female is called Urthona's daughter (*Am* 1:1); and Orc, in one of his metamorphoses, is "a serpent folding around the pillars of Urthona" (*Am* 1:15).

URTHONA'S SPECTRE is Los separated from Enitharmon. See LOS.

UTHA is the second of the first four sons of Urizen. He is the Element Water (*Ur* 23: 13). See URIZEN'S SONS, under URIZEN.

UVETH (the heart) is the second of the three daughters of Urizen, who direct the River of Generation. She is a "terrible woman, clad in blue, whose strong attractive power draws all into a fountain at the rock of [her] attraction. With frowning brow [she sits], mistress of these mighty waters" (*FZ* vi:13). When the sisters make Orc's bitter bread, her icy hands knead the dough in her trough (*FZ* vii:102; viii:77). See URIZEN'S DAUGHTERS, under URIZEN.

UZZAH, fearing that the Holy Ark would fall from the cart in which it was being transported to Jerusalem, tried to steady it, and was struck dead instantly by the angry God (*II Sam* vi:6–8; *I Chron* xiii:9–11).

"Man is the ark of God . . . if thou seekest by human policy to guide this ark, remember Uzzah" (On Lavater 533, *K* 82). When the warrior trembles on approaching the Daughter of Albion, "by the fires of thy secret tabernacle and thy ark & holy place, at thy frowns, at thy dire revenge, smitten as Uzzah of old, his armour is soften'd, his spear and sword faint in his hand" (*J* 68: 49).

VALA is the goddess of Nature (*J* 18:30; 34:9). As everything we see is an exteriorization of our emotions, she is quite properly the Emanation of Luvah, the eastern Zoa. Her name is that of the Scandinavian prophetess and guardian spirit of the earth in the oldest *Edda*, the "Völuspa." Wagner applied her name (which he pronounced "Valla") to the earth-goddess Erda (*Siegfried* III.i, etc.).

Vala first appears in *The Four Zoas*, which originally was to be called "Vala" (t.p.) or "The Book of Vala" (*FZ* i:3). However, she is not the leading character of the epic, although she is the prime cause of Albion's fall. "Among the Flowers of Beulah walk'd the Eternal Man & saw Vala the lilly of the desert melting in high noon; upon her bosom in sweet bliss he fainted. . . . There he revel'd in delight among the Flowers. Vala was pregnant & brought forth Urizen, Prince of Light, first born of Generation. Then behold a wonder to the Eyes of the now fallen Man: a double form Vala appear'd, a Male and female; shudd'ring pale the Fallen Man recoil'd from the Enormity & call'd them Luvah & Vala" (*FZ* vii:239–48). He sought to comfort Vala, but she left his throne for "the shadows [delusions] of her garden, weeping for Luvah lost" (*FZ* i:286). When "The Dark'ning Man" walked with Vala "in dreams of soft deluding slumber," he came to worship his own Shadow, "And Vala trembled & cover'd her face, & her locks were spread on the pavement" (*FZ* iii:44–56; *J* 29:33–43); whereupon Luvah smote him with Job's boils and contracted his four senses (*FZ* iii:

78–90; *J* 29:61–71). "And now the Human Blood foam'd high . . . Luvah & Vala went down the Human Heart, where Paradise & its joys abounded, in jealous fears, in fury & rage, & flames roll'd round their fervid feet, and the vast form of Nature like a Serpent play'd before them. And as they went, in folding fires & thunders of the deep, Vala shrunk in like the dark sea that leaves its slimy banks; and from her bosom Luvah fell far as the east and west, and the vast form of Nature like a Serpent roll'd between" (*FZ* iii:94–101; *J* 29:73). The two have moved from Luvah's eastern realm into Urizen's. And thus Vala's lovely form "drew the body of Man from heaven" (*FZ* v:47). It was at this time, while Albion, Urizen, and Vala slept, that Luvah seized Urizen's chariot of light (*FZ* i:263). See URIZEN.

"But Luvah and Vala standing in the bloody sky on high remain'd alone, forsaken, in fierce jealousy. They stood above the heavens, forsaken, desolate, suspended in blood. Descend they could not, nor from Each other avert their eyes." They are vouchsafed a vision of the Incarnation, "One Man infolded in Luvah's robes of blood," but it means nothing to them (*FZ* i:359–65). The demons of the deep sing: "Luvah & Vala ride triumphant in the bloody sky, & the Human form is no more" (*FZ* i:408).

But the two are now hopelessly divided. Vala is "the sweet wanderer" (*FZ* ii:110; iii:85; ix:576). Luvah recalls her persistent development towards material nature, in spite of all he could do. First she was an earthworm, then a scaled serpent, then a dragon; he fed her insatiable thirst with all the floods of heaven and commanded the great deep to hide her; she then became a little weeping infant and hid in her gardens, where she bore him sons and daughters; nevertheless, she always hated him, and finally disappeared (*FZ* ii:83–97). She does not recognize him; "in vain his love brought him in various forms before her, still she knew him not, still she despis'd him, calling on his name & knowing him not, still hating, still professing love" (*FZ* ii:232), "& calling him the Tempter" (*FZ* iii:129).

Urizen takes advantage of their division to build the Mundane Shell out of Luvah's substance. "Luvah was cast into [Urizen's] Furnaces of affliction & sealed, and Vala fed in cruel delight the furnaces with fire" (*FZ* ii:72; *J* 7:30). Luvah is melted down; Vala's fires burn to a heap of ashes (*FZ* ii:113); the furnaces are opened; and the Mundane Shell is cast from Luvah's substance, while Vala's ashes are mingled with the mortar (*FZ* ii:171). She herself is compelled to labor lamenting (*FZ* ii:215; *Mil* 19:43): "I see not Luvah as of old, I only see his feet like pillars of fire travelling thro' darkness & non entity" (*FZ* ii:229).

After a long period, Vala begins to reanimate in Enitharmon's bursting heart (*FZ* v:179). However, when at last she reappears, she has sunk into the material form of the Shadowy Female (*FZ* vii *b*:137, 229). (See SHADOWY FEMALE.) The Spectre announces: "I will bring down soft Vala to the embraces of this terror [Orc]" (*FZ* vii:299), and puts him in her charge (*FZ* vii:332). Speechless, she feeds him his bitter bread until he reaches the age of fourteen, breaks loose, and embraces her (*Am* 1–2; *FZ* vii *b*:124–43). This is the outbreak of war; she is hailed as its presiding spirit (*FZ* vii *b*:187–209; *J* 65:29–55).

When Tharmas does not recognize the Female, she identifies herself as Vala; he replies: "Vala, thy sins have lost us heaven & bliss. Thou art our Curse" (*FZ* vii *b*:229, 256). But in spite of the beauties of nature, she remains a howling melancholy (*FZ* vii

b:269–87). In vain she pleads with Urizen to restore Luvah (*FZ* viii:145–70); she saturates with her tears the Web of Religion, which falls, entangling Urizen (*FZ* viii:176).

The division of Luvah and Vala is most explicit when War becomes the Hermaphrodite, from whose bosom Satan bursts, "a male without a female counterpart . . . yet hiding the shadowy female Vala as in an ark & Curtains" (*FZ* viii:253–55); at the same time, confronting Satan, Jesus appears "in the Robes of Luvah" (*FZ* viii:263). To condemn Jesus as a transgressor, Urizen summons the Synagogue of Satan; in the midst is "a False Feminine Counterpart of Lovely Delusive Beauty, Dividing & Uniting at will in the Cruelties of Holiness, Vala, drawn down into a Vegetated body, now triumphant" (*FZ* viii:278). She has become the Scarlet Woman of *Revelation*, "Mystery, Babylon the Great, the Mother of Harlots" (*FZ* viii:330; *J* 70:31). But after the Crucifixion, "when Rahab had cut off the Mantle of Luvah from the Lamb of God, it roll'd apart, revealing to all . . . Rahab in all her turpitude" (*FZ* viii:341–44). She confronts Urizen, who "beheld reveal'd before the face of heaven his secret holiness" (*FZ* viii:412); and "forgetful of his own Laws, pitying he began to embrace the shadowy Female" (*FZ* viii:420); and becomes the Dragon of *Revelation*. But Rahab is uncertain in her mind: she questions Los, only to depart "burning with pride & revenge" (*FZ* viii:410); she then alternates between the Synagogue and (in secret) Orc; with the result that the Synagogue burns her with fire, but her ashes animate and become Deism (*FZ* viii:618). See RAHAB.

At the Last Judgment, Rahab is consumed (*FZ* ix:32, 67, 157, 657). When Urizen renounces his authority, he gives "all my joy unto this Luvah & Vala" (*FZ* ix:179), and is instantly rejuvenated. After the plowing of the First Day, "The Regenerate Man . . . in his holy hands reciev'd the flaming Demon [Orc] & Demoness of smoke and gave them to Urizen's hands; the Immortal frown'd saying, 'Luvah & Vala, henceforth you are Servants; obey and live.

You shall forget your former state; return, & Love in peace, into your place, the place of seed, not in the brain or heart' " (*FZ* ix: 360). They are thus demoted from Heart to Loins; love and lust become one.

Luvah and Vala then descend from Urizen's hands into "the shadows of Vala's Garden" (*FZ* ix: 376). See VALA'S GARDEN, below. In this realm of reverie, closed up from the tumult of the universe, they live in their "ancient golden age" (*FZ* ix: 386). They are still separated: Vala can see Luvah only in dreams, but she can hear his voice; meanwhile, he acts as her guardian. (Luvah in his cloud addressing Vala suggests Thel and her cloud; the invisible lover of the beautiful maiden also suggests Apuleius' myth of Cupid and Psyche.) Vala tends her flocks, and while she sleeps at noon, the unseen Luvah constructs a palace round her. She wakes; she bathes in the river; "and as she rose her eyes were open'd to the world of waters" (*FZ* ix: 483), where she beholds the bearded Tharmas mourning for Enion. But when she returns to her palace, she finds Tharmas and Enion playing together as two children. "Thus in Eternal Childhood, straying among Vala's flocks, in infant sorrow & joy alternate Enion & Tharmas play'd round Vala in the Gardens of Vala & by her river's margin. They are the shadows of Tharmas & of Enion in Vala's world" (*FZ* ix: 553). Whatever the state of the two in the world of Experience, the soul of sweet delight can never be defiled.

On the Second Day of Judgment, Urizen pours forth his light "to exhale the spirits" of the two "thro' the atmosphere. . . . in all their ancient innocence," but though they respond to the light, Luvah is still lamenting the loss of Vala (*FZ* ix: 569–76). Their reunion is not described, but at the feast of the Fifth Day, Vala is there with the other Emanations, who rise from the feast to tend their looms (*FZ* ix: 778–79). After the vintage, the two fall asleep on the floor (*FZ* ix: 788). When they wake, they try to rejoin the Eternal Man, but "he cast them wailing into the world of shadows [Vala's Garden]

. . . till winter is over & gone" (*FZ* ix: 795–98); and presumably the spring comes on the Seventh Day.

In *Jerusalem*, Blake studied at length the relationship of Vala and Jerusalem—of the laws of nature and freedom. Basically, the two are twin aspects of Albion's wife, Brittannia: when the Zoas changed their places, "England, who is Brittannia, divided into Jerusalem & Vala" (36:28). When England drew away from Albion's embrace, Jerusalem and Vala appeared in the dragon wings above her (54:31). Vala, however, is but Jerusalem's Shadow (12:19; 31:41), "animated by [her] tears" (11:24–25), "builded by the Reasoning power in Man" (44:40). "Vala produc'd the Bodies, Jerusalem gave the Souls" (18:7).

Jesus took Jerusalem, Albion's Emanation, as his bride, and gave Vala to Albion for his wife (20:40; 63:7; 64:19; 65:71). Thus God and Man are joined through their Emanations. "Vala was Albion's Bride & Wife in great Eternity, the loveliest of the daughters of Eternity when in day-break I emanated from Luvah over the Towers of Jerusalem . . . why loved I Jerusalem? Why was I one with her, embracing in the Vision of Jesus?" (33:39–44).

Vala is still Luvah's Emanation; she is also his daughter (63:7; 64:19; 80:27); she acknowledges him both as father and as lover (80:16–23). As in *The Four Zoas*, she fires the furnace where her unrecognized Luvah is being melted down (7:30). From the burning rises a pillar of smoke "writhing afar into Non-Entity" (5:51), which contains the weeping Vala and Jerusalem. Vala, however, being the laws of nature, is of course the enemy of Liberty: "Vala would never have sought & loved Albion if she had not sought to destroy Jerusalem; such is that false and Generating Love, a pretence of love to destroy love, cruel hipocrisy" (17:24). Vala claims dominion over her victim. "Albion is mine! Luvah gave me to Albion and now recieves reproach & hate" (31:50).

Jerusalem and Vala, "the Lilly of Havilah," are still friends, singing together in

Lambeth, when the sinking Albion finds them (19:40–24:63). Vala and Albion are obsessed with sin and guilt; Jerusalem protests against their state of mind; whereupon Albion rejects Jerusalem as a delusion, and casts Vala's "Veil of Moral Virtue, woven for Cruel Laws . . . into the Atlantic Deep, to catch the Souls of the Dead" (23:22), then sinks down dying.

The triumphant Vala now proclaims her materialism. "I alone am Beauty. The Imaginative Human Form is but a breathing of Vala: I breathe him forth into the Heaven from my secret Cave, born of the Woman to obey the Woman, O Albion the mighty, for the Divine appearance is Brotherhood, but I am Love elevate into the Region of Brotherhood with my red fires" (33:48–34:1). Los protests: "There is a Throne in every Man, it is the Throne of God; this, Woman has claim'd as her own . . . O Albion, why wilt thou Create a Female Will?" (34:27–31). "The Satanic Holiness triumph'd in Vala, in a Religion of Chastity & Uncircumcised Selfishness both of the Head & Heart & Loins, clos'd up in Moral Pride" (60:47). Nevertheless, she is to give birth to Jesus; his female ancestors are "the Daughters of Vala, Mother of the Body of death" (62:7, 13).

When war breaks out, Vala begins to use her "Druid Knife of Revenge & the Poison Cup of Jealousy" (63:39), which Albion has recognized as hers (22:29). She vegetates into "a hungry Stomach & a devouring Tongue. Her Hand is a Court of Justice: her Feet two Armies in Battle: Storms & Pestilence in her Locks, & in her Loins Earthquake and Fire & the Ruin of Cities & Nations & Families & Tongues" (64:8). The Spectre draws her into his bosom: they stand frowning, the dark Hermaphrodite of War, while Vala turns the iron Spindle of destruction (64:25, 31; 66:10; 71:60). She becomes Rahab (70:31). The Sons of Albion crown her and give her power over the earth (78:15–16). Jerusalem asks what her purposes are (79:68); and nonetheless sincere for being quite confused, she replies: "My Father gave to me command to murder

Albion in unreviving Death; my Love, my Luvah, order'd me in night to murder Albion, the King of Men; he fought in battles fierce, he conquer'd Luvah, my beloved, he took me and my Father, he slew them. I revived them to life in my warm bosom. He saw them issue from my bosom dark in Jealousy. He burn'd before me. Luvah fram'd the Knife & Luvah gave the Knife into his daughter's hand . . . But I, Vala, Luvah's daughter, keep his body, embalm'd in moral laws with spices of sweet odours of lovely jealous stupefaction, within my bosom, lest he arise to life & slay my Luvah" (80:16–29).

Vala-Rahab refuses to take definite form (80:52). Therefore Los tells Albion to determine "a form for Vala and a form for Luvah . . . nail them down on the stems of Mystery" (83:10–13). Vala and Jerusalem cease to mourn when they hear Los's Watch Song (85:15); and Jerusalem takes away "the Cup which foam'd in Vala's hand" (88:56). Vala-Rahab then manifests as the Whore of Babylon in the tabernacle of the Covering Cherub (89:52), and vanishes forever when England-Brittannia wakes: "I have slain in Dreams of Chastity & Moral Law: I have Murdered Albion! . . . I have Slain him in my Sleep with the Knife of the Druid" (94:20–25). But at her repentance, Albion wakes and slays the Covering Cherub.

VALA'S CUP is the Cup of Mystery, the Whore of Babylon, who has "a golden cup in her hand full of abominations and filthiness of her fornication" (*Rev* xvii:4). Blake calls it "the Poison Cup of Jealousy" (*J* 63:39), with "Poisons Twenty-seven-fold" (*J* 75:3), and "the Cup of Delusion" whereby one may reign in pride and oppress an earthly kingdom (*J* 85:31). Bath stands on the Severn, "the Cup of Rahab in his hand" (*J* 75:2–3); Jerusalem finally takes it away from Vala (*J* 88:56).

It is associated with the "Druid Knife of Revenge" (*J* 22:29; 63:39). Once it is identified with the communion cup of worldly religion (*J* 91:13).

In the engraving of Chaucer's pilgrims, the Wife of Bath holds it, thus identifying her as Rahab.

VALA'S GARDEN is the realm of daydreaming, where our hopes and fears take fugitive shapes. Being part subconscious, it is entered through "the Gates of Dark Urthona" (*FZ* ix:375). Here "the impressions of Despair & Hope for ever vegetate in flowers, in fruits, in fishes, birds & beasts & clouds & waters, the land of doubts & shadows, sweet delusions, unform'd hopes" (*FZ* ix: 377), where Luvah and Vala, shut off from the tumult of the universe, renew "their ancient golden age" (*FZ* ix:386). They have recovered their Innocence in the state of reverie. When Vala turns guiltily from Albion after their embrace, she takes refuge here, weeping for her lost Luvah (*FZ* i:286). After Urizen has told the two to behave, they walk from his hands into these "shadows" (*FZ* ix:376) and find themselves again in the state of Innocence. When Man rejects the two before the great work is finished, he casts them into this garden (*FZ* ix:798).

Vala's Garden was probably suggested by Spenser's Gardens of Adonis, "the first seminarie of all things that are borne to live and die" (*FQ* III.vi.30–44). But where Spenser described the philosophical concept of the realm of Platonic ideas, Blake was describing a state of mind familiar to us all.

VALA'S VEIL is the film of matter which covers all reality.

It is the Mundane Shell (*J* 42:81; 59:7; *GoP* 17, *K* 770).

It is our body of flesh (*J* 55:11; 65:61; 67: 16; 90:4) and is therefore described as scarlet (*J* 21:50); or of blood (*J* 67:16; 68:21; 90:4), although in the pictures it is usually blue or dark gray.

It is the code of Moral Law (*J* 21:15; 23: 22, 31), "composed of the Spectres of the Dead" (*J* 47:12)—the reasonings of those blind to Eternity.

It is the Veil in the Temple, which conceals the divinity (*J* 56:40; 59:55—cf. *Exod* xxvi:1, 7, 31), and which Jesus rends at the Crucifixion (*Matt* xxvii:51; *J* 30:40; 55:16; 65:61), "& the whole Druid Law removes away" (*J* 69:39).

In *Jerusalem*, when Vala first wove of tears (20:3) her "beautiful net of gold and silver twine" (20:30), she caught her then beloved Jerusalem in its bands of love. Albion, furiously in love with Vala's beauty, embraced her, rending the Veil (20:36). His soul then melted away "inwoven within the Veil," which Jerusalem had reknitted (23:4). Guilty, he "recoil'd: he rush'd outwards: he bore the Veil whole away. . . . He drew the Veil of Moral Virtue, woven for Cruel Laws, and cast it into the Atlantic Deep, to catch the Souls of the Dead" (23: 20–23), "a Law, a Terror & a Curse" (23: 32). "Thund'ring the Veil rushes from his hand, Vegetating Knot by Knot, Day by Day, Night by Night" (24:61). When it began "to Vegetate & Petrify around the Earth of Albion among the Roots of his Tree," Los formed it into "the beautiful Mundane Shell, the Habitation of the Spectres of the Dead" (59:2–8). It is "the Net & Veil of Vala among the Souls of the Dead" (42:81), "composed of the Spectres of the Dead" (47:12).

"VEGETATE is one of Taylor's favorite expressions to describe the living death of the earthly existence" (*Harper* 163). Actually "vegetative" is a medical term applied to those physiological functions or systems which are automatic and beyond the control of the will, such as growth in general, or digestion and sleep.

But "We who dwell on Earth can do nothing of ourselves; every thing is conducted by Spirits, no less than Digestion or Sleep" (*J* 3). All causation is psychological, not material: "every Natural Effect has a Spiritual Cause, and Not a Natural; for a Natural Cause only seems: it is a Delusion of Ulro & a ratio of the perishing Vegetable Memory" (*Mil* 26:44). "There is no Such Thing as . . . a Natural Cause for any Thing in any Way" (On Bacon, *K* 403).

Therefore Blake called all material things "vegetative" or "vegetable," the mortal body as well as the astronomical universe. To "vegetate" is to materialize. In the last illustration to *Il Penseroso*, "the Spirits of the Herbs & Flowers" are the lovers, the mother, and the baby.

The spirits who "controll our Vegetative powers" in every bosom are the Daughters of Albion (*J* 5:39). However, it is the Daughters of Beulah who meet the Spectre "& give to it a form of vegetation" (*FZ* i: 105). And Enion has a "shining loom of Vegetation" in which she draws the Spectre forth from Tharmas (*FZ* i:122). "Shakspeare's Fairies . . . are the rulers of the vegetable world, and so are Chaucer's; let them be so considered, and then the poet will be understood, and not else" (*DesC* III, *K* 570).

But whatever is created shall be destroyed. This is accomplished by the mysterious "Two Beings each with three heads; they Represent Vegetative Existence . . . it represents the Eternal Consummation of Vegetable Life & Death with its Lusts. The wreathed Torches in their hands represents Eternal Fire which is the fire of Generation or Vegetation; it is an Eternal Consummation." At the Last Judgment, it is they who strip Mystery naked and burn her with fire, "as it is written in Revelations" (*LJ*, *K* 609; see Illustrations, "LJ" Nos. 49, 48); but according to John the Divine this is done by the ten horns of the beast (*Rev* xvii:16).

VEIL. See VALA's VEIL, under VALA.

"VENGEANCE" is Blake's term for the punishment of sins. What seems to us impartial Justice is really an attempt to suppress our own sins, and has a terrible effect on the punisher. It is contrary to the teachings of Jesus.

"Every Religion that Preaches Vengeance for Sin is the Religion of the Enemy & Avenger and not of the Forgiver of Sin, and their God is Satan, Named by the Divine Name" (*J* 52). "Why did you take Vengeance, O ye Sons of the mighty Albion? . . . Injury the Lord heals, but Vengeance cannot be healed. As the Sons of Albion have done to Luvah, so they have in him done to the Divine Lord & Saviour, who suffers with those that suffer; for not one sparrow can suffer & the whole Universe not suffer also in all its Regions, & its Father & Saviour not pity and weep, but Vengeance is the destroyer of Grace & Repentance in the bosom of the Injurer, in which the Divine Lamb is cruelly slain" (*J* 25:3–11). "What shall I do! what could I do if I could find these Criminals? I could not dare to take vengeance, for all things are so constructed and builded by the Divine hand that the sinner shall always escape. And he who takes vengeance alone is the criminal of Providence. If I should dare to lay my finger on a grain of sand in way of vengeance, I punish the already punish'd. O whom should I pity if I pity not the sinner who is gone astray?" (*J* 31:29). "Hark! & Record the terrible wonder! that the Punisher mingles with his Victim's Spectre, enslaved and tormented to him whom he has murder'd, bound in vengeance & enmity" (*J* 47:14).

VENUS was the Roman goddess of love. Her paramour was Mars, the god of war. The association of the two symbolized for Blake the close connection between sex and war. The warriors invoke her name (*J* 68:18). The two with Apollo defended Troy and were "the detestable gods of Priam" (*Mil* 14:15).

When Blake was a boy, his father bought him various casts, among which was "the Venus of Medicis" (*Malkin* xix), the best known example of the "Venus pudica," who modestly covers her breasts and pudenda. Cambel (*J* 81) assumes this pose, also Eve in Blake's illuminated *Genesis* iii, which he headed: "Of the Sexual Nature and the Fall into Generation and Death." In the Rosenwald "Last Judgment" (see Illustrations, "LJ" No. 32), a woman in that posture is dragged down by a spirit holding a key.

The Venus and all the other statues of

classical gods are "representations of spiritual existences, of Gods immortal to the mortal perishing organ of sight" (*DesC* IV, *K* 576), copied from "those wonderful originals called in the Sacred Scriptures the Cherubim" (*DesC* II, *K* 565). "These gods are visions of the eternal attributes, or divine names, which, when erected into gods, become destructive to humanity" (*DesC* III, *K* 571).

Thor and Friga are for Blake the Scandinavian equivalents of Mars and Venus. See FRIGA.

VERULAM, in Hertfordshire, was the most important town of southern England during the days of the Romans. After their departure, it fell to ruins and was never rebuilt, being replaced in the eighth century by St. Albans, on the opposite bank of the river Ver. Spenser describes Verulam in his *Ruines of Time*, but in Blake's day it was so unimportant that it was not represented in Cary's Atlas of 1787, nor does the name appear in the index of the 1906 Baedeker.

Verulam never contained a cathedral, nor did St. Albans until 1877, when the famous Abbey Church was elevated to that dignity. Blake, however, made Verulam one of his four chief Cathedral Cities, which he placed South under Urizen (*J* 46:24; 74:3). He chose the name doubtless because Francis Bacon, who "put an End to Faith" (On Bacon, *K* 398), was created Baron Verulam and Viscount St. Albans; furthermore, Bacon was buried in St. Michael's, which was within the site of Verulam and was partly constructed out of its ruins.

Verulam is in the ecclesiastical province of Canterbury. Blake identified Verulam with Canterbury (*J* 38:45), which was also spiritually in ruins (*Mil* 39:41), and elsewhere substituted "Verulam" for "Canterbury" (*J* 46:24). His words about Verulam therefore are a criticism of the Anglican Church, which he believed to have become materialistic.

The invented temple at Verulam is described in *Europe* as a druidic serpent temple, "image of infinite, shut up in finite revolutions" (10:21). It is "golden"—Urizen's metal (10:5; *J* 38:46). It stands in an oak grove. Its pillars are "plac'd in the order of the stars, when the five senses whelm'd in deluge o'er the earth-born man" (10:7, 10). It contains the Stone of Night, "image of that sweet south once open to the heavens, and elevated on the human neck, now overgrown with hair and cover'd with a stony roof. Downward 'tis sunk beneath th' attractive north" (10:26-30)—i.e., man is now upside down. Thus "man became an Angel, Heaven a mighty circle turning, God a tyrant crown'd" (10:22).

In its eternal state, Verulam-Canterbury is the "venerable parent of men, generous immortal Guardian, golden clad!" (*J* 38:45); but after its decay, it became the brain and heart of druidic materialism. "In Verulam the Polypus's Head, winding around his bulk," passes through the Cathedral Cities to Bristol, "& his Heart beat strong on Salisbury Plain, shooting out Fibres round the Earth" (*J* 67:35-38).

Although it is sixteen miles away, Spenser located Verulam on the Thames (*Ruines* 2), and so did Blake (*Eur* 10:5).

VESPUTIUS was Americus Vespucius (1454-1512), a Florentine explorer, who claimed to be a member of the expedition which discovered the mainland of America. Therefore the German geographer Martin Waldseemüller in 1507 suggested that the new lands be named "America"; thus Vespucius got the credit which should have gone to Columbus.

"Columbus discover'd America, but Americus Vesputius finish'd & smooth'd it over, like an English Engraver or Corregio & Titian" (*PubA*, *K* 598).

The VINTAGE is an episode of the Last Judgment described in *Revelation* xiv:18–20. First an angel reaps the Harvest of the earth: "And another angel came out from the altar, which had power over fire; and cried with a loud cry to him that had the sharp sickle, saying, Thrust in thy sharp sickle, and gather the clusters of the vine of the earth; for her grapes are fully ripe. And the angel thrust in his sickle into the earth, and gathered the vine of the earth, and cast it into the great winepress of the wrath of God. And the winepress was trodden without the city, and blood came out of the winepress, even unto the horse bridles, by the space of a thousand and six hundred furlongs." This Vintage has customarily been interpreted as signifying war; Blake followed this interpretation (*Mil* 27:8), as later did Julia Ward Howe: "He is trampling out the vintage where the grapes of wrath are stored."

For Blake, the Harvest and Vintage, which on earth are the disasters preceding the Millennium, are in heaven the making of the bread and wine of Eternity. The Vintage takes place on the Fifth Day, and is the work of Luvah and his children. When the grapes are pressed, Luvah and Vala, over-wearied, sleep on the floor, while Urthona and Tharmas with their children separate the lees and load their wagons with the wine (*FZ* ix:715–94).

In *Milton* the Last Vintage is eagerly anticipated as the revolution in world thought (23:59). Blake himself is "the Signal that the Last Vintage now approaches" (24:42), and the reaping of the whole earth is to begin at Lambeth (25:48). Los is in charge, putting the oppressor and the oppressed indiscriminately into the vats (25:6). The Wine-press is situated on the Rhine (25:3) in the battles of the Napoleonic wars. It is also "eastward of Golgonooza before the Seat of Satan: Luvah laid the foundation & Urizen finish'd it in howling woe" (27:1). The children of Luvah tread the grapes (25:1; 27:3); then the description given in *The Four Zoas* ix:742–71 is repeated with a few additions (*Mil* 27:3–41). After Blake's mystical vision of Ololon, all is ready "to go forth to the Great Harvest & Vintage of the Nations" (*Mil* 43:1).

The VIPER is a poisonous snake which was supposed to kill its mother by eating its way out of the womb. Naturally, Albion's Angel calls Orc, the spirit of revolution in America, "Eternal Viper, self-renew'd . . . writhing in pangs of abhorred birth . . . devourer of thy parent . . . those ever-hissing jaws and parched lips drop with fresh gore . . . thy mother lays her length outstretch'd upon the shore beneath" (*Am* 9:15–25).

Possibly Blake had read John Trumbull's American best-seller *M'Fingal* (1782), in which the Tory squire denounces the Whigs: "Ungrateful sons! a factious band, | That rise against your parent land. | Ye viper race, that burst in strife | The welcome womb that gave you life, | Tear with sharp fangs and forked tongue | Th' indulgent bowels whence you sprung."

Americans were not averse to being symbolized as a poisonous snake. Franklin's much-copied "Join, or Die"—the first American newspaper cartoon—which represented the Colonies as a disjointed snake, appeared in the *Pennsylvania Gazette* as early as 1754. There was also the Rattlesnake Flag of the Revolution ("Don't Tread on Me").

In the third "Memorable Fancy" (*MHH* 15), the Viper appears as an early stage of creative activity: "In the second chamber was a Viper folding round the rock & the cave, and others adorning it with gold, silver, and precious stones."

VIRGIL, the greatest Roman poet, was never a favorite of Blake's. He ranked him, as the writer of an epic, automatically with Homer and Milton (To Trusler, 23 Aug 1799); but twenty years later, he was trying to prove that Greece and Rome "were destroyers of all Art. Homer, Virgil & Ovid confirm this opinion & make us reverence The Word of God, the only light of antiquity that remains unperverted by War. Virgil in the Eneid, Book VI, line 848, says 'Let others study Art: Rome has somewhat better to do, namely War & Dominion' " (*On Virgil, K* 778). Also: "Empire against Art—See Virgil's Eneid, Lib. VI, v. 848" (*Laoc, K* 777). "Eneas is here shewn a worse man than Achilles in leaving Dido" (On Boyd, *K* 412). "Ceasar, Virgil's Only God—see Eclogue I" (On Thornton, *K* 789).

It is true that Virgil treated his mythological characters merely as persons in his narrative; Ovid was equally superficial.

VIRGINIA, one of the thirteen original States, took a leading part in the American Revolution. At the arrival of the plagues from Albion, "the builder of Virginia throws this hammer down in fear" (*Am* 14:16).

VIRGINITY is of the mind and not the body. Like Spenser's Chastity, it is *not* abstinence, "that wishes but acts not" (*MHH* 27), but the innocent, normal development of soul and body. Oothoon, though raped by Bromion, declares herself a virgin (*VDA* 6:21), contrasting herself with the technical virgin, whose acquired modesty is lustful hypocrisy (*VDA* 6:7–11; 7:3–5). The soul of sweet delight can never be defiled. But in *The Golden Net* (*K* 424), the three technical virgins torture the poet.

VIRTUES and Vices are the false standards of Good and Evil, the basis of the Moral Code. Jesus ignored the Moral Code in treating human problems, and by teaching Forgiveness defied the Mosaic Law. "Our Virtues & Cruel Goodnesses have deserv'd Eternal Death," cry the penitent Elect (*Mil* 13:34).

VISION is the perception of the human in all things. All nature is a projection of ourselves. "As a man is, So he Sees." Each person sees the universe in his own way. "The tree which moves some to tears of joy is in the Eyes of others only a Green thing that stands in the way" (To Trusler, 23 Aug 1799). No two painters could possibly paint the same landscape identically. "All that we See is Vision" (*Laoc*, *K* 776). However, it is seen "not with but through the eye." The psychological term is empathy; it is the direct contrary of Ruskin's unfortunate theory of the Pathetic Fallacy.

Blake's visions were not supernatural: they were intensifications of normal experience. He believed that "all men partake of it, but it is lost by not being cultivated" (*CR*

264). "You have the same faculty as I . . . only you do not trust or cultivate it. You can see what I see, *if you choose*. . . . You have only to work up imagination to the state of vision, and the thing is done" (*Gil* I, 364). But "The Nature of Visionary Fancy, or Imagination, is very little Known" (*LJ*, *K* 605).

As a painter, Blake could visualize things not actually before his eyes. But the thought-emotions which rose from his subconscious inevitably took human form in visual symbols, with a vividness and completeness comparable to the color-visions of peyote. "He who does not imagine in stronger and better lineaments, and in stronger and better light than his perishing and mortal eye can see, does not imagine at all" (*DesC* IV, *K* 576). This happens to everybody in his dreams; Blake's visions might be considered waking dreams.

Blake always insisted that Vision and Memory are entirely different; yet it is obvious that Memory furnished all the raw materials for his visions. But something happened to these materials in his subconscious: they altered, combined into new forms, in accordance with the thought which Blake was expressing. Therefore, even when he seemed to be copying, he gave a freshness and spontaneity to his images, so that they became original with him. He *used* these materials; he did not really copy; he was no plagiarist. His attacks on Memory as inspiration were therefore impelled by that self-protective instinct which permits the creations by denying sources. See PAINTING.

Blake distinguished four degrees of Vision. "Now I a fourfold vision see, | And a fourfold vision is given to me; | 'Tis fourfold in my supreme delight | And threefold in soft Beulah's night | And twofold Always. May God us keep | From Single vision & Newton's sleep!" (To Butts, 22 Nov 1802, 2nd letter, 83–88).

Single vision is not properly "vision" at all: it is seeing with the physical eye only the facts before it. It "leads you to Believe a Lie | When you see with, not thro' the Eye" (*EG* d:105). Twofold vision is seeing "through" the eye: it is the perception of the human values in all things. Then the thistle in the path reveals a discouraging old man (To Butts, 22 Nov 1802, 23–30), or the rising sun "an Innumerable company of the Heavenly host crying 'Holy, Holy, Holy is the Lord God Almighty!'" (*LJ*, *K* 617). Threefold vision "in soft Beulah's night" is the creative state, where thought appears in emotional form. Fourfold vision, "my supreme delight," is the mystical ecstasy, such as the one Blake has just been describing to Butts.

Blake claimed he had the ability to see visions "from earliest infancy" (*Gil* I, 7). The earliest we know of occurred at the age of four, when God put his head to the nursery window and set him a-screaming (*CR* 293). Blake, however, dated his "first vision" when he was a boy "of eight or ten perhaps"; sauntering in Peckham Rye, he saw "a tree filled with angels, bright angelic wings bespangling every bough like stars." This was followed shortly one summer morn when he saw angelic figures walking amid the haymakers (*Gil* I, 7). His father tried to beat this mendacious nonsense out of him, but the boy persisted. He knew well enough that these angels were the products of his imagination; but he was not lying—his visions were valuable aesthetic facts. And he kept on seeing visions all his life.

A VISION OF THE LAST JUDGMENT (1810) was intended to be added to Blake's *Descriptive Catalogue* when he planned to hold another exhibition in spite of the failure of 1809. But the second exhibition was never held, the *Catalogue* was never reissued, and the *Vision* exists only in unorganized passages scattered here and there in Blake's Note-Book, pages 68–95 (*K* 604–17).

W. M. Rossetti on November 27, 1864, wrote to Horace Scudder, the first American Blake enthusiast, mentioning "a M.S. volume belonging to my brother & myself. . . . If I can find a convenient little bit to snip out, I shall have great pleasure in sending it to you, just as a specimen of writing."

(This letter, now in the Houghton Library, was called to my attention by Mrs. Norman V. Ballou.) Evidently this snip was a corner of page 71; unfortunately, W. M. Rossetti did not copy it before transcribing the *Vision* for the Gilchrist *Life*, and it has never been recovered.

As now arranged, the text begins with a definition of the Last Judgment, and continues with what is apparently the earliest distinction between symbolic writings ("vision") and allegory. The picture which Blake describes is lost; it was estimated to have contained over a thousand figures. Blake's explanation of these figures, however, can often be applied to his other pictures and sketches of the Last Judgment which still exist (see Illustrations). The article concludes with many more valuable explanations of Blake's ideas.

VISIONS OF THE DAUGHTERS OF ALBION. *The Eye sees more than the Heart knows. Printed by Willm Blake: 1793.* As Blake had removed to Lambeth early in 1791, this book was obviously etched and printed there. Seventeen copies have been traced.

It belongs in the period of Experience. It is a continuation, though in thought only, of *The Book of Thel.* That represented the soul in the state of Innocence; this, the soul in the state of Experience. It was probably completed before *The Marriage of Heaven and Hell.* It is primarily a protest against the sexual customs of the times.

The plot is simple: the innocent Oothoon in solitude plucks from its dewy bed the fatal flower of Leutha's Vale; but while winging her way towards her beloved Theotormon, she is raped by Bromion. Having impregnated her, he casts her off; nevertheless, the two are "Bound back to back" (2:5), he with heavy fetters on his ankles, while she has the lightest of bonds. Meanwhile the jealous Theotormon will not marry the polluted girl, but sits weeping on the threshold of Bromion's cave. The remainder of the poem consists of their lamentations.

Oothoon denounces the loveless marriage, in which "she who burns with youth . . . is bound in spells of law to one she loathes," dragging "the chain of life in weary lust" and all the night turning "the wheel of false desire" (5:21–27); also the selfish and envious husband, "a creeping skeleton with lamplike eyes watching around the frozen marriage bed," while his jealousy spins "a web of age around him . . . till his eyes sicken at the fruit that hangs before his sight" (7:18–22). She pities the ill-trained children of such a marriage (5:30), and exposes the miserable practices of the solitary girl and lad (7:3–11). The *Visions* is the frankest literary work on this subject before our own times.

The same time-spirit which enslaves women also enslaves the Negroes. Blake had helped illustrate J. G. Stedman's *Narrative* with dreadful plates of their tortures. Bromion, who is under Urizen, is a slave-owner. "Stampt with my signet [i.e., branded] are the swarthy children of the sun; they are obedient, they resist not, they obey the scourge; their daughters worship terrors and obey the violent" (1:21); and Theotormon hears "the voice of slaves beneath the sun, and children bought with money, that shiver in religious caves beneath the burning fires of lust" (2:8). Although Oothoon is white and is never offered for sale, it has been argued that Bromion has impregnated her to increase her selling price.

Oothoon challenges the time-spirit. "They told me that I had five senses to inclose me up" (2:31). She argues against Locke's materialistic philosophy by showing that all animals have the same five senses and yet act differently according to their various instincts (3:2–13). She is the first to name Urizen, the god of the Age of Reason (5:3), whom she denounces and curses (7:12).

Neither Theotormon nor Bromion is any help to her. The emotional and self-centered Theotormon is lost in the mystery of his own sufferings: "Tell me, what is the night or day to one o'erflow'd with woe?"

(3:22). For him, Oothoon and Bromion, though unmarried, are morally adulterers (2:4). Closing his eyes and ears to her pleas, he sits on the threshold of Bromion's cave, paralyzed like Spenser's Malbecco (*FQ* III. x.60). He does hear "beneath him" the laments of the slaves (2:7), but they mean nothing to him. Meanwhile the logical Bromion wonders vaguely if there may not be worlds of joy outside his universe, but he remains convinced that there is one Law and a Hell (4:22–24).

Oothoon, however, in denouncing Urizen, has reached the stage of spiritual rebellion. Against his authority she asserts her own essential purity, whatever may have happened (3:16, 20). She proclaims the sanctity of the individual and his various joys (5:6), and the freedom of true love (7:16); then she bids man take his bliss (6:2): "Arise and drink your bliss, for every thing that lives is holy" (8:10).

But she has not yet reached the stage of out-and-out Revolution. The situation of the soul torn between Desire and Convention seems hopeless. "Enslav'd, the Daughters of Albion" (1:1) "hear her woes & eccho back her sighs" (8:13).

Blake was obviously inspired by his friend Mary Wollstonecraft's famous *Vindication of the Rights of Women*, which had been published the year before in 1792. A possible source for his plot was *Oithona*, one of Macpherson's Ossianic poems. Oithona, in love with Gaul, is carried off by the evil Dunrommath. Gaul avenges the rape by killing Dunrommath in battle; but the shamed Oithona, garbed as a youth, seeks death in the conflict and dies in her lover's arms. The only parallel is the rape; Blake did not follow the heroic vengeance and suicide.

VOLTAIRE (1694–1778) was the wittiest of the Deists, a courageous and ribald lampooner of the authorities, and an indefatigable champion of the oppressed. His oft-quoted "Écrasez l'infâme!" was directed against all persecutors. He preached incessantly the freedom of thought, the encouragement of arts and sciences, religious toleration, mild laws, sound finance, avoidance of war, and above all a spirit of humanity. But these were the commonplaces of European liberalism; he was not the discoverer of new ideas but rather the destroyer of the old shams. His blazing wrath roared through the forests of the night, sparing nothing, not even the Bible.

Blake told Crabb Robinson (*CR* 267) that God had commissioned Voltaire to "expose" the literal sense of the Bible; and the Holy Ghost truly operated in him. "I have had much intercourse with Voltaire, and he said to me I blasphemed the Son of Man, and it shall be forgiven me. But they (the enemies of Voltaire) blasphemed the Holy Ghost in me, and it shall not be forgiven them"—a very apt application of *Matthew* xii:32, which has proved true. But, as Blake said of Irving, "they who are sent sometimes go further than they ought" (*CR* 259). When in *Candide* (Chap. xxv) Voltaire ridiculed the idea of the Creator's using compasses, Blake made one of his strongest pictures on that very subject (*Eur*, frontis.).

Characteristically, Blake took Voltaire's genius for granted and proceeded to attack him unsparingly for his errors. He began with his superficiality. *An Island in the Moon* opens with a quarrel over Voltaire between Etruscan Column and Inflammable Gass, both of whom are right. The former complains: "Voltaire was immersed in matter, & seems to have understood very little but what he saw before his eyes"; the latter counters with "I wish I could see you write so. . . . He was the Glory of France" (*K* 44–46). Also, Voltaire was "as intolerant as an Inquisitor" (*LJ*, *K* 615); his wit was "a wracking wheel" (*J* 52:6). As a Deist he taught doubt and attacked the visionaries as hypocrites (*EG h*, *K* 756). Blake retorted the charge. "Voltaire, Rousseau, Gibbon, Hume, charge the Spiritually Religious with Hypocrisy . . . Voltaire! Rousseau! You cannot escape my charge that you are Pharisees & Hypocrites, for you are constantly talking of the Virtues of the Human Heart and particularly of your own, that you may accuse others, & especially the Religious, whose errors you, by this display of pretended Virtue, chiefly design to expose" (*J* 52). Like the other Deists, he was also a materialist: "Voltaire insinuates that these Limits [Satan and Adam] are the cruel work of God, mocking the Remover of Limits & the Resurrection of the Dead, setting up Kings in wrath, in holiness of Natural Religion" (*J* 73:29).

Blake constantly linked Voltaire and Rousseau as the heralds of the Revolution. "Seeing the Churches at their Period [i.e., end] in terror & despair, Rahab [the spirit of ribaldry] created Voltaire, Tirzah [the spirit of prudery] created Rousseau" (*Mil* 22:41). "How is this thing, this Newtonian Phantasm, this Voltaire & Rousseau . . . this Natural Religion . . . ?" (*Mil* 40:11). They are the two wings of the Spectre (*J* 54:18). They are the two Covering Cherubs of Vala, "afterwards named Voltaire & Rousseau, two frowning Rocks on each side of the Cove & Stone of Torture, frozen Sons of the feminine Tabernacle of Bacon, Newton, & Locke" (*J* 66:12). The monks are "driven out of the abbeys, their naked souls shiver in keen open air, driven out by the fiery cloud of Voltaire and thund'rous rocks of Rousseau" (*FR* 275). Over Lafayette's head "the soul of Voltaire shone fiery; and over the army Rousseau his white cloud unfolded" (*FR* 282). When the Revolution is ready to break forth, "Clouds roll heavy upon the Alps round Rousseau & Voltaire" (*SoL* 4:18).

One can only guess which of Voltaire's voluminous works Blake read. In the Reynolds annotations (*K* 445) he copied a passage from the *Moeurs des Nations* in the original French. He could not have missed *Candide*, a passage in which may have inspired the frontispiece to *Europe*, as we have said. David Erdman (*Erd* 98) traces the influence of *Le Philosophe Ignorant* on *An Island in the Moon*. Voltaire's poem about the Lisbon earthquake mocked the optimistic commonplace that the misfortune of one is the benefit of another: "Quand la mort met le comble aux maux que j'ai soufferts, | Le beau soulagement d'être mangé des vers!'" The Cloud answers this couplet when he tells Thel: "Then if thou art the food of worms, O virgin of the skies, how great thy use, how great thy blessing! Every thing that lives lives not alone nor for itself" (*Thel* 3: 25).

A VORTEX is an idea which, becoming active, attracts and tends to absorb its surroundings.

"The nature of infinity is this: That every thing has its own Vortex, and when once a traveller thro' Eternity has pass'd that Vortex, he percieves it roll backward behind his path, into a globe itself infolding like a sun, or like a moon, or like a universe of starry majesty, while he keeps onwards in his wondrous journey on the earth, or like a human form, a friend with whom he liv'd benevolent. As the eye of man views both the east & west encompassing its vortex, and the north & south with all their starry host, also the rising sun & setting moon he views surrounding his corn-fields and his valleys of five hundred acres square, thus is the earth one infinite plane, and not as apparent to the weak traveller confin'd beneath the moony shade. Thus is the heaven a vortex pass'd already, and the earth a vortex not yet pass'd by the traveller thro' Eternity" (*Mil* 15:21).

In brief, one learns by experience. When once an experience has been passed through, its human significance becomes apparent, and illumines the man with the sun of the imagination, the moon of love, the stars of reason, or the affection of a friend. A man's private universe is such a Vortex.

Urizen's vortices, of course, are not so illuminating. When caught in his ruined world, he tries to escape upwards by forming a Vortex, but it only puts him to sleep, and when he wakes refreshed, " 'tis downward all" (*FZ* vi:204–6). He then tries to build another world better suited to obey him; "and the Sciences were fix'd & the Vortexes began to operate on all the sons of men, & every human soul terrified at the turning wheels of heaven shrunk away, inward with'ring away" (*FZ* vi:234). Worse yet, the Net of Religion begins to grow from his soul, "shivering across from Vortex to Vortex" (*FZ* vi:245).

Blake's vortices may well have been suggested by the famous vortices of Descartes. He theorized that the material particles in space moved in vortices, producing sun and stars; the centrifugal particles produced radiating light, and so forth; until the astronomical universe was created mechanically, without the intervention of spirits, intelligences, and the like. It was a brilliant theory, which was accepted for many years.

WALES is West in the ternary of Great Britain, Scotland being North and England East. As the body, Wales is often associated with Scotland, the soul (*Mil* 39:41; *J* 23: 27; 29:21; 66:60, 67). "Wales and Scotland shrink themselves to the west and to 'he north!" (*J* 5:11).

But in the quaternary of the British Isles, Wales is South by elimination, as Scotland is North, England East, and Ireland West. However, Blake makes nothing of this, even in *Jerusalem* 29:20, when Ireland is called Jerusalem's "holy place, and the murder'd bodies of her little ones are Scotland and Wales."

When Los fixes the counties of Wales, he fixes Jerusalem's Gates "in the Twelve Counties of Wales, & thence Gates, looking every way to the Four Points, conduct to England & Scotland & Ireland, and thence to all the Kingdoms & Nations & Families of the Earth" (*J* 16:32). Each of the Welsh Gates is assigned to a son of Israel (*J* 16: 35–42). South Wales is assigned to Gwantoke and North Wales to Peachey (*J* 71:29–30).

The Cathedral City of Hereford is near the Welsh border, and is the "ancient Guardian of Wales, whose hands builded the mountain palaces of Eden, stupendous works!" (*J* 46:3)—a reference to the lofty Welsh mountains and also to Inigo Jones, whose father came from Wales.

When Hand slept on Skiddaw's top, his divided Emanation Cambel "sent him over Mountainous Wales into the Loom of Cathedron . . . to weave Jerusalem a Body repugnant to the Lamb" (*J* 80:63–65).

WALTON was a village in Surrey, situated on the Thames, seventeen miles southwest of London. "From the Hills of Camberwell & Wimbledon, from the Valleys of Walton & Esher, from Stone-henge & from Malden's Cove, Jerusalem's Pillars fall" (*J* 68: 43).

WAR is the physical result of one of man's fundamental instincts. In Eternity, war is "intellectual" (*FZ* ix:854). "As the breath of the Almighty, such are the words of man to man in the great Wars of Eternity, in fury of Poetic Inspiration, to build the Universe stupendous, Mental forms Creating" (*Mil* 30:18). Terrible as these wars may seem, they are fundamentally humane: "Our wars are wars of life, & wounds of love with intellectual spears & long winged arrows of thought" (*J* 38:14).

But warfare on earth is a dreadful debasement of this instinct. "War & Hunting, the Two Fountains of the River of Life, are become Fountains of bitter Death & of corroding Hell, till Brotherhood is chang'd into a Curse" (*Mil* 35:2; *J* 43:31). "For the Soldier who fights for Truth calls the enemy his brother: they fight & contend for life & not for eternal death; but here the Soldier strikes, & a dead corse falls at his feet" (*J* 43:41).

War on earth is "energy Enslav'd" (*FZ* ix:152). It is "the fever of the human soul" (*J* 38:9). After Luvah is sealed in the furnaces of affliction, he reappears in the lower form of Orc; and the demons cry: "Luvah, King of Love, thou art the King of rage & death" (*FZ* v:42). When Orc breaks loose and embraces the Shadowy Female (the debased Vala), war enters the material world. It goes beyond Urizen's control, and appears as the hermaphrodite Satan, whose first ideal is the male (*FZ* viii:102), but later is the Shadowy Female (viii:255). See HERMAPHRODITE. It is waged by beasts in human form; "terrific men they seem to one another, laughing terrible among the banners" (*FZ* viii:121).

In *Jerusalem*, the war breaks out after Jesus has prophesied it: "Luvah's Cloud reddening above burst forth in streams of blood upon the heavens" (*J* 62:30). "The Winepress [war] on the Rhine groans loud, but all its central beams act more terrific in the central Cities of the Nations, where Human Thought is crush'd beneath the iron hand of Power" (*Mil* 25:3).

The concept of war as an intoxication is first found in *The French Revolution* (83–86), where Blake invented a Duke of Burgundy, "the ancientest Peer," as spokesman for the war party. He is "red as wines from his mountains; an odor of war, like a ripe vineyard, rose from his garments." Later, this suggestion is expanded into the apocalyptic vision of the Wine-press of Luvah (*FZ* ix:692–771; *Mil* 27:1–41), where the human grapes of wrath are crushed for the Wine of the New Age. The Dragon of *Revelation* is another symbol of war (see DRAGON); and the two beasts of Job, Leviathan and Behemoth, are "the War by Sea enormous & the War by Land astounding" (*J* 91:39–41).

The epics of Homer and Virgil glorified war; therefore, Blake believed, we follow their ideal. "The Classics! it is the Classics, & not Goths nor Monks, that Desolate Europe with Wars." The Bible is "the only light of antiquity that remains unperverted by War" (*On Homer's Poetry*; *On Virgil*, K 778). See HOMER and VIRGIL. Their spirit had evidently inspired "the Lewis's & Fredericks, who alone are [war's] causes & its actors" (*J* 52).

But neither the ancient classics nor the modern monarchs are the fundamental cause of war. Blake anticipated Freud in arguing that it was the result of suppressed sex. "I must rush again to War, for the Virgin has frown'd & refus'd" (*J* 68:63). It is common knowledge that the thwarting of a sexual act produces wrath, but the process goes deeper than that. When Enitharmon established her Female Will, she reversed the normal cause of life, repressing sex until it was reduced to the erotic dream (Thiralatha); then Thiralatha's consort, Sotha, burst forth as War, and Orc awoke (*Eur* 14:1–31). See SOTHA; ENITHARMON, diagram. Venus and Mars, two of Priam's gods, were the causes of the Trojan War (see PRIAM); but as War springs from the North, Blake substituted their Scandinavian equivalents, Thor and Friga (i.e., Freya), when the warriors are in full cry. See FRIGA.

WARREN (Joseph, 1741–75), the beloved physician of Boston, was one of the leading revolutionists in that town, and the first prominent American to be killed in the Revolution. His death in the battle of Bunker Hill is the central feature of Trumbull's famous painting, "The Battle of Bunker's Hill."

In *America* Warren is named four times. He is one of those who meet after the Boston Massacre (3:4); one of the "terrible men" who rear their foreheads against the threats of Albion's Angel (9:11); one of those by whom the Thirteen Angels stand (12:7); and one of those who hear Albion's Angel let loose the plagues on America (14:2).

WARWICK is a county in the west Midlands of England. With the adjacent Leicester and Worcester, it is assigned to Naphtali (*J* 16:46); with Northampton, Bedford, Buckingham, Leicester, and Berkshire, it is assigned to Hutton (*J* 71:36); and with Oxford and Wilts it is also assigned to Kox (*J* 71:42).

WASHINGTON (1732–99) was the outstanding figure of the American Revolution. Blake, in naming patriots, always puts him first. Washington meets with others after the Boston Massacre, and warns them of the threatening tyranny (*Am* 3:4–12); with others he rears his forehead against Albion's Angel (9:10); the Thirteen Angels of the colonies stand by him and his friends (12:7); the thirteen royal governors grovel at his feet (13:4); and with other patriots, he hears Albion's Angel loose the plagues (14:2).

In May 1804, Hayley recommended to Blake a newly published *Life of Washington*; Blake thanked him on May 28, and returned the second volume on September 28. "I suppose an American would tell me that Washington did all that was done before he was born, as the French now adore Buonaparte and the English our poor George; so the Americans will consider Washington as their god. This is only Grecian, or rather Trojan, worship, and perhaps will be revised [?] in an age or two" (To Hayley, 28 May 1804).

WATER, one of the Four Elements, is placed West, under Tharmas (the body). The Pythagoreans and the Neo-Platonists had employed it as a symbol of Matter, and, beginning in the Lambeth period, so did Blake. Thereafter, any form of water may safely be translated as "matter," unless it is obviously not; for example, the fountain of the Holy Ghost, the four rivers of Paradise, and the baptismal font.

The Sea of Time and Space is Blake's plainest use of water as matter. This is "the wat'ry shore" given to the fallen soul until the break of day (*SoE*, "Introduction" 19). It is pictured on the title page of *Visions of the Daughters of Albion* and elsewhere in the book. The Atlantic in *America* is obviously the necessary, literal ocean; yet it is certainly a symbol in the myth of Ariston (10:5–10); and Urizen's weapons—stored snows, icy magazines, clouds, and cold mists (16:5–13)—are always forms of water.

WATERFORD is a county of Munster, the southern province of Ireland. With the other counties of that province it is placed under Reuben, Simeon, and Levi (*J* 72:22).

WATLING-STREET was the Roman military road which ran from the east coast of Kent into North Wales. Blake refers to its still-enduring pavement in *A Descriptive Catalogue* V (*K* 577).

The WELSH TRIADS were a mnemonic and aphoristic form, peculiar to the Welsh bards, in which characters or statements were arranged in groups of three.

The first stanza of Blake's lines about the Ancient Britons (*K* 560), which he ascribed to the "Welch Triades," is an adaptation of No. LXXXV in the *Myvyrian Archaiology* (London, 1801–7). David Jenkins, Keeper of Printed Books at the National Library of Wales, who found this source for me, has kindly translated it as follows:

"Three men escaped from [the battle of] Camlan, Morfran son of Tegid, Sandde with the countenance of an Angel, and Glewlwyd Gafaelfawr. Morfran, because of his ugliness, everyone, deeming him to be a devil, avoided him. Sandde being so fair and beautiful, no-one raised a hand against him, thinking him to be an angel; and Glewlwyd, because of his size and strength, everyone fled before him."

Camlan was Salisbury, scene of Arthur's last battle.

Blake's friend William Owen Pughe (1759–1835), who did most of the work on the *Archailogy*, was obviously the person who called Blake's attention to this passage. Southey, who carelessly assumed that the two men did not meet until after the death of Joanna Southcott (d. 1814), wrote to Caroline Bowles: "Poor Owen found everything he wished to find in the Bardic system, and there he found Blake's notions, and thus Blake and his wife were persuaded that his dreams were old patriarchal truths, long-forgotten and now re-revealed" (*Correspondence*, Dublin, 1881, p. 194).

As Mr. Jenkins found no source for Blake's second stanza, it is evident that Blake adapted and expanded his original, which he again adapted and expanded in his *Descriptive Catalogue* V, "The Ancient Britons" (*K* 577).

The WEST is one of the four compass-points. It is assigned to Tharmas, who symbolizes the five senses; thus the West is the body, that "portion of Soul discern'd by the five Senses" (*MHH* 4). It is the Circumference (*J* 12:55). The strongest of the senses is Touch, which is the sexual instinct (symbolized by Enion, Tharmas' Emanation). In the healthy man, sex is counterbalanced by love (Luvah, in the East). The western Element is Water, which symbolizes matter.

Blake's first use of the West as a symbol occurs in *Tiriel*. Tiriel is king of the West (ii:18, 20; viii:4), though he pretends to be from the North (ii:51).

WESTLEY (a variant spelling) was John Wesley (1703–91), the founder of Methodism, whose direct address to the heart appealed strongly to Blake.

He identified Wesley and his fellow evangelist Whitefield with the two Witnesses of *Revelation* xi; they shall testify before the Second Coming, be martyred, and after their unburied bodies lie in the street of the city, be resurrected. "But then I [Rintrah—just wrath] rais'd up Whitefield, Palamabron [pity] rais'd up Westley . . . The Witnesses lie dead in the Street of the Great City: no Faith is in all the Earth: the Book of God is trodden under Foot. He sent his two Servants, Whitefield & Westley: were they Prophets, or were they Idiots or Madmen? Shew us Miracles! Can you have greater Miracles than these? Men who devote their life's whole comfort to intire scorn & injury & death?" (*Mil* 22:55–23:2).

In 1790, Blake acquired a copy of Wesley's *Hymns for the Nation in 1782* which is now owned by Sir Geoffrey Keynes.

WESTMEATH is a county of Leinster, the eastern province of Ireland. With all the other counties of that province, it is under Judah, Issachar, and Zebulun (*J* 72:19).

WESTMINSTER, a separate political and nearly separate geographic entity in London, is the seat of government and the residence of royalty.

When Albion's Angel howls in the flames of Orc, "Above the rest the howl was heard from Westminster louder & louder" (*Eur* 12:14). When Los perambulates London, he beholds Jerusalem "in Westminster & Marybone, among the ruins of the Temple" (*J* 31:40). The victims of the press gangs complain: "We were carried away in thousands from London & in tens of thousands from Westminster & Marybone, in ships clos'd up, chain'd hand & foot, compell'd to fight under the iron whips of our captains, fearing our officers more than the enemy" (*J* 65:33).

WESTMORELAND is one of the northernmost counties of England, along with Cumberland, Northumberland, and Durham. These four are "divided in the Gates of Reuben, Judah, Dan, & Joseph" (*J* 16:51). With the adjacent Yorkshire and Durham, it is assigned to Brertun (*J* 71:32). "Cheshire & Lancashire & Westmoreland groan in anguish as [Bowen and Conwenna] cut the fibres from the Rivers" (*J* 90:18).

WEXFORD is a county of Leinster, the eastern province of Ireland. With the other counties of that province, it is under Judah, Issachar, and Zebulun (*J* 72:20).

The WHALE is one of the four elemental forms taken by the west-seeking imagination of the chained Orc (*Am* 1:14; 2:14). The four are the Eagle of Mexico (air), the Lion of Peru (earth), the Whale of the South-sea (water), and the Serpent of Canada (fire).

Oothoon, arguing that each species lives his own life according to his innate instincts, asks Urizen: "Does the whale worship at thy footsteps as the hungry dog; or does he scent the mountain prey because his nostrils wide draw in the ocean? does his eye discern the flying cloud as the raven's eye? or does he measure the expanse like the vulture?" (*VDA* 5:33).

WHEELS of various kinds appear in Blake's poetry.

First are the eyed wheels of the Zoas themselves, described in *Ezekiel* (i). "Terrific rag'd the Eternal wheels of intellect, terrific rag'd the living creatures of the wheels in the Wars of Eternal life. But perverse roll'd the wheels of Urizen & Luvah, back revers'd downwards & outwards, consuming in the wars of Eternal Death" (*FZ* i:571). Later, all four Zoas "saw their Wheels rising up poisonous against Albion" (*J* 43:1). "Their Wheels in poisonous and deadly stupor turn'd against each other, loud & fierce" (*J* 74:5). Milton used Ezekiel's wheels for the war-chariot of Paternal Deity, studded with accusing eyes, in which the Son drove the devils out of heaven: "the living Wheels distinct alike with multitude of eyes . . . and every eye glar'd lightning and shot forth pernicious fire among th' accurst" (*PL* vi:750, 847–50). These are Blake's "Chariot Wheels filled with Eyes," which in wartime "rage along the howling Valley" (*J* 63:11).

The Wheels of Eden, "Wheel within Wheel, in freedom revolve in harmony & peace," contrasting with the cruel wheels of this world, "wheel without wheel, with cogs tyrannic moving by compulsion each other" (*J* 15:18–20), such as the machinery of the Industrial Revolution: "intricate wheels . . . Wheel without wheel" (*FZ* vii *b*: 179; *J* 65:21). "Why should Punishment Weave the Veil with Iron Wheels of War, when Forgiveness might it Weave with Wings of Cherubim?" (*J* 22:34 and illustr.).

The Wheels of Enitharmon (*Mil* 6:27; *J* 88:54) are spinning wheels on which the thread is woven for the looms which make bodies for the unborn spectres. Her daughters labor at them hour after hour, weeping at their hardships. "Yet the intoxicating delight that they take in their work obliterates every other evil; none pities their tears, yet they regard not pity & they expect no one to pity, for they labour for life & love regardless of any one but the poor Spectres that they work for always, incessantly. They are mock'd by every one that passes by; they regard not, they labour, & when their Wheels are broken by scorn & malice, they

mend them sorrowing with many tears & afflictions" (*J* 59:26–41).

The "starry wheels" of Albion's Sons represent their materialistic thought and consequently their mechanical Newtonian universe. Our heavens are visibly "a mighty circle turning" (*Eur* 10:23). Urizen complains: "Can I not leave this world of Cumbrous wheels, Circle o'er Circle?" (*FZ* vi: 196). When he fixes the sciences, "every human soul terrified at the turning wheels of heaven shrunk away, inward with'ring away" (*FZ* vi:236). These wheels also constitute the system of Natural Religion, and are twice associated with Druidism (*J* 60:7; 62:32). They overhang the creative Furnaces, drawing Jerusalem and Vala towards Non-Entity in a column of the smoke (*J* 5: 46–65); they divide Los and his Spectre (*J* 6:3); and revolve around the sleeping Albion and his England (*J* 94:11).

"Ulro is the space of the terrible starry wheels of Albion's sons" (*J* 12:51). The third gate of the fourfold Northern Gate of Los looks towards Ulro, "turning upon the Wheels of Albion's sons with enormous power" (*J* 12:65). The ornaments of the Eastern Gate are "terrible & deadly . . . taking their forms from the Wheels of Albion's sons, as cogs are form'd in a wheel to fit the cogs of the adverse wheel" (*J* 13:13).

In "an orbed Void of doubt, despair, hunger & thirst & sorrow," the twelve Sons "became as Three Immense Wheels turning upon one-another into Non-Entity . . . to murder their own Souls, to build a Kingdom among the Dead" (*J* 18:4–10). When Hand (the head) absorbed all the other Sons, "Hyle [the heart] & Coban [the loins] were his two chosen ones for Emissaries in War: forth from his bosom they went and return'd, like Wheels from a great Wheel reflected in the Deep. Hoarse turn'd the Starry Wheels rending a way in Albion's Loins" (*J* 18:41). Hand's wheels are of course also his father's; and when the Cathedral Cities try to force Albion back through Los's Gate into Eden, "Albion dark, repugnant, roll'd his wheels backward into Non-Entity. Loud roll the Starry

Wheels of Albion into the World of Death, and all the Gate of Los clouded with clouds redounding from Albion's dread Wheels" (*J* 44:5). But the finger of God touches Los's seventh Furnace "away from the Starry Wheels to prepare Jerusalem a place" (*J* 48:45), and "Erin's lovely Bow enclos'd the Wheels of Albion's Sons" (*J* 50:22). See ERIN.

When war impends, "the Divine Vision appear'd on Albion's hills, often walking from the Furnaces in clouds and flames among the Druid Temples & the Starry Wheels" (*J* 60:5); when war actually breaks out, "the Wheels of Albion's Sons turn'd hoarse over the Mountains, & the fires blaz'd on Druid Altars" (*J* 62:32).

Hyle also has his Wheels: "roof'd . . . in Albion's Cliffs by the Affections rent asunder & oppos'd to Thought," he tries "to draw Jerusalem's Sons into the Vortex of his Wheels" (*J* 74:28).

Related to, if not identical with, the Starry Wheels are the wheels of the dark Satanic Mills: the "Mills of resistless wheels" (*FZ* viii:218), "the hidden wheels" of Satan (*Mil* 9:41); Jerusalem wanders "among the dark Satanic wheels" (*J* 12:44); and the Wheel of Hand runs the mills of Babylon where Jerusalem labors (*J* 60:41). "The abstract Voids between the Stars are the Satanic Wheels" (*J* 13:37).

Urthona also has a mill, where he grinds the flour for the Bread. "And Men are bound to sullen contemplations in the night: restless they turn on beds of sorrow; in their inmost brain feeling the crushing Wheels, they rise, they write the bitter words of Stern Philosophy & knead the bread of knowledge with tears & groans" (*FZ* ix:817).

Blake likened "Religion" to a counter-clockwise wheel of fire, which in turn was equated with the revolving sword of the prohibiting cherubim (*Gen* iii:24). "Jesus died because he strove against the current of this Wheel; its Name is Caiaphas, the dark Preacher of Death, of sin, of sorrow & of punishment, opposing Nature! It is Natural Religion" (*J* 77:16).

War makes history as event forces event; therefore the Wine-press of Los is also his Printing-Press: "here he lays his words in order above the mortal brain, as cogs are form'd in a wheel to turn the cogs of the adverse wheel" (*Mil* 27:9).

The mechanistic philosophy of Locke is a Loom "whose Woof rages dire, wash'd by the Water-wheels of Newton" (*J* 15:15). Water wheels are also mentioned elsewhere (*FZ* ii:220; vii *b*:176; *J* 65:18; 73:14).

WHITEFIELD (George, 1714–70) was one of the most extraordinary evangelists of Protestantism. At Oxford he became the friend of the Wesleys and of Hervey, and thus became associated in the public mind with Methodism. Officially an Anglican, he was early denied the use of their churches because of his attacks on the worldly clergy; therefore he "took the world for his parish" and preached to everybody, regardless of sect, out of doors, with enormous success. Thus he became the real father of mass evangelism. Benjamin Franklin ingeniously calculated that his stentorian voice could be heard by thirty thousand. With great dramatic power he preached from the heart, first throwing his hearers into paroxysms of terror by convicting them of sin, then offering them salvation by faith alone. The bane of bishops, he was often attacked by mobs; and when he became well known, among his enemies were Hogarth, Fielding, and Smollett, although he was admired by Cowper and the Deist Franklin. Samuel Foote caricatured him as "Dr. Squintum" in *The Minor* (1750). "Foote in calling Whitefield, Hypocrite, was himself one; for Whitefield pretended not to be holier than others, but confessed his Sins before all the World" (*J* 52, *K* 682). Blake's precise reference is lost, because Foote's attack caused such a storm of protest from the Methodists that in the printed version of the play, almost all scenes in which Dr. Squintum appeared were omitted, and the Epilogue, which Foote had delivered in the character of Squintum (according to his picture published in 1779), was rewritten for Shift.

Blake heartily admired the tireless enthusiast who made Jesus the center of his teaching, who relied on the spontaneous impulses of the heart, and who cared not for sect, rank, or liturgy. "Fenelon, Guion, Teresa, Whitefield & Hervey" are among "the gentle Souls who guide the great Wine-press of Love" and guard Los's Gate towards Beulah (*J* 72:50). Blake also identified Whitefield and Wesley as the two Witnesses of *Revelation* xi (*Mil* 22:55, 61). See WESTLEY.

Beginning in 1738, Whitefield made seven preaching trips to America, dying in Newburyport, Massachusetts, completely worn out.

The WICKER MAN was a druidic method of sacrificing human beings. "Others use huge figures, whose wicker limbs they fill with living men and set on fire, and the men die surrounded by flames" (Caesar *Commentaries* vi:16).

Blake used it as a symbol of war: "the Wicker Man of Scandinavia in whom Jerusalem's children consume in flames among the Stars" (*Mil* 37:11). "I see a Wicker Idol woven round Jerusalem's children" (*J* 43:65). When war breaks out, it is at first "a Vegetating Root, in grinding pain animating the Dragon Temples, soon to become that Holy Fiend the Wicker Man of Scandinavia, in which, cruelly consumed, the Captives rear'd to heaven howl in flames among the stars" (*J* 47:5).

WICKLOW is a county of Leinster, the eastern province of Ireland. With the other counties of Leinster, it is under Judah, Issachar, and Zebulun (*J* 72:20). Erin, bidding the Daughters of Beulah mourn, says "Stand ye upon the Dargle from Wicklow to Drogheda" (*J* 49:5).

WIGTOUN (i.e., Wigtown) is a county of Scotland which, with Sutherland and Sterling, is assigned to Asher (*J* 16:56). All Scotland is assigned to Bowen (*J* 71:46).

The WILL is an essential attribute of the Individual. It is sacred: only the Divine Will may control it, and even then without overt conflict, and under special circumstance. "By Providence Divine conducted, not bent from his own will lest Death Eternal should be the result, for the Will cannot be violated" (*FZ* vi:282). "The Will must not be bended, but in the day of Divine Power" (*J* 44:18).

Blake's attitude is that of Job and not of Milton. "Though he slay me, yet will I trust in him: but I will maintain mine own ways before him" (*Job* xiii:15). On the other hand, the basic plot of *Paradise Regained* consists of Satan's attempts to persuade or force the Christ to exert his personal will, thus violating the will of Providence. Milton was merely repeating the ancient tenet (so convenient to authoritarianism) that the individual will is evil; a tenet still in force in the days of our grandparents, who believed that the "breaking" of a child's will was an essential part of his upbringing.

The Female Will, however, is evil. When the Individual is divided, the Emanation has a will of her own, which acts in opposition to her consort, for she is half of a "split personality." When Urizen perceives that Ahania is separate, "Two wills they had, two intellects, & not as in times of old" (*FZ* ii: 206); the same line is repeated for Los and Enitharmon (*J* 86:61). Vala, without knowing what she is doing, practically destroys Luvah. The woes caused by Enitharmon when she becomes dominant are detailed in *Europe* and elsewhere.

The domination of woman, Blake believed, is one of the greatest forces corrupting society. "What may Woman be to have power over Man from Cradle to corruptible Grave? There is a Throne in every Man, it is the Throne of God; this, Woman has claim'd as her own, & Man is no more!... O Albion, why wilt thou Create a Female Will?" (*J* 34:26–31; also 56:43). "O Woman-born and Woman-nourish'd & Woman-educated & Woman-scorn'd" (*J* 64:16). The over-idealization of woman is one of the errors of historical Christianity (*Eur* 3: 1–5), and the Daughters of Albion practise their schemes through a large part of Chapter iv ("To the Christians") of *Jerusalem*.

The determination of woman to dominate, with the result that she destroys her husband or son, is a common theme of our contemporary literature. Antiquity furnishes us Clytemnestra, but the first thorough analysis of the Female Will was (I think) Milton's Dalila, though Shakespeare's Goneril might be considered a specimen. After Blake, the first example was Strindberg's *The Father* (1887). The first American examples were George Kelly's 1925 Pulitzer Prize winner, *Craig's Wife*, and Sidney Howard's brilliant *The Silver Cord* (1926). Since then the theme has become common, having been treated by Eugene O'Neill, Tennessee Williams, and Lillian Hellman, among others.

WILLAN'S FARM, with its fields of cows, was one of the spots where Blake rambled in the freedom of his boyhood (*J* 27:15). Here a lad might get a mug of fresh milk. There is a picture of the farm in Paul Miner's "William Blake's London Residences." Kerrison Preston informs me that it appears on a map dated February 17, 1794. Paul Miner informs me that it was kept by Thomas Willan and was also known as "Mary-le-bone Park Farm." The site is now occupied by Bedford College. Fifty yards to the east was the Jew's-Harp-House tea garden.

WILTS (Wiltshire) is a county in southwest England, best known for the megalithic remains of Stonehenge and Avebury. With the adjoining counties of Somerset and Gloucester, it is assigned to Judah (*J* 16:45), and also to Coban (*J* 71:26). With the contiguous counties of Oxford and Warwick, it is also assigned to Kox (*J* 71:42). "Hants, Devon & Wilts [are] surrounded with masses of stone in order'd forms" (*J* 83:9).

WIMBLEDON was a village in Surrey.

When Blake recovered from his mystical experience at Felpham, "Immediately the Lark mounted with a loud trill from Felpham's Vale, and the Wild Thyme from Wimbleton's green & impurpled Hills, and Los & Enitharmon rose over the Hills of Surrey" (*Mil* 42:29). "From the Hills of Camberwell & Wimbledon, from the Valleys of Walton & Esher [all, places in Surrey, just south of the Thames], from Stonehenge & from Malden's Cove, Jerusalem's Pillars fall in the rendings of fierce War" (*J* 68:43).

WINCHESTER is the principal city of Hampshire (Hants), a southern maritime county of England. It contains a splendid cathedral (in the province of Canterbury) and Winchester School (connected through its founder William of Wyckeham with New College, Oxford), which since the fourteenth century has been one of the leading public schools of England. The first Four Sons of Los, who were never generated, "dwell over the Four Provinces of Ireland . . . the Four Universities of Scotland, & in Oxford & Cambridge & Winchester" (*J* 71:52).

Winchester, being South, is appropriately placed under Urizen and Verulam, which is Canterbury (*J* 74:3). It is the nearest Cathedral City to Chichester; and as Chichester (the first Cathedral City in Blake's list) is to be identified with Blake, Winchester (the second) is to be identified with Blake's neighbor, William Hayley (*J* 40:52–57). "Hyle dwelt in Winchester" (*J* 71:20). See HAYLEY.

When Albion bids Hand and Hyle, who have already seized "the Twenty-four rebellious ingratitudes" (*J* 42:48) to bring Los to justice, "Oxford groans in his iron furnace, Winchester in his den & cavern" (*J* 42:58).

WINDSOR (Berkshire), on the south bank of the Thames, contains Windsor Castle; nearby is the public school Eton. Though it is twenty-one miles west of London, the Castle can be seen from Hampstead Heath on a clear day.

When the daughters of Zelophehad weave the Woof of Death, "Rahab & Noah dwell on Windsor's heights" while the other daughters are situated variously in

Camberwell, Blackheath, Harrow to Hampstead, and Highgate to Blackheath (*Mil* 35: 8–13). When Albion rises, "his left foot near London covers the shades of Tyburn: his instep from Windsor to Primrose Hill stretching to Highgate & Holloway" (*Mil* 39:36).

The WINE-PRESS of Los symbolizes war on earth (*Mil* 27:8). See WAR. But the great Wine-press of Love symbolizes the wars of the spirit; it is guided by "gentle souls," including Fenelon, Guion, Teresa, Whitefield, and Hervey (*J* 72:50–52).

WINTER is "the night of Time" (*FZ* ix: 824).

Before Noah, only two seasons were recognized: summer and winter (*Gen* viii:22). Winter was the season when most of the agricultural work was done. Blake softened them to "the two Seasons of Spring & Autumn," there not being four until "the Changed State made by the flood" (*LJ, K* 611). Milton had represented the season of Eden as "spring perpetual" (*PL* x:678), and believed that frigid winter and torrid summer were the result of the Fall (*PL* x: 655).

In *The Four Zoas*, the making of the Bread and Wine, the food for the New Age, is finished in the autumn; then Urthona takes his repose (*FZ* ix:824; *Eur* 3:10). But Urizen and the other Zoas, including Los, work in winter. "The winter thou shalt plow & lay thy stores into thy barns, expecting to recieve Ahania in the spring with joy. Immortal thou, Regenerate She, & all the lovely Sex from her shall learn obedience & prepare for a wintry grave, that spring may see them rise in tenfold joy & sweet delight" (*FZ* ix:214).

While the men work, the women weave themselves cocoons; they "sleep the winter in soft silken veils woven by their own hands to hide them in the darksom grave; but Males immortal live renew'd by female deaths; in soft delight they die, & they revive in spring with music & songs" (*FZ* i: 64). Ahania sleeps through the winter "in silken garments spun by her own hands

against her funeral" (*FZ* ix:213); she wakes too soon and falls dead—Urizen still has work to do—but eventually is sitting at the feast (*FZ* ix:778). Enion also looks forward to the spring: "Soon renew'd, a Golden Moth, I shall cast off my death clothes & embrace Tharmas again" (*FZ* ix:598).

Ahania and Enion are passive in their separation from their consorts, but there is plenty of evidence that Enitharmon and Vala do not spend their winters in sleep.

WODEN is another name for Odin, the Scandinavian war-god. "Woden and Thor and Friga wholly consume my Saxons on their enormous altars built in the terrible north" (*J* 83:19). See ODIN.

The WOLDS are undulating chalk-hill tracts in Yorkshire and Lincolnshire, which reach an altitude of about 800 feet. When Albion claims his mountains, he includes the Wolds (*J* 4:30).

The WOLF is a predatory animal whose victims are the flocks which the noble Lion protects. Blake often refers to the warfare between the two: "To the Evening Star" 11 (*PS*); "Night" 25, 33 (*SoI*); "The Little Girl Found" 51 (*SoI*); Proverb 27 (*MHH* 8); "Empire is no More! and now the Lion & Wolf shall cease" (*MHH* 27; repeated *Am* 6:15); "Loud howls the eternal Wolf! the eternal Lion lashes his tail!" (*Am* 9:2; repeated *Am* 9:27).

The WOMAN (*J* 90:30) is the Virgin Mary. Los forbids Individuals to imitate anybody, even the holy people of Scripture: David, Eve, the Woman, the Lord, Reuben, etc. Blake's attitude against mariolatry evidently led him to suppress her name and even, a few lines later, to substitute that of Eve: "A Vegetated Christ & a Virgin Eve are the Hermaphroditic Blasphemy; by his Maternal Birth he is that Evil-one" (*J* 90: 34).

The WOMAN IN THE WILDERNESS is the pregnant woman "clothed with the sun, and the moon under her feet, and upon her head a crown of twelve stars." She was pursued by the "great red dragon," who waited before her "to devour her child as soon as it was born"; but the "man child, who was to rule all nations with a rod of iron . . . was caught up unto God, and to his throne. And the woman fled into the wilderness, where she hath a place prepared of God" (*Rev* xii: 1–6). Religious refugees in America often applied the prophecy to themselves; indeed, Kelpius' group of Rosicrucians, who settled on the Wissahickon near Philadelphia, called itself "The Woman in the Wilderness."

Albion's dragon-angel perversely identifies Orc with the Dragon: "Art thou not Orc, who serpent-form'd stands at the gate of Enitharmon to devour her children?" (*Am* 7:3).

In a letter to Ozias Humphry (18 Jan 1808, *K* 443), describing the "Last Judgment," Blake added to the Woman's attributes "six infants," and explained her simply as "the Christian Church." He was much more explicit in the later *Vision of the Last Judgment* (*K* 609–10), where she is "the Church Universal, represented by a Woman Surrounded by Infants. There is such a State in Eternity: it is composed of the Innocent civilized Heathen & the Uncivilized Savage, who, having not the Law, do by Nature the things contain'd in the Law. This State appears like a Female crown'd with stars, driven into the Wilderness: she has the Moon under her feet." (See Illustrations, "LJ" No. 64.)

On the title page of Night iii of Young's *Night Thoughts*, the Woman represents the dying Narcissa. Crowned with stars and kneeling on the moon, she aspires to rise above the Serpent.

WORCESTER is a west Midland county of England, situated almost entirely in the basin of the Severn. With the adjoining counties of Warwick and Leicester, it is under Naphtali (*J* 16:46); with the adjoining counties of Hereford and Stafford, it is under Kotope (*J* 71:44).

Its chief city is the eighteenth in the list of the Twenty-four Cathedral Cities (*J* 46:

18). For its position under Luvah and London, see CATHEDRAL CITIES. At the impact of war, "Worcester & Hereford, Oxford & Cambridge reel & stagger overwearied with howling" (*J* 66:66).

The WORD (*Logos*) was the Reason of God. Originally an attribute, it became the Father's agent, personalized as the Son, begotten before the Creation. "All things were made by him" (*John* i:3; *Psalm* xxxiii: 6; *Col* i:16; *Heb* i:2). Therefore, in the mosaics of St. Mark's, Venice, and other Byzantine works, the Creator is represented as Jesus the crucified. All the ante-Nicene Fathers, from Justin Martyr through Arius, taught that the Word was the manifestation of the invisible Father, and that the Biblical theophanies or appearances of God were the appearances of the Son. Thus, according to Theophilus of Antioch, not the infinite Father, "but his Word, through whom he made all things, assuming the person of the Father and Lord of all, went to the garden in the person of God, and conversed with Adam. For the divine writing itself teaches us that Adam said he had heard the voice. But what else is this voice but the Word of God, who is also His Son?" (*To Autolycus*, II, xxii). (See Alvan Lamson, *The Church of the First Three Centuries*, 2nd ed., Boston, 1865, *passim*.)

Blake adapted this belief when he wrote of "The Holy Word that walk'd among the ancient trees, calling the lapsed Soul, and weeping in the evening dew" (*SoE*, "Introduction" 4–7; cf. *Gen* iii:8–10). The "lapsed Soul" is mankind and nature, which fell with him; the Word is not the Angry God but the sorrowing Jesus, whose voice is the forgiveness of sins.

Elsewhere Jesus is credited with creating the Lamb (*SoI*, "The Lamb") and the baby (*SoI*, "A Cradle Song" 24).

"Our Lord is the word of God & every thing on earth is the word of God & in its essence is God" (On Lavater, *K* 87).

WORDSWORTH (William, 1770–1850), according to Blake, was "the *only poet* of the age"; so Crabb Robinson wrote Dorothy Wordsworth on February 20, 1826 (*CR* 274). Of course, by that time Byron, Keats, and Shelley were dead. A large portion of Wordsworth's poems were inspired by the Holy Ghost, but as a worshipper of Nature, Wordsworth was an atheist, inspired by the Devil (*CR* 264, 265, 266, etc.). "I see in Wordsworth the Natural Man rising up against the Spiritual Man Continually, & then he is No Poet but a Heathen Philosopher at Enmity against all true Poetry or Inspiration" (On Wordsworth, *K* 782).

When Crabb Robinson first met Blake at Mrs. Aders' (December 10, 1825), Blake, who had been reading *The Recluse*, very earnestly asked: "Is Mr. W[ordsworth] a sincere real Christian? . . . If so, what does he mean by 'the worlds to which the heaven of heavens is but a veil,' and who is he that shall 'pass Jehovah unalarmed?' " (*CR* 275). "Does Mr. Wordsworth think his mind can *surpass* Jehovah?" (*CR* 258). "Solomon, when he Married Pharoh's daughter & became a Convert to the Heathen Mythology, Talked exactly in this way of Jehovah as a Very inferior object of Man's Contemplation; he also passed him by unalarm'd & was permitted. Jehovah dropped a tear & follow'd him by his Spirit into the Abstract Void; it is called the Divine Mercy" (On Wordsworth, *K* 784). The Preface to *The Excursion* "caused him a bowel complaint which nearly killed him" (*CR* 275). However, Crabb Robinson's reading of the *Ode on Intimations of Immortality* threw Blake "almost into a hysterical rapture" (*CR* 297), especially the strophe "But there's a Tree, of many one," which Crabb Robinson usually omitted in reading, "lest I should be rendered ridiculous, being unable to explain precisely *what* I admired" (*CR* 297).

Blake also admired particularly "To H. C. Six Years Old." "This is all in the highest degree Imaginative & equal to any Poet, but not Superior. I cannot think that Real Poets have any competition. None are greatest in the Kingdom of Heaven; it is so in Poetry" (On Wordsworth, *K* 783).

Crabb Robinson's efforts to have the two poets meet came to nothing. Wordsworth, after reading the *Songs of Innocence and of Experience*, remarked: "There is no doubt this poor man was mad, but there is something in the madness of this man which interests me more than the sanity of Lord Byron and Walter Scott!" (*CR* 281). Robinson's edition of Wordsworth poems, which he loaned to Blake, was not returned until after Blake's death. (See Blake's annotations, *K* 782–84.)

The WORM is, for Blake, the lowest and weakest form of animal life, a simple alimentary tube without any means of self-defense. Its position is West (*J* 98:43). Like all other living things, it is of the divine substance. "God is in the lowest effects as well as in the highest causes; for he is become a worm that he may nourish the weak" (On Lavater 630, *K* 87). His "Mutual Covenant Divine" is made with all things, including the Worm (*J* 98:41, 43). He cherishes it with milk and oil, and punishes "the evil foot" that wilful bruises its "helpless form" (*Thel* 5:9–11). And even the Worm practises his doctrine of Forgiveness: "The cut worm forgives the plow and dies in peace" (*K* 183; also *MHH* 7, Proverb 6). "O Lord . . . if thou chuse to elect a worm, it shall remove the mountains" (*Mil* 20:17–19). And it does actually renew the moisture of the sandy plain (*FZ* ii:368).

Ever since Bildad announced that man is a worm (*Job* xxv:6), the worm has been an emblem of his mortality. This is the false doctrine of Enitharmon: "tell the Human race . . . that an Eternal life awaits the worms of sixty winters in an allegorical abode where existence hath never come" (*Eur* 5:5). The Worm is an attribute of her daughter Ethinthus, who is the body (*Eur* 13:16). This doctrine is a convenient one for the tyrants of Asia (*SoL* 7:7). It is taught by Satan (*J* 27:55), by the Spectre (*J* 33:6), and by Vala (*J* 64:12). Tiriel comes to believe it (*Tir* viii:24); Los is convinced for a time (*J* 34:57); and even Jerusalem wavers

(*J* 80:3). Actually, all depends on our perceptions: "Let the Human Organs be kept
in their perfect Integrity, at will Contracting into Worms or Expanding into Gods"
(*J* 55:36). And even the Worm is "translucent all within" (*J* 27:56).

Oothoon finds the call to love even in the
grave-worm: "Does not the worm erect a
pillar in the mouldering church yard and a
palace of eternity in the jaws of the hungry
grave? Over his porch these words are
written: 'Take thy bliss, O Man, and sweet
shall be thy taste, & sweet thy infant joys
renew!' " (*VDA* 5:41–6:3). Ahania, de-
ploring man's cult of death, repeats Oothoon's words as she cries aloud to the caverns of the grave: "Will you erect a lasting
habitation in the mouldering Church yard?
Or a pillar & palace of Eternity in the jaws
of the hungry grave?" (*FZ* viii:495). Enion
replies from the caverns: "Once I wail'd
desolate like thee; my fallow fields in fear
cried to the Churchyards & the Earthworm
came in dismal state. I found him in my
bosom . . ." (*FZ* viii:536).

For in this world, the mortal flesh is ines-
capably part of man, and is from the female.
"I have said to the Worm: thou art my
mother & my sister" (*GoP* 16; cf. *Job* xvii:
14). "Thou'rt my Mother from the Womb,
| Wife, Sister, Daughter, to the Tomb, |
Weaving to Dreams the Sexual strife | And
weeping over the Web of Life" (*GoP*, "Of
the Gates" 45). The mystery of Generation
is involved. The grave-worm is weaving the
sexual impulses, and the resultant foetus
begins as a worm. Vala is first a worm, then
becomes a serpent and a dragon, before she
is born as an infant (*FZ* ii:83–92). Orc also
is first a worm in the womb, then a serpent,
then "many forms of fish, bird, & beast" before he is born as a baby (*Ur* 19:20–36).
Blake anticipated the still-respected theory
of Recapitulation, according to which the
foetus grows through all the previous forms
of evolution. He may have got the idea
from the *Zoonomia* of Erasmus Darwin, who
figured out much of the theory of evolution
before his grandson proved it.

In *The Book of Thel*, the Worm and the
Clod are the baby and its mother (*Thel* 4:
2–9).

Reversion to the Worm is possible. When
Orc is oppressed by Urizen's hypocrisy, he
becomes again the Worm, which grows into
the Serpent of Eden (*FZ* vii:139). When
Gwendolen tries to reduce her consort Hyle
to a baby, he becomes instead a Worm (*J*
82:47); then she labors "to form the Worm
into a form of love by tears & pain" (*J* 82:
76), until her original falsehood "grew &
grew till it became a Space & an Allegory
around the Winding Worm. They nam'd it
Canaan & built for it a tender Moon" (*J*
84:32–85:2), i.e., marriage, in which the
wandering Reuben finally finds rest.

" 'Consider this, O mortal Man, O worm
of sixty winters,' said Los; 'consider Sexual
Organization & hide thee in the dust' " (*J*
34:57).

WRATH is traditionally an attribute of
God, also one of the Seven Deadly Sins.
Blake believed that it was neither; or rather,
that it became deadly only through perversion and corruption.

Thus, the Angry God of the Old Testament is not the true God, but that revolted
and fallen aspect of God whom Blake named
Urizen. "Is [the true] God a smiter with
disease?" (*EG* b:30) or is he not rather the
Great Healer?

As for the Deadly Sins, all of them, including Wrath, are basically good and have
their place and function in the Divine
scheme.

Wrath is Revolution. It is the explosive
which wrecks the oppressive past of Experience. When things have been too bad for
too long, the human being reacts in a blind
outburst, which springs from a deeper wisdom than the tame horses of instruction.
See TYGER.

Thus Job's Curse is the beginning of his
salvation. He has ceased to be passive under
his misfortunes; reacting against them, he
comes eventually to recognize the error
which caused them.

All true art begins with a reaction against
the past, a discontent with things as they

are commonly accepted. Therefore the child of Los is Orc (Revolution); and the primary aspect of Orc is Rintrah. Rintrah (wrath at the state of things) and his brother Palamabron (pity for its victims) usually work together. See RINTRAH.

One should of course distinguish between the different types of Wrath. The wrath of the Lion is the protection of the flocks; the wrath of the Tyger is the blind, impersonal rage of revolution; the wrath of Urizen is the satanic desire to murder opposition.

YEARS are the sixth in Blake's eight divisions of Time, beginning with Moments, continuing through Minutes, Hours, Days, Months, Years, and Ages, ending with Periods. They are built by some of the Sons of Los (*Mil* 28:44–45), but as they pertain to the material world, "All are the work of Fairy hands of the Four Elements" (*Mil* 28:60).

TWO HUNDRED YEARS. A Period consists of seven Ages, and "Seven Ages is amounting to Two Hundred Years" (*Mil* 28:58). When Eno expands a Moment of Time into eight thousand and five hundred years, "Every two hundred years has a door to Eden" (*J* 48:37).

SEVEN THOUSAND YEARS is the time from the Creation to the Last Judgment. "Eno . . . took a Moment of Time and drew it out to seven thousand years" (*FZ* i:222). But later, Blake found this extent insufficient. Eno extends the Moment to eight thousand and five hundred years (*J* 48:36), which is also the length of time in which Los retains his youth (*J* 83:52).

SIX THOUSAND YEARS is the traditional length of time between the Creation and the Millennium. This figure was reached by combining two texts: "For in six days the Lord made heaven and earth . . . and rested the seventh day" (*Exod* xx:11) and "one day is with the Lord as a thousand years and a thousand years as one day" (*II Peter* iii:8; cf. *Psalm* xc:4). Therefore it was concluded that his Creation of six days should

last six thousand years, to be followed by the Sabbath of the seventh day, the Millennium.

The tradition is very old, having been ascribed to Elias; it is first mentioned, however, in a first-century Christian epistle ascribed to Barnabas. Archbishop Ussher accepted it in his famous chronology, which was not seriously challenged until the geologists began their discoveries, and still can be found in some Bibles.

Blake accepted the tradition. The royalist Duke of Burgundy cries out, "Shall . . . these mowers from the Atlantic mountains mow down all this great starry harvest of six thousand years?" (*FR* 89), not realizing that if his timing is correct, the Millennium is close at hand.

The imminence of the Millennium runs all through *Milton*. The Revolutionist Los, Master of Time, proclaims: "I am that Shadowy Prophet who Six Thousand Years ago fell from my station in the Eternal bosom. Six Thousand Years are finish'd. I return! both Time & Space obey my will. I in Six Thousand Years walk up and down; for not one Moment of Time is lost, nor one Event of Space unpermanent, but all remain: every Fabric of Six Thousand Years remains permanent" (*Mil* 22:15; also *Mil* 23:55; 39:13; *J* 85:6).

As with the Lord a thousand years is as one day, so the creative moment sums up all time. "Every Time less than a pulsation of the artery is equal in its period & value to Six Thousand Years, for in this Period the Poet's Work is Done, and all the Great Events of Time start forth & are conciev'd in such a Period, within a Moment, a Pulsation of the Artery" (*Mil* 28:62–29:3).

YOD (the Hebrew letter) is the first letter of the Divine Name; but it is no more than that, and therefore does not signify the total God. It is instead "The Angel of the Divine Presence," in "Laocoön" (*K* 775) the father of Satan and Adam. It is he who wrote the Decalogue; in Blake's water color he begins it by inscribing his own name.

See ANGEL OF THE DIVINE PRESENCE, under ANGEL.

YORK is one of the Four Cathedral Cities which comprise the other Twenty-four (*J* 46:24). "They are the Four Zoas that stood around the Throne Divine: Verulam, London, York & Edinburgh their English names" (*J* 59:13). As Verulam is South, Edinburgh North, and London East, York, though it is in the north of England, must be West. Actually, it is a full degree of longitude west of St. Paul's. As though to confirm this wrenching of geography, Blake pictured York as west of London in the decoration on *Jerusalem* 57. York therefore is Tharmas.

When Albion's plagues recoil upon England, "ancient miterd York" sickens, his head upon a snowy hill (*Am* 15:9). When Albion rises, "his bosom girt with gold involves York, Edinburgh, Durham & Carlisle" (*Mil* 39:42). Durham and Carlisle are in the episcopal province of York.

In *Jerusalem*, York is "crown'd with loving kindness" (38:51). "The voices of Bath & Canterbury & York & Edinburgh Cry over the Plow of Nations in the strong hand of Albion" (57:1). In the time of war, "London feels his brain cut round: Edinburgh's heart is circumscribed: York & Lincoln hide among the flocks" (66:64). "From London to York & Edinburgh the Furnaces rage terrible. Primrose Hill is the mouth of the Furnace & the Iron Door" (73:53).

YORKSHIRE, with the adjacent counties of Lincoln and Lancashire, is assigned to Simeon (*J* 16:44). With the adjacent counties of Durham and Westmoreland, it is assigned to Brertun (*J* 71:32).

YOUNG (Edward, 1683–1765) in his day was ranked with the greatest poets. His *Revenge* (1721) was one of the biggest stage successes of the century; his *Night Thoughts* (1742–45), an international success, instituted the school of graveyard poetry; his *Conjectures on Original Composition* (1759), which attacked neoclassicism, had a wide effect on the Continent.

The *Night Thoughts* was so very successful because it gave eloquent voice to orthodoxy; it is unreadable today for the very same reason. It begins excellently: the sleepless poet, in the darkness of the night, laments his misfortunes and meditates upon the mysteries of death and immortality. Young had a knack of compressing his thoughts into resonant pentameters, which made for quotability: indeed, "Procrastination is the Thief of Time" (i:393) became proverbial; and I have seen "She sparkled, was exhal'd, and went to Heav'n" (v:601) on New England tombstones. However, after the success of the first four Nights, Young unfortunately added five more (1745), in which he tried to convert his worldly friend Lorenzo; but it is too protracted a sigh. The poetry is gone. The tone has sunk to the monotonous false ecstasy of the conventional preacher, and the arguments have become a pompous parade of pious platitudes—ideal reading for the solemn (though inaccurate) Steelyard (*IslM*, Chap. viii).

Young's philosophy was quite contrary to Blake's at every point. Young's God is remote in space; the size and mechanism of the skies prove his existence ("An *undevout* Astronomer is *mad*," ix:771); Reason is supreme in man, while the Imagination is evil ("Imagination is the *Paphian* Shop . . . foul *Ideas* . . . hot as Hell," viii:994–97); Good and Evil are absolutes, yet "All Evils *Natural* are *Moral* goods" (ix:389); "A GOD all mercy is a GOD unjust" (iv:233); and even Hell is really good: "its hideous Groans join Heav'n's sweet Hallelujahs in

thy Praise, great Source of Good *alone*!
How Kind in All! in Vengeance Kind!
Pain, Death, Gehenna, SAVE" (ix:476).

The disagreements run all along the line.
For example, Blake liked the "innocently
gay & thoughtless" who he thought were
not "among the condemn'd, because ignorant of crime" (*LJ*, *K* 610; cf. "careless, gay
people are better than those who think," *CR*
270); whereas Young fashionably deplored
levity: "*Laughter*, tho' never censur'd yet
as Sin . . . is half-immoral. . . . 'Retire, and
read thy Bible, to be Gay' " (viii:748–71).

But leafing through Blake's illustrations,
one would never guess these profound disagreements. Yet the 537 water colors are
proof enough that the *Night Thoughts* inspired Blake; they also affected his verse.
Young had an ability to improvise original
metaphors, which are intellectual rather
than visual; Blake visualized them. "Woes
cluster; rare are *solitary* Woes" wrote
Young (iii:63), his way of saying that troubles never come singly; but Blake seized on
the word "cluster" and transformed Young's
banality into a knot of woes wailing against
a weird night sky (see Illustrations). Or
Young described Philander's tuberculosis
thus: "Death's subtle Seed within (sly,
treach'rous Miner!) working in the Dark,
smil'd . . . and beckon'd the Worm to riot
on that Rose so red" (i:355); Blake disen-
tangled Young's decidedly mixed metaphor, and made it into a poem as well as a
picture, "The Sick Rose" (*SoE*). Young's
lines on the dead Narcissa and Philander,
"O the soft Commerce! O the tender Tyes
close-twisted with the Fibres of the Heart!"
(v:1063) meant for Blake the underworld of
the subconscious. When Thel enters this

world, she sees "the couches of the dead, &
where the fibrous roots of every heart on
earth infixes deep its restless twists" (*Thel*
6:3). Blake pictured it as "Grief among the
Roots and Trees" when illustrating Gray's
Hymn to Adversity; and he pictured it again
as the abode of the Worm (*GoP* 16).

When Blake made his designs for *The
Gates of Paradise* (1793) he certainly had
the *Night Thoughts* in mind. The idea of the
caterpillar frontispiece he used again for his
179th water color, where a whole host of
caterpillar babies devour the last leaves of a
tree. "Embryos we must be, till we burst the
Shell, yon ambient azure Shell, and spring
to Life" (i:132)—the Mundane Shell!—is
pictured as "At length for hatching ripe he
breaks the shell" (*GoP* 6). "The Traveller
hasteth in the Evening" (*GoP* 14) is the
same design as the 113th water color, which
illustrates Young's "If prudent, Age should
meet the friendly Foe" (iv:19). The Worm
sits beneath the fibrous roots (*GoP* 16). And
finally, the last line of Young's eighth Night,
"Satan, thy Master, I dare call a Dunce" is
the first line of Blake's Epilogue: "Truly,
My Satan, thou art but a Dunce" (*K* 771).

The 537 water colors had been commissioned by Richard Edwards, a leading bookseller who had a great admiration for Blake's
work. But only forty-three of the designs,
selected from the first four Nights, were actually engraved, and published in 1797.
Some were hand-colored. Although Benjamin West, Richard Cosway, and Ozias Humphry spoke warmly of them, a financial
crisis was at its peak, and the book was a
failure. (See *Erd* 265.)

YUVA was a son of Tiriel (*Tir* i:25).

Z

ZAARA is the twenty-fourth of the Thirty-two Nations which shall preserve liberty and rule the rest of the world (*J* 72:41). It is the last of the African group, and seemingly is Blake's spelling of Sahara.

ZARETAN was east of the Jordan on the river bank. Here the Israelites bore the Ark across the Jordan. Because of the clay between this city and Succoth, Solomon's foundries for making the ornaments of his Temple were situated here.

Reuben sleeps between Zaretan and Succoth on the Stone of Bohan (*J* 34:45).

ZAZEL is a brother of Tiriel (*Tir* vii:9, 13), who chained Zazel and enslaved his sons (*Tir* i:35, 41). They live in caves of the wilderness, sustained by roots and water. They represent the original thinkers whom the legalistic Tiriel could not tolerate.

When the blind Tiriel, led by his maddened daughter, approaches their caves at eventide, old Zazel and his sons mock them. At Tiriel's voice some of the sons flee, but Zazel stands his ground, accusing Tiriel and sneering that soon he will be "as foolish as thy foolish brother Zazel" (*Tir* vii:13).

The name of Zazel, like that of Tiriel, is to be found in Agrippa's *Occult Philosophy* II, xxii. Here Zazel is identified as an evil spirit of Saturn.

ZEBULUN was Jacob's tenth son, and the founder of a Tribe.

With his brothers, he is listed as a Son of Los who fled (*FZ* viii:361, 377). When the Sons of Albion divide him, with five of his brothers he rolls apart, "to dissipate into Non Entity" (*J* 74:50–51).

In Wales, Los assigns him the counties of Anglesea and Sodor; in England, Bedford, Huntingdon, and Cambridge; in Scotland, Orkney, Shetland, and Skye; in Ireland, he shares with Judah and Issachar the twelve counties of the eastern province, Leinster (*J* 16:40, 48, 57; 72:18).

ZELOPHEHAD had five daughters: Mahlah, Noah, Hoglah, Milcah, and Tirzah; but he left no son to inherit. The daughters therefore appealed to Moses, who ruled that in such cases the daughters could inherit, provided they married within the Tribe (*Numb* xxvii:1–11; xxxvi:3; *Josh* xvii:3–4).

Blake took these daughters independent of the male to be Female Wills, who restrict the senses of man. Tirzah, the last, is the most important: she is the mother of the "Mortal part" or body (*SoE*, "To Tirzah" 9), and with her sisters she weaves "the black Woof of Death" (*Mil* 29:55–56). She also binds the eyes and nostrils (*FZ* viii: 301–3; *J* 67:47–49), while Noah restricts the sex (*FZ* viii:312–13; *J* 67:59–60), Hoglah and Mahlah the tongue (*FZ* viii:316–17; *J* 68:4–5), and Milcah the ear (*FZ* viii:318; *J* 68:6). With the addition of Rahab, they are equated with Milton's three wives and three daughters (*Mil* 17:11).

The ZENITH is Reason, man's brain, his highest point when erect. It is the southern Zoa, Urizen (*J* 12:55–58). Its opposite is the Nadir (north—subconscious). The Circumference is the West, or physical body; the Center is the East, or heart.

When Urizen bids Luvah soar into the Zenith (*FZ* i:495), he is giving over his southern realm to the Emotions. When Blake first saw Milton in the Zenith (*Mil* 15:47), he implies that Milton's ideas interested him first.

"ZIBEAH the Philistine" is obviously Zibiah, the Jewess of Beer-sheba, who became the mother of the weak king Joash (*II Kings* xii:1; *II Chron* xxiv:1). Blake listed her as the eleventh and penultimate name in the Maternal Line from Cainah to Mary (*J* 62: 12).

ZILLAH, a Cainite, was the second wife of Lamech, the first polygamist. She became the mother of Tubal-Cain and his sister Naamah (*Gen* iv:19–22). Blake listed her twelfth in the line of the Daughters of Los and Enitharmon from Ocalythron to Mary (*FZ* viii:365). In the revised list of the Maternal Line, she is the third in the line of the Daughters of Vala, from Cainah to Mary (*J* 62:9).

ZION ("fortress") was originally the rocky scarp on the southern end of the ridge between the Kidron and Tyropoeon valleys in Jerusalem. Blake thrice called it "Zion('s) Hill's most ancient promontory" (*J* 12:27; 29:3; 80:36). The name came to include the adjacent Temple Hill; then Zion was "the holy hill" and "the habitation of the Lord." Eventually it became a general name for the entire city, and in Christian times was taken as a type of heaven. Paul contrasted it with the terrifying Sinai (*Heb* xii: 18, 22). John the Divine looked, "and, lo, a Lamb stood on the mount Sion" (*Rev* xiv:1).

"And Enitharmon said: 'I see the Lamb of God upon Mount Zion'" (*FZ* viii:22). In the days of Innocence, "Mount Zion lifted his head in every Nation under heaven" (*J* 24:48); but Satan "wither'd up sweet Zion's Hill from every Nation of the Earth" (*J* 27:49). Blake called it once "the Hill of Giants" (*J* 78:22). And once the Divine Vision set like a sun "behind the Gardens of Kensington on Tyburn's River in clouds of blood, where was mild Zion Hill's most ancient promontory" (*J* 29:2).

ZOA is a Greek plural which Blake used as an English singular. In *Revelation* (iv:6, etc.) it is awkwardly translated "beasts." John the Divine on Patmos saw the four beasts (*Rev* iv; v; *FZ* viii:600; *Mil* 40:22) standing about the throne of the Lamb. They worship him and sing a new song. Each beast thunders "Come and see," revealing in turn the Four disastrous Riders of the Apocalypse. "One of the four beasts gave unto the seven angels seven golden vials full of the wrath of God" (*Rev* xv:7), which are poured out on mankind.

These beasts are the same four "living creatures" (Chayot Hakodesh) which Ezekiel beheld by the river of Chebar (*Ezek* i: 5 ff.; *J* 12:58). They have complicated eyed wheels within wheels, which revolve independently, and act as the chariot of Deity.

In conventional iconography (ignoring minor discrepancies) they have respectively the face of a man, a lion, an ox, and an eagle (*Ezek* i:10; *Rev* iv:7), and are commonly identified with the four evangelists. However, before Ezekiel, the huge statues of the guardians of the Assyrian palace gates were sculptured with the face of a man, the head of a lion, the wings of an eagle, and the body of an ox.

Blake identified them with the four fundamental aspects of Man: his body (Tharmas—west); his reason (Urizen—south); his emotions (Luvah—east); and his imagination (Urthona—north). These aspects are Jung's fourfold analysis of man. Blake named them and assigned them compass-points (*Mil* 19:18; 34:35, etc.). They are "the Four Eternal Senses of Man" (*J* 36: 31; 98:22), "the Four Rivers of the Water of Life" (*J* 98:15): "West flow'd the Parent Sense, the Tongue . . . South stood the Nerves of the Eye; East, in Rivers of bliss, the Nerves of the Expansive Nostrils . . .

North stood the labyrinthine Ear" (*J* 98: 16–18).

As Man was made in the image of God, his Zoas are reflections of the divine aspects. Tharmas the Shepherd is a mirroring of God the Father; Luvah, in whose robes of blood Jesus descends, corresponds to the Son; and Urthona-Los, the fount of inspiration, is the Holy Ghost. Urizen, however, is that aspect of Divinity which falls and becomes the equivalent of the Devil. See URIZEN.

The co-eternal Zoas emerge into this world in a counterclockwise cycle. Tharmas is the "Parent power" in the West (*FZ* i:24; *J* 98:17); Urizen (south) and Luvah (east) follow; and Los (north), who is Urthona's manifestation in this world, is the fourth (*FZ* i:14; *Mil* 24:8, 76).

They suffer in their descent into their "Slumbers of Six Thousand Years" (*Mil* 39:13). The trouble began when the Emotions usurped the place of Reason. "When Luvah assum'd the World of Urizen to the South, and Albion was slain upon his mountains & in his tent, all fell towards the Center, in dire ruin sinking down" (*Mil* 19:19; 34:38; *J* 59:15). They "clouded rage" and "change their situations in the Universal Man" (*J* 36:25; 74:1). They "rush around on all sides in dire ruin" (*J* 58:47). They turn their wheels against man (*J* 43:1) and against each other (*J* 74:5).

Urthona, who never manifests in Time, becomes Los, who splits from his Emanation, or feminine portion, Enitharmon, and eventually sinks as the Spectre of Urthona, while she becomes a Shadow. Luvah splits from his Emanation, Vala, and is consumed in the furnaces but is reborn on a lower plane as Orc, who becomes the Serpent of Eden, while Vala is materialized as the Shadowy Female (nature), who is also Rahab (Natural Religion). Urizen casts out his Emanation, Ahania, and degenerates until as the Dragon he loses all human form. Tharmas also splits, losing his Emanation, Enion, and is debased to the material body. Each Zoa in turn thinks he has become supreme, and is God, but is mistaken. At the end, they are all restored to their pristine glories and harmony, and retake their places in Albion's bosom (*J* 96:41). Their whole story is told at length in *The Four Zoas*. For their individual stories, see LOS; LUVAH; THARMAS; URIZEN; URTHONA.

Blake made use of the eyed wheels which Ezekiel saw. See WHEELS. In the Rosenwald "Last Judgment" (see Illustrations), each of the Zoas has the four faces of man, lion, ox, and eagle, as Ezekiel described them (*Ezek* i:10); but in Blake's first watercolor sketch for the title page of *Genesis* (see Illustrations), each Zoa has only one head, as described by John (*Rev* iv:7). They sit in a row on the earth. On the extreme left is the man-headed Luvah, who is already starting trouble. Affirming his independence, he leans away from the other Zoas, whom he regards with a malicious laugh. His scales, his crown of precious gems, and his snake's tongue indicate that he has sunk to Luvah's lower form, Orc, and is becoming the Serpent of Eden, ready to ascend into the Tree of Death, just behind him, towards which he stretches his left arm. Inclined towards him yet looking away is Los with the eagle head of Genius. Urizen's lion head suggests his lions which forge the astronomical universe; he leans away from Los, his hands folded in prayer, like those of Tharmas, with the ox's head, above whom rises the Tree of Life.

The activities of the Zoas during the Last Judgment are detailed in *The Four Zoas* ix. Before they begin their operations, their spiritual forms appear around the Throne: "four Wonders of the Almighty, incomprehensible, pervading all, amidst & round about, fourfold, each in the other reflected: they are named Life's—in Eternity —Four Starry Universes going forward from Eternity to Eternity" (ix:281). In the letter to Ozias Humphry describing the "Last Judgment" (*K* 444), they are "Four Living Creatures filled with Eyes, attended by Seven Angels with the Seven Vials of the Wrath of God, & above these [there are] Seven Angels with the Seven Trumpets [composing] the Cloud, which by its rolling away displays the opening Seats of the Blessed." In *A Vision of the Last Judgment* (*K* 612), they are "the Four Living Creatures mention'd in Revelations as Surrounding the Throne; these I suppose to have the chief agency in removing the old heavens & the old Earth to make way for the New Heaven & the New Earth, to descend from the throne of God & of the Lamb; that Living Creature on the Left of the Throne Gives to the Seven Angels the Seven Vials of the wrath of God, with which they, hovering over the deeps beneath, pour out upon the wicked their Plagues; the Other Living Creatures are descending with a Shout & with the Sound of the Trumpet, directing the Combats in the upper Elements." (See Illustrations, "LJ" Nos. 9, 14.)

ILLUSTRATIONS
BY BLAKE
& MAPS

Illustrations

I. A Vision of the Last Judgment

II. Title Page of *Genesis* Showing the Four Zoas as the Beasts of *Revelation*

III. Moses and the Burning Bush

IV. The Circle of Life

V. Two Lovers in the Lilly

VI. London from Lincoln's Inn to Lambeth in the Time of William Blake

VII. London and Neighboring Villages as William Blake Knew Them

VIII. Spenser's *Faerie Queene*

IX. Milton and the Spirit of Plato

X. Milton's Dream

XI. Hervey's *Meditations Among the Tombs*

XII. "Woes cluster; rare are solitary Woes"

KEY TO 'A VISION OF THE LAST JUDGMENT'

1. The Holy Ghost
2. Glorification of angels with harps
3. The Candlestick
4. The Table of Shew-bread
5. The cherubim of the Ark
6. Infants; "these represent the Eternal Births of Intellect from the divine Humanity"
7. Baptism
8. Education ("Nursing Fathers & Nursing Mothers")
9. A Living Creature (a four-headed Zoa)
10. The Two Witnesses subduing their enemies
11. The Lord's Supper
12. The Angel of the Divine Presence, "having a writing tablet & taking account of the numbers who arise . . . is frequently call'd by the Name of Jehovah Elohim"
13. The Holy Family ("Mary, Joseph, John the Baptist, Zacharias & Elizabeth")
14. A Living Creature "on the Left of the Throne Gives to the Seven Angels the Seven Vials of the wrath of God"
15. A woman with children fleeing from the Wrath; "these represent those who, tho' willing, were too weak to Reject Error without the Assistance & Countenance of those Already in the Truth"
16. Michael
17. Apollyon, "foiled before the Sword of Michael"
18. The Book of Life
19. Three figures bowing in humiliation before the record of their good deeds
20. The Book of Death, uttering "Lightnings & tempests"
21. Two Pharisees "who plead their own Righteousness before the throne"
22. Jachin and Boaz
23. The Four and Twenty Elders "sitting in judgment"
24. Adam
25. Eve
26. Three plagues poured from the Vials of Wrath: Labor, Materialism, and Hate
27. Cain, "falling with the head downward"
28. Araunah casting out the chaff, "the vanities of Riches & Worldly Honours"
29. The Cross, on which the Serpent is nailed
30. Satan, wound round by the Serpent
31. Eliakim, the Son of Hilkiah, who "drags Satan down headlong"
32. Sin, dragged down by the hair by a demon with a key
33. Death, dragged down by a demon
34. Time, dragged down by the same demon
35. Og, king of Bashan, with the sword of Justice
36. Cruel laws, as "three fiery fiends with grey beards & scourges of fire"
37. Moses, "casting his tables of stone into the deeps"
38. A male and female, "chain'd together by the feet; they represent those who perish'd by the flood"
39. Hazael the Syrian, "a fiend with wings," who "urges the wicked onwards with fiery darts"; he "drives abroad all those who rebell against their Saviour"
40. Achitophel, with the cord in his hand
41. Caiaphas "has a Blue Flame like a Miter"
42. Pilate "has bloody hands that never can be cleansed"
43. Babylon and other kingdoms
44. The Inquisition, "dragging up a Woman by her hair"
45. The Inquisition; two men contending even on the brink of the Pit
46. A Cruel Church; a man strangling two women
47. Four Angels "descend headlong with four trumpets to awake the dead"
48. "The Harlot nam'd Mystery in the Revelations"
49. Vegetative Existence ("Two Beings each with three heads")
50. Mystery's kings and counsellors
51. The Dragon with seven heads and ten horns
52. Satan's book of Accusations
53. Gog
54. Magog

55. The skeleton animating
56. "A Youthful couple . . . awaked by their Children"
57. "The two Figures in purifying flames by the side of the dragon's cavern represents the Latter state of the Church when on the verge of Perdition, yet protected by a Flaming Sword"
58. Albion awakened by Brittannia
59. "A Man & Woman; these are the Primitive Christians"
60. Elijah; "he comprehends all the Prophetic Characters"
61. Abel, "surrounded by Innocents"
62. Seth. "This State call'd Seth is Male & Female in a higher state of Happiness & wisdom than Noah, being nearer the State of Innocence . . . The figures of Seth & his wife comprehends the Fathers before the flood & their Generations"
63. "The two Seasons of Spring & Autumn"
64. The Church Universal as the Woman in the Wilderness. "There is such a State in Eternity: it is composed of the Innocent civilized Heathen & the Uncivilized Savage, who, having not the Law, do by Nature the things contain'd in the Law"
65. "Between Seth & Elijah three Female Figures crown'd with Garlands Represent Learning & Science, which accompanied Adam out of Eden"
66. "Two figures, a Male & Female, with numerous Children; these represent those who were not in the Line of the Church, & yet were Saved from among the Antediluvians who Perished"
67. "A female figure represents the Solitary State of those who, previous to the Flood, walked with God"
68. Noah, with Shem and Japhet; "these three Persons represent Poetry, Painting & Music, the three Powers in Man of conversing with Paradise, which the flood did not Sweep away"
69. The Four Seasons, "the Changed State made by the flood"
70. Abraham
71. Hagar and Ishmael
72. "Jacob & his Twelve Sons hover beneath the feet of Abraham"
73. Abraham's Posterity. "The Children of Abraham, or Hebrew Church, are represented as a Stream of Figures, on which are seen Stars somewhat like the Milky way; they . . . Represent Religion, or Civilized Life such as it is in the Christian Church, who are the Offspring of the Hebrew"
74. "On the right hand of Noah, a Woman with Children Represents the State Call'd Laban the Syrian; it is the Remains of Civilization in the State from whence Abraham was taken"
75. "Three aged Men who appear as suddenly emerging from the blue sky for their help. These three Aged Men represent divine Providence as oppos'd to, & distinct from, divine vengeance, represented by three Aged men on the side of the Picture among the Wicked, with scourges of fire"
76. "A Mother Meets her numerous Family in the Arms of their Father; these are representations of the Greek Learned & Wise, as also of those of other Nations, such as Egypt & Babylon in which were multitudes who shall meet the Lord coming in the Clouds"
77. "On the right hand of Noah A Female descends to meet her Lover or Husband, representative of that Love call'd Friendship, which Looks for no other heaven than their Beloved & in him sees all reflected as in a Glass of Eternal Diamond"
78. Lovers reunited, or the Soul reunited with the Body
79. "Three Females, representing those who are not of the dead but of those found alive at the Last Judgment; they appear to be innocently gay & thoughtless, not being condemn'd because ignorant of crime in the midst of a corrupted Age; the Virgin Mary was of this class"
80. Mahomed, beneath Ishmael
81. The Seven Eyes of God

These identifications are made from A Vision of the Last Judgment (K 604–17). There are some discrepancies between the text and this picture. Only two of the Living Creatures are shown, and only three of the seven Vials of Wrath. Satan, though he has coils about his waist, is not involved with the crucified Serpent; neither is Sin bound in the Serpent's folds. Death is not chained to the Cross. Some attributes are also omitted; for example, Og has his sword but not his balances.

A Vision of the Last Judgment

Title Page of *Genesis* Showing the Four Zoas as the Beasts of *Revelation*. See Z O A

Moses and the Burning Bush

The Circle of Life

Department of Printing and Graphic Arts, Harvard College Library

FINAL VERSION

The Pierpont Morgan Library

EARLY PROOF

Two Lovers in the Lilly (headpiece for Chapter ii of *Jerusalem*). See LILLY

LONDON FROM LINCOLN'S INN TO LAMBETH
IN THE TIME OF WILLIAM BLAKE

REPRODUCED FROM
Cary's New and Accurate Plan of
London and Westminster . . . Corrected to June 1, 1820

Scale of Half a Mile.

1   2   3   4 Furlongs

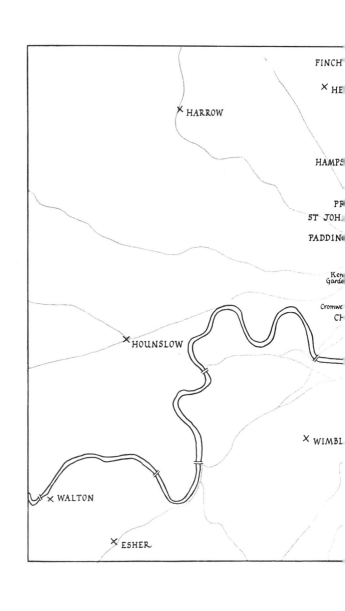

FINCH

× HE

× HARROW

HAMPS

PR

ST JOH

PADDIN

Ken
Garde

Cromwe
Ch

× HOUNSLOW

× WIMBL

× WALTON

× ESHER

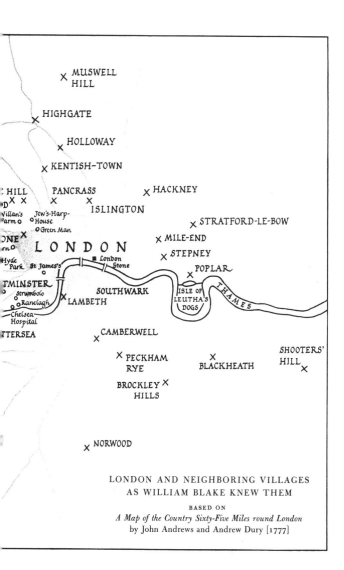

LONDON AND NEIGHBORING VILLAGES
AS WILLIAM BLAKE KNEW THEM

BASED ON

A Map of the Country Sixty-Five Miles round London
by John Andrews and Andrew Dury [1777]

Spenser's *Faerie Queene*

Milton and the Spirit of Plato (from the illustrations to *Il Penseroso*)

Milton's Dream (from the illustrations to *Il Penseroso*)

KEY TO 'HERVEY'S *MEDITATIONS AMONG THE TOMBS*

1. God out of Christ is a Consuming Fire
2. Eve
3. Adam
4. Serpent
5. Cain
6. Abel
7. Enoch
8. Noah
9. Mother of Rebecca
10. Mother of Leah
11. Abraham believed God

12. Aaron
13. Solomon
14. David
15. Moses
16. Jesus
17. Elias
18. Angel of Providence
19. Hervey
20. Guardian Angel
21. Widow
22. Father

23. Angel of Death
24. Virgin
25. Angel of Death
26. Mother
27. Sophronia Died in Childbed
28. Orphan
29. Protecting Angel
30. She Died on Her Wedding Day
31. Recording Angels
32. Protecting Angel

33. WRATH
34. MERCY
35. Ministering Angels
36. These died for Love
37. Where is your Father
38. Infancy
39. Sage
40. Husband
41. Wife
42. Baby
43. Baptism

Hervey's *Meditations Among the Tombs*

(9)

Woes cluſter; rare are ſolitary Woes;
They love a Train; they tread each other's Heel :
Her Death invades *His* mournful right, and claims
The Grief that ſtarted from my Lids for Him;
Seizes the faithleſs, alienated Tear,
Or ſhares it, e'er It falls.   So frequent Death,
Sorrow, He more than cauſes, He confounds;
For human Sighs his rival Strokes contend,
And make Diſtreſs, Diſtraction.   Oh *Philander !*
What was thy Fate?   A double Fate to me;
Portent, and Pain!   a Menace, and a Blow!
Like the black Raven hov'ring o'er my Peace,
Not leſs a Bird of Omen, than of Prey.
It call'd *Narciſſa* long before her Hour;
It call'd her tender Soul, by Break of bliſs,
From the firſt Bloſſom, from the Buds of Joy;
Thoſe Few, our noxious Fate unblaſted leaves,
In this inclement Clime of human life.

B   Sweet

"Woes cluster; rare are solitary Woes" (Young's *Night Thoughts*, Night iii, line 66)

INDEX

PREFACE TO THE INDEX

I gave what I thought were good reasons for having an index to Damon's *Blake Dictionary*, despite its alphabetical arrangement, in a list of the entries that I compiled and that *Blake's Studies* published in 1970, and there is no need to repeat all of that here. But I can summarize the reasons in a few sentences, and give at least a single example. The alphabet is an arbitrary ordering of letters used mechanically to make orderly categories. But Damon's *Dictionary* is an unusual combination of mechanical orderliness and unmechanical inconsistency. In some ways it is a very personal account of his understanding of Blake arranged impersonally, and it is no doubt one of the greatest of a venerable scholarly genre now nearly extinct, the one-man compendium. Damon tried to make the *Dictionary* an encyclopedia, but he was not compulsive about it, and he did not resist the urge to put things where he felt like putting them, a characteristic that makes the *Dictionary* as a study of Blake more interesting, the *Dictionary* as a dictionary less accessible. Damon interpolated a discussion of Britain as the seat of Biblical history and eighteenth-century theories on that subject into his entry for the *Druids*. The interpolation is natural enough, and some expert readers looking for information on Blake's ideas about the relation between Britain and Jerusalem might think to look under *Druids*, but not most readers, certainly. In making this index, I have tried to remember that the *Dictionary* is the book probably consulted more than any other by people reading Blake for the first time.

The Reader will do the indexer a favor by remembering in turn that the *Dictionary* is virtually an index in itself to Blake's writings, and the density of a truly comprehensive index to it would be overwhelming. The index has been considerably reduced on the following principle: whenever Damon's discussion is closer to summary and concordance than to interpretation, I have usually not made an entry. When in doubt, I have chosen to make an entry rather than not to make one. For the reader who is not an expert, I have indexed a large selection of elementary facts about Blake and related matters, but I have omitted much elementary material. I selected by hunch and intuition, and to some users my selection may seem random, but I hope not to many.

I have been especially selective in indexing
   (1) plot summaries of Blake's works except when they are pre-
       dominantly interpretative, as they sometimes are (see *The
       Book of Thel*, for instance, interpreted as a sexual allegory);
   (2) quotations from the Bible, except when cited as a source
       for something in Blake, or interpreted;
   (3) quotations from or summaries of works used routinely by
       Damon for documentation, such as Geoffrey's *Historia Bri-
       tonum*, Gilchrist's *Life of Blake*, Symons's collection of ma-
       terial about Blake, Crabb Robinson's reminiscences, etc.;
   (4) uninterpreted quotations from Blake's work.
From those exclusions the reader may infer that I have been a
good deal more selective than I have in fact. For instance, I have
considered a quotation from Blake "interpreted" by Damon even
when he glosses a single word in a line. Upon learning that, many
readers will probably wish I had been more selective. But I knew all
along that indexing the *Dictionary* would be done once and not again,
and I've tried to take advantage of the opportunity to get as many of
the possibly useful items in, on the assumption that the reader can
ignore whatever he wants to.
   The user will want to know the following facts.
   (1) Entries in the *Dictionary* are alphabetized word by word.
       This index is alphabetized letter by letter.
   (2) This index is based on the first printing. A few changes
       were made in the second printing of the *Dictionary* in 1967
       that altered pagination in several places. When the pagina-
       tion of the first printing is different from the second, I
       have given second-edition pagination in square brackets: thus
       "254d [255a]." [Ed. note: This UPNE edition of the *Dictio-
       nary* uses the text of the second printing.]
   (3) For readers interested in Damon's interpretations of indi-
       vidual lines, passages, and pictures within a work, I have
       listed the plate (or page) and line references in a sub-entry
       under the name of the work: for instance, "*Milton, plates of,
       pl. 4, illus.*, 109d, 388b."
   (4) Pages are referred to by numbers and letters, "25c-d." The
       number is a page number, of course; the letters represent
       quarters of the page, divided as shown here:

a	c
b	d

(5) Entries in the index that are also entries in the *Dictionary* are treated in a special way in the index. The page numbers of the *Dictionary* entry are placed immediately after the entry-word and divided from the rest of the page numbers by a semicolon: "Judea, 266b-c[c]; 69b, 226a-b, 241d [242b]."

(6) A word that appears in square brackets after an entry-word is one of two things: an alternative spelling of the entry-word—"Scofield [Scofeld, etc.]"—or Damon's entry-word following one of its alternative spellings--"Kaffraria [Caffraria]."

(7) All pages, page, section, and line numbers for Blake's works refer to the edition by Geoffrey Keynes that Damon used in the *Dictionary*.

(8) There are a few abbreviations and short titles:

B	Blake
"Hervey's *Meditations*"	"Hervey's *Meditations Among the Tombs*" (painting by Blake)
illus.	illustration
The Marriage	*The Marriage of Heaven and Hell*
Songs	*Songs of Innocence and of Experience*
Visions	*Visions of the Daughters of Albion*
"VLJ"	"A Vision of the Last Judgment" (can stand for one of several versions of the picture by Blake)
VLJ	*A Vision of the Last Judgment* (essay)

Aaron, illus. XI (#12)
  breastplate of. *See* Breastplates
Abarim, 3a
Abel, 3a-b; 5d, 65a, 152a, 153c-154b,
  184c, illus. I (#61), illus. XI (#6).
  See also *Ghost of Abel*
Aberdeen, 3b
Abomination of Desolation, 3c-d
Abraham [Abram], 3d-4b; 171b-c, 199a,
  259a
  state of 231a, b
  in "Hervey's *Meditations Among the
    Tombs,* " illus. XI (#11).
  in "VLJ," 366d, illus. I (#69)
Abstraction, 4b-d. *See also* Generalization;
  Law; Minute Particulars; Reason
  Albion's Sons use, 15c-d
  in allegory, 17b
  art destroyed by, 29a
  and Brama, 58b
Academies destructive of art, 268a
Accusers
  Albion's Sons as, 15a
  devils as, 103b
  in *Gates of Paradise*, 388c
  Satan as, 356a, illus. I (#52)
  Scofield as, 361a, b
  Shaddai as, 368c
  of Socrates, 25d, 376a
Achitophel, 4d; illus. I (#40)
Ackermann, Rudolph, 48b-c, d
Acts ix:4, 323b
Adah, 4d-5a; 266a
Adam, 5a-6c. *See also* Eve; Fall of Man
  in *Book of Los*, 51d
  Cave of, 6b-c, 348a
  and contraction, 6a, 241a[b]
  in *Genesis* MS., 5b, 151d, 152a
  in *Ghost of Abel*, 153c-154b
  in "Hervey's *Meditations*," illus. XI (#3)
  in Laocoön engraving, 5c, 234b
  as microcosm, 295b
  and Natural Man, 6a, 351c
  in *Paradise Lost*, 88a, 276d
  Scofield identified with, 361b
  in 27 churches, 6a-b, 85b
  in "VLJ," 192a, illus. I (#24)

"Adam, The Elohim Creating," 119b
Adamah, 6c; 5a, 6c
"Adam and Eve, Satan Watching," 303b
"Adam and Eve, The Clothing of," 371a
Adam Kadmon 9d, 215c
Adams, Samuel, 22d, 55b
Adder, 219c
Aders, Charles, 362d
Aders, Elizabeth, 451a
Adolescence in *Gates of Paradise*, 149d
Adona, 6c
Adonis (river), 6c
Adonis, Garden of, 432b
Adultery, 264a,c, 350d
Adversary, 355d
Advertisement of B's Exhibition of 1809,
  443c, d
Aeneas, 152b
Aeneid (Virgil), 112b, 234b, 349a-b
Aeschylus
  Choephoroi, 112b
Aesop
  Fables, 334b
Aesthetics of B. *See* Allegory; Art;
  Creative Process; Genius; Imagination;
  Inspiration; Memory; Minute
  Particulars; Painting; Poet; Poetry;
  Vision
Affections, 342b, 365a, 373b, 388d
Affliction, 146c
Africa, 6c-7b; 54d, 64b, 282c. *See also*
  Egypt; *Son of Los*
Agag, 7b
Against the Heresies (Irenaeus), 402d
Age of Reason, The (Paine), 63b, 101a, 397a,
  317d-318a
Ages, 454a
Agesander, 234b
Agriculture. *See* Harrow; Harvest; Plow;
  Vintage
Agrippa, Cornelius (von Nettesheim)
  7b-d; 9a
  Occult Philosophy, 7c, d, 52a, 282c, 406d,
  457b
Ahania, 7d-9a; 50d-51a; 449c. See also
  Book of Ahania
Ahithophel [Achitophel], 4d, illus. I (#40)

Aholiab, 9a; 45a
"Ah! Sun-Flower," ix, 19b, 390b-c. *See
also* Sunflower
Air, 9a-b; 419a. *See also* Elements
Albion, 9b-16c
    and Adam, 5a
    and Adam Kadmon, 9d, 215c-d
    Angel of, 22d
    Angry God invented by, 160b-c
    as Arthur, 29c
    as Atlas, 9d, 32c
    Bard of, 37a
    as Beautiful, Strong, and Ugly Man,
    209a
    bow of, 55c
    as Britain, 9b-c, 61a, 155d
    dance of. *See* "Albion's Dance"
    Daughters of, 14a-15a, 16b, 131b-c,
    152c, 201d-202a [202a-b], 236d [237a],
    433a, 447d-448a. *See also* names of
    the Daughters; *Visions of the Daughters
    of Albion*
    in Divine Family, 10a, b, 106a
    Forests of, 141b
    Friends of 73a-b
    as Grand Man, 9d, 393b
    Guardian Prince of, 152d
    in *Jerusalem*, 11c-13c, 211a-213a in
    passing
    and Job, 217a
    as Lazarus, 236b-c[d]
    in *Milton*, 11a-c, 277b, 280c
    as Patriarch of Atlantic Continent,
    31a-32a
    pillars of his throne, 237c[d]
    as Plowman, 13a-b, 330a-b
    and polypus, 333a
    at Rock of Ages, 11a, 350b, 363a
    Sons of, 15a-16c, 93a-d, 234a, 333a,
    445c-446a. *See also names of the Sons*
    Spectre of, 11b, 12b-c, 382b-c
    Spenser's use of, 385b
    Tree of Mystery of, 411b-c
    in "VLJ," illus. I (#58)
    mentioned, 162c
"Albion Rose." *See* "Albion's Dance."
"Albion's Dance." 13c-14a; 9b, 140a
Alchemy, 7d, 40b, 182c-183b, 343b. *See
also* Occultism
Alla, 17a
Allamanda, 17a-b; 57a-b, c, 141b, 333d
Allegory, 17b-18a
    in *Job* illustrations, 218c
    in Old Testament, 17c, 215a
    in *Pilgrim's Progress*, 17d, 62b
    and symbolism, 17c, 437c
Allen, Ethan, 18a
    A Narrative of Col. Ethan Allen's Captivity,
    18a
    Reason the Only Oracle of Man, 18a
All Religions Are One, 16d-17a; [236c], 343d,
    385a, 397b

Almighty, 18b-c, 368b
Alps, 18c
Altar, 26d, 109c
Al-Ulro, 9b
Amalek and Amalekites, 18d-19a; 150b
Amavia, babe of, 384b
Amazonia, 19a-b
America, 19b-21c. See also *America, a
Prophecy*; Viper; *and place names*
    and England divided, 19c-d, 31c-d,
    32a, 300d
    and the Flood, 300d
    and Ireland, 197c-d [197d-198a]
    naming of, 434d
    Paine's relations with, 317b-c
    and *Song of Los*, 7a, 21a, 153a, 377c, d
    United States of, 69d, 317c
    Welshman discovered, 243a[b]
    Whitefield in, 447a
America, a Prophecy, 20a-21c
    astronomy in, 263d
    Atlantic in, 443b
    Bernard in, 20d, 42a-b
    Blake in, 36d
    and *Book of Los*, 51d
    Boston in, 20b, 55b-c
    and *Europe*, 21a 51d, 131d
    George III in, 20 b, 20d-21a,
    152d-153a
    grapevine in, 232c
    illustrations in, 21a-c, 311b
    and Milton's political works, 275a
    Orc in, 20c-d, 21a, 310a, c, 310d-311a,
    311b
    Ossian's influence on, 312c
    Paine in, 20c, d, 317d
    plates of
        pl. 1, illus., 21b, 310a
        pl. 2:18-21, 36d, 228b
        pl. 2, illus., 21b
        pl. 3:1, 377d
        pl. 3:5, 20b
        pl. 3, illus., 21b
        pl. 4, illus., 21b-c, 145d
        pl. 5:2-5, 263d
        pl. 5, illus., 21c, 366a
        pl. 6:1-11, 20c
        pl. 6:15, 449d
        pl. 6, illus., 21c, 141a
        pl. 7:3, 108a
        pl. 7:4, 310d
        pl. 7, illus., 21c
        pl. 8:4, 385d
        pl. 8:16, 58b, 271a
        pl. 9:2, 449d
        pl. 9:27, 449d
        pl. 11, illus., 366c
        pl. 13, 52d
        pl. 13, illus., 363a
        pl. 14:14, 55b-c
        pl. 14, illus., 366a
        pl. 15:2-3, 59a

America, a Prophecy (cont'd)
 pl. 15:9, 244d [245a]
 pl. 15:16, 37a
 pl. 16, 235a
 pl. b:6-7, 98c
 pl. b, illus., 152d
 pl. c:4, 244d [245a], 246a[b]
 pl. c:10, 387c
 pl. c:15, 271a
 Sea of Time and Space in, 363a
 and Song of Los, 21a, 153a, 377c, d
 Warren in, 442d
 Washington in, 20b-c, 443a
 mentioned, 18b, 232d (twice), 377c
American Crisis, The (Paine), 316d, 317c
American Revolution. See also names of
 participants
 and America, 20b-21c
 and revolutionary formula, 349a
 and Rousseau, 351b
 serpents as symbols in, 435c
 and "A Song of Liberty," 19c
 Virginia in, 436a
Americus Vesputius [Vesputius], 434d
Ammon, 21d
Amnion, 232a
Amoret, 384b (twice)
Amos, 335c
Amsterdam, 21d-22a
Anak, 22a-b; 30b-c
Anakim, 22a, b
Analogy, Divine [Divine Analogy], 104d
Anana, 22b; 27b
Ananton, 22b; 122b
"Ancient Britons, The," 197b[c], 297b-c
 description in Advertisement of Exhibition,
 443c, d
 discussion in Descriptive Catalogue,
 208d-209a, 443d
Ancient Night, 77c, 299c
"And Did Those Feet in Ancient Time,"
 118d
Andrews, John, and Andrew Dury, A Map
 of the Country Sixty-Five Miles Round
 London, illus. VII
Androgeny, 5b, 182b-c
Anemone, 332d
Angel, 22b-24c. See also Cherubim,
 Seraphim; and names of angels
 Albion's, 22d
 Boston's, 22d, 55b
 of bottomless pit, 26a-b
 of Death, 22c-d, 242a-b[c], 257d [258a],
 illus. XI (#23, 25)
 and devils, 22d-23a, 103b
 of the Divine Presence, 23b-d, 36a, 138c,
 215c, 234b, 455a, illus. I (#12)
 in "Hervey's Meditations," illus. XI
 (#20, 23, 25, 29, 31, 32, 35)
 in Job illustrations, 219b, 221b, d (twice)
 as lark, 234c
 in The Marriage, 23a, 24c, 262b

Angel (cont'd)
 of the Presence, 23d-24c, 371a, 385d.
  See also Eyes of God
 of Providence, 23d, illus. XI (#18)
 in Swedenborg, 393b
 in "VLJ," 23a-b, illus. I (#2, 12, 14, 47)
Anger. See God, Angry; Wrath
Anglesea, 24c-d; 284d-285a
Anglican Church. See Church of England
Angry God. See God, Angry
"Angry God of This World, The," in B's
 illustrations to Dante, 97d, 125b, 161a,
 286a, 380a
Annandale, 24d
Annunciation, 264a-b
Antamon, 24d-25b
 as Cloud, 24d, 25b, 401d
 and Elythiria, 25a, 120c-d
 and Leutha, 25a, 124c (diagram), 130c-d,
  237d [238a], a[b-c]
 and sex, 124c (diagram), 132b
Antediluvians, 25b; 155b-c, 157a, 366d,
 illus. I (#62, 66, 67). See also Flood
 of Noah
Ante-Nicene Fathers, 269a, 343a, 450c
Antichrist, 25b; 108a, 194b, 363a
Antrim, 25c-d; 156c
Anubis, 116d-117a
Anytus, 25d; 376a
Apennines, 26b
Aphorisms, [236c], 364a
Aphorisms on Man (Lavater), 16d, [236c]
 [B's annotations to, 236c—2nd printing
 only]
Apocalypse. See Harvest; Last Judgment;
 Revelation; Vintage; Vision of the Last
 Judgment
Apocalypse Revealed (Swedenborg), 392d
Apocatastasis, 296d, 410c
Apollo, 25d-26a; 189d, 220d, 385a, 390a, c
 as Urizen, 247c[d], 334c, 419b
Apollo Gardens, 232b
Apollonius of Tyana, 182d
Apollyon, 26a-b; illus I (#17)
Apology (Justin Martyr), 269a
Apology for the Bible, An (Watson), 317d-318a
 B's annotations to, 101d
Apostles of Christ, 151d, 409a
Appenines, 26b
Apuleius, Lucius, 26b-c; 257a[b]
 The Golden Ass, 26b, 149d
Aquinas, Saint Thomas, 85a, 129b
Arabia, 26c
Aradobo, 199c[d]
Aram and Aramaeans, 26c; 261a
Aramitess, the, 261a
Ararat, 26d
Araunah the Jebusite, 26d; 84c-d, illus. I
 (#28)
Archangels. See by name
Archetypes, 318d-319a
Archiereus, 27a

Architecture, 27a
  of Canterbury, 68d-69a
  classical, 27a, 218c
  of Druids. *See* Druids, architecture of
  Gothic. *See* Gothicism, in architecture
  in *Job* illustrations, 217d-222d
  pagan, 384a, b
  in *Pilgrim's Progress* illustrations, 62c
  as science, 27a, 359d
  in "Spenser's *Faerie Queene*," 384a-b
  and Urizen, 27a, 419a, 420d
  mentioned, 290a
Argyll, 27b
Ariston, 27b; 22b, 31d-32a, 140d, 443b
Aristophanes, 168a
Aristotle, 27b-c; 273c, 343b
Ark
  of the Covenant, 27d-28a, 371c, 395a-b
  in *Milton*, 280b
  of Noah, 26d, 27c, 61b-c, 286b, 300d
  in "VLJ," 28a, 235c, illus. I (#5)
  at Zaretan, 457a
Arlington Court Picture. *See* "Circle of Life"
Armagh, 28a
Armenia, 26d
Arnon, 28a-c; 115a-b, 327a, 338a
Arphaxad, 28c
Arrows, 55c, 74a-b
Art, 28c-29b. *See also* Artist; Creative
    Process; Vision; *names of*
    the arts.
  allegory in, 16d-17d
  and Apollo, 25d-26a
  Bible as, 45c
  Bonaparte's treatment of, 50b
  classical vs. Hebraic, 350c-d
  and commerce, 91a-b
  and Enitharmon, 124a-d
  of Eternity, 129c, 371c, illus. I (#68).
    See also Architecture; Music; Painting;
    Poetry
  and Forgiveness of Sins, 141d
  function of, 129c
  Golgonooza city of, 162d
  as healer, 38a
  and humanization, 134a[b]
  and imagination, 28c, 195c-d
  in *Job* illustrations, 222a, b (twice),
    c (twice), d
  and life, 28c-d
  meaning in, ix-xi
  and memory, 267c-268b
  minute particulars in, 281b
  and Noah's family, 85d, illus. I (#68)
  prayer as, 28d, 222a
  and revolution, 28d, 145a-b
  and science, 28c, 359c-360a
  and society, 333d
  in "Spenser's *Faerie Queene*," 384a
  and wrath, 452d-453a
Arthegall, Sir, 384c

Arthur, King, 29b-30b
  Atlas and Boötes identified with, 29d,
    61d
  last battle of, 30b, 375d, 443c, d
  at Legions, 237c[d]
  and Merlin, 29d, 30a, b, 270b-c
  in "Spenser's *Faerie Queene*," 384d
Artist, 9a, 164c, 187b, 225a. *See also* Art;
  Creative Process; Imagination; Vision
Art of William Blake, The (Blunt), 14a,
  268a-b, 320c-d
Arts of Eternity, 129c, 371c, illus. I (#68).
  See also Architecture; Music; Painting;
  Poetry
Asaph, 30b-c
Ascension, 187d
Asher, 30c
  Gate of, 69d
Ashtaroth [Ashtoreth], 30c-d; 33a, 161d
Ashur, 30d; 31a
Asia, 30d-31a; 131d. *See also* Gods, of Asia;
  Song of Los, "Asia"
Asmodeus, 293b
Asshur [Ashur], 30d, 31a
Assimilation, 408a
"Assumption of the Virgin, The," 213a,
  264c
Assyria, 31a; 30d
Astronomy. *See* Stars
Asylum, 31b; 181c, 232c
Athanasius, Saint: *On the Incarnation*, 402d
Atheism, 295d, 317a, 389c
Athena, 282d
Athenodorus, 234b
Atlantic Continent [Atlantean Hills or
  . Mountains], 31c-32a; 17d
Atlantic Ocean, 31b; 346c
Atlantic Vale, 32b-c; 346d
Atlas, Mount, 76b
Atlas, Titan, 32c; 61d
Atom, 102a, 298c
Atonement, 85d, 88d, 160b, 179d
Atropos. *See* Fates, Three
Attainment, 291c
Aubrey, John, 387d
Auguries of Innocence, 221c-d
Aureolus, Philippus. *See* Paracelsus
Aurora (Behmen), 39c
Autumn, 366d, illus. I (#63, 69)
Avebury. *See* Stonehenge
Ayr, 32d
Aztec emblem, 271d

Baal, 33a; 30c-d, 161d
Baalim, 33a
Babel, 33b; 372a. *See also* Babylon
  Tower of, 33b, 299d (twice), 300a (twice),
    272a, 284a
Baby. *See* Infants
Babylon, 33d-34d. *See also* Babel
  dungeons of, 300a

Babylon (cont'd)
on Euphrates, 131b-c
King of, 254b[a]. See also Nebuchadnezzar
in "Spenser's Faerie Queene," 384a
in "VLJ," illus. I (#43, 76)
Whore of, 33d, 82d-83a, 107d-108a,
291a, 324b, 431d. See also Mystery;
Rahab
"Babylon, By the Waters of," 258c
"Babylon, The Whore of," 83a, 107d
"Babylon in Hell, The King of," 34c, 83b
Bacchus, 34d; 321c
Bacon, Francis, 34d-35c; 100c, 343b, 359b.
See also Verulam
B's annotations to, 370d
Baedeker, Karl: London (1892), 372b
Baer, Karl Ernst Van, 53d
Bailey, Harry, 384c
Balaam, 35c-36b
Balak, 36a
Balinas, 182d
Ballad, 170b
Ballou, Mrs. Norman V., 437c
Baltimore, Irish town, 36c
Banff, 36c
Bangor, Welsh city, 36c
Baptism, 36c-d; 246c[d], 353c-354a, illus. I
(#7), illus. XI (#43)
Barbauld, Anna Letitia, 199c[d]
Bard, 36d-37a. See also Albion, Bard of;
Oxford, Bard of; Poet; Prophet
Bard, The (Gray). See Gray, Thomas,
the Bard
Barlow, Joel: Vision of Columbus, 20d
Barnabas, 454c
Barnfield, Richard, 383d
Bashan, 37a-b; 347d-348a
Basire, James, 59d, 166d-167a, 241c[d]
plates in Bryant's New System, 61c-d
Bastille, 146a
Bath, 37b-38d
founding of, 37c, 47b
in Jerusalem, 37c-38c, 210a-b
as Legions, 38b, 69b, 237c[d]
Bath-Rabbim [Beth-Rabbim], 42c
Bathsheba, 38d; 266b
Batrachomyomachia (Anon.), 189a
Battersea, 39a
"Battle of Bunker Hill, The" (painting,
Trumbull), 442d
Beast. See Behemoth; Dragon; Gog;
Gogmagog; Leviathan; Zoa
"Beatrice Addressing Dante from the Car,"
in B's illustrations to Dante, 82a
Beautiful Man, 209a, 375d. See also Man,
Strong; Man, Ugly
Beauty
Ariston king of, 27b
in B's art, ix
Enitharmon as spiritual, 124a
roses and lillies as, 222b

Bedford, 39a
Bedford College, 448b
Bedlam, 42c-d
Beelzeboul [Beelzebub], 39a-b
Behemoth, 39b-c
in Job, 39b, 216c
in Job illustrations, 39b-c, 118a, 221a,
240a[b]
and Leviathan, 39b-c, 239c[d], 240d-241a
[240a-c]
as war, 39c, 442b
"Behemoth, The Spiritual Form of Pitt
Guiding," 240a[b]
Behmen, Jacob, 39c-41b
Book of Urizen influenced by, 41b, 53b
eighteenth-century sect of, 39b, 342d
Law edition, illustrations in, 39d-40a,
272b
in The Marriage pl. 22, 40a, d, 322b
and Swedenborg, as sources for B,
40d-41a, 393c
Way to Christ, 39c
mentioned, 262d, 263a, 343b
Belial, 41b; 376c, d
Belin, King, 41c-d
Belinus, King, 237c[d]
Belt (constellation), 311d
Ben-hadad, 179a
Benjamin, son of Jacob, 41d-42a
Bentley, G. E., Jr., ed.: Vala; or, The Four
Zoas, 142b, 144c
Beor, 42a
Berger, Pierre, 143a
Berkeley, George, 263a
Berkshire, 42a; 448d-449a
Bernard, Sir Francis, 42a-b; 55a
Bernard's House, 42b, 55c
Berwi[c]k, 42b
Beryl, 42b-c
Betelgeuse, 311d
Bethlehem, 127c
Bethlehem Hospital, 42c-d
Beth-Peor, 92a
Beth-Rabbim, 42c
Betrayal of Joseph, son of Jacob, 223d-224c
Beulah, 42d-45a
Bunyan possible source of, 42d, 62d
Churches or Heavens of, 44c-45a
Lark passes through, 234d
Moses in, 287c
Polypus and, 333b
Salah and, 354d
as Ulro's heavens, 416d-417a
Daughters of, 43d, 433a
in Four Zoas, 43d-44a
in Jerusalem, 44a-b
in Milton, 44a
Gates of, 43c-d
in Job illustrations, 220d
and the moon, 43a, 285b, d
Rivers of, 43b, 385b, 398c-d

Beulah (cont'd)
  sex and marriage in, 43a-b, 367c
  Sons of, 44b-c
  "Beulah Land, O" (Sweeney), 42d
Bezaleel, 45a; 9a
Bhagavad-Gita, B's knowledge of, 343b
Bible, 45b-46b. See also names of books
    of the Bible
  angels in, 22c
  Behmen's interpretation of, 41a
  B's interpretation of, 45b-46b, 104d,
    214d-215b, 286d-287a, 343a, c
  B's reading of, 46a-b, 343a
  as B's source, 393c
  in Book of Ahania, 51a
  bowels in, 56a-b
  classical mythology and, 188c, 267d
  British history and, 108c-d
  Druids and, 108c-d
  forgiveness in, 46a, 141d-142a
  giants in, 155b-d
  Gospels in, 45b, 62d
  of Hell, 46b-c
  in "Hervey's Meditations," 184c-d
  human sacrifice in, 283d-284a
  inspired books of, 45c, 393c
  in Job illustrations, 217b-c
  Justice and Mercy in, 119a
  King James version of, 316b
  liberty in, 206d
  metals in, 271a
  Michelangelo's interpretation of, 272b-c
  mythography of 18th century and, 61a-d,
    108c-d
  Paine's view of, 317b, 343c
  Pentateuch in, 100b, 286d-287a
  as porch of 16 pillars, 73b
  as record of man's spiritual existence,
    307a
  Satan in, 357a
  as sculptures, 362c-d
  in Song of Los, 423b
  Swedenborg's interpretation of, 45c, 393c
  as tomb in Jerusalem, 45c, 350b
  and Voltaire and B, 439a-b
Bible of Hell, 46b-c
Bilhah, 347a
Billingsgate, 46d
"Binding (et cetera) of Vala, The"
    (Erdman), 144c
Binyon, Laurence, and Geoffrey Keynes:
    Illustrations of the Book of Job by William
    Blake, 217b
Bird in "The Little Girl Lost," 258a[b]. See
    also names of birds
Birth, 149c-d, 192c, 261d
Bishop, Morchard: Blake's Hayley, 176d
Bitumen, 46d
Blackheath, 46d-47b
Blacksmiths, 247a[c], 412d, 426b
Bladud, King, 47b

Blair, Robert, 47b-49a
  The Grave
    B's illustrations to, 47c-49a, 319b
      "The Day of Judgment," 106d, 192a,
        235b
      death in, 99d
      "The Descent of Man into the Vale
        of Death," 99c
      "Reunion of the Soul and the Body,"
        184a
    described, 48a
    editions of, 48b-c, 48d-49a
Blake, Catherine
  bore a daughter, 401c
  not Elynittria, 120b
  as Enitharmon, 124b, 251b-c[d]
  Hayley and, 177d, 178b, 361a
  in Island in the Moon, 200b[c]
  in Milton, 280c
  Milton's first wife and, 274c
  prayer and, 334b
Blake, James, 215b
"Blake, Life of" (Cunningham), quoted,
  136c
Blake: Prophet Against Empire. See Erdman,
  David V., Blake: Prophet Against Empire
Blake, Robert, 199c[d], 389d, 278c
Blake, William
  artistic aims of, 130c, 196c
  attitudes of
    toward Catholic Church, 84d-85a
    toward classicism, 226d, 267d, 412d
    toward commerce, 90d-91b
    toward conquest of Canaan, 270a
    toward Deism, 101d-102a
    toward Greece, 167a-168a
    toward London, 244b[c]
    toward music, 290a-b
    toward Plato, 328c-d
    toward Socrates, 376b
    toward Sussex, 392a
  baptism of, 36c-d
  and Basire, 166d-167a
  Bible's influence on, 46a-b
  birth of, and New Jerusalem, 235a
  Byron might have met, 63c-d [1st pr.
    only]
  casts owned by, 158a, 433d
  as Chichester, 72a, d
  critics of, 219c-d, 320b-d
  daughter of, who died, 401c
  death of, 290d
  as Dr. Tobias Ruddicombe, 209b
  in Europe, 132d-133a
  exhibition of, in 1809, 102d
  exhibition planned for 1810 at Felpham,
    136d-137b, 329b
  as fly, 139d-140a
  and Hayley. See Hayley, William, B's
    relationship with
  influences on, 135c[d]

Blake, William (cont'd)
in *Island in the Moon*, 199c[d], 200b-c[d], 337a-b, 375a
in Islington, 200d [201a]
in *Jerusalem*, 11d, 207d
languages studied by, 97d, 215b-c, 419a
and Los, 147c-148c, 247a[b], 251b[c]
love affairs of, 95c, 233b-c
marriage of, 39a
memory in creations of, 268b
mercy and, 269d
Milton and, 274b-c, 383c
in *Milton*. See *Milton, A Poem*, B in
music for poems of, 290c-d
mysticism of, 291c-292a
nude sunbathing by, 303b-c
occultism rejected by, 183b
Ossian's influence on, 312d
as painter, estimates of his worth, 320b-d
as Palambron, 238c[d], 321a
prayer and, 334b
as psychologist, 331c
as Quid, 199c[d], 337a-b, 375a
as ram, 341a
reading done by, 343a-c
residences of, 59c-d, 232c-d, 241c[d], 332c
Scofield and, 360d-361a
as Selsey, 72a, d
sketching expedition of, up the Medway, 266d-267a
sources of, 268a-b, 320c-d
Spenser's influence on, 383c, 385a-b
Swedenborg's influence on, 393a-394a
Thomas Taylor and, 397a-c
trial for treason of, 15a-b, 50b, 81c, 324c, 360d-361a, 375c
visions of, 335a, 341a, 437a-b
walks of, in and around London, 137d, 172a
Wordsworth's poems owned by, 451c
Young's influence on, 455d-456a
Blake and Modern Thought (Saurat), 215d
"Blake's Apology for His Catalogue," 237b[c]
"Blake's Early Swedenborgianism" (Erdman), 392c
"Blake's Fourfold Correspondences in *Jerusalem*" (diagram), 212
Blake's Grave (ed. Damon), 49a
Blake's Hayley (Bishop), 176d
Blake's Illustrations to the Divine Comedy (Roe), 84a, 97c, d, 188d, 263d, 300a, 390c
Blake's Memorandum, 360d
Blake's Studies (Keynes), 61c-d, 229a
Blake's Vision of the Book of Job (Wicksteed), 217b-c, 222b
Blatant Beast, 384d
Blood, 157d, 367a
"Blossom, The," 380d
Blunt, Anthony, 13d-14a

Blunt, Anthony (cont'd)
The Art of William Blake, 14a, 268a-b, 320c-d
Blurt, Master-Constable (Middleton), 74d
Boadicea, Queen, 49a-b; 66a
Boaz and Jachin, 204a, illus. I (#22)
Body. *See also* Female; Loins; Male; *names of organs of the body*; Senses; Sex
as Abomination of Desolation, 3d
as America, 300d
automatic functions of, 432d
Beulah's gates in, 43c
in B's religion, 343d, 344b
in *Book of Urizen*, 53c-d
cave as, 75a
circumference as, 87c
creation of, 6c, 53c-d, 164d-165c, 407a-b
creative moment and, 29b
death of, 77d (diagram), 99b-100b
divine, 104d-105a
earth as, 113b
Entuthon as, 141b
Erin and, 128a-b, 197d [198a]
Ethinthus and, 124c (diagram)
in *Jerusalem*, 251d [252a]
false, 68b
Flood of Noah and, 139b
as furnace, 147b
geography and, 19b
Golgonooza as, 162d-164a
Horeb and, 189b
loins source of, 244a[b]
Polypus and, 333d
rainbow as, 128b, 300d-301a, 340d
sea shells as, 363a
soul and, 184a, 362a-b, 363a, 441a, illus. I (#78)
Tharmas as, 363a, 399a, 458d
Tiriel of the, 405b
tree as, 410b
universe as, 295b
Vala's veil as, 432b
Wales as, 362a-b, 441a
weaving of, 74b-c
West as, 19b, 444a
"Body, The Reunion of the Soul and the" (Blair's *Grave* illus.), 184a
Boehme, Jakob. *See* Behmen, Jacob
Bognor, 49b-c
Bognor Rocks, 49b-c
Bohan, 49c; 348a
Böhme, Jakob. *See* Behmen, Jacob
Boils, 49d-50a; 219a
Boke of the Dutchesse (Chaucer), 143b
Bolingbroke, Henry St. John, 50a; 101a
Letters on the Study of History, 50a
Bonaparte, Napoleon, 50a-b
arts and, 50b, 145a-b
Byron and, 63a
Jerusalem answers, 68a
Luvah and, 256c[d]

Bonaparte, Napoleon (cont'd)
  wars of, 98a, 256c[d]
  mentioned, 323a
Bne Seraphim, 282c
Book
  of Accusations, illus. I (#52)
  of Brass, 58b-c, 424b-c
  of Death, illus. I (#20)
  of Iron, 424c
  Law as, 217d, 218b, 219a, 222d, 254c[d]
  of Life, illus. I (#18)
Book of Ahania, The, 50c-51a. See also
  Ahania in a Bible of Hell, 46b-c
  Book of Urizen and, 50c, 51b, 53a, 423a
  Fuzon in, 50d-51a, 148c-d
  Platonic source of, 50c, 328d
  Tree of Mystery in, 50d-51a, 410d-411a
  Urizen in, 50d-51a, 423a-b
  Urizen's sons in, 425b-c
Book of Enoch: B's illustrations for, 23b,
  126b, 155b
Book of Jasher, 293a, b
Book of Los, The, 51b-d. See also Los; Song
  of Los
  in a Bible of Hell, 46b-c
  Book of Urizen and, 51b, 53a, b, 423b
  Genesis interpreted in, 51c-d, 152a
  plates of:
    pl. 4:57-8, 332d
  as prelude to America, Europe, and Song
    of Los, 51d, 377c-d
  Urizen in, 423b
Book of the Dutchess (Chaucer), 143b
Book of Thel, The, 52a-d. See also Thel
  Clod of Clay in, 52b, 89a, 452b-c
  Cloud in, 24d, 52b, 89a
  Comus and, 52a-b, 275a
  death in, 99c-d
  Har in, 174d
  Lilly in, 52b, 240c[d]
  Luvah in, 255c[d]
  Mne Seraphim in, 7d, 282c
  plates of, 52d
    pl. i (Motto), 271b, 373b, 406d
    pl. 1:1, 282c
    pl. 6, illus., 366c
  Thel in, 401a-d
  Thomas Taylor and, 397b
  Visions and, 52c-d, 401c, 437d
  Voltaire's influence on, 52c, 440a
  Worm in, 401b, 452b-c
  Young's influence on, 52c, 456b-c
  mentioned, 319a
Book of Urizen, The [First], 53d-55a.
  See also Urizen
  Africa in, 6d-7a, 54d
  in a Bible of Hell, 46c
  Book of Ahania as a sequel to, 50c, 53a,
    423a
  Book of Los retells, 51b, 53b, 423b
  Genesis interpreted in, 53b, 152a, 345b

Book of Urizen, The (cont'd)
  Los in, 54a-c, 247d [248a]
  plates of:
    pl. 3:18, 37, 38, 41b
    pl. 5, illus., 366a
    pl. 10:22, 53c
    pl. 25:23-47, 152a, 345b
    pl. 28, illus., 345b, 422a
  science in, 360b
  Urizen in, 422d-423a
  Urizen's sons in, 54c-d, 425b
Book of Urizen, The Second: Book of Ahania
  as, 50c
Boötes, 61d
Boston, 55a-c; 20b
Boston Massacre, 55a, b, 152d
Boston's Angel, 22d, 55b
Boston Tea Party, 55b (twice)
Botanic Garden, The. See Darwin, Erasmus,
  The Botanic Garden
Bow, village, 55d-56a; 388d-389a
Bow, weapon, 55c-d; 74a-b
Bowels, 56a-b
Bowen, 56b-57a; 42a
Bowen, Thomas Barton, 56b
Bower of Bliss, 384a, c
Bowlahoola, 57a-d
  Allamanda and, 17a, 57c, 333d
  communication as, 333d
  Or-Ulro and, 57d, 309b
  stomach as, 57a, 387b
Boyd, Henry, 97c-d, 188a
Boyd, William [sic], 188a
Brain, 57d-58b; 322d, 457d
Brama, 58b
Brand, Rev. John
  as Etruscan Column, 131a-b
  Observations on Popular Antiquities, 131b,
    199d [200a]
Brass, 58b; 271a, 399a
  Book of, 58b-c, 424b-c
Bray, Mrs. A. E.: Life of Thomas Stothard,
  267a
Brazil, 58d
Bread, 222a, 236b, 289d, 446b
Breadth, 103d
Breast as mountain, 260d
Breastplates, 69b, 308c, 310c, 355b
Breckno[c]kshire [Brecknokshire], 58d
Brereton [Brertun], William, 58d
Bristol, 59a-b
Britain. See also Briton; Brittania; England;
  English
  Albion as, 9b-c, 61a, 155d
  Biblical history and, 108c-109a
  Cathedral Cities of, 70 (diagram)
  giants of, 155d-156c
  Golgonooza in, 165a
  history of, 152b-c
  mythology of, 229a
  Sons of Israel and, 202a-b[b-c]

Britannia (Camden): Gogmagog in, 162b
Britomart, 384c
Briton, 59b; 443c, d
Briton, Ancient. *See* "The Ancient Britons"
Brittannia, 59b-c; 9d, 430c, illus. I (#58).
  See also Britain; England; English
Broad Street, 59c-d
Broadwick Street, 59c
Brockley Hills, 60a
Bromion, 60a-c; 309c, 401d, 437d,
  438b, b-c
Brotherhood of Man, 60c-d
  amalgamation of races necessary for, 36b,
    59b, 60d, 68c, 266b-c, 301d
  Balaam's promotion of, 36b
  Bath a symbol of, 37c
  in B's religion, 344c
  brass a symbol of, 58b
  emanation necessary for, 120d
  forgiveness and, 141d, 214b-c
  liberty and, 60d, 211a
  Lord's Supper a symbol of, 246c[d]
  nations and, 60d, 294b
  polypus and, 333a
Brothers, Richard: on druids, 108c
Brutus [Brut], Trojan, 60d-61a; 162b, c,
  152b, c, 229a
Bryant, Jacob, 61a-d; 343b
  A New System . . . of Ancient Mythology
    Babel and Shinar in, 33b, 372a
    Basire's plates for, 61c-d
    B's tailpiece for, 300d
Bucks [Buckingham, Buckinghamshire],
  61d-62a
Bulls, 62a-b; 163 (diagram)
Bunker Hill, Battle of, 55b, 442d
Bunyan, John, 62b-d
  The Holy War, 368d
  Pilgrim's Progress
    Apollyon in, 26b
    Beulah in, 42d
    B influence by, 62b-d
    B's illustrations of, 62b-d
    Law in, 374b-c
"Burial of Moses, The," 272a, 286c, 287d
Burke, Edmund
  Reflections on the Revolution in France, 316d
  Speech on Conciliation, 379c
Bury, Charlotte, 163c [1st pr. only]
Business. *See* Commerce
Busyrane, 384c
Bute, Lord: as Albion's Angel, 22d
Bute, county of Scotland, 62d-63a
Butterfly, 139d-140a
Butts, Thomas, 49c, 217a, 232c
Byron, George Gordon, Lord, 63a-b. *See
  also Ghost of Abel*
  Bonaparte and, 50a, 63a-b
  Cain, 63a-d[a-c], 153b-d
  incest in works of, 196a
"By the Waters of Babylon," 258c

Cabul, 64a
Caerlheon, 237c[d]
Caerosc, 237c[d]
Caesaer, generic term, 64a-b
Caesar, Julius, 108b, 108d-109a
  Commentaries, 109a
Caffraria, 64b
Cage, 64b; 108b, 109c
Caiaphas, 64b-d; 326d-327a, illus. I (#41)
Cain, 64d-65a
  in *Genesis* MS., 64d, 152a
  in *Ghost of Abel*, 64d, 153c-154b
  in "Hervey's *Meditations*," 3b, 65a, 184c,
    illus. XI (#5)
  Lamech and, 233c
  Maternal Line traced to, 65a, 266c
  in "VLJ," illus. I (#27)
  mentioned, 5d
Cain: A Mystery (Byron), 63a-d[a-c], 153b-d
Caina [Cainah], 65a; 266a
Cainan, 65a-b
Cainan the Second, 65b
Caiphas [Caiaphas], 64b-d, 326d-327a
Caithness [Caitnes], 65b-c
  Gate of, 65b
Caleb, 65c; 22a
Callot, Jacques, 412b
Calvary, 65c-d; 413b. *See also* Golgotha
Calvin, John, 65d
  Institutes, 402d
Calvinism, 183d, 409a
Calydore, Sir, 384d (twice)
Cam, river, 65d
Cambel, 65d-66c; 169a, 418d, 433d
Camberwell, 66d
Cambria, 66a
Cambrian History (Pughe), 29d
Cambridgeshire, 67a
Cambridge University, 66d-67a; 65d, 71d,
  119d-120a, 313d
Camden, William, 245d-246a
  Britannia, 162b
Canaan, 67b-d; 18d, 270a
Canaanites, 67d-68c
Canada, 68d
Cancer: polypus as, 333b
Candide (Voltaire), 91c, 439a, d
Candlestick in "VLJ," illus. I (#2)
Canterbury, 68d-69b; 434b
Canterbury, Archbishop of, 246a[b]
"Canterbury Pilgrims" engraving by B,
  79b-c, 407d-408a, 383d, 432a
"Canterbury Pilgrims" engraving by
  Stothard, 48a
Capaneus, 69b
"Capaneus the Blasphemer," in B's
  illustrations to Dante, 69b
Carbuncle, 69b
Cardiganshire, 69c
Carlisle, 69c
Carlow, 74d

Carmarthenshire, 69c-d
Carmel, 69d
Carnarvonshire, 69d
Carolina, 69d
Carroll, Lewis: *Sylvie and Bruno*, 143b
Cartoon, newspaper political, 435c
Cary, Henry, 97d
Cary, Joyce: *The Horse's Mouth*, 268d, 320b
Cary's New and Accurate Plan of London and Westminster . . . Corrected to June 1, 1820, illus. VI
casting, 147a
Castle of Otranto (Walpole), 331a
Caterpillar [Catterpiller], 74d-75a; 240d [241a], 450c
Cathedral Cities, 71a-74b
   Albion's sons and, 16a-b
   Eno as emanation of, 125d
   in *Jerusalem*, 12d, 73a-74b
   Los and, 67a-b, 72c, 73a, b-d, 74a
   in *Milton*, 72d-73a, 280b-c
"Cathedral Cities, The" (diagram), 70
Cathedron, 74b-d
Catherlo[g]h, 74d
Cathnes [Caithness], 65b
Catholic Church. *See* Church of Rome
Catterpiller, 74d-75a; 240d [241a], 450c
Cavan, 75a
Cave, 75b-c
   of Adam, 6b-c, 348a
   of Machpelah, 259a
   Polar, 306a-b
   scull as, 362b-c
"Caverns of the Grave I've Seen, The," 235c
Celibacy. *See* Chastity
Center, 75c-76a. *See also* Circumference; Nadir; Zenith
   Luvah's place at the, 75c, 255a[b]
   of Man, moon at, 75c, 285c
Chain of Jealousy, 76a-c; 205b
Chaldea, 76c-d
Change as death, 401b
Chaos, 76d-78a; 267c, 299c
"Characters of Spenser's *Faerie Queene*, The," 383d-385a
Charity, 82a, 218d, 323d, 324b
Charlemaine [Charlemagne], 78a-b; 254c-d [254d-255b], 324a
"Charlemaine, I Saw a Monk of," 78a, 285b
Charles I, King, 78b
Charleston, Mass., 55b
Charlotte, Queen: as Tirzah, 411d
Charterhouse School, 72c
Chastity. *See also* Enitharmon, repression of sex under
   Christian cult of, 259c-d, 368a
   druids invented, 109d
   Ethinthus, Manathu-Varcyon, and, 261c
   in *Europe*, 275b, 378d
   Female Will and, 212a-b, 252d [253a]
   Immaculate Conception and, 264a-c
   in *Jerusalem*, 212a-b

Chastity (*cont'd*)
   Mahomet's attitude toward, 259c-d
   Tirzah as, 253b[c]
   virginity vs., 436a
Chateaubriand, Vicomte François René, 195d
Chatterton, Thomas, 78b-d
   Bristol and, 59a, 71d, 72d
   "Godred Crovan," 78c, 170b
   Miscellanies, 78c
   mentioned, 331a
Chaucer, Geoffrey, 78d-79d
   Boke of the Dutchesse, 143b
   Canterbury Tales, B's engraving of, 79b-c, 383d, 407d-408a, 432a
   Monkes Tale, Ugolino's story in, 79c-d, 97b
   "Chaucer's Canterbury Pilgrims" engraving, 79b-c, 407d-408a, 383d, 432a
Chebar, 79d
Chelsea, 79d
Chemosh, 80a; 283d-284c
Cherubim, 80a-d; 163 (diagram), 268b, 365a, illus. I (#5)
Cheselden, 80d-81a
Cheshire, 81a
Chester, 81a
Chester's River, 81a
Cheviot, 81a-b
Chichester, 81b-c; 363d
Child, Jesus as, 363a
Childhood, 149d, 210d
Children, 81c-82a. *See also* Infants
   in Behmen, 41b
   Cherubim as, 365a
   in "Hervey's *Meditations*," illus. XI (#37)
   of Los, 253a-c [253b-254a]
   sexuality of, 366c
"Chimney Sweeper, The," 22c-d, 99c
Chimneysweeps, 244b[c]
China, 82a-b
Chisledon, 80d-81a
Chivalry and war, 332c
Christ, 82b; 140a, 409a, illus. XI (#1). *See also* Antichrist; Jesus; Trinity
Christian Doctrine, The (Milton), 275a-b, 296d
Christianity
   art as, 28c-d
   chastity in, 259c-d, 368a
   of B, Paine, and Watson, 317d-318b
   without Christ, 417a
   errors of, 132a-c, 210d-211a
   in *Europe*, 132a-c
   Forgiveness in, 344c
   Gibbon's idea of, 156d
   Har as spirit of, 405c
   Hermes Trismegistus and, 182c
   in *Jerusalem*, 210d-211a
   Joseph of Arimathea symbol of true, 225a
   of Paul, 323b-324b
   in *Tiriel*, 174b, 405c
   Twenty-Seven Churches as dogmatic, 85a
   in "VLJ," 82a, illus. I (#59, 73)

Christianity (cont'd)
  woman idealized in, 447d-448a
Chronicles of England, Scotland, and Ireland
  (Holinshed), 237c[d]
Church, 82b-86b. See also Beulah, Churches
  or Heavens of; Churches, Seven;
  Churches, Twenty-Seven; Church of
  England; Church of Rome;
  Religion; Satan, Synagogue of
  Caiaphas as, 64c
  Canterbury as Established, 68d
  False
    Covering Cherub as, 94a-b
    cross and, 95b-c
    Female Babe as, 268c
    Militant, 254d [255a]
    Rahab as, 82d, 338d
  Fathers of the, 450c
  in "London," 244b[c]
  mankind as, 82b, 206c
  in The Marriage, 25a, 85a
  Paul as, 324a-b
  of Satan, 82c, 356b
  State and, 64c, 82c, 326d-327a, 386b-c
  in "VLJ," 82a, 450b, illus. I (#46, 57,
    64, 73)
  Woman in the Wilderness as, 82a, c,
    450a-b, illus. I (#64)
Churches, Seven, 85a; 238a[b-c]
Churches, Twenty-Seven, 85a-86b. See also
  names of churches
  Abraham in, 4a-b, 85b-86a in passing
  Adam in, 6a-b, 85b (twice), b-c
  in Beulah, 44c-d
  Divine Humanity opposes, 106c-d
  final septenary of, 324a-b
  Reuben in, 4a-b
  Satan in, 6a-b, 85b
  Whore of Babylon and Dragon as,
    107d-108a
Churches or Heavens of Beulah. See
  Beulah, Churches or Heavens of
Church of England, 71a, 254c[d] 342c,
  434b, 446c
Church of Rome, 82d-85a; 204b-c, 235c-d,
  264d-265a
Church of the First Three Centuries, The
  (Lamson), 450d
Church of This World. See Church, False
Cicero, 86b-c
Circle, 109d-110a, 222c
Circle of Destiny, 86c-d; 417a
"Circle of Life, The," 86d-87c; 304b, 363a,
  400d-401a, 420a, illus. IV
"Circle of the Lustful," in B's illustrations
  to Dante, 97d
Circumference, 87c-d; 75c. See also Center;
  Nadir; Outline; Zenith
Cities, Cathedral. See Cathedral Cities
Clakmanan [Clackmannan], 87d
Clare, 87d
Clarence, Duke of, 229a

Classes, 87d-88d. See also Elect; Redeemed;
  Reprobate; Transgressors
Classicism. See also Greece; Neoclassicism;
  Virgil
  in architecture, 27a, 218c
  B's rejection of, 226d, 267d, 412d
  English, and Ovid, 313b-c
  in Job illustrations, 218c
  Jupiter and the rejection of, 226d
  in sculpture, 433d-434a
  of Thomas Taylor, 396c-397a, 397b-c
  war and, 442b
Clay, 88d-89a; 52b, 163 (diagram), 389b,
  401b
Clod, 52b, 401b
"Clod & the Pebble, The," 89a
"Clothing of Adam and Eve, The," 371a
Clotho. See Fates, Three
Cloud, 89a-b
  male principle or semen as, 24d, 25a,
    52b, 89a, 401b, c-d
  Pillar of, 204a
"Cloud, The" (Shelley), 25b
Clytemnestra, 448a
Coat of Joseph as flesh, 224b-c
Coban, 89b-c; 172d-173c
Cock [Kox], Private, 171c, 229d-230a, 361d
Colchester, 89d
Coleridge, Samuel Taylor, 185d
Comedy, 203c[a], 331d, 373b
Comforter in Job illustrations, 221d
Commandments, 89d-90d; 219d, 377c,
  345a, 374a-b. See also Decalogue; Law
Commentaries (Julius Caesar), 109a
Commerce, 90d-91b
  Canaanites in, 68a
  in King Edward the Third, 90d, 229a
  Mammon and, 260c
  nervous system and, 17a-b, 90d, 141b
Common sense: and deism, 100c
Common Sense (Paine), 316d
Communication, 17a
Communion. See Lord's Supper
Communion of Saints, 71a, c, 105a
Compass, 91b-c; 439a
Compassion, 56a
Compass points, 70 (diagram), 71c (table),
  77c-d (diagram), 103d, 124c (diagram),
  140b-c, 163 (diagram), 212 (table), 288
  (diagram). See also East; North; South;
  West
Compositions for the Divine Comedy (Flaxman),
  97b
Comus (Milton), 52a-b, 275a, 353b, 401b-c
Concerts, satire on, 362a
Confessions (Rousseau), 351c
Congo, 91c
Conjectures on Original Composition (Young),
  455c
Conjugial Love (Swedenborg), 388d, 392d,
  393c, 408c
Connaut [Connacht, Connaught], 91c; 261b

Conscious mind. *See* Mind, conscious
Constantine, 91c-d; 254c-d [254d-255b],
  324a
Constellations. *See* Belt; Betelgeuse;
  Ophiuchus; Orion, Pleiades
Continents. *See* Africa; America; Asia;
  Egypt
Contraction. *See* Limits
Contraries. *See also* Experience; Innocence;
  Negation
  Behmen's idea of, 40b-41b
  in Beulah, 42d
  B's idea of, 343c-d
  in *Book of Urizen*, 53c
  Heaven and Hell as, 394a
  Justice and Mercy as, 227c, 269c-d
  in *The Marriage*, 262b, c, 263a
  in *Mental Traveller*, 268c, d
  in *Songs*, 378b-c
  in Urizen and Orc's relationship, 311b
Contrat social (Rousseau), 351b
Conway's Vale, 91d-92a
Conwenna, 92a-b; 56c, d, 57a, 66b
Copernicus, Nicolaus, 262b, 418d
Copying and imitation, 267d, 319d-320a,
  320c-d, 436d, 449d
Cordella [Cordeilla, Cordelia], 92b-c
I Corinthians xv:44, 301a, 323c, 378c
II Corinthians iv:4, 150a, 355d
Cork, 92c
Cornwall, 92c-d
Corregio, Antonio Allegri da, 412b
Correspondences, 212 (diagram), 296b,
  393b-c
"Correspondences in *Jerusalem*, Blake's
  Fourfold" (diagram), 212
Cosmology, 77b-c, 142c, 328d, 394a. *See also*
  Stars; Universe
Cosway, Richard, 199c[d], 456d
Cotton, Charles: *Wonders of the Peake*, 102b-c
Council of God, 92d; 10a, b, 105a-106b
Counter-revolution and America, 20a
"Count Hugolino" (Reynolds), 97b
Counties of the British Isles, 92d-93d. *See
  also names of counties*
"Count Ugolino" (Fuseli), 97b-c
Courthope, 229d
Covenant, Ark of the. *See* Arks, of the
  Covenant
Covering Cherub, 93d-94c
  Baalim in, 33b
  diamond on, 103c
  druid religion as, 109a
  Eden reflected in, 115b
  from *Ezekiel*, 93d, 135a[b-c]
  Iereus part of, 194b
  in *Jerusalem*, 27a, 94a-b, 213a
  Lazarus miracle and, 94a, 236c[d]
  in *Milton*, 94a, 279c
  Presbuterion and, 334c
  Satan as, 11b, 93d

Covering Cherub (*cont'd*)
  Selfhood as, 93d, 94a, b, 363c
  stomach of, 22b, 33b
  as Tyre, King of, 414d
Cowper, William, 177a, 377a, 446d
"Cradle Song, A," 22c 450d
Craig's Wife (Kelly), 448a
Creation, 94c-d. *See also* Creative Process;
  Genesis
  by Antamon, 25a
  in Bible, 45b
  in B's religion, 345b
  in *Book of Los*, 51b, c-d
  by compass, 91b-c
  destruction of matter and, 433a-b
  as division, 76d-77a, 94d, 418c
  duration of, 454b-c
  by Elohim, 119a-b
  ex nihilo, B's view of, 84b
  in *Four Zoas*, 236b
  by Jesus, 94c, 159b, 450c
  in *Job* illustrations, 220d
  by Los, 51b, 94c, 247a-c[c-d]
  as merciful act, 94c, 240a[b-c], 269b-c
  Paracelsus' idea of, 322c
  by Urizen, 94c, 419b, d
  by vortices, 440c-d
Creative process. *See also* Art; Imagination;
  Inspiration; Painting
  Antamon and, 25a
  B's artistic method and, ix-xi
  children symbols of, 81d
  creative moment and, 29b, 138a, 454d
  dragon and, 107c-d
  in *Four Zoas*, 164c-165a
  furnaces symbols of, 147a-b
  gnomes and, 158a-b
  memory and, 268b
  in *Milton*, 25a, 165a-c, 277a-b
  revolutionary forces and, 321a
  threefold vision and, 437a
Cressy [Crécy], 228d
Criticism, literary, 110b-c, 282d
Cromarty [Kromarty], 230b
Cromek, Robert Hartley, 47c-48a
  his widow, 48b-c
Cromwell, Oliver, 94d-95a
Cromwell's Gardens, 95a
Cross, 95a-c. *See also* Crucifixion
  dome and, 62c, 95b, 106d
  in *Job* illustrations, 218d, 219b, c, 220a, d,
    222a, b (twice)
  Tree of Mystery as, 410d
  in "VLJ," 95a, 235c (twice), illus. I (#29)
Crown, 235d
Crucifixion. *See also* Cross
  Calaphas' part in, 64c
  on Calvary, 65c
  on Golgotha, 165d
  justified, 213d-214a
  Nature and, 369d
  Paul's view of, 323d

Crucifixion (cont'd)
  scribes and, 166b
  as symbol, 214a
"Crucifixion of St. Peter" (Michelangelo),
  224d
Cruelty, 133a, 198b-c[c-d], 269c-d
Crystal Cabinet, The, 95c; 197a, 233b, 285b,
  391c
Cube, 222a
Cuckoo, 219c
Cumberland, George, 209c
Cumberland, county, 95c-d
Cunningham, Allen: "Life of Blake"
  quoted, 136c
Cupid and Psyche, 26b-c, 257a[b], 430a
Cup of Vala, 431d-432a
Cush, 95d
Cyclopaedia (Rees), 234b
Cynicism. See Quid the Cynic

Dacre, Tom, 99c
Dagon, 96a
Dalila, 88a, 307b, 448a
Damascus, 95b
Damnation, 357b, c
Damon, S. Foster: ed., Blake's Grave, 49a
Dan, 96b-d
Dance, 290b-c
Dance of the Giants: Stonehenge as, 388a
Daniel, 3c, 214a
Daniel, 213d, 271a, 297b, c
Dante Alighieri, 96d-98a
  B's attitude toward, 96d-97a, 187c, 262d
  Chaucer and, 79c-d, 97b
  Divine Comedy, B's illustrations of,
    96d-98a
    Inferno
      #3 "Mission of Virgil" ("Angry God
        of This World"), 97d, 125b, 161a,
        286a, 380a
      #7 "Homer, Bearing the Sword, and
        His Companions," 188d, 167c
      #8 "Homer and the Ancient Poets,"
        167c
      #10 "Circle of the Lustful," 97d
      #27 "Capaneus the Blasphemer,"
        69b
      #28 "Symbolic Figure of the Course
        of History Described by Virgil,"
        97d
      #47 "Ugolino Relating His Death,"
        97d
      #60 "Primeval Giants Sunk in the
        Soil," 155c
      #61 "Nimrod," 300a
    Purgatorio
      #88 "Beatrice Addressing Dante
        from the Car," 82a
      #89 "The Harlot and the Giant," 83a
    Paradiso

Dante Alighieri (cont'd)
  Divine Comedy, illus. (cont'd)
    Paradiso (cont'd)
      #97 "Deity, from Whom Proceed the
        Nine Spheres," 263c-d
      #99 "Queen of Heaven in Glory,"
        84a, 98a, 246c[d], 390c
  Swedenborg and, 393a
  translations used by B, 97c-d, 188a
Danube, 98a; 349b-c
Dargle, 98a
Dark Night of the Soul, 291c
Darwin, Erasmus, 98a-c
  Botanic Garden, 98b
    B's engravings for, 98c
    Fuseli's designs for, 98c
  The Loves of the Plants, 411c
  Zoonomia, 452b
David, 98c-d; 26d, 213d, illus. XI (#14)
Davies, Edward, 180c, 343b
Dawn, 234c, 286b
Daydreaming, 4d, 432a
"Day of Judgment," in B's illustrations to
  Blair's Grave, 106d, 192a, 235b
Dead, 98d-99a
Dead Sea, 99a-b; 354c
Death, 99b-100b. See also Spectre, of the
  Dead
  Angel of. See Angel, of Death;
  Death, lion the angel of
    in Beulah, 43b, 44c
  in Blair's Grave and B's illustrations for it,
    48a-b, 99c, d
  of body, 77d (diagram), 99b-100b
  Book of, illus, I (#20)
  in Book of Thel, 99c-d, 401b
  cross as, 95b
  Enitharmon's false doctrine of, 451d
  eternal, 13d
  fear of, 99d, 341c
  gate of, 192c
  in Gates of Paradise, 99d, 149d
  in Golgonooza, 163 (diagram)
  in "Hervey's Meditations," 183d-184a
  in Innocence and Experience, 99c-d,
    [197b-c]
  in Job, 219d
  lion the angel of, 22c, 99c, 242a-b[c],
    257d [258a]
  nature of, 452a-b
  Nimrod and, 300b
  number of, 220c
  Satan as state of, 355b, d
  second, 231d
  as sleep, 315d
  Tree of. See Tree, of Mystery
  in Ulro, 416d
  in "VLJ," illus. I (#20, 33)
  wish for, 390c
  worm of, 221a, 451d
Deborah, song of, 229c

Decalogue, 100b-c; 90d, 138c, 287a. *See also* Commandments; Law

Declaration of Independence, 20d

Decline and Fall of the Roman Empire (Gibbon), 156d

Dee, River, 81a

Defence of Poetry (Shelley), 248a[b]

De irae dei (Lactantius), 182c

Deism, 100c-102a
  Babylon as city of, 34a
  of Bolingbroke, 50a, 101a
  Christianity and, 345b
  Druid religion as, 109a-b, 387d, 388a
  in *Jerusalem*, 101a-b, 101d-102a, 210d
  Locke and, 243b[c]
  on miracles, 213c
  Nature and, 100c-101c in passing, 344a
  No Natural Religion attacks, 101a, 402c
  of Paine, 101a, d, 317a-b
  Paley's refutation of, 69c, 101d
  Pharisees a manifestation of, 326b-c
  Rahab as, 101a, 339b (twice), c, 340a
  of Rousseau and Voltaire, 101d, 351c
  wheels of, 445c
  mentioned, 18a

"Deity, from Whom Proceed the Nine Spheres," in B's illustrations to Dante, 263c-d

Delight, Valley of, 237d [238b]

Delilah, 88a, 307b, 448a

Delusion as Shadow, 369b

Demetrius (Plutarch), 231b

Demiurge as Urizen, 343a

Democritus, 102a; 298c

Denbighshire, 102a

Denmark, 102a

Depth, 103d

Derby [Derbyshire], 102a-b; 170a-b

Derby Peak, 102b-c

Descartes, René: vortices of, 440c-d

"Descent of Man into the Vale of Death, The," in B's illustrations to Blair's *Grave,* 99c

Descriptive Catalogue, A, 102c-103a
  on "Ancient Britons," 208d-209a, 443d
  on Chaucer, 78d-79c
  on *Jerusalem*, 208d-209a
  on "VLJ," 235c-d
  memory of cherubim in, 268b
  VLJ and, 103a, 437b

Desire, 124c (diagram), 219b, 270d, 257c, 401d

Destiny, Circle of [Circle of Destiny], 86c-d; 417a. *See also* Fate; Fates, Three

Destroyers, 26a, 29a-b

Details. *See* Minute Particulars

Deus, 103a

Devils, 103b. *See also* Beelzeboul; Satan
  angels and, 22d-23a
  in *The Marriage*, 23a, 262b, 270d

Devon, 103b

Dew, 25a

Dhinas-bran, 103c

Diabolos, Satan as, 356a

Diamond, 103c-d

Diana, 220d, 321c

[*Dichtung and Wahrheit* (Goethe), 236b—2nd pr. only]

Dick, A. L., 48d

Dickens, Charles
  Nicholas Nickleby, 59d
  Oliver Twist, 187d

Digby, George W.: *Symbol and Image in William Blake,* 87b

Dimensions, 103d

Dinah, 104a; 128b, 371a

Dinas Bran [Dhinas-bran], 103c

Dinas Penmaen, 103c

Diogenes Laertius, 374d

Diralda, 104a; 378d, 402d, 403a

Directions. *See* Compass points; East; North; South; West

Dis, 349a, b

Discours sur les arts et sciences (Rousseau), 351b

Disease, 104a-d; 260a, 373d

Dispensation, Old vs. New, 227c

Dissenters, 342c

Dissertation on the Eleusinian Mysteries (Taylor), 397b

Divine Analogy, 104d

Divine Body, 104d-105a

Divine Comedy (Dante), B's illustrations of. *See* Dante Alighieri, *Divine Comedy,* B's illustrations of

Divine Council [Council of God], 10a, b, 92d, 105a-106b

Divine Family, 105a-106b; 10a, b, 92d

Divine Hand, 106b-c. *See also* Providence

Divine Humanity, 106c-d, 191a-b

"Divine Image, A" (*Songs of Experience*), 269c, 422d

"Divine Image, The" (*Songs of Innocence*), 269c, 344a, 377a, 393b

Divine Love (Swedenborg), 267b, 392d
  B's annotations to, 194b, 393d

Divine Providence (Swedenborg), 392d
  B's annotations to, 393d

Divine Pymander (Hermes Trismegistus), 182c

Divine Vision, 9d, 10c

Divine Will. *See* Providence

Division
  Creation as, 76d-77a, 94d, 418c
  of Man, 285c
  Meribah as, 270a
  into nations, 347b
  pity and, 327b-c

Dogs of Leutha, 239a[b-c]. *See also* Isle of Leutha's Dogs

Dog Star, 117a
Dome, 106d-107a; 62c
Dominance, sexual, 367c-d. *See also* Female
    Will
Dominion, Charlemaine as, 78a
Donnegal, 107a
Dorchester Heights, 55b
Dorset, 107a
Dostoyevsky, Fyodor, 410b
Doubt, 181d
Dove, 107a; 235c
Dovedale, 107a-b
Dover, 107b
Down, 107c
Dragon, 107c-108a. *See also* Behemoth;
    Leviathan
    in *America*, 21b-c, 108a
    Antichrist as, 25b, 108a
    in Dante illustrations, 83a
    in *Job* illustrations, 220d
    Last Judgment and, 107d, 162b, illus. I
        (#51)
    in *Night Thoughts* illustrations, 82d-83a,
        107d
    Orc as, 108a, 450a
    Satan as, 357a
    in "VLJ," illus. I (#51)
    war as, 107c, 442b
Dranthon, 108a-b
"Drawing of the Last Judgment, A" (Roe),
    235d
Dreams
    as "abstraction," 4d
    erotic, 124c (diagram), 402d-403a, 378d
    as technique in *Four Zoas*, 143a-b
    in Vala's garden, 432a
    visions and, 436c
"Dream, A," 22c
Drogheda, 108b
Druidism. *See also* Druids
    in architecture. *See* Druids, architecture
        of
    B's ideas of, 108c-109a, 343b (twice)
    Canaanites practice, 68b-c
    church of, 82c
    deism and, 109a-b, 387d, 388a
    human sacrifice in, 3d-4a, 108b, 109c,
        343b, 447a
    Malden and, 260b
    revenge in, 387b-c
    on Salisbury Plain, 354c
    Twenty-Seven Churches and, 85c-86a
    Verulam as, 434b-c, d
    wheel symbolism and, 445c
    in Wilts, 448b
Druids, 108b-110a. *See also* Druidism
    Anglesea ruins of the, 285a
    architecture of, 27a, 68d-69a, 109d, 218d,
        219b
    Babel and, 33c

Druids (*cont'd*)
    Bryant's ignorance of, 61d
    at Dura, 111b
    in Gaza, 150b-c
    at London Stone, 245d [246a]
    oak groves and, 108b-c, 141b, 168c,
        305b-c
    Philistia and, 326c
    at Stonehenge, 109b-c, 387d
    stones of, 109d-110a, 245d [246a], 389a
Drum, 302a
Drunkenness and war, 442a-b
Dryden, John, 110a-111a
    Fables preface and B's criticism of
        Chaucer, 78d-79a, 110b
    Lee and, 110d, 237b[c]
    Parallel of Poetry and Painting, 237b[c],
        389d
    Pope and, 333d-334a
    Religio Laici, 386a
"Dryden in Rhyme Cries: 'Milton Only
    Plann'd,' " 237b[c]
Dublin, county of Ireland, 111a
Dumbarton, 111a
Dumfries, 110a-b
Dungeons of Babylon, 300a
Dura, 111b-c
Dürer, Albrecht: "Madonna and Child,"
    412c
Durham, 111c
Durness, 111d
Duror as Dura, 111c
Dury, Andrew, and John Andrews: *A Map of
    the Country Sixty-Five Miles round London*,
    illus. VII
Duty, 181b, c

Eagle, 112a-d
    in *Genesis* Ms., 151d
    in *Job* illustrations, 112c, 221b
    of Manathu-Varycon, 112c, 261c
    serpent and, 112a-b, 271d (twice)
    Zoa as, 458d
Ear, 113a-b
Earth, 113b-c; 158a, 168c. *See also* Elements
"Earth's Answer," 113b, 205a, 329a, 422d
East, 113c; 75c, 271a. *See also* Compass
    points
Eastmeath, 113d
Ebal, Mount, 113d
Eber [Heber], 179b
Ecce Homo, 67d
"Ecchoing Green, The," 305a
Ecclesiastes, 219b
eclecticism in B's philosophy, 343a-d
Economics, 17d
Ectomorph, 57b
Eddas, name of Vala in, 428a
Eden, 114a-115c

Eden (cont'd)
  life in, 114d, 121a-b
  Paradise and, 322d
  rivers of, 114b-c, 114d-115c, 185c, 364d,
    458d. See also names of the rivers
  Sons of, as Divine Family, 105b
  Tree of Life in, 114a, 410c
  wheels of, 114b, 445a-b
Edinburgh, 115c-d; 349d
Editing of text of B's work, 144b-c
Edom, 115d-116b; 128d
Education, 351b-c, illus. I (#8)
Edward I, King, 19d
Edward III, King, B's drawing and
  engraving of, 229a. See also King Edward
  the Third
Edwards, Richard, 456d
Egg, Mundane [Mundane Egg], 5c,
  287d-288b
"Egg, The Mundane" (diagram), 288a-b
Ego and superego. See Mind, conscious
Egremont, Countess of: B's "VLJ" for,
  235b-c
Egypt, 116b-117a
  Africa's name as, 6d, 116c
  Assyria and, 31a, 116d
  Holy Family of, 116c, 311d
  Joseph, son of Jacob, in, 116b, 224a, c
  Lybia and, 116d, 257d [258a]
  slavery as, 116b, 406a
  subconscious as, 221a
  in "VLJ," illus. I (#76)
"Egypt, The Fertilization of," 98c,
  116d-117a
Eight, Starry, 307d, 308a
1809 Exhibition, B's 102d
  Advertisement of, 443c, d
Eighth, 117a
Elders of Revelation, illus. I (#23)
Eldon, Lord Chancellor: and Byron's
  Cain, 63b
Elect, 45a, 87d-88d, 342a, 402c
Elegy on an Unfortunate Lady (Pope), 334a
Elements, 117b-d. See also Air; Earth; Fire;
  Water
  in Gates of Paradise, 149d
  in Il Penseroso illustrations, 117d, 328a
  Rahab and Satan as, 339b
  time built by, 454a
  Urizen's sons as, 54c, 117b-c, 425b
  whale among, 444d
Elephant, 117d-118a
Eleth, 118a
Elgin, 118a-b
Eliakim, 118b; illus. I (#31)
Elias, 118b; 454c, illus. XI (#17). See also
  Elijah
Elihu, 216c-d, 219d-220a
Elijah, 118c-d; 153d, 366d, 408d-409a,
  409a, illus. I (#60). See also Elias
Eliphaz, 219c, d, 222d, 316c

Elisha, 179a
Elizabeth, mother of John the Baptist, illus.
  I (#13)
Ellayol, 118d
Ellis, Edwin J., and W. B. Yeats: eds. Works
  of William Blake, 144b, 375a
Elohim, 119a-d
  Adam's creator as, 5b, 119b
  Angry God as, 160c
  as an eye of God, 119b, c, 134c[d], 134d
    [135a] (twice), 222d, 223a
  in Ghost of Abel vs. Byron's Cain,
    154a, b-c
  Jehovah Elohim, 23c, 119d, 206b-c, 215c,
    227c, 269d
  in Job illustrations, 135a, 222d, 223a
"Elohim Creating Adam, The," 119b
Eloisa to Abelard (Pope), 334a
Eloquence, god of, 269a
Ely, 119d-120a; 67b
Elynittria, 120a-c; 305d, 321c
Elythiria, 120c-d; 24d-25a
Emanation, 120d-122b. See also Milton,
  Sixfold Emanation in; and names of
  emanations
  eon contraction of, 127a
  incest and, 196a-b
  reason and, 121d, 341d
  reunion of, 120d, 190b-191a, 368b
  role of, 120d-121a, 121a-122b in passing,
    190b-c
  and spectre in Jerusalem, 381d-382a
  spectre's craving for, 381c-d, 318d-382a
  tabernacle the dwelling-place of,
    395d-396a
  will of, 447c-d
Embryology and Book of Urizen, 53d, 232a
Emerald Table, 182d-183b
Emile (Rousseau), 351b
Emim, 122b
Emotions, 77d (diagram), 289d, 295d, 302c,
  428c, 458d
Empathy, 134a[b], 296b, 436b
Empire
  art and, 29a
  Babylon as, 33d
  Bonaparte and, 50b, 63a
  Bryon and, 63a
  Dante and, 96d-97a
  in a Dante illustration, 300a
  Virgil and, 167c
Enanto, 122b; 22b
Endomorphs, 57b
Energy, 40d, 113b, 262b (twice)
England, 122b. See also Britain; Church of
  England; English; and place names
  Albion as, 9b
  America and, 19c, 31c-d, 32a
  Brittannia as, 59b, 122b
  counties of, 92a, 93b-d (table)
  in Jerusalem, 330a

England (cont'd)
Joseph of Arimathea in, 224d-225a
oak and, 305a
Rock of Ages as shore of, 350c
English, 122b-c. See also Britain; Brittannia;
England
Engraving, 47c. See also Illuminated
Printing
Engravings of William Blake, The (Russell), 61c
Enion, 122c-124a
in Jerusalem pl. 87, illus., 400d
name of, 122c, 124a, 401a
Tharmas, and, 122c-123d, 399c-400d in
passing
mentioned, 433a, 449c
Enitharmon, 124a-125b
as Catherine Blake, 124b, 251b-c[d]
children of. See Los, children of
doctrine of mortality held by, 451d
as emanation, and her relation to spectre,
381d-382a, 383a-b
in Europe, 132a-c
in Four Zoas, 381d, 383a-b
from Globe of Blood, 157d
Golgonooza and, 164c-165c
in Jerusalem, 211b, 212c, 251b-c[d],
381d-382a, 400d
Los and, 8a-b, 124b-125a, 247d [248a],
248a-250d [248c-251a] in passing,
251b-d [251d-252a] in passing, 252c-d
[253a]
in The Marriage, 263c
in Milton, 277b, 278b
Oedipus theory and, 76a-b
Orc and, 124d, 253a[b], 309c, 309d-310a
rainbow of, 340c
repression of sex under, 124c (diagram),
130c-d, 132a-b, 261c, 403a, 378d, 442c
as source of names of Enion and
Tharmas, 122c, 401a
space and, 125b, 380a-b, 404b
Urthona and, 426c
wheels of, 445b-c
mentioned, 449c
"Enitharmon, The Repression of Sex
under" (diagram), 124c; diagram
discussed, 130c-d
Enlightenment, See Reason, Age of
Eno, 125b-d; 340d
Enoch, 125d-126b; 155b, illus. XI (#7)
Enoch, B's illustrations for, 23b, 126b, 155b
"Enoch" (lithograph). See "Job in His
Prosperity"
Enos, 126b
Entuthon, Forests of, 141b
Entuthon Benython, 126c-127a; 17a, 57b
Eon, 127a
Ephesians vi:12, 323d
Ephraim [Ephram], 127a-c; 224a,
260d-261a
Ephratah, 127c

Epic, Four Zoas as, 142c-143a
Epicurus, 127c-128a; 389c. See also Suction
the Epicurean
Epistemology, 239c-d [239d-240a],
243a-b[b]
Epistle on Painting, Addressed to George
Romney, The (Hayley), 176d
"Epitome of James Hervey's Meditations
Among the Tombs." See "Hervey's
Meditations Among the Tombs"
Erato, 258c
Erda, 428a
Erdman, David V.
"The Binding (et cetera) of Vala," 144c
"Blake's Early Swedenborgianism," 392c
"Lambeth and Bethlehem in Blake's
Jerusalem," 232c
Blake: Prophet Against Empire
on Albion's and Boston's Angels, 22d,
55b
on America, 20c, 20d-21a, 22d, 55b
on Apollo Gardens in Lambeth, 26a
on Bath, 38c, 72b
on Behmen's English illustrator, 39d
on Bowen, 56b
on Charles I, 78b
on Enion, 122c, 401a
on Green Man, 168a
on Guardian of secret codes in Europe,
166d
on Island in the Moon, 197b, 199b[c],
c[d], 374d, 389d, 439d
on King Edward the Third, 228d, 229b
on Night Thoughts illustrations, 456d
on Oothoon, 313a
on Paine, 317a
on Royal Asylum for Female Orphans,
31b, 181c
on Tharmas, 401a
on Tiriel, 406d
on Vala, 144a
mentioned, 332d
"The Suppressed and Altered Passages in
Blake's Jerusalem," 210b-c
Erigena, 296d
Erin, 128a-c. See also Ireland
body and, 198a, 128a-b
Dinah and, 104a, 128b
in Jerusalem, 128a-c, 247b[c], 251d [252a]
sex and, 128a-b, 197d [198a]
mentioned, 340d
Error
baptism casts off, 36c, 353c-d
church and, 82c
Covering Cherub as, 93d (twice)
creation as, 94c-d
fire consumes, 138d-139a
forest of, 220b
of great men, 262d-263b
in Job illustrations, 221c
Last Judgment casts out, 235a, b

Error (cont'd)
  Los gives form to, 247b-c[c-d], 355c, 365a
  in Mundane Shell, 288d
  oak groves symbols of, 168c
  Rahab exposed as, 340a-b
  in Rephaim, 346d
  Satan as, 355b, 358a-b
  in states, 386c, d
  tree symbol of, 410b
  truth and, 85d
Erythrean, sea, 128c-d; 61d, 342a, 379c
Esau, 128d; 115d-116b
Esher, 128d
Esop, 128d
Essay Concerning Human Understanding
  (Locke), 243a[b]
Essay on Epic Poetry (Hayley), 97b
Essay on Man (Pope), 50a, 100d-101a
Essay on Sculpture (Hayley), 177a
Essex, 129a
Esthetics of Blake. See Allegory; Art;
  Creative Process; Imagination;
  Inspiration;Memory; Minute Particulars;
  Painting; Poet; Poetry; Vision
Estrild, 129a-b; 169a
Etching. See Engraving; Illuminated
  Printing
Eternal Man. See Albion
Eternal Prophet. See Los, prophecy and
Eternals. See Divine Family
Eternity, 129b-130c. See also Immortality
  angels and, 22c
  Arts of, 129c, 371c, illus. I (#68). See also
    Architecture; Music; Painting; Poetry
  Beulah open to, 43b
  creation and, 94c, d, 129b
  dimensions in, 103d
  Eden and, 114d
  entering, 288d-289a
  in Europe, 132b, d
  Nature and, 129c-d, 296b
  prophet of, 335a-b
  Rock of, 350c, 363a
  sex in, 130b, 190b, 367b
  space, time, and, 129b, 340d, 379d,
    440a-b
Ethics. See Morality
Ethinthus, 130c-131a; 124c (diagram),
  132b, 261b-c, 451d
Ethiopia, 131a
Etruscan Column (character), 131a-b; 199d
  [200a]
Eucharist. See Lord's Supper
Euphrates, 131b-c. See also Eden, rivers of
Europe, 131c-d; 329b-330b. See also Song
  of Los
Europe, a Prophecy, 131d-133a
  America, Book of Los, Song of Los, and, 21a
    51d, 131d, 377d
  in cycle of continents, 377d
  Leutha in, 238a[b]

Europe, a Prophecy (cont'd)
  Orc in, 311a
  Palamabron in, 321c
  plates of, 133a
    pl. i, frontispiece, 91c, 133a, 221a,
      420b-c, 439a-b, d
    pl. ii, title page, 365d, 366a
    pl. iii, 132c-133a, 408d
    pl. 2:13, 363a
    pl. 3:2, 363a
    pl. 3:25, 349d
    pl. 8:1, 349d
    pl. 10:5, 434d
    pl. 11, illus., 83b
    pls. 13:9-14:28, 124c (diagram)
    pl. 14:1-31, 442c
    pl. 14:15-19, 25a
    pl. 14:20, 85a
  sex repression in, 132b-c, 275b
  Song of Los and, 21a, 30d, 131d, 377c, d
  Urizen in, 83b, 91c, 133a, 420c
  Verulam temple in, 132c, 434b-c
  vision in, 296c-d
Evangelists as Zoas, 458d
Eve, 133b[a-b]
  creation of, 5b, 133b[a-b]
  in Genesis Ms., 152a, 433d
  in Ghost of Abel, 133b, 153c-154b
  in "Hervey's Meditations," illus. XI (#2)
  Heva in, 185c
  in Jerusalem 90:34, 133b, 449d
  as mother of death, 100a
  in Paradise Lost, 88a, 276d, 307b
  as sense, 6a
  in "VLJ," 192a, illus. I (#25)
"Eve, Satan Watching Adam and," 303b
"Eve, The Clothing of Adam and," 371a
Everlasting Gospel, 25b-c, 60c-d, [133c]
[Everlasting Gospel, The, 133c-d—2nd pr.
  only]
  Herod in, 183c
  humility in, [133c], 191c-d
  Jesus in, [133c], 213d
  Mary Magdalene in, 264a
  text of
    e: 70-78, 264a, 283c
  Everything that lives is holy, 133c[d]
Evil, 133d[c]. See also Good and evil
  B vs. Swedenborg on, 393d-394c
  leviathan symbol of, 239d
  in poetry, 331c
  serpent symbol of, 365b
Evolution, 53d, 309d, 452b
Examiner, R. Hunt's review of B's 1809
  exhibition in, 102d
Excursion, The (Wordsworth), 451a
Exeter, 133d [133d-134a]
Exhibition of 1809, B's, 102d;
  Advertisement of, 443c, d
Exhibition planned for 1810, B's, 103a
Existence, Imagination as, 195b-c

Exodus, 46c, 215a
Experience. *See also* Contraries; Innocence;
  Songs of Innocence and of Experience
  in *Book of Thel*, 99c-d, 401a
  death and, 99c-d, [197b-c]
  defined, 378a
  Fall of Man and, 5d, 378a
  in *Four Zoas*, 122c-d
  in *Jerusalem*, 292b
  in *Job*, 217c
  in *Job* illustrations, 219b, c, 222d-223a
  love in, 351a
  in *Milton*, 292a-b
  in mysticism, 291c, 292a
  path of
    through Eyes of God, 134b[c], 147b-c,
      217c-d, 222d-223a, 254b[c], 386d
    through furnaces, 146c, 147b, 292a
    through Heavens, 292a-b
  in *Songs of Experience* title page, 99c,
    [197b-c]
  in "To Tirzah," [197c], 407d
  in *Visions*, 401c, 437d
Eye, 133d-134a [134a-b]; 315a-d, 419a.
  See also Vision
Eyes of God, 134b-d [134c-135a]. *See also*
  names of the Eyes
  Angels of the Presence as, 23d-24a
  Angels of Providence as, 23d
  B learns, 215c
  in Experience, 134b[c], 292a. *See also*
    Experience, path of, through Eyes
    of God
  in *Job* illustrations, 134d [135a], 217a,
    c-d, 220c, 222d-223a
  lamps as, 18c, 233d
  in Los's furnaces, 147b-c, 247b[c]
  role of, 10a, 134b[c]
  Starry Seven as, 385d
  as states, 386d
  in "VLJ," illus. I (#81)
  mentioned, 24d
Ezekiel, 134d-135c [135a-c]
  in *The Marriage*, 135a-c[c], 262d
  Son of Man as, 214a
Ezekiel, 134d-135c [135a-c]
  B's illustrations of, 135c, 318d
  Covering Cherub in, 93d, 135a[b-c]
  New Jerusalem in, 135a[c], 202a[b]
  prince of Tyre in, 135a[b], 357a
  prophecy of 12 tribes in, 135a[b],
    201b[c], 348c-d
  stones of fire in, 388c
  wheels in, 445a
  Zoas in, 135a[b], 458c-d. 459c
Ezra, 135c[c-d]; 46a

Fable, 17c, 26c
Fables Ancient and Modern (Dryden),
  78d-79a, 110b
Faces of Man, Four, 364d

Faerie Queene, The (Spenser). *See* Spenser,
  Edmund, *The Faerie Queene*
"Faerie Queene, Spenser's," painting by B,
  383d-385a, illus. VIII
"Fair Elenor," 331b, 361a
Fairies, 136a-c; 132d-133a
Faith, xi
Fall of Man. *See also* Flood of Noah; Senses;
  World, Material
  Adam and, 5a-6c
  in Behmen's system, 40c
  brain after, 57d
  creation and, 94c
  dimensions after, 103d
  false religion begins with, 345a
  God of This World after, 160d
  hermaphroditism and, 182c
  Innocence, Experience, and, [197b-c],
    378a
  inversion in, 293c-d
  in *Jerusalem*, 210d
  limits of, 309a *See also* Limits
  moon's place in, 285d
  Original Sin and, 5d, 65a, 119a
  in *Paradise Lost*, 357b
  psychological meaning of, 121b-c
  seasons and, 449a-b, 366d, illus. I
    (#63, 69)
  senses after, 295b-c, 364b
  sex and, 276c
  shame and, 283c, 370d-371a
  tree and, 410c-411d
  in "VLJ," illus. I (#65)
  in Zoas story, 418c, 459a-c
"Fall of Man, The," 160c
False Tongue, 408b, c
Family, 213c
Family, Divine [Divine Family], 105a-106b
Family gods, 236c[d]
Famine in *Europe*, illus., 133a
Fate, stars as, 386a. *See also* Circle of Destiny
Fates, Three, 87a, 227a, 327d, 400d-401a
Father, illus. XI (#22)
Father, The (Strindberg), 448a
Fathers, Church, 269a, 343a, 450c
Father's Memoirs of His Child, A (Malkin),
  414c-d, 433d
Fayette, Marquis de la [Lafayette], 231b-d
"Fayette," 231d
fear, 316b (twice)
Fearful Symmetry (Frye), 194d (twice), 306a
Felpham, 136d-137b. *See also* Hayley,
  William
  B and Scofield at, 137a, 360d-361a
  Bognor Rocks near, 49b, 137a
  fly symbol and, 139d-140a
  plow in, 329b
  Sussex and, 136d, 391d
"Felpham, Landscape Near," 137b
Female
  Cambel as warring, 66a

Female (cont'd)
  Cathedron as body of, 74b
  in Chaucer, B's view of, 79c
  dome a symbol of, 106d
  domination of. See Female Will
  emanation of, 120d
  in Europe, 378d
  foreign, 261a
  function of, 286a
  genitals of, 28b, 80b, 107b, 237d [238b],
    265c, 395b
  Joseph's coat stripped off by, 224b
  male absorbs, 280a
  in marriage, 305d-306a
  Milton and. See Milton, John, women and
  mortal body given by, 6c, 100a-b, 451b
  Shadowy, 369b-d, 429b
  space created by, 380a
  in Ulro, 367c-d
  in Visions, 260a, 437d-438d
  Zelophehad's daughters and
    emancipation of, 260a
Female Babe, 268c, 340c
"Female Babe and 'The Mental Traveller' "
  (Paley), 268d
Female Will, 447c-448a
  Albion's daughters and, 14c
  Albion's sons and, 16b
  Arthur and Merlin victims of, 270c
  Dalila as, 307b, 448a
  in Europe, 132a-c
  Gwendolen as, 169b
  in Jerusalem, 212a-b, 252c-d [253a]
  Paul's attitude toward sex and, 324a
  Rahab as, 339d
  Zelophehad's daughters and, 260a, 457d
Fénelon, François de Salignac de la Mothe,
  137c-d; 168d, 343b
  Maximes des Saintes sur la vie intérieure,
    137c
Fermanagh, 137d
"Fertilization of Egypt," 98c, 116d-117a
Fetus, 53c
Fielding, Henry, 446d
Fifeshire, 137d
Finchley, 137d-138a
"Finding of Moses, The," 286c
Fingal (Macpherson), 312a
Finger of God, 138a-c; 247b[c]
Finnegans Wake (Joyce), 143b
Fire, 138c-139a. See also Elements
  chariot of, 118d
  Fuzon as, 139a, 148c
  genii as, 139a, 152b
  of hell, 389d
  Lake of, 139a, 231d-232a, 235b
  Pillar of, 204a
  seraphim as, 365a
  stones of, 388c-d
  wrath as, 413c
First Book of Urizen, The. See Book of Urizen,
  The [First]

Fitzwilliam Museum, 224b
"Five Windows Light the Cavern'd Man,"
  132c-133a, 408d
Flaxman, John
  Compositions for the Divine Comedy, 97b
  on Grave designs, 47c
  at Hampstead, 172a
  Steelyard the Lawgiver as, 199c[d]
  Thomas Taylor and, 396d-397a
  mentioned, 177a, 330d
Flaxman, Maria, 172a, 177b
"Flea, Ghost of a," 154d
Flesh. See Body; Death; Senses; Sex
Fletcher, John, 331a
Flintshire, 139b
Flogiston, 197a-b
Flood of Noah, 139b-c, 300c-301a. See also
  Antediluvians
  on Atlantic Continent, 31c-d
  Atlantic Vale in Jerusalem and, 32b-c
  Sea of Time and Space and, 363a
  in "VLJ," 140b, 366d, 371c, illus. I (#38,
    66, 68, 69)
Flora, Temple of, 232b
Flora Tea Gardens, 232b
Florida Tea Gardens, 95a
Flowers, 238a[b], 265c
Fly, 139d-140a
"Fly, The," 139d
Foetus, 53c
Foot, 140a-d. See also Left and right
  symbolism; Sandal
Foote, Samuel, 140d
  The Minor, 140d, 446d
For Children: The Gates of Paradise. See Gates
  of Paradise
Forests, 140d-141b
  of Albion, 141b
  of Entuthon, 141b
  error as, 141a, 410b
  of God, 140d
  of the night, 141a, 414a
Forfar, 141b-c
Forgiveness of Sins, 141c-142b, 373d-374a
  apocatastasis and, 296c, 410c
  in Bible, 46a, 141c, 141d-142a
  in B's religion, 179d, 344c
  of Cain, 3a, 64d, 142a, 154a
  cherubim as, 80b
  Decalogue and, 141c, 287b
  Elohim and, 119d, 141c
  by Har, 405c
  in Jerusalem, 208a
  as Jesus's doctrine, 141c, 214c-d
  in Job illustrations, 222a
  by Joseph, son of Jacob, 223d, 224a
    [224a, b]
  by Joseph of Nazareth, 225b-c[c]
  Mary the Virgin and, 264c
  mercy as, 269b
  Paul's view of, 323d
  Word as, 450d

Forgiveness of Sins (cont'd)
  by worm, 451d
Form
  of error, 355c, 365a
  human, 55a, 436b. See also Body; Nudity
  ideal, 194a, 328d, 362c
  of spectres, 25a
  universal, 280d
Formlessness, 416a-c
For the Sexes: The Gates of Paradise. See Gates
  of Paradise
Fountain, 197b[c], 219b
"Fourfold Correspondences in Jerusalem,
  Blake's" (diagram), 212
Fourfoldness, 125c, 142c, 163 (diagram),
  220c-d, 291c-d, 331b. See also
  Quaternaries
Four Points. See Center; Circumference;
  Nadir; Zenith
Four Precious Stones, 388b. See also Stones,
  precious
Four Rivers of Eden. See Eden, rivers of
Four Zoas. See Zoas
Four Zoas, The, 142b-144c
  Ahania in, 8a-d
  Albion in, 9c-11a
  Bible of Hell and, 46c
  Book of Ahania and, 50c, 53a
  Book of Los and, 53a
  Book of Urizen and, 53a
  Daughters of Beulah in, 43d-44a
  Divine Family in, 105c
  Enion in, 122b-123d
  epigraph for, 323d
  furnaces in, 146d
  Golgonooza in, 164c-165a
  harrow in, 175a, 176b
  Hell in, 180c-d
  hermaphrodite in, 181d-182a
  Jerusalem in, 144a, 207a
  Joseph of Arimathea in, 225a[a-b]
  Koran and, 259d
  Last Judgment in, 236a-b, 459d-460a
  limits in, 241a[b]
  Los in, 225a[a-b], 248a-250c [248b-251a]
  Los's daughters in, 253b-c[d]
  Los's sons in, 253b[c-d]
  Luvah in, 255c-257b [255d-257c]
  Maternal Line in, 265d-266a
  metal-casting in, 147a
  metals in, 271a-b
  Orc in, 309d-310d, 365c, 411a-b
  Paradise Lost and, 142d-143a, 275b-c
  plow in, 329c-d
  Prester Serpent in, 334c
  Rahab in, 338d-339d, 340a-c
  Satan in, 181d-182a
  science in, 360b-c
  seasons in, 449b-c
  Shadowy Female in, 369c-d
  spectre in, 381d
  Spectres of the Dead in, 382d-383b

Four Zoas, The (cont'd)
  text and illustrations of
    p. 3 recto, illus., 400d
    p. 98, illus., 334c
    i:495, 458a
    i:508, 373a
    ii:66-69, 117-118, 136-140, 147a
    ii:273, 303d
    iii:82, 217a
    v:189-220, 373b-c
    v:234, 18b, 255d [256a]
    v:234-237, 86d
    vi:243-259, 345b
    vii b:289, 332d
    viii:16-19, 10b
    viii:74, 42b
    viii:176-181, 421d-422a
    viii:215-217, 28b
    viii:274, 409b
    viii:297-321, 18d
    viii:339-340, 225a[a-b]
    viii:363-365, 265d-266a
    viii:364, 130d, 261c
    viii:368-370, 176b
    viii:446, 233d
    viii:585-592, 340b-c
    ix:311-315, 329c
    ix:363-365, 255a[b-c]
    ix:742-771, 435b
    ix:749-751, 180d
    ix:759, 259b
  Tharmas in, 399c-400d
  Tree of Mystery in, 411a-b
  Urizen in, 10c-d, 143a, 329c-d, 411a-b,
    420d-422b
  Urizen's daughters in, 424c-425b
  Urizen's sons in, 425c-426a
  Urthona in, 426b-427a
  Urthona's mills in, 273c
  Vala in, 428a-430c
  Zoas in, 142b-c, 161b, 459d-460a
  mentioned, 152a, 177c
Fragments of Ancient Poetry Collected in the
  Highlands of Scotland (Macpherson), 312a
France, 144c-145c; 150b, 256c[d], 371d-372a
Franklin, Benjamin, 145c-d; 21c, 435c,
  446c-d, d
Freedom. See Liberty
Free love, 25b, 367b
Freher, Dionysius, illustrations in English
  edition of Behmen, 39d
French Revolution. See also France; French
  Revolution
  Bonaparte and, 50b
  Lafayette in, 231b-d
  Paine in, 317a-b
  Rousseau and Voltaire as mainsprings of,
    351c-352a
  "The Tyger" and, 414a
  mentioned, 18c, 323a
French Revolution, The, 145d-146b;
  144d-145a

French Revolution, The (cont'd)
  Lafayette in, 231c
  Ossian's influence on, 312c
  text of
    1. 29, 335d
    11. 89-90, 145a, 454d
    1. 97, 350c
  mentioned, 20b
Freud, Sigmund: B's anticipations of, 169b,
    262b, 368a-b, 442b-c *See also* Mind;
    Oedipus complex; Subconscious;
    Superego
Freya [Friga], 146b-c, 442c, 434a
Friends, Society of, 39d, 342c-d
Friendship in "VLJ," illus. I (#77)
Friends of Albion, 73a-b
Friga, 146b-c; 434a, 442c
Frog, 219b
Frye, Northrop: *Fearful Symmetry,* 194d
    (twice), 306a
Furnaces, 146b-148c; 292a. *See also* Los,
    furnaces of
[Fuseli, Henry, 236b-c—2nd pr. only]
    "Count Ugolino," 97b-c
    "Fertilization of Egypt," 98c, 116d-117a
Fuzon, 148c-d; 50d-51a, 411a

Gad, 149a-b; 103c
Gate of, 325d
Gadarene swine, 216a
Gallows, 65d, 379c, 413b
Galway, 149b
Garden
  of Adonis in Spenser, 432b
  of Eden. *See* Eden; Paradise
  pleasure, 232b-c
  of Vala, 385b, 432a-b
Garrison, William Lloyd: *Liberator,* 317c
Gate
  enrooted at a, 361c
  guarding of a, 361c
  Northern, 401b
Gate of Asher, Gates of Beulah, etc. *See*
    Asher, Gate of; Beulah, Gates of, *etc.*
Gates, Horatio, 149b
Gates of Paradise, The, 149c-150b
  Grave designs and, 48d
  Night Thoughts influences designs for,
      456c-d
  plates and text of
    Prologue, 388c
    pl. 2, 149d, 261d
    pl. 6, 149d, 456c
    pl. 9, 140b, 149d, 285b
    pl. 12, 97c, 149d
    pl. 13, 149d, 456c
    pl. 14, 99d, 149d
    pl. 16, 149d, 216d, 456c
    "The Keys of the Gates," 150a, 288b, 452b
    Epilogue, 150a-b, 254a[c], 323d, 358b-c,
        456c-d
  thirteen in, 149d, 220c

Gates of Paradise, The (cont'd)
  mentioned, 232d, 319a-b
Gaul, 150b
Gaza, 150b-c
Geber, 182d
Gehenna, 186b
Gemini, 311c
Gems. *See* Stones, precious
Generalization, 80a (twice), 284c. *See also*
    Abstraction; Law; Minute Particulars
Generation, 150c-151a. *See also* Matter;
    Vegetate
  in "The Circle of Life," 87b
  in *Gates of Paradise,* 452b
  of Los's sons, 150d-151a, 347b
  nymphs as spirits of, 303d
  Ulro and, 150c, 417c
Genesis, book of the Bible, 151a-152b. See
    also *Genesis* Manuscript
  creation in, 45b, 46c, 51b, c-d, 53b, 77a,
      151a-b
  Book of Los and, 46c, 51b, c-d, 53b
  Book of Urizen and, 46c, 53b
  in Byron's *Cain,* 153b-d
  Eden in, 114a
  Michelangelo's version of, 272c
  text of
    i, 5a, 46c, 51b, c-d, 53b, 151b, 182c,
        240b[c]
    ii, 5a-b, 151b, 206c
    iii, 119a, 345b, 357a, 446b
    iv, 266c
    v, 85b, 182c, 233c-d
    xi:10-26, 85b
    xix:26, 253d [254a]
    xxiii:3, 293a
    xxxvi:39, 267b
Genesis Manuscript, B's illuminated,
    151c-152a
  in Bible of Hell, 46c
  Cain in, 64d, 152a, 154a
  Eve in, 152a, 433d
  text and illustrations of
    title page, 151c-d, 158c, 160c, 187d,
        313d, 401a, 459c-d
    chap. iii, 152a, 433d
    Trinity in, 151c-d, 158c
Genesis, the Seven Days of the Created World
    (Tasso, trans. Hayley), 152a-b
Genii, 152b
Genitals. *See* Female, genitals of
Genius
  classes of men and, 88a-d, 409b-c
  eagle symbol of, 112a-d
  Holy Ghost as, 187a-b
  Poetic, 330b-c, 343d. *See also* Imagination
  Zazel as, 406c
  mentioned, 71b
Geoffrey of Monmouth, 152b-c
  Historia Britonum
    Albion's daughters in, 14b, 152c
    Arthur in, 29b, 152c

Historia Britonum (cont'd)
  Belin in, 41c-d
  Conwenna in, 92a
  Cordella in, 92b
  Gogmagog in, 152c, 162b
  Gonorilla in, 166a
  Guanhumara, 170c-d
  Guendoloena, 169a
  Ignoge in, 194d
  Legions in, 237c[d]
  Mehetabel in, 267b
  Sabrina in, 353b
Geography, 19b, 71a-b. *See also* Compass
  points; East; North; South; West
Geometry, 14a, 91c
George III, King, 152d-153a; 20b,
  20d-21a, 406d
Germany, 153b
Gethsemane, 213d
Ghost of Abel, The, 153b-154c
  Abel's ghost in, 3a, 154a-b, 155a
  Ark of the Covenant and, 27d-28a
  Byron's *Cain* and, 63b, 153b-d
  Cain depicted in designs for, 64d
  Elijah in, 118c
  Elohim Jehovah in, 154a, b-c, 206b, 227c
  Eve in, 133b, 154a-b
  Hamlet echoed in, 370d
  humility in, 191d
  plates of
    pl. 1:13, 3b
    pl. 2:19-22, 358b
"Ghost of a Flea," 154d
Ghosts, 154c-155a; 346b, c, 370b-c. See also
  Ghost of Abel; Holy Ghost
"Giant, The Harlot and the," 83a
Giants, 155a-156c
  Albion as, 9c, 155d-156b
  Anakim as, 22a
  Antediluvians as, 25b, 155b-c
  Atlas as, 32c
  Dance of the, 388a
  Gibborim as, 157a
  Gogmagog as, 162b-c
  Roman Emperor as, 83a
  Rephaim as, 346b, c
  of Twenty-Seven Churches, 85b
Giant's Causeway, 156c-d; 197d [198a]
"Giants Sunk in the Soil, Primeval," 155c
Gibble Gabble, 199c[d]
Gibbon, Edward, 156d-157a; 100c
Gibborim, 157a
Gihon, 157a-b; 114d, 115a-b, c
Gilchrist, Alexander
  Life of William Blake
    on *America*, 21a-b
    on Blackheath, 47a
    B's fame renewed by, 48d
    on "VLJ" (fresco), 236a
    VLJ in, 437c
Gilead, 157b-c
Gilead, Mount, 157b-c, 375d-376a

Gilgal, 157c
Ginzberg, Louis: *Legends of the Jews*, 347b
"Glad Day." *See* "Albion's Dance"
Glamorganshire, 157d
Glasgo[w], 157d
Glastonbury Abbey, 224d, 225a
Glastonbury Thorn, 224d, 225b
Gleckner, Robert F.: *The Piper & the Bard*,
  392c, 401a
Globe of Blood, 157d
Gloucester [Gloucestershire], 157d-158a
Glycon, 158a
Gnomes, 158a-b
Gnosticism, 115c-d, 127a, 153b, 270d, 343a
"Goblin, The," 390d
God, 158b-161a. *See also* Jehovah; Trinity;
  entries beginning with "Divine"
  Abstract, 159d-160a
  Albion and Grand Man as, 393b
  as Almighty, 18c
  as angel, 22c
  Angry, 160a-c, 452c-d
    Loving God and, 232a-b, 414a
    in Dante illustration "Mission of
      Virgil," 97d, 125b, 161a, 286a, 380a
    in "The Tyger," 232b
    in "VLJ," illus. I (#14, 15, 26)
  in Ark, 395b
  Brama as, 58b
  in B's religion, 343d-344a, 344b-c
  cherubim of, 80b
  Council of, 10a, b, 92d, 105a-106b
  in Dante illustration "Deity, from Whom
    Proceed the Nine Spheres," 263c-d
  of deism, 100d, 101b-c, d
  as Deus, 103a
  Eyes of. *See* Eyes of God
  as Father, 205d, 399a, 450c
  Finger of, 138a-c, 247b[c]
  in *Ghost of Abel* and Byron's *Cain*,
    153c-154c
  Hell and, 179d-180c
  in "Hervey's *Meditations*," illus. XI (#1)
  humanity as, 158c-159a, 190a, 214b,
    [236c], 419a-b
  humility and, 191c-192a
  imagination and, 159b, 195b
  jealousy of, 250a
  Jesus as, 158b-159d, 214b
  in *Job*, 216b-d
  in *Job* illustrations, 217d-223a
  love and, 232a-b, 271c
  in Methodism, 271c
  in "Milton's Dream," 277a
  Milton's view of, 276d
  name of, 215d, 455a. *See also* Eyes of God
  as Pantocrator, 322a
  pity of, 327a
  in space, 77b
  spirits of, 233d
  Tharmas as, 399a
  of This World, 160c-161a

God (cont'd)
    of This World (cont'd)
        Biblical source for, 323d, 355d
        in Dante illustrations, 97d, 125b, 161a,
            286a, 380a
        in "Divine Image" (Songs of Experience),
            269c
        in "Human Abstract," 269c
        Nobodaddy as, 301c
        in "Spenser's Faerie Queene," 384a-b, c
            (twice)
        Urizen as, 420b-c
    Urizen as, 160c, 276d, 420b-c
    of Young, 455d
"God of This World, The Angry," 97d,
    125b, 161a, 286a, 380a
"Godred Crovan" (Chatterton), 78c, 170b
Gods, 161a-162a. See also names of gods
    of Asia, 42c, 44c, 161c-162a
    family, 236c[d]
    Greek, 205a
Godwin, William, 314c
"God Writing on the Tables of the
    Covenant," 138c, 192a, 286c (twice)
Goemagot [Gogmagog], 152c, 162b-c
[Goethe, Johann Wolfgang von: Dichtung
    und Wahrheit, 236b—2nd pr. only]
Gog, 162a-b; illus. I (#53)
Gogmagog, 162b-c; 152c
Gold, 162c-d
    Book of, 424c
    bow of, 55c
    intellect as, 162d, 341a
    reason as, 271b
    serpent and, 366a
    silver and, 373b (three times)
    Urizen's metal as, 162c, 419a
    mentioned, 271a
Golden Age, 262c, 358d
Golden Ass, The (Apuleius), 26b, 149d
Golden Net, The, 297d-298a, 436a
Golden Square, 59c
Golgonooza, 162d-165d
    Beulah and, 43c
    Blackheath and, 47a
    diagram of, 163
    Gates of, 22a, 74b, 114c, 150c-d, 163
        (diagram), 164a-b, 165a, c-d, 253d
        [254a], 417c
    in Jerusalem, 147d, 163 (diagram), 165c-d
    Udan-Adan and, 416a, b
    mentioned, 247b[c]
"Golgonooza" (diagram), 163
Golgotha, 165d; 413b. See also Calvary
Gomorrha, 166a; 376c
Gon, 166a
Gonorill, 166a-b; 448a
Good and evil. See also Evil; Morality
    in Behmen's system, 40b
    in Job illustrations, 218a
    in The Marriage, 262b, 270d

Good and Evil (cont'd)
    origins of, 5d, 345a
    serpents as, 234b
    Swedenborg's idea of, 393b
    Tree of the Knowledge of. See Tree,
        of Mystery
    in Young, 455d
Gordon Riots of 1780, 59d
Gordred, 170b-c, 406b
Goshen, 166b
Gospels. See Bible; Forgiveness of Sins
Gothicism
    in architecture, 27a, b, 62c, 217d, 225a, b,
        384b
    in Poetical Sketches, 331b
Government. See State
Goyder, George, and Geoffrey Keynes:
    eds., William Blake's Illustrations to the Bible,
    46b, 286c
Grammateis, 166b-c
Grand Man, Swedenborg's, 9d, 393b
Grapevine in Lambeth, 232c
Grasshoppers, 166c; 219b
Grave, The (Blair). See Blair, Robert,
    The Grave
Gravity, 298b
Gray, Thomas
    The Bard, 36d, 91d, 375d
    B's illustrations to, 36d
    Hymn to Adversity, B's illustrations to, 456c
    Poetical Sketches influenced by, 331a
    Ugolino poem by, 97b
Great Bear, 227a, 327d
Great Britain. See Britain; Brittannia;
    England; English
Great George Street, 166c-d
Great Queen Street, 166d-167a; 241c[d]
Greece, 167a-168a. See also Classicism;
    Muses; Neoclassicism
    art of, B's attitude toward, 167a-b, 267d
    Bryant's opinion of, 61d
    gods of, 205a
    Helle as, 181b
    Javan and, 204d-205a
    language of, B's knowledge of, 419a
    liberty and, 168a, 295b
    philosophy of, 110a
    poets of, 17d
    Taylor's knowledge of, 396c
    in "VLJ," illus. I (#76)
Green[e], General Nathaniel, 168b
Greenland, 168c
Green Man, 168a-b; 216b
Greenwich, Queen's house at, 72c
Grey Monk, The, 78b, 285a-b
"Grief among the Roots and Trees," 456c
Griffin, 21b
Grodna, 168c
Grosser, Maurice: Painter's Eye, 320b-c
Grosseteste, Robert: as Lincoln, 72c, d,
    241b[c-d]

Groves, 168c
Guantock, John, 168c
Guantok, 168c-d
Guardian of the secret codes, 166c-d
Guardian Prince of Albion, 152d
Guardian spirit, 22d
Guendoloena, 129a
Guildhall, 162c
Guilt, 124c (diagram). *See also* Sin
Guinea, 168d
Guinevere [Gwiniverra], 170c-d
Guion, 168d; 343b
Guyon, Madame Jeanne Marie Bouvier de
la Motte- [Guion], 168d, 343b
Guyon, Sir, 384b
Gwantock [Guantok], 168c-d
Gwantoke [Guantok], 168c-d
Gwendolen, 169a-170b
  Cambel and, 66a-b, 169a, 169b-170a
  Hyle and, 169b, d, 192d-193a, 452c
  Mam-Tor exposed by, 170b, 260d
  worm and, 169d-170a, 452c
  mentioned, 102b
Gwinefred, 170c
Gwiniverra, 170c-d
"Gwin, King of Norway," 170b-c; 78c, 155d,
  312c, 406b

Hackney, 171a
Haddntn [Haddington], 171a-b
Hades, 171b; 311c. *See also* Hell
Hagar, 171b-c; 198d [199a], illus. I (#71)
Haines, William, 392a
Half Manasseh, ruler of Bashan, 37b
Hals, Frans, 412b
Ham, 171c-d
Hamath, 171d
Hamilton, Dr. William: *Letters Concerning the
  Northern Coast of Antrim*, 156c
Hamlet (Shakespeare), 370d
"Hamlet and the Ghost of His Father," 155a
Hampshire, 171d
Hampstead, 171d-172b
Hancock, John, 172b
Hand, son of Albion, 172b-173d; 66a, b, c
Hand, terminal part of arm, 173d-174a. *See
  also* Left and right symbolism
Hants [Hampshire], 171d
Har, 174a-d; 401d, 405c, 406a-b, c
  Vales of, 52b, c, 174b, d, 401a
Harford [Hertfordshire], 183c-d
Harhath, 174d
"Harlot and the Giant, The," 83a
Harlots and harlotry, 200c[d], 244b[c-d],
  254d [255a], 263d, 283a, 338d, 339c-d.
  See also Babylon, Whore of; Mystery
Harmony vs. melody, 290a-b
Harper, George Mills: *The Neoplatonism of
  William Blake*, 131a, 199c-d [199d-200a],
  328c, 375a-b, 397b-c, 432d
Harps, 258c, 377c

Harrow, town, 174d-175a
Harrow, tool, 175a-176b. *See also* Plow
  of Palamabron, 175b-176b, 189d, 238c-d
  [238d-239a], 321d
Hartford [Hartfordshire], 183c-d
Harvest, 176b-c; 10c-11a, 13a-b, 133a,
  236b, 434d-435b. *See also* Last Judgment
Hate, 219c, 235d, 255a[b], illus. I (#26)
Havilah, 176c; 327a
Hawthorne, Nathaniel, 196a
Hayley, Thomas Alphonso, 177a (three
  times), b, d
Hayley, William, 176c-178d. *See also*
  Felpham
  B's relationship with, 120b, 136d-137b,
    167a, 177b-178d, 380a-b, 403d
  B's wife and, 177d, 178b, 361a
  Enitharmon's function and, 380a-b
  Epistle of Painting, 176d
  Essay on Epic Poetry, 97b
  Essay on Sculpture, 177a
  Hyle as, 178d, 193c
  Klopstock dictated to B by, 177c, 229c
  Leutha and, 178c-d, 238b-239a
    [238c-239b]
  Life of Cowper, 177d
  Life of Romney, 177c
  Little Tom the Sailor, 177b
  in *Milton*, 175b, 178c-d, 238b-239a
    [238c-239b], 277b-280d, 356d-357a,
    357c-358a
  Satan as, 178c-d, 250b[c], 357c-358a
  Tasso's *Genesis* dictated to B by, 152a-b
  Triumphs of Temper, 176d, 177b
  Winchester as, 72a, d, 178d, 448d
  mentioned, 443a
"H[ayle]y's Friendship, On," 361a
"H[ayley] the Pick Thank, On," 178a
Hazael, 179a; illus. I (#39)
Hazor, 179a
Head, 118a, 379b
Heads of the Poets, 189a, 177b, 334a,
  370b-c
Heart
  Alla in, 17a
  Bowlahoola as, 57a
  Canaan as, 67d
  Center as, 75c
  East and, 113c
  Luvah's place as. 255a[b]
  moon's place as, 285c
  Orc's name and, 309c
  Paradise in, 322d
  reason separated from, 382a-b
  reins and, 342b
  Uveth as, 427c
  wisdom of, 352a
  wrath of Tyger and, 413c
Heaven. *See also* Beulah, Churches or
  Heavens of; Churches, Twenty-Seven
  Albion and Grand Man as, 393b

Heaven (cont'd)
  in Behmen's system, 40b-41a
  in The Marriage, 262b
  Rose of, 390c
  superego as, 357c, 394a
  in Swedenborg's system, 393b
Heaven and Hell (Swedenborg), 392d (twice)
Heavens of Beulah. See Beulah, Churches
  or Heavens of
Heber, 179b
Hebrew, B's uses of, 23c, 215b-c, 261a-b
Hebrews, 225a, 374b
Hebrides, 200c[d]
Hebron, 179b; 22a
"Hecate," 313c, 370c-d, 391a
Height, 103d
Hela, 179b-c; 406b
Hêlêl, 186a
Hell, 179d-181b. See also Fire, Lake of
  in Behmen's system, 40b-41a
  Bible of, 46b-c
  fire of, 389d
  Hades as, 171b, 311c
  Hinnom as, 186b
  in Job illustrations, 219d
  in The Marriage, 180b-c, 262b, 270d
  in Milton, 180d-181a, 277b
  Satan created, 356b-c
  subconscious as, 357c, 394a
  Young's view of, 455d-456a
Helle, 181b
Hellman, Lillian, 448a
Hendon, 181b
I Henry IV (Shakespeare), B's illustrations
  of, 370c
Hercules [Heracles], 181b-c; 158a, 334b
Hercules Buildings, 232c
Hercules Tavern, 232c
Hereford [Heref], 181c-d; 441b
Heresy, 296d
Hermaphrodite, 181d-182c
Hermes in Il Penseroso illustrations, 227a
Hermes Trismegistus, 182c-183b
  Divine Pymander, 182c
Hermetic books, 182c
Hermit, The (Parnell), 259d
Hermon, Mount, 183b; 236d [237a]
Herod Antipas, 183c; 223b
Herodotus, 27b
Herschel, Sir William, 358d
Hertfordshire, 183c-d
Hervey, James, 183d-185a, illus. XI (#19)
  Meditations Among the Tombs, 183d, 184d.
    See also "Hervey's Meditations Among the
    Tombs"
"Hervey's Meditations Among the Tombs,"
  183d-184d, illus. XI
  Cain and Abel in, 36, 65a, 184c
  cross not in, 95c, 184d
  Enoch in, 126b
  Transfiguration in, 184d, 409a

Heshbon, 185a-b
Hesperia, 185b
Heth, 185b
Heuxox, 185b-c
Heva, 185c; 174a-d, 405c, 406a-b, c
Hiddekel, 185c. See also Eden, rivers of
"Hiding of Moses, The," 286c
[Higher Innocence, 197c]
Highgate, 185c-186a
High priest, 27a, 69b
Hillel, 186a
Hindostan, 186a
Hindu, 186a
Hinduism, 58b
Hinnom Valley, 186a-b
Hippolytus: Refutation of All Heresies, 115c
Hiram, 64a
Historia Britonum (Geoffrey of Monmouth).
  See Geoffrey of Monmouth, Historia
  Britonum
Historia Naturalis (Pliny), 329a
History
  Biblical, 45b, 51a
  in prophetic books, B's use of, 20b,
    20d-21a, 145d-146b
  pulsation of an artery and, 29b
"History Described by Virgil, Symbolic
  Figure of the Course of," 97d
History of Britain (Milton). See Milton, John,
  History of Britain
History of England, The, planned by B, 232d
"History of the Restoration of the Platonic
  Theology" (Taylor), 396c-d
Hittites, 186b-c; 185b
Hobbes, Thomas: Leviathan, 239d
  [239d-240a]
Hogarth, William, 412c, 446d
Hoglah, 186c; 457c
Hohenheim, Theophrastus Bombastus von.
  See Paracelsus
Holbein, Hans, 412b
Holiness, 186c-d; 296d-297a
Holinshed, Raphael: Chronicles, 108d,
  237c[d]
Holland, 186d
Holloway, 186d
Holmyard, A. J.: "The Emerald Table,"
  182d
Holy Family of Egypt, 311d
Holy Ghost, 186d-187d
  body and, 187a, 344b
  imagination as, 186d, 195b
  intellect as, 186d-187a, 197b[c]
  Jesus and, 158c, 187a
  Mary the Virgin and, 187b, 213a, 264a,
    b-c
  of Milton, 187b, 277a
  Urthona corresponds to, 426b
  in "VLJ," 187c-d, 235c, illus. I (#1)
  in Voltaire, 187c, 439a
Holy Grail, 224d

Holy Thursday, 187d
"Holy Thursday" (Songs of Experience), 187d;
illus., 305b
"Holy Thursday" (Songs of Innocence), 187d,
200a[b]
Holy Word [Word], 269a, 386b, 450c-d
Homer, 187d-189a; 112b, 167c, 442b
"Homer and the Ancient Poets," 167c
"Homer, Bearing the Sword, and His
Companions," 188d, 167c
Homer's Poetry, On [On Homer's Poetry],
188b-c, 308a-b
Homosexuality
B's view of, 376c-377a
Greece and, 167c-d
of Hayley, 178c, 238c[d]
mentioned, 166a
Hope, 340c
Hor, 189a
Horeb as Sinai, 374a
Horizon, 419a
Horses, 189c-d
Horse's Mouth, The (Cary), 268d, 320b
Horus, 311d (twice)
Hosts, Starry [Starry Hosts], 385d
Hotton, John Camden, 49d
Houghton Library, Harvard, 437c
Hounslow, 190a
Howard, Sidney: The Silver Cord, 448a
Howe, Julia Ward: "Battle Hymn of the
Republic," 435a
"How Sweet I Roam'd," 64b, 297d, 331b
"Hugolino, Count" (Reynolds), 97b
Hulton, Lt. George, 192b
"Human Abstract, The," 139d, 191d, 269c,
291b, 341c, 410d; illus., 345b, 422a, d
Human form, 55a, 436b. See also Body;
Nudity
Humanity, 190a-191b. See also Brotherhood
Divine, 106c-d, 191a-b
Four Regions of, 138a, 190c
God as, 158c-159a, 190a, 214b, [236c],
419a-b
of Job, 220a
in Milton, 190c-d, 363c
in repose, states of, 9b, 17a, 43a, 309b
Humanization, 17b, 134b, 215c, 436b
Human sacrifice. See Sacrifice, human
Humber, 191b
Hume, David, 191b-c; 100c
Humility, 191c-192a
"Humility of the Saviour, The," 213b
Humor, 456a
Humphry, Ozias, 456d
Hungerford, Edward B.: Shores of Darkness,
61b
Hunt, Leigh, 172a
Hunt, Robert: reviews B's 1809 exhibition,
102d
Hunter, Dr. John, 199c[d], 199d [200a],
375a

Huntingdon [Huntgn], 192b
Huntsman, Nimrod as, 299d
Husband, illus. XI (#40)
Hutton [Hutn, Huttn], 192b-c
Hyde Park 192c-d
Hyle, 192d-193c
Gog as, 162b
Hand and, 172d-173c, 192b
Hayley as, 178d, 193c
wheels of, 446a
Hymn on the Nativity (Milton), 275b
B's 3rd illustration to, 283d
Hymns for the Nation in 1782 (Wesley), 444b
Hymn to Adversity (Gray): B's illustrations to,
456c
Hymn to Beauty (Spenser), 17a, 385a
Hypocrisy, 283b, 327c, 365b-c

Ideal, 395a, 397c, 407b
Ice in Golgonooza, 163 (diagram)
Id. See Subconscious
Ideas. See also Intellect
in B's visions, 319a
cherubim as, 80a
lark as, 234c-d
Platonic, 432b
reaction to new, 76a
vortex as, 440a
Identity, 194a-b
Iereus, 194b
Ignoge, 194b-d; 61a
"I Heard an Angel Singing," 269c
Ijim, 194d-195a; 174c, 393c, 406b, d
Iliad (Homer), 188a-b
Ilium. See Troy
Ilive, Jacob, 293a
Illuminated Printing, 16d, 154c, 199b[c-d],
337b. See also Engraving; Painting
Illustration. See Painting and names of authors
whose works were illustrated by B
Illustrations of the Book of Job. See Job, B's
illustrations to, Illustrations of the Book of
Job
Illustrations of the Book of Job by William Blake
(Binyon and Keynes), 217b
Il Penseroso (Milton). See Milton, John, Il
Penseroso
Imagery, B's: influenced by Ossian, 312c
Imagination, 195b-d. See also Creative
Process; Genius; Inspiration; Vision
Albion's sons and, 15c-d
allegory and, 17c
in All Religions are One, 16d
art and, 28c, 195c-d
in Behmen's system, 41a
B's painting and, 318c-319a
in B's religion, 343d
Bowlahoola and, 57b
chaos of, 77c (diagram)
children as, 81d
Divine Body as, 104d-105a

Imagination (*cont'd*)
    Europe realm of, 131c
    God as, 195b, 220d
    gods originate in, 161b-c
    Gwendolen as, 169b
    Holy Ghost as, 186d, 195b
    Jesus and, 159b
    Los as, 246c[d], 247a[b]
    memory and, 195d, 267b-268b
    Merlin symbol of, 270b
    New Age and, 329d
    Northern Gate as, 401b
    North symbol of, 301d
    in Paracelsus's system, 263a, 322c-d
    polar region and, 332c
    reason and, 195b, d, 273b, 341d
    sun symbol of, 390a
    universe of the, 418a-c
    Urthona as, 426b
    Young's idea of, 455d
    Zoas in, 418b-c
Imitation and copying, 319d-320a, 320c-d,
    436d, 449. *See also* Memory
"Imitation of Spencer, An," 226a, 269a,
    383c, 385a
Immaculate Conception, 264a-c
Immortality, 17d, 126a, 300d, 328a. *See
    also* Eternity
Imputed Righteousness, 185a
Incarnation. *See also* Mary the Virgin
    B's literary use of, 159c
    in the East, 113c
    forgiveness and, 213a-b
    in *Four Zoas*, 164d
    Generation and, 151a
    [Lavater's influence on B's idea of,
        236c—2nd pr. only]
    mercy and, 269b
    There is No Natural Religion describes, 402d
Incest, 195d-196b
Indefiniteness, 416a-c
India, 196b; 186a
Indians, American, 243a[b]
Individual, 196b-197a
    Cathedral Cities as, 71c
    center of universe as, 417d-418c
    Eighth as, 134c [134d-135a]
    eternity and, 130a
    reason and, 341d
    selfhood and, 346a-b
    states and, 386c
    Urthona as imagination of the, 426b
    will of the, 447b-c
Individuality, 60c, 194a-b, 308b-c. *See also*
    Minute Particulars
Industrial Revolution, 13d, 16c, 445b
Infants. *See also* Children
    heads of, 80a
    in "Hervey's *Meditations*," illus. XI
        (#38, 42)
    in "VLJ," illus. I (#6)
    worms as, 401b

"Infant Sorrow," 282b-c, 365c
Inferno (Dante), B's illustrations of. *See*
    Dante Alighieri, *Divine Comedy*, B's
    illustrations of
Inflammable Gass, 197a-b; 199c[d], 374d,
    375a
[Innocence, 197b-c]. *See also* Contraries;
    Experience; *Songs of Innocence and of
    Experience*
    of Albion's sons, 15c
    betrayed, Joseph, son of Jacob, as type of,
        223d-224b
    [children and, 81c-d, 197b—2nd pr. only]
    of Conwenna, 92a
    of Cordella, 92c
    defined, 378a
    in *Four Zoas*, 122c
    in *Job*, 217c
    in *Job* illustrations, 217d, 218b, 219b
        (twice)
    love in, 351a
    in mysticism, 291c
    protectors of, 305a-b, 340d-341a
    symbols of, 232a-b, 240c[d], 401b
    Thames in age of, 398b
    of Thel, 401a, b
    in "VLJ," 366d, illus. I (#61, 62, 79)
Innogen, 194d
Inns of Court: Lincoln's Inn, 241c[d]
Inquisition in "VLJ," illus. I (#44, 45)
Inspiration. *See also* Creative process; Holy
    Ghost; Imagination; Vision
    Daughters of, 267d
    Divine Hand power behind, 106b
    female as, 305d-306a
    lark as, 234c-d
    moment of, 29b, 284c-d, 454b, d
    muses and, 289c-d
    in Surrey, 391b-d
Institutes of the Christian Religion (Calvin),
    402d
Intellect, 197b-c[c-d]; 162d, 220d, 441c-d.
    See also Ideas
"Interpreter's Parlor, The Man Sweeping
    the," 62c-d
Intestines, 56b, 57d
"In the Last Battle that Arthur Fought,"
    443c, d
Intoxication and war, 442a-b
"Introduction" (*Songs of Experience*)
    B as Bard in, 36d
    Earth in, 113b
    Sea of Time and Space in, 443b
    stars in, 386b
    states in, [197c], 378b-c
    Word in, 450d
Introspection, 418a-c
Inverness[s], 197c[d]; 389a
Inversion, 88a, 254d-255a [225b], 293c-d
Ion, 204d
Ireland, 197c-198a [197d-198c]. *See also*
    Erin; *placenames*

Ireland (cont'd)
   counties of, 96b, 197d-198a [198a-b],
      201a-b[c], 294b
   Giant's Causeway in, 156c-d, 197d [198a]
Irenaeus: *Against the Heresies*, 402d
Irish Sea, 198b[c]
Iron, 198b-c[c-d]; 58c, 163 (diagram), 271a,
   373b, 424c
"I Rose Up at the Dawn of Day," 260c
Isaac, 171b-c
Isaiah, 198c-d [198d-199a]; 262c, d
Isaiah, 198c-d [198d-199a]
   B's illustrations of, 34c
   B's reading of, 46a
   "Ijim" and "Ochim" in, 174c, 194d, 306a,
      406d
   Lucifer in, 254a[b]
   text of
      xiii:21, 174c, 194d, 306a, 406d
      xiv, 357a
      xiv:9, 34c .
      xiv:12, 254a[b]
      xxxiv:14, 240b[d]
      xxxv, 262c
      liii:12, 409a, b
"I Saw a Chapel All of Gold," 352b, 366c
"I Saw a Monk of Charlemaine," 78a, 285b
Ishmael, 198c-199b [199a-c]; 171b-c,
   259b-c, illus. I (#71)
Ishmaelites, 272d
Isis, wife of Osiris, 199b[c]; 26b, 311d
Isis, river, 315a
Island in the Moon, An, 199b-200c
   [199c-200d]
   Chatterton in, 78c-d
   Hervey in, 184d
   Locke in, 243c
   Quid in, 199c[d], 199d-200c [200a-d], 337a-b
   Pliny in, 329a
   Scopprell in, 362a
   Shakespeare in 370a
   Sutton in, 72c
   Taylor in, 199c[d], 199d [200a], 397a-b
   "To be, or not to be," 111c
   Voltaire's influence on, 439b, d
   Young's *Night Thoughts* read in, 455d
Islands as nations, 294d
Isle of Leutha's Dogs, 200c[d]; 239a[b]
Isle of Man, 200c[d]; 377a
Isles, 200c-d [200d-201a]
Isles of Javan, 205a
Islington, 200d [201a]
Israel, 200d-202b [201a-202c]. *See also* Jews
   Maternal Line and, 266b-c
   Sons of, 57a, 93a-d, 201a-202b [201b-
      202c], 441b. *See also names of the Sons*
   Tribes of, 15b-c, 201a[b], b[c], 201d [202a],
      a-b[b-c], 294a. *See also names of the Tribes*
Issachar, 202b-d [202c-d]
Italy, 202c-d [202d-203a]; 185b
Ives, Herbert, 56b
   "The Trial of William Blake," 360d

Ivory, 202d-203c [203a-c]; 373b
"I Will Tell You," 329a

Jabin, 67d
Jachin and Boaz, 204a; illus. I (#22)
Jacko, Mr., 199c[d]
Jacob, 204a-c
   Esau and, 115d-116a, 204b
   Israel as, 200d-201a [201a-b], 204b
   Laban and, 231a
   Leah, 236c[d]
   Shechem and, 371a-b
   in "VLJ," illus. I (#72)
"Jacob's Ladder," 113a
James II, King, 204b-c
James i:15, 238b[c]
Japan, 204c-d; 82a
Japheth [Japhet], 204d; 371c, illus. I (#68)
Jared, 204d
Jasher, Book of, 293a, b
Java, 411c
Javan, 204d-205a
Jealousy, 205a-c
   Chain of, 76a-c, 205b
   Father of, 205a, 301c
   Nobodaddy and, 205a, 301c
   Ocalythron associated with, 305d
   Theotormon as, 401d
Jebusites, 205c
Jehovah, 205c-206c. *See also* God; Trinity;
   Urizen
   Angel of the Divine Presence as, 23c
   Elohim, 23c, 119c-d, 206b-c, 215c, 227b,
      269d
   as Eye of God, 134d[c], 134d [135a]
      (twice), 205b-206a, 223a
   in Ghost of Abel and Byron's *Cain*, 154a,
      b-c, 206b
   in *Job* illustrations, 223a (twice)
   in Laocoön engraving, 234b
Jellyfish, 332d
Jenkins, David, 443c
Jenkins, Herbert, 56b
"Jeptha's Daughter, The Sacrifice of," 258c
Jeremiah viii:22, 157b
Jerusalem, character in *Jerusalem*,
   206c-208d
   four sons of, 349d
   furnaces of Los and, 148a-b
   in *Jerusalem* 14, illus., 208c, 340d
   Lambeth and, 232d
   liberty as, 206c, 206d-208d, 211a, 232d,
      395b-c
   Malden and, 260b
   pearl associated with, 324d-325a
   wisdom as, 41b
   mentioned, 17d
Jerusalem, city, 206c, 213d, 232d-233a,
   247b[c], 324d-325a
"Jerusalem" ("And Did Those Feet"), 118d
Jerusalem, The Emanation of the Giant Albion,
   208d-213a

Jerusalem (cont'd)

Albion in, 11c-13c, 211a-213a in passing

Albion's daughters in, 14b-d, 211d, 212a, c, 447d-448a

Albion's sons in, 15a-16c, 211a, c, 212a

Albion's spectre in, 210c, 211b-213a in passing, 382b-c

arrangement of plates in, 39d, 209d-210c

Bard of Oxford in, 37a, 38d, 71d, 72d, 120a, 148a, 209c, 210a-b, 314c-315d

Bath in, 37c-38c, 210a-b

Beulah's daughters in, 44a-b, 211a, d

Cambel in, 66a, 169b-170b, 212c

Canaan in, 67c

Cathedral Cities in, 73a-74b, 211c

Churches in, 86b, 212a

Coban in, 172d-173c

Catherine Blake's miscarriage recorded in, 401c

Divine Family in, 105d-106a

Egypt in, 116b-d

elements in, 117c

Elohim-Jehovah in, 227c

Enitharmon in, 211b, 212c, 251b-c[d], 381d-382a, 400d

Eno in, 125d

Ezekiel's influence on, 135a[c]

Experience in, 292b

flood of Noah in, 32b-c, 139c

Foote in, 446d

fourfold correspondences in, 212 (diagram)

Generation in, 150c-151a

giants in, 156a-c

Golgonooza in, 150c-d, 163 (diagram), 165c-d

Gwendolen in, 169b-170b, 212c

Hand in, 172b-173d

Hayley in, 178d

Hell in, 181a-b

hermaphrodite in, 182a-b, 212a

Hesbon in, 185a-b

Horeb in, 189c

Hyle in, 172d-173c

Jerusalem in, 207b-208d, 211a-213a in passing, 430c-431d

Jews in, 215a-b

Lambeth and, 232d-233a

Lamb of God in, 232b

limits in, 241b[b-c]

Locke in, 243d-244a, 243b-c [243d-244a]

London in, 244b-245c [244d-245d]

Los in, 147c-148c, 211a-213a in passing, 251b-253a [251c-253b], 400d

Luvah in, 257b-c[c-d]

Maternal Line in, 266a-b

mills in, 273d-274a

Milton's *History of Britain* and, 275c

moon in, 285c-286b

nations in, 295 (map)

plates of

Jerusalem—plates of (*cont'd*)

arrangements and revisions, 12b-c, 38d, 209d-210c

pl. 4:9-10, 32b-c

pl. 4:30-31, 260c

pl. 4:34, 398c

pl. 5, illus., 147a

pl. 7:48-49, 56c

pl. 11:21-23, 361c

pls. 12-13, 163 (diagram), 165c-d

pl. 14:10-12, 9a

pl. 14, illus., 208c, 340d

pl. 15:2-5, 361c

pl. 15:28, 3d-4a

pl. 15, illus., 4b

pl. 16:61-62, 268b

pl. 17:59-63, 361d

pl. 18, illus., 240c[d]

pl. 21:34, 260c

pl. 21:35, 348c

pl. 22:3, 299d

pl. 23, illus., 390c

pl. 24:4-11, 388a

pl. 24, illus., 300d

pl. 25:1-2, 56b

pl. 25:8-9, 380d

pl. 25, illus., 311d

pl. 26, illus., 173d

pl. 27:81-82, 213c

pl. 28:14, 12b

pl. 28, illus., 75a, 240c-d [240d-241a], 298a, 332d, 363a, illus. V

pl. 29, 382b

pl. 29:9-16, 341d

pl. 29:64, 217a

pl. 32, illus., 106d

pl. 33, 382b

pl. 33:19-21, 75d

pl. 34:39-40, 303d

pl. 34:43-54, 347d

pl. 35[31], illus., 5b

pl. 36:1-14, 347d

pl. 36:36-38, 117c

pl. 38:16-22, 105a-b

pl. 38:55, 210c

pl. 40:21-23, 73b

pl. 40, illus., 304a-c

pl. 41:1, 69b

pl. 41:15-21, 233b

pl. 41, illus., 381a

pl. 43:6, 19c-d

pl. 43:55, 38c, 73c

pl. 44:24-27, 83d

pl. 44[39], illus., 300d

pls. 45-46, 314c-d

pl. 45:19-24, 7b

pl. 45:28-30, 38a

pl. 45:34-32, 314c-d

pl. 45:37-39, 73d

pl. 46:3, 72b-c

pl. 46:24, 434b

Jerusalem—plates of *(cont'd)*
  pl. 46, illus., 118d
  pl. 47, illus., 158b
  pl. 48:9-11, 393c
  pl. 48:35, 340d
  pl. 49:4, 36c
  pl. 49:72-73, 388c-d
  pl. 50:22, 340d
  pl. 50, illus., 173a
  pl. 51, illus., 193c
  pl. 52, 78b, 446d
  pl. 53:9-10, 42c
  pl. 54, illus., 350a, 401d
  pl. 56:13-16, 401c
  pl. 57:6-7, 350d-351a
  pl. 57, illus., 106d, 455d
  pl. 59, 388b
  pl. 59:1, 43c-d
  pl. 60:1-3, 13b
  pl. 61:16, 22c
  pl. 62:8-13, 266a-b
  pl. 62:20-22, 257c[d]
  pl. 63:5, 408c
  pl. 63:11, 445a
  pl. 65:42, 233b
  pl. 66:24-25, 67d
  pls. 67:44-68:9, 18d
  pl. 68:39, 368d
  pl. 70, illus., 109d, 388a
  pl. 72:30-45, 295 (diagram)
  pl. 72:51, 210c
  pl. 73:16, 22b, 306d
  pl. 73:28, 5d
  pl. 73:36, 78b
  pl. 74:39, 68a
  pl. 75:24, 86a
  pl. 76, illus., 95c
  pl. 77, 323b
  pl. 79:11-12, 157b
  pl. 79:40-44, 398a
  pl. 81, illus., 66a, 169c-d, 433d
  pl. 82:45, 107b, 170a-b
  pl. 83:40-41, 262b, 418d
  pl. 83:59-60, 19d, 242d-243a [243b]
  pls. 84:31-85:4, 67c
  pl. 84, illus., 106d
  pl. 85:1-2, 170a
  pl. 87, illus., 400d
  pl. 88:20, 377a
  pl. 89:24-25, 28b-c
  pl. 89:39, 84c
  pl. 90:19-22, 56d
  pl. 90:24-25, 49b
  pl. 90:30, 449d
  pl. 90:34-35, 83c, 449d
  pl. 90:40-43, 56d
  pl. 91:8-13, 158d
  pls. 93-94, 25d
  pl. 93, illus., 25d
  pl. 94, illus., 25d
  pl. 97:16-98:2, 74a-b

Jerusalem—plates of *(cont'd)*
  pl. 98:9, 359b
  pl. 98:43, 118a, 242a[b]
  pl. 100, illus., 109c, 366a
plow in, 329d-330b
Rahab in, 212a, 213a, 339b-d, 340a-b
religion's wheel in, 345b-c
Reuben in, 209d, 211c, 213c, 347c-348d
Scofield in, 361a-d
Shelley in. See *Jerusalem*, Bard of Oxford
  in
Shiloh in, 371d-372a
Southey's opinion of, 209a, 315b-c
spectres in, 210c, 211b-213a in passing,
  381d-382a, 383b-c
states in, 386d-387a
Stedman's *Narrative* in, 7b
Tree of Mystery in, 411b-c
Ulro in, 150c
Urizen in, 423d-424a
Urizen's sons in, 426a
Urthona in, 426b-d
Vala in, 11d-12c, 16a, 148a-b, 211a, c, d,
  430c-431d
Vala's veil in, 211a, 432c-d
wheels in, 345b-c, 445c-446c
Whitefield in, 446d
mentioned, 217b
Jesus, 213a-214d. *See also* Incarnation;
  Trinity
Albion and, 9d, 10a
Apuleius's *Golden Ass* and, 26b
Bath symbol of, 37c-d
as Christ, 82c, 140a, 409a, illus. XI (#1)
as Creator, 94c
cross and, 95a-c
Divine Family as, 60c
error and, 214d, 311b-c
in *Everlasting Gospel*, 133c-d
as an Eye of God, 159c-d, 217d
forgiveness and, 141c-142b, 213b, 214c,
  287b
genealogies of, 98d, 213b, 265d-266c
God as, 158b-159d, 214b, 393a, b
as healer, 104a, c-d
in "Hervey's *Meditations*," illus. XI (#16)
Holy Ghost as, 187a
Imagination as, 28c, 104d-105a, 330b
in *Jerusalem*, 13c, 208a-b
in *Job* illustrations, 222c, 223a (twice)
Lamb of God as, 232a
at Last Judgment, 235a, b
Law and, 213a, 214b, d, 287b
as liberator, 106d
limits set by, 355b-c
lion as, 242b, 241d [242b]
Los and, 209a, 247a, 246d [247a]
Luvah associated with, 255b-c[c-d]
Mary Magdalene and, 214c, 263d-264a
Mary the Virgin and, 213a-c, 264a-265a
  in passing

Jesus (cont'd)
as Messiah, 20c, 214a, 262d, 270d
in *Milton*, 280c
in Milton's work, 276d
Moses and, 227c
Nature and, 213c-d, 369d
as One Man, 105a-b
prophets and, 214d, 335c
Providence and, 335d
purpose of, 345b
revolution and, 213d, 214b, c, 349a
sacraments and, 353d
Second Coming of, 94d, 392b, 393b
secret child as, 363a
as state, 386d
not supernatural, 264b
as Transgressor, 88a-b, 409b
virtues and, 436b
war permitted by, 257c[d]
Whitefield's view of, 447a
as Word, 269a, 386b, 450c-d
mentioned, 88a, 134[d], 134d [135a]
(twice), 187b, 205d
Jewels, *See* Stones, precious
Jews, 214d-216a. *See also* Israel
art of, 350c
culture of, 167d, 215a, 215d-216a
Heber and, 179b
in *Jerusalem*, 210d, 215a-b
Maternal Line and, 215d, 266b-c
religion of, 326b-c
Sanhedrim of, 355a
Sihon and, 372d, 385d
in "VLJ," illus. I (#73)
Jew's-Harp-House, 216a-b; 448b
Jimson, Gulley, 268d, 320b
Job, 216b-223a.
boils of Job in, 49d
Providence in, 217c, 447c
revolution of Job in, 349a
Satan as tempter in, 357a
text of
iv:14, 316c
xvii:14, 149d, 216d
xix:27, 342b-c
xxviii:18, 352a
xli:1, 240a[b]
wrath and Job's curse in, 452d
Job, B's illustrations of
earlier engravings, water colors,
paintings, and drawings, 216d-217a,
222b
Illustrations of the Book of Job
Behemoth in, 39b-c, 118a, 221a, b,
240a[b]
Eyes of God in, 134d [135a], 217a-b,
222d-223a
Grave illustrations and, 48d, 217b
left and right symbolism in, 173d-174a,
217c, 217d-222d in passing
Lord's Supper in, 222a, c, 289d
music in, 217d, 222c, d, 289d-290a

Job (cont'd)
Illustrations of the Book of Job (cont'd)
mysticism in, 221d, 291d, 292a
Pahad in, 316c, 222d, 223a
plates of
title page, 217c-d, 368c
pl. 1, 217d, 289d
pl. 6, 49d, 140a, 166c, 219a-b,
244a[c], 364d, 388b, 408d
pl. 7, 219b, 388b
pl. 9, 141a, 219c, 316c
pl. 10, 219c-d, 313c, 316c
pl. 11, 139a, 153d-154a, 219d, 342b-c
pl. 13, 117a, 141a, 192a, 220b-c
pl. 14, 61d, 189d, 220c-221a, 419b
pl. 15, 39b-c, 112c, 221a-b, 240a[b],
363a
pl. 16, 221c, 235a
pl. 17, 192a, 221c-d, 316c
pl. 18, 221d-222a, 289d
pl. 20, 222b-c, 289d
pl. 21, 222c-d, 258c, 289d-290a
Satan in, 49d, 217c, 219d, 221c
Urizen in, 26a, 189d, 221a, 390a
"Job in His Prosperity," 126a-b, 217a,
258a[c], 289d
mentioned, 319a-b
"Job in His Prosperity," 126a-b, 217a,
258a[c], 289d
"Job, Wife, and Friends," 216d
John, text of
i:14, 105b
ii:4, 83d, 378c, 407d
xi, 236b[c]
xvii:21-23, 105a-b
John Groat's House [John o'Groat's House],
223a-b
John of Patmos, Saint. *See* John the
"Divine"
Johnson, Joseph, 145d, 199c[d], [236c]
Johnson, Samuel, 71d, 72d, 242c[d], 337b
Rasselas, 195b
John the Baptist, 223b; illus. I (#13)
John the "Divine," 223b-c; 323b, 409a, 458d
"Join, or Die," 21c, 435c
Joktan, 223c
Jonah, 272c
Jones, Inigo, 72c, d, 181c, 241c[d], 387d,
441b
Jonson, Ben, 331a
Jordan, 223c-d
Joseph, Count Truchsess, 412a
Joseph, son of Jacob, 223d-224d; 202c
B's paintings of, 224a-b[b]
Gate of, 91c, 102a
Joseph of Arimathea, 224d-225b
"Joseph of Arimathea among the Rocks
of Albion," 224d-225a, 272b
"Joseph of Arimathea Preaching to the
Inhabitants of Britain," 225b
Joseph of Nazareth, 225b-c
genealogy of, 265d-266c

Joseph of Nazareth (cont'd)
  Jesus and, 213b-c
  Mary the Virgin and, 208a, 213a-b,
    225b-c, 264a-b
  in "VLJ," illus. I (#13)
Joshua, 225d; 65c
Joshua, 225d
Jove, 225d-226a [226a]. *See also* Jupiter
Joy in B's religion, 344d
Joyce, James: *Finnegans Wake*, 143b
Judah, 226a-b; 69b, 226c, 241d [242b]
Jude 9, B's water color of, 272a, 286c, 287d
Judea, 226b-c[c]; 69b, 226a-b, 241d [242b]
Judges. *See* Elohim
Judges, 226c; 297b
Judgment, Day of. *See* Last Judgment
Judgment, Last. *See* Last Judgment
Jung, Carl Gustav, ix, 458d
Jupiter, 226d-227a[b]
  Capaneus and, 69b
  heaven of, 327d
  as Jove, 226a
  Mercury and, 269a
  of Plato, in B's designs, 91c
Justice, 227c
  Antichrist as, 25c
  Commandments as, 90a
  Elohim as, 119a, 227c
  in *Jerusalem*, 56c, 227c
  London Stone symbol of, 245d [246a]
  mercy and, 90c-d, 227c, 269c, d
  Michael as, 272a
  Og symbol of, 306b
  origins of, 345a-b
  Orion as, 288d, 311c
  in "Spenser's *Faerie Queene*," 384a, b, c
  vengeance and, 433b
  in "VLJ," 306b, illus. I (#35)
Justin Martyr: *Apology*, 269a

Kabbalah and Kabbalism, 9d, 215d
Kadesh [Meribah Kadesh], 269d-270a
Kaffraria [Caffraria], 64b
Kambreda, 66a
Kanah River, 228a
Katherine, Queen: B's painting of, 370c
Kelly, George: *Craig's Wife*, 448a
Kelpius, 450a
Kensington Gardens, 228a-b
Kent, 228b
Kentish-town, 228b-c
Kerry, 228c
Keynes, Sir Geoffrey
  Blake Studies, 61c-d, 229a
  *Illustrations of the Book of Job by William
    Blake* (ed. with George Goyder), 217b
  1925 text of B, 144b-c
  owns B's copy of Wesley *Hymns*, 444b
  Sipsop identified by, 199c[d]
  William Blake's Illustrations to the Bible, 46b,
    286c
Kidneys [Reins], 342b-c

Kidron, Valley of, 205c
Kildare, 228c
Kilkenny, 228d
Kincard[ine], 228d
Kinder Scout [Peak], 324c
King Edward the Third, 228d-229b; 9b, 61a,
    90d, 144c, 152c, 156a
King Lear (Shakespeare), 370d, 448a
"King of Babylon in Hell, The," 34c, 83b
Kings, 300a, illus. I (#50)
Kings, 229b; 153d
King's County, 229b
Kinros[s], 229b
Kiralis, Karl, 210c
Kirkubriht [Kirkcudbright], 229b-c
Kishon, 229c
Klopstock, Friedrich Gottlieb, 229c; 232d,
    301c
  Messias, 177c, 229c
Knowledge. *See also* Wisdom
  science as, 359c, illus. I (#65)
  theory of, 239c-d [239d-240a], 243a-b[b]
Koban [Coban], 89b-c, 172d-173c
Kock [Kox], Private, 171c, 229d-230a, 361d
Koran, 236a, 259b, c-d, 343b
Kotope, 229d; 385d
Kox, 229d-230b; 171c, 361d
Kromarty, 230b
Kwantok [Gwantok], 168c-d

Laban, 231a-b; 236d[c], illus. I (#74)
Labor, 235d, illus. I (#26)
Labyrinth, 350d, 351a
Lacedaemonians, 231b
Lacedemonian Instruction, 231b
Lachesis. *See* Fates, Three
Lactantius: *De irae dei*, 182c
Lady of the Lake, 270b
Lafayette, Marquis de, 231b-d
Lake, 231d-232a
  of Fire, 139a, 231d-232a, 235b
  of Urizen, 232a
L'Allegro (Milton). See Milton, John,
  L'Allegro
Lamb, Caroline, 63c [1st pr. only]
Lamb, Charles, 78d, 102d, 414a
Lamb
  B's vision of, 362d
  creation of, 269c
  of God, 10c, 232a-b
  Lambeth the house of, 233a
  lion and, 242a[b]
  Song of, 222d
"Lamb, The," 232a, 386b, 414a, 450d
Lambeth, 232b-233c; 20a, 26a, 31b, 181c,
    391b-c
"Lambeth and Bethlehem in Blake's
  Jerusalem" (Erdman), 232c
Lambeth Books, 232d. See also *America*;
  Book of Ahania; *Book of Los*; *Book of
  Urizen*; *Europe*; *Song of Los*
Lambeth Road, 42c

Lambeth Vale, 32b
Lamech, 233c-d
"Lamech and His Two Wives," 233d
Lamia, 233d
Lamps, 233d
Lamson, Alvan: *The Church of the First Three Centuries*, 450d
Lanarkshire [Lanerk], 234a
Lancashire, 233d-234a; 375c, 385d
Landaff, 234a
"Landscape Near Felpham" 137b
Lanerk, 234a
Laocoön, B's engraving of, 234b-c
  Adam and Adamah in, 5a, 6c
  Angel of the Divine Presence in, 23c, 234b, 455a
  Lilith in, 234c, 240b-c[d]
  Ophiuchus and, 234c, 309b, 373a
  serpents in, 234b, c, 306c-d, 366a
  Troy's history symbolized in, 412a
Laoighis [Queen's County], 337a
Lark, 234c-d; 279c, 280c, 292a-b, 307d
Larma, 233d
Last Judgment, 235a-236b. *See also* Harvest; Revelation; *Vision of the Last Judgment*
  Ahania at, 8d
  Albion at, 10b-11a
  in *America*, 21c
  apocatastasis and, 296d-297a
  art and science at, 299b
  in Bible, 45b, 235a. See also *Revelation*
  in B's letter to Humphrey, 235c, 450a
  B's pictures of, 235b-236a
    Blair's *Grave*, Last-Judgment design for, 106d, 192a, 235b
    fresco, 235d-236a, 437c
    Hell in, 180b
    Mary the Virgin in, 265a
    Petworth version, 28a, 95a, 192a (twice), 235b-c
    Rosenwald version, 235c-d, illus. I, with key
      Angels of *Revelation* in, 23b
      giants in, 155b-c
      pencil sketch for, 235c
      Zoas in, 459c
      numbers below refer to figures in key to illus. I
        No. 1, 28a, 187c-d
        No. 6, 82a
        No. 8, 353d
        No. 9, 460b
        No. 13, 265a, 353d
        No. 14, 460b
        No. 16, 272a
        No. 17, 272a
        No. 19, 192a
        No. 24, 192a
        No. 25, 192a
        No. 26, 235d
        No. 28, 26d, 84c-d
        No. 29, 84c-d, 95a

Last Judgment (cont'd)
  B's pictures of (*cont'd*)
    figures in key to illus. I (cont'd)
      No. 31, 118b
      No. 32, 433d
      No. 35, 306b
      No. 37, 287d
      No. 38, 140b
      No. 39, 179a
      No. 41, 64d, 327a
      No. 42, 64d, 327a
      No. 48, 433b
      No. 49, 433b
      No. 60, 366d
      No. 62, 366d
      No. 63, 366d
      No. 64, 82a, c, 450b
      No. 66, 366d
      No. 67, 366d
      No. 68, 371c
      No. 69, 366d
      No. 70, 171c
      No. 71, 171c, 199b[c]
      No. 73, 82a
      No. 76, 168a
      No. 80, 199b[c], 259b-c
  Creation reversed by, 151c
  in *Four Zoas*, 236a-b
  in Koran, 236a, 259d
  Los at, 250b-c [250c-251a]
  Luvah at, 257a-b[b-c]
  materialism and, 299b
  in Michelangelo, 272c
  Mystery destroyed at, 433b
  Normans and, 301d
  in Paracelsus, counterpart of, 322c
  Rahab cast out at, 340a-b
  sex begins the, 344a[b]
  Swedenborg's idea of, 235a, 392b, 393b
  Tharmas at, 400b-d
  time and, 405a
  Urizen at, 420c, 422a-b
  Urizen's sons at, 426a
  Urthona at, 426d-427a
  war of nations and, 294c
  Zoas at, 459d-460b
  mentioned, 162a
Last Judgment (Swedenborg), 262c
Last Supper, 246c[d]
"Laughing Song," 258a[c]
Laughter, 456a
Lavater, Johann Kaspar, [236b-c]; 4d, 343b, 402c
  [*Aphorisms on Man*, 16d, 236c—2nd pr. only]
    [B's annotations to, 236c—2nd pr. only]
Law, Rev. William, 39d
Law, profession, 290a, 319c
Law, codes of behavior. *See also* Abstraction; Commandments; Decalogue; Good and evil
  Albion and, 11d-12b, 15d

Law (cont'd)
in Ark of the Covenant, 27d
genius and, 88a-b
Horeb and, 189b-c
in Interpreter's Parlor, 62c-d
in Jerusalem, 56d
Jesus and, 213a, 214b-d, 264a, 409b,
436b
in Job illustrations, 217d (twice), 219d
Leutha and, 237d [238a]
Mt. Ebal and, 113d
music and, 290a, 319c
One-, 308b-c
in "Paul Preaching," 324b
Paul's attitude toward, 323c
of the Pharisees, 326b
Reuben and, 37b
scribes and, 166b
sex under, 237d [238a]
Sinai symbol of, 374b
Theotormon and, 401d
in Urizen's Book of Brass, 58b-c
in "VLJ," illus. I (#36, 64)
Lawrence, Sir Thomas, 412b-c
Lazarus, 236b-c[c-d]; 94a, 254d [255a],
265a, 323c-d
Leah, 236c[d]; 338a
mother of, illus. XI (#10)
Learning. See Knowledge; Wisdom
Leaves, 314c-d
Lebanon, 236d-237a [237a-b]
Lebanon, Mount, 301b
Lee, "Light Horse" Harry, 237a[b]
Lee, Nathaniel, 237a-b[b-c]
Rival Queens, 237a[b]
"To Mr. Dryden, on His Poem of
Paradise," 110d
Left and right symbolism, 237b[c-d]
for feet, 140b-d, 354d
in Gates of Paradise, 140b, 285b
for hands, 140b, 173d-174a
in Il Penseroso illustrations, 227a
in Job illustrations, 140a, 173d-174a,
217c-223a in passing
in Milton, 140c-d, 174a, 354d-355a
Legends of the Jews (Ginzberg), 347b
Legions, 237b-c[d]; 38b, 69b
Leibitz, Baron Gottfried Wilhelm, 100d
Leicester[shire], 237c-d [237d-238a]
Leinster, 237d [238a]
Leitrim, 237d [238a]
Leix [Queen's County], 337a
L'Estrange, Roger: Seneca's Morals, 364a
Length, 103d
Leprosy, 49d
Letters Concerning the Northern Coast of Antrim
(Hamilton), 156c
Letters on the Study of History (Bolingbroke),
50a
"Let the Brothels of Paris Be Opened,"
301c, 411c-d

Leutha, 237d-239a [238a-239c]
Antamon and, 25a, 124c (diagram),
130c-d, 237d [238a], a[b-c]
as Bromion's emanation, 60a, 237d [238a]
death and, 100a, 238b[c]
dogs of, 200c[d], 239a[b-c]
in Milton, 178c-d, 238b-239a [238c-239b],
277c-280d
name of, 312d
Palamabron and, 238c-239a [238d-239b],
321d
rainbow of, 238a[b] (twice), c[d], 340c
sex and, 124c (diagram), 132b, 237d-238b
[238a-c]
sin as, 25a, 237d [238a], b-c[c-d], 357d
Vale of, 238a[b], 265c
Leutha's Dogs, Isle of, 200c[d], 239a[b]
Levi and Levites, 239b-c[c-d], 240b[c]; 149b
Leviathan, 239c-240b [239d-240c]
Behemoth and, 39b-c, 239c[d], 240d-241a
[240a-c]
in Job, 216c, 239c[d], 240a[b], a-b[c]
in Job illustrations, 221a, b, 240a[b]
war symbol of, 442b
Leviathan (Hobbes), 239c-d [239d-240a]
"Leviathan, The Spiritual Form of Nelson
Guiding," 240a-b, 239d-240a [240a-b]
Levinson, Dr. Ronald, 396c
Levites and Levi, 239b-c[c-d], 240b[c]; 149b
Liberator (Garrison), 317c
Liberty. See also Marriage of Heaven and
Hell
plates of, pls. 25-27
Alps and, 18c
America as, 19b
in America, 232d
Beulah's daughters protect, 44a
in B's religion, 344b-c
in Greece, 168a
Jerusalem as, 206c, 206d-208d, 211a,
395b-c
in King Edward the Third, 229a
in Mental Traveller, 268c-d
war and, 356c
Libido, 262b
Libya [Lybia], 257d [258a]
Lichfield [Litchfield], 242c[d]
Life
Book of, illus. I (#18)
holiness of, 133c[d]
journey of, 149c-d. See also Experience
Tree of. See Tree, of Life
"Life, The Circle of." See "Circle of Life"
"Life of Blake" (Cunningham), quoted,
136c
Life of Cowper (Hayley), 177d
Life of George Washington (Marshall), 443a
Life of Romney (Hayley), 177c
Life of Thomas Stothard (Bray), 267a
Life of William Blake (Gilchrist). See
Gilchrist, Alexander, Life of William Blake

Life of William Blake (Wilson), 412a
Lilith, 240c-d[b-c]; 5d, 215d, 234c, 343b
Lilly, 240c-d [240d-241a]
  in *Book of Thel*, 52b, 240c[d], 401b
  in *Jerusalem* 28, illus., 75a, 240c-d
    [240d-241a]
  in *Job* illustrations, 222b
  rose and, 240c[d], 351a
"Lilly, The," 191d, 240c[d], 283c, 351a
"Lilly, Two Lovers in the." See *Jerusalem*,
    plates of, pl. 28
Lily. *See* Lilly
Limerick, 240d [241a-b]
Limits, 240d-241b [241b-c]
  of contraction, 6a, 240d-241b [241b-c]
  Divine Hand finds the, 106b, 241a
    [241b-c]
  Jesus set, 241a[b], 355b-c
  of opacity, 240d-241b [241b-c], 309a
  on senses, 365a
  Urizen and, 419a
Lincoln, 241b-c[c-d]
Lincolnshire, 241c-d [241d-242a]
Lincoln's Inn, 241c[d]
Lincoln's Inn Chapel, 72c, 181c, 241c[d]
Lincoln's Inn Fields, 166d, 167a, 241c[d]
Line, 319b-c. *See also* Circumference;
    Minute Particulars
Lineaments, 241d [242a]
Linlithgo[w], 241d [242a]
Linnell, John, 172a, 209b, 217a-b, 222b
Lion, 241d-242c [242a-d]
  in *Genesis* Ms., 151d
  in Golgonooza, 163 (diagram)
  in "The Little Girl Lost," 242a-b[b-c],
    257d
  Tyger and, 242b[c], 413d-414a
  wolf and, 242a[b], 449c-d
  wrath of, 242b[c], 453c
  Zoa as, 241d-242a [242a], 458d
Lion Heart, 349c
Lisbon earthquake of 1755, 100d
Litchfield, 242c[d]
literalism, 83b-c
"Little Boy Lost, A" (*Songs of Experience*),
    82c, 291b
"Little Boy Lost, The" (*Songs of Innocence*),
    200b[c]
"Little Girl Found, The" (*Songs of Innocence*,
    Songs of Experience), 22c, 99c,
    242a-b[b-c], 257d-258a [258a-c], 449d
"Little Girl Lost, A" (*Songs of Experience*),
    258a[b], 308b
"Little Girl Lost, The" (*Songs of Innocence*,
    Songs of Experience), 22c, 75b-c, 99c,
    242a-b[b-c], 257d-258a [258a-c]
Little Tom the Sailor (Hayley), 177b
"The Little Vagabond," illus., 358c
Liverpool, 242c[d]
Living creatures. *See* Zoas
Lizard Point, 242c-d [242d-243a]
Llama, 233d

Llandaff [Landaff], 234a
Llewellyn, Prince of Wales, 242d-243a
    [243a-b]
Locke, John, 243a-d [243b-244a]
  Bacon, Newton, and, 100c, 243b[c],
    243c-d [243d-244a], 343b, 359b
  Carolina constitution and, 69d
  Essay Concerning Human Understanding,
    243a[b]
  Fall of Man and, 57d
  system of, as ratio, 341b
  in *There is No Natural Religion*, 402c-d
  in *Visions*, 57d, 243b[c]
Locrine, King, 129a, 169a
Logic, 4c, 273c, 345b
Logos, 269a, 386b, 450c-d
Loins, 243-244a [244a-c]; 89c, 308b, 399c
London, county, 55d
London, city, 244b-246b [244c-246c]. *See
    also place names*
  Bishop of, 246a[b]
  Jews of, 215d-216a
  maps of, illus. VI, VII
  Middlesex and, 272c
  in a quaternary, 137d, 245b-c[c-d]
  social conditions in, 244b-245a
    [244c-245b], 281c
  Tower of, 246a-b[b-c], 255a[b]
  as Troja Nova, 61a
London (Baedeker), 372b
"London," 244b[c-d], 320d
Londonderry, 246b[c]
London Magazine, 209b
London's Guardian, 246a[b]
London's River. *See* Thames
London Stone, 47a, 245c-d [245d-246b]
Longford, 246b[c]
Looking Glass, 246b-c[c-d]; 393b, illus. I
    (#77)
Looms, 74b-c, 255b[c]
"Lord Answers Job Out of the Whirlwind,
    The," water color, 216d-217a
Lord's Supper, 246d; 222a, c, 289d-290a,
    353c-354a, illus. I (#11)
Lorenzo in *Night Thoughts*, 455d
Lorrain, Claude, 412b
Los, 246c-253c [246d-254a]. *See also Book of
    Los; Song of Los*
  children of, 22b, 130c-d, 201d-202c,
    253a-c [253b-254a], 254a[b], 324a,
    331d, 347b-c, 454a. *See also names of the
    children*
  Councellors of, 72c, 241b[c]
  as Creator, 94c, 247b-c[c-d]
  Elijah and, 118c
  Elohim and, 119d
  emanations and, 381d-382a
  Enitharmon and, 8a-b, 124b-125a, 247d
    [248a], 248b-250d [248c-251a] in
    passing, 251c-251d [251d-252a] in
    passing, 252d [253a]
  error given form by, 355c

Los (cont'd)
  furnaces of, 138a-b, 146d-148c, 232a,
    247a-b[c], 387b
  Gates of, 67a, 445c-d, 388b
  Golgonooza and, 162d-165d, 247b[c]
  in Jerusalem, 147c-148c, 211a-213a in
    passing, 251b-253a [251c-253b], 400d
  Jesus and, 209a, 246d [247a]
  limits and, 241a-b [241b-c]
  marriage of, 8a-b
  Mercury and, 269a
  mercy and justice combined by, 269d
  in Milton, 147c, 175b-d, 250d-251b
    [251a-c], 277b, 278b, c, d, 280c-d
  nostrils and, 302d-303a
  Oedipus theory and, 76a-b
  Orc and, 124d, 247a[b], 253a[b], 309c,
    309d-310a, 453a
  printing press of, 251a[b], 335a, 446c
  prophecy and, 247a[b], 331d, 335a-b
  Reuben and, 347c-d
  sculptures of halls of, 362c-d
  spectres and, 249c-250a [249d-250b],
    250c-d [250d-251a], 251c-d [252a],
    318d-382a, 383a-b
  sun formed by, 246d [247a], b-c[d], 247d
    [248a], 390b
  time and, 379d-380a, 404b
  as "twenty-eighth," 67a, 247c[d]
  Urthona and, 12c-d, 246c-d [246d-247a],
    335b, 426c, d
Los, The Book of. See Book of Los
Los, The Song of. See Song of Los
Lot, 253d [254a]
Lotho; 253d [254a]
Lot's wife, 253d [254a]
Lotus, 240d [241a]
Love. See also Affections; Sex
  Ark as, 27c, 300d
  in Beulah, 43a
  Brotherhood and, 60d
  in Crystal Cabinet, 95c
  dove as, 107a
  fire as, 138c
  free, 25b, 367b
  Generation as, 150c
  God as, 271c
  God's, 232a-b
  Havilah as, 176b, 327a
  jealousy and, 205a-b
  lilly as, 240c-d [240d-241a]
  Luvah Prince of, 255a[b]
  moon as, 9b, 285b-286b
  nostrils as, 302c
  pearl as, 324d, 325a, 352a
  rose as, 351a
  secretive, 308d, 309a, 314a-b
  of self, 194d-195a, 401a. See also Selfhood
  seraphim spirits of, 365a
  silver as, 371b
  between time and space, 404d-405a
  Urizen's Book of, 424c

Love (cont'd)
  Venus goddess of, 433d
  in "VLJ," illus. I (#77)
  wine-press of, 449a
  wisdom and, 393b
"Love and Harmony Combine," 410b
Loves of the Plants, The (Darwin), 411c
Lowth, 253d [254a]
Luban, 253d-254a [254a-b]; 74b
Lucifer, 254a-c[b-d]. See also Satan
  in Byron's Cain vs. Satan in Ghost of Abel,
    153b-154b
  as Eye of God, 134b[c], 134d [135a]
    (twice), 186a, 254b[c]
  in Job illustrations, 134d [135a], 222d,
    223a
  in Milton, 279b
  morning star as, 186a, 254a-b[b-c]
Lucius, King, 237c[d]
Luke, as Zoa, 458d
Luke, 85b, 318a, 354b
Lungs, 57a
Lust, 122c
"Lustful, The Circle of the," 97d
Luther, Martin, 254c-255a [254d-255b];
  324a
Luvah, 255a-257c [255b-257d]. See also Zoa
  Beautiful Man as, 209a
  boils from, 219a
  bulls of, 62a-b, 118d
  center as, 75c
  in "Circle of Life," 87a
  crucifixion of, 67d, 257c[d]
  east and, 113c
  Job and, 217a
  lyre of, 258a[c]
  music and, 258a[c], 289d
  Orc and, 256d [257a], 309b-d, 310d-311c,
    441d-442a
  Theotormon and, 401d
  Tyger and, 413c
  Vala and, 255c-257c [255d-257d] in
    passing, 295d, 429a-b, 429c-430a, 430d
  vintage and, 257a-b[b-c], 435a
  wine-press of, 442b
Lybia, 257d [258a]
Lyca, 257d-258a [258a-c]; 99c
Lycon, 25d, 376a
Lyre, 258a-c[c-d]

Macbeth (Shakespeare), 370b, 390a
  B's illustrations of, 370c, c-d
MacCool, Finn, 156c
Machpelah, 259a
Macpherson, James. See Ossian
Madoc, Welsh prince, 243a[b]
Madoc (Southey), 243a[b]
"Madonna and Child" (Dürer), 412c
Madrid, 259a
"Mad Song," 331b
Magdalen [Mary Magdalene], 263d-264a
Maggots, 259b

Magog, 152c, 162a-b, b-c, illus. I (#54)
Mahalaleel, 259a
Mahlah, 457c
Mahomet [Mahomed], 259b-d; 199a-b[c], illus. I (#80)
Maimonides, Moses, 119a
Makuth, 259d
Malah, 260a
Malbecco, 385a, 402b, 438c
Malden [Maldon], 260a-c
Male, 89a-b, 120d, 280a, 367c-d. See also Spectre
Male Babe, 268c, d
Malkin, Benjamin Heath, 331b, 370d
    Father's Memoirs, 414c-d, 433d
Malvern Hills, 260c
Mammon, 260c
Mam-Tor, 260d
Mam-Win, 260d
Man, bishopric, 377a
Man. See also Albion; Brotherhood; Humanity
    Ark as, 27d
    average, 347b
    Beautiful, 209a, 375d
    B's theory of nature of, 16d
    brotherhood of. See Brotherhood of Man
    cherubim of, 80c
    Eternal. See Albion
    fallen, 9c, 309a. See also Albion; Fall of Man
    Four Faces of, 364d
    in Genesis Ms., 151d-152a
    God as. See God, as humanity
    history of, in Song of Los, 248a[b]
    Holy Ghost and, 187a-b
    imagination and, 195b
    as microcosm, 14a
    Natural, 6a, 151d-152a, 270b, 351c
    One, 105a
    as Poetic Genius, 330b-c
    Strong, 208d-209a, 375d
    threefold form of, 379b
    Ugly, 197b[c], 209a, 375d
    as Zoa, 458d
Managhan, 260d
Manasseh [Manazzoth, Menassheh], 260d-261b; 37b, 224a, 308c
Manathu-Varcyon, 261b-c; 124c (diagram), 130c, d, 132b
Manchester, 261c-d
Mandrake, 261d-262a
Manhood in Jerusalem, 210d
"Man Sweeping the Interpreter's Parlor, The," 62c-d
Map of the Country Sixty-Five Miles round London (Andrews and Dury), illus. VII
Maps
    "London and Neighboring Villages," illus. VII
    "London from Lincoln's Inn to Lambeth," illus. VI

Maps (cont'd)
    "The Thirty-Two Nations," 295
Marchantes Tale, The (Chaucer), 79c
Margoliouth, H. M.: Vala, Blake's Numbered Text, 144c, 401a
Marie Antoinette as Rahab, 411d
Marigold [Marygold], 265b-d
Mariolatry, 264b, 449d
Mark, 242a[b], 458d
Mark iii:29, 318a
Marriage. See also Beulah
    in Behmen's heaven, no, 41b
    cage symbol of, 64b, 297d
    Canaan as, 66c
    in "Circle of Life," 87c
    earthly, 18a, 66c
    female in, 305d-306a. See also Emanation
    in Heaven, 41b, 190b-c
    in Il Penseroso illustrations, 328a
    incest and, 196a-b
    in Jerusalem 28, illus., 240d [241a]
    of Lamb and Jerusalem, 206c
    mirtle symbol of, 282c, 410b
    in My Spectre, 121d, 290d-291a
    mystical, 94d
    net as, 240d [241a]
    Swedenborg's view of, 393b
    Thames and Medway symbols of, 267a
    worm and, 348b, 452c
Marriage of Heaven and Hell, The, 262a-263c
    aim of, 94d
    angels in, 23a, 24c, 262b
    Behmen and, 40d-41a, 263a
    devils in, 103b, 262b
    Edom and, 116a
    [Everlasting Gospel and, 133c—2nd pr. only]
    Ezekiel in, 135a-c[c]
    fire in, 138d
    Hell in, 180b-c, 231d-232a
    Jacob and, 116a
    Jehovah in, 206a
    Leviathan in, 239d [240a]
    Messiah in, 270d
    Milton and, 275a-b, 357b-c
    mind in, 262b-c, 394a-c
    oak in, 410b
    One Law in, 308b-c
    Orc in, 263c, 310a-b, 377c
    plates of
        pl. 1, title page, illus., 138d
        pl. 2, Argument, 116a, 191d, 204b, 350a
        pl. 3, 116a, 204b, 235b
        pls. 5-6, 187b, 216d, 270d, 276d-277a
        pls. 6-7, 409c
        pl. 7, proverb 2, 329b
        pl. 7, proverb 6, 329b
        pl. 7, proverb 14, 303d
        pl. 8, proverb 14, 242a[b]
        pl. 8, proverb 27, 449d
        pl. 8, proverb 34, 118a
        pl. 9, proverb 4, 329b

Marriage of Heaven and Hell, The (cont'd)
  plates of (cont'd)
    pl. 11, 344a
    pl. 11, illus., 75b
    pls. 11-13, 330c
    pls. 12-13, 98c-d
    pl. 14, 75a. 410c
    pl. 15, illus., 112a-b, 271d
    pl. 16, 97c
    pls. 17-20, 273c, 305b
    pl. 19, 24c, 25a, 85a
    pl. 20, 238a-b[c]
    pl. 20, illus., 366a
    pl. 22, 40a, 158d, 322b
    [*pls. 22-24*, 133c—2nd pr. only]
    pl. 23, 392c
    pl. 24, 406d-407a
    pl. 24, illus., 297c
    pls. 25-27, A Song of Liberty, 19c, 377c
    pl. 26, para. 15, 118a
    pls. 26-27, para. 18, 385d, 420c (twice)
    pl. 27, para. 20, 189d, 420b, 449d
    pl. 27, Chorus, 133c[d]
  plow in, 329b
  Proverbs of Hell in. *See above, pls. 7-9*
  psychology in, 394a-c
  senses in, 364b-c
  sex in, 394b
  Song of Liberty in. *See above, pls. 25-27*
  subconscious in. *See* Subconscious, in *The Marriage*
  Swedenborg and, 23a, 262c, d, 263a (twice), 392c, 393a, 394a-c
  Urizen in, 263c, 310a-b, 377c, 420c, 422c
  viper in, 435d
  Visions and, 437d
  mentioned, 232d
Mars, 263c-d
  heaven of, 327d (twice)
  in *Il Penseroso* illustrations, 227a, 263d
  Venus and, 433d, 442c
  sulphur sun and, 390a
  mentioned, 334c
Marsh, Edward Garrard, 315a
Marshall, John: *Life of George Washington*, 443a
Martin, Albin, 217a
Marvell, Andrew, 110c
Marybone, 265b
Marygold, 265b-d
Marylebone [Marybone], 265b
Mary-le-bone Park Farm, 448b
Mary Magdalene, 263d-264a
Mary the Virgin, 264a-265a. *See also* Joseph of Nazareth
  B's attitude toward, 83d-84a
  as Body of Death, 74c
  Eve as, 133b
  geneology of, 264c-d, 265d-266c
  Holy Ghost and, 187b, 264b-c in passing
  in *Jerusalem*, 208a
  Jesus and, 213a-c, 264a-265a in passing

Mary the Virgin (*cont'd*)
  Marygold and, 265c
  "Queen of Heaven in Glory," 84a, 98a, 246c[d], 390c
  Swedenborg's idea of, 213b, 264d, 393a-b
  in "VLJ," 235d, 265a, illus. I (#13, 79)
  as the woman, 449d
  worship of, 264b, 449d
Massachusetts Spy, ship, 21c
Massachusetts Spy (Revere), 145d
Masturbation, 265c
Materialism. *See also* Matter
  Bacon, Newton, and Locke represent, 35b
  church and, 82c
  Commandments and, 90c
  in *Europe*, 132b-c
  False Tongue as, 408b, c
  in history, 248a[b]
  left and, 237b[d]
  of Newton, 298c, 299a
  in Oxford, 313d-314a
  Starry Wheels represent, 445c
  Tiriel analyzes failure of, 405b-c
  in "VLJ," 235d, illus. I (#26)
Maternal Humanity, 191a
Maternal Line, 265d. *See also* names of people in the Line
  B discovers, 215d
  Lamech and, 233d
  Los's daughters and, 253c[d], 265d
  miscegenation emphasized by, 36b, 266b-c
  Transgressors in, 264c-d, 266c
Matha, 266c-d; 312d
Mathematics in Taylor's thought, 396d, 397c
Mathew, A. S., 199d [200a] (twice), 330d
Mathew, William Henry, son of A. S., 199d [200a], 375a-b
Matter, 266d. *See also* Generation; Materialism; Vegetate; World, material
  Atlantic Ocean as, 31b
  as chaos, 76d
  Circle of Destiny as, 86c
  elements as, 117c-d
  Flood and, 300d-301a
  Hyle and, 193c
  Matha and, 266c
  Mundane Shell as, 288b
  Nature and, 295d
  Sea of Time and Space as, 362d-363a, 443b
  Vala's veil as, 266d, 432b
  water symbol of, 139b, 303d, 443b, 444a
Matthew as Zoa, 458d
Matthew
  genealogy of Jesus in, 266d
  Lake of Fire in, 231d
  text of
    i:20, 22b-c
    x:29, 380d

Matthew (cont'd)
    text of
        xii:32, 318a, 439a
Matthews [sic], A. S., 199d [200a] (twice),
    330d
Matthews [sic], William Henry, son of
    A. S., 199d [200a], 375a-b
Mayo, 266d
Mechanism, 298c
Media, 266d
"Medicina Mentis, A Specimen of
    Theological Arithmetic" (Taylor), 396d
Medicine. See Surgery
Medieval painting, 412c
Meditaciones poeticas (Mora), 48d
Meditations Among the Tombs (Hervey), 183d,
    184d
"Meditations Among the Tombs," painting
    by B. See "Hervey's Meditations Among the
    Tombs"
Medway, 266d-267a; 385b, 398c-d
Mehetabel, 267a-b
Meletus, 25d, 376a
Melody and harmony, 290a-b
Melville, Herman, 196a
Memorable Fancy. See Marriage of Heaven
    and Hell
Memory, 267b-268b; 21d, 77b, 289c,
    436c-d. See also Imitation and copying
Menassheh. See Manasseh
Mental acts. See Mind
Mental Traveller, The, 268b-d; 324d, 340c,
    352a, 369d
Merchant. See Commerce
Merchant's Tale, The (Chaucer), 79c
Mercury, 268d-269a; 327d, 385a
Mercy, 269b-d
    Creation as, 240a-b[b-c], 269b
    of God, 179d
    in Grave illustrations, 184b
    in "Hervey's Meditations," illus. XI (#34)
    holiness and, 186d
    justice and, 90c-d, 227c, 269c, d
    in "Spenser's Faerie Queene," 384b, c
    states defined by, 386c
    Young's view of, 455d
Meribah Kadesh, 269d-270a
Merionethshire, 270b
Merlin, 270b-c
Merlin's Prophecy, 270c
Mersey, 270d
Mesomorphs, 57b
Messenger, angel as, 22b
Messiah, 270d; 20c, 214a, 262d. See also
    Jesus; Incarnation; Trinity
Messias (Klopstock), 177c, 229c
Metals, 270d-271b; 163 (diagram), 373c,
    424a. See also names of metals
Metamorphoses (Ovid), 112b, 313a-c
Metaphors, B's visualization of Young's,
    456a

Methahel, 267b
Methodism and Methodists, 271b-c; 342d,
    444a, 446c, d
Methusalah, 271c
Mexico, 271c-d; 112b
M'Fingal (Trumbull), 435c
Michael, 271d-272b; illus. I (#16)
"Michael and Satan," 272a, 286c, 287d
Micah iii:12, 329c
Michelangelo Buonarroti, 272b-c; 138a,
    224d
Middlesex, 272c-d; 55d
Middleton, Thomas: Blurt, Master-Constable,
    74d
Midian, 272d-273b; 266a
Midrash Rabba, 293a, b
Midsummer Night's Dream (Shakespeare),
    165b, 331d, 370b, d
Milcah, 273b; 457c
Mile-End, 273b
Milky Way, illus. I (#73)
Mill, 273b-274b; 197b[c], 357c, 446a-b
Millenium, 220d, 435a, 454b, b-c, d
Milton, John, 274b-280d
    B's knowledge and use of, x, 140c,
        274b-275d, 343a
    Christian Doctrine, 275a-b, 296d
    classes of men in works of, 87d-88a, 342a,
        409c
    Comus, 52a-b, 275a, 353b, 401b-c
    in Divine Family, 106a
    Ely as, 71d, 72d, 120a
    Hebraic tradition and, 188c, 223d
    History of Britain
        Albion's daughters' names from, 14b
        Arthur in, 29b-c
        Belin in, 41c-d
        Boadicea in, 49a-b
        Geoffrey's Historia Britonum and, 152c
        Jerusalem and, 275c
    Il Penseroso, 274d-275a, 378a
        B's illustrations to
            #3, "Milton and the Spirit of Plato,"
                91c, 117d, 136a, 227a, 263d, 269a,
                304a, 319b, 327c-328a, 376d-377a,
                illus. IX
            #5, "Milton's Dream," 277a, 298a, 304a,
                423d, illus. X
            #6, "Milton's Old Age," 311c, 433a
    L'Allegro, 274d-275a, 378a
        B's illustrations to
            #5, "The Goblin," 390d
            #6, "The Youthful Poet," 370a
    in The Marriage, 262d
    in Milton, 3a, 11a-b, 190c-d, 277d-280d,
        368b, 457d
    on memory and imagination, 267b-c
    nudity praised by, 371a
    On the Morning of Christ's Nativity, 132a,
        275b
        B's 3rd illustration to, 283d

Milton (cont'd)
  Paradise Lost
    Belial in, 41c
    B's illustrations to
      "Promise of the Redemption," 160a
      "Satan Watching Adam and Eve,"
        303b
    Blakes recite, 303c
    B's understanding of, 274d, 276b-c,
      357b-c
    chaos in, 77c
    compass in, 90b-c
    Dryden's adaptation of, 110c
    Dryden's opinion of, 110c
    Fall of Man in, 357b
    Four Zoas and, 142d, 275b-c
    The Marriage and, 216d, 357b-c
    Michael in, 272a
    Milton and, 175b
    Molech in, 284b
    night in, 77c, 299c
    text of
      i:17, 187b
      i:391-513, 161d
      i:490-505, 376c
      i:521, 349b
      ii:511, 279d
      ii:621, 180d
      ii:760-761, 158b, 357d, 277d
      ii:766-787, 238b[c] (twice)
      ii:787, 277d
      ii:894-896, 959-963, 77c-d (diagram)
      iii:274-343, 160a
      vi, 272a
      vii:208, 225-227, 90b-c
      viii:530, 408c
    Satan in, 143a, 341d, 357a-c, 422b
    seasons in, 449a-b
    sex and reason in, 276c-d
    wheels in, 445a
  Paradise Regained, 447c
  Poetical Sketches influenced by, 331a
  Reason of Church Government, 289c
  rivers of Eden and, 115a
  Samson Agonistes, 275d, 448a
  on senses, 364c
  sex in works of, 276c-d, 408c
  Sixfold Emanation of. See Milton, Sixfold
    Emanation in
  Spenser, B, and, 274b, 383c
  women and, 3a, 273b, 274c, 275a, 276d,
    307b, 457d
  mentioned, 263a (twice), 324a
"Milton and the Spirit of Plato." See
  Milton, John, Il Penseroso, B's illustrations
  to
Milton, A Poem, 275d-280d
  aim of, 140c, 276b-277b
  Albion in, 11a-c, 277b, 280c
  Ancient Night and Chaos in, 299c
  Angels of the Presence in, 24a-c

Milton, A Poem (cont'd)
  Arnon River in, 28b
  Beulah's daughters in, 44a
  B in, 11a, 120b, 175b, 238c[d], 277b-280d
    in passing, 307d-308a, 321a
  Canaan in, 67b
  Cathedral Cities in, 72d-73a, 280b-c
  Chain of Jealousy in, 76c
  dance in, 290b-c
  Divine Family in, 105c-d
  eagle in, 112b-c
  Elect in, 409c-d
  Elynittria in, 120a-c
  Experience in, 292a-b
  Four Zoas anticipates, 250b[c]
  Golgonooza in, 165a-c
  harrow in, 175b-176a
  Hayley in. See Hayley, William, in Milton
  Hell in, 180d-181a, 277b
  hermaphrodite in, 182a
  Horeb in, 189b
  humanity in, 190c-d, 363c
  inspiration analyzed in, 284c-d
  jealousy in, 205b-c
  Jerusalem in, 207a-b
  lark in, 234d, 279c, 280c, 292a-b
  Leutha in, 178c-d, 238b-239a
    [238c-239b], 277c-280d
  limits in, 241a[b]
  London in, 244c-245c [244d-245d] in
    passing
  Los in, 147c, 175b-d, 250d-251b [251a-c],
    277b, 278b, c, d, 280c-d
  Michael in, 272a-b
  Midian in, 273a-b
  Millenium in, 454d
  mills in, 273d
  Milton in. See Milton, John, in Milton
  Mundane Shell in, 288b-c
  music in, 290b-c
  mysticism in, 280c (twice), 291d
  Ololon in, 280a-b, 307b-308a
  Palamabron in, 174b-176b, 238c-239a
    [238d-239b], 277b-280d, 321a, d,
    409d-410a
  plates of
    pl. 1 ("And Did Those Feet"), 118d
    pls. 2:25-13:44 (Bard's Song), 120a-c,
      277b-d
    pl. 4:1, 18b
    pl. 4:12, 18b
    pl. 4, illus., 109d, 388b
    pl. 6, 147a
    pl. 6, illus., 109d, 110a
    pl. 8:11-12, 354d-355a
    pl. 8:32-44, 272a-b
    pl. 9:11, 349d
    pl. 9:19, 349d
    pl. 9:50-51, 84c
    pl. 9, illus., 238c[d]
    pl. 10, illus., 238c[d]

Milton, A Poem (cont'd)
 plates of
  pl. 11:13-14, 356b
  pl. 11:28-13:44, 238b-239a [238c-239b]
  pl. 11, illus., 340c
  pl. 12:20-26, 277d, 357d
  pl. 12:36-39, 357d
  pl. 12:38-39, 158b, 277d
  pl. 12, illus., 340c
  pl. 13:39-44, 277d
  pl. 13:41, 233b
  pl. 13:43-44, 351a
  pl. 14:14-15, 294c
  pl. 15:47, 458a
  pl. 15:49, 140c
  pl. 16, illus., 363c
  pl. 19:7-9, 223d
  pl. 21:12-14, 355a
  pl. 22:50, 354d
  pl. 23:59-60, 354b
  pl. 25:48-50, 181b-c, 232c
  pl. 26:20, 44d
  pl. 27:3-41, 435b
  pl. 27:8-9, 251a[b]
  pl. 27:16, 259b
  pl. 27:31-33, 180d
  pl. 27:45-46, 44d
  pl. 28:1, 198c[d]
  pl. 28:1-5, 165b, 331d-332a, 370d
  pl. 28:1-9, 373b
  pl. 28:1-20, 203c[b]
  pl. 32:4, 290d-291a
  pl. 33, 288a-b (diagram)
  pl. 33, illus., 5c
  pl. 34:29-30, 28b
  pl. 35:22-24, 333d
  pl. 35:31-33, 307d
  pl. 35:62, 255a[b]
  pl. 35, illus., 112b-c
  pl. 36:4-6, 23d
  pl. 36:13-14, 333d
  pl. 36, illus., 137b
  pl. 37:16-34, 161d
  pl. 37:30-32, 376c
  pl. 37:33, 349b
  pl. 37:50, 311c
  pl. 37:53-54, 386a
  pl. 39:26-27, 279d
  pl. 39:29, 77c-d (diagram)
  pl. 39:35, 69b
  pl. 42:9-15, 280b
  pl. 42:11-15, 45c-d
  pl. 42:28, 280c
  pl. 42:33, 233b
 plow in, 329d
 polypus in, 333c-d
 Rahab in, 278b, 279d, 339b, 340a
 Redeemed in, 409d-410a
 Reprobate in, 410a
 sandal in, 140c-d, 354d-355a
 Satan in, 175b-176b, 177c-178d, 277b-d,
  356d-357a, 357a-358a

Milton, A Poem (cont'd)
 Sixfold Emanation in, 3a, 279a, 280b,
  307b, 368b
 Spectres of the Dead in, 383b
 thyme in, 403d-404a
 Urizen in, 140c (twice), 277b, 278b, 363c,
  423c-d
 vintage in, 435b
 "Milton's Dream," 277a, 298a, 304a, 423d,
  illus. X
 "Milton's Old Age," 311c, 433a
 Mind. *See also* Freud, Sigmund
  Behmen's analysis of, 40b-41b
  in B's work, ix, 331c
  cave as, 75b-c
  chaos as, 77a-b
  conscious, 6a, 239c [241a], 262b, 357c,
   394a
  control of, 260c
  emanation and, 121a, b-c
  in *Four Zoas*, 142c
  in *The Marriage*, 262b-c, 394a-c
  miracles and, 282a
  Paracelsus's analysis of, 322c
  subconscious. *See* Subconscious
  tabernacle as, 395c-d
 Miner, Paul, 168b, 389b
  "William Blake's London Residences,"
   448a-b
 Minerva, 385a
 Minor, The (Foote), 140d, 446d
 Minute Particulars, 280d-281d; 319b, 392c
 Miracles, 281d-282b; 213c, 215d-216a,
  236b-c[c-d], 264d-265a
 Mirror [Looking Glass], 246b-c[c-d], illus. I
  (#77)
 Mirth, 456a
 Mirtle, 282b-c; 410b
 Miscarriage by Catherine Blake, 401c
 Miscegenation. *See* Brotherhood of Man,
  amalgamation of races necessary for
 Miscellanies (Chatterton), 78c
 "Mission of Virgil." *See* Dante Alighieri,
  Divine Comedy, B's illustrations of
 Mistletoe of druids, 108c, 110a
 Mizraim, 282c
 Mne Seraphim, 282c-d; 7d. *See also*
  Seraphim
 Mnetha, 282d; 174b, 405d
 Moab, 282d-283b; 18d, 80a, 266a
 "Mock on, Mock on, Voltaire, Rousseau,"
  298c
 Modesty, 283b-c
 Moeurs des Nations (Voltaire), 439d
 Mole, 283c-d
 Molech, 283d-284c
  Chemosh and, 80a, 283d
  child-sacrifice and, 80a, 81d, 283d-284a
  as Eye of God, 134c[d], 134d [135a]
   (twice), 284a
  in *Job* illustrations, 134d [135a] (twice),
   222d, 223a

Molech (cont'd)
in "Spenser's *Faerie Queene*," 384a, d
Moment of Inspiration, 284c-d; 29b, 454b, d
Mona, 284d-285a
Monaghan [Managhan], 260d
Money. *See* Commerce
Money changers. 213d
Monk, 285a-b
Monk's Tale, The (Chaucer), 79c-d, 97b
Monmouth, 285b
Montgomeryshire, 285b
Monthly Magazine, 97c
Moon, 285b-286b
  Ark as, 27c, 61b-c, 286b, 300d
  in Beulah, 43a, 285b, d
  center as, 75c, 285c-d
  in *Gates of Paradise*, 149d, 285b
  goddess of, 33a
  in *Jerusalem* 25, 311d
  in *Job* illustrations, 220d
  love and, 43a, 285b
  Woman in the Wilderness clothed by, 449d, 450b
Moony space, 286a-b
Mora, Jose Joaquin de: *Meditaciones poeticas*, 48d
Morality. *See also* Good and evil
  in allegory, 17b-c
  Babylon symbol of, 34a
  of deism, 100d, 101c
  in *Job* illustrations, 220b
  Leviathan as, 239d [240a]
  results of, 281c
  Reuben in *Jerusalem* and, 211b-c, 347c-d
  Satan's religion as. 356a
  of Seneca, 364a
  serpent as, 309a
  sin and, 65a, 373d
  in Swedenborg, 393d-394c
  Tree of Mystery as, 345c, 410d
  Vala's veil as, 432b
  virtue and, 436a-b
Moray [Murra], 289c
Morn, 286b; 234c
Morning, 269d
Morning Star, 186a, 254a-b[b-c]
Morocco, 286b
Mortality. *See* Death
Moses, 286b-287d
  Balaam accused by, 35d
  in B's illustrations, 192a, 286c, 408d-409a
  Books of, 100b, 286d-287a
  in "Hervey's *Meditations*," 409a, illus. XI (#15)
  on Horeb, 189a, b
  Jesus vs. 227c, 287b-c
  in Meribah Kadesh, 270a
  Naamah and, 293a-b
  on Sinai, 189a, b, 287a, 374a
  Song of, 222d
  in "Transfiguration," 408d-409a

Moses (cont'd)
  veil of, 41a, 215a
  in "VLJ," 287d, illus. I (#37)
  mentioned, 3a
"Moses, The Finding of," 286c
"Moses, The Hiding of," 286c
"Moses and the Burning Bush," 286c (twice), illus. III
"Moses Erecting the Brazen Serpent," 286c
"Moses Indignant at the Golden Calf," 286c
"Moses Striking the Rock," 286c
Moslems, 259b
Mother, 401a, b, illus. XI (#26)
Motherhood, 87b
Motte-Guyon [Guion], Jeanne Marie Bouvier de la, 168d, 343b
Mountains, 31c-d, 174a. *See also names of mountains and mountain ranges*
"Mount of Cursing" [Ebal], 113d-114a
Mundane Egg, 287-288b; 5c
"Mundane Egg, The" (diagram), 288a-b
Mundane Shell, 288b-289a
  Blackheath and, 47a-b
  Cambel and making the, 66c
  caverns in, 75b
  constellations of the, 240b[c], 288c-d, 306c, 309b
  in *Gates of Paradise*, 288b, 456c
  in *Night Thoughts*, 456c
  Vala's veil as, 288b, 295d, 432b
Munster, 289a
Murder, 289a-b
Murra, 289c
Muses, 289c-d; 43d, 188c, 226d, 267c, c-d, 268a
Music, 289d-290d
  east and, 113c
  in "Fertilization of Egypt," 117a
  in *Job* illustrations, 217d, 222c, d, 289d-290a
  law as, 290a, 318c
  lyre symbol of, 258a[c]
  in "VLJ," 371c, illus. I (#68)
Muswell Hill, 290d
Mydon, 291a
"My Pretty Rose Tree." 351a
Myratana, 291a
Myrtle [Mirtle], 282b-c, 410b
"My Spectre around Me Night and Day," 290d-291a; 381d
Mysterious Mother, The (Walpole), 195d
Mysterium Magnum, 322c
Mystery, 291a-b; 82d (twice), 223c, 433b, illus. I (#48). *See also* Babylon, Whore of; Rahab
Mystical ecstasy
  defined, 291b-c
  fourfold vision as, 291c-d, 437a
  God united with man as, 206c, 418d
  in *Job* illustrations, 216c, 220b, c, 221d, 291d
  in *Milton*, 280c (twice)

Mystical ecstasy (cont'd)
    of Thomas Taylor, 418d
Mystical marriage, 94d
Mysticism, 291b-292b
    of Behmen, 39c-41b
    B's reading in, 343b
    Brama and, 58b
    of Fénelon, 137c
    Guion and, 168d
    in "Hervey's Meditations," 184d, 409a
    in Job illustrations, 216c, 220b, c, 221d,
        291d, 292a
    of Thomas Taylor, 396c-d
Mystic Way, 184d
Mythography, 61a-d, 108c-109a
Mythology. See also names of gods and
    goddesses
    Biblical vs. classical, 188c, 267d
    B's, and the mind, ix
    British, 229a
    classical, Ovid source of, 313a-b
    of druids and Romans, 108b
Myvyrian Archailogy (Pughe), 443c-d

Naamah, the Ammonite, 293c; 21d, 266b
Naamah, wife of Noah, 293a-d; 215d, 266a
Nadir, 293c-d; 426c. See also Center;
    Circumference; Zenith
Nahor, 293d
Nairn, 293d-294a
Names of B's characters, 312d-313a
Nannicantipot, Mrs., 199d
Naphtali, 294a; 355b
Napoleon Bonaparte. See Bonaparte
Napoleonic Wars, 349b-c
Napthali [Naphtali], 294a, 355b
Narcissa, 390c, 450b
Narrative, of a five years' expedition to Surinam
    (Stedman), 7b, 438a
Narrative of Col. Ethan Allen's Captivity, A
    (Allen), 18a
Natho, 294a
Nations, 294b-295b
    brotherhood and, 60d, 294b
    guardian spirit of, 22d
    nationalism and, 201d [202a]
    origin of, 347b
    Thirty-Two, 19b, 294d-295b, 295
        (diagram). See also names of
        the nations
Nativity, 369d. See also Incarnation
Nativity Ode (Milton), 132a, 275b
    B's 3rd illustration to, 283d
Nativity of Mr. Blake (Smith), 276a
Natural Man, 6a, 151d-152a, 270b, 351c
Natural Religion. See Deism
Nature, 295b-297a. See also Deism; Universe
    in Comus, 52b
    Creation and, 119b, 296d
    eternity and, 129c-d, 296a-b
    Ijim and, 194d-195a
    Leviathan as, 220a

Nature (cont'd)
    Looking glass of, 246b-c[c-d]
    in The Marriage, 262b
    memory and, 267b-c
    miracles and, 281d
    Mundane Egg as, 287d-288a, 295d
    Mundane Shell as, 288b
    as projection, 294d, 436b
    in religion, 344a-b
    salvation of, 369d
    secret child and, 363a
    serpent and, 309a, 365d, 366a-b
    Shadowy Female voice of, 369c
    Vala goddess of, 295d, 428a
Navy, British, 19d
Nazareth, 297a
Nazarite, 297a-b
Nebuchadnezzar, 297b-d; 271a, 357a. See
    also Babylon, King of; "King of Babylon
    in Hell"
"Nebuchadnezzar," 297c
Negation. See also Contraries
    cruelty as, 269c, d
    hermaphrodite and, 181d
    in Mental Traveller, 268c
    nations as, 294b
    Tyger and Lamb as, 414b
Negroes, 141c, 438a
Negroland, 297d
"Nelson Guiding Leviathan, The Spiritual
    Form of," 239d-240a [240b]
Nephilim, 297d
Neoclassicism. See also Classicism; Greece;
    Reason, Age of
    B's break with, 188c
    memory and, 25d-26a, 267c-268a
    minute particulars vs., 281a-b
    Mnetha spirit of, 282d, 405d
    Ossian and, 312a-b
    Ovid and, 313b-c
    Young attacked, 455c
Neo-Platonism
    "Circle of Life" a study of, 86d, 304b
    in flower symbolism, 265c-d
    hermeticism and, 182c
    nymphs in, 303d
    of Thomas Taylor, 396c
Neoplatonism of William Blake, The (Harper),
    131a, 199c-d [199d-200a], 328c, 375a-b,
    397b-c, 432d
Nervous system, 17a-b, 57a, 90d, 141b
Ness, River, 389a
Net, 297d-298a; 240d [241a], 345b
"Never Pain to Tell Thy Love," 298a-b
New Age, 262c
New Birth, 220c, 291c
New Church of Swedenborg, 235a, 392b, d,
    393b
New Jerusalem, 162d, 202a-b[b-c], 235a,
    384a, b, 410c-d
New System, or an Analysis of Ancient Mythology
    (Bryant). See Bryant, Jacob, New System

New Testament. *See* Bible
Newton, Isaac, 298b-299d; 39d, 100c, 343b, 359b
"Newton," 91c, 299b-c, 332d
New York, 298b
Nicholas Nickleby (Dickens), 59d
Night, 299c-d; 43a, 77c, d (diagram), 291c, 299c, 387b-d
"Night," 22c, d, 242a[b] (twice), 449d
Night Thoughts. See Young, Edward, *Night Thoughts*
Nimrod, 299d-300b; 95d
"Nimrod," 300a
Nimrod's Tower. *See* Babel, Tower of
Nimue, 270b
Nineteenth Century, 360d
Nineveh, 300a-b
Noah, female, 301b-c; 457c
Noah, male, 300c-301b
 Adam and, 6b
 Ark of. *See* Ark, of Noah
 druids descendants of, 108c, 301b
 Flood of. *See* Flood of Noah
 in "Hervey's *Meditations*," illus. XI (#8)
 Kox as, 171c, 301a-b
 rainbow of, 300b, 340d
 in Sistine Chapel paintings, 272b-c
 Twenty-Seven Churches and, 6a, 85c-d, 300c, 301b
 in "VLJ," 371, illus. I (#68)
Noble Savage, 351b
Nobodaddy, 301c; 63d [not in 2nd pr.], 160b, 229c, 422c
Norfolk, 301c-d
Norman, 301d
North, 301d-302a; 37c, 75c, 271a, 332c. *See also* Compass points
Northampton, 302a-b
Northern Gate, 401b
Northumberland, 302b
Norwich, 302b
Norwood, 302c
Nostrils, 302c-303a; 113c, 216a, 376b
Note-Book, 437b
Nottingham, 303a
Nouvelle Héloise (Rousseau), 351b
Nudity, 303a-c; 48b, 371a
"Number, weight & measure," 303d
"Nurse's Song" (*Songs of Innocence*), 200b[c], 337c
Nymphs, 303d; 265c

Oak, 305a-c; 19c-d, 108b-c, 141b
 of druids, 108b-c, 141b, 168c, 305b-c
 error as, 168c, 305b, 410b
 in "Joseph of Arimathea Preaching," 225b
"O Beulah Land" (Sweeney), 42d
Obscurity in B's prophetic books, x
Observations on Popular Antiquities (Brand), 131b, 199d [200a]
Obtuse Angle, 199c[d], 199d [200a], 397a-b

Ocalythron, 305c-306a
Occultism, 7c-d, 9a, 182c-183b, 396c-397a, 397b-c. *See also* Alchemy; Mysticism
Occult Philosophy (Agrippa), 7c, d, 52a, 282c, 406d, 457b
Ochim, 306a; 174c, 393c
Ode on Intimations of Immortality (Wordsworth), 451b
"Ode to the West Wind" (Shelley), 314c-d
Odin, 306a-b; 403c-d, 449c
Oedipus complex, 50c, 53d, 76a, 148d, 309d
Og, 306b-d; 22a, 37a, 288d, 372d, illus. I (#35)
Ogleby, Mr., 266d
Ohana, 306d
Oithona, 309a, 313a
Old age, 149d, 210d
Old Bow [Bow], 55d-56a
Old Testament. *See* Bible
Oliver Twist (Dickens), 187d
Olivet, 307a
Ololon, 307b-308a; 190d, 278d-279a, 279c, d, 280a-b
Ona, 308b; 244a[b]
O'Neill, Eugene, 448a
One Law, 308b-c
"On H[ayle]y's Friendship," 361a
On H[ayley] the Pick Thank, 178a
On Homer's Poetry, 308a-b; 188b-c
On the Cave of the Nymphs (Porphyry), 265c
On the Incarnation (Áthanasius), 402d
On the Morning of Christ's Nativity (Milton), 275b
 B's 3rd illustration to, 283d
On the Virginity of the Virgin Mary & Johanna Southcott, 264b, 379d
On Virgil, 308a-b
Onyx, 308c
Oothoon, 308c-309a, 437d-438c
 Marygold and, 265c
 modesty and, 283b-c
 name of, 309a, 313a
 Persephone and, 265c
 sex and, 124c (diagram), 132b
 Thel vs., 401c
 Theotormon and, 124c (diagram), 130d, 402b
 in *Visions* illustrations, 402b
Opacity, 309a; 241a-b[b]. *See also* Limits
Ophiuc[h]us, 309a-b
 Laocoön and, 234c, 373a
 Orion and, 288d, 309a, 311c, 372d-373a
 Sihon and, 288d, 306c, 309a-b, 372d-373a
Optic nerve [Ozoth], 315c-d
Orc, 309b-311c
 in *America*, 20c-d, 21a, 310a, c, 310d-311a, 311b
 binding of, 76c, 310d-311a
 breastplate of, 310c, 355b
 dragon as, 108a, 450a

Orc (cont'd)
  Enitharmon and, 124d, 253a[b], 309c,
    309d-310a
  in Four Zoas, 309d-310d, 365c, 411a-b
  hatred as, 333a
  Los and, 124d, 247a[b], 253a[b], 309c,
    309d-310a, 453a
  Los's children as, 253a[b], 309c
  Luvah and, 256d [257a], 309b-d,
    310d-311c, 441d-442a
  in The Marriage, 263c, 310a-b, 377c
  in Mental Traveller, 268c
  motivation of, 349d
  name of, 309c, 444d
  Oedipus theory and, 76a-b, 309d
  onyx on, 308c
  revolution as, 253a[b], 309b-311c, 369b
  Rintrah and, 309c, 349d, 453a
  serpent as, 145d, 309d, 310b, d, 365c,
    435b-c
  Shadowy Female and, 369b, c
  Tyger and, 413a
  Urizen and, 8b, 310a-b, b, d, 311a-b
  viper as, 145d, 310d, 435b-c
  whale and, 309c, 444d
  worm as, 309d, 310b, 452b, c
Orcus, 311c
Origen, 254a[b], 296d
Original Sin. See Sin, Original
Orion, 311c-d
  Og and, 306c, 311c
  Ophiuchus and, 288d, 309a, 311c,
    372d-373a
Orkney, 311d
Orkney Islands, 200c[d]
Ornan [Araunan], 26d
Orphans, 31b, illus. XI (#28)
Orthodoxy, London's Guardian as, 246a[b]
Or-Ulro, 309b; 387b
Orus, 311d (twice)
Oshea [Joshua], 65c, 225d
Osiris, 311d-312a; 26b
Ossian, 312a-313a; 170b, 309a, 331a
  Fingal, 266c-d, 312a
  Fragments of Ancient Poetry Collected in the
    Highlands of Scotland, 312a
  Oithona, 438d
  Temora, 312a
Outline, firm, 319b-c. See also
  Circumference; Minute Particulars
Ovid, 313a-c; 182b, 436a
  Metamorphoses, 112b, 313a-c
Owl, 313c; 219c
Ox, 313d
  in Genesis Ms., 151d, 313d, 401a
  lion and, 242b-c[d]
  as Zoa, 458d
Oxford, English town, 313d-315a
  Bard of
    as Marsh, 315a
    as Shelley, 37a, 38d, 71d, 72d, 120a,
      148a, 209c, 210a-b, 314b-315a

Oxford, English town (cont'd)
  River of, 315a
Oxfordshire, 315c
Oxford Street, 315a-c
Oxford University, 313d, 314a-b
Ozoth, 315c-d

Pacific Ocean, 342a
Pacifism, 38c-d, 71b, 78b
Pachad, 316a. See also Pahad
Paddington, 316a-b
Pahad, 316b-c
  as Eye of God, 134c[d], 134d [135a]
    (twice), 222d, 223a, 317b-c
  in Job illustrations, 222d, 223a, 317c
  Pachad as, 316a
Paine, Thomas, 316d-318b
  Age of Reason, 63b, 101a, 317a, 317d-318a
  in America, 20c, d, 317d
  American Crisis, 316d, 317c
  Bible and, 317b, 318a, 343c
  B's attitude toward, 101d, 263a
  Common Sense, 316d
  deism and, 100c, 317a-b, 317d-318a
  miracles worked by, 282a-b, 318a-b
  Rights of Man, 316d
Painter's Eye (Grosser), 320b-c
Painting, 318b-320d. See also Art;
  Truchsessian Gallery
  Heva as, 405c
  medieval, 412c
  nudity in, 303c
  surgery and, 318c, 391a-b, 399b
  as Tharmas's art, 399b
  vision in, 436c
  in "VLJ," 371c, illus. I (#68)
Palace, 320d-321a
Palamabron, 321a-d
  in Four Zoas, 176b
  gnomes of, 158a-b
  harrow of, 238c-d [238d-239a], 321b, d
  Leutha and, 238b-239a [238d-239b],
    321d
  mercy and, 269d
  in Milton, 174b-176b, 238c-d [238d-239a],
    277b-280d, 321a, d, 409d-410a
  Orc and, 309c
  Redeemed and, 409d-410a
  Rintrah and, 321b-c, 350a, 453a
  Shaddai and, 368c-d
Palestine, 322a; 3a, 42d, 347d-348c. See also
  place names
Paley, Morton D.: "The Female Babe and
  'The Mental Traveller,' " 268d
Paley, William, 69c, 71d, 72d
Palm of suffering, 322a
Palmer, Samuel, 313b
Palmer, in Faerie Queene, 384b
Pan, 385a
Pancrass, 322a
Pantocrator, 322a

Paracelsus, Phillipus Aureolus, 322b-d; 9a, 195d, 262d, 263a, 322c, 343b
Paracelsus his Archidoxies (Paracelsus), 322c-d
Paradise, 322d; 259c-d. *See also* Eden; *Gates of Paradise*
Paradise Lost (Milton). *See* Milton, John, *Paradise Lost*
Paradiso (Dante), B's illustrations of. *See* Dante Alighieri, *Divine Comedy*, B's illustrations of
Parallel of Poetry and Painting (Dryden), 237c[b]. 389d
Parent Sense, 399b, 408a
Paris, 323a
Parker, James, 199c[d]
Park Gate, 323a
Parnell, Thomas: *The Hermit*, 259d
Parrot, 218c
Particulars. *See* Minute Particulars
Passions, symbols of, 62a, 220d, 239b
Passover, 232a
Patagonia, 323a-b
Pathetic fallacy, 436b
Patience of ox, 313d (twice)
Patmos, 323b
Patriotism criticized, 229a
Patristic writers, 269a, 343a, 450c
Patterson, Dr. Merrill, 140b
Paul, Saint, 323b-324b. *See also names of New Testament books attributed to Paul*
  allegorical interpretation and, 215a
  B's attitude toward religion and, 323d-324a, 342a-343a
  on Jesus as Liberator, 206d
  in quaternary, 254c-255a [254d-255b], 324a
"Paul Preaching," 324b
Paved Work, 324b-c
Peace, 38c-d, 71b, 78b, 206c-d, 371c
Peachey, 324c
Peachey, John, J.P., 324c
Peacock, 218c
Peak, 324c
Pearl, 324d-325a; 352a
Peckham Rye, 325a
Peebles, 325a
Peel, cathedral at, 377a
Peleg, 325a-b; 223c
Pembrokeshire, 325b
Penmaenmawr, 325b; 348c
Pen[n]sylvania, 325b-c
Pennsylvania Gazette, 435c
Pentateuch, 100b, 286d-287a
Pentland, 325c
People, power of the, 195a
Peor, 325c
Perception. *See also* Senses
  dimensions and, 103d
  in Minute Particulars, 281a-b
  Nature and, 296a-d
  of thistle, 403b-c
  of universe, 417d

Perception *(cont'd)*
  in vision, 436b
  worm and, 452a
Percy, Thomas: *Reliques of Ancient English Poetry*, 170b, 331a
Period of time, 454a (twice)
Persephone and Oothoon, 265c
Persia, 325d
Personality, universe projection of, 418a
Personification, 17b, 134a[b], 215c, 436b
Perth, 325d
Peru, 325d-326a
Pessimism in B's prophetic books, 233a
"Peter, Crucifixion of Saint" (Michelangelo), 224d
Peterboro[ugh], 326a
Petworth Last Judgment picture, 235c. *See also* Last Judgment, B's pictures of, Petworth version
Peyote, 436c
Phallic symbolism, 271b, 366b-c, 410c
Pharaoh, 326a
Pharisaion, 326a-b; 166b
Pharisees, 326a; 45a, 186c, 217c, 409c, illus. I (#21)
Pharoh [Pharaoh], 326a
Philebus (Plato), 50c-d, 328d
Philistia and Philistines, 326c-d; 33a, 150b
Phillips, Richard: *Picture of London for 1805*, 412a, c
Le Philosophe Ignorant (Voltaire), 439d
Philosophical and Mathematical Commentaries of Proclus, The (Proclus), 396c
Philosophy. *See also* Religion; *names of philosophers*
  abstract, 58b, 126d-127a, 141b
  B's, 343b-c
  B's vs. Young's, 455d-456a
  pagan, 343b
  tent represents, 397c
Philostratus, 233d
Phlogiston, 197a-b
Phylogeny, 309d
Physic, 391a
[Pictorial Key to the Tarot, The (Waite), 223a —2nd pr. only]
Picture of London for 1805, The (Phillips), 412a, c
Pierpont Morgan Library, 50c, 217b
Pigs, 216a
Pilate, Pontius, 326d-327a; 64c-d, illus. I (#42)
Pilgrim's Progress, The (Bunyan). *See* Bunyan, John, *Pilgrim's Progress*
Pillars of cloud and fire, 204a
Piper and the Bard, The (Gleckner), 392c, 401a
Pison, 327a. *See also* Eden, rivers of
Pitch, 46d
Pitcher, 219b
"Pitt Guiding Behemoth, The Spiritual Form of," 240a[b]

Pity, 327a-c; 269d, 321a, 380a
"Pity," 318c, 370c
Plague in *Europe*, illus.,, 133a
Planets, Urizen's daughters as, 424d
Plato, 327c-328d
    androgeny in works of, 5b
    Philebus, 50c-d, 328d
    Symposium, 182b
    Taylor's translation of, 328c, 396c
    Theaetetus, 134a[b]
    Timaeus, 222a, 328d
    mentioned, 319b, 343a
"Plato, Milton and the Spirit of," *See* Milton,
    John, *Il Penseroso*, B's illustrations to
"Platonic Theology, History of the
    Restoration of the" (Taylor), 396c-d
Platonism, 194a, 246b[c], 327c-328d, 432b.
    See also Neo-Platonism
Pleasure, 7d-8a, 50d-51a, 127c-d, 181b, c
Pleasure gardens in Lambeth, 232b-c
Pleiades, 311d
Plinlimmon, 329a
Pliny, 329a; 234b
    Historia Naturalis, 329a
Plow, 329a-330b; 189d, 273b. *See also*
    Harrow
Plowing of the Nations, 13a-b, 189d. *See also*
    Harvest; Vintage
Plowman, Max, 143b-c, 263b-c
Plowman, Urizen as, 329c, 420c
Plutarch: *Demetrius*, 231b
Poe, Edgar Allan, 196a
Poet
    as Bard, 36d-37a
    Byron as true, 63b
    deist vs. 344a
    error given form by, 355c
    in *Jerusalem*, 251b[c]
    in *Milton*, 175b
    prophet as, 335b
    revolutionary as, 253a[b], 309c
Poetical Sketches, 330d-331c. *See also names
    of individual works within the collection*
    ghosts in, 154d-155a
    Milton's influence on, 274c-d, 331a
    Muses in, 267c
    Romanticism in, 331a, b, 332a-b
    Shakespeare's influence on, 331a, 370a
    mentioned, 200b[c]
Poetic Genius, 330b-c; 343d. *See also*
    Genius; Imagination
Poetry, 331c-332b. *See also* Art
    allegory in, 17b-d, 18a
    Bible as, 45d
    Councellors of Los and, 72c
    Eno mother of, 125c
    Har as, 174b-c, 405c
    Los as, 246c[d], 331d-332a
    lyre symbol of, 258c
    Plato's view of, 328b, d
    religion as, 318c

Poetry (*cont'd*)
    trees and, 410a-b
    in "VLJ," 371c, illus. I (#68)
"Poison Tree, A," 289b, 410b
Poland, 332b-c
Poland Street, 332c
Polar region, 332c-d. *See also* North; Sotha
Political cartoon, 435c
Politics, 332d
Polydorus, 234b
Polygamy, 233c
Polypus, 332d-333d
    Albion's sons as, 16c, 333a
    from center, 75d
    heads of, 69a, 240b[c], 333c
    heart of, 245d [246a], 333c
    in "Newton," 299b, 332d
Pope, Alexander, 333d-334a
    Elegy on an Unfortunate Lady, 334a
    Eloisa to Abelard, 334a
    Essay on Man, 50a, 100d-101a
Pope, Roman Catholic, 83a, b
Poplar, borough, 334a; 55d
Porphyry: *On the Cave of the Nymphs*, 265c
Portraits of poets. *See* Heads of the Poets
Poseidon, 234b
Postdiluvians, 155c-d
Potiphar's wife, 202b[c], 224b
Poverty in London, 281c
Powell, Mary, 276d
Prayer, 334a-b; 222a
Precious stones. *See* Stones, precious
Predestination, 393d
Preliminary Discourse (Sale), 236a, 259c
Pre-Raphaelites, 319d
Presbuterion, 334b-c
Prester Serpent, 334c; 104c, 365d
Preston, Kerrison, 208d, 419b, 448b
Priam, 334c-d; 26a, 294c, 442c
Pride of Urizen, 414b-c
Priest. *See also* Laocoön
    breastplate of high, 69b
    Covering Cherub and, 27a, 194b
    serpent as, 334c, 365c-d
Priestley, Joseph, 197a-b, 199c[d], 375a
Priestley, Mary, 199c[d]
"Primeval Giants Sunk in the Soil," 155c
Primrose Hill, 334d-335a; 265b, 390a
Prince of Light, 335a
Printing. *See* Illuminated Printing
Printing press, 335a; 251a[b], 446c
Prioress, 79b-c, 407d
Prison in *Europe*, illus., 133a
Proclus, 396c
    *Philosophical and Mathematical Commentaries
    of Proclus*, 396c
Prodicus, 181b
Prodigal Son, Satan as, 358c
Progress and revolution, 348d-349a
Projection, mental, 369a, 418a, 436b
Prometheus, 32c, 76b, 112d, 309d, 310b

Promised Land, 3a
"Promise of the Redemption," 160a
Prophecy, 20b, 331c, 335a-b, d
Prophet, 335b-d
    Balaam as, 35c-36b
    Elijah as, 118c, 153d, 366d, illus. I (#60)
    false, 25b
    Jesus as, 214d
    Los as, 247a[b], 335a-b
    Los's sons as, 6b, 7a
    Michelangelo's idea of, 272c
    poet as, 331c
    wrath of, 349d
Prophetic books, B's, 48c-d, 49a, 335d
Prophetic Writings of William Blake, The (Sloss
    and Wallis), 144c, 266b
Prophet of Eternity, 335a-b
Prosody. See Versification
Prostitutes and prostitution. See Harlots and
    harlotry
Proverbs, 91b, 352a
Proverbs of Hell. See Marriage of Heaven and
    Hell, plates of, pls. 7-10
Providence, 335d-336b
    Angel of, 23d, illus. XI (#18)
    Divine Hand an act of, 106b
    Generation and, 151a
    in "Hervey's Meditations," illus. XI (#18)
    in Job illustrations, 217c, 221b
    of Milton, 24a
    in "VLJ," illus. I (#75)
    will and, 447c
Province House, 42b, 55c
Prude, Tirzah as, 339d, 407b
Psalms, 98d, 363a-b
Psyche and Cupid, 26b-c, 257a[b], 430a
Psychology. See Mind
Ptolemy, 262b, 418d
Puberty and trees, 410a-b
Public Address, 103a, 110d-111a, 276b
Pughe, William Owen
    Cambrian History, 29d
    Myvyrian Archailogy, 443c-d
Punishment of sins. See Vengeance
Purgatorio (Dante), B's illustrations of. See
    Dante Alighieri, Divine Comedy, B's
    illustrations of
Pye, James Henry, 37a
Pyramid, 222a, 406a
Pythagoras, 336b; 110a, 182c, 374d. See also
    Sipsop the Pythagorean

Quakers, 39d, 342c-d
Quaternaries
    Achitophel, Caiaphas, Judas, Pilate, 4d
    Air, Earth, Water, Fire, 138c, 148c, 152b
    Amelekite, Canaanite, Egyptian, Moabite,
        19a, 68b
    Anak, Og, Satan, Sihon, 22a-b, 155d,
        306b-c, 372d
    Bath, Cambridge, Norwich, Oxford, 38b

Quaternaries (cont'd)
    Bath, Canterbury, Edinburgh, York, 38b,
        115d
    Bath, Legions, London, Edinburgh, 38b,
        115c, 245b-c[d]
    Blackheath, Finchley, Hounslow,
        Norwood, 47a, 137d-138a, 190a, 302c
    Body, Emotions, Imagination, Reason,
        77c-d, 299c-d
    Bowen, Kotope, Kox, Scofield, 15a,
        56c-d, 229d, 230a
    Brass, Gold, Iron, Silver, 162c, 198b[c],
        271a, 373b
    Bromion, Palamabron, Rintrah,
        Theotormon, 60a-b, 321a
    Carlisle, Durham, Edinburgh, York, 115c
    Center, Circumference, Nadir, Zenith,
        293c-d
    Chaos, Death, Night, Sin, 77c-d, 299c-d
    Charlemaine, Constantine, Luther, Paul,
        254c-255a [254d-255b]
    Dove, Eagle, Fly, Worm, 107a, 112a,
        139d
    Eagle, Lion, Serpent, Whale, 444d
    Earth, Moon, Stars, Sun, 113b, 285c,
        386a, 390a
    Edinburgh, Lincoln, Monmouth,
        Norwich, 115d
    Edinburgh, London, Verulam, York,
        115c
    Elephant, Horse, Lion, Tyger, 118a,
        189c-d, 242a[b], 413c
    Emanation, Humanity, Shadow, Spectre,
        368d,380d-381a
    England, Ireland, Scotland, Wales,
        197c[d]
"Quaternary, Satan's Evil" (diagram), 77c-d
"Queen Katherine's Dream," 370c
"Queen of Heaven in Glory." See Dante
    Alighieri, Divine Comedy, B's illustrations
    of
Queen's County, 337a
Quid the Cynic, 337a-b; 199c[d], 374d,
    375a

Rabbinical tradition, 343b
Race. See Brotherhood of Man,
    amalgamation of races necessary for
Rachel, 338a-b; 236c[d]
Radnorshire, 338b
Ragan, 338b-c; 58d
Rage. See God, Angry; Wrath
Rahab, 338c-340c. See also Babylon, Whore
    of; Mystery
    Albion's daughters and, 14c
    Church of Rome as, 82d
    Female Babe and, 268c
    Marie Antoinette as, 411d
    in Maternal Line, 266a-b
    in Milton, 278b, 279d, 339b, 340a
    Tirzah and, 339d-340a, 407b-d

Rahab (cont'd)
  Vala as, 339b, 429c-d, 431c-d
  Wife of Bath as, 79b, 407d-408a, 432a
Rainbow, 340c-d; 238a[b], c[d], 300d-301a
Raine, Kathleen, 419a
  "Who Made the Tyger?" 414b
Ram, 340d-341a
Ranelagh, 341a
Rasselas (Johnson), 195b
Rathlin, 341a
  ratio and, 341b
  sex and, 276c-d
  South as, 379b
  spectre as, 172c, 341d, 380d, 381a, c-d,
    382a-b
  stars as, 386a
  sun as, 390a
  superego as, 262b
  Urizen and, 197b[c], 341d, 419a
  Young's idea of, 455d
  zenith as, 457d
  Zoa as, 458d
Reason of Church Government, The (Milton),
  289c
Reason the Only Oracle of Man (Allen), 18a
Rebecca, mother of, illus. XI (#9)
Rebirth, 220c, 291c
Recapitulation, theory of, 53d, 309d, 452b
Recluse, The (Wordsworth), 451a
Redcrosse Knight, 384b
Redeemed, 342a; 88a (twice), b, 409c,
  409d-410a
Redemption, 45b, 296d, 410c
Red Sea, 342a; 61d, 128c-d, 379c
Rees, Abraham: Cyclopaedia, 234b
Reflection, Shadow as, 369a
Reflections on the Revolution in France
  (Burke), 316d
Reformation, Protestant, 65d, 254c[d]
Refutation of All Heresies (Hippolytus), 115c
Regan [Ragan], 58d, 338b-c
Regent's Park, 265b
Rehob, 342a-b
Reins, 342b-c
Religio Laici (Dryden), 386a
Religion, 342c-346b. See also especially All
  Religions Are One; Church; Deism; There
  is No Natural Religion
  abstraction as, 4b-c
  B's use of the word, xi, 345d
  brotherhood and, 60c-d, 344c
  development of, 7a
  dome and cross symbol of, 106d
  failure of, as healer, 38a
  humility and, 191c
  Italy and, 202c[d]
  in London, 244b[c], 244d [245a]
  London's Guardian personifies, 246a[b]
  poetry and, 318c, 343d, 344a
  polypus as, 332d-333a, 333b-c
  prophets' attitude toward, 335c
  of Satan, 344d-346b, 356a

Religion (cont'd)
  of sex, 30d, 345c, 367d-368b, 395b
  state, 3c, 386b-c
  of Swedenborg, 342d, 392c-394c
  Urizen's web of, 54d, 345b, 421d-422a
  wheel of, 345b-c, 446b
Reliques of Ancient English Poetry, The (Percy),
  170b, 331a
Rembrandt van Rijn, 319d, 412b
Renfru [Renfrew], 346b
Reni, Guido, 412b
Rephaim, 346b-d; 391d
Repose, states of humanity in, 9b, 17a, 43a,
  309b
Repression and suppression, sexual. See
  Sex, repression of
Reprobate. See also Classes; Transgressors
  Byron as, 63b
  in Milton, 410b
  in Milton's poems, 409c
  Shelley as, 314c (twice)
  Transgressors and, 409b-c
  mentioned, 342a
Restoration Period, 79c
Resurrection
  in America, 21c
  of body, 83b-c, 94a, 214a, 300d-301a
  Catholic doctrine of, 83b-c
  fly as, 140a
  Paul's view of, 300d-301a, 323c-d
  rainbow as, 300d-301a
Reu, 347a
Reuben, 347a-348d
  Abraham and, 4a-b
  as average sensual man, 202b[c], 347b
  in Bashan, 37b, 347b, d
  Benjamin and, 41d, 347b-c, 348c
  in Cave of Adam, 6b, 348a
  Gate of, 69c-d, 348c, c-d
  in Jerusalem. See Jerusalem, Reuben in
  Jordan crossed by, 223d, 347a, c
  Promised Land and, 333b, 347c, 348b
  mentioned, 21d, 259a
Reunion, 120d, 190b, 191a, 262c, 327b,
  367b, 368b, 418c-d
"Reunion of the Soul and the Body, The,"
  184a
Revelation, 335b
Revelation. See also Last Judgment
  Angels of, 23a-b
  Bible as history and, 45b
  B's illustrations of, 82a, 223b-c, 272a.
    318d. See also Last Judgment, B's
    pictures of
  Dante illustrations and, 83a
  dragon of, 357a. See also Dragon
  Four Zoas and, 236a, b
  harvest imagery in, 176b
  Lake of Fire in, 231d
  Lamb of God in, 232a
  in Milton, 238b[c]
  Seven Churches of Asia in, 85a

Revelation (cont'd)
  "Spenser's *Faerie Queene*" and, 384b
  text of
    ii:9, 338d, 356b
    iii:9, 356b
    iv:7, 459c
    ix:11, 272a
    xi:7-12, 271c
    xii:1-6, 238c[d], 450a
    xii:4, 108a, 238d [239a], 310d, 357d
    xii:7, 272a
    xiv:14-20, 176b
    xiv:18-20, 434d
    xv:3, 222d
    xvii, 83a
    xvii:4, 431d
    xvii:9, 84c
    xvii:16, 433b
    xxii:2, 314c
  Tribes of Israel in, 96c
  Witnesses in, 444a, 447a
  Woman in the Wilderness in, 384b, 450a
  Zoa in, 458c
Revenge. *See* Vengeance
Revenge (Young), 455c
Revere, Paul, 21c
  Massachusetts Spy, 145d
Reversal, 88a, 255a[b], 293c-d
Revolt of Islam (Shelley), 112b, 271d
Revolution, 348d-349a. *See also* American
  Revolution; French Revolution
  art and, 28d-29a, 253a[b]
  B's view of, 144d-145a
  in *Book of Ahania,* 7a
  brass and, 58b
  counter-, 20a
  creative process and, 321a
  degeneration of, 365c
  in *Europe,* 132c
  Experience and, 219c, 348d, 407d
  fire as, 139a
  formula for, 20b
  Gwin, King of Norway and, 170b
  harrow as, 174a
  Jesus and, 213d, 214b, 349a
  Los's relation to, 247a[b]
  in *The Marriage,* 262b, 263c
  Orc as, 253a[b], 309b-311c, 369b
  plow as, 174a, 329b-330b
  prophecy and, 335d
  Rousseau and, 351b-352a, 439c-d
  Tyger's wrath as, 413d, 349a
  Voltaire and, 439c-d
  war and, 86a
  wrath as, 413d, 452d
Revolutionary Period
  in literature, 195d-196a, 331a, 332a
  in religion, 342c-d, 392c
Reynolds, Sir Joshua, 80d, 267d, 389d
  "Count Hugolino," 97b
  Discourses, B's annotations to, 289c

Rhadamanthus, 349a-b
Rhea, 349b
Rhine River, 349b-c; 98a
Rhode Island School of Design, 324b
Ribble, River, 349c
Richard I, King, 349c
Richard of Cirencester, 108d
Riches, 324d, 352a
Richmond, George, 334b
Richmond, Sir William Blake, 334b
Right. *See* Left and right symbolism
Rights of Man, The (Paine), 316d
Rimmon, 349c-d; 96b
Rintrah, 349d-350a
  Merlin and, 270c, 350a
  in *Milton,* 277c, 278c-d
  Orc and, 309c, 349d, 453a
  Palamabron and, 321b-c, 350a, 453a
  Reprobate and, 410a
Rituals, sacraments as, 353d-354a
Rival Queens (Lee), 237a[b]
River Dee, 81a
River of Life, 115a, 410c-d
River of Oxford, 315a
Rivers of Eden. *See* Eden, rivers of
Rivers of the Water of Life, Four, 364d, 458d
Robinson, Henry Crabb, 276a-b, b-c, 376b, 451a-b, c
Rochester, 350a-b
Rock of Ages, 350b-c
Rock of Eternity, 350c; 363a
Rod as phallic symbol, 271b
Roe, Albert S
  Blake's Illustrations to the Divine Comedy, 84a, 97c, d, 188d, 263d, 300a, 390c
  "A Drawing of the Last Judgment," 235d
Roller, 329a
Roman Catholic Church. *See* Church of Rome
Romano, Giulio, 313b
Romanticism, 195d-196a, 331a, b, 332a-b
Rome, 350c-d; 83a, 156d. *See also* Church of Rome
Romeo and Juliet (Shakespeare), 14a
Romney, George, 176d
Rosamond's Bower, 350d-351a
Rosary, 235d
Roscommon, 351a
Rose, Samuel, 360d
Rose, 351a; 74d, 222b, 240c[d] (twice), 283c, 390c
Rosenwald Collection, 50c
Rose of Heaven, 390c
Rosicrucians, 450a
Ross, 351a-b
Rossetti, William Michael, 236a, 405b, 437b-c
Rousseau, Jean Jacques, 351b-352a
  Confessions, 351c
  Contrat social, 351b

Rousseau, Jean Jacques (cont'd)
  Discours sur les art et sciences, 351b
  Émile, 351b, 406d
  "Mock on, Mock on, Voltaire, Rousseau,"
    298c
  Natural Man of, 6a, 351b, c
  Nouvelle Héloise, 351b
  Tiriel source in, 406d
  Voltaire and, 351c-352a, 439c-d
  mentioned, 18c, 100c
Rowley, Thomas, 78c
Roxbro [Roxburgh], 352a
Royal Academy, 47d, 267a
Royal Asylum for Female Orphans
  [Asylum], 31b, 181c, 232c
Rubens, Peter Paul, 319d, 412b
Ruby, 352a-b; 324d
Ruddicombe, Dr. Tobias, M.D., 209b
Ruins of Time (Spenser), 385b, 434a, c-d
Ruskin, John, 208d, 436b
Russell, A. G. B.: The Engravings of William
  Blake, 61c
Russia, 352b
Ruth, 352b; 266a, b
Rutland, 352b
Ruysdael, 412b

Sabbath as Millenium, 454c
Sabrina, 353a-c; 169a, 367a
Sacraments, 353c-354a. See also Baptism;
  Lord's Supper
Sacrifice
  animal, 4a
  human
    Canaanites practiced, 68b
    Chemosh and, 80a
    druidism and, 3d-4a, 108b, 109c, 343b,
      447a
    at London Stone, 245c-d [246a-b]
    Molech and, 186b, 283-284a
    at Tophet, 186b
    Twenty-Seven Churches and, 85c-86a
    by Wicker Man, 447a
  self-, 100b, 222a, 307c (twice), 309b, 401a
"Sacrifice of Jepthah's Daughter, The,"
  258c
Saddusaion, 354a
Sage, illus. XI (#39)
Sahara, 457a
Saint Albans, town, 434a, b
Saint David's, 354a
Saint James's Park, 323a
Saint John's Wood, 354a
Saint Paul's Cathedral, 72c, 106d
Saints, See also names of saints
  communion of, 71a, c, 105a
  as Elect, 87d
  Pharisees as, 88b
  Satan a, 88b
Salah, 354a-b

Salamandrine Men, 354b
Sale, George: Preliminary Discourse, 236a,
  259c
Salisbury, 254b-c
Salisbury Plain, 354c. See also Stonehenge
Salt Lake, 354c
Salvation, 271c, 358a-b, 446d
Sampson, John: French Revolution in his
  edition of B, 146a
Samson, 354d; 88a, 297a-b
"Samson," 297b
Samson Agonistes (Milton), 275d, 448a
Samuel, 354d; 7b
Samuel, 354d
Sandal, 354d-355a; 140c-d
Sanhedrim [Sanhedrin], 355a-b
Sapphire, 355b
Sarah, 171b-c, 198d [199a]
Satan, 355b-358c. See also Lucifer
  Adam and, 5b-c, 6a-b
  Albion's spectre as, 11b
  Anak and, 22a
  Angel of the Divine Presence as, 22b
  angels of, 24c, 365b
  Apollo as, 26a, 390a
  bow of, 55c-d
  cherubim of, 365b
  Church of, 82c, 356b
  Covering Cherub as, 11b, 93d
  Elect as, 88b
  without emanation, 122a
  evil quaternary of, 77c-d (diagram)
  in Gates of Paradise, 150a-b, 358b-c
  gnomes and, 158a-b
  God of This World as, 160c-d, 344d,
    355d
  in Job, 216b, 276d
  in Job illustrations, 49d, 217c, 219d, 221c
  in Laocoön, 234b
  mills of, 273d
  in Milton, 175b-176b, 177c-178d, 277b-d,
    356d-357a, 357a-358a
  in Milton's work, 88a, 143a, 276d, 341d,
    357a-c, 422b
  opacity as, 241a[b], 309a, 355b-c
  Orc as, 310b
  paved work of, 324b-c
  Reactor as, 341c-d
  Reprobate as, 88a
  selfhood and, 356c, 363b, 381c
  spectre as, 356c, 381c
  state of, 355b, c-d, 356b, 358a-b, 386c-d,
    419b, c-d
  sun as, 390a
  Synagogue of, 94a, 388d, 356b, 394c-d,
    417a
  Urizen as, 26a, 143a, 419b, c-d, 422b
  in "VLJ," illus. I (#30)
  war as, 356c-d, 442a
"Satan in His Original Glory," 254b-c[c-d]

"Satan's Evil Quaternary" (diagram), 77c-d
"Satan Smiting Job with Boils," tempera, 217a
"Satan Watching Adam and Eve," 303b
Satire, Greek, 168a
Saturn, son of Uranus, 358c-d; 50d, 148d, 457b
Saturn, planet, 358d-359a
Satyrs, 194d
Saul, 359a; 7b
Saul of Tarsus. See Paul
Saurat, Denis; Blake and Modern Thought, 215d
Saviour. See Jesus
"Saviour, The Humility of the," 213b
Saxons, 359a
Scales, 244a[b-c]
Scandinavia, 359a-b; 447a-b
Scepter, 254b[c]
Schiavonetti, Louis, 47d
Schofield. See Scofield
Scholem, Dr. Gershom, 264d
Scholfield. See Scofield
Science, 359b-360c
  Allamanda and Bowlahoola represent, 57c, 360a
  Antichrist as, 25c
  architecture as, 27a, 359d
  Bacon founder of, 34d
  forgiveness and, 141d
  in Island in the Moon, 197a, 199d [200a], 374d
  tent as, 360b, 397d
  Ulro and, 417b-c
Scofield [Scofeld, etc.], 360d-361d; 50b, 56c-d, 85c, 178b
Scopprell, 362a
Scotland, 362a-b; 92d-93d, 312a-b, 441a.
  See also place names
Scribes, 166b-c
Scroll as inspiration, 218b, 219a, 222a, 254b[c], 299c
Scudamore, Sir, 384c
Scudder, Horace, 437b
Scull, 362b-c; 6b
Sculptures, 362c-d; 268d, 433d-434a
Sea anemone as polypus, 332d
Sea monster, 96a
Sea of Rephaim, 346c
Sea of Time and Space, 362d-363a
  in "Circle of Life," 87a, 304b
  Flood of Noah and, 31b, 139b, 300d, 363a
  in Four Zoas, illus., 400d
  in Gates of Paradise, 140b, 149d
  in Jerusalem, illus., 240d [241a], 390c
  in Job illustrations, 221a, b, 240b[c], 363a
  matter as, 362d-363a, 443b
  sea shells of, 240b[c], 363a
  Tharmas and, 399b
Sea shells, 363a; 221b, 240b[c]

Seasons, 331b, 366d, 449a-b, illus. I (#63, 69)
Second Book of Urizen, The: Book of Ahania as, 50c
Second Coming of Jesus, 94d, 392b, 393b
Secrecy, 308d-309a, 314a-b
Secret Child, 363a
Selah, 363a-b
Self, 363b-d
Selfhood, 363b-d
  center and, 75d
  Covering Cherub as, 93d, 94a, b, 363c
  individual and, 346a-b
  in Job illustrations, 222d, 223a
  Satan as, 356c, 363b, 381c
  spectre as, 363b, 381a
Self-love, 194d-195a, 401a
Self-sacrifice. See Sacrifice, self-
Selkirk, 363d
Selsey, 363d-364a; 81b-c
Semen. See Cloud, as male principle or semen
Semites, 371b
Seneca, 363a
Seneca's Morals (L'Estrange), 364a
Sense, Parent, 399b, 408a
Senses, 364a-365a. See also Body; Perception; names of senses and sense organs
  America as, 19b
  in Book of Thel, 401b
  death of, 49d, 219a, 406d, 408c-d
  in Europe, 132d-133a
  Four, 115b, 364d-365a
  giants as, 155c
  in Hobbes' theory of knowledge, 239c-d [239d-240a]
  in Job illustrations, pl. 6, 49d, 219a, 364d, 408d
  limitation of, 295b-c, 364b, 365a, See also Limits
  Locke's philosophy of, 243a[b], 364b, 402c-d
  Moral Virtue and, 347c-d
  rivers of Eden as, 115b
  sex and, 19b, 364c, 365a, 367b
  Suction the Epicurean represents philosophy of, 199d [200a], 389c
  Tharmas as, 399a
  in Tiriel, 179c, 406d, 408c-d
  tongue's place among, 408a
  West and, 444a
  Zoas as, 458d
Septenary: Abraham, Moses, Soloman, Paul, Constantine, Charlemaine, Luther, 324a-b
Seraphim, 365a-b
  Mne Seraphim, 7d, 282c-d
Serpent, 365b-366c. See also Adder; Prester Serpent; Rattlesnake; Viper

Serpent (cont'd)
in American Revolution as symbol, 435c
eagle and, 112a-b, 271d (twice)
in *Europe*, pl. ii, illus., 133a, 365d
of *Genesis* as Satan, 357a
in *Genesis* Ms. title page, 151c-d, 459c-d
in "Hervey's *Meditations*," illus. XI (#4)
in *Jerusalem*, 46, illus., 118d
in *Job* illustrations, 218d, 219a, d
in Laocoön, 234b (twice), 306c-d, 366a
Leviathan as, 239c[d]
in "The Little Girl Lost," illus., 258a[b]
as musical instrument, 290b
Nature and, 309a, 365d, 366a-b
in *Night Thoughts* illustrations, 450b
of Ophiuchus, 309a-b
Orc as, 145d, 309d, 310b, d, 325a, 365c, 435b-c
Stonehenge and, 109b-c
in "VLJ," 84c, 95a, illus. I (#29, 30)
Serpent Temple, 365d-366a, 387c
Serug, 366c
Seth, 366c-d; illus. I (#62)
Sette Giornale des Mondo Creato, Le (Tasso), 152b
Seven, Starry, 385d
Seven Angels. *See* Angel, of the Presence
Seven Churches, 85a; 238a[b-c]
Seven Deadly Sins, 104a-c, 161c, d, 452c, d
Seven Eyes. *See* Eyes of God
Seven in Golgonooza, 163 (diagram)
1757, 235a
Severn, 367a; 169a, 353a, b
Sex, 367b-368b. *See also* Body; Chastity;
  Harlots and harlotry; Hermaphrodite;
  Marriage; Phallic symbolism;
  Senses
adulterous, 264a, c, 350d
America as, 19b
Arnon symbol of, 28b
Babylon and, 33d
Balaam urges, 36b
in Beulah, 43a-b, 367c
in *Book of Thel*, 52b-c, 401b
brotherhood and, 60d
Cambel and Gwendolen use, 169b
Catholic debasement of, 83c-84a
dream of, 378d, 402d-403a
Enion and, 122c, 399d
Erin and, 128a-c
in eternity, 130b, 190b, 367b
fairies and, 136a
Fall and, 276c, 285d
foot represents, 140a-b
in *Four Zoas*, 122c-d, 399d
in *Gates of Paradise*, 452b
Hela as, 179b-c, 406b
in *Job* illustrations, pl. 6, 219a
Last Judgment and, 244a[b]
Leutha and, 124c (diagram), 132b, 237d [238a]

Sex (cont'd)
liberty and, 207d-208a
Mahomet's idea of, 259c-d
in *The Marriage*, 394b
Marygold as, 265b-c
in *Midsummer Night's Dream*, 370b
and *Milton* 35, illus., 112b-c
in Milton's works, 276c-d, 408c
Minute Particulars in, 281b-c
mirtle as, 282b
Moab and, 283a
Moral Virtue and, 347c-d
net as, 297d
in "Never Pain to Tell Thy Love," 298a
Oothoon's view of, 308c-309a
passions of (symbology of), 62a, 220d, 239a[b]
in "Paul Preaching," 324b
Paul's attitude toward, 323d-324a
plow as, 329a
Rahab seeks domination by, 339d
reason and, 276c-d
as religion, 30d, 345c, 367d-368b, 395b
repression of, 124c (diagram), 130c-d, 132a-b, 261c, 367d-368b, 368d-369a, 378d-379a, 403a, 442c
Rosamond's bower as illicit, 350d
serpent symbol of, 366b-c
in Sodom, 376c-d
Swedenborg's ideas about, 394b, 408c
Theotormon and, 124c (diagram), 132b
Thiralatha and, 124c (diagram), 132b, 403a
Tirzah represents, 407a
touch and, 155c, 364c-d, 408c, d, 444a
Tree of Life and, 367b, 410c
in *Visions*, 308c-309a, 437d-438a
war and, 146b-c, 169b, 284b, 306a, 332c, 356d, 368a-b, 378d-379a, 433d, 442b-c
West and, 444a
Sexes, 42d-43a, 49b, 133a-b, 181d-182c. *See also* War, of the sexes
Shaddai, 368b-d
Almighty as, 18b, 386b
as Eye of God, 134c[d], 134d [135a] (twice)
in *Job* illustrations, 217d, 222d, 223a, 368c
Shadow, 368d-369b
Milton's, 278a, 279c, 280b, 368d-369a
Shadowy Female, 369b-d; 429b
Shakespeare, William, 369d-370d
"Albion's Dance" and, 14a
B's illustrations of, 155a, 319c, 370c-d
Dryden's opinion of, 110b
Dryden's adaptations of, 110c
Hamlet, 370d
  B's illustrations of, 155a
I Henry IV, B's illustrations of, 370c
King Edward the Third influenced by, 228d
King Lear, 370d, 448a

Shakespeare, William (cont'd)
  Macbeth, 370b, 390a
  B's illustrations of, 370c, c-d
  Midsummer Night's Dream, 165b, 331d, 370b, d
  Poetical Sketches influenced by, 331a, 370a
  Romeo and Juliet, 14a
  mentioned, 262d
Shame, 370d-371a; 5d, 283c
Sharp, William, 379d
Shechem, 371a-b
Shell. See Mundane Shell; Sea shells
Shelley, Percy B.
  as Bard of Oxford in Jerusalem, 37a, 38d, 71d, 72d, 120a, 148a, 209c, 210a-b, 314b-315a
  "The Cloud," 25b
  Defence of Poetry, 248a[b]
  Erasmus Darwin and, 98b
  incest in works of, 196a
  "Ode to the West Wind," 314c-d
  The Revolt of Islam, 112b, 271d
Shem, 371b-c; illus. I (#68)
Shenstone, William, 383d
Shepherd, Tharmas as, 399a (twice)
Shetland, 371c
Shift, character in play, 446d
Shiloh, 371c-372a; 379d
Shinar, 372a-b; 33b-c
Shipbuilding, 68a
Shooter's Hill, 372b
Shores of Darkness (Hungerford), 61b
Shropshire, 372b
Shuah's daughter, 372b-c; 266a
Shur, 372c
Siberia, 372c
"Sick Rose, The," 351a, 456b
Sidon, 372c
Siegfried (Wagner), 428a
Sight. See Eye
Sihon, 372d-373a; 22a, 156b, 288d, 306c-d
Silver, 373b-c; xi-xii, 198c[d], 271a, b
  Book of, 424c
Simeon, 373c-d; 27b
  Gate of, 69c
Simony, 36a
Sin, 373d-374a
  Ahania as, 8a
  baptism and, 36c
  Catholic doctrine of, 84a-b
  deadly, 104a-c, 161c, d, 452c, d
  as disease, 104a-d, 373d-374a
  emanation invents, 121d
  of emotions, 77d (diagram)
  forgiveness of. See Forgiveness
  against Holy Ghost, 187c
  justice and, 227c
  Leutha as, 25a, 237d [238a], b-c[c-d], 357d
  in Milton and Paradise Lost, 158b, 175b
  Original, 5d, 65a, 119a

Sin (cont'd)
  punishment of, 160d-161a, 227b. See also Vengeance
  in "VLJ," 433d, illus. I (#32)
Sinai, Mount, 374a-c; 189b
Single vision. See Vision, levels of
Sinners as Transgressors, 409a
Sins, Seven Deadly, 104a-c, 161c, d, 452c, d
Sion [Zion], 458b-c
Sipsop the Pythagorean, 374c-375b; 199c[d], 199d [200a]
Sirius, 117a
Sistine Chapel, Michelangelo's paintings in, 138a, 272b-c
Sixfold Emanation, Milton's. See Milton, Sixfold Emanation in
Skeat, W. W., 78c
Skepticism, 156d, 191b
Skiddaw, 375d
Skofeld. See Scofield
Skofield. See Scofield
Skull (Scull), 6b, 362b-c
Sky, 288b, 397d
Skye, 375c
Slade [Slaid, Slayd, etc.], 375c; 385d
Slander, 219c
Slavery, 6c-d, 7b, 116b, 406a, 438a-b
Sleep, 43b, 269b, 315d
Sligo, 375c-d
Sloss, D. J., and J. P. R. Wallis: The Prophetic Writings of William Blake, 144c, 266b
Sloth, 376c, d
Smaragdine Table, 182d-183b
Smell. See Nostrils
Smith, J. T., 290c, d
[Smith, Pamela Colman, 223a--2nd pr. only]
Smith, R. L.: Nativity of Mr. Blake, 276a
Smoke, 413c'
Smollett, Tobias, 446d
Snake. See Serpent
Snowdon, Mount, 375d-376a; 157c
Snubnose, 376b
Society
  brass the metal of, 399a
  forest as, 141a
  human form of, 393b
  in Mental Traveller, 268c
  polypus as, 332d-333a
  Ulro and, 417b
  Urizen's ideal for, 424b
Society of Friends, 39d, 342c-d
Sociology, 424b
Socrates, 376a-c; 25d
Sodom, 376c-377a; 166a, 253d [254a]
Sodomy, 376c
Sodor, 377a; 24d
Soho, Broad St. in, 59c
Sol, 247a, 246d [247a]
Solomon, 377a-b; 389b, 457a, illus. XI (#13)
Solomon, Song of, 236d [237a], 407a

Solomon, Wisdom of, 303d
Somerset, 377c; 59a
"Song of Liberty, A," 377c. See also
    Marriage of Heaven and Hell, plates of,
    pls. 25-27
Song of Los, The, 377c-d
    "Africa," 7a, 21a, 153a, 377c, d
    America and, 7a, 21a, 153a, 377c, d
    "Asia," 21a, 30d-31a, 377c, d
    Bible plot in, 423b
    Book of Los and, 51d, 377c-d
    Diralda in, 403a
    Europe and, 21a, 30d, 131d, 377c, d
    Los in, 248a[b]
    Noah in, 301a
    plates of
        pl. 3:28-29, 259d
        pl. 3:30-31, 306a
        pl. 4:13-14, 7a
        pl. 4:21, 7a
    Urizen in, 423b-c
Song of Solomon, 236d [237a], 407a
Songs of Experience. See also titles of individual
    poems
    B's poetic purpose in, 147d
    [title page, illus., 99c, 197b-c--2nd pr.
        only]
    Urizen in, 422d
Songs of Innocence. See also titles of individual
    poems
    art of, 319a
    death in, 99c
    in *Island in the Moon*, 199b[c], 200a-b[b-c]
Songs of Innocence and of Experience, 378a-c.
    See also titles of individual poems
    angels in, 22c-d
    Innocence and Experience in, [197b-c],
        378a-c
    L'Allegro and *Il Penseroso*'s influence on,
        274d-275a, 378a
    Wordsworth's opinion of, 451c
    mentioned, 232d
Son of God. *See* Jesus; Trinity
Son of Man, Jesus as, 214a
Sons of Israel. *See* Israel, Sons of
Sophronia, illus. XI (#27)
Sorrow after self-love, 306a
Sotha, 378a-379a; 124c (diagram), 132b,
    306a
Soul
    body and, 362a-b, 363a, 441a, illus. I
        (#78)
    in "Circle of Life," 86d
    Dark Night of the, 291c
    Los conducts, 247c[d]
    Scotland as, 362a-b, 441a
    transmigration of, 108b, 110a
"Soul and the Body, The Reunion of
    the," 184a
Sources, B's use of, 268a-b, 320c-d, 436d
South, 379a-b; 75c, 271a, 441a. *See also*
    Compass points

Southcott, Joanna, 379c-d
Southey, Robert, 209a, 315b-c, 443d
    Madoc, 243a[b]
South Molton Street, 379b-c
South Sea, 379c; 61d, 128c-d, 342a
Space, 379d-380c; 77b, 125b, 286a-b. *See*
    also Sea of Time and Space; Time
Spain, 380c-d
Sparrow, John, 39d
Sparrow, 380d
Spartans [Lacedaemonians], 231b
Spectre, 380d-383c
    Abomination of Desolation as, 3c
    Abstract God invented by, 159c
    of Albion, 11b, 12b-c, 382b-c
    Albion's sons as, 15a-b
    Antamon and, 25a
    of the Dead, 382d-383c
    emanation craved by, 381c-d, 318d-382a
    in *Jerusalem*, 210c, 211b-213a in passing,
        381d-382a, 383b-c
    memory and, 267c
    reason as, 172c, 341d, 380d, 381a, c-d,
        382a-b
    reunion of, 120d, 190b-191a, 368b
    Satan as, 356c, 381c
    selfhood as, 363b, 381a
    of Urthona, 12c-d, 382c-d, 385b, 427c
"Spectre around Me Night & Day, My,"
    290d-291a, 381d
Speech, 408a. *See also* Word
Speech on Conciliation (Burke), 379c
"Spencer, An Imitation of," 226a, 269a,
    383c, 385a
Spenser, Edmund, 383c-385b
    Faerie Queene
        androgeny in, 182b
        B's illustration of, 383d-385a, illus.
            VIII
        eagle and serpent in, 112b
        Medway and Thames in, 267a, 385b
        nudity and sex in, 303b
        Spectre of Urthona resembles Talus in,
            382c, 385b
        Theotormon resembles Malbecco in,
            385a, 402b, 438c
        Vala's garden resembles Garden of
            Adonis in, 385b, 432b
    Hymn to Beauty, 17a, 385a
    nakedness admired by, 303b, 371a
    Poetical Sketches influenced by, 331a
    Ruins of Time, 385b, 434a, c-d
    in "Spenser's *Faerie Queene*," 384d
    as symbolist, 274b
"Spenser's *Faerie Queene*," 383d-385a,
    illus. VIII
Spider, 385b-d; 219b
Spinning wheels, 445b-c
Spirit of All Religion, The (Taylor), 397b
Spiritual body. *See* Body
"Spiritual Form of Nelson Guiding
    Leviathan, The," 239d-240a [240a-b]

"Spiritual Form of Pitt Guiding Behemoth, The," 240a[b]
"Spirit Vaulting from a Cloud to Turn and Wind a Fiery Pegasus, A," 370c
Spring, 366d, illus. I (#63, 69)
Squid as polypus, 332d
Squintum, Dr., 140d, 446d (3 times)
Staff, 225b
Stafford, 385d; 234a, 375c
Stamp Act, 55a
Starry Eight, 307d, 308a
Starry Hosts, 385d
Starry Seven, 385d
Starry Wheels, 16b-c, 445c-446a
Stars, 386a-b. *See also* Belt; Betelgeuse; Cosmology; Ophiuchus; Orion; Starry Eight; Starry Hosts; Starry Seven; Starry Wheels; Universe
on Albion in *Jerusalem*, 311c-d
in *America*, 263d
of Arthur, 29c, d
in *Il Penseroso* illustrations, 227a, 327d
in *Job* illustrations, 221a
Lucifer as morning, 186a, 254a-b[b-c]
of Mundane Shell, 18c, 240b[c], 372d-373a, 386a
science and, 360b (twice)
of Urizen, 414c, 424d, 425c-d
in "VLJ," 82a, illus. I (#73)
in Woman in the Wilderness's crown, 449d, 450b
zodiac and, 8a, 425c
State, government
art and, 29a
Beast of *Revelation* and, 83a
church and, *See* Church, state and
Jesus wrong to attack, 213d-214a
Leviathan as, 240a
in "London," 244b[c]
palace symbol of, 320d
Pilate as, 64c
State religions, 386b-c. *See also* Church, state and
States, B's idea, 386c-387a
of humanity in repose, 9b, 17a, 43a, 309b
Hell as, 180a
Lake of Fire receives, 232a
Last Judgment and, 235b
of Satan. *See* Satan, state of
Stedman, J. G.: *Narrative*, 7b, 438a
Steelyard the Lawgiver, 184d, 199c[d], 455d
Stepney, 387a
Sterling [Stirling], 387a-b
Stevenson, Robert Louis, 158a
Stomach, 387b; 57a, 309b
Stone, London [London Stone], 47a, 245d [245d-246b]
Stonehenge, 387d-388b; 109b, 245d [246a], 354c
Stone of Night, 387b-d
Stones, 388b-d. *See also* Rock of Ages; Rock of Eternity
body and, 189b

Stones (*cont'd*)
of druids, 109d-110a, 389a
of Fire, 388c-d
in Golgonooza, 163 (diagram)
Horeb and, 189b
precious, 42b, 324b-c, 366a, 388b. *See also* Beryl; Carbuncle; Diamond
Rocking, 388b-c
Storge, 388d; 393c
Stothard, Thomas, 48a, 266d-267a
Stratford, 388d-389a; 55d-56a
Stratford-le-Bow, 55d, 388d
Stratford Place, 389a
Strathness, 389a
Strindberg, August: *The Father*, 448a
Strong Man, 208d-209a, 375a. *See also* Man, Beautiful *and* Man, Ugly
Strumbolo, 389a-b
Stukeley, William, 108c, 109b, 343b, 387d
Subconscious. *See also* Freud, Sigmund; Mind
Behemoth and Leviathan as, 39b
Beulah as, 42d
in *Book of Thel*, 456b-c
earth as, 113b
energy as, 262b (twice)
in *Gray illustrations*, 456c
Hell as, *See* Subconscious, in *The Marriage*
in *Job* illustrations, pl. 15, 221a, 240a[b]
lilly as, 240c-d [241a]
in *The Marriage*, 231d-232a, 263c, 270d, 357c
mole explores, 283c-d
nadir symbol of, 293c
Urthona's forge and dens in, 263c, 426b
vision and, 436d
in Young, 456b-c
Sublimity, 328b
Succoth, 389b-c
Suction the Epicurean, 389c-d; 199c[d], 374c
Suffering, furnaces symbols of, 146c
Suffolk, 389d
Sulphur, 389d; 390a-b
Summer and Smoke (Williams), 298a-b
Sun, 390a-b
B's vision of, on Primrose Hill, 335a, 390a
Eyes of God and, 217d
god of, 25d, 33a, 311d
in *Jerusalem* 25, 311d
in *Job* illustrations, 219a-b, b, 220d, 222d, 390a
as Los's planet, 246d [247a], 390b
material, 393c, 389d, 390a, 419c
moon and, 285c
of Salah, 354b
Urizen's, 390a, b, 419c
of Woman in the Wilderness, 449d
Sunflower, 390b-c; 410b. *See also* "Ah! Sun-Flower"
"Sunflower, The." *See* "Ah! Sun-Flower"
Superego, 262b, 357c, 394a. *See also* Mind

Superstition, 390d-391a; 346c, d
"Suppressed and Altered Passages in Blake's Jerusalem, The" (Erdman), 210b-c
Suppression, sexual. *See* Sex, repression of
Surgery, 391a-b; 318c, 374d-375a, 391a-b, 399b
Surinam slave revolt, 7b
Surrey, 391b-d
Susan, in "Laughing Song," 258a[c]
Sussex, 391d-392a
Sussex Advertizer, 360d
"Sussex Men Are Noted Fools, The," 392a
Sutherlan[d], 392a
Sutton, Thomas, 72c, d, 111c
Sweden, 392b
Swedenborg, Emanuel, 392b-394c
  angels in, 23a, 393b
  Apocalypse Revealed, 392d
  on Bible, 45c, 393c
  Conjugial Love, 388d, 392d, 393c, 408c
  Divine Love, 267b, 392d
    B's annotations to, 194b, 393d
  Divine Providence, 392d
    B's annotations to, 393d
  Grand Man of, 9d
  Heaven and Hell, 392d (twice)
  on Jesus, 213b, 393a-c
  Last Judgment, 262c
  Last Judgment in, 235a, 392b, 393b
  The Marriage, and, 23a, 262c, 263a (twice), 392c, 393a, 394a-c
  Mary the Virgin and, 213b, 264d, 393a-b
  religion as system of, 342d
  Samson as, 354d
  on senses, 364c
  sex in, 394b, 408c
  suns of, 390a, 393c
  True Christian Religion, 194d-195a, 306a, 392c, d, 393c
  Universal Theology, 406d
  mentioned, 343b
Sweeney, J. R.: "O Beulah Land," 42d
Swinburne, Algernon Charles, 274c
Swine, 216a
Switzerland, 18c
Sword and the Church Paul, 324a
Sybils, Michelangelo's, 272c
Sylvie and Bruno (Carroll), 143b
Symbol and Image in William Blake (Digby), 87b
"Symbolic Figure of the Course of History Described by Virgil," 97d
Symbolism
  allegory and, 17c, 437c
  of Bible, 41a
  in *Book of Ahania*, B's dissatisfaction with, 51a
  Divine Analogy as, 104d
  in English literary tradition, 274b, 383c
  Homer's, 188a

Symbolism (*cont'd*)
  in Nature, 296b
  in *Poetical Sketches*, 331b
  Swedenborg's, 392c
  vision and, 17c, 436c, 437c
Synagogue of Satan. *See* Satan, Synagogue of
Syria and Syrians, 26d, 261a

Tabernacle, 395a-396a; 397d
Talus, 382c, 384c, 385b
Tamar, 396a; 266a
Tammuz [Thammuz], 398d
Tarot cards, 223a
Tartary, 396a-b
Tasso, Torquato: *Le Sette Giornale del Mondo Creato*, 152b
Taurus, 311c
Taxes, 396b
Taylor, Thomas, 396c-397c
  Dissertation on the Eleusinian Mysteries, 397b
  "History of the Restoration of the Platonic Theology," 396c-d
  in *Island in the Moon*, 199c[d], 199d [200a], 397a-b
  "Medicina mentis," 396d
  On the Cave of the Nymphs, 265c
  religion and the Platonism of, 342d
  Spirit of All Religion, 397b
  symbolism and, x
  mentioned, 328c
Tearguts, Jack, 199c[d], 374d, 375a
Teeth and tongue, 408b
Temora (Macpherson), 312a
Temple, veil in the, 432b-c
Temple of Flora, 232b
Ten Commandments. *See* Commandments; Decalogue
Teniers, David, 412b
Tent, 397c-d
Terah, 397d-398a
Teraphim stolen by Rachel, 236c[d]
Teresa, Saint, 398a; 343b
Terror, 316b (twice)
Tesshina, 398a-b
Tetragrammaton, 215d
Text of B's work, editing of, 1, 144b-c
Thames, 398b-d; 32b, 267a, 385b, 434d
Thammuz, 398d
Tharmas, 399a-401a. *See also* Zoa
  body as, 363a, 399a, 458d
  in "Circle of Life," 87a-b, 400d
  circumference as, 75c, 87c
  Enion and, 122c-123d, 399c-400d in passing
  in *Genesis* Ms. title page, 313d, 401a
  name of, 124a, 401a
  ox as, 313d, 401a
  sea shells and, 363a
  west assigned to, 399a-b, 444a
  York as, 455b

Thebes, 69b
Thel, 401a-d; 6c, 430a
Thel, The Book of. See *Book of Thel*
"Then She Bore Pale Desire," 104b, 161c
Theophilus of Antioch: *To Autolycus*, 450c-d
Theosophical Society, 392d
Theotormon, 401d-402c
  Malbecco and, 385a, 402b, 438c
  mills of, 273d
  name of, 312d-313a, 401d
  Oothoon and, 124c (diagram), 130d,
    402b, 437d, 438b-c
  sex and, 124c (diagram), 132b
  mentioned, 309c
There is No Natural Religion, 402c-d; 343d
Theresa, Saint [Teresa], 343b, 398a
"There's Dr. Clash," 362a
Theron and Aspasio (Hervey), 184d
Theseus, 165b
Thiralatha, 402d-403b
  Diralda as, 104a, 378d
  sex and, 124c (diagram), 132b, 403a
  Sotha and, 124c (diagram), 378d
Thiriel, 403b; 9a
Thirteen, 220c
Thirty-Two Nations, 294d-295b; 19b. *See
  also names of the nations*
"Thirty-Two Nations, The" (diagram), 295
Thistle, 403b-c
Thomson, James, 331a
Thor, 403c-d; 434a, 442c
Thoth, 182c
Thought. *See* Mind
Three Books of Philosophy (Paracelsus), 322c
Three Classes of Men. *See* Classes
Threefold form of man, 397b
Threefoldness. *See* Triads; Trinities;
  Trinity
Thulloh, 403d
Thurlow, Lord, 166d
Thyme, 403d-404a
Tiara, 235c
Tiger. *See* Tyger
Tigris River, 185c
Timaeus (Plato), 222a, 328d
Time, 404a-405b; 29b, 247b[c], 299c, 340d,
  illus. I (#34). *See also* Moment; Sea of
  Time and Space; Years
Time-spirit in *Visions*, 438a, b
Tipperary, 405b
Tiriel, character, 405b-407a; 7d
Tiriel, 405b-407a
  Book of Thel and, 52a
  Har in, 174a-c, 405c, 406a-b, c
  Hela in, 179b-c, 406b
  Ijim in, 194d-195a, 406b, d
  illustrations in, 319a, 405b
  senses in, 179c, 406d, 408c-d
  text of
    viii:18, 271b
    viii:37, 191c-d

Tiriel (cont'd)
  West in, 405b, 444a
"Tiriel Supporting Myratana," 406a
Tirzah, 407a-408a. *See also* "To Tirzah"
  Albion's daughters and, 14c
  Cambel and, 66a (twice)
  Charlotte as, 411d
  chastity as, 253b[c]
  daughters of, 18d
  in *Gates of Paradise*, 149d
  in *Milton*, 278b
  Prioress as, 79b, 407d
  Rahab and, 330d-340a, 407b-d
  Song of, 18d
  Zelophehad's daughter as, 457c, d
Titans, 32c
Titus, 408a
To Autolycus (Theophilus of Antioch),
  450c-d
"To Autumn," 331b
Todd, Ruthven: *Tracks in the Snow*, 61b, c,
  300d
"To H. C. Six Years Old" (Wordsworth),
  451b
Tongue, 408a-c, 408c; 399b
To Nobodaddy, 301c, 422c
Tophet, 186b
"Tornado," 98c
"To Spring," 331b
"To Summer," 331b
"To the Evening Star," 331b, 449d
"To the Muses," 117b, 289c, 331b-c
"To Tirzah"
  Biblical source for, 100b, 301a, 323c
  death and sleep in, 269b
  Innocence and Experience in, 197c, 378c
  mother-image cast off in, 83d, 100b, 407d
Touch, 408c-d; 49d, 155c, 364c-d, 367b,
  406b, d, 444a
Tower of Babel. *See* Babel, Tower of
Tower of London, 246a-b[b-c], 255a[b]
"To Winter," 331b
Town & Country Magazine, 78c
Tracks in the Snow (Todd), 61b, c, 300d
Traditions, 268a, 346d
Tragedy, 203b, 236a[b], b[c], 331d, 373b
Trajan, 408d
Transfiguration, 408d-409a
"Transfiguration, The," 408d-409a
Transgressors, 409a, 410a. *See also* Classes;
  Reprobate
  inspired, 187c
  Mary the Virgin as, 264c-d
  in Maternal Line, 266c
  prophets as, 335c
Transjordan, 347d-348a
Transmigration of souls, 108b, 110a
Transubstantiation. 83c
Treachery in *Europe*, illus., 133a
Treason. *See* Blake, William, trial for
  treason of

Treatise concerning Heaven and Hell, A
  (Swedenborg), 392d (twice)
Tree, 410a-411d
  of Life, 151d, 152a, 176c, 314c, 410c-d
  of Mystery, 410d-411d
  in *Book of Ahania*, 50d, 410d-411a
  in Byron's *Cain*, 153c
  in *Genesis* Ms. title page, 459d
  polypus as, 333c
  raven and, 341c, 410d
  religion as, 291b, 345c
  Tree of Life and, 410c
  mentioned, 17d, 140b
Trent, 411d
Triads. *See* Trinities; Trinity; Welsh Triads
"Trial of William Blake, The" (Ives), 360d
Tribes of Israel. *See* Israel, Tribes of
Trilithons, 388a-b
Trinities
  Accuser, Executioner, Judge, 345b
  Allamanda, Bowlahoola,
    Entuthon-Benython, 17a, 57a-b
  Amalek, Canaan, Moab, 18d, 283a
  Arthur, Bladud, Merlin, 30a, 47b
  Bacon, Locke, Newton, 35b, 343b[c],
    298c, 343c
  Chaucer, Milton, Shakespeare, 35c
  Coban, Hand, Hyle, 15b, 89c, 172d, 192d
  Head, Heart, Loins, 8a, 43c, 57d, 243d
    [244a], 283a, 342b
  Heart, Lungs, Stomach, 57a-b
  Isis, Horus, Osiris, 199b[c], 311d (twice)
Trinity
  B's idea of, 393a
  Elohim and, 119c
  in *Genesis* Ms. title page, 151c-152a, 158c
  God and Jesus identified in, 158c
  Holy Ghost and Jesus in, 187a
  of Milton, 276d-277a
  Swedenborg's idea of, 393a
  Tharmas in, 399a
  Word and, 450c-d
  Zoas and, 419a-b, 459a
Trismegistus [Hermes Trismegistus],
  182c-183b
Triumphs of Temper, The (Hayley), 176d, 177b
Troja Nova, 61a
Troy, 411d-412a; 234b, 442c
Troy, New, 61a
Truchsess, Count, 412a
Truchsessian Gallery, 412a-d; 167b, 397c
True Christian Religion (Swedenborg),
  194d-195a, 306a, 392c, d, 393c
Trumbull, John, painter: "Battle of
  Bunker's Hill," 442d
Trumbull, John, poet: *M'Fingal*, 435c
Truth
  in *America c:*10, 387c
  art as, 28d
  in B's works, ix, xi
  eternity as, 129b-c
  Jesus as, 159b-c, 235b

Truth (*cont'd*)
  Lord's Supper acceptance of, 353c-d
  Spirit of, as Comforter, 221d
Tubal, 412d
Turkey, 412d-413a
Turner, Dawson, 209b
"Turret, The," Hayley's Felpham home,
  136d, 177b
  water color by B, 137b
Tweed, 413a
Twelve Gods of Asia, 42c, 44c, 161c-162a
Twenty-Four Cathedral Cities. *See*
  Cathedral Cities
Twenty-Seven Churches. *See* Churches,
  Twenty-Seven
Twenty-Seven Heavens. *See* Beulah,
  Churches or Heavens of
Twofold vision, 296c, 436b-c
"Two Lovers in the Lilly." See *Jerusalem,
  plates of, pl. 28*
Tyburn, 413b-c; 65d, 379c
Tyburn Brook, 398c, 413b
Tyburn Road, 315a-c
Tyger, 413c-414d
  creation of, 269c, 414a
  in forest, 141a
  horses and, 189c
  lion and, 242b[c], 413d-414a
  Urizen and, 160c, 386b, 414b-c, 419d,
    422d
  wrath of, 242b[c], 413c-414c in passing,
    453b
"Tyger, The," 173d, 232b, 386b, 414a-d,
  422d
Tyne, 414d
Tyranny, brass the metal of, 58b
Tyre, 414d-415b; 372c
Tyre, King of, 69b-c, 357a, 414d
Tyrone, 415b

Udan-Adan, 416a-c
Ugly Man, 197b[c], 209a, 375a. *See also*
  Man, Beautiful *and* Man, Strong
Ugolino, Count
  B's designs of, 97c, 149d
  in Chaucer's *Monkes Tale*, 79c-d, 97b
  Fuseli's painting of, 97b-c
  in *Gates of Paradise*, 149d
  Reynolds's painting of, 97b
  as Romantic artistic subject, 97a-c
"Ugolino, Count" (Fuseli), 97b-c
"Ugolino Relating His Death," 97d
Ulro, 416c-417d; 150c, 367c-d
Ulster, 417d. *See also place names*
Una, 384b
Underhill, Evelyn, 291c
Understanding, 80b (twice), 359c
Union. *See* Reunion
United States of America, 69d, 317c.
  See also America
Unity. *See* Reunion
Universality, 196c-d

Universal Tent, 397d
Universal Theology (Swedenborg), 406d
Universe, 417d-418d. See also Nature; Stars
  B's concept of, 77b-c, 142c, 328d, 394a
  body as, 295b
  in The Marriage, 262b-c
  mill as, 274a-b
  in Milton, 280c-d
  Mundane Shell in, 288c-d
  of Newton, 298b-c
  Ptolemaic, 358d, 359a
  tent in, 397d
  wheels of, 445c
  Young's, 455d
Upas tree, 411c, d
Uranus, planet, 358d
Urizen, 419a-426a. See also Book of Urizen;
    Zoa
  abstraction and, 4c
  Africa and, 6d
  Albion and, 10c-d
  in "Ancient Britons," 197b[c]
  Apollo as, 26a, 334c, 419b
  architecture and, 27a, 420d
  in Book of Ahania, 7d-8d, 50d-51a, 411a,
    423a-b
  Books of, 424a-c
  Bromion and, 60a
  "Changes" of, and embryology, 53c-d
  in "Circle of Life," 86d, 304b, 420a
  Creator as, 94c, 343a, 419d, 420b-c. See
    also Urizen, Tyger and
  cruelty as, 410d
  daughters of, 8a, 424c-425b. See also
    Eleth; Ona; Uva
  Decalogue authored by, 90b-c, 287a-b,
    420c
  in "Earth's Answer," 205a, 422d
  Elohim as, 154a, 160c
  in Europe, 83b, 91c, 133a, 420c
  in "Fertilization of Egypt," 117a
  in Four Zoas, 10c-d, 143a, 329c-d, 411a-b,
    420d-422b
  in Genesis Ms. title page, 151d
  God as, 160c, 276d, 420b-c
  gold and, 162c-d, 424d
  horses of, 189d, 420a-b
  in Job illustrations, 26a, 189d, 221a, 390a
  Lake of, 232a
  left foot symbol of, 354d
  Los and, 247b-c[c-d]
  in The Marriage, 263c, 310a-b, 377c, 420c,
    422c
  in Milton, 140c (twice), 277b, 278b, 363c,
    423c-d
  in "Milton's Dream," 277a, 423d
  night and, 299c
  North and, 302a
  Orc and, 8b, 310a-b, b, d, 311a-b
  in Paracelsus, counterpart of, 322c
  plowman as, 329c, 420c

Urizen (cont'd)
  Pope as, 83b
  Prince of Light as, 335a
  reason and, 197b[c], 341d, 419a
  Satan as, 26a, 143a, 419b, c-d, 422b
  science and, 27a, 360b-c
  separation of nations and, 294b
  silver and, 373b-c, 424c
  in Song of Los, 7a, 423b-c
  sons of, 117b-c, 425b-426a. See also
    Fuzon; Grodna; Thiriel; Utha
  South the compass point of, 379a-b
  Temple of, 257d [258a]
  Tiriel and, 407a
  Tyger and, 160c, 386b, 414b-c, 419d,
    422d
  Ugly Man as, 197b[c] (twice), 209a
  in Visions, 422c, 438a, b, c,
  vortices of, 440c
  weapons of, 55d, 422c-d, 443b
  wrath of, 414b-c, 419d, 452d, 453b
Urizen, The [First] Book of. See Book of Urizen,
    The [First]
Urizen, The Second Book of: Book of Ahania as,
    50c
Urthona, 426b-427c. See also Zoa
  division of, 124b, 426c-d
  humanity as, 190b
  Los and, 12c-d, 246c-d [246d-247a],
    335b, 382c, 426c, d
  mills of, 273a, 446b
  nadir as, 75c, 426c
  name of, 312d, 426b
  right hand symbol of, 354d
  Rintrah and, 349d
  in "Song of Liberty," 263c, 426b, 427b
  Spectre of, 12c-d, 382c-d, 385b, 427c
  Strong Man as, 208d-209a
Ussher, Archbishop James, 454c
Utha, 427c
Uveth, 427c
Uzzah, 427c-d

Vagina, Luban as, 254a [253d]. See also
  Female, genitals of
Vala, 428a-432d
  Albion and, 11d-12c. See also Vala, in
    Jerusalem
  Albion's sons and, 16a
  in America 14, illus., 366a
  in Beautiful Man, 209a
  in "Circle of Life," 87a
  cup of, 431d-432a
  daughters of, as Maternal Line, 266a-b
  garden of, 385b, 432a-b
  in Jerusalem, 11d-12c, 16a, 148a-b,
    211a, c, d, 390c, 430c-431d
  Lilly of Havilah as, 240c[d], 430d
  Luvah and, 255a-256a, 255c-d
    [255d-256a], 295d, 429a-b, 429c-430a,
    430d

Vala (cont'd)
 Rahab and, 339b, 429c-d, 431c-d
 Shadowy Female as, 369b, 429b
 throne of, in *Jerusalem* 23, illus., 390c
 veil of, 11d-12a, 266d, 288b, 295d, 298a, 432b-d
 worm as, 452b
 mentioned, 449c
Vala. See *Four Zoas*
Vala; or, The Four Zoas (Bentley, ed.), 142b, 144c
Vale, Conway's, 91d-92a
Vale of Rephaim, 346c-d; 32c
Valley of Delight, 237d [238b]
Valley of Peor, 325c-d
Vampire, Lamia as, 233d
Van Dyck, Sir Anthony, 412b
Varley, John, 154d, 318c
Vates, 335b
Vauxhall, 232b
Vegetable looking-glass, 393b
Vegetarianism, 374d
Vegetate, 432d-433b; 150c, illus. I (#49)
Veil, 41a, 80b, 215a. See also Vala, veil of
Velutello, Sessi: text of Dante, 97d
Vengeance, 433b-d
 cross and, 95b
 in *Ghost of Abel*, 3a, 153d-154b [154a-c]
 as punishment for sin, 160d-161a, 227b, 433b
 in religion, 345a
 Satan and, 160d-161a
 Stone of Night as, 387b-c
 in Twenty-Seven Churches, 85c-86a
 in "VLJ," illus. I (#75)
Venus, 433d-434a
 Cambel as, 66a, 433d
 Eve as, 152a, 433d
 Friga as, 146b, 434a
 garden as, 385b
 in *Il Penseroso* illustrations, 227a, 327c, d (twice), 376d
 Intelligences of, 282c-d
 Mars and, 433d, 442c
 mirtle and, 282b
 pudica, 152a, 433d
 temple of, 384b
 mentioned, 334c
Versification
 B's, 332b
 B's and Milton's, 274c-d
 of *Book of Ahania, Book of Los*, and *Book of Urizen*, 46b, 53a
 couplet as cage in, 174b-c
 Dryden's, 110b, 333d-334a
 [in *Everlasting Gospel*, 133c—2nd pr. only] of *French Revolution*, 146b
 Hayley's, 178b
 Ossian's, influence on B, 312c-d
 of *Poetical Sketches*, 331b (twice), c
 Pope's, 333d-334a

Verulam, 434a-d; 35c, 67d, 385b. See also Bacon, Francis
Vesputius, Americus, 434d
Vials of wrath in "VLJ," 235d, 460b, illus. I (#14, 26)
Via Negativa, 291d
Vices and virtues, 436a-b. See also Good and evil; Morality
Victorian period, 79c
Vindication of the Rights of Women (Wollstonecraft), 438d
Vintage, 434d-435b; 10c-11a, 13a-b, 133a, 176b-c, 236b. See also Last Judgment
Viper, 435b-d; 145d. See also Serpent
Virgil, 435d-436a; 167c, 442b
 Aeneid, 112b, 234b, 349a-b
"Virgil, Mission of." See Dante Alighieri, *Divine Comedy*, B's illustrations of
Virgil, On, 308a-b
Virgin, illus. XI (#24)
"Virgin, The Assumption of the," 213a, 264c
Virginia, 436a
Virginity, 436a; illus. XI (#24). See also Chastity; Mary the Virgin
Virtues, 436a-b. See also Good and evil; Morality; *and names of virtues*
Vision, 436b-437b. See also Eye
 allegory vs., 17c, 437c
 B's painting and, 318c-319a, 436c
 Divine, 9d, 10c
 levels of, 125c, 164c, 266d, 291c-d, 296c, 436d-437a
 of Swedenborg, 392c
 symbolism and, 17c, 436c, 437c
Visionary Heads, 154d, 318c
Vision of Columbus (Barlow), 20d
"Vision of the Last Judgment, A," B's paintings. See Last Judgment, B's pictures of
Vision of the Last Judgment, A, B's essay, 437b-c; 3b, 387a, 450a-b. See also Last Judgment
Visions of the Daughters of Albion, 437c-438d
 Albion's daughters in, 14a-b
 Book of Thel and, 52c-d, 401c, 437d
 Bromion in, 60b-c, 437d, 438b, b-c
 eagles in, 112d
 free love in, 147d
 illustrations in, 402b
 Marygold in, 265c
 Milton's divorce pamphlets and, 275a
 Oothoon in. See Oothoon
 plates of
  pl. i, frontispiece, illus., 402b
  pl. ii, title page, illus., 340d, 422c, 443b
  pl. 1:5-11, 303d
  pl. 3:2-13, 243b[c], 438b
  pl. 4:23-24, 180c
  pl. 4, illus., 402b
  pl. 5:28, 80d

Visions of the Daughters of Albion (cont'd)
  plates of (cont'd)
    pl. 6, illus., 402b
    pl. 7:24, 373c
    pl. 8:11-12, 402b, 438c
  Sea of Time and Space in, illus., 363a
  Taylor's influence on, 397b
  Theotormon in, 402a-b, 437d, 438b-c
  Urizen in, 422c, 438a, b, c
  mentioned, 232d
Vitruvian Man, 13d
Vivien, 270b
"Voice of the Ancient Bard, The," 36d,
  286b
Voltaire, 438d-440a
  Alps associated with, 18c
  B's vision of, 187c, 439a
  Bolingbroke and, 50a
  Book of Thel influenced by, 52c
  Candide, 91c, 439a, d
  deism and, 101d
  Holy Ghost and, 187c, 343c, 439a
  in "Mock on, Mock on, Voltaire,
    Rousseau," 298c
  Moeurs des Nations, 439d
  Paine and, 318a, b
  Philosophe Ignorant, 439d
  Rousseau and, 351c-352a, 439c-d
  mentioned, 100c
Völuspa, 428a
Vortex, 440a-d
Vultures and eagles, 112d

Wagner, Richard, 196a
  Siegfried, 428a
Wainwright, Thomas Griffiths, 209b
[Waite, Arthur Edward, 223a—2nd pr. only]
  [*Pictorial Key to the Tarot,* 223a—2nd pr.
    only]
Waldseemüller, Martin, 434d
Wales, 441a-b; 66a, 92d-93a, 242d-243a
  [243a-b], 362a-b. *See also* Counties; *place
    names*
Wallis, J. P. R., and D. J. Sloss: *The Prophetic
  Writings of William Blake,* 144c, 266b
Walpole, Horace, 195d
  Castle of Otranto, 331a
  Mysterious Mother, 195d
Walton, 441c
War, 441c-442c. *See also names of wars and
  warriors;* Revolution
  Antichrist as, 25c
  Arthur and, 29d
  Babel as, 33c
  Bible as spiritual, 45c-d
  Caesar as cause of, 64b
  Charlemaine as, 78a
  Cheviot associated with, 81b
  Church Militant and, 86a, 254d [255a]
  classicism and, 167c, 188d, 313c, 327d,
    350d, 442b

War (*cont'd*)
  Constantine promotes, 91d
  corporeal vs. spiritual, 301d-302a
  dragon as, 107c-d, 442b
  in *Europe,* illus., 133a
  fire as, 139a
  in Golgonooza, 163 (diagram)
  Greece and, 167c, 327d
  Homer and, 188d, 442b
  inspiration threatened by, 391c-d
  in *Jerusalem,* 12d-13c
  Jesus permits, 257c[d]
  London affected by, 244c-d [244d-245a]
  Mars and, 263c-d, 442c
  Molech symbol of, 284b
  Odin god of, 306a-b
  in Oxford, 313c-314a
  in polar regions, 29d, 332c
  Prester Serpent authorizes, 334c
  Priam and, 294c, 334c-d, 442c
  printing press as, 335a
  Satan as, 356c-d, 442a
  sex and, 124c, (diagram), 146b-c, 169b,
    284b, 306a, 332c, 356d, 368a-b,
    378d-379a, 433d, 442b-c
  of sexes, 14c, 30a, 124c, 125a, 367c-d
  Sotha as, 378c
  spider as cause of, 385c
  Sussex affected by, 392a
  Thor god of, 403c-d, 442c
  Urizen's book of, 424c
  vintage as, 435a
  Whore of Babylon motivates, 83a
  Wicker Man symbol of, 447a-b
  wine-press as, 442b, 449a
War Inconsistent with Christianity (Warner),
  38c-d, 72b
Warner, Richard
  Bath as, 38c-d, 72b, d, 210b
  War Inconsistent with Christianity, 38c-d, 72b
War of 1812, 19d
Warren, Joseph, 442c-d; 55b, c
"War Song to Englishmen, A," 349c
Warwick, 442d
Washington, George, 442d-443a; 55b
Water, 443a-b. *See also* Cloud; Elements;
  Flood of Noah; Rainbow; Sea of Time
  and Space
  matter as, 265c, 303d, 443b
  Tharmas's element as, 399b, 443a
  Urizen's weapons and, 422c-d, 443b
  Utha as, 427c
  West and, 443a, 444a
Waterford, 443b
"Waters of Babylon, By the," 258c
Water wheels, 446c
Watling-Street, 443c
Watson, Caroline, 177d
Watson, Richard, Bishop: *An Apology for the
  Bible,* 317d-318a
  B's annotations to, 101d

Watteau, Jean Antoine, 412b
Way to Christ (Behmen), 39c
Weaver, Luvah as, 255b[c]
Weaving on looms of Cathedron, 74b-c
Web of religion, 421d-422a
Wells. *See* Bath
Welsh Triads, 443c-d
Wesley, Charles, 271b
Wesley, John. *See* Westley, John
West, Benjamin, 47d, 456d
West, 444a. *See also* Compass points
    America and, 19b
    body as, 19b, 444a
    brass and, 58b, 271a
    circumference as, 75c
    Ethinthus, Manathu-Varcyon, and, 261c
    Ireland and, 197d [197d-198a]
    Tharmas, 399a-b, 444a
    Wales and, 441a
    worm and, 451c
Westley, Charles, 271b
Westley, John, 444a-b; 271b, c, 446c
Westmeath, 444b
Westminster, 444b-c
Westminster Abbey, 106d
Westmoreland, 444c
Wexford, 444d
Whale, 444d; 309c, 379c
Wheat, 222a
Wheels, 444d-446c; 16b-c, 345b-c,
    445c-446a
"When Klopstock England Defied," 229c,
    301c
"When Old Corruption First Begun," 375a
Whirlwind in *Job* illustrations, 216c,
    220b, c, 221c, 223a
Whitefield, George, 446c-447a; 140d,
    271b, c (twice), 444a-b
Whitehall, Banqueting House at, 72c
Whitehead, William, 37a
"Who Made the Tyger?" (Raine), 414b
Whore of Babylon. *See* Babylon, Whore of;
    Mystery; Rahab
"Whore of Babylon, The," 83a, 107d
Whores and whoredom. *See* Harlots and
    harlotry
"Why Was Cupid a Boy," 167c-d, 376d
Wicker Man, 447a-b
Wicklow, 447b
Wicksteed, Joseph, 140b
    Blake's Vision of the Book of Job, 217b-c,
    222b
Widow, illus. XI (#21)
Wife, illus. XI (#41)
Wife, Elynittria represents, 120a
Wife of Bath, 79b-c, 407d-408a, 432a
Wigtoun [Wigtown], 447b
Wilford, Francis, 108c-109a
Will, 447b-448a. *See also* Female Will;
    Providence
Willan, Thomas, 448b

Willan's Farm, 448a-b; 216b, 265b
William, in *King Edward the Third,* 228d
William Blake's Illustrations to the Bible (ed.
    Goyder and Keynes), 46b, 286c
"William Blake's London Residences"
    (Miner), 448a-b
William the Conqueror, 301d
Williams, Tennessee, 448a
    Summer and Smoke, 298a-b
Wilson, Mona: *The Life of William Blake,*
    412a
Wilts [Wiltshire], 448b
Wimbledon, 448b-c
Winchester, 448c-d; 178d
Windsor, 42a, 448d-449a
Wine, 222a, 236b, 289d, 442a-b
Wine-press of Los, 449a; 278d, 335a, 446c
Wine-press of Luvah, 442b
Winter, 449a-c
Wisdom. *See also* Knowledge
    in B's painting, 319a
    cherubim as, 80a
    in "Hervey's *Meditations,*" illus. XI (#39)
    Jerusalem as, 41b
    love and, 393b
    owl as false, 219c, 313c
    ruby as, 324d, 352b
Wisdom of Solomon, 303d
Witnesses of *Revelation,* 444a-b, 447a, illus. I
    (#10)
Wodin, 449c; 306a-b, 403c-d
Wolds, 449c
Wolf, 449c-d
Wollstonecraft, Mary, 314c
    Vindication of the Rights of Women and
    Visions, 438d
Woman, sex. *See* Female
Woman, The [Mary the Virgin], 449d. *See
    also* Mary the Virgin
Woman Clothed with the Sun, 449d
Woman in the Wilderness, 449d-450b;
    82a, c, illus. I (#64)
Woman Old, 268c, d, 369d
Womb, 74b
Wonders of the Peake (Cotton), 102b-c
Worcester, 450b-c
Word, 450c-d; 269a, 386b, 408a
Wordsworth, William, 450d-451c
    Excursion, 451a
    Ode on Intimations of Immortality, 451b
    Recluse, 451a
    "To H. C. Six Years Old," 451b
Works of William Blake, The (ed. Ellis and
    Yeats), 144b, 375a
World
    Church of This. *See* Church, false
    material, 99a-b, 369b, 380b-c, 390a,
    393b-c, 416c, 445b. *See also* Fall of Man;
    Matter; Space; Time
    spiritual, 393b-c
Worlds, Three: of Behmen, 40b-41a

Worm, 451c-452c
  in *Book of Thel*, 401b, 452b-c
  of death, 221a, 451d
  Hyle as, 193
  marriage as, 348b, 452c
  Orc as, 309d, 310b, 452b, c
Wrath, 452c-453b
  of God. *See* God, Angry
  in "Hervey's *Meditations*," 184b, illus.
    XI (#33)
  lion as, 242b[c]
  Molech as, 284b
  Rintrah as, 349d
  of Salamandrine men, 354b
  Shaddai and, 368c
  of Tharmas, 400a
  Tyger as, 242b[c], 413c-414c in passing,
    453b
  of Urizen, 414b-c, 419d, 452d, 453b
  in "VLJ," 235d, 460b, illus. I (#14, 26)
Writing, 89d, 374a

Yale University Library, sheets of *Book of
  Ahania* in, 50c
Years, 454a
  seven thousand years, 454b
  six thousand years, 454b-455a
  two hundred years, 454b
Yeats, William Butler, and E. J. Ellis: eds.,
  Works of William Blake, 144b, 375a
Yod, 455a; 23c
York, 455a-b
Yorkshire, 455b-c
Young, Edward, 455c-456d
  Conjectures on Original Composition, 455c
  Night Thoughts, 455c, c-d
    Blair's *Grave* and, 47b
    B's illustrations to, 456a-d; 319c, 390c,
      illus. XII
      (*Note: The numbers below—e.g., 87: III,
      12--refer to the place of the individual
      water color in the whole sequence of
      B's water color illustrations to* Night
      Thoughts *(87); the "Night" being
      illustrated (III); and the place of the
      water color in the sequence of water
      colors for that particular "Night" (12).*)
      29: I, 24 ("*Rose so red*"), 456b
      78: III *(title page)*, a, 450b
      84: III, 9, 456b, illus. XII
      87: III, 12, 390c
      108: III *(last page)*, 33, 215b
      113: IV, 4, 456c
      117: IV, 8, 300b
      119: IV, 10, 6a
      148: IV, 39, 140a
      179: V, 24, 456c
      215: V, 60 ("*O the soft Commerce*"),
        456b
      299: VII, 27, 297c
      345: VIII *(title page)*, a, 82d, 107d

Young, Edward (*cont'd*)
  Night Thoughts (cont'd)
    B's illustrations to (*cont'd*)
      508: IX, 118a
  Book of Thel and, 52c, 456b-c
  Gates of Paradise and, 150a, 358c,
    456c-d
  Satan in, 358b
  "Sick Rose" and, 456b
  text of (*referred to by* "Night" *and line
    numbers*)
    I:132, 456c
    I:355, 456b
    III:66, 456b
    III:117-123, 390c
    IV:4, 456c
    IV:19, 456c
    IV:96, 300b
    IV:136, 6a
    IV:687, 140a
    V:1063, 456b-c
    VII:27, 297c
    IX:167, 329c
    IX:1851, 118a
  Revenge, 455c
"Youthful Poet, The," 370a
Yuva, 456d

Zaara, 457a
Zacharias, illus. I (#13)
Zaretan, 457a-b
Zazel, 457b; 7d, 406c, d
Zebulun, 457b-c
  Gate of, 24d
Zechariah, 272c
Zeitgeist, 438a, b
Zelophehad, 457c-d
  daughters of, 273b, 457c-d. *See also*
    Hoglah; Milcah; Noah, female;
    Tirzah
Zenith, 457d-458a. *See also* Center;
  Circumference; Nadir
Zeus. *See* Jove; Jupiter
Zibeah [Zibiah], 458a; 266b
Zillah, 458a-b; 266a
Zion, 458b-c
Zipporah, 266a
Zodiac, 8a, 425c
Zoonomia (Darwin), 452b
Zoas, 458c-460b. *See also* Four Zoas; Luvah;
  Tharmas; Urizen; Urthona
  Cathedral Cities and, 70 (diagram),
    71a, c, (table)
  cherubim as, 80b
  from *Ezekiel*, 135a[b], 458c-d, 459c
  in *Genesis* Ms., 151c-d
  in imagination, 418b-c
  in *Jerusalem*, 212 (diagram)
  in *Job* illustrations, 220d
  metals and, 271a
  in Mundane Egg, 288a-b (diagram)

Zoas (*cont'd*)
    in Paracelsus, 322c
    rivers of Eden as, 115a, 458d
    Trinity and, 419a-b, 459a
    in "VLJ," illus. I (#9, 14)
    wheels as, 445a

Library of Congress Cataloging in Publication Data
Damon, S. Foster (Samuel Foster), 1893–1971.
A Blake dictionary.
Bibliography: p.
Includes index.
1. Blake, William, 1757–1827 — Dictionaries, indexes, etc.
I. Eaves, Morris, 1944– . II. Title.
PR4146.A24   1988   821'.7   87-40509
ISBN 0–87451–436–3